MW01054129

Mexico at War

Mexico at War

FROM THE STRUGGLE FOR INDEPENDENCE TO THE 21ST-CENTURY DRUG WARS

David F. Marley

 ABC-CLIO

Santa Barbara, California • Denver, Colorado • Oxford, England

Library of Congress Cataloging-in-Publication Data

Marley, David, 1950–
  Mexico at war : from the struggle for independence to the 21st-century drug wars / David F. Marley.
    pages cm
  Includes bibliographical references and index.
  ISBN 978–1–61069–427–8 (hard copy : acid-free paper) — ISBN 978–1–61069–428–5 (ebook)   1. Mexico—History, Military.   2. Social conflict—Mexico—History.
3. Mexico—History—1810– I. Title.
F1227.5.M37   2014
972′.03—dc23   2014006614

ISBN: 978–1–61069–427–8
EISBN: 978–1–61069–428–5

18 17 16 15 14   1 2 3 4 5

This book is also available on the World Wide Web as an eBook.
Visit www.abc-clio.com for details.

ABC-CLIO, LLC
130 Cremona Drive, P.O. Box 1911
Santa Barbara, California 93116-1911

This book is printed on acid-free paper (∞)

Manufactured in the United States of America

In memory of
Helen Wilkinson
who is hopefully herself once again.

Contents

Guide to Related Topics

Independence (1810–1821)

Acapulco, Insurgent Siege

Aculco, Battle of

Alhóndiga de Granaditas, Assault on the

Allende, Ignacio de

América, Ejército de

Calderón Bridge, Battle of

Calleja del Rey, Félix María

Cuautla, Siege of

Ejército Trigarante

gachupín

Guerrero Saldaña, Vicente Ramón

Hidalgo y Costilla Gallaga, Miguel Gregorio Antonio Ignacio

Huajuapan, Royalist Siege of

Iguala, Plan de

Iturbide Arambúru, Agustín Cosme Damián de

Mina's Expedition

Monte de las Cruces, Battle of

Morelos Pavón, José María Teclo

Oaxaca, French Siege of

Oaxaca, Insurgent Occupation of

Peninsular

"Pípila," El

Texas, Insurgency in Spanish

Three Guarantees

Tres Palos, Battle of

Valladolid, Battle of

Postindependence Turbulence (1822–1834)

Academia de Cadetes

Acordada Mutiny

Barradas's Invasion

Ejército Libertador

Ejército Trigarante

Guerrero Saldaña, Vicente Ramón

Iturbide Arambúru, Agustín Cosme Damián de

Parián Riot

Perote, Fort of

San Juan de Ulúa

Santa Anna, Antonio López de

Veracruz, Spanish Retention of

Woll, Adrián

Zacatecas, Sack of

Loss of Texas (1835–1836)

Alamo, Siege of the

San Jacinto, Battle of

Santa Anna, Antonio López de

Woll, Adrián

War of the Cakes (1835–1836)

First French Intervention

San Juan de Ulúa

Santa Anna, Antonio López de

Veracruz, French Blockade and Assault on

Internal Turmoil (1840–1845)

Ampudia Grimarest, Pedro

Jones's War

Santa Anna, Antonio López de

Yucatán, Separation of

Mexican-American War (1846–1848)

Ampudia Grimarest, Pedro

Buena Vista, Battle of

Cerro Gordo, Battle of

Chapultepec, Battle of

Churubusco, Battle of

Contreras, Battle of

flying artillery

Monterrey, Battle of

Niños Héroes

Palo Alto, Battle of

Puebla, American Defense of

San Patricio Battalion

Santa Anna, Antonio López de

Veracruz, U.S. Bombardment and Occupation of

Zuloaga Trillo, Félix María

Liberal Revolution and War of the Reform (1854–1860)

Ahualulco de los Pinos, Battle of

Ayutla, Revolution of

blusas

Calpulalpan, Battle of

campechana

Cangrejos, Marcha de los

Degollado Sánchez, José Nemesio Francisco

Ejército Restaurador

Escobedo Peña, Mariano Antonio Guadalupe

Estancia de las Vacas, Battle of

González Ortega, José Canuto de Jesús

Guadalajara, Sieges of

joven Macabeo

Márquez Araujo, Leonardo

Miramón Tarelo, Miguel Gregorio de la Luz Atenógenes

Ocotlán, Battle of

Osollo Pancorbo, Luis Gonzaga

pintos

Puebla, Conservative Revolt and Liberal Sieges of

Puerto de Carretas, Battle of

Salamanca, Battle of

Santa Anna, Antonio López de

Silao, Battle of

Tacubaya, Battle of

Tacubaya, Plan de

Veracruz, Conservative Sieges of

Zaragoza Seguín, Ignacio

Zuazua Esparza, Juan Nepomuceno

Zuloaga Trillo, Félix María

French Intervention (1862–1867)

Aculcingo, bataille d'

Barranca Seca, Battle of

Bazaine, François Achille

Borrego Hill, Battle of

Camerone, Battle of

Cinco de Mayo, Battle of the

Corona Madrigal, Ramón

Cumbres de Acultzingo, Battle of the

Díaz Mori, José de la Cruz Porfirio

Escobedo Peña, Mariano Antonio Guadalupe

First French Intervention

French Foreign Legion in Mexico

La Carbonera, Battle of

las armas nacionales se han cubierto de gloria

Lorencez, Charles Ferdinand Latrille, Comte de

Márquez Araujo, Leonardo

Maximilian, Emperor of Mexico

Miahuatlán, Battle of

Miramón Tarelo, Miguel Gregorio de la Luz Atenógenes

Puebla, French Siege of

Puebla, Republican Recapture of

Querétaro, Siege of

San Jacinto, Battle of

San Lorenzo, Battle of (1863)

San Lorenzo, Battle of (1867)

Santa Gertrudis, Battle of

Sedgwick's Intervention

Zaragoza Seguín, Ignacio

Zouaves

Porfirian Era (1876–1910)

ametralladora

Buatachive, Campaign of

Cananea Strike

Colt-Browning heavy machine gun

Díaz Mori, José de la Cruz Porfirio

Ejército Federal

Hotchkiss heavy machine gun

Kosterlitzky, Emilio

ley fuga

Madsen light machine gun

Mauser

Mondragón rifle

Rexer light machine gun

Río Blanco Strike

rurales

Schneider-Canet 75mm field gun

Tecoac, Battle of

Yaqui War

Mexican Revolution (1910–1930)

adelita

Ángeles Ramírez, Felipe de Jesús

Arisaka Type 38 rifle

Aultman, Otis A.

Bierce, Ambrose Gwinett

Carabina 30-30

Modern Era (1931–Present)

List of Maps

Preface

This book attempts to reveal and detail numerous aspects of the military history of Mexico as of 1810, from its struggle to win its independence from Spain until the drug wars of the current day, which required the active deployment of 50,000 soldiers in 2006. Earlier centuries of cruel tribal warfare, which had culminated with the ascendancy of the Aztec empire—as well as their epic conquest by a small army of Spanish soldiers under Hernán Cortés—have of necessity been omitted from this work, along with the three centuries of colonial administration that produced the Mexican militia battalions, guerrilla bands, and weaponry that would campaign for freedom under the insurgency's leaders.

Many broader aspects of this country's rich cultural history have also been forsaken, in order to focus in some depth upon the military commanders, armies, and weaponry that actually fought the battles that have shaped modern Mexico. Too often, generalized accounts have glossed over details that were important to the outcome of certain important events: for example, the French army that was defeated at the famed Battle of the Cinco de Mayo outside the city of Puebla on May 5, 1862, was suffering from disease and hunger as it approached, so its commander chose to drive straight into the teeth of its republican defenses with his initial assault in a desperate bid to win through—a tactical blunder that would cause his relieved Mexican opponent Zaragoza to observe that "the French soldiers fought very bravely; their commander, clumsily."

Significant historical figures such as Presidents Anastasio Bustamante, Benito Juárez, and Venustiano Carranza have also been omitted for this reason, while many worthy battlefield commanders such as Gen. Tomás Mejía had not received their own entry simply for considerations of space, although they are frequently mentioned in the text. Certain surprising facts nonetheless emerge, such as the fact that Mexico's national army has been officially dissolved twice—in 1860 and 1914—and forced to rise from the ashes, reconstituting itself from those defeats.

The roughly 275 encyclopedic entries of this book are arranged in alphabetical order (with entries beginning with the same name arranged chronologically), providing breakdowns on the careers of the most famous officers—who often participated in numerous different actions over a span of decades, so any particular action can be quickly located. The entries also offer many insights into the daily life of soldiers, beyond the usual listing of famous battles: the rank-and-files' preferred music, their uniforms, their weaponry, their humor. The eight sections of the Appendix provide highly detailed summaries of the evolution of the Mexican Army, from the royal Spanish army and its loyalist militia auxiliaries who were actively defending the viceroyalty of New Spain in September 1816, to the peacetime Porfirian Army of 1900, which would soon be destroyed during the coming Mexican Revolution.

The Appendix provides detailed statistical "snapshots" of the strength and distribution of army units throughout the country during the 19th century, just as the 10 Primary Documents offer glimpses into Mexico's military history; such as the fourth document, a letter written by an American visitor at Acapulco in March 1854 who personally witnessed the spread of the Revolution of Ayutla through that port; or the seventh document, an account written by another American visitor who was escorted through the state of Jalisco by a squadron of liberal cavalrymen, providing a wealth of details as to their dress, equipment, and diet. The Glossary further rounds out the text, by offering many unusual technical terms used by Mexican soldiers as well as clever nicknames. Finally, the Chronology and Bibliography provide a great deal of supplementary information, helpfully broken down according to time period.

Introduction

Long live Ferdinand VII!
Long live religion!
Death to bad government!
— Miguel Hidalgo's *grito* for
independence at Dolores, dawn
of September 16, 1810

When a Napoleonic army crossed the Pyrenees into northern Spain in March 1808, seizing its royal family and occupying several major cities, the Mexican viceroyalty was a vast trans-Atlantic dependency that sprawled for thousands of miles, from outposts as far north as Texas and Upper California to the Panamanian border. Millions of subjects lived within its jurisdiction, many of whom could not speak Spanish, but only one of a dozen diverse tribal tongues, and were loyal to their own immediate community or region. When the French emperor installed his brother, Joseph Bonaparte, on the throne in occupied Madrid in June 1808, this coronation supposedly asserted title over its American colonies as well, although this usurpation was virtually ignored in Mexico and the rest of Spanish America. Instead, its sitting Bourbon-appointed officials heeded the emergency *junta* or "council" that was convened that same September 1808 at Aranjuez in Spain to spearhead resistance against the French occupiers of the motherland.

Over the ensuing couple of years, the privileged minority of Peninsula-born Spaniards, who dominated the best administrative and military posts in the viceroyalty of New Spain, jealously demanded loyalty to the Bourbon monarch Ferdinand VII, who was being held captive in France, while their Mexican Creole peers—many of whom were wealthy owners of vast estates, mines, or business enterprises in Mexico—wished for a greater say and easier access to these closed circles of power. When a few regional *juntas* began sprouting in South America as well, some Mexican leaders expressed the feeling that they too could govern themselves without supervision from Madrid until the French were expelled and Ferdinand VII restored to his throne—and a few even came to entertain the notion of outright independence.

Difficult Struggle against Colonial Rule (1810–1821)

The well-to-do and erudite village priest at the tiny parish of Dolores in the highland province of Guanajuato, 57-year-old Miguel Hidalgo y Costilla, secretly began planning an insurrection with some colleagues in February 1810, intending to launch his revolt at the annual San Juan de los Lagos religious festival that same December 1st, when more than 100,000 pilgrims would be in attendance. But when this plot was revealed prematurely to the Crown authorities, Hidalgo roused a few hundred supporters around his rural church by pealing its bells at dawn on September 16, 1810, and calling for an immediate uprising.

Although today remembered as the *grito de la Independencia* or "cry for Independence," according to eyewitnesses Hidalgo actually began his harangue to the assembled throng by shouting: "Long live Ferdinand VII! Long live religion! Death to bad government!" A few local monarchists were thereupon arrested, and 800 rebels started a march through the district, attracting thousands more peasant adherents as they progressed. Royal offices and buildings were looted, and many Peninsula-born Spaniards were arrested or murdered, as the unchallenged throng of 20,000–25,000 rebels overran the provincial capital of Guanajuato only a dozen days later.

Hidalgo's call had unleashed a torrent of plebeian anger, whose excesses would cloud the reputation of his movement among other segments of Mexican society. One month later, his horde of 80,000 undisciplined followers—the grandly self-styled "Army of America"—was defeated outside Mexico City, after which smaller but better-armed loyalist regiments under the Spanish general Félix María Calleja broke the back of his initial insurrection, vengefully executing thousands of rebels. Hidalgo and his fugitive lieutenants were betrayed to the Crown authorities by March 1811, their severed heads being left exposed in iron cages to overlook the city of Guanajuato for the next 10 years, even though their rebellion did not fade away.

Instead, hundreds of poorly armed bands continued to fight on as guerrillas, defending their own districts and occasionally coalescing under a recognized leader to conduct combined operations: commanders such as Jose María Morelos, another rebel priest who fought on in the south. He even came to occupy Oaxaca with his army to serve as an insurgent capital and convened an insurgent Congress that declared independence from Spain, before he too was finally defeated and executed in late 1815—having failed to dislodge the smaller, but better-armed and -disciplined royalist regiments that controlled most major cities. Yet despite Morelos's death and the collapse of his short-lived government, resistance still continued. Calleja himself, now elevated to viceroy, acknowledged as much when he wrote to Madrid requesting that 8,000 Spanish regulars be sent to reinforce his command because of "the difficulty of recruiting in a country, where the great mass of the population are decidedly in favor of the revolution."

His viceregal successor, Adm. Juan Ruiz de Apodaca, witnessed the insurgency's strength as he ran a gauntlet of large guerrilla formations before reaching Mexico City to assume office in September 1816 and therefore implemented a more benign policy of amnesties and reduced military offensives over the next four years, which helped to reduce the level of violence—but not the desire for independence. This stalemate was finally broken when the ruthless royalist colonel Agustín de Iturbide was assigned the thankless task of campaigning against Vicente Guerrero's elusive forces in the pestilential lowlands of southern Mexico during the winter of 1820–1821 and instead proposed an accommodation to that guerrilla chieftain on terms that would satisfy both sides.

Codified as the *Plan de Iguala* on February 24, 1821, Iturbide's proposal was designed to appeal to loyalists by maintaining the primacy of the Catholic Church and retaining all colonial property titles, substituting a new national monarchy to govern Mexico. Insurgent demands were in turn met by declaring outright independence from Spain and convening a congress to draft a constitution that would enshrine individual rights and impose limits upon this new Mexican monarchy. To adhere, commanders on both sides simply had to agree to stop fighting one other and instead join a unified *Ejército de las Tres Garantías* or "Army of the Three Guarantees," whose tricolor flag represented religion, independence, and the union of all Mexicans.

Over the next few months, more and more Creole loyalist battalions and insurgent guerrilla bands joined this alliance, so when the last viceroy-designate, Juan O'Donojú, reached Veracruz from Madrid in late July 1821, he realized that New Spain was essentially lost. Insurgents controlled the entire viceroyalty except for Veracruz, Mexico City, and Acapulco, and with only 4,200 widely scattered Spanish troops still loyal to the Crown, it was militarily impossible to reverse this situation. O'Donojú consequently procured a safe conduct from the local insurgent commander (a youthful ex-monarchist named Lt. Col. Antonio López de Santa Anna) to proceed inland and conclude a treaty with Iturbide that recognized Mexico's de facto independence by mid-September 1821.

Troubled Young Nation (1821–1853)

Yet despite attaining this goal, many thorny issues still remained. When Iturbide crowned himself emperor in July 1822 and attempted to rule as Agustín I, mutinies and rebellions quickly erupted, so he was forced to depart by March 1823. The Mexican Congress appointed Nicolás Bravo, Guadalupe Victoria, and Pedro Celestino Negrete to govern temporarily as a triumvirate until a republican constitution could be drafted. But with no political experience, the legislators' debates soon splintered into two contending factions: those favoring a strong central authority (known as *escoceses* or "Scots"), opposed by those wishing for a looser federal system (the *yorkinos* or "Yorkists"). Strife spread, as a ready resort to arms now seemed justified to all in light of the recent struggle for liberty. The fledgling nation would endure frequent *pronunciamientos*, regional coups, and countercoups.

Meanwhile, the imperial army that Iturbide had sent to submit the former viceregal dependencies in Central America caused those freed colonies to break away as independent republics, while separatist sentiments were also being openly expressed in Oaxaca and Yucatán. Mexico was contracting, and its war-ravaged economy struggled to revive without its traditional trade outlets. A die-hard royal Spanish regiment still held out in the island fortress of San Juan de Ulúa, while Madrid refused to recognize Mexico's unstable new government or even to acknowledge its very existence, instead planning the dispatch of a military expedition to attempt their viceroyalty's *reconquista* or "reconquest" with the help of local sympathizers.

Mexico's national elections in August 1828 revealed yet more deep-seated problems. With no experience as a democracy, or even any clearly defined political parties, the results failed to reflect the popular will. The lowborn insurgent hero Vicente Guerrero had been the clear choice of a majority of voters, yet because he was a mulatto who had begun his career as a teamster, he was deemed unworthy to occupy such high office by the Creole elites that dominated public institutions—and since raw popular-vote tallies had to be weighed by each state legislature before casting their decisive electoral votes,

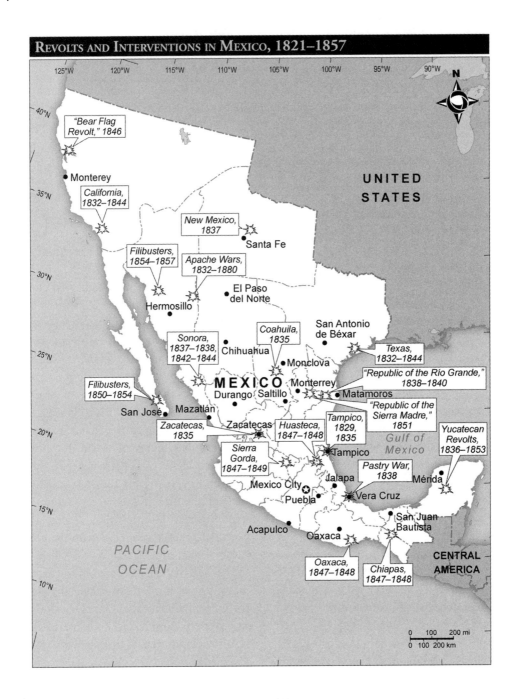

REVOLTS AND INTERVENTIONS IN MEXICO, 1821–1857

"Bear Flag Revolt," 1846

California, 1832–1844

New Mexico, 1837

Filibusters, 1854–1857

Apache Wars, 1832–1880

Sonora, 1837–1838, 1842–1844

Coahuila, 1835

Texas, 1832–1844

"Republic of the Río Grande," 1838–1840

Filibusters, 1850–1854

Zacatecas, 1835

Huasteca, 1847–1848

Tampico, 1829, 1835

"Republic of the Sierra Madre," 1851

Yucatecan Revolts, 1836–1853

Sierra Gorda, 1847–1849

Pastry War, 1838

Oaxaca, 1847–1848

Chiapas, 1847–1848

UNITED STATES

MEXICO

PACIFIC OCEAN

Gulf of Mexico

CENTRAL AMERICA

Monterey · Santa Fe · El Paso del Norte · Hermosillo · San Antonio de Béxar · Chihuahua · Monclova · Monterrey · Matamoros · Durango · Saltillo · San José · Mazatlán · Zacatecas · Tampico · Jalapa · Mérida · Mexico City · Puebla · Vera Cruz · Acapulco · Oaxaca · San Juan Bautista

0   100   200 mi
0   100 200 km

the winner emerged as the former royalist officer, highborn Gen. Manuel Gómez Pedraza, with Guerrero relegated to serve as his vice president. Within days, Santa Anna launched a military protest in Veracruz and—with Guerrero looking on—Gómez Pedraza was driven from office by the additional Acordada Mutiny in the national capital by early December 1828.

Mexico would undergo a further quarter century of hundreds of internal coups, *pronunciamientos*, and rebellions, even a strongman such as Santa Anna enduring repeated removals. States such as Yucatán and Texas would break away, while others such as Guanajuato and Zacatecas would have their autonomy subdued by military campaigns launched by the federal government. In addition, foreign invaders such as the French would punitively blockade Veracruz in 1838, while a U.S. army would penetrate into the very heartland and seize the national capital, demanding the northern borderlands as the price for a return to peace.

The nation emerged debilitated from this defeat, struggling to revive its army and other federal institutions, while foreign filibusters and regional collaborators held sway in northern Mexico. The will for unity nonetheless remained intact, so despite its many problems and pressures, Mexico did not fragment any further. With the reincorporation of the breakaway state of Yucatán in 1848, its borders became fixed at what they are today.

Emergence of Liberal Power (1854–1875)

When a military coup in 1853 brought Santa Anna back from exile in Colombia to once again impose a traditional conservative regime with all the trappings of royalty, a deep-seated resistance arose. For decades, the wealthy Creole elites who had emerged triumphant from the War of Independence, had insisted upon retaining their colonial-era social stranglehold over all lands, education, and high office. However well deserving, no lowborn individual could hope to rise above menial duties in agriculture, business, the government, the Church, or the military. Even such a gifted commander as Ignacio Zaragoza had been repeatedly rejected for service in his youth, not being admitted as a sergeant into the lowly militia

until he was 22 years of age—in contrast to the well-born Miguel Miramón, who was promoted to brigadier general in the regular army shortly after he turned 26.

Faced with Santa Anna's reintroduction of an administration in which he was to be addressed as "His Most Serene Highness" and surrounded by a revived "Order of Guadalupe" of appointed nobles, a military insurrection at the remote outpost of Ayutla in 1854 proclaimed a plan to instead remove him in favor of a truly republican government. Santa Anna marched with his large army to crush this poorly armed rebel force, yet found that he could not come to grips with them in such torrid terrain, so further liberal insurrections erupted.

Without any direct battlefield confrontation, the dictator was driven from power by August 1855, and a liberal administration took office. Their efforts to reform the Constitution by doing away with entrenched traditional privileges were so resented by conservatives that repeated military mutinies finally exploded in January 1858 into the War of the Reform. Self-taught liberal generals raised armies in the north and west, which defeated the conservative regulars within three years and occupied Mexico City on Christmas Day 1860—at which time the victorious Jesús González Ortega ordered the entire federal force dissolved for its unquestioning service to the conservative cause (see the document titled "Dissolution of the Mexican Army" in the Primary Documents at the end of this book).

The conservatives subsequently aligned themselves with the French, whose well-armed and disciplined regiments invaded in early 1862, and despite being thrown back at the Battle of the Cinco de Mayo of May 5, 1862, eventually succeeded in driving the liberal government of Pres. Benito Juárez out of Mexico City by the summer of 1863.

Yet their occupation of central Mexico and installation of the Austrian archduke Maximilian on the throne as emperor by June of 1864 could not subdue republican resolve. Stubborn guerrilla resistance and American diplomatic pressure compelled the French to withdraw by early 1867, after which Maximilian and his last loyal imperial army were besieged in Querétaro, captured, and executed.

Porfirian Era and Mexican Revolution (1876–1920)

Dissatisfied after the death of Benito Juárez by the policies pursued by his liberal successor Sebastián Lerdo de Tejada, the military hero, Gen. Porfirio Díaz, rose in revolt in October 1876, and the next month succeeded in winning a victory at the Battle of Tecoac, which caused that president to flee. Greeted with ringing church bells and enthusiastic crowds when his train pulled into Buena Vista station on the afternoon of November 23, 1876, Díaz was launched on a lengthy political career. He was careful to only briefly accept the temporary title of "interim president" from November 28 to December 6, 1876, before ceding it to the venerable liberal general Juan N. Méndez.

However, Díaz easily won the ensuing presidential elections so was sworn in officially as of February 17, 1887, vowing to serve only one term. At the end of his tenure, though, he engineered the election of his trusty subordinate—one-armed Gen. Manuel González—to succeed him on December 1, 1880, maintaining his influence over governmental affairs. Four years later, Díaz got himself reelected to succeed González on December 1, 1884, and would hold onto that office uninterruptedly for the next 26 years.

Díaz used the stability and power of his prolonged rule to impose an interlude of relative peace upon the war-weary country, during which Mexico prospered and modernized through the advent of railways, telegraphs, and more-productive industries, yet whose greatest benefits were to be reserved for members of the upper classes and foreign investors. The increasingly autocratic and inflexible Porfirian regime was moreover sustained by federal army garrisons distributed around every region, plus mounted police squadrons known as *rurales* who patrolled the roads and small towns.

When the 79-year-old Díaz stood for an eighth term in the summer of 1910 and arrested the high-minded reformer who dared to run against him, this unleashed a wave of pent-up anger and frustration against his entrenched regime. So many local revolts exploded in the north and south that his vaunted federal army and *rurales* could not contain them, and Díaz was driven from power within six months. His inexperienced successor, Francisco I. Madero, failed to resolve the national chaos, being betrayed and murdered in February 1913 by the hardened general Victoriano Huerta, who promised a return to law and order and commenced a huge military buildup.

But even more powerful revolutionary armies arose out of the north, in particular Pancho Villa's *División del Norte*—which annihilated several large federal armies in a string of victories in early 1914—as well as Álvaro Obregón's Army of the Northwest, which entered the national capital triumphantly in August 1914 (after demanding the dissolution of the entire federal army: see the document titled "Dissolution of Mexico's Federal Army, According to the Terms Laid Out in the Treaties of Teoloyucan (August 1914)" in the Primary Documents at the end of this book). Villa and Obregón subsequently fought a trio of climactic battles in the Bajío during the summer of 1915, the biggest in Mexico's modern history, in which the smaller but much better equipped and disciplined *obregonista* army destroyed Villa's larger horde, as well as his reputation. Obregón went on to become president, while Villa was assassinated.

Modern Repression (1920–Present)

Having fought its last set-piece battles during the early 1920s and performed little more than police duties during World War II, the Mexican Army gradually evolved into an instrument of the ruling *Partido Revolucionario Institucional* or "Revolutionary Institutional Party" (PRI), which ruled Mexico for 71 uninterrupted years. Army officers were treated well and granted many privileges so as to retain their loyalty to the regime, and military detachments were employed to root out rural protests or outbreaks of banditry.

Such actions became more brutal and protracted during the 1960s and 1970s, when thousands of troops were deployed to hunt socialist guerrillas in the countryside as well as their urban supporters in large towns or cities: the so-called dirty war in which torture and murder were routinely inflicted upon helpless detainees in order to extract information or influence the elusive guerrillas. In modern times, entire army regiments have conducted sweeps through remote jungle areas to eradicate clandestine drug fields, while strike units from highly trained special forces such as the GAFE or Parachute Brigade have been used to overwhelm criminal strongholds. (About 30 of these expert marksmen also defected to serve the Gulf Cartel, becoming a vicious new gang called the Zetas.)

Amid a spreading wave of drug-related violence, the newly elected president, Felipe Calderón, inaugurated his administration in 2006 with the deployment of what would eventually total 50,000 soldiers—fully one-quarter of the Mexican Army's fighting strength—and 10,000 federal police officers in a bid to rein in this slaughter. Some initial successes were achieved, but the violence spread into other, less-patrolled states such as Veracruz, Nuevo León, and Guerrero, while army units vainly sweep former hotbeds in search of opponents, becoming daily more tempted by the corrupting influences of cartel money.

— David F. Marley
Windsor, Ontario, Canada
December 2013

Who is your perfect guide? Mary.
Who rules in your heart? Religion.
Who defends her cause? Allende.

— popular chant during Mexico's initial
revolt against Spanish rule (1810)

Academia de Cadetes
(1822–1823)

Name given to the institution temporarily created for instruction of military cadets prior to the establishment of Mexico's permanent *Colegio Militar* or "Military College."

During the late-colonial period, the Spanish engineer and brigadier general Diego García Conde had proposed in 1817 to the royal ministers in Madrid the establishment of a school in Mexico City so as to instruct local cadets in the production and proper usages of artillery pieces. His suggestion had been ignored at that time by the Crown, but a few short weeks after Mexico's independence was attained, García Conde swore the oath of fealty so as to become a Mexican citizen as of October 13, 1821, and (as a valuable specialist) was retained in the service of the new Mexican Army with the rank of *mariscal de campo* or "field marshal."

García Conde was formally appointed as the army's director general of engineers effective on January 12, 1822, and among his many organizational efforts, he once more proposed the creation of an institute for proper military instruction. But the Mexican imperial legislature postponed any immediate decision on this matter; so García Conde unilaterally gathered a small group of cadets and began giving engineering classes as early as May 1822 in some rooms in the former inquisitorial headquarters at the corner of Brasil and Venezuela Streets in Mexico City, a vast building that had been expropriated for military use.

His extemporized *Academia de Cadetes* or "Academy of Cadets" was formally recognized by a government decree issued on September 3, 1823, and its faculty and students were subsequently assigned space in the vast Fortress of Perote on October 11, 1823, and transferred there to have it serve as the young republic's new *Colegio Militar* or "Military College" with cavalry colonel Juan Domínguez y Gálvez acting as its first director (until 1824, when he was succeeded by Lt. Col. José Manuel Arechega). Less than four years later, the entire faculty and students were transferred back into Mexico City from the state of Veracruz as of March 1828.

See also: Perote, Fort of.

Further Reading

Anna, Timothy E. *Forging Mexico: 1821–1835*. Lincoln: University of Nebraska Press, 1998.

Anna, Timothy E. *The Mexican Empire of Iturbide*. Lincoln: University of Nebraska Press, 1990.

Kahle, Günter. *El ejército y la formación del Estado en los comienzos de la independencia*

Captured Mexican military cadets being marched into confinement during the military uprising against Pres. Francisco I. Madero, February 1913. (Library of Congress)

de México. Mexico City: Fondo de Cultura Económica, 1997.

Acapulco, Insurgent Siege of (1810–1813)

Protracted encirclement of this isolated royal garrison during the early phase of Mexico's War of Independence by guerrilla forces under the command of the ex-teamster and rebel priest José María Morelos.

Failed Initial Attempt (November 1810–April 1811)

Less than six weeks after Fr. Miguel Hidalgo's revolt had first erupted in central Mexico, his lieutenant (and former seminary student) Morelos arrived in the vicinity of Acapulco with a few hundred poorly armed adherents in early November 1810, to help spread the insurgency into this torrid coastal region. Having driven Capt. Juan Antonio Fuentes's royalist company out of Tecpan on November 7, 1810, the rebel firebrand was then joined by contingents under the brothers José and Antonio Galeana, roaming together over the next couple of days through the hamlets of El Zanjón, Coyuca, and Aguacatillo, gaining further strength.

Reinforced by some Indian allies from Atoyac, Morelos finally invested the port of Acapulco itself on November 9, 1810, whose vast harbor and small town were dominated by a strong castle named Fort San Diego. Normally, its economy depended on the arrival of a royal ship from the Philippines every year known as the "Manila galleon," whose rich cargo attracted thousands of traders and teamsters to its commercial fair for a few months before Acapulco reverted to a somnolent state once this vessel cleared on its return voyage. Otherwise, communication overland with Mexico City remained slow and difficult for the small Crown garrison.

After withstanding an initial sally by its royal commander Luis de Calatayud on November 14, 1810, Morelos left 600 men behind to harry Fort San Diego's defenders while visiting nearby Veladero with his main body. The impoverished region proved ripe for rebellion, just as Morelos had anticipated, so he soon commanded a force of roughly 3,000 guerrillas. He clashed with Acapulco's royal defenders again on December 1, 1810. His forces were scattered with minor losses on both sides, although more volunteers still continued to join his rebel ranks.

On December 13, 1810, Morelos's subordinate Julián de Ávila ambushed a strong royalist column at Paso Real de la Sabana, which was slowly trudging to Acapulco's relief from Oaxaca under Capt. Francisco Paris. After this host of conscripts reached the seaport and was reinforced by local levies into a total strength of 3,000 men, Morelos—shrewdly judging the low morale and inexperience of this monarchist rank and file—led slightly more than 1,000 of his own men in an attack on the night of January 4–5, 1811, surprising their foes as they lay encamped at Tres Palos Ranch near Acapulco. The rebel chieftain's assault inflicted 400 casualties and took 700 royalist prisoners, in addition to 700 muskets, five artillery pieces, ammunition, and supplies, while scattering the entire force of unhappy levies back into their homes.

Inspired by this success, Morelos attempted another assault against Fort San Diego on February 8, 1811, believing that he had bribed its royalist gunner, José Gago, into crippling its artillery. Instead, he and his rebels were received with grapeshot, suffering 14 deaths from a blast before retreating back into their camp at La Sabana. Morelos temporarily ceded command of his forces to Col. Francisco Hernández while traveling to Tecpan to recuperate.

During his absence, Fort San Diego's *sargento mayor* or "military adjutant" Nicolás Cosío resumed the royalist sallies against Morelos's guerrillas, defeating some of them at Las Cruces Point on April 4, 1811. However, a more ambitious assault against the rebels' main encampment at La Sabana was repelled on April 30, 1811, and a second attempt the next day was also defeated, costing the royalist *sargento mayor* his command.

Fall of Acapulco (April–August 1813)

Morelos would not renew his efforts to take this stubborn royalist stronghold until a couple of years later. After barely escaping from the besieged city of Cuautla, he managed to gather some new adherents and resume guerrilla strikes against isolated Spanish garrisons in the vicinity of Jalapa and Veracruz. Eventually, Morelos marched out of Tehuacán at the head of a resurrected insurgent army of 5,000 men and 40 crude guns on November 10, 1812, pretending to be marching to assail Acapulco once more—although he instead carried the city of Oaxaca two weeks later.

But despite the palpable weakness of the royal forces holding on in central Mexico, Morelos then led his victorious army out of Oaxaca on February 7, 1813, and slowly wended his way west toward the Pacific shores rather than threaten the viceregal capital. Strategists and historians have wondered ever since about his choice of investing this remote and unessential port.

Upon coming within sight of Acapulco again on April 6, 1813, his 1,500 rebel troops occupied the Iguanas and Mira Heights, bombarding its buildings over the next six days with a few fieldpieces, obliging the royalists to evacuate their Casamata and Hospital bulwark and to withdraw inside 90-gun Fort San Diego under its garrison commander,

Pedro Vélez. The insurgents thereupon settled in for a lengthy siege, further seizing Roqueta Island offshore on June 9, 1813, so as to hamper access by water. However, it was not until they closed in and tightened their siege lines around Fort San Diego as of August 17, 1813, that the flow of supplies could be entirely cut off and enough hardship exerted so as to compel the defenders to capitulate three days later.

Morelos's victory nonetheless proved a hollow one, as the fall of Acapulco did not directly threaten any major royal interest, although it did allow the insurgent chieftain to address the Mexican Constitutional Congress at Chilpancingo from a position of political strength when it convened on September 13, 1813.

Royal Recuperation and Aftermath (1814–1821)

Yet between Christmas Day 1813 and New Year's Day of 1814, Morelos suffered crushing defeats at the twin disasters of Valladolid and Puruarán, straggling back into Acapulco by early March 1814 with only 100 demoralized survivors still under his direct command. Learning one month later that a strong royalist force under Col. José Gabriel de Armijo was closing in on his stronghold, Morelos burned his hard-won prize on April 9, 1814, hanged over 100 royalist prisoners, and then disappeared into the Atijo Mountains one week later with a few adherents.

Armijo's division reoccupied devastated Acapulco on April 14, 1814, and it would remain under undisputed monarchical control for the remaining seven-and-a-half years of the War of Independence, while Morelos was captured and executed some 18 months afterward—around the same time that the annual reception of Manila galleons was shifted to San Blas.

It was not until preparations commenced for the viceroyal capital of Mexico City to be surrendered to Mexico's triumphant insurgent armies under Agustín de Iturbide that a detachment under Isidro Montes de Oca and Juan N. Álvarez besieged the last royalist holdouts garrisoning Fort San Diego, who accepted the capitulation of all Crown authority and surrendered to Álvarez by October 15, 1821.

See also: Hidalgo y Costilla Gallaga, Miguel Gregorio Antonio Ignacio; Independence, War of; Morelos Pavón, José María Teclo; Tres Palos, Battle of; Valladolid, Battle of.

Further Reading

Hamnett, Brian R. *Roots of Insurgency: Mexican Regions, 1750–1824*. Cambridge, England: Cambridge University Press, 1986: 142–45.

Ibarra, Ana Carolina. *El cabildo catedral de Antequera, Oaxaca y el movimiento insurgente*. Morelia: El Colegio de Michoacán, 2000.

Lemoine, Ernesto. *Morelos: su vida revolucionaria a través de sus escritos y otros testimonios de la época*. Mexico City: UNAM, 1991.

McFarlane, Anthony. *War and Independence in Spanish America*. New York: Routledge, 2014.

Acordada Mutiny (1828)

Military coup resulting from broad-based political discontent that finally toppled the newly elected president, Manuel Gómez Pedraza, in favor of the more popular choice, lowborn Vicente Guerrero.

Failed Electoral Exercise (August–September 1828)

With no experience as a democracy, or even any clearly defined political parties, the national elections held in August 1828 failed to reflect the popular will. The insurgent hero Guerrero had been the preferred choice by a majority of Mexicans, yet because he was a mulatto who had begun his career as a common teamster, he was deemed unworthy to occupy such high office by the Creole elites that dominated all public institutions—and since the raw voting results had to be weighed by each state legislature in turn before these bodies cast their decisive electoral votes, the final outcome proved to be quite unexpected.

The former royalist officer and sitting minister of war, Gómez Pedraza, had received 11 out of 36 electoral votes; only 8 went to Guerrero, the clear winner of the popular vote; and the remaining electoral votes were split up among Anastasio Bustamante, Ignacio Godoy, and Melchor Múzquiz. Gómez Pedraza was consequently proclaimed the winner and next president on September 1, 1828, with Guerrero relegated to serving as his vice president. Both men were in fact members of the *yorquino* or "Yorkist" Masonic faction, but whereas the new president-elect favored a restrained policy against the large numbers of Spaniards still residing in Mexico, Guerrero was spearheading a movement calling for their removal through mass expulsions out of fear of an attempted *reconquista*—an anti-Spanish policy with considerable support throughout the country.

Santa Anna's Uprising (September 1828)

A couple of days after Gómez Pedraza had been declared the winner, the 34-year-old vice governor of Veracruz, Gen. Antonio López de Santa Anna, began engineering a revolt in that state: first, by persuading the municipal government of its capital city of Jalapa to challenge the electoral vote cast by the Veracruzan legislature in favor of Pedraza, against the popular returns that had been recorded throughout that state. Suspended from office as vice governor for this act on September 5, 1828, Santa Anna rebelled openly two days afterward, by assuming command over Lt. Col. Mariano Arista's 80 men of the 2nd Cavalry Regiment and Lt. Col. José Antonio Heredia's 500 soldiers of the 5th Permanente Infantry Regiment (whose commander, Col. Juan M. Azcárate—a brother-in-law of President Gómez Pedraza—had been arrested while attempting to leave its San José barracks).

Santa Anna then sent out calls for support from his regional allies and marched his small force—including two small fieldpieces and 150 urban militiamen—out of Jalapa on the night of September 11–12, 1828, heading toward the strategically placed Fort of Perote. Riding on ahead with an advance party of only eight riders, Santa Anna persuaded its 290-man garrison to arrest their *pedrazista* commander, Lt. Col. José Manuel Arechega and admit his mutinous brigade on September 13, 1828, thereby joining his rebellion. Once ensconced in Perote, Santa Anna issued a *pronunciamiento* on September 16, 1828—Mexico's Independence Day—addressed to the "peoples of Anáhuac" in the name of his so-called *Ejército Libertador* or Liberating Army, calling for the annulment of Gómez Pedraza's installation as president, the immediate substitution of Guerrero, as well as enactment of effective legislation to remove all Spaniards from Mexican soil.

Some local units joined Santa Anna's command at Perote, and supportive uprisings ensued when Gen. Isidoro Montes de Oca and Col. Juan N. Álvarez seized the garrison at Acapulco, as well as lesser outbreaks at Chalco and Apám, but not the broad-based national insurrection that he had been expecting. Instead, the Gómez

Pedraza administration remained firmly in control of most major garrisons and cities, quickly declaring Santa Anna an outlaw and assembling an army of almost 3,000 soldiers under Brig. Gen. Manuel Rincón at Mexico City to invest the rebels within Perote.

This army approached that fort by the afternoon of September 28, 1828, and dug in nearby. Santa Anna sallied from Perote with a column of 300 men shortly after midnight on the night of October 1–2, 1828, circling around via the Santa Gertrudis road to surprise and capture an 800-man *pedrazista* detachment under Col. Pablo Unda that was holding Aguatepec, most of whom thereupon deserted from government service. Santa Anna wrote to fellow conspirators in Mexico City, encouraging them to foment an uprising, while continuing to make feints from Perote in hopes of goading Rincón into mounting a costly assault with his larger army, to no avail. Finally, one rebel sortie on October 13–14, 1828, was bloodied by Rincón's cavalry, so the mutineers persuaded Santa Anna to escape from Perote toward Oaxaca City in a bid to spread their insurrection.

Leaving behind 150 troops, 40 gunners, and 63 convalescents to hold Perote, Santa Anna slipped out with 626 troopers and infantrymen at 7:00 p.m. on October 19, 1828, making for San Andrés Chalchicomula. He arrived there two days later, sending out couriers to Orizaba, Córdoba, and Oaxaca in hopes of raising money and supporters. Allowed passage through the Pass of Cuicatlán into Oaxaca by Col. Pedro Pantoja, Santa Anna was eventually able to enter its state capital uncontested on November 6, 1828, as its *pedrazista* governor fled, bringing his total strength to 1,400 rebel troops and four guns. Rincón had meanwhile accepted the submission of

Perote and followed Santa Anna at a slow pace, arriving outside Oaxaca City one week later.

Both generals met at San Juan and seemingly agreed to allow the mutiny to be resolved peaceably before the legislature, but Santa Anna failed to evacuate his defenses as promised. So Rincón assaulted Oaxaca on November 14, 1828, defeating the rebel forces and driving Santa Anna back into its stone Santo Domingo Convent to become besieged once more.

Acordada Mutiny (November 30–December 3, 1828)

Finally, the unpopular administration of President Gómez Pedraza was challenged directly in Mexico City when the urban militia captain Lucas Balderas declared himself in favor of Guerrero assuming the presidency from the Inquisition building on the evening of November 30, 1828, and a body of mutineers under Col. Santiago García of the Tres Villas Battalion and militia colonel José María de la Cadena seized the old Acordada tribunals, which housed a large arsenal of weaponry and ammunition. Although well armed because of this coup, the rebels remained very disorganized, falling into disputes among themselves after Brig. Gen. José María Lobato arrived and tried to assume command over their movement, only to be rebuffed—at which point Colonel de la Cadena left to rejoin the government ranks.

However, Gómez Pedraza's supporters were likewise gripped with uncertainty and confusion, so no confrontation immediately ensued. Eventually, after two chaotic days the fugitive governor of the neighboring state of Mexico—40-year-old Dr. Lorenzo de Zavala—took charge of the mutineers, instructing Lobato to assume command over the *Ciudadela* or "Citadel," while

Colonel García led probes through the city streets toward the *pedrazista* loyalists holding the Presidential Palace, as well as other adjoining buildings. They opened fire on these rebel patrols at noon on December 2, 1828, some heavy exchanges of gunfire ensuing that killed Colonel García as well as cavalry colonel Gaspar López on the government side.

Vice President Guerrero, who had exited Mexico City and continued monitoring the progress of events from its outskirts, thereupon departed toward Tláhuac, while Gómez Pedraza remained ensconced in the Presidential Palace for only another day before resigning from office and departing toward Guadalajara on the evening of December 3, 1828. With the capital devoid of any recognized authority the next morning, a mob chanting *Mueran los españoles* or "Death to the Spaniards" broke into the padlocked commercial stalls of the Parián in the city center, stripping them bare.

Aftermath (January–August 1829)

Order was gradually restored, and the precedent had unfortunately been set for many future revolts against unpopular administrations. Guerrero was not actually voted into the presidency by the reconvened Congress until January 12, 1829, and even before officially assuming office issued an executive order on March 20, 1829, that expelled all Spaniards from Mexico. Guerrero was then inaugurated on April 1, 1829, with Anastasio Bustamante as his vice president and Santa Anna as governor of Veracruz. A Spanish expeditionary force disembarked in Tamaulipas that same August to attempt the reconquest of Mexico.

See also: Barradas's Invasión; Ejército Libertador; Guerrero Saldaña, Vicente Ramón; Perote, Fort of; *pronunciamiento*; Santa Anna, Antonio López de.

Further Reading

Arrom, Sylvia M. "Popular Politics in Mexico City: The Parián Riot, 1828." *Hispanic American Historical Review* 68, no. 2 (May 1988): 245–68.

Rivera, Manuel. *Historia antigua y moderna de Jalapa y de las revoluciones del estado de Veracruz*. Mexico City: Ignacio Cumplido, 1869, 2: 481–509.

Vázquez, Josefina Zoraida. "Los primeros tropiezos." In *Historia General de México*, edited by Josefina Zoraida Vázquez, 525–82. Mexico City: Colegio de México, 2009.

Vázquez, Josefina Zoraida. "Political Plans and Collaboration between Civilians and the Military, 1821–1846." *Bulletin of Latin American Research* [UK] 15, no. 1 (January 1996): 19–38.

Acteal Massacre (1997)

Atrocity in which 45 peaceful natives were murdered, possibly with the complicity of the Mexican Army.

This attack occurred against a backdrop of a government crackdown against the activities of the *Ejército Zapatista de Liberación Nacional (EZLN)* or "Zapatista Army of National Liberation," a leftist movement in Mexico's southernmost state of Chiapas. Members of a separate, broad-based pacifist group of displaced natives known as *Las Abejas* or "The Bees" were attending a Roman Catholic prayer meeting on December 22, 1997, in the small village of Acteal in the municipality of Chenalhó when they were viciously attacked by a gang of armed men. Nine Abejas, 21 of their women, 14 children, and a baby were butchered in an indiscriminate bloodbath that lasted for four hours during which no troops from the army garrison stationed near this Chiapan village moved to the rescue.

The horrifying nature of this atrocity created a public outcry, both at home and abroad, so federal authorities in Mexico City launched an investigation, initially attributing this slaughter to a sinister paramilitary group known as the *Máscara Roja* or "Red Mask." Eventually, some 57 suspects were rounded up and brought to trial in mid-1999, while the next year the retired army general Julio César Santiago Díaz—who had been serving as chief of the auxiliary police forces of the state of Chiapas when this crime had occurred—was tried and sentenced to eight years' imprisonment for his willful neglect of duty. Court records revealed that Santiago Díaz had remained beside the highway outside of Acteal for several hours with his men, doing nothing despite the gunshots and machine gun fire that could be plainly heard emanating from the village. When contacted by phone by his superiors, Santiago Díaz had furthermore reported "that there was no news, when asked about the situation in the community."

Eventually, 18 of the actual Tzotzil perpetrators of this massacre were convicted and sentenced to 40-year prison terms apiece in July 2007—yet questions still lingered as to which higher authorities had cleared this brutal operation for action in the first place or whether the army had been advised beforehand that it would occur so as to turn a blind eye to its execution.

See also: Ejército Zapatista de Liberación Nacional.

Further Reading

Lacey, Marc. "10 Years Later, Chiapas Massacre Still Haunts Mexico." *New York Times*, December 23, 2007.

Moksnes, Heidi. "Factionalism and Counter-insurgency in Chiapas: Contextualizing the Acteal Massacre." *Revista Europea de Estudios Latinoamericanos y del Caribe* 76 (April 2004): 109–17.

activo

Nineteenth-century designation for a Mexican militia battalion, each usually maintained by a state, region, or city—as opposed to a *permanente* regiment, which was the term applied to a regular unit comprising soldiers of the standing national army.

When independent Mexico's armed forces were first organized in 1823, at least 30 different *batallones activos* were recognized by its government, based at: Acayucan, Alvarado, Celaya, Chiapas, Chilpancingo ("Del Sur"), Colima, El Carmen, Guadalajara, Guanajuato, Jamiltepec, Mestitlán (or Mextitlán), Mexico City, Michoacán, Morelia, Oaxaca, Ometepec, Puebla, Querétaro, San Blas, San Luis Potosí, Tabasco, Tampico, Tehuantepec, Tlaxcala, Toluca, Tuxpan, Tres Villas, Valladolid (modern Morelia), Yucatán, Zacatecas, and Zacatula. Several of these units—such as those at Mexico City and Yucatán, for example—consisted of more than one battalion.

The number of *activo* units was reduced over the next dozen years, as can be seen in the "Mexico's Armed Forces in 1835" section in the Appendix, although they would remain a regular feature of the country's military establishment well into the 19th century.

Further Reading

De Palo, William A., Jr. *The Mexican National Army, 1822–1852*. College Station: Texas A&M University Press, 1997.

Memoria del Secretario de Estado y del Despacho de Guerra y Marina, leída ... en marzo de 1835. Mexico City: Ignacio Cumplido, 1835.

Aculcingo, bataille d' (1862)

French name for the encounter better known in Mexico as the Battle of Barranca Seca—not to be confused with a skirmish that had been fought earlier at Cumbres de Acultzingo while Maj. Gen. Charles, Comte de Lorencez's army was still pushing inland during the opening phase of the War of the French Intervention.

This misidentification occurred because the stone bridge at Barranca Seca lies near to Acultzingo, so French accounts recorded their victory near that place on May 18, 1862, as the *combat de la barranca seca d'Aculcingo*. It should furthermore be noted that the correct modern spelling for this tiny Mexican hamlet's name—which lies at the foot of the Malintzin Volcano in the state of Puebla—is Acultzingo.

For a more complete description of this particular clash, when the 99th Line Regiment succeeded in capturing a Mexican flag, *see* Barranca Seca, Battle of (1862).

See also: Cinco de Mayo, Battle of the; Cumbres de Acultzingo, Battle of the; French Intervention, War of the; Lorencez, Charles Ferdinand Latrille, Comte de; Zaragoza Seguín, Ignacio.

Further Reading
Bibescu, Georges. *Au Mexique 1862: combats et retraite des six mille*. Paris: Plon, Nourrit, et Cie., 1887.

Aculco, Battle of (1810)

Unimpressive yet significant royalist victory that dispersed Miguel Hidalgo's initial insurrection against Spanish rule, thereby forcing his rebellion over onto the defensive.

Prelude (October 1810)

Having mushroomed into a mass movement within the span of six short weeks, Hidalgo's huge throng of followers had begun a slow migration toward the Valley of Mexico, intending to cap their revolt by storming the viceregal capital. However, after fighting all day to defeat a heavily outnumbered royalist force of scarcely 2,000 men at the Battle of Monte de las Cruces on October 30, 1810, Hidalgo had unexpectedly given the order for his undisciplined throng to then veer around northwestward, heading away from defenseless Mexico City, and instead proceed toward Querétaro. The reasons for discontinuing his offensive to mount a decisive assault against the viceregal capital have never been fully explained.

Battle of Aculco (November 7, 1810)

Having traveled for only a short distance in this new direction, his 55,000 followers were resting in sprawling camps around the rural village of San Jerónimo Aculco when they were suddenly surprised on November 6, 1810, by reports of the arrival at Arroyo Zarco—a mere five miles away—of a 15,000-man royalist force under 55-year-old brigadier general Félix María Calleja del Rey, who was hastening down from San Luis Potosí to help relieve the viceregal capital and confront the rebels.

Despite their vast numbers, Hidalgo's following included only some 4,000 ill-equipped provincial militiamen among their ranks out of a total of roughly 40,000 volunteer fighters with scant training or battlefield experience, backed by eight poorly manned fieldpieces. Calleja himself commanded only 2,000 reliable infantry regulars, 7,000 mostly untried militia cavalry troopers and a dozen guns, as well as a mixed assortment of loyalist volunteer companies of dubious military value.

However, the superiority of his core of regular Spanish officers and soldiers allowed Calleja to organize a coordinated attack in five columns on the morning of November 7, 1810, approaching the green insurgents who were drawn up to await him around Aculco Hill. The opening bombardment by the royalists' guns started around 9:00 a.m., and soon sowed panic among the waiting rebel ranks, which broke and dissolved into wholesale flight within an hour, once the royalist infantry columns began to press forward to engage at close range.

Hidalgo fled from the scene of this spiraling disaster with a handful of retainers, escaping through Villa del Carbón toward the distant city of Valladolid (modern Morelia), while his military *teniente general* or "lieutenant general," the Creole militia captain Ignacio de Allende, fell back through Maravatío and Acámbaro with whatever demoralized stragglers he could regroup around his flag. According to the postaction report that Calleja sent from the strewn battlefield to the viceroy, Francisco Javier Venegas, in Mexico City, his royalist army—at a cost of merely 1 dead and 2 wounded—had slain 85 insurgents and wounded another 53, plus seized their eight fieldpieces, 300 muskets, 50 iron cannonballs, 120 cases of gunpowder, 40 of ammunition, 200 horses, 1,300 cattle, 1,600 sheep, and 11 carriages.

Aftermath (November 1810–January 1811)

The next day—November 8, 1810—Calleja resumed his pursuit, intending to fully disperse the rebels before resting his troops in the city of Querétaro. As he advanced, hundreds more insurgent runaways were captured over the next few days, some being summarily executed along the way. Then, after resting in Querétaro for about a week, Calleja would resume his chase of Allende's shrunken remnants, in the process restoring royal rule throughout central Mexico. Eventually, he would take Guanajuato without much of a fight on November 25, 1810, and Allende would retreat to join Hidalgo at Guadalajara. Their combined insurgent army would be defeated at the Battle of Calderón Bridge early the next year, both leaders fleeing (soon to be betrayed, captured, and executed), and no insurgent threat would be mounted against the viceregal capital for the remaining 11 years of the War of Independence.

See also: Allende, Ignacio de; Calderón Bridge, Battle of; Calleja del Rey, Félix María; Hidalgo y Costilla Gallaga, Miguel Gregorio Antonio Ignacio; Independence, War of; Monte de las Cruces, Battle of.

Further Reading

Bustamante, Carlos María de. *Campañas del general D. Félix María Calleja*. Mexico City: Imprenta del Águila, 1828.

Frías, Heriberto. *Episodios militares mexicanos: primera parte, guerra de Independencia*. Mexico City: Viuda de C. Bouret, 1901.

Hamill, Hugh M., Jr. "Royalist Counterinsurgency in the Mexican War for Independence: The Lessons of 1811." *Hispanic American Historical Review* 53, no. 3 (August 1973): 470–89.

Acultzingo, Battle of (1862). *See* Cumbres de Acultzingo, Battle of the (1862).

adelita

Nickname that translated literally means "Little Adele" but during the Mexican Revolution came to be applied to the women who accompanied soldiers on their campaigns, specifically those tending to rebel forces operating out of northern states.

It had long been common practice for Mexican armies to be trailed by the wives or female companions of its troops, known as *soldaderas*, who prepared meals whenever their companies encamped, as well as attended to any injured or wounded, washed laundry, etc. During the initial burst of revolutionary warfare, which quickly toppled the dictator Porfirio Díaz as early as the spring of 1911, a northern contingent of Maderista troops under the self-proclaimed "generals" Domingo and Mariano Arieta had marched triumphantly into Mexico City, singing a lively piece called *La Adelita*, which would become instantly popular. Its words described a soldier's undying love for his little Adele, its opening verse being:

> If Adelita should go off with another,
> I'd follow her by land and by sea,
> If by sea, aboard a warship,
> If by land, aboard a military train.

As the Revolution dragged on for the remainder of that same decade, it became usual to refer to all of the long-suffering young women who trailed along behind its many armies as Adelitas.

See also: *soldaderas.*

Further Reading

Arrizón, Alicia. "Soldaderas and the Staging of the Mexican Revolution." *TDR* 42, no. 1 (Spring 1998): 98–112.

de María y Campos, Armando. *La Revolución mexicana a través de los corridos populares.* Mexico City: INEHRM, 1962.

Herrera-Sobek, Maria. *The Mexican Corrido: A Feminist Analysis.* Bloomington: Indiana University Press, 1990.

Ahualulco de los Pinos, Battle of (1858)

Conservative triumph during the War of the Reform that won its youthful victor, Miguel Miramón, promotion to major general, and the presidency of Mexico only a few months afterward.

Prelude (June–August 1858)

During the summer of 1858, the prostrate state of San Luis Potosí in central Mexico was being contested by liberal forces pressing down out of Nuevo León and Coahuila under long-range directives issued by the northern politician-soldier, Gov. Santiago Vidaurri. On June 29, 1858, a detachment of 3,400 *blusas* under his liberal subordinate, Col. Juan Zuazua, had surprised and captured the 1,500-man conservative garrison holding the state capital of San Luis Potosí. Its bishop, Pedro Barajas, was thereupon expelled along with most other clergymen, while numerous buildings were ransacked by these captors.

The conservative government in Mexico City consequently decided to respond to this seizure by ordering some 4,000 troops to begin marshaling at the city of Querétaro so as to march northward under the veteran 38-year-old brigadier general Leonardo Márquez and counter this liberal gain. Because of the sparse resources available along their route of march through this inhospitable terrain, Márquez set out from Querétaro with the first conservative brigade on July 28, 1858, to advance up one road; a second conservative brigade departed via another route two days later under the 37-year-old brigadier general Tomás Mejía; and a third brigade left along a third path on August 1, 1858, under Brig. Gen. José Maria Moreno.

As they made slow progress though, overall command of this *Ejército del Norte* or "Northern Army" was to be entrusted to the 26-year-old Miramón, himself a recently promoted brigadier and colleague of the late commander for that disputed region, Luis G. Osollo. Immediately upon being given this commission, Miramón had hastened northward from Mexico City to overtake his advancing columns, assuming command on what would prove to be his first large-scale campaign in command of other generals. Joining Mejía's brigade at Celaya, Miramón had cautiously pushed into the city of San Luis Potosí by September 12, 1858—whose liberal occupiers had disappeared without a fight two nights previously, withdrawing northward under the overall command of the recently arrived Vidaurri, in the general direction of Zacatecas.

Battle of Ahualulco de los Pinos (September 25–29, 1858)

Miramón, with Márquez as his second-in-command, installed a conservative garrison in the city of San Luis under its ex-governor, Juan Othón, before reemerging with his army on September 25, 1858, to press his pursuit of the vanished liberal force. He did not have far to go, for later that very same day the conservative vanguard under Mejía contacted a 500-man liberal rearguard at nearby Puerto de Carretas—who again offered but a token resistance before melting away so as to rejoin Vidaurri's main force, which had taken up a strong defensive position only a few miles beyond at the tiny rural hamlet of Ahualulco de los Pinos to await the advancing conservatives on this advantageous ground. Miramón immediately closed in on this liberal concentration with Mejía's Third Division alone, reaching a place named Lagunillas where 20 liberal artillery

pieces suddenly opened up a cross-river bombardment—yet so poorly executed that the conservative general would record in his journal that "of more than 300 rounds which they fired, I only had to lament the loss of seven men and a few horses."

Still, a closer inspection of Vidaurri's position the next morning revealed its great strength, almost 5,000 liberals having entrenched themselves behind earthworks and stockades on the far banks of the fast-flowing Bocas River, their battle line extending right up to the very top of an adjacent peak on their left. Realizing that any frontal assault would be suicidal, Miramón ordered a reconnaissance made around the liberals' left flank by Col. Felipe Chacón, who circled around the mountain range and reported back that the river could be forded some 15 miles farther east, near the Bocas Ranch. Miramón therefore drew his army out of their encampments directly opposite Ahualulco at 6:00 a.m. on September 27, 1858, causing the liberals to jubilantly mistake this redeployment as a retreat until he wheeled around and began marching for Bocas Ranch. Riding on ahead of his trudging columns, Miramón ordered Colonel Chacón to ford the river with his reconnaissance force (the Toluca Battalion and a cavalry squadron) so as to secure Los Trojes high ground a few miles on its far side, while the main conservative body would bivouac overnight at Bocas Ranch.

Drenched by heavy rainfall during the night and awakened at 4:00 a.m. on September 28, 1858, Miramón's soldiers toiled for four hours so their artillery pieces and supply train could accompany them across this river ford before resuming their push westward, up into the mountains behind the liberals' left flank. By 11:00 a.m., the conservative army began to draw long-range cannon fire from their opponents' guns, who had begun redeploying their battalions into new defensive positions up above, so Miramón's troops formed into attack columns and charged uphill two hours later, driving Vidaurri's men back from the first line of peaks. The liberals attempted a counterenvelopment of their own, massing several hundred troops, only to be thrown back around 4:00 p.m. by the timely intervention of Márquez.

Both armies spent a miserable night camped out in the cold, and the next morning, thick fog blanketed the terrain. Miramón delayed giving the order to resume the conservative offensive until visibility could improve, despite repeated requests from an impatient Márquez, whose advance elements began drawing artillery fire from the liberal guns as early as 7:00 a.m. on that September 29, 1858. The liberals even made a thrust of their own against the conservative left before Miramón finally gave the order for all his columns to charge into battle at 11:30 a.m. Their assaults overran some liberal positions before they were met by a huge liberal cavalry countercharge, which in turn was checked by the commitment of the conservative reserves under the personal leadership of Márquez and Miramón.

By 2:00 p.m. on that September 29, 1858, all organized resistance by the liberals was at an end, their army disintegrating into headlong flight while leaving behind 672 dead, 91 prisoners, 23 fieldpieces, 1,200 rifles, and an immense number of mules, wagons, and supplies. Miramón had suffered 143 officers and soldiers killed, plus another 200 wounded, in winning the Battle of Ahualulco.

Aftermath (October 1858)

Delegating the tedious chore of policing up its bloody aftermath to Márquez, Miramón galloped off the next day with a small escort toward San Luis Potosí, arriving there by 2:00 a.m. on October 1, 1858, to be acclaimed as that city's savior. Conversely, Vidaurri's reputation as a leader was destroyed by this defeat, his liberal subordinates blaming him for the crippling loss, so many ceased to obey his orders or pose any kind of cohesive military threat.

See also: *blusas*; Márquez Araujo, Leonardo; Miramón Tarelo, Miguel Gregorio de la Luz Atenógos; Osollo Pancorbo, Luis Gonzaga; Reform, War of the; Zuazua Esparza, Juan Nepomuceno.

Further Reading

Cambre, Manuel. *La guerra de Tres Años: apuntes para la historia de la Reforma.* Guadalajara, Jalisco: Gobierno del Estado, 1949.

"Important from Mexico: Particulars of the Engagement between Vidaurri and Miramón." *New York Times*, October 25, 1858.

Alamo, Siege of the (1836)

Last in a series of victories won during Santa Anna's yearlong military campaign to impose a centralized, conservative regime over Mexico's fractious states.

Background (June 1834–December 1835)

Disapproving of the liberal reforms that had been enacted by his civilian vice president, Valentín Gómez Farías, and the Mexican Congress during his six-month leave of absence from the presidency, Santa Anna reassumed office and dissolved that legislative body in mid-June 1834. He then called for new elections and set about rescinding many liberal measures that had been based on the federalist Constitution of 1824, while Gómez Farías fled into exile in the United States by September 8, 1834, leaving

Fighting during the fall of the Alamo on March 6, 1836, as depicted in a modern painting by Percy Moran. (Library of Congress)

Santa Anna to continue directing his political machinations toward imposing a strong central government over the disordered young republic—monopolistic measures that would be resented in many outlying states such as Zacatecas, Yucatan, and Texas.

On February 14, 1835, Santa Anna's new conservative Congress furthermore passed a law reducing each state's militia forces to just one soldier for every 500 inhabitants, thus ensuring that his regular army would be the preeminent military force in the nation. Zacatecas, with 4,000 militiamen already under arms and another 16,000 in reserve, was the best-armed state and openly defied this decree, increasing its armament production and appointing Gen. Francisco García Salinas as its militia commander-in-chief in anticipation of an armed confrontation. However, Santa Anna struck fast by suddenly materializing with 4,000 soldiers less than nine miles east of the Zacatecan capital on May 10, 1835, easily defeating García Salinas the next day near Guadalupe, in the process killing 81 of his men and capturing 2,700 before penetrating into the defenseless city and plundering it as a wanton act of punishment.

Farther north, federalist officials of the combined states of Coahuila and Texas—alarmed by reports of Santa Anna's swift strike against Zacatecas—fled from their capital of Monclova into Texas on May 21, 1835, leaving Col. Martín Perfecto de Cos (a longtime retainer of Santa Anna) in command of the centralist garrison stationed at Saltillo. The latter would soon be reinforced and ordered to Matamoros by the beginning of July 1835 so as to lead an expedition into Texas to stamp out anticentralist dissent. Cos duly disembarked with 500 soldiers at the tiny port of Copano, about 30 miles north of present-day Corpus Christi, on September 20, 1835, pushing some 50 miles up the San Antonio River to occupy the small presidio town of Goliad by October 2, 1835. Leaving behind a garrison of 30 soldiers, he then pressed on with his main force into San Antonio.

One week afterward, Cos's detachment at Goliad was surprised and overwhelmed by 50 Texian volunteers from nearby Victoria under George M. Collinsworth, and by the end of October 1835 a small Texian army under Stephen F. Austin—after a few clashes—imposed a loose siege on Cos's unhappy garrison, comprising only the regular Morelos Battalion plus five companies of conscripts. On November 3, 1835, a Texian convention at San Felipe resolved to oppose Santa Anna as loyal Mexican citizens, upholding its federal constitution of 1824 while furthermore calling on other Mexican states to oppose his dictatorship.

One month later, "Colonel" Benjamin R. Milam led the Texian besiegers in an assault into the streets of San Antonio, pressing Cos's men back inside the Alamo on December 5, 1835. Four days later, Cos sued for terms, and soon more than 1,100 Mexican troops would begin marching south, evacuating Texas. Winter now having set in, many of the victorious Texians decamped in the erroneous belief that the campaign had largely ended.

Approach of Santa Anna's Army (January–February 1836)

However, the Mexican president reached Saltillo in the state of Coahuila by January 7, 1836, and quickly began organizing a large army so as to invade Texas and reimpose his rule. Within three weeks, Santa Anna was heading north with one cavalry and two infantry brigades, plus a siege train, to join Brig. Gen. Joaquín Ramírez y Sesma's army, which was already operating near the Río Grande. The Mexican order of battle for the forthcoming campaign had Maj. Gen. Vicente Filisola serving as Santa Anna's second-in-command with Brig. Gen. Juan Arago as chief of staff, plus Brigadier Generals Manuel Fernández Castrillán, Cos, and Juan Valentín Amador, as well as Colonels Juan Nepomuceno Almonte, Juan Dríngas, and José Bates all serving as aides-de-camp. Quartermaster duties would be handled by Col. (brevet brigadier general) Adrián Woll, while the artillery was under Lt. Col. Tomás Requena, and Capt. (brevet lieutenant. colonel) Ignacio Labastida was the chief of engineers.

Ramírez y Sesma's army or "Vanguard Brigade" comprised the Matamoros and Jiménez Permanent Infantry Battalions; San Luis Potosí Active Infantry Battalion; Dolores Permanent Cavalry Regiment; plus eight artillery pieces. Col. Antonio Gaona's 1st Brigade was composed of the Aldama Permanent Infantry Battalion; 1st Toluca, Querétaro, and Guanajuato Active Infantry Battalions; the Río Grande Presidial Company; 185 *zapadores* or "sappers"; plus six guns. Col. Eugenio Tolosa's 2nd Brigade was made up of the Morelos and Guerrero Permanent Infantry Battalions; 1st México, Guadalajara, and Tres Villas Active Infantry Battalions; as well as six artillery pieces. Brig. Juan José Andrade's Cavalry Brigade comprised the Tampico Permanent Cavalry Regiment and Guanajuato Active Cavalry Regiment. Brig. Gen. Juan José Urrea also commanded a separate division made up of the Yucatán Active Infantry Battalion, Cuautla Permanent Cavalry Regiment, an auxiliary cavalry troop, and a single artillery piece.

In total, Santa Anna had 6,045 soldiers at his disposal for the invasion of Texas: 4,500 infantrymen, 1,120 cavalrymen, 190 artillerymen, and 185 sappers under 50 staff officers. Meanwhile, 26-year-old William B. Travis—a newly appointed lieutenant colonel in the Texian cavalry—arrived at unwary San Antonio on February 3, 1836, to assume command over the 150 men of its Alamo garrison.

13-Day Siege (February 23–March 6, 1836)

News was suddenly received on February 11, 1836, of Santa Anna's advance on the Río Grande with a large army before a heavy snow fell two days later. Although expected to delay him, the Mexican commander-in-chief nevertheless drove his men through on an epic march and continued to approach swiftly. Unaware of the imminence of this danger, San Antonio's defenders held a vote on February 14, 1836, at which most of its volunteers elected "Colonel" James Bowie to replace Travis as garrison commander, and a drunken celebration ensued. The next day, both commanders worked out a compromise.

At dawn on February 23, 1836—sooner than anticipated—the first 1,500 mounted elements of Santa Anna's 2,500- to 3,000-man main column were sighted, only a mile and a half outside of San Antonio. Its 150 surprised Texian defenders and 25 non-combatants sent a courier with a message requesting help from James W. Fannin's force at Goliad before gathering inside the fortified Alamo, east of San Antonio's river. They were invested that same afternoon by the vanguard of Mexican cavalrymen, and Bowie collapsed the next day, suffering from an advanced case of tuberculosis. A Mexican battery consisting of two eight-pounders and a seven-inch howitzer also opened fire on February 24, 1836, at which time a loose siege was imposed, while further batteries were being installed to jointly weaken its defenses—Santa Anna's intent apparently being to cow its heavily outnumbered garrison into capitulation.

Skirmishes occurred on February 25 and 27, 1836. Then just after midnight of February 29–March 1, 1836, 32 more volunteers slipped into the Alamo from Gonzales, led by Lt. George Kimball (or Kimbell, originally a New York hatter). At last realizing that its defenders were willing to fight to the death, Santa Anna sent 1,700 men in four assault columns at 5:00 a.m. on March 6, 1836, to storm the Alamo's walls: Cos led the Aldama Battalion and three companies of the San Luis Potosí Battalion against its northwestern corner; the northeastern was attacked by Col. Francisco Duque and Brig. Fernández Castrillán's Toluca Battalion, plus the balance of the San Luis Potosí troops; from the east came Col. José María Romero's Matamoros and the Jiménez Fusilier Companies; while the light companies of the Matamoros, Jiménez, and San Luis Potosí units advanced from the south under Col. Juan Morales. In reserve, Santa Anna held back five grenadier companies and his sappers, approximately 385 men in total, plus 350 cavalrymen.

After charging through the Texian artillery fire, which killed Duque and numerous others, the Mexicans gained the outer walls and eventually scaled the Alamo's north side, forcing its defenders back inside their sleeping quarters—known as the "Long Barracks"—where the last few Texians were slaughtered by 6:30 a.m. Mexican casualties totaled 70 men killed and 300 seriously wounded, while 182 of the 183 Texians inside the Alamo had been put to death.

Aftermath (March–April 1836)

The very next day after the massacre of the Alamo's defenders, Santa Anna began sending out detachments to stamp out any remaining pockets of resistance throughout Texas. He would personally lead one column in pursuit of Gen. Sam Houston's retreating Texian army until he overconfidently confronted this opponent at the Battle of San Jacinto on April 21, 1836, only to be surprised and defeated by enemies charging across the battlefield to annihilate his army with shouts of "Remember the Alamo!"

See also: Cos Muñóz, Martín Perfecto de; San Jacinto, Battle of (1836); Santa Anna, Antonio López de.

Further Reading

Benson, Nettie Lee. "Texas Viewed from Mexico, 1820–1834." *Southwestern Historical Quarterly* 90, no. 3 (1987): 219–91.

Chartrand, René, *Santa Anna's Mexican Army 1821–48*. Oxford: Osprey, 2004.

de la Peña, José Enrique. *With Santa Anna in Texas: A Personal Narrative of the Revolution*. College Station: Texas A&M University Press, 1975.

Hardin, Stephen L. *Texian Iliad: A Military History of the Texas Revolution*. Austin: University of Texas Press, 1997.

Haythornthwaite, Philip. *The Alamo and the War of Texan Independence, 1835–1836*. London: Osprey, 1986.

Nofi, Albert A. *The Alamo and the Texas War of Independence, September 30, 1835 to April 21, 1836*. Conshohocken, PA: Combined Books, 1992.

Procter, Ben H. *The Battle of the Alamo*. Austin: Texas State Historical Association, 1986.

Santos, Richard G. *Santa Anna's Campaign against Texas, 1835–1836*. Salisbury, NC: Documentary Publications, 1982.

Todish, Tim and Terry S. *The Alamo Sourcebook, 1836*. Austin, TX: Eakin Press, 1997.

Alhóndiga de Granaditas, Assault on the (1810)

First major bloodshed in Mexico's struggle for independence, a pitiless slaughter of several hundred royalists that would cloud the insurgency's reputation.

When the village priest at the rural hamlet of Dolores, Miguel Hidalgo y Costilla, had summoned his parishioners with pealing church bells at dawn on September 16, 1810, to call for Mexico's independence, he unleashed a torrent of pent-up anger that could scarcely be controlled. Marching toward nearby Atotonilco and San Miguel el Grande at the head of 800 volunteers, Hidalgo not only encountered no resistance but was joined by hundreds more adherents, many bent on vengeful violence. Crown offices and churches were ransacked as they advanced; prominent local royalists were manhandled and incarcerated, many even being executed as rebels arbitrarily assumed their offices and imposed new laws on their own initiative, etc.

As Hidalgo's swelling throng swept through the countryside, he sent messages on ahead to the Spanish intendant at the provincial capital of Guanajuato, Juan Antonio Riaño y Bárcena (a personal acquaintance of Hidalgo), calling for this royal official's surrender—demands that went unheeded. Eventually, after having overrun the towns of Celaya, Salamanca, Irapuato, Silao, Retiro, and Marfil, Hidalgo's 20,000–25,000 ill-disciplined adherents appeared above Guanajuato City on the morning of September 28, 1810, circling around Cuarto and San Miguel Hills to descend into its streets by 1:00 p.m. As this tide of insurgents came swarming down Nuestra Señora de Guanajuato Avenue, Intendant Riaño took shelter inside its recently completed royal granary—a formidable stone building called the *Alhóndiga de Granaditas*—with a few loyal troops plus most of Guanajuato's Peninsular-born Spaniards.

Firing erupted, but after a few hours of desperate resistance, the building was breached when a young miner named Juan José María Martínez (alias the "Pípila") tied a thick stone slab to his back and under its protective covering crawled through a hail of bullets to set the granary's wooden doors ablaze with a torch. As evening fell, the Alhóndiga's doors slowly crumbled, allowing the aroused insurgents to fight their way into its darkened interior, slaughtering some 600 monarchists by dawn of September 29, 1810. This pitiless massacre of virtually everyone inside—men, women, the elderly—would cloud the rebels' reputation, horrifying and alienating many segments of Mexican society who might otherwise have been sympathetic to their cause.

One year later, after Crown rule had been reestablished over Guanajuato, the severed heads of Hidalgo and his subordinates Allende, Jiménez, and Aldama were brought back into the city and put on public display in iron cages at the four corners of the Alhóndiga, dangling them over the ensuing decade until Mexico's independence was achieved.

See also: Allende, Ignacio de; Hidalgo y Costilla Gallaga, Miguel Gregorio Antonio Ignacio; Independence, War of.

Further Reading

Archer, Christon I. "Bite of the Hydra: The Rebellion of Cura Miguel Hidalgo, 1810–1811." In *Patterns of Contention in Mexican History*, edited by Jaime E. Rodríguez O., 69–93. Wilmington, DE: Scholarly Resources, 1992.

Hamill, Hugh M., Jr. *The Hidalgo Revolt: Prelude to Mexican Independence*. Gainesville: University of Florida Press, 1966.

Landavazo, Marco Antonio "El asesinato de gachupines en la guerra de independencia mexicana." *Estudios mexicanos* 23, no. 2 (Summer 2007): 253–82.

Allende, Ignacio de (1769–1811)

Creole officer who provided military leadership for Miguel Hidalgo's initial uprising against Spanish rule.

Birth and Youth (1769–1794)

He was born on January 21, 1769, in the province of Guanajuato in Mexico's central highlands, in a beautiful town then known as San Miguel el Grande—but since 1951 renamed as the city of San Miguel de Allende, in honor of its famed native son. His parents were the prosperous Basque merchant and rancher Domingo Narciso Allende Ayerdi and his Creole wife, Mariana Josefa Unzaga Menchaca. The fifth child and fourth son of what would eventually be a total of seven children, his parents baptized him as Ignacio José de Allende y Unzaga.

His first studies were made in the San Felipe Neri Oratorio, and then in the local Colegio de San Francisco de Sales under the tutelage of his uncle, José María Unzaga; some of his schoolmates included such future rebel colleagues as Juan Aldama. Comfortably off thanks to his family wealth, Allende was able to idle away his teenage years indulging in horsemanship, bullfighting, and country sports. At 23 years of age, he sired a son named Indalecio out of wedlock in 1792 with a woman called Antonia Herrera.

Early Military Career (1795–1809)

Three years afterward, Allende was commissioned as lieutenant of the 3rd Company of the newly created provincial *Dragones de la Reina* or "Queen's Dragoons" cavalry regiment. (Ignacio's older brothers, José María and Domingo Pedro, were simultaneously appointed as captain of its 7th Company and lieutenant of its 1st Company, respectively.) When a gang of highwaymen led by an outlaw nicknamed *Máscara de Oro* or "Golden Mask" began terrorizing roads near the city of San Luis Potosí in 1800, Allende's company was detached there on patrol duties under Col. Félix María Calleja. The young lieutenant also participated in the consecration of that city's Santuario de Guadalupe, in a religious ceremony presided over by Fr. Miguel Hidalgo y Costilla.

Allende participated in the initial stages of the campaign northward during the winter of 1800–1801 to hunt for the American interloper Philip Nolan but had returned home to San Miguel in time to marry María de la Luz Fuentes by April 10, 1801 (who would tragically die the next year). When the viceroyalty's militias were mobilized because of fears of a British invasion, Allende served in Mexico City and Jalapa in 1806, and was still in the province of Veracruz two years later when news arrived of the Napoleonic invasion of Spain and capture of the royal family. His regiment was rotated away from the coast in September 1808, first to San Juan de los Llanos and then to San Agustín del Palmar before finally returning home to San Miguel early in 1809—where after 14 years as a lieutenant, the 40-year-old Allende was promoted to captain.

Insurgent Captain General (September 1810–January 1811)

It is believed that while on this extended deployment among other Creole militia officers, Allende came to aspire for a greater say by Mexicans in their affairs and began meeting with like-minded individuals—including Fr. Miguel Hidalgo of nearby Dolores. When that priest ran his church bells to summon the first insurgents at dawn on September 16, 1810, Allende quickly assumed command over military operations as Hidalgo's lieutenant. But the torrent of rebels proved almost impossible to control, and only a small fraction were trained militiamen. When the unwieldy throng—some 60,000 strong—swarmed into the city of Valladolid (modern Morelia, Michoacán) on October 17, 1810, an orgy of looting and murders ensued for the next three days, which Allende could not quell despite firing cannon blasts to disperse the crowds.

Consequently, the undisciplined insurgent migration into the Valley of Mexico was bloodied by a much smaller royalist force at Monte de las Cruces on October 30, 1810, and then (after Hidalgo ordered a change in direction) was scattered altogether one week later by a royalist force under Brig. Gen. Félix María Calleja at the Battle of Aculco. Allende gathered up dispersed units and tried to make a stand in the city of Guanajuato, but Calleja pushed him out two-and-a-half weeks later.

Allende rejoined Hidalgo at Guadalajara, and the royalists soon followed. Early in the new year, Hidalgo—against the advice of Allende—opted to exit from that city with their untried, ill-armed host and dig in 20 miles to its east, atop the heights overlooking the stone Bridge of Calderón across the Colorado River, which seemed to offer a naturally defensible position. Yet only 1,200 of the 35,000 green insurgents were bearing muskets, so despite six hours of stout resistance on January 17, 1811, they were soundly beaten once again, suffering 3,000 killed and wounded before scattering in many directions, having inflicted only 400 casualties among Calleja's royalist troops.

Flight, Capture, and Execution (January–July 1811)

Allende never got a chance to exercise proper command. Following their rout at the Puente de Calderón, he and Hidalgo met with other fugitive insurgent leaders at the Hacienda de San Blas de Pabellón outside of the city of Zacatecas in late January 1811, where the former was stripped of all military authority in favor of Allende. They then continued retreating north with the remnants of their army, reaching Saltillo by early March 1811.

A couple of weeks later, with royalist forces moving slowly yet inexorably in their wake, Allende and Hidalgo decided to leave behind 4,000 insurgents to garrison Saltillo under Ignacio López Rayón, while they resumed their progression northward with another 1,300 men on March 16, 1811, hoping to find support in the United States. Four days afterward, they met up with retired militia captain Francisco Ignacio Elizondo and rode along unsuspectingly with his 342 followers until they were suddenly arrested at Acatita de Baján on March 21, 1811, and conveyed into Monclova to be handed over to the Spanish governor, Manuel María de Salcedo, the next day in exchange for a royalist reward. Allende was executed on July 25, 1811, and his pickled head forwarded to Guanajuato City to be displayed in an iron cage at one corner of the Alhóndiga de Granaditas for the next 10 years until Mexico's independence was won.

See also: Aculco, Battle of; Alhóndiga de Granaditas, Assault on the; Calderón Bridge, Battle of; *gachupín*; Hidalgo y Costilla

Gallaga, Miguel Gregorio Antonio Ignacio; Monte de las Cruces, Battle of; Peninsular.

Further Reading

Barajas Becerra, Antonio. *Generalísimo don Ignacio de Allende y Unzaga, fundador de la Independencia de México*. Mexico City: Editores Mexicanos Unidos, 1969.

Frías, Heriberto. *Episodios militares mexicanos: primera parte, guerra de Independencia*. Mexico City: Viuda de C. Bouret, 1901.

Hamill, Hugh M. "Early Psychological Warfare in the Hidalgo Revolt." *Hispanic American Historical Review* 41, no. 2 (May 1961): 206–35.

Hamill, Hugh M. *The Hidalgo Revolt: Prelude to Mexican Independence*. Gainesville: University of Florida Press, 1966.

Sosa, Francisco. *Biografías de mexicanos distinguidos*. Mexico City: Porrúa, 2006.

América, Ejército de (1810–1815)

Name that translated literally means the "Army of America" and was adopted by Miguel Hidalgo for his mass of armed followers during the earliest stages of their insurrection against Spanish rule.

After issuing his call for independence at the rural parish of Dolores, Hidalgo departed from that tiny village on September 16, 1810, with 35 troopers of the Reina Provincial Dragoon Regiment under Capt. Ignacio de Allende plus 800 ill-armed civilian volunteers, half of them afoot. By the time that his movement entered Celaya four days later, this rebel throng had swollen to some 20,000 adherents, including several hundred provincial militiamen who had foresworn their allegiance to the Crown.

In that town, Hidalgo was also acclaimed as *capitán general* or "captain general" of the so-called *Ejército de América* or Army of America, with Allende and Juan Aldama designated as his *tenientes general* or "lieutenant generals." When this host swarmed into Acámbaro a month later, their numbers exceeded 80,000 men, so Hidalgo's title was elevated to that of "generalissimo of America" as of October 24, 1810, while Allende succeeded him as captain general or military commander for the insurgency. Of course, even though scores of commissions would be subsequently issued to volunteer militia or guerrilla chieftains to operate as officers in the "Army of America," it never constituted a formal military organization but rather remained an agglomeration of unpaid irregulars whose appointments were not even recognized by the royalist forces that opposed them.

And to further complicate matters, Crown ministers in Madrid routinely referred to the royal regiments that were being dispatched across the Atlantic to suppress the independence movements through all of Spanish America as their own *Ejército de América*.

See also: Allende, Ignacio de; Hidalgo y Costilla Gallaga, Miguel Gregorio Antonio Ignacio; Independence, War of; Peninsular.

Further Reading

Hamill, Hugh M., Jr. *The Hidalgo Revolt: Prelude to Mexican Independence*. Gainesville: University of Florida Press, 1966.

Horgan, Paul. *Great River: The Rio Grande in North American History*. Middletown, CT: Wesleyan University Press, 1984, 1: 423.

Meyer, Jean A. *Los tambores de Calderón*. Mexico City: Editorial Diana, 1993.

ametralladora

Generic term for a "machine gun" in the Spanish language, derived from the same Latin root origin as the 19th-century French word *mitrailleuse*.

During the modernization phase of the Mexican Army under the regime of Pres. Porfirio Díaz, more advanced weaponry was purchased from European and American armaments manufacturers so as to upgrade unit firepower, including tripod-mounted heavy machine guns for use on the battlefield. Such pieces required specialized training, so a subbranch of the federal artillery was created as of July 1900, designated as the *compañía de ametralladoras* or "machine gun company" and intended to train select gunners in the operation and maintenance of these powerful firearms. Various different foreign models were tested for potential acquisition, but the French-made Hotchkiss M.1897 and American Colt-Browning M.1895 proved to be the preferred choices.

Although not as lethal or inexhaustible as the weapons that would be developed a couple of decades later for use in the trenches of World War I, these machine guns nonetheless proved formidable pieces during the battles of the Mexican Revolution, many of which still featured cavalry charges. *Ametralladoras* were coveted prizes for all the factions involved in this struggle but most especially by the *Ejército del Noroeste* or "Army of the Northwest" commanded by Gen. Álvaro Obregón, which deployed them to great effect in defeating the much larger División del Norte of Pancho Villa in the two Battles of Celaya and at Trinidad in 1915.

Obregón's army emerged triumphant from the Revolution, largely because of its superior weaponry and organization, and became the core of the modern Mexican Army. In late April 1918, the U.S. military attaché in Mexico City, Capt. Robert M. Campbell, estimated that this force included one regiment armed with 40 Hotchkiss heavy machine guns; 10 smaller units, each armed with 5 Hotchkiss machine guns apiece; 4 more small units, equipped with 5 Colt machine guns apiece; plus another 10 small units, each armed with 10 Rexer light machine guns—a total of 110 heavy and 100 light machine guns, which had proven decisive in winning the Revolution.

See also: Celaya, Battles of; Colt-Browning heavy machine gun (M.1895); Hotchkiss heavy machine gun; Madsen light machine gun; Trinidad, Battle of.

Further Reading

Fitzsimmons, Bernard. *Illustrated Encyclopedia of Weapons and Warfare*. London: Phoebus, 1978.

Hughes, James B., Jr. *Mexican Military Arms: The Cartridge Period, 1866–1967*. Houston, TX: Deep River Armory, 1968.

Jowett, Philip, and Alejandro de Quesada. *The Mexican Revolution, 1910–20*. Oxford: Osprey, 2006: 14–16.

"Rexer Automatic Machine Gun." *Scientific American*, August 19, 1905.

Ampudia Grimarest, Pedro (1805–1868)

Royalist subaltern during his youth who after Mexico's independence was attained served in its national army for decades, fighting against the Americans in Texas and northern Mexico.

Birth and Introduction to Royal Service (1805–1821)

He was born on January 30, 1805, in Havana, Cuba, the youngest of five sons and two daughters of a 46-year-old Spanish officer named Francisco Ampudia Valdés and his French-born wife, Emmanuelle Valentine or "Manuela Valentina" LeGallois Grimarest. When his father was transferred to the garrison at Campeche, young Pedro

was enrolled in its Colegio de la Misericordia and spent his youth in that city.

Late during the War of Independence, he became a cadet in a Spanish infantry regiment and was sent to Veracruz in the summer of 1821 to serve as an *alférez* or "ensign" on the staff of the newly arrived viceroy, Juan O'Donojú, accompanying him inland when he went to conclude a treaty with Agustín de Iturbide recognizing Mexican independence.

Entering Mexican Service (1821–1829)

The 16-year-old Ampudia enthusiastically embraced Iturbide's Plan of Iguala and paraded triumphantly into Mexico City in late September 1821 as a member of the *Ejército Trigarante* or "Army of the Three Guarantees." He was subsequently posted to military duty at Veracruz, maintaining watch over the Spanish royal garrison that

Pedro de Ampudia, second in command of the Army of the North when the Mexican-American War began in April 1846, who then mounted an epic defense of Monterrey. (Library of Congress)

was still stubbornly holding out in its off-shore island of San Juan de Ulúa. During the ensuing few years, he often came into contact with the ambitious young general Antonio López de Santa Anna.

A year after these Spanish holdouts had at last capitulated and departed, Ampudia—still stationed at Veracruz—married 17-year-old María Barbara González in that city's Jesucristo de los Santos Church on September 30, 1826, their marriage certificate noting that he had resided in that city "for six years" (and also recording his age as 23, instead of the correct 21). They would have a son together the next year and a daughter almost 15 years later. When the Spanish general Isidro Barradas disembarked a royal army farther up the Gulf coast in the summer of 1829 to attempt the *reconquista* or "reconquest" of Mexico, Ampudia remained on active duty at Veracruz.

Services in Northeastern Mexico and Campeche (1830–1845)

Details of Ampudia's advancement in rank under Santa Anna remain sketchy, but he arrived outside the Alamo in March 1836 as a lieutenant colonel of the *permanente* or "regular" artillery branch, in direct command of the 62 gunners of the *Ejército del Norte* or "Army of the North" who would bombard its Texian garrison with their four howitzers. Two years after Santa Anna had been captured at San Jacinto and disgraced himself by capitulating, Ampudia was still commanding the centralist garrison at Matamoros against local federalist forces, defeating them at Cruz Verde in 1838. The next year, he penetrated as far as the city of Monterrey in battles against its separatist leader Pedro Lemus, and in 1842 participated in the defeat of the Mier Expedition out of Texas.

Ampudia was then ordered far south to Campeche by Santa Anna (who had regained the presidency), where a centralist Mexican army had become bogged down by late May 1843 in its attempts to reverse the separatist movement in Campeche and Yucatán. Ampudia had been chosen to relieve that army's defeated commander, in part because he had grown up in Campeche and thus was familiar with its terrain and people. Yet despite arriving outside that beleaguered city with 500 fresh troops and better guns, he could not immediately reduce it either and was soon distressed by the appearance of Texan privateer warships out in the Gulf, which attacked his vessels as allies of the Yucatecans.

Ampudia consequently entered into discreet talks with the local authorities, agreeing to end his siege and withdraw if the separatist Yucatecan government would send a delegation to Mexico City to resume negotiations toward their state's reincorporation into the republic. This was agreed to, so Ampudia retired with his siege force back out to sea from Campeche toward El Carmen on June 26, 1843, and hostilities ceased. However, the governor of Tabasco subsequently complained about the presence of this sickly centralist army at El Carmen, demanding its evacuation. Ampudia angrily occupied the state capital, then chased down and decapitated its defiant governor, leaving his head exposed in a cage while assuming office as military governor of Tabasco from September 1, 1843, until June 30, 1844, and again from September 5, 1844, until January 2, 1845.

Opening Campaign of the Mexican-American War (April–November 1846)

When a U.S. army moved into Texas to ensure its annexation as an American state, Ampudia was transferred back north in anticipation of an outbreak of hostilities. Now a brigadier general, he reentered his old base of Matamoros with 1,000 cavalry troopers and 1,500 infantrymen on April 11, 1846, constituting the vanguard of Maj. Gen. Mariano Arista's approaching army. Two days later, Ampudia wrote to direct U.S. general Zachary Taylor to begin retiring his forces back toward Corpus Christi and tensions escalated. Eventually, Mexico declared a "defensive war" against this American presence on April 23, 1846, and Arista crossed the Río Grande to engage Taylor's forces in their rear. Ampudia remained in command of Matamoros's garrison, bombarding the U.S. troops holding Fort Brown until the defeats suffered at Palo Alto and Resaca de la Palma obliged the Mexican army to evacuate, enduring a grueling 45-day trek through the northern wastelands before reaching Linares on June 29, 1846.

Arista faced a court-martial, after which Ampudia was appointed to succeed him in command of the Army of the North, reaching Monterrey with 3,500 fresh soldiers from San Luis Potosí on August 30, 1846, to incorporate its city garrison into his forces. But rather than then retreat into Saltillo as instructed, he decided to make a stand in Monterrey and mounted an epic defense from September 19 to September 24, 1846, against Taylor's smaller, yet more powerfully armed forces before Ampudia finally had to request terms. The capitulation nonetheless permitted his army to march out with their arms and six guns over a number of days, retreating beyond Rinconada Pass, after which both sides would observe a two-month cessation of offensive operations.

Both Taylor and Ampudia were criticized for this agreement, and the Mexican general furthermore failed to mount any defense of Saltillo when the U.S. occupiers pushed southwestward out of Monterrey to take it as well in mid-November 1846 once this truce had lapsed. Ampudia nonetheless commanded a light-infantry brigade in Santa Anna's main army, which marched back north and fought the Battle of Buena Vista (or La Angostura) in February 1847, performing well during that losing encounter. He brought his contingent of the Army of the North back through Querétaro into central Mexico to help fight against Maj. Gen. Winfield Scott's invasion force at the Battle of Cerro Gordo in April 1847, successfully conducting the retirement of the remnants of Santa Anna's cavalry through Puebla after that defeat.

Liberal Supporter (1853–1868)

As Mexico's government began to resurrect itself after the disastrous Mexican-American War, Ampudia was appointed as chief of staff for its penniless Federal Army in February 1853, then subsequently served as governor and military *comandante general* or "commanding general" of the state of Nuevo León from June 23, 1853, until October 22, 1854, and as governor of Yucatán from February 6 until November 24, 1855. Although he had received these postings through Santa Anna, Ampudia was not a supporter of the restored dictator and instead came to firmly embrace the liberal cause.

During the War of the Reform, he served in defense of Benito Juárez's displaced government in Veracruz, when the rival conservative president and major general Miguel Miramón led an army of 5,000 men down out of Orizaba on March 2, 1859, to descend into the torrid coastal zone and besiege that city. Three days later, Ampudia and Ignacio de la Llave succeeded in checking Miramón's vanguard briefly at Jamapa Ravine before falling back under pressure.

The conservatives nonetheless pushed through, arriving in the vicinity of Veracruz by March 18, 1859, only to discover that its 2,500-man liberal garrison was too strongly dug in, while Ampudia was prowling through the nearby maze of dunes with a division of 2,600 troops, threatening their lines of communication.

By now in his mid-fifties, Ampudia served as Juárez's minister of war at Veracruz from April 29 to September 20, 1860, before resigning from that position to take up a field command for one last time by leading one of the liberal armies that closed in on central Mexico and snuffed out the last conservative resistance that same December 1860. Although no longer capable of commanding in the field, Ampudia remained loyal to the liberal cause throughout the War of the French Intervention from 1862 to 1867, dying in Mexico City the year after its conclusion on August 7, 1868, his remains being interred in the Panteón San Fernando.

See also: Cerro Gordo, Battle of; Monterrey, Battle of; San Patricio Battalion; Veracruz, Conservative Sieges of (1859–1860).

Further Reading

Bauer, K. Jack. *Zachary Taylor: Soldier, Planter, Statesman of the Old Southwest.* Baton Rouge: Louisiana State University Press, 1993.

Dana, Napoleon J. T. *Monterrey Is Ours! The Mexican War Letters of Lieutenant Dana, 1845–1847.* Lexington: University Press of Kentucky, 1990.

Dimmick, Gregg J. "A Newly Uncovered Alamo Account: By Pedro Ampudia, Commanding General of the Mexican Army over Texas Artillery." *Southwestern Historical Quarterly* 114, no. 4 (April 2011): 379–86.

Sosa, Francisco. *Biografías de mexicanos distinguidos.* Mexico City: Porrúa, 2006.

Tucker, Spencer C. *The Encyclopedia of the Mexican-American War.* Santa Barbara, CA: ABC-CLIO, 2013.

Ángeles Ramírez, Felipe de Jesús (1868–1919)

Widely admired Porfirian military officer who fought and died as a rebel general during the Mexican Revolution.

Born in the tiny rural hamlet of Zacualtipán in the state of Hidalgo on June 13, 1868, he was the second son and third of four children sired by a small-time, 45-year-old rancher named Felipe Ángeles Melo with his second spouse, Juana Ramírez. As a boy, young Felipe studied in the local schools of nearby Huejutla and Molango, and then later at the Instituto Literario in the city of Pachuca.

Because his father had served against the American invasion of 1847–1848, and most especially as a "colonel" in the regional militia under Porfirio Díaz against the French Intervention during the 1860s, his sons, Eduardo and Felipe, were both offered scholarships by that president to attend the Colegio Militar in Chapultepec Castle, which at that time overlooked the national capital.

Early Military Career (1883–1909)

Fourteen-year-old Felipe Ángeles followed his older brother, Eduardo, in being enrolled into Mexico's prestigious military academy as of January 26, 1883, and although quiet and shy, he would prove to be an outstanding student. Excelling in mathematics and physical sciences, he took so many additional classes and performed extra teaching assignments at the Colegio Militar de Aspirantes and Escuela Nacional Preparatoria that he did not actually graduate until November 29, 1892, when he was commissioned as a lieutenant on the staff of the Corps of Engineers.

After serving two years with the *Batallón de Zapadores* or "Sapper Battalion" on such projects as digging the Duero River Canal in Zamora, Michoacán, Ángeles returned to the Military Academy at Chapultepec to take an artillery course, being promoted upon its completion to *capitán segundo* or "second captain" in the Artillery Corps. Ángeles furthermore distinguished himself by his outspoken public views on the moral obligations of Mexican Army officers, believing that they should set an example of integrity in the defense of human rights and honoring of democratic decisions. On November 25, 1896, he married Clara Krause Sánchez—a schoolteacher and American citizen—in the Parroquia de la Santa Veracruz in Mexico City. They would have four children together: Isabel, Alberto, Julio, and Felipe Jr.

A lieutenant colonel by 1905, Ángeles was sent to France that same year to study the finer details of artillery practice at Fointainebleu and Camp de Mailly, and on his return to Mexico three years later was promoted to full colonel and given command of the army's *Escuela de Tiro* or "Marksmanship School."

Maderista Adherent (1910–1913)

When the idealistic young reformer Francisco I. Madero drove Porfirio Díaz from power and reached Mexico City by early June 1911, he would spend the next five months preparing to run in a special presidential by-election, during which interlude he came to regard Ángeles as one of the most promising officers in the Mexican Army. Therefore, a month after being officially inaugurated on November 6, 1911, Madero named Colonel Ángeles to command of the 1st Artillery Regiment and

simultaneously appointed him director of the Military College at Chapultepec as of January 8, 1912.

With Emiliano Zapata having once again risen in open rebellion against the central government and his native state of Morelos was being terrorized by brutal federal countersweeps, the new president dispatched the high-minded Ángeles into that troubled region on a fact-finding mission early that same year. Eventually, he would promote Ángeles to brigadier general on June 2, 1912, so as to place him in command of the turbulent 7th Military Zone, which encompassed Morelos as of August 3, 1912, where Ángeles implemented a much more humane campaign in hopes of placating its Zapatista rebels.

He was still employed on such duties when a military coup against Madero erupted in the capital on February 9, 1913. The president temporarily appointed Gen. Victoriano Huerta (who had been dismissed from the army so happened to be in the crowd) as interim commander at the Presidential Palace, while Madero himself traveled by train to Cuernavaca that same afternoon so as to summon a further 1,000 troops under the more reliable and honorable Ángeles. He and his men arrived in Mexico City the next day, bringing the combined total of loyal soldiers to 6,000 (compared to only 1,800 trapped rebels)—but Huerta was senior to Ángeles in the military hierarchy and so remained in overall command of the presidential defense.

Huerta subsequently seemed incapable of reducing the rebel forces, coming under growing suspicion among Madero's followers until he finally betrayed and arrested the president nine days later. Ángeles was detained at that same time and held in the military prison at Santiago Tlatelolco by the Huertista conspirators until they could decide what to do with him. A trumped-up charge of ordering a civilian executed during the Decena Trágica was discarded, as well as the notion of appointing Ángeles as Mexico's military attaché to Belgium, so he was eventually released from detention on July 29, 1913, and simply ordered to France two days afterward to supposedly continue his artillery studies. However, shortly after arriving in Europe, Ángeles contacted the exiled opposition leader Miguel Díaz Lombardo and traveled back to the United States by late September 1913 so as to reenter Mexico and join the fight against the usurper Huerta.

Villista General (1913–1915)

Ángeles crossed the border from Arizona at Nogales on October 17, 1913, and because of his excellent reputation as a military specialist was enrolled less than a month later as an officer in the high command of the constitutionalist forces—even being named "subsecretary of war" by the presidential challenger Venustiano Carranza, despite some resentments expressed by other Carrancista subordinates against this elevation of an ex-Porfirian officer. And in an unusual combination, Ángeles came into contact with the revolutionary commander Pancho Villa in the wilds of Chihuahua and by early 1914 was advising him on a wide variety of military matters.

The organizational and operational focus provided by Ángeles, a first-rate trained professional, helped the charismatic and impulsive ex-bandit Villa to channel his horde of devoted irregulars into a devastating fighting force. As early as mid-March 1914, his División del Norte departed Chihuahua City to reconquer Torreón with a vanguard division of 8,200 men aboard a convoy of 15 trains, which deposited their troops before returning empty so as to bring in thousands more reinforcements, maintaining steady Villista strength as their assault against that city evolved over the next couple of weeks. Ángeles furthermore commanded Villa's two artillery regiments during this successful attack and subsequent campaigns.

He would serve as one of Villa's most trusted subordinates at the victorious Battles of San Pedro de las Colonias, Paredón, and Zacatecas during the spring of 1914, and sided with his commander during the falling-out with Carranza. Ángeles represented Villa at the Convention of Aguascalientes, which by the first week of November 1914 recognized Gen. Eulalio Gutiérrez as Mexico's "true" interim president and appointed Villa as "head of military operations" to drive Carranza from Mexico. Ángeles led the vanguard of the Villista army into the national capital on December 2, 1914, but their ensuing clashes against the tough, well-disciplined Carrancista army of Gen. Álvaro Obregón at the Battles of Celaya and Trinidad in the spring of 1915 ended in abject defeat. The Villistas retreated northward until the División del Norte was disbanded by Christmas 1915 and its commanders dispersed, Ángeles escaping across the border into exile in the United States.

Return and Death (1918–1919)

After three years of political debates and writing, Ángeles returned to Mexico on the night of November 11, 1918, crossing the Rio Grande at San Belisario to meet up with Villa at Tosesihua three days later and jointly call for an uprising against the Carrancista government. Yet it quickly became apparent that no mass support would be forthcoming for the two former generals, so they were reduced to a few pinprick attacks with small guerrilla bands—operations in which Ángeles was very much out of his element and unsuccessful. In June 1919, they succeeded in briefly capturing the border city of Ciudad Juárez, only to be driven out by U.S. troops from adjacent El Paso, Texas.

Parting company with Villa, Ángeles was soon left with only a dozen followers, leading a nomadic existence as a wanted outlaw. Finally, he was betrayed to the Carrancista authorities in Chihuahua and tracked down on November 15, 1919, by a posse to a cave in Las Moras Hill, in San Tomé Canyon near Balleza in the Valle de los Olivos, who carried him into the state capital to claim a reward of 10,000 *pesos*. Brought to trial nine days later in the Teatro de los Héroes before a five-man military tribunal, he was found guilty of "rebellion" and sentenced to death, although many pleas for clemency were made, both from within Mexico and abroad.

At 6:00 a.m. on November 26, 1919, he was taken from his cell and shot by a firing squad in the courtyard of the 21st Cavalry Regiment's barracks. His widow, Clara, died in New York City on December 7, 1919, without knowing that her husband had already been executed. Their four children, ranging in ages at that time from 21 to only 10, had been left orphaned within the span of a couple of weeks.

See also: Celaya, Battles of; *Decena Trágica*; Díaz Mori, José de la Cruz Porfirio; División del Norte; Paredón, Battle of; Revolution, Mexican; San Pedro de las Colonias, Battle of; Torreón, Villa's Second Capture of; Trinidad, Battle of; Zacatecas, Battle of.

Further Reading

Ángeles Contreras, Jesús. *Felipe Ángeles: su vida y su obra*. Pachuca, Hidalgo: Universidad Autónoma del Estado de Hidalgo, 1996.

Gilly, Adolfo. *Felipe Ángeles en la Revolución*. Mexico City: Ediciones Era, 2005.

Mena Brito, Bernardino. *El lugarteniente gris de Pancho Villa*. Mexico City: Casa M. Coli, 1938.

Sosa, Francisco. *Biografías de mexicanos distinguidos*. Mexico City: Porrúa, 2006.

Angostura, Battle of La (1847).

Name in Mexico for the encounter known to American military history as the "Battle of Buena Vista." *See* Buena Vista, Battle of (1847).

Añil, Battle of El (1886). *See* Buatachive, Campaign of (1886).

Arango Arámbula, Doroteo.

Real name of Pancho Villa. *See* Villa, Pancho (1878–1923).

Arisaka Type 38 rifle (1910)

Japanese bolt-action rifle, several thousand of which were purchased for the Mexican Army during the late Porfirian era.

As unrest mounted in Mexico during 1910, the government sought a way to quickly acquire more field service rifles, so an order was placed for 14,000 Arisaka Type 38 rifles and carbines to be manufactured at the Koishikowa Arsenal in Japan. However, only about 5,000 of these could be delivered before Pres. Porfirio Díaz was driven from power in the spring of 1911, the remainder being warehoused in Japan and eventually sold off to Russia during World War I.

See also: Carabina 30-30; Máuser; Mondragón rifle.

Further Reading

Fitzsimmons, Bernard. *Illustrated Encyclopedia of Weapons and Warfare*. London: Phoebus, 1978.

Hughes, James B., Jr. *Mexican Military Arms: The Cartridge Period, 1866–1967*. Houston, TX: Deep River Armory, 1968.

Jowett, Philip, and Alejandro de Quesada. *The Mexican Revolution, 1910–20*. Oxford: Osprey, 2006.

armas nacionales se han cubierto de gloria. *See las armas nacionales se han cubierto de gloria.*

Army of the Three Guarantees (1821–1822). *See* Ejército Trigarante (1821–1822).

Arroyo Feo, Battle of (1858). *See* Salamanca, Battle of (1858).

aspillera

Generic term in the Spanish language for any gun slit, loophole, or embrasure in a fort or defensive position.

For example, during the desperate nocturnal assault by Pancho Villa's army after nightfall of March 25, 1914, against federal emplacements that had been installed atop La Pila Hill outside of Torreón's satellite city of Gómez Palacio, the fighting moved into such close range that some eyewitnesses even reported seeing Villista soldiers grappling with rifle muzzles that were being aimed by the defenders out of their *aspilleras*.

See also: Torreón, Villa's Second Capture of.

Aultman, Otis A. (1874–1943)

American photographer whose presence in El Paso, Texas, permitted him to capture many firsthand views of the Mexican Revolution.

He was born on August 27, 1874, in Holden, Missouri, the son of a Union Army veteran. His mother suffered from tuberculosis, so the family moved to Trinidad in the state of Colorado in 1887 when Otis was only 14 years old. He learned photography from his older brother, Oliver, who was self-taught, and they opened a studio together. Aultman married a woman named Lela Whiscarver and they had two children, a daughter and son, but this marriage ended in permanent separation as of 1908, after which he moved to Texas.

Recording the Mexican Revolution (1911–1917)

Upon first settling in El Paso, Aultman was employed by the Scott Photo Company, and the Mexican Revolution erupted only two years later, one of its earliest major actions being the two-and-half-week rebel siege in April–May 1911 of Ciudad Juárez, just on the opposite side of the Rio Grande. With requests pouring in from news agencies for a photograph of Pancho Villa, Aultman traveled into Mexico and with considerable difficulty located him at San Pedro, only to have his request to photograph the subject turned down with the words:

> I will not allow any *gringo* to make pictures of me. I don't want my picture shown in the United States. I want my friends, the Mexicans, to make all the money there is to be made by taking pictures of me.

Yet despite this inauspicious start, Aultman persisted and eventually became a favorite and friend of Villa, who referred to the diminutive photographer as the "Banty Rooster" because he was only 5'4" tall.

He accompanied the revolutionary leader on several campaigns, even being allowed to set up a darkroom in a railroad boxcar.

In March 1916, Aultman was one of the first photographers to arrive at Columbus, New Mexico, after the infamous raid on that town by Villa. It was recorded of Aultman that "he drove 75 miles from El Paso in record time; the town was still smoldering ruins, and people still hysterical." He also accompanied Gen. John Pershing's subsequent "Punitive Expedition" into northern Mexico, which did not withdraw until February 1917, after which Aultman gradually settled down to a conventional career as a commercial photographer in El Paso.

Death (1943)

Active in many circles, Aultman died tragically when he fell from a seven-foot platform into the alley by his studio at 204 San Francisco Street on March 6, 1943. The El Paso Chamber of Commerce subsequently purchased his thousands of negatives from his estate, which were moved from one storage place to another over the next 20 years, some disappearing in the process. In the 1960s, the remaining 6,000 negatives were purchased, prints of each were made, and both negatives and prints were placed in the El Paso Public Library with a second set of prints in the Library of the University of Texas at El Paso, preserving this rich resource on the history of the Mexican Revolution.

See also: Tierra Blanca, Battle of; Villa, Pancho.

Further Reading

Núñez, Aurora, and Amanda Taylor. "Otis A. Aultman Captured Border History in Pictures." *Borderlands* 21 (2002).

Sarber, Mary A. *Photographs from the Border: The Otis A. Aultman Collection.* El Paso, TX: El Paso Public Library Association, 1977.

Ayutla, Revolution of (1854–1855)

Liberal insurrection that spread throughout the country and toppled Santa Anna for the final time, replacing his regime with republican rule—yet failing to extinguish conservative resistance altogether, so this rivalry would continue into the Wars of the Reform and French Intervention as well.

Background (1853)

Despite being exiled in Colombia, Santa Anna was to be reinstalled as president of troubled Mexico in April 1853, following a military coup in the capital engineered by Gen. Manuel María Lombardini. His conservative backers hoped that their

Variety of Mexican soldiers and guerrillas in the field, as depicted in the August 1852 edition of "Gleason's Pictorial Drawing-Room Companion" of Boston. (Anne S. K. Brown Military Collection, Brown University Library)

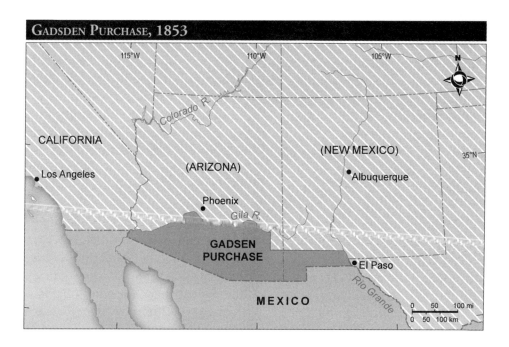

GADSDEN PURCHASE, 1853

strongman's return would restore some semblance of order to a country that remained wracked and angry in the wake of its defeat by the United States. However, its weak and bankrupt central government meant that Santa Anna would initially experience difficulties raising sufficient funds through traditional tax measures, while his authority was furthermore being openly flouted or ignored by some state or regional leaders. Simultaneously, Santa Anna had to negotiate territorial claims being pressed by the U.S. ambassador, James Gadsen, increasing worries among Mexicans about more concessions being demanded of their national sovereignty.

Santa Anna prepared to meet such challenges by recalling and promoting many loyalists into high-ranking military positions and starting to rebuild the army's strength before at last blatantly assuming dictatorial powers as of December 16, 1853—when he proclaimed that he would henceforth dispense with any kind of legislature, abolish all political parties, create an order of nobility, and demand to be addressed as "Most Serene Highness."

Two weeks afterward he signed the Gadsen Treaty, which granted the United States free passage for mail, merchandise, and troops across the Isthmus of Tehuantepec, as well as added a readjustment to the boundaries established earlier by the Treaty of Guadalupe Hidalgo, giving Washington almost 30,000 more square miles of territory in New Mexico and Arizona—in exchange for 10 million desperately needed dollars, which Santa Anna used to help finance his massive military buildup. (The size of Mexico's standing army shot up from 6,000 men in 1852 to roughly 46,000 by March 1854, although the vast majority of these new recruits proved to be unreliable and ill-trained conscripts; see the section "Mexico's Reconstituted Army, 1851," in the Appendix.)

Pronunciamiento at Ayutla
(March 1854)

The Mexican public was outraged by Santa Anna's actions, for both assuming an imperial crown as well as signing away more Mexican territory, so various mutinies flared up in protest. Among these insurrections, one called not only for Santa Anna's removal but for a complete replacement of the limited democracy that had been imposed on the nation ever since colonial days in favor of a more inclusive form of liberal republican government. On March 1, 1854, Col. Florencio Villarreal rose against Santa Anna with his 400-man militia battalion at Ayutla, Guerrero, publishing the so-called *Plan de Ayutla*—a liberal program drawn up by his 63-year-old regional superior, ex-governor and general Juan Nepomuceno Álvarez and the illiterate Brig. Gen. Tomás Moreno, aimed not only at deposing Santa Anna but furthermore empowering a national congress to enact a less restrictive constitution.

Ten days later, the 500-man garrison at Acapulco under Col. Rafael Solís also embraced this plan (persuaded by its 41-year-old ex-customs collector, Col. Ignacio Comonfort), while calling on Álvarez and Moreno to assume command over all rebel contingents. Álvarez wrote accepting Comonfort's recommendation on March 15, 1854, suggesting that this nation-wide armed movement should be named the *Ejército Restaurador de la Libertad* or "Restorer of Liberty Army."

Santa Anna's Opening Campaign into Guerrero (March–April 1854)

Having anticipated that resistance might erupt in Guerrero, Santa Anna had already stationed Maj. Gen. Ángel Pérez Palacios with 3,000 troops at Chilpancingo, while another brigade of more than 1,000 soldiers was marching out of Oaxaca toward Omotepec under Brig. Gen. Luis Noriega and a regiment under Col. Francisco Cosío Bahamonde was headed toward Huetamo. These preemptive deployments allowed Santa Anna to respond very swiftly to Álvarez's *pronunciamiento*, as the dictator personally marched out of Mexico City at the head of 5,000 troops on March 16, 1854, to wend through the Sierra Madre range down to the Pacific shores and stamp out this uprising.

Santa Anna reached Chilpancingo with his main *división de operaciones* or "operational division" by March 30, 1854, having brushed aside a force of poorly armed *pinto* militiamen under Faustino Villalba while crossing the Mezcala River. Santa Anna resumed his push from Chilpancingo deeper into insurgent territory on April 9, 1854, weathering an ambush at Cajones and some losses four days later in Coquillo Canyon before his cavalry scattered and chased off the shadowing guerrilla bands. Ominously, though, no supplies or messengers were able to follow his army down this long primitive road to the coast, as rebel riders closed in behind Santa Anna and cut off his lines of communication. A detachment of 400 soldiers under his subordinate, Col. Francisco Suárez, was furthermore checked in its attempt to raid the private country estate of General Álvarez, while Noriega's brigade was scarcely able to crawl into Ayutla before collapsing, its men not having had anything to eat or drink for two days.

By the time Santa Anna came within sight of Acapulco on April 20, 1854, his own soldiers were already suffering from thirst, hunger, and exhaustion in the oppressive heat, while disease was thinning their ranks. His initial overture to present his terms for the garrison's surrender was greeted with gunfire from Comonfort's artillery, so Santa Anna sent a column of

900 men to assault the principal harbor castle called Fort San Diego, but they became caught in a crossfire for four hours and failed to reach its walls. Santa Anna reluctantly encamped for a siege, although his army could not encircle Fort San Diego, so he sent Gen. Manuel Céspedes to negotiate with Comonfort—even offering the rebel garrison commander a 100,000-*peso* bribe to submit, which was rejected.

Acapulco's defenders were surprised to see Santa Anna's army break camp on April 26, 1854, and begin to retreat back toward Chilpancingo. Guerrilla forces under General Moreno followed at a safe distance, while the rebel commander-in-chief's son—Col. Encarnación Álvarez—hastily entrenched several *pinto* militia units atop the hill above Peregrino Pass (where the highway zigzagged up in a steep incline) and contested Santa Anna's retreat through that chokepoint on April 30, 1854. Hearing the sound of heavy guns, Moreno hurried two of his trailing regiments forward to join in on this battle and found Santa Anna's rearguard drawn up atop Agua del Perro but could not best them before the retreating army pushed through Peregrino Pass two hours later. The rebels nonetheless seized 360 loaded pack animals, making the last stage of Santa Anna's crippled retreat even more miserable.

He finally reached safety at Chilpancingo on May 4, 1854, spending the next three days refreshing his survivors as they arrived. Santa Anna then rode off to the capital with his staff and an elite escort, returning to Mexico City by May 16, 1854—entering through a triumphal arch, trying to give the impression of great success. Santa Anna would shrug off his failed campaign by attributing it to his lowly *pinto* opponents, native peasants inured to those torrid coastal lowlands, whose faces were marred with splotches from local contagions.

Punitive Strikes into Guerrero (June 1854–June 1855)

Santa Anna's failure to crush the Ayutla rebellion inspired other revolts, so rural bands in neighboring Michoacán and Morelos soon began rising against his regime as well as in such northern states as Nuevo León and Coahuila. The dictator reacted by proclaiming on June 5, 1854, that any department, district, city, or town that switched allegiance to adhere to the Plan of Ayutla would be subjected to the full rigors of martial law, and in order to make a fearsome example, Santa Anna instructed General Pérez Palacios to unleash detachments from his advance base at Chilpancingo, to punish rebels and noncombatants alike throughout Guerrero.

Col. Félix María Zuloaga was placed in command of one of the first such punitive missions, leading a flying column of 1,500 men and two fieldpieces, which arrived below the rebel fortification atop Limón Hill outside of Iguala and carried it by storm on July 12, 1854. The defeated rebel chieftain Villalba was thereupon executed and his head left exposed in an iron cage at Mezcala, winning Zuloaga promotion to brigadier.

However, this cruel strategy not only failed to break rebel spirits, it would soon be undone by the evasive tactics adopted by both the guerrillas and their civilian supporters. When Gen. Severo del Castillo was sent by Santa Anna's minister of war, Gen. Santiago Blanco, with two brigades to destroy the remote Hacienda de la Providencia, which was home and headquarters to the rebel leader Álvarez, this expedition forged with great difficulty through hot jungle approaches and arrived to find the estate empty, leaving them isolated far from safety while subjected to thirst, hunger, disease, desertions, and vengeful pursuers.

Zuloaga was subsequently ordered by Del Castillo to split off in November 1854 and proceed alone toward Coyuca de Benítez with his own brigade, deeper inside the rebel territory south of the Balsas River, whose capture would supposedly cut off the provisions sustaining the insurgent garrison at Acapulco. But after fighting past a rebel force under Brigadier Moreno entrenched at El Calvario on December 9, 1854, Zuloaga turned away in weary distress for the relative safety of Tecpan. Instead, though, he was cornered four days later with his 1,000 surviving men and five fieldpieces in the Hacienda de Nuxco by a convergence between Álvarez and Moreno that left the *santannistas* surrounded by 4,000 rebels. After holding out for 37 days, beyond hope of rescue, Zuloaga's officers and soldiers surrendered to the besiegers on January 18, 1855, most joining the rebel ranks, while Zuloaga would remain a prisoner over the next four months.

The regime's inability to crush these impoverished coastal rebels meant that their insurgency not only had taken root in Guerrero, Michoacán, and Morelos but would also begin spreading into central and northern Mexico. Soon, other regional leaders were announcing their adherence to the Plan de Ayutla, attacking Santa Anna loyalists and tax collectors, although not seeking to coalesce into any unified army. Local caudillos or chieftains merely acknowledged Álvarez's nominal leadership, so long as it did not infringe on their own activities or prerogatives. An American correspondent for the *New York Daily Tribune* reported from Mexico City how "Álvarez and his adherents have a great number of men scattered about in small bodies in the mountainous country and neighborhood of the towns occupied by Government troops," attacking small detachments and fleeing from larger formations.

Santa Anna attempted a second punitive march through the center and north of the state of Guerrero in the spring of 1855, encountering no opponents on the battlefield and torching as many empty communities as he could, to no avail. He returned to Mexico City on June 9, 1855—once again proclaiming his campaign a triumph, yet to scant enthusiasm. With his government now bankrupt and support falling away, Santa Anna quietly appointed three men to temporarily assume his presidential duties on August 8, 1855, then at 3:00 a.m. the next morning slipped out of Mexico City with an escort of a regiment of lancers, headed toward Veracruz. He paused at Perote to issue a public proclamation on August 12th, formally resigning from the presidency, and six days afterward sailed away from Veracruz aboard the ship *Iturbide* toward Cuba to proceed back into exile at Turbaco (Colombia).

See also: *pintos*; Santa Anna, Antonio López de.

Further Reading

"From Mexico." *New York Times*, July 7, 1854.

Haworth, Daniel S. "The Mobile National Guard of Guanajuato, 1855–1858." In *Forced Marches: Soldiers and Military Caciques in Modern Mexico*, edited by Ben Fallaw and Terry Rugeley, 49–80. Tucson: University of Arizona Press, 2012.

"Important from Mexico: Progress of the Revolution." *New York Times*, April 19, 1854.

"Interesting from Mexico: Santa Anna's Return to the Capital." *New York Times*, June 3, 1854.

Johnson, Richard A. *The Mexican Revolution of Ayutla, 1854–1855*. Westport, CT: Greenwood Press, 1974.

"Later from Mexico: Probable Destruction of Santa Anna and His Army." *New York Times*, May 19, 1854.

"Mexico: From Our Own Correspondent." *New York Daily Tribune*, April 19, 1855, 8.

B

As to me, I leave here tomorrow for an unknown destination.

— closing line from Ambrose Bierce's last letter, written from Chihuahua City on December 26, 1913

Bajío

Traditional name for the expanse of flat, fertile farmlands that are enclosed by the mountain ranges of central Mexico and were to be militarily contested for more than a century because of their abundant resources.

Although averaging roughly a mile in elevation, this arable plateau was long ago dubbed the *Bajío* or "Lowland" because of the even greater height of its surrounding mountains. It had proven attractive for settlement as far back as the earliest nomadic tribes, as well as by the first Spanish *conquistadores* who arrived to subdue them and who claimed large *haciendas* or "estates" during the 16th century. By the end of the colonial era, the Bajío was a well-developed agricultural breadbasket, dotted with medium-size cities and roads. It stretched from the city of Aguascalientes in its north to the city of Querétaro in its south, encompassing lower-lying portions of the states of Aguascalientes, Guanajuato, Querétaro, the *Altos* or "Highlands" of Jalisco, and northern Michoacán. During the 20th century, it furthermore came to be bounded by a triangle made up of the country's three major metropolises: Mexico City, Guadalajara, and Monterrey.

Because of its economic and logistical importance, control of the Bajío proved to be a recurrent strategic priority throughout Mexico's many wars—beginning with Miguel Hidalgo's struggle for independence, which erupted in its very heartland in September 1810. Royalist counteroffensives would temporarily reclaim its cities for the Crown, but the Bajío's hamlets and farms and highways would remain under insurgent control. After independence was won, the region would be repeatedly swept by Santa Anna's centralist forces, as well as by liberal and conservative armies marching and countermarching during both the Wars of the Reform and French Intervention, as they contested its bounty. It would be fought over even yet again by Porfirian and various rebel factions during the Mexican Revolution of 1910.

See also: French Intervention, War of the; Hidalgo y Costilla Gallaga, Miguel Gregorio Antonio Ignacio; Independence, War of; Mexican Revolution; Reform, War of the.

Further Reading

Kirkwood, Burton. *The History of Mexico.* Santa Barbara, CA: ABC-CLIO, 2009.

Barradas's Invasion (1829)

Failed attempt by the Spanish monarchy to reconquer its former Mexican viceroyalty by landing a military expedition so as to foment a popular uprising in favor of a return to colonial rule—an unrealistic prospect.

Preliminaries (January–June 1829)

For the seven years since its former colony had broken away and asserted its independence, Madrid had refused to acknowledge this fact, or to even diplomatically recognize Mexico's new republican government. As political, financial, and social chaos gripped the fledgling nation, Ferdinand VII and his ministers came to believe reports that they were receiving from exiles, who assured them that a royal expedition would be welcomed back by many now-disillusioned Mexicans as a means of restoring the peace, stability, and prosperity of viceroyal rule. As a result, secret orders began to be issued as of October 1828 to marshal a small fleet at the royal naval base at Havana, Cuba, in order to transport an armed contingent across the Gulf and disgorge it into Mexico so as to attempt its *reconquista* or "reconquest."

The administration of Pres. Vicente Guerrero began learning of these preparations through newspaper reports from New Orleans in January 1829 and maintained an uneasy watch on the preparations in Cuba. Finally, the veteran Spanish brigadier general Isidro Barradas Valdés reached Havana on June 2, 1829, bearing the king's order (dated April 7, 1829) to proceed with this operation—despite the fears that were thereupon openly expressed by Cuba's captain general, Francisco Dionisio Vives, and other local authorities of being stripped of men, materiel, and resources.

After heated discussions, the Spanish expedition departed Havana on July 5, 1829, consisting of the naval ship of the line *Soberano*, the frigates *Lealtad* ("Loyalty") and *Restauración* ("Restoration"), and two brigs under Adm. Ángel Laborde, escorting 50 small transports bearing the so-called Vanguard Division of the Royal Army that was expected to follow: 3,000 infantrymen of the "Rey Fernando," "Reina Amalia," and "Real Borbón" Battalions, plus 300 dragoons without mounts and 200 artillerymen without guns (it being expected that both horses and artillery could be procured after landing in Mexico). Three days later, this fleet was struck and scattered by a storm in the Bay of Campeche and took almost two weeks to reassemble off Lobos Island before proceeding on to its destination.

Spanish Disembarkation (July 27–September 11, 1829)

The expedition sighted Cape Rojo in the state of Veracruz on July 26, 1829, and its 3,500 troops began coming ashore the next day at Santander Beach, the landing being completed by the afternoon of July 28, 1829. The first actual clash occurred three days afterward at La Aguada, and again on August 1, 1829, while Barradas's invaders were attempting to traverse Corchos Pass, after which they skirted the burning, abandoned fortress at La Barra before occupying Tampico without resistance on August 6, 1829. Two days previously, Brig. Gen. Antonio López de Santa Anna had landed farther south at Tuxpan with the first 1,000 men of a 3,750-troop counterexpedition from Veracruz, proceeding northwestward on foot. Tampico's small garrison meanwhile withdrew northward into the village of Altamira, where it was joined on August 8, 1829, by another 1,800 Mexican soldiers under Gen. Felipe de la Garza.

Learning of this latter concentration, Barradas left his subordinate, Col. José Miguel Salomón, to hold Tampico with a small garrison, while advancing a week later against De la Garza with his main body. The Mexicans braced to receive the Spaniards at Altamira, being reinforced from Matamoros on August 15, 1829, by another contingent under Gen. Manuel Rafael Simón de Mier y Terán. Nevertheless, after only a brief exchange of long-range fire two days later, the defenders abandoned Altamira to Barradas.

Having meanwhile circled around the Pánuco River, Santa Anna joined Mier y Terán and De la Garza by August 20, 1829, then slipped a detachment across by boat that same night to attack Salomón the next dawn within Tampico. He was unable to carry the town by storm though, so retired toward Pueblo Viejo once Barradas returned to rescue his subordinate. Still, the Spanish incursion had been checked, and after a further buildup of Mexican strength, action resumed.

On September 3, 1829, Col. Carlos Beneski captured a Spanish schooner offshore; four days later, Mier y Terán advanced from recently reinforced Altamira with 1,000 men and three fieldpieces to the Hacienda Doña Cecilia and Carpintero Lagoon to block the last remaining road inland. On September 8, 1829, Santa Anna sent a demand for unconditional surrender to Barradas, who responded with a request for free passage to evacuate his increasingly sickly army from Tampico. Santa Anna refused, and both sides prepared the next day for battle, although such a heavy tropical storm arose that same afternoon of September 9, 1829, that both camps were swamped and the Pánuco River overflowed its banks.

Even though it was still raining on the morning of September 10, 1829, and many Mexican militiamen had deserted, Santa Anna sent in a 1,000-man assault column that same afternoon under Lt. Col. Pedro Lemus, who vainly tried to fight their way up the slippery, muddy slopes and carry the Spanish strongpoint. Yet despite having

held off these attackers, Spanish colonel Salomón and Lt. Col. Fulgencio Salas requested terms by 3:00 p.m. on September 11, 1829, which were agreed to and signed in Santa Anna's headquarters at Pueblo Viejo. The Mexicans had suffered 127 killed and 191 wounded during their prolonged assaults, compared to 102 Spaniards slain and 66 injured.

Aftermath (September 12–20, 1829)

Barradas and Santa Anna ratified this agreement, after which the Spanish brigadier departed for New Orleans on September 13, 1829, to hire vessels and buy provisions for his men. His 1,800 demoralized survivors would be allowed to reembark and sail away on condition that they never again took up arms against the Mexican republic. Santa Anna sent a detailed report on September 14, 1829 to President Guerrero, who received it six days later while attending a play in Mexico City, amid much applause.

In retaliation for this invasion, the Mexican government would later commission Gen. José Ignacio Basadre to travel to Haiti and recruit black guerrillas to infiltrate Cuba in hopes of fomenting a slave revolt against Spanish rule, while Madrid would commence preparations for another, even larger expedition to reconquer Mexico by late 1829, but this project was set aside when the monarchy in neighboring France was deposed that following summer.

See also: Santa Anna, Antonio López de.

Further Reading

Frasquet, Ivana. "Milicianos y soldados: la problemática social mexicana en la invasión de 1829." In *Las ciudades y la guerra, 1750–1898*, edited by Salvador Broseta Perales, 115–32. Castelló de la Plana: Universitat Jaume, 2002.

Langrod, Witold. "The Ups and Downs of Charles Beneski: An Attempt to Reconstruct a Distant Life History." *Polish Review* 26, no. 2 (1981): 64–75.

Sims, Harold. *The Expulsion of Mexico's Spaniards, 1821–1836.* Pittsburgh, PA: University of Pittsburgh Press, 1990.

Barranca Seca, Battle of (1862)

Republican setback in the immediate aftermath following their Cinco de Mayo victory at Puebla, early during the War of the French Intervention, which would swing the strategic balance back in favor of the foreign invaders and their Mexican conservative collaborators.

French Retirement toward Orizaba (May 8–18, 1862)

Having been defeated in their initial attempt to storm the city of Puebla on May 5, 1862, the invasion force under Maj. Gen. Charles, Comte de Lorencez recuperated for two days atop the nearby Amalucan heights, still hoping to be reinforced from distant Izúcar de Matamoros by their Mexican allies. However, when no conservative help had appeared by the third morning, Lorencez began leading his battered 6,000-man army east toward Orizaba at 2:00 p.m. on May 8, 1862, trailed with some difficulty by the ill-supplied 7,500-man *Ejército de Oriente* or "Eastern Army" under Puebla's victorious republican defender, Brig. Gen. Ignacio Zaragoza. (Annoyed by the lack of support that he had received from inhabitants of that conservative city upon exiting in pursuit of the French, Zaragoza would angrily note on May 9, 1862: "How good it would be to burn Puebla!")

The French Army retreated slowly over roads that were soon waterlogged by heavy rains, hampered by their 300 wounded from that battle plus many other soldiers who were falling sick. Zaragoza chose to rest his own weary and hungry column for a few days around San Andrés Chalchicomula, in anticipation of being joined by the Zacatecas Division under Brig. Gen. Jesús González Ortega. But when Lorencez's army also encamped for the night of May 17, 1862, at the Hacienda de Tecamalucan, the French commander was surprised to receive a visit at 5:00 p.m. that same evening from the Mexican conservative general Leonardo Márquez, who informed him that his reinforcements were at last nearby. Márquez had brought 2,500 riders from Izúcar de Matamoros, covering 100 miles in four days of hard travel in hopes of joining the French column.

Battle of Barranca Seca (May 18, 1862)

Márquez had left these 2,500 cavalrymen resting for the night at the Rancho El Potrero under his second-in-command, Gen. José Domingo Herrán. Heartened, the French resumed their retreat the next morning, May 18, 1862, expecting to regain the safety of Orizaba by that same afternoon. When about halfway there, Lorencez detached from his column the French 99th Line Regiment under Col. Edmond-Aimable l'Hérillier to wait at El Ingenio de Nogales with two field howitzers, acting both as a rearguard for his own army as well as to cover the conservatives' arrival and amalgamation into the French Army, if the need should arise.

And indeed, Zaragoza had already learned of the proximity of these reinforcements; so his republican subordinate, Gen. Santiago Tapia, raced on ahead from Acultzingo with 662 cavalrymen, reaching the stone bridge at the lonely rural crossroads of Barranca Seca by 10:00 a.m. that same morning of May 18, 1862, deploying into a battle formation so as to impede the conservatives from crossing over and reaching the French, who were already headed on their final stage into Orizaba.

Since advance elements of Herrán's straggling column of 2,500 riders were already descending out of the Acultzingo Heights into this valley near the Hacienda of Tecamalucan, Tapia sent an urgent message to Zaragoza, requesting liberal infantry support. Receiving this missive at his Cañada de Ixtapa field headquarters around noon on May 18, 1862, Zaragoza hastened five companies on ahead of his main army as reinforcements: 1,190 light-infantrymen under the liberal republican colonel José Mariano Rojo. They did not arrive at Barranca Seca until around 5:00 p.m. but immediately attacked in two columns with a cavalry squadron screening their right flank.

However, while thus engaged, the republicans were suddenly surprised by two relief columns of the 2nd Battalion of the French 99th Line Regiment, who had marched 12 miles in three hours from El Ingenio de Nogales to rescue Márquez's men. The 99th promptly drove into Tapia's left, killing 100 republicans, wounding 200, and capturing 600. Allied casualties totaled 214 men, among them only 2 French dead and 26 injured. The French would therefore record this victory as the *bataille d'Aculcingo* and accord the 99th the distinction of a Cross of the Legion of Honor for having captured an enemy standard—allegedly a Mexican flag that liberal forces had captured almost two years previously from Miguel Miramón's conservative army at the Battle of Silao.

See also: Cinco de Mayo, Battle of the; French Intervention, War of the; Márquez Araujo, Leonardo; Silao, Battle of; Zaragoza Seguín, Ignacio.

Further Reading

Cambre, Manuel. *La guerra de Tres Años: apuntes para la historia de la Reforma.* Guadalajara, Jalisco: Gobierno del Estado, 1949.

Chartrand, René. *The Mexican Adventure, 1861–67.* Oxford: Osprey, 1994.

Sánchez Lamego, Miguel A. "El combate de Barranca Seca." *Historia Mexicana* 14, no. 3 (January–March 1965): 469–87.

Bazaine, François Achille (1811–1888)

Foreign Legion general noted for his bravery who would further distinguish himself and be promoted to marshal during the War of the French Intervention in Mexico.

He was born at 9, boulevard de l'Impératrice (modern 33, boulevard de la Reine)

The fearless François Achille Bazaine, who had risen from the ranks as a private in the French Foreign Legion to become a general. (Library of Congress)

in Versailles on February 13, 1811, the third illegitimate child and second son from an unsanctified union between the young Napoleonic engineer Pierre-Dominique Bazaine and a former linen maid and seamstress named Marie-Madeleine "Mélanie" Vasseur. Shortly before the infant Achille's birth, his father had been sent by the emperor to help establish an engineering institute for Czar Alexander I in Russia.

However, when Napoleon subsequently invaded that country the next summer, Pierre-Dominique Bazaine was interned by the Russians in Siberia, and payment of his salary ceased. Achille's mother was consequently compelled to reveal her children's existence to the remainder of the family at Metz, to a lukewarm reception. Young François was given a modest education at the Bardet Institution and the Collège Saint-Louis before failing to pass the entrance exam into the École polytechnique at the age of 19, so he instead enlisted as a fusilier private in the 37th Line Infantry Regiment at Auxonne on March 28, 1831.

Early Military Career (1831–1861)

Within a year, Bazaine had been promoted to sergeant and transferred with that rank in August 1832 into the recently created *Légion Étrangère* or "Foreign Legion," which at that time was still only a single regiment of ill-equipped and expendable non-French soldiers who were being used to fight the unglamorous colonial pacification campaign in North Africa. Bazaine fit in well among these outcasts, as well as proving to be remarkably brave and cool under fire, and so was promoted from sergeant major to *sous-lieutenant* or "sublieutenant" as of November 2, 1833. After being wounded while fighting in the bloody Battle of Macta in June 1835, he was promoted to full lieutenant as of July 22, 1835, and

awarded a Knight's Cross in the *Légion d'honneur.*

Five days afterward, the entire 4,000-man French Foreign Legion was loaned out to fight in Spain for Queen Isabel II, so Bazaine would spend the next three years campaigning in Iberia. He rejoined the French 4th Light Infantry Regiment in 1838 and was promoted to captain in the Legion again as of October 20, 1839, campaigning with distinction in Algiers and becoming fluent in Arabic. His service culminated with the rank of colonel of the 1st Foreign Legion Regiment as of February 4, 1851, stationed at its headquarters in Sidi bel Abès.

At 41 years of age, while on leave in Versailles, Bazaine married the Spanish-born María Juana de la Soledad Tormo of Murcia on June 12, 1852. He led two Legion regiments during the Crimean campaign of 1854, being appointed military governor of Sebastopol on September 10, 1855, and promoted to major general. After a brief stint in command of the 19th Military Division at Bourges upon his return to France, Bazaine received command of the 3rd Infantry Division for the Italian campaign, remaining stationed in that country for a further year after the conclusion of those hostilities.

Service in Mexico (1862–1867)

Bazaine did not participate in the first French expedition sent to Mexico, which was defeated at the Battle of the Cinco de Mayo outside of Puebla and driven back into Orizaba. Instead, on July 1, 1862, he was given command of the 1st Infantry Division of the 23,000-man second expedition under Gen. Elie Frédéric Forey and arrived in Mexico during its disembarkation and deployment that same autumn. It was recorded that as early as November 7, 1862, the republican general Ignacio de la

Llave had abandoned the Fortress of Perote at the approach of Bazaine's probing division, who brushed aside the few Mexican irregulars who remained roaming outside its defenses under republican Gen. Aurelio Rivera.

Bazaine would distinguish himself during the subsequent two-month siege of Puebla, most particularly when Forey was informed on May 5, 1863, that the disperse republican formations of Maj. Gen. Ignacio Comonfort's *Ejército del Centro* or "Army of the Center"—which had been observing the French siege operations from a safe distance—were concentrating for a relief attempt. Hoping to slip supplies into the city's exhausted garrison, Comonfort's 6,000 men advanced in three divisions onto the surrounding plains, pausing about 25 miles southeast of Puebla. When nothing more occurred by the evening of May 7, 1863, Forey ordered Bazaine to take four select battalions of French infantry from the 51st Line Regiment, 3rd Zouaves, and *Tirailleurs algériens*; four cavalry squadrons from the 2nd Regiment de Marche; and eight fieldpieces, on a nocturnal march to surprise Comonfort's army the next dawn.

Departing the French camps via the road leading toward Mexico City between 1:00 and 2:00 a.m. on May 8, 1863, Bazaine moved swiftly but silently through the night, before veering right and coming within sight of the encamped republican army at 5:00 a.m. Comonfort had installed his 1st Division under Gen. Ignacio Echegaray at the hamlet of San Lorenzo Almecatla, his 2nd Division under Gen. Ángel Trías Álvarez at nearby Panzacola, and his 3rd Division under Gen. Plácido Vega Daza at Santo Toribio. The French were already less than a mile away when the republicans spotted them in the early morning light, Echegaray's 1st Division hastily standing to their guns and opening fire.

Behind covering fire from his own field-pieces, Bazaine's infantry double-timed into action at San Lorenzo, breaking the overmatched 1st Division, which after a brave stand reeled back toward Panzacola. Trías's 2nd Division was also mauled there, after which Vega's 3rd Division was directed to cover the retreat of both shattered formations toward the city of Tlaxcala. Márquez descended from San Juan Hill with some of his conservative troops to complete Comonfort's rout.

Bazaine reported leaving some 800–900 dead or wounded republicans on the battlefield, as he immediately returned toward Puebla (having ordered his own personal field tent set up and left behind at San Lorenzo, so as to provide some shelter for the republican wounded until they could be rescued). French losses totaled only 11 dead and 89 injured during this clash, thanks largely to the element of surprise and their superior weaponry. Returning into base camp, Bazaine presented Forey with more than 1,000 prisoners, along with eight guns, three flags, and the entire supply train that had been intended to relieve Puebla's republican garrison The next day, Forey had many of these prisoners released into the city so as to provide convincing proof of Comonfort's defeat, hastening the despairing garrison's surrender by May 17, 1863.

Bazaine departed Puebla nine days later with Castagny's brigade, some light infantry, and a body of conservative cavalry to seize the vital bridges leading toward Mexico City, meeting with such negligible republican opposition that his vanguard even continued as far as Ayutla by June 1, 1863, causing President Benito Juárez and his government to abandon their capital and flee northward. Forey's main army followed Bazaine's vanguard and paraded triumphantly into Mexico City by June 10, 1863, creating an interim government five days later which would soon offer the title of "Emperor of Mexico" to the Archduke Maximilian of Austria, as planned. Meanwhile, Bazaine was rewarded from France on July 2, 1863 with the title of Knight Grand Cross in the Legion of Honor for his victory at San Lorenzo.

And as a reward for Forey, he was promoted to field marshal on October 1, 1863, and ordered home to France, being succeeded as commander-in-chief of the expeditionary force in Mexico by Bazaine. The latter's promotion was greeted favorably by the French occupation troops, Bazaine having risen from the ranks and being very popular among his soldiers. He subsequently directed their campaigns in securing much of the Mexican interior aided by their conservative allies, personally entering the city of Guadalajara at the head of one such combined army on January 6, 1864.

Bazaine bluntly dealt with the issue of the ex-dictator Santa Anna returning from eight years of exile in Colombia, when he arrived at Veracruz aboard a British vessel on February 27, 1864. Initially, Bazaine allowed the ex-President ashore after extracting a loyalty oath to the new conservative regime and a promise not to take part in any political activity, but Santa Anna almost immediately began issuing calls to his adherents through the *Indicador* newspaper, so that Bazaine promptly had him deported aboard the French corvette *Colbert*.

That same month of March 1864, Bazaine also directed the conservative Mexican general and former president Miguel Miramón to serve under a French colonel at Guadalajara, removing him from command when he refused and bundling him off to study military science in Europe. Bazaine's

efforts thus cleared the way for a smooth coronation of Maximilian as Mexico's new Emperor in June 1864, for which he received his marshal's baton from France on October 7, 1864. That same winter Bazaine descended into the state of Oaxaca to personally assume command over the 4,000 infantrymen and 1,000 troopers closing in upon its capital as of January 17, 1865, directing a siege operation that caused its republican garrison under Gen. Porfirio Díaz to surrender by February 8, 1865, being marched off wholesale into captivity.

Bazaine's 35-year-old Spanish-born wife having died of pleurisy at Croisy sur Seine on October 17, 1863, the 54-year-old General became engaged to the 17-year-old Mexican beauty Maria Josefa Pedraza de la Peña y Barragán on May 28, 1865, ignoring complaints from conservative allies because her family were prominent liberal supporters. The Emperor bestowed Buena Vista Palace upon the married couple and continued to shower Bazaine with honors. Yet despite ordering increasingly severe measures against republican guerrillas, the French commanding General could not stamp out resistance against the imperial regime, especially in the arid northern and western states where campaigning conditions were extremely difficult.

The conclusion of the American Civil War in April 1865 further complicated matters, as Washington began exerting intense diplomatic pressure on Paris to remove the large French army from along its southern borderlands, while furnishing large amounts of arms and supplies to their republican opponents. With military victory no longer possible and disapproval growing in France, Napoleon finally issued a public statement on January 22, 1866, declaring the intervention in Mexico a success, while dispatching a delegation to inform Maximilian that

French troop withdrawals would have to be accelerated.

Bazaine would be criticized at home for prolonging this retirement, taking his time in reassembling all French forces for evacuating Mexico in accordance with his instructions, so as to give the emperor a few months' grace to stabilize his regime. Nonetheless, most of the French line regiments had been gathered around Mexico City by December 28, 1866, and Bazaine finally hauled down his colors and marched the last of his 27,000 troops down toward Veracruz on February 5, 1867, setting sail for France by March 12th. Without Bazaine's troops, Maximilian was doomed, being quickly besieged, captured, and executed at Querétaro.

See also: French Foreign Legion in Mexico; French Intervention, War of the; Oaxaca, French Siege of.

Further Reading

Chartrand, René. *The Mexican Adventure, 1861–67.* Oxford: Osprey, 1994. "Correspondence between Gens. Bazaine and Santa Anna." *New York Times*, March 27, 1864.

Dabbs, Jack A. *The French Army in Mexico, 1861–1867: A Study in Military Government.* The Hague: Mouton, 1963.

García, Genaro. *El sitio de Puebla en 1863, según los archivos de d. Ignacio Comonfort.* Mexico City: Viuda de C. Bouret, 1909.

La Bédollière, Émile de. *Histoire de la guerre du Mexique 1861 à 1866.* Paris: Georges Barba, 1866.

Montbarbut Du Plessis, Jean-Marie. *L'armée de Napoléon III au Mexique, 1862–1867.* Paris: Éditions Nouvelles, 2009.

Bierce, Ambrose Gwinett (1842–1914)

Noted American man of letters who vanished while visiting revolutionary Mexico—presumably killed and buried unnoticed amid its chaotic violence.

He was born on June 24, 1842, at Horse Cave Creek in Meigs County, Ohio, to Marcus Aurelius and Laura Sherwood Bierce, a poor but literary couple who imbued him with a lifelong love of books and writing. He was the 10th of 13 children, who were all given names beginning with the letter "A": Abigail, Amelia, Ann, Addison, Aurelius, Augustus, Almeda, Andrew, Albert, Ambrose, Arthur, Adelia, and Aurelia. Details about Ambrose's childhood remain sketchy, but he was known to have left the family home at age 15 to work as a "printer's devil" for a small abolitionist newspaper in Indiana. He also lived for a spell with his uncle, Lucius Verus, in Ohio (a man who would supply John Brown with some of the weapons used in his failed slave uprising at Harper's Ferry), then attended the Kentucky Military Institute for a year before dropping out.

Civil War Service (1861–1866)

Ambrose worked a few odd jobs until the outbreak of the American Civil War in April 1861 when he enlisted in the 9th Indiana Volunteer Infantry Regiment. He participated that same spring in the Western Virginia campaign, was present at the so-called first battle at Philippi, and received some newspaper coverage for his daring rescue under fire of a badly wounded comrade at the Battle of Rich Mountain in July 1861. Because of his great literacy and intellectual capabilities, 19-year-old Ambrose also came to be commissioned as a first lieutenant in February 1862, serving as a topographical engineer on the staff of Gen. William B. Hazen. The young officer furthermore fought in the Battle of Shiloh that same April 1862, a terrifying experience that he would later use as source material for several short stories and a memoir.

Bierce was disappointed when his engagement to his childhood sweetheart, Bernice "Fatima" Wright, was broken off. He then sustained a serious head wound at the Battle of Kennesaw Mountain in June 1864, spending the rest of that summer on furlough before he could return to active duty by September 1864. He was officially discharged from the U.S. Army in January 1865 with the brevet or temporary rank of major, and after the conclusion of the Civil War a few months later, he worked for the Treasury Department in the postbellum South for almost another year. Disgusted by Reconstruction's blatant corruption, he would rejoin his former commander, Hazen, in mid-1866 to take part in an inspection tour of U.S. military outposts across the Great Plains. This expedition departed from Omaha, Nebraska, proceeding by horseback and wagons until they arrived toward year's end in California.

Journalistic and Literary Career (1867–1913)

Disappointed at still being only a second lieutenant in the regular U.S. Army, Bierce resigned his commission to take a job in 1867 at the mint in San Francisco. Toward the end of the next year, the 26-year-old also began writing a part-time column for one of its local newspapers and quickly showed a real talent for journalism. Acidic, cynical, and literate, Bierce soon won great local fame and a growing national notoriety, so by 1871 he was able to court and wed Mary Ellen "Mollie" Day, a socialite from one of the best families in San Francisco. A wedding gift took them to live in England the next year, where Bierce continued writing while his first two children were born: sons Day in 1872 and Leigh two years afterward.

Early in 1875, Mollie returned to San Francisco with their young family, Bierce following reluctantly later that same year, arriving just before the birth of their third child, a daughter named Helen. He continued writing as a newspaper columnist, interrupted by a brief interlude during 1879–1880 when he ventured to Rockerville and Deadwood in the Dakota Territory to act as manager for the New York–owned Black Hills Placer Mining Company. When this operation folded, Bierce returned to San Francisco and resumed work as a columnist. In 1887, he joined the *San Francisco Examiner* newspaper of William Randolph Hearst.

Although professionally successful, Bierce's personal life was marred by tragedy as he separated from his wife in 1888 after finding "improper" letters addressed to her from a European admirer, and the next year their 17-year-old son, Day—his pride and joy—died of a gunshot. His columns subsequently became even more biting and his behavior more prickly, earning him the nickname of "Bitter Bierce," although his prose remained as popular as ever. Bierce was one of the few journalists brave enough to oppose the railroad interests that controlled the politics of that day.

When Collis P. Huntington directed a U.S. congressman to quietly introduce a bill that would excuse the Union Pacific and Central Pacific companies from having to repay the $130 million they had been loaned to build the Transcontinental Railroad, Hearst dispatched Bierce to Washington in January 1896 to foil this swindle. With national coverage in the *Examiner* and *New York Journal*, Bierce was able to expose this scheme and get the bill killed. An angry Huntington reportedly confronted Bierce on the steps of the U.S. Capitol and asked him to name his price, to which Bierce replied:

My price is one hundred thirty million dollars. If, when you are ready to pay, I happen to be out of town, you may hand it over to my friend, the Treasurer of the United States.

His later years were filled with writing, although Bierce's son Leigh died of pneumonia related to alcoholism in 1901 and his wife, Mollie, finally filed for divorce on the grounds of "abandonment" three years afterward, dying before these proceedings could be finalized in 1905. Late in life, the 71-year-old Bierce—suffering from asthma and his old war wounds—departed his Washington, D.C., home in October 1913 to make a tour of the old Civil War battlefields of his youth. By December of that same year, he had passed through Louisiana and was into West Texas, where he learned that Pancho Villa's revolutionary army had recently seized the border town of Ciudad Juárez opposite El Paso and was preparing to do battle against a federal force rushing north from Chihuahua City to confront these rebels.

Disappearance in Mexico (Late December 1913)

Like other curiosity seekers, Bierce was able to obtain passage across the loosely guarded border at El Paso and travel about 10 miles south of Ciudad Juárez to witness Villa's victory over the *federales* and their *colorado* auxiliaries at the Battle of Tierra Blanca in late November 1913. With their main army defeated, the surviving federal forces in that state subsequently abandoned Chihuahua City, offering no resistance when Villa pushed south to occupy it on December 8, 1913.

It seems certain that Bierce must have accompanied Villa's army as far as Chihuahua City, as the last known communication from him, dated December 26, 1913, referred to the departures of several revolutionary troop trains under Villa's subordinate Pánfilo Natera to begin offensive operations against the surviving federals who had taken refuge in the border town of Ojinaga (opposite Presidio, Texas). Yet Bierce was never heard from again, presumably having died unnoticed and his body being disposed of in an unmarked grave amid the lawless chaos of the Revolution. His worried daughter, Helen, soon petitioned the U.S. government for help in locating her famous father, but no trace of Bierce was ever found. He had simply vanished, fueling many fanciful theories as to his true fate.

See also: Ojinaga, Battle of; Tierra Blanca, Battle of; Villa, Pancho.

Further Reading
Fuentes, Carlos. *The Old Gringo*. New York: Noonday Press, 1997.
Morris, Roy. *Ambrose Bierce: Alone in Bad Company*. New York: Oxford University Press, 1999.

blusas

Word that translated literally means "blouses" or "tunics," yet during the mid-19th century was applied as a nickname to the militiamen of the so-called *Ejército del Norte* or Army of the North, irregulars fighting on behalf of the liberal states of Nuevo León and Coahuila.

This nickname had arisen from the simple fact that this army's sketchy, state-issued "uniforms" consisted merely of red tunics with matching hatbands, plus a general directive to all troopers to tuck their trousers into their boot tops—such a casual, unmilitary style of dress that these riders were often looked down on as amateurs (or bandits) by officers of the regular Mexican Army. For example, after Col. Juan Zuazua had overwhelmed the 800-man regular garrison holding the city of Zacatecas with a surprise descent by 2,000 of his mounted *blusas* on April 27, 1858, the defeated general Antonio Manero wrote complainingly to his captor:

> Mr. Zuazua:
>
> I protest against the defeats suffered by the "Restorer of Guarantees" Army [the conservatives' name for their army during the War of the Reform] at Puerto de Carretas and Zacatecas, because your troops do not go into battle in columns, but rather dispersed, crawling on the ground and jumping around; I protest, because in moments of danger, they do not maintain the requisite circumspection and moderation, but rather to the contrary, give off shouts and whoops in a Comanche style; and lastly I protest, because their method of subduing opponents with clubs is very indecent and against regulations.

See also: Ahualulco de los Pinos, Battle of; Puerto de Carretas, Battle of; Zuazua Esparza, Juan Nepomuceno.

Further Reading

García, Luis Alberto. *Guerra y frontera: el Ejército del Norte entre 1855 y 1858*. Monterrey: Fondo Editorial y Archivo General del Estado de Nuevo León, 2006.

"Mexico: A Peculiar People." *New York Times*, October 5, 1858.

boina

Generic Spanish word for "beret," a type of headgear that became widely adopted by the Mexican Army during the last few decades of the 20th century.

Paratroopers traditionally wear red or *carmesí*-colored berets, while elite units such as the Presidential Guards or Special Forces wear black berets. Occasionally, berets of different colors have been worn by certain units on special ceremonial occasions or parades, although these unique *boinas* do not constitute part of their standard dress uniform.

See also: *blusas*.

Further Reading

Hefter, Joseph. *Crónica del traje militar en México, del siglo XVI al XX*. Mexico City: Artes de México, 1968.

Borrego Hill, Battle of (1862)

Failure of Mexico's republican armies, in the wake of their Cinco de Mayo victory, to dislodge the defeated French expeditionary force that was recuperating in Orizaba.

After stealing up on Lorencez's army in two columns, Zaragoza and González Ortega arrived outside Orizaba on June 13, 1862, the latter quietly occupying *Cerro del Borrego* or "Sheep Hill" overlooking the suburban hamlet of Tlalchichilco. Learning of this deployment, the French commander sent a 150-man company under the recently promoted captain Paul Alexandre Détrie of the 99th Line Regt to reconnoiter. Détrie ascended this height before sunup on June 14th and discovered sleeping sentinels from the 4th Zacatecas Battalion.

A skirmish thereupon erupted, after which a second 99th company under Captain Leclerc joined this nocturnal clash. Despite heavily outnumbering their opponents, the raw Mexican troops fired wildly on each other in the darkness, suffering 250 casualties and 200 captured, an even greater number deserting during the subsequent retreat. French losses totaled 7 killed and 28 wounded. At dawn, Lorencez skirmished with Zaragoza's main body outside La Angostura Gate leading into Orizaba, prompting the latter to withdraw his entire army toward El Retiro.

See also: Barranca Seca, Battle of; González Ortega, José Canuto de Jesús; Zaragoza Seguín, Ignacio.

Further Reading

Chartrand, René. *The Mexican Adventure, 1861–67*. Oxford: Osprey, 1994.

Buatachive, Campaign of (1886)

Major operation marking the renewal of the Yaqui Wars under the Porfirian regime conducted by several army columns that converged to assault a fortified native stronghold high in the mountains of northwestern Mexico.

Historical Background (1821–1884)

Since colonial times, the seminomadic tribes of this stark mountainous region had resisted assimilation, so only a few Mexican settlements had ever been established along the coasts of the Sea of Cortés or Gulf of California. An uneasy truce prevailed for many decades between the Mexican residents of these coastal pockets and various inland tribes, occasionally flaring into open warfare as different bands fought against one another or resisted territorial encroachments, during which they often attacked each other's allies as well. Fierce warriors who spoke Tarahumara, they were feared by the Mexicans, just as the natives in turn mistrusted and resented the coastal strangers' incomprehensible demands and designs.

As Mexico began to modernize and prosper during the last quarter of the 19th century under Pres. Porfirio Díaz, unscrupulous local developers tried to expand their claims inland by selling titles to agricultural properties on apparently unused native lands—which the developers had had legally reclassified before compliant Mexican courts as *tierra baldía* or "empty wasteland." The affected Yaqui nomad bands challenged these incursions into their traditional territory, refusing to sign away their rights as various treaties were presented to them by Sonoran officials and thus remaining a threat to the scattered farms and settlements that were being sold and cleared ever farther inland from the coast.

Renewed Hostilities (January 1885–April 1886)

In late January 1885, elements within the Sonoran state government secretly provided boats to transport a raiding party led by Loreto Molina upriver from Guaymas to make a surprise attack against the ranch of his bitter rival, the "captain general for the Yaqui and Mayo Indians," José María Leyva—who was more commonly known by his native name of "Cajeme." But since this chieftain happened to be absent, the attackers instead beat his family, looted and torched his house, and carried away several captives, prompting a furious Cajeme to declare war against these rival tribesmen and, after discovering and seizing the Guayman boats that had transported them on their murderous mission, holding those for ransom.

As scattered Yaqui bands began to rally at Cajeme's summons to war, reports of depredations and violence soon began to multiply with Mexican settlers fleeing back into the coastal towns. Gen. Col. Bonifacio Topete sallied from Hermosillo with 50 cavalry troopers and 80 infantrymen on February 23, 1885, to protect a group of civilians who had fortified themselves within the Hacienda de la Misa. Five days later, the Ministry of War in Mexico City ordered reinforcements sent into the troubled theater, while the state authorities began raising large numbers of militiamen and hiring mercenaries.

An expedition totaling 2,200 men—1,400 federal troops and 800 state militiamen—was assembled and divided into two columns, one advancing under Brig. Gen. José Guillermo Carbó on May 1, 1885, the other under Topete. While the former remained patrolling around Guaymas, the latter penetrated into the Sierra Madre range until checked by a Yaqui mountain fortress named El Añil near Vicam, Sonora. Despite bombarding its moat, stakes, and palisades with a small fieldpiece, Topete was unable to carry this stronghold, having to retire by July 1885 because of the onset of torrid summer weather.

Then Carbó died unexpectedly from a stroke at Hermosillo on October 30, 1885, being temporarily succeeded in command of the 1st Military Zone by Gen. Marcos Carrillo. The latter agreed to allow a peace delegation to meet in early December 1885 with Yaqui and Mayo spokesmen at Pótam, but they could not reach a written accord with the suspicious Cajeme. Several months of patrols and pursuits failed to quell the widespread Yaqui unrest, so the Mexican Army's veteran general Ángel Martínez arrived at Álamos in January 1886 with orders from the ministry to assume command over all forces in Sonora and Sinaloa and to pacify the Mayo before penetrating into the Yaqui heartland. Having completed the first part of his instructions, Martínez then marshaled some 3,700 troops in four columns for his campaign to pacify the Yaqui:

- Brig. Gen. Marcos Carrillo near the mouth of the Yaqui River with 1,200 soldiers
- Gen. Diego M. Guerra with 300 troopers and the 11th Infantry Regiment at Buenavista
- Gen. José T. Otero advancing out of Navojoa with another 1,300–1,400 men
- Martínez's own smaller force moving in from Álamos

Guerra's detachment was the first to advance into hostile territory, capturing Cócorit against token resistance on April 26, 1886, where Martínez and Carrillo arrived two days afterward.

Assault on El Añil (May 5, 1886)

Then at 4:00 p.m. on May 2, 1886, Carrillo's column resumed its push from Cócorit up the right bank of the Yaqui River, resting at Teracoba before reaching a river bend the next afternoon atop which sat the fortified Yaqui stronghold of El Añil, held by Cajeme with some 800 warriors. Martínez overtook Carrillo's column and ordered a reconnaissance made of this stronghold's defenses on May 4, 1886, after which the Mexican troops the next day began cutting swathes through the trees obstructing the approaches to El Añil's earthen ramparts, which were further palisaded with heavy timber.

Suddenly Cajeme sallied from El Añil with about 600 men at 3:00 p.m. on this same May 5, 1886, only to be repelled by gunfire from a skirmish line of soldiers from the Sonora Militia Battalion, who were guarding the tree-cutting efforts. Having beaten off this sortie, Carrillo ordered a probe of El Añil's parapet as that afternoon began to wane and discovered that the Yaquis had silently retired out of its far side, leaving their fort empty except for 14 bodies left inside. Mexican casualties totaled 7 wounded.

Martínez immediately dispatched two cavalry columns to trail the escaping Yaquis at 6:00 p.m. that same May 5, 1886. The column of Col. Juan Hernández took the left bank of the Yaqui River and was obliged to turn back the next day; but the second column of 5th Cavalry Regiment troopers and the 1st Álamos Militia Squadron under Col. Lorenzo Torres got as far as Omteme Pass, from where this officer requested reinforcements on May 6, 1886, to probe the nearby Bacatete range into which the natives had disappeared. Having since been joined at El Añil by Otero's force, Martínez sent him on ahead that same day to occupy the town of Tórim with the 12th Battalion under Lt. Col. Gonzalo del Valle and two companies of the Sonora Battalion under Col. Francisco Miranda y Castro, while General Martínez followed with his main body and they all reunited at that town on May 7, 1886.

That same afternoon, Martínez directed Otero to take 350 infantrymen and 25 troopers to probe a small earth fortification named Chumampaco erected by the Yaqui on the left bank of the river leading toward Vícam. Its 200 defenders retired into the hills rather than resist, although the Mexican commander learned from a prisoner who could speak a bit of Spanish that Cajeme was ensconced 10 miles farther north with 4,000 tribesmen in an impregnable stronghold named Buatachive.

Battle of Buatachive (May 11, 1886)

Martínez struggled on and finally approached that sprawling camp with his 1,400 troops on May 11, 1886, finding its three-and-a-half-mile perimeter protected by a system of trenches and stone walls. That night, however, Col. Lorenzo Torres was able to lead 300 Mexican soldiers to the heights above Buatachive, and when Martínez saw Torres's company becoming engaged the next dawn, he attacked at various other points with his own main army divided into four assault columns supported by artillery. The Yaqui were defeated, suffering 100–200 dead and more than 2,000 noncombatants captured, while Cajeme escaped even deeper into the mountains with a band of survivors.

Mexican casualties from this campaign totaled 21 dead and 48 wounded, and the prisoners were marched back to the coast, eventually being paroled against promises of their good behavior. Future operations would quickly grow more ruthless, though, with wholesale massacres of poorly armed warriors and the deportation of any survivors to Yucatán as slaves.

Aftermath (June 1886–May 1887)

Less than six weeks later, Colonel Torres encountered Cajeme once again on June 22, 1886, at Guichamoco Beach, leading 1,500 warriors across open country for an intended surprise attack against Gen. Juan Hernández's garrison at nearby Médano in hopes of gaining some desperately needed weapons. Torres charged and easily scattered this poorly armed host, killing 62 and effectively bringing an end to organized Yaqui resistance under Cajeme.

Almost 10 months later, the chief himself was arrested—living under an assumed name in Guaymas—on April 12, 1887, and taken aboard the steam frigate *Demócrata* to be sailed up the Yaqui River and publicly executed at Cócorit 13 days afterward. His second-in-command, Antonio Cuca, was furthermore extradited the next month from Tucson, Arizona, to share this same fate.

See also: Yaqui War.

Further Reading

"A Butchery: The Mexican Victory over Chief Cajeme and the Yaquis." *Daily Alta California* 40, no. 13,424, May 29, 1886, 5.

Hernández, Fortunato. *Las razas indígenas de Sonora y la guerra del Yaqui*. Mexico City: Elizalde, 1902.

Troncoso, Francisco de Paula. *Las guerras con las tribus yaqui y mayo del Estado de Sonora*. Mexico City: Departamento de Estado Mayor, 1905.

Buena Vista, Battle of (1847)

Decisive defeat suffered by Santa Anna against the U.S. invaders of northern Mexico, leaving Zachary Taylor in uncontested occupation of that region for the remainder of the Mexican-American War.

Background (January 1847)

After Taylor had seized the northern cities of Monterrey and Saltillo during the opening phase of this conflict, a recently restored Pres. Antonio López de Santa Anna spent the next few months massing his main strength at the central city of San Luis Potosí for a major counteroffensive. In mid-January 1847, he learned through intercepted intelligence that his opponent's army was being reduced in numbers to help constitute a new expedition under Gen. Winfield Scott, which was to be transported down the Gulf coast and disembarked at Veracruz for a thrust inland toward Mexico City.

Hoping to surprise Taylor's diminished force with a quick strike in the window of opportunity before Scott's expedition could land and pose a strategic threat, Santa Anna issued orders for his 20,000-man army to begin breaking camp around San Luis Potosí on January 28, 1847, so as to march northward—in four divisions at one-day intervals—through the harsh desert landscape. They were to rendezvous south of Saltillo at the village of Encarnación, but a

The Battle of Buena Vista, known in Mexico as La Angostura or "The Narrows," as the outnumbered U.S. Army was able to defeat Santa Anna's superior numbers because of their concentrated position at this chokepoint on February 22–23, 1847. (Library of Congress)

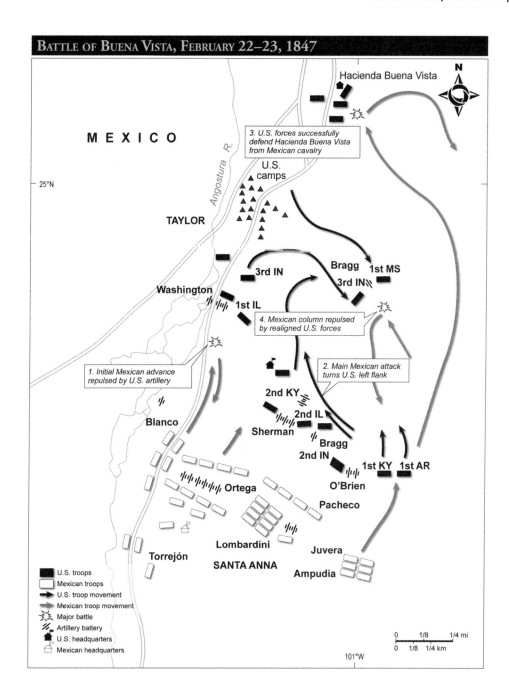

BATTLE OF BUENA VISTA, FEBRUARY 22–23, 1847

Hacienda Buena Vista

N

MEXICO

Angostura R.

25°N

U.S.
camps

3. U.S. forces successfully
defend Hacienda Buena Vista
from Mexican cavalry

TAYLOR

Bragg   1st MS

3rd IN

3rd IN

Washington

1st IL

4. Mexican column repulsed
by realigned U.S. forces

1. Initial Mexican advance
repulsed by U.S. artillery

2. Main Mexican attack
turns U.S. left flank

2nd KY

2nd IL

Blanco

Sherman

Bragg

2nd IN

1st KY   1st AR

Ortega

O'Brien

Pacheco

Lombardini

Juvera

Torrejón

SANTA ANNA

Ampudia

■ U.S. troops
□ Mexican troops
➡ U.S. troop movement
➡ Mexican troop movement
✺ Major battle
⚔ Artillery battery
🏠 U.S. headquarters
⌂ Mexican headquarters

| 0 | 1/8 | 1/4 mi |
| 0 | 1/8 | 1/4 km |

101°W

few thousand Mexican troops would drop out from fatigue and deprivation during this grueling trek, so only 14,000 effectives would participate in the forthcoming battle.

Battle of La Angostura or Buena Vista (February 22–23, 1847)

On February 21, 1847, an unsuspecting Taylor was encamped with 4,800 troops in an advanced position at Agua Nueva, Coahuila, when he was suddenly informed by his scouts of Santa Anna's arrival at nearby Encarnación with thousands of soldiers after a grueling march from San Luis Potosí. While Taylor quickly visited Saltillo to ensure that Santa Anna had not slipped around behind him, Wool dug in, facing southward down the San Luis Potosí road with almost 3,000 infantrymen, 1,450 cavalrymen, and 267 gunners for 18 fieldpieces.

Shortly after sunrise on February 22, 1847, Santa Anna's 14,000 troops and 17 guns appeared, and the Mexican commander-in-chief sent a surrender demand on ahead at 11:00 a.m. under a flag of truce. Taylor, who had just returned from Saltillo, rejected it. Around noon, Ampudia's light-infantry brigade and Juvera's cavalry were detached to occupy the high ground east of the plateau, prompting the American commander to send two cavalry regiments and a battalion of infantry to contest this flanking maneuver. After an indecisive firefight, these Americans withdrew at nightfall, the only other action being a long-range exchange between Blanco's lead Mexican division and Taylor's main battle line.

Early the next morning, February 23, 1847, the Mexicans resumed the action, Blanco being repulsed by Washington's battery and the 1st Illinois. However, Ampudia and Juvera repelled a second attempt by Yell's Arkansas and Marshall's Kentucky cavalry to gain the eastern high ground, after which Pacheco's division hit Bowles's 2nd Indiana, sending it reeling back out of Wool's line. By the time Taylor returned from Saltillo around 9:00 a.m., the situation had grown precarious, although it was soon rectified when the 1st Mississippi and 3rd Indiana plugged the hole.

As in previous encounters, the American horse-drawn artillery proved too much for the attackers, repeatedly smashing any threatened Mexican breakthroughs. Taylor's army was compressed by the attackers' pressure, yet did not break, while Santa Anna had a horse shot out from under him. A flanking maneuver by Pacheco's division was intercepted atop a ridge at 1:00 p.m. by the Mississippians, 3rd Indiana, and Bragg's artillery, resulting in heavy Mexican losses. By nightfall, the Americans had suffered 267 killed, 456 wounded, and 1,500 deserters but still held the field. They were further encouraged by the arrival of Brig. Gen. Thomas Marshall's and Col. George W. Morgan's two fresh regiments from Saltillo.

The Mexicans, in contrast, had had enough, having endured 1,800 dead or injured and another 300 captured. After conferring with his staff that evening, Santa Anna ordered a stealthy retreat toward Agua Nueva, so the Americans awakened on the morning of February 24, 1847, to find the plain overlooked by their positions virtually empty. Satisfied with his hard-won victory, Taylor retired northeast shortly thereafter into Monterrey, allowing Santa Anna to limp away.

See also: flying artillery; *rancho*.

Further Reading

Salisbury, Richard V. "Kentuckians at the Battle of Buena Vista." *Filson Club History Quarterly* 61, no. 1 (1987): 34–53.

Tucker, Spencer C. *The Encyclopedia of the Mexican-American War*. Santa Barbara, CA: ABC-CLIO, 2013.

C

What [Texians] desire is what I and all Federalists desire, that is the Constitution of 1824, and that we should not be governed either by friars or aristocrats.

— Gen. José Antonio Mexía, northern opponent of Santa Anna's conservative regime, December 1835

Cabañas Barrientos, Lucio (1938–1974)

Leftist guerrilla leader who was hunted down and killed by the Mexican Army.

Birth and Politicization (1938–1967)

He was born on December 12, 1938, in the hamlet of El Porvenir in the municipality of Atoyac de Álvarez in the coastal state of Guerrero. His grandfather had served under Emiliano Zapata during the Revolution, and several members of the family were politically inclined. Shortly after enrolling in the Preparatoria Normal at Ayotzinapa in February 1956, the 18-year-old Lucio had himself become embroiled in student politics and joined the Communist Party's youth organization. He then met the older Genaro Vázquez through the activist *Asociación Cívica Guerrerense* or "Civic Association of Guerrero" and upon graduating in 1964 with a teacher's certificate was assigned to the rural school at Mexcaltepec, barely six miles from Atoyac.

After assisting the natives of Mexcaltepec to reassert their logging rights over the adjoining forests, Cabañas was briefly reassigned to a school in the distant state of Durango in 1965 before being returned to Atoyac. Continuing his political activities, he helped organize a political rally in Atoyac's main square on May 18, 1967, which was broken up with considerable gunfire by the state judicial police, resulting in deaths and injuries.

Guerrilla Campaigner (1967–1973)

Now wanted by the authorities, Cabañas fled into the mountains and lived as a fugitive but was supported by his friends and soon proved popular among the region's impoverished rural peasants as well, coming from a similar background and having their interests genuinely at heart. He formed his *Partido de los Pobres* or "Party of the Poor" that same year of 1967 and later added a *Brigada de Ajusticiamiento* or "Rough-Justice Brigade"—armed followers who would intervene against official brutality or corruption. At his peak, it is estimated that Cabañas commanded about 350 guerrillas.

Within a couple of years, his activities were proving too much for local authorities or the state police, so Cabañas came to the attention of the army officers responsible for the *27a. Zona Militar* or "27th Military Zone," who also tried in vain to capture him. Having escalated his depredations to include bank and payroll robberies as well as kidnappings of wealthy victims, Cabañas had gained such notoriety by 1971 that the newly inaugurated president, Luis Echeverría Álvarez, secretly authorized his secretary of defense, Gen. Hermenegildo Cuenca Díaz, to implement a stepped-up military operation code-named *Telaraña* or "Cobweb" to run him down. Yet despite deploying at least 3,100 soldiers into a front-line base at El Ticui and providing three helicopters operated by the federal police to assist, they failed to find their quarry.

Emboldened, Cabañas and 20 guerrilla companions ambushed a Mexican Army convoy one year later at Arroyo Las Piñas near San Andrés de la Cruz, Guerrero, killing 10 soldiers and wounding 18 on June 25, 1972. This attack, coupled with a second ambush at nearby Arroyo Oscuro on August 23, 1972, that left 18 more soldiers dead, 9 wounded, and 11 captured, goaded the army into a series of increasingly brutal reprisals throughout the region. Convinced that Cabañas's band must number at least 150 active members at any given time, the authorities deployed five fresh infantry battalions as well as thousands of state policemen, in another vain effort to capture him.

The next year, faced with increased hostility from Cabañas's growing guerrilla movement throughout the Atoyac range, the Mexican Army began pushing in columns to relieve its isolated garrisons. On November 11, 1973, one such 300-man convoy was ambushed and suffered 4 soldiers killed between the hamlets of Yerbasantita and Las Compuertas, so the authorities replied yet again by launching *Operación Luciérnaga* or "Operation Firefly," which involved sending a trio of heavily armed, mobile columns in a sweep through this remote district. But Cabañas merely shifted from one jungle camp to another with his followers, so after a week of fleeting

skirmishes, the army wound down this fruitless chase.

Last Strike (June–October 1974)

The guerrilla leader's final act began after three days of secret negotiations between Cabañas and the senator (soon to be elected governor) for the state of Guerrero, Rubén Figueroa Figueroa, which concluded with him abruptly seizing this guest on June 2, 1974, and holding the senator for ransom. This sparked more massive military sweeps and roundups throughout the region, which once again failed to corner Cabañas or his 60 fighters, so Gen. Salvador Rangel Medina was relieved of command as of August 5, 1974, and replaced by Gen. Eliseo Jiménez Ruiz. A ransom of 50 million *pesos* was eventually paid for the captive Figueroa, although 60 elite troops under Lt. Col. Juan López Ruiz then intercepted his guerrilla guards as they approached El Huicón to release the senator on September 8, 1974, killing three and scattering the remainder.

With his hostage freed and Cabañas's location more precisely known, the manhunt by 5,000 Mexican troops intensified until the guerrilla leader and 14 of his companions were surprised shortly after noon on October 11, 1974, near Los Toronjos in the Tecpan range. Making his escape over Achotla Mountain after nightfall, Cabañas was left with only 4 followers. Even his mother, wife, and three-week-old daughter were captured two weeks afterward at Tixtla by an army detachment.

Eventually, Mexican troops of the 19th Battalion under Capt. Pedro Bravo Torres—guided by a captive—overtook Cabañas's small fugitive band near El Ototal, 12 miles northwest of Tecpan de Galeana, at 9:00 a.m. on December 2, 1974. After a firefight during which two soldiers were slain and five wounded, Cabañas killed himself rather than surrender, virtually ending all revolutionary activity in the mountains of Guerrero.

See also: *Telaraña, Operación.*

Further Reading

Bartra, Armando. *Guerrero bronco: campesinos, ciudadanos y guerrilleros en la Costa Grande.* Mexico City: Era, 200.

Montemayor, Carlos. *Guerra en el paraíso.* Mexico City: Seix Barral, 2008.

Suárez, Luis. *Lucio Cabañas: el guerrillero sin esperanza.* Mexico City: Grijalbo, 1976.

caja

Generic word in the Spanish language for any kind of "box" but that in military parlance is used as the nickname for a drum.

For example, when the wounded captain Manuel María Giménez witnessed Santa Anna's impending counterattack against the French disembarkation at Veracruz on the morning of December 5, 1838, he later described it as follows:

> At eleven a.m., we saw coming from the direction of La Carnicería, a force of about 200 men with low-slung arms, led by General Santa Anna; shortly before reaching the gate into the docks, they formed up by companies, shouldered arms, and their *cajas*—which until then had been tapping a low *sordina*—beat out double-time.

Charging through the gate, Santa Anna and his men were still wheeling into firing position when a blast of grapeshot from a French boat gun killed nine of the Mexican soldiers and blew off Santa Anna's lower-left leg.

Further Reading

Giménez, Manuel María. *Memorias.* Mexico City, 1863, 70.

Hefter, Joseph. *Crónica del traje militar en México, del siglo XVI al XX.* Mexico City: Artes de México, 1968.

Cakes, War of the (1838–1839)

Mocking name given in 19th-century Mexico to a punitive French expedition that blockaded and attacked Veracruz in an effort to extort compensation for commercial losses suffered by its citizens.

**Historical Background
(September 1837–March 1838)**

In the chaotic decades immediately following Mexico's independence from Spain, foreign traders and investors often complained to their home governments about losses suffered due to the many insurrections, military coups, and lawlessness that plagued the young republic. France consequently sent Antoine-Louis, Baron Deffaudis, to Mexico City as a special plenipotentiary in September 1837 to demand compensation for the sacking of French businesses and forced loans extorted from French merchants during the latest disturbances. The Mexican government rejected such claims, arguing that it lay beyond the scope of any nation to protect foreign visitors from the vicissitudes that even its own citizenry must endure.

Unsatisfied, Deffaudis quit these talks on January 1, 1838, and 15 days later took ship from Veracruz, returning by March 21, 1838—with 10 French warships. Anchoring off Sacrificios Island, he sent an ultimatum ashore from its flagship *Herminie*, demanding 600,000 *pesos'* compensation for a long list of wrongs. (When this note was

Crude lithograph depicting the French capture of the offshore Castle of San Juan de Ulúa after its bombardment by the squadron of Vice-Admiral Baudin, November 1838. (DeAgostini/Getty Images)

delivered in Mexico City, popular opinion erroneously believed it to include a claim for pastries taken by Santa Anna's troops in 1832 from the French-owned "Remontel" Restaurant in Tacubaya, so the subsequent hostilities would become derisively known among Mexicans as the *Guerra de los Pasteles* or the "War of the Cakes.")

French Blockade (April–October 1838)

The allotted time period for satisfaction having elapsed on April 15, 1838, the French squadron the next day imposed a limited naval blockade on Veracruz, restricting entry for many items in order to deprive the Mexican government of revenues. The 53-year-old rear admiral Charles Baudin was sent out from France to assume command over this operation, while other nations also dispatched men-of-war to look after their own nationals' interests.

After six months' blockade, Admiral Baudin set another communication ashore

at Veracruz on October 21, 1838, which led to a face-to-face meeting with the Mexican foreign minister, Luis G. Cuevas, at the inland town of Jalapa on November 17, 1838—who was willing to concede most points—yet the French admiral then demanded an additional 200,000 *pesos* to compensate the French government for its expeditionary costs, which Cuevas refused, so Baudin departed back toward Veracruz at 5:00 a.m. on November 21, 1838.

Bombardment of San Juan de Ulúa (November 27, 1838)

Six days later at 9:00 a.m., the Mexican officers Valle and Díaz Mirón boarded Baudin's flagship *Néréide* with a last-minute offer from Minister Cuevas to renew negotiations, only to have the French admiral dismiss this proposal five-and-a-half hours later. Five minutes afterward—while Valle and Díaz Mirón were still being rowed ashore—the frigates *Néréide*, *Iphigénie*, *Gloire*, corvette

Créole, and bombs *Cyclope* and *Vulcain* opened fire on Veracruz's 153-gun, 1,186-man harbor castle of San Juan de Ulúa, using the newly developed Paixhans explosive shells.

This exchange persisted until 6:00 p.m. when the bombardment slackened and finally ceased at nightfall two hours later, after garrison commander Antonio Gaona had requested a truce so as to attend to his wounded. During the course of that afternoon's exchange of salvoes, the French squadron had suffered a mere 4 killed and 39 injured; San Juan de Ulúa, in comparison, had endured 224 casualties and 20 dismounted guns.

Overnight, the French informed Gaona that his fortress would be leveled the next day if he did not surrender. After consulting with Gen. Manuel Rincón in Veracruz at 3:30 a.m. on November 28, 1838, the garrison commander agreed to capitulate at eight o'clock the next morning, at the same time surrendering a corvette, two sloops, and three brigs that were moored beneath San Juan de Ulúa's walls. By midday of that same day, the French were in possession of the fortress, while Rincón—with the intervention of the disgraced ex-president and general Antonio López de Santa Anna, who had arrived from his nearby Manga de Clavo Hacienda—agreed to a cessation of hostilities. Baudin's vessels were to be allowed to refresh their provisions ashore, French citizens were promised some measure of compensation, and the blockade was to be lifted for eight months so as to allow for a diplomatic resolution to each nation's grievances.

Mexican Declaration of War (November 30, 1838)

When news of Rincón's and Gaona's capitulation reached Mexico City on November 30, 1838, an infuriated government ordered both officers arrested and their agreement voided, then took a vote that declared that a state of war existed against France. Santa Anna was informed of this rejection on the night of December 3, 1838, and given command over the 700–800 soldiers remaining in that port city (out of a nominal garrison of 1,353 men) with orders to resist the French invaders. The next morning, he informed Baudin of this rejection of the truce, and both leaders agreed to refrain from a resumption of hostilities until 8:00 a.m. on December 5, 1838.

That same night, the 36-year-old general Mariano Arista entered Veracruz, having ridden ahead of an 871-man relief column that he had left encamped seven to eight miles away at Santa Fe so as to consult with Santa Anna. The latter ordered Arista's contingent to plan on advancing on Veracruz's outlying town of Los Pocitos by dawn before both commanders turned in at 2:00 a.m. A few hours later, they were awakened by gunfire, as Baudin swept down on Veracruz's waterfront in a three-pronged assault. Boatloads of French marines and sailors occupied the Santiago and Concepción Bastions at the city's southeastern and northwestern corners, spiking their few guns, while other French forces advanced from the wharf into the city's main square.

Santa Anna narrowly escaped from his headquarters at the corner of Coliseo and Damas Streets, but Arista was taken, surrendering his sword to the prince of Joinville. Baudin then besieged Veracruz's garrison within their fortress-like barracks in La Merced Square, vainly firing on its doors with the small artillery pieces that he had brought along in a bid to gain entry. After an hour of fruitless exchanges though, the French decided to retreat, hoisting a white flag to call for a truce, which the Mexicans refused to honor.

Baudin managed to fight his way back to the wharf with his wounded by 10:00 a.m., beginning his reembarkation. Santa Anna arrived on the scene an hour later with 200 men that he had hastily formed up into a company, only to receive a blast from a French boat gun covering the beach, which killed nine of his men and blew off Santa Anna's left leg below the knee as well as a finger from his right hand. Baudin, having suffered 8 men killed and 60 wounded during his foray ashore, retired to his warships and continued bombarding Veracruz for another two hours, while the Mexicans retreated out of their devastated city that afternoon to take up safer positions in the dunes beyond.

Diplomatic Settlement (December 1838–March 1839)

With passions at last beginning to cool on both sides after this bloodletting, Baudin two weeks later dismissed part of his blockading squadron from outside Veracruz on December 16, 1838, and six days afterward the British ambassador, Richard Pakenham, arrived to help mediate an ending to this extended Franco-Mexican dispute. He was reinforced by the appearance offshore of a Royal Navy squadron under Vice Adm. Sir Charles Paget on December 26, 1839, consisting of:

- The 74-gun flagship *Cornwallis* of Capt. Sir Richard Grant and *Edinburgh* under William Honyman Henderson
- The 46-gun frigate *Madagascar* of Provo William Perry Wallis, 36-gun *Pique* of Edward Boxer, 28-gun *Andromache* of Robert Lambert Baynes, and 26-gun *Vestal* of Thomas Wren Carter
- The 18-gun sloop *Rover* of Cmdr. Thomas Matthew Charles Symonds,

Modeste of Harry Eyres, and *Racehorse* of Henry William Craufurd
- The 16-gun sloops *Snake* of Alexander Milne and *Ringdove* of acting Cmdr. Keith Stewart

After consulting for a few days with Baudin, the British furthermore agreed to withdraw part of their own squadron from the anchorage so as to leave its numbers on a par with the remaining French force.

Pakenham then departed inland toward Mexico City on January 8, 1839, eventually arranging a meeting between Baudin and the Mexican delegates Manuel Eduardo de Gorostiza and Guadalupe Victoria for March 7, 1839. Two days after that, the Mexican and French representatives signed a peace treaty whereby the former agreed to pay the original 600,000-*peso* compensation while the latter restored San Juan de Ulúa to Mexican control, and the War of the Cakes drew to a close. One of its unexpected consequences was that Santa Anna's personal prestige was greatly restored on account of his painful maiming in the line of duty, leading to his return to power a few years later.

See also: Santa Anna, Antonio López de.

Further Reading

Aquino Sánchez, Faustino A. *Intervención francesa, 1838–1839: la diplomacia mexicana y el imperialismo del librecambio.* Mexico City: INAH, 1997.

"Blockade of the Mexican Ports." *Niles' National Register* 54, no. 1,389 (May 12, 1838): 163–64.

Calderón Bridge, Battle of (1811)

Lopsided royalist victory that marked a final end to Miguel Hidalgo's initial uprising against viceregal rule.

Preliminary Deployments
(January 12–16, 1811)

On January 12, 1811, Hidalgo had learned while reassembling a second vast throng of insurgent followers around the city of Guadalajara that Calleja's main monarchist army—after its own six-week respite following their victory at Aculco, recapture of Guanajuato, and restoration of Crown rule throughout the central highlands—was now advancing on the rebel host, having already reached nearby San Juan de los Lagos. Over the objections of his second-in-command, Allende, Hidalgo decided to sortie away from Guadalajara two days later so as to offer battle 20 miles farther to its east, near the village of Zapotlanejo—specifically, from atop the heights looking down on the 200-foot-long, 17th-century stone *Puente de Calderón* or "Calderón's Bridge" over the Colorado River, a naturally defensible position.

Despite having twice been defeated in the field by smaller, yet better-disciplined royalist forces, Hidalgo ordered this position fortified and reached it himself with many of his followers by January 15, 1811. Allende arrived the next day with his own forces, bringing total insurgent strength to 35,000 men (although only 1,200 were actually armed with muskets), plus a few fieldpieces.

Battle of Puente de Calderón
(January 17, 1811)

On January 17, 1811, Calleja's 14,000 royalists began a series of assaults against these rebel positions, suffering considerable losses before an insurgent grenade accidentally detonated one of their own ammunition wagons, creating widespread panic among the defenders' ranks. The monarchists took advantage of this confusion by launching a heavy cavalry charge. Despite sustaining 3,000 casualties and being driven from the field after six hours of fighting, Hidalgo and Allende retired in good order. Calleja, on the other hand—despite having had only 400 men killed or wounded—was slow to pursue, not occupying Guadalajara until four days later. Still, his victory proved a serious reverse for the insurgency and would earn him ennoblement with the title of conde de Calderón.

See also: Allende, Ignacio de; Calleja del Rey, Félix María; Hidalgo y Costilla Gallaga, Miguel Gregorio Antonio Ignacio; Independence, War of; Monte de las Cruces, Battle of.

Further Reading

Guzmán, Moisés. "Miguel Hidalgo y la artillería insurgente." *Revista Ciencia [Academia Mexicana de Ciencias]* LXI, no. 3 (July–September 2010): 30–39.

Meyer, Jean A. *Los tambores de Calderón.* Mexico City: Editorial Diana, 1993.

Calleja del Rey, Félix María
(1753–1828)

Veteran Spanish officer who defeated Miguel Hidalgo's initial insurrection against colonial rule and was rewarded with the office of viceroy, although he subsequently proved incapable of stifling Mexico's drive toward independence.

Birth and Services in New Spain
(1753–1809)

He was born on November 11, 1753, at Medina del Campo in the province of Valladolid, Spain, the son of Juan Cayetano Calleja and Eugenia Severina del Rey. Enrolled as a cadet in the Saboya Infantry Regiment at 20 years of age, he served two years later in the disastrous expedition against Algiers and then participated in the siege of Gibraltar and siege of Minorca. A full captain by 1784, he was appointed director of the Military College at the Puerto de Santa María until it closed its doors four years later.

Unemployed, Calleja attached himself in 1789 to the train of the second conde de Revillagigedo, who was traveling out to New Spain as its newly appointed viceroy. Calleja had his captain's rank confirmed and served Revillagigedo on numerous military commissions: as an instructor at Puebla, on inspection tours to remote provinces, and most especially in organizing new militia companies in diverse northern provinces. The next viceroy, Marqués de Branciforte, retained Calleja for such work in 1795, dispatching him into Nuevo Santander and Nuevo León.

By 1798, Calleja was a lieutenant colonel when he was appointed to command the 10th Brigade of the Militia Corps, headquartered in the city of San Luis Potosí. His conduct of the expedition northward during the winter of 1800–1801 to hunt for the American interloper Philip Nolan won him promotion to colonel. Now fully settled into Mexican life, the 54-year-old Calleja married the wealthy 21-year-old *criolla* María Francisca de la Gándara y Cardona in San Sebastián Church in San Luis Potosí on January 26, 1807, receiving the Hacienda de Bledos as part of his wife's dowry. When news arrived one year later of Napoleon's invasion of France and detention of its royal family, Calleja was one of the Peninsular Spaniards who gathered in Mexico City to ensure loyalty to the Bourbon monarchy and was an active participant in the removal of Viceroy José de Iturrigaray and substitution by the ultra-loyalist Pedro Garibay.

Savior of the Viceroyalty (1810–1812)

A couple of years later, Calleja first heard rumors of a possible Creole insurrection when he was summoned from San Luis Potosí at 10:30 a.m. on September 19, 1810, to ride some 25 miles into the Valley of San Francisco and learn details from an informant about Hidalgo's planned uprising. The priest had actually already launched his rebellion three days previously at the village of Dolores in the province of Guanajuato, so by the time confirmation of this outbreak reached San Luis Potosí, Calleja was already taking the steps to mobilize his brigade.

As reports of the insurgency's spread poured into San Luis in early October 1810, he furthermore imposed martial law and arrested scores of individuals suspected of possible disloyalty, plus casted a few crude cannon and raised an additional 600 light infantrymen, all the while training his small army on the grounds of the suburban Hacienda de la Pila. Leaving behind a garrison of 700 loyalists under Toribio Cortina, Calleja departed from San Luis Potosí on October 24, 1810, with 3,000 cavalrymen, 600 infantrymen, and four small fieldpieces.

Having traveled only a short distance in this new direction though, his 55,000 remaining followers were sprawled around the rural village of San Jerónimo Aculco when they were suddenly surprised on November 6, 1810, by the arrival at Arroyo Zarco—a mere five miles away—of a 15,000-man royalist force under 55-year-old brigadier general Félix María Calleja del Rey, who had hastened from San Luis Potosí to help relieve the viceregal capital and confront the rebels.

Despite their vast numbers, Hidalgo's following included only some 4,000 ill-equipped provincial militiamen out of a total of roughly 40,000 volunteer fighters with scant battlefield training or experience among them, backed by eight poorly manned fieldpieces. Calleja himself commanded only 2,000 reliable infantry regulars, plus 7,000 mostly untried militia cavalry troopers and a dozen guns, as well as a mixed assortment of loyalist volunteer companies of very dubious military value.

However, the superiority of his core of regular Spanish officers and soldiers allowed Calleja to organize a coordinated thrust in five columns on the morning of November 7, 1810, approaching the green insurgents who were drawn up to await them around Aculco Hill. The opening bombardment by the royalists' guns started around 9:00 a.m. and soon sowed panic among the rebel ranks, which broke and dissolved into wholesale flight within an hour as the royalist columns pressed forward to engage at close range.

Hidalgo fled from the scene of this spiraling disaster with a handful of retainers, traveling via Villa del Carbón toward the distant city of Valladolid (modern Morelia), while his military *teniente general* or "lieutenant general," the Creole militia captain Ignacio de Allende, fell back through Maravatío and Acámbaro toward the city of Guanajuato with a depleted contingent of demoralized stragglers, which he gradually managed to regroup around his flag.

According to the postaction report that Calleja sent from the strewn battlefield to the viceroy, Francisco Javier Venegas, in Mexico City, his royalist army—at a cost of merely 1 dead and 2 wounded—had slain 85 insurgents and wounded another 53, plus seized their 8 guns, 300 muskets, 50 iron cannonballs, 120 cases of gunpowder, 40 of ammunition, 200 horses, 1,300 cattle, 1,600 sheep, and 11 carriages. Calleja resumed his march that very next day—November 8, 1810—

intending to fully disperse the rebels before resting his troops in the city of Querétaro. As he advanced, hundreds more insurgent runaways were captured over the next few days, some being summarily executed along the way by the monarchists.

After resting in Querétaro for about a week, Calleja would resume his pursuit of Allende's shrunken remnants, in the process restoring royal rule throughout central Mexico as he marched. He would take Guanajuato without much of a fight on November 25, 1810, and eventually defeat Hidalgo's main force for good at the Battle of Calderón Bridge early the next year.

Viceroy of New Spain (1813–1816)

When Calleja assumed office on March 4, 1813, he found the royalist regiments dispersed among cities and large towns, some reduced to such desperate financial straits that their men were unpaid, barefoot, starving, and deserting, while guerrilla bands controlled the intervening countryside and made communications uncertain. The treasury was empty and the economy at a standstill, although his predecessor, Venegas, had sailed for Spain aboard the warship *San Pedro de Alcántara* with more than 2 million *pesos* in minted Mexican silver for the distant Crown.

Calleja therefore ordered the scattered royal regiments to forsake garrison duties in peripheral territories in favor of reconcentrating into two main *ejércitos de operaciones* or "operational armies": an Army of the North based in either Querétaro or Guanajuato to restore some measure of stability and trade throughout the vital Bajío region, and an Army of the South stationed at Puebla to recuperate Antequera (modern Oaxaca City) from Morelos and contest his insurgents' hold over much of its adjacent southern provinces.

Despite losing Acapulco shortly thereafter, royalist strength gradually revived, one of Calleja's columns arriving in time to prevent Morelos's capture of Valladolid (modern Morelia) in December 1813 and dispersing his main insurgent following soon after. The city of Antequera or Oaxaca was abandoned by its insurgent occupiers without a fight on March 29, 1814, while Acapulco was recovered for the Crown that very next month, and Morelos was captured and executed by December 1815. Yet notwithstanding these successes, the will for independence remained strong among the Mexican people, to the extent that Calleja even asked that 8,000 Spanish regulars be sent to reinforce his government because of "the difficulty of recruiting in a country, where the great mass of the population are decidedly in favor of the revolution."

By the time Calleja relinquished the office of viceroy to his successor, Adm. Juan Ruiz de Apodaca, on September 19, 1816, he claimed that his three years of pacification efforts had succeeded in restoring communications throughout central Mexico, as well as reviving royalist fortunes and the taxation system—yet the admiral's own trip inland from Veracruz to Mexico City had been a grueling trek as part of a convoy escorted by 1,000 Spanish troops, shadowed and constantly harassed by large formations of insurgent guerrillas. Calleja may have prevented the viceroyalty from being lost outright, but the independence movement remained very much alive.

Last Years in Spain (1818–1828)
Upon returning to Madrid in 1818, Calleja was ennobled as the *conde* or "count" of ̄ ́n, as well as receiving Grand ́n the orders of Isabel la Católica ̄rmenegildo. Next year, he was ̄ptain-General of Andalucia

and Governor of Cadiz, but when named to command the army departing for Spanish America in early 1820, he was imprisoned for three years on Mallorca as a result of the liberal revolt launched by Rafael del Riego. Released in 1823, he was appointed Captain-General of Valencia, dying in that post on July 24, 1828.

See also: Aculco, Battle of; Allende, Ignacio de; Bajío; Calderón Bridge, Battle of; Ejército de Operaciones; Hidalgo y Costilla Gallaga, Miguel Gregorio Antonio Ignacio; Independence, War of.

Further Reading
Archer, Christon I. "Years of Decision: Félix Calleja and the Strategy to End the Revolution of New Spain." In *Birth of Modern Mexico*, edited by Christon I. Archer, 125–49. Wilmington, DE: Scholarly Resources, 2003.

Bustamante, Carlos María de. *Campañas del general D. Félix María Calleja, comandante en jefe del ejército real de operaciones, llamado del Centro.* Mexico City: Imprenta del Águila, 1828.

Calpulalpan, Battle of (1860)

Climactic liberal victory won on the outskirts of Mexico City marking an end to the War of the Reform.

Prelude (Summer–Autumn 1860)
After three years of warfare, the conservative commander-in-chief and "substitute president," Maj. Gen. Miguel Miramón, had raced a liberal army and interrupted its assault against the city of Guadalajara in late May 1860. However, even after drawing off, this liberal army remained so strong that Miramón hesitated to attack when he found it dug in shortly thereafter, while another 10,000-man liberal army under the

Zacatecan general Jesús González Ortega then crushed his 3,000 conservative reinforcements in the state of Aguascalientes, so Miramón hastened out of Jalisco into the Bajío of central Mexico in order to concentrate his dwindling strength for a showdown with this new threat.

But with a rising tide of liberal armies closing in from various directions on his depleted forces at León, Guanajuato, Miramón ordered a retreat southeastward in early August 1860, during which his 3,300 demoralized soldiers, 1,300 militia auxiliaries, and 18 guns were overtaken outside Silao on August 9, 1860, by González Ortega's pursuing 8,000 liberal soldiers and 38 fieldpieces. They pulverized his army in a short, sharp encounter the next morning, Miramón being lucky to escape in the chaos, although losing his entire army and reaching safety with only a handful of riders.

Guadalajara fell by November 3, 1860, so all liberal armies begin closing in on Mexico City for a final confrontation with the conservatives, whose fortunes were clearly faltering. Miramón's administration was by then so bankrupt that it was reduced to extorting or stealing funds from commercial interests so as to mount its defense of the capital. His tactical skill nonetheless allowed Miramón to surprise and capture the liberal generals Santos Degollado and Felipe Berriozábal at Toluca on December 8, 1860, along with more than 1,300 of their men and 12 guns, although other liberal columns still continued to close in regardless.

Battle of Calpulalpan (December 22, 1860)

Soon González Ortega began drawing near to the Valley of Mexico out of the east, bringing a total of 11,000 men and 14 fieldpieces in various detached columns under the command of his liberal brigadiers

Ignacio Zaragoza, Leandro Valle, Nicolás de Régules, and Francisco Alatorre. On the morning of December 19, 1860, Miramón sortied from the capital with 8,000 conservative troops and 30 guns under his brigadiers Leonardo Márquez, Francisco A. Vélez, Miguel Negrete, and Marcelino Cobos, intending to march up and occupy the high ground around the rim of the Valley of Mexico so as to give battle from a ridge overlooking the rolling plains around the village of San Miguel Calpulalpan in the municipality of Jilotepec some 30 miles east of the capital.

By December 21, 1860, the liberal army had assembled in the vicinity of Arroyo Zarco, and Brigadiers Valle and Álvarez even suggested a tactic to González Ortega on the very eve of battle whereby Miramón's main thrust would be drawn down off the heights by a feigned retreat by some liberal units, only to then become engulfed by flanking attacks, allowing the liberals' superior numbers to tell. The commander-in-chief approved, and when Miramón began the action at 8:00 a.m. the next morning, December 22, 1862, by leading a charge down against the liberal left wing and center, these conservatives would be struck on both flanks by Zaragoza and Régules.

While the main conservative assault columns were thus checked, González Ortega sent Valle's and Alatorre's cavalry in a wide circling movement, riding up into the mountains and routing the conservatives at 10:00 a.m. by unexpectedly charging into them from the rear at the head of 1,000 lancers. An eyewitness account of the battle later reported how:

> Márquez on the right, had made an impression on the Liberal lines and had even broken them in some places, and Miramón was pushing on hard for the

center, where Ortega was posted personally, but the left of the Liberals had penetrated the Conservative right, which was opposed to them, and that rendered the fortunes of the day nearly equal. At this critical moment, Ortega changed his front so as to relieve his right from the hot impetuosity of Márquez and bring the weight of his heavy troops upon the enemy's wavering right. The maneuver was a successful one, and at once fixed the fortunes of the day. For a while the enemy showed a brave front, but the frequent gaps made in his lines by our heavy artillery, at point-blank range, soon cooled his ardor and he began his retreat sullenly and slowly at first, but a cavalry brigade being ordered up, helped him to quit the field with greater alacrity, and the steady, orderly retreat soon became a pell-mell breakneck race, each one striving, if possible, to get away with his own life.

The conservatives broke and fled, most of this action having actually been fought around the village of San José Deguedo in the municipality of Soyaniquilpan, although it would go down in history as the Battle of Calpulalpan.

Aftermath (December 23, 1860–January 11, 1861)

A staggered Miramón rode back into Mexico City from this defeat with only Márquez and some 60 riders around midnight on December 22–23, 1860, and spent the next morning entertaining options from his military advisers. Some suggested further resistance, but with only 2,500 outnumbered soldiers of dubious resolve still left under his command and no rescuers marching to his aid, a majority of Miramón's officers convinced him to request terms. The Spanish and French ambassadors, along with the paroled prisoner Berriozábal, left on this commission that very same afternoon of December 23, 1860, and reached González Ortega's headquarters at Tepejí del Río by midnight to ask for his conditions. The liberal general-in-chief replied that he was not empowered to negotiate, so he could offer the conservatives only the choice to either unconditionally surrender or fight it out.

Informed of this stark choice, Miramón and his followers prepared for flight. Looting what little was left in the treasury, he officially delegated control of the capital to his captive Berriozábal as of 9:00 p.m. on Christmas Eve 1860, then departed two hours later into the darkness with about 1,200 men and a few fieldpieces. The first advancing liberal troops appeared in the city streets by 5:00 a.m. on Christmas morning, followed into the unresisting capital by regiment after regiment, González Ortega himself being cheered all the way into the empty Presidential Palace by noon. By 7:00 p.m. on that Christmas Day, December 25, 1860, there were an estimated 10,000 liberal troops resting within Mexico City. Two days afterward, González Ortega used his temporary powers to issue a decree dissolving the *permanente* army regiments that had upheld the conservative cause, deeming this institution to have long been a "sucker fish."

A grand parade was scheduled for New Year's Day 1861, to include even more liberal forces, which continued to arrive, so as many as 30,000 men were to march in celebration of the triumph of the liberal cause—Mexico City being firmly in their hands and no conservative challengers left to contest its ownership. Juárez departed Veracruz on January 5, 1861, and six days later assumed his duties as president in Mexico City, officially marking an end to the conflict.

Miramón was meanwhile secretly whisked down to Veracruz through the intervention of the French ambassador, Alphonse Dubois de Saligny, and set sail for Havana aboard a Spanish warship before the month was out, eventually proceeding into exile in Europe. A few conservative diehards such as Márquez, Cobos, and Mejía withdrew into the hills of Mexico to continue the struggle on behalf of the fugitive conservative president Zuloaga, but their cause seemed essentially lost.

See also: Márquez Araujo, Leonardo; Miramón Tarelo, Miguel Gregorio de la Luz Atenógenes; Reform, War of the; Zuloaga Trillo, Félix María.

Further Reading

"Important from Mexico: Confirmation of the Defeat of Miramón and Occupation of the City of Mexico by the Liberals." *New York Times*, January 14, 1861.

"Letter from Mexico." *Sacramento Daily Union* 20, no. 3075 (February 4, 1861).

"Mexico: The Triumph of the Liberals." *Harper's Weekly*, January 26, 1861, 55.

Camerone, Battle of (1863)

Heroic stand by a heavily outnumbered detachment of Foreign Legionnaires during the War of the French Intervention.

Preliminaries (Autumn 1862– Spring 1863)

Originally, France's *Régiment Étrangèr* or "Foreign Regiment" had not been assigned to the expedition sent to Veracruz in early 1862 under Maj. Gen. Charles, Comte de Lorencez, to help Mexico's conservatives install a puppet monarchy; nor to the second larger expedition that began to depart as reinforcements during the summer and autumn of 1862 under Maj. Gen. Elie Forey after this first expedition had been repulsed at the Battle of the Cinco de Mayo outside of Puebla. But determined to take part in this overseas campaign, the Foreign Legion officers stationed at their Algerian base of Sidi-bel-Abbès convinced their colonel, Pierre Joseph Jeanningros, to petition the war minister, who in turn finally issued the desired orders for the regiment to prepare to deploy.

The five battalions of Legionnaires set sail from Oran aboard the ships *Saint Louis* and *Wagram* on February 9, 1863, arriving off Veracruz by March 25th and disembarking the next day. Shortly after arriving though, Jeanningros and his men were disappointed to learn that they would not be joining Forey's main siege army, which was already deep inland attempting to subdue the city of Puebla but rather were assigned the more mundane duty of protecting the supply route that stretched from Tejería through La Soledad and Chiquihuite as far as the city of Córdoba.

Battle of Camerone (April 30, 1863)

At 1:00 a.m. on April 30, 1863, 34-year-old captain Jean Danjou—his left arm having been blown off 10 years previously by an exploding musket and replaced with a wooden prosthesis—departed the town of Chiquihuite with 61 men of the 3rd Company of the recently arrived 1st French Foreign Legion Battalion to reconnoiter the road leading inland from Paloverde toward the city of Puebla, in advance of a scheduled payroll shipment bound toward the main army.

While breakfasting at 8:00 a.m., Danjou's Legionnaires were surprised by 650 Mexican riders under Col. Francisco de Paula Milán, who had massed undetected at nearby La Joya. They chased Danjou's company into the hamlet of Camarón, where the desperate French fortified themselves one hour later inside its abandoned hacienda. By that same afternoon, another 1,000 Mexican militiamen of the Veracruz, Jalapa, and Córdoba Mounted Infantry Battalions joined Milán and by evening overwhelmed the hacienda's few dozen defenders in a massive assault. Despite repeated calls for their surrender, Danjou's handful fought gallantly to the end, suffering 30 killed and 32 severely wounded, while inflicting heavy casualties.

The next day, Col. Pierre-Jean Joseph Jeannigros reached this site with his main Foreign Legion column and, in honor of such spirited resistance, removed Danjou's wooden arm before his body was buried, which is today preserved as a sacred relic at the Legion's headquarters in Aubagne, France. Every April 30th, the Legion holds its regimental parade on "Camerone Day," Danjou's wooden arm receiving the salute after a recitation of his brave act.

See also: Bazaine, François Achille; French Foreign Legion in Mexico.

Further Reading

Porch, Douglas. *The French Foreign Legion: Complete History of the Legendary Fighting Force.* New York: Harper Perennial, 1992.

Rickards, Colin. *Hand of Captain Danjou: Camerone and the French Foreign Legion in Mexico, 30 April 1863.* Marlborough, Wilshire, England: Crowood Press, 2008.

Ryan, James W. *Camerone: The French Foreign Legion's Greatest Battle.* New York: Praeger, 1996.

campechana

Nineteenth-century Mexican artillerymen's slang expression for a combination of a round shot and a canister shell.

Normally, a canister shell consisted of some 100 musket balls packed inside a tin enclosure and nailed atop a tapered wooden block known as a *sabot*, which was fired at close range as an antipersonnel projectile because it would disintegrate and scatter its contents during flight. However, in his account of the Battle of Silao in August 1860, Col. Jesús Lalanne described how the liberal forces managed to maneuver their guns under cover of a dark, rainy night to within 700 yards of the waiting conservative lines, and "since these pieces were loaded with a mixture which we called *campechana*, which is a can of small-shot atop a round, we waited with great confidence" for the fighting to erupt at dawn because of the devastating effects from this special double-charged combination.

See also: Reform, War of the; Silao, Battle of.

Further Reading

Cambre, Manuel. *La guerra de Tres Años.* Guadalajara, Jalisco: Biblioteca de Autores Jaliscienses, Gobierno del Estado, 1949, 473.

Cananea Strike (1906)

Labor protest by Mexican miners that was promptly put down with military and American intervention.

In the northern state of Sonora, 5,360 Mexican workers went on strike on June 1, 1906, against the policies exercised by the Consolidated Copper Company at their Cananea mining operation, specifically protesting against the higher wages and shorter work hours enjoyed by its 2,200 American employees. While union leaders were meeting with the company managers, some 2,000 strikers marched through the streets of the mining camp, then headed toward the

Col. William C. Greene addressing a crowd of striking miners at Cananea, June 1906. (Library of Congress)

company lumberyard on the mesa above—where most of the Americans worked. The lumberyard manager, George Metcalf, and his brother, William, shut its gates and turned a fire hose on the advancing marchers. Incensed, they charged the gates and gunfire broke out, the Metcalf brothers continuing to fire out of an office window until the building was set ablaze and they were forced out and killed amid the conflagration. Riot ensued in which 23 mostly Mexicans died and another 22 were wounded. The strikers were thereupon chased out of Cananea and into the mountains by armed American riders, yet not before they torched numerous buildings.

The company owner, Col. William C. Greene, requested intervention from the Mexican authorities, who not only dispatched state troops and *rurales* (federal policemen) under Col. Emilio Kosterlitzky but also allowed 400 gun-toting American "volunteers" to enter the country from

nearby Naco (Arizona), greatly offending Mexican sensibilities. Some 50 strikers were subsequently identified and transported into penal servitude on the island fortress of San Juan de Ulúa (Veracruz).

Finally, Kozterlitzky arrived with 75 *rurales* at dusk on June 2, 1906, after having made a hard ride from Magdalena. Immediately, he imposed martial law and his men moved through the town, breaking up crowds by killing several dozen people and hanging seven union leaders. He also ordered Rynning's volunteers to leave Mexico, which they did, taking the 10:00 p.m. train that same night back to Naco.

Federal regulars disgorged from a train the next morning—Sunday, June 3, 1906—and their commander, Gen. Luis E. Torres, addressed a crowd of 2,000 miners, telling them that anyone not back at work on Monday morning would be subject to conscription into the army and sent to fight against the Yaqui Indians. When Greene furthermore announced that he knew which American miners had sympathized with the strikers and would deal with them separately, about 300 left.

Aftermath (1906–1909)

Eight union leaders were arrested two days later, although they would not be brought to trial until July 1908, at which time they were sentenced to 15 years' hard labor in the fetid fortress of San Juan de Ulúa. It would take another year for the unfortunate convicts to be transported to distant Veracruz in August 1909, where they would languish until released by the new Mexican president, Francisco I. Madero, in 1911.

See also: Kosterlitzky, Emilio; *rurales*.

Further Reading

Gonzales, Michael J. "United States Copper Companies, the State, and Labour Conflict in Mexico, 1900–1910." *Journal of Latin American Studies* 26, no. 3 (October 1994): 651–81.

Truett, Samuel. "Transnational Warrior: Emilio Kosterlitzky and the Transformation of the U.S.-Mexico Borderlands." In *Continental Crossroads*, edited by Samuel Truett and Elliott Young, 241–70. Durham, NC: Duke University Press, 2004.

Cangrejos, Marcha de los (1854–1867)

Satirical song whose title translates literally as the "March of the Crabs," originally composed in the mid-19th century by the liberal man of letters Guillermo Prieto to mock the hollow promises of social progress being extended by the conservatives toward the common people.

A lifelong liberal, Prieto was a witty writer who tirelessly published newspaper articles, poems, songs, plays, and books in Mexico City, calling for genuine sociopolitical reforms that would open up better opportunities for the country's lower classes. His "March of the Crabs" appeared around 1854, apparently composed when the Revolution of Ayutla was first erupting against Santa Anna's entrenched and discredited conservative regime, which had not furnished any significant changes or improvements in Mexican society after decades in power. To underscore the lack of hope in continuing to follow their policies, the opening verse and refrain of this catchy tune can be loosely translated as:

> Cassocks and cowls,
> Predominate everywhere,
> Wise men in their high hats,
> Shall make us all happy.
>
> Like crabs following the lead,
> Let's all march backward,
> Zis, zis y zás,
> Let's all march backward.

Los Cangrejos proved instantly popular, being quickly spread throughout the nation by street performers and adopted as an anthem by the advancing liberal armies, who even began alluding to their conservative foes as *cangrejos* or "crabs." And to mark an end of the War of the Reform, it was recorded how Gen. Jesús González Ortega's victorious army had marched into Mexico City in January 1861 behind bands playing this cheerful tune.

Los Cangrejos proved equally popular a few years later in many anti-imperial variants during the War of the French Intervention.

See also: Ayutla, Revolution of; Santa Anna, Antonio López de.

Further Reading

Prieto, Guillermo. *Viajes de orden suprema: años de 1853, 1854 y 1855*. Mexico City: Bibliófilos Mexicanos, 1968.

Sosa, Francisco. *Biografías de mexicanos distinguidos*. Mexico City: Porrúa, 2006.

Carabina 30-30

Name in Spanish for a Winchester rifle, a lightweight sporting and hunting weapon that was to serve as the standard firearm for many rebel soldiers during the earliest phases of the Mexican Revolution.

Background (1894–1909)

This famous rifle was designed in 1894 by John M. Browning for the Winchester Repeating Arms Company of New Haven, Connecticut, and was originally intended to fire a half dozen black-powder cartridges, which would be fed into its chamber one after the other by lever action from an internally encased tube magazine. That following year though, the company had further upgraded this firearm's manufacturing specs by including a superior steel composition so it would be capable of handling higher-pressure smokeless rounds as well, which were to be offered to purchasers in two different cartridge weights.

The .30-30 Winchester or .30WCF (Winchester Centerfire) cartridge quickly became the preferred round, so this particular model of repeating rifle would become universally famous as a Winchester 30-30, Winchester 94, Win 94, or simply as a 30-30—in Mexico, translated into *treinta-treinta*.

Makeshift Revolutionary Firearm (1910–1911)

Eventually manufactured by the millions, when the insurrection against the dictatorship of Pres. Porfirio Díaz erupted in November 1910, many Mexican civilians initially went off to fight against the government forces armed only with their *treinta-treintas* and hand pistols. The professional soldiers in the Federal Army derided such lightweight weaponry, typically used only in peacetime against such nuisance scavengers as coyotes or for hunting game, as being utterly lacking in the penetrating power or range of their heavier military-grade Máusers or machine guns, which fired high-compression rounds with lethal effects on the battlefield. Yet despite being thus badly outgunned, thousands upon thousands of poorly armed rebels would nonetheless risk their lives in fights against better-armed federal soldiers and succeeded in toppling the Porfirian government, albeit at considerable cost.

The first verse of "*Carabina 30-30*," one of the most enduring *corridos* or ballads to emerge from the Mexican Revolution, opened with these melancholy lines:

Carabina 30-30, which the rebels carried,
And which the Maderistas said,
That with those, you could not kill.
Yet with my 30-30 I'm going to fight,
Amid the ranks of the rebellion,
And if asked for my blood, I'll give it,
For the inhabitants of our nation.

Eventually, Álvaro Obregón's well-equipped and disciplined army would use heavy artillery, machine guns, and modern weaponry to annihilate the hordes of irregulars serving under Pancho Villa, bringing an end to any effective participation by such lightly armed soldiery in the Revolution.

See also: *corridos*; Máuser; Mondragón rifle; Obregón Salido, Álvaro; Villa, Pancho.

Further Reading

Fitzsimmons, Bernard. *Illustrated Encyclo-pedia of Weapons and Warfare*. London: Phoebus, 1978.

Hughes, James B., Jr. *Mexican Military Arms: The Cartridge Period, 1866–1967*. Houston, Texas: Deep River Armory, 1968.

Jowett, Philip, and Alejandro de Quesada. *The Mexican Revolution, 1910–20*. Oxford: Osprey, 2006.

Carbonera, Battle of La (1866).

See La Carbonera, Battle of (1866).

Celaya, Battles of (1915)

First two of three smashing victories won by Gen. Álvaro Obregón over his revolutionary rival, Pancho Villa, which—taken together— would break the military power of Villa's División del Norte forever.

Prelude (March 7–April 5, 1915)

After a few months of friction and scattered confrontations between lesser detachments of their widespread armies following the contentious Convention of Aguascalientes, Obregón began gathering his well-organized force of *constitucionalistas* and preparing to challenge Villa's sprawling *convencionista* hordes to a showdown. An Obregonista brigade under Col. Eugenio Martínez advanced out of Mexico City and was attacked on March 7, 1915, near the rural Peón railway station in the state of Querétaro, by three Villista cavalry columns under Generals Agustín Estrada, Canuto Reyes, and Joaquín de la Peña. Despite being outnumbered, Martínez emerged victorious after a hard-fought engagement, and three days later Obregón began departing northward from Tula, Hidalgo, with his own main army—now renamed the *Ejército de Operaciones* or "Operational Army" of the constitutionalist government of Venustiano Carranza—aboard a stream of train convoys, heading into the mountainous central state of Guanajuato to confront Villa.

Reaching the small city of Celaya by April 4, 1915, Obregón soon learned that Villa had hastened south from Torreón to seek battle, his main concentration now only 30 miles farther to the west of Celaya around Irapuato where the Villista forces were rendezvousing at their staging area. The next day, April 5th, Obregón sent a scouting force under Alejo G. González and Alfredo Elizondo to reconnoiter the town of Acámbaro, while a cavalry column under Jesús S. Novoa and Porfirio G. González was dispatched to tear up the San Luis railway tracks at Empalme González. But Villa then abruptly began to close the distance between both armies, departing Salamanca by the morning of April 6, 1915, with 20,000 men and 22 artillery pieces aboard three train columns hurtling across the final 20 miles toward the waiting Obregonistas.

First Battle of Celaya (April 6–7, 1915)

Although Obregón commanded only a total of 6,000 cavalrymen and 5,000 infantrymen, backed by 86 heavy machine guns and 13 cannon under the German immigrant colonel Maximilian Kloss, his compact army was much better disciplined and battle ready than Villa's unwieldy mass. By later that same Tuesday morning of April 6, 1915, advance elements of the huge Villista force were detraining on the plains west of Celaya and preparing to decimate Fortunato Maycotte's 1,800-man brigade, which had been quartered some 10 miles in advance of Obregón's main body at the rural El Guaje railway station.

Realizing that he would soon be heavily outnumbered, Maycotte telegraphed Obregón in Celaya, who instructed his subordinate Manuel Laveaga to begin transferring the 1,500 men of his 1st Brigade aboard an armored train as reinforcements so as to sally and rescue Maycotte. Meanwhile, Obregón recalled his long-range cavalry patrols, then personally boarded Laveaga's train to accompany and supervise the withdrawal back into his lines of both these detachments. His train pulled out of Celaya at noon on April 6, 1915, comprising flatcars with sandbagged machine gun emplacements, gondolas bristling with riflemen, and Brig. Gen. Martín Triana's 700 cavalry troopers riding along beside the track to act as scouts.

Halfway to El Guaje, Obregón's men began to sight retreating constitutionalist cavalrymen who were being pursued by Villistas, so pressed on cautiously. Nearing Maycotte's trapped brigade by around 2:00 p.m. on April 6, 1915, the locomotive engineer repeatedly blew his whistle and Laveaga's men opened up long-range fire, distracting the swarms of Villistas so Maycotte and his survivors could clamber aboard and the train be reversed and run back toward Celaya.

It backed into Celaya's station about two hours later, the troops immediately detraining to run to their positions along a three-mile firing line that Obregón's trusted subordinate, Gen. Benjamín G. Hill, had laid out around the western perimeter of the city. Triana's cavalry brigade meanwhile fought a brief delaying action three miles farther west, at the Crespo station, until the sheer weight of Villa's approaching horde pushed them back: Agustín Estrada leading three full brigades of Villista riders north of the track, while Abel Serratos was bringing another two brigades south of the line, and

Villa himself was advancing in between at the head of four infantry brigades and six batteries under his artillery commander, Gen. Felipe Ángeles.

The "First Battle of Celaya" became fully joined once Villa's advance riders charged headlong into Obregón's battle line shortly after 4:00 p.m. on April 6, 1915, being checked by heavy counterfire and barbed-wire entanglements. Estrada's Villista cavalry brigades nonetheless threatened to overwhelm Obregón's right an hour later until beaten back when he committed his last reserves. By 6:00 p.m., Villa could see that his initial attack had not broken through anywhere, so he ordered a halt to such assaults overnight, intending to make a renewed concerted thrust at dawn (although his ill-disciplined followers continued mounting piecemeal attacks well into the night, pointlessly enduring losses).

Therefore, both armies blazed away at each other in the darkness throughout much of that night, and Obregón was heartened when a couple of thousand of his dispersed cavalrymen managed to rejoin his main body in good order. Villa's 22 artillery pieces opened up a bombardment at 4:00 a.m. on the morning of April 7, 1915, and he tried to use their covering fire to send in four attack columns, each comprising an infantry brigade to clear a path for a cavalry brigade that was following along behind—but the Villista artillery shells proved to be of such low quality that the bombardment was ineffective, even when their guns were moved in so close that Villa noted how "the enemy machine-gun bullets rang on our gun-shields." Repeated waves of attackers were consequently cut down in swathes by Celaya's entrenched defenders until a general assault was attempted by Villa at 9:00 a.m.—resulting only in more deaths, including Estrada and many of his horsemen as they tried to charge across the muddy terrain at heavy machine gun nests.

Realizing by 11:00 a.m. on April 7, 1915—after having withstood some 40 disparate cavalry charges—that Villa had committed and expended his entire strength, Obregón finally countered by sending Maycotte's and Novoa's cavalry brigades at noon on a wide flanking movement to the south, plus González's brigade around to the north, thereby threatening to circle around and close in on Villa's rear. When this move was at last detected by Villa, it proved too late: the double-pincer envelopment collapsed his left wing, and the Villista retirement toward their trains—waiting for them nine miles in the rear—turned into a rout by 2:30 p.m.

Galloping around the battlefield protected by his escort of Dorados, Villa managed to extricate his artillery and assisted in making a fighting retreat through the pursuing Obregonista cavalry, reboarding his train by evening and departing in complete disarray for Salamanca and Irapuato. He left behind 1,800 dead, 3,000 wounded, 500 prisoners, cattle, and heaps of materiel. Obregón's losses totaled 558 killed and 365 injured (313 and 157, respectively, lost during the rescue of Maycotte's trapped contingent at El Guaje).

Obregón thereupon rested his victorious but exhausted troops in Celaya, while calling in fresh formations from Querétaro and Tula to bolster his army's strength now that he had found and come to grips with the main enemy force. His 1st *División de Oriente* or "Eastern Division" furthermore arrived by rail from the state of Veracruz, along with three full cavalry regiments and an infantry battalion, plus fragments of the Gavira, Novoa, and Joaquín Amaro Brigades, and even a couple of "red battalions" of volunteer workers. A large

munitions train under Norzagaray furthermore steamed into Celaya on April 12, 1915, by which time Obregón's total strength had risen to 15,000 well-equipped soldiers, although with his 8,000 cavalrymen remaining carefully hidden farther to its east in a forest. According to one of his biographers, Obregón was content to lie in wait on the defensive, confident that he could count on the "impulsive character of his adversary."

Villa had likewise spent that week feverishly recalling his own contingents so as to hastily rebuild his battered army. Large formations began heading toward Salamanca over the next few days, the mounted brigades of José I. Prieto, José Ruiz, and César Moya reaching the Villista concentration from Nuevo León, while infantry and artillery under Francisco Carrera Torres and Pánfilo Natera traveled by rail from Jalisco, and Villa's brother, Hipólito, sent shipments of arms and ammunition down from the bordertown of Ciudad Juárez. Finally, Villa ordered a mass parade of 30,000 men on Monday, April 12, 1915, and at the next dawn began sending out his infantry and 36 guns aboard trains once again toward Celaya, while his masses of cavalry followed, riding along beside the rails.

Second Battle of Celaya (April 13–15, 1915)

The first Villista troops began disgorging from their trains at 6:00 a.m. that same morning of April 13, 1915, five miles outside Celaya at the rural Crespo station. It took them a couple of hours to form up and limber their artillery batteries before advancing in three columns across the arid landscape toward the city, their smoke and dust columns plainly visible to Obregón, who was watching from his advance observation post atop "La Internacional" factory on the western outskirts of Celaya. Villa deployed his men more prudently for this second confrontation, his artillery stopping to take up firing positions about two-and-a-half miles from the defenders' outer lines behind a screen of his foot soldiers.

It was not until 5:00 p.m. that Tuesday afternoon that the first Villista companies moved within range (approximately 400 yards) of the constitutionalist trenches, a brief exchange of gunfire erupting against elements of Obregón's 1st Infantry Brigade before dying off and giving way to a much heavier round of generalized rifle and artillery fire an hour later. By 9:00 p.m., more than seven miles of the defenders' lines were fully engaged by Villa's regiments, who had circled around and surrounded Celaya's entire perimeter, looking for any weak points. Around midnight, fierce fighting erupted at the city bridge leading in from the Apaseo highway, but its constitutionalist defenders succeeded in beating back this assault with heavy losses.

All day on April 14, 1915, Villa's field commanders launched furious attacks against selected spots along Obregón's lines, suffering many casualties due to the flat and open terrain, which left their troops exposed to murderous counterfire from machine gun nests and entrenched riflemen whenever they broke cover. At 1:00 p.m., Villa even tried phoning from his field headquarters at the Hacienda de Trojes to speak with Obregón, but the latter ordered his subaltern to simply give him "a brief and energetic reply, which must have disconcerted the bandit."

Cavalry charges proved especially costly to the Villistas, so as the day wore on, the attackers' morale began to wane. Then suddenly at dawn on Thursday, April 15, 1915, Obregón surprised Villa's exhausted army by launching a massive prearranged cavalry movement to the north with Gen. Cesáreo Castro's division, prompting Villa's weary followers to break and flee westward by that same nightfall, leaving behind another 4,000 dead, 5,000 wounded, 6,000 prisoners, 1,000 fully saddled horses, and all their artillery. Obregón, in comparison, had lost only 138 officers and soldiers killed, plus another 276 wounded.

Aftermath (May–June 1915)

Within days, Obregón would resume his pursuit of Villa, pressing northwestward to inflict another heavy defeat on the Villistas at the Battle of Trinidad in May–June 1915, destroying any further military threat from the shattered División del Norte. These two decisive battles at Celaya are often referred to jointly to this day as the *combates de Celaya*.

See also: División del Norte; Dorados; Ejército de Operaciones; Madsen light machine gun; Obregón Salido, Álvaro; Trinidad, Battle of; Villa, Pancho.

Further Reading

Gilliam, Ronald R. "Turning Point of the Mexican Revolution." *MHQ: The Quarterly Journal of Military History* 15, no. 3 (Spring 2003): 40–51.

Obregón, Álvaro *Partes oficiales de las batallas de Celaya: 6, 7, 13, 14 y 15 de abril de 1915.* Celaya, Guanajuato: Confederación Revolucionaria, 1915.

Cerro Gordo, Battle of (1847)

Defensive stand made by Santa Anna in an attempt to halt any penetration inland from the coast by Maj. Gen. Winfield Scott's recently disembarked U.S. Army so as to deny these invaders access into central Mexico.

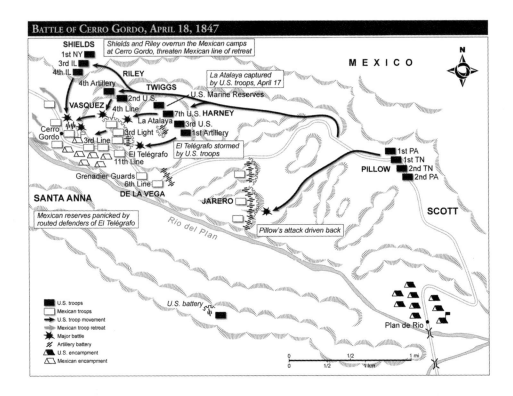

BATTLE OF CERRO GORDO, APRIL 18, 1847

SHIELDS
1st NY
3rd IL
4th IL
RILEY
4th Artillery
TWIGGS
2nd U.S.
VASQUEZ 4th Line
La Atalaya
Cerro
Gordo
3rd Line 3rd Light
El Telégrafo
11th Line
Grenadier Guards
6th Line
SANTA ANNA DE LA VEGA
JARERO

7th U.S. HARNEY
3rd U.S.
1st Artillery

U.S. Marine Reserves

1st PA
1st TN
PILLOW 2nd TN
2nd PA

SCOTT

MEXICO

N

Shields and Riley overrun the Mexican camps
at Cerro Gordo, threaten Mexican line of retreat

La Atalaya captured
by U.S. troops, April 17

El Telégrafo stormed
by U.S. troops

Mexican reserves panicked by
routed defenders of El Telégrafo

Río del Plan

Pillow's attack driven back

U.S. battery

Plan de Rio

U.S. troops
Mexican troops
U.S. troop movement
Mexican troop retreat
Major battle
Artillery battery
U.S. encampment
Mexican encampment

0 1/2 1 mi
0 1/2 1 km

Preliminary Maneuvers (April 8–14, 1847)

Scott's 2,600-man vanguard division under Brig. Gen. David E. Twiggs had departed occupied Veracruz on April 8, 1847, to be followed up the road in stages by the remaining 6,000 soldiers of the American army. The Mexican president and commander-in-chief, Antonio López de Santa Anna, hoped to prevent this force from marching up out of the coastal lowlands into the cooler and healthier highlands, instead confining them to endure a hot and pestilential summer around Veracruz. For this reason, he had already rejected a previous site selected by Gen. Valentín Gómez to fight a defensive battle in favor of directing Gen. Ciriaco Vázquez to prepare a more forward position: an expanse around a waystation known as Plan del Río, a well-chosen stretch of terrain that tapered upward into a narrow defile. Santa Anna had therefore begun to encamp some 12,000 troops, many of them raw conscripts, and 43 fieldpieces just west of a 1,000-foot prominence called Cerro Gordo (today known as El Telégrafo Hill).

Three days later, Twiggs's vanguard had detected this large Mexican force dug in four miles northwest of the hamlet of Plan del Río, seemingly barring any further progress up the road leading toward the city of Jalapa, which lay four miles beyond the Mexican positions. Twiggs's engineer—Lt. Pierre G. T. Beauregard—reconnoitered and reported that the defenders' emplacements could be flanked if an assault column first took a hill in front of Cerro Gordo, called La Atalaya, but Twiggs instead prepared to launch a direct frontal assault, underestimating Santa Anna's strength at only 4,000 men. However, when Maj. Gen.

Robert Patterson's division of volunteers overtook Twiggs at Plan del Río on April 12, 1847, his brigade commanders, Gideon Pillow and James Shields, talked him out of such an attempt. The decision was postponed until Scott arrived two days later to assume direct command over his combined force of 8,500 effectives.

The American commander ordered another reconnaissance made by Capt. Robert E. Lee, who discovered that Santa Anna had deployed relatively few men to hold his left flank, relying instead on the rough terrain in that sector to act as a natural buffer. But Lee reported that a column could bypass these positions undetected along a hidden path, emerging behind Cerro Gordo to cut off the road behind the entire Mexican Army and envelop them wholesale.

Battle of Cerro Gordo (April 17–18, 1847)

Scott agreed, dispatching Twiggs on the Saturday morning of April 17, 1847, to circle north around the Mexican positions with Col. Bennett Riley's 2nd Infantry, Smith's Mounted Rifles—temporarily commanded by Col. William S. Harney—and Brig. Gen. James Shields's brigade, composed of 3rd and 4th Illinois, plus the New York Regiment. Although intended only as a preliminary movement, this column blundered into some skirmishers and was then hit by a Mexican counterattack, diverting Harney into veering around so as to engage Santa Anna's main force holding La Atalaya Hill before the outnumbered Americans finally withdrew at nightfall. Santa Anna mistook this flanking maneuver as an attempt to secure the dominant Cerro Gordo heights, despite receiving intelligence overnight from a U.S. deserter as to Scott's true objective.

The next morning, Harney did indeed move forward again from La Atalaya and eventually claimed the summit of Cerro Gordo. But the real blow was struck when Twiggs emerged unexpectedly much farther west with Shields's and Riley's brigades, directly threatening the Mexican encampments. Fearful of having their escape cut off in the rear, Santa Anna's disorganized battle line quickly dissolved into panic, with thousands of troops fleeing south and west toward Orizaba, leaving behind about 1,000 casualties, more than 3,000 prisoners, all 43 fieldpieces, complete with their artillery and baggage trains. Even Santa Anna's personal luggage (including a spare prosthetic leg) was seized, while he had to ride away hastily on horseback from this battlefield as his carriage and six-mule team had been riddled by American shots. American losses from these two days of fighting totaled 63 killed and 367 wounded, but the road into healthy cantonments at Jalapa now lay open, the invaders entering that city uncontested by April 20, 1847.

Further Reading

Johnson, Timothy D. *A Gallant Little Army: The Mexico City Campaign.* Lawrence: University Press of Kansas, 2007.

Tucker, Spencer C. *The Encyclopedia of the Mexican-American War.* Santa Barbara, CA: ABC-CLIO, 2013.

chaco

Phonetic spelling in the Spanish language of the word "shako," itself a generic name for the typical early 19th-century military headgear, which in later decades would be superseded by the smaller kepi.

In one of many examples, the liberal brigadier general Nicolás de Regules wrote from Silao on August 15, 1860, to his immediate superior, Gen. Manuel Doblado, reporting that his men:

> of the 2nd Brigade came on this campaign almost naked, and consequently remain lacking smocks, many soldiers without *chacos* [shakos], and many without *fornituras* [leather straps and cartridge-belts].

Further Reading

Doblado, Manuel. *La guerra de Reforma*. San Antonio, TX: Lozano, 1930, 213–14.

Hefter, Joseph. *Crónica del traje militar en México, del siglo XVI al XX*. Mexico City: Artes de México, 1968.

Chapultepec, Battle of (1847)

Final assault by the U.S. invaders clearing the way for the capture of Mexico City the next day, which would bring to an end almost all major military action during the Mexican-American War.

Preamble (August 16–September 11, 1847)

Having disembarked at Veracruz and trudged inland to occupy Puebla, the 7,200-man army of U.S. major general Winfield Scott circled around Santa Anna's main defensive concentration at El Peñón de los Baños—10 miles east of the capital, on the rim of the Valley of Mexico—on August 16, 1847, instead doubling back in order to descend into the valley by a less strongly defended route. The invaders then continued slipping around other southeastern outposts as well, all the while drawing ever closer to Mexico City. Santa Anna had tried to counter these flanking maneuvers by hastily redeploying his forces and mounting unsuccessful stands at the Battles of Contreras and Churubusco, after which his Mexican troops fought a stubborn yet costly defensive action at the Molino del Rey complex and its adjacent stone Casa Mata on September 7, 1847, which briefly checked Scott's approach.

Contemporary painting of the storming of Chapultepec Castle on September 13, 1847, a victory that allowed the U.S. army of Gen. Winfield Scott to sweep past and claim Mexico City the next day. (Library of Congress)

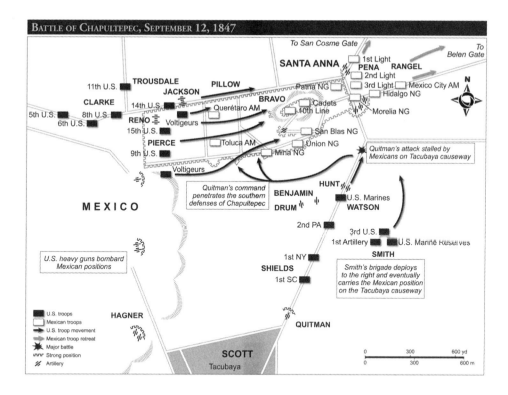

BATTLE OF CHAPULTEPEC, SEPTEMBER 12, 1847

To San Cosme Gate

To Belen Gate

SANTA ANNA

1st Light
PENA   RANGEL
2nd Light
3rd Light   Mexico City AM
Hidalgo NG

11th U.S.   TROUSDALE   PILLOW   Patria NG
JACKSON

CLARKE   14th U.S.   BRAVO
5th U.S.   8th U.S.   Querétaro AM   Cadets
6th U.S.   RENO   Voltigeurs   40th Line   Morelia NG
15th U.S.   San Blas NG
PIERCE   Toluca AM   Union NG
9th U.S.   Mina NG

N

Voltigeurs

Quitman's attack stalled by
Mexicans on Tacubaya causeway

Quitman's command
penetrates the southern
defenses of Chapultepec

MEXICO

HUNT

BENJAMIN   U.S. Marines
DRUM   WATSON

2nd PA
3rd U.S.
1st Artillery   U.S. Marine Reserves

U.S. heavy guns bombard
Mexican positions

1st NY   SMITH

SHIELDS   Smith's brigade deploys
1st SC   to the right and eventually
carries the Mexican position
on the Tacubaya causeway

HAGNER

QUITMAN

U.S. troops
Mexican troops
U.S. troop movement
Mexican troop retreat
Major battle
Strong position
Artillery

SCOTT
Tacubaya

0   300   600 yd
0   300   600 m

Rather than resume their assault directly into the teeth of Mexico City's defenses out of its south though, the Americans subsequently began sliding around yet again, edging still farther west. Realizing that his capital lay quite defenseless from that direction since most of the intervening canals and waterways were at their lowest levels because it was the dry season, Santa Anna ordered that 200-foot-high Chapultepec Hill and its surrounding woods be hurriedly prepared to serve as a defensive strongpoint.

Elderly Maj. Gen. Nicolás Bravo and the engineer, Brig. Gen. Juan Cano, had consequently begun distributing some 1,300 troops into the following positions:

- One hundred and fifteen men of the Querétaro Activo Battalion and 27 of the Toluca Activo Battalion into trenches around its lower levels to the west

- Two hundred and seventy-seven men of the Mina, 211 of the Unión, and 300 of the San Blas National Guard Militia Battalions into a similar line of trenches to its south

- Two hundred and fifty regulars of the 10th Line Regiment and seven artillery pieces under Cmdr. Manuel Gamboa into the frail hilltop castle up above

(Despite its imposing appearance, the castle had originally been designed as a viceregal residence and therefore lacked the thick walls of a proper military fortress.)

While these defensive preparations were being made, an order was also issued for the 100 or so cadets of the Military College that it housed to be evacuated, although its director, Gen. Col. Mariano Monterde, and a dozen staff officers intended to remain to assist in the defense. Parents arrived from nearby Mexico City to pick up their children from among the students, but some cadets refused to depart (such as 15-year-old Miguel Miramón), while others hailed from more distant parts of the country and therefore had nowhere to go. Eventually, 46 cadets stayed on with their instructors, constituting part of the Mexican defenders who intended to hold Chapultepec Castle itself.

American Bombardment and Assault (September 12–13, 1847)

Scott ordered his artillery to begin bombarding the hilltop castle at 5:00 a.m. on September 12, 1847, intending to soften up this strongpoint so as to take it by storm and then drive straight past with his main army into Mexico City (although he simultaneously detached some regiments to feint a return southeastward as well to divide Santa Anna's forces). Chapultepec's young cadets and other defenders endured this barrage all day and again the next dawn until the American guns suddenly fell silent around 8:00 a.m. on the morning of September 13, 1847.

At that hour, a column of assault troops advanced from Brig. Gen. John A. Quitman's division to the south, charging into the Mexican defenders around the base of the hill and breaking through after intense hand-to-hand combat. Other U.S. columns also forged out of the west from Brig. Gen. Gideon J. Pillow's division, Franklin Pierce's and George Cadwalader's brigades smashing through the Querétaro and Toluca positions. All the vanguard American units then had to pause at the base of the Chapultepec heights until scaling ladders could be brought forward in order to launch their final assault against the castle up above.

But these ladders were soon received and the attackers resumed their advance, swarming up and overwhelming the last defenders in a hail of bullets, during which some

6 cadets were believed to have been killed, 5 wounded, and 45 captured before all shooting ceased. By 9:30 a.m. on that September 13, 1847, Col. Joseph E. Johnston's gray-coated Voltigeur Regiment was unfurling the Stars and Stripes atop the lofty fortress, while below other columns swept on past toward Mexico City's western gates.

Aftermath (September 14–15, 1847)

By nightfall on that same September 13, 1847, Santa Anna had suffered 1,800 casualties, compared to Scott's 450, so at 1:00 a.m. the Mexican general-in-chief gave the order for his surviving troops to evacuate the capital northward via Guadalupe. The invaders pushed their way through sporadic resistance into its main square by noon of September 14, 1847, after which a couple of days' looting and rioting gutted many buildings. Brig. John A. Quitman was appointed military governor and restored order, U.S. forces remaining in possession of the sparsely populated capital for the next eight months.

See also: Molino del Rey, Battle of; Niños Héroes.

Further Reading

Frías, Heriberto. *Episodios militares mexicanos: segunda parte, invasión norteamericana.* Mexico City: Viuda de C. Bouret, 1901, 227–41.

Tucker, Spencer C. *The Encyclopedia of the Mexican-American War.* Santa Barbara, CA: ABC-CLIO, 2013.

chivo

Among many other meanings, a slang expression among Mexican soldiers for their salary or wages, *día del chivo* or "day of the goat" being a term used to denote "payday."

For example, the revolutionary soldier Hermelindo Santos Ramos would recall with pride, many years later in his memoirs, how as a 13-year-old recruited into the military ranks at Pachuca in December 1914 he thereupon received his first "*chivo*, that is my salary, as this was a very common word used among the troops."

Further Reading

Santos Ramos, Hermelindo. *Así construimos una nueva sociedad*. Mexico City: INAH, 1998.

Churubusco, Battle of (1847)

Second battle won in quick succession outside Mexico City in the immediate wake of the U.S. Army victory at Contreras.

The subsequent American pursuit of this broken formation from Contreras carried as far northeastward as San Angel and Coyoacán, spreading panic among other Mexican units. Brig. Gen. William J. Worth took advantage of this breakthrough to send Clarke's brigade (consisting of the 5th, 6th, and 8th Infantry Regiments) wheeling behind the San Antonio stronghold, causing its Mexican garrison to flee northward into Churubusco as well rather than risk being cut off. Santa Anna's disperse contingents now utterly collapsed as a cohesive fighting force, every man struggling to recross the river at either Coyoacán or Churubusco. Scott directed Shields and Pierce to attack the former bridgehead while sending Worth and Pillow against the latter around noon.

After more than two hours of heavy fighting, the 2,600 troops of Clarke's and Cadwalader's brigades, plus Duncan's Artillery Battalion, overcame the Churubusco bridgehead; then Alexander's 3rd

Infantry stormed its last stronghold, the fortified San Mateo Convent. This building's defenders—Irish-American deserters from the U.S. Army who had joined the so-called San Patricio Battalion—resisted desperately but were eventually overwhelmed (30 of their 69 survivors later being court-martialed and executed). By mid-afternoon of August 20, 1847, Santa Anna had fled back into the capital, his army in ruins. Mexican casualties totaled 4,000 killed or wounded and another 3,000 captured—including two former presidents and six generals. Scott's losses were 139 killed and more than 900 wounded or missing.

Aftermath

Although having Mexico City at his mercy, Scott hesitated to move against the capital the next morning, instead allowing Santa Anna time to request a truce—which the Americans granted on Sunday, August 22, 1847, hoping that it would lead to a general armistice.

See also: San Patricio Battalion.

Further Reading

Tucker, Spencer C. *The Encyclopedia of the Mexican-American War*. Santa Barbara, CA: ABC-CLIO, 2013.

Cinco de Mayo, Battle of the (1862)

Unexpected victory won by Puebla's republican defenders over an invading French Army—whose military forces were at that time deemed to be the best and most advanced in the world.

Preliminary Movements (April 1862)

Recognizing the route inland that these foreigners must take when they pushed up out of the torrid coastal region (where they had been disembarked three months previously) so as to penetrate into Mexico's central highlands and threaten the national capital with their opening offensive of the War of the French Intervention, the commander of the republican *Ejército de Oriente* or "Eastern Army"—33-year-old bespectacled general Ignacio Zaragoza—chose to concentrate his overmatched troops into defensive positions around the city of Puebla. His choice to fight a potentially destructive action from within this beautiful 16th-century city, the intellectual core of Mexico's conservative movement, had appealed to longtime liberals in Pres. Benito Juárez's government.

In order to buy time so as to complete his defensive preparations, Zaragoza then personally led the 2nd Infantry Division under his 29-year-old subordinate, Gen. José María Arteaga, in a foray that ambushed the approaching French column on April 28, 1862, surprising the invaders as they began ascending the winding highway just outside of the town of Acultzingo—a delaying action that would be remembered as the Battle of the *Cumbres* or "Heights" of Acultzingo.

Yet the 6,100-man French Army of Gen. Charles, Comte de Lorencez, had continued its advance undeterred, passing through the villages of San Agustín del Palmar, Quecholac, and Acatzingo without meeting any further opposition from the republicans until his columns entered the eerily quiet town of Amozoc at 3:00 p.m. on May 4, 1862—only 12 miles short of Puebla.

Lorencez's Tactical Decision (May 4, 1862)

The French leadership had been repeatedly assured by their Mexican conservative allies that they would be greeted as liberators into this anti-Juarista heartland and, more importantly, reinforced by the arrival from distant Izúcar de Matamoros by large contingents of conservative guerrillas and troops that had deserted from the Mexican Army, all under the command of the antirepublican general Leonardo Márquez—neither of which events transpired.

Worried by this evident lack of popular support in the region and with dysentery already appearing among the ranks of his French units, Lorencez decided to consequently march due west along the highway directly toward Puebla the next dawn, May 5th—in Spanish, the *cinco de mayo*—intending to drive straight into its republican defenses and pierce through at a single focal point in order to carry the city in a *coup d'audace* or "audacious blow" thanks to his superior firepower and the shock of his assault. Otherwise, he feared that his 6,000-man army might prove too small to effectively besiege the defenders and would deteriorate from disease and lack of supplies during any protracted encirclement.

Republican Defensive Dispositions (May 5, 1862)

Awaiting the French arrival were some 6,000 republican defenders, ensconced into various strongpoints within and to the east of the city of Puebla. Zaragoza himself had established his field headquarters at the monastery of Los Remedios, a suburban cluster of stout stone buildings that sat directly beside the highway leading in from Amozoc and was being held by Gen. Porfirio Díaz's 1,020-man 3rd Infantry Brigade—comprising the Patria, Morelos, and Guerrero Battalions, as well as the 1st and 2nd National Guard Battalions of Oaxaca—plus a company of sappers.

A ridge of hills rose just to the north of Los Remedios whose two peaks were manned by a total of 1,200 defenders from the 2nd Infantry Division under Brig. Gen.

Miguel Negrete (Arteaga's replacement, as the latter had had to have a leg amputated from the wound that he had received one week previously at the Battle of Cumbres de Acultzingo). Negrete's division was distributed into a series of trenches around both hilltop strongholds, which were religious chapels that had been fortified over the previous few weeks under the supervision of the engineer, colonel Joaquín Colombres, who had strengthened their walls and directed the digging of a maze of staggered, overlapping defenses all the way up the hillside from the plains below. The first stronghold of Guadalupe was held by the:

- "Cazadores de Morelia" Battalion
- Mixed Battalion of Querétaro
- 2nd Active Battalion of Puebla
- 6th Line Battalion
- Two batteries of artillery

The second, neighboring stronghold of Loreto—located farther northwest of Guadalupe—was manned by the:

- Fixed Battalion of Morelia
- "Tiradores de Morelia" Battalion
- 6th National Guard State Battalion of Puebla
- Four militia companies from Tetela de Ocampo
- One militia company each from Zacapoaxtla and Xochiapulco
- Plus another two artillery batteries

Hidden out of sight still farther to the northwest along the riverbank directly behind and beneath Loreto, were 550 cavalrymen under Gen. Antonio Álvarez, including the Carabineros de Pachuca Regiment, plus a few assorted squadrons under Col. Miguel Solís.

Another 60 well-mounted irregulars—the self-proclaimed *Exploradores de Zaragoza* or "Scouts of Zaragoza"—were patrolling across the plains in the direction of Amozoc, intending to bring in intelligence of the enemy approach, while another two cavalry brigades had been detached days earlier under Generals Tomás O'Horan and Francisco Carvajal to detect any attempted movement from Izúcar by the turncoat conservative formations and prevent their reinforcement of the French expedition.

Still more republican troops were stationed in reserve within the city itself, ready to sally at Zaragoza's command from behind Puebla's protective walls and buildings, consisting of the:

- 1st Infantry Brigade under Brig. Gen. Felipe Berriozábal, composed of 1,082 soldiers of the Fixed Battalion of Veracruz, plus the 1st and 2nd Light-Infantry Battalions from Toluca who were resting in Puebla's Plazuela de San José
- the 2nd Infantry Brigade, 1,000 soldiers of the "Reforma" and "Rifleros" Battalions from San Luis Potosí under Brig. Gen. Francisco Lamadrid, who were deployed in Cárdenas Street and around the city's San Juan de Letrán College (more commonly known as the Hospitalito)

Finally, Puebla's military governor, Santiago Tapia, commanded a subsidiary force of three battalions from the Michoacán Brigade under Brig. Gen. José Rojo, roughly 1,200 men who were distributed in the city's Plazuela de San Francisco and around its Jesuit College ready to join in and assist Zaragoza in the city's defense.

Battle of the Cinco de Mayo (May 5, 1862)

At 10:45 a.m. on that Monday morning, May 5, 1862, the principal "María" church bell in the cathedral tower began to peal, announcing that the dust columns being thrown up by the approaching French Army could be seen in the distance. Lorencez had broken camp at Amozoc before dawn, a squadron from the 2nd *Chasseurs d'Afrique* Regiment leading his columns in the van. The main body had reached Los Álamos Hacienda by 9:00 a.m., then disgorged out onto the plain and trudged toward Puebla, which still remained largely shielded from view to them beyond its surrounding hills and woods except for a few protruding church spires. A few Mexican cavalry patrols fired token shots against the French Army at long range before galloping off to report.

Lorencez allowed his troops to rest for about three-quarters of an hour and brew up some coffee before wheeling two Zouave battalions and a Marine Fusilier battalion over onto his right at 11:30 a.m. in order to circle forward and occupy Rementería Ranch, where 10 of the French fieldpieces could be unlimbered and installed by gunners from the 9th Artillery Regiment. Zaragoza's own heavy guns fired a few counterrounds from atop Guadalupe Hill, at their maximum range of almost a mile-and-a-half, while farther below them, republican soldiers began deploying into their first line of trenches around the base of the hill, intending to contest any French assault by slowly retiring uphill through a series of prepared defenses while keeping up a steady counterfire on the enemy below them. By midday, the three French columns veered toward Rementería and shortly thereafter unlimbered their field guns and opened fire 15 minutes later.

By 1:15 p.m. though, Lorencez (who had been observing the development of this action from nearby Oropeza Ranch) realized that his artillery was having no effect because it was positioned at a range of a mile and a third, too far to achieve much toward weakening the Mexican defenses, so he ordered that these guns be moved forward—only to learn that the intervening terrain was so difficult to maneuver over, that the range could be closed by only a few hundred yards. The French general consequently ordered a direct assault against Guadalupe Hill by midafternoon.

Two extended lines of Zouaves advanced through a heavy counterfire, led by their commanders Morand and Cousin, the right-hand thrust being followed by the Marine Fusiliers and the left-hand one by a battalion from the 99th Line Regiment. Berriozábal reinforced Negrete's Division at the most threatened section atop Guadalupe Hill, the Mexicans twice checking the French assault waves, killing the few invaders who succeeded in nearing its summit. One French participant later recorded how as their assault lines advanced higher up the slope, "the defense multiplied, the fire redoubled; soon there was nothing in the air but the uninterrupted whistling of bullets and balls."

When Lorencez finally committed two more Zouave companies, a sudden rainstorm made it impossible for them to ascend the slippery slopes of Guadalupe Hill, after which they were hit in the right flank by Álvarez's cavalry and a bayonet charge by Berriozábal. The defeated attackers were subsequently allowed to begin an orderly retreat at 4:00 p.m. toward Los Álamos, having suffered 117 killed and 305 wounded. Mexican losses totaled 83 dead and 232 injured.

Aftermath (May 6–18, 1862)

After recuperating for three days atop the nearby Amalucan heights, still vainly hoping to be reinforced by his Mexican conservative allies, Lorencez finally gave the order at 2:00 p.m. on May 8, 1862, for his battered army to begin trudging wearily back east toward Orizaba. They would be trailed with some difficulty by Zaragoza's *Ejército de Oriente*, which, although augmented to 7,500 men thanks to the arrival of republican reinforcements, emerged from Puebla very ill-supplied. The French retreated slowly over roads that soon became waterlogged from heavy rains, hampered by their 300 wounded plus many other soldiers who were sick. Zaragoza rested his own weary and hungry column for a few days around San Andrés Chalchicomula in anticipation of being joined by the fresh Zacatecas Division under Brig. Gen. Jesús González Ortega.

Lorencez, while also encamped for the night at the Hacienda de Tecamalucan, was surprised to receive a visit at 5:00 p.m. on May 17, 1862, from the long-overdue Mexican conservative general Leonardo Márquez, who had brought 2,500 riders from Izúcar de Matamoros that were resting nearby. Zaragoza was unable to prevent these reinforcements from joining the French the next day despite rushing republican detachments forward to attempt to bar their path at Barranca Seca. Lorencez was therefore able to ensconce himself impregnably within Orizaba, assisted by Mexican cavalrymen to patrol his supply lines and communications down to the coast until a much larger expedition could be sent out from France by early the next year.

See also: Barranca Seca, Battle of; Cumbres de Acultzingo, Battle of the; Díaz Mori, José de la Cruz Porfirio; French Intervention, War of the; González Ortega, José Canuto de Jesús; Lorencez, Charles Ferdinand Labrille, Comte de; Zaragoza Seguín, Ignacio.

Further Reading

Arroyo Llano, Rodolfo. *Ygnacio Zaragoza: defensor de la libertad y la justicia.* 2nd ed. Puebla: Colegio de Puebla and Gobierno del Estado de Puebla, 2012.

Bibescu, Georges. *Au Mexique 1862: combats et retraite des six mille.* Paris: Plon, Nourrit, et Cie., 1887.

González Lezama, Raúl. *Cinco de mayo: las razones de la victoria.* Mexico City: Instituto Nacional de Estudios Históricos de las Revoluciones de México, 2012.

Palou, Pedro Ángel. *5 de mayo, 1862.* Puebla: Benemérita Universidad Autónoma de Puebla, 2007.

Paz, Ireneo. *Datos biográficos del general de división C. Porfirio Díaz, con acopio de documentos históricos.* Mexico City: Imprenta de Ireneo Paz, 1884, 35–39.

Ramos, Patricio. *Descripción de la batalla del 5 de mayo de 1862.* 2nd ed. Puebla: Colegio de Puebla, Gobierno del Estado de Puebla, and INAH Puebla, 2012.

Salazar Exaire, Celia. *Los fuertes de Loreto y Guadalupe.* Puebla: Colegio de Puebla, Gobierno del Estado de Puebla, and INAH Puebla, 2012.

ciudadano

Word that simply denotes a "citizen" but since shortly after Mexico had achieved its independence became an honorific embellishment used by military officers to underscore their supposed egalitarianism and acceptance of civilian rule by inserting the initial "C." before their rank in all official documents.

This practice had originated as long ago as 1822, when the insurgent champion

Guadalupe Victoria adopted the title of "citizen General Don Guadalupe Victoria" in all of his correspondence, soon abbreviated as a simple "C."—and that stood in stark contrast to the grandiose title of "emperor" that had been assumed by the recently deposed Agustín de Iturbide, along with an order of nobility and many other grandiose imperial trappings.

Victoria's example, which was in keeping with the democratic ideals then still in vogue during his age, stemming from the French and American Revolutions, would be subsequently emulated by many other officers, right up to the present day. It was featured routinely in almost every published work as well, such as:

- Mariano Arista's 1840 treatise *Teoría para el manejo del sable a caballo por el general de brigada del Ejército mexicano C. Mariano Arista, con ocho láminas litográficas*
- Manuel Z. Gómez's 1862 *Biografía del Gral. de división C. Ignacio Zaragoza*
- Ireneo Paz's 1884 book *Datos biográficos del general de división C. Porfirio Díaz, con acopio de documentos históricos*
- The official 1871 report *Parte oficial de la toma de Tampico por las fuerzas del supremo gobierno al mando del C. general S[óstenes] Rocha*
- The 1873 *Memoria que el C. General de División Ignacio Mejía, Ministro de Guerra y Marina, presenta al 7. Congreso Constitucional*
- Bernardo Reyes's 1879 *Conversaciones militares escritas para las academias del 6° regimiento de caballería permanente, por el jefe del mismo, coronel C. Bernardo Reyes, San Luis Potosí*

See also: Iturbide Arambúru, Agustín Cosme Damián de; Victoria, Guadalupe.

clarín de órdenes

A military designation that can be translated literally as the "clarion of orders," signifying a staff trumpeter who served as "command bugler" in 19th-century Mexican armies relaying signals to units in the field or deployed on a battlefield by playing certain prearranged *toques* or "calls" that could be heard over a considerable distance.

It was recorded that when Gen. Porfirio Díaz found the lines of his detached republican ally, Gen. Jesús Lalannc, in the evening gloom near the town of San Lorenzo on April 9, 1867, he was mistakenly attacked by a Mexican lancer—who was called off at the very last moment by warning cries from Díaz's accompanying *clarín de órdenes* and a captain of his escort.

See also: San Lorenzo, Battle of (1836).

Further Reading

Hefter, Joseph. *Crónica del traje militar en México, del siglo XVI al XX*. Mexico City: Artes de México, 1968.

Colt-Browning heavy machine gun (M.1895)

One of several tripod-mounted machine guns acquired from different foreign manufacturers during the modernization of the Porfirian army and that would see active service during the Mexican Revolution of 1910.

In 1889, John M. Browning of Utah had conceived of the first "gas-operated" machine gun, whose muzzle flashes were designed to activate a lever so as to instantly chamber succeeding rounds. Improved and patented by 1892, Browning offered this design to the Colt Manufacturing Company of Hartford, Connecticut. Initial prototypes required a very heavy, straight "contour" barrel because of the heat that would build up whenever protracted bursts were fired. The Colt-Browning's closed bolt mechanism meant that additional rounds in its chamber might be accidentally discharged or "cooked off" if its barrel grew too hot, so the gun had to be quickly unloaded once heat built up, while extended bursts of fire meant that bullets would eventually begin tumbling out of control.

For this reason, initial purchases of the Model 1895 Colt-Browning were rejected by the U.S. Army, who preferred going with Colt's older-vintage .45-caliber Gatling guns, updated that same year into a new version featuring 10 rotating barrels. Yet the U.S. Navy did purchase several hundred of the new Colts, using them to arm detachments of Marines for swift disembarkations ashore, obtaining satisfactory field results during the Spanish-American War of 1898 in Cuba—where the army's more cumbersome Gatlings had to be hauled overland behind mule teams, while the Colt-Brownings (each weighing only 35 pounds apiece, plus 56 pounds for its tripod) proved much more maneuverable.

When an improved version of the Colt-Browning was introduced after that war, the U.S. Army bought 140 of them in 1904, and the Mexican government acquired 150 in its 7x57mm-cartridge version. They proved to be relatively reliable and mobile, yet with a significantly slower rate of fire than competitors such as Maxim guns.

See also: *ametralladora*; Hotchkiss heavy machine gun; Madsen light machine gun; Rexer light machine gun.

Further Reading

Fitzsimmons, Bernard. *Illustrated Encyclopedia of Weapons and Warfare*. London: Phoebus, 1978.

Hughes, James B., Jr. *Mexican Military Arms: The Cartridge Period, 1866–1967*. Houston, TX: Deep River Armory, 1968.

Jowett, Philip, and Alejandro de Quesada. *The Mexican Revolution, 1910–20*. Oxford: Osprey, 2006, 15–16.

"Rexer Automatic Machine Gun," *Scientific American*, August 19, 1905.

Columbus Raid (1916)

Cross-border attack launched by Pancho Villa, seemingly in hopes of restoring his former prominent position in the Mexican Revolution after his string of defeats at the hands of Álvaro Obregón.

Approach and Strategic Goal (March 3–8, 1916)

Having seen his once-proud army (the *División del Norte*) destroyed and disbanded by Christmas 1915, Villa had spent the next six weeks hiding out in the mountains of Chihuahua with a few hundred followers. He emerged and reunited at Las Cruces with his subordinates Candelario Cervantes, Francisco Beltrán, and Pablo and Martín López on March 3, 1916, leading some 300–400 riders through Ojitos Ranch three days afterward and reaching Boca Grande to encamp by the afternoon of March 8, 1916—with the intent of striking across the U.S. border the next dawn against the small American town of Columbus, New Mexico.

Villa's motivation for this unprovoked attack has never been clearly explained. Contemporary accounts suggested that he wished to precipitate a diplomatic crisis between the governments of Presidents Venustiano Carranza and Woodrow Wilson by giving the lie to the Carrancista claim of having pacified the war-torn neighboring country. During any resultant military pursuit, Villa could once again begin

Photograph of some of the destruction left in Columbus, New Mexico, after Pancho Villa's raid on March 9, 1916. (Library of Congress)

patriotically rallying followers so as to replenish his ranks while denigrating his opponents as collaborators with the Americans. Modern research has furthermore suggested that his raid may have been encouraged as well by German agents as a means of diverting the American public's interest away from joining the ongoing World War I in Europe, but the real reasoning behind Villa's thinking has never been firmly established.

Columbus Raid (March 9, 1916)

In the predawn hours, Villa crossed the border a few miles west of Columbus, sending his 400 or so riders to storm this town from three directions at 4:00 a.m. In the process, his followers also assaulted the encampment of six troops—200 soldiers in total—of Col. H. J. Slocum's 13th U.S. Cavalry Regiment, in addition to looting numerous buildings and corrals and setting fire to Columbus's business district before hastily withdrawing. Yet despite being surprised, the defenders

nonetheless killed about some of the Villistas. Eighteen Americans—10 of them civilians—were left dead, another 8 wounded.

Villa's raid was calculated not only to vault his name back into prominence in Mexico but also to belie the Carrancista claim of having pacified the war-torn country. Any American pursuit onto Mexican soil would furthermore be resented by many Mexicans for purely patriotic reasons because of the recent Veracruz intervention, thereby drawing new recruits into Villa's ranks while alienating Carranza from popular opinion if he helped to hunt down the raiders.

See also: División del Norte; Obregón Salido, Álvaro; Villa, Pancho.

Further Reading

Braddy, Haldeen. *Pancho Villa at Columbus: The Raid of 1916.* El Paso: Texas Western College Press, 1965.

de Quesada, Alejandro. *The Hunt for Pancho Villa: The Columbus Raid and Pershing's*

Punitive Expedition, 1916–17. London: Osprey, 2012.

Katz, Friedrich. "Pancho Villa and the Attack on Columbus, New Mexico." *American Historical Review* 58, no. 1 (February 1978): 101–30.

Sandos, James A. "German Involvement in Northern Mexico, 1915–1916: A New Look at the Columbus Raid." *Hispanic American Historical Review* 50, no. 1 (February 1970): 70–89.

combates de Celaya. Popular name in Mexico for the two major set-piece battles fought during the Mexican Revolution between the powerful armies of Pancho Villa and Álvaro Obregón in the state of Guanajuato, in April 1915.

For its full entry, *see* Celaya, Battles of (1915).

Contreras, Battle of (1847)

First of a pair of quick successive victories won by the invading American army on the outskirts of Mexico City, facilitating its penetration into the Valley of Mexico so as to directly threaten Santa Anna's capital out of its more lightly defended south.

Preliminary Maneuvers (August 16–19, 1847)

After having fought their way inland from Veracruz past Cerro Gordo and through Puebla, Gen. Winfield Scott's small but potent army of 7,200 men maneuvered around the concentration of 7,000 Mexican troops and 30 cannon massed atop El Peñón Hill, 10 miles due east of their capital. Instead, the divisions of Brigadier Generals William J. Worth, Gideon J. Pillow, and John A. Quitman veered southwest around this strongpoint on the morning of August 16, 1847,

leaving Brig. Gen. David E. Twiggs's division alone at Ayotla to hold Santa Anna in check. Scott's circling vanguard reached the town of San Agustín two days later and turned north, only to have its advance cavalry screen draw fire from a heavy Mexican battery ensconced at San Antonio, three miles south of Churubusco. Unable to outflank this position because of an impassable lava field to its west called El Pedregal, the Americans decided to again slip farther around (along a road reconnoitered by Capt. Robert E. Lee).

Santa Anna, meanwhile—having been alerted at El Peñón as to this movement around his southern flank—redeployed Maj. Gen. Gabriel Valencia's 5,500 veterans of the *Ejército del Norte* or "Army of the North" into San Ángel; Gen. Francisco Pérez Arévalo's 3,500 two miles farther to its east at Coyoacán; perhaps 2,000 of the former president Nicolás Bravo's *Ejército del Centro* or "Army of the Center" into Churubusco; while Gen. Manuel Rincón remained at El Peñón with the reserve. Fearing that his troops would see no action, however, Valencia disobeyed and took up station five miles southwest of his allotted position, in the village of Padierna.

On the morning of August 19, 1847, Twiggs set out westward from San Agustín to lead Pillow and Worth in their latest flanking maneuver. Early that afternoon, while approaching the San Angel-Contreras highway at its Padierna crossroads, his advance elements came under artillery fire, prompting Twiggs to deploy Capt. John Magruder's two field batteries to counter this threat. When it became evident that they were dueling against Valencia's 22 heavy guns and not some minor outpost, Pillow committed 3,500 men of Riley's, Cadwalader's, and Morgan's contingents into capturing vacant San Gerónimo, hoping to thereby isolate Valencia from the principal Mexican body.

Instead, Santa Anna moved southwestward late in the day with another 3,500 Mexican troops to extricate Valencia, in the process unwittingly threatening to crush the American thrust between two pincers. Realizing this danger, Smith followed Riley, Cadwalader, and Morgan into San Gerónimo by nightfall, directing them to leave a screen facing northward against Santa Anna while continuing with him behind Valencia's positions under cover of darkness with their combined strength. The next dawn, Santa Anna unexpectedly began retiring northeastward, so when Riley suddenly launched his surprise attack from Valencia's rear at 6:00 a.m., the latter's men were already feeling lost. They scattered after only 17 minutes' fighting, suffering 700 killed and 813 captured, along with losing all of their artillery.

The subsequent American pursuit of this broken formation from Contreras carried as far northeastward as San Angel and Coyoacán, spreading panic among other Mexican units. Worth took advantage of this breakthrough to send Clarke's brigade (the 5th, 6th, and 8th Infantry Regiments) wheeling behind the San Antonio stronghold, causing its Mexican garrison to flee northward into Churubusco as well rather than risk being cut off. Santa Anna's disperse contingents now utterly collapsed as a cohesive fighting force, every man struggling to recross the river at either Coyoacán or Churubusco. Scott directed Shields and Pierce to attack the former bridgehead while sending Worth and Pillow against the latter around noon.

Further Reading

Frías, Heriberto. *La batalla de Padierna.* 2nd ed. Mexico City: Fondo de Cultura Económica, 2000.

corneta de órdenes

Expression that translated literally means "cornet of orders" but more accurately denotes a "command bugle" that in the 19th-century Mexican Army referred to a staff trumpeter who relayed signals and commands to units deployed on a battlefield by playing certain prearranged *toques* or "calls."

For example, after the conservative brigadier general Miguel Miramón had refrained all morning from giving the signal to storm his liberal opponents' positions at Ahualulco on September 29, 1858, he finally gave this order at 11:30 a.m. and noted in his journal that upon doing so, "the *corneta de órdenes* played the *toque* to attack, which was repeated all down the line," so his forces thereupon opened up a general fire and advanced to engage the enemy.

See also: Ahualulco de los Pinos, Battle of; *clarín de órdenes*; Miramón Tarelo, Miguel Gregorio de la Luz Atenógenes.

Further Reading

Hefter, Joseph. *Crónica del traje militar en México, del siglo XVI al XX.* Mexico City: Artes de México, 1968.

Corona Madrigal, Ramón (1837–1889)

Liberal republican general who distinguished himself during the War of the French Intervention.

He was born on October 18, 1837, at Puruagua Ranch outside the town of Tuxcueca, on the southern shores of Lake Chapala in the state of Jalisco, the first of three children sired by Esteban Corona Sánchez with his wife, María Dolores

Madrigal Navarro. Details about Ramón's boyhood and early education remain sketchy, although he reportedly was sent to live with relations and to study in Guadalajara in 1845, but the eruption of the Mexican-American War that following year meant he was returned home. It is known that his mother died before he reached the age of 11, after which he was again sent by his father to live with his relations, this time to learn the rudiments of business.

Early in 1851, his father had taken him to Tepic but abandoned him there the next year. The 15-year-old worked briefly in a store before being helped by the wealthy Gómez Cuervo family, who gave the bright young Corona a job as administrator at their Montage mines in 1856, although young Ramón was still only a teenager. The next year, Corona was listed as a volunteer infantry lieutenant in the local "Degollado" Militia Battalion and became a staunch liberal supporter like his patrons.

Local Liberal Campaigner (1858–1863)

When the War of the Reform between liberal and conservative factions erupted in central Mexico during the spring of 1858, Corona saw his first fighting that same autumn in an assault against the fortified compound of the local conservative leader, Manuel Lozada, on November 18, 1858. Thanks to his wealthy backers, Corona would be able to recruit numerous followers and rise to the rank of colonel (despite being involved in only local skirmishes), he and made his first major forays to participate in the failed liberal assault against Guadalajara in late May 1860 and its eventual capture that same September.

But Corona's focus remained mostly parochial, in Tepic. Even after the War of the Reform had concluded elsewhere, he departed on March 7, 1861, on yet another

campaign in pursuit of Lozada. This rivalry continued into the War of the French Intervention, and a large expeditionary force disembarked in far-off Veracruz early the next year, whose Mexican conservative collaborators called for revolts in the invaders' support so as to help drive the republican administration of Pres. Benito Juárez from power. As early as May 30, 1862, Lozada's conservative irregulars clashed with some of Corona's forces at the base of Ceboruco Hill in the state of Nayarit. However, their clashes took on greater importance when a French squadron under Cmdr. Thomas Louis Le Normant de Kergrist seized the Pacific port of Mazatlán without opposition on November 12, 1863, backed by a military column arriving overland the next day under Lozada.

Liberal Champion (1864–1867)

As the Franco-imperial regime of the emperor Maximilian sought to expand its influence from the capital into this distant region, Corona was thrust into the forefront of liberal resistance. With 600 lightly armed guerrillas, he attempted on New Year's Day 1865 to dispute passage through the Sierra Madre range from Durango toward Mazatlán of Col. Isidore T. Garnier's 18th *Chasseur* and 31st Line Regiments, backed by their respective artillery trains and Lozada's irregulars. Despite having chosen a highly defensible position at the *Espinazo del Diablo* or "Devil's Spine," his republican militiamen were eventually enveloped and scattered.

Undeterred, Corona surprised part of a French supply convoy a fortnight later at Veranos station, this time defeating its escort of 150 soldiers from the 7th *Chasseurs de Vincennes* Regiment plus 50 armed teamsters. The 60 French and 40 teamster prisoners were thereupon hanged, prompting the

French garrison commander in Mazatlán—Gen. Armand Alexandre de Castagny—to issue a decree on January 25, 1865, that ordered the execution of all republican guerrillas. Hostilities persisted between the Franco-imperial garrison hemmed inside their port and the republican guerrillas who controlled the countryside. On April 1, 1865, a sally by Lozada bested Corona in a skirmish at Concordia, Sinaloa, and again 17 days later near Cacalotán.

In early January 1866, two columns of 1,000 French and 1,200 imperial troops sortied from Mazatlán in a major attempt to chase away Corona's will-o'-the-wisp guerrillas; but only Lozada succeeded in surprising Col. Perfecto Guzmán's company at Guapicori, Sonora, on March 24, 1866, dispersing them before skirmishing against Corona himself at Concordia and retiring back into Mazatlán by April 11, 1866.

Eventually, the French abandoned that port on November 7, 1866, allowing Corona to reoccupy it five days later. As imperial fortunes waned and Paris ordered the recall of its expeditionary force, Maximilian's only reliable support, Corona was able to go over onto the offensive and began marching toward Central Mexico, gathering strength along the way. He entered Morelia, Michoacán, by February 20, 1867, raising the number of his republican troops to 6,000–7,000 before departing five days later to strike into the interior via Acámbaro and Celaya. At this latter city, his army was joined by an additional 3,000 men and 10 artillery pieces under Colonels Franco and Bermúdez on February 27, 1867, and at Chamacuero he agreed with Mariano Escobedo on March 5, 1867, to advance jointly against Maximilian's stronghold of Querétaro the next day, in parallel columns of approximately 10,000 men apiece.

Advance republican cavalry units confined the imperial defenders inside this city, allowing the approaching main bodies to encircle and besiege Querétaro. Corona's column arrived on March 8, 1867, seizing San Juanico and Celaya Gate just as Escobedo's contingent appeared out of the north. Corona's command was to be designated as the II or Western Corps and composed of the Jalisco Infantry Division under Manuel Márquez, the Sinaloa Infantry Division under Félix Vega, the Michoacán Infantry Division under Nicolás Régules, plus the Third Division from the I (Northern) Corps under Saturnino Aranda; and an artillery train under Francisco Paz.

Eventually, the republican host swelled to 32,000 troops and 100 guns, besieging 12,000 imperial defenders whose numbers and morale quickly dwindled as the weeks slipped past. Corona played a prominent role in this siege and personally captured the Emperor when resistance finally collapsed on May 15, 1867.

Later Years (1868–1889)

Corona served in political roles under the liberal Pres. Benito Juárez, and after his death was dispatched to Europe in 1874 by his successor Sebastián Lerdo de Tejada, serving as Mexico's ambassador for a decade—first to Portugal and then to Spain—until he returned to Mexico in 1884. Three years afterward, he was elected governor of Jalisco, assuming office on March 1, 1887. He introduced several reforms before he was unexpectedly stabbed by a madman on November 10, 1889, while walking through the streets of Guadalajara toward the Teatro Principal with his family. He died the next day, and lies buried in the Rotunda of Hombres Ilustres Jaliscienses.

See also: Escobedo Peña, Mariano Antonio Guadalupe; French Intervention, War of the; Maximilian, Emperor of Mexico; Querétaro, Siege of.

Further Reading

Beltrán y Puga, Emilia. *Apuntes biográficos del general de división Ramón Corona.* Mexico City: Tipografía "Diario del Hogar," 1885.

Message of the President of the United States of January 29, 1867, Relating to the Present Condition of Mexico. Washington, DC: U.S. Government Printing Office, 1867, 256–58, 271–75.

Sosa, Francisco. *Biografías de mexicanos distinguidos.* Mexico City: Porrúa, 2006.

corridos

Mexican ballads—popular songs that were sung by street performers during the 19th and early 20th centuries near gathering spots such as taverns or markets, often narrating stories about noteworthy events or figures.

As so many irregulars without uniforms had joined the ranks of different armies during the Mexican Revolution, one distinguishing feature became the music played by each particular faction. Northern rebels had become identified as early as the spring of 1911 with *La Adelita*, a lively piece sung by Maderista troops under "Generals" Domingo and Mariano Arieta as they had come marching into Mexico City. It would later be adopted by Pancho Villa's armies. His own personal favorite would be *Las tres pelonas*, a ribald ballad about three women on a balcony cheering passing troops: first those of Villa, then of his bitter rival Álvaro Obregón, then of his ally Tomás Urbina, then of his hated opponent Carranza, and finally of Villa again.

Obregón's well-disciplined army from Sonora would be recognized by *La Valentina*. *El abandonado* had been favored by conservative backers of the Díaz regime and later of Victoriano Huerta. Patrick O'Hea, a transplanted young Irishman who would meet many of the Revolution's chieftains, recorded in his *Reminiscences* the last request made by Jesús "Cheché" Campos, leader of a bloodthirsty pack of right-wing *colorados*. Standing before the execution wall, Campos had asked for a three-finger shot of *sotol* and for the band to play *El abandonado*. He had then "closed his eyes and given the sign to the firing squad."

Hundreds of ballads known as *corridos*, sung in restaurants or public places by street musicians, would narrate the great clashes of the war. *La toma de Zacatecas*, for example, would give an account of Villa's capture of that city in June 1914, while *Nuestro México, febrero veintitrés* satirized Pershing's cross-border incursion of two years later. Troubadours would also note the passing of famous personages such as *Benjamín Argumedo* and *Gabino Barrera*. The suffering of the anonymous soldiery would be described in *Carabina 30-30*, *Soldado de levita*, and many other songs. Eventually, these simple yet enduring tunes—favorites of revolutionary armies—would pass into the very fabric of Mexico's culture.

See also: *adelita*; Carabina 30-30.

Further Reading

Cardozo-Freeman, Inez. "José Inés Chávez García: Hero or Villain of the Mexican Revolution?" *Bilingual Review* 18, no. 1 (January–April 1993): 3–13.

Sánchez, Enrique. *Corridos de Pancho Villa.* Mexico City: Editorial de Magisterio, 1952.

Simmons, Merle E. *The Mexican Corrido as a Source for Interpretive Study of Modern Mexico (1870–1950).* New York: Kraus Reprint, 1969.

Cos Muñóz, Martín Perfecto (1805–1854)

Military officer affiliated since youth with the López de Santa Anna family and who would play a leading role in the ill-fated campaign that lost Texas.

Birth and Early Life (1805–1821)

Born in the port city of Veracruz in 1805, Martín Perfecto was the eldest of what would eventually be eight children (seven sons and one daughter) sired by the colonial functionary and notary Martín María Cos Cortés with his wife, María del Carmen Muñóz Hesaín. Young Martín's uncle— José Cos Cortés, older brother of his father—owned several businesses in that city and also held high command in its Regimiento de Infantería de Nueva España, into which his teenaged nephew would be duly enrolled as a cadet when he turned 15 years of age in 1820.

Antonio López de Santa Anna, an older friend of the family, had already been serving in that same regiment for a decade and was a veteran captain by the time that the teenager joined. The youthful Cos was promoted to lieutenant in 1821, the same year in which most remaining royalist units and officers in the country switched their allegiance over from the Spanish Crown to an independent Mexico.

Early Political Activity (1822–1829)

It is possible that in 1822, the 17-year-old subaltern was among the opponents of the newly crowned Emperor Iturbide who were jailed, as the name "Martín Cos" figured among a list of 52 political prisoners— including the congressional deputies José Joaquín Herrera, Francisco María Lombardo, "Servando Mier," "José Ugartechea," etc.— who were being detained in various convents around Mexico City on December 8, 1822, shortly before this would-be imperial government collapsed altogether.

Little else is known about Cos's early political-military career, although he may have been incarcerated again among the retinue of Veracruz's governor, Miguel Barragán, and Col. Manuel López de Santa Anna when those two officers were arrested and held in the offshore fortress of San Juan de Ulúa on orders from Pres. Guadalupe Victoria in late January 1828 for planning to support a stillborn insurrection by Nicolás Bravo. After a summary trial in Mexico City, most of those conspirators would be condemned to six years' exile and deported that same summer to widely scattered destinations.

Cos's name appeared among a list compiled on July 4, 1828, as having been sentenced to be sent—along with five other fellow prisoners, including José Urrea (his future enemy)—to Guayaquil, Ecuador. Many of these deportees would manage to reassemble in the United States, and when all were amnestied the next year by the new president, Vicente Guerrero, Cos was mentioned in a document dated November 6, 1829, as having been among the exile group aboard the American sloop *Splendid* that brought Bravo and Barragán home to Veracruz.

Santa Anna Loyalist (Early 1830s)

Cos was next identified as a loyal Santa Anna staff officer with the rank of colonel, who was riding alongside this president when the division with which they were marching together toward Cuautla Amilpas mutinied in favor of Gen. Mariano Arista on June 6, 1833, seizing and briefly detaining Santa Anna and his retainers—although they were released shortly thereafter. When this strongman subsequently led a 4,000-man army in a punitive strike against the autonomous movement in the state of Zacatecas, sacking its capital city in mid-May 1835, his loyal retainer Cos was in command of the centralist garrison stationed farther north at Saltillo.

When the federalist officials governing the combined states of Coahuila and Texas—alarmed by the report of Santa Anna's sack of Zacatecas—fled from their capital of Monclova into Texas on May 21, 1835, Cos assumed control from his base at Saltillo. He would soon be reinforced by Santa Anna, promoted to brigadier, and ordered to Matamoros by the beginning of July 1835 in order to lead an expedition into Texas, to stamp out its anticentralist dissenters.

Loss of Texas (1835–1836)

Cos duly disembarked with 500 soldiers at the tiny Texan port of Copano, about 30 miles north of present-day Corpus Christi, on September 20, 1835, pushing some 50 miles up the San Antonio River to occupy the small presidio town of Goliad by October 2, 1835. Leaving behind a garrison of 30 soldiers, he then pressed on with his main force into San Antonio.

One week afterward, Cos's detachment at Goliad was surprised and overwhelmed by 50 Texian volunteers from nearby Victoria under George Collingsworth, and by the end of October 1835 a small Texian army under Stephen F. Austin—after a few clashes—imposed a loose siege upon Cos's unhappy garrison, comprising only the regular Morelos Battalion plus five companies of unhappy conscripts. On November 3, 1835, a Texian convention at San Felipe resolved to oppose Santa Anna as loyal Mexican citizens upholding Mexico's federal constitution of 1824 while furthermore calling on other Mexican states to oppose his dictatorship.

One month later, "Colonel" Benjamin R. Milam led the Texian besiegers in an assault into the streets of San Antonio, pressing Cos's men back into the Alamo on December 5, 1835. Four days later Cos sued for

terms, and soon more than 1,100 Mexican troops would begin marching south, evacuating Texas. Winter now having set in, many of the victorious Texians decamped in the erroneous belief that the campaign had largely ended. However, Santa Anna suddenly materialized and crossed the border with a large invasion force during the first week of February 1836, driving upon San Antonio.

Cos figured as an aide-de-camp on Santa Anna's staff in this 6,000-man army, whose vanguard besieged and massacred the Alamo's outnumbered defenders by March 6, 1836. (It has long been erroneously maintained that Cos was the dictator's brother-in-law, although historical records indicate Cos had not yet been married at this time, nor would he ever marry any of Santa Anna's sisters.) Detachments were subsequently sent deeper into Texas to pursue fleeing Texian formations, Santa Anna himself leading one such column into Harrisburg by April 16, 1836, narrowly missing the fugitive Texian government.

Four days later, Santa Anna discovered the 900-man Texian army under Gen. Sam Houston encamped on the banks of the San Jacinto River and deployed for battle. Cos with 500 men reinforced Santa Anna's 900 troops on the morning of April 21, 1836, giving him superiority of numbers, so that the Mexican president confidently rested his army that same afternoon. But Houston silently charged at 4:30 p.m., quickly overwhelming the unprepared Mexicans, and capturing Santa Anna and Cos while annihilating their army. Texas had to be evacuated as a result, with the senior Mexican commanders being retained as prisoners of war.

Cos was not released until 14 months later, as according to Manuel Rivera Cambas's *Historia antigua y moderna de Jalapa*

(Mexico City: Ignacio Cumplido, 1870, 3: 327):

At Boca del Río, a North-American sloop dropped anchor on June 23 [1837], bringing on board various chiefs and officers who had been prisoners in Texas, and shortly thereafter another ship arrived, bringing General Martín Perfecto Cos.

Later Career (1837–1854)

With Santa Anna in disgrace, Cos could only find employment in his native state of Veracruz. During general Urrea's federalist uprising, Cos was listed as being in command of the centralist garrison at Túxpan, which was defeated when Mejía took that city on March 15, 1839. In his personal life, Cos would marry María Crispina Guillén Bello in the Sagrario of Tampico, Tamaulipas, on May 3, 1840, their only child—a daughter named María de la Soledad Jacobina Cos Guillén—being born the next year. Otherwise, there is little notice of his activities.

In Juan Nepomuceno Almonte's *Guía de forasteros* for 1852, Col. Martín Perfecto de Cos (with the acting rank of general) was mentioned as having headed the Comandancia General of Veracruz until September 30, 1852, when he reverted to second-in-command upon the resumption of this position by the naval commodore Tomás Marín. Two years later, Mariano Galván Rivera's *Guía de forasteros* for 1854 would list Cos as a general, by then in command of the department at Tehuantepec, a position which he was holding at the time of his death.

See also: Iturbide Arambúru, Agustín Cosme Damián de; San Jacinto, Battle of (1836); Santa Anna, Antonio López de; Texas Revolution.

Further Reading

Sosa, Francisco. *Biografías de mexicanos distinguidos*. Mexico City: Porrúa, 2006.

Cristero Rebellion (1926–1929)

Rural uprising led by conservative elements against the leftist social reforms implemented by Pres. Plutarco Elías Calles.

Troubled Prelude (January–June 1926)

This low-grade struggle slowly evolved after radical new policies, which had been drafted yet never enacted during the turbulence of the Mexican Revolution, began to be introduced by Calles as of January 1926. A tough political fixer who wished to transform Mexico's society and modernize its economy by improving prospects for urban laborers and rural peasants through better educational opportunities, greater equality of justice, and an end to class restrictions, Calles soon became frustrated by entrenched opposition from conservative leaders. When Archbishop José Mora y del Río of Mexico City responded to the administration's policies with a pastoral letter restricting religious services, Calles (an avowed Freemason and atheist) expanded his campaign.

With the promulgation of new anticlerical legislation on June 24, 1926, religious orders became outlawed; all priests had to be native Mexicans; religious schools were decertified; monasteries and other Church properties were nationalized; clergymen were denied the right to trial by jury and the vote; etc. Ecclesiastical leaders, with the backing of the Vatican, suspended all religious services as of July 31, 1926, and called for an economic boycott of the government.

Cristero Rebellion (1926–1929)

Feelings quickly escalated in remote rural areas, the first antigovernment attack being launched by the guerrilla chief Pedro Quintanar at Huejuquilla el Alto in the state of Jalisco on August 29, 1926. Soon, similar outbursts began to occur in neighboring Zacatecas, Guanajuato, Colima, and Michoacán. Exiles living in the United States, headed by René Capistrán Garza, organized the *Liga Nacional para la Defensa de la Libertad Religiosa* or "National League for the Defense of Religious Liberty" and had furthermore created a "war committee" by November 26, 1926, which instructed its followers to officially inaugurate hostilities against the Calles administration as of January 1, 1927. Their antipathy deepened when Mexico's reelection law was amended early in the new year to allow an ex-president (such as Obregón, whom they greatly abhorred) to run for a second term.

A band of rebels waylaid the Laredo-to-Mexico City train at San Miguel Allende on March 20, 1927, killing its conductor and guards and reputedly stealing 100,000 *pesos* in government funds. Since these Catholic irregulars—mostly impoverished, poorly armed peasants—displayed symbols of the Virgin of Guadalupe, called themselves *defensores* or "defenders" of the faith, and often shouted *Viva Cristo rey!* or "Long live Christ the King!" as their rallying cry, they would soon become more widely known as *cristeros*. Another 400 intercepted the Mexico City-to-Guadalajara train the next month near La Barca, Jalisco, not only killing its guards and crew but moreover setting it ablaze—113 innocent passengers dying in the resultant conflagration, many of them already wounded from the initial attack.

The government of Calles retaliated by expelling all archbishops and bishops from Mexico and sending the army on brutal sweeps throughout the state of Jalisco. Its mountainous backcountry would nonetheless prove to be a difficult maze and remain a hotbed of guerrilla activity, spearheaded by the well-regarded local leader Anacleto González Flores. In Mexico City, Obregón's reelection campaign provoked a short-lived military mutiny in October 1927 as well as an assassination attempt the next month by pro-Catholic fanatics, which resulted in a round of many executions. Eventually, Obregón won the election but was murdered at a public banquet on July 17, 1928, before being sworn in for his second term.

Three months afterward, the *cristero* leader González Flores was captured and executed by federal troops on October 28, 1928, being succeeded in command of the Catholic *Ejército Nacional Libertador* or "National Liberator Army" by the military veteran Enrique Gorostieta (a graduate of West Point).

At 4:00 a.m. on March 17, 1929, a column of 500 government troops under Gen. Pablo Rodríguez and 4,000 of Saturnino Cedillo's militia auxiliaries reached Españita on the outskirts of the slumbering town of Tepatitlán, Jalisco, penetrating into its streets to engage a concentration of some 4,000 *cristeros* who had gathered under the leadership of the priest José Reyes Vega. More than 100 of the attackers were killed in the resultant shootout, along with Reyes Vega himself and some two dozen *cristeros*, before Rodríguez was compelled to withdraw.

Gorostieta was betrayed to federal soldiers by a colleague on June 2, 1929, and killed. His successor proved to be less intractable, so with the mediation of U.S. ambassador Dwight W. Morrow, the Mexican Church and government were finally able to resolve their differences and a general amnesty was declared. Still, sporadic hostilities would persist in the hinterland for many years to come.

See also: Obregón Salido, Álvaro.

Further Reading

Bailey, David C. *Viva Cristo Rey! The Cristero Rebellion and the Church-State Conflict in Mexico.* Austin: University of Texas Press, 1974.

Butler, Matthew. *Popular Piety and Political Identity in Mexico's Cristero Rebellion: Michoacán, 1927–29.* New York: Oxford University Press, 2004.

Castillo Girón, Víctor Manuel. "La cristiada: desarrollo y efectos en el suroeste de Jalisco." *Estudios jaliscienses* 18 (November 1994): 47–62.

Jrade, Ramón. "Inquiries into the Cristero Insurrection against the Mexican Revolution." *Latin American Research Review* 20, no. 2 (1985): 53–69.

Meyer, Jean A. *The Cristero Rebellion: The Mexican People between Church and State, 1926–1929.* New York: Cambridge University Press, 1976.

cuartelazo

Slang expression used in Mexico and throughout Latin America to denote a military mutiny or coup, it was derived from the word *cuartel*, which simply means "barracks" or "quarters."

The term *cuartelazo* was usually applied to any surprise strike or seizure originating out of a single base or unit directed against an authority figure such as a government leader or military superior, rather than emanating from a more broad-based insurrection. A classic example of a *cuartelazo* would be the coup attempted when Brig. Gen. Juan José Urrea was broken out of confinement in Mexico City at 2:00 a.m. on July 15, 1840, then led the 5th Battalion and *Comercio* Militia Regiment in a quick occupation of the nearby Presidential Palace, capturing Pres. Anatasio Bustamante asleep in bed. At dawn, Urrea proclaimed the liberal ideologue Valentín Gómez Farías as Mexico's new president, but a loyalist counterattack out of the Ciudadela Barracks pinned his rebel followers inside the palace, from which Bustamante furthermore managed to cut his way free that same night with the help of a squadron of dragoons. After a fortnight of gunfire being rained down on the isolated rebels, and with no one else rising in his support, Urrea was compelled to surrender.

A more common form of mutiny was the *pronunciamiento* or "pronouncement," such as the insurrection initiated in March 1854 by the tiny garrison at remote Ayutla in the state of Guerrero. The small number of troops involved, and their geographic remove, made this revolt seem inconsequential—yet the manifesto that they published calling for the removal of the dictator Santa Anna and entrenched conservative rule, the so-called Plan de Ayutla, proved to be so broadly appealing that it spread to other garrisons. When Santa Anna failed to check this expanding insurrection with his army, more and more generals, governors, and cities began adhering to this plan, eventually making the Revolution of Ayutla impossible to extinguish and driving him from office.

See also: Ayutla, Revolution of; plan; *pronunciamiento*.

Further Reading

Finer, Samuel E. *The Man on Horseback: The Role of the Military in Politics.* 3rd ed. New Brunswick, NJ: Transaction, 2009.

Cuautla, Siege of (1812)

Protracted encirclement of José María Morelos's insurgent army that ended with his personal escape but the annihilation of his military force.

Preamble (Christmas 1811–February 7, 1812)

Having already secured most of the torrid southwestern coastal region (roughly equivalent to the modern state of Guerrero) by late 1811, this rebel chieftain dispatched columns to attempt Antequera de Oaxaca and the mining city of Taxco, while he entered the town of Cuautla de Amilpas with a sizeable contingent of followers on Christmas Day 1811. He departed shortly thereafter to attack a royalist band at Tenancingo, leaving his subordinate Leonardo Bravo in charge of Cuautla with orders to begin converting it into a fortified stronghold.

Having triumphed at Tenancingo, Morelos hastened back into Cuautla on February 7, 1812, realizing that a large royalist army under Gen. Félix María Calleja del Rey was about to attack his base. In finalizing its defensive preparations, he assigned Cuautla's San Diego district to Col. Hermenegildo Galeana, its Santo Domingo district to Leonardo Bravo, and the Buenavista district to Mariano Matamoros.

Initial Assault (February 17–19, 1812)

On February 17, 1812, Calleja's 2,000 royalists encamped at Pazulco—two-and-a-half miles northeast of Cuautla—having cornered Morelos inside with 2,000 riders, 1,000 infantry, and 1,300 auxiliaries under his subordinate colonels Hermenegildo Galeana, Miguel Bravo, and 41-year-old Mariano Matamoros (originally a village

priest from Jantetelco). The next day, the royalists advanced to probe Cuautla's defenses, only to have Morelos launch a surprise cavalry charge against their rear. In heavy fighting, the insurgent leader was almost captured before being rescued by Galeana.

At dawn of February 19, 1812, Calleja launched a four-pronged attack against Cuautla's San Diego Convent, which was being defended by Galeana. The insurgents waited until the royalists drew within 100 yards then opened up a withering fire. Despite heavy losses, Calleja's men overran the city's northeastern trench system, only to be blown off its northern parapets by the heroic 12-year-old gunner Narciso Mendoza, stationed at the Encanto Street battery. After six hours' close-quarter combat, the royalists retreated, leaving behind 200 dead (including Colonels Conde de Casa Rul and Juan N. Oviedo).

Six-Week Siege (February 20–May 1, 1812)

Having been thus bloodily repulsed in a direct assault, Calleja opted to impose a siege. In late February 1812, he was reinforced by 5,000 additional troops of the Puebla Division under Ciriaco de Llano. Royalist batteries also opened fire on Cuautla from Zacatepec and Calvario Hills by March 4, 1812, and siege lines were begun the next day from both the north and south. Over the ensuing few weeks, Calleja cut off the city's water supply, to which the insurgents responded by recapturing Juchitengo Dam and holding it against all royalist counterattacks.

On April 21, 1812, Matamoros led a desperate, 10-dragoon sally from Santa Inés Gate to contact an insurgent relief column that was bringing food under Miguel Bravo at Tlayacac Ravine (*Barranca Hediohonda*) but was then unable to escort these supplies back into Cuautla, instead being ambushed at Amazingo by Llano's cavalry and compelled to flee toward Tlacalaque (where Matamoros was eventually defeated by Mateo Nieto).

Desperate Escape (May 2, 1812)

One week later, provisions within the beleaguered city were finally exhausted, so at 2:00 a.m. on May 2, 1812, Morelos led a dash toward freedom. The starved insurgents quietly wended their way down Cuautla's riverbank until they encountered the royalist picket lines, at which point they charged and fought their way through as best they could. Losses were heavy on both sides, some of Calleja's royalist formations mistakenly firing on each other in the gloom. Morelos escaped to Ocuituco, but his insurgent army was nevertheless broken and dispersed, units being chased for many miles by royalist cavalry while Cuautla itself was given over to the sack.

See also: Calleja, Félix María; Morelos Pavón, José María Teclo.

Further Reading

Archer, Christon I. "Years of Decision: Félix Calleja and the Strategy to End the Revolution of New Spain." In *The Birth of Modern Mexico*, edited by Christon I. Archer, 125–49. Wilmington, DE: Scholarly Resources, 2003.

Bustamante, Carlos María de. *Campañas del general D. Félix María Calleja*. Mexico City: Imprenta del Águila, 1828.

Hamill, Hugh M., Jr. "Royalist Counterinsurgency in the Mexican War for Independence: The Lessons of 1811." *Hispanic American Historical Review* 53, no. 3 (August 1973): 470–89.

Lemoine, Ernesto. *Morelos: su vida revolucionaria a través de sus escritos y otros testimonios de la época*. Mexico City: UNAM, 1991.

Cucaracha, La

Popular 19th-century *corrido* or street ballad that took on a special meaning and underwent many interpretations—often with political overtones—during the Mexican Revolution of 1910.

This uncomplicated, catchy tune had existed since at least the year 1883, although its origin and composer remain unknown. The words of its first verse begin simply:

> The cockroach, the cockroach,
> Can no longer walk,
> Because it's missing,
> Because it doesn't have,
> Its principal little leg.

Over the decades, people had invented their own unique verses for every conceivable occasion or event, many of these extemporized versions having a mocking air—especially whenever directed as a subtle protest or complaint against the actions of public figures.

For example, the betrayal and murder of Pres. Francisco I. Madero in February 1913 by the man who would then usurp his position, Gen. Victoriano Huerta, had made the latter, sustained in office by random arrests or murders of any opponents who dared speak out against him, a hated and feared figure among the population at large. The frightened citizenry of Mexico City took to greeting news reports of Huerta's armies being destroyed one after another up in the north by playing *La Cucaracha*—its connotation being that as each "leg" or army propping up his regime disappeared, his administration was becoming less and less able to "walk."

The infectious *Cucaracha* has since gone through countless more adaptations and interpretations and still remains today universally recognized as a quintessential Mexican tune.

See also: *corridos*; Huerta Márquez, José Victoriano.

Further Reading

de María y Campos, Armando. *La Revolución mexicana a través de los corridos populares*. Mexico City: INEHRM, 1962.

Mendoza, Vicente T. *El corrido mexicano*. Mexico City: Fondo de Cultura Económica, 1954.

Cuerpo del Ejército Constitucionalista del Noroeste (1913–1914)

Literally translated as "Corps of the Constitutionalist Army of the Northwest," this was the official designation for one of seven revolutionary corps whose creation had been authorized as of July 4, 1913, by the insurrectionist *primer jefe* or "first chief" of the anti-Huertista movement, Gov. Venustiano Carranza of Coahuila.

In theory, rebels in every part of the country were supposed to coalesce into regional corps of his nationwide "Constitutionalist Army," whose organization he had compartmentalized into a:

- *Cuerpo de Ejército del Noroeste* (Northwest)
- *Cuerpo de Ejército del Noreste* (Northeast)
- *Cuerpo de Ejército del Este* (East)
- *Cuerpo de Ejército del Occidente* (West)
- *Cuerpo de Ejército del Centro* (Center)
- *Cuerpo de Ejército del Sur* (South)
- *Cuerpo de Ejército del Sureste* (Southeast)

In reality, though, only a few northern leaders ever chose to fully recognize Carranza's authority, much less submit to this organizational scheme. The "Corps of the Army of the Northwest," for example, was

Portrait of Gov. Venustiano Carranza of Coahuila, dressed in his uniform as "First Chief" of the movement against Huerta; humorless and autocratic, he would be resented by almost all the revolutionary chieftains. (Library of Congress)

supposed to encompass all rebel troops in the states of Chihuahua, Durango, Sinaloa, and Sonora, and the territory of Baja California—although the huge *División del Norte* or "Northern Division" of Pancho Villa operated with its own separate agenda in neighboring Chihuahua and Durango, only rarely heeding Carranza's directives.

Nevertheless, the smaller but very potent *Cuerpo del Ejército Constitucionalista del Noroeste* or "Army of the Northwest" under Brig. Gen. Álvaro Obregón would not only help to topple the regime of Victoriano Huerta but eventually defeat Villa as well.

See also: División del Norte; Ejército del Noroeste; Obregón Salido, Álvaro; Revolution, Mexican; Teoloyucan, Treaties of; Villa, Pancho.

Further Reading

Hall, Linda B. *Álvaro Obregón: Power and Revolution in Mexico, 1911–1920.* College Station: Texas A&M University Press, 1981.

Jowett, Philip, and Alejandro de Quesada. *The Mexican Revolution, 1910–20.* Oxford: Osprey, 2006.

Salmerón, Pedro. *Los carrancistas: la historia nunca contada del victorioso Ejército del Noroeste.* Mexico City: Planeta, 2010.

Cumbres de Acultzingo, Battle of the (1862)

Initial encounter of the War of the French Intervention, a fleeting clash between a Mexican division waiting in a roadside ambush and the advancing French expeditionary force.

French Approach (April 27, 1862)

After pushing inland from the Gulf coast, the invaders under Maj. Gen. Charles, Comte de Lorencez had entered the city of Orizaba unopposed on April 27, 1862. Leaving behind two infantry companies and a naval battery as its garrison (as well as 463 ill or convalescent men), the French general then continued his march inland the next morning at the head of 6,150 troops which included:

- 11 companies of the 99th Line Regiment under Col. Edmond-Aimable l'Heriller
- Two battalions of the 2nd Zouave Regiment under Col. Pierre G. E. Gambier
- The 1st Battalion of the *Chasseurs à Pied* Regiment under Lt. Col. Léon Mangin
- Two battalions of French Marines under Col. Agathon Hennique
- Four companies of *Marins Fusiliers* under Frigate Captain Allègre
- The sixth company of the 2nd Engineers under Captain Barillon
- Various auxiliaries
- An artillery train of 16 small pieces under Capt. Maximilien C. C. Bernard of the 3rd Artillery Regiment

When the regional commander for Mexico's republican *Ejército de Oriente* or "Eastern Army," Gen. Ignacio Zaragoza, learned that the French had resumed their penetration deeper into the country, he ordered 29-year-old general José María Arteaga to take his 2nd Division, along with 200 dragoons and a dozen small field howitzers, to occupy the *cumbres* or "heights" above the town of Acultzingo and challenge the French as they trudged up its steep, winding highway into the central highlands. Arteaga's main body consisted of 2,000 infantrymen from four brigades:

- The 1st Brigade under Brig. Gen. José Rojo
- The 2nd Brigade under Col. Mariano Escobedo
- The 3rd Brigade under Brig. Gen. Domingo Gayoso
- The 4th Brigade under Brig. Gen. Miguel Negrete

However, Zaragoza accompanied Arteaga on this detached service and instructed him to mount only a transitory resistance (a *"defensa meramente pasajera"*) before drawing his outnumbered division off so as to rejoin the main republican concentration that was already marshaling to make its stand in the city of Puebla.

Battle at the Cumbres de Acultzingo (April 28, 1862)

As Lorencez's vanguard—a squadron of the 2nd *Chasseurs d'Afrique*—emerged onto the plain outside Acultzingo at 9:00 a.m. on the morning of April 28, 1862, they spotted some Mexican riders in the distance who promptly wheeled about and disappeared. Soon after, as the main French body began disgorging out onto this same plain, the abandoned town burst into flames, so the invaders had to bivouac in open ground by 10:00–11:00 a.m. to prepare their midday meal, their numbers and composition plainly visible to republican scouts and observers looking down from the nearby mountains.

When the 2nd Zouave Battalion subsequently resumed its march around smoldering Acultzingo toward the *Puente Colorado* or "Red Bridge" beyond, at the base of the upward-winding highway, they suddenly drew fire at 1:30 p.m. from hidden republican riflemen who had stealthily moved into position with a small battery; and when the French light infantry failed to chase away these ambushers and their shooting instead intensified, Lorencez deployed his entire army so as to engage in strength.

While a main body of 3,000 French troops pushed directly up the highway, twin flanking columns of 1,000 soldiers apiece worked up into the mountains on either side of it, all three columns preceded by screens of *tirailleurs*. Unable to clearly discern his opponents' formations, Lorencez believed that he had engaged a republican army rather than a single detached division and so moved upward cautiously. The Mexicans managed to stall his main central thrust, but while Zaragoza was inspecting the distant right flank of the far-flung republican positions, Arteaga was wounded in a leg and his staff gave the prearranged signal for a general retirement. After three hours of sniping and exchanges of long-range volleys, the republicans withdrew and the French gained the heights above Acultzingo as evening fell, seeing their foes retiring back in the direction of San Agustín del Palmar.

Aftermath (April 29–May 3, 1862)

Curiously, both sides were convinced that they had inflicted heavy casualties on their enemies during this indecisive engagement, although losses were in fact minimal on either side. Zaragoza, whose intent had been to merely take a toll on the invaders at this vulnerable highway ascent and slow their advance, reported to his superiors in Mexico City that the French had "suffered greatly from dead and wounded, whose number was considerable"—but in fact, French regimental returns recorded only 2 dead and 32 wounded from this action. Lorencez in turn, convinced that he had beaten off a major republican army rather than simply endured an ambush by a single division, estimated Mexican losses to run into many hundreds—although their total casualties scarcely reached 50 (among them Arteaga, whose leg had to subsequently be amputated).

Naturally, neither commander lingered on this mountainside battlefield to verify their claims. Instead, a satisfied Zaragoza returned into Puebla by May 3, 1862, to complete his defensive dispositions, and one week later he defeated Lorencez's direct assault on that city during the Battle of the Cinco de Mayo.

See also: Cinco de Mayo, Battle of the; Escobedo Peña, Mariano Antonio Guadalupe; French Intervention, War of the; Lorencez, Charles Ferdinand Latrille, Comte de; Zaragoza Seguín, Ignacio.

Further Reading

Bibesco, Prince Georges. *Au Mexique 1862: combats et retraite des six mille*. Paris: E. Plon, Nourrit, et Cie., 1887, 116–32.

D

Here are your wrappers back,
send me more tamales.
— taunting note sent by Pascual Orozco
to Pres. Porfirio Díaz, along with bloody
khaki uniforms taken from dead federal
soldiers (December 1910)

Decena Trágica (1913)

The "Tragic Fortnight," the name popularly
applied to the violent military coup that
deposed the inexperienced president
Francisco I. Madero, in the process inflicting
heavy civilian casualties and damage amid
the crowded confines of Mexico City.

Uprising and Standoff (February 9–17, 1913)

After months of mounting dissatisfaction
against the ineffectual administration of the
political neophyte Madero, Generals
Manuel Mondragón and Gregorio Ruiz initiated a mutiny against the increasingly
unpopular president at 2:00 a.m. on February 9, 1913, by marching into Mexico City
from nearby Tacubaya at the head of the
1st, 2nd, and 5th Cavalry Regiments—
being joined en route by the 1st Artillery
Regiment, for a total of 2,400 rebel soldiers
under their command, backed by six cannon
and 14 machine guns. Some 600 cadets from
Mexico's *Escuela de Aspirantes* or military
"Preparatory School" in Tlalpan also commandeered streetcars, leading the way into
the heart of the capital that quiet Sunday

morning so as to help support this insurrection. Meanwhile, one column of mutineers
released Gen. Bernardo Reyes from imprisonment at Santiago Tlatelolco, while
another freed Brig. Gen. Félix Díaz from
Lecumberri Penitentiary.

By the time that the mutineers began converging on the Presidential Palace, it had
already been briefly occupied by the cadets,
who in turn were overwhelmed by 500 troops
of the 24th Battalion under the elderly general
Lauro Villar, loyal to Madero. Lauro then
furthermore arrested General Ruiz when the
latter entered the main square, at which point
a shootout erupted during which exchange of
gunfire the mutinous General Reyes and
another 300 people—including many curious
civilian onlookers—were killed and another
200 wounded.

Repelled from the Presidential Palace, the
mutineers withdrew and at 1:00 p.m. forced
their way into the *Ciudadela* or "Citadel"
arsenal less than a mile away, executing its
commanding general, Rafael Dávila, and
numerous other defenders before digging in
to fight it out against loyalist forces. In the
meantime, Madero had descended from
Chapultepec Castle at midday and appointed
Gen. Victoriano Huerta (who had been dismissed from the army and so was in the
crowd) as interim commander of the Presidential Palace in place of Villar, who had
since been badly wounded. Huerta summarily ordered the captive General Ruiz
and all rebel cadets to be shot by firing
squads, while Madero traveled toward
Cuernavaca that same afternoon to summon

a further 1,000 loyal troops under the more reliable and honorable 43-year-old brigadier general Felipe Ángeles.

Monday, February 10, 1913, passed in tense silence in the capital, although the quiet was shattered at 10:00 a.m. on Tuesday morning when an artillery duel erupted against the mutineers still holding out inside the surrounded *Ciudadela* during which another 500 civilians were killed. (Eventually, 5,000 would perish over the course of the days of fighting in this densely packed urban landscape.) Upon Ángeles's arrival on the scene, he and his superior, Huerta, commanded a combined total of 6,000 troops, while only 1,800 remained to the trapped rebels Mondragón and Díaz; still, Huerta seemed incapable of reducing this ancient fortress, soon provoking doubts as to his loyalty.

Betrayal and Murder (February 18–22, 1913)

After five more days of long-range shelling, President Madero's youngest brother, Gustavo, arrested Huerta at 2:00 a.m. on February 18, 1913, accusing him before the president of treacherously delaying any military resolution. Unconvinced, the latter ordered the general released, and at 1:30 that same afternoon, Huerta in turn detained Gustavo Madero (who was soon put to death and his body dismembered), while sending Gen. Aureliano Blanquet's 29th Battalion to capture the president, who after a brief struggle was seized along with his vice president, José María Pino Suárez, and most of the cabinet.

By 9:30 p.m. on February 18, 1913, Huerta was meeting with Díaz at the residence of the U.S. ambassador, Henry Lane Wilson—a vocal critic of Madero—to sign a pact whereby Huerta would temporarily assume the presidency on the understanding that he would subsequently support the ex-Porfirian dictator's son during forthcoming elections. As for Francisco Madero, after resigning from office and being promised safe conduct into Cuban exile, he was taken out behind Lecumberri Penitentiary on the edge of Mexico City on the night of February 22, 1913, and cruelly murdered.

Aftermath (Spring 1913)

This brutal usurpation of the office of president made Huerta a widely hated figure, so many states refused to acknowledge his authority and revolutionary armies resurged in greater strength than ever before, united in their desire to drive him from power. Despite a massive buildup of the Federal Army, Huerta would be defeated and exiled from Mexico in a little over a year.

See also: Ángeles Ramírez, Felipe de Jesús; Huerta Márquez, José Victoriano; Mondragón Mondragón, Manuel.

Further Reading

Aguilar, José Ángel. *La decena trágica*. No. 89, 2 vols. Mexico City: Biblioteca del INEHRM, 1981–1982.

Hanrahan, Gene Z. *Documents on the Mexican Revolution, Volume 4: The Murder of Madero and Role Played by U.S. Ambassador Henry Lane Wilson*. Salisbury, NC: Documentary Publications, 1981.

Hidalgo, Dennis R. "The Evolution of History and the Informal Empire: La Decena Trágica in the British Press." *Mexican Studies/Estudios Mexicanos* 23, no. 2 (Summer 2007): 317–54.

Villalpando César, José Manuel. *La decena trágica*. Mexico City: Diana, 2009.

Degollado Sánchez, José Nemesio Francisco (1811–1861)

Amateur liberal general who endured repeated defeats during the War of the

Reform before his cause eventually emerged triumphant.

Birth and Early Life (1811–1835)

He was born in the city of Guanajuato on October 30, 1811, and baptized two days later as José Nemesio Francisco Degollado Sánchez by his parents, the Spanish-born Francisco Degollado and his Mexican wife, María Sánchez—but because that particular baptismal date of November 1st coincided with the *día de Todos los Santos* or "All Saints Day" on the Church calendar, the infant would later be commonly called José Santos Degollado or simply Santos Degollado throughout most of his lifetime. A second son, christened Rafael, would be born into this small family the next year, although the parents then suffered the confiscation of their goods by the Crown authorities because of their insurgent proclivities, and the two boys were left orphaned by 1817.

Six-year-old Francisco "Santos" Degollado was sent to live with his uncle, the presbyter Mariano Garrido, who in turn was dispatched by the Church to serve as assistant village priest at San Diego Cocupao (modern Quiroga, Michoacán). Young Santos consequently received his early education and grew up there, and two weeks short of his 17th birthday married Ignacia Castañeda Espinoza on October 14, 1828, moving with her to live and work in Morelia as the scribe at its cathedral. Soon, they would have two sons, named Joaquín and Mariano.

Initial Political-Military Activities (1836–1857)

In the turbulent times following the defeat and capture in Texas of the centralist dictator, Pres. Antonio López de Santa Anna, in early 1836, the 25-year-old Santos Degollado briefly joined the federalist forces in Michoacán as a sublieutenant under Col. Felipe Angón, whose movement was quickly crushed. As a liberal sympathizer though, Degollado was incarcerated again for eight months in 1840, but his abilities and inclinations proved to be of a more scholarly nature so he instead shined as a gifted scholar, educator, and bureaucrat. When the literate Melchor Ocampo became governor of the state of Michoacán, he appointed Degollado to numerous high institutional positions, and when Ocampo resigned from the governorship, Degollado served out the rest of his term from March 27 to July 6, 1848.

Upon the eruption of the *anti-santannista* Revolution of Ayutla in the spring of 1854, Degollado figured once again among the ranks of liberal supporters. The June 28, 1854, edition of the *New Orleans Picayune* newspaper even included a paragraph stating that:

On the first of June [1854], Señores Santos Degollado and Octaviano Ortiz, accused "by public opinion" of being the principal instigators of the insurrection in this department, were arrested. The law of conspirators was not enforced against them, however, but they were banished to distant points.

Santa Anna was driven from office by August 1855, at which time Degollado was appointed to serve as interim governor and militia general-in-chief for the state of Jalisco, a position that he would occupy from August 31, 1855, until May 30, 1856. During this term, the acting president of Mexico, Gen. Juan N. Álvarez, furthermore conferred on him the rank of *general de brigada* or "brigade general."

Service during the War of the Reform (1858–1860)

Degollado was elected that same February 1856 as a *diputado* or "delegate" from

Michoacán to the national Congress in Mexico City, which would set out to reform the Constitution by controversially eliminating many ancient privileges and laws. A leading liberal figure, he was voted governor of Michoacán in the elections of November 1857 and named as a Supreme Court justice, although conservative opposition quickly flared into open conflict after the moderate president Ignacio Comonfort was deposed by a coup in January 1858. Subsequently, a conservative army under the youthful brigadier generals Luis G. Osollo and Miguel Miramón defeated a concentration of liberal militia formations under Gen. Anastasio Parrodi (who was also the governor of Jalisco) at the Battle of Salamanca in March 1858, entering Guadalajara without resistance before that same month was out.

Prior to fleeing from that city, the fugitive liberal president Benito Juárez had appointed Degollado on March 27, 1858, as the minister of war and general-in-chief of his government. After the main conservative army departed on further commissions, Degollado returned to besiege Guadalajara with his 1st Liberal Division on May 21, 1858, parleying with its conservative garrison commander, Gen. Francisco García Casanova, at the tiny hamlet of San Pedro during a brief ceasefire on June 4, 1858. Unable to reach an accord, Degollado closed with his liberals and they fortified themselves around the Hospicio de Santo Domingo, exchanging desultory gunfire until it was learned that Miramón was marching to the garrison's relief with an army of regulars, so the ill-armed liberals raised their siege nine days afterward.

Disaster at Estancia de las Vacas (November 1859)

By early November 1859, Degollado was leading a liberal army of 6,000 men and 29 fieldpieces through the Bajío region of central Mexico with such well-known field commanders as José Justo Álvarez, Manuel Doblado, Miguel Blanco, José María Arteaga, and Santiago Tapia serving as his subordinate brigadiers. They easily bested a small conservative contingent near Silao and then chased another out of the city of Guanajuato. To personally counter this growing threat, Miramón left Mexico City on the night of November 5–6, 1859, to assume command over a scratch army that was being thrown together at Querétaro, totaling only 2,600 conservative troops armed with 19 guns.

Degollado's advancing army had reached Apaseo by November 11, 1859, from where the liberal commander sent an emissary into Querétaro to propose a meeting between himself and Miramón. The two generals met between La Calera and the Hacienda del Rayo at 4:30 p.m. on November 12, 1859, but failed to arrive at any understanding. Degollado consequently ordered his second-in-command, Doblado, to deploy the liberal army overnight into defensive battle lines atop the hills of Estancia de las Vacas, less than six miles west of Querétaro.

Miramón's smaller conservative army also moved out of the city, and his guns opened up long-range fire against the liberal positions at 7:00 a.m. on November 13, 1859. After two hours of exchanges, attack columns swarmed out of both liberal wings, yet the difficult terrain hampered their efforts to charge in a single mass. Miramón managed to check the danger on both his flanks until Degollado sent his liberal 1st and 2nd Light San Luis Battalions under Tapia and Blanco directly into the conservative center. They overran some guns, and when Miramón countered with his reserve, the liberals broke up these formations as well, seeming to be on the verge of carrying the day.

Desperate, Miramón personally led his last 120 reserves into the center while calling for a general counterattack all along his battle line. At this crucial juncture, Tapia and Col. Albino Espinosa of the liberal 1st Light San Luis Battalion both fell severely wounded, so their leaderless men began to shrink back out of the firefight in confusion. Then, as more and more liberal troops began retreating, Degollado tried to stabilize the situation by issuing an order around 11:00 a.m. for his reeling army to withdraw and reassemble within their strong defensive positions atop the Estancia de las Vacas hills. However, their jumbled retirements out of the battle line quickly turned into outright flight, officers' shouted commands being ignored as their soldiers scattered in every direction. Many of these runaways appropriated horses and mules from the artillery and supply trains so as to make good their escape. A furious Doblado even wanted to fire grapeshot at these deserters but discovered that the liberals' guns already lay abandoned by their crews.

Despite being outnumbered by more than two to one, Miramón had emerged victorious, although his army had suffered 89 killed and 114 wounded during this quick, sharp encounter, compared to 275 casualties among the liberals. The conservatives nonetheless retained 120 prisoners, 29 fieldpieces, a forge, 63 loaded wagons, and some 500 firearms, while Doblado led the tattered remnants of his liberal army away toward Salvatierra. Degollado, who escaped through Celaya toward San Luis Potosí, would henceforth become known derisively as the *héroe de las derrotas* or "hero of the defeats" among liberals and conservatives alike.

But the victorious liberals would not immediately close in on Mexico City. González Ortega gained the city of Querétaro against scant opposition, only to then install a garrison of 4,000 men and 14 artillery pieces under Generals Berriozábal and Benito Quijano before reversing his main army and marching back westward on September 7, 1860—in obedience of Degollado's orders, as "general-in-chief of the Federal [constitutionalist] Army"—to first subdue Guadalajara, the last major conservative-held stronghold before commencing any final push toward the national capital.

Death (June 1861)

Although the War of the Reform had ended in a liberal victory, small contingents of conservatives continued to carry out isolated attacks. One such group captured Degollado's predecessor as foreign minister, the scholarly Melchor Ocampo, on June 1, 1861, at the latter's Hacienda de Pomoca near Maravatío, Michoacán, taking him before the fugitive generals Leonardo Márquez and Félix Zuloaga at Tepejí del Río in the state of Hidalgo. They ordered Ocampo summarily shot by a firing squad on June 3, 1861, and left his body hanging from a tree.

Incensed by this brutal murder of his lifelong friend, Degollado and liberal general Leandro Valle rode in pursuit of these conservatives so as to avenge his death. However, while riding from Lerma across the Salazar plains toward the old battlefield of Monte de las Cruces on June 15, 1861, Degollado was suddenly struck in the head by shots fired from the nearby trees. As he lay wounded on the ground, the conservative gunmen emerged from their hiding spots and finished him off, his body being interred at nearby Huixquilucan.

See also: Márquez Araujo, Leonardo; Monte de las Cruces, Battle of; Reform, War of the; Tacubaya, Plan de; Zuloaga Trillo, Félix María.

Further Reading

Cambre, Manuel. *La guerra de Tres Años: apuntes para la historia de la Reforma.* Guadalajara, Jalisco: Gobierno del Estado, 1949.

"From Mexico." *New York Times*, July 7, 1854.

"From Mexico: Further Success of the Conservative Cause." *New York Times*, December 14, 1859.

Sosa, Francisco. *Biografías de mexicanos distinguidos.* Mexico City: Porrúa, 2006.

diana

Centuries-old Spanish name for a trumpet flourish, usually referring to the tune played at dawn to announce reveille, although also used by 19th- and early 20th-century Mexican armies to highlight special moments or events throughout the day.

For example, when Brig. Gen. Miguel Miramón's conservative Carabinero and Toluca Battalions charged uphill against the strongpoint on liberals' left flank during the Battle of Ahualulco de los Pinos at 1:00 p.m. on September 28, 1858, their commander would note with some relief in his journal the moment when he at last heard the *dianas* that their distant bands "made resound throughout the air, in signal of triumph."

See also: Ahualulco de los Pinos, Battle of; Miramón Tarelo, Miguel Gregorio de la Luz Atenógenes.

Further Reading

Hefter, Joseph. *Crónica del traje militar en México, del siglo XVI al XX.* Mexico City: Artes de México, 1968.

Díaz Mori, José de la Cruz Porfirio (1830–1915)

Hero of the War of the French Intervention who would subsequently serve as president of Mexico for nine terms, eventually being expelled as a hated despot.

Birth and Education (1830–1854)

He was born and baptized on September 15, 1830, in the southern city of Oaxaca, the sixth child and eldest surviving son of José Faustino Díaz Orozco and his wife, María Petrona Cecilia Mori Cortés. His father was a Creole who owned a modest inn, while his mother was of Zapotec descent. Three years later, one final child—a boy christened as Felipe Santiago—would be born into this family, but the father died that same year, leaving them in straitened circumstances.

Porfirio's widowed mother would succeed in getting her 15-year-old son admitted to that city's Seminario Conciliar in 1845, where he studied over the next four years. Upon graduating, he was enrolled in the state-run *Instituto de Ciencias y Artes* or "Institute of Sciences and Arts," studying for the law until the Revolution of Ayutla erupted against the ostentatious regime of President Santa Anna in the spring of 1854, when funding was suspended and several teachers arrested.

Liberal Militia Commander during the War of the Reform (1855–1860)

The 24-year-old Díaz joined a band of irregulars under the local liberal leader Francisco Herrera, making raids in the Mixteca region until they were dispersed by *santannista* troops. Díaz lived as a fugitive in the wilderness with a few companions until the dictator was driven from power by early August 1855, when he emerged from hiding

and was rewarded with appointment as sub-
prefect of the district of Ixtlán, located just
north of Oaxaca City. He participated
actively in the rough-and-tumble of politics,
and after Benito Juárez was elected state
governor and conservative outbursts
erupted, Díaz was appointed a captain in
the 1st *Guardia Nacional* or "National
Guard" Battalion of Oaxaca on December 22, 1856.

He was badly wounded during a clash at
Ixcapa on August 13, 1857, convalescing
over the next four months. He commanded
the Santa Catarina district of Oaxaca City
when it was besieged in December 1857
by a force led out of Tehuantepec by
conservative Gen. José María Cobos, who
was defeated and driven off on January 16,
1858. Sent in pursuit with 600 troops, Díaz
beat the Tehuantepecans again at Jalapa on
February 25, 1858, and remained as military
governor of their city with a garrison of only
150 liberal troops. They soon became isolated within its Santo Domingo Convent
because of the locals' hostility, but Díaz succeeded in surprising the Tehuantepecan
militia leaders at a ranch called Las Jícaras
after a swift, stealthy approach on April 13,
1858, killing most of them and easing the
pressure on his occupying force. For this,
he was promoted to *comandante* or "commander" in the Oaxaca state militia as of
July 22, 1858.

He was still troubled by the bullet in his
body that had wounded him almost a year
earlier at Ixcapa. It was removed that same
summer of 1858 by some American sur-
geons who were attending to the workers
engaged on a private road project across the
isthmus of Tehuantepec. By the next spring,
Díaz was able to pursue and defeat a
conservative force on June 17, 1859, at La
Mixtequilla, a few miles west of the city of
Tehuantepec, which won him promotion to

lieutenant colonel in the Oaxacan state militia. He was still serving on this detached service, though, when the main 3,000-man
Oaxacan army under Gen. Ignacio Mejía
was beaten by Cobos at Teotitlán del
Camino, and Oaxaca City was abandoned
to the conservatives on November 5, 1859.
A detachment thereupon advanced on
Tehuantepec as well, which Díaz also abandoned, but he returned stealthily with 300
troops to reclaim it briefly through a surprise
attack against its conservative garrison on
the night of November 24–25, 1859, winning promotion to full colonel.

Nonetheless, he soon evacuated that city
to join the fugitive liberal government at Ixtlán, whose forces remained dispersed and
under strength throughout that winter. It
was not until Colonels Cristóbal Salinas
and Díaz finally marched with 1,000 men
and three small fieldpieces on July 31,
1860, that they were able to reconquer
Oaxaca City from Cobos one week later.
Díaz was recognized as a full colonel in the
national army fighting for the liberal cause,
and by late October 1860 he marched as
one of the commanding officers of a brigade
intended to join Gen. Pedro Ampudia's division at Tula, Hidalgo, for the final push
against Mexico City. This Oaxacan contingent did not arrive until after the last
conservative army had been defeated at
the Battle of Calpulalpan, but they did
participate in the grand parade into the
national capital a couple of weeks later
before returning home to be disbanded in
January 1861.

Rise to National Prominence (1861–1865)

Shortly thereafter, Díaz was elected a *diputado* or "deputy" for Oaxaca to the new
national Congress and returned to Mexico
City. While in session on June 24, 1861,

word suddenly arrived that the fugitive conservative general Leonardo Márquez had materialized with 2,600 troops and five small guns and was penetrating the capital along its San Cosme *calzada* or "causeway." Díaz hastened from the chamber to the Oaxaca Brigade's quarters in the San Fernando Convent and helped organize a hasty counterattack that drove away this danger. He then marched in pursuit of the retreating conservatives as part of a converging liberal division under the command of Maj. Gen. Jesús González Ortega, overtaking and scattering Márquez's small army on August 13, 1861, while it was resting at the town of Jalatlaco. His role in the forefront of these events won Díaz promotion to *general de brigada* or "brigade general."

When the fugitive conservatives reemerged a couple of months later to seize the Mineral del Chico, just beyond the city of Pachuca in the state of Hidalgo, Díaz marched as a senior commander of the liberal army that defeated them on October 20, 1861. And that same December 17, 1861, some 5,800 Spanish soldiers disembarked to occupy the city of Veracruz with demands for compensation from Mexico's bankrupt republican government, so Díaz was placed in command of the 2nd Oaxaca Brigade as the *Ejército de Oriente* or "Army of the East" was mobilized to confront these foreign invaders.

He would see distinguished service during the ensuing conflict known as the War of the French Intervention, his 1,020-man 3rd Infantry Brigade playing a central role and fighting bravely in the initial victory at Puebla on May 5, 1862, the famed Battle of the Cinco de Mayo. When a second, much larger French Army succeeded in capturing that city a year later, the 32-year-old Díaz commanded the division that escorted President Juárez out of the capital on May 31, 1863, to set up a government in exile at San Luis Potosí. And as French columns and their Mexican conservative collaborators spread inexorably throughout central Mexico, he worked his way back toward his home state of Oaxaca with a 7,000-man army so as to sustain conservative resistance.

On October 27, 1863, Díaz attacked the rich mining town of Taxco in the state of Guerrero with:

- Two battalions of Oaxaca chasseurs under Gen. José María Ballesteros, constituting his detached army's 1st Infantry Brigade
- Two battalions of the México Regiment under Col. Manuel González, acting as his 2nd Infantry Brigade
- Three battalions of the Sinaloa Regiment under Col. Apolonio Angulo, serving as his 3rd Infantry Brigade
- Three squadrons of the San Luis Potosí Cavalry Regiment under Gen. Mariano Escobedo
- An artillery battery under Lt. Col. Martiniano Ruiz

He overwhelmed its defenders by the next day, taking 269 prisoners, before resuming his march and eventually reaching Oaxaca City on December 1, 1863, to establish it as his headquarters and base of operations.

Because of its inaccessibility and numerous other distractions, the French and their imperial consorts did not attempt Oaxaca until the next year. Inevitably though, a four-pronged penetration was initiated in early August 1864, but Díaz slipped with 2,000 men between the two main French columns that were approaching, falling on a small garrison that they had left to hold San Antonio Teotitlán in their rear. Compelled to double back in the steamy summer heat in order to rescue their detachment, the

French then resumed their advance, only to discover that Díaz had meanwhile heavily fortified Nochistlán (60 miles northwest of Oaxaca City). The overall French commander-in-chief, Marshal Achille Bazaine, consequently sent orders from Mexico City that prohibited any direct storming of this stronghold as he lacked sufficient reserves to send a relief column should this assault miscarry, so their expedition retired into its original bases.

Hero of the War of the French Intervention (1866–1867)

Having recuperated the city of Oaxaca from its Franco-imperial occupiers by the end of October 1866, Díaz then received a shipment of American war surplus armaments in early December 1866, arranged through the offices of Pres. Benito Juárez (whose government was still displaced in northern Mexico). This weaponry allowed Díaz to sortie from Oaxaca toward Tehuacán with his self-proclaimed *Ejército de Oriente* or "Army of the East" on December 19, 1866, so as to begin clearing the Isthmus of Tehuantepec of its last Franco-imperial garrisons.

On March 9, 1867, Porfirio Díaz arrived at San Juan Hill west of this city with 3,000 republican troops to lay siege to its 3,000-man imperial garrison under Gen. Manuel Noriega. After being reinforced by local contingents and cutting off all communications inland, the republicans began formal siege proceedings.

Within the next couple of weeks, General Carrión seized both San Javier and Penitenciaría redoubts through costly assaults, as the republicans gradually fought their way into the city limits. However, Díaz was unable to completely subdue the defenders, and on March 31, 1867, he received word that Leonardo Márquez had quit Mexico City the preceding day with a relief column of 3,000 imperial troops and 17 fieldpieces.

Reacting swiftly, the republican general gathered three assault columns of 300 men apiece to storm Puebla's main stronghold—El Carmen Convent—plus 13 companies of approximately 100 men each to stealthily approach other points around the city's defenses. At 2:00 a.m. on April 2, 1867, the three-pronged attack was launched against El Carmen. After an hour and a half of noisy fighting—long enough for Noriega to commit his reserves—Díaz signaled from San Juan Hill, directing his 1,300 hidden soldiers to rise and mount simultaneous attacks. They broke through everywhere, only the Siempreviva trenches and El Carmen Convent offering much resistance before surrendering.

Noriega's remaining defenders sought refuge in the Loreto and Guadalupe Convents, being compelled to capitulate two days later. This assault had cost Díaz 253 dead and 233 wounded, as opposed to much higher casualties among the defenders, plus 2,000 captives. The republican commander quickly detached Colonel Lalane with 900 troopers on April 4, 1867, to monitor the approach of Márquez's imperial relief column.

Unhappy Retirement and Seizure of Power (1868–1876)

Dissatisfied after learning that Benito Juárez's liberal successor, Sebastián Lerdo de Tejada, was intending to run for a second presidential term in 1876, Díaz had again risen in revolt, issuing his "Plan of Tuxtepec" on January 10th of that same year, which called for an anti-reelectionist revolt in southern Mexico—yet failed to shake the Lerdista administration's grip on power. Díaz's uprising was quickly smothered, and a second attempt after reentering the country from Brownsville, Texas, in order to foment a similar insurrection in the North, also failed. Yet despite his defeats in both theaters and his followers' lack of heavy weaponry or materiel, Díaz and his allies sustained a series of guerrilla raids and strikes against isolated army detachments until Lerdo de Tejada was controversially declared the winner of a very tight presidential election in late September 1876.

The next month Díaz joined the challenges that arose on all sides against this decision, hastening to rejoin his rebel forces as they reassembled in the region of Tlaxcala and Puebla. On November 16, 1876, his 4,000 lightly armed irregulars—grandly titled the *Ejército Regenerador de la República Mexicana* or "Regenerative Army of the Mexican Republic"—managed to defeat a Lerdista army of 3,000 government regulars under Gen. Ignacio R. Alatorre at the Battle of Tecoac, thanks to the timely arrival of reinforcements under Díaz's faithful subordinate, one-armed general Manuel González. News of this victory prompted Lerdo de Tejada to slip out of the capital on the night of November 19–20, 1876, leaving behind a vacuum of power. Díaz was able to enter unchallenged, being greeted with ringing church bells and enthusiastic crowds when his train pulled into Buena Vista station at 3:15 p.m. on the afternoon of November 23, 1876.

Presidential Terms (1876–1911)

He was careful to only briefly accept the temporary title of "interim president" from November 28 to December 6, 1876, before ceding it to the venerable liberal general Juan N. Méndez. However, Díaz easily won the ensuing presidential elections and was sworn in officially as of February 17, 1887, vowing to serve only one term. At the end of his tenure though, he engineered the election of his trusty subordinate—one-armed general González—to succeed him on December 1, 1880, so as to maintain his influence over the course of governmental affairs. Four years later, Díaz got himself reelected to succeed González on December 1, 1884, and would hold onto that office uninterrupted for the next 26 years.

Coming to firmly embrace the principles of order and progress, Díaz used the stability and power of his prolonged rule to create an interlude of relative peace for the country, during which Mexico prospered and modernized through the advent of railways, telegraphs, and more productive industries, yet whose greatest benefits were to be reserved for members of the upper classes and foreign investors. The increasingly autocratic and inflexible Porfirian regime was moreover sustained by Federal Army garrisons distributed around every region and mounted police squadrons known as *rurales* who patrolled the roads and small towns.

Downfall (November 1910–May 1911)

During the summer of 1910, President Díaz—now approaching 80 years of age—announced that he would stand for an eighth term, and the wealthy, high-minded northerner landowner Francisco I. Madero declared that he would run against him on an "anti-reelectionist" ticket. Intolerant by now of any show of opposition, Díaz had arranged for Madero to be arrested, and by the time the primaries were held on June 21, 1910, 5,000 of his challenger's adherents had joined him in prison; when the final elections were held on July 8, 1910, an estimated 60,000 were behind bars. A compliant Congress duly certified the results and proclaimed Díaz reelected on September 27, 1910—11 days after the celebrations that had marked the centennial of Mexico's uprising against Spanish colonial rule.

Madero was then allowed to escape from loose confinement at San Luis Potosí on October 4, 1910, riding across the border to seek asylum in San Antonio, Texas; but incensed by Díaz's machinations, he issued a call for a nationwide uprising to start on November 20, 1910, so as to drive the dictator from power. Numerous outbreaks erupted throughout northern Mexico, almost exclusively confined to remote towns and villages, where rebels would overrun isolated federal outposts and then defeat the detachments of troops or *rurales* sent in by rail to suppress them. Although larger cities remained under government control, there were not enough soldiers to confront every outburst, so sentiment began to turn more openly against the regime.

Then a second popular insurrection exploded in the southern state of Morelos in March 1911, spearheaded by the charismatic Emiliano Zapata fervently demanding *tierra y libertad* or "land and liberty" for his thousands of peasant followers. The next month, Madero managed to marshal some 3,500 of his freelancing northern rebels into a ragtag "army" to besiege the 700-man federal garrison holding Ciudad Juárez (opposite El Paso, Texas), whose defenses were finally overwhelmed by the first week of May 1911 by "Gen." Pascual Orozco and "Col." Pancho Villa.

Having failed to mount any kind of rescue for Ciudad Juarez's doomed federal defenders, the increasingly hard-pressed Díaz proved equally powerless to prevent another 1,700 of his troops from being chased out of the city of Torreón on May 15, 1911, or to ensure that the fortified city of Cuautla in the southern state of Morelos did not to fall to Zapata's peasant army six days afterward. Sensing the dictator's weakness, antigovernment riots broke out in the main square of Mexico City itself on the evening of May 24, 1911, so the octogenarian Díaz finally decided to relinquish the presidency the next day and depart for Veracruz, sailing away into European exile aboard the German liner *Ypiranga*.

See also: Ayutla, Revolution of; Cinco de Mayo, Battle of the; Oaxaca, French Siege of; Tecoac, Battle of.

Further Reading

"Affairs in Mexico: Reported Capture of Puebla by Gen. Díaz." *New York Times*, March 6, 1867.

Paz, Ireneo. *Datos biográficos del general de división C. Porfirio Díaz, con acopio de documentos históricos.* Mexico City: Imprenta de Ireneo Paz, 1884.

Sosa, Francisco. *Biografías de mexicanos distinguidos.* Mexico City: Porrúa, 2006.

División del Norte (1913–1915)

Traditionally, the standard military designation for the Mexican Army formation stationed in the northern border states, which translates as the "Division of the North" or "Northern Division"—but a title that would be co-opted and made world famous as that of the revolutionary horde commanded by Pancho Villa.

Historical Background (1846–1875)

The term "División del Norte" had been used since the early decades of the 19th century. For example, just prior to the invasion of northern Mexico by U.S. general Zachary Taylor's army out of Texas, the 3,500 Mexican troops patrolling that region under Generals Mariano Arista and Pedro de Ampudia bore that designation (and even published a short-lived newspaper in Matamoros called the *Boletín de la División del Norte* in April and May of 1846 before their numbers were augmented as the war broke and their formation became reclassified as the *Ejército del Norte* or "Army of the North").

During Mexico's frequent civil wars, it often happened that two rival factions would use the same appellation within their contending forces. When the liberal general Santos Degollado of Jalisco drove through the Bajío to threaten Mexico City with more than 6,000 troops in March 1859, his army included an attached "División del Norte" under the command of his northern subordinate Ignacio Zaragoza. However, Degollado's army was also being pursued and harried since passing through Querétaro by a 2,400-man conservative "División del Norte" under Brigadier Generals Gregorio del Callejo and Tomás Mejía, who managed to circle around this larger liberal army and enter the threatened capital on March 24, 1859, augmenting the strength of its defenders to 4,000 men. Having weathered a liberal assault, they then helped defeat Degollado at the Battle of Tacubaya and scatter his broken army—although Zaragoza's "División del Norte" was the only liberal formation to escape intact from this disaster, and retreat back northward into its original theater of operations.

Porfirian *División del Norte* (1876–1910)

Under the prolonged dictatorship of Pres. Porfirio Díaz, the overall size of Mexico's Federal Army was reduced from 37,500 officers and men in 1876 to 25,400 by 1910. However, the Porfirian soldiers were better armed with modern weaponry and distributed throughout Mexico in a planned and rational pattern. The senior staff of its peacetime Federal Army compartmentalized the country's administration into 10 major "military zones," the vast and barren northern states of Chihuahua and Durango being designated as the *Segunda Zona Militar* or "Second Military Zone," which were to be patrolled by a federal División del Norte operating out of Chihuahua City. With railway and telegraph lines now radiating throughout the country, the strategy was for detachments to be rushed to any rural disturbance by train, after which further instructions and coordination could be provided through directives wired from headquarters.

Upon the outbreak of the Mexican Revolution on November 20, 1910, the federal *División del Norte*, commanded by *General de Brigada* or "Brigade General" Manuel M. Plata, consisted of 1,420 officers and men of the 12th Infantry Battalion and 3rd Cavalry Regiment based in Chihuahua City with small detachments at Ciudad Juárez and Ciudad Guerrero. Shortly after the insurrection erupted, an additional 440 officers and men of the 20th Infantry Battalion were dispatched by rail into Chihuahua. However, with scores of attacks occurring simultaneously throughout that vast state, even this augmented federal *División del Norte* could not contain the rapidly spreading rebellion, and its performance would come to be criticized.

To add to the confusion, the Revolution's inexperienced civilian leader Francisco I. Madero—after being wounded during his failed attack against Casas Grandes, Chihuahua, on March 6, 1911—retired to the Hacienda de Bustillo and temporarily created his own *Primera División del Norte del Ejército Libertador* from among his 3,000 armed rebel followers, appointing Pancho Villa as one of its colonels.

Almost two years later, after Madero had been deposed and murdered by Gen. Victoriano Huerta, this new dictator resurrected a more robust federal *División del Norte*, so as to combat revolutionary activities in Chihuahua. Its strength augmented to 6,300 troops, the force operated under the direct supervision of a military governor installed in the state capital (an unwelcome intrusion into local politics that would be held for little more than a month by the unpopular general Antonio Rábago, then— as of May 30, 1913—by Gen. Salvador R. Mercado). The strategic aims of this new federal *División* were described in a work of propaganda written by the right-wing author Juan José Tablada and printed that same year by the government press in Mexico City, under the title of *La defense social: historia de la campaña de la División del Norte*.

Creation of Pancho Villa's *División* (September 1913)

Nonetheless, the reality was that raw federal recruits being hustled north into Chihuahua would prove no match for its aroused guerrilla bands, who soon began picking off isolated garrisons and roaming that state with impunity. By autumn, federal forces retained control over only a few large cities in Chihuahua, while the 1,200-man rebel "brigade" of Pancho Villa—loaded with booty aboard three trains, including two heavy 75mm Mondragón artillery pieces and some machine guns taken after defeating Gen. Félix Terrazas at the hamlet of San Andrés, just south of Chihuahua City—met up with 400 riders under Maclovio Herrera at Santa Rosalía de Camargo on September 15, 1913, and then traveled together to be joined by another 600 men under Tomás Urbina at Jiménez. The latter had just returned from sacking the city of Durango, so these three chieftains jointly discussed the possibility of doing the same against Torreón, despite its 3,100-man

federal garrison under Gen. Eutiquio Munguía.

Villa, Herrera, and Urbina led their followers to the Hacienda de la Loma, on the banks of the Nazas River 15 miles west of Torreón in the state of Durango, where they were joined by a gathering of more and more rebel formations until their numbers swelled to around 10,000 undisciplined men under such varied leaders as Orestes Pereyra, Calixto Contreras, Toribio Ortega, Manuel Chao, among others. Villa convinced them that some sort of military hierarchy would be necessary in order to successfully launch a coordinated assault against Torreón, so it was agreed to coalesce the diverse regional bands into rough "brigades" under their own individual leaders then select an overall commander from among them. At a meeting held in the Hacienda de la Loma on September 26, 1913, Villa was acclaimed commanding general over this makeshift army, which— to underscore the rebels' repudiation of the usurper Huerta and the illegitimacy of his regime—was dubbed the *División del Norte Constitucionalista* or "Constitutionalist Division of the North," a rival to the federal force with this same name that was holding Chihuahua.

Three mornings later, an unexpected sally by the Huertista garrison out of Torreón started shelling the sprawling rebel encampments, and Villa's new *División del Norte* counterattacked in an unstoppable wave that carried that city by October 1, 1913. However, his unwieldy formation's lack of battlefield discipline and heavy weaponry meant that it proved incapable of dislodging the main Huertista concentration from Chihuahua City in early November 1913, and instead took the border town of Ciudad Juárez (opposite El Paso, Texas) by a stealthy penetration at dawn on November 15, 1913.

String of Victories (November 1913–December 1914)

Observers were then surprised when the ex-bandit deployed his amateurish *División* for a setpiece battle south of that occupied city, and clumsily defeated a federal relief force at the Battle of Tierra Blanca one week later. With additional input from the trained professional soldier Felipe Ángeles (who was put in charge of Villa's artillery train), a proper organizational structure came to be created for the *División*, and Villa soon learned to concentrate his disperse brigades swiftly against any chosen target by transporting them by rail. This tactic allowed him to easily rout the federal defenders out of Ojinaga (opposite Presidio, Texas) within 30 minutes of launching his opening charge on the afternoon of January 10, 1914.

His prestige now soaring, Villas *División del Norte* swelled into a powerful force of more than 15,000 rebel troops, which he led aboard a convoy of 15 trains to reclaim Torreón from the 7,000 federal defenders and 6,000 *colorado* auxiliaries who vainly tried to hold ònto that city in late March and early April 1914. After pulverizing the surviving formations a fortnight later at the nearby San Pedro de las Colonias railway station, Villa hoped to be rewarded by having his huge and triumphant *División* accorded the status of a full army by the Constitutionalist political figurehead, *primer jefe* or "first chief" Venustiano Carranza—which was denied.

A month after his triumph at San Pedro de las Colonias, Villa routed another Huertista army at the Battle of Paredón on May 17, 1914, and seized Saltillo uncontested. When Carranza thereupon ordered him to detach several brigades from his *División* to

assist another general in capturing Zacatecas, Villa asked permission to lead his own troops personally, which Carranza spitefully refused. Angry, Villa struck out southward with his entire *División* on June 16, 1914, massing 25,000 troops and 50 guns around the city of Zacatecas six days later, which carried it in a massive assault amid great slaughter and destruction on June 23, 1914.

Carranza retaliated for this disobedience by denying Villa's *División* coal for his trains, so that the more loyal general Álvaro Obregón might have the honor of advancing with his Army of the Northwest and accepting the capitulation of Mexico City by mid-August 1914. Bitter, Villa broke with Carranza that same autumn, leading his mighty *División* southward so as to unite with Emiliano Zapata and parade a combined total of 50,000 armed men into a brief occupation of the national capital on December 6, 1914.

Disintegration (1915)

Yet as rapidly as the *División* had risen to fame, its fall would be equally swift. Obregón moved northward on March 7, 1915, with his smaller but much better-equipped and disciplined army, which inflicted thousands of casualties against the wild charges launched by Villa's hordes of followers. Two huge battles at Celaya in April 1915, plus a third crushing defeat next month at Trinidad, destroyed the *División*'s fighting power and reputation.

Villa kept retreating northward under pressure, his numbers steadily dwindling and resources evaporating as his *División* was destroyed piecemeal. After venturing into the state of Sonora in the vain hope of diverting Obregón's pursuit, Villa gave up all hopes of attaining military victory by late November 1915, limping away with only 1,400 survivors to disband the bedraggled remnants of his *División* in

Chihuahua City, and disappear to become a fugitive in the mountains once again by Christmas Eve 1915.

See also: Ángeles Ramírez, Felipe de Jesús; Bajío; Celaya, Battles of; Degollado, Sánchez, José Nemesio Francisco; Dorados; Ojinaga, Battle of; San Pedro de las Colonias, Battle of; Tacubaya, Battle of; Tierra Blanca, Battle of; Torreón, Villa's First Capture of; Torreón, Villa's Second Capture of; Trinidad, Battle of; Villa, Pancho; Zaragoza Seguín, Ignacio.

Further Reading

Aguirre Benavides, Luis and Adrián. *Las grandes batallas de la División del Norte al mando del general Francisco Villa.* Mexico City: Diana, 1967.

Chávez M., Armando B., and Francisco R. Almada. *Visión histórica de la frontera norte de México, tomo V.* Mexicali: Universidad Autónoma de Baja California y Editorial Kino, 1994, 6–12.

Salmerón, Pedro. *La División del Norte: la tierra, los hombres y la historia de un ejército del pueblo.* Mexico City: Editorial Planeta Mexicana, 2006.

Tablada, Juan José. *La defensa social: historia de la campaña de la División del Norte.* Mexico City: Universidad Iberoamericana, 2010 ed.

Dorados

Nickname that translated generally means the "Golden Ones" or "Gilt Ones" but during the Mexican Revolution came to be applied to a select squadron or troop of cavalrymen who served as personal bodyguards for Pancho Villa.

Villa's army, known as the *División del Norte* or "Northern Division," had been originally drawn together out of separate revolutionary bands operating under their individual guerrilla commanders, and its organizational table would soon come to include a single squadron of elite riders chosen for their bravery and skill from among all of these groups who were to serve as the *escolta personal* or "personal escort" for their "general-in-chief." They were organized into three companies of 32 riders apiece, each of these units commanded by a first and second captain. Members were appointed to the Dorados because of their recognized courage, skillful riding, and marksmanship, and each were armed with a pair of .44 Colts or other similar weaponry.

They were not so much a military force, though, as a protective group who accompanied their commander on his wide-ranging battlefield forays. The transplanted Irishman Patrick O'Hea, on pages 146–47 of his *Reminiscences of the Mexican Revolution*, recorded an eyewitness account of seeing the Dorados in action, surrounding Villa as he personally brought the first of his water-starved locomotives in from the Durango desert into the roundhouse at recently captured Gómez Palacio to be refilled on March 27, 1914:

> Villa himself, his eyes bloodshot, his cheeks more than ever unshaven and his misfitting clothes askew, swung down from the first locomotive that, in its elephant-grey coat of dust, nosed cautiously into our station-yards over the patched-up permanent way. We reported the water, to his relief ... At that, there came on the wind the crackle of firing on the south side of our town, towards Torreón. Almost on the instant, after only a few orders shouted to his aides, Villa was in the saddle of his horse, that had been brought up, and riding down our streets toward the sound of the outbreak, at the head of his thundering troop of bodyguards.

A famous group photograph showed Villa posing proudly with his Dorados beside a railway car while traveling to attend the revolutionary Convention at Aguascalientes in autumn of 1914. A little more than a year later, after repeated defeats at the hands of Álvaro Obregón's army, Villa dissolved his División del Norte around Christmas 1915, although many of his Dorados would continue to serve him loyally as a fugitive in the hills.

See also: División del Norte; Obregón Salido, Álvaro; Torreón, Villa's Second Capture of; Villa, Pancho.

Further Reading

Ortiz, Orlando. *Los dorados: Pancho Villa y la División del Norte*. Mexico City: Nueva Imagen, 1982.

Drug War (1980s–present)

Originally a nonmilitary campaign conducted by various different police agencies and customs border patrols but that has since deteriorated into a difficult security operation embroiling the bulk of the Mexican Army.

Background (1975–2005)

During the late 1970s, Mexico's army was not directly employed in the United States' "War on Drugs," which was primarily conducted by law enforcement agencies focused on intercepting cocaine shipments reaching the United States from Colombia and the millions of dollars flowing back in profits. However, cartels in distant Medellín, Cartagena, and Cali soon noticed the ready access that small-time smuggling rings in northern Mexico enjoyed into their four adjoining American states, so they began diverting their consignments—which were growing

increasingly vulnerable to detection in the air or on the high seas by U.S. patrols—into Mexican ports during the early 1980s. There, they could easily circumvent a cursory custom inspection and be transported by truck so as to be safely stockpiled in warehouses along the border until an opportune time came to move them across by local intermediaries, disappearing into the vast unregulated American highway system.

The incredible profits to be had from this lucrative traffic meant that Mexican gangs began focusing their efforts on subverting border security within their districts so as to better handle the Colombians' coveted business. Formerly small-time operators, these criminals were soon pouring money into charting more remote and undetectable desert routes as well as bribing or recruiting hundreds of ill-paid Mexican police and customs officers. The high profit margins from even relatively small loads of cocaine—bundles that could fit comfortably into the bed of a single pickup truck—ensured ample funds for effective operations.

Displeased by this strategic shift into its porous southwestern borderlands, Washington pressured Pres. Miguel de la Madrid (who was in office from 1982 to 1988) to declare drug trafficking a "national security problem" for Mexico, providing him with funds and equipment in order to better outfit its federal police and Coast Guard forces. Yet the relatively small volumes of cocaine being transited were difficult to detect and skirted densely populated areas, so drug imports into the United States from Mexico grew instead of contracting under De la Madrid as well as during the term of his successor Carlos Salinas de Gortari from 1988 to 1994. In fact, it has been estimated that the share of cocaine passing through Mexico into the United States escalated from about

30 percent during the mid-1980s to at least 50 percent (if not more) by the 1990s.

As the Colombian cartels started fading from power during that era, Mexican gangs began adding their own homegrown narcotics into this illicit flow, especially opium and potent strains of marijuana. Although trans-shipments of foreign cocaine had proven difficult to intercept, the administration of Pres. Ernesto Zedillo could deploy the army to stamp out the cultivation of such illicit products within Mexico, whole battalions backed by helicopters making sweeps through remote areas during his term in the late 1990s so as to burn thousands of acres of hidden crops. Elite forces such as the *Grupo Aeromóvil de Fuerzas Especiales* or "Aeromobile Group of Special Forces" (GAFE) and *Brigada de Fusileros Paracaidistas* or "Brigade of Parachutist Fusiliers" were also used to make arrests of heavily guarded drug lords, while individual army companies were also assigned to police certain communities whose administration had fallen prey to corruption, violence, and fear.

These military interventions, especially the vigorous eradication of large swathes of illicit crops, intensified the competition between the various gangs—and also produced the first overt instances of army corruption. Since the earliest days of the trade, traffickers had commonly resorted to such treacherous schemes as denouncing rival operators to the authorities in hopes of seeing their competitors crippled by a strike from the Federal Police or Army. But on February 18, 1997, Maj. Gen. Jesús Gutiérrez Rebollo—the head of Mexico's federal drug agency, recently praised by Washington—was arrested and it was revealed that he had actually been directing his antidrug sweeps to benefit his covert cartel backer, Amado Carrillo Fuentes. (General Gutiérrez Rebollo's criminal

activities would be subsequently depicted in the Hollywood movie *Traffic*.) One month later, Brig. Gen. Alfredo Navarro Lara was likewise arrested for offering a bribe of a million dollars a month to a fellow brigadier on behalf of the Arellano Félix brothers of the Tijuana Cartel so as to facilitate their own drug shipments through Baja California.

Selective murders had also been a commonplace feature of the ongoing clandestine struggles to dominate regional distribution networks on both sides of the border. That same September 1997, Osiel Cárdenas Guillén—locked in a power struggle for leadership over the Gulf Cartel in the border state of Tamaulipas—hired a group of highly trained deserters from Mexico's Special Forces to become his personal bodyguards and hit men, whose skill with the most sophisticated types of modern military-grade weaponry available—machine guns, assault rifles, rocket-propelled grenades, and explosives—as well as their cruel ferocity under their code name of *Los Zetas* would terrify and defeat larger gangs. Soon, though, these rivals also began acquiring similar personnel and ordnance of their own, such as AK-47s and AR-15s, to match the Zetas' firepower, making confrontations all the more dangerous and their firepower too great for regular police forces.

President Zedillo's government struggled to recuperate from these betrayals within the army ranks, and the ensuing administration of Vicente Fox also endured worsening bouts of public lawlessness occasioned by the spiraling drug violence that left some parts of states such as Baja California, Chihuahua, and Sinaloa in the grip of silent fear and complicity with the drug lords. In certain cities, towns, and districts, cartels operated openly and with complete impunity, unchallenged by the fearful and inadequate local policemen, municipal leaders, and media.

Full Deployment (2006–Present)

As a result of this deteriorating situation, Pres. Felipe Calderón inaugurated his administration in December 2006 with the deployment of what would eventually be 50,000 soldiers (fully one-quarter of the Mexican Army's fighting strength) and 10,000 Federal Police officers in a bid to rein in cartel violence. Some initial successes were achieved, but critics pointed out that this more forceful strategy by its very nature had failed to reduce casualties or restore peace among terrified segments of the civilian population. The arrival of troops from outside any affected region inevitably led to shootouts with local cartel gunmen, while any arrests or casualties inflicted among the cartel leadership created a power vacuum during which underlings would fight desperately among themselves to inherit the lucrative operation while at the same time staving off encroachments into their territory or personnel by hostile gangs. During such periods of instability, reckless young gangsters would descend into ever more brutal acts of public cruelty in order to retain their strangleholds through sheer fear.

Turf wars spread into other, less-patrolled states such as Veracruz, Nuevo León, and Guerrero, while army units vainly swept former hotbeds of bloodshed in search of any remaining opponents, becoming ever more tempted by the corrupting influences of cartel money the longer that the modestly paid soldiers remained deployed. Meanwhile, narcotics still continued to flow across the border with relative ease, and millions were still to be made from shipping drugs across the 1,100-mile desert expanse.

See also: Guzmán Loera, Joaquín Archivaldo "El Chapo"; Zetas.

Further Reading

Díez, Jordi, and Ian Nicholls. *The Mexican Armed Forces in Transition.* Carlisle, PA: Strategic Studies Institute, January 2006.

Grayson, George W., and Samuel Logan. *The Executioner's Men: Los Zetas, Rogue Soldiers, Criminal Entrepreneurs, and the Shadow State They Created.* Piscataway, NJ: Transaction, 2012.

Preston, Julia. "Another Mexican General Is Arrested and Charged with Links to Drug Cartel." *New York Times*, March 18, 1997.

The War on Mexican Cartels: Options for U.S. and Mexican Policy-Makers. Cambridge, MA: Harvard University Institute of Politics, September 2012.

E

Part of the tragedy which the Mexican people have to experience has to do with the fact that we live beside the biggest consumer of drugs in the world, and the largest supplier of weapons.

— Pres. Felipe Calderón, commenting on cartel violence in Mexico, March 2009

Ejército de América (1810–1815).

A name that translates literally as the "Army of America" and was adopted by the rural priest Miguel Hidalgo for his mass of volunteer followers at the beginning of their War of Independence against Spanish colonial rule—proving to be more of an armed movement, though, than a disciplined fighting force.

For a more complete description of this army, *see* América, Ejército de (1810–1815).

Ejército del Noroeste (1913–1914)

Literally the "Army of the Northwest," which was a small, short-lived, yet potent revolutionary fighting force organized out of the state of Sonora by Álvaro Obregón and that within a year helped to topple the federal regime of Victoriano Huerta and capture the national capital.

Background (Spring 1913)

The Revolution's initial uprising in late 1910 had quickly driven Pres. Porfirio Díaz from power, replacing him in office with the idealistic and inexperienced reformer Francisco I. Madero. When the latter had been betrayed and murdered by General Huerta in February 1913, open warfare soon resumed, as rebel forces once again assembled to drive out this new usurper. In the remote border state of Sonora, its interim governor, Ignacio L. Pesqueira, quickly rejected the notion of Huerta's succession and in preparing for an armed confrontation appointed the unknown militia colonel Álvaro Obregón as chief of the Sonoran government's *Sección de Guerra* or "War Section."

Obregón quickly organized 1,500 troops and led them out of the state capital of Hermosillo on March 6, 1913, seizing the border town of Nogales one week later by an assault that drove the survivors of its garrison of 100 federal soldiers under army colonel Manuel Reyes, plus 300 *rurales* under Col. Emilio Kosterlitzky, to seek asylum in Arizona. Within a month, every federal outpost in Sonora had been taken by Obregón or one of his subordinates, and Governor Pesqueira thereupon joined the "constitutionalist" anti-Huertista alliance that was being formed by Gov. Venustiano Carranza of Coahuila.

Creation (Summer 1913)

The dictator Huerta countered the gains made from this northwestern insurrection by sending a seaborne expedition of 3,000 federal soldiers to occupy the Pacific port of Guaymas and attempt to march a detachment 85 miles inland to threaten the Sonoran capital. Obregón, though, managed to check their overland advance at the Battle of Santa Rosa on May 13, 1913, winning himself promotion to the rank of state brigadier general as of June 29th. When Carranza subsequently issued a directive from Monclova calling for the raising of a "constitutionalist army" on July 4, 1913, Pesqueira was appointed commander of one of its seven corps with Obregón as his second-in-command of what was to be called the *Cuerpo del Ejército Constitucionalista del Noroeste* or "Corps of the Army of the Northwest." In theory, Carranza's appointment meant that its commanders were to direct all rebel activities throughout the states of Coahuila, Chihuahua, Sinaloa, and Sonora, and the territory of Baja California, although in reality many regional leaders simply refused to recognize this authority.

Quiet and bookish, Obregón nonetheless threw himself into studying military tactics and logistics so as to at least organize his Sonoran troops into an effective fighting force, which would soon become more commonly known as the *Ejército del Noroeste* or "Army of the Northwest." The veteran Swedish soldier-of-fortune Ivor Thord-Gray, who joined Obregón's staff as an instructor and artillery officer around this time, noted approvingly that his diminutive commander, "unlike many other generals, was very keen to learn, and he did." Obregón furthermore proved highly receptive to such modern innovations as machine guns and aircraft, while the open border into Arizona allowed the constitutionalists to acquire good equipment and materiel. And being humbly born himself, Obregón welcomed all classes of people into his ranks and issued assignments and promotions based on merit. Thus even contingents of Yaqui Indians would come to join his army and march away with him toward Mexico City.

Campaign (September 1913–July 1914)

Shortly after Carranza transferred his headquarters into Hermosillo on September 18, 1913, Obregón was given full command over the Ejército del Noroeste and went on the offensive. Leaving the federal garrison inside Guaymas bottled up by 3,000 Sonoran besiegers, he led his main body south into neighboring Sinaloa, capturing its capital of Culiacán by November 14, 1913, and cutting off all overland communications for the Huertista garrison, which was left isolated within the port city of Mazatlán. The Army of the Northwest remained encamped around the Sinaloan capital during the winter of 1913–1914, growing in strength as more and more volunteers joined and became properly assimilated into its units.

The next spring, after Pancho Villa had won a series of spectacular victories in the north and Emiliano Zapata had captured Cuautla in the south, Obregón resumed his drive deeper into central Mexico by departing Culiacán with his Ejército del Noroeste at the end of April 1914. First, his six infantry battalions and two cavalry regiments traveled by rail through Modesto station and Venadillo to invest the Huertista garrison in Mazatlán as of May 4, 1914. Detachments under Manuel M. Diéguez and Lucio Blanco meanwhile captured Acaponeta in the adjoining state of Nayarit on May 5th, followed by Tepic nine days afterward, securing it as an advance base for continuing into Jalisco. Obregón consequently left 3,000 Sinaloan militiamen with five cannons and three machine guns to maintain a siege of Mazatlán under Gen. Ramón F.

Iturbe, while he and the Army of the Northwest marched away on May 17, 1914, to prepare to penetrate into Jalisco.

Since there was no railway line running through the Sierra Madre mountains between Tepic and San Marcos, Obregón carefully marshaled his reserves and supplies at Tepic before dispatching all his cavalry on ahead under Blanco and a vanguard under Diéguez, then following with the bulk of the Army of the Northwest's infantry and artillery on June 10, 1914, their munitions and supplies being carried by 200 wagons and 2,000 pack mules. It took two weeks for this main body to trudge through the mountain range, lashed by frequent rains, until they at last passed wearily through San Marcos at noon on June 24th and reunited with their vanguard contingent that evening at Etzatlán. Numerous local guerrilla leaders were also awaiting Obregón to propose joint operations against the 12,000-man federal *División de Occidente* or "Western Division" under Maj. Gen. José María Mier, which was holding Guadalajara.

Obregón was further informed that a strong column of several thousand federal defenders had exited from that city westward under Brig. Gen. Miguel Bernard and were probing in the vicinity of La Vega railway station, hoping to engage his army as they emerged from their mountain traverse. He nevertheless pressed into Ahualulco the next day (45 miles west of Guadalajara), reuniting his Army of the Northwest with its waiting cavalry by June 25, 1914, and then contacting the federal probe that following day near Hacienda El Refugio, only 12 miles from his main camp.

Yet this federal force refused to venture farther away from its main concentration inside Guadalajara, thus giving Obregón's Army of the Northwest a week to recuperate

from its trek. Then, in an intricately planned and executed envelopment maneuver, he directed two columns to circle around the unwary *federales* over the next few days before striking simultaneously in a three-pronged attack at dawn on July 6, 1914. Only a well-disciplined and veteran army could carry out such coordinated attacks, which utterly confused and routed the disperse Huertista forces by July 8, 1914. This bewildering series of strikes inflicted losses totaling 2,000 dead, 1,000 wounded, and 5,000 captured among the federal ranks, along with the seizure of 16 fieldpieces, 18 trains, and 40 locomotives.

Triumph and Transformation (August–December 1914)

A week after this victory, Huerta resigned from the presidency and fled Mexico City, so the road into the national capital now lay open. Carranza took steps to ensure that Obregón would have the honor of being the first to arrive. Meeting with elements of Pablo González's subordinate Army of the Northeast at Querétaro on August 1, 1914, they drove on together toward Mexico City without encountering any opposition. Those who witnessed the Army of the Northwest's triumphal march up Avenida de la Reforma into the heart of Mexico City two weeks later could not help but comment on how different its uniforms were compared to the federal army's, for these northern rebels wore olive-green tunics, khaki pants, brown gaiters, and broad-brimmed Texas-style felt hats (some with a peacock feather thrust into the left side of their hatbands).

Soon after its triumphal entry into Mexico City, the Army of the Northwest would begin to undergo a series of changes that effectively dissolved its original organization, redirecting much of its fighting strength into a new formation. Some regiments were detached immediately to supplant federal units still defending the region, which were now scheduled for demobilization. Then in October 1914, various subordinate commanders of the Ejército del Noroeste—such as its former cavalry commander, Lucio Blanco—decided to withdrew their participation altogether, having realigned themselves instead with the anti-Carrancista confederation emerging from the Convention of Aguascalientes.

By the time Carranza transferred his government out of Mexico City and into the port of Veracruz in December 1914 and appointed Obregón as "general-in-chief" charged with rearranging and creating a wholly new constitutionalist field force, the 17-month-old Army of the Northwest had virtually ceased to exist. Yet many of its officers and units still remained loyal to Obregón and—now armed with the choicest weaponry extracted from federal arsenals— would reamalgamate into a new force dubbed the *Ejército de Operaciones* or "Operational Army" of the constitutionalist government. And a scant three months afterward, Obregón would lead this compact, well-disciplined force into central Mexico, where it would destroy the much larger army of Pancho Villa in three decisive battles.

See also: *Cuerpo del Ejército Constitucionalista del Noroeste*; Huerta Márquez, José Victoriano; Obregón Salido, Álvaro; Orendáin, Battle of; Revolution, Mexican; Teoloyucan, Treaties of; Villa, Pancho.

Further Reading

Gilliam, Ronald R. "Turning Point of the Mexican Revolution." *MHQ: The Quarterly Journal of Military History* 15, no. 3 (Spring 2003): 40–51.

Hall, Linda B. *Álvaro Obregón: Power and Revolution in Mexico, 1911–1920*. College Station: Texas A&M University Press, 1981.

Jowett, Philip, and Alejandro de Quesada. *The Mexican Revolution, 1910–20*. Oxford: Osprey, 2006.

Salmerón, Pedro. *Los carrancistas: la historia nunca contada del victorioso Ejército del Noroeste*. Mexico City: Planeta, 2010.

Thord-Gray, Ivor. *Gringo Rebel*. Coral Gables, FL: University of Miami Press, 1960.

Fjército de Operaciones

Generic term in the Spanish language that translates simply as "Operational Army" and was used to describe any large force or concentration of units that was actively engaged on a major offensive or other strategic duty—as opposed to reserve units, static garrisons, or forces on a reduced peacetime status.

Many examples abound of this term being applied throughout Mexico's military history, such as:

- The main loyalist army that the Spanish general Félix María Calleja commanded early during Mexico's struggle for independence, which although officially designated as the *Ejército del Centro* or "Central Army" was more commonly referred to as the *ejército real de operaciones* or "royal operational army" because of its mobility and offensive capabilities
- The army that Antonio López de Santa Anna personally led northward a quarter century later to crush the revolt in Texas, referred to as the *Ejército de Operaciones* in all official reports and correspondence related to that campaign during the winter of 1835–1836—just as Santa Anna himself was titled "His Excellency the General-in-Chief of the

Operational Army and President of the Mexican Republic"

- Pres. Ignacio Comonfort, who marched from the national capital against the conservative mutineers who had seized the city of Puebla in March 1856 with the joint titles of *general de división y en jefe del ejército de operaciones sobre Puebla* or "major-general and [general]-in-chief of the Operational Army against Puebla"
- Two years later, the young conservative commander Luis G. Osollo would serve during the early months of the War of the Reform with the official title of *general en jefe del ejército de operaciones del interior* or "general-in-chief of the Operational Army of the Interior"
- The next spring during that very same conflict, the liberal brigadier general Juan Zuazua would be appointed as general-in-chief of their combined *ejército de operaciones* or "operational army" in the Bajío on April 25, 1859, with Ignacio Zaragoza serving as his second-in-command
- After having captured Mexico City, Álvaro Obregón's revolutionary *Ejército del Noroeste* or "Army of the Northwest" would be expanded and reorganized into a powerful new field force renamed as the main *Ejército de Operaciones* or "Operational Army" for the entire constitutionalist movement, which he then led northward in early March 1915 to pulverize Pancho Villa's División del Norte

See also: Appendix, section titled "Viceroyal Mexico's Spanish and Loyalist Forces"; División del Norte; Ejército del Noroeste.

Further Reading

Bustamante, Carlos María de. *Campañas del general D. Félix María Calleja,* *comandante en jefe del ejército real de operaciones.* Mexico City: Del Águila, 1828.

García, Genaro. *Causa mandada formar a D. Leonardo Márquez por desobediencia e insubordinación como general en jefe del primer cuerpo del Ejército de Operaciones.* Mexico City: Vda. de Ch. Bouret, 1906.

Villareal, Florencio. *Parte oficial que dirige al Exmo. Sr. presidente de la República y general en jefe del ejército de operaciones.* Mexico City: J. M. Macías, 1856.

Ejército Federal (1876–1914)

Term that translates simply as "Federal Army" and was initially ascribed to the national army created to serve Mexico's First Republic from 1823 to 1835—yet a name that would become much more famously associated with the army reconstituted and modernized under the prolonged tenure of Pres. Porfirio Díaz, only to be destroyed by the Mexican Revolution of 1910.

Porfirian Army (1876–1911)

The liberal administration under Benito Juárez's successor, Pres. Sebastián Lerdo de Tejada, whom Díaz defeated and supplanted in November 1876, had maintained a large standing national army of 37,500 officers and men, although its members were only indifferently trained and equipped with outdated weaponry. During his initial four-year presidential term, Díaz achieved little toward modernizing Mexico, but upon being returned into office for a second term as of 1884, he set about implementing a series of long-term measures intended to improve many of Mexico's institutional deficiencies.

One of the organizations that would benefit the most from these Porfirian reforms would be the *Ejército Federal* or Federal Army. Although its overall size was steadily reduced to only 25,400 officers and soldiers by 1910, they were much better trained and armed with modern weaponry such as Mauser rifles, Hotchkiss and Colt heavy machine guns, and French artillery pieces. Their regiments were strategically distributed in bases throughout Mexico, so as to be able to quickly travel by rail to any trouble spot, where they would then receive telegraphed intelligence and instructions so as to better direct their actions. Military officers also commanded the highly regarded mounted police force known as the *rurales*, who supplemented their patrols.

The Porfirian *Ejército Federal* was admired as an organization, its soldiers being proud of their crack regiments, and also feared by lowly civilians as agents of repression. It therefore came as a shock at how easily this modern force was overwhelmed by the widespread insurrection of ragtag, ill-armed rebels that exploded against the government in November 1910, and triumphing through sheer weight of numbers. For example, the federal *División del Norte*—comprised of 1,860 officers and men of the 12th and 20th Infantry Battalions, and 3rd Cavalry Regiment—found itself incapable of dealing with the scores of attacks that erupted throughout the vast state of Chihuahua, while in the southern state of Morelos, the splendid 5th Cavalry Regiment (known as the *Regimiento de Oro* or "Golden Regiment") was likewise driven out of Cuautla by swarms of *zapatista* peasants, so that—against all expectations—the Porfirian regime fell within a few weeks' time.

Overambitious Resurrection (1912–1913)

The Federal Army continued functioning on a more restrained basis both before and after the reform-minded Francisco I. Madero was elected president in November 1911, but he was deposed and brutally murdered 15 months later by Gen. Victoriano Huerta. Assuming office himself, Huerta began the most notable military buildup in Mexico's history with the aim of augmenting the Federal Army to such a size that it could stamp out the Revolution in every region. Between June and September 1913 alone, the number of generals in the *Ejército Federal* rose from 128 to 182, total membership of active-duty officers rose from 4,464 to 5,537, while the number of rank-and-file soldiers ballooned from 63,500 to 85,000. Huerta furthermore reassigned all 31 police regiments of *rurales* away from the secretariat of the interior to the Ministry of War by a decree dated August 15, 1913, and increased the number of each regiment's riders so as to create an auxiliary *cuerpo de exploradores* or "scout corps" of 12,400 troopers for the Federal Army. He even demanded that supplementary military services be performed by the 31,000 poorly trained and ill-armed members of Mexico's regional militias.

Yet this rapid buildup on such a scale was achieved mostly through rounding up raw conscripts for the Federal Army and hastening them north to defend stark, unfamiliar territories against committed forces of local revolutionaries, who were becoming ever better equipped and organized. Many of these recruits were drafted unwillingly and thus prone to desert, while they furthermore lacked the years of training of Porfirian veterans, and proved useless on the battlefield. After a string of reverses during the winter of 1913–1914 had lost thousands of these new recruits to death or desertion, Huerta informed his docile Congress in a speech on April 1, 1914 that—in order "to achieve a reestablishment of peace" throughout the country—he was proposing to more than double his already-expanded army into an even more massive force of 250,000 men.

Yet this enormous escalation would never even be attempted, as later that same month a U.S. landing force seized the port of Veracruz against feeble opposition; Pancho Villa destroyed a major federal army at the Battle of Zacatecas on June 23, 1914; and Álvaro Obregón pulverized another at the Battle of Orendáin outside of Guadalajara on July 6–8, 1914, dooming Huerta's regime.

Defeat and Dissolution (1914)

One week later, the failed dictator resigned from office and fled Mexico City along with his minister of war, Gen. Aureliano Blanquet, to sail away into European exile. Huerta's interim successor—the head of the Supreme Court and minister of foreign relations, the civilian lawyer Francisco S. Carvajal—sought to arrange a peaceful surrender of the government and national capital to the rapidly approaching *Cuerpo del Ejército Constitucionalista del Noroeste* or "Corps of the Constitutionalist Army of the Northwest" under the victorious Obregón.

The latter's vanguard under his subordinate Alfredo Robles Domínguez met with the interim minister of war, Maj. Gen. José Refugio Velasco, on August 9, 1914, persuading him to withdraw the federal garrison from Mexico City without attempting any kind of resistance against such overwhelming odds. Two days later, after Carvajal had formally stepped down as acting president, the military governor, Eduardo Iturbide of Mexico City, and various foreign diplomats were driven out toward the revolutionary encampment and—halfway between Cuautitlán and Teoloyucan, on the fender of a mud-spattered car—signed a preliminary agreement with Obregón.

The formal "treaties of Teoloyucan" were actually concluded in the Ejército del Noroeste camp on August 13, 1914, and were to become known by this pluralized name as this agreement encompassed two separate documents: one detailing the conditions for the peaceful surrender and occupation of Mexico City, another laying out the terms for the remnants of its defending garrison to evacuate the capital and for the entire Federal Army to thereupon be dissolved.

The next dawn, demoralized regiments of the once-proud Federal Army exited their bases and shuffled disconsolately through the streets to board various trains, then were transported eastward in the direction of Puebla and dropped off by the thousands at different remote stations with vouchers to find their way home. Meanwhile, Obregón's triumphant Army of the Northwest—now 18,000 strong—paraded into the capital at noon on August 15, 1914, occupying the vacated federal quarters and arsenals by nightfall. Porfirio Díaz's *Ejército Federal* had ceased to exist.

See also: Appendix, section titled "The Federal Army of Porfirio Díaz"; División del Norte; Mauser; Mondragón Mondragón, Manuel; Orendáin, Battle of; *rurales*; Teoloyucan, Treaties of; Zacatecas, Battle of.

Further Reading

Escalafón general del Ejército: cerrado hasta 30 de junio de 1910. Mexico City: Secretaría de Guerra y Marina, 1910.

González, Manuel. *Ordenanza general para el Ejército de la República Mexicana*. Mexico City: Ignacio Cumplido, 1882.

Hernández Chávez, Alicia. "Origen y ocaso del Ejército Porfiriano." *Historia Mexicana* 39, no. 1 (1989): 257–96.

Janvier, Thomas A. "The Mexican Army." *Harper's New Monthly Magazine* 79, no. 474 (November 1889): 812–27.

Memoria de la Secretaría de Estado y del Despacho de Guerra y Marina. Mexico City: Departamento de Estado Mayor, Palacio Nacional, 1909.

Ramírez Rancaño, Mario. *El ejército federal, 1914: semblanzas biográficas.* Mexico City: Universidad Nacional Autónoma de México, 2012.

Ramírez Rancaño, Mario. "La logística del ejército federal: 1881–1914." *Estudios de Historia Moderna y Contemporánea de México* 36 (July–December 2008): 183–219.

Ejército Libertador (1828)

Grandiose name chosen by Santa Anna for the armed movement that he hoped to foment in order to overturn the results of Mexico's second presidential election.

With no experience as a democracy, this vote held in August 1828 had ended badly. For although the war hero Vicente Guerrero had prevailed in Mexico's popular vote, many aristocratic state legislators had subsequently balked at casting their official electoral ballots in favor of a mulatto ex-teamster, so the highborn Manuel Gómez Pedraza—a former royalist officer and sitting minister of war—was instead proclaimed the winner on September 1, 1828, despite having received only 11 out of 36 electoral votes (with Guerrero's number now being reduced to a mere 8).

Veracruz had been one state whose legislators had ignored the poll results so as to shift their electoral votes in favor of Gómez Pedraza, so its vice governor—34-year-old general Antonio López de Santa Anna—mutinied a few days afterward at Jalapa and led a small force of 750 soldiers and two small fieldpieces to occupy the lonely fort at Perote. Its 290-man garrison had arrested their *pedrazista* commander and admitted Santa Anna's brigade on September 13, 1828, thereby joining his rebellion.

Three days later (timed to coincide with Mexico's Independence Day celebrations), he issued a *pronunciamiento* addressed to the "peoples of Anáhuac" from the headquarters of his so-called *Ejército Libertador* or Liberating Army within Perote, calling for the annulment of Gómez Pedraza's election and immediate substitution by Guerrero. Some small units would join his command, and a few supportive uprisings ensued at Acapulco, Chalco, and Apám, but not the broad-based national insurrection that he had hoped for; so rather than see his "Liberating Army" swell in size, Santa Anna became confined within his fort that same month by an approaching *pedrazista* army of almost 3,000 men under Brig. Gen. Manuel Rincón.

Santa Anna retreated into Oaxaca with the remnants of his still-born "Liberating Army" by mid-October 1828, and an entirely separate mutiny was launched by the Acordada garrison in Mexico City on November 30, 1828, driving Gómez Pedraza from the presidency after two days of street fighting. Almost unnoticed, Santa Anna dissolved what was left of his short-lived "Liberating Army" so as to resume his service under Guerrero and got a chance to distinguish himself the next summer in repelling Barradas's Spanish invasion.

See also: Acordada Mutiny; Barradas's Invasion; Guerrero Saldaña, Vicente Ramón; Perote, Fort of; *pronunciamiento*; Santa Anna, Antonio López de.

Further Reading

Arrom, Sylvia M. "Popular Politics in Mexico City: The Parián Riot, 1828." *Hispanic American Historical Review* 68, no. 2 (May 1988): 245–68.

Moctezuma, Esteban. *Detall que el señor general D. Estévan Moctezuma dirije al Exmo. Señor D. Antonio López de Santa Anna, general de división y en gefe del ejército libertador*. Mexico City: Imprenta Liberal, 1832.

Rivera, Manuel. *Historia antigua y moderna de Jalapa y de las revoluciones del estado de Veracruz*. Mexico City: Ignacio Cumplido, 1869, 2: 481–509.

Vázquez, Josefina Zoraida. "Los primeros tropiezos." In *Historia General de México*, 525–82. Mexico City: Colegio de México, 2009.

Vázquez, Josefina Zoraida. "Political Plans and Collaboration between Civilians and the Military, 1821–1846." *Bulletin of Latin American Research* [UK] 15, no. 1 (January 1996): 19–38.

Ejército Libertador del Sur (1911–1920)

Name of Emiliano Zapata's armed following that could be translated literally as the "Liberating Army of the South," although it was in reality more of a rebel movement than an organized military force.

Zapata's insurrection in the spring of 1911 against the heartless indifference and exploitative policies under Pres. Porfirio Díaz's entrenched dictatorship unleashed a mass peasant movement behind his simple rallying cry of *Tierra y libertad* or "Land and Liberty." Poor, ill-armed, and mostly illiterate, his disparate bands of followers knew only a rudimentary discipline and battle tactics, yet succeeded in initially overwhelming the few federal garrisons scattered throughout the state of Morelos through sheer weight of numbers and raw courage.

However, when the post-Porfirian interregnum retaliated by dispatching 1,000 regulars into Cuernavaca under hard-bitten Gen. Victoriano Huerta, who began a series of brutal sweeps as of August 1911, the Zapatistas proved powerless to challenge these federal forces in battle. A more humane policy ensued once Francisco I. Madero was installed as president, who replaced Huerta with the high-minded Gen. Felipe Ángeles early in 1912, but Zapata nonetheless realized that to achieve his main political goal of reclaiming and legitimizing his followers' landholdings, he would have to harness his disparate groups into a more effective fighting force.

Zapata consequently tried to impart some sort cohesion to these formations that same year of 1912 by appointing seven major subchieftains to serve as "generals" in a crude chain of command (to be headed up by his own brother Eufemio), plus 27 "colonels" and a host of lesser officers for perhaps 12,000 men in total—without uniforms, standard-issue weapons, pay, or rations beyond those that they could acquire by themselves. These troops moreover retained their traditional loyalty to their individual leaders, only cooperating in joint campaigns for short periods of time while expecting to be on active duty for three months a year and otherwise allowed to tend to their fields.

After Huerta betrayed and murdered Madero in February 1913, Zapata resumed his military offensives, although the "Instructions" that he issued as general-in-chief of the "Liberating Army of the South and Center of Mexico" to his field commanders in June and July of 1913 revealed the very loose nature of this organization, as officers were charged with:

- Operating independently in the absence of any communications from headquarters
- Removing all civilian authorities who were "not pleasing to the people"

- Demanding forced loans from wealthy hacienda owners "in accordance with the importance of their properties"
- Obtaining provisions through confiscations supervised by municipal authorities
- Helping local townspeople to reclaim their lands "through a resort to force of arms, whenever necessary"
- Sending in action reports every 15 days, maintaining proper discipline upon entering captured towns, etc.

Huerta having been defeated, Zapata commanded perhaps 25,000 troops by late 1914, when he and Pancho Villa paraded into Mexico City at the head of their respective revolutionary armies and visited the vacant Presidential Palace—but even Villa noted the poverty of the weaponry and equipment available to the humble Zapatista soldiery when compared to his own División del Norte. And the constitutionalist forces under Venustiano Carranza were even better armed and battle ready, so his subordinate, Gen. Álvaro Obregón, decimated Villa's División del Norte in three huge battles during the summer of 1915, after which his other subordinate, Gen. Pablo González, led another army into Morelos and over the course of three years eradicated the Liberating Army of the South and assassinated its charismatic leader.

See also: Díaz Mori, José de la Cruz Porfirio; Revolution, Mexican; Zapata Salazar, Emiliano.

Further Reading

Brunk, Samuel. *Emiliano Zapata: Revolution and Betrayal in Mexico*. Albuquerque: University of New Mexico Press, 1995.

Jowett, Philip, and Alejandro de Quesada. *The Mexican Revolution, 1910–20*. Oxford: Osprey, 2006, 46–51.

MacGregor, Josefina, and Guillermina Palacios Suárez. *Ejército Libertador del Sur,* *1911–1923*. Mexico City: Cuadernos del Archivo Histórico de la UNAM, 1988.

McNeely, John H. "Origins of the Zapata Revolt in Morelos." *Hispanic American Historical Review* 46, no. 2 (May 1966): 153–69.

Rosovsky, Mirta, et al. *Documentos inéditos sobre Emiliano Zapata y el Cuartel General*. Mexico City: Archivo General de la Nación, 1979.

Ejército Regenerador

A name that translates loosely as "Regenerative Army" and was often self-applied by 19th-century mutineer or rebel forces to justify their intent of removing a particular leader or administration.

Many such revolts began with a *pronunciamiento* or "declaration of principles" intended to attract adherents to their cause—just as their choice of a name for their movement or "army" was also meant to express their goals or sentiments, in the most broadly appealing terms. For example:

- In March 1849, the rebel chieftain Eleuterio Quiroz grandly renamed his few surviving fugitive companies in the state of Querétaro as the *Ejército Regenerador de la Sierra Gorda* or "Regenerative Army of the Sierra Gorda," while demanding the restoration into office of federalist authorities throughout the state and the utter prohibition against any future return to power by the exiled Santa Anna.
- In mid-December 1857, Gen. Félix María Zuloaga staged a phony "mutiny" at Tacubaya outside of Mexico City in support of Pres. Anastasio Bustamante, aimed at merely replacing his liberal Congress, and so named the mutinous regiments that

Mexican street scene, ca. 1854: two army officers talking to a peasant teamster with his oxcart. (Anne S. K. Brown Military Collection, Brown University)

backed this coup the *Ejército Regenerador.*

- Porfirio Díaz, in his rebellion to prevent the reelection of liberal president Sebastián Lerdo de Tejada in 1876, dubbed his assorted throng of southern followers the *Ejército Regenerador de la República Mexicana* or "Regenerative Army of the Mexican Republic."

Other equally self-serving names chosen for such insurrections would be *Ejército Libertador* or "Liberating Army," *Ejército Restaurador* or "Restorative Army," etc.

See also: Ejército Restaurador; *pronunciamiento.*

Further Reading

Fowler, Will. *Malcontents, Rebels, and* Pronunciados: *The Politics of Insurrection in Nineteenth-Century Mexico.* Lincoln: University of Nebraska Press, 2012.

Thomson, Guy P. C., and David G. LaFrance. *Patriotism, Politics, and Popular Liberalism in Nineteenth-Century Mexico.* Wilmington, DE: Scholarly Resources, 1999.

Ejército Restaurador

A name that can be translated loosely as "Restorer Army" or "Restorative Army," used by some 19th-century rebel forces to suggest a return to earlier bedrock values in the hopes of attracting like-minded individuals to their cause.

Just as with *Ejército Regenerador* (see preceding entry), the choice of name for any armed movement was meant to express the goals and sentiments of its participants, in broadly appealing terms. Therefore, the insurgent hero Gen. Juan N. Álvarez deliberately chose the name *Ejército Restaurador de la Libertad* or "Restorer of Liberty Army" for the liberal insurrection that he helped foment at Ayutla in the spring of 1854—which was intended to not only drive the dictator Santa Anna from office but moreover remove or reduce the entrenched conservative impediments in government and society left over from colonial times.

The resultant Revolution of Ayutla ended in triumph for the liberals' Ejército Restaurador, driving Santa Anna from office by August 1855 and replacing him with Álvarez. Consequently, when a conservative coup two-and-a-half years later wrested the presidency back, their leadership selected the name *Ejército Restaurador de las Garantías* or "Restorer of Guarantees Army" for the force that they dispatched north into the Bajío at the beginning of the War of the Reform to stamp out all liberal opposition.

See also: Ayutla, Revolution of; Bajío; Reform, War of the; Santa Anna, Antonio López de.

Further Reading

Cuentas de la comisaría y sub-comisaría del Ejército Restaurador de la Libertad. Mexico City: Vicente García Torres, 1856.

Fowler, Will. *Malcontents, Rebels, and Pronunciados: The Politics of Insurrection in Nineteenth-Century Mexico.* Lincoln: University of Nebraska Press, 2012.

"The Insurrection in Mexico." *New York Times*, September 29, 1854.

Thomson, Guy P. C., and David G. LaFrance. *Patriotism, Politics, and Popular Liberalism in Nineteenth-Century Mexico.* Wilmington, DE: Scholarly Resources, 1999.

Ejército Trigarante (1821–1822)

A name that translates literally as the "Army of the Three Guarantees," yet did not really represent a structured army in the classical sense of the word but rather a voluntary association of disparate regional units—some previously antagonistic—that had been brought together by the common goal of resolving Mexico's War of Independence.

Background (1816–1820)

After the explosiveness of Miguel Hidalgo's initial uprising against Spanish rule in September 1810, and then the gradual defeat and dispersal of José María Morelos's insurgent concentrations by late 1815, the four years of desultory struggle that ensued between 1816 and 1819 had degenerated into a stalemate between royalist garrisons holding most major cities and the guerrilla bands that ignored proffered amnesties and still controlled much of the countryside and threatened most roads—yet, despite outnumbering the royalist garrisons, were too weakly armed and parochially inclined to mount any major offensives, assaults, or siege operations.

However, the commitment to Crown rule by many Creole royalists was suddenly shaken in the spring of 1820 after an army mutiny in Spain had reimposed a liberal constitution on Mexico's viceroyal administration, including certain provisions aimed at curtailing or eliminating outdated prerogatives of the aristocracy and clergy and military. Displeased by this development, which seemingly undermined the royalists' hopes of retaining their traditional conservative values and privileged statuses intact from the 18th century, many loyal Creoles began to waver and openly consider some measure of separation from Madrid but on less radical terms than those suggested by the insurgent leadership.

The Three Guarantees (1821)

Surprisingly, a solution was proposed to Mexico's rebels by a royalist Creole officer with a reputation for implacable ruthlessness toward his foes, Col. Agustín de Iturbide. Having been assigned the thankless task of campaigning during the winter months of 1820–1821 against Vicente Guerrero's elusive guerrilla bands in the lowlands of southern Mexico, Iturbide unexpectedly contacted that insurgent chieftain on January 10, 1821, to suggest that they suspend hostilities and instead forge a coalition to achieve Mexico's independence on terms that would satisfy both factions. Guerrero suspected a trap, but Iturbide compiled and issued a public proclamation from his base at Iguala on February 24, 1821, that incorporated broad principles that most of the antagonists could accept.

According to the articles of Iturbide's so-called *Plan de Iguala*, conservative values would be upheld by declaring the Catholic Church the paramount religious institution of the newly emergent nation, while furthermore specifying the creation of a constitutional monarchy to govern it, which would in turn recognize and respect the already-existing colonial titles regarding land grants, private property, etc. Insurgent demands would be met by declaring outright independence from Spain and then convening a congress of Mexicans to draft a national constitution, which at that point could address such questions as individual rights and impose limits on the powers of the constitutional monarchy.

Although a lengthy document, Iturbide's *pronunciamiento* was fixed on three focal conditions or "guarantees"—predominance of the Catholic faith, separation from Spain, and unity among Mexicans—and furthermore included several articles prescribing the immediate formation of "a protecting army, which shall be called the Army of the Three Guarantees," so as to carry out this design. Simply put, royalist and insurgent commanders who agreed to adhere to this plan would cease campaigning against one other while retaining their military rank in this ephemeral new organization, whose command structure would be devised later by the national congress.

This truce between combatants began when Guerrero agreed to merge his insurgent forces with Iturbide's loyalists at a conference held at Acatempan near Teloloapan on March 10, 1821, thereby laying the foundation for a unified *Ejército de las Tres Garantías*. Although the Plan of Iguala was bitterly denounced and disavowed four days later in Mexico City by the Spanish viceroy, Juan Ruiz de Apodaca, Iturbide's proposal turned into an unstoppable movement over the next several months, as more and more royalist Creole militia commanders and insurgent guerrilla chieftains agreed to subscribe to this notion of an "Army of the Three Guarantees" under its new tricolor flag: whose white segment represented religion, green stood for independence, and red for the union of all Mexicans.

Bloodless Victory (August–September 1821)

As such defections spread, fighting soon contracted into sporadic skirmishes between ever-larger Mexican formations, against fewer and fewer monarchical adherents. By the time that the next viceroy designate, the liberal lieutenant general Juan O'Donojú, arrived from across the Atlantic at the end of July 1821 to assume office, he discovered that the only troops remaining loyal to Spain were trapped within their depleted garrisons at Mexico City, Veracruz, and Acapulco. With the rest of the country in insurgent hands, O'Donojú felt that he had no choice but to agree to Iturbide's terms and consequently signed a treaty at Córdoba in

August 1821 that recognized Mexican independence (albeit while still holding out a promise of maintaining some tenuous links to Spain, although this latter arrangement was to be rejected out of hand by Madrid).

Despite never having fought in battle, the "Army of the Three Guarantees"—this loose coalition of diverse royalist regiments, insurgent battalions, and rural guerrilla bands that had subscribed to Iturbide's Plan of Iguala—converged on Mexico City to celebrate their almost-bloodless joint victory with a grand parade on September 27, 1821, marking Mexico's independence. It was recorded that the army consisted of 7,616 infantrymen, 7,755 cavalrymen, and 763 artillerymen for 68 pieces of various calibers.

See also: Guerrero Saldaña, Vicente Ramón; Iguala, Plan de; Independence, War of; Iturbide Arambúru, Agustín Cosme Damián de.

Further Reading

Anna, Timothy E. *The Fall of Royal Government in Mexico City*. Lincoln: University of Nebraska Press, 1978.

Hefter, Joseph. *Crónica del traje militar en México*. Mexico City: Artes de México, 1968.

Rodriguez O., Jaime E. *"We Are Now the True Spaniards": Sovereignty, Revolution, Independence, and the Emergence of the Federal Republic of Mexico, 1808–1824.* Stanford, CA: Stanford University Press, 2012.

Vázquez, Josefina Z. "Iglesia, ejército y centralismo." *Historia mexicana* 39, no. 1 (July–September 1989): 205–34.

Ejército Zapatista de Liberación Nacional (1994)

Name chosen by a modern armed movement in the state of Chiapas.

Rafael Sebastián Guillén Vicente, the melodramatic leader known as "Subcomandante Marcos" of the Zapatista National Liberation Army (EZLN), speaking to reporters in Chiapas in December 1994. (Gerardo Magallon/AFP/Getty Images)

On New Year's Day 1994, in a move timed to embarrass the Mexican government by coinciding with that nation's entry into the North American Free Trade Agreement or NAFTA, guerrilla bands of the heretofore unknown *Ejército Zapatista de Liberación Nacional* or "Zapatista Army for National Liberation" (EZLN) seized government offices in the towns of San Cristóbal de las Casas, Las Margaritas, and Ocosingo, all located in the impoverished southern border state of Chiapas. Thousands of troops were rushed into that region on orders from Pres. Carlos Salinas de Gortari, yet they could not crush the elusive 2,000 guerrillas, who disappeared into jungle hideaways—despite various clashes in which several hundred people perished, while tens of thousands of peasant refugees sought to escape from the fighting. Salinas de Gortari consequently called a halt to military operations on January 12, 1994, and sent his foreign minister, Manuel Camacho Solís, to negotiate a truce with the mysterious rebel leader, who was known by the *nom de guerre* "Subcomandante Marcos." These talks continued until the scheduled change of federal administrations at the end of that year.

However, the newly installed president, Ernesto Zedillo Ponce de León, on February 9, 1995, ordered the army to resume its offensive against the rebel stronghold of Guadalupe Tepeyac, deep within the Lacandona jungles, and moreover identified the rebel leader as a university graduate named Rafael Sebastián Guillén, born into a middle-class family 37 years previously at Tampico, Tamaulipas. Five days afterward, military operations were once again halted, and a year of more negotiations ensued, producing an accord that was signed by February 16, 1996. Upon assuming office on December 1, 2000, the next president, Vicente Fox, ordered the army withdrawn altogether from Chiapas, even allowing Marcos to tour the country giving leftist speeches.

Further Reading

Harvey, Neil. *The Chiapas Rebellion: The Struggle for Land and Democracy.* Durham, NC: Duke University Press, 1998.

Muñoz Ramírez, Gloria. *The Fire and the Word: A History of the Zapatista Movement.* San Francisco: City Lights, 2008 translation.

Womack, John. *Rebellion in Chiapas: A Historical Reader.* New York: New Press, 1999.

El Añil, Battle of (1886). *See* Buatachive, Campaign of (1886).

escalafón general

Generic term in the Spanish-language military lexicon for "chain of command" referring to a recognized hierarchical structure of ranks and grades, from highest down to lowest.

Generally, *escalafón* signifies any kind of "scale," "ranking," or series of steps in the Spanish language: for example, *escalafón de salarios* means "wage scale"; *ascender el escalafón* means to "work one's way up the ladder," etc. According to the Mexican Army's *Ordenanza general* or "General Ordinances" for 1882, the descending order of military ranks at that time consisted of:

- *General de división* or "division general"
- *General de brigada* or "brigade general"
- *General coronel* or "general colonel"
- *Coronel* or "colonel"
- *Teniente coronel* or "lieutenant colonel"
- *Mayor* or "major"
- *Ayudante* or "adjutant"
- *Capitán primero* or "first captain"
- *Capitán segundo* or "second captain"
- *Sub-ayudante* or "subadjutant"
- *Teniente* or "lieutenant"
- *Alférez* or "ensign"
- *Subteniente* or "sublieutenant"
- *Sargento de banda* or "band sergeant"
- *Sargento primero* or "first sergeant"
- *Sargento segundo* or "second sergeant"
- *Cabo de cornetas y trompetas* or "cornet or trumpeter corporal"
- *Cabo* or "corporal"
- *Soldado de primera clase* or "private first-class"

- *Soldado de guardia* or "guard private" (a soldier capable of manning a guard post)
- *Soldado* or "private"

Some older 19th-century ranks, such as *general coronel* or "general colonel" and *alférez* or "ensign," as well as the various grades within each rank, would disappear by the early 20th century. For example, Article 5 of the *Ordenanza general del Ejército* issued on January 5, 1912, more simply described the "hierarchical structure of the Army" as follows:

I. Troops
Soldado or "soldier"
Cabo or "corporal"
Sargento segundo or "second sergeant"
Sargento primero or "first sergeant"
II. Officers
Subteniente or "sublieutenant"
Teniente or "lieutenant"
Capitán segundo or "second captain"
Capitán primero or "first captain"
III. *Jefes* or chiefs
Mayor or "major"
Teniente coronel or "lieutenant colonel"
Coronel or "colonel"
IV. Generals
General brigadier or "brigadier general"
General de brigada or "brigade general"
General de división or "division general" (i.e., major general)

Further Reading

Escalafón general del Ejército y Armada nacionales. Mexico City: Oficina Impresora del Timbre, 1897

Escalafón general que comprende a los Exmos. Sres. capitán general, generales de división, a los de brigada efectivos y

graduados, a los Sres. coroneles de todas armas, etc. Mexico City: Ignacio Cumplido, 1854.

Escalante, Constantino (1836–1868)

Political illustrator and satirist who produced accurate depictions of Mexican soldiers among his works during the 1860s.

Relatively little is known about Escalante's early life beyond the fact that he was born in Mexico City in 1836 and at the age of 24 cofounded a popular newspaper named *Mi Sombrero* or "My Hat" in 1860, the last year of the conservative hold on power in the national capital under Maj. Gen. and "substitute president" Miguel Miramón. The next year, following the restoration of the liberal administration of Pres. Benito Juárez, Escalante joined his cousin Carlos R. Casarín and Manuel C. de Villegas in launching a satirical publication in March 1861 that was called *La orquesta* or "The Orchestra" and that would continue to appear over the next 13 years.

But when the French intervention led to foreign invasion and a renewed round of warfare in the spring of 1862, patriotic pride generated by Gen. Ignacio Zaragoza's successful defense of Puebla at the Battle of the Cinco de Mayo and subsequent actions led Escalante to begin producing some special drawings (beyond his regular journalistic output), which were lithographed by the talented Hesiquio Iriarte for publication in August 1862 in a slim album entitled *Las Glorias Nacionales* or "The National Glories." When the French invaders succeeded in gaining Mexico City in the summer of 1863, this album was withdrawn from circulation but was reissued upon the republican triumph in 1867 with two additional lithographs depicting Gen. Vicente Riva Palacios's attack at Zitácuaro and Gen. Porfirio Díaz's victory at La Carbonera.

These 11 meticulously detailed depictions offer a rare, accurate portrayal of Mexican soldiers in action during that era. Tragically, more were to have been produced, but the 32-year-old Escalante died during a railway accident while traveling from Mexico City to nearby Tlalpan on October 29, 1868.

See also: Cinco de Mayo, Battle of the; La Carbonera, Battle of; Reform, War of the.

Further Reading

Escalante, Constantino, and Hesiquio Iriarte. *Las glorias nacionales: el álbum de la guerra*. Puebla: Gobierno del Estado de Puebla and SEP, 2012.

Grabados Mexicanos: An Historical Exhibition of Mexican Graphics. South Hadley, MA: Mount Holyoke College, 1974.

Sosa, Francisco. *Biografías de mexicanos distinguidos*. Mexico City: Porrúa, 2006, 260–65.

Escobedo Peña, Mariano Antonio Guadalupe (1826–1902)

Liberal republican general who fought in the War of the Reform and captured the emperor Maximilian at the siege of Querétaro, thus bringing an end to the War of the French Intervention.

He was born on January 16, 1826, at the hamlet of San Pedro de los Labradores (modern Galeana) in the northern state of Nuevo León, the fifth and final child of Manuel Escobedo and María Rita Peña. After commencing their educations in the local school, Mariano's three older brothers had all been sent to continue their studies in the city of Monterrey, but Mariano was kept home to help with his parents' farming businesses. Although bespectacled, young Mariano would become an excellent rider and teamster.

Early Service during the Mexican-American War (1846–1847)

At 20 years of age and with the U.S. Army of Brig. Gen. Zachary Taylor penetrating into northern Mexico, Escobedo joined the staff of Col. José López Uraga and was appointed to the rank of *alférez* or "ensign" in the *Guardia Nacional* or "National Guard" militia by Gen. Pedro Ampudia as of September 14, 1846, just in time to take part in the three-day defense of Monterrey against these American invaders one week later, as well as in the subsequent evacuation of that city's Mexican garrison beyond Rinconada Pass and two-month suspension of hostilities.

Returning to his hometown during this interval, Escobedo was assigned as of October 21, 1846, to the 1st Militia Company of Galeana, serving under its commander, Francisco Martínez Salazar, during an ambush in Santa Rosa Canyon of a detachment of American soldiers, as well as later fighting in Santa Anna's defeat at the Battle of Buena Vista or La Angostura in February 1847.

Campaigns against the Indians (1848–1854)

Escobedo continued to serve as an ensign in the 1st Militia until January 10, 1848, by which time the Mexican-American War was virtually over, and the next day he was transferred to the *Compañía Activa* of Galeana, campaigning sporadically against native war parties in that region over the next four years, while privately engaged in raising cattle and running the family farms. He was promoted to lieutenant of cavalry in the *Guardia Nacional* or "National Guard" by Gov. Agapito García of Nuevo León on August 31, 1852. Escobedo was also appointed *segundo jefe* or "second chief" for the canton of Galeana, his responsibilities being expanded to include the adjoining cantons of Iturbide and Rayón when he was promoted to captain by Ampudia—in his capacity as liberal military governor—on April 22, 1854.

Rise to Prominence (1855–1857)

Escobedo participated in Col. Juan Zuazua's offensive against the 2,000-man *santannista* concentration that had gathered at Rancho de las Varas outside Saltillo under Gen. Francisco Güitián, the liberal army coming within sight of that city by July 22, 1855. Under cover of darkness, three columns led by Escobedo, Ignacio Zaragoza, and Pedro Hinojosa then mounted a coordinated assault that same night which captured almost its entire garrison and their armaments, for which success Escobedo (like Zaragoza and Hinojosa) was promoted four days later to the rank of *comandante* or "commander" of the 4th and 5th Squadrons.

When Nuevo León's cantankerous Gov. Santiago Vidaurri annexed Coahuila in February 1856 and then angrily rebuffed all objections raised against this unilateral expropriation by the fledgling national government under interim president Ignacio Comonfort, the latter finally authorized the use of military force on August 8, 1856, to remove the defiant Vidaurri from office. Two armies began converging on Nuevo León: one out of Tamaulipas to its east, advancing in twin columns through the towns of Villagrán and Mier under Gen. Juan José de la Garza, plus a second army out of San Luis Potosí to its south, moving under Gen. Vicente Rosas Landa.

Escobedo (now bearing the rank of lieutenant colonel since February 21, 1856), rushed in late September 1856 to hold Villagrán with 100 cavalrymen, being reinforced shortly thereafter by infantry and artillery contingents under Zaragoza. The state capital of Monterrey was briefly besieged for two days as of November 1, 1856, after which a peace was arranged whereby Vidaurri agreed to resign as governor and recognize the authority of the national government. Naturally, he did not resign, although he did mobilize against the conservative coup that deposed the liberal President Comonfort in Mexico City on January 22, 1858, during which mobilization Escobedo was once again activated as a lieutenant colonel on March 20, 1858.

War of the Reform (1858–1860)

Less than a month later, he commanded Col. Juan Zuazua's right at the Battle of Puerto de Carretas on April 17, 1858, and participated in the capture of Zacatecas nine days afterward. Escobedo then rode as second-in-command under Col. Miguel Blanco at the head of 800 mounted riflemen of the 2nd *Regimiento de Rifleros* and seven field-pieces that were sent south to reinforce Santos Degollado in the state of Jalisco, where they combined with regional irregulars into a formation known as the 1st Liberal Division and besieged Guadalajara as of May 21 until June 13, 1858 when it was learned that conservative brigadier general Miguel Miramón was marching to the garrison's relief with an army of regulars. After the liberals redeployed, Escobedo distinguished himself at the defensive action fought against Miramón at Atenquique on July 2, 1858, receiving a light wound and having his horse killed before taking part in another thrust toward Guadalajara one week later.

His northern detachment then returned homeward, during which Escobedo was promoted to full cavalry colonel and placed in command of Coahuila's frontline base at Saltillo as of August 15, 1858, a position which he would hold for more than a year, although remaining active in the heartland of the country. Indeed, he took part in the unsuccessful assault by a small liberal army against the San Cosme Gate outside of Mexico City on October 14–15, 1858, and commanded the rearguard which helped this defeated force to escape from the pursuit by Miramón. Escobedo then ended this year by participating in the liberal capture of Irapuato on December 30, 1858, and campaigning early next spring against the conservative commanders Antonio Taboada, Joaquín Miramón, and Tomás Mejía in the state of Guanajuato.

In April 1859, the cantankerous Gov. Santiago Vidaurri of Coahuila ordered the recall of his liberal contingents that were operating on detached service with Degollado's army in the Bajío, so that Escobedo was commissioned to return to Monterrey and request that this recall be rescinded. He was instead instructed to remain in Galeana and take charge of the *Legión del Norte* or "Northern Legion" as of September 2, 1859, but Escobedo conspired with Zaragoza to distract the governor three weeks later with a military mutiny, during which Vidaurri was arrested and deported toward the U.S. border to be expelled—only to be rescued en route by his adherents, so that Coahuila's political crisis dragged on for several more months and Escobedo remained idle.

Because of this internal dissension, he did not take part in any more military actions during the War of the Reform, beyond a few minor skirmishes in the state of San Luis Potosí in mid-October 1860, as conservative strength collapsed and the

liberal Pres. Benito Juárez was restored into office by the end of that same year. Ironically, Escobedo was surprised and captured after this conflict had concluded, when the diehard Mejía overran Río Verde with a column of conservative renegades in January 1861. Escobedo was lucky to escape from his captors while wending their way through the Sierra de Querétaro, and played an active role in subsequently hunting them down from February to late April 1861.

War of the French Intervention (1862–1866)

As a 36-year-old republican colonel, Escobedo fought in the Battle of Cumbres de Acultzingo on April 28, 1862, against the initial French expeditionary force which penetrated into Central Mexico, as well as commanding the Santa Inés reserve one week later during the famous Cinco de Mayo defense of Puebla. Escobedo was then promoted to brigadier general during the French siege of this same city one year later (on April 25, 1863) by its liberal garrison commander, Gen. Jesús González Ortega, and designated as "Major General of Cavalry Formations" during the retreat toward Toluca by the survivors once that city fell in mid-May 1863.

He led this extemporized cavalry brigade to join Porfirio Díaz's scratch army at San Luis Potosí, so as to continue republican resistance. Escobedo and his three squadrons of the San Luis Potosí Cavalry Regiment took part in Díaz's successful attack on October 27, 1863, against the imperial garrison holding the mining town of Taxco in the state of Guerrero. However, after separating from Díaz and being driven out of southern Mexico altogether into the United States, Escobedo recrossed the Texas border and with a handful of followers occupied Nuevo Laredo on March 7, 1864. He fought under

Miguel Negrete's command in the delaying action at La Angostura on May 30, 1865, which allowed the republicans to slip away from converging Franco-imperial columns.

Once that summer's heat abated, Escobedo began gathering an army with an 11-gun siege train on September 28, 1865, to besiege Mejía's imperial garrison, which was holding Matamoros and its Gulf outlet at Bagdad. The French admiral Cloué responded to this latter threat by landing reinforcements from his anchored squadron, yet this did not deter Escobedo from pressing in to besiege Matamoros itself on October 23, 1865. He installed an eight-gun battery and siege lines southwest of its walls by the next day, then mounted a three-pronged assault at dawn of October 25, 1865, which was checked by heavy counterfire. After settling down to a brief siege, the republicans' ammunition and patience ran low, so Escobedo retired by November 14, 1865.

Unfazed by this setback, he quickly gathered another small army outside of Monterrey, whose French troops had already departed, leaving only a Mexican imperial garrison under Felipe Tinajero and Julián Quiroga. These conservative commanders made a sudden sally on November 23, 1865, being checked from atop Guadalupe Hill by Col. Jerónimo Treviño's republican cavalry. Two days later, Escobedo sent in twin assault columns to storm the city's Carlota and Pueblo redoubts, who succeeded in gaining Monterrey's main square within two hours, only to be interrupted by the unexpected arrival of a French relief column from Saltillo under Foreign Legion major Hubert de La Hayrie. Learning that General Jeanningros was also coming along behind with another 800 soldiers, Escobedo broke off the action and withdrew his men in two

separate directions, bloodying a pursuit column that followed as far as Los Lermas.

Escobedo's troops reemerged from the mountains to overrun the tiny Gulf port of Bagdad below Matamoros on January 4, 1866, chasing its few Austrian defenders aboard an anchored French vessel. Because looting subsequently threatened some American properties, 150 U.S. Army regulars were dispatched across the border to restore order; they were withdrawn three weeks later amid protests from the imperial and French authorities. By this time, Napoleon in Paris was succumbing to diplomatic pressure and preparing to accelerate French troop withdrawals, so a few Foreign Legion companies would be left to fight rearguard actions in northern Mexico.

On April 1, 1866, Escobedo struck against Matehuala in the state of San Luis Potosí, and then detached his subordinate Col. Ruperto Martínez westward to loot the rich mining camp of Real de Catorce. Two and a half months later, Escobedo won a major victory when his 1,500 troops ambushed a large mule train in mid-June 1866 near Santa Gertrudis, escorted by 2,000 Austrian and imperial troops. His victory was so decisive, 368 of the surprised enemy being killed and another 1,000 captured, that the half-starved imperial garrison evacuated Matamoros without a fight shortly thereafter. Soon, the French began withdrawing their outposts from the North as well, so that Escobedo was promoted to *general de división* or "major general" on November 2, 1866, by a grateful President Juárez.

Triumph Over Miramón (February 1867)

With northern Mexico cleared of imperial garrisons and the French retiring down to Veracruz so as to sail away for Europe,

Escobedo was at last free to launch an offensive into the country's heartland. On January 16, 1867, he reached San Luis Potosí with a 10,000-man republican army, pausing there to refresh. Two weeks later, he caught the formerly invincible conservative Gen. Miguel Miramón hastening southeastward out of Zacatecas, hoping to unite with an approaching 2,000-man imperial army under Gen. Severo del Castillo.

Escobedo engaged Miramón on February 1, 1867, at San Diego Hacienda on the road between San Jacinto and San Francisco de Adames. The outnumbered imperial infantrymen positioned themselves within the hacienda, their cavalry on both flanks. But Escobedo's superior force easily overwhelmed these defenses, driving their enemies back into Cuisillo Ranch. Miramón was fortunate to escape toward Querétaro with a handful of followers, leaving behind 100 dead, 800 captives, his artillery and supply train, plus countless turncoats and deserters. After this battle, Escobedo executed 103 French prisoners for violating the decree recalling them to Europe.

Siege of Querétaro and Capture of the Emperor (March–May 1867)

After conferring at Chamacuero on March 5, 1867, Escobedo and the northwestern republican commander Ramón Corona agreed to jointly begin their final offensive against Maximilian's stronghold of Querétaro the next day in parallel columns of approximately 10,000 men apiece.

Díaz (who had already revised the terms of his original Plan de Tuxtepec on a couple of occasions so as to accommodate to these changing circumstances) was among the first to heed this call. As early as November 2, 1876, his rebel forces had seized the railroad station at tiny Apizaco, Puebla, and began dismantling its rails and trestle bridge so as to cut communications from the national capital. President Lerdo and his Ministry of War, now under the direction of Gen. Mariano Escobedo, had responded by dispatching 600 soldiers from Mexico City to reinforce the regional commander, Gen. Ignacio R. Alatorre, with orders to confront these upstarts in battle.

See also: Ampudia Grimarest, Pedro; Cinco de Mayo, Battle of the; Corona Madrigal, Ramón; Cumbres de Acultzingo, Battle of the; French Intervention, War of the; González Ortega, Jesús; Maximilian, Emperor of Mexico; Miramón Tarelo, Miguel Gregorio de la Luz Atenógenes; Puerto de Carretas, Battle of; Querétaro, Siege of; Reform, War of the; Santa Gertrudis, Battle of; Zaragoza Seguín, Ignacio; Zuazua Esparza, Juan Nepomuceno.

Further Reading

Message of the President of the United States of January 29, 1867, Relating to the Present Condition of Mexico. Washington, DC: U.S. Government Printing Office, 1867, 28–29, 76–77, 225–33.

Sosa, Francisco. *Biografías de mexicanos distinguidos.* Mexico City: Porrúa, 2006.

Estancia de las Vacas, Battle of (1859)

Unexpected victory won by the conservative general Miguel Miramón during the War of the Reform.

Early in November 1859—late during the second year of this national conflict between liberals and conservatives—a swelling upsurge in support meant that several liberal armies had suddenly materialized in the Bajío region of central Mexico. One large force of 6,000 men and 29 fieldpieces under Gen. Santos Degollado, with such well-known field commanders as José Justo Álvarez, Manuel Doblado, Miguel Blanco, José María Arteaga, and Santiago Tapia serving as his subordinate brigadiers, easily bested a small conservative contingent under Gen. Francisco Pacheco near Silao and then chased Gen. Francisco A. Vélez out of the City of Guanajuato.

Preliminary Movements (November 5–12, 1859)

With few significant conservative formations now standing between this liberal concentration and the national capital, Miramón (in his joint capacity as acting "substitute president" and army commander-in-chief) issued orders for Vélez to fall back and incorporate his 800 survivors into Gen. Tomás Mejía's 1,500-man garrison at Querétaro. Then, after further instructing the conservative generals Adrián Woll at Zacatecas and Leonardo Márquez at Guadalajara to detach reinforcements to his relief, Miramón and his staff left Mexico City by stagecoach on the night of November 5–6, 1859, to personally assume command over the scratch army that was being thrown together at Querétaro. The 4th Infantry Battalion was to furthermore follow Miramón from the capital, its 300 men escorting some additional artillery pieces so as to comprise a combined force totaling 2,600 conservative troops armed with 19 guns.

Degollado's advancing army had reached Apaseo by November 11, 1859, from where the liberal commander sent Col. Benito Gómez Farías on ahead as an emissary into Querétaro to propose a meeting between the liberal chieftain Degollado and conservative commander Miramón. The two generals, each accompanied by only a single aide-de-camp, met in the no-man's-land between the liberals' advance outpost at La Calera and the conservatives' outpost

in the Hacienda del Rayo, at 4:30 p.m. on November 12, 1859. But having failed to arrive at any kind of an understanding by the time evening fell, Degollado left and ordered his second-in-command Doblado to deploy the entire liberal army overnight into a series of three defensive battle lines atop the hills of Estancia de las Vacas, less than six miles west of Querétaro.

Battle of Estancia de las Vacas (November 13, 1859)

Miramón's smaller conservative army had also moved out of that city to prepare for the forthcoming battle, so his guns opened up long-range fire against the liberal positions at 7:00 a.m. on Sunday morning, November 13, 1859. After two hours of exchanges, attack columns swarmed out of both liberal wings, the Morelia and Tamaulipas Infantry Battalions emerging from the liberal left under Arteaga, while a rifle regiment and the Aguascalientes Battalion simultaneously pushed out from their right under Col. Julián Quiroga. Cavalry squadrons under Gen. Emilio Langberg followed on the liberal left and Col. Vicente Vega's squadrons on their right—yet difficulties presented by irregularities in the terrain hampered their efforts to form up properly and charge in a single large mass.

Miramón therefore managed to check the danger on his left flank but only by committing Mejía into shoring it up with 400 cavalrymen, the Alfaro Brigade, the Guanajuato and León Battalions, plus six small howitzers. Over on the conservative right, the Silao Battalion and a field battery also helped to fight off the liberal onslaught on that flank until Degollado sent his liberal 1st and 2nd Light San Luis Battalions under Tapia and Blanco directly into the conservative center. These columns overran some guns, and when Miramón countered with his reserve—the Sierra Gorda Battalion and 200 chasseurs—the liberals broke up these formations as well, seeming to be on the verge of carrying the day.

Desperate, Miramón personally led his last 120 reserves into the center while calling for a general counterattack all along his battle line—and at this crucial juncture, Tapia and Col. Albino Espinosa of the liberal 1st Light San Luis Battalion both fell severely wounded, so their leaderless men began to shrink back out of the firefight in confusion. Then, as more and more liberal troops began retreating, Degollado tried to stabilize the situation by issuing an order around 11:00 a.m. for his reeling army to withdraw and reassemble within their strong defensive positions atop the Estancia de las Vacas hills. However, their jumbled retirements out of the battle line quickly turned into outright flight, officers' shouted commands being ignored as their soldiers scattered in every direction. Many of these runaways appropriated horses and mules from the artillery and supply trains so as to make good their escape. A furious Doblado even wanted to fire grapeshot at these deserters but discovered that the liberals' guns already lay abandoned by their crews.

Aftermath (November 14–19, 1859)

Despite being outnumbered by more than two to one, Miramón had emerged victorious, although his army had suffered 89 killed and 114 wounded during this quick, sharp encounter, compared to 275 casualties among the liberals. The conservatives nonetheless retained 120 prisoners, 29 fieldpieces, a forge, 63 loaded wagons, and some 500 firearms, while Doblado led the tattered remnants of his liberal army away toward Salvatierra. Degollado, who escaped through Celaya toward San Luis Potosí,

would henceforth become known derisively as the *héroe de las derrotas* or "hero of the defeats" among liberals and conservatives alike.

As for the triumphant Miramón, he inspected the damages inflicted throughout Apaseo and Guanajuato by this liberal incursion before proceeding on to Guadalajara by stagecoach. Arriving there unexpectedly at 2:00 p.m. on Saturday afternoon, November 19, 1859, he was greeted by a 21-gun salute and pealing church bells. His conservative rival, General Márquez—who had never sent the requested reinforcements—was just then absent, having marched westward at the head of a division, but was promptly recalled by the angry Miramón and arrested on a vindictive charge of misappropriation of funds.

See also: Bajío; Degollado Sánchez, José Nemesio Francisco; Márquez Araujo, Leonardo; Miramón Tarelo, Miguel Gregorio de la Luz Atenógenes; Reform, War of the; Woll, Adrián.

Further Reading

Cambre, Manuel. *La guerra de Tres Años: apuntes para la historia de la Reforma.* Guadalajara, Jalisco: Gobierno del Estado, 1949, 332–39.

"From Mexico: Further Success of the Conservative Cause." *New York Times*, December 14, 1859.

EZLN (1994–present).
Acronym that stands for the *Ejército Zapatista de Liberación Nacional* or "Zapatista Army of National Liberation," a leftist revolutionary movement that operates in Mexico's southernmost state of Chiapas.

See Ejército Zapatista de Liberación Nacional.

F

The bane of Mexico has been, and is, militarism. Very few civilians have become President. Always generals ... and what generals! This has to end, for the good of Mexico.

> Pres. Venustiano Carranza, ca. April 1920, one month prior to his deposal and murder

First French Intervention (1838–1839)

In Spanish *Primera Intervención Francesa*, the name given by many modern Mexican scholars to the punitive naval expedition that was sent from France to blockade, bombard, and seize the port city of Veracruz during the winter of 1838–1839 so as to exact compensation for economic losses suffered by their country's business interests during Mexico's chaotic infighting. However, this foreign aggression was more popularly known during its day as the *Guerra de los Pasteles* or the "War of the Cakes" and is still commonly referred to by that same name today.

See also: Cakes, War of the.

flying artillery (1846–1848)

Significant tactical advantage enjoyed by U.S. armies during their invasion of Mexico in the Mexican-American War because of the superior speed and mobility of their field artillery batteries.

During the early 1840s, the U.S. Army had developed a separate artillery branch, which began adapting and creating some promising new armaments and techniques. In particular, a few mobile batteries of light artillery were armed with six-pound howitzers, designed to carry their gunners on horseback instead of on foot so as to be able to speed around and swiftly deploy on a battlefield rather than remain fixed in static positions with heavier guns. Mexican officers first experienced the devastating effectiveness of this mobile artillery in the very opening battle of that conflict, at Palo Alto on May 8, 1846.

Having interposed his army between Zachary Taylor's column and his forward base at Brownsville, Texas, the Mexican commander Mariano Arista deployed his 3,200 men across the road in a battle line a mile-and-a-half long, his flanks anchored behind a swamp and a cluster of woods.

Further Reading

Tucker, Spencer C. *The Encyclopedia of the Mexican-American War.* Santa Barbara, CA: ABC-CLIO, 2013.

Foreign Legion. *See* French Foreign Legion in Mexico (1863–1867).

fornitura

Name in Spanish for the leather cartridge belts and straps typically worn by soldiers to carry their accessories and gear.

In one of many examples of this term's usage, the liberal brigadier general Nicolás de Regules wrote from Silao on August 15, 1860, to his immediate superior, Gen. Manuel Doblado, complaining that his men:

> of the 2nd Brigade came on this campaign almost naked, and consequently remain lacking smocks, many soldiers without *chacos* [shakos], and many without *fornituras*.

Further Reading

Doblado, Manuel. *La guerra de Reforma*. San Antonio, TX: Lozano, 1930, 213–14.

Heftcr, Joseph. *Crónica del traje militar en México, del siglo XVI al XX*. Mexico City: Artes de México, 1968.

French Foreign Legion in Mexico (1863–1867)

A unique military unit that was to greatly enhance its reputation—and fight an epic losing battle—while campaigning in Mexico during the War of the French Intervention.

Early History (1831–1859)

Soon after France had conquered Algiers during the summer of 1830, whose subsequent occupation was promising to be a dirty and difficult affair with little appeal among regular regiments, King Louis-Philippe had authorized the creation of a *Légion Étrangère* or "Foreign Legion" on March 9, 1831. Through this measure, all non-French royal battalions scattered among France's standing army were to be regrouped into a single regiment, into which new foreign volunteers could then also be allotted so as to be deployed instead of French units on this unpleasant and unpopular Algerian service. All of these

foreign troops were moreover prohibited by law from operating on Continental French soil, in the uneasy aftermath of the July 1830 Revolution.

The Legion's original 1st, 2nd, and 3rd Battalions had therefore been cobbled together out of the already-serving Swiss (*Gardes Suisses*) and German (*Hohenlohe*) units; the 4th Battalion from Spanish and Portuguese units; the 5th from Sardinians and Italians; the 6th from Belgians and Dutchmen; and the 7th from Poles. New recruits were allotted into these units according to their nationality aftcr a simple verbal declaration as to their name and country of origin. Under such a rudimentary system of admission, even a hardened criminal could disappear into the Legion's ranks under an assumed name, and many did so in order to put themselves beyond the reach of the law.

The first contingents of legionnaires had reached Algiers by August 1831, undergoing their baptism of fire on April 27, 1832. Poorly equipped, ill-paid, and expendable, morale had initially plummeted so low that many members of this early Legion had deserted. When civil war threatened in Spain two years later, the entire 4th Battalion was disbanded so as to repatriate them to their Iberian homelands, and when that conflict finally did erupt, France had transferred its entire 4,000-man Legion over to Spain's Queen Isabel II as of June 29, 1835, so as to fight for her cause.

A brand-new Foreign Legion therefore had to be created at Algiers as of December 16, 1835. This new force was to initially be made up of only three battalions, but these were rejoined more than three years later by 500 or so survivors from the *Ancienne Légion* sent into Spain. Two more battalions had consequently been formed out of these survivors at Pau and Perpignan in 1840, after which the reunited Legion was divided up into two regiments designated the *1er. et 2e. Régiments de la Légion Étrangère*. Both had departed Algiers to fight during the Crimean War from 1854 to 1856, serving well at the Battle of Alma and siege of Sebastopol, at the conclusion of which they had been amalgamated into a single formation dubbed the *Régiment Étrangèr* (they would not be called the "Foreign Legion" again until two decades later). They also performed well at the Battles of Magenta and Solferino during the Italian campaign of 1859.

Deployment to Mexico (February–March 1863)

However, it was to be the legionnaires' conduct during the War of the French Intervention in Mexico that would establish their reputation as tough, elite troops in the most inhospitable of environments. The regiment had initially not been assigned to the first expedition sent to Veracruz in early 1862 under Maj. Gen. Charles, Comte de Lorencez, nor to the second larger force that began to depart as reinforcements during the summer and autumn of 1862 under Maj. Gen. Elie Forey. Yet the Foreign Legion officers at their Algerian base of Sidi-bel-Abbès convinced their colonel, Pierre Joseph Jeanningros, to petition the war minister, who in turn issued the desired orders for the regiment to participate.

The five battalions of Legionnaires set sail from Oran aboard the ships *Saint-Louis* and *Wagram* on February 9, 1863, arriving off Veracruz by March 25th and disembarking the next day. Jeanningros and his men were disappointed to learn that they would not be joining Forey's main siege army, which was attempting to subdue the city of Puebla, but rather were assigned the more mundane duty of protecting the supply route that stretched inland from Tejería

through La Soledad and Chiquihuite as far as the city of Córdoba.

Their heroism at Camerone impressed officers of the French high command, although the legionnaires nonetheless remained employed on their usual unglamorous duties: escorting convoys, patrolling roads, chasing elusive guerrilla bands, and enduring the boredom of occupation. By February 1864, they had become so decimated by initial bouts of disease that only 800 of its original 2,000 men remained fit for service, and the five undermanned infantry battalions had been reorganized down into four, bolstered by a company of Mexican volunteers and a mounted scouting company, plus a field artillery battery armed with six small howitzers carried by mules. At Colonel Jeanningros's suggestion, the Legion was allowed to request more volunteers from Algiers, and the Legion's home base was furthermore temporarily shifted from Sidi-bel-Abbès to Aix-la-Chapelle in France so as to recruit more volunteers to replace its losses in Mexico.

By June 1864, official returns indicated that regimental strength had rebounded to "a total of 2,682 men (2,263 under arms) who were stationed in the city of Puebla with detachments at San Juan de los Llanos, Zacatlán, Tlaxcala, Tepejí de la Seda, and Acatlán"—see the Appendix in the section titled "The Imperial (Combined Franco-Mexican) Army under Maximilian."

Campaign in Northern Mexico (May 1865–January 1867)

Given the toughest assignments, 1,500 Franco-imperial troops under Jeanningros reached San Buenaventura, Coahuila, on May 25, 1865, part of a pincer operation intended to break up republican concentrations around Saltillo under Negrete and Escobedo. One week later, his Legionnaires encountered the republicans at La Angostura, who repulsed the initial assaults and then slipped away into the mountains on the night of June 6–7, 1865, before the pincer could close in from Parras. The Legion companies would remain deployed in the stark landscape of northern Mexico for the next year and a half.

Mariano Escobedo's attempt to storm Monterrey on November 25, 1865, was interrupted by the timely arrival of a relief column of legionnaires from their base at Saltillo. And by January 1866, Napoleon was succumbing to diplomatic and political pressures in Paris and so began issuing instructions to prepare to accelerate the French troop withdrawals from Mexico, which meant that Foreign Legion companies would be expected to fight increasingly desperate rearguard actions, while the departure of all other units was already inevitable. As usual, the Legionnaires fought stoically and well, even in a doomed cause.

When Parras was seized by emboldened republican forces on February 12, 1866, four companies of the 2nd Foreign Legion Battalion marched from Saltillo to the rescue under Maj. Amable Brian de Foussieres-Founteneuille, recuperating that town without opposition eight days later. However, when Brian subsequently learned on February 25th that the 300 republican raiders had withdrawn only seven miles north to the Santa Isabel Hacienda atop La Cruz Hill in the nearby mountains, the major celebrated his 38th birthday and then sallied at midnight on February 27–28 to attack—little realizing that the republicans had been heavily reinforced in the interim by Colonels Treviño and Naranjo.

Before first light on February 28, 1866, Brian's two companies of 188 legionnaires and 250 imperial partisans approached the hacienda, only to be greeted by heavy volleys fired from the darkness. The French commander fell severely wounded, his auxiliaries fled, and Captain Moulinier led the surviving Legionnaires in a hopeless series of assaults, which ceased at dawn when the republican cavalry circled behind the attackers, cutting off their escape. Eventually, a single Legionnaire managed to crawl back into Parras from this disaster, 82 others having been killed and more than 100 captured.

By the time that it was withdrawn in February 1867, the Legion had suffered 31 officers and 1,917 men killed during its four-year tour of duty in Mexico. The Legion's tenacity, enduring such brutal losses even in a doomed cause, would further burnish its fame.

See also: Bazaine, François Achille; Camerone, Battle of; Lorencez, Charles Ferdinand Latrille, Comte de.

Further Reading

Chartrand, René. *The Mexican Adventure, 1861–67.* Oxford: Osprey, 1994.

Montbarbut Du Plessis, Jean-Marie. *L'armée de Napoléon III au Mexique, 1862–1867.* Paris: Éditions Nouvelles, 2009.

Porch, Douglas. *The French Foreign Legion: Complete History of the Legendary Fighting Force.* New York: Harper Perennial, 1992.

Rickards, Colin. *Hand of Captain Danjou: Camerone and the French Foreign Legion in Mexico, 30 April 1863.* Marlborough, Wilshire, England: Crowood Press, 2008.

Ryan, James W. *Camerone: The French Foreign Legion's Greatest Battle.* New York: Praeger, 1996.

French Intervention, War of the (1861–1867)

Continuation of the decades-old struggle between Mexico's liberals and

French lithograph, showing their forces carrying Puebla's defenses in the spring of 1863. (Library of Congress)

conservatives, although this time with the defeated conservatives receiving assistance from a French military expedition so as to drive the liberals from power and replace Mexico's republican government with an imperial regime.

Background (July–November 1861)

The conservative cause had seemingly spiraled into outright defeat, their final loss occurring at the Battle of Calpulalpan in late December 1860, which had resulted in the detention or dispersal of their leadership abroad and ended the three-year War of the Reform. The administration of liberal president Benito Juárez had returned triumphantly into Mexico City from exile and assumed office, only to be obliged within six months to declare bankruptcy due to the dislocations of the war-ravaged national economy. On July 17, 1861, they had suspended payments for a period of two years

on a foreign debt totaling 82.2 million *pesos*, 70 million of which were owed to British interests, 9.4 million to Spanish interests, and 2.8 million to French interests. Both the English and French ambassadors had severed diplomatic relations in protest, while their home governments cast about for means to punish this default.

The most direct method seemed to be armed intervention, so London, Paris, and Madrid signed a pact on October 31, 1861, in which they agreed to jointly send an expedition to occupy Veracruz and garnishee its customs dues until Mexico's obligations were met. However, since the earliest days of independence from Spain, Mexican conservatives had also been proposing the adoption of a constitutional monarchy as a way of stabilizing its administration. Consequently, José Manuel Hidalgo—a Mexican conservative who in September 1861 had been living at the

French empress Eugénie's court at Biarritz—suggested that this intervention might furthermore be used to implement just such a scheme, even proposing the 29-year-old archduke Ferdinand Maximilian of Austria as an ideal neutral candidate. Napoleon III agreed, and the archduke in turn was persuaded to assume the mantle of Mexican emperor should it ever be offered.

Cooperative Multinational Effort (December 1861–March 1862)

On December 10, 1861, a Spanish squadron bearing 5,800 soldiers dropped anchor southeast of Veracruz, and four days later delivered a demand for that city's republican Gov. Ignacio de la Llave to surrender his port. Instructed from Mexico City not to resist, his garrison retired inland and allowed the Spaniards to occupy both the city and its off-lying island fortress of San Juan de Ulúa by December 17, 1861. English and French squadrons then joined this Spanish force by January 7, 1862, and all three leaders sent a joint offer inland to Mexico City a week later, hinting at a resolution. The Mexican foreign minister, Manuel Doblado, had responded in kind, but excessive demands by the French delegation hampered any further progress. The French were also secretly allowing Mexican conservatives to return from exile and begin calling on their sympathizers inland to mutiny against Juárez's republican regime. Such sedition prompted the Mexican government to proclaim the death penalty for any citizens found collaborating with these occupiers.

Then on February 2, 1862, the foreign commanders informed the authorities in Mexico City that their joint expedition was suffering from disease in that coastal city so would have to advance inland to healthier cantonments. This warning caused Foreign Minister Doblado to reopen negotiations, and a preliminary accord was even signed two weeks later at the city of Orizaba. Yet before this agreement could be received, much less ratified, in Europe, the French contingent unilaterally moved inland from Veracruz on February 25, 1862, and was further reinforced by the disembarkation a fortnight later of 4,500 more French troops under Gen. Charles, Comte de Lorencez. One month later, the British and Spanish governments dissolved their association with the French, who were plainly pursuing their own separate agenda for the installation of a puppet regime in Mexico.

Initial French Penetration and Repulse (April–May 1862)

As France's former partners prepared to depart Veracruz, Lorencez struck inland from his base camp at Córdoba on April 19, 1862, with 6,800 French troops and 16 guns. After traveling only five miles, they skirmished at El Fortín against a Mexican republican cavalry screen under Col. Félix Díaz, who was able to warn Gen. Ignacio Zaragoza to begin evacuating nearby Orizaba. But in a coordinated move, Gen. Antonio Taboada also revolted that same day against Juárez's government, soon being joined by other conservative sympathizers stationed throughout the country—Leonardo Márquez, Tomás Mejía, Juan Vicario, etc.—who together intended to bring as many as 8,000 mutinous Mexican soldiers to join the advancing French.

Leaving a garrison in Orizaba, Lorencez continued marching inland on April 27, 1862, with his 6,150 troops, reaching the outskirts of Acultzingo by the next morning. His well-armed and veteran French force then exchanged long-range fire with a division of 2,200 republicans and a dozen field howitzers hidden atop the nearby *cumbres* or "heights" that same afternoon of April 28, 1862, who melted away after three hours rather than engage in a set-piece battle, leaving the winding highway ascent up into the central highlands clear for Lorencez to press on toward the city of Puebla with his column and 260 supply wagons.

Upon reaching deserted Amozoc without encountering any further opposition on May 4, 1862, the entire French Army paused to rest, while vainly awaiting the arrival of Mexican conservative reinforcements under Márquez. These failed to appear despite repeated assurances that the invaders could expect wholehearted support from many Mexicans, so Lorencez had to send his vanguard of *Chasseurs d'Afrique* on ahead alone the next dawn, May 5th (in Spanish: *cinco de Mayo*), reaching Los Álamos Hacienda by 9:00 a.m. and clearing the way for his main body to assault the nearby city of Puebla.

Invasion and Imperial Imposition (1863–1865)

Deeming Mexico City to be untenable against this resumed French advance, despite its 12,000 republican defenders, President Juárez reverted to his tactic from the War of the Reform of a few years earlier by departing his capital on May 31, 1863, to set up a government in exile at San Luis Potosí, escorted by a division under 32-year-old brigadier general Porfirio Díaz. Four days later, the *Chasseurs de Vincennes* Battalion—in the forefront of Forey's vanguard—reached the suburb of San Lázaro just outside Mexico City, and Bazaine penetrated into its streets on June 7, 1863, paving the way for Márquez to lead a triumphal parade into the national capital with his Mexican conservative allies three days afterward.

The French army occupied Mexico City, and a new administrative body known as the "Superior Junta" was temporarily installed by Forey on June 15, 1863, who in turn were instructed to appoint the puppet general Juan N. Almonte as "provisional president" of Mexico the next day. This same Junta subsequently elevated the country's status into a "Catholic empire" on July 10, 1863, and voted to offer its imperial crown to Maximilian. In the meantime, Franco-conservative detachments were fanning out to occupy such nearby cities as Toluca by July 5, 1863, and Cuernavaca on July 29, 1863, encountering little organized resistance.

After a pause to let the summer heat pass, Franco-conservative columns resumed their operations to subdue more of the country in October 1863, general Charles Douay marching north from Mexico City with a powerful French division toward Querétaro to take control of the Bajío. Another such imperial column spearheaded by general Armand de Castagny's 1st Infantry Division occupied Morelia, Michoacán, on November 30, 1863, while Douay seized Guanajuato, Celaya, and San Miguel Allende nine days afterward. Threatened by Castagny's and Mejía's parallel drives northward, the republican president Juárez abandoned his provisional capital of San Luis Potosí in favor of Saltillo on December 20, 1863, while Guadalajara fell to a concentration of forces directed by the French commander-in-chief Bazaine on January 6, 1864.

The city of Aguascalientes was occupied by Franco-conservative forces on February 2, 1864, followed by Zacatecas five days later. Mejía and the French colonel Edouard, Baron de Aymard, drove the republican Gen. Manuel Doblado out of the northern town of Matehuala on May 17, 1864, and 11 days afterward Maximilian reached Veracruz aboard the Austro-Hungarian frigate *Novara*, to proceed triumphantly inland to assume the throne. Napoleon III has promised to support his regime for three years, while gradually reducing the size of the French occupation force from 38,000 to 20,000 men. A four-pronged offensive against Oaxaca—the last major pocket of republican resistance—was launched on August 1, 1864, but then postponed four and a half months until the advent of cooler winter weather, resulting in the wholesale surrender of its garrison by early February 1865.

Deterioration and Republican Triumph (1866–1867)

Yet although the French divisions were unstoppable, they were too few in numbers to garrison more than a few major cities and towns, while their conservative allies were despised for collaborating with these foreign invaders. Roads and the countryside remained at the mercy of guerrilla bands, while tough republican units began to multiply in the stark desert landscapes of northern Mexico, far from the imperial reach. As the months dragged on, morale among the professional French soldiers dipped due to the boredom of thankless garrison duties, and the unpopularity of their occupation efforts among the citizenry.

Worse still, the end of the American Civil War in April 1865 ushered in mounting diplomatic pressure from Washington for the removal of all French forces from its neighbor Mexico, and the supplying of better weaponry to republican forces. Unrest also grew in France about the costly and unending overseas operation, until finally Napoleon was obliged to issue a public statement that declared the intervention in Mexico a "success" on January 22, 1866, while quietly giving the order to begin drawing down French forces. Bazaine reassembled his far-flung regiments in as measured a fashion as possible, so as to give the emperor time to stabilize his regime, but most were gathered by December 28, 1866, and had marched down to Veracruz to reembark by early February 1867. With his strongest support removed, large republican armies converged within a few weeks' time to besiege Maximilian in Querétaro, and bring an end to the War of the French Intervention.

See also: Calpulalpan, Battle of; Cumbres de Acultzingo, Battle of the; Lorencez, Charles Ferdinand Latrille, Comte de; Márquez Araujo, Leonardo; Reform, War of the; Zaragoza Seguín, Ignacio.

Further Reading

Chartrand, René. *The Mexican Adventure, 1861–67.* Oxford: Osprey, 1994.

Hanna, Alfred J. and Kathryn A. *Napoleon III and Mexico: American Triumph over Monarchy.* Chapel Hill: University of North Carolina Press, 1971.

Montbarbut Du Plessis, Jean-Marie. *L'armée de Napoléon III au Mexique, 1862–1867.* Paris: Éditions Nouvelles, 2009.

Rivera Cambas, Manuel. *Historia de la intervención europea y norteamericana en México y del imperio de Maximiliano de Hapsburgo.* Mexico City: INEHRM, 1987.

G

Not even Death can stop us, but if it should surprise us, welcome it shall be.

— motto of the Grupo Aeromóvil de Fuerzas Especiales (1990s)

gachupín

Mexican slang expression for any Peninsular Spaniard, a social group that was to be vindictively targeted during the War of Independence.

One of the most deep-seated grievances held by a vast majority of Creoles in the viceroyalty of New Spain, whether highborn aristocrats or lower-caste members of the colonial hierarchy, was reserved for the privileged elite of Peninsula-born Spaniards who arrived from across the Atlantic to monopolize the best bureaucratic, military, and ecclesiastical appointments. Such entitlements were made exclusively by Crown ministers in Madrid, so virtually all were filled by Spanish place seekers—often avaricious individuals who sought to wring as much profit as possible from their brief tenures in office before returning to Spain to enjoy the proceeds. Overseas trade was also monopolized by Crown license holders, any foreign goods being subject to denunciation and seizure by the king's officers, while all important legal matters had to be appealed to high courts in Spain as well.

When the rural priest Miguel Hidalgo called for a popular uprising against Spanish misrule on September 16, 1810, he unleashed a torrent of this pent-up anger. From its very first days, his followers murdered *gachupines* and looted royal offices as they advanced on the provincial capital of Guanajuato, where some 20,000–25,000 rebels swarmed into its streets around midday on September 28, 1810, and slaughtered the 600 monarchists who had taken refuge inside its royal granary—the *Alhóndiga de Granaditas*—by the next dawn. Hidalgo furthermore ordered another 100–200 Peninsula-born Spaniards, who had been rounded up from their homes in Guanajuato to be marched away and quietly butchered in an out-of-the way spot, their bodies left stripped and exposed to the elements.

Such excesses continued when Hidalgo's tumultuous throng—now numbering 60,000 followers—entered the city of Valladolid (modern Morelia, Michoacán) on October 17, 1810, killing numerous *gachupines* during an orgy of looting that lasted for three days and could not even be quelled by the insurgent military commander captain Ignacio Allende, who ordered cannon blasts fired in a vain attempt to disperse the euphoric rioters. Such violence might have been expected during the rebellion's initial outburst of unbridled lawlessness, yet the deliberate murders of Peninsular Spaniards would continue, even after Hidalgo's throng was defeated by royalist forces outside the capital of Mexico City and retreated back into Valladolid with a much smaller and more subdued following on November 10, 1810.

Naturally, royalist officers responded in kind against these insurgent executions, field commanders such as Capt. Agustín de Iturbide—the son of a Peninsular father and Mexican Creole mother who managed to escape from Valladolid—routinely ordering wholesale shootings of any insurgents who happened to fall into his hands as prisoners.

See also: Alhóndiga de Granaditas, Assault on the; Hidalgo y Costilla Gallaga, Miguel Gregorio Antonio Ignacio; Iturbide Arambúru, Agustín Cosme Damián de; Peninsular.

Further Reading

Archer, Christon I. "Bite of the Hydra: The Rebellion of Cura Miguel Hidalgo, 1810–1811." In *Patterns of Contention in Mexican History*, edited by Jaime E. Rodríguez O., 69–93. Wilmington, DE: Scholarly Resources, 1992.

Culebrina bien cargada para la cachupinada. Puebla: Oficina Nacional, 1832.

Hamill, Hugh M., Jr. *The Hidalgo Revolt: Prelude to Mexican Independence.* Gainesville: University of Florida Press, 1966.

Herrerón Peredo, Carlos. *Hidalgo: razones de la insurgencia y biografía documental.* Mexico City: SEP, 1987.

Landavazo, Marco Antonio. "El asesinato de gachupines en la guerra de independencia mexicana." *Estudios mexicanos* 23, no. 2 (Summer 2007): 253–82.

Sims, Harold D. *The Expulsion of Mexico's Spaniards, 1821–1836.* Pittsburgh, PA: University of Pittsburgh Press, 1990.

gavilla

Noun with various similar applications in the Spanish language, all usually referring to a "group" or "bunch"—*gavilla de trigo*, for example, being the term for a "sheaf" or "bundle of wheat."

In Mexico's history though, the word *gavilla* has often been applied by the authorities

Colored lithograph of a Mexican irregular cavalryman, ca. 1860, based upon an earlier painting by Carlos de Paris. (Anne S. K. Brown Military Collection, Brown University Library)

to describe a lawless "gang" and was also to be favored by regular army officers to deride the unmilitary rebel bands the they pursued during wartime. For example, when the conservative general Francisco García Casanova sallied from the city of Guadalajara with 1,500 troops and seven fieldpieces at dawn on September 18, 1858, he publicly proclaimed to its citizenry that he was off to "exterminate the *gavillas*" to its south—only to return four days later with scarcely 60 survivors, having been ambushed and utterly routed while marching along the highway near the Cuevas or Cuevitas of Techaluta by hidden military companies of the 1st Division under liberal general Santos Degollado.

See also: Degollado Sánchez, José Nemesio Francisco; Guadalajara, Sieges of.

Further Reading

Cambre, Manuel. *La guerra de Tres Años: apuntes para la historia de la Reforma.* Guadalajara, Jalisco: Gobierno del Estado, 1949, 141.

González Ortega, José Canuto de Jesús (1824–1881)

Liberal politician and self-taught general who played a prominent military role during the Wars of the Reform and of the French Intervention.

Birth and Education (1824–1851)

Although family recollections would later suggest that he was born on January 19, 1822, on the Hacienda San Mateo de Valparaíso in the *partido* of Fresnillo (today known as the municipality of Valparaíso in the state of Zacatecas), a baptismal record indicates that his birthdate was actually on October 9, 1824. Young Jesús was the eldest son of a lowly ranch foreman and bookkeeper named Laureano Filomeno González de Ávila and his wife, María Francisca Mateos Ortega, who had originally been from Morelia before settling in nearby Monte Escobedo. The family apparently moved into the city of Guadalajara around 1832, where Jesús was enrolled at 11 years of age in its Seminario Conciliar for almost a decade, proving to be an apt pupil.

The González family thereupon returned to the district of Valparaíso and by 1845 had resettled in San Juan Bautista del Teúl, where among various other ventures they would come to establish a boarding school, and well-educated young Jesús would work as the *escribiente* or "scribe" at its local courthouse. Inexplicably, rather than follow conventional practice and call himself Jesús González Mateos—adopting the surnames of both his parents, as was the usual custom—he instead chose to refer to himself throughout his lifetime as "Jesús González Ortega" or even "Jesús G. Ortega," to the point of signing his name in this latter fashion.

Having turned 21 years of age, González Ortega had also embraced many federalist and liberal ideals during his years of study in Guadalajara and consequently began writing numerous articles and helping to publish such anticentralist local weeklies as *El Pobre Diablo* or "The Poor Devil"; *El Espectro* or "The Specter"; *El Guardia Nacional* or "The National Guard"; and *La Sombra de García* or "García's Shadow" (named in honor of the federalist Francisco García Salinas, who had successfully served as Zacatecas's state governor from 1828 to 1835 until his administration was crushed by Santa Anna's centralist army).

Early Political Career (1852–1857)

When a conservative coup spearheaded by Col. José María Blancarte seized Jalisco's state government and issued the Plan del Hospicio from Guadalajara on October 20, 1852, calling for the removal of Pres. Mariano Arista and return from Colombian exile of Santa Anna so as to reassume the presidency, González Ortega helped the local liberal militia colonel José María Sánchez Román disarm some regular troops who happened to be in Tlaltenango, in transit through Zacatecas from Durango with the intent of joining the conservative insurrection at Guadalajara. As a result, González Ortega and Sánchez Román would be hunted for the next two-and-a-half years by the conservative authorities, often hiding in the hilly countryside so as to evade capture.

When the Revolution of Ayutla finally drove Santa Anna from office for the last time in early August 1855, González Ortega not only was able to return to his civilian occupation as a newspaper publisher (being later nicknamed the *tinterillo de la Reforma* or "inkwell of the Reform"), he was moreover rewarded for his patent loyalty to the liberal cause by being appointed by Col. Victoriano Zamora as *jefe politico* or "political chief" for the district of Tlaltenango on August 29, 1855. He threw himself into this work with a reformer's zeal and was elected as a representative to the national Constituent Congress that was convened the next year, although he did not attend. He was subsequently appointed "political chief" of the larger city of Fresnillo and its district as of May 14, 1857, and that same December was incensed by the moderate president Ignacio Comonfort's staged "Plan of Tacubaya" in Mexico City, which aimed to displace the elected liberal Congress that had begun reforming the national Constitution with a more conservative body.

Liberal Political Leader (1858)

When a coup deposed President Comonfort in January 1858 and a conservative army under the youthful brigadier generals Luis G. Osollo and Miguel Miramón struck north from Mexico City into the Bajío, to stamp out liberal opposition in what would become known as the War of the Reform, González Ortega initially remained in his role as politician and propagandist, trying to help raise men and materiel to resist. But the main conservative army smashed a liberal concentration outside the city of Salamanca in the first week of March 1858, then sent detachments to occupy most major cities in the region, including Zacatecas on April 17, 1858. However, the northern liberal colonel Juan Zuazua surprised and defeated its conservative garrison with a counterattack 10 days later, followed

by San Luis Potosí, so a major conservative offensive was sent back to recuperate this theater under Miramón that same autumn.

Inflicting a crushing defeat on the combined liberal forces at the Battle of Ahualulco de los Pinos in late September 1858, the victorious conservatives once again sent detachments fanning out into the region. Zacatecas's civilian governor, Javier de la Parra, resigned from office and was succeeded on October 5, 1858, by González Ortega, who evacuated that city upon the approach of an occupying column 17 days later.

Field Commander (1859–1861)

For lack of any competent military leader in his state, the untutored González Ortega's role evolved from that of a civilian organizer into an active campaigner. Always able to rouse and direct large numbers of people for political ends, he now relied upon trusted advisers and his studious nature to attract, assemble, and command ever larger military formations. What his troops lacked in training and proper weaponry, they more than made up for by their zeal and overwhelming numbers.

González Ortega's organizational skill and charismatic leadership doomed conservative hopes of retaining the fertile Bajío. In a three-hour battle on June 15, 1860, he led 10,000 men to victory over Silverio Ramírez's and Domingo Cajén's 3,000-man division at the Hacienda of Peñuelas, less than a dozen miles south of the city of Aguascalientes, while the latter were marching southwest toward Guadalajara to reinforce Miramón. This victory prompted the conservative commander-in-chief to leave a 5,000-man garrison under Gen. Severo del Castillo in Guadalajara and hasten out of the crucial state of Jalisco two weeks afterward, so as to concentrate his slender forces in a desperate bid to bar the road into Mexico City.

He fell back further as another large liberal division under Gen. Ignacio Zaragoza closed in on his southwestern flank to unite with González Ortega in July 1860, then was overtaken and pulverized at Silao on August 10, 1860. (Just before this climactic battle, it was learned that González Ortega did not actually hold any military rank, and he rebuffed the one that was hastily offered to him by Juárez.) González Ortega treated his prisoners magnanimously after the battle, releasing most, and had sufficient strategic vision to reverse his army from Querétaro and march westward—at Degollado's order as "general-in-chief of the Federal [constitutionalist] Army"—to first subdue Guadalajara before commencing any final push upon the national capital.

After a wearying and rain-sodden march, González Ortega's army arrived on September 22, 1860, to besiege the conservative garrison holding Guadalajara, his bringing total liberal strength to 20,000 besiegers and 125 fieldpieces. The 5,000 defenders under Severo del Castillo put up a stout resistance until October 29, 1860, when the starving civilian populace was allowed to evacuate. The last conservative hope of relief was extinguished two days later when Márquez was defeated on the main highway at Tepetates Ranch near Zapotlanejo, leaving his 3,000 men and 18 cannon to surrender to Zaragoza. Del Castillo also capitulated to González Ortega's subordinate Zaragoza two days later, on generous terms (the liberal commander-in-chief having been ill throughout most of these operations).

December 21, 1860, Calpulalpan: All liberal armies began closing in on Mexico City for a final confrontation. González Ortega was the first to approach, with a total of 11,000 men and 14 fieldpieces in various columns under the command of his brigadiers Zaragoza, Valle, Régules, and Alatorre. Miramón—who was so desperately short of cash that a month earlier his chief of police, Lagarde, broke into the British Legation and commandeered 630,000 *pesos* over the objections of Ambassador Charles Lennox Wyke—sortied to occupy the high ground around the rim of the Valley of Mexico with 8,000 troops and 30 guns under his brigadiers Márquez, Vélez, Miguel Negrete, and Cobos, intending to give battle amid the rolling plains around San Miguel Calpulalpan, some 30 miles east of the capital.

Liberal brigadiers Valle and Álvarez suggested a tactic to González Ortega on the eve of battle whereby Miramón's main thrust would be drawn out by a feigned retreat by some liberal units, only to then become engulfed by flanking attacks, allowing the liberals' superior numbers to tell. The commander-in-chief approved, and when Miramón began the action by leading a charge down against the liberal left wing at 8:00 a.m. the next morning, December 22nd, the conservatives were struck on both flanks by Zaragoza and Régules. While thus checked, González Ortega led Valle and Francisco Alatorre in a wide encircling march, routing the conservatives by unexpectedly charging into them from the rear at the head of 1,000 lancers.

Miramón staggered back into Mexico City with only 1,500 soldiers still under his command, pausing long enough to release his prisoner, Berriozábal, before fleeing and being secretly whisked down to Veracruz through the intervention of the French ambassador, Alphonse Dubois de Saligny, setting sail for Europe aboard a Spanish warship by January 1861. A few conservative diehards such as Márquez, Cobos, and Mejía withdrew into the hills to continue the struggle, but their cause was lost. González Ortega's victorious army made its triumphal entry into Mexico City on Christmas Day 1860, to mark the end of the resultant War of the Reform.

Shortly thereafter, Díaz was elected a *diputado* or "deputy" for Oaxaca to the new national Congress, and returned to Mexico City. While in session on June 24, 1861, word suddenly arrived that the fugitive conservative Gen. Leonardo Márquez had materialized with 2,600 troops and five small guns and was penetrating into the capital along its San Cosme *calzada* or "causeway." Díaz hastened from the chamber to the Oaxaca Brigade's quarters in the San Fernando Convent and helped organize a hasty counterattack that drove away this danger. He then marched in pursuit of the retreating conservatives as part of a converging liberal division under the command of Maj. Gen. Jesús González Ortega, overtaking and scattering Márquez's small army on August 13, 1861, while it was resting at the town of Jalatlaco.

The French Army retreated slowly over roads that were soon waterlogged by heavy rains, hampered by their 300 wounded from that battle and many other soldiers who were falling sick. Zaragoza chose to rest his own weary and hungry column for a few days around San Andrés Chalchicomula, in anticipation of being joined by the Zacatecas Division under Brig. Gen. Jesús González Ortega. But when Lorencez's army also encamped for the night of May 17, 1862, at the Hacienda de Tecamalucan, the French commander was surprised to receive a visit at 5:00 p.m. that same evening from the Mexican conservative general Leonardo Márquez, who informed him that his reinforcements were at last nearby.

June 10, 1862: After being reinforced by 6,000 conscripted troops under republican general Jesús González Ortega, Zaragoza's 14,000-man army marched out of Acultzingo to attack the French in Orizaba.

After stealing in on Lorencez's army in two columns, Zaragoza and González Ortega arrived outside Orizaba on June 13, 1862, the latter quietly occupying *Cerro del Borrego* or "Sheep Hill" overlooking the suburban hamlet of Tlalchichilco.

Zaragoza died of typhoid fever in Puebla on September 8, 1862, and González Ortega succeeded him in command of the Army of the East.

Despite stubborn patriot resistance, Franco-conservative armies gained Mexico City by the summer of 1863, then spread out to subdue the entire country. One such column forged slowly northwestward under the French general Charles-Abel Douay, compelling González Ortega to abandon the unfortified city of Zacatecas by February 5, 1864, and retreat toward Fresnillo with his 3,000 troops. Douay entered unopposed the next afternoon, his 600 French troops and conservative auxiliaries being greeted festively with pealing church bells. Two months later, Col. Edmond L'Heriller was appointed as imperial governor and inaugurated a two-and-a-half year occupation.

On December 30, 1864, Juárez granted González Ortega permission to take a temporary leave of absence from his duties, which he used to travel into the United States in an effort to raise support and supplies for the republican cause. When he did not report back for active service within the allotted time though, González Ortega was declared to be in dereliction of his duties on November 8, 1865, for having abandoned the country and his troops without any additional permission from the republican Congress or president, and proceedings were instituted against him. When he attempted to return to Mexico one year later, González Ortega was briefly detained by U.S. officials on November 3, 1866.

Released, he was arrested again upon reentering Mexico on orders from the acting governor of Zacatecas and imprisoned in Saltillo on January 8, 1867. Transferred that same April 1867 to the prison in the Obispado at Monterrey, Nuevo León, he was nonetheless elected to Congress during this incarceration but declined to serve.

Final Years and Death (1868–1881)

After his release from prison on August 1, 1868, González Ortega retired to private life in Saltillo. On July 11, 1869, he was elected *diputado proprietario* from Tlaltenango to the Congreso de la Unión. He was named enviado extraordinario y ministro plenipotenciario to Spain on March 11, 1874. On January 6, 1881, President Manuel González conferred on him the rank of general. González Ortega died in Saltillo on February 28, 1881.

See also: Ahualulco de los Pinos, Battle of; Márquez Araujo, Leonardo; Miramón Tarelo, Miguel Gregorio de la Luz Atenógenes; Reform, War of the; Zaragoza Seguín, Ignacio.

Further Reading

Apuntes biográficos del ciudadano Jesús González Ortega. Mexico City: Manuel Castro, 1861.

Cambre, Manuel. *La guerra de Tres Años: apuntes para la historia de la Reforma.* Guadalajara, Jalisco: Gobierno del Estado, 1949.

"Important from Mexico: Confirmation of the Defeat of Miramón and Occupation of the City of Mexico by the Liberals." *New York Times,* January 14, 1861.

"Important from Mexico: Defeat and Dispersion of the Reactionary Army." *New York Times,* September 15, 1861.

Sosa, Francisco. *Biografías de mexicanos distinguidos.* Mexico City: Porrúa, 2006.

Guadalajara, Sieges of (1858–1860)

Capital of the wealthy state of Jalisco and thus a city that was to be repeatedly contested between liberal and conservative forces during the War of the Reform.

When this conflict had first erupted early in 1858, the city of Guadalajara was politically a liberal stronghold and therefore became briefly the seat of the displaced national government of Pres. Benito Juárez as of February 15, 1858, after he had been driven out of the city of Guanajuato by the approaching conservative army of 5,400 regulars under Gen. Luis G. Osollo. This pursuing force had then continued to draw near and defeated the main liberal army at the Battle of Salamanca on March 9–10, 1858, occupying Guadalajara without resistance two weeks later, after Juárez and his cabinet had fled to the Pacific coast. (They would eventually circle around through Panama, Cuba, and New Orleans to resurrect their fugitive government in the port city of Veracruz.)

Osollo had meanwhile installed the civilian Urbano Tovar in Guadalajara on March 24, 1858, to act as Jalisco's new conservative governor, an appointment that would be contested by Pedro Ogazón Rubio—the state's liberal governor-designate—who was temporarily headquartered at Ciudad Guzmán, as well as Gen. Santos Degollado, the liberal general-in-chief for southern Jalisco.

First Liberal Siege (May–June 1858)

A combination of regional irregulars known as the 1st Liberal Division, bolstered by

800 mounted riflemen and seven fieldpieces under Col. Miguel Blanco and Lt. Col. Mariano Escobedo—which had been detached out of northern Mexico to reinforce Santos Degollado as his allies—arrived to jointly besiege Guadalajara as early as May 21, 1858, the city being defended by conservative Generals Francisco García Casanova and José María Blancarte. The latter two initially sortied to intercept these approaching liberals out in the open field but subsequently returned into their defensive trenches without engaging, instead leaving Degollado and Casanova to discuss terms at the tiny hamlet of San Pedro during a ceasefire on June 4, 1858.

Unable to reach any kind of accord, the liberals closed in and fortified themselves around the Hospicio de Santo Domingo, both sides exchanging desultory long-range gunfire until it was learned that conservative brigadier general Miguel Miramón was marching to the garrison's relief with an army of regulars, so the ill-armed liberals raised their siege and vanished on June 13, 1858.

Second Liberal Siege (July 1858)

After relieving the city, Miramón was diverted into fighting a heavy but indecisive battle on July 2, 1858, farther south at the bottom of Atenquique Ravine (near modern Ciudad Guzmán, Jalisco), against a combination of liberal commanders, during which distraction a separate liberal force arrived to attempt to besiege Guadalajara once again on July 3, 1858. However, when these besiegers learned that Miramón was returning from his southern foray, they too hastily departed without a fight on July 21, 1858. The city remained in conservative hands over the next couple of months until Miramón had to leave Jalisco altogether to bolster the hard-pressed conservative army of Gen. Leonardo Márquez in central Mexico.

Third Liberal Siege (September–October 1858)

During Miramón's absence, Casanova sallied with 1,500 troops and seven guns at dawn on September 18, 1858, to "exterminate" the liberals to its south. However, while marching along the highway three days later past Techaluta, about 50 miles away—with the 2nd Regiment and a company of the 1st Line Battalion in their van; the 1st and 2nd Guadalajara Battalions, a company from the San Blas Battalion, and the mounted "Seguridad Pública" Squadron as their main body in the center; plus the Santa Ana and Portillo militia companies guarding the supply trains in their rear—the conservatives spotted a liberal formation seemingly retreating along the road far ahead of them.

Pressing their pace, they failed to notice that rifle companies of Degollado's 1st Division were hidden behind a long stone fence beside the highway until the ambush was sprung. Casanova's army was shot to pieces over the next couple of hours, so he returned to Guadalajara with scarcely 60 survivors on September 22, 1858, to resign his commission in disgrace. He was succeeded in command of the city garrison by Blancarte, who had only about 400 regulars and 1,000 militiamen left to defend Guadalajara, yet nonetheless managed to check the 4,000 triumphant liberals who arrived to take back their state capital five days later under Degollado and Ogazón with their subordinate commanders Leandro Valle, Esteban Coronado, José Silverio Núñez, and many other chieftains.

Unwilling to brave the defenses in a direct assault, this liberal army formally instituted a third siege of Guadalajara as of September 27, 1858. After a month of artillery exchanges, the besiegers suddenly detonated mines beneath two conservative strongpoints at 10:00 p.m. on October 27, 1858, storming into the city's central square and subduing all resistance within the hour—except for the San Francisco Convent, the last refuge of Blancarte and a few loyal followers. Surrounded and facing impossible odds, he agreed to capitulate at 10·45 a.m. the next morning to Degollado, who now styled himself as the "minister of war and general-in-chief of the Federal Army of the constitutional government."

But after having his surrender duly accepted and being released into his home, Blancarte was "arrested" and summarily murdered by the former bandit turned liberal militia "colonel" Antonio Rojas on October 30, 1858, to avenge this guerrilla chief's own personal grievances. A couple of conservative colonels were publicly lynched in retribution for their past repressive acts as well, while many other prominent figures and priests were mistreated, churches were pillaged, and other anticonservative excesses were committed.

Conservative Recuperation (December 1858)

After only six weeks of liberal occupation, the main conservative army under Miramón, Márquez, and Marcelino Cobos returned and routed Degollado and his liberal subordinates in a series of clashes along the banks of the Santiago River, culminating with their final defeat at San Miguel Ranch, three miles from Poncitlán, on December 14, 1858—which allowed the conservative troops to reoccupy Guadalajara that very same day and for local survivors to unleash a vengeful pogrom of their own against liberal partisans in reprisal for their recent sufferings.

Miramón meanwhile quickly proceeded to again best Degollado in a skirmish on December 20, 1858, at San Joaquín Ranch, 15 miles from the state line with Colima, so he had driven the liberal army completely out of the state of Jalisco by Christmas 1858. War-weary Guadalajara endured yet another blow when an ammunition dump accidentally exploded on January 10, 1859, causing extensive damage to its municipal palace.

However, the focus of the war subsequently shifted into central Mexico, where Degollado led a drive on the national capital, so Márquez had to hasten off to its relief with a considerable portion of Guadalajara's conservative garrison in March 1859. Liberal resistance slowly revived in Jalisco, so Miramón was obliged to lead another sweep through the state in December 1859, besting Ogazón after a long pursuit at Beltrán and Juan Rocha at Tonila or Albarrada in neighboring Colima.

Uraga's Assault (May 1860)

Nevertheless, as part of a renewed liberal offensive the next spring throughout the entire Bajío, an undaunted Ogazón encamped three miles east of Guadalajara at San Pedro Tlaquepaque on May 11, 1860, with more than 3,000 men and 15 fieldpieces of the 1st Division, composed of the following units:

- 1st, 2nd, and 3rd Line Battalions
- Hidalgo, Morelos, and Mina *Guardia Nacional* or "National Guard" Battalions
- Progreso, Fijo de Jalisco, Herrera, Cairo, and Lanceros de Jalisco cavalry regiments

- 1st Brigade of Michoacán, which included the Activo Infantry Battalion of Morelia, and the Huerta, Arista, and Ayutla lancer squadrons

The conservatives' military governor for the city, Gen. Adrián Woll, mobilized his 2,700 troops of the Fijo de Guadalajara, Activo de San Blas, and 2nd Line Battalions, with the 1st and 2nd mounted *Seguridad Pública* or "Public Security" squadrons serving as his cavalry. In addition, he could count on 600 volunteers of the Blancarte Battalion, led by their civilian lieutenant colonel (and lawyer) Remigio Tovar.

A stalemate ensued, as Ogazón had hoped to lure a conservative sally out from behind their defenses into the open countryside, while Woll had orders not to exit the city until a relief column could arrive under Miramón. A liberal "Central Division" of 5,000 men under Gen. José López Uraga meanwhile raced from Lagos de Moreno to reinforce Ogazón's effort, en route detaching its La Luz and Figueroa Battalions under Col. Ignacio Álvarez—after the main body had crossed over Tololotlán Bridge—so as prevent being followed across that structure by Miramón's army, which was coming along only two days behind.

Reaching Zapotlanejo by the afternoon of Tuesday, May 22, 1860, López Uraga issued a general order for his division to merge the next day with Ogazón's at Tlaquepaque and together close in on Guadalajara forthwith, assaulting the city with their combined 8,000 men and 42 guns by Thursday morning, May 24th. Woll meanwhile received a message from Miramón on that same Tuesday, May 22, 1860, and so ordered his military engineer, Col. Genaro Noris, to barricade the streets in hopes of being able to resist the liberal attacks for two days until relief could arrive.

The liberal army duly appeared outside Guadalajara on May 24, 1860, and called on Woll to surrender. When he refused, López Uraga proceeded with his assault, only to be badly wounded and captured. His bespectacled, 31-year-old brigadier general Ignacio Zaragoza temporarily assumed command and withdrew the assault columns on news of Miramón's approach with the main conservative army. Two days later, the repulsed liberals reassembled at Zacoalco, a review revealing that—despite their recent setback—they still numbered 5,000 infantrymen and 1,500 riders, with 40 artillery pieces.

Ogazón was selected to succeed López Uraga as overall commander, and when Miramón learned that the liberals had retreated in the direction of Manzanillo and sortied from Guadalajara in pursuit with his 6,000 soldiers, he hesitated to attack when he found Ogazón's army dug in along Zapotlán Crest between Ciudad Guzmán and Sayula on June 8, 1860, as it still remained so strong. And then one week later, another 10,000-man liberal army under Gen. Jesús González Ortega crushed Miramón's anticipated 3,000 reinforcements from the state of Aguascalientes, so the conservative commander-in-chief instead left a 5,000-man garrison under Gen. Severo del Castillo to hold Guadalajara on June 27, 1860, before hastening into Lagos de Moreno three days afterward to begin concentrating his dwindling strength for a showdown in central Mexico. A mere six weeks later, his army was pulverized at the Battle of Silao by the combined forces of González Ortega and Zaragoza.

Fall of Guadalajara (September–November 1860)

Fresh from this victory, González Ortega's liberal army arrived near Guadalajara on

September 22, 1860, after a wearying and rain-sodden march through central Mexico to assist in besieging this last major conservative-held stronghold. Four days later, he was joined at San Pedro Tlaquepaque by Ogazón's corps, bringing their total strength to 20,000 men and 125 fieldpieces, the first of which opened fire by September 27th. The 5,000 defenders under Severo del Castillo put up a stout resistance until October 29th, when the starving civilian populace was allowed to evacuate.

The last conservative hopes of relief were extinguished when Márquez was defeated on the main highway at Tepetates Ranch near Zapotlanejo on November 1, 1860, leaving his 3,000 men and 18 cannon to surrender to Zaragoza's encircling army, while Márquez himself made good his escape in the direction of Tepatitlán. Del Castillo therefore capitulated to González Ortega's subordinate Zaragoza two days later, receiving generous terms. Six weeks later, the last conservative army was defeated at the Battle of Calpulalpan, and Mexico City was occupied by Christmas Day 1860, marking an end to the War of the Reform.

See also: González Ortega, José Canuto de Jesús; Márquez Araujo, Leonardo; Miramón Tarelo, Miguel Gregorio de la Luz Atenógenes; Osollo Pancorbo, Luis Gonzaga; Reform, War of the; Salamanca, Battle of; Zaragoza Seguín, Ignacio.

Further Reading

"The Battle of Guadalajara: Full Particulars of Uraga's Defeat." *New York Times*, June 29, 1860.

Cambre, Manuel. *La guerra de Tres Años: apuntes para la historia de la Reforma.* Guadalajara, Jalisco: Gobierno del Estado, 1949.

Guerrero Saldaña, Vicente Ramón (1782–1831)

Surviving hero from Mexico's War of Independence whose claim to the presidency would be contested by conservative resentments because of his low birth.

He was born in the "Zapateros de las Cuatro Esquinas" neighborhood of the town of Tixtla on August 9, 1782, and baptized the next day in its San Martín Church, the fourth and final child of Juan Pedro Guerrero Campos and his wife, María Guadalupe Saldana Rodríguez (although some sources would indicate that his father's surname was actually Tescucano). Little is known about his early life with any certainty, beyond the fact that he worked as a teamster and would marry María Guadalupe Hernández in that same church on July 9, 1804, with whom he would have a single child, a daughter born less than four years later and christened as Dolores Guerrero Hernández on February 27, 1808.

Insurgent Champion (1811–1821)

When the rebel priest and firebrand José María Morelos entered the coastal region in December 1810 to raise the banner of revolt, Guerrero and his friend Nicolás Catalán traveled to join this rebellion's ranks. Guerrero consequently participated in the siege of Acapulco and Battle of Tres Palos, as well as in the freeing of Chilpancingo on May 22, 1811, and of his own hometown of Tixtla four days afterward. By the time that Morelos marched into Izúcar with two companies of insurgents and 800 Indian archers on December 10, 1811, Guerrero was a veteran captain and so left in charge as its garrison commander. He fended off a royalist attack on February 9, 1812, but could do nothing to help Morelos when his army became trapped in Cuautla.

He subsequently rejoined the insurgent chieftain on May 15, 1812, and by the time that the insurgent army marched on Oaxaca in November of that same year, Guerrero held the rank of lieutenant-colonel. He commanded a column which intercepted a rich consignment of tobacco and cocoa bound from Acapulco toward Mexico City, carrying this rich booty into Oaxaca to great acclaim on January 15, 1813. He campaigned independently as a guerrilla leader in his own right over the next two years, until he joined Morelos, Nicolás Bravo, and other commanders in late September 1815 to escort the insurgent Congress from Uruapan to Tehuacán.

Guerrero managed to get his caravan across the Mezcala River at Tenango on November 3, 1815, but Morelos was captured two days later at Tezmalaca and shot by a firing squad before that year was out, around the same time as the demoralized congressional congress also disbanded. Guerrero nonetheless fought on, forcing the surrender of the royalist garrison holding Acatlán under Antonio Flon, conde de la Cadena on December 15, 1815, although put to flight shortly thereafter by monarchist reinforcements.

November 1816	The Mexican guerrilla leader Guerrero was driven back in a skirmish in Los Naranjos Canyon by the royalist Carlos Moya.
September 15, 1818	The Mexican guerrilla leader Guerrero defeated his royalist pursuer Armijo at Tamo, wresting sufficient arms and ammunition to furbish 1,800 men.
November 16, 1820	The royalist Iturbide quit Mexico City for Teloloapan, having been appointed commander of New Spain's southern district with orders to subdue the last vestiges of guerrilla activity under Guerrero and Pedro Ascencio Alquisiras.
January 2, 1821	Guerrero defeated a small loyalist contingent at Zapotepec.
January 5, 1821	The Mexican guerrilla leader Ascencio defeated a royalist force at Tlatlaya. On January 10, 1821, Iturbide contacted the insurgent leader Guerrero, proposing that rather than continue to skirmish against each other, they instead should join forces so as to forge a new alliance leading toward Mexico's independence, based on Spain's liberal constitution of 1812.
February 24, 1821	Iturbide, Guerrero, and other Mexican insurgent leaders announced the "Plan of Iguala," whereby their nation would proclaim its freedom from Spain subject to three conditions or "guarantees": the predominance of Catholic faith, total independence (although under the continuing symbolic rule of Spain's royal family), and a union or reconciliation between Mexico's embittered Creoles and Peninsulars. Viceroy Ruiz de Apodaca rejected this

arrangement and declared Iturbide an outlaw on March 14th.

March 10, 1821 At a conference held at Acatempan (near Teloloapan, Mexico), Guerrero agreed to merge his insurgent forces with Iturbide's loyalists, thus creating the patriotic *Ejército de las Tres Garantías* or "Army of the Three Guarantees" (representing Catholicism, independence, and union, better known as the *Ejército Trigarante*).

November 6, 1829 Yucatán rebelled against Guerrero's government. On December 4, 1829, Vice President Bustamante—still in command of the large army raised that summer to repel Barradas's Spanish invasion—mutinied at Jalapa against Guerrero. The latter quickly found himself without supporters (Bravo defeating his troops at Chilpancingo, then occupying Acapulco) so the president fled the capital two weeks afterward to establish a tenacious guerrilla campaign in southern Mexico. His rival, Bustamante, assumed office as president by January 1, 1830, while sending General Armijo to fight Guerrero.

January 15, 1831 After a year of successful guerrilla forays, Guerrero was lured aboard the Genoese brigantine *Colombo* at Acapulco, its captain, Francesco Picaluga, having been offered a 50,000-*peso* bounty by President Bustamante to kidnap his intransigent predecessor. Instead of the lunch that he had been promised, Guerrero was sailed around to the port of Huatulco in the state of Oaxaca and handed over to Capt. Miguel González, who executed him by firing squad at nearby Cuilápam on the morning of February 14, 1831.

See also: Acapulco, Insurgent Siege of; Cuautla, Siege of; Morelos Pavón, José María Teclo; Tres Palos, Battle of.

Further Reading

Sosa, Francisco. *Biografías de mexicanos distinguidos*. Mexico City: Porrúa, 2006.

Guzmán Loera, Joaquín Archivaldo "El Chapo" (1957–)

Longtime leader of the powerful Sinaloa drug cartel, who was eventually captured by Mexican Marines.

Birth and Early Life (1957–late 1970s)

He was born on April 4, 1957, into a poor family in the rural mountain community of La Tuna, in the municipality of Badiraguato in the northwestern state of Sinaloa, the second eldest surviving son of Emilio Guzmán Bustillos and María Consuelo Loera Pérez. Educational opportunities were rare in this remote, stark setting high up in the Sierra Madre, so young Joaquín did not receive more than a third-grade level of education before going to work with his father, who is believed to have eked out a meager existence as a *gomero* or low-level opium poppy grower.

Disapproving of his father's dissolute and irresponsible lifestyle, Joaquín had allegedly begun cultivating and harvesting his own more profitable marijuana crops by the age of 15, with the help of his cousins. He also worked for the local smuggling kingpin Héctor Luis "El Güero" Palma Salazar, proving himself to be ruthless in overseeing the shipments of low-grade drugs out of that highland region, via aircraft to urban areas near the U.S. border. Widely known by his nickname of "El Chapo" (a contraction of the word *chaparro* or "shorty"), the five-foot, six-inch Guzmán Loera was introduced sometime during the early 1980s to the regional crime boss—Miguel Ángel Félix Gallardo of Culiacán—as a promising young operator suitable to be recruited and groomed for bigger jobs.

Discreet Rise to Power (1980s)

Guzmán Loera initially began working as a chauffeur for Félix Gallardo, but was soon put in charge of coordinating the stealthy importation of increasingly large shipments of high-value Colombian drugs into Mexico. The Colombian cartels' established traffic patterns through the Caribbean were becoming compromised during the early 1980s by American countermeasures, so they began diverting millions of dollars' worth of their cocaine through Mexico, from where it could be more easily smuggled across the land border into the United States. Criminal middlemen such as Félix Gallardo grew rich and powerful from this traffic, and his young subordinate Guzmán Loera distinguished himself by the variety of different land, air, and sea routes that he used for moving these shipments, as well as for his "piecemeal strategy" of dividing up large consignments so as to minimize financial losses from any single interception.

The business changed in November 1984, when a raid by 450 Mexican soldiers backed by helicopters destroyed a 2,500-acre marijuana plantation owned by Félix Gallardo, who in retribution had a suspected informant named Enrique Camarena Salazar kidnapped, viciously tortured, and murdered in early February 1985—unaware that Camarena was actually an undercover DEA agent. The resultant manhunt by enraged American and Mexican authorities led to many arrests, leaving some syndicates vulnerable. Félix Gallardo convened a summit meeting of all Mexican drug bosses in Acapulco in 1987 so as to establish clear territorial boundaries and thus ensure a continuation of profitable operations, but shortly after he himself was arrested on April 8, 1989, the gangs began fighting among themselves for power.

Emergence (Early 1990s)

In particular, the Tijuana Cartel of the Arellano Félix brothers went to war against the Sinaloa Cartel, feeling that their territory had been infringed upon when Félix Gallardo assigned the border towns of Tecate, Mexicali, and San Luis Río Colorado to the Sinaloans for running their drugs into California and Arizona. Palma lost his wife and children to a series of cruel attacks, making way for Guzmán Loera to emerge as the Sinaloa Cartel's leader. Low-key, cunning, and distrustful, Guzmán Loera lived furtively in numerous different residences, although he was almost killed when Ramón Arellano Félix and four henchmen riddled his vehicle with AK-47 rounds while he was being driven through the streets of Guadalajara in November 1992.

This wave of murders and countermurders between both gangs climaxed when a 20-man hit squad under Francisco Javier Arellano Félix mistakenly attacked a chauffer-driven car at the Guadalajara

International Airport on May 24, 1993, murdering the cardinal and archbishop Juan Jesús Posadas Ocampo instead of Guzmán Loera (who was seated in a nearby car). The manhunt resulting from this outrage sent Guzmán Loera fleeing across the southern border into Guatemala, after first giving $200 million to a trusted employee for running his cartel's day-to-day activities during his absence and a like amount to a friend to look after his family.

Despite lavishing bribes on both Mexican and Guatemalan officials, the fugitive drug lord was promptly arrested in the border town of Tapachula on June 9, 1993, and flown back aboard a military airplane to be interned in the "La Palma" or "Altiplano" maximum-security prison at Almoloya in the state of Mexico, where he was tried and sentenced to serve 20 years. Yet because of his immense wealth, loyal underlings, and discreet financial backing of numerous influential people, he lived royally while in this penitentiary and continued to direct the operations of his cartel, especially after being transferred to the "Puente Grande" maximum-security prison in Jalisco.

Escape and Recapture (2001–2014)

After seven years of being incarcerated, a ruling by the Supreme Court of Mexico made the prospect of extradition to the United States easier, so Guzmán Loera bribed almost 80 prison employees in order to escape on January 19, 2001. Once free, he revived his former furtive lifestyle, moving frequently among many residences (often up the Sierra Madre mountains), in no small part because of the violent warfare between rival cartels. In response to the Gulf Cartel's employment of ex-military commandos known as the Zetas, the Sinaloa Cartel hired as hit men similar deserters,

who were dubbed *Los Negros* or "The Black Ones." In a bid to take over the border crossings at Ciudad Juárez, Guzmán Loera sent this hit squad to murder that city's drug boss, Rodolfo Carrillo Fuentes, while he was shopping with his wife and two children on September 11, 2004. This assassination set off a bloodbath as rival cartels fought to take over his hub, resulting in thousands of deaths.

While every bit as ruthless and vicious as his rivals, Guzmán Loera also realized that the brazen public attacks and grotesque filmed beheadings perpetrated by the Zetas were counterproductive. Preferring to discreetly bribe public officials and conduct low-profile murders, his rivals were soon complaining that their leaders were being killed and their syndicates dismantled by Pres. Felipe Calderón's military crackdown as of 2006, while the Sinaloa Cartel remained relatively unaffected—free to take over other gangs' territories once they were dismembered, including the coveted Ciudad Juarez-El Paso corridor. Suspicions were even raised that Calderón was intentionally allowing the less sadistic Sinaloa Cartel to win the drug war, a charge that the president denied in newspaper ads, pointing to his administration's killing of the top Sinaloa deputy Ignacio "Nacho" Coronel as evidence.

Eventually, armed with intelligence from the DEA and U.S. Marshals' Service, 10 pickup trucks of the Mexican Navy carrying more than 65 Marines approached the beachfront Miramar condominiums in Mazatlán, Sinaloa, at 3:45 a.m. on February 22, 2014, quietly overpowering a bodyguard before stealing upstairs to burst into apartment 401 by 6:40 a.m. Inside they captured Guzmán Loera, who was visiting with his young third wife and twin baby daughters. Wanted for many crimes in diverse Mexican states, it is uncertain whether he will be extradited to the United States before he has answered to these charges. It has further been pointed out that his arrest "is a thorn in the side of the Sinaloa Cartel, but not a dagger in its heart."

See also: Drug War; Zetas.

Further Reading

Beith, Malcolm. *The Last Narco: Inside the Hunt for El Chapo, the World's Most Wanted Drug Lord*. New York: Grove Press, 2010.

Longmire, Sylvia. *Cartel: The Coming Invasion of Mexico's Drug Wars*. New York: Macmillan, 2011.

H

All here is confusion, fear, and disorder.

— in a letter to liberal general Manuel Doblado from Mexico City on August 14, 1860, four days after news had arrived of the conservative defeat at the Battle of Silao

Halcones

Code name meaning "Hawks" assigned to a shadowy paramilitary group of thugs raised by the Mexican government and trained by army officers to suppress popular dissent.

Background (December 1970– May 1971)

Luis Echeverría Álvarez, elected and sworn in as Mexico's new president on December 1, 1970, was the *secretario de gobernación* or "secretary of the interior" under the preceding administration of Gustavo Díaz Ordáz and therefore the man in charge of national security when the massacre at Tlatelolco had occurred scarcely two years earlier—a repressive action that had left dozens of protesters dead at the hands of the police and military and tainted Echeverría's reputation. Consequently, during his recent presidential campaign, he had reached out to young people and promised to head up a kinder, gentler government that would seek to repair relations with the nation's disaffected students.

Nonetheless, a mere month after being sworn into office, the newly inaugurated Echeverría also quietly instructed his secretary of foreign relations, Emilio Rabasa, to approach U.S. ambassador Robert McBride and inquire whether Washington would be willing to arrange police training for an already-existing "special security group." The leader of this irregular force, Col. Manuel Díaz Escobar Figueroa—an active-duty officer in the Mexican Army—subsequently explained during a visit with the American officials that he particularly wished for his men to be instructed in:

> crowd control, dealing with student demonstrations, and riots. They would also be interested in training in physical-defense tactics and hand-to-hand combat.

Uneasy, the U.S. officials learned that this group was code-named the *Halcones* and had already been employed in breaking up a purported student rally with bamboo sticks on November 4, 1970, which was being held to celebrate the election of Chile's Marxist president Salvador Allende. Described as "army-trained toughs" by victims of this attack, it was believed that the *Halcones* numbered about 2,000 young men who were maintained, trained, and directed by subalterns on detached duty from the military.

Political strife shut down the Autonomous University of Nuevo León in Monterrey on May 1, 1971, amid angry demonstrations after the conservative state Congress altered that university's bylaws, greatly reducing its autonomy. Gov. Eduardo Elizondo further sent police forces to occupy parts of the campus, exacerbating student outrage, so Echeverría intervened by annulling the offending law and restoring full autonomy to the university—a decision that prompted Elizondo to resign from office.

Attack by the Halcones (June 10, 1971)

Yet despite this favorable settlement, students in Mexico City decided to proceed with a march already planned for June 10, 1971, in support of the struggle in Monterrey. This protest was to be the first major student demonstration since the massacre of Tlatelolco, and organizers hoped that it would revive Mexico's student movement, which had been hard hit by the repression of 1968.

June 10, 1971: To quell a wave of violent leftist street protests gripping Mexico City, President Echeverría unleashed a shadowy paramilitary group nicknamed the *Halcones* or "Hawks," a mixture of 800 active-duty soldiers and hired thugs who had been secretly raised and trained by Col. Manuel Díaz Escobar, a member of the capital's municipal administration. They were allowed to bypass ranks of riot police and fall on a mob of protesters on the Avenue of Los Maestros, killing 23 and injuring some 200–300 in a clash that was photographed by newsmen. Embarrassed by this disclosure, Colonel Díaz's group was quickly disavowed and dissolved.

See also: Tlatelolco Massacre.

Further Reading

Adler Hellman, Judith. *Mexico in Crisis*. New York: Holmes & Meier, 1978.

Schmidt, Samuel. *The Deterioration of the Mexican Presidency: The Years of Luis Echeverría*. Tucson: University of Arizona Press, 1991.

Hallström, Thord Ivar. *See* Thord-Gray, Ivor (1878–1964).

Hidalgo y Costilla Gallaga, Miguel Gregorio Antonio Ignacio (1753–1811)

A vigorous and widely read village priest who launched Mexico's War of Independence against Spanish colonial rule, proving to be an inspirational figurehead—if not a particularly gifted military commander.

Early Life and Clerical Career (1753–1808)

He was born on May 8, 1753, at the Hacienda of San Diego de Corralejo, near the city of Pénjamo in the mountainous central province of Guanajuato, the second of five sons resulting from the first marriage of Cristóbal Hidalgo y Costilla, manager of

Portrait of Miguel Hidalgo y Costilla, the rural priest who launched Mexico's War of Independence. (DeAgostini/Getty Image)

that estate. Young Miguel's mother, Ana María Gallaga, had died when he was only nine. Three years later he and his older brother, José Joaquín, were sent to the Jesuit College of San Francisco Xavier in the city of Valladolid (modern Morelia in the state of Michoacán), where their studies were interrupted when the Jesuit order was suddenly expelled from the viceroyalty of New Spain in the summer of 1767, so their father came to retrieve them.

Yet by that same year's end, both boys had been reenrolled in San Nicolás Obispo College at Valladolid, Miguel proving to be such a clever student that he was nicknamed *El Zorro* or "The Fox" by his classmates. He received his bachelor's degree before the age of 17 and continued to excel while studying for the priesthood, learning the native Otomí, Tarasco, and Náhuatl languages in addition to Latin, French, and Italian. He received full religious orders as a presbyter in September 1778 and taught at San Nicolás for the next 13 years, rising to become college rector. During this same interlude, he also expanded his common name from "Miguel Hidalgo" into "Miguel Hidalgo y Costilla," even signing this way so as to differentiate himself from another contemporary priest named Miguel Hidalgo, an older cleric who was serving in Durango.

Hidalgo y Costilla had also become quite wealthy, stocking his personal library with expensive foreign books and even buying three ranches near the town of Irimbo for family members. He had moreover sired at least two children out of wedlock and enjoyed gambling. Finally, gossip obliged him to renounce his college rectorship on February 2, 1792, and he went to serve for eight months as the priest at the Pacific port of Colima. Although his scandalous past would prevent his return to Valladolid, Hidalgo's wealth, urbane education, and

local connections had ensured a warm welcome when he was allowed to transfer to the San Felipe parish near Guanajuato City. Soon, his parties were being attended by such local luminaries as the immensely rich marqués de Rayas and the royal Spanish intendant for that province, Juan Antonio Riaño y Bárcena.

When Hidalgo's older brother, José Joaquín, who had been serving as village priest at Dolores, died on September 19, 1802, Miguel had arranged to take over this post himself two weeks later. He arrived at Dolores with two more illegitimate daughters, as well as several other family members, soon becoming so immersed in pet projects such as a pottery, tannery, saddler's works, forge, carpentry shop, weavers' looms, and even bee-keeping that he had delegated his religious duties to an assistant.

Revolutionary Firebrand (1809–1810)
Still vigorous at 55 years of age, Hidalgo had been among the Creole leaders who in the summer of 1808 believed that Mexico could govern itself until the French invaders were expelled from Spain and Ferdinand VII was restored to the throne. Yet from talks that he had held over the next year and a half, he came to embrace the notion of outright Mexican independence. He and Capt. Juan Aldama secretly visited Dr. Manuel Iturriaga at Querétaro in February 1810, agreeing to lead his proposed insurrection. The revolt had been planned to occur on December 1st of that same year at San Juan de los Lagos, when more than 100,000 pilgrims would be attending its annual religious festival.

Returning to Dolores, Hidalgo had ordered his workshops to begin discreetly producing thousands of blades and spears as well as experimental cannons (supposedly to accompany religious celebrations).

During a second visit to Querétaro in early September 1810, the plotters had agreed to move up their date to October 2, 1810. But when their plot was revealed prematurely to the Crown authorities, Hidalgo responded boldly.

He roused the few hundred supporters around his rural church by pealing its bells at dawn on September 16, 1810, calling for an immediate uprising. Although today remembered as *el grito de la Independencia* or "the cry for Independence," Hidalgo actually began his address to the assembled throng by shouting: "Long live Ferdinand VII! Long live religion! Death to bad government!" A few local monarchists were thereupon arrested, and 800 rebels started out on a march through nearby Atotonilco and San Miguel el Grande during which Hidalgo removed a religious banner with a painted figure of the Virgin of Guadalupe from the church sacristy at Atotonilco to serve as his standard.

His progression attracted thousands more peasant adherents as it advanced, numbering in the thousands by the time it swarmed into Celaya on September 20, 1810, where Hidalgo was acclaimed "captain general" of his movement (a military title normally reserved for the viceroy) and installed a Creole government. Looting royal offices and buildings as they overran Salamanca, Irapuato, and Silao, they closed in on the provincial capital of Guanajuato. On the morning of September 28, 1810, his 20,000–25,000 ill-disciplined adherents appeared above that terrified city, circling around Cuarto and San Miguel Hills to descend into its streets by 1:00 p.m. The Spanish provincial intendant, Juan Antonio Riaño y Bárcena (a personal acquaintance of Hidalgo's), had taken refuge inside its recently completed royal granary—a formidable stone building called the *Alhóndiga de Granaditas*—with a few loyal troops, plus all of Guanajuato's Peninsula-born Spaniards, but its wooden doors were burned down and the 600 monarchists were pitilessly slaughtered by the next dawn. Hidalgo furthermore ordered another 100–200 Spanish captives who had been rounded up in Guanajuato to be marched away and quietly butchered in an out-of-the-way spot, their bodies being stripped and left exposed to the elements.

News of this slaughter would horrify and alienate many segments of Mexican society who might otherwise have proven sympathetic to the insurgent cause. Returning to Dolores, Hidalgo learned on October 8, 1810, that the Spanish authorities in the neighboring province of Michoacán had been detained on orders from the woman insurgent María Catalina Gómez de Larrondo, so he sent José Mariano Jiménez with 3,000 armed men in support of her. Hidalgo soon followed with his mass of followers and occupied its capital of Valladolid (modern Morelia) nine days later without any resistance, just the usual excesses and executions. He then continued on through Zinapécuaro and Maravatío, deciding on October 23, 1810, to lead his unwieldy host to assault the viceregal capital of Mexico City.

Military Setbacks (1810–1811)

Within the span of six short weeks, Hidalgo's insurrection had mushroomed into a mass movement, yet so cumbersome and unwieldy that it proved of negligible martial value. His self-styled *Ejército de América* or "Army of America" consisted of more than 80,000 followers, yet scarcely 3,000 had any kind of proper weaponry or training (mostly members of turncoat provincial militia regiments). His military colleague, Capt. Ignacio de Allende, had organized some 14,000 of the best-mounted rebel riders into a large mass of irregular cavalry, but they lacked the ability to perform even the most basic battlefield maneuvers, such as forming and charging as a body.

Consequently, this vast insurgent throng progressed clumsily and blindly into the Valley of Mexico by late October 1810 and with great difficulty bested a much smaller royalist force that tried to bar its path. The young Spanish lieutenant colonel Torcuato Trujillo commanded a mere 1,000 loyalist infantry, 200 dragoons, 150 militia lancers, and another 1,000 or so auxiliaries when he checked Hidalgo's advance and inflicted so many casualties at the Battle of Monte de las Cruces on October 30, 1810, that Hidalgo subsequently gave the order for his host to veer around and exit northwestward back out of the Valley of Mexico, away from the viceregal capital. And one week later, his huge following would be surprised and dispersed at the Battle of Aculco by a royalist army hastening down from San Luis Potosí under Brig. Gen. Félix María Calleja, so the insurgency's best chance of toppling the viceregal government in its initial stages was lost forever.

All thoughts of resuming any kind of offensive were ended, Hidalgo retreating into Guadalajara and learning on January 12, 1811, that Calleja's 14,000-man monarchist army was bearing down on that city. The insurgent chieftain—against the advice of Allende—opted to exit and dig in 20 miles east of Guadalajara atop the heights overlooking the stone Calderón Bridge across the Colorado River, a naturally defensible position. Yet only 1,200 of Hidalgo's 35,000 men were bearing muskets, so despite six hours of stout resistance there on January 17, 1811, the result proved to be the same: after enduring 3,000 killed and wounded, the insurgents were broken and

fled from the battlefield in scattered bands, having inflicted only 400 casualties among Calleja's troops.

Flight and Capture (January–March 1811)

Following their rout at Puente de Calderón, Hidalgo, Allende, and other defeated insurgent leaders met at the Hacienda de San Blas de Pabellón outside of the city of Zacatecas by late January 1811, where the former was stripped of all military authority in favor of Allende. The fugitive leaders then continued retreating north with the remnants of their army, reaching Saltillo by early March 1811.

A couple of weeks later, with royalist forces moving slowly but inexorably in their wake, Allende and Hidalgo decided to leave behind 4,000 insurgents to garrison Saltillo under Ignacio López Rayón, while they resumed their progression northward with another 1,300 men on March 16, 1811, hoping to find support in the United States. (The next day, the 30-year-old colonel José Bernardo Gutiérrez de Lara was detached from their column to ride on ahead to Washington, where he would eventually meet with Sec. of State James Monroe, yet refuse to agree to any concessions in exchange for American aid.)

Three days after Gutiérrez de Lara had parted company with Allende, Hidalgo, and the rebellion's other leaders, they met up with retired militia captain Francisco Ignacio Elizondo, riding along in the company of his 342 followers until they were suddenly and treacherously arrested at Acatita de Baján on March 21, 1811, and conveyed into Monclova to be handed over the next day to the Spanish governor Manuel María de Salcedo in exchange for a royalist reward.

Execution (July 30, 1811)

Five days after Allende, Jiménez, Aldama, and several of his other subordinates had already been executed, Hidalgo was shot by a 12-man firing squad in Chihuahua City at dawn on July 30, 1811. His body was exhibited on public view all day, tied into a chair, then beheaded after nightfall. While his corpse was taken for internment by the local Franciscan friars, Hidalgo's head—along with those of the other executed insurgent leaders—was pickled in salt and forwarded to Guanajuato City by October 1811 to be displayed in iron cages at the four corners of the Alhóndiga de Granaditas over the next 10 years until Mexico's independence was at last won.

See also: Aculco, Battle of; Calderón Bridge, Battle of; Calleja del Rey, Félix María; *gachupín*; Independence, War of; Monte de las Cruces, Battle of; Peninsular.

Further Reading

Archer, Christon I. "Bite of the Hydra: The Rebellion of Cura Miguel Hidalgo, 1810–1811." In *Patterns of Contention in Mexican History*, edited by Jaime E. Rodríguez O., 69–93. Wilmington, DE: Scholarly Resources, 1992.

Hamill, Hugh M., Jr. *The Hidalgo Revolt: Prelude to Mexican Independence*. Gainesville: University of Florida Press, 1966.

Herrerón Peredo, Carlos. *Hidalgo: razones de la insurgencia y biografía documental*. Mexico City: SEP, 1987.

Sosa, Francisco. *Biografías de mexicanos distinguidos*. Mexico City: Porrúa, 2006.

Hotchkiss heavy machine gun (1897–1914)

Powerful antipersonnel weapon that was first purchased during the modernization of the Porfirian Army and would prove decisive in some of the biggest battles of the Mexican Revolution.

A weapon first introduced in France in 1897 with an export version being produced the next year and then another model appearing by 1900. A heavy gas-operated machine gun with five distinctive cooling rings encircling its barrel and a metal-strip feed system of 8mm rounds. Robust and serviceable weapons, they weighed 52 pounds apiece, so were cumbersome to reposition while under fire and therefore were usually installed into static emplacements.

As of July 1900, there was a separate entity designated as the *Compañía de Ametralladoras* or "Machine Gun Company" listed in the organizational charts of the Federal Army.

37mm Automatic Cannon

Hotchkiss also manufactured a scaled-up version of this machine gun, resulting in a larger antipersonnel weapon designed to fire one-pound 37mm x 94mm "revolving-cannon rounds" from eight-round clips while mounted either atop a light field carriage or on a cone (the latter for naval use). A light fieldpiece on a gun carriage, it was designed to fire one-pound shells, which were fed into its chamber in eight-round clips.

Obregón's army emerged triumphant from the Revolution largely because of its superior weaponry and organization and became the core of the modern Mexican Army. In late April 1918, the U.S. military attaché in Mexico City, Capt. Robert M. Campbell, estimated that this force included one regiment armed with 40 Hotchkiss heavy machine guns; 10 smaller units, each armed with 5 Hotchkiss machine guns apiece; 4 more small units, equipped with 5 Colt machine guns apiece; plus another 10 units, each armed with 10 Rexer light machine guns—a total of 110 heavy and 100 light machine guns, which had proven decisive in winning the Revolution.

See also: Celaya, Battles of; Colt-Browning heavy machine gun (M.1895); Trinidad, Battle of.

Further Reading

Jowett, Philip, and Alejandro de Quesada. *The Mexican Revolution, 1910–20*. Oxford: Osprey, 2006, 15–16.

Mellichamp, Robert A. *A Gun for All Nations: The 37mm Gun and Ammunition*. Vol. 1. Houston, TX: Privately published, 2010.

Huajuapan, Royalist Siege of (1812)

Resolute insurgent defense of this village in northwestern Oaxaca that helped to sustain rebel hopes during a difficult period early in the War of Independence.

With José María Morelos and his main insurgent army besieged inside Cuautla de Amilpas (120 miles to the northwest) and royalist forces in the ascendancy throughout the southeastern province of Oaxaca, the Spanish lieutenant colonel Francisco Caldelas appeared before the town of Huajuapan on Sunday, April 5, 1812, with more than 2,000 men and 14 fieldpieces to besiege its insurgent garrison under Col. Valerio Trujano. After his initial assault was repelled, Caldelas instituted a formal siege, camping north of this town atop Calvario Heights, while his subordinate Gabriel Esperón occupied its western side, Juan de la Vega the southern, and José María Régules the eastern bank of the Huajuapan River with his *Batallón de la Mermelada* or "Marmalade Battalion" (so called because of its purple-colored uniforms). Siege batteries were installed by April 10, 1812, opening fire against Trujano's defenders, who had no artillery of their own with which to reply. Opposing trenches encircle the town, and the royalists settle down to starve its garrison into submission.

A hastily assembled insurgent force approached Huajuapan from Tehuacán on May 17, 1812, hoping to lift its royalist siege, only to be ambushed near Chilapilla by black royalist troopers under Caldelas, who scattered this relief column while compelling them to abandon their nine fieldpieces and supply train. Two months later, the same occurred when the first division of Morelos's army under Miguel Bravo also appeared southwest of Huajuapan on July 22, 1812, being scattered by a sharp sally from Caldelas, who seized two of Bravo's small fieldpieces.

The next day, however, Morelos and Galeana arrived from Tlapa with 1,800 additional men, reinforcing Bravo so he was able to attack Esperón's camp west of Huajuapan, while Galeana assaulted Caldelas's positions to its north, and the beleaguered garrison emerged eastward out of Huajuapan to distract Regules. Divided by this multiprong effort, the royalists were quickly overwhelmed, Caldelas being killed along with 400 of his men and another 200 captured—along with 14 guns, more than 1,000 muskets, and considerable materiel. Morelos remained for two weeks in the aftermath of this victory before marching toward Tehuacán de las Granadas to enter it triumphantly on August 10, 1812.

See also: Independence, War of; Morelos Pavón, José María Teclo.

Further Reading

Lemoine, Ernesto. *Morelos: su vida revolucionaria a través de sus escritos y otros testimonios de la época*. Mexico City: UNAM, 1991.

McFarlane, Anthony. *War and Independence in Spanish America*. New York: Routledge, 2014.

Sosa, Francisco. *Biografías de mexicanos distinguidos*. Mexico City: Porrúa, 2006.

Huerta Márquez, José Victoriano (1850–1916)

Hard-bitten career officer notorious for his ruthlessness, a quality that both helped him to claw his way into the presidency and would accelerate his downfall.

He was born at Agua Gorda Ranch in the municipality of Colotlán in the state of Jalisco on December 22, 1850, the first child of Jesús Huerta Córdoba and María Lázara del Refugio Márquez Villalobos. Four sisters would follow in succession

The hard-bitten ex-Porfirian general and presidential usurper Victoriano Huerta (center), in civilian clothes, ca. 1914. (Library of Congress)

over the next seven years, so Victoriano would grow up as the only son in the family. Both his parents were reportedly ethnic Huichols, and young Victoriano identified himself as indigenous, learning to read and write at a school run by the local priest. In 1869, the teenaged Victoriano was employed by the visiting liberal general Donato Guerra to serve as his personal secretary, who three years later obtained his admission to the national Military Academy at Chapultepec.

Early Military Career (1872–1910)

Enrolled in 1872, it has been recorded that Huerta was noticed among the ranks of cadets during an inspection made by Pres. Benito Juárez, who singled him out for praise and commented that the Mexican Army needed more officers of indigenous origins. Upon graduating in 1877, Huerta was commissioned into the Corps of Engineers, spending the early years of his career undertaking topographic studies in the states of Puebla and Veracruz, where he met Emilia Águila Moya, his future wife. They were married a month before his 30th birthday, in the Santa Veracruz Parish Church in Mexico City on November 21, 1880, and with whom he would eventually have nine children.

He attained the rank of Colonel of Engineers by 1890, and a decade later participated in military sweeps against the Yaqui Indians in Sonora, as well as Mayan tribesmen in Yucatan in 1902, for which he was promoted to brigadier general and received the Medal of Military Merit. Three years afterward, Huerta was appointed to head a committee overseeing the redesign of uniforms for the Federal Army, and retired from the military in 1907 on grounds of ill-health, having developed cataracts.

Maderista General (1910–1912)

After serving briefly as the Head of Public Works in Monterrey, Nuevo León, and planning a new street layout for that city, Huerta was teaching mathematics in Mexico City when the Mexican Revolution erupted in November 1910. He applied successfully to rejoin the Federal Army with his former rank of brigadier general, but did not play a major role in the early fighting, although he did command the military guard which escorted the deposed Pres. Porfirio Díaz down to Veracruz in May 1911 so as to sail away into exile. And before the idealistic Francisco I. Madero could assume office, Huerta was dispatched by the interim ex-Porfirian government to Cuernavaca in August 1911, to monitor and contain Emiliano Zapata's followers through heavy-handed actions by his 1,000 soldiers.

By the time Madero finally won a special by-election and assumed the vacant presidency in early November 1911, Zapata was again in open rebellion because of these brutal sweeps, so that Madero replaced Huerta early next year with the high-minded general Felipe Ángeles, who implemented a much more humane campaign. But when the disaffected Pascual Orozco rose in rebellion against Madero in early March 1912, accusing him of having failed to carry out the Revolution's promise, his 6,000 well-equipped irregulars promptly defeated the initial Maderista army sent into Chihuahua to put down this uprising. Its commander, Gen. José González Salas—a relative of Madero by marriage who had resigned his post as war minister in order to lead this failed venture—brought his demoralized survivors back into Torreón, Coahuila, before committing suicide.

Under pressure from his shaken cabinet, Madero had little choice but to recall Huerta to active duty and offer him command of the defeated expedition on April 1, 1912. Eleven days later, Huerta arrived at Torreón to assume command, reorganizing this division so as to be able to push northward again within a month's time, penetrating into Orozquista territory with 4,000 troops, five batteries of field artillery, four machine guns, and two Blériot XI monoplanes for reconnaissance purposes (flown by the hired American "captain" John H. Worden and Francisco Álvarez).

Huerta brushed past one force at the rural Los Conejos railway station on May 12, 1912, then inflicted a summer-long series of defeats on the rebel leader's 7,000 men: first at Los Conejos on May 12th; then at Rellano on May 22nd–23rd; at La Cruz in Bachimba Canyon by late June; at Bermejillo, Chihuahua City, and finally at Ciudad Juárez on August 16th. By late September 1912, Orozco had been wounded and driven to seek refuge in the United States.

Treacherous Seizure of Power (February 1913)

At dawn on February 9, 1913, some 3,000 troops under the mutinous Generals Manuel Mondragón and Gregorio Ruiz attempted to depose Madero, although their assault failed to carry the National Palace. When the president descended from Chapultepec Castle to review the situation, he noticed the unemployed Huerta in the crowds of onlookers, and so appointed him as interim commander of the loyal Maderista forces in Mexico City, while travelling to Cuernavaca that same afternoon to summon a further 1,000 troops under the more reliable and honorable brigadier general Ángeles.

Upon Ángeles's arrival with reinforcements next day, though, he had to serve under Huerta as his superior officer, who despite commanding a combined total of 6,000 troops (compared to only 1,800 mutineers trapped in the Ciudadela) could seemingly not reduce that ancient fortress. Suspected of disloyalty and briefly arrested, Huerta suddenly turned the tables by detaining the president and his vice president on the afternoon of February 18, 1913.

That same evening, to give his coup the appearance of legitimacy, Huerta had the compliant foreign minister—constitutionally third in line for the presidency—assume this vacant office and appoint him as interior minister (fourth in line), then resign from the presidency 15 minutes afterward so that Huerta would succeed. During a special late-night session of Congress, the legislators—surrounded by Huerta's troops—endorsed his assumption of power, after which Madero and his vice president were taken from their prison cells four nights later and murdered.

The Usurper (February 1913–July 1914)

Huerta's crude seizure of power was widely viewed with disgust, so that rebellions against his regime sprang up everywhere. Among many others, the northern Gov. Venustiano Carranza called for the creation of a "Constitutional Army" to oust the usurper and restore legal government, while huge well-equipped rebel armies began winning victories under such talented self-taught commanders as Pancho Villa and Álvaro Obregón. After repeated field defeats of Huerta,s expanded Federal Army, he bowed to circumstances and resigned the presidency on July 15, 1914, sailing away into exile aboard the German cruiser S.M.S. *Dresden*.

Exile and Death (August 1914–January 1916)

After residing briefly in Britain and Spain, Huerta arrived in the United States in April 1915, hoping to plot a return to power in Mexico. World War One having since erupted, his negotiations with a German intelligence agent in New York were monitored by the U.S. Secret Service, so that when Huerta then took a train towards El Paso, Texas, it was stopped in Newman, New Mexico, and he was arrested together with Pascual Orozco on June 27, 1915, and charged with conspiracy to violate U.S. neutrality laws. After some time spent in a U.S. Army prison at Fort Bliss, Texas, Huerta was released on bail but remained under house arrest, before being returned to jail and dying there of cirrhosis of the liver on January 13, 1916.

See also: *Decena Trágica*; Obregón Salido, Álvaro; Revolution, Mexican; Villa, Pancho.

Further Reading

Meyer, Michael C. *Huerta: A Political Portrait*. Lincoln: University of Nebraska Press, 1972.

Rausch, George J., Jr. "The Early Career of Victoriano Huerta." *Americas: Academy of American Franciscan History* 21, no. 2 (October 1964): 136–45.

Sosa, Francisco. *Biografías de mexicanos distinguidos*. Mexico City: Porrúa, 2006.

I

You command a fortress that exists in absolutely nothing more, than name alone.

— Spanish brigadier General Fernando Mijares to the royal governor of dilapidated Veracruz (June 1815)

Iguala, Plan de (1821)

Proposal for a merger between Mexico's long-contending royalists and insurgents to come together by the common goal of resolving Mexico's War of Independence.

Background (1816–1820)

After the explosiveness of Miguel Hidalgo's initial uprising against Spanish rule in September 1810, and then the gradual defeat and dispersal of José María Morelos's insurgent concentrations by late 1815, the four years of desultory struggle that ensued between 1816 and 1819 had degenerated into a stalemate between royalist garrisons holding most major cities, who remained outnumbered by the guerrilla bands that ignored proffered amnesties and still controlled much of the countryside and threatened most roads—yet were too weakly armed and parochially inclined to mount any major offensives, assaults, or siege operations.

However, the commitment to Crown rule by many Creole royalists was suddenly shaken in the spring of 1820, after an army mutiny in Spain had reimposed a liberal constitution on Mexico's viceroyal administration, including certain provisions aimed at curtailing or eliminating outdated prerogatives of the aristocracy, clergy, and military. Displeased by this development, which seemingly undermined the royalists' hopes of retaining their traditional conservative values and privileged statuses intact from the 18th century, many loyal Creoles began to waver and openly consider some measure of separation from Madrid but on less radical terms.

The Three Guarantees (1821)

Surprisingly, a solution was proposed to Mexico's rebels by a royalist Creole officer with a reputation for implacable ruthlessness toward his foes, Col. Agustín de Iturbide. Having been assigned the thankless task of campaigning during the winter months of 1820–1821 against Vicente Guerrero's elusive guerrilla bands in the lowlands of southern Mexico, Iturbide unexpectedly contacted that insurgent chieftain on January 10, 1821, to suggest that they suspend hostilities and instead forge a coalition to achieve Mexico's independence, on terms that would satisfy both factions. Guerrero suspected a trap, but Iturbide compiled and issued a public proclamation from his base at Iguala on February 24, 1821, which incorporated broad principles that most of the antagonists could accept.

According to the articles of Iturbide's so-called *Plan de Iguala*, conservative values would be upheld by declaring the Catholic Church the paramount religious institution of the newly independent nation, while furthermore specifying the creation of a constitutional monarchy to govern it that would respect existing rights regarding land grants, private property, etc. Insurgent demands would be met by declaring outright independence from Spain and then convening a congress of Mexicans to draft a national constitution, which in turn could address such questions as individual rights and impose limits on the powers of the constitutional monarchy.

Although a lengthy document, Iturbide's *pronunciamiento* was fixed on three focal conditions or "guarantees"—predominance of the Catholic faith, separation from Spain, and unity among Mexicans—and furthermore included several articles prescribing the immediate formation of "a protecting army, which shall be called the Army of the Three Guarantees," so as to carry out this design. Simply put, royalist and insurgent commanders who agreed to adhere to the plan would cease campaigning against one other, while retaining their military rank in this ephemeral new organization, whose command structure would be devised later by the national congress.

This truce between combatants began when Guerrero agreed to merge his insurgent forces with Iturbide's loyalists at a conference held at Acatempan near Teloloapan on March 10, 1821, thereby laying the foundation for a unified *Ejército de las Tres Garantías*. Although the Plan of Iguala was bitterly denounced and disavowed four days later in Mexico City by the Spanish viceroy, Juan Ruiz de Apodaca, Iturbide's proposal turned into an unstoppable movement over the next several months as more and more royalist Creole militia commanders and insurgent guerrilla chieftains agreed to subscribe to this notion of an "Army of the Three Guarantees" under

its new tricolor flag: whose white segment represented religion, green stood for independence, and red for the union of all Mexicans.

Bloodless Victory (August–September 1821)

As such defections spread, fighting soon contracted into sporadic skirmishes between ever-larger Mexican formations, against fewer and fewer monarchical adherents. By the time that the next viceroy-designate, the liberal lieutenant general Juan O'Donojú, arrived from across the Atlantic at the end of July 1821 to assume office, he discovered that the only troops remaining loyal to Spain were trapped within their depleted garrisons at Mexico City, Veracruz, and Acapulco. With the rest of the country in insurgent hands, O'Donojú felt that he had no choice but to agree to Iturbide's terms and consequently signed a treaty at Córdoba in August 1821 that recognized Mexican independence (albeit while still holding out a promise of maintaining some tenuous links to Spain, although this latter arrangement was to be rejected out of hand by Madrid).

Despite never having fought in battle, the "Army of the Three Guarantees"—this loose coalition of diverse royalist regiments, insurgent battalions, and rural guerrilla bands that had subscribed to Iturbide's Plan of Iguala—converged on Mexico City to celebrate their almost-bloodless joint victory with a grand parade on September 27, 1821, marking Mexico's independence. It was recorded that the army consisted of 7,616 infantrymen, 7,755 cavalrymen, and 763 artillerymen for 68 pieces of various calibers.

See also: Guerrero Saldaña, Vicente Ramón; Independence, War of; Iturbide Arambúru, Agustín Cosme Damián de.

Further Reading

Anna, Timothy E. *The Fall of Royal Government in Mexico City*. Lincoln: University of Nebraska Press, 1978.

Anna, Timothy E. "The Rule of Agustín de Iturbide: A Reappraisal." *Journal of Latin American Studies* 17, no. 1 (May 1985): 79–110.

Robertson, William S. *Iturbide of Mexico*. Durham, NC: Duke University Press, 1952.

Independence, War of (1810–1821)

Insurrection that was begun to overthrow the rule by Peninsular Spaniards in Mexico, yet concluded with many colonial-era institutions and observances still preserved intact.

Background (1789–1806)

The late-18th century intellectual movement known as the Enlightenment, which spread through learned circles in Europe, played a negligible role in sparking the uprising that eventually brought independence to colonial Mexico. Followers among Spain's conservative ruling classes accepted certain facets of enlightened thought—especially in scientific and technological matters—yet not in any broader political or social context. Charles III enacted his own brand of enlightened despotism by selectively introducing reforms throughout his empire, aimed at overhauling outdated administrative practices or increasing commercial and manufacturing output. A few more liberal concepts eventually came to be entertained during the reign of his successor, Charles IV, such as abolishing entailed estates or revoking certain ancient privileges, yet the "Spanish Enlightenment" was to remain a relatively restrained and pragmatic movement, primarily focused on practical improvements.

The American and French Revolutions were viewed with misgiving and some distaste, particularly the violent emergence and radical doctrines broadcast by the First French Republic, which were greeted throughout Spain and Spanish-America by a purge of their few Francophile or republican sympathizers. Controlled newspapers such as the *Gazeta de México* reported on the dramatic events in Paris, yet simply to contrast them unfavorably with Spain's seemingly more stable monarchy and comfortable Catholicism. Considerable surprise had been felt at the French Revolution's triumphs over the crowned heads of Europe, resulting in a weakened Spain being pulled into an uneasy alliance with the radical young republic by August 1796, followed by a crippling trans-Atlantic blockade imposed by Britain's Royal Navy.

But the wealthy viceroyalty of New Spain was not militarily threatened during the ensuing six years of hostilities, so Mexico's internal commerce continued unaffected and some overseas trade was even possible aboard neutral carriers. A brief restoration of peace in Europe had led to a resumption of direct rule from Madrid in 1803, only to again be severed as Spain was drawn back into the global conflict as an unequal partner of France by the next autumn. A further three years of reverses ensued until at last Napoleon contemptuously sent an army across the Pyrenees to depose the failed Charles IV, seize his youthful heir, Ferdinand VII, and install his own brother, Joseph Bonaparte, on the throne of Spain.

Stirrings of Autonomy (1808–1809)

When Joseph Bonaparte was crowned in occupied Madrid in June 1808, this coronation supposedly asserted title over Spain's American colonies as well, although this usurpation was virtually ignored in Mexico and throughout the rest of Spanish America. Instead, its sitting Bourbon-appointed officials heeded instructions from the emergency *junta* or "council" that was convened that same September 1808 at Aranjuez in Spain to spearhead resistance against the French occupiers of the motherland.

Over the ensuing couple of years, the privileged minority of Peninsula-born Spaniards who dominated the best administrative and military posts in Mexico jealously demanded loyalty to the captive Bourbon monarch Ferdinand VII, while their Mexican Creole peers—many of whom were wealthy owners of vast estates, mines, or business enterprises in Mexico—wished for a greater say in their own governance and easier access to the closed circles of power. When a few regional *juntas* began sprouting in South America, some Mexican leaders expressed the opinion that they too could govern themselves without supervision from Madrid until the French were expelled and Ferdinand VII restored to his throne— and a few even came to entertain the notion of outright independence.

Revolt against Colonial Rule (1810–1815)

The well-to-do and erudite village priest at the tiny parish of Dolores in the highland province of Guanajuato, 57-year-old Miguel Hidalgo y Costilla, had secretly begun planning a popular insurrection with some colleagues in February 1810, intending to launch his revolt at the annual San Juan de los Lagos religious festival that same December 1st, when more than 100,000 pilgrims would be in attendance. But when this plot was revealed prematurely to the Crown authorities, Hidalgo roused a few hundred supporters around his rural church by pealing its bells at dawn on September 16, 1810, calling for an immediate uprising.

Although today remembered as the *grito de la Independencia* or "cry for Independence," according to eyewitnesses Hidalgo actually began his harangue to the assembled throng by shouting: "Long live Ferdinand VII! Long live religion! Death to bad government!" A few local monarchists were thereupon arrested, and 800 rebels started marching through the district, attracting thousands more peasant adherents as they went. Royal offices and buildings were looted, and many Peninsula-born Spaniards were arrested or murdered, as the unchallenged throng of 20,000–25,000 rebels overran the provincial capital of Guanajuato a dozen days later.

Hidalgo's call had unleashed a torrent of plebeian anger, whose excesses would cloud the reputation of his initial movement. One month later, his horde of 80,000 undisciplined followers—the self-styled "Army of America"—was defeated outside of Mexico City, after which smaller but better-armed loyalist regiments under the Spanish-born brigadier general Félix María Calleja broke the back of his movement, vengefully executing thousands of rebels. Hidalgo and his fugitive lieutenants were betrayed to the Crown authorities in March 1811, their severed heads being left exposed in iron cages in the city of Guanajuato for the next 10 years, although their rebellion did not fade away.

Instead, hundreds of poorly armed bands continued to fight on as guerrillas, defending their own districts and occasionally coalescing under a recognized leader to conduct combined operations: commanders such as Jose María Morelos, another rebel priest who fought on in the south. He occupied Oaxaca with his army to serve as an insurgent capital and convened a Congress that declared outright independence from Spain before he too was finally defeated and executed in late 1815—having failed to dislodge the smaller, yet better-armed and -disciplined Spanish and royalist regiments that controlled most major cities.

Stalemate (1816–1820)

Yet despite Morelos's death and the collapse of his short-lived government, resistance still continued. Roads, smaller towns and cities, and the countryside were dominated by an intractable insurgent spirit. Concerned by the difficult communications between the main seaport of Veracruz and Mexico City, the Spanish Crown had sent a division of 2,000 troops drawn from the Regiments of Órdenes Militares and Navarra under Brig. Gen. Fernando Mijares y Mancebo, who disembarked in June 1815 and made a sweep through its torrid coastal region. As usual, the insurgent guerrilla bands had simply fled out of this Spanish army's path to then return and reoccupy their fortified roadblocks, where they continued openly charging tolls and taxes on all transients.

Calleja himself, now elevated to viceroy for his past military successes against rebel concentrations, acknowledged the unflagging nature of this opposition when he wrote to Madrid requesting that an additional 8,000 Spanish regulars be sent to reinforce his command because of "the difficulty of recruiting in a country, where the great mass of the population are decidedly in favor of the revolution."

His viceregal successor, Adm. Juan Ruiz de Apodaca, personally witnessed the insurgency's undying strength as he ran a gauntlet of large guerrilla formations with an escort of 1,000 troops before reaching Mexico City to assume office in September 1816. He consequently implemented a more benign policy of amnesties and reduced military offensives over the next four years, which in fact helped to bring in many converts and reduce the level of violence—but not the desire for independence.

Resolution (1821)

The stalemate was finally broken when the ruthless royalist Col. Agustín de Iturbide was assigned the thankless task of campaigning against Vicente Guerrero's elusive guerrillas in the pestilential lowlands of southern Mexico during the winter of 1820–1821 and instead proposed an accommodation to that chieftain on terms that would satisfy both sides. Codified as the *Plan de Iguala* on February 24, 1821, Iturbide's proposal was designed to appeal to loyalists by maintaining the primacy of the Catholic Church and retaining all colonial property titles, merely substituting a new national monarchy to govern Mexico. Insurgent demands were to be met by declaring outright independence from Spain and convening a Congress to draft a constitution that would enshrine individual rights and impose limits on this new Mexican monarchy. To adhere, commanders on both sides simply had to agree to stop fighting one other and join a unified *Ejército de las Tres Garantías* or "Army of the Three Guarantees," whose tricolor flag represented religion, independence, and the union of all Mexicans.

Over the next few months, more and more Creole loyalist battalions and insurgent guerrilla bands joined this alliance, so when the last viceroy-designate, Juan O'Donojú, reached Veracruz from Madrid in late July 1821, he realized that New Spain was essentially lost. Insurgents controlled the entire viceroyalty except for Veracruz, Mexico City, and Acapulco, and with only 4,200 widely scattered Spanish troops still loyal to the Crown, it was militarily impossible to reverse this situation. O'Donojú consequently procured a safe conduct from the local insurgent commander (a youthful ex-monarchist named Lt. Col. Antonio López de Santa Anna) to proceed inland and conclude a treaty with Iturbide, which recognized Mexico's de facto independence by mid-September 1821.

See also: Alhóndiga de Granaditas, Assault on the; Calleja del Rey, Félix María; Hidalgo y Costilla Gallaga, Miguel Gregorio Antonio Ignacio; Monte de las Cruces, Battle of; Morelos Pavón, José María Teclo.

Further Reading

Frías, Heriberto. *Episodios militares mexicanos: primera parte, guerra de Independencia.* Mexico City: Viuda de C. Bouret, 1901.

Hamnett, Brian R. *Roots of Insurgency: Mexican Regions, 1750–1824.* Cambridge: Cambridge University Press, 1986.

Henderson, Timothy J. *The Mexican Wars for Independence.* New York: Hill and Wang, 2009.

Rodriguez O., Jaime E. *"We Are Now the True Spaniards": Sovereignty, Revolution, Independence, and the Emergence of the Federal Republic of Mexico, 1808–1824.* Stanford, CA: Stanford University Press, 2012.

Van Young, Eric. *The Other Rebellion: Popular Violence, Ideology, and the Mexican Struggle for Independence, 1810–1821.* Stanford, CA: Stanford University Press, 2001.

Iturbide Arambúru, Agustín Cosme Damián de (1783–1824)

Staunch royalist officer who eventually engineered a unification between Mexico's factions in 1821 that allowed for the consummation of national independence,

Portrait of Agustín de Iturbide as independent Mexico's self-anointed emperor, 1822. (Library of Congress)

although his real aim was to impose a monarchy.

He was born on September 27, 1783, in the colonial city of Valladolid (later renamed Morelia, Michoacán), the sixth child and third son of a Peninsular Spaniard originally from Pamplona named José Joaquín de Iturbide Arrequi and his Mexican wife, María Josefa Arambúru Carrillo-Figueroa. Three more siblings would follow, for a total of nine births in the family— although Agustín was only the second child and eldest son to survive infancy so he would be doted on from an early age as the heir apparent. He began his education in the city's Colegio de San Nicolás and in 1800 was furthermore enrolled as a *Segundo alférez* or "second ensign" in the Provincial Infantry Regiment of Valladolid.

Early Militia Activities (1805–1809)

Shortly before departing his native city to participate in a concentration of military units at Jalapa from throughout the viceroyalty of New Spain in 1805, the 21-year-old Iturbide married the wealthy Ana María Huarte Muñíz on February 27, 1805. Her dowry of 100,000 *pesos* would allow the young couple to purchase the Hacienda de Apeo near Maravatío, and they would eventually have 10 children together.

In 1806, Iturbide would be promoted from second to first lieutenant in Valladolid's Provincial Infantry Regiment, and two years afterward he happened to be in Mexico City (on a legal matter that was being argued before its Royal Audiencia), when 300 armed Peninsular Spaniards led by the wealthy merchant Gabriel de Yermo penetrated into its viceregal palace on the night of September 16, 1808, and deposed the viceroy, José de Iturrigaray, because of their doubts regarding his total commitment to Spain in the wake of the motherland's occupation by France. The 25-year-old Iturbide did not actually participate in this coup, although he was known to have been among those who subsequently signed an *acta de lealtad* or "loyalty oath" and volunteered to support the substitute viceroy, 80-year-old retired field marshal Pedro de Garibay.

Royalist Champion (1810–1815)

He was a lieutenant in the Provincial Infantry Regiment of Valladolid when Hidalgo's uprising exploded in mid-September 1810. When the insurgent throng, tens of thousands strong, swept into his native Valladolid early that following month, Iturbide and his regiment departed before their arrival. After conducting several local sweeps, Iturbide arrived in Mexico City with 32 of his troops by mid-October 1810 and was immediately dispatched with his company toward Toluca, to become incorporated into the small loyalist army of Lt. Col. Torcuato Trujillo.

Iturbide fought bravely and well in the Battle of Monte de las Cruces on October 30, 1810, commanding the three companies that comprised the royalist right before being driven from the field and retreating through Cuajimalpa into the safety of Tacubaya.

Himself the son of a Peninsular Spaniard, he would fight the insurgency with a grim resolve, matching their killings of *gachupines* with mass executions of any prisoners who fell into his hands. Promoted to captain, Iturbide was transferred north into Guanajuato in July 1812 to pursue rebels in that province, which he did with much zeal. In December 1813, he was ordered to rush and help reinforce Valladolid's threatened royalist garrison, and his bold evening sally on Christmas Eve proved crucial in confusing and collapsing Morelos's undisciplined insurgent throng outside that city, after which they dispersed and those who regrouped were crushed at Puruarán.

Once more back in Guanajuato, Iturbide even mounted a long-range strike against the fugitive Morelos and his insurgent Congress—who were rumored to be gathering at Ario, Michoacán—when he secretly led 420 of his royalist troopers and 100 mounted infantrymen out of Yuriria at dawn on May 2, 1815. Traveling almost 120 miles over the next two-and-a-half days, they burst into Ario at dawn on May 6, 1815, only to learn that the insurgent leadership had been warned and scattered in various different directions that previous night, so Iturbide had to satisfy himself with executing as many rebel sympathizers as he could find and then do the same eight days afterward at Pátzcuaro before returning to his base in Guanajuato.

Dismissal from Royal Command (1816–1820)

Given the emergency powers exercised by royal field commanders and military governors during the War of Independence, many enriched themselves, none more so than Iturbide. In April 1816, the commercial guilds of both Querétaro and Guanajuato appealed for his removal to Viceroy Calleja, so he was suspended from command and brought up on charges in June 1816. However, no one dared testify against Iturbide in open court, so the charges were dropped and it was ordered on September 3, 1816, that he could once again resume command over the *Ejército del Norte* or "Army of the North."

However, that force had actually been dissolved in the interim, while Calleja was succeeded as viceroy by Adm. Juan Ruiz de Apodaca—who would implement a more benign policy of amnesties and reduced military offensives against the scattered bands of insurgents—so Iturbide was to remain unemployed. He brought suit before the royal courts to demand a full exoneration, even buying a hacienda outside Mexico City in 1818, to fully pursue this legal recourse—to no avail. It would not be until the royalist colonel José Gabriel de Armijo resigned as *comandante general del sur y de Acapulco* or "commander-in-chief of the south and of Acapulco" in the autumn of 1820 that Iturbide would be offered military employment once again.

The "Three Guarantees" (1821)

Iturbide departed Mexico City for Teloloapan to take up this new command on November 16, 1820, with orders to subdue the will-o'-the-wisp guerrilla activities of Vicente Guerrero and Pedro Ascencio Alquisiras. These leaders proved impossible to find, but they defeated one of Irurbide's contingents at Zapotepec on January 2, 1821, then another three days later at Tlatlaya. Rather than continue such fruitless

pursuits, Iturbide instead surprised Guerrero by contacting him on January 10, 1821, proposing that they join forces and forge a new alliance that would lead to Mexico's independence.

Like many other Creole royalists, Iturbide's commitment to Crown rule had been shaken by an army mutiny in Spain in the spring of 1820, which reimposed the liberal constitution of 1812 on Mexico's viceroyal administration. Displeased with its threat to traditional values and privileged statuses, he and other Creole conservatives began to consider some measure of separation from Madrid, albeit on less radical terms than those suggested by the insurgent leadership. Guerrero suspected a trap, yet Iturbide compiled and issued a public proclamation from his base at Iguala on February 24, 1821, which incorporated broad principles (the "Three Guarantees") that most of the antagonists could accept.

At a conference held at Acatempan near Teloloapan on March 10, 1821, Guerrero agreed to merge his insurgent forces with Iturbide's loyalists so as to lay the foundation for a patriotic *Ejército Trigarante* that would uphold Catholicism, independence, and the union of all Mexicans. Viceroy Ruiz de Apodaca rejected this arrangement and declared Iturbide an outlaw four days afterward, to no effect. Iturbide's proposal quickly spread across New Spain, so by the time the next viceroy-designate—Lt. Gen. Juan O'Donojú—arrived from across the Atlantic at the end of July 1821, he discovered that the only troops remaining loyal to Spain were trapped around their depleted garrisons at Mexico City, Veracruz, and Acapulco. O'Donojú consequently felt that he had no choice but to agree to Iturbide's terms and signed a treaty at Córdoba in August 1821 that recognized de facto Mexican independence.

Self-Coronation as Emperor (May–July 1822)

Iturbide headed up a temporary Junta, which in turn convened a Congress to begin drafting a constitution and creating a new monarchical government, but he soon grew concerned by this body's deliberations. After assigning sovereignty to itself as of February 1822—rather than to any future monarch—this Congress thereupon turned to considering such liberal measures as restrictions on the power of the landed elite, as well as lowering military pay and decreasing the size of the army. Such contemplated policies moved Iturbide to act.

After learning two weeks previously that Spain had categorically refused to recognize Mexico's independence, much less any terms leading toward the creation of a limited constitutional monarchy in its former colony as defined by the Treaty of Córdoba, Iturbide moved to assume the title for himself. In a staged gesture, troopers from the 1st Cavalry Regiment left their San Hipólito barracks in Mexico City at 8:00 p.m. on the evening of May 18, 1822, and marched through the darkening streets to Iturbide's splendid home. Assembled outside by torchlight, a sergeant named Pío Marcha delivered a prepared speech urging the insurgent hero to accept the title of emperor, to which Iturbide finally assented, after a show of reluctance.

The next morning, Congress was bullied by the presence of soldiers inside its chambers into ratifying this arrangement, so the reign of "Agustín I" was proclaimed. A grand coronation was celebrated in Mexico City's cathedral on July 21, 1822, during which Iturbide—like Napoleon—took the emperor's crown from the presiding Archbishop's hands and placed it on his own head, while his wife was also crowned as "Empress Ana María." Iturbide furthermore proposed creating a new order of Mexican nobility that was to be called the "Order of Guadalupe," so his decrees would henceforth bear the official heading of "Agustín, through Divine Providence and the Congress of the Nation, first Constitutional Emperor of Mexico, and Grand Master of the Imperial Order of Guadalupe."

Resistance and Deposal (August 1822–March 1823)

Mexicans of all classes were offended by such presumption, and opposition to Iturbide's reign soon arose. One month afterward, a series of arrests of military officers began throughout the country on August 26, 1822, because of suspicions of a plot to overthrow Agustín I. The next month, the emperor dispatched Brig. Gen. Juan José Zenón Fernández from San Luis Potosí to put down a republican mutiny in Tamaulipas initiated by Brig. Gen. Felipe de la Garza. In Mexico City itself, Iturbide dissolved Congress with the help of Gen. Luis de Cortazar's troops on October 31, 1822, replacing them with a *junta* appointed by and thus answerable only to himself.

Four days earlier, the imperial governor at Veracruz—28-year-old brigadier general Antonio López de Santa Anna—had attempted to lure 400 troops from Spanish-occupied San Juan de Ulúa ashore to be ambushed, only to have his scheme fail. The captain general for that district, Gen. José Antonio de Echávarri, secretly informed Iturbide that this planned deception had been deliberately sabotaged by Santa Anna, so the emperor summoned him to an award ceremony in Jalapa the next month, intending to pretend to offer Santa Anna a new posting in Mexico City—where he might be quietly arrested afterward for his failed ambush as well as for harboring republican sentiments.

However, it was recorded that upon seeing the *veracruzanos'* euphoria as their native son Santa Anna entered Jalapa on a white horse, Iturbide promptly informed his suspect general that he was being removed from military command and must accompany the emperor's party back to the capital. Santa Anna insisted on first disposing of his personal affairs, so after Iturbide departed Jalapa on December 1, 1822, Santa Anna immediately galloped back to Veracruz and proclaimed himself in revolt the next day against the imperial regime.

Before that same month was out, its 600-man garrison was besieged by 3,000 imperial troops under Generals Echávarri and José Gabriel de Armijo. Nevertheless, resentment against the autocratic misrule of Agustín I broke out elsewhere as well, with such famous figures as Nicolás Bravo and Vicente Guerrero rising against the emperor. Despite having their rebel contingents bested at Almolonga during the last week of January 1823 by Armijo's imperial subordinate, Brig. Gen. Epitacio Sánchez, sentiment against Iturbide continued to mount.

Echávarri and Armijo agreed to lift their siege of Veracruz on February 1, 1823, formalizing their support of Bravo's anti-imperial rebellion by signing the "Plan of Casamata." Now led by senior commanders, this mutiny quickly spread to most other army units, including virtually all troops in Mexico City by February 12, 1823, when Iturbide shifted his headquarters out of the capital to Ixtapalucan, while the congressmen whom he had imprisoned were released. Finally, with the rebellious generals Echávarri, Bravo, José Morán, and Miguel Barragán closing in, Iturbide agreed to abdicate as emperor on March 19, 1823.

In order to avert any further bloodshed, Gen. Manuel Gómez Pedraza arranged a safe conduct for the fallen ruler to be escorted to the port city of Antigua under Bravo's protection, from where he was eventually deported aboard the frigate *Rawlins* on May 11, 1823. The Mexican Congress had already decided six weeks previously that a triumvirate composed of Bravo, Guadalupe Victoria, and Pedro Celestino Negrete would rule the country temporarily until a constitution could be drafted creating a republican form of government.

Exile and Death (August 1823–July 1824)

After traveling across the Atlantic, Iturbide eventually disembarked in August 1823 at Liorna, Italy, residing briefly at Villa Fornier before proceeding on to Florence and then into England. After a year's exile abroad, Iturbide decided to depart London in May 1824 so as to return into Mexico, unaware that he had been declared a traitor and an outlaw that previous month by its Congress.

Arriving incognito at Soto la Marina on July 14, 1824, Iturbide was promptly recognized, arrested, and executed five days later at the village of Padierna in the state of Tamaulipas, at only 40 years of age. Almost a decade later, Santa Anna would have his remains brought to Mexico City and reinterred with full military honors in November 1833, honoring him as one of the "First Heroes of the Independence."

See also: *gachupín*; Guerrero Saldaña, Vicente Ramón; Monte de las Cruces, Battle of; Peninsular; Santa Anna, Antonio López de.

Further Reading

Anna, Timothy E. *The Mexican Empire of Iturbide*. Lincoln: University of Nebraska Press, 1990.

Archer, Christon I. "Royalist Scourge or Liberator of the Patria? Agustín de Iturbide and Mexico's War of Independence, 1810–1814." *Estudios Mexicanos* 24, no. 2 (Summer 2008): 325–61.

Correspondencia y diario militar de don Agustín de Iturbide, 1810–1813. Mexico City: Archivo General de la Nación, 1923.

Kahle, Günter. *El ejército y la formación del Estado en los comienzos de la independencia de México.* Mexico City: Fondo de Cultura Económica, 1997.

Ortiz Escamilla, Juan. *Veracruz, la guerra por la Independencia de México, 1821–1825: antología de documentos.* Jalapa, Veracruz: Comisión Estatal del Bicentenario de la Independencia, 2008.

Robertson, William S. *Iturbide of Mexico.* Durham, NC: Duke University Press, 1952.

Rodriguez O., Jaime E. *"We Are Now the True Spaniards": Sovereignty, Revolution, Independence, and the Emergence of the Federal Republic of Mexico, 1808–1824.* Stanford, CA: Stanford University Press, 2012.

J

It became urgent to prevent the enemies' reunion, putting fear into them with an armed action.

— Gen. Adrián Woll reporting on his attack against the Texians at Salado Creek, September 1842

Jones's War (1842)

Jesting nickname for the premature attack launched against Mexico's distant province of California by the commander of the U.S. Navy's Pacific squadron.

While lying at the Peruvian port of Callao in September 1842, the veteran commodore Thomas ap Catesby "Tac" Jones received seemingly reliable information as to an outbreak of hostilities having erupted between the United States and Mexico on account of border frictions involving the Republic of Texas. Concerned in case California should be peremptorily seized during the distractions ensuing from this diplomatic confrontation, by British or French interests with rival designs on that sparsely populated territory, Jones hastened northwestward with his peacetime squadron, which was composed of Capt. James Armstrong's 44-gun, 1,600-ton frigate *United States* and the 20-gun, 790-ton sloop *Cyane*.

At 2:45 p.m. on October 19, 1842, Jones dropped anchor off Monterey, determined to immediately launch a preemptive strike. The few ships at anchor were consequently taken as prizes of war, and Armstrong was sent ashore under a flag of truce at 4:00 p.m. to demand the surrender of its Mexican garrison. Ex-governor Juan B. Alvarado and Capt. Mariano Silva were in command of only 29 soldiers and 25 raw recruits within their tiny redoubt, armed with 11 nearly useless cannon, so agreed to capitulate that same night.

The next morning, October 20, 1842, the American commodore landed with 150 men and a band, marching inland to occupy this surrendered Mexican position, which was renamed Fort Catesby. By the following morning though, it became obvious—even to Jones—that no state of belligerency existed between the two nations, so he restored all of his captures. Notwithstanding this unwarranted intrusion, his subsequent stay in California was not altogether unfriendly, although Jones was eventually recalled by an embarrassed (yet not altogether reproving) government in Washington.

Further Reading

Gapp, Frank W. *The Commodore and the Whale: The Lost Victories of Thomas ap Catesby Jones.* New York: Vantage Press, 1996.

Smith, Gene A. *Thomas ap Catesby Jones: Commodore of Manifest Destiny.* Annapolis, MD: U.S. Naval Institute Press, 2000.

joven Macabeo

Nickname given to the youthful general Miguel Miramón by his ardent conservative backers, meaning the "young Maccabee."

Judah Maccabee was a biblical figure of great military prowess, the third son chosen by his father, Matthias, on his deathbed to assume leadership of the revolt against Antiochus Epiphanes, which he conducted brilliantly by winning a string of victories against heavy odds. Mexican conservative leaders began euphorically acclaiming Miramón as a *joven Macabeo* because of the defeats that he routinely inflicted on larger liberal formations during the War of the Reform, while still only in his twenties—implying that Miramón was specially chosen for this destiny, graced by his dashing talents to become president and general-in-chief at the age of 27.

His liberal opponents commonly referred to him by this nickname as well, although less adoringly. Among many examples that could be quoted, the civilian Justo R. Arroyo wrote secretly from conservative-held Mexico City to his friend, the liberal general Manuel Doblado on August 14, 1860—four days after Miramón's resounding defeat at the Battle of Silao—reporting how the young beaten president had returned:

> on the night of the 12th [August 1860], and immediately Muñoz Ledo, Corona, Díaz, and the Spanish Ambassador had met with their defeated hero. After much arguing, that the *Macabeo* must resign, that Pavón, President of the Court of Justice, shall assume power, as he in effect did yesterday at four in the afternoon

However, the "young Maccabee's" aura remained intact, and the conservative leadership reelected Miramón as their president two days afterward.

Further Reading

Doblado, Manuel. *La guerra de Reforma*. San Antonio, TX: Lozano, 1930, 211.

K

I was attacked by a multitude of sailors, with pistols and boarding cutlasses; they took a shot at me at point-blank range, which fortunately did not discharge; but I fell from eight wounds, most of them grave, and the loss of blood made me lose consciousness.

— from the memoirs of Capt. Manuel María Giménez, Santa Anna's aide-de-camp at Veracruz, December 5, 1838

kepi or quepi

Generic name for a neat style of military cap that became standard-issue headgear among most armies around the world during the 19th century, including Mexico's.

Its unusual name originated in Germany, where the tall and cumbersome hats (known as shakos) that had been worn throughout the Napoleonic era were being replaced early on in the 19th century by more practical, snug-fitting caps for nonceremonial work details or drill purposes—the original German word *Käppi* or "little cap" being the diminutive form in that language of *Kappe* or "cap." French units had soon adopted this handy and more comfortable German style of headgear for their own campaigns in the harsh environment of North Africa during the 1830s, their designation of *képi* being simply a phonetic French derivation of the original German term *Käppi*. This style of headgear had

quickly proven so popular among soldiers because of the caps' easy fit and maintenance that its usage had spread to other armies under the French version of that name (*kepi* sometimes being furthermore written phonetically in Spanish as *quepi*).

Technically referred to as "forage caps" in British and American armies, kepis typically featured a sloping visor, a welt around the crown, a leather chin strap held on by two small buttons, and a loop consisting of two leather slides and a brass buckle. Inside, the interior top of each kepi held a cardboard stiffener, while its sweatband consisted of an inner reinforcing layer made of a material such as buckram, covered in a lining of black cloth, both enclosed in leather. The Porfirian Federal Army would additionally order small cloths stitched in around the backs of their kepis, which could be tucked up inside the cap until needed and then let down so as to provide shade for the neck against scorching sunshine.

Variants of 19th-century kepis still remain in use as part of the dress uniform of modern Mexican Army units, although they have been largely supplanted by berets and other caps.

Further Reading

Hefter, Joseph. *Crónica del traje militar en México, del siglo XVI al XX*. Mexico City: Artes de México, 1968.

Rankin, Robert H. *Military Headdress: Pictorial History of Military Headgear from 1660 to 1914*. London: Arms & Armour Press, 1976.

Kosterlitzky, Emilio (1853–1928)

Russian-born adventurer who became a legendary commander of *rurales* during the Porfirian era.

He was born in Moscow on November 16, 1853, to a Russian father named Ernst Kosterlitzky—believed to have been a Cossack cavalry officer who had lost a leg during the Crimean War—and a German mother named Emily Lendert. At the age of 10, young Emil's family had moved to Charlottenburg, just outside of Berlin. Four years later, they would return to Russia so he could be enrolled in a military school at St. Petersburg in 1867, later transferring into the Royal Naval College in Moscow.

Upon graduating in 1872, the teenaged Kosterlitzky had been shipped out as a midshipman cadet for a world cruise aboard a training vessel but deserted on December 3, 1872, while it was lying at anchor during a layover at Puerto Cabello, Venezuela. He then apparently wandered through the Caribbean and perhaps as far north as New York City over the next three months until the vessel on which he was traveling up the Pacific coast toward California paused on April 29, 1873, off the port of Guaymas on the west coast of Mexico.

Allegedly, the 19-year-old Kosterlitzky spotted a troop of Mexican dragoons exercising ashore, and—being the first cavalry that he had seen since leaving Russia—he impulsively decided to go ashore and enlist.

Service with the *Rurales* (1873–1910)

Kosterlitzky was indeed noted in official Mexican Army records as having enrolled as a private in this cavalry unit at noon on May 1, 1873, his name being Hispanicized from Emil into "Emilio." Given his military upbringing, he adapted well and rose through its ranks, being promoted to corporal by June 3, 1874, then to second sergeant early in 1876, quickly followed by first sergeant on July 2, 1876, and ensign by the end of that same year. He became a first lieutenant as of 1880 and captain in the National Guard by 1883, while fighting against the Apaches under Col. Ángel Elías.

During these campaigns in the mountains of northern Mexico, Kosterlitzky would come to meet and cooperate with U.S. Cavalry squadrons in their pursuits of war bands across the border, according to the terms laid out in the 1882 U.S.-Mexico reciprocal border-crossing treaty. These American officers, troopers—and especially reporters—would find the presence of a multilingual white Russian officer in command of crack Mexican cavalrymen to be quite exotic and attributed great feats of daring to Kosterlitzky, referring to him by such vivid nicknames as the "Mexican Cossack" or the "Eagle of Sonora." He always disavowed such exaggerated tales, though, deeming them distasteful and unprofessional.

In April 1885, Kosterlitzky was transferred into the *Gendarmería Fiscal* to serve for a few years in the customs service, settling with his wife Francesca into a home in Magdalena, Sonora, but he was to achieve his greatest fame as a field commander of *rurales* or federal mounted policemen under the Porfirio Díaz regime, patrolling in that same state. He earned the military rank of lieutenant colonel by 1890 and became a full colonel as of December 28, 1906, the same year in which he had led 75 *rurales* on an epic ride from Magdalena, Sonora, to help restore order during the miners' strike in June 1906 at Cananea.

Revolutionary Upheaval (1910–1912)

Kosterlitzky was promoted to command of the 3rd Corps of *rurales* as of July 10, 1910, having 250 men under his command and headquartered at his long-time home-town of Magdalena, Sonora. When the defrauded presidential challenger Francisco I. Madero launched an insurrection against the Porfirian regime in the state of Chihuahua that same November of 1910, Kosterlitzky led his mounted policemen in pursuit of small bands of rebels so as to arrest them as lawbreakers as this insurgency spread, but he was not involved in any military actions.

Kosterlitzky clearly preferred the strongman Díaz as his national commander, having communicated with him on numerous occasions, but he nonetheless continued serving under Madero when the old administration was swept away in May 1911. The *rurales* were sufficiently well regarded by the new government as to be retained in service, although unrest continued and Kosterlitzky retired from active duty effective as of February 12, 1912, after having been temporarily blinded by a hand grenade while fighting some rebels at the Battle of La Dura. Nevertheless, president Madero requested his return to service and he obliged on September 11, 1912.

Defeat at Nogales (March 1913)

Kosterlitzky may have admired Díaz more than Madero, Colonel Kosterlitzky was in command of 280 *rurales* and 120 federal troops, based in the small town of Nogales on the border between Sonora and Arizona, when Madero was murdered in Mexico City during the *Decena Trágica* of February 1913 and the presidency was usurped by Gen. Victoriano Huerta. disapproved of Madero, but he hated Huerta, deeming the new administration in the national capital to be barely legitimate.

However, Kosterlitzky quickly found that the state authorities in Sonora not only had rejected Huerta's claim to office but were furthermore targeting federal garrisons for removal. As early as March 5, 1913, Kosterlitzky began sending worried telegrams to the regional military commander, Gen. Pedro Ojeda, who had another 700 soldiers under his command at the nearby town of Naco; 600 more were at the mining camp of Cananea. And indeed within days, the Sonoran colonel Álvaro Obregón suddenly arrived at Lomas outside of Nogales at midday on March 12, 1913, with 500 militiamen of the 4th Irregular Battalion of Sonora and about 50 turncoats from two companies of *rurales* (the 47th and 48th Cuerpos Rurales), demanding the surrender of its garrison.

Kosterlitzky refused, and the rebels attacked early on the morning of March 13, 1913, striking simultaneously out of both east and west in twin 150-man assault columns. Obregón's militiamen gradually pressed the defenders back from their outer lines as the day wore on, so by 5:00 p.m., demoralized *rurales* began emerging from their last trenches into the town square in front of the customs house where Kosterlitzky formed up 209 survivors and led them across the Bonillas Bridge into Nogales, Arizona, where he surrendered his command and sword to Capt. Cornelius C. Smith of the 5th U.S. Cavalry Regiment. The latter congratulated Kosterlitzky on having survived the battle, to which the colonel allegedly replied, "I wish it were otherwise."

The victorious Obregón reported to Sonora's interim governor, Ignacio L. Pesqueira, that his militiamen had suffered only 6 men killed and 9 injured during their assault, finding 24 dead and a like number of wounded among Nogales's defenders, while pouring scorn on Kosterlitzky for having escaped "without spilling a drop of his blood" to seek the protection of a foreign flag.

Internment (1913–1914)

Kosterlitzky and his survivors were interned at Fort Rosecrans in San Diego, he and his officers being allowed to give their paroles shortly thereafter, so they could live in rented houses in town and even be joined by their families from Mexico. The enlisted men, however, were kept living under canvas behind barbed wire, while the U.S. and Mexican governments argued over who was responsible for their pay, clothing, and food. The new Mexican administration did not wish to pay for the upkeep of ex-*rurales*, while the American authorities were uneasy about attracting even more refugees through providing handouts. American papers had a field day editorializing about "paid vacations courtesy of Uncle Sam" for every "gun toting thug" who could sneak across the border. The career of camp commandant F. W. Benteen was badly damaged when he bought new uniforms for the internees out of his own pocket. There was a prolonged outcry over his "mollycoddling" the Mexicans.

Things got so bad that 60 of the frustrated *rurales* tunneled out and escaped. Kosterlitzky was shocked and offended. He felt that since he had given his parole, the escape of the enlisted men had broken his word. He mounted up with the American troops and helped run down most of the escapees. And when he caught up with his men he talked them all in, ensuring that force would not be needed. Eventually, Mexico's new president, Venustiano Carranza, declared a general amnesty and

Kosterlitzky's command returned home, but not Kosterlitzky.

U.S. Service (1917–1926)

He decided it would be safer to stay in the United States, so he moved to Los Angeles, where he had no visible means of support until March 26, 1917, when he was hired by the U.S. Justice Department as a "special employee." As a counterspy, Kosterlitzky seems to have spent most of his time wandering around Los Angeles, making incendiary comments, pretending to be an anti American agitator, and luring German agents into revealing themselves. In this work he was helped by the fact that he read, wrote, and spoke Spanish, French, English, Russian, German, Italian, Polish, and Chinese.

His knowledge of the borderlands, as well as his intelligence and professionalism, led to an appointment as special employee of the U.S. Department of Justice's "prohibition team," spending the next four years running down bootleggers and rumrunners along the California coast. In the words of J. Edgar Hoover, he rendered services "of great value in investigations along the Mexican border and on the West Coast" before resigning this position because of failing health on September 4, 1926, and living in Los Angeles until his death on March 2, 1928, being buried in the Calvary Cemetery. He was survived by his Mexican widow, Francisca López, three sons, and three daughters.

See also: Cananea Strike; *Decena Trágica*; Huerta Márquez, José Victoriano; Obregón Salido, Álvaro; Revolution, Mexican; *rurales*.

Further Reading

Smith, Cornelius C. *Emilio Kosterlitzky: Eagle of Sonora and the Southwest Border.* Glendale, CA: A. H. Clark Company, 1970.

Truett, Samuel. "A Mexican Cossack in Southern California." *Huntington Frontiers* 1, no. 2 (2005), 14–17.

Truett, Samuel. "Transnational Warrior: Emilio Kosterlitzky and the Transformation of the U.S.-Mexico Borderlands." In *Continental Crossroads*, edited by Samuel Truett, 241–70. Durham, NC: Duke University Press, 2004.

L

A traitor to God, to the King, and to the Pope.

> — verdict handed down against the ex-priest and insurgent chieftain José María Morelos, November 28, 1815

La Carbonera, Battle of (1866)

Second of a pair of republican victories won in quick succession outside the city of Oaxaca during the War of the French Intervention.

After four years of active campaigning on behalf of its Mexican conservative allies and their foreign figurehead, the emperor Maximilian, Paris had finally announced during the summer of 1866 that it was preparing to withdraw its expeditionary forces from this conflict. Heartened by such news, the republican general Porfirio Díaz had lured a portion of the imperial garrison holding the capital city of the remote, southeastern state of Oaxaca into the open field and defeated it on October 1, 1866, at the Battle of Miahuatlán.

Preliminaries: Siege of Oaxaca (October 6–16, 1866)

His younger brother, Col. Félix Díaz, had thereupon led his cavalry detachment directly into the streets of Oaxaca four days later, securing most of that city before being joined by Porfirio's victorious main army on October 6, 1866, so together the two brothers could besiege the remaining imperial defenders under Gen. Carlos Oronoz within the Santo Domingo, El Carmen, and La Soledad strongholds.

However, 10 days later, Porfirio Díaz learned through an intercepted message that 1,500 Austro-Hungarian mercenaries and Mexican imperial troops under Col. Johann Carl, Graf (Count) Khevenhüller of the Red Hussars, were hastening to the relief of Oaxaca's beleaguered garrison. As a result, Díaz silently broke off his siege operations on the night of October 16–17, 1866, and regrouped his army around the Hacienda de Aguilera before marching northwestward unseen through the hills to meet this approaching enemy column.

First, Díaz proceeded to Etla, fearful that some 350 reinforcements coming to join him from Teotitlán under Brig. Gen. Luis Pérez Figueroa might unwarily blunder into this enemy force, but instead the two republican columns chanced upon each other safely at the town of San Juan del Estado at 9:00 a.m. on October 17, 1866. Detaching his cavalry so as to feint a return toward Oaxaca (with orders to double back and rejoin him after dark) in order to keep that city's imperial garrison on the defensive, Díaz led his infantry and artillerymen out of Etla after midnight on October 17–18, 1866, making a forced march through Tenexpa and Huitzo in hopes of gaining the *meseta* or plateau around the rural hamlet of La Carbonera, the highest stretch of ground along the main highway coming through the mountains.

Battle of La Carbonera (October 18, 1866)

But his 3,000-man republican army and Khevenhüller's smaller force gained the plateau simultaneously the next morning, although Díaz was able to deploy his battle lines facing northeastward, looking up the highway from slightly beneath the Carbonera hamlet. Figueroa's brigade was positioned on the republican right; on the left were the Patria and Morelos Battalions under Col. Fidencio Hernández; in the center, the Chiautla and *Cazadores* Battalions [350 men under Col. Juan Espinosa]; while in the rear were the cavalry from the Fieles, Montaña, Guerrero, and Costa Chica Regiments, plus the Tlaxiaco militia, and some artillery.

Around noon on October 18, 1866, Díaz's scouts discovered the Austro-imperial army approaching, who despite being outnumbered two to one, immediately deployed for battle. After marshalling on a nearby height, two companies of 300 Austro-imperial troops apiece advanced on the republican lines, only to be repelled. Both armies then closed and fought a general action. Eventually, the Austro-imperial right was outflanked and their cohesion disintegrated. Díaz's victorious troops pursued their vanquished foe for 12 miles until evening halted the chase at Las Minas by 7:00 p.m. and Díaz could report that he had "captured 396 Austrian, Polish, and Hungarian prisoners, among whom are seven officers; four mountain rifled guns; over 600 carbines; and great abundance of munitions."

See also: Díaz Mori, José de la Cruz Porfirio; Miahuatlán, Battle of.

Further Reading

U.S. Congressional Serial Set. Vol. 1294, 309.

La Cucaracha. *See* Cucaracha, La.

las armas nacionales se han cubierto de gloria

Popular catchphrase in Mexico that can be translated literally as "the national arms have covered themselves in glory" and was inspired by the battlefield report from Gen. Ignacio Zaragoza announcing his victory over a French invasion force during the famous "Cinco de Mayo" battle at Puebla on May 5, 1862.

On that day, all of Mexico waited anxiously as a string of telegrams describing this action arrived from Zaragoza until finally one was received toward evening that began: *Las armas del Supremo Gobierno se han cubierto de gloria* or "The arms of the Supreme Government [i.e., the republican administration of Pres. Benito Juárez] have covered themselves in glory." Joyful celebrations erupted, as this triumph had been quite unexpected, and this sentence passed into the popular lexicon. A comparable example from American history would be Commo. Oliver Hazard Perry's report after his victory at the Battle of Lake Erie on September 10, 1813: "We have met the enemy, and they are ours."

In modern times, both sentences are still instantly recognizable among the public at large, although their exact origins might be only vaguely remembered. Thus a petty triumph in Mexico today might be facetiously greeted with the compliment of "the national arms have certainly covered themselves in glory."

See also: Cinco de Mayo, Battle of the; Zaragoza Seguín, Ignacio.

Further Reading

Echenique, Rafael. *Batalla del 5 de Mayo de 1862 en Puebla: telegramas oficiales relativos a la mencionada batalla.* Mexico City: Eusebio Sánchez, 1894.

Legión de Honor (1862–1863)

Designation given to the 6,000 or so conservative collaborators who formed around the initial expedition that France landed in Mexico at the start of the War of the French Intervention motivated by their desire to help remove its liberal republican government.

Despite this grandiose title, membership consisted of a patchwork of random companies brought in haphazardly by turncoat Mexican Army officers, or bands of irregulars riding under their own chosen leaders with no hierarchical structure or military cohesion. Lacking any kind of official standing, they furthermore received no regular pay or supplies and so were reduced to pillaging the villages around Orizaba for their subsistence, the priest Francisco J. Miranda reporting how even their "very own Generals would go in person to rustle cattle, so as to later sell them to the French commissariat." Such undisciplined actions and outright criminality meant that they were soon dubbed the "Legión de Horror" by the long-suffering civilian populace of the state of Veracruz.

Behavior improved a bit after Gen. Elie Frédéric Forey succeeded Charles Lorencez as French commander-in-chief and began issuing regular pay and rations to the best 2,000 of these Mexican auxiliaries, while recognizing Leonardo Márquez and Antonio Taboada as their de facto leaders. Still, the cruel vagaries of war meant that looting and violence would nonetheless persist, although the priest Miranda at least acknowledged that in this, he could discern

no difference between the soldiers "of Juárez, and [the Legion] of Márquez. Both armies are identical in their lack of training, in their indiscipline, in their immorality, in everything."

See also: French Intervention, War of the; Lorencez, Charles Ferdinand Latrille, Comte de; Márquez Araujo, Leonardo.

Further Reading

Bassols Batalla, Ángel. *Temas y figuras de la intervención.* Mexico City: Sociedad Mexicana de Geografía y Estadística, Sección de Historia, 1963.

Chartrand, René. *The Mexican Adventure, 1861–67.* Oxford: Osprey, 1994.

Dabbs, Jack A. *The French Army in Mexico, 1861–1867: A Study in Military Government.* The Hague: Mouton, 1963.

Légion Étrangère. *See* French Foreign Legion in Mexico (1863–1867).

ley fuga

A ruthless military measure transferred into police practice as early as the mid-19th century signifying the summary execution of a criminal suspect or detainee without arrest or trial.

This expression translates literally as "flight law" or "law of flight," its implicit intent being to explain away the deliberate killing of a detainee by justifying this extra-legal death as a simple case of a prisoner having been "killed while attempting to escape" from a duly constituted authority. In 1909, the author Carlo de Fornaro would observe:

The "*ley fuga*" is not in truth a law, nor anything which might count as one, but rather a Mexican euphemism. It has been in use for the elimination of bandits, over the past two or three generations.

Indeed, this policy of applying *ley fuga* to criminals caught in the act of committing a felony is known to have been practiced since at least the mid-19th century. For example, the frustrated liberal government of the state of Jalisco is known to have decreed as long ago as 1857 that any high-waymen caught in the act could be *pasado por las armas* by local authorities within 24 hours after only the very sketchiest of hearings to serve as his trial.

Ironically, even young Gen. Porfirio Díaz would complain in his Plan de la Noria issued on November 8, 1871, that his opponents within Pres. Benito Juárez's liberal administration

have calculated the inviolability of human life, converting horrible murders into daily practice, to the point where the grim phrase *ley fuga* has become a common saying.

During his three decades in power, though, Díaz's administration would become even more notorious in its own right for its ready recourse to this same measure. Determined to stamp out banditry as part of his vision of modernizing Mexico, he seconded young officers from the army to train and lead a mounted police force known as the *rurales* on their patrols, giving them free rein to execute on the spot any criminal caught red-handed or who resisted arrest.

Naturally, such a callous policy could also be extended to other kinds of offenders as well, so government critics, union organizers, peasant or native leaders, political agitators, and the like might find the *ley fuga* being applied to them by various different

authorities under Díaz (the phrase *se le aplicó la ley fuga* or "the *ley fuga* was applied to him" becoming a common catchphrase for such sanctioned murders). On pages 151–52 of his 1908 book entitled *Barbarous Mexico*, the crusading American journalist John Kenneth Turner explained it thus:

The Ley Fuga, or law of flight, is a method of killing resorted to by all branches of the Mexican police power. It was originated by order of General Diaz, who decreed that his police might shoot any prisoners who should try to escape while under guard. While it may not have originated for that purpose, this rule came to be used as one of the means of putting to death persons against whom the government had not the shadow of another excuse for killing. The marked man is simply arrested, taken to a lonely spot, and there shot. The matter is kept quiet, if possible; but if a situation should arise that demands an explanation, the report is given out that the victim had attempted to escape and had brought his fate upon himself.

De Fornaro concluded his own observations by writing that in its beginnings, "the *ley fuga* was nothing more than a fruitless attempt to rid the country of bandits," but went on to point out that while banditry had been virtually eradicated by 34 years of Díaz's iron-fisted rule, this policy still

remained in full force, being used for private vengeance, for political purposes, and is one of the most dangerous, cowardly, and execrable weapons of the many used by Porfirio Díaz and his political Mafia.

Unfortunately, the military defeat and removal of the Porfirian regime by the Mexican Revolution would not bring an end to the practice of *ley fuga*.

See also: *rurales.*

Further Reading

Fornaro, Carlo de. *México tal cual es*. New York: International Publishing Company, 1909.

"Kill Mexican Officers Under the 'Ley Fuga,' " *New York Times*, November 6, 1919.

Lomas de San Lorenzo, Battle of the (1867). *See* San Lorenzo, Battle of (1867).

Lomas de Santa María, Battle of the (1813). *See* Valladolid, Battle of (1813).

Lorencez, Charles Ferdinand Latrille, Comte de (1814–1892)

Commander of the first military expedition sent out to commence the French Intervention in Mexico who would be defeated at the Battle of the Cinco de Mayo outside of Puebla and resign his position rather than be superseded.

He was born in Paris on May 23, 1814, the first child of the Napoleonic major general Guillaume Latrille, Comte de Lorencez, and his wife, Nicolette Caroline Oudinot de Reggio, daughter of the famed imperial marshal Nicolas Charles, Comte Oudinot. A sister baptized as Adèle would be born that following year, these being the only two children born of this union.

Military Background (1832–1861)

At the age of 16, young Charles had been enrolled as a student cadet in the *Ecole spéciale militaire* or "Special Military School" at Saint-Cyr in December 1830, graduating to be commissioned as a sublieutenant in the 11th Light Infantry in 1832. Assigned to the already-ongoing campaign in Algiers, it took Lorencez six years to be promoted to lieutenant, then another two to become a captain by 1840. He would serve in that rank with the 2nd *Chasseurs à pied* Battalion from June 1841 until January 1850, when he was promoted to lieutenant colonel of the 7th Line Regiment. During his two decades of service in North Africa, Lorencez was wounded once and mentioned in dispatches on three separate occasions.

He returned to France to become colonel of the 49th Line Regiment as of December 1852, which a year-and-a-half later would sail as part of the French Army that was sent to fight in the Crimean War. While engaged in the yearlong siege of the major Russian seaport of Sebastopol, Lorencez was promoted to brigadier general on June 11, 1855, and then wounded one week later during a failed assault against that city's advance stronghold, named Malakoff.

While recuperating from this injury, Lorencez's personal circumstances also changed due to the death of his father on October 1, 1855, which meant that he inherited his title and estate. This inheritance furthermore allowed the 41-year-old Lorencez the financial means to marry Euphémie Caroline Lloret on November 27, 1856.

Departure for Mexico (January 1862)

Following his wedding, Lorencez remained on peacetime duty at various army bases throughout France—Paris, Pau, Chalons, Vesoul, and Metz—for the next five years

French lithograph showing Spanish general Juan Prim's division paraded in the main square of Veracruz in January 1862, initiating the foreign intervention into Mexico. (Anne S. K. Brown Military Collection, Brown University Library)

before being appointed on January 20, 1862, to assume command over the military expedition that was being dispatched across the Atlantic to reinforce Mexico's conservatives and install an imperial regime. Departing Cherbourg eight days later aboard the steam corvette *Forfait*, Lorencez arrived off Veracruz by the afternoon of March 5, 1862, coming ashore the next day with his 14 staff officers to begin preparing for the disembarkation of the 4,811 soldiers who were following along behind aboard seven other warships, along with their artillery train, munitions, firearms, supplies, 613 horses, etc. Assuming command of the French naval contingent that was already ashore, Lorencez was promoted from brigadier to *général de division* or "major general" as of March 20, 1862, eight days before the last of his straggling transports finally appeared off Veracruz.

The French alliance with their increasingly uneasy British and Spanish allies was officially dissolved as of April 9, 1862, allowing Lorencez the freedom to act openly in consort with the anticipated Mexican collaborators, whom he had been sent to support in toppling the republican government of Pres. Benito Juárez. Ten days later, he struck inland from his forward base of Córdoba with 6,800 French soldiers and marines, optimistically expecting to be reinforced by conservative contingents as he pushed deeper into Mexico—and even to be greeted as a liberator in certain cities or regions.

Republican patrols shadowed the invaders' progress from afar as the French Army entered Orizaba uncontested on April 27, 1862. Pausing only long enough to install a small garrison (as well as to leave behind 463 ill men to convalesce), Lorencez resumed his march the next morning, proceeding up into the central highlands at the head of 6,150 troops, which included the 99th Line Regiment, two battalions of the 2nd Zouave Regiment, the 1st Battalion of the *Chasseurs à Pied* Regiment, two battalions of French Marines, and numerous lesser companies.

Cumbres de Acultzingo (April 28, 1862)

At 9:00 a.m. on April 28, 1862, Lorencez's vanguard—a squadron of the 2nd *Chasseurs d'Afrique*—emerged out onto the plain below the town of Acultzingo, being spotted by some distant Mexican riders who wheeled about and then torched this small town as the main French body followed their scouts out onto the plain. Lorencez let his men rest and consume their midday meal before resuming his route march. However, when his forward-most unit (the 2nd Zouave Battalion) passed through smoldering Acultzingo and neared its *Puente Colorado* or "Red Bridge" beyond, at the base of the highway that wound still higher up into the mountains, they suddenly drew fire at 1:30 p.m. from hidden republican riflemen, who had stealthily moved into concealed positions along with a small battery. And when the French light infantry failed to chase these ambushers away and shooting instead intensified, Lorencez deployed his entire army for battle, believing that he had encountered the main republican *Ejército de Oriente* or "Eastern Army" under its regional commander, Gen. Ignacio Zaragoza.

Looking to engage, Lorencez sent a column of 3,000 French troops to forge directly up the highway, while twin columns of 1,000 soldiers apiece groped up into the surrounding mountains on either flank seeking to make contact with their opponents'

army—all three columns preceded by skirmish lines of *tirailleurs*. But in fact, only a single republican division had lain in concealment to spring this ambush, 2,000 infantrymen and 200 cavalry troopers brought from Puebla by Zaragoza so as to bloody and delay the French advance while the defensive preparations around Puebla were being completed.

These outnumbered Mexicans even managed to stall Lorencez's main central thrust before Zaragoza's divisional commander, Gen. José María Arteaga, was wounded in a leg and his staff prematurely gave the pre-arranged signal for a general retirement. Therefore, after three hours of sniping and some exchanges of long-range volleys, the republicans withdrew and Lorencez gained the heights above Acultzingo as evening fell, glimpsing his foes as they retired in the direction of San Agustín del Palmar.

Curiously, both commanders emerged from this indecisive engagement convinced that they had inflicted heavy casualties on their enemies, although losses were actually minimal on both sides. Zaragoza reported to his superiors in Mexico City that the French had "suffered greatly from dead and wounded, whose number was considerable," although French regimental returns recorded only 2 dead and 32 wounded from this affray. Lorencez in turn was convinced that he had beaten off a major republican army, rather than merely enduring an ambush by a single division, and so estimated Mexican losses to run into many hundreds—although their casualties scarcely totaled 50.

Yet despite encountering no further resistance as his army moved on up through the silent villages of El Palmar, Quecholac, and Acatzingo, Lorencez grew increasingly worried by the invaders' lack of popular support as well as the dysentery that began appearing among his ranks. His conservative partners had repeatedly assured him that the French would be greeted into the anti-Juarista heartland around Puebla as liberators and furthermore be reinforced by thousands of irregulars and deserting Mexican Army units that were coming from Izúcar de Matamoros under Gen. Leonardo Márquez—neither of which was proving to be true.

Therefore, as his weary columns entered the silent town of Amozoc at 3:00 p.m. on May 4, 1862, now only 12 miles short of the city of Puebla, Lorencez decided to strike due west the next dawn, marching straight down the highway leading from Amozoc into that city so as to quickly punch through at a single focal point of its defenses, thanks to his superior firepower and the shock of his assault—hoping to carry Puebla by a sudden *coup d'audace* or "audacious blow" rather than settle in for a more protracted siege operation.

Defeat outside Puebla (May 5, 1862)

Departing Amozoc at dawn on that Monday morning, May 5, 1862, Lorencez's 6,100-man army reached Los Álamos Hacienda by 9:00 a.m., then trudged due west toward Puebla, which lay almost hidden from view amid its surrounding hills. As the city's 6,000 defenders manned their outer lines of defenses at 10:45 a.m., Lorencez halted his own troops and gave them time to eat a light refreshment before wheeling his two Zouave battalions and Marine Fusilier battalion over onto his right at 11:30 a.m., so as to move forward and occupy Rementería Ranch, installing a battery of 10 French fieldpieces there. The French commander intended to bombard the main Mexican stronghold of Guadalupe atop its commanding hill, then send his well-armed troops sweeping up its slopes in serried battle lines so as to secure this eminence, forcing the evacuation of the city that lay exposed behind it.

But Lorencez was unaware that his swift tactical decision would send his troops marching directly uphill through serried rows of defensive trenches, invisible from lower down. The republican defenders slowly fell backward uphill, all the while keeping up a steady counterfire which caused the French 50 dead, 304 wounded, and 128 captured soldiers—482 total casualties—compared to the Mexican republican losses of 83 dead, 132 wounded, and 12 deserters.

Retreat and Resignation (1862–1863)

After being repulsed, Lorencez recuperated his battered army for two days atop the nearby Amalucan heights, still hoping to be joined by his long-overdue Mexican allies. However, when no conservative help appeared by the third morning, he began leading his 6,000 men back east toward Orizaba at 2:00 p.m. on May 8, 1862, trailed at a safe distance by Zaragoza's recently reinforced but ill-supplied army. The French retreated slowly over roads that were soon waterlogged by heavy rains, hampered by their 300 wounded and many other soldiers who had fallen sick.

When Lorencez encamped for the night of May 17, 1862, at the Hacienda de Tecamalucan, he was surprised to receive a visit that same evening from the Mexican conservative general Leonardo Márquez, who had brought 2,500 riders to join the French column. The next day, they fought their way past a liberal force that interposed themselves at the stone bridge across Barranca Seca with the help of the French 99th Line Regiment, detached from Lorencez's main force.

That same day, his soldiers and their Mexican collaborators gained the safety of

Orizaba, where they would entrench for a protracted stay. A much larger expedition was sent out from France under General Forey, and Lorencez was named to be his second-in-command, but declined. Instead , he departed Veracruz in late November 1862 aboard the French steamer *Floride*, which touched at Santiago de Cuba before proceeding across the Atlantic.

Later Career (1863–1894)

Returning to France on December 15, 1862, still suffering the debilitating effects from the yellow fever that he had contracted in Orizaba, Lorencez was not employed again in any military capacity until 1864 when he was appointed an inspector general. Retiring from the French Army at 65 years of age as of July 16, 1879, he died almost 15 years later at Laao in the Pyrenees on April 23, 1894.

See also: Barranca Seca, Battle of; Cinco de Mayo, Battle of the; Cumbres de Acultzingo, Battle of; French Intervention, War of the; Zaragoza Seguín, Ignacio.

Further Reading

Bibescu, Georges. *Au Mexique 1862: combats et retraite des six mille*. Paris: Plon, Nourrit, et Cie., 1887.

Bibescu, Georges. *Le corps Lorencez devant Puebla 5 mai 1862: retraite des cinq mille*. London: British Library, 2011 reedition.

"The American Question in France." *New York Times*, July 17, 1862.

"Mexican Affairs." *New York Times*, May 13, 1862.

M

It is eight at night, all doors are shut, except the one leading to Heaven.

— Miguel Miramón's last letter to his wife, written from his execution cell in Querétaro on June 18, 1867

Macabeo. Nickname given to the youthful general Miguel Miramón by his ardent conservative backers, referring to the biblical warrior Judah Maccabee; for a more complete description, *see* joven Macabeo.

Madsen light machine gun (1902–1911)

An advanced infantry weapon for its day, some of which were purchased during the modernization phase of the early 20th-century Mexican Army.

The initial prototype of this sophisticated weapon was designed in 1896 by the Danish inventors Julius A. Rasmussen and Theodor Schoubue. With the enthusiastic endorsement of that nation's minister of war, Vilhem H. O. Madsen, it was adopted for use by the Royal Danish Army six years later, the first production models of "Madsen light machine guns" appearing by 1904. It featured a complex firing mechanism and was therefore quite expensive to manufacture but proved very reliable and, given its compact dimensions (measuring only 45 inches in length and weighing 20 pounds), could be easily carried into battle and operated by a single soldier in the prone position—unlike other contemporary machine guns, which were heavier and had to be mounted on an exposed tripod in order to be fired.

Over 1,200 export models of the Madsen LMGs (light machine guns) were purchased that same year by the Imperial Russian Army and performed very well during the Russo-Japanese War. In 1905, a British firm named the Rexer Arms Company began manufacturing an unlicensed copy of the Madsen, and the Porfirian government purchased several dozen of these less-expensive models before Rexer was obliged to halt production because of a lawsuit filed by Madsen. In 1911, the Mexican Army did apparently acquire at least 100 of the M.1911 Madsen light machine guns directly from the Danish manufacturer, although most sources continued to describe all their weapons as "Rexers."

For example, the U.S. military attaché in Mexico City, Capt. Robert M. Campbell, estimated in late April 1918 that the postrevolutionary Mexican Army's machine guns were distributed as follows: 1 regiment armed with 40 Hotchkiss heavy machine guns; 10 smaller units, each armed with 5 Hotchkiss machine guns apiece; 4 more small units, equipped with 5 Colt machine guns apiece; plus another 10 small units, each armed with 10 Rexer light machine guns—a total of 110 heavy and 100 light machine guns.

See also: *ametralladora*; Colt-Browning heavy machine gun; Hotchkiss heavy machine gun; Rexer light machine gun.

Further Reading

Fitzsimmons, Bernard. *Illustrated Encyclopedia of Weapons and Warfare*. London: Phoebus, 1978.

Hughes, James B., Jr. *Mexican Military Arms: The Cartridge Period, 1866–1967*. Houston, TX: Deep River Armory, 1968.

Jowett, Philip, and Alejandro de Quesada. *The Mexican Revolution, 1910–20*. Oxford: Osprey, 2006, 15–16.

"Rexer Automatic Machine Gun." *Scientific American*, August 19, 1905.

Malpaso Canyon, Ambush in (1910)

Small but spectacular rebel victory won early during the Mexican Revolution that publicly signaled the weakness of Porfirio Díaz's military grip on the country.

Critical Situation in Chihuahua (November–December 1910)

The normal peacetime garrison of 1,900 federal troops in the vast northern state of Chihuahua had quickly become overextended by the scores of small insurrections that began erupting throughout its district as of mid-November 1910 in support of the defrauded presidential candidate Francisco I. Madero. The high command in Mexico City consequently telegraphed orders to Col. Martín Luis Guzmán in the city of Querétaro on December 13, 1910, directing him to take his 6th Infantry Battalion by rail so as to reinforce that troubled region.

Guzmán departed that very same day with 19 officers and 440 soldiers of his 6th Battalion, but his train did not manage to crawl into the station at Chihuahua City until dawn on December 17, 1910, because of the numerous obstructions encountered along the way.

Ordered to proceed immediately so as to deliver supplies and reinforce the federal garrison that was beleaguered by rebel forces at Pedernales, it took Colonel Guzmán a few hours to find railway crews who were willing to make this perilous run, so he did not depart Chihuahua with his convoy until 11:00 a.m. on that same December 17, 1910. The original train with his 6th Battalion on board was now outfitted with an armored flatcar out front, carrying the engineer, Maj. Vito Alessio Robles, and 30 men so as to keep watch along the line ahead for any dangers, and was trailed along behind by a second train bearing a squadron of federal cavalrymen and their mounts under First Capt. Julio A. Cerda, plus a pair of mountain howitzers.

Ambush in Malpaso Canyon (December 18, 1910)

Having been forewarned of the *federales*' intent, the rebel forces under Pascual Orozco prepared an ambush in Malpaso Canyon, positioning their men in the heights overlooking an exposed stretch of track before destroying a nearby section. Therefore, when the two federal trains halted to effect repairs on December 18, 1910, they found themselves under fire from above as they attempted to alight—while the bridge that they had just crossed behind them was being set ablaze in their rear, trapping them in between. Guzmán and his men endured scores of casualties as they fought for six long hours to extricate themselves from this predicament, eventually repairing the bridge sufficiently behind them so as to escape and retreat into the rural Bustillos railway station to tend to their wounded. The colonel himself had been hit in a leg and died 11 days later in Chihuahua City.

News of this shootout created a sensation throughout Mexico, especially as it was rumored that in the aftermath to his victory, Orozco had instructed his men to gather up the bloodied light-khaki caps and uniforms of the dead soldiers and sent them to Díaz with a taunting note that read: *"Ahí te van las hojas, mándame más tamales"* or "Here are your wrappers back, send me more tamales." Whether true or not, the regime's aura of invincibility had been diminished, notwithstanding the fact that a federal column succeeded shortly thereafter in dislodging Orozco's rebels from Malpaso Canyon in early January 1911.

See also: Orozco Vázquez, Pascual; Revolution, Mexican.

Further Reading

Chávez M., Armando B., and Francisco R. Almada. *Visión histórica de la frontera norte de México, tomo V.* Mexicali: Universidad Autónoma de Baja California y Editorial Kino, 1994, 8–11.

"Official Report on Fight at Malpaso." *The Daily Colonist* 103, no. 323, December 21, 1910, front page.

manco de Celaya (1915)

An expression that translates literally as the "one-armed man of Celaya" and that became the popular nickname given to the revolutionary general Álvaro Obregón after he had the lower portion of his right arm blown off during one of his epic battles against Pancho Villa.

Curiously, though, it was widely known that this injury had not been suffered during either one of Obregón's two major victories over Villa at the city of Celaya but rather

six weeks later at the Battle of Trinidad on June 3–5, 1915. Yet since all three of these huge and decisive encounters had been fought within a span of only two months, the nickname *manco de Celaya* somehow took root in the public imagination, possibly because it slides so smoothly off the tongue.

See also: Celaya, Battles of; Obregón Salido, Álvaro; Revolution, Mexican; Trinidad, Battle of; Villa, Pancho.

máquina loca

Mexican colloquialism that translated literally means a "crazy machine" and is used to describe any runaway engine—but in the military history of this country was specifically applied to the tactic of unleashing a runaway locomotive filled with explosives to smash into an enemy target.

During the Mexican Revolution, lightly armed irregulars would sometimes commandeer a train, fill it with explosives and combustibles, then unleash it to careen unmanned down a track and smash into an oncoming enemy train or plunge destructively into a crowded railyard or siding. The rebel chieftain Emilio P. Campa was credited with having introduced this tactic, most famously when a 6,000-man Maderista army under Gen. José González Salas was advancing northward aboard a train convoy from Torreón into the state of Chihuahua in March 1912 to put down Pascual Orozco's anti-Maderista rebellion.

Dug in awaiting them at the rural Rellano railway station, the rebel Campa decided to surprise the approaching Maderistas by unleashing a runaway—jocularly dubbed a *loco loca*, a rhyming-slang expression meant as a punning phrase for *locomotora loca* or "crazy locomotive"—which gained speed over the next several miles until it came barreling down on González Salas's convoy. His troops had seen the approaching engine smoke and so had sufficient time to detrain and even dislodge some of the intervening track, but to no avail. The speeding runaway hurtled off the rails, yet still carried sufficient momentum to crash into the lead Maderista train and explode. Although relatively few casualties were inflicted by this smash-up, the advance of González Salas's army had been effectively halted and his men were forced to abandon their convoy, soon coming under fire from more than 1,000 rebels as they started trudging toward the surrounding hills. Hemmed in on the low ground in this harsh environment, the Maderista general had no choice but to make a fighting retreat back into Torreón, where he committed suicide.

Because of this widely publicized success, Campas's tactic would come to be employed on numerous other occasions during the Revolution. Another noteworthy case occurred when Pres. Venustiano Carranza fled from Mexico City at dawn on May 7, 1920, aboard a 15-mile-long train convoy bearing 10,000 adherents and the national treasury. At the nearby station of Guadalupe that very same afternoon, a dynamite-laden locomotive had smashed into his lead train, the resultant explosion killing 200 people and injuring hundreds more, thereby hampering Carranza's escape so that he was eventually run down on horseback and murdered. This particular crash was later memorialized by a popular *corrido* or ballad entitled *La máquina loca*, composed by Melquiades C. N. Martínez.

See also: *corridos*; railroads.

Further Reading

Jowett, Philip, and Alejandro de Quesada. *The Mexican Revolution, 1910–20*. Oxford: Osprey, 2006, 13.

Knight, Alan. *The Mexican Revolution*. New York: Cambridge University Press, 1986, 55: 322.

LaFrance, David G. *Revolution in Mexico's Heartland*. Wilmington, DE: Scholarly Resources, 2003, 49.

Márquez Araujo, Leonardo (1820–1913)

Conservative officer who mutinied and fought against the liberal government throughout the War of the Reform and then served the imperial regime during the War of the French Intervention.

Upbringing (1820–1835)

Born in Mexico City toward the end of the colonial era on January 8, 1820, he was the first child and only son of First Sgt. Cayetano Márquez Huerta of the viceregal Light Battalion of Querétaro and his wife, María de la Luz Araujo Arces. Their son would be baptized with the full name of Leonardo Teófilo Guadalupe Ignacio del Corazón de Jesús, and a daughter would be born eight years afterward who would be christened as María Dolores Isabel Zacarías Cayetana.

As a child, young Leonardo had accompanied his father on military campaigns into Chiapas, as well as on the major expedition that contained and defeated a Spanish expeditionary force under Gen. Isidro Barradas that landed near Tampico in 1829. One week after turning 10 years of age, Leonardo's name had been enrolled on the lists as a cadet as of January 15, 1830, in the *compañía presidial* at Lampazos in the northern state of Nuevo León (which his father was commanding as a captain), and the youngster then traveled with his father again to campaign against Juan José Codallos's revolt in the states of Michoacán and

Guerrero in 1831. The next year, the 12-year-old Leonardo was listed on the books of the Active Battalion of Querétaro—another of his father's units—as of June 1, 1832.

Early Career and First Mutiny (1836–1849)

However, Márquez did not actually see active service until after he turned 16 years of age, when (over his father's objections) he obtained appointment as a *subteniente* or "sublieutenant" of fusiliers in the militia Battalion of Mextitlán as of October 1, 1836. He was subsequently transferred into the 11th Regiment and rose to become a captain, seeing some action in Texas before joining the 1st Light Infantry as of July 1, 1844, and fighting with that regiment a couple of years later against the U.S. invasion of northern Mexico during the Mexican-American War.

As a member of Santa Anna's huge army, his conduct at the losing Battle of La Angostura or Buena Vista on February 22–23, 1847, earned Márquez promotion to the command of a battalion. But then, in the chaotic aftermath following Mexico's national defeat and capitulation to the invading U.S. forces, Márquez mutinied in support of the disgraced and exiled Santa Anna when he rose with his 1st Line Battalion in the city of Querétaro in early February 1849—an insurrection that was quickly crushed, so at 29 years of age, Márquez was compelled to retire to private life on a rural hacienda named Huehuechoca.

Reactivation and Second Mutiny (1853–1856)

Four years later, after Gen. Manuel María Lombardini engineered a coup in Mexico City to temporarily seize the presidency on February 7, 1853, holding it until Santa Anna could return from Colombia and reassume office, Márquez was one of the *santannista* loyalists who early on were rewarded. Even before the dictator's return to Mexico, Márquez was amnestied for his mutinous conduct of four years previously, recalled to active duty in the Mexican Army, and promoted to lieutenant colonel as of March 26, 1853, with orders to resurrect the Active Battalion at Toluca. He became its colonel as of that same August 11, 1853, and when the liberal Revolution of Ayutla erupted the next spring, he once more campaigned in support of Santa Anna.

However, this insurrection spread nationwide and drove the dictator from office for the final time by August 1855. Márquez was able to reconcile with the new liberal administration under Pres. Ignacio Comonfort and so was in command of an army unit in the city of Toluca when a conservative uprising led to the seizure of Puebla early in 1856, and he joined this rebellion as well. After being defeated at the Battle of Ocotlán on March 8, 1856, Márquez was among the mutineers who managed to flee abroad. A report from a Havana newspaper, reprinted on page 2 of the May 15, 1856, edition of the *Times-Picayune* newspaper of New Orleans, indicated:

> The *Diario de la Marina*, of the 8th inst. announces the arrival there of H. B. M. ship *Penelope*, at Havana, on the previous day from Vera Cruz. She took, as passengers, a number of the parties to the late revolution at Puebla, among them Señor D. Antonio Haro y Tamariz, Gen. Leonardo Marquez, Col. Luis G. de Osollo, Lieut. Cols. Ángel López Santa Anna, and Juan Bautista Legarde, Chief of Battalion, Manuel Cano, Capt. Rafael González, and Lieut. Manuel Fontenecha.

Outbreak of the War of the Reform (1857–1858)

Márquez eventually managed to return and secured command of a contingent in the conservative army that marched north from Mexico City early in 1858 under the youthful brigadier Osollo to inaugurate the War of the Reform. After their initial success, the situation in the Bajío worsened when the cities of San Luis Potosí and Guanajuato were overrun by a large republican counteroffensive out of the north, so Osollo briefly resumed command in the field—before suddenly falling ill of typhoid fever and dying.

Márquez succeeded to command of the 4,000 conservative troops who were being marshaled at Querétaro to begin marching northward in three separate brigades by early August 1858 with the intent of reversing these liberal gains. However, when he initially made slow progress, the 26-year-old Miramón convinced the conservative leadership in Mexico City to make him commander-in-chief of this *Ejército del Norte* or "Northern Army," relegating Márquez to serve as one of his brigade commanders. Thus it was Miramón who encountered and defeated the main republican concentration at the Battle of Ahualulco de los Pinos on September 29, 1858, galloping off the next day with a small escort to be acclaimed as the savior of San Luis Potosí, while delegating the tedious chore of policing up the battle's bloody aftermath to Márquez. Miramón subsequently rushed off to rescue the threatened conservative garrison at Guadalajara as well, and by year's end had been promoted to major general and was being offered the presidency.

Tiger of Tacubaya (March–April 1859)

Márquez's brigade helped relieve Guadalajara, so he was still stationed in that city early the next year when Miramón—in his joint capacity as "substitute president" and senior conservative field commander—led his main army out of Mexico City in mid-February 1859 to besiege the rival liberal administration of Pres. Benito Juárez down on the Gulf coast in Veracruz. During his absence, the liberal general Santos Degollado began marshaling forces from throughout the Bajío to threaten the national capital, so Márquez was instructed on March 12, 1859, to assume command as *general en jefe* or "general-in-chief [i.e., commanding general]" of a *Primer Cuerpo* or "First Corps" composed of virtually every conservative garrison in that region, with authorization to draw on the necessary units to march and prevent the success of this liberal offensive.

Leaving Col. Luis Tapia with 1,500 troops behind at Guadalajara to act as its military governor, Márquez departed at the head of 1,200 men and nine guns by March 18, 1859, working his way through the mountains toward Mexico City. (With this reduction of conservative strength in Jalisco, the local liberal commander Ogazón was able to reclaim Colima before that same month was out.)

Degollado meanwhile appeared outside Mexico City with more than 6,000 liberal troops by March 22, 1859, occupying its suburbs of Tacubaya and Chapultepec, while the 2,400 conservatives of the pursuing División del Norte under Brigadier Generals Gregorio del Callejo and Tomás Mejía—who had been harrying this liberal army's progression since Querétaro—managed to circle around and enter the capital as well two days later, augmenting the strength of Maj. Gen. Antonio Corona's defenders to 4,000 men. They remained well entrenched behind their defenses and were heartened by the news that Márquez was hastening to their relief.

His column had in fact reached Lagos by March 26, 1859, and entered the beleaguered capital on April 7, 1859, to go over onto the offensive three days thereafter. Márquez and his second-in-command, Brig. Gen. Tomás Mejía, held a mass review in its Zocalo or main square at 6:00 a.m. on that Sunday morning of April 10, 1859, then led out 10 infantry battalions organized into three brigades under Brigadier Generals Francisco Vélez, José Quintanilla, and Ignacio Orihuela, plus two cavalry brigades for a total of 5,500 soldiers and 22 guns. Exiting through San Cosme Gate, Márquez's conservative army passed through Hacienda de los Morales and wound its way around the foothills so as to emerge from the woods beside Chapultepec Hill, cresting the western ridge overlooking Tacubaya by 4:00 p.m. Half an hour later, Márquez opened up a long-range bombardment with some 20 pieces against the distant liberal entrenchments below, who replied—equally ineffectually—with their fewer guns. Firing ceased on both sides as evening fell.

The next dawn, Monday, April 11, 1859, Márquez paraded his troops at 6:00 a.m., then one hour later launched a column of some 2,000 soldiers behind heavy covering fire from his batteries toward the Molino de Valdés, a liberal strongpoint "in the highest part of Tacubaya." Degollado's few artillery pieces could make little response to this shelling, the liberals instead waiting until their advancing foes had come within rifle range before checking this opening charge with their counterfire. A second conservative infantry assault against this stronghold met the same fate, so Márquez shifted his batteries farther forward into Molino del Rey, the folds of Chapultepec Hill, and La Condesa.

His bombardments from this closer range and the inexorable pressure from his infantry finally wore down liberal resistance over the next three hours, so their lines began to waver by 10:00 a.m. and gave way entirely an hour later. Their retirement from the battlefield quickly turned into a rout, surviving units streaming southwestward out of the Valley of Mexico to flee haphazardly back toward Jalisco and Michoacán. Márquez wrote immediately from his field headquarters in Chapultepec Castle to General Corona in Mexico City, reporting on this victory:

The arms of the Supreme Government have triumphed completely over the bandits who were threatening the capital of the Republic. The brave troops whom I am proud to command, have obtained this victory, fighting hand-to-hand over the ground and not only defeating the enemy, but also wrenching from them all their artillery, ammunition, wagons, armaments, and other war-implements, including the tunic with Major-General's insignia worn shamelessly by the infamous Degollado, who has never served the nation, nor even belonged to the noble calling of the arms.

Among the prisoners which were taken, are the ex-[army] General Marcial Lazcano and many other officers, who have already paid at the execution-spot [*patíbulo*] for the crime which they have committed.

Márquez's callous order that every liberal captive be executed—including medical personnel and civilian and foreign detainees, among them at least three American neutrals—would mar his reputation and earn him the sobriquet of the *Tigre de Tacubaya* (an expression roughly equivalent to the "Beast of Tacubaya" in the English language), although years later he would insist rather unconvincingly that this brutal directive had been given without his knowledge by the conservative president Miramón during an inspection that he made of the field immediately after fighting ceased.

Miramón had in fact belatedly regained the Valley of Mexico that same Monday afternoon, having withdrawn his main conservative army from its siege of Veracruz and hastened on ahead of its marching columns to help defend the capital. Entering Mexico City by stagecoach from Puebla, he immediately secured a mount and galloped to the scene of the Battle of Tacubaya, just after this engagement had concluded and the liberal survivors were fleeing in defeat. His own army still being many miles distant, Miramón was annoyed to discover that his old rival Márquez would reap all the accolades for defeating Degollado and saving the national capital.

Shortly past noon on Tuesday, April 12, 1859, Márquez marched triumphantly back into the cheering capital with his victorious army and even received the "blue band" signifying promotion to major general from the hands of Miramón himself. Meanwhile, the defeated Degollado—escorted by his loyal subordinate, Brig. Gen. Leandro Valle, and the Lanceros de Jalisco cavalry regiment—overtook Zaragoza's retreating División del Norte that same Tuesday, both formations reabsorbing detached liberal fragments as they trudged away to Maravatío, where Degollado ordered Zaragoza to split off for Guanajuato with his northern contingent while Degollado continued toward Morelia with his western forces.

Márquez did not emerge from Mexico City with 3,000 soldiers in pursuit until April 17, 1859, pushing uncontested into Morelia 12 days afterward, long after Degollado had departed (its 2,000-man liberal garrison commander, Brig. Gen. Epitacio

Huerta, simply exiting that city and then reclaiming Morelia once the conservative army passed on through toward Guadalajara). Márquez returned to Jalisco to discover that his rescue of the national capital had weakened conservative strength, leading to a liberal revival, so he spent the next few months pursuing elusive enemy strike forces.

Incarceration and Reactivation (November 1859–August 1860)

Márquez was absent on one such campaign into western Jalisco when Miramón sent him instructions from Mexico City early in November 1859 to detach reinforcements for a scratch conservative army that was being thrown together at Querétaro to counter a liberal upsurge in that region. When Miramón arrived at Querétaro shortly thereafter to personally assume command of this small army, he found himself outnumbered by more than two to one by the liberal general Santos Degollado and barely managed to win a miraculous victory at the Battle of Estancia de las Vacas on November 13, 1859. Immediately thereafter, Miramón arrived unexpectedly at Guadalajara by stagecoach at 2:00 p.m. on Saturday afternoon, November 19, 1859, to be greeted by a 21-gun salute and pealing church bells.

Learning that Márquez was still absent on campaign at the head of his division and had never sent the requested reinforcements, Miramón angrily recalled and arrested him on a vindictive charge of misappropriation of funds. Márquez would remain imprisoned in the national capital for the next nine months until Miramón finally returned to that city—almost alone and defeated—on the evening of August 12, 1860, having lost the bulk of his army at the Battle of Silao. Because of this resounding loss, he was obliged to temporarily relinquish his office as "substitute president" until a vote of confidence could be held by the conservative power brokers known as the *Junta de Notables*, who were left to choose between Miramón and Márquez.

Miramón was restored to power by their vote two days later, although Márquez was also released from prison, restored to his full military honors, and given a command in the field. However, conservative fortunes were by now on the verge of collapse, so when the victorious González Ortega besieged Guadalajara with a huge liberal army of 20,000 men and 125 fieldpieces by the end of September 1860, Márquez was sent in a last desperate hope of relieving its trapped conservative garrison. Vastly outnumbered, he was defeated on the main highway at Tepetates Ranch near Zapotlanejo on November 1, 1860, abandoning his 3,000 men and 18 cannon to surrender to the encircling enemy, while making good his own escape in the direction of Tepatitlán. Guadalajara capitulated two days later, and Mexico City fell to the liberals by Christmas Day 1860, bringing an end to the War of the Reform.

Conservative Diehard (1861)

Some of the defeated and fugitive conservatives such as Márquez, Marcelino Cobos, Juan Vicario, and others managed to reunite and recognize Félix M. Zuloaga as the "legitimate" president of Mexico on May 23, 1861, intending to fight on against the restored liberal administration of Benito Juárez. One of their conservative bands captured the scholarly Melchor Ocampo, ex-liberal foreign minister, at his Hacienda de Pomoca near Maravatío on June 1, 1861, bringing him before Márquez and Zuloaga two days later at Tepejí del Río in the state of Hidalgo, who ordered Ocampo summarily shot by a firing squad and his body left hanging from a tree.

A few weeks after this cruel act, Márquez surprised Mexico City's liberal garrison by suddenly materializing on June 24, 1861, with 2,600 troops and five small guns along its San Cosme *calzada* or "causeway," only to be driven away by hastily converging liberal forces. Pursued by González Ortega's 5,000-man liberal division, his small conservative force was overtaken while resting at the town of Jalatlaco on August 13, 1861, at which point Márquez and Zuloaga simply rode away with a few retainers, abandoning their troops to their fate.

The conservative leaders managed to escape up into the mountains of Querétaro, eventually finding shelter with partisans commanded by the skillful general Tomás Mejía. But when these fugitives reemerged a couple of months later to seize the Mineral del Chico, just beyond the city of Pachuca in the state of Hidalgo, they were soon challenged and defeated by another pursuing liberal army on October 20, 1861.

See also: Ahualulco de los Pinos, Battle of; Bajío; Barradas's Invasion; Calpulalpan, Battle of; *compañías presidiales*; Miramón, Miguel; Puebla (1856), Conservative Revolt; Reform, War of the; Tacubaya, Battle of.

Further Reading

Cambre, Manuel. *La guerra de Tres Años: apuntes para la historia de la Reforma.* Guadalajara, Jalisco: Gobierno del Estado, 1949.

Díaz Reyes Retana, Fernando. *Vida militar y política del señor general de división don Leonardo Márquez Araujo.* Querétaro: Editorial Libras de México, 1978.

Hernández Rodríguez, Rosaura. "Leonardo Márquez: de cadete a capitán." In *Estudios de historia moderna y contemporánea de México,* 5: 53–62. Mexico City: UNAM, 1976.

Pola, Ángel. *Manifiestos (el imperio y los imperiales) por Leonardo Márquez, lugarteniente del imperio.* Mexico City: Vázquez, 1904.

Mauser (1895–1907)

Well-designed German rifle imported by the thousands during the rearming of the Mexican Army under Pres. Porfirio Díaz and that would later prove to be a highly prized weapon on the battlefields of the Mexican Revolution.

First Imported Versions (1895–1907)

As part of the upgrading and modernization of the Porfirian Army, the Mexican government placed its first order in 1895 for Mauser rifles that fired 7x57mm rounds, in both its carbine and long-rifle versions. The very early deliveries of this Model 1895 weapon that were received the next year were marked "Ludwig Loewe," but as of December 1896 the weapons were stamped "DWM" for the name of their factory outside Berlin: *Deutsche Waffen und Munition* or "German Weapons and Munitions." Highly pleased with this initial shipment, the Mexican Army placed a second order in 1897, although the German authorities were offended by the bribes demanded by officers and government officials for this deal to be consummated. (It has been suggested that some *Modelo 1893* Mauser rifles and *Modelo 1895* Mauser carbines were also purchased from the German subsidiary in Spain, including some marked "Oviedo," but these firearms actually came into Mexico from stocks captured by the U.S. Army during the Spanish-American War that were sold off as secondhand weapons by brokers in El Paso.)

Because the high-powered, precision Mauser rifles—deemed the best in the world at that time—were so expensive, the Porfirian military simultaneously purchased Remington Model 1897 carbines and rifles in fairly large numbers as an economy measure to supplement the Mausers (three Remington carbines costing the same as one Mauser). As regiments were gradually outfitted with Mausers, these Remington rifles and carbines were handed down to police units such as the *rurales*.

In 1902, under the more honest supervision of Gen. Bernardo Reyes as secretary of war (who was rewarded with a medal from a grateful German government), another large contract was signed and about 38,000 more Mausers were delivered by 1904. Two years later, an additional consignment was requested and assigned by the Mauser Rifle Cartel to be manufactured by Steyr in Austria, who duly delivered 40,000 more M1902 versions. Mexico also ordered some of the simpler, more economical Model 1907 Mausers that were being supplied to various Latin American armies in a long-barreled, standard-action version with a pistol-grip stock at that time.

Mexican Manufacture (1910)

As early as 1902, the Mexican government had begun construction on a new complex for its *Fábrica Nacional de Armas* or "National Arms Factory" at Santa Cruz, in the municipality of Atizapán outside of Mexico City, followed by the erection four years later of a new cartridge factory at Santa Fe. In a bid to make the country less dependent on foreign suppliers, the Porfirian administration entered into protracted negotiations to arrange for the establishment of a Mauser subsidiary in Mexico. Machinery for a small production plant duly arrived, along with foreign technicians to help set it up and train Mexican workers in its operation.

Various problems delayed production until 1910 when the first few *Máuser Mexicano Modelo 1910* appeared, a copy of the M.1902 that was to be called the "M.1910." However, the Revolution erupted and Diaz was forced from office by the spring of 1911 before any significant numbers could be manufactured. The Federal Army would fight throughout the ensuing decade of warfare with its imported German firearms, which were also highly coveted by their rebel opponents. Some production resumed at Santa Cruz under the regime of Gen. Victoriano Huerta in 1913–1914, whose administration also attempted to buy more Mauser M.1912 long rifles and carbines direct from Steyr in Austria, but no significant additional amounts of weaponry resulted.

Prized Battlefield Weapon (1910–1920)

After Pancho Villa defeated a federal contingent with his ill-equipped guerrilla band at the Hacienda de Bustillos railway station on June 13, 1913, he specifically mentioned in his official report to his political superior, Venustiano Carranza, how his captured booty included a locomotive and "sixty Máuser rifles with a small amount of ammunition, which I distributed among the troops under my command."

See also: Carabina 30-30; *rurales*; Villa, Pancho.

Further Reading

Hughes, James B., Jr. *Mexican Military Arms: The Cartridge Period, 1866–1967.* Houston, TX: Deep River Armory, 1968.

Maximilian, Emperor of Mexico (1832–1867)

Foreign prince installed on the throne at the behest of Mexico's conservative faction to

The young Austrian idealist Maximilian, chosen by the French government and Mexican conservatives to be imposed as emperor of Mexico, 1864. (Library of Congress)

serve as a figurehead toward creating a monarchy that—it was hoped—would stabilize and better control the fractious young country.

Birth and Early Education (1832–1849)

He was born in Schönbrunn Castle outside of Vienna on July 6, 1832, the second son of Archduke Franz Karl of Austria and his wife, Sophie of Bavaria, being christened the next day as Ferdinand Maximilian Joseph von Habsburg-Lothringen. The young boy's education was rigorously conducted through tutors, the 32 hours per week of classes at age 7 being steadily increased until it reached 55 hours per week by the time that he had turned 17. In addition to his native German, he would also learn to speak Hungarian, Slavonic, English, French, Italian, and Spanish to varying degrees. Young Ferdinand Max was described as being an open, joyful, charming, and popular child, unlike his more aloof and self-contained older brother Franz Joseph, who was being groomed to succeed their grandfather, Francis II, on the throne.

In 1848, a wave of protests and riots swept Europe, causing the Austrian emperor to abdicate by December 2, 1848, in favor of Maximilian's 18-year-old brother, who thus ascended the throne as Franz Joseph I. Himself only 16, Maximilian accompanied this new monarch on his campaigns that had put down most rebellions throughout Austria by 1849 but at a cost of hundreds of rebels executed and thousands imprisoned. The sensitive Maximilian was horrified by such brutality and complained openly, later remarking: "We call our age the Age of Enlightenment, but there are cities in Europe where, in the future, men will look back in horror and amazement at the injustice of tribunals, which in a spirit of vengeance condemned to death those whose only crime lay in wanting something different to the arbitrary rule of governments which placed themselves above the law."

Naval Career (1850–1856)

Upon turning 18 years of age, Maximilian was made a lieutenant in the Austro-Hungarian Navy and began having dalliances with actresses and dancers. In 1851, he fell in love with the German countess Paula von Linden, who was the daughter of the ambassador from Würtemberg—but she was deemed beneath him, so it was arranged to have her father recalled from Vienna and Maximilian dispatched on a naval cruise to Spain and Portugal. There he became engaged early in 1852 with the 20-year-old Portuguese princess María Amalia of Braganza (a distant relation), but she fell ill

and died of tuberculosis by February 1853 before they could become married.

Throwing himself into naval affairs, Maximilian sailed as commander of the corvette *Minerva* on an exploring expedition along the coasts of Albania and Dalmatia in 1854 and that same year was promoted to rear admiral and became commander-in-chief of the small Austro-Hungarian Navy. Despite being only 22 years old, he had won over career officers by his genuine zeal for maritime life, and they realized that his influential position at court would greatly benefit the development of a proper naval force, which had never been an imperial priority and remained chronically underfunded. Thanks to Maximilian's leadership, its squadrons were soon being modernized and expanded, and new port installations were created at Trieste and Pola. By 1857, preparations were complete for the dispatch of the 42-gun, 2,600-ton frigate *Novara* on a major scientific expedition, which would become the first Austrian warship to circumnavigate the globe.

Marriage and Italian Residence (1857–1861)

After a state visit to Belgium, the archduke Maximilian married its 17-year-old princess, Charlotte, in Brussels on July 27, 1857, and was named by his brother as viceroy over the Italian states of Lombardy and Venice (*Lombardo Veneto*), which at that time were restless Austrian dependencies. Maximilian adopted quite liberal policies in their governance, and although well liked by his Italian subjects, they persisted in wishing to throw off foreign rule. After two years, he was dismissed from that office by his brother Franz Joseph, after which most of the Italian provinces won their independence in 1859.

Maximilian and Charlotte had meanwhile retired from public life and moved to Trieste, where they completed a splendid new residence named Miramare by 1860. He also made a scientific expedition to Brazil that same year and was being considered by a few leading Mexican conservatives living in exile as a potential royal figurehead for their turbulent country. Since the earliest days of Mexico's independence from Spain, some conservatives had suggested the adoption of a constitutional monarchy as a means of stabilizing its government, providing continuity from one administration to the next.

This notion took concrete shape when José Manuel Hidalgo—a Mexican conservative who in September 1861 was living as an exile at the French empress Eugénie's court at Biarritz—proposed that an armed intervention by France might be used to implement just such a scheme, further proposing the 29-year-old archduke Ferdinand Maximilian of Austria as an ideal neutral candidate. Napoleon III, eager to expand French influence overseas and support a Catholic cause, agreed to this suggestion and the archduke himself was persuaded to eventually assume the mantle of Mexican emperor, should it ever be offered.

The first expedition that landed in Mexico was repulsed at the Battle of Cinco de Mayo outside of Puebla on May 5, 1862, and so had to be reinforced over that ensuing winter by a much larger army under Maj. Gen. Elie Frédéric Forey. After a lengthy siege of Puebla in the spring of 1863, its republican garrison surrendered and the Franco-conservative army pushed the government of Pres. Benito Juárez out of Mexico City by June 10, 1863. Under Forey's guidance, an interim government was created five days later, which in turn officially voted to offer the title of "Emperor of Mexico" to Maximilian on July 10, 1863.

A delegation was named that formally made this representation to him at Miramare on October 3, 1863, to which Maximilian replied with a request that a plebiscite be held to determine the true will of the Mexican people. It took a few months to carry out this exercise, so it would not be until April 10, 1864, that Maximilian—having the previous day renounced all claims to the Austrian throne—formally accepted the offer of Mexico's crown and prepared to sail. Napoleon promised to support him militarily for the next three years, gradually reducing the size of the French expeditionary force already deployed in Mexico from 38,000 down to 20,000 men.

Emperor of Mexico (1864–1867)

Maximilian and Charlotte (who would become universally known throughout Mexico by her Hispanicized name of "Carlota") reached Veracruz aboard the Austro-Hungarian frigate *Novara* on May 28, 1864, and after a ceremonious progression inland entered Mexico City to a generally warm reception on June 12, 1864. Many Mexican conservatives, however, would soon become offended by some of their idealistic young monarch's more liberal opinions, while republicans would continue to regard him as an unwanted foreign puppet. Well-meaning and sincere, the young emperor would be confined to ceremonial duties in and around the capital, while his French allies and imperial subjects attempted to stamp out republican resistance throughout the country.

This became increasingly difficult after the American Civil War ended in April 1865 and Washington began complaining to Paris about the presence of a large French army along its southern borderlands, while furnishing arms and supplies to the republican resistance. With military victory no longer attainable, Napoleon issued a public statement on January 22, 1866, that declared the intervention in Mexico a success, while quietly dispatching a delegation to inform Maximilian that French troop withdrawals would have to be accelerated. The young Austrian and Belgian volunteers who offered to serve under their young monarchs in Mexico, while well armed and trained, could not replace the professional French line regiments.

Discouraged by this drawdown and his failure to win the hearts of the Mexican people, Maximilian quit Mexico City on October 16, 1866, intending to sail from Veracruz back to Europe because of his imperial government's flagging fortunes. Five days later, he reached the city of Orizaba, where he was met by Gen. Henri Pierre Abdon Castelnau—an aide-de-camp to Napoleon III—who had been sent to Mexico as a plenipotentiary to attempt to persuade the emperor to abdicate his throne and return home.

However, after repeated importuning by such conservative leaders as Márquez and Miramón, Maximilian agreed on December 1, 1866, to remain on as emperor, even after all his supporting French forces had been withdrawn. Twelve days later, he departed Orizaba to return into Mexico City escorted by two infantry regiments, 400 cavalry troopers, and his contingent of Austrian volunteers, determined to hold onto his throne. Bazaine was meanwhile reassembling all the French forces in anticipation of evacuating Mexico in accordance with his instructions from Paris, most of whom had been gathered by December 28, 1866, although the expeditionary commander then delayed hauling down his colors and marching the last of his 27,000 troops down toward Veracruz until February 5, 1867, so as to give the emperor a few weeks' grace to stabilize his defenses.

Five days afterward, the emperor privately told his physician to prepare for a two-week expedition to Querétaro, having become convinced by his Mexican advisers that his personal presence was required there so as to counteract the demoralizing effects of Miramón's recent defeat at the Battle of San Jacinto in the state of Zacatecas. Maximilian consequently set out northwestward from Mexico City on February 13, 1867, with Márquez and an escort of 1,600 Mexican troops, augmented along the road toward Querétaro by another 2,500 men under Vidaurri. Skirmishes occurred against republican guerrillas under Catarino Fragoso at Lechería and Calpulalpan before the emperor's column finally reached San Juan del Río on February 16, 1867. He wrote to a European friend during this trip:

> As you will already have learned through the newspapers, our friends, the French, have at last left Mexico, and—having once more obtained liberty of action—we have exchanged the butterfly net for the sword. Instead of bugs and beetles, we now pursue other game. Bullets instead of bees now buzz about our heads. Twice between Mexico and Querétaro we were in action, and had a number of our men killed and wounded.

Capture and Execution (February–June 1867)

Maximilian entered the city of Querétaro with his 1,600 troops and a dozen fieldpieces on February 19, 1867, being well received by its garrison commander, General Escobar, as well as the populace at large. After a *Te Deum* at the cathedral, the Spanish casino was prepared as his residence and a banquet held that evening. Three days later, the imperial general José Ramón Méndez arrived from Morelia with 3,500 more troops, bringing the total number of the city's defenders to 12,000 men.

However, advance republican cavalry units began appearing outside the city on March 6, 1867, being joined two days later by their main bodies under the northern Gens. Mariano Escobedo and Ramón Corona. Eventually, this host would swell to 32,000 troops and 100 guns, laying siege to the city. Maximilian was headquartered in La Cruz Convent,

The captive Maximilian was put on trial at the Iturbide Theater in Querétaro on May 24, 1867, along with Miramón and Mejía.

At 4:00 a.m. on June 19, 1867, a priest arrived at Maximilian's cell within Las Capuchinas, finding him already awake and neatly dressed. After attending Mass an hour later, the emperor ate a light meal of coffee, bread, some chicken, and red wine at 5:45 a.m., after which republican colonel Miguel Palacios entered at 6:00 a.m. to escort him to the execution ground. Maximilian, Miramón, and Mejía each boarded one of three separate carriages, accompanied by a priest and a companion or two, which were driven toward the Cerro de las Campanas. Heavily escorted, this procession was observed quietly as it moved through the streets by civilian onlookers.

When the carriages reached the grounds, 4,000 republican troops were drawn up in silent ranks. The three prisoners were led to an execution wall that had been extemporized out of adobe bricks, where Maximilian distributed gold coins among the firing squad, asking them to aim at his chest. At the last moment, he allowed Miramón the honor of standing at the center of their group, and all three spoke a few last words.

The emperor thereupon separated his long, blond beard and draped its tips over his shoulders, so as to leave his chest exposed. At the command, the squad fired six bullets into him so that he fell backward and remained with an upraised arm feebly moving about and mumbling inaudibly until a *coup-de-grace* was quickly added at point-blank range into his heart. His clothing caught fire briefly before being extinguished with a dash of water, after which Maximilian was pronounced legally dead at 7:05 a.m.

See also: Escobedo Peña, Mariano Antonio Guadalupe; French Intervention, War of the; Márquez Araujo, Leonardo; Miramón Tarelo, Miguel Gregorio de la Luz Atenógenes; San Jacinto, Battle of (1867).

Further Reading

Causa de Fernando Maximiliano de Hapsburgo y sus generales Miguel Miramón y Tomás Mejía. Guadalajara: Instituto Jalisciense de Historia y Antropología, 1967.

de la Peza, Ignacio, and Agustín Pradillo. *Maximiliano y los últimos sucesos del imperio en Querétaro y México.* Mexico City: Imprenta de Ignacio Cumplido, 1870.

McCornack, Richard Blaine. "Maximilian's Relations with Brazil." *Hispanic American Historical Review* 32, no. 2 (May 1952): 175–86.

"Mexican Affairs: Departure of Maximilian from Orizaba." *New York Times*, January 10, 1867.

Moreno, Daniel. *El sitio de Querétaro, según protagonistas y testigos.* Mexico City: Porrúa, 1982.

Mexican-American War (1846–1848)

Unsuccessful struggle to retain Mexico's claim over its breakaway province of Texas

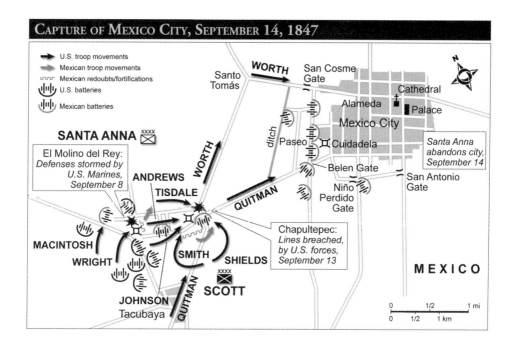

CAPTURE OF MEXICO CITY, SEPTEMBER 14, 1847

and that resulted in the further loss of its sparsely populated northern provinces of New Mexico, Arizona, and California.

Rising Tensions (March 1845–March 1846)

Because of internal divisions, Mexico's government by late 1844 was militarily powerless to reverse the separations of both Yucatán and Texas. Beset by mutinies and revolts, Santa Anna gave up all hopes of retaining the presidency and fled toward the coast by early January 1845, being captured en route and detained in the Fort of Perote, leaving Gen. José Joaquín de Herrera and others to dispute the title of president. As a result, when the U. S. Congress voted on March 1, 1845, to accede to American settlers' wishes and annex the Republic of Texas, the Mexican ambassador, Juan Nepomuceno Almonte, could do little more than depart in protest, while declaring that his government still regarded Texas as a breakaway province. Three weeks afterward, Mexico also severed diplomatic relations, to no effect.

On April 18, 1845, a U.S. naval squadron anchored off Antón Lizardo, southeast of the main seaport of Veracruz, while another arrived at Galveston in early May for a two-month visit. After the Anglo-Texans accepted the terms for annexation on July 4, 1845, the Mexican Army began a buildup near the mouth of the Río Grande, to which the U.S. government responded by dispatching 1,500 troops from Fort Jesup in Louisiana under Brig. Gen. Zachary Taylor, who disembarked and was encamped by July 31, 1845, at Corpus Christi, near the mouth of the Nueces River (traditionally regarded by Mexico as marking its border with Texas).

In order to help facilitate a reconciliation with Mexico, the U.S. naval squadron was withdrawn from near Veracruz on October 31, 1845, and the ex-Louisiana

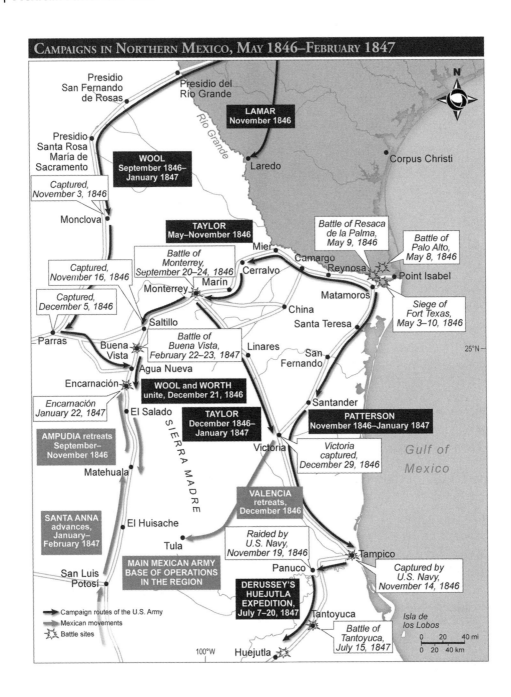

CAMPAIGNS IN NORTHERN MEXICO, MAY 1846–FEBRUARY 1847

congressman John C. Slidell arrived one month afterward to reopen diplomatic contacts with the Mexican government. Yet little progress was made as a military revolt against President Herrera erupted at San Luis Potosí on December 14, 1845, resulting in his being driven from office in favor of Gen. Mariano Paredes by January 2, 1846. Eventually, the Mexican troops stationed along the Río Grande were surprised when Taylor suddenly materialized at Point Santa Isabel on March 24, 1846, having pushed south from Corpus Christi with his 3,500 troops—deeper into disputed territory.

Border Confrontation (April–May 1846)

When Taylor's vanguard reached the northern banks of the Río Grande on March 28, 1846, he was given a frosty reception by Col. Francisco Mejía, the Mexican commander in Matamoros opposite, who considered this American advance from the Nueces River to be an invasion of national territory. But despite having a 3,000-man garrison under his orders, Mejía was not empowered to do anything more than observe as Taylor erected a star-shaped fortified camp for his 2,200 troops. Two days later, Slidell—having failed to reach any agreement with the government in Mexico City—departed Veracruz, and the war minister, José María Tornel, appointed Maj. Gen. Mariano Arista on April 4, 1846, to begin organizing an *Ejército del Norte* or "Army of the North" at Monterrey to confront Taylor's incursion.

The vanguard of this force—1,000 cavalry troopers and 1,500 infantrymen under Gen. Pedro de Ampudia—reached Matamoros one week later, who then directed Taylor on April 13, 1846, to begin retiring north toward Corpus Christi within 24 hours. The American general refused and in turn instructed his warships out in the Gulf to blockade the Río Grande, cutting off seaborne supplies for the Mexican garrison. President Paredes declared a "defensive war" against the American incursion, so Arista sent 1,600 cavalrymen across the Río Grande on April 23, 1846, a few miles upstream of Taylor's encampment, who the next day clashed with an American patrol.

Fearful that he was about to be encircled, Taylor left a single regiment and two artillery batteries to hold his fort, while marching with 2,300 soldiers back toward Point Santa Isabel on May 1, 1846. During his absence, the Mexican guns in Matamoros opened fire, so Taylor marched back to the rescue. He encountered Arista's 3,200 men drawn up at Palo Alto and defeated them on May 8, 1846, then again the next day at Resaca de la Palma. Because of the earlier clashes, Pres. James Polk officially asked Congress on May 11, 1846, for a declaration of war, which was passed the next day and signed by May 13th.

Northern Penetration (May 1846–February 1847)

Arista retreated out of Matamoros, so Taylor was able to push across the Río Grande and occupy this border city without resistance on May 18, 1846. A U.S. naval blockade was also imposed on Tampico and Veracruz, while Mexico's woes worsened when a revolt against President Paredes erupted at Guadalajara on May 20, 1846, amid growing dissatisfaction about his handling of affairs. The first contingent of a 6,000-man government army arrived to besiege that rebel city on June 12, 1846, and a protracted encirclement ensued. Meanwhile, a U.S. warship dropped anchor three weeks later off Monterey, California, to assist its American settlers in gaining their independence from Mexico. And just as Paredes was preparing to depart Mexico City on August 5, 1846, to invigorate his siege of Guadalajara, he was arrested and deposed by a mutiny in the capital's *Ciudadela* or "Citadel." Santa Anna returned 11 days later to Veracruz from his exile in Cuba, being allowed to enter that port by its U.S. naval blockaders because Washington erroneously believed that he would help conclude a peace.

Taylor, his army having been reinforced, advanced from Camargo toward Cerralvo with 3,200 regulars and 3,000 volunteers on

August 19, 1846, resting there for three weeks before striking out on September 12th across the 60 miles of burning desert for Monterrey, Nuevo León. Its 5,300 defenders and 1,500 local militiamen had been fortifying that city all summer against an anticipated American assault and so were able to resist for five days inside their thickly walled buildings before finally requesting terms on September 24, 1846. Taylor agreed to permit its garrison to march out with their arms and six guns over a number of days, retreating beyond Rinconada Pass, after which a two-month cessation of offensive operations would be observed. Both commanders were criticized by their governments for this outcome.

A stalemate ensued as Santa Anna departed Mexico City northward on September 28, 1846, traveling to San Luis Potosí to begin marshalling a 21,500-man army to dispute any deeper penetration toward central Mexico by Taylor. But once the truce lapsed, this American general merely pushed 60 miles west-southwest out of Monterrey to occupy undefended Saltillo, while the Gulf port of Tampico was also taken over by a U.S. Navy landing force on November 14, 1846. The leadership in Washington—having failed to bring the Mexican government to the bargaining table, despite occupying the northern portion of their country—now decided on a different strategy: rather than order Taylor to march south across the desert into the teeth of Santa Anna's waiting army, the U.S. Navy would instead transport another army to Veracruz so as to disembark closer to the enemy capital.

But before this second front could be inaugurated, Santa Anna struck. Learning through an intelligence windfall in mid-January 1847 that Taylor's army was being reduced so as to help constitute this new seaborne expedition under Gen. Winfield Scott, Santa Anna broke camp at San Luis Potosí in hopes of surprising Taylor's diminished force with a quick strike. However, despite an epic trek through the desert to rendezvous south of Saltillo, his 14,000 Mexican troops could not defeat Taylor on February 22–23, 1847, at the Battle of Buena Vista or La Angostura.

Eastern Invasion (March–October 1847)

Scott's 8,600 troops and a 1,200-man naval contingent came ashore southeast of Veracruz on March 9, 1847, encircling and securing that city 20 days afterward. Santa Anna meanwhile regained Mexico City from San Luis Potosí with his two best surviving divisions and prepared to confine this enemy invasion force in the pestilential coastal lowlands, rather than permitting them to march up into the cooler and healthier highlands. Therefore, when Scott's divisions started departing occupied Veracruz in stages on April 8, 1847, aiming to take the city of Jalapa, Santa Anna positioned himself four miles to its east with 12,000 troops (many of them raw conscripts) and 43 fieldpieces, only to be outflanked and driven back at the Battle of Cerro Gordo on April 17–18, 1847.

Suffering the Americans to occupy Jalapa, and Puebla one month later without resistance, Santa Anna began concentrating his forces in the Valley of Mexico so as to defend the national capital. He was relieved when seven of Scott's volunteer regiments, representing 3,000 men, quit the expedition because their terms of enlistment had expired, leaving the American commander with only 5,820 effectives—too few to push on toward Mexico City. Instead, Scott would have to wait for three months in Puebla until sufficient reinforcements arrived to resume his offensive.

Learning that the invaders had been reinforced and were at last moving out of Puebla during the first week of August 1847, Santa Anna ordered his brigades to begin entering the prepared defensive works atop El Peñón de los Baños—a prominence 10 miles east of the capital, on the rim of the Valley of Mexico—so as to make their stand. But Scott's 7,200-man army bypassed this strongpoint on August 16, 1847, instead descending into the valley by a less strongly defended route. The invaders then continued slipping around other southeastern outposts as well, all the while drawing ever closer to Mexico City. Santa Anna tried to counter these flanking moves by hastily redeploying his forces and mounting unsuccessful stands at the Battles of Contreras and Churubusco, after which his Mexican troops fought a stubborn defensive action at the Molino del Rey complex on September 7, 1847, that briefly checked Scott's approach.

But the Americans subsequently began sliding around yet again, edging still farther west and overrunning Chapultepec Castle by September 13, 1847, while other columns swept on past toward Mexico City's western gates. Having suffered 1,800 casualties that day, Santa Anna gave the order at 1:00 a.m. on September 14, 1847, for his surviving troops to evacuate the capital northward via Guadalupe, so the Americans entered the next morning to negligible opposition. Santa Anna meanwhile ordered Brig. Gen. José Joaquín de Herrera to march the scattered remnants of their defeated army north to begin reconstituting a military force at Querétaro, then resigned the presidency in favor of Chief Justice Manuel de la Peña y Peña on September 15, 1847. Santa Anna subsequently proceeded over the mountain range with a small force and attempted to overwhelm Puebla's U.S. Army garrison at Puebla in late September–early October,

1847, thereby threatening Scott's supply lines, to no avail.

Occupation (November 1847– July 1848)

Unable to resist further, delegates from eight unoccupied Mexican states met on November 18, 1847, agreeing to undertake the thankless chore of reaching a peace accord with the victorious Americans. After fitful negotiations by this faction-plagued rump of a government, the Treaty of Guadalupe Hidalgo was signed on February 2, 1848. By its terms, the provinces of California, Nevada, Utah, Colorado, Arizona, and New Mexico were ceded to the Americans, while all Mexican claims to Texas were abandoned forever. This agreement was ratified by the U.S. Congress on March 10, 1848, and by the Mexican Congress on May 19, 1848. Veracruz was restored to Mexico's control one month later, and the last of 18,300 American troops departed through there by the end of July.

See also: Ampudia Grimarest, Pedro; Buena Vista, Battle of; Cerro Gordo, Battle of; Chapultepec, Battle of; Churubusco, Battle of; Contreras, Battle of; flying artillery; Monterrey, Battle of; Niños Héroes; Palo Alto, Battle of; Puebla, American Defense of; San Patricio Battalion; Santa Anna, Antonio López de; Veracruz, U.S. Bombardment and Occupation of.

Further Reading

Bauer, Karl J. *The Mexican War, 1846–1848.* Lincoln: University of Nebraska Press, 1992.

Butler, Stephen R. *A Documentary History of the Mexican War.* Richardson, TX: Descendants of Mexican War Veterans, 1995.

Field, Ron. *Mexican-American War, 1846–1848.* London: Brassey's, 1997.

Fowler, Will. *Santa Anna of Mexico*. Lincoln: University of Nebraska Press, 2009.

Frías, Heriberto. *Episodios militares mexicanos: segunda parte, invasión norteamericana*. Mexico City: Viuda de C. Bouret, 1901.

Levinson, Irving. *Wars within Wars: Mexican Guerrillas, Domestic Elites, and the United States of America, 1846–1848*. Fort Worth: Texas Christian University Press, 2005.

Santoni, Pedro. *Mexicans at Arms: Puro Federalists and the Politics of War, 1845–1848*. Fort Worth: Texas Christian University Press, 1996.

Tucker, Spencer C. *The Encyclopedia of the Mexican-American War: A Political, Social, and Military History*. Santa Barbara, CA: ABC-CLIO, 2013.

Mexican Revolution (1910–1920).

See Revolution, Mexican (1910–1920).

Miahuatlán, Battle of (1866)

First in a pair of republican victories won in quick succession outside the city of Oaxaca over a Franco-conservative pursuit column during the War of the French Intervention.

Background (Summer 1866)

Having failed to stamp out all liberal resistance throughout Mexico, despite more than four years of active campaigning with full military support from their French allies, the imperial garrisons began to dwindle in strength once Paris announced that it was preparing to withdraw its expeditionary force from this conflict. Heartened by this development, Gen. Porfirio Díaz had devised a strategy in the remote state of Oaxaca whereby his recently reconstituted *Ejército de Oriente* or "Eastern Army" would harass the imperial defenders of its capital city out of the south, while his

brother Félix did the same with a detachment striking out of the Sierra of San Felipe del Agua to its north. Their aim was for one or the other brother to lure away a portion of its imperial defenders, so the remaining, unengaged republican force could then make a descent on the city's understrength garrison during this absence.

Porfirio Díaz's 1,100-man army had consequently been chased by a similar-sized imperial column under the conservative general Carlos Oronoz, although the latter force consisted of a well-armed Chasseur battalion and the 9th French Line Infantry Regiment, several cavalry squadrons under Gen. Mariano Trujeque, and two 12-inch fieldpieces. Since the republicans could not match the superior firepower of these disciplined French formations, they had to keep a wary distance. On October 1, 1866, Díaz's vanguard under Lt. Col. Feliciano García Bustamante reached the town of Miahuatlán, followed by the remainder of his force the next day, settling down to await reinforcement by a republican cavalry brigade, as Oronoz's pursuit column was believed to be likewise resting 24 miles farther northwest at Ejutla.

However, suddenly at dawn on October 3, 1866, Díaz—who had scheduled a *revista de comisario* or "formal inspection" of his army for that same afternoon—was informed by his frantic scouts that the 1,200 French and imperial troops had stolen a march and were fast closing in, their dust clouds now plainly visible from the republican encampment. Díaz sallied with 30 cavalrymen to observe the enemy approach, while giving orders for his infantry commander, Col. Manuel González, to immediately lead the foot soldiers across the Miahuatlán River and dig in atop the Nogales Hills, facing northwestward. His force consisted of Col. Manuel

González's 130-man brigade; Lt. Col. Juan J. Cano's 100-man Morelos Battalion; Cmdr. Felipe Cruz's 230 *Tiradores de Montaña* or "Mountain Rangers"; Col. José Segura's 96-man Patria Battalion; an 80-man militia company from Chiautla; the 130-man "Fieles de la Patria" Battalion; and 40 local militiamen known as the *Cuerudos* under Capt. Apolinar García.

They were attacked by 1,100 French and imperial troops under Gen. Carlos Oronoz, consisting of an infantry brigade (a Chasseur battalion and the 9th French Line Regiment), several cavalry squadrons under General Trujeque, and two 12-inch fieldpieces. They closed in on the republican positions from Matadero Rise in three columns, preceded by a skirmishing line and long-range bombardment.

Díaz checked them along Nogales Ravine, then sent his cavalry—spearheaded by the Tepejí squadron—across the Miahuatlán River to circle behind and fall on the enemy's right rear. Oronoz fled the battlefield, leaving behind some 70 dead (including his French second-in-command, Col. Henri Testard) as well as 400 prisoners and two artillery pieces. Republican losses totaled 59 killed and 140 wounded.

Aftermath (October 5–16, 1866)

Taking advantage of this crushing victory, Col. Félix Díaz's cavalry occupied most of Oaxaca City on October 5, 1866, being joined the next day by Porfirio Díaz's main army, which besieged Oronoz's remaining followers within its Santo Domingo, El Carmen, and La Soledad strongholds. Learning on October 16th that another 1,500 Austrian and imperial troops were marching to the garrison's relief, Porfirio Díaz sortied and defeated them as well at the Battle of La Carbonera.

See also: Díaz Mori, José de la Cruz Porfirio; La Carbonera, Battle of; French Intervention, War of the.

Further Reading

House Documents. Washington, DC, 1867, vol. 4, no. 2, 304–9.

Tamayo, Jorge L., compiler. *Benito Juárez: documentos, discursos y correspondencia.* Mexico City: Universidad Autónoma Metropolitana Azcapotzalco, 2006.

Mina's Expedition (1817)

A young Spanish adventurer and an avowed antimonarchist, Mina recruited Spanish, Italian, English, and American followers during a cruise from Liverpool to Norfolk (Virginia), Baltimore, Saint Thomas in the Virgin Islands, Port-au-Prince, Galveston, and New Orleans, sailing aboard the hired American ships *Cleopatra*, *Neptuno*, and *Congreso Mexicano*.

After riding out a brief storm in the Gulf of Mexico, Mina disembarked on April 15, 1817, at Soto la Marina with 500 foreign mercenaries under Henry Perry to bolster the Mexican insurgency's flagging fortunes. He erected a fort on the eastern side of Soto la Marina's plaza using artillery from his ships before dispatching them for supplies and reinforcements.

On May 17, 1817, the Spanish frigate *Sabina*, plus the schooners *Belona* and *Proserpina*, appeared from Veracruz under Commo. Francisco Berenguer and sank one of Mina's remaining ships, drove another aground, and forced the remainder to flee. Thus cut off at sea, Mina decided to strike inland one week later with 300 men to join forces with other insurgents, while leaving behind a 200-man garrison under Maj. José Sardá to hold Soto la Marina. After rustling

700 horses from Cojo Hacienda, fording the Tamesí River, and emerging into the Valle del Maíz, Mina defeated a force of 152 royalists under Captain Villaseñor.

June 11, 1817: The royalist commander Arredondo arrived from Veracruz with 666 foot soldiers, 850 riders, and 109 gunners to besiege Mina's garrison remaining under Major Sardá at Soto la Marina, compelling its 93 men to surrender five days later. The prisoners were conducted into captivity at San Juan de Ulúa and the fortress at Perote near Jalapa.

While continuing his march toward San Luis Potosí, Mina defeated 2,000 royalists drawn up at the Hacienda of Peotillos under Col. Benito Armiñán on June 15, 1817, then four days later surprised and occupied Real de Pinos with a nocturnal attack. He then linked up with some Mexican insurgents on June 22nd, reaching Fort Sombrero in the Comanja range two days afterward to join forces with the guerrilla chieftains Pedro Moreno and Encarnación "El Pachón" Ortiz.

Mina and Moreno sortied from Fort Sombrero with 330 followers on June 29, 1817, mauling a royalist force under Col. Cristóbal Ordóñez at Ferrero Ranch on the Hacienda of San Juan de los Llanos, killing this commander and capturing 152 of his men. This victory allowed the insurgents to seize 140,000 pesos in silver bars at the Jaral Hacienda on July 7th before moving on to attempt the city of León.

Failing in this endeavor, Mina and Moreno became besieged within their Fort Sombrero base camp on August 1, 1817, by 3,500 royalists under *mariscal de campo* or "field marshal" Pascual Liñán. These forces stormed the fort's defenses three days later, only to be repelled; then the insurgents in turn failed to cut their way out of their encampment on August 7, 1817. Mina and Moreno managed to slip away that following night with part of their small army, then attempted to rescue their trapped colleagues by attacking Liñán's positions from the rear on August 12, 1817. When this failed, Mina and Moreno withdrew five days later to reinstall themselves at Remedios Fort near Pénjamo, leaving their beleaguered associates to surrender to the royalists by August 19th.

October 10, 1817: While returning toward their base camp at Remedios after raiding San Luis de la Paz, Mina and Moreno are defeated in a clash at the Caja Hacienda by royalists under Col. Francisco Orrantia.

On October 25, 1817, Mina and other insurgent leaders attempted to attack the royalist garrison within Guanajuato City with 1,400 men, only to be repulsed. Two days afterward, while sleeping at Venadito Ranch, Mina and Moreno were surprised with their aides by a monarchist column under Orrantia, all being slain except Mina, who was carried into Liñán's encampment near Fort Remedios to be shot on November 11th atop Bellaco Hill. Because of this royalist success, the Mexican viceroy, Juan Ruiz de Apodaca, was rewarded from Madrid with the title of "Conde de Venadito."

See also: Appendix, section titled "Viceroyal Mexico's Spanish and Loyalist Forces, September 1816."

Further Reading

Guzmán R., José R. "Francisco Javier Mina en la isla de Gálveston y Soto la Marina." *Boletín del Archivo General de la Nación* [Mexico], 2nd series, 7, no. 4 (October–December 1966): 898–1081.

Guzmán R., José R. "La correspondencia de don Luis de Onís sobre la expedición de Javier Mina." *Boletín del Archivo General de la Nación* [Mexico], 2nd series, 9, nos. 3–4 (July–December 1968): 509–44.

Ortuño Martínez, Manuel. *Brush, Webb, Bradburn y Terrés: diarios*. Mexico City: Trama Editorial, 2011.

Ortuño Martínez, Manuel. *Expedición a Nueva España de Xavier Mina*. Pamplona: Universidad Pública de Navarra, 2006.

Miramón Tarelo, Miguel Gregorio de la Luz Atenógenes (1831–1867)

Dashing conservative commander during the War of the Reform who became the youngest-ever president of Mexico and was executed beside the emperor Maximilian.

He was born in Mexico City on November 17, 1831, the fifth child and second son out of what would eventually be 13 children sired by Lt. Col. Bernardo Miramón Arrequívar with his wife, María del Carmen Tarelo Segundo de la Calleja. In his childhood, young Miguel studied at the prestigious San Gregorio College until his father was assigned to a tour of duty in Tlaxcala, at which time he enrolled his 15-year-old son, Miguel (like his older brother Joaquín before him), in the Military College at Chapultepec Castle on February 10, 1846, which then stood overlooking the western outskirts of the capital.

Early Military Career (1847–1855)

As a cadet, the teenaged Miramón chose to remain and take part in the academy's unsuccessful defense against the American invasion of September 1847, being slightly wounded and captured during its final assault. Released on February 29, 1848, along with almost 50 of his classmates, he would return to his interrupted academy studies once hostilities ceased that same June, graduating by November 1851. The next year, he would be posted as a sublieutenant of artillery to the 2nd Division at the Fortress of Perote in the state of Veracruz.

Smart, well connected, and able, Miramón quickly won promotion to captain, then rejoined the academy as an infantry-tactics instructor on April 13, 1853. Staunchly conservative, he supported Santa Anna's return from exile and so was given command of the 2nd Active Battalion of Puebla later that same year, as part of the massive military buildup launched by the restored conservative dictator.

Miramón served against the liberal Revolution of Ayutla, which erupted in March 1854, although not immediately deployed. Put in command of the Baja California Activo Battalion, which was stationed at Toluca, Miramón wounded a civilian in a duel and had consequently been detained until this opponent recovered, at which point he was allowed to belatedly join Santa Anna's unsuccessful campaigns down into the state of Guerrero. Miramón subsequently participated in the clashes at Mescala, Xochipala, and Zopilote Canyon before winning field promotion to lieutenant colonel as a result of his conduct during the Battle of Tepemajalco.

Conservative Mutineer and Renegade (1856–1857)

Santa Anna was overcome militarily and exiled once again by August 1855, yet the new liberal administration of interim president Ignacio Comonfort would nonetheless confirm the 24-year-old Miramón's promotion to lieutenant colonel and second-in-command of the 11th Line Regiment that same December 10, 1855. But when this unit was sent out four days later to help put down a conservative uprising at Zacapoaxtla, Miramón mutinied and arrested his superior, Col. Rafael Benavides, at Tatlaquitepec on Christmas Day 1855, instead leading his contingent to join this revolt with shouts of *¡Viva la religión!* or "Long live Religion!"

The conservative general Antonio Haro y Tamariz thereupon escaped from confinement to assume military leadership of this rebellion, and the mutineers pushed their way into the city of Puebla by January 23, 1856, fortifying themselves against the inevitable liberal counteroffensive. Miramón figured among such men as Leonardo Márquez, Luis G. Osollo, Severo del Castillo, among others, who would all become prominent generals during the War of the Reform. However, the 4,000 conservative rebels holding Puebla were soon challenged by a 16,000-man liberal army under President Comonfort, and a sally by Haro was bested at the Battle of Ocotlán on March 8, 1856. As a result, the conservatives surrendered Puebla two weeks later, Haro and other commanders fleeing the country through the port of Veracruz, while Miramón remained hidden by sympathizers within the city.

That same autumn, the 24-year-old fugitive participated in another bold venture when Capt. Leónides Campo arrived unannounced at Puebla's municipal palace at 1:00 a.m. on October 20, 1856, declaring that he was bringing in two prominent captives: the conservative renegades Miramón and Francisco A. Vélez. Awakening the liberal military governor, Gen. José María García Conde, Campo requested that these prisoners be incarcerated in the same cell as Lt. Col. Luis Reyes; but when the governor complied, it proved to have been a ruse. He was suddenly disarmed by Campo, and the four conservative officers allowed their fellow conspirator Col. Joaquín

Francisco Orihuela to gain entry into the palace and assume command over the city garrison.

Six days later, the liberal general Tomás Moreno arrived outside Puebla with 4,000 troops and 30 artillery pieces, laying siege to the city once more, being superseded the next month by the 23-year-old brigadier general Leandro Valle Martínez. Conservative resistance finally collapsed on December 15, 1856, their leaders once again scattering. Orihuela was overtaken and executed at San Andrés Chalchicomula, but Miramón—an academy classmate of Valle—was apparently allowed to escape along with Vélez, Manuel Ramírez Arellano, and 100 men.

Shortly thereafter, Miramón attempted an assault against his old military base at Toluca, only to be repulsed. Wounded during this attack, he was sheltered by a friend in Mexico City until eventually found out and arrested by the authorities. Incarcerated in the ex-Acordada prison, Miramón managed to escape from there on September 13, 1857, and this time avoided recapture by hiding out at the rural hacienda of his friend Raymundo Mora.

Stroke of Fortune (January–May 1858)

When the moderate Comonfort—uneasy at continuing in office as reelected president under the newly "reformed" liberal Constitution—staged a false "coup" on December 17, 1857, with the assistance of his trusted aide at Tacubaya, Brig. Gen. Félix M. Zuloaga, their proclamation suggested that Comonfort remain as president, while dissolving Congress and drafting a less-radical Constitution. However, three weeks of confusion ensued, during which liberals throughout Mexico resoundingly rejected this proposition.

Gen. José de la Parra consequently led the Tacubaya garrison in a second, authentic conservative mutiny on January 11, 1858, aimed at removing the ineffectual president from office altogether. These mutineers seized the Ciudadela and San Agustín Church, while Comonfort held out in the Presidential Palace with perhaps 3,000 men, and independent liberal forces occupied the Santísima and San Francisco Churches as their own separate strongholds. After 10 days of this three-sided standoff, the youthful conservative colonels Osollo and Miramón led an assault against Comonfort's positions at dawn on January 21, 1858, defeating his dwindling band of followers and driving him from the city. The next day, an extemporized body of 22 leading conservatives dubbed the *Junta de Notables* chose Zuloaga as their "interim president," with Parra as his minister of war, who in turn rewarded Osollo and Miramón with promotion to brigadier general as of January 25, 1858.

Miramón immediately led a column due west from the capital toward his old base of Toluca, the mere threat of his approach chasing out its liberal garrison, so he installed a detachment before returning into Mexico City. Miramón then marched out of the capital for a second time on February 5, 1858, heading northwest with a vanguard brigade of 1,200 regulars to spearhead an army that was to push up into the Bajío and disperse the liberal militia forces that were gathering there in support of the legitimate presidential successor, Benito Juárez. An even larger contingent followed out of Mexico City a few days later under Osollo, the conservatives' chosen commander-in-chief, whose column merged with Miramón's and then met up with a third brigade under Brig. Gen. Tomás Mejía,

together entering the city of Querétaro uncontested on February 12, 1858.

Miramón served under Osollo in their subsequent victory at Salamanca on March 10, 1858, and triumphantly entered to Guadalajara two weeks afterward. Later that same month, the victorious occupiers learned that the liberal colonel Juan Zuazua was cautiously leading a small *Ejército del Norte* or "Army of the North" down from Monterrey to threaten the feeble 1,500-man conservative garrison holding the city of San Luis Potosí, so Miramón was hastily ordered from Guadalajara with 2,200 infantrymen, 400 cavalry troopers, and 12 guns in relief. Zuazua ambushed Miramón's column with 1,100 mounted riflemen as it came through *Puerto de Carretas* or "Wagons' Pass" on the night of April 17, 1858, inflicting several hundred casualties, although Miramón pushed past and gained San Luis, bracing for a liberal assault—which Zuazua deferred by instead disappearing westward with his entire army and surprising the city of Zacatecas on April 27, 1858.

Osollo was consequently obliged to depart the national capital on May 14, 1858, scraping together another army by the time that he entered San Luis Potosí in early June 1858. Miramón was detached with a strong force to rescue the conservative garrison at Guadalajara, whose ill-armed liberal besiegers simply vanished at the news of his approach on June 13, 1858. Miramón therefore continued farther south to fight a heavy but indecisive battle against a combination of liberal forces at the bottom of Atenquique Ravine (near modern Ciudad Guzmán, Jalisco), during which he learned that Osollo had died of typhoid fever at San Luis Potosí.

Conservative Savior (September 1858–January 1859)

Miramón returned to Guadalajara from his southern foray on July 21, 1858, chasing away yet another liberal siege force. Meanwhile, the situation in the Bajío had deteriorated for the conservative cause, both San Luis Potosí and Guanajuato falling to Zuazua's northern forces in the wake of Osollo's demise. The conservative leadership in Mexico City countered by ordering 4,000 troops to marshal at Querétaro and begin marching northward in three separate brigades by early August 1858, under the command of the veteran 38-year-old brigadier general Leonardo Márquez.

But when the latter made slow progress, Miramón used his influence to persuade the conservative leaders to entrust him with this campaign, despite being only 26 years of age. Hurrying to overtake Márquez's advancing columns, he assumed command and pushed cautiously into evacuated San Luis Potosí by September 12, 1858. The main concentration of 5,000 liberal troops was encountered two weeks later, entrenched at nearby Ahualulco de los Pinos, and soundly beaten in a two-day battle. Since Guadalajara had also fallen to Jalisco's liberals during Miramón's absence, he returned there with the main conservative army and routed them in a series of clashes along the banks of the Santiago River on December 14, 1858, reclaiming Guadalajara and driving the liberal army entirely out of Jalisco by Christmas 1858.

Commander-in-Chief (February 1859–December 1860)

For these feats, Miramón would be promoted to major general, and after the conservatives' "interim president" Zuloaga was toppled by a coup in the capital, this office would also be offered to him by a narrow vote in early January 1859, although he refused. The thoroughly discredited Zuloaga was consequently reinstalled on January 24, 1859, although one week later he appointed Miramón as his "substitute president," who reached Mexico City to be sworn in as the country's youngest-ever president on February 2, 1859.

As commander-in-chief, his strategy was to march down from the national capital and directly challenge Juárez's rival liberal administration in its transplanted headquarters at Veracruz, so Miramón left Mexico City on February 16, 1859, to personally supervise the assembly of 5,000 men and 46 artillery pieces at Orizaba. This army began departing in segments on March 2, 1859, so as to move through the torrid coastal zone in manageable groups, followed at a safe distance by its munition train. Harried by liberal guerrillas, Miramón's single vanguard brigade did not come within sight of Veracruz until 16 days later, and he did not gather sufficient strength to invest its defenses until March 24, 1859—when he learned that his vital powder train had never even departed Mexico City, so he had to order an abrupt about-face and retreat.

While retiring from this failure toward the national capital, Miramón furthermore heard that a liberal army under Gen. Santos Degollado was threatening to attack Mexico City during his absence and galloped back in on the afternoon of April 11, 1859—just in time to witness his bitter rival Márquez driving off the remnants of the shattered liberal army, having won all the accolades for rescuing the capital's conservative garrison and triumphed in the Battle of Tacubaya. Miramón's retreat from Veracruz had also assured American recognition of Juárez as the legitimate president of Mexico, so his liberal government began issuing even more drastic "reform laws," deepening worries among conservative supporters.

Miramón resumed field command that same autumn of 1859, as an unmistakable upsurge in liberal strength meant that several of their armies had suddenly materialized in the Bajío region of central Mexico, the largest—of 6,000 men and 29 fieldpieces—under an undaunted Degollado. Smaller conservative garrisons having been chased back out of Silao and Guanajuato City by his advance, Miramón ordered his own regiments to marshal at Querétaro and left Mexico City by stagecoach with his staff on the night of November 5–6, 1859, to personally assume command over a scratch army of 2,600 troops and nineteen guns.

He did not have to go in search of Degollado, whose army had reached Apaseo—18 miles west of Querétaro—by November 11, 1859. The liberal commander sent an emissary on ahead to propose a meeting between Degollado and Miramón; so the two generals met in the no-man's-land between La Calera and the Hacienda del Rayo at 4:30 p.m. on November 12, 1859. Unable to arrive at an understanding, Degollado left and positioned his liberal army overnight atop the hills of Estancia de las Vacas—less than six miles west of Querétaro—where Miramón confronted and unexpectedly beat them the next day, despite being outnumbered by more than two to one.

He continued on to Guadalajara, arriving to pealing church bells and a 21-gun salute on Saturday afternoon, November 19, 1859, arresting his conservative rival Márquez shortly thereafter on a charge of misappropriation of funds. Miramón then swept Jalisco of its own resurgent liberals, besting Ogazón at Beltrán on December 24, 1859,

and Juan Rocha at Tonila or Albarrada in neighboring Colima before returning triumphantly into the national capital.

In the new year, Miramón marched out from Mexico City at the head of a large army once again on February 8, 1860, to attempt a second siege of Juárez's government at Veracruz. Pushing his way down into the coastal lowlands and establishing his headquarters at Antón Lizardo by March 6, 1860, Miramón was joined offshore by two blockaders, secretly hired at Havana to supplement his siege efforts. However, these vessels were promptly captured by the U.S. warship *Saratoga* as suspected "pirates," additionally costing the conservative besiegers a pair of mortars and 1,000 shells that they were also transporting on board, so when Miramón began his bombardment of Veracruz on March 15, 1860, he soon ran out of heavy ammunition and was compelled to withdraw six days later.

His next crisis arose at Guadalajara, which was threatened with a renewed liberal offensive in early May, 1860. While planning his campaign to relieve its garrison, Miramón was annoyed when the sidelined Zuloaga circulated an "official" decree on May 9, 1860, revoking his long-ago appointment of the "substitute president." Miramón summoned Zuloaga to the Presidential Palace, and after ignoring him for hours, contemptuously informed his unfortunate predecessor that he would be taking Zuloaga along as a prisoner on this campaign, to "show him how the presidential chair is won."

At the head of 6,000 troops, Miramón raced liberal Gen. José López Uraga's 5,000-man division to Guadalajara, arriving just in time behind them to interrupt the liberal assault against that city on May 24, 1860. However, even after drawing off, this liberal army remained so strong that Miramón hesitated to attack it, once he

found these opponents dug in along Zapotlán Crest between Ciudad Guzmán and
Sayula on June 8, 1860. And one week
later, another 10,000-man liberal army
under Gen. Jesús González Ortega crushed
Miramón's anticipated 3,000 reinforcements
in the state of Aguascalientes; so the
conservative commander-in-chief left a
5,000-man garrison under Gen. Severo del
Castillo to hold Guadalajara on June 27,
1860, before hastening into Lagos de
Moreno three days afterward, to begin
concentrating his dwindling strength for a
showdown in central Mexico.

Defeat (August–December 1860)

With a rising tide of liberal armies closing in
on his depleted forces from various directions by early August 1860, Miramón
ordered a retreat southeastward out of the
city of León, Guanajuato, hoping to reach
Querétaro. However, his 3,300 demoralized
soldiers, 1,300 militia auxiliaries, and 18
guns were quickly overtaken while resting
outside of Silao on August 9, 1860, by
González Ortega's and Zaragoza's pursuing
8,000 liberal soldiers and 38 fieldpieces,
who the next morning pulverized the
conservatives in a short, sharp encounter.
Miramón was lucky to escape in the chaos
of his army's collapse, although his whereabouts remained unknown for a couple of
days, during which it began to be rumored
that he had been killed. Zuloaga, who had
been held captive in Miramón's train, managed to regain the national capital and
attempted to reclaim the office of president,
only to fail because of his utter lack of
conservative support.

Miramón himself reappeared in Mexico
City on the night of August 12, 1860, and
although temporarily obliged to relinquish
office as "substitute president" by the
conservative leadership, was restored

to power by a vote of confidence two
days later and desperately began seizing
money and men, so as to raise a new
army. His aura of invincibility now shattered, though, it was left to his bitter rival
Márquez to attempt to save the conservative
garrison at Guadalajara when it became
encircled by a huge liberal concentration as
of late September 1860. But Márquez failed
as well, being defeated at Tepetates Ranch
on the main highway near Zapotlanejo on
November 1, 1860, abandoning his
3,000 men in order to make good his own
escape.

Miramón was to consequently resume
field command, although his conservative
administration was by then so bankrupt that
it was reduced to extorting or stealing
funds from commercial interests to mount
any kind of defense. (For example, his
chief of police, Lagarde, broke into the
warehoused properties of the British Legation and commandeered 630,000 *pesos*,
over the heated objections of Ambassador
Charles Lennox Wyke.) Miramón's tactical
skill nonetheless reasserted itself when he
surprised and captured the liberal generals
Degollado and Felipe Berriozábal at Toluca
on December 8, 1860, although other liberal
armies still continued to close in on the
capital irregardless.

On the morning of December 19, 1860,
Miramón exited Mexico City with 8,000
conservative troops and 30 guns, intending
to give battle from the advantageous position overlooking the rolling plains around
San Miguel Calpulalpan, some 30 miles
east of the capital. González Ortega's
11,000 liberals and 14 fieldpieces nevertheless beat Miramón within the span of
two hours the next morning, so he staggered
back into Mexico City with only a small
group of retainers by midnight of December 22–23, 1860, and spent that day

entertaining grim options from his military advisers.

Some suggested further resistance, but with only 2,500 soldiers of dubious resolve left under his command and no one marching to his rescue, Miramón's officers convinced him to request terms. The Spanish and French ambassadors, along with the paroled prisoner Berriozábal, left that same afternoon of December 23, 1860, reaching González Ortega's headquarters at Tepejí del Río by midnight to ask for his conditions. The liberal general-in-chief replied that he was not empowered to negotiate so could offer only that the conservatives capitulate unconditionally or fight it out.

Informed of this stark choice, Miramón prepared for flight. Taking what little money was left in the Treasury, he officially delegated control of Mexico City to his captive, Berriozábal, at 9:00 p.m. on Christmas Eve 1860, then departed two hours later with about 1,200 men and a few fieldpieces, eventually being whisked out of Veracruz in January 1861 through the intervention of the French ambassador, Alphonse Dubois de Saligny, setting sail for Havana aboard a Spanish warship.

Exile (January 1861–November 1866)

The December 21, 1861, edition of the *New York Times* published the following item under "General City News":

Gen. Miramón, of Mexican celebrity, has very quietly arrived in our City, and has rooms at the Metropolitan Hotel, where he will remain until the departure of the next Havana steamer, on which he will embark for that port, en route to Mexico. The present intervention of Spain, France, and England in the political affairs of his native country, is the chief object of the General's attention, and the cause of his presence here at this time.

Miramón did indeed travel through Havana to reappear off Veracruz as a passenger aboard the British steamer *Avon* by January 27, 1862, only to be intercepted before stepping ashore by a Royal Navy boarding party and deported one week later back to Havana aboard the British steamer *Phaeton*, after which he continued across the Atlantic for Cadiz.

Miramón consequently pressed on to Mexico City, where he arrived by July 28, 1863, and on the advice of Archbishop Antonio de Labastida offered his services the next day to the commander-in-chief of the French expeditionary forces, Maj. Gen. François Achille Bazaine. As a very belated volunteer, he was only grudgingly accepted and not given any kind of military assignment until November 1863, when Miramón was ordered to begin organizing a division of 3,400 Mexican auxiliaries to assist Colonel Garnier of the 52nd Line Regiment in its advance on Guadalajara.

Displeased at finding himself subordinated to a French colonel, Miramón appealed in December 1863 to the Ministry of War in Mexico City, but Bazaine's opinion weighed against him. Miramón therefore threatened to resign his commission altogether in March 1864 and retire into private life, which was not allowed due to the impending arrival of Maximilian. Once crowned as emperor, the young monarch approved a suggestion of sending Miramón to study military science in Berlin, so he was sent to Germany with his family, where they remained for the next two years.

Return, Defeat, and Death (December 1866–June 1867)

According to an American observer, Miramón returned to Veracruz from Europe aboard a French steamer in mid-November 1866, accompanied by his aides and family. The emperor was then at Orizaba, considering abdication because of the imminent departure of the entire French expeditionary force upon which his regime depended. However, Miramón and Márquez, along with numerous other conservative leaders, convinced the young monarch to remain in Mexico and defend his title. Maximilian agreed to stay by December 1, 1866, and 12 days later departed for Mexico City so as to resume his imperial duties. Shortly thereafter, Miramón was appointed to command the army at Querétaro, which he then led on a typically bold venture.

Learning that the republican president Juárez was at Zacatecas, Miramón led his small army out of Querétaro, riding ahead with 2,000 imperial horsemen on a daring 250-mile dash northwestward to burst into Zacatecas five days later—Sunday, January 27, 1867—only to find that his quarry had been alerted and decamped for Fresnillo. Four days later, Juárez reappeared from Mexquitic with a much larger republican army under Generals Mariano Escobedo and Jerónimo Treviño, who chased down the retreating Miramón and crushed his column on February 1, 1867, between the Haciendas de Ledesma and San Jacinto on the road leading toward Aguascalientes. Escaping from this debacle with only 15 surviving cavalry troopers, the conservative general managed to ride out through the Hacienda de San Marcos at 8:00 p.m. that same night, leaving behind about 800 prisoners in republican hands (including Miramón's older brother Joaquín and 107 French troops, who were all executed on Escobedo's orders over the next four days).

His prestige diminished by this crushing failure, Miramón returned into Querétaro along with Del Castillo during the first week of February,1867 and awaited the emperor's arrival there. Maximilian entered with Márquez at his side on February 19, 1867, and two days later appointed Miramón's old rival as chief of staff for the city's defense, thereby subordinating Miramón under Márquez's orders as commander of the infantry alone, with his headquarters located atop the Cerro de las Campanas west of the city. Advance elements of a huge republican army then began to appear on March 6, 1867, taking a week to fully deploy into siege positions that encircled Querétaro. This host eventually swelled to 32,000 troops and 100 guns, heavily outnumbering the 12,000 initial defenders.

Márquez and Mejía commanded the few initial counterattacks against republican probes, until Miramón led a successful sally with the imperial *Guardia municipal* and *Cazadores* Battalions at dawn on March 22, 1867, supported by a half dozen fieldpieces and a cloud of cavalry, that surprised an approaching republican supply train that had just reached the Hacienda of San Juanico, capturing and carrying it intact into Querétaro with scarcely any losses. This strike furthermore allowed Márquez and Vidaurri to slip out of the besieged city that same evening with 1,100 cavalry troopers, having been ordered by Maximilian to cut their way through to Mexico City and bring back reinforcements.

Miramón sortied again on April 1, 1867 with eight infantry battalions and 1,000 dragoons to attack the republican siege lines extending from the San Sebastián Convent, northwest of Querétaro, but was quickly contained. A third sally with 3,000 troops in two columns at 5:00 a.m. on April 27, 1867, broke the republican encirclement at Cimatario and seized 21 guns and valuable provisions from supply parks in their rear, although the imperial troops then could not transfer these into the city before a massive response by republican cavalry drove them back into Querétaro empty-handed.

Three more sorties by Miramón were repelled on May 1, 3, and 5, 1867, while the effective strength of the imperial garrison was reduced to only 5,000–6,000 men, and civilians starved. Morale within the city fell, until a commander betrayed Maximilian's headquarters to a surprise assault by the republicans at dawn on May 15, 1867, and the emperor surrendered after reaching Miramón's defenseless Las Campanas camp. Both men, along with general Mejía, were put on trial in the Iturbide Theater nine days later, and condemned to death by mid-June 1867.

As a result, after attending a Mass and eating a light breakfast at dawn on June 19, 1867, Miramón, Maximilian, and Mejía each separately boarded a carriage with a few companions, to be driven through the silent city streets toward the Cerro de las Campanas under heavy escort. The prisoners found 4,000 paraded republican troops awaiting them, being led through their rigid ranks to an execution wall which had been extemporized out of adobe bricks. Miramón apparently fainted upon first approaching this site, and had to be helped to his feet, after which Maximilian at the last moment allowed him to stand at the center of their group. All three spoke a few last words, then the squad fired, the trio being declared dead shortly after 7:00 a.m.

See also: Ahualulco de los Pinos, Battle of; Ayutla, Revolution of; Estancia de las Vacas, Battle of; Márquez Araujo, Leonardo; Niños Héroes; Osollo Pancorbo, Luis Gonzaga; Puerto de Carretas, Battle of; Querétaro, Siege of; Reform, War of the; Salamanca, Battle of; Tacubaya, Battle of; Tacubaya, Plan de; Veracruz, Conservative Sieges of; Zuloaga Trillo, Félix María.

Further Reading

"Affairs in Mexico: Arrival of Miramón and the Meaning of His Movements." *New York Times*, December 6, 1866.

Cambre, Manuel. *La guerra de Tres Años: apuntes para la historia de la Reforma.* Guadalajara, Jalisco: Gobierno del Estado, 1949.

Daran, Victor. *Le général Miguel Miramon: notes sur l'histoire du Mexique.* Rome: Edoardo Pereno, 1886.

"From the Capital of Mexico: The Excesses of Miramón's Government." *New York Times*, July 26, 1859.

Galeana, Patricia. "Los conservadores en el poder: Miramón." *Estudios de Historia Moderna y Contemporánea de México* 14 (1991): 67–87.

"Important from Mexico: Miramón a Prisoner on Board the English Frigate *Challenger.*" *New York Times*, February 14, 1862.

"Latest Mexican News: The Flight of Miramón." *New York Times*, March 19, 1861.

Teixidor, Felipe, ed. *Memorias de Concepción Lombardo de Miramón.* Mexico City: Porrúa, 1980.

Molino del Rey, Battle of (1847)

Defensive stand that inflicted the heaviest toll on the invading U.S. Army during the series of encounters that were fought around the national capital in the closing stages of the Mexican-American War.

Prelude (August 1847)

Having pushed into the central highlands from occupied Puebla, the 7,200-man army of Maj. Gen. Winfield Scott then circled around Pres. Antonio López de Santa Anna's main defensive concentration at El Peñón de los Baños, 10 miles east of Mexico City, so as to instead descend into its valley via a less strongly defended route.

Crude American lithograph depicting the hard-fought assault on the Molino del Rey complex on the outskirts of Mexico City, September 1847. (Interim Archives/Getty Image)

On August 19–20, 1847, the Americans defeated the redeployed Mexican forces at the Battles of Contreras and Churubusco, so the next day Santa Anna sent emissaries to propose a truce for a discussion of terms.

Scott agreed to this request on Sunday, August 22, 1847, hoping that it might lead to a general armistice, so talks commenced two days later. But after nine days of fruitless exchanges, the U.S. representative presented an ultimatum to his Mexican counterparts on September 2, 1847, and meetings were adjourned for another four days. Hearing rumors that the Mexican commander-in-chief had recommended to his ministers during this lull that the city's defenses should be bolstered ("in gross violation of the third article of the armistice," according to Scott), the American general informed Santa Anna on September 6, 1847, that negotiations would be broken off the next day at noon, after which his American army would resume its offensive operations.

Believing that the U.S. forces would strike almost immediately after this armistice lapsed, the Mexican president ordered the brigade of Gen. Antonio de León—comprising the Libertad, Unión, Querétaro, and Mina militia battalions of the *Guardia Nacional* or "National Guard"—to take up positions in the complex of thickly walled, stone colonial-era buildings known as the *Molino del Rey* or "King's Mill" on September 6, 1847, to hold them as the left for a new Mexican battle line. The brigade of Gen. Rómulo Díaz de la Vega, consisting of the 4th Light Infantry and 11th Line Regiments under Gen. Francisco Pérez Arévalo, then arrived the next morning to take up positions in the Casamata out on the Molino's right flank, while in between the brigade of Gen. Gregorio Gómez Palomino—made up of the Fijo Battalion of Mexico

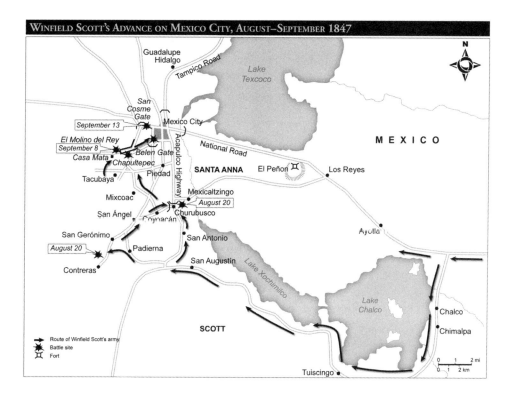

WINFIELD SCOTT'S ADVANCE ON MEXICO CITY, AUGUST–SEPTEMBER 1847

City, 2nd Light Infantry, and 1st and 12th Line Regiments under Gen. Simeón Ramírez, plus a field battery with six pieces commanded by Gen. Antonio Carona— entrenched themselves in a dry agricultural ditch running across the fields between both clusters of buildings.

Some 4,000 cavalrymen of the *Ejército del Sur* or "Army of the South" furthermore waited under Gen. Juan N. Álvarez in the middle distance near the Hacienda de los Morales, beyond cannon range west-northwest of the Casamata, while the 3rd Light Infantry and 4th Line Regiment were held back as a hidden reserve in the Chapultepec Woods.

Battle of Molino del Rey (September 8, 1847)

However, the Americans did not launch an immediate attack on September 7, 1847, so

Santa Anna began reconsidering his tactical dispositions and repositioning a few units in anticipation of a possible enemy drive against San Antonio Abad. But the U.S. major general had learned that same afternoon of the 4,000 Mexican infantrymen who were taking up defensive positions between the Casamata and Molino del Rey, scarcely a mile-and-a-third from his Tacubaya headquarters, with several thousand more looming in support beyond.

Consequently, wishing to drive back this concentration before his main army continued to circle around so as to take the commanding heights of Chapultepec, then initiate its final assault against Mexico City out of the west, Scott ordered brevet major general William J. Worth to employ his division and Brig. Gen. George Cadwallader's brigade, plus some 300 dragoons and a battery of heavy artillery—perhaps 3,500 men in total—to engage this line the next dawn.

Expecting the Mexicans to simply fall back before this show of strength, the U.S. guns deployed and opened fire on the morning of September 8, 1847, then their infantry swept forward in a frontal assault. The defense proved to be much more tenacious than anticipated, though, so this first wave of attackers faltered and had to retreat, prompting Scott to order Brig. Gen. Franklin Pierce's brigade to begin moving up from three miles behind, in case it should be needed in support. A second wave of attackers encountered the same stubborn resistance around the Molino del Rey and Casamata, so a fierce two-hour firefight developed, and a concerned Scott instructed brevet Brig. Gen. Bennett Riley's brigade to start moving up in support as well.

The outgunned Mexican defenders were meanwhile enduring heavy casualties, while frustrated because none of Álvarez's mass of waiting troopers moved to take the Americans in the flank. Conflicting directives and a breakdown in communications meant that the Mexican cavalry failed to intervene, so the defenders finally broke, and the U.S. infantry rooted them out of their trenches and strongholds.

Aftermath (September 9–17, 1847)

American losses nonetheless totaled 116 killed and 671 wounded for that day, as well as 18 missing, proving to be their costliest engagement of the war. Worth came in for much of the blame for such a high casualty figure, having failed to determine the true strength of the Mexican defenses before launching his headlong assaults. Mexican losses were comparably high as well: 269 killed (including General de León and Colonels Lucas Balderas and Gregorio Gelati), approximately 500 wounded—Miguel María de Echegaray, Díaz de la Vega, and Anastasio Parrodi among them—and 852 taken prisoner, along with four guns. Generals Manuel Andrade and Antonio María Jáuregui would be subsequently court-martialed for their cavalry's failure to intervene at an opportune moment.

With this obstacle removed, Scott's army continued to circle westward, assaulting and overrunning Chapultepec Hill by September 13, 1847, and occupying Mexico City two days later.

See also: Mexican-American War.

Further Reading

An Artillery Officer in the Mexican War, 1846–7: Letters of Robert Anderson, Captain 3rd Artillery, U. S. A. New York: G. P. Putnam's Sons, 1911.

Butler, Stephen R. A Documentary History of the Mexican War. Richardson, TX: Descendants of Mexican War Veterans, 1995, 228–29.

Frías, Heriberto. Episodios militares mexicanos: segunda parte, invasión norteamericana. Mexico City: Viuda de C. Bouret, 1901, 213–26.

To Mexico with Scott: Letters of E. Kirby Smith to His Wife. Cambridge, MA: Harvard University Press, 1917.

Tucker, Spencer C. The Encyclopedia of the Mexican-American War. Santa Barbara, CA: ABC-CLIO, 2013.

Mondragón Mondragón, Manuel (1861–1922)

Gifted weapons designer who eventually became stigmatized and exiled from Mexico for participating in the plot that deposed and murdered Pres. Francisco I. Madero.

He was born in the town of Ixtlahuaca, in the state of Puebla, the younger of two sons of José María Mondragón Esquivel and his wife, Concepción Mondragón Tello. Sources do not agree as to year of his birth, some variously citing 1858 or 1859, although it appears most likely that Manuel was born in 1861, the year after his older brother, José Jr. They were to be the only two children in this family, and both were enrolled in Mexico's *Colegio Militar* or "Military College" in the national capital during the late 1870s. Manuel, a brilliant student, graduated and received a *patente* or "commission" as a captain in the 4th Artillery Battalion dated December 7, 1881, the same day on which his older brother, José, was also appointed to serve as a lieutenant on the Army's senior staff.

Manuel married 25-year-old Mercedes Balseca Santos-Coy in La Candelaria Church in Tacubaya on April 22, 1885, with whom he would eventually have eight children. His commission as lieutenant colonel was dated March 1, 1894, and three years later he traveled to Paris with his family to supervise the production of his 75mm field gun. He remained there from 1897 until 1905, being listed on Mexican Army returns for 1899 as being officially still in charge of the Fábrica de Armas, although detached on a commission in Europe.

Decena Trágica (1913)

At 2:00 a.m. on February 9, 1913, Mondragón and Gen. Gregorio Ruiz initiated a mutiny against the increasingly unpopular president by marching into Mexico City from nearby Tacubaya at the head of the 1st, 2nd, and 5th Cavalry Regiments being joined en route by the 1st Artillery Regiment, for a total of 2,400 rebel soldiers under their command, backed by six cannon and 14 machine guns. Some 600 cadets from Mexico's *Escuela de Aspirantes* or Military

Preparatory School in Tlalpan also commandeered streetcars, leading the way into the heart of the capital that quiet Sunday morning so as to help support this insurrection. Meanwhile, one column of mutineers released Gen. Bernardo Reyes from imprisonment at Santiago Tlatelolco, while another freed Brig. Gen. Félix Díaz from Lecumberri Penitentiary.

By the time the mutineers began converging on the Presidential Palace, it had already been briefly occupied by the cadets, who in turn were overwhelmed by 500 troops of the 24th Battalion under elderly Gen. Lauro Villar, loyal to Madero. Lauro then furthermore arrested General Ruiz when the latter entered the main square, at which point a shootout erupted during which exchange the mutinous General Reyes and another 300 people—including many curious civilian onlookers—were killed, and another 200 wounded.

Repelled from the Presidential Palace, the mutineers withdrew and at 1:00 p.m. forced their way into the *Ciudadela* or "Citadel" arsenal less than a mile away, executing its commanding general, Rafael Dávila and numerous other defenders before digging in to fight it out. In the meantime, Madero had arrived from Chapultepec Castle at midday and appointed Gen. Victoriano Huerta (who had been dismissed from the army, so was in the crowd) as interim commander of the Presidential Palace in place of Villar, now badly wounded. Huerta summarily ordered the captive general, Ruiz, and all rebel cadets shot by firing squads, while Madero traveled toward Cuernavaca that same afternoon to summon a further 1,000 loyal troops under the more reliable and honorable 43-year-old brigadier general Felipe Ángeles.

Monday, February 10, 1913, passed in tense silence in the capital, which was shattered at 10:00 a.m. on Tuesday morning when an artillery duel erupted against the mutineers still holding out inside the surrounded *Ciudadela*, during which another 500 civilians were killed. (Eventually, 5,000 perished over the course of this urban fighting.) Upon Ángeles's arrival, he and his superior, Huerta, commanded a combined total of 6,000 troops, while only 1,800 remained to the trapped rebels Mondragón and Díaz; still, Huerta seemed incapable of reducing this ancient fortress, soon provoking doubts as to his loyalty.

After five more days of long-range shelling, the president's youngest brother, Gustavo, arrested Huerta at 2:00 a.m. of February 18, 1913, accusing him before Madero of treachery. Unconvinced, the latter ordered the general released. At 1:30 that same afternoon, Huerta in turn detained Gustavo Madero, then sent Gen. Aureliano Blanquet's 29th Battalion to capture the president, who after a brief struggle was seized along with his vice president, José María Pino Suárez, and most of the cabinet. By 9:30 p.m. on February 18, 1913, Huerta met with Díaz at the residence of the U.S. ambassador, Henry Lane Wilson—a vocal critic of Madero—to sign a pact whereby Huerta temporarily assumed the presidency, on the understanding that he would support the ex-Porfirian dictator's son during forthcoming elections.

Mondragón served briefly as secretary of war under Huerta, but given the many failures in stamping out the resurgent revolutionary armies, resigned this ministry in June 1913 and was dispatched to France by the government. He never returned. When World War I erupted, Mondragón moved from Paris with his family to San Sebastián in neutral Spain, where he would eventually die on September 28, 1922.

Further Reading

Prida, Ramón. *From Despotism to Anarchy: Porfirio Díaz to Victoriano Huerta.* El Paso, TX: El Paso Printing Company, 1914.

Sosa, Francisco. *Biografías de mexicanos distinguidos.* Mexico City: Porrúa, 2006.

Mondragón rifle (1891–1908)

Semiautomatic rifle designed and refined in stages by the military officer Manuel Mondragón to be produced in Europe.

As early as 1891, the 30-year-old Mondragón had come up with his original design for a bolt-action firearm featuring a gas piston that would automatically feed additional rounds into its chamber. The government of Pres. Porfirio Díaz encouraged further development of this weapon, in no small part for national prestige, so Mondragón was relieved of other duties and promoted to lieutenant colonel so as to devote himself to its refinement. A working model was officially unveiled on December 22, 1894, to be manufactured by SIG at Neuhausen, Switzerland and receiving US Patent 557079 as a new "Breech loading bolt gun."

In 1908, the Mexican Army officially placed an order with SIG for the purchase of 4,000 Mondragón rifles designed to fire 7x57mm Mauser rounds, the first 400 being ceremoniously stamped "Fusil Porfirio Díaz, Sistema Mondragón, Modelo 1908" in honor of this occasion. However, such precision weapons would prove unamenable to the lower-grade ammunition available in Mexico or any unusually difficult field conditions, so only 1,000 had been delivered by the time that the Porfirian regime was deposed in the spring of 1911. SIG managed to sell the remainder off a few years later to the German Army, who assigned these weapons for use by their air corps.

See also: Carabina 30-30; Mauser.

Further Reading

Fitzsimmons, Bernard. *Illustrated Encyclopedia of Weapons and Warfare.* London: Phoebus, 1978,18: 1933–35.

Hughes, James B., Jr. *Mexican Military Arms: The Cartridge Period, 1866–1967.* Houston, TX: Deep River Armory, 1968.

Mondragón 75mm field gun (1897)

Artillery piece originally designed by the Porfirian armaments specialist Manuel Mondragón, to be manufactured in France.

When the youthful lieutenant colonel Mondragón drew up plans for this sophisticated new weapon in the mid-1890s, Mexico lacked the industrial specialists necessary to cast and produce such a gun, so the Porfirian government entered into an arrangement with the French armaments company of Saint-Chamond to craft its initial prototype and then manufacture the first production-run. Mondragón moved to Paris with his family in 1897, and supervised the development of this new piece along with Saint-Chamond's own technical director, Lt.-Col. Emile Rimailho.

Unlike many 19th-century artillery-pieces which had heavy recoils, requiring them to be repositioned and re-aimed after each shot, this powerful new weapon featured "a hydraulic recoil absorber with a pneumatic recuperator" underneath its barrel that absorbed the heavy discharges, thereby minimizing the need for repeated adjustments. Mondragón remained in France for eight years until a working version was finally completed by 1905, of which some 100 guns were then produced and delivered to the Mexican Army. The 75 mm St. Chamond-Mondragón was considered a very fine piece, capable of firing 15 high-explosive rounds a minute, with great stability. The initial 1905 model was intended to be towed into action behind a team of six horses, while also drawing along a limber which contained 36 rounds of ammunition.

Service History (1910–1948)

This gun proved to be one of the highly prized heavy weapons of the Mexican Revolution. One of Pancho Villa's earliest victories as commander of an independent rebel "brigade"—over Gen. Félix Terrazas at the hamlet of San Andrés, just south of Chihuahua City in the autumn of 1913—was crowned by the capture of two heavy 75mm Mondragón guns, which his 1,200 ragtag followers then dragged aboard their three trains and proudly carried away as part of their booty, even though they did not know how to operate them. After capturing Ciudad Juárez a few weeks later, Villa challenged the Swedish-born mercenary Ivor Thord-Gray to make the pair functional, who had the requisite firing-pins (which had been removed) made across the river in El Paso, Texas, so as to command them in battle.

This artillery proved so decisive shortly thereafter to Villa's victory at the Battle of Tierra Blanca, that the delighted revolutionary rewarded Thord-Gray with promotion to "Major" as of Christmas Day 1913, and even named a nearby railway junction as *El Sueco* or "The Swede" in his honor. The 75 mm Mondragón gun was to be featured in many major battles over the next couple of years, especially in the well-equipped army of Gen. Álvaro Obregón.

Large numbers of a modified 1914 version were also produced in France during World War One, proving highly effective on the battlefields of Europe. Capt. Harry S. Truman of the 129th U.S. Field Artillery commanded a battery of these same 75 mm guns at Vosges and Verdun during the autumn of 1918. And even three decades afterward, Israel purchased 32 of these St. Chamond-Mondragón guns from Mexico in 1948, using them in defense of their new country. Still outfitted with wooden wheels, the Israelis nicknamed them *Cucarachas* or "Cockroaches," three of which survive in museums there today.

See also: Schneider-Canet 75mm field gun.

Further Reading

Estudio comparativo de los cañones de 75mm. de tiro rápido, Schneider-Canet, St. Chamond-Mondragón y Krupp. Mexico City: Secretaría de la Defensa Nacional, 1902.

Jowett, Philip, and Alejandro de Quesada. *The Mexican Revolution, 1910–20.* Oxford: Osprey, 2006, 16–18, 50.

Monte de las Cruces, Battle of (1810)

Costly insurgent victory during the triumphal opening phase of Miguel Hidalgo's uprising against Spanish rule, which apparently caused him to reconsider any direct assault against the viceregal capital.

Rebel Threat (September–October 1810)

Within the span of six short weeks, Hidalgo's insurrection had mushroomed into a mass movement, so by the time his so-called *Ejército de América* or Army of America began migrating southward out of Ixtlahuaca toward Toluca on the morning of Saturday, October 27, 1810, he was leading more than 80,000 armed followers on a slow progression into the Valley of Mexico. However, only 3,000 of his rebels were actually trained soldiers, mostly members of turncoat provincial militia regiments that had heeded his call to mutiny against the Crown.

Hidalgo's military second-in-command, Capt. Ignacio de Allende, had furthermore organized some 14,000 of the best-mounted volunteer riders into a large mass of irregular cavalry, but his wish to employ thousands of the barefoot natives as porters or laborers had been vetoed by Hidalgo—who instead acceded to their desire of being deployed into the main battle line, although they were armed with little more than machetes and bows and arrows. As this vast insurgent throng moved along, Peninsular Spaniards, Crown officials, and monarchist supporters fled out of their destructive path.

Defensive Maneuvering (October 27–29, 1810)

In order to check this threat, a small royalist force had been hastily sent more than 45 miles due west out of the capital into the city of Toluca, to dig in there under the youthful Torcuato Trujillo, a newly promoted Spanish lieutenant colonel. Several royal regiments having earlier been dispatched on counterinsurgency duties into the disturbed interior of the viceroyalty, Trujillo was left in command of only the Tres Villas Infantry Regiment under José de Mendivil and Dragones de España cavalry regiment, totaling scarcely 1,300 regulars and without any artillery. Some 5,000 monarchist militiamen, volunteers, and auxiliaries had also attached themselves to this small army but were of little military value, while Mexico City was reduced to being defended by the Viceroy Francisco Xavier Venegas at the head of its "Urban Commerce" and "Distinguished Patriots" regiments alone—two units composed of well-to-do civilians with no martial abilities whatsoever.

Hoping to check this rebel advance by entrenching his vastly outnumbered army into a strong riverbank position behind the Don Bernabé Bridge, Trujillo exited northward from Toluca that same Saturday, October 27, 1810—yet before he could reach the naturally defensible spot afforded by the Don Bernabé Bridge, his column was met at 7:00 p.m. that same evening by his advance detachment of dragoons, who were now retreating in sheer fright after having seen the enormous size of the approaching insurgent vanguard under Mariano Jiménez.

The young Spanish lieutenant colonel consequently turned his column about and made a forced march in the opposite direction, arriving so as to instead dig in at Lerma (east of Toluca) by midnight on October 27–28, 1810. The next day, Sunday, October 28, 1810, Hidalgo was greeted jubilantly into Toluca, a Te Deum being sung in his honor in its Parroquia de San Francisco before he retired to rest comfortably overnight on October 28–29, 1810 (in a house that is still preserved today as Toluca's Museo José María Velasco).

Trujillo, in the meantime—after waiting anxiously all day at Lerma without any further news of rebel movements—learned from a priest on Monday, October 29, 1810, that the insurgents were intending to traverse the river a couple of miles south of his position by crossing the Atenco Bridge so as to circle in behind the royalists and take Cuajimalpa in their rear, thereby cutting off any hopes of reinforcement or escape into Mexico City. Too late, the young lieutenant colonel detached some troops and auxiliaries toward Santiago Tianguistengo to destroy the Atenco Bridge, little realizing that Jiménez's insurgent vanguard was already streaming across it.

Furthermore, Hidalgo and Allende appeared shortly thereafter to the north and west of Lerma itself at the head of two huge rebel formations, which obliged Trujillo's few thousand royalists to make a desperate, daylong fighting retreat into a new position by 5:00 p.m. on that same Monday, October 29, 1810, atop a low wooded tabletop named Monte de las Cruces, astride the *camino real* or "royal highway" near La Marquesa in the municipality of Ocoyoacac.

Battle of Monte de las Cruces (October 30, 1810)

Both armies encamped within distant sight of one another overnight, and Trujillo received a despairing message from Viceroy Venegas in Mexico City at dawn on Tuesday, October 30, 1810, which concluded:

> Victory or death is our motto. If you must pay this price where you are, you will have the glory of anticipating me by a few hours in consuming such a welcome holocaust; for I shall not survive the discredit of being defeated by such vile and false people.

As daylight broke that Tuesday morning, an insurgent assault column led by Mariano Abasolo probed Trujillo's outer defenses, charging three times in the gloom until repeated volleys from the royalist infantry and countersallies by their mounted dragoons ensured the rebel commanders that the monarchists intended to stand and fight where they were, rather than continue retreating. Firing thereupon died down, as both sides retired to have breakfast around 8:00 a.m.

During that brief interval of rest, Trujillo's small army was reinforced by the timely arrival of 150 mounted militia lancers and two small 4-inch fieldpieces manned by a party of 50 men under naval lieutenant Juan Bautista de Uztariz. Trujillo ordered these two small cannon concealed with branches at the center of his battle line, in hopes of revealing their presence after luring the next insurgent attack into point-blank range. The forward-most loyalist pickets, mostly militia auxiliaries, were thereupon recalled back into the main battle line and the monarchists sat back to await the commencement of action. They totaled approximately 1,000 infantrymen, 200 dragoons, 150 militia lancers, and another 1,000 or so auxiliaries.

Around 11:00 a.m. on that October 30, 1810, the principal rebel assault column finally bore down on them, headed by four fieldpieces manned by the turncoat Guanajuato Battalion, backed by the Celaya and Valladolid Infantry Regiments, and protected on their flanks and rear by the Pátzcuaro, Reina, and Príncipe Dragoon Regiments. These 3,000 rebel soldiers were backed by thousands of mounted irregulars, and armed peasants intermingled among their formations. Trujillo recorded how a "great multitude of Indians" charged on ahead of the approaching rebels to howl at his lines "with no other object, I believe, than to intimidate my brave soldiers."

Several blasts of grapeshot from his concealed pair of cannons surprised and halted this insurgent advance, who thereupon countered by redeploying behind their own fieldpieces, after which a heated exchange of gunfire ensued. An attempt by companies on the rebel left to climb up a heavily wooded hill on the royalist right was countered by a monarchist detachment of three companies stationed atop that high ground under the 27-year-old lieutenant Agustín de Iturbide.

Trujillo's right was nevertheless pressed back through sheer weight of numbers, so he retired and re-formed his central battle line beyond an expanse of open ground to await the next enemy charge, hoping that they would consequently "have to emerge from the woods, where grapeshot might be used." However, while keeping the loyalist front fully engaged, the insurgents over the next three hours used the superior size of their army to continuously infiltrate riders and companies behind the monarchists by circling around through the adjoining forests. Rebel spokesmen also repeatedly called on their opponents to switch allegiance, so—much to his disgust—the haughty Trujillo was twice obliged to order a ceasefire so as to listen to appeals from their emissaries.

On the third occasion, the Spanish lieutenant colonel lured the insurgent messengers near to his ranks then ordered the banner of Our Lady of Guadalupe wrested from their "sacrilegious hands" and

> gave the order to fire to my nearby infantry, with which I finished off these dogs that I had before me and their seductions, freeing myself of being bothered any further with such matters.

Fighting raged on until 5:30 p.m., when royalist resistance finally collapsed. Trujillo managed to cut his way free from the battlefield with a couple of companies of riders (including Iturbide), reaching Cuajimalpa closely pursued by insurgent cavalrymen, so the Spanish lieutenant colonel rode on with his few retainers to gain the safety of Santa Fe by that same night.

Aftermath (October–November 1810)
Exact casualty figures are unknown, although it is believed that some 500 royalists were killed or wounded during the Battle of Monte de las Cruces, while many

more deserted into the rebel ranks, so Trujillo's small army virtually ceased to exist. Insurgent losses were perhaps 1,000 dead or injured, but the most surprising consequence of the rebels' victory was to occur in its immediate aftermath: for despite occupying Cuajimalpa uncontested with his Army of America on October 31, 1810, Hidalgo unexpectedly gave the order for his undisciplined throng to then veer around northwestward, heading out of the Valley of Mexico and away from the viceregal capital, toward Querétaro. One week later, his huge following would be dispersed at the Battle of Aculco by a royalist army out of San Luis Potosí under Brig. Gen. Félix María Calleja del Rey, and the insurgents' chance of toppling the viceregal administration was lost.

See also: Aculco, Battle of; Calleja del Rey, Félix María; Hidalgo y Costilla Gallaga, Miguel Gregorio Antonio Ignacio; Independence, War of; Iturbide Arambúru, Agustín Cosme Damián de.

Further Reading

Archer, Christon I. "Bite of the Hydra: The Rebellion of Cura Miguel Hidalgo, 1810–1811." In *Patterns of Contention in Mexican History*, edited by Jaime E. Rodríguez O., 69–93. Wilmington, DE: Scholarly Resources, 1992.

González Betancourt, Jorge. *Batalla del Monte de las Cruces*. Mexico City: Comisión Nacional para las Celebraciones del 175º. Aniversario de la Independencia Nacional, 1985.

Hamill, Hugh M., Jr. "Early Psychological Warfare in the Hidalgo Revolt." *Hispanic American Historical Review* 41, no. 2 (May 1961): 206–35.

Hamill, Hugh M., Jr. *The Hidalgo Revolt: Prelude to Mexican Independence*. Gainesville: University of Florida Press, 1966.

Monterrey, Battle of (1846)

Stubborn defensive action fought by this city's garrison early during the Mexican-American War, being eventually overcome by the U.S. invaders after three days of bloody street fighting.

Preparations (July–August 1846)

When Maj. Gen. Mariano Arista's defeated *Ejército del Norte* or "Army of the North" had retreated out of the border town of Matamoros, they endured a grueling 45-day trek through the northern wastelands before reaching Linares on June 29, 1846, where this officer—in one of his final acts as commander—ordered Lt. Col. Félix María Zuloaga to proceed into Monterrey with Lt. Col. Mariano Reyes's sappers and begin fortifying that city against an inevitable American assault. Arista was recalled shortly thereafter to face a court-martial, so his subordinate, Brig. Gen. Francisco Mejía, slowly marched the remaining 1,850 soldiers of the Ejército del Norte into this city as well, resting for two weeks at Cadereyta before finally entering Monterrey on July 21, 1846. Some defensive work had already begun under Zuloaga and Reyes and would continue to strengthen the city's most strategically placed buildings.

One month later, Gen. Pedro Ampudia—newly appointed commander-in-chief for the Army of the North—reached Monterrey from San Luis Potosí via Saltillo at midnight on August 29–30, 1846, bringing in 3,500 fresh soldiers and orders to supersede Mejía. Meeting at dawn with Nuevo León's Gov. Juan N. de la Garza Evia and other local commanders to discuss Monterrey's already-ongoing defensive labors, Ampudia decided to incorporate Mejía's division into his own army and make a stand at

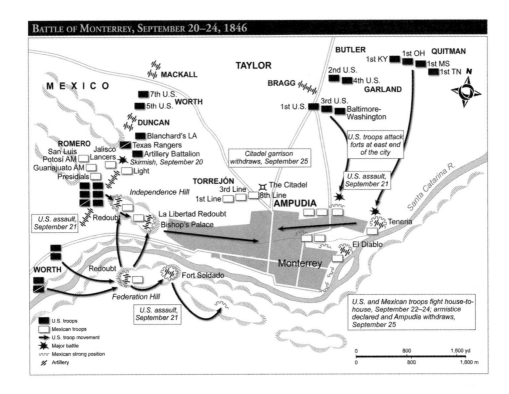

BATTLE OF MONTERREY, SEPTEMBER 20–24, 1846

Monterrey, rather than tear down its defenses and retreat so as to reconcentrate all of his strength at Saltillo, some 60 miles farther west-southwest. Nonetheless, the Mexican commander had personal doubts as to the loyalty of Monterrey's citizenry in support of the centralist government headed by Santa Anna, fears that were seemingly confirmed when Governor de la Garza Evia and several other officials resigned shortly thereafter, in protest against the demotion of their favorite, Mejía.

Yet Ampudia's 3,500 troops, plus Mejía's 1,850 and some 1,500 local militia auxiliaries, allowed the defenders to fortify themselves strongly in thick-walled buildings inside and around the city. Two weeks later, Brig. Gen. Zachary Taylor's vanguard began moving southwestward out of Cerralvo, his army exiting at intervals over the

next three days so as to traverse the 60 miles of burning desert to Monterrey in a spread-out formation.

Battle of Monterrey (September 19–23, 1846)

One week later—on Saturday morning, September 19, 1846—the first of Taylor's 6,645 troops came within sight of the city, being fired on as they closed the distance by its dark, formidable, eight-gun *Ciudadela* or "Citadel" (quickly dubbed the "Black Fort" by the advancing Americans). The next afternoon, Worth swung west in a flanking maneuver with Col. John C. "Jack" Hays's Texas Cavalry Regiment, Lt. Col. Thomas Staniford's 1st Infantry Brigade, and Col. Persifor F. Smith's 2nd Brigade.

Early on Monday, September 21, 1846, a mixed body of 1,500 Mexican cavalrymen and infantry under Lt. Col. Juan N. Nájera confronted this American column, suffering 100 casualties—including their commander—before retiring 15 minutes later, having killed or wounded only a dozen invaders. Thus, Worth sat astride the Saltillo road by 8:00 a.m., cutting off Monterrey's supply lines. At noon, he continued eastward up the nearby Blanca Hill to overrun its Federación and El Soldado strongpoints by nightfall. Taylor's main body also launched an assault against Monterrey's northeastern suburbs this same September 21st, during which Twiggs's 1st Division—temporarily commanded by Lt. Col. John Garland—and other units become enfiladed by various Mexican redoubts, suffering 394 casualties. Despite such punishment, the Americans captured the 200-man *Tenería* or "Tannery" stronghold and five Mexican artillery pieces.

While Taylor's main force recuperated on the rainy night of September 22nd, Worth stole up Independencia Hill and surprised its defenders. Lt. Edward Deas's 50 gunners manhandle a 12-pound howitzer to its 800-foot summit by noon, opening fire on the 200 Mexican troops holding the fortified *Obispado* or "Bishopric" under Lt. Col. Francisco Berra. They were finally overwhelmed by 4:00 p.m., prompting a discouraged Ampudia to call in all of his outposts that same night.

By the morning of September 23, 1846, the principal American army noticed that the Rincón or Diablo strongpoint lay abandoned, so they quickly occupied it with the 1st Mississippi Rifle Regiment under the 38-year-old colonel and congressman Jefferson Davis (Taylor's former son-in-law and later to become the Confederate president). Supporting units then began fighting their way into northeastern Monterrey house to

house, joined that afternoon by a similar offensive out of the west under Worth.

Aftermath (September–November, 1846)

By dawn of September 24, 1846, most of Monterrey was in American hands and Ampudia requested terms. The capitulation was signed the next morning, Taylor agreeing to permit the Mexican Army to march out with their arms and six guns over a number of days, retreating beyond Rinconada Pass, after which both sides would observe a two-month cessation of offensive operations. The conquest of this city had cost 120 American dead and 368 wounded, while the defenders had suffered 700 casualties.

See also: Ampudia Grimarest, Pedro; Mexican-American War; Zuloaga Trillo, Félix María.

Further Reading

Dana, Napoleon J. T. *Monterrey Is Ours! The Mexican War Letters of Lieutenant Dana, 1845–1847.* Lexington: University Presses of Kentucky, 1990.

Dilworth, Rankin. *The March to Monterrey: The Diary of Lt. Rankin Dilworth.* El Paso: Texas Western University Press, 1996.

Dishman, Christopher D. *A Perfect Gibraltar: The Battle for Monterrey, Mexico, 1846.* Norman: University of Oklahoma Press, 2010.

Rocha, Sóstenes. *Enquiridión para los sargentos y cabos del ejército mexicano.* Vol. 7. Mexico City: El Combate, 1892.

Spurlin, Charles. "Texas Volunteers in the Monterrey Campaign." *Military History of Texas and the Southwest* 16, no. 1 (1980): 5–22, and no. 2, 137–42.

Tucker, Spencer C. *The Encyclopedia of the Mexican-American War.* Santa Barbara, CA: ABC-CLIO, 2013.

Morelos Pavón, José María Teclo (1765–1815)

Rugged village priest turned guerrilla chieftain who would become the Mexican insurgency's most charismatic figurehead following the execution of Miguel Hidalgo.

Morelos was born on September 30, 1765, in the city of Valladolid (modern Morelia, Michoacán, later renamed in his

Modern depiction of the fiery rural priest and insurgent leader José María Morelos. (Library of Congress)

honor). He was the second son and third child of what would eventually be a family totaling nine children sired by a native carpenter named José Manuel Morelos Robles and his wife, Juana María Pavón-Pérez Estrada. It has long been claimed that Morelos was of mulatto descent, although this fact has never been clearly established or confirmed. And although most commonly referred to today throughout Mexico as José María Morelos y Pavón, his baptismal christening was actually recorded in Valladolid's cathedral registry on October 4, 1765, showing him as having been named José María Teclo Morelos Pavón y Pérez.

Working-Class Upbringing and Priesthood (1779–1809)

After his father died in 1779, the teenaged José was entrusted to the care of his uncle Felipe, a teamster who operated out of Tahuejo near Apatzingán. The 14-year-old had worked as a shepherd on nearby estates until he was old enough to join his uncle on his regular transport runs between Mexico City and the isolated Pacific port of Acapulco. After almost a decade in this employment, nearly 25 years of age and already the father of three children by three different women, Morelos had given in to his mother's insistence that he accept his great-grandfather's vacant bequest in April 1790 and study for the priesthood.

Morelos had thereupon been enrolled in San Nicolás Obispo College at Valladolid, whose rector was Fr. Miguel Hidalgo. The former teamster proved to be an apt pupil, graduating first in his class by March 1795, then receiving minor religious orders. On January 31, 1798, he had been temporarily appointed as village priest at Churumuco. Arriving there with his mother, Juana, and next-youngest sister, María Antonia, they soon found this locale to be so hot and unhealthy that he had requested a transfer. By the time that Morelos was reassigned to the parish of San Agustín Carácuaro on March 12, 1799, his mother had died.

Opening Campaign in the South (1810–1811)

More than a decade would pass in his priestly duties in this provincial backwater until word had arrived at Carácuaro during the autumn of 1810 of Hidalgo's insurrection against Spanish rule in the distant province of Guanajuato. Morelos had immediately returned to his native city of Valladolid to join his former mentor's cause. During a reunion held while riding between Charo and Indaparapeo on October 20, 1810, Hidalgo had commissioned his onetime student to "raise troops on the southern coast, acting in accordance with the verbal instructions which I have given him."

Morelos promptly rode on to Carácuaro and left there with 25 poorly armed adherents. At Coahuayutla, he was joined by several ranchers, the militia cavalry captain Marcos Martínez subsequently adding his 50 troopers to this small force at Zacatula as well as enlisting all the volunteer workers from Petatlán. Morelos had therefore appeared in the vicinity of the port of Acapulco with a couple of hundred followers by early November 1810 to raise the banner of revolt throughout that torrid coastal region.

Articulate, passionate, and with the common touch among people whom he had known ever since his youth, the 45-year-old priest would excel as an insurgent leader. Thousands would rally to his side to besiege royalist outposts and ambush their couriers and supply columns. Even after Hidalgo's betrayal and arrest in the north, Morelos would continue to campaign well in the southwest. His army overran Tixtla (modern Ciudad Guerrero) on May 26, 1811, defeating its 1,500 royalist defenders while netting 600 prisoners, 200 muskets, and eight fieldpieces; and when the royalist lieutenant colonel Juan Antonio Fuentes attempted to recapture this town on August 15, 1811, Morelos rode to the rescue of its insurgent garrison the next day with 300 riders from Chilpancingo, inflicting so many casualties among the demoralized royalists that they withdrew from the theater altogether, retreating up into the highlands around Mexico City.

Morelos consequently tried launching a three-pronged offensive out of his territory in early November 1811, sending one column toward Oaxaca under Miguel Bravo, while Hermenegildo Galeana took another toward Taxco, and Morelos himself marched with two companies of insurgents and 800 Indian archers to overrun Izúcar without opposition by December 10, 1811, followed by Cuautla de Amilpas on Christmas Day. However, one week later a 5,000-strong royalist army under Gen. Félix María Calleja destroyed Zitácuaro in a counteroperation, and within a month compelled Morelos to retreat into Cuautla with his main force on February 7, 1812.

Defeat at Cuautla (February 17– May 2, 1812)

Ten days later, Calleja's vanguard division of 2,000 royalists encamped two-and-a-half miles northeast of Cuautla at the hamlet of Pazulco, cornering Morelos inside the small city with 2,000 riders, 1,000 infantrymen, and 1,300 auxiliaries. The loyalist van advanced to probe Cuautla's defenses on February 18, 1812, only to have Morelos launch a surprise cavalry charge against their rear, during which he was almost captured but was rescued by his subordinate,

Col. Hermenegildo Galeana. Calleja launched a four-pronged attack against Cuautla's defenses the next dawn, only to be bloodily repulsed after six hours of desperate fighting, so he imposed a siege.

He was reinforced by an additional 5,000 troops under Brig. Gen. Ciriaco de Llano in late February 1812, and royalist batteries opened fire on Cuautla from its nearby hills while siege lines were begun from both north and south by March 5, 1812. Calleja also attempted to cut off the city's water supply, but the insurgents responded by recapturing Juchitengo Dam and held it against all royalist assaults. Nevertheless, hunger grew among the defenders as weeks passed, Mariano Matamoros leading a cavalry sally to contact an insurgent relief column that was approaching with food on April 21, 1812, only to fail to win his way back into Cuautla.

One week later, provisions within the beleaguered city were utterly exhausted, so Morelos decided on a desperate dash for freedom. At 2:00 a.m. on May 2, 1812, he led his starved insurgents quietly down Cuautla's riverbank until they encountered the royalist picket lines, at which point everyone charged and fought their way through as best they could. Losses were heavy on both sides, some of Calleja's royalist formations mistakenly firing on each other in the gloom, but Morelos's insurgent army was completely broken, disperse units being chased for many miles by royalist cavalry, while what remained of Cuautla was given over to a pitiless sack.

Renewed Guerrilla Warfare (Summer–Autumn 1812)

Injured during this escape from Cuautla, Morelos reached Ocuituco and went on to recuperate at Izúcar, while his surviving followers resumed making a few minor guerrilla strikes in that district. Once recovered, he united forces with Miguel Bravo and the Galeana brothers, using their combined strength of 800 insurgents to defeat a small monarchist force at Citlala on June 4, 1812, then moved southward into western Oaxaca so as to relieve Col. Valerio Trujano, who was being besieged within Huajuapan by royalist forces. This town was relieved by July 24, 1812, after which Morelos resumed his guerrilla operations against isolated Spanish garrisons in yet another theater, the region of Jalapa and Veracruz.

By early November 1812, his strength had resurged to 1,000 armed men, although Morelos failed to carry the city of Orizaba as planned. Therefore, upon being joined at his base of operations at Tehuacán by his subordinates Matamoros and Miguel Bravo, each bringing in an additional 2,000 followers apiece, Morelos marched away on November 10, 1812—pretending to be bent on attempting the royalist garrison holding Acapulco once more, although his real intent was to surprise the city of Antequera (modern Oaxaca).

Seizure of Oaxaca City (November 1812)

Morelos suddenly appeared in the Valley of Etla, only a dozen miles northwest of Antequera, with his 5,000 rebels and 40 crude guns on the afternoon of November 24, 1812. He sent a message on ahead the next dawn, calling on the city's royal governor to surrender within three hours. Having 2,000 monarchist defenders and 36 guns under his own command to defend this well-fortified city, the Spanish official rejected this demand, so the insurgent columns closed in and began their assault by 10:00 a.m.

They easily broke through everywhere, resistance by the unready monarchists proving so feeble that insurgent casualties totaled a mere 12 men. When Morelos entered the city triumphantly at 1:00 p.m. that same afternoon of November 25, 1812, he ordered summary executions of most of its remaining royal officials, dispatched detachments to subdue lesser outlying towns, and then set about installing an insurgent government for the entire province. Antequera would become his capital city for the next 16 months, an administration being formally constituted, all loyalist goods were confiscated, Morelos even personally supervised the recasting of its church bells into artillery pieces, and a short-lived newspaper was issued.

Capture of Acapulco (February–August 1813)

In a decision that has been questioned by strategists and historians, Morelos led a division out of Oaxaca on February 7, 1813, intending to invest the unessential and marginalized royal garrison at Acapulco rather than threaten the viceregal administration in central Mexico during a period of its greatest weakness. Instead, though, Morelos slowly took his 1,500 rebel troops west toward the Pacific shores, coming within sight of Acapulco by April 6, 1813, occupying its nearby heights and bombarding its buildings with a few fieldpieces until the royalists withdrew into their citadel of Fort San Diego six days later.

The insurgents thereupon settled down for a lengthy siege, eventually tightening their lines as of August 17, 1813, so the flow of supplies was cut off and enough hardship exerted for the defenders to capitulate three days later. Morelos's victory nonetheless proved a hollow one, as the fall of Acapulco did not directly threaten any major royal interest, although it did at least allow the insurgent chieftain to address the Mexican Constitutional Congress at Chilpancingo from a position of political strength when it convened on September 13, 1813.

Congress of Chilpancingo (September 13–November 6, 1813)

Fresh from his victory, Morelos arrived at Chilpancingo to preside over a meeting that he had called to provide structure and purpose to Mexico's struggle for freedom. It was attended by rebel representatives from New Galicia, Michoacán, Guanajuato, Puebla, Mexico City, Zacatecas, Tlaxcala, Oaxaca, and Técpan, and after some debate, they formally declared independence from Spain, while retaining the Catholic faith. A constitution was to be drawn up establishing legislative, executive, and judicial branches of government; private property was to be respected (although large landholdings were to be broken up and Peninsular Spaniards were to be deprived of their goods); slavery, torture, and payment of tributes were to be abolished; monopolies and class distinctions were to be eliminated; etc.

Morelos himself was offered the title of "generalissimo" with a formal style of address as "Your Highness," yet he refused, saying that he preferred to be called the *Siervo de la Nación* or "Servant of the Nation." After a brief recess, the Congress reconvened at Apatzingán on October 22, 1813, where a "Constitutional Decree for the Liberty of Mexican America" was promulgated, theoretically establishing an insurgent government with a weak executive branch and powerful legislature—the opposite of what Morelos had wished, although he accepted it as the best arrangement that he could hope for under the circumstances. Once the deputies signed a "Solemn Act of Declaration of Independence" from Spain on November 6, 1813, Morelos prepared to resume his military campaigns.

Defeats at Valladolid and Puruarán (December 1813–January 1814)

Gathering forces while advancing north-westward through Mezcala, Cutzamala, Huetamo, and Tzitzio, Morelos intended to assault his native city of Valladolid (modern Morelia), so as to conquer it as the capital for his new government. In Mexico City the viceroy, Calleja, learned of this design and countered by issuing orders on December 8, 1813, for 3,000 royalist troops to rush under General de Llano to reinforce its garrison. Morelos's subordinate Ramón López Rayón attempted to check this relief column at Jerécuaro on December 21, 1813, only to be badly beaten.

The next day, Morelos appeared south of Valladolid with 5,600–5,700 rebel cavalry-men and infantrymen, plus some 30 guns, deploying for battle onto its adjoining plains by December 23, 1813. However, his assaults were beaten back by the defenders, and his inexperienced troops—while retiring into their encampments for the night on Christmas Eve—were surprised by royalist infiltrators under Col. Agustín de Iturbide, whose unexpected volleys caused the insurgents to begin firing into each other's ranks by mistake and eventually dissolve into panic-stricken flight.

His army having disintegrated outside Valladolid, Morelos fled through Chupio with a handful of followers, ordering his forces to regroup 60 miles southwest around the Hacienda de Santa Lucía at Puruarán. De Llano exited in pursuit five days later, while Morelos's loyal subordinate Matamoros persuaded the insurgent generalissimo to avoid the upcoming battle. Indeed, the disorganized insurgents were once again surprised on the night of January 4, 1814, by De Llano's cavalry and completely routed by his main body the next day with Matamoros being carried into Valladolid as a captive. Morelos wrote from Coyuca offering to exchange 200 Spanish prisoners for his second-in-command, but this offer was ignored and Matamoros was executed by a firing squad on February 3, 1813—for which act Morelos angrily retaliated by ordering the deaths of his Spanish captives.

Demotion (January 1814)

In the wake of his twin defeats at Valladolid and Puruarán, the Congress sitting at Chilpancingo voted to remove Morelos as chief executive on January 17, 1814, assuming many of his powers for themselves and appointing his rival, Ignacio López Rayón, as commander-in-chief of the surviving insurgent garrisons at Tecpan and Oaxaca. Morelos consequently staggered back into Acapulco with only 100 demoralized survivors by early March 1814 and one month later learned that a royalist division under Col. José Gabriel de Armijo was closing in on this stronghold.

Morelos therefore torched Fort San Diego on April 9, 1814, hanged over 100 royalist prisoners, then disappeared into the Atijo Mountains one week later with a few loyal adherents. He continued operating out of the mountains against Spanish forces on a diminished basis for the next year until he was tasked by members of Congress to transfer their fugitive insurgent government from Uruapan in Michoacán to the rebel stronghold at Tehuacán in Veracruz—a distance of almost 450 miles. Morelos gathered 1,000 well-armed riders and stealthily led the legislators' convoy away from Uruapan on September 29, 1815.

Capture (November 1815)

One month later, a report was received at the royalist base of Iguala on November 2,

1815, that this slow-moving congressional expedition was near the town of Tenango, seeking a spot to cross over the Mezcala River. The next day, Morelos—finding that the rafts that he had been promised to covertly transport them across to the far bank did not arrive—was obliged to capture Tenango itself, in the process killing its native chieftain and burning every building except its church to the ground so as to compel its boats and boatmen into ferrying his large convoy and military escort over to the far shore.

Realizing that this attack would alert every monarchist formation in the district, Morelos then drove his expedition hard along the road on the far side for another 20 miles, staggering into the hamlet of Tezmalaca by nightfall. Heavy downpours fell overnight, rendering the roads so impassable by dawn of November 4, 1815, that Morelos allowed his exhausted troops and travelers a day's rest. The next morning, though, royalist pursuers appeared, so he had to fight a rearguard action with about 30 men to allow his charges to escape and was taken alive.

Execution (December 1815)

News of Morelos's capture reached Mexico City at 2:30 p.m. on November 9, 1815, being greeted with pealing church bells by Crown and Church officials, although with muted sadness throughout the population as a whole. Fearful of sparking a riot, he was smuggled into the capital inside a closed carriage at dawn on November 22, 1815, and incarcerated in the secret jails of the Inquisition. After two days of interrogation, Morelos was stripped of his religious orders as a "traitor to God, to the King, and to the Pope," then handed over on November 28,

1815, to receive his final sentencing from a secular court.

Three weeks later, Morelos was made to kneel before the Crown tribunal while his execution order was read to him on December 21, 1815. He was conveyed at 6:00 a.m. the next morning out of the capital (once again in a closed carriage) to the abandoned estate of San Cristóbal Ecatepec, which was being used by the royalist army as a military base. After a light lunch, the 50-year-old insurgent champion was made to kneel beside a wall that afternoon of December 22, 1815, then shot in the back by a four-man firing squad. A second volley of four more rounds was fired into his lifeless body, after which it was carried away to be buried anonymously in the local churchyard.

See also: Acapulco, Insurgent Siege of; Calleja del Rey, Félix María; Hidalgo y Costilla Gallaga, Miguel Gregorio Antonio Ignacio; Independence, War of; Tres Palos, Battle of; Valladolid, Battle of.

Further Reading

Archer, Christon I. "Years of Decision: Félix Calleja and the Strategy to End the Revolution of New Spain." In *The Birth of Modern Mexico*, 125–49. Wilmington, DE: Scholarly Resources, 2003.

Ibarra, Ana Carolina. *El cabildo catedral de Antequera, Oaxaca y el movimiento insurgente*. Morelia: El Colegio de Michoacán, 2000.

Lemoine, Ernesto. *Morelos: su vida revolucionaria a través de sus escritos y otros testimonios de la época*. Mexico City: UNAM, 1991.

McFarlane, Anthony. *War and Independence in Spanish America*. New York: Routledge, 2014.

Sosa, Francisco. *Biografías de mexicanos distinguidos*. Mexico City: Porrúa, 2006.

N

Tremble, murderers and arsonists.
We shall see you soon.
—— note left nailed to a post at Gen. Juan
N. Álvarez's hacienda, found by Santa
Anna's troops in November 1854

Niños Héroes (1847)

Literally the "Boy Heroes," a popular name given to the half dozen teenage cadets who laid down their lives to help defend their military college during the assault against Chapultepec Castle by U.S. troops in the Mexican-American War.

Background (August 16–September 11, 1847)

On August 16, 1847, the 7,200-man army of U.S. major general Winfield Scott—which had been approaching Mexico City from occupied Puebla—circled around Santa Anna's main defensive concentration at El Peñón de los Baños, 10 miles east of the capital on the rim of the Valley of Mexico. Instead, these invaders descended toward the valley floor via a less heavily defended route, and then furthermore continued slipping past other southeastern outposts as well, all the while drawing ever closer to Mexico City. Santa Anna tried to counter these flanking maneuvers by hastily redeploying his forces and mounting unsuccessful stands at the Battles of Contreras and Churubusco, after which his Mexican troops had fought a stubborn yet costly defensive action at the Molino del Rey complex and its adjacent stone Casa Mata on September 7, 1847, which briefly checked Scott's inexorable approach.

At that point, the Americans—rather than resume their drive directly into the teeth of Mexico City's defenses out of its south—began sliding around Santa Anna's dispositions once again, edging still farther west. Realizing that his capital lay quite vulnerable from that direction, especially since most of the intervening canals and waterways were at their lowest levels due to it being then the dry season, the Mexican president ordered 200-foot-high Chapultepec Hill and its surrounding woods hurriedly prepared as a defensive strongpoint.

Consequently, elderly major general Nicolás Bravo and the engineer, Brig. Gen. Juan Cano, began digging in with some 1,300 troops, specifically instructing:

- The 115 men of the Querétaro Activo Battalion and 27 of the Toluca Activo Battalion to begin preparing trenches around its lower levels to the west
- The 277 men of the Mina, 211 of the Unión, and 300 of the San Blas National Guard Militia Battalions to do the same along its south
- While 250 regulars of the 10th Line Regiment and seven artillery pieces under Cmdr. Manuel Gamboa were to be installed into the frail hilltop castle up above

(Despite its imposing appearance, this structure had originally been designed as a viceregal residence, therefore lacked the thickly buttressed walls of a military fortress.)

While these defensive preparations were being made, an order was also issued for the 100 or so cadets of Mexico's *Colegio Militar* or Military College—which was housed within the castle—to be evacuated, although its director, Gen. Col. Mariano Monterde, and a dozen staff officers intended to remain behind so as to assist in the defense. Parents hurried from nearby Mexico City to pick up their children from among the student body, but some cadets refused to depart (such as 15-year-old Miguel Miramón), while others hailed from more distant parts of the country and therefore had no place to go. Eventually, 46 cadets stayed on with their instructors, constituting part of the Mexican defenders who were to hold Chapultepec Castle against its attackers.

American Bombardment and Assault (September 12–13, 1847)

Scott directed his artillery to begin bombarding the hilltop castle at 5:00 a.m. on September 12, 1847, intending to soften up this strongpoint (while simultaneously detaching some regiments to feint a return southeastward as well so as to confuse and divide Santa Anna's forces) with the aim of taking Chapultepec by storm the next day and then driving straight past with his main army toward Mexico City. Chapultepec's young cadets and other defenders therefore had to endure this barrage all day and again the next dawn—until the American guns suddenly fell silent around 8:00 a.m. on the morning of September 13, 1847.

At that hour, a column of assault troops pushed out from Brig. Gen. John A. Quitman's division to the south of Chapultepec,

charging into the Mexican defenders around the base of its hill and breaking through after intense hand-to-hand combat. Other U.S. columns also charged out of the west from Brig. Gen. Gideon J. Pillow's division, Franklin Pierce's and George Cadwalader's brigades smashing through the Querétaro and Toluca positions. All these vanguard American units then paused at the base of Chapultepec's heights until scaling ladders could be brought forward so as to launch their final assault against the castle up above.

These ladders were soon received and the attackers swarmed up, overwhelming the last defenders in a hail of bullets during which some 6 cadets were killed, 5 wounded, and 45 captured before all the shooting finally ceased. By 9:30 a.m. on that September 13, 1847, Col. Joseph E. Johnston's gray-coated Voltigeur Regiment was unfurling the Stars and Stripes atop the lofty fortress, while below them other U.S. columns swept on past toward Mexico City's western gates. That same nightfall, Santa Anna decided to abandon his capital altogether, leaving it open for Scott to push into its streets uncontested next day.

Honors and Myth Making (1871–1946)

In the chaotic few days after this defeat, Mexican burial parties tentatively identified six young bodies from among the heaps of 600 dead or dying that were strewn throughout Chapultepec Castle and its surrounding woods as having been cadets: Fernando Montes de Oca, Francisco Márquez Paniagua, Vicente Suárez, Juan Escutia, and Lieutenants Juan de la Barrera and Agustín Melgar. All six would later be remembered as the *Niños Héroes* or "Boy Heroes," although recent historical research has revealed that Escutia was actually a young soldier from the San Blas National Guard Battalion.

Their fellow cadets who had been captured were released from U.S. detention in the spring of 1848, once hostilities ceased, eventually resuming their studies. Twenty years after this particular class had graduated from the Military College, their surviving members would form an association in 1871 to commemorate the sacrifices made by their classmates who had fallen on that day. They petitioned the government of Pres. Porfirio Díaz, and a remembrance ceremony was duly authorized as of 1880. A small obelisk (designed by the military engineer Ramón Rodríguez Aragoity, himself a surviving cadet from that battle) was erected four years later, atop one of the trenches where many of the dead were believed to have been buried in a common grave.

Yet since Mexico during the early 1870s had only recently emerged from several decades of bitter conflict between its liberals and conservative factions, many of the latter criticized the liberal president Benito Juárez's decision to honor the lowborn cadets, derisively reciting a refrain that said that *ni eran niños, ni eran héroes* ("they were not children, nor were they heroes"). To counter such disparaging criticism, myths were elaborated by liberal commentators that eulogized the young cadets: for example, by asserting that one of them—either Juan de la Barrera or Juan Escutia—had wrapped himself in the castle's large Mexican flag and flung himself from the battlements rather than allow it to fall into the invaders' hands.

Modern Veneration (1947–Present)

Another controversy erupted during the centennial year marking their deaths, when the American president Harry S. Truman—on a goodwill visit to Mexico City in March 1947—placed a floral wreath on the Boy Heroes' obelisk in Chapultepec Park and gave a brief speech during which he innocently suggested that the ensuing minute of silence would do much to heal the hundred years of hostility between both countries. Although well intentioned, his words so offended certain people that a pair of Military College cadets came galloping up on horseback that same evening to wrench his wreath from the obelisk and toss it into the garbage.

In order to placate inflamed military sensibilities, Pres. Miguel Alemán announced that same September 1947 that the remains of the six young cadets had been positively identified as lying beneath the obelisk and so would be removed and reinterred atop tall columns in a magnificent new marble "Monument to the Boy Heroes," which was erected in the city's beautiful Alameda Park with Chapultepec Castle as its backdrop.

See also: Churubusco, Battle of; Contreras, Battle of; Mexican-American War; Miramón Tarelo, Miguel Gregorio de la Luz Atenógenes; Molino del Rey, Battle of.

Further Reading

Frías, Heriberto. *Episodios militares mexicanos: segunda parte, invasión norteamericana*. Mexico City: Viuda de C. Bouret, 1901, 227–41.

Sosa, Francisco. *Biografías de mexicanos distinguidos*. Mexico City: Porrúa, 2006.

Tucker, Spencer C. *The Encyclopedia of the Mexican-American War*. Santa Barbara, CA: ABC-CLIO, 2013.

In this country, if Cain had not killed Abel, then Abel would have killed Cain.

— attributed to the revolutionary general Álvaro Obregón

Oaxaca, Insurgent Occupation of (1812–1813)

Surprise attack that resulted in the easy capture of this southern city by an army led by José María Morelos, whose forces thereupon retained it as their capital for the next year and a half.

Preliminary Operations (Summer–Autumn 1812)

Antequera, as this city of roughly 17,500 inhabitants was still known during the late-colonial period, had failed to rise in response to Miguel Hidalgo's initial insurrection in distant Guanajuato against Spanish Crown rule in mid-September 1810. Indeed, when rebel forces under his subordinate, the ex-priest Morelos, had finally penetrated into southeastern Mexico more than a year later, they had become besieged and eventually defeated within the city of Cuautla by royalist forces.

But Morelos managed to escape from that disaster and gather new adherents so as to resume his guerrilla strikes against isolated Spanish garrisons in the region of Jalapa and Veracruz. By early November 1812, his strength had resurged to 1,000 armed men, although he had failed to carry the city of Orizaba as planned. Therefore, when he was joined at his base of operations at Tehuacán by his subordinates Mariano Matamoros and Miguel Bravo, each bringing in an additional 2,000 followers apiece, Morelos marched away on November 10, 1812—pretending to be bent on once more attempting the royalist garrison holding the Pacific port of Acapulco with his combined strength of 5,000 rebels and 40 crude guns, although his real intention was to surprise Antequera.

Capture and Occupation (November 1812–March 1814)

Morelos's large rebel army suddenly appeared in the Valley of Etla, only a dozen miles northwest of Antequera on the Tuesday afternoon of November 24, 1812, from where Morelos sent a message on ahead the next dawn, calling on the city's royal governor—Lt. Gen. Antonio González Sarabia—to surrender within three hours. Having 2,000 monarchist defenders and 36 guns under his command to defend his well-fortified city, the Spanish official rejected this demand, so the insurgent columns duly closed the distance and began their assault by 10:00 a.m. the next morning.

With Morelos observing the action from just outside the city's *garita* or "gatehouse" del Marquesado, Eugenio Montaño led a cavalry charge into Antequera's suburb of Xochimilco so as to cut off the road leading northeastward to Tehuantepec before storming and penetrating through the city defenses proper around La Merced.

Meanwhile, Ramón Sesma drove against the fortified La Soledad Church with his San Lorenzo Battalion under covering fire provided by Manuel de Mier y Terán's artillery, while the rebel priest Matamoros assaulted El Carmen, and Hermenegildo Galeana carried the huge Santo Domingo Convent.

The resistance mounted was only feeble, monarchist leaders such as Bishop Antonio Bergoza and the royalist militia commander Bernardo Bonavia having already fled, so insurgent casualties totaled a mere 12 men. When Morelos entered the city at 1:00 p.m. on the afternoon of November 25, 1812, he ordered summary executions of most of its remaining royal officials, then installed an insurgent government for the entire province that was to be jointly headed by José María Murguía y Galardi and the new insurgent garrison commander, Benito Rocha, while Manuel Nicolás Bustamante was to administer the city itself as its *presidente del ayuntamiento* or "municipal president." Detachments were soon dispatched to subdue lesser outlying towns as well, while Morelos supervised the recasting of Antequera's church bells into artillery pieces; the confiscation of all loyalist goods; and even began issuing a short-lived newspaper, initially called *Sud* and then subsequently renamed *El Correo Americano del Sur* or "The Southern American Mail" as of January 1813.

By February 7, 1813, the rebel commander was ready to march westward with the bulk of his army to attack Acapulco, leaving Rocha behind with a 1,000-man garrison. Antequera remained in rebel hands for another year, Matamoros fending off a feeble royalist counterthrust out of Guatemala under the Italian-born lieutenant colonel Manuel Servando Danbrini in the spring of 1813. But insurgent defeats elsewhere eventually sapped the defenders' resolve, so when Col. Melchor Álvarez advanced from Tepeaca with 2,000 monarchist troops early in 1814, Antequera's occupiers simply stripped and abandoned the city, allowing Alvarez to enter uncontested on March 29, 1814.

Aftermath (1815–1821)

Ruined by this ordeal, as well as by their lost overseas trade, the city populace found itself reduced to 15,700 people by 1815, whose prospects scarcely improved during the remaining six years of the War of Independence. Eventually, monarchist fortunes contracted throughout Mexico until the royalist captain Antonio de León revolted against Crown authority in June 1821 with his Huajuapan garrison, marching against Antequera and defeating its last loyalist defenders under Col. Manuel Obeso at Etla on July 29, 1821, so the city fell two days afterward.

And despite the fact that national freedom had been secured, Antequera and its district would continue to suffer as its cochineal exports could no longer compete with cheaper produce emanating out of Guatemala, while Mexico was furthermore plunged into prolonged factional strife, handicapping all its recuperation and modernization efforts.

See also: Acapulco, Insurgent Siege of; Hidalgo y Costilla Gallaga, Miguel Gregorio Antonio Ignacio; Independence, War of; Morelos Pavón, José María Teclo.

Further Reading

Ibarra, Ana Carolina. *El cabildo catedral de Antequera, Oaxaca y el movimiento insurgente*. Morelia: El Colegio de Michoacán, 2000.

Montiel, Rosalba, ed. *Documentos de la guerra de independencia en Oaxaca.*

Oaxaca City: Archivo General del Estado de Oaxaca, 1986.

Oaxaca, French Siege of (1865)

Successful campaign by Franco-imperial forces during the War of the French Intervention against a republican garrison that could hold out for only a few weeks when cornered within their southern capital.

Preliminary Approaches (August–December 1864)

Because of its inaccessibility due to the few roads through its mountainous landscape, no French force had been detached to subdue the state of Oaxaca during their initial conquest of central Mexico. Consequently, its native son, Gen. Porfirio Díaz, had retreated into his home state with a small republican army, digging in to preserve the republican cause. A four-pronged French offensive into this region in August 1864 under Brig. Gen. Augustin Brincourt had been obliged to turn back when Díaz made several strikes in their rear.

Four months later the French artillerist, Maj. Gen. Courtois Roussel d'Hurbal, returned for a second attempt with a contingent of engineers and a siege train, who

Watercolor of a mounted French soldier employed on counterguerrilla sweeps in Mexico, ca. 1865. (Anne S. K. Brown Military Collection, Brown University Library)

patiently cleared a road which allowed him to reach the town of Yanhuitlán—only 60 miles from Oaxaca City—by December 12, 1864. Two more columns then penetrated into the region as part of a renewed, three-pronged effort to subdue this region for the emperor Maximilian.

The commander-in-chief of all the French forces in Mexico, Marshal François Bazaine, reached Etla on January 17, 1865, to personally assume command over the 4,000 infantrymen who were closing in on Oaxaca City, consisting of two battalions of the 3rd Zouave Regiment, 12 companies of Foreign Legionnaires, and a battalion of *Infanterie Légère d'Afrique*. They were furthermore supported by 1,000 troopers—a company of mounted Zouaves, three squadrons of French cavalrymen, and four squadrons of Mexican imperial riders—as well as a dozen 12-pound siege guns, eight 4-pound fieldpieces, and six mortars manned by a total of 80 gunners, with 200 sappers and 500 auxiliaries rounding out this force.

Siege of Oaxaca (January 21–February 8, 1865)

Within a couple of days, advance French elements began harrying the republican defenders just north of Oaxaca City, prompting Díaz to order his own cavalry—700 dragoons under his younger brother, Col. Félix Díaz—to exit, while preparing the remainder of his 3,000 regulars and 4,000 local militiamen to withstand a siege. On January 21, 1865, Col. José Guillermo Carbó's Morelos Battalion sallied from the city and fell upon some French units at the Hacienda of Aguilera, this action eventually embroiling two other companies of the Sinaloa Battalion and one from the Sierra Juárez Battalion.

However, the defenders otherwise mounted no more counterattacks once Colonel Dutretaine commenced his siege

works on February 1, 1865, installing batteries opposite Oaxaca City as well as atop Mogote and Pelado Hills. One week later, republican morale collapsed and Díaz surrendered, being carried off into captivity along with Colonels Juan Espinosa, Manuel González, and Francisco Carrión.

See also: Bazaine, François Achille; Díaz Mori, José de la Cruz Porfirio; French Intervention, War of the.

Further Reading

"From Mexico: Porfirio Diaz Strongly Fortified at Oaxaca." *New York Times*, January 26, 1865.

"Important from Mexico: Particulars of the Capture of Oajaca." *New York Times*, March 10, 1865.

"Our Havana Correspondence: Details of the Siege of Oaxaca." *New York Times*, March 18, 1865.

Obregón Salido, Álvaro (1880–1928)

A humble participant at the beginning of the Mexican Revolution who would rise to become its greatest general.

He was born on February 19, 1880, at Siquisiva Ranch near Navojoa in the torrid northwestern state of Sonora, the 18th and final child of Francisco Obregón Gámez and Cenobia Salido Palomares. His 64-year-old father had died a few months after his birth, so following a basic education at Álamos and the school of Huatabampo in southern Sonora (where the family had moved and which was run by his brother José), the teenaged Álvaro started work as a lathe operator and mechanic at the Novolato mill, then briefly taught primary school himself at the village school of Moroncárit before turning his hand to farming.

At the age of 23, Obregón had married María del Refugio Urrea in 1903, and two years later bought his own small ranch on the Mayo River banks near Huatabampo, which he named Quinta Chilla. A daughter christened with her mother's name was born that same year of 1905, and a son named Humberto followed in 1906, when Obregón also began planting crops of *garbanzos* or "chick-peas" and even invented a special harvester that he manufactured and sold to other farmers, so he became modestly prosperous. However, his quiet domestic life would be saddened by his wife's accidental death a few months after giving birth to twin boys in 1907, who also did not survive this tragedy.

Early Militia Career (1912–1913)

The outbreak of the Revolution elsewhere throughout Mexico in November 1910 had not at first involved Obregón, a widower left with the responsibility for two small children. Still, after failing in his first attempt to win public office, he was elected municipal president of Huatabampo by its few score voters in 1911. His military career began equally modestly after Pascual Orozco rebelled in neighboring Chihuahua against Pres. Francisco I. Madero in March 1912. In the ensuing fighting, Obregón offered to raise a unit for the state militia, quickly attracting 300 volunteers. This force was designated as the 4th Irregular Battalion of Sonora, and he became its lieutenant colonel. The 32-year-old Obregón had thereupon campaigned into the mountains of Chihuahua under Brig. Gen. Agustín Sanginés, distinguishing himself during an encounter at Ojitos so he was even formally introduced to the federal general Victoriano Huerta at the rural Sabinal railway station near Casas Grandes on September 1, 1912.

Obregón's battalion was subsequently rushed back into Sonora by train to save the town of Agua Prieta 11 days later from an Orozquista attack, after which he also relieved the mining camp of Nacozari and drove these marauders off after a clash at San Joaquín. Once Orozco's rebellion was ended, Obregón had dissolved his battalion and resigned his commission as of January 1913, returning to office as municipal president of Huatabampo. That very next month, though, Madero's betrayal and murder in Mexico City by the turncoat Huerta had revived fighting throughout Mexico. Sonora's interim governor, Ignacio L. Pesqueira, soon rejected any notion of accepting Huerta's accession to the presidency, and in preparing for armed conflict, the governor recalled Obregón to militia duty, promoted him to colonel, and appointed him as chief of staff of the Sonoran government's *Sección de Guerra* or "War Section."

Obregón quickly proved his worth by gathering 1,500 troops and leading them out of the state capital of Hermosillo as early as March 6, 1913, to seize the border town of Nogales one week later—after a brisk assault that utterly routed its garrison of 100 federal soldiers under army colonel Manuel Reyes and 300 *rurales* under Col. Emilio Kosterlitzky, sending the survivors fleeing across the river to seek asylum in Arizona. Within a month, every federal outpost in northern Sonora had been taken over by Obregón or one of his subordinates, while preparations began to invest the only major federal base remaining in that state of 1,400 regular soldiers stationed at the port of Guaymas in its south.

Governor Pesqueira furthermore aligned himself with the "constitutionalist" anti-Huertista alliance that was being formed by Gov. Venustiano Carranza of Coahuila, so Huerta moved to counter these developments on April 22, 1913, by sending a seaborne expedition of an additional 1,200 federal soldiers under Brig. Gen. Luis Medina Barrón to reinforce the garrison already in Guaymas and jointly mount an offensive by pushing 85 miles inland to remove the defiant Sonoran government from its capital of Hermosillo. Obregón, however, managed to check this overland push at the Battle of Santa Rosa on May 13, 1913, inflicting considerable losses among the federals and thus winning promotion for himself to the rank of state brigadier general on June 29th.

Creation of the Army of the Northwest (1913)

Five days later, Carranza issued a directive from Monclova on July 4, 1913, that called for raising a nationwide "constitutionalist army" to be composed of seven regional corps, and subsequently appointed the 46-year-old entrepreneur Pesqueira as titular commander of one such unit—officially designated as the *Cuerpo del Ejército Constitucionalista del Noroeste* or "Corps of the Constitutionalist Army of the Northwest" but that was to become much more commonly known as the *Ejército del Noroeste* or "Army of the Northwest"—with Obregón as his second-in-command.

The latter threw himself into studying military science and logistics so as to organize the most effective fighting force possible, proving to be an intelligent and gifted leader. The veteran Swedish soldier of fortune Ivor Thord-Gray, who joined Obregón's staff as an instructor and artillery officer around this time, would note approvingly that his diminutive commander "unlike many other generals, was very keen to learn, and he did." Obregón was furthermore highly receptive to such modern innovations as machine guns, armored trains,

and aircraft, while the open border with Arizona allowed the constitutionalists to acquire good equipment and materiel. The result would eventually be a disciplined, compact army capable of defeating much larger foes.

In theory, Carranza's appointment meant that the Army of the Northwest's commander was to direct all rebel activities in Sonora as well as throughout the adjoining states of Coahuila, Chihuahua, and Sinaloa, and the territory of Baja California, although in reality many leaders in those regions simply refused to recognize this authority. Shortly after Carranza retreated into Hermosillo on September 18, 1913, Obregón was given full command over the Ejército del Noroeste and went on his first major offensive. Leaving the federal garrison inside Guaymas bottled up by 3,000 Sonoran besiegers, he led his main army south by rail into neighboring Sinaloa, capturing its capital of Culiacán by November 14, 1913, while isolating another garrison of Huertista defenders within the coastal city of Mazatlán.

Obregón then remained encamped around the Sinaloan capital over the winter of 1913–1914, his Army of the Northwest growing in strength as more and more volunteers continued to join, being trained and properly assimilated. The next spring, after Pancho Villa had won a series of spectacular victories in the north and Emiliano Zapata had captured Cuautla in the south, Obregón resumed his drive into central Mexico by first capturing the city of Tepic on May 14, 1914, where he prepared to abandon his trains so as to lead his 14,000 men on an epic march through the mountain range and penetrate into the state of Jalisco.

Drive on the National Capital (1914)

After a two-week trudge through the Tepic range, lashed by frequent rains, Obregón's

14,000-man army reunited at Ahualulco on June 25, 1914, where he learned that the 12,000-man federal *División de Occidente* or "Western Division" of Maj. Gen. José María Mier was awaiting his emergence from the mountains, only 45 miles farther east within Guadalajara. A contingent of 5,000 *federales* under Brig. Gen. Miguel Bernard had even sallied from that city by train, venturing as far as La Vega railway station in hopes of catching the constitutionalists as they descended wearily and in disarray from this trek. Obregón, however, remained out of sight and so regrouped his army in the rocky terrain between the Tequila and Ameca ranges before planning and launching a well-coordinated attack that surprised the divided federals at two places on July 6, 1914, virtually annihilating Guadalajara's entire garrison over the next two days in what was to become known as the Battle of Orendáin.

With Pancho Villa's victorious rebel army restrained in the north by a lack of coal for his trains (on Carranza's spiteful orders), and Zapata's forces reluctant to push out of their southern stronghold, the path now lay open for Obregón to drive on toward Mexico City and claim the national capital from the Huertista regime, which was plainly tottering on the verge of collapse. Defeated on every side, the dictator fled in disgrace on July 15, 1914, leaving a makeshift administration to meet with Obregón three weeks later on the outskirts of the capital at Teoloyucan and arrange for the capitulation of the city and entire federal government. Among the terms imposed was to be the outright dissolution of the once-proud Federal Army, whose soldiers were transported eastward in the direction of Puebla with orders to simply find their own way home, while Obregón's triumphant Army of the Northwest—now 18,000 strong—

paraded into the capital's streets on August 15, 1914.

Obregón made a point of securing as much heavy weaponry as possible from the surrendered federal arsenals, as it soon became apparent that powerful rivals such as Villa and Zapata were voicing serious objections against the newly self-proclaimed president, Carranza. He used Obregón in an attempt to mediate, but after a convention held at Aguascalientes ended in rancorous rupture by mid-November 1914, Obregón openly declared war against Villa from Mexico City on November 19th, and five days later withdrew from the capital toward Veracruz with what remained of his Army of the Northwest to protect Carranza's government, which also shifted down to the coast shortly thereafter.

Villa and Zapata formed a nominal alliance, professing that they would march together into Puebla and Veracruz with their armies—a combined total of 60,000 men—so as to confront the *constitucionalistas* on behalf of the Convention, but such an offensive never materialized. Instead, Obregón (who had been promoted to "general-in-chief" by Carranza) recuperated the city of Puebla from its Zapatista occupiers on January 5, 1915, and the national capital three weeks later, while his subordinate, Gen. Manuel M. Diéguez, contested the Villista claim over Guadalajara.

Defeat of Villa (1915)

Obregón spent five weeks assembling a new field force in and around Mexico City that was to be officially designated as the *Ejército de Operaciones* or "Operational Army" of the constitutionalist government, then sent a vanguard unit probing northward on March 7, 1915, which soon clashed with three Villista cavalry brigades near the rural

Peón railway station in the state of Querétaro. Obregón followed this pathfinder unit three days later with his main body, heading up into the mountainous central region of Mexico aboard a stream of trains in a direct challenge to Villa for a showdown.

Reaching the small city of Celaya in the state of Guanajuato by April 4, 1915, Obregón learned that Villa had indeed hastened south from Torreón to meet him, eager for battle. Villa quickly closed the distance between both armies, departing Salamanca on the morning of April 6th with 20,000 men and 22 artillery pieces aboard three train columns, hurtling across the final 20 miles against the entrenched constitutionalists. Although Obregón commanded only 6,000 cavalrymen and 5,000 infantrymen, his smaller army was much better disciplined and had greater firepower than Villa's unwieldy mass, especially as Celaya's defensive lines featured 86 heavy machine gun emplacements.

The Villistas began detraining 10 miles west of the city that same afternoon of April 6, 1915, and spent the next 24 hours enduring heavy losses in repeated but fruitless charges against Obregón's infantry, who were well dug in. Finally, he unleashed the unengaged constitutionalist cavalry, sending them on a vast prearranged encircling move so when their closing pincers began materializing in Villa's rear on the afternoon of April 7th, the attackers broke and fled in panic toward their trains, leaving behind 1,800 dead, 3,000 wounded, 500 prisoners, plus heaps of abandoned materiel. Obregón's losses totaled 558 killed and 365 injured in this, the First Battle of Celaya.

Shrewdly judging his opponent's impulsive character, Obregón remained in Celaya, resting his victorious troops while calling in fresh formations to bolster his army's strength to 7,000 infantrymen and 8,000 cavalry troopers now that he had come to grips with the enemy. Villa spent the next few days feverishly rebuilding his battered army as well by summoning large detachments into his marshaling area at Salamanca. Finally, Villa ordered a mass parade of a new army of 30,000 men on Monday, April 12, 1915, and the next dawn began sending out his infantry and guns aboard trains toward Celaya once again, while his masses of cavalry rode along beside the rails. Having been bloodied previously, the Villistas took several hours to unlimber their artillery five miles west of the city and form up into proper attack columns before advancing across the arid landscape toward Celaya.

The result was nonetheless the same: despite their two-to-one superiority in numbers, the attackers spent themselves over the next two days in costly attacks against Obregón's well-positioned infantry until his cavalry emerged from concealment in a forest to his rear on April 15, 1915, and launched another massive envelopment to the north, which caused Villa's disheartened followers to break and flee westward by that same nightfall, leaving behind a further 4,000 dead, 5,000 wounded, 6,000 prisoners, 1,000 saddled horses, and all their artillery. Obregón, in comparison, had lost only 138 officers and soldiers killed, plus another 276 wounded.

Bested once more in this Second Battle of Celaya, Villa disappeared northward to León, so after resting for a fortnight, Obregón pressed ever deeper into Villista territory in pursuit. Grown more cautious, Villa now hoped to lure his opponent out into the flat Trinidad plains between Silao and León where the Villistas' numerical advantage in cavalry might work to his advantage. Obregón obliged by pushing northwest from Silao on May 7, 1915, reaching the lonely Trinidad railway station and entrenching his 14,300 infantrymen and 9,400 cavalry troopers into a huge defensive square over the next few days, which extended for 10 miles from corner to corner.

Villa was reduced to commanding only 19,500 riders and 6,000 infantrymen on this occasion, his numerical edge having been eroded. He used 8,000 of his cavalrymen to make an initial strike against Obregón's lines on May 12, 1915, and after 10 days of probes and long-range exchanges left his artillery commander, Gen. Felipe Ángeles, to maintain pressure on Obregón's main army while personally leading another 8,000 fresh riders through the hills to surprise the main constitutionalist supply base at Silao, destroying numerous trains, bridges, and telegraphs in his opponent's rear. Obregón found this disruption worrisome, especially after he learned that Villa had returned into Duarte by the morning of June 2, 1915, and was preparing to an all-out assault with his entire strength.

When the first Villista wave of three infantry battalions broke cover the next morning and charged directly at Santa Ana del Conde Hacienda, behind an artillery barrage laid down by Ángeles's batteries, Obregón was unexpectedly wounded—his right arm being shredded by a shell. Yet his second-in-command, Hill, immediately took over and decimated the advancing Villistas with counterfire from well-placed machine guns and sharpshooting troops. After two days of exhausting their strength and ammunition in fruitless charges, Villa and Ángeles finally gave the order to retreat at dawn on June 5, 1915, their army disintegrating during the resultant pursuit, suffering 8,000 casualties—triple those of the Obregonistas, whose discipline remained intact despite their leader's grievous wound—and the loss of all their materiel.

Despite having the remnants of his right forearm surgically amputated, Obregón resumed command over his army after only a one-month convalescence, continuing to drive northward in pursuit of Villa. His forces defeated Villa's rearguard at Calvillo Ravine on July 8, 1915, then occupied the city of Aguascalientes two days later. Almost three weeks afterward, a detachment of 4,000 riders under Villa's henchman Rodolfo Fierro—retiring northward after a successful raid into central Mexico—blundered into Obregón's army in the Mariscala Hills near the city of Querétaro and were badly beaten at Jerécuaro.

Obregón seized Saltillo during the first week of September 1915, after which Villa desperately tried to distract his relentless pursuer by raiding into his home state of Sonora, only to be defeated at every turn. Beaten and discouraged, Villa disbanded the remnants of his once proud *División del Norte* in Chihuahua City and disappeared into the mountains with a few loyal retainers on Christmas Eve 1915, leaving Obregón victorious. As the main Carrancista focus then shifted south against Zapata, Obregón was freed of his military obligations and spent more time with his family.

Political Candidacy and Revolt (1919–1920)

On June 1, 1919, Obregón announced from his Quinta Chilla ranch near Nogales, Sonora, that he intended to run in that coming year's presidential election. He tentatively began a political campaign that same fall, although as yet having no formal affiliation with any organization. His candidacy nonetheless incurred the disapproval of Carranza, who had long deplored the uninterrupted string of military men who had monopolized the office of president of Mexico, so the first chief was instead aligning the civilian Ignacio Bonillas, Mexico's ambassador in Washington, to inherit his post.

Carranza's opposition grew more ominous after Obregón accepted an offer in March 1920 from the head of the Liberal Constitutionalist Party, the union manipulator Luis N. Morones, to sponsor his candidacy as the head of his party's ticket. Very shortly thereafter, Obregón was ordered to appear before a military tribunal in Mexico City on April 11, 1920, in which he was informed that charges of treason and conspiracy were being prepared against him based on the confession of Col. Roberto Cejudo (one of Félix Díaz's minions, recently released from jail by Carranza's police).

Knowing that he stood in danger, the one-armed Obregón fled from the capital disguised as a railway man on April 13, 1920, and traveled to Iguala in the state of Guerrero to be given sanctuary by his former subordinates, Generals Fortunato Maycotte and Rómulo Figueroa. One week later, Obregón issued a proclamation from Chilpancingo calling for an uprising to depose the unpopular Carranza. Supporters rallied to his side from every corner of the country, generals mutinying with entire divisions to join his cause. Even Pancho Villa, Obregón's former battlefield foe, helped capture Chihuahua City from its Carrancista garrison on April 29, 1920.

Within a couple of weeks, large Obregonista armies were closing in on Mexico City, prompting Carranza to abandon the capital at dawn on May 7, 1920, aboard a 15-mile-long train convoy bearing 10,000 adherents and the national treasury. Attacked from every side, the fugitive president was reduced to a few score followers by the time he rode up into the Puebla mountain range one week later. He was murdered in a mountain hut on May 21, 1920.

Reelection Campaign and Assassination (January 1927–July 1928)

In January 1927, Mexico's reelection law was amended to allow an ex-president such as Obregón to stand for a second term (although not in direct succession from one term into the next). The administration of his successor, Calles, was already embroiled in a contentious dispute with the Catholic Church over his anticlerical legislation, and their antipathy also extended to include Obregón. Shortly after he announced in June 1927 that he would be actively seeking reelection, other opponents began to appear as well.

On October 2, 1927, military maneuvers scheduled to be held in Balbuena Park east of Mexico City were abruptly canceled by President Calles on suspicion that he and Obregón—who were both scheduled to be in attendance—were to be seized in a coup. Indeed, approximately 1,000 men of the 48th and 50th Infantry Battalions, plus the 25th and 26th Cavalry Regiments, did mutiny under Gen. Héctor Ignacio Almada and march east toward Veracruz. Fearing a more widespread conspiracy, Calles ordered numerous suspect generals executed throughout the country, while most of Almada's mutinous troops soon surrendered to loyal forces a short distance outside Mexico City and the remainder were hunted down.

Resuming his electoral campaign, Obregón was sitting in his Cadillac in Mexico City's Chapultepec Park on Sunday, November 13, 1927—awaiting the start of a bullfight—when four pro-Catholic fanatics tossed a pair of bombs at his vehicle. He emerged unscathed, his attackers being captured and killed, along with the Jesuit priest Miguel Pro, plus other conspirators who were implicated in this plot. But the next summer, Obregón—having been reelected although not yet inaugurated into office for his second term as president—was assassinated while attending a political banquet at La Bombilla restaurant in the capital's suburb of San Ángel on July 17, 1928, shot by a 27-year-old itinerant artist and Catholic fanatic named José de León Toral who was innocently sketching people in the room.

Less flashy than Villa or Zapata, Obregón's *Ejército Invicto* or "Undefeated Army" had ended the Revolution by beating all of its rivals. His body lies buried today at his home of Huatabampo.

See also: Ángeles Ramírez, Felipe de Jesús; Celaya, Battles of; Ejército del Noroeste; Huerta Márquez, José Victoriano; Orendáin, Battle of; *rurales*; Santa Rosa, Battle of; Teoloyucan, Treaties of; Thord-Gray, Ivor; Trinidad, Battle of; Villa, Pancho.

Further Reading

Buchenau, Jürgen. *The Last Caudillo: Álvaro Obregón and the Mexican Revolution.* Chichester, England: Wiley-Blackwell, 2011.

Hall, Linda B. *Álvaro Obregón: Power and Revolution in Mexico, 1911–1920.* College Station: Texas A&M University Press, 1981.

Sosa, Francisco. *Biografías de mexicanos distinguidos.* Mexico City: Porrúa, 2006.

Ocotlán, Battle of (1856)

Liberal victory that helped their newly installed government to regain control over the mutinous city and state of Puebla during the turbulent period immediately prior to the outbreak of the War of the Reform.

Background (November 1855–January 1856)

Santa Anna having been driven from office for the final time in early August 1855, a new administration and Congress dominated by liberals were installed into office, which promptly set about drafting a new constitution. One of the first pronouncements issued by this body on November 23, 1855—by Justice Minister Benito Juárez, a former political prisoner and exile—called for the abolition of the traditional tribunals reserved for members of the military and clergy, so conservative protests erupted in various parts of the country.

The strongest revolt broke out on December 12, 1855, in the mountain hamlet of Zacapoaxtla in the state of Puebla, led by its village priest, Francisco Ortega y García. Mexico's interim president, the moderate liberal general Ignacio Comonfort, responded two days later from the national capital by ordering that a couple of cavalry detachments keep this uprising under observation, but their commanders—the conservative-leaning colonels Luis G. Osollo and Juan Olloqui—instead joined the rebels' ranks. Comonfort therefore directed that an army brigade begin penetrating into that region under the command of the politically appointed governor of Veracruz, Ignacio de la Llave; but when this brigade's first unit (the 11th Line Regiment) marched from Mexico City and reached Tatlaquitepec on Christmas Day 1855, the regimental second-in-command—24-year-old lieutenant colonel Miguel Miramón—arrested his superior, Col. Rafael Benavides, and his contingent also joined the rebellion to shouts of *¡Viva la religión!* or "Long live Religion!"

De la Llave was lucky to return into the capital alive a few days later with only a handful of staff officers. Then the 45-year-old conservative general Antonio Haro y Tamariz escaped from confinement at Córdoba in the state of Veracruz on January 5, 1856, riding into the state of Puebla to assume command over its insurrectionists, while one week later a second, even more robust brigade of 2,000 men sent by the liberal government under Brig. Gen. Severo del Castillo also defected. The conservatives used this combined strength to push into the city of Puebla and expel its liberal National Guard garrison under 34-year-old militia colonel Juan Nepomuceno Méndez on January 23, 1856, tacitly assisted and welcomed by Bishop Pelagio Antonio de Labastida.

Government Reaction (February–March 1856)

Now faced with a rebel army ensconced inside a major fortified city, Comonfort summoned militia regiments from numerous liberal states to the capital so as to reinforce those army regulars who had remained reliable supporters of his administration. The militia units continued to stream into Mexico City throughout January and February 1856 until the president was able to order an army of 10,345 troops and 36 guns to marshal under the command of Maj. Gen. Florencio Villareal at three separate staging points, in anticipation of advancing over the mountain range into Puebla. Villareal's army consisted of three infantry divisions, a cavalry division, and a "mobile brigade" of light cavalry.

This liberal force was given the order to march on February 27, 1856, their columns penetrating into the plains around Puebla and occupying the city of Tlaxcala, while driving back conservative patrols so Comonfort was able to depart Mexico City with his personal staff on February 29, 1856, and the next day establish his headquarters as

"general-in-chief" at San Martín Texmelucan, some 20 miles northwest of the city of Puebla. Because of what was perceived to be the conservatives' superiority in cavalry, the next few days were spent erecting field fortifications and reconnoitering the intervening terrain, as well as offering amnesty to rebel officers before the liberal army (whose numbers would steadily increase to an eventual total of 16,000 men through the arrival of even more reinforcements) resumed its drive southeastward on Puebla on March 7, 1856.

Battle of Ocotlán (March 8, 1856)

Villareal's three large infantry divisions closed to within nine miles of Puebla before beginning to encamp around 1:00 p.m. that same afternoon of March 7, 1856, with:

- The 1st Division under Anastasio Parrodi resting between Río Prieto and Montero Hill
- The 2nd Division under Tomás Moreno on the grounds of the Hacienda de Santa Inés, along with the "mobile brigade" of light cavalry under Italian-born Luigi Ghilardi
- The 3rd Division under Félix M. Zuloaga, which camped on the farmland surrounding the Hacienda de San Isidro, with Manuel Doblado's brigade holding the vital center atop Ocotlán Hill
- Villareal's headquarters established in the forefront at the hamlet of San Miguel Xoxtla, protected by Portilla's cavalry

That evening, Comonfort instructed his generals to prepare to send out an advance cavalry force to seize Coronango by 6:00 a.m. the next morning, which would allow the slower-moving liberal infantry divisions to pass through that village and then split up so as to take Cholula and Santorum in turn, thereby beginning the envelopment of Puebla itself.

However, it was the conservatives who struck first. With only 4,000 soldiers to defend the city, General Haro had emerged that same night under cover of darkness with 2,500 infantrymen, 1,000 cavalry troopers, and a half dozen fieldpieces hoping to surprise the liberal columns piecemeal before they had a chance to mass into battle formation. Haro succeeded in engaging Doblado's brigade atop Ocotlán Hill by 8:00 a.m. on March 8, 1856, driving it off this prominence after two hours of fighting with losses on both sides. But as Villareal continued to bring up more and more liberal formations, a truce was arranged at 10:00 a.m. to gather up the wounded and dead.

During this interlude, Haro (a lifelong friend and colleague of the president) also requested to have a personal interview with Comonfort, so the two met beneath the shade of a tree at noon on March 8, 1856. During this conversation, the liberal president renewed his amnesty offer, and Haro requested three hours to discuss the matter with his colleagues. When he failed to return after the allotted time though, Comonfort sent a staff rider to investigate, who returned to report that the outnumbered and demoralized conservatives were by then streaming back into Puebla in disarray.

Aftermath (March 9–23, 1856)

The liberal army therefore followed and bottled them inside, besieging the city until the rebels agreed to capitulate by March 22, 1856. Upon surrendering the next day, Haro, Leonardo Márquez, Del Castillo, and Osollo succeeded in escaping from the country through the port of Veracruz, while Miramón remained well hidden among sympathizers within Puebla. All other rebel officers were stripped of their ranks two days later and humiliated by being incorporated into the liberal army to serve as lowly privates. Many Church properties were moreover expropriated to defray the costs of this campaign, while Bishop Lamadrid was deported from Mexico, actions that only fueled further resentment among the faithful.

See also: Miramón Tarelo, Miguel Gregorio de la Luz Atenógenes, Osollo Pancorbo, Luis Gonzaga; Zuloaga Trillo, Félix María.

Further Reading
"Additional from Mexico: The Puebla Revolution-Conditions of the Surrender." *New York Times*, April 12, 1856.

Álvarez, José J. *Parte general que sobre la campaña de Puebla dirige al ministerio de la Guerra el Sr. general ayudante general.* Mexico City: Vicente García Torres, 1856.

Bazant, Jan. "La iglesia, el estado y la sublevación conservadora de Puebla en 1856." *Historia mexicana* 35, no. 1 (1987): 93–109.

"Important from Mexico: The Rebels Beaten—Capitulation of Puebla." *New York Times*, April 19, 1856.

Villareal, Florencio. *Parte oficial que dirige al Exmo. Sr. presidente de la República y general en jefe del ejército de operaciones, como su segundo el de división D. Florencio Villareal, de la batalla del día ocho del presente en el puerto de Montero y San Francisco Ocotlán.* Mexico City: J. M. Macías, 1856.

Ojinaga, Battle of (1914)

Lopsided victory won by Pancho Villa in which he crushed the last remaining federal army in the state of Chihuahua.

Over the span of three short months in late 1913, during the anti-Huertista phase

Mexican soldiers in the act of chambering an artillery round at Ojinaga, December 1913; Pancho Villa would overrun this city in 30 minutes on January 10, 1914. (Corbis)

of the Mexican Revolution, numerous rebel bands had coalesced into a huge fighting force under Villa's mercurial leadership, being dubbed the constitutionalist *División del Norte* or "Northern Division" (an ill-disciplined horde, although it included a few field batteries and heavy machine guns).

Preceding Operations (November–December 1913)

Villa had taken this swarm of 6,200 irregulars and in mid-November 1913 seized the border city of Ciudad Juárez (opposite El Paso, Texas) with ease, executing hundreds of members of its Huertista garrison. And when a 5,500-man army of federal troops and their *colorado* allies had hastened northward out of Chihuahua City under Gen. José Jesús Mansilla and Brig. Gen. Manuel Landa, traveling by train to help the ex-Orozquista militia general José Inés Salazar recuperate Ciudad Juárez, Villa's force— rather than melt away as had been the

previous rebel practice—instead deployed into a ragged battle line that extended for 12 miles around the rural Tierra Blanca railway station, south of Ciudad Juárez, and defeated these *federales* and *colorados* in a pitched battle that cost them 1,000 dead.

Salazar had reeled southeastward after this defeat, leading his surviving men into the border town of Ojinaga (population: 3,000) opposite Presidio, Texas, where he was to be joined by the 2,900-man Huertista garrison evacuating Chihuahua City under the state's military governor, Gen. Salvador R. Mercado. Several thousand civilians also joined this flight from the state capital, despite the grave difficulties in traversing the stark desert during wintertime. The victorious Villa meanwhile made an orderly entry into half-empty Chihuahua City on December 8, 1913, even magnanimously declaring that the 200 federal troops who had been left behind were "brave men," granting them safe conduct to travel to

Ciudad Juárez so as to seek asylum in the United States.

That same day, Mercado's vanguard began staggering into Ojinaga, and his main force arrived five days later on December 13, 1913, to join Salazar in digging defensive trenches. All of Mexico had been shocked by this revelation of Villa's new-found power, his scruffy bandit groups now proving capable of defeating federal armies or of taking over a state capital unopposed. On the other hand, Mercado was angrily derided in the Mexico City press as the "Great Evacuator," while Pres. Victoriano Huerta threatened to have him court-martialed for cowardice—invective that further demoralized Ojinaga's already-shaky defenders.

Battle of Ojinaga (December 31, 1913–January 10, 1914)

In late December 1913, Villa detached his subordinates Pánfilo Natera and Toribio Ortega with 3,000 troops from Chihuahua City to expel Mercado's and Salazar's Huertista remnants at Ojinaga. After detraining and overrunning the defenders' outlying posts at El Mulato, Candelaria, and San Juan, these Villista contingents launched a multipronged attack against Ojinaga itself on December 31, 1913. However, despite charging into battle and exchanging artillery salvoes and small-arms fire all day long, they found that they could not penetrate its defenses—which were being stoutly held by some 3,000 federal soldiers and 2,000 *colorado* irregulars, backed by 18 artillery pieces and several heavy machine gun emplacements.

Therefore, after falling back and spending several days in long-range exchanges, Natera and Ortega launched a second major assault out of the west and northwest of Ojinaga at 2:00 p.m. on January 4, 1914—which once again failed to pierce its barricades. And as that evening fell, a federal cavalry column even emerged from the town and circled around to the south to drive into the *villista* flank and scatter them with heavy losses.

Natera and Ortega consequently regrouped their men at the nearby hamlet of San Juan and telegraphed news of their repulse to Villa in Chihuahua City, who decided to end his monthlong stint as "governor" by formally resigning from office, then ordering a couple more brigades (1,500 men in total) to accompany him against Ojinaga. Villa detrained at San Juan by January 9, 1914, in bitterly cold weather, and after conferring with Natera and Ortega, prepared to assault Ojinaga out of a different direction next day. Its federal defenders knew that Villa had arrived with reinforcements and so expected the worst.

After maneuvering into new attack positions atop the ridgeline looking down on Ojinaga's outer perimeter, a general bombardment erupted on the afternoon of January 10, 1914, to provide cover for several Villista probing charges. While thus engaged, federal troops at one particular sector of the defenders' lines were ordered to fall back to reload—and the sight of them running toward the rear set off a wholesale panic among the jittery defenders. Within a matter of 30 minutes, the entire federal army poured across the Rio Bravo into Texas in a frenzy, where U.S. officials rounded up and confined these refugees into a large camp. Only the auxiliary brigadier general Marcelo Caraveo Frías managed to evade the U.S. authorities and recross the river back into Mexico with about 100 of his *colorados*, eventually reaching safety in the Bolsón de Mapimí from where he would then ride on to join the large federal garrison at Torreón.

(Caraveo would later be commissioned as second-in-command of a reconstituted federal "División del Norte" under Gen. Carlos García Hidalgo and go on to serve under Emiliano Zapata as well.)

Aftermath (January 1914)

The U.S. Army officials in Presidio, Texas—whose command had just been taken over by 53-year-old general John Joseph "Black Jack" Pershing—would eventually report to Washington how they sent 509 federal officers, 3,212 soldiers, plus 1,081 women and 533 children to internment at Fort Bliss outside of El Paso, leaving another 100 wounded *federales* behind at Presidio to convalesce—more than 3,800 fighting men in total.

This victory ended all Huertista resistance in the state of Chihuahua.

See also: División del Norte; Huerta Márquez, José Victoriano; Orozco Vázquez, Pascual; Revolution, Mexican; Tierra Blanca, Battle of; Villa, Pancho.

Further Reading

Elam, Earl. "Revolution on the Border: The U.S. Army in the Big Bend and the Battle of Ojinaga, 1913–1914." *West Texas Historical Association Yearbook* (1990): 5–25.

Guzmán, Martín Luis. *Memoirs of Pancho Villa*. Austin: University of Texas Press, 1976.

Raun, Gerald G. "Refugees or Prisoners of War: The Internment of a Mexican Federal Army after the Battle of Ojinaga, December 1913–January 1914." *Journal of Big Bend Studies* 12 (2000): 133–65.

Orendáin, Battle of (1914)

Major victory won by Álvaro Obregón's army during the Mexican Revolution in its drive inland from the Pacific coast to expel the government of Victoriano Huerta from the national capital.

Traverse over the Mountains (June 1914)

Having pushed hundreds of miles down the Pacific coast from his native state of Sonora during previous months and captured the city of Tepic in Nayarit by mid-May 1914, Obregón's *Ejército del Noroeste* or "Army of the Northwest" then spent the next four weeks marshaling its strength and supplies at that railhead in anticipation of marching on foot up through the trackless Tepic mountain range and then down into the state of Jalisco.

After a two-week trek in four separate columns, his 14,000 men had emerged from various mountain passes and reunited by June 25, 1914, at Ahualulco—a town located 45 miles west of the city of Guadalajara—where they were greeted by a number of local rebel leaders who wished to jointly operate and coordinate attacks against the 12,000-man federal *División de Occidente* or "Western Division" of Maj. Gen. José María Mier, which was garrisoning the capital of Jalisco.

Foiled Ambush (late June 1914)

Obregón was furthermore informed by his local allies that 5,000 of these *federales* under Brig. Gen. Miguel Bernard had sallied westward from Guadalajara with four artillery pieces shortly before, hoping to confront his constitutionalist army as it came descending wearily and disarticulated after its difficult passage over the mountains. However, this federal force had ventured only as far as La Vega railway station before it had then unconcernedly halted to repair some nearby rail lines, its trains meanwhile left idling in plain view—affording Obregón time to regroup over the next couple of days and conceal his own undetected army in the rocky terrain between the Tequila and Ameca ranges, from where he hoped to goad Bernard into pursuing his cavalry scouts and draw the *federales* into a trap.

But the local guerrilla chieftain Julián Medina had unthinkingly burned a railway bridge behind the resting federal train convoy on June 28, 1914, prompting the Huertistas to fall back to repair that damage as well, in the process relocating their encampment onto the plains just south of Orendáin (alternate modern spelling: Orendain). His original design thus frustrated, Obregón devised a second plan involving two roundabout strikes: one to attack the rear of Bernard's detachment and thereby cut it off from its avenue of retreat (as well as receiving any reinforcements out of Guadalajara); plus another simultaneous descent on the rail lines south of the city itself so as to freeze Mier's garrison in position and discourage any attempted rescue of his colleague, who would be caught out in open country.

Stealthy Approach (July 1–5, 1914)

All of Obregón's constitutionalist cavalry was therefore gathered unseen between Ameca and La Vega under Brig. Gen. Lucio Blanco and dispatched from there on July 1, 1914, with orders to make a long circuitous ride eastward over the next four days, slipping between Guadalajara and Tlacomulco so as to materialize unexpectedly at dawn on July 6, 1914, launching a surprise attack against the federal outposts at El Castillo and La Capilla. Likewise, Brig. Gen. Manuel M. Diéguez also departed Obregón's camps on July 2, 1914, leading the 1st, 5th, 13th, 14th, 15th, 16th, and 17th Sonora Battalions and the 2nd Sonora Regiment under Lieutenant Colonels Eugenio Martínez, Esteban B. Calderón, Pablo

Quiroga, Juan José Ríos, Severiano A. Talamante, Fermín Carpio, and Alfredo Murillo, and Colonel Jesús Trujillo to make their own stealthy three-day trudge northward around the eastern end of the Tequila range, as far as Amatitlán before circling round to emerge atop La Venta Hills—appearing abruptly at dawn on July 6, 1914, directly in Bernard's rear.

Battle of Orendáin (July 6–8, 1914)

Obregón himself waited at the Hacienda El Refugio until Diéguez's column had engaged the Huertistas on July 6, 1914, before bombarding their paralyzed train convoy from the west with his own army's artillery and four machine guns, starting at midnight. The federal army was disintegrating into panic by dawn of July 7, 1914, individual units breaking off in hopes of regaining Guadalajara. Rather than indulge in diverse chases, Obregón continued swiftly into Zapopan, arriving that same evening and barring all access into the capital, thereby preventing the disperse Huertistas from reinforcing its garrison.

When Mier attempted to quit Guadalajara on July 8, 1914, with his remaining 3,000-man garrison, he found Blanco already blocking his escape route at El Castillo, being killed while attempting to fight his way through. Over the course of these three days of fighting, Huertista losses totaled 2,000 dead, 1,000 wounded, and 5,000 captured, along with 16 seized fieldpieces, 18 trains, and 40 locomotives. Obregón's constitutionalists entered Guadalajara that very same day of July 8, 1914, and its native son Diéguez assumed office as state governor.

Aftermath (July 9–August 15, 1914)

A week after the Battle of Orendáin, Huerta resigned the presidency and fled Mexico City, appointing Francisco S. Carvajal as his interim successor. With the road into the national capital now open, Carranza took steps to ensure that his reliable subordinate Obregón would be the first to arrive. Pablo González's constitutionalist Army of the Northeast took the city of San Luis Potosí without opposition on July 20, 1914, and his advance elements met Obregón at Querétaro 12 days later, driving on together toward Mexico City. On August 15, 1914, the victor of Orendáin and his Ejército del Noroeste paraded triumphantly into its streets.

See also: Ejército del Noroeste; Huerta Márquez, José Victoriano; Obregón Salido, Álvaro.

Further Reading

Cumberland, Charles C. *Mexican Revolution: The Constitutionalist Years.* Austin: University of Texas Press, 1972.

Jowett, Philip, and Alejandro de Quesada. *The Mexican Revolution, 1910–20.* Oxford: Osprey, 2006.

Knight, Alan. *The Mexican Revolution.* New York: Cambridge University Press, 1986.

Obregón, Álvaro. *Ocho mil kilómetros en campaña.* Mexico City: Secretaría de la Defensa Nacional, [n.d.], 2: 311–19.

Orozco Vázquez, Pascual (1882–1915)

Major rebel commander early on during the Mexican Revolution who later switched allegiances and fell from grace, dying as an outcast.

He was born on the Hacienda de Santa Inés near the village of San Isidro in the municipality of Guerrero in the northern state of Chihuahua on January 28, 1882, and baptized four days later as the son of Pascual Orozco and Amada Orozco y Vásquez. Shortly thereafter, the family moved into San Isidro proper, where Orozco attended school for four or five years. At the age of 12 or 13 he went to work in his father's store, and in his late teens he married Refugio Frías. From 1902 to 1910 Orozco worked as a muleteer, transporting precious metals, mostly silver, for several large mining companies in the Chihuahua mountains. He also opened a mercantile store in Estación Sánchez and eventually bought a gold mine. He soon acquired a substantial fortune.

Revolutionary Commander (1910–1911)

When the idealistic reformer and defrauded presidential candidate Francisco I. Madero issued a call from exile in Texas for a series of uprisings to erupt throughout Mexico on November 20, 1910, Orozco would be among the first to respond. He formed part of a small group under the leadership of his father-in-law, Albino Frías—including Orozco and his own father, Pascual Orozco Sr.; Orozco's brothers-in-law Antonio and Pablo Frías; as well as José, Marcelo, and Samuel Caraveo—which seized the tiny federal outpost at Miñaca on November 19, 1910, and then the next day carried San Isidro and the entire municipality of Guerrero.

One week later, a portion of this scratch force also ambushed the vanguard of an approaching federal column under Gen. Juan N. Navarro at Pedernales, after which Orozco personally led a descent against the federal garrison at Ciudad Guerrero, 100 miles west of Chihuahua City, capturing it by early December after a brief siege. In announcing this victory to the public, he signed himself the "*jefe de armas* Pascual Orozco, Jr."

Cerro Prieto and La Mojina were also attacked, while a federal column was ambushed in Mal Paso Canyon on January 2, 1911. After this latter victory, Orozco famously ordered his men to gather up the light-khaki caps and uniforms of the dead soldiers, to be sent to Díaz with the taunt: *Ahí te van las hojas, mándame más tamales* or "Here are your wrappers back, send me more tamales." Early next month, Orozco and 400 of his followers commandeered a freight- and two passenger-trains, using these to approach the federal garrison holding Ciudad Juárez on February 2, 1911, although unable to then subdue its outnumbered defenders before a federal relief-column under Col. Antonio M. Rábago fought its way in three days later from Bauche.

Orozco served as a "general" among the 3,500 ill-disciplined revolutionaries which Madero brought to besiege Ciudad Juárez on April 19, 1911, and along with "colonel" Pancho Villa was disappointed when a 10-day truce was arranged with its 700-man federal garrison under General Navarro to meet some plenipotentiaries sent by President Díaz from Mexico City. Two days after these talks broke off, the impatient Orozco and Villa arranged for their rebel troops to precipitate a firefight against the trapped *federales* on May 8, 1911, furnishing an excuse to storm Ciudad Juárez and push the outnumbered defenders back inside their cavalry barracks, where they surrendered two days afterward.

Orozco and Villa subsequently challenged Madero, demanding that Navarro and his federal officers—infamous for their harshness—be executed, but Madero refused and instead released the captives into the United States. Both rebel commanders, after grudgingly acquiescing with Madero's decision, left his service shortly thereafter. Orozco, in particular, entered Chihuahua City triumphantly at the head of his own small army on June 22, 1911, transforming it into his personal headquarters while Madero was being greeted into the national capital, and preparing to run again in a specially arranged presidential by-election five months later.

Anti-*Maderista* Rebellion (1912)

Inexperienced politically, Madero found it difficult to govern, both before and after he was elected into office. Orozco was among the most disaffected of his former followers, and so rose against Madero in Chihuahua City on March 3, 1912, accusing him of failing to carry out "the Revolution's promise" (although Orozco was actually resentful at being passed over for preferment). A vanguard of 1,000 *orozquista* cavalrymen struck southward from Chihuahua a few days later under Generals José Inés Salazar and Emilio P. Campa aboard two trains, to be followed by Orozco himself with 6,000 well-equipped irregulars, prompting Gen. José González Salas—a relative of Madero by marriage—to resign his post as war minister in Mexico City and march northward to confront this rebellion.

On March 25th near Rellano station in southern Chihuahua, González's vanguard was devastated by a runaway Orozquista locomotive sent flying down the track filled with dynamite by Campa, then the Maderista army was attacked from its rear by Campa's rebel cavalry. During this fighting, a federal battalion even mutinied, having to be fired uon by other federal contingents. Wounded and despondent, González ordered a retreat into Torreón (Coahuila) before committing suicide at Bermejillo.

April 12, 1912: Huerta reached Torreón (Coahuila) to take over González Salas's defeated army. After reorganizing this formation—and nearly executing "brigadier" Villa for insubordination—he advanced northward into Chihuahua to confront Orozco.

In a summer-long campaign, Huerta inflicted a series of defeats on the rebel leader's 7,000 men: first at Los Conejos on May 12th; then at Rellano on May 22nd–23rd; at La Cruz, in Bachimba Canyon, by late June; at Bermejillo, Chihuahua City, and finally at Ciudad Juárez on August 16th. Although Orozco and his surviving followers won an isolated victory on September 11th against the federal garrison holding the border town of Ojinaga, the rebel leader was wounded during this affray so sought refuge in the United States.

June 1, 1912: With 60 riders, Huerta defeated a 400-man Orozquista garrison at Parral (Chihuahua).

March 17, 1913: In Chihuahua, Orozco accepted the rank of brigadier in Huerta's federal army.

Exile in the United States (September 1914–July 1915)

Bested at every turn, Orozco headed back into Texas by September 1914. After visiting San Antonio, he went on to St. Louis, Washington, and New York. In early May 1915, he returned to New York to confer with Huerta, discussing plans for relaunching a campaign into northern Mexico from American soil. But he and Huerta were subsequently arrested on June 27, 1915, in Newman, New Mexico, being charged with conspiracy to violate the U.S. neutrality laws. Taken to El Paso, they were both briefly held at Fort Bliss before being freed on bonds of $15,000 for Huerta and $7,500 for Orozco, although still confined under house arrest. After Orozco somehow contrived to escape on July 3, 1915, though, Huerta was incarcerated once more.

Death (August 1915)

For almost two months, Orozco avoided recapture by the American authorities. However, on the morning of August 29, 1915, he and four companions—reputedly intending to ride across the border to meet some supporters at Bosque Bonito in Mexico—approached Dick Love's ranch near Sierra Blanca in Hudspeth County, Texas, and ordered its cook to begin preparing breakfast for them while their horses were being reshod. But before either task could be completed, the intruders saw Love and two of his men driving up in an automobile so helped themselves to other mounts in the stables and fled with Love and his men in pursuit. That night, some 15 marshals, deputy sheriffs, Texas Rangers, and troopers from the U.S. 13th Cavalry Regiment were organized into a posse and caught up to Orozco and his comrades on the afternoon of August 30, 1915, eight miles south of Lobo in the Van Horn Mountains. They were shot to death from the rims of Green River Canyon and only on viewing their bodies did the posse realize that their quarry had not been common bandits.

Orozco's body was carried into Van Horn, where it was embalmed, and there were unfounded fears for some weeks afterward that reprisals might occur in El Paso, San Antonio, or other centers of pro-Orozquista sentiment. Villa announced that his family could bury him in Mexico, but Orozco's widow disdained this offer, so he was instead buried in El Paso's Concordia Cemetery on September 3, 1915. Orozco was interred wearing the uniform of a major general of the Mexican Army with a Mexican flag draped over his coffin and about 3,000 mourners in attendance. The members of the posse that killed him were indicted on October 7, 1915, but found not guilty after a brief hearing the next day. In 1923, Orozco's remains were removed and reinterred in Chihuahua.

See also: Malpaso Canyon, Ambush in.

Further Reading

Meyer, Michael C. *Mexican Rebel: Pascual Orozco and the Mexican Revolution, 1910–1915.* Lincoln: University of Nebraska Press, 1967.

Sosa, Francisco. *Biografías de mexicanos distinguidos.* Mexico City: Porrúa, 2006.

Ortega, Jesús G. *See* González Ortega, José Canuto de Jesús (1824–1881).

Osollo Pancorbo, Luis Gonzaga (1828–1858)

Youthful general who early during the War of the Reform became the champion of the conservative cause, only to die prematurely from typhoid fever on the day before his 30th birthday.

He was born in a house located at 13 Calle de la Palma in Mexico City on June 19, 1828, the only son and second of two children of Francisco Osollo Iriarte and Gabriela Pancorbo Samaniego, his older sister, María Estefana Genoveva, having been born two years previously. Two days after his own birth, the infant boy was baptized in the Sagrario de la Parroquia de la Asunción as José Luis Silverio Pascual Osollo Pancorbo, but he would become much more commonly known throughout his short lifetime as Luis Osollo, Luis Gonzaga Osollo, or Luis G. Osollo.

While still scarcely a year old, his family had been forced to relocate to the Biscayan port city of Bilbao in Spain—his father's birthplace—after the expulsion of Spaniards from Mexico had resurged during 1829,

during which purge his father was ordered to be deported. Osollo had consequently first attended school in Bilbao and proved a bright student. It remains uncertain when his father died, but it is known that his Mexican mother had returned home to enroll her 10-year-old Luis in the *Colegio Militar* or "Military College" by April 28, 1839, and that she remarried shortly thereafter, giving birth to another daughter and two sons with her second husband between 1840 and 1842.

Early Military Career (1842–1854)

Because he was still only 13 years of age when he graduated from Mexico's military institute, Osollo was not immediately assigned to any army unit, being instead commissioned as a *subteniente de infantería permanente suelto* or "unattached [*suelto*] sublieutenant of permanent [regular] infantry." Wishing for a chance, he appealed in writing to Pres. Antonio López de Santa Anna for a posting in a letter dated January 29, 1842, and was rewarded one week later by being given command of the 1st Company of the Active Battalion of Zacatecas. He served with this state militia unit during its difficult campaign against the separatists in Yucatan and Tabasco, being promoted to lieutenant as of April 28, 1843, and to captain by the time he was granted four months' sick leave on November 22, 1843, so as to return home and recuperate from an illness.

Because of his excellent conduct during that miserable campaign, when the 15-year-old Osollo reported back to active duty, he was elevated to captain of the 6th Company of the 2nd Battalion, 1st Light Infantry Permanent Regiment as of April 2, 1844. His role during the Mexican-American War remains somewhat hazy, one document dated August 9, 1846, indicating that he was to be assigned to Gen. Pedro Ampudia's

Ejército del Norte or "Army of the North" in checking Zachary Taylor's invasion force, although this order was rescinded only two days later. When Santa Anna returned from exile and resumed the presidency in 1853, initiating a considerable military build-up, Osollo was among his loyalists and promoted to lieutenant colonel as of October 5, 1853, and to full colonel as of September 8, 1854.

Conservative Mutineer (1855–1856)

Displeased by the ejection of Santa Anna upon the triumph of the liberal Revolution of Ayutla, as well as his own recall into Mexico City by the acting president, Gen. Martín Carrera, Osollo deliberately disabled more than 1,000 firearms in his military stores at Iguala before returning into the national capital with a few of his troops on September 5, 1855, to resign his commission. He was nonetheless reinstated to command under the incumbent liberal administration of interim president Ignacio Comonfort, so that when a reactionary revolt broke out in the village of Zacapoaxtla in the mountains of Puebla on December 12, 1855, Osollo mutinied one week afterward and joined his battalion to this movement.

President Comonfort responded by ordering that a small army converge on this region under the overall command of a political appointee, the acting liberal governor Ignacio de la Llave of Veracruz, but when the first regiment marching from Mexico City reached Tatlaquitepec on Christmas Day 1855, its second-in-command—24-year-old lieutenant colonel Miguel Miramón—also arrested his superior, Col. Rafael Benavides, and this whole force joined the rebellion as well. De la Llave was lucky to return alive to the capital a few days later with only a handful of loyal officers. Another liberal brigade sent out

under Brig. Gen. Severo del Castillo joined the rebel ranks as well, while the 45-year-old conservative general Antonio Haro y Tamariz escaped from confinement at Veracruz next month to assume military leadership over this rebellion.

Thus Osollo was an officer in the mutinous conservative army of Haro, Del Castillo, and Miramón that pushed its way into the city of Puebla on January 23, 1856, tacitly assisted by Bishop Pelagio Antonio de Labastida y Dávalos.

March 1, 1856, Ocotlán: Comonfort arrived at San Martín Texmelucan, personally commanding 12,000 liberal troops. The president halted his advance to offer amnesty to Haro's rebel forces, ensconced inside nearby Puebla. When no answer was received within six days, Comonfort ordered his brigadiers Moreno and Italian-born Luigi Ghilardi to close on the city at dawn of March 8th.

Haro (a lifelong friend and colleague of the president) sallied to meet this liberal attack from atop Ocotlán Hill. Fighting raged until 10:00 a.m., when a truce was arranged to gather up the wounded and dead. The conservative commander also requested an interview with Comonfort, so they met beneath a tree at noon. The president renewed his amnesty offer, and Haro requested three hours to discuss the matter with his colleagues.

He failed to return at the appointed hour, though, and when Comonfort sent a rider to investigate, the scout reported that the outnumbered and demoralized conservatives were in full retreat back into Puebla. The liberal army therefore followed and bottled them inside until the rebels agreed to capitulate by March 23rd. Haro was carried off to prison in Mexico City, where he died shortly thereafter; Osollo and Del Castillo succeeded in escaping, while Miramón hid within Puebla. All other rebel officers were stripped of their rank two days later and incorporated into the liberal army as privates. Many Church properties were moreover expropriated to defray the costs of this campaign, while Bishop Lamadrid was deported from Mexico, actions that fueled resentment among the faithful.

Exile and Injury (1856–1857)

Osollo, along with Haro and Márquez, escaped through Veracruz on April 27, 1856, sailing away aboard the French vessel *Pénélope*. The *Times-Picayune* newspaper of New Orleans reported on page 2 of its May 15, 1856, edition how news from Havana indicated:

> The *Diario de la Marina*, of the 8th inst. [May 8, 1856] announces the arrival there of H. B. M. ship *Penelope*, at Havana, on the previous day from Vera Cruz. She took, as passengers, a number of the parties to the late revolution at Puebla, among them Señor D. Antonio Haro y Tamariz, Gen. Leonardo Marquez, Col. Luis G. de Osollo, Lieut. Cols. Ángel López Santa Anna, and Juan Bautista Legarde, Chief of Battalion, Manuel Cano, Capt. Rafael González, and Lieut. Manuel Fontenecha.

Subsequently going ashore at New Orleans, Osollo worked as a waiter in a restaurant in order to survive, proudly turning down the 1,000 *pesos* that were sent to him as a conciliatory gesture by President Comonfort. When Gen. Manuel María Calvo led the garrison of San Luis Potosí in yet another conservative revolt on December 10, 1856, Osollo contrived to return into Mexico and join its ranks.

The liberal general Anastasio Parrodi having been sent from Guadalajara with a large army to crush Calvo's insurrection, the latter abandoned San Luis Potosí and retired toward Querétaro on January 10, 1857. Overtaken two weeks later, the conservatives were defeated at Tunas Blancas and trapped atop Magdalena Hill until the night of February 6, 1857, when they managed to slip away under cover of darkness. Run down the next day while fleeing toward Magdalena, Osollo fought a rearguard action and was badly wounded in his right arm during a clash at the Hacienda de La Esperanza. Upon surrendering to Parrodi, the badly injured young officer was well treated, although his arm required amputation on February 9, 1857, after which Parrodi petitioned Comonfort for the young rebel to be pardoned, which was granted.

Conservative Coups (December 1857–January 1858)

Recuperated from his convalescence, Osollo was still in Mexico City 10 months later when Comonfort staged a fake "coup" with the help of his trusted subordinate, Brig. Gen. Félix M. Zuloaga, on December 17, 1857, intended to retain him in the presidency while dissolving his liberal Congress and revoking their "radical" constitutional reforms. After more than three weeks of confused uncertainty during which liberals across the country voiced angry opposition and few hard-core conservatives rose in support of Comonfort's middle-of-the-road course, Gen. José de la Parra led the Tacubaya garrison in a second authentic coup on January 11, 1858, aimed at removing the ineffectual Comonfort altogether in favor of the figurehead Zuloaga.

These mutineers seized the Ciudadela and San Agustín Church, while Comonfort managed to hold out in the Presidential Palace with perhaps 3,000 men, and independent liberal forces occupied the Santísima and San Francisco churches as their own separate strongholds. This tense three-sided standoff was broken 10 days later when Osollo and the equally youthful conservative lieutenant colonel Miguel Miramón led successful assaults against Comonfort's positions at dawn on January 21, 1858, defeating and scattering his last disheartened followers, so he fled the capital into foreign exile.

An extemporized body of 22 leading conservatives dubbed the *Junta de Notables* then convened in Mexico City the next day and elected Zuloaga as "interim president," with Parra as his minister of war. The latter in turn promoted the 29-year-old Osollo to the rank of brigadier general as of January 25, 1858 (conferring the same rank on 26-year-old Miramón), and shortly thereafter Zuloaga furthermore appointed the one-armed Osollo to be commander-in-chief of the main *Ejército Restaurador de las Garantías* or "Restorer of Guarantees Army," which was to march north into the Bajío and put down all liberal opposition.

Youthful Conservative Champion (February 1858)

Resistance to the conservatives' forced revocation of the Constitution in the national capital had caused numerous liberal states to begin mobilizing their militias for war. Comonfort had ordered the incarcerated Benito Juárez, president of the Supreme Court, released before fleeing Mexico City, who—being legally next in line to the presidency—had traveled clandestinely to the city of Guanajuato and become the figurehead for liberal resistance.

By the second week of February 1858, Osollo departed Mexico City northwestward with a large contingent of regular troops, following a vanguard brigade of 1,200 men

that was already advancing under his subordinate, Brig. Gen. Miguel Miramón, with orders to push into the Bajío and disperse any liberal militia forces that might be gathering there in support of their rival, Pres. Benito Juárez.

While penetrating into this hostile territory, a third conservative brigade under Brig. Gen. Tomás Mejía fell back from San Juan del Río and incorporated itself into Osollo's army, bringing his total strength up to some 5,400 men. Expecting to be defied by the liberal general José María Arteaga at Querétaro, Osollo was surprised to enter that city uncontested on February 12, 1858, this liberal commander having withdrawn due west in the direction of Celaya with his 2,000 troops. (Two days later, the very threat posed by Osollo's drive northwestward would also cause Juárez to evacuate his government-in-exile from Guanajuato in favor of Guadalajara.)

Learning that as many as 6,000 liberal militiamen were marshaling under Gen. Anastasio Parrodi—the governor of Jalisco—around Celaya, only 30 miles from Querétaro, Osollo carefully planned his approach with the intention of attacking this superior force from two directions. It took him until February 24, 1858, to bring his lone division into Apaseo (nine miles east of Celaya), while the brigades of his conservative subordinates Francisco García Casanova and Mejía had circled around and were coming down the road from Chamacuero (modern Comonfort), 15 miles to the north.

The next day, February 25, 1858, Osollo's advance scouts exchanged fire with the liberal defensive lines some three miles outside Celaya, their combined strength now totaling over 7,000 men, who were dug into strong positions behind the banks of the Laja River. Once again, Osollo prudently waited for his trailing siege train of 40 pieces and supply caravan to close up before attempting to brave these redoubts. And he tricked some liberal brigades into withdrawing from their Laja entrenchments with a feint on March 7, 1858, so his regulars were able to stream across its stone bridge and drive through this gap toward Celaya, while Parrodi's outmaneuvered liberal army had to hastily retreat by forced marches into Salamanca, 30 miles farther west, arriving there exhausted on the night of March 8, 1858.

Battle of Salamanca (March 10, 1858)

Casanova's pursuing conservative brigade clashed with some liberal cavalrymen at the Hacienda de Cerro Gordo on March 9, 1858, so Parrodi—realizing Osollo's main body would be coming along close behind—ordered his weary and disorganized liberal army to retrace their steps from their Salamanca encampments to make a stand a half dozen miles outside that city, behind a small watercourse known as Arroyo Feo or "Ugly Creek." Some 7,300 liberal troops had deployed into a shaky battle line by that same afternoon behind its banks, while Osollo's 5,400 regulars arrived on the far side. As darkness fell, the artillery batteries that had been exchanging long-range gunfire fell silent, in anticipation of a major encounter the next day.

On the morning of March 10, 1858, the gun duel resumed as the conservative infantry closed on the waiting liberal lines, Parrodi responding by launching a charge around his left flank with two full cavalry regiments. Watching from his command post, Osollo instructed his artillery commander, Col. Ceferino Rodríguez, to redirect his heavy gunfire to break up this mass formation with grapeshot, then a

countercharge by Mejía's cavalry chased these broken squadrons back into the liberal left.

Meanwhile, Osollo's regular army infantry continued to steadily close on the liberal militia throng. The Fieles de Guanajuato Battalion was the first liberal unit to give way and run, after which Parrodi's army rapidly disintegrated. Only the liberals' 1st and 5th Line Regiments, 1st Light Infantry Regiment, Tiradores de Guerrero Battalion, Rifleros de Policía Battalion, and parts of their Guanajuato Brigade— 2,800 men in all—managed to trudge off the battlefield in formation, retreating west toward Irapuato with 18 guns and part of their artillery train. Parrodi led these remnants of his army in a further retreat through Silao to Lagos, where they arrived by March 13, 1858, closely shadowed by Mejía's pursuing cavalry.

Osollo had been left victorious on the battlefield with another 12 captured liberal guns and perhaps as many as 4,000 prisoners, plus countless horses and wagons. With no major concentration of militiamen left to oppose him, the conservative general resumed his march and entered the city of León uncontested on March 12, 1858, and the next day received the surrender at Romita of Guanajuato's Manuel Doblado and his 800 survivors from Arroyo Feo.

When news of this crushing defeat at Salamanca reached Guadalajara on the morning of March 13, 1858, Lt. Col. Antonio Landa of the 5th Line Regiment mutinied and seized President Juárez and his liberal cabinet, parading them before a firing squad the next day, only to be spared at the last moment by the eloquence of the minister Guillermo Prieto, who persuaded the soldiers to lower their weapons and spare their lives. Landa's men nonetheless ransacked the palace before decamping on March 15,

1858, the day before the beaten Parrodi brought his surviving troops back home into Guadalajara.

On March 20, 1858, Juárez and his ministers fled toward the Pacific coast with an escort of only 90 liberal troopers, leaving Parrodi to arrange the surrender of the liberal city the next day to Osollo's approaching army. The conservatives occupied it triumphantly on March 23, 1858, in accordance with the terms of the capitulation agreement worked out two days previously and soon after departed to continue campaigning in the state of San Luis Potosí.

Last Campaign and Unexpected Death (May–June, 1858)

Osollo returned triumphantly into Mexico City from his sweep through the Bajío on April 22, 1858, but news reached him only a week later that the liberal colonel Juan Zuazua had surprised and overwhelmed the conservative force left to garrison the city of Zacatecas. Osollo consequently departed the national capital again on May 14, 1858, at the head of 500 men and six guns. While proceeding northward, he was to incorporate Gen. Luis Pérez Gómez's 1,000 men and half dozen guns into his column as he passed through Querétaro, plus another 600 men and six guns from Guanajuato, as well as be overtaken en route by the 500-man Orizaba Battalion so as to arrive at San Luis Potosí with these additional 2,600 men and 18 guns to engage the northern liberals.

Reaching San Luis by early June 1858, Osollo was then obliged to detach Miramón with a strong force to rescue the threatened garrison at Guadalajara. While awaiting the outcome of this diversion, Osollo suddenly sickened from typhoid fever and his health declined rapidly. He died in the city of San Luis Potosí at 5:15 p.m. on June 18, 1858, the day before his 30th birthday. Miramón would subsequently inherit his mantle as conservative commander-in-chief.

See also: Ampudia Grimarest, Pedro; Ayutla, Revolution of; Barradas's Invasion; Guadalajara, Sieges of; Miramón Tarelo, Miguel Gregorio de la Luz Atenógenes; Reform, War of the; Salamanca, Battle of; Tacubaya, Plan of; Zuazua Esparza, Juan Nepomuceno.

Further Reading

Hernández Rodríguez, Rosaura. *El general conservador Luis G. Osollo*. Mexico City: Editorial Jus, 1959.

"Interesting from Mexico: Particulars of the Suppression of the San Luis Insurrection." *New York Times*, March 12, 1857.

Sosa, Francisco. *Biografías de mexicanos distinguidos*. Mexico City: Porrúa, 2006.

P

The palace filled with all kinds of people; the government, weak and without prestige, no longer served to even give an illusion of power.

— Pres. Manuel Gómez Pedraza,
describing his removal by the
Acordada Mutiny (December 1828)

Padierna, Battle of (1847). Mexican name for the engagement called the "Battle of Contreras" by the U.S. invaders during the Mexican-American War. *See* Contreras, Battle of (1847).

Palo Alto, Battle of (1846)

Opening encounter of the Mexican-American War, a decisive victory for the U.S. invaders thanks to their superior horse artillery, which would remain a significant tactical advantage throughout the ensuing conflict.

Preliminary Maneuvers

Learning that Fort Texas had been attacked, Taylor departed Point Santa Isabel with 2,300 men at 3:00 p.m. on May 7, 1846, to relieve his beleaguered detachment. After camping overnight, he encountered Arista's and Torrejón's 3,200 Mexicans on May 8,

American lithograph depicting U.S. staff officers at the Battle of Palo Alto on May 8, 1846. (Library of Congress)

1846, who were blocking the road at Palo Alto Pond in a mile-and-a-half-long battle line.

Having secured their baggage train, the Americans advanced early that afternoon with the 8th Infantry and Capt. James Duncan's light-artillery battery on the left; the 4th and 3rd Infantry in the center, supported by heavy 18-pounders; plus the 5th Infantry and Capt. Samuel Ringgold's light field artillery on the right. The Mexican guns opened fire as Taylor advanced, making poor execution due to their weak powder and the fact that they had no high-explosive shells. The horse-drawn "flying" American light batteries, in contrast, wrought fearful havoc by swiftly deploying ahead of Taylor, pouring a heavy fire into the static Mexican lines.

Arista ordered Torrejón's lancers to charge the American left, but this attack was broken before it could even develop by Ringgold's accurate counterfire. Having endured more than 400 casualties without ever coming to grips with their enemies, as well as being blinded by a dense brushfire that was raging through the chaparral, the Mexicans withdrew by evening. American losses totaled 9 dead—among them, Ringgold—44 wounded, and 2 missing.

Further Reading

Tucker, Spencer C. *The Encyclopedia of the Mexican-American War.* Santa Barbara, CA: ABC-CLIO, 2013.

Paredón, Battle of (1914)

Lightning victory won by Pancho Villa, sweeping away the remnants of a federal army that had already been rendered jittery by its recent defeats.

Having smashed major Huertista concentrations at Torreón and San Pedro de las Colonias only a few weeks previously, Villa was unhappy at not being rewarded with command of his own army corps by the constitutionalist *primer jefe* or "first chief," Venustiano Carranza—nor being authorized to drive on south toward the city of Zacatecas, the most direct route leading into the national capital.

Instead, since the rebels' more feeble *Ejército del Noreste* or "Army of the Northeast" under Gen. Pablo González had failed to push 60 miles southwestward down a parallel rail line out of Monterrey to take the smaller city of Saltillo, thereby cutting off the arrival of any more federal troops out of central Mexico to reconstitute their surviving regional forces, Carranza ordered Villa to veer his victorious División del Norte eastward from Torreón, pursuing the remnants of his retreating Huertista opponents following in their tracks and fighting his way onward to seize Saltillo.

Villa's Approach (May 12–16, 1914)

Villa's artillery commander and professional military strategist, Gen. Felipe Ángeles, consequently departed Torreón eastward on May 12, 1914, with three dozen guns and the entire *villista* artillery train aboard railway flatcars, reaching the lonely Saucedo railway station next day. There he discovered that the 12 miles of track leading on to the next station of Amargos had been torn up by the retreating Huertistas, who were reassembling six miles beyond there at the Paredón station with a mixed force of 5,000 federal troops and raw conscripts under Maj. Gen. Ignacio Muñoz and Brig. Gen. Francisco Osorno, while still farther beyond at Saltillo another 15,000 federal soldiers and auxiliaries were marshalling under Maj. Gen. Joaquín Maass Águila (a nephew of the dictator Victoriano Huerta).

As the Villista trains began piling up behind Ángeles's halted artillery convoy, he sent his aide, Col. Vito Alessio Robles, 12 miles back from Saucedo aboard a locomotive to suggest a plan to Villa—whose headquarters car was stopped at Hipólito—whereby all the cavalry and infantry would be detrained so:

- A detachment could be sent overland to seize the station at Zertuche, thus preventing any possible reinforcement of the Huertista army gathering at Paredón from a force of 2,000 *colorado* irregulars known to also be stationed at Ramos Arizpe.
- Villa would meanwhile lead the main body of his cavalry and infantry through Josefa Canyon, following the ruined tracks so as to head straight at the federal concentration at Paredón.
- Ángeles would circle around to the north through La Tortuga, Treviño, Leona, and Las Norias with his artillery convoy so as to rejoin Villa with his 36 guns in time for an all-out assault against Paredón.

Villa agreed, ordering his troops to detrain, and began his own advance through Josefa Canyon by the afternoon of Friday, May 15, 1914.

Battle of Paredón (May 17, 1914)

At 5:00 a.m. on the following Sunday morning, May 17, 1914, Ángeles departed the Hacienda de las Norias overland with four mule-drawn batteries of guns, struggling to reach Villa's main body five hours later, which was already in the act of deploying for the impending battle. The outnumbered Federal Army under Generals Muñoz and Osorno had been caught by surprise by Villa's sudden appearance and were utterly unprepared to mount any kind of proper defense, their artillery opening up an erratic fire that fell well short as the Villista columns churned up huge dust clouds while wheeling and forming up to attack.

Shortly after 10:30 a.m., before Ángeles's guns could even be unlimbered, Villa gave the signal to begin the battle by launching a massive cavalry charge with 6,000 riders, who galloped straight at the federal positions. Panic gripped their demoralized soldiers, who broke and within 15 minutes were fleeing in all directions. Hundreds of Huertistas were slain (many summarily by firing squads as they were overtaken), while 2,100 were captured along with 10 cannon and all their supply trains. Their commanding general, Muñoz, had fallen on the battlefield, while Osorno managed to escape only as far as one of the trains before being caught and killed. In the euphoria of victory, Villa's subordinates Maclovio Herrera and Tomás Urbina even fell to exchanging gunfire against each other in a dispute over who would get to keep a band of musicians captured from among the *federales*—an issue resolved by Ángeles through a coin toss, won by Herrera.

Only the 1,000 Huertista cavalrymen under Brig. Gen. Miguel Álvarez succeeded in escaping through Mesillas and Valle Perdido toward Saltillo, closely pursued by the riders of *villista* brigadier general José Isabel Robles. Maass subsequently evacuated Saltillo without a fight, retreating overland toward San Luis Potosí with considerable difficulty and losing many stragglers because the rail lines through this district were so badly damaged, while behind him Villa triumphantly occupied Saltillo on May 20, 1914.

See also: Ángeles Ramírez, Felipe de Jesús; División del Norte; Huerta Márquez, José Victoriano; San Pedro de las Colonias, Battle of; Torreón, Battle of; Villa, Pancho.

Further Reading

Campobello, Nellie. *Apuntes sobre la vida militar de Francisco Villa*. Mexico City: EDIAPSA, 1951.

Guzmán, Martín Luis. *Memoirs of Pancho Villa*. Austin: University of Texas Press, 1976 translation.

Parián Riot (1828)

Looting spree in Mexico City directed against Spanish monopolists in the immediate wake of Pres. Manuel Gómez Pedraza's expulsion from office.

Background (August–November 1828)

With no experience as a democracy, or even any clearly defined political parties, the national elections that had been held in August 1828 failed to reflect the popular will. The lowborn insurgent hero Vicente Guerrero had been the preferred choice by a clear majority of Mexican voters, yet because he was a mulatto who had begun his career as a common teamster, he was deemed unworthy to occupy such high office by the Creole elites that dominated public institutions—and since raw popular-vote results had to be weighed by each state legislature before casting their decisive electoral votes, the winner was instead declared to be the former royalist officer and sitting minister of war, General Gómez Pedraza, with Guerrero relegated to serving as his vice president.

A military insurrection erupted in distant Veracruz under Gen. Antonio López de Santa Anna a few days after Gómez Pedraza had assumed the presidency on September 1, 1828, although it did not spread. Adding to the tension between both factions was the fact that the newly elected president favored a restrained policy against the large numbers of Spaniards still residing in Mexico, while Guerrero was spearheading a movement calling for their removal through mass expulsions out of fear of an attempted *reconquista*—an anti-Spanish policy with considerable support among the lower classes.

Parián Riot (December 4, 1828)

Eventually, a confused military uprising dubbed the "Acordada Mutiny" broke out in Mexico City on the evening of November 30, 1828, whose disorganized members finally attacked the *pedrazista* loyalists holding out in the Presidential Palace around noon on December 2, 1828, resulting in volleys of gunfire and numerous deaths in the city streets. With his fledgling government incapable of acting, Gómez Pedraza resigned from office and departed toward Guadalajara on the evening of December 3, 1828, leaving the capital devoid of any recognizable authority.

Therefore, on the morning of December 4, 1828, a mob chanting *Mueran los españoles* or "Death to the Spaniards" broke into the padlocked commercial stalls of the Parián in the city center, stripping them bare. Order was gradually restored, although Guerrero was not officially voted into office as president by the reconvened Congress until January 12, 1829.

See also: Acordada Mutiny; Guerrero Saldaña, Vicente Ramón; Santa Anna, Antonio López de.

Further Reading

Arrom, Sylvia M. "Popular Politics in Mexico City: The Parián Riot, 1828." *Hispanic American Historical Review* 68, no. 2 (May 1988): 245–68.

parte official

Generic designation used in the Mexican bureaucracy for any kind of "official report" and long employed in the Mexican Army to refer to the account submitted to headquarters by a field commander on the conclusion of a major action or campaign, reports that were then often published for widespread consumption.

Hundreds of examples of famous *partes oficiales* abound from Mexico's military past, such as:

- The *parte oficial* written by the imperial Col. Juan Domínguez on December 21, 1822, and printed one week later in Mexico City, describing his successful defense of Xalapa against Santa Anna
- The *parte oficial* written "at seven at night" on April 18, 1847, by Gen. Valentín Canalizo of the Ejército de Oriente and printed two days later in Mexico City as a broadside by José María Rivera, describing the defeat of Santa Anna's army by Winfield Scott at the Battle of Cerro Gordo
- The *parte oficial* written by Gen. Ignacio Zaragoza of his famous defense of Puebla on May 5, 1862, which was very widely published
- The *parte oficial* completed by Maj. Gen. Gustavo A. Maass on May 17, 1914, and published eight days later in Mexico City, giving a detailed account of the U.S. occupation of the port of Veracruz

Further Reading

Parte oficial de la toma de Tampico por las fuerzas del supremo gobierno al mando del C. general S. Rocha. Mexico City: Imprenta del Gobierno, 1871.

Villareal, Florencio. *Parte oficial que dirige al Exmo. Sr. presidente de la República y general en jefe del ejército de operaciones, como su segundo el de división D. Florencio Villareal, de la batalla del día ocho del presente en el puerto de Montero y San Francisco Ocotlán.* Mexico City: J. M. Macías, 1856.

Pasteles, Guerra de los (1838–1839). *See* Cakes, War of the (1838–1839).

patente

A generic term in the Spanish language for any kind of official "certificate" issued for public use but that in the Mexican Army was reserved for the "commission" given to an officer on being promoted to a new rank.

For example, Article 32, Section III of the military *Ordenanza general* or "General Ordinances" of January 5, 1912, specified that the "seniority of each class or employment" among army officers of equal rank was to depend on "the date of the *patente* issued by the President of the Republic or by the Secretary of War."

See also: *escalafón general.*

pecho a tierra

Expression that translates literally as "chest to ground" but was used by soldiers to indicate a prone position.

When the liberal general Jesús González Ortega later wrote to report on his stealthy, nocturnal deployment of twin assault columns to within close range of the conservative artillery prior to the Battle of Silao in August 1860, he added that his soldiers had been instructed to lie down "*pecho a tierra*, and for our encampment to remain in silence" so their presence would remain undetected and allow them to surprise their enemy at dawn.

See also: González Ortega, José Canuto de Jesús; Silao, Battle of.

pelón

Word literally meaning someone with a "shaved head" or a crew cut, often used as a slang expression to describe a soldier.

This term became especially commonplace when referring to members of Pres. Porfirio Díaz's federal army in the early 20th century, so many examples abound in historical texts. For example, the American observer John Reed recorded on pages 209–10 of his book *Insurgent Mexico* how, upon departing a Villista encampment with some soldiers at dawn in March of 1914, heading toward the audible gunfire of battle around the outskirts of the city of Torreón, the rebel sentries had called after them: "Adios! Don't kill them all! Leave a few *pelones* for us!"

And the famous *corrido* or "ballad" on the death of Emiliano Zapata also features the verse:

> From Cuautla to Amecameca,
> Matamoros and the Ajusco,
> with the *pelones* of old Don
> Porfirio, he had a good time.

The expression *pelón* still remains current in Mexico today.

See also: *corridos*; Torreón, Villa's Second Capture of.

Further Reading
Reed, John. *Insurgent Mexico*. New York: Appleton, 1914.

Peninsular

Nickname during the late colonial and early independence eras for Spanish-born subjects from the Iberian Peninsula, as opposed to native-born Mexican *criollos* or "Creoles."

The latter resented the special privileges and status accorded under the viceregal system to these trans-Atlantic appointees, who received their titles and grants directly from Crown ministries in Madrid that were inaccessible to American-born subjects and then arrived to profit from their brief tenures in the New World before returning home enriched to Spain. The more vituperative form of address for such individuals was *gachupines*, and the resentments accumulated against their overbearing presence did much to fuel the violent eruption of Mexico's War of Independence in September 1810.

See also: *gachupín*; Independence, War of.

Further Reading
Hernández Sáenz, Luz María. "Médicos Criollos y Cirujanos Peninsulares: Criollo Nationalism and the Medical Profession in Colonial Mexico." *Canadian Journal of Latin American and Caribbean Studies* 25, no. 49 (2000): 33–51.

perfumao

Contraction in Spanish of the adjective *perfumado* or "perfumed one," a derisive slang expression often used by Mexican soldiers or country folk to describe fashionable city dwellers.

This term was a favorite pejorative often employed by the former bandit and rough-hewn revolutionary general Pancho Villa whenever speaking about high-ranking federal officers, government officials, or others of his opponents. In particular, he commonly referred to his great battlefield foe Álvaro Obregón as "El Perfumado," and furthermore called Obregón's political chieftain Venustiano Carranza a *chocolatero perfumao* or "perfumed chocolate drinker."

Apparently Villa's gibe rankled with the humbly born, self-made man Obregón, for it was recorded how prior to his second great battle against Villa at the city of Celaya in mid-April 1915, Obregón had not worn his customary khaki field uniform on the day of battle but instead appeared before his soldiers dressed in the traditional broad-brimmed hat, silver-studded trousers, and chamois goatskin jacket of a Mexican *charro*. When asked after his victory about his change of garb, Obregón had allegedly replied: "Villa gave me the not-very-manly nickname of 'El Perfumado,' and to prove him wrong, I had to smell like a goat."

See also: Obregón Salido, Álvaro; Villa, Pancho.

Further Reading

Gilliam, Ronald R. "Turning Point of the Mexican Revolution." *MHQ: The Quarterly Journal of Military History* 15, no. 3 (Spring 2003): 40–51.

Katz, Friedrich. *The Life and Times of Pancho Villa*. Stanford, CA: Stanford University Press, 1998, 480.

Perote, Fort of (1770–2007)

Enormous colonial-era stronghold that saw relatively little military action, serving briefly as the home of Mexico's first Military College, then later as a prison.

Construction and Royal Service (1770–1821)

Following Spain's easy defeat at the hands of Great Britain in 1762, during the final disastrous year of the French and Indian War, a major upgrade was ordered for all military defenses throughout Spanish America. The viceroyalty of Mexico's principal seaport of Veracruz began having its fortifications strengthened very shortly thereafter, but differences arose as to adding an extended new line of coastal batteries. Instead of beginning such a costly project, the viceroy, Marqués de Croix, instructed *mariscal de campo* or "Field Marshal" Antonio Ricardos y Carrillo to conduct a survey during the summer of 1766 of the two highways leading up into the central highlands from the torrid coastline and then submitted a report to Madrid that same October 25, 1766, that recommended the erection of a single new strategic fort far inland in the vicinity of Perote.

This village, nestled 35 miles west of the city of Jalapa, had long served as a waystation along the *camino real* or "royal road" that circled around the extinct Cofre de Perote volcano and lay a full three days' march inland from Veracruz. Its remove so far from the coast meant that Perote would be safe from any surprise attack following an enemy disembarkation, and since it was at 8,000 feet above sea level, it enjoyed a cool climate, abundant water, and fertile farmland. In the event of a seaborne invasion, a stronghold installed at that spot would provide a safe "depot [*almacén general*] to assist San Juan de Ulúa," as well as a bountiful marshaling area for the thousands of troops who would be summoned to muster there from throughout "the interior of the kingdom." Perote's highway was moreover considered the fastest descent down to the coast, in comparison to the alternate route passing through Orizaba.

The royal engineer Manuel de Santisteban, already engaged in improving Veracruz's defenses, was consequently ordered to draw up plans for construction of a major new strategic fortress at Perote. He chose some high ground about a mile northwest of its town and submitted a proposal by late February 1769, which was approved by a royal decree issued from Madrid in late August 1769—although calling for an increase in the size of its structure. Santisteban's revised design was submitted by April 1770, intended for an enormous fort covering 26 acres, with embrasures for 75 heavy guns lining its four bastions, capable of housing 1,000 troops. Ground was broken and work officially began on June 25, 1770, its main structure being completed by December 1775. Its interior buildings and details were completed by late 1777, and 54 artillery pieces mounted, at which time it was christened as the *Fuerte de San Carlos de Perote* in honor of Spain's ruling king Charles III. Its four bastions were named San Carlos at its eastern point, San Julián at its northern point, San Antonio at its southern point, and San José at its western point.

At the time of its completion, the Fort of Perote was one of the largest and most imposing military structures in the Americas. Gen. Thomas J. Green, a Texan who would be imprisoned inside its compound for a few months, later described his first impression upon coming within sight of the distant fort on March 25, 1843:

> Upon our arrival at the village of Perote, in looking north about one mile we could see the massive walls of the castle, with its numerous portholes and dark-mouthed artillery. The great extent of ground covered by the castle wall and the earthen embankment around the outer *"chevaux de frize"* gave this fortification a low appearance, and, at first sight, we were not struck with the

magnitude of its strength. Upon nearer approach, in making our way through its winding entrance, and across the drawbridge over the great moat, thence through an archway into the great *plaza* fronting the governor's quarters, amid the bugle's blast and the roll of drums, the din of arms and the clank of chains opened our eyes to the reality of imprisonment, and showed us what abler pens than mine have described as the most approved fortification of the eighteenth century.

No enemy disembarkation ever tested Perote's military strength during the remainder of the colonial era, nor was its royal garrison ever directly challenged during Mexico's War of Independence, although the long, lonely highways running throughout its jurisdiction were often infested with insurgent guerrilla bands. On June 8, 1812, Perote's military governor—the Spanish brigadier general Antonio Olazábal—apparently uncovered a plot to deliver his fortress into rebel hands, and so he ordered 13 men arrested and court-martialed, executing 9 of them in the moat beneath its walls with firing squads on June 16, 1812.

Eventually though, after Agustín de Iturbide's "Plan of Iguala" spread and was widely accepted throughout the viceroyalty, even being embraced by the townspeople of the nearby town of Perote, the royal garrison simply marched out of their fort on October 10, 1821, so as to assemble with the other Crown regiments who were waiting to be repatriated to Spain next spring.

Military College (1823–1828)

In the immediate postindependence era, the fort was entrusted to Iturbide's imperial brig general, Rafael Ramiro, and used briefly as a staging area for the 3,000-man army that descended on Veracruz in

January 1823 in an unsuccessful campaign to put down an early insurrection by Antonio López de Santa Anna. Following the emperor's removal, the fledgling Academy of Cadets—which had been created a few years earlier in Mexico City by Gen. Diego García Conde to train young officers for the Mexican Army—was assigned the Fortress of Perote on October 11, 1823, to serve as the young republic's new *Colegio Militar* or "Military College."

Perote was duly occupied for this purpose, with cavalry colonel Juan Domínguez y Gálvez acting as its first director until 1824, when he was succeeded by Lt. Col. José Manuel Arechega. Its garrison of troops from the 10th Battalion under Capt. Agustín Terán was suspected of conspiring to facilitate a Spanish *reconquista* in 1827 and so were arrested before the college's entire faculty and students were transferred back into Mexico City as of March 1828. The fort thereupon resumed its former military role, being garrisoned by two companies (120 soldiers) of the Tres Villas Infantry Regiment under Capt. Domingo Huerta, 90 cavalrymen of the Jalapa Regiment under Lt. Col. José María Zomosa, and 80 artillerymen under Capt. Ignacio Ortiz.

Siege of Autumn 1828

With no experience as a democracy, or even any clearly defined political parties, the national elections held in August 1828 failed to reflect the popular will. The insurgent hero Guerrero had been the preferred choice by a majority of Mexicans, yet because he was a mulatto who had begun his career as a common teamster, he was deemed unworthy to occupy such high office by the Creole elites who dominated all public institutions—and since the raw voting results had to be weighed in turn by each state legislature, before these bodies cast their decisive electoral votes, the final outcome proved to be quite unexpected.

The former royalist officer and sitting minister of war, Gómez Pedraza, had received 11 out of 36 electoral votes; only 8 went to Guerrero, the clear winner of the popular vote; and the remaining electoral votes were split up among Anastasio Bustamante, Ignacio Godoy, and Melchor Múzquiz. Gómez Pedraza was consequently proclaimed the winner and next president on September 1, 1828, with Guerrero relegated to serving as his vice president. Both men were in fact members of the *yorquino* or "Yorkist" Masonic faction, but whereas the new president-elect favored a restrained policy against the large numbers of Spaniards still residing in Mexico, Guerrero was spearheading a movement calling for their removal through mass expulsions, out of fear of an attempted *reconquista*—a policy with considerable support throughout the country.

Santa Anna's Uprising (September 1828)

A couple of days after Gómez Pedraza had been declared the winner, 34-year-old general and vice governor of Veracruz, Antonio López de Santa Anna, began engineering a revolt in that state: first, by persuading the municipal government of its capital city of Jalapa to challenge the electoral vote cast by the Veracruzan legislature in favor of Pedraza, against the popular returns that had been recorded throughout that state.

Suspended from office as vice governor in retaliation on September 5, 1828, Santa Anna openly rebelled two days later by assuming command over Lt. Col. Mariano Arista's 80 men of the 2nd Cavalry Regiment and Lt. Col. José Antonio Heredia's

500 soldiers of the 5th Permanent Infantry Regiment (whose commander, Col. Juan M. Azcárate—a brother-in-law of President Gómez Pedraza—had been arrested while attempting to leave the San José barracks). Santa Anna then sent out calls for support to his regional allies and marched his small force—including two small fieldpieces and 150 militiamen from Jalapa—out of that city on the night of September 11–12, 1828, heading toward the strategically placed Fort of Perote.

Riding on ahead with an advance party of only eight riders, he convinced the officers of its 290-man garrison to arrest their *pedrazista* commander, Lt. Col. José Manuel Arechega, and admit Santa Anna with his brigade on September 13, 1828, thereby joining his rebellion. From Perote, he subsequently issued a *pronunciamiento* three days later—Mexico's Independence Day—addressed to the "peoples of Anáhuac" in the name of his so-called *Ejército Libertador* or Liberating Army, calling for the annulment of Gómez Pedraza's installation as president, the immediate substitution of Guerrero, and enactment of effective legislation to remove all Spaniards from Mexico's soil.

Some small units marched to join Santa Anna at Perote, and supportive uprisings ensued at Acapulco, Chalco, and Apám but not the broad-based national insurrection that he was expecting. Instead, the Gómez Pedraza administration remained firmly in control of most major garrisons and cities, quickly declaring Santa Anna an outlaw and assembling an army at Mexico City of almost 3,000 men under Brig. Gen. Manuel Rincón to invest the rebels within Perote.

This army approached that fort by the afternoon of September 28, 1828, and dug in nearby. Santa Anna sallied from Perote shortly after midnight on October 1–2, 1828, capturing an 800-man *pedrazista* detachment under Col. Pablo Unda that was holding Aguatepec, most of whom thereupon deserted from government service.

August 8, 1841: In a prearranged coup, the 44-year-old Mexican brigadier Mariano Paredes y Arrillaga—military commander at Guadalajara—rose against President Bustamante, being joined shortly thereafter by Santa Anna at Veracruz. Paredes marched on Guanajuato with 600 men and received the defection of Brig. Pedro Cortázar. They then proceeded together toward Querétaro to incorporate Gen. Julián Juvera's garrison into their ranks, swelling rebel numbers to 2,200 men.

Santa Anna meanwhile occupied Perote with a few hundred troops, while General Valencia mutinied with another 1,200 inside Mexico City itself, seizing the Ciudadela and Acordada Barracks. The beleaguered president fought back with 2,000 loyal troops and a dozen guns, calling for reinforcements from the countryside, while civilians fled out of the line of fire. Although his following eventually numbered 3,500 men, Bustamante was driven out of the capital by September 20th, resigning nine days later to go into exile in Europe.

Prisoners at Perote (1841–1845)

Starting in late 1841, groups of foreign detainees were brought to this isolated fort for incarceration. First, some 300 survivors of a Texan wagon train that had attempted to cross the desert and set up a colony in New Mexico surrendered to its governor, Manuel Armijo, in October 1841 and were marched deep into Mexico to be confined at Perote over that ensuing winter, most being released in April or June 1842. Then, after Gen. Adrián Woll led a large Mexican force into Texas that briefly seized San Antonio in September 1842, and a Texan counterraid was subsequently defeated at Mier, another 250 prisoners began arriving at Perote in various batches as of December 1842.

Forced to perform common labor, their lonely plight aroused considerable sympathy in both the Republic of Texas and the United States. Prisoners were allowed to write and receive letters, though, as well as to be sent gifts and money with which to purchase supplies outside the fort, but the funds voted by the Texas Congress for their relief never reached the detainees. In April 1843, U.S. president John Tyler instructed the American ambassador in Mexico City to inquire whether any U.S. citizens might be among their number and to negotiate toward the release of all the captives, while a group of 16 Texan prisoners took a more direct approach by escaping through a hole bored through Perote's walls on July 2, 1843, 8 being soon recaptured.

Eight-and-a-half months later, a few dozen of the prisoners taken by Woll at San Antonio were released on March 23, 1844—and two days afterward, another 16 prisoners escaped from Perote again through a tunnel, 7 of whom were promptly recaptured. Eventually, all the remaining prisoners (about 105 in number) were amnestied and released from the fort during Mexico's Independence Day celebrations of that same year, September 16, 1844. The exact number of those who had perished from disease or ill-treatment, or escaped or secured their release through influential means, was never clearly established. The next year, two prisoners—Thomas J. Green and William P. Stapp—published separate accounts in the United States of the cruel hardships and sufferings that they had endured during their incarceration.

And ironically, a military uprising erupted throughout central Mexico against Santa Anna's misrule in November 1844, so he was overwhelmed and driven from power by early January 1845, abandoning his shrunken army so as to ride toward Veracruz with only a small cavalry escort. However, attempting to avoid capture en route— allegedly by disguising himself as a lowly teamster—he was recognized upon reaching Naolinco and therefore arrested and detained in Perote over the next five months until he could be banished to Cuba on June 3, 1845, aboard the gunboat *Victoria*.

U.S. and French Occupations (1847–1867)

The castle was taken without resistance during the Mexican-American War, as Maj. Gen. Winfield Scott's invading army penetrated deeper inland from the coast after winning the Battle of Cerro Gordo on April 18, 1847. Four days later, the 1st Regiment of Pennsylvania Volunteers under Col. F. M. Winkoop occupied Perote, while the main U.S. Army swept on to seize Puebla and eventually conquered Mexico City. On May 27, 1847, Maj. Samuel H. Walker's 1st Regiment of Texas Mounted Riflemen (more commonly known as the "Texas Rangers") was also assigned to duty within the castle, using it as a base to patrol the stretch of highway running between Perote and Jalapa against Mexican guerrilla activity.

Having been incarcerated within the castle himself, Walker bore a special grudge because of this past mistreatment, it being recorded about his local antipartisan sweeps:

> Should Captain Walker come upon guerrillas, God help them, for he seldom brings in prisoners. The captain and most all of his men are very prejudiced

and embittered against every guerrilla in the country.

When Maj. Gen. Joseph P. Lane came through Perote on October 5, 1847, escorting a large group of reinforcements and supplies that was headed toward Puebla (under threat from a small die-hard Mexican army under Santa Anna), he took along Walker and a goodly portion of Perote's garrison to help defeat that enemy concentration a few days later at Huamantla. (*See* Puebla, American Defense of [1847].)

Once hostilities ceased and its American occupiers departed, the 7th Line Battalion was assigned to Perote as its new garrison in 1849, and the stronghold resumed its former military role. For example, when young Miguel Miramón graduated from the academy at Chapultepec Castle in Mexico City in November 1851, his first posting that following year was as a sublieutenant of artillery with the 2nd Division at Perote. Its installations were upgraded during Santa Anna's huge military buildup of 1853–1855 but saw no action before he was driven out of the national capital with a regiment of lancers as his escort, pausing at Perote to issue a public proclamation formally resigning the presidency on August 12, 1856, then sailing away from Veracruz to return into exile in Colombia.

November 7, 1862: De la Llave abandoned Perote Fortress at the approach of Forey's spearhead, the 1st Div. under the French general's 51-year-old second-in-command, Gen. François Achille Bazaine. The invaders brushed aside the few Mexican irregulars roaming outside under Gen. Aurelio Rivera, although not actually bothering to garrison this fortification until September 9, 1863.

Modern Era (1939–Present)

Its value as a military installation long since passed, Perote was repaired in 1939 to temporarily house refugees fleeing from the Spanish Civil War, then used to hold German and Italian internees when Mexico entered into World War II as an Allied nation in May 1942. The vast complex was subsequently remodeled to serve as the main penitentiary for the state of Veracruz as of August 1949 before finally being officially abandoned by the state government in March 2007. Nevertheless, the municipal authorities in the town of Perote managed to get the derelict building entrusted to their care three months later and commenced some restoration work as of September 2008 with the aim of resurrecting it as a tourist attraction.

See also: Iguala, Plan de; Independence, War of; Santa Anna, Antonio López de; Woll, Adrián.

Further Reading

Calderón Quijano, José Ignacio. *Historia de las fortificaciones en Nueva España*. Seville: Escuela de Estudios Hispanoamericanos, 1953, 124–30.

Green, Thomas J. *Journal of the Texian Expedition Against Mier*. Austin, TX: Steck, 1935 reedition.

Haynes, Sam W. *Soldiers of Misfortune: The Somervell and Mier Expeditions*. Austin: University of Texas Press, 1997.

Sánchez Lamego, Miguel A. *El castillo de San Carlos de Perote*. Jalapa: Colección Suma Veracruzana, 1939.

Stapp, William P. *The Prisoners of Perote*. Austin: University of Texas Press, 1977 reedition.

Tucker, Spencer C. *The Encyclopedia of the Mexican-American War*. Santa Barbara, CA: ABC-CLIO, 2013.

Pershing's Pursuit of Pancho Villa (1916)

Punitive expedition that invaded northern Mexico in retaliation for Villa's violent cross-border raid against Columbus, New Mexico.

Six days after this bloody strike, two columns composed of 3,000 troops of the 13th U.S. Cavalry; the 6th and 16th U.S. Infantry Regiments; and the 1st U.S. Artillery Battery, crossed the border on March 15, 1916, at Palomas in the state of Chihuahua so as to pursue Villa and punish his attack. Mexico's president Venustiano Carranza offered the American president Woodrow Wilson very grudging cooperation in this matter, while urging his own field commanders to capture the renegade themselves as soon as possible so as to end any further excuse for this foreign intervention.

Villa proved elusive though, his troops disappearing into the hilly desert terrain with which they were so familiar and adopting hit-and-run guerrilla tactics. The local Mexican populace also viewed the U.S. incursion with undisguised hostility. Less than a month later, an American scouting party—two troops of the 13th Cavalry under Maj. Frank Tompkins—approached the city of Parral on April 12, 1916, only to be set on by a mob shouting "Viva Villa!" and "Viva México!" This encounter resulted in a melee in which 3 American soldiers were killed and 7 wounded, as compared to some 40 Mexican casualties.

Still more units continued to cross the border and join Pershing, though, so by the time he reached the rural hamlet of Casas Grandes in late April 1916, he had 9,000 soldiers under his command: eight cavalry and five infantry regiments, five artillery

Generals John J. Pershing and Tasker Bliss inspecting a U.S. Army camp in northern Mexico, during their failed expedition to capture Pancho Villa, 1916. (Library of Congress)

batteries, and numerous other auxiliaries (including eight Jenny biplanes of the 1st Provisional Aero Squadron flown out of San Antonio, Texas). In May 1916, an American detachment managed to skirmish against a small Villista force at Ojos Azules Ranch, but the latter quickly disappeared. Then in early June 1916, Villa emerged from hiding to overrun the Carrancista garrison under Gen. José Cavazos holding the town of Guerrero, Chihuahua, but was wounded in his right leg. Villa therefore ordered his men to disperse once again and reassemble at San Juan Bautista on the Durango border by July 6, 1916, while he himself retired into a remote mountain cave to convalesce.

Shortly thereafter, Carranza's government informed Pershing that any deeper penetrations westward, southward, or eastward into Mexico would be contested by force of arms. On June 20, 1916, two troops of the 10th Cavalry—84 black troopers under Capt. Charles T. Boyd—probed east toward Villa Ahumada, erroneously believing that Villa might be there. At Carrizal, they collided with a Carrancista garrison under Gen. Félix U. Gómez, who deployed his troops for battle and forbade the Americans to advance. Boyd nonetheless insisted and lost his life in the ensuing exchange of gunfire, during which 9 of his men were also killed, 10 wounded, and 23 captured. Mexican losses totaled 74 dead—among them, Gómez.

This bloody clash brought an effective halt to all of Pershing's pursuit operations, as Washington had to placate an incensed Mexican government. Over the next seven months, the American expeditionary force—now numbering 12,000 men, and sarcastically dubbed the "Perishing Expedition"—remained largely immobile, 150 miles inside Mexico. Eventually, the U.S. government announced its withdrawal on January 28, 1917, and the last American troops departed Chihuahua eight days later.

See also: Columbus Raid; Revolution, Mexican; Villa, Pancho.

Further Reading

de Quesada, Alejandro. *The Hunt for Pancho Villa: The Columbus Raid and Pershing's Punitive Expedition, 1916–17.* London: Osprey, 2012.

Hurst, James W. *Pancho Villa and Black Jack Pershing: The Punitive Expedition in Mexico.* Westport, CT: Greenwood, 2008.

Thomas, Robert S., and Invez V. Allen. *The Mexican Punitive Expedition under Brigadier General John J. Pershing, United States Army, 1916–1917.* Washington, DC: Office of the Chief of Military History, Department of the Army, 1954.

Welsome, Eileen. *The General and the Jaguar: Pershing's Hunt for Pancho Villa, a True Story of Revolution and Revenge.* New York: Little, Brown, 2006.

pienso y agua

Generic expression used by Mexican cavalrymen or horsemen to refer to the "feed and water" for their mounts.

For example, in describing his army's movements prior to their victory over the conservatives at the Battle of Silao on August 10, 1860, liberal general Jesús González Ortega later wrote how he had approached and carefully positioned his forces by 4:30 p.m. on that previous afternoon, at which time he ordered that his mounted regiments should—one squadron at a time—give "feed and water to the horses, and *rancho* for all the corps."

See also: González Ortega, José Canuto de Jesús; *rancho*; Silao, Battle of.

pintos

Nickname that can be translated as "spotted ones" or "dappled ones," applied derisively by Santa Anna to his rebel opponents in 1854–1855 during the Revolution of Ayutla.

This term had actually existed since colonial times, referring to a skin disease prevalent around the Balsas River Basin and commonly known as *jirícua* or *mal de pinto* (the "dappled ailment") that was spread by insect bites and caused severe infections, leaving its victims with permanent blemishes in shades ranging from whitish to bluish or reddish. Due to the torrid climate and many other contagions, the coastal lowlands of the southwestern state of Guerrero had a long-standing reputation for being unhealthy and unproductive, so they still remained sparsely populated by the mid-19th century—and mostly by impoverished local peasant bands known as *pintos* because so many of their members bore such blotches. (As recently as the 1940s, before proper treatments were introduced, almost 90 percent of some river towns' inhabitants showed vestiges of this disease.)

Therefore, when the 400-man militia battalion of Col. Florencio Villarreal rose in revolt on March 1, 1854, in the remote backwater of Ayutla, Guerrero, intending to depose Santa Anna's grandiose regime in the national capital, the autocratic president had derided these rebels as lowly *pintos* before departing two weeks later on a military campaign that was intended to crush their insolent insurrection. However, his large army soon became cut off and endured much hardship in that trackless region before staggering back into Chilpancingo in defeat. When Santa Anna himself regained Mexico City on May 16, 1854, he would try to shrug off this failure by attributing it

to the *pintos'* immunity to the coastal diseases that had decimated his soldiers, while adding that the rebels' backwardness and primitive poverty meant that they represented no real threat to his administration. Yet his subsequent inability to quell the spread of this revolt would encourage other outbreaks elsewhere throughout the country and bring down his government within a year's time.

After his departure into exile abroad, the victorious 5,000 man *pinto* army of elderly general Juan N. Álvarez approached Mexico City from Cuernavaca in early October 1855 so their leader might assume the vacated presidency. An American visitor in the capital named Robert A. Wilson, a circuit court judge from the Sacramento District in California who happened to be conducting historical research in the National Palace at that time, was an eyewitness to the *pintos'* arrival and recorded his impressions:

A strange army was this of the Pintos. Their dusky skins were covered with spots, as though they had been sprinkled with indigo. An old straw hat—a striped blanket, with a slit for the head to pass through, serving as covering by night and coat by day—together with a pair of ragged cotton drawers, constituted their uniform. Now and then one rejoiced in the luxury of shoes, but the majority contented themselves with sandals. They strode along like persons unaccustomed to military exercise, but with a self-possession which showed that they saw nothing to fear in the elegant city they had captured.

When these men reached the Plaza [*sic*; Zocalo], and took possession of the [National] Palace, it was curious to mark the strong contrast of present appearances with the scenes that took place here when [Santa Anna's] "Royal and Imperial Order" of Guadalupe was installed, a few months before. The guards that then kept the Palace had more lace and more brilliant armor, but less courage. Then, despotic power waited on the caprice of a turbulent soldiery; but now, the new President [Álvarez] rested securely under the guard of his faithful Pintos, whose courage none could doubt, and whose faithfulness all admired.

See also: Ayutla, Revolution of; Santa Anna, Antonio López de.

Further Reading

Johnson, Richard A. *The Mexican Revolution of Ayutla, 1854–1855: An Analysis of the Evolution and Destruction of Santa Anna's Last Dictatorship.* Westport, CT: Greenwood Press, 1974.

Lambert, Dean P. "Regional Core-Periphery Imbalance: The Case of Guerrero, Mexico, since 1821." *Yearbook of the Conference of Latin Americanist Geographers* 20 (1994): 59–71.

"Pípila," El (1810)

Nickname for a young miner in the city of Guanajuato whose real name was Juan José María Martínez.

He achieved fame when the initial insurgency raised by Miguel Hidalgo y Costilla swarmed into that city on September 28, 1810, and attempted to attack its small Spanish royalist garrison and citizenry, who had taken refuge inside the formidable stone granary called the Alhóndiga de Granaditas. Held at bay by musket fire from its windows, El Pípila tied a thick stone slab onto his back and then crawled through a hail of bullets under its protective covering to set the granary's wooden doors ablaze with a torch. As evening fell, these slowly crumbled and gave way, allowing the insurgents to fight their way inside and slaughter some 600 monarchists by dawn.

See also: Alhóndiga de Granaditas, Assault on the; Hidalgo y Costilla Gallaga, Miguel Gregorio Antonio Ignacio.

plan

A generic word in the Spanish language, but in terms of 19th- and early 20th-century Mexican military history, it was a synonym for a "declaration of principles"—a proclamation that was issued and disseminated as widely as possible whenever an insurrection was attempted so as to attract more adherents to the rebels' or mutineers' particular cause.

The "Plan de Ayutla" of 1854, for example—emanated by a tiny garrison in an insignificant provincial backwater—consisted of only six articles, yet they so succinctly encapsulated the people's desire for change that it swept away Santa Anna's grandiose conservative government and powerful army, despite providing few successes on the battlefield.

Conversely, the liberal revolt that had been attempted 14 years earlier by a group in Mexico City at dawn on July 15, 1840, was criticized by contemporaries for "not having issued any plan whatsoever, only saying: that their rebellion was for the Federation, with the constitution of the year 1824"—the implication being that these particular rebels had not clearly thought out or prepared their action beforehand.

Mexican lithograph lampooning Santa Anna's many failed plans and programs, December 1844. (Anne S. K. Brown Military Collection, Brown University Library)

See also: Ayutla, Plan of.

Further Reading

Fowler, Will. *Celebrating Insurrection: The Commemoration and Representation of Nineteenth-Century Mexican Pronunciamiento*. Lincoln: University of Nebraska Press, 2012.

Fowler, Will. *Forceful Negotiations: The Origins of the Pronunciamiento in Nineteenth-Century Mexico*. Lincoln: University of Nebraska Press, 2010.

Potrero del Llano, Sinking of (1942)

International incident precipitated by the destruction of a neutral Mexican tanker by a German submarine, leading to Mexico's entry into World War II as an Allied nation.

Background (1939–1941)

When that conflict had first erupted with the invasion of Poland in distant Europe in September 1939, neither the Mexican government nor a majority of its citizenry had felt particularly concerned or affected by these remote affairs. The United States' abrupt embroilment after the Japanese bombardment of the U.S. naval base at Pearl Harbor far out in the Pacific on December 7, 1941, had likewise not elicited any great apprehension or offers of support from Mexico.

However, in going over onto a full wartime footing, the administration of Pres. Franklin D. Roosevelt nonetheless hoped to forge a continental alliance throughout the Americas so as to at least deny Axis raiders any opportunities for resupply in neutral ports throughout the Western Hemisphere, or to receive any kind of trans-Atlantic trade. Ironically, Washington's aim in this regard would be considerably bolstered by the offensives unleashed in American waters by long-range German U-boats, especially the campaign initiated in the Caribbean Sea as of mid-February 1942 code-named Operation *Neuland* or "New Land." Suddenly, merchantmen of all nationalities stood in danger of being torpedoed without warning while merely going about their business.

Submarine Attacks (May 14–20, 1942)

While sailing unescorted past Miami, the neutral 4,000-ton Mexican oil-tanker *Potrero del Llano*—bound from its home port of Tampico, Tamaulipas, with 6,100 tons of petroleum in its bunkers destined for New York City—was spotted at 7:17 a.m. on May 14, 1942, by the Type-VIIC German submarine *U-564* of Lt. Cmdr. Reinhard "Teddy" Suhren. Although a large Mexican flag had been painted and was illuminated on both flanks of the tanker, this display lacked a central eagle crest (which only Mexican Navy vessels were allowed to display), so Suhren mistook this identification as a ruse, believing that the ship was trying to masquerade as an Italian vessel—Germany's Axis partner in the war—so as to avoid attack. The tanker was consequently torpedoed and left ablaze with the loss of 15 of its 35-man crew, eventually sinking after burning for hours.

The Mexican consul in Miami telegraphed a report of this attack to the Foreign Office in Mexico City, and that same evening the secretary of foreign relations, Ezequiel Padilla, filed a "formal and energetic protest" through the Swedish Legation with the government of Nazi Germany. It gave the Axis power one week to provide full satisfaction and pay compensatory damages for this attack, or else Mexico would take "the necessary measures." In a display of public anger, the German Club and several businesses in Mexico City were stoned by angry crowds, and the Mexican government's protest was ignored by Berlin.

Then one week later, the 6,000-ton Mexican tanker *Faja de Oro*—returning in ballast toward its home port of Tampico, Tamaulipas, after making a delivery to Marcus Hook, Pennsylvania—was torpedoed near Key West at 4:21 a.m. on May 20, 1942, by the German submarine *U-106* of Capt. Lt. Hermann Rasch, resulting in the deaths of 8 of its 36-man crew. Two days afterward, the Mexican government declared that a "state of war" existed with the Axis powers—not an outright declaration of war, but enough to legally impound German vessels and properties, and actively assist the Allied war efort.

Further Reading

Paz Salinas, María Emilia. *Strategy, Security, and Spies: Mexico and the U.S. as Allies in World War II*. University Park: Pennsylvania State University Press, 1997.

Primera Intervención Francesa (1838–1839)

A title that can be translated literally as "First French Intervention," the name given by many modern Mexican scholars to the punitive naval expedition that was sent from France to blockade, bombard, and seize the port city of Veracruz during the winter of 1838–1839 so as to exact compensation for economic losses suffered by their country's business interests during Mexico's chaotic infighting. However, this foreign aggression was more popularly known during its day as the *Guerra de los Pasteles* or the "War of the Cakes" and is still commonly referred to by that same name today.

See also: Cakes, War of the (1838–1839).

pronunciamiento

Word that translates simply as "pronouncement" and in 19th- and early 20th-century Mexican military history meant a public "declaration of principles"—a proclamation issued and disseminated as widely as possible so as to attract adherents to a particular insurrection or cause.

The "Plan de Ayutla" of 1854, for example—emanated by a tiny garrison in an insignificant provincial backwater—consisted of only six articles, yet they so succinctly encapsulated the people's desire for change that it swept away Santa Anna's grandiose conservative government and powerful army, despite providing few successes on the battlefield.

Conversely, the liberal revolt that had been attempted 14 years previously by a group in Mexico City at dawn on July 15, 1840, was criticized by contemporaries for "not having issued any plan whatsoever, only saying: that their rebellion was for the Federation, with the constitution of the year 1824"—the implication being that these particular rebels had not clearly thought out or prepared their action beforehand.

See also: Ayutla, Plan of.

Further Reading

Fowler, Will. *Celebrating Insurrection: The Commemoration and Representation of Nineteenth-Century Mexican Pronunciamiento.* Lincoln: University of Nebraska Press, 2012.

Fowler, Will. *Forceful Negotiations: The Origins of the Pronunciamiento in Nineteenth-Century Mexico.* Lincoln: University of Nebraska Press, 2010.

Puebla, American Defense of (1847)

Mexican siege of this U.S.-occupied city, a vital waystation along the supply route that extended between Veracruz and the national capital during the Mexican-American War.

Background (May-August 1847)

After being bested at the Battle of Cerro Gordo in mid-April 1847, Pres. Antonio López de Santa Anna and his subordinate, Gen. Pedro de Ampudia, had led their scattered formations in retreat both around and through Puebla, leaving that city of roughly 60,000 inhabitants to fall without a struggle to U.S. major general Winfield Scott's resumed advance on May 15, 1847. However, when the American commander found himself left shortly thereafter with barely 5,800 effectives (following the departure of several volunteer regiments whose terms of enlistment had expired), he chose to remain in Puebla for the next three months awaiting reinforcements before resuming his offensive into the Valley of Mexico.

Finally, Scott's first brigade exited Puebla northwestward on August 7, 1847, followed by his main army in an ascent into the central highlands to invest Mexico's capital. A small 400-man garrison under brevet colonel Thomas Childs, well provided with artillery, was left behind to hold Puebla and guard its 3,000 American convalescents. But shortly after the main U.S. forces had departed, local guerrillas began harassing the American defenders under the direction of militia general Joaquín Rea, who had been specially detached into that region to raise partisan forces and threaten Scott's supply lines and communications.

Soon, Rea's irregulars began ambushing American wagon trains and even destroyed the aqueduct that brought water into the city. They also captured most of the garrison's livestock in a raid on August 25, 1847, threatening them with starvation. Childs countered by fortifying his troops within the *ciudadela* or "citadel" beside the central Plaza de San José as well as in Fort

19th-century American engraving, showing U.S. troops entering the city of Puebla on May 15, 1847, prior to advancing over the mountains to capture Mexico's capital that same autumn. (DeAgostini/Getty Images)

Loreto and Guadalupe convent on the heights overlooking Puebla.

Siege (September 14–October 12, 1847)

In an attempt to divert Scott from his inexorable drive on Mexico City, Rea ventured into Puebla and probed the American street barricades around the Plaza de San José on the night of September 13–14, 1847, before raising his strength fully up to 2,000 men and calling on Childs to surrender unconditionally two days later. When the American officer refused, Rea attempted two separate attacks against the Plaza de San José defenses, both of which were repulsed thanks in no small part to the devastating volleys of grapeshot fired by their artillery pieces.

Mexico City had meanwhile fallen to Scott on September 14, 1847, Santa Anna escaping into the satellite town of Guadalupe, where he ordered Brig. Gen. José Joaquín de Herrera to march the scattered remnants of their defeated army north so as

to begin reconstituting their formations at Querétaro. Santa Anna then resigned the presidency in favor of Chief Justice Manuel de la Peña y Peña (who was legally next in line for that office, according to the chain of succession) on September 15, 1847, before proceeding over the mountain range in his military capacity alone and with a small force to assume command over Rea's operation and attempt to threaten Scott's supply lines.

Santa Anna appeared outside Puebla on September 21, 1847, his arrival bringing total Mexican strength up to 3,200 irregular cavalrymen and 2,500 militiamen, so he stormed its American defenses the next day without success. After vainly calling on Childs to surrender again, Santa Anna did not resume any assaults until September 27, 1847, continuing them in a more measured fashion for the next couple of days.

Realizing that Scott would not be able to send any relief from recently occupied

Mexico City to the beleaguered Americans holding out in Puebla because of the state of the rain-soaked roads in the intervening mountain passes, Santa Anna decided to redeploy his forces so as to challenge any American reinforcements that might be coming up from the coast. Consequently, he left Rea to maintain the siege of Childs's garrison while shifting about half the total Mexican strength northeast of Puebla on September 30, 1847, encamping just outside of the town of Huamantla with two artillery pieces so as to be in a position to confront any rescue column approaching from Jalapa.

Eight days later, some of Santa Anna's pickets were chased back into Huamantla on October 8, 1847, by a party of "Texas Rangers" under Maj. Samuel H. Walker, who were acting as advance scouts for an approaching 3,000-man brigade (of volunteers) under Maj. Gen. Joseph P. Lane. This force was bringing reinforcements and supplies for the trapped contingent in Puebla and engaged Santa Anna's alerted army the next day. After a round of heavy fighting, which included several U.S. cavalry charges and infantry assaults, the overmatched Mexicans were driven from the field in disarray, leaving behind their two guns. Nevertheless, Walker fell mortally wounded in this action, so his Texans and numerous other ill-disciplined American volunteers took their revenge by sacking and torching helpless Huamantla.

Final Hostilities (October 12, 1847)

The next day, Lane's army continued on toward Puebla, arriving there to engage the remaining Mexican besiegers under Rea by October 12, 1847, and driving them off after another brief but hard-fought engagement, which lifted the 28-day encirclement of its brave U.S. garrison. The Americans had suffered 22 killed, 52 wounded, and

1 missing during the course of this month-long siege, which was the last major operation fought during the Mexican-American War. Shortly thereafter, Santa Anna was informed by President Peña that he was to turn over military command to Gen. Manuel Rincón so as to prepare to stand trial for his conduct of Mexico's national defense.

See also: Santa Anna, Antonio López de.

Further Reading

Levinson, Irving. *Wars within Wars: Mexican Guerrillas, Domestic Elites, and the United States of America, 1846–1848.* Fort Worth: Texas Christian University Press, 2005.

Tucker, Spencer C. *The Encyclopedia of the Mexican-American War.* Santa Barbara, CA: ABC-CLIO, 2013.

Winders, Richard B. "Puebla's Forgotten Heroes." *Military History of the West* 24, no. 1 (Spring 1994): 1–23.

Puebla, Conservative Revolt and Liberal Sieges of (1856)

Uprisings involving this opposition stronghold during the troubled interlude between the fall of Santa Anna and the outbreak of the War of the Reform.

Background (August–November 1855)

Upon the conservative dictator Santa Anna's resignation from the presidency for the final time in August 1855, Mexico had been left with a power vacuum that was to be resolved among five liberal contenders: Gen. Ignacio Comonfort in the country's south, west, and around Veracruz; Gen. Martín Carrera in the central Valley of Mexico and national capital; Gov. Manuel Doblado in the state of Guanajuato; the former finance secretary, Gen. Antonio Haro y Tamariz, in the state of San Luis Potosí; and Gov. Santiago Vidaurri in the northern states of Nuevo León, Coahuila, and Tamaulipas. On August 20, 1855, the moderate general Carrera in Mexico City had arranged for elections to a new Congress, which was to draft a new constitution—elections from which clerics were barred, both as voters and as candidates.

The elderly liberal general Juan N. Álvarez had been elevated to interim president as of October 4, 1855, with the moderate Comonfort holding the influential cabinet post of minister of war. Two weeks later, a Congress was elected that included numerous liberal ideologues, bent on implementing their long-delayed reforms as they set about rewriting Mexico's Constitution. One of the very first pronouncements issued by this body on November 23, 1855—from its justice minister Benito Juárez, a former political prisoner and exile—called for the abolition of the exclusive tribunals reserved for members of the military and clergy, so conservative protests erupted in various parts of the country.

Conservative Takeover and Liberal Response (January–March 1856)

The strongest revolt broke out on December 12, 1855, in the mountain hamlet of Zacapoaxtla in the state of Puebla, led by its village priest Francisco Ortega y García. The moderate interim president, Ignacio Comonfort, responded two days later from Mexico City by ordering that a couple of cavalry detachments keep this uprising under observation, but their commanders—the conservative-leaning colonels Luis Gonzaga Osollo and Juan Olloqui—instead joined the rebels' ranks. Comonfort thereupon directed that an army brigade begin penetrating that region under the overall command of the politically appointed governor of Veracruz, Ignacio de la Llave; but

when its first regiment marched from Mexico City and reached Tatlaquitepec on Christmas Day 1855, the regimental second-in-command—24-year-old lieutenant colonel Miguel Miramón—arrested his superior, Col. Rafael Benavides, and this unit also joined the rebellion to shouts of *¡Viva la religión!* or "Long live Religion!"

De la Llave was lucky to return into the capital alive a few days later with only a handful of staff officers still left loyal to him. Then the 45-year-old conservative general Antonio Haro y Tamariz escaped from confinement at Córdoba, Veracruz, on January 5, 1856, riding into the state of Puebla to assume military command over its insurrection, while one week later a second, even more robust brigade of 2,000 men under Brig. Gen. Severo del Castillo also defected. The conservatives used this combined strength to push their way into the city of Puebla and expel its liberal "National Guard" garrison under 34-year-old militia colonel Juan Nepomuceno Méndez on January 23, 1856, tacitly assisted by Bishop Pelagio Antonio de Labastida.

Now faced with a rebel army ensconced inside a major fortified city, Comonfort summoned militia regiments from liberal states to the capital so as to reinforce the army regulars who had remained reliable supporters of his liberal government. Such units reached Mexico City throughout January and February 1856 until the president was able to march out at the head of 10,345 troops and 36 guns on February 29, 1856, establishing his headquarters the next day at San Martín Texmelucan (some 20 miles from the city of Puebla).

They were given the order to march on February 27, 1856, their columns penetrating into the plains around Puebla, occupying the city of Tlaxcala, and driving back conservative patrols, so Comonfort was able to depart Mexico City with his personal staff on February 29th and the next day establish his headquarters as "general-in-chief" at San Martín Texmelucan, some 20 miles northwest of the city of Puebla. Because of the conservatives' superior strength in cavalry, the next few days were spent erecting field fortifications and reconnoitering the intervening terrain as well as offering amnesty to the rebel officers before the liberal army (whose numbers would steadily increase to an eventual total of 16,000 men through more reinforcements) resumed its drive southeastward on Puebla on March 7, 1856.

Villareal's three large infantry divisions closed to within nine miles of Puebla before beginning to encamp around 1:00 p.m. that same afternoon of March 7, 1856: the 1st Division under Anastasio Parrodi resting between Río Prieto and Montero Hill; the 2nd Division under Tomás Moreno on the grounds of the Hacienda de Santa Inés, along with the "mobile brigade" of light cavalry under Italian-born Luigi Ghilardi; while the 3rd Division under Félix M. Zuloaga camped on the farmland surrounding the Hacienda de San Isidro, with Manuel Doblado's brigade holding the vital center atop Ocotlán Hill, and Villareal's headquarters established in the forefront at the hamlet of San Miguel Xoxtla, protected by Portilla's cavalry. That evening, Comonfort instructed his generals that a cavalry force was to seize Coronango by 6:00 a.m. the next morning, allowing the slower-moving infantry divisions to pass through there and split up so as to take Cholula and Santorum, beginning the envelopment of Puebla.

However, it was the conservatives who struck first. With only 4,000 soldiers to defend the city, General Haro had emerged under cover of darkness with 2,500 infantry, 1,000 cavalry troopers, and a half dozen fieldpieces, hoping to surprise the liberal columns piecemeal before they had a chance to mass into battle formation. Haro succeeded in engaging Doblado's brigade atop Ocotlán Hill by 8:00 a.m. on that March 8, 1856, driving it off this prominence after two hours of fighting with losses on both sides. But as Villareal continued to bring up more and more liberal formations, a truce was arranged at 10:00 a.m. to gather up the wounded and dead.

A truce was arranged to gather up the wounded and dead, during which the conservative commander Haro (a lifelong friend and colleague of the president) also requested an interview with Comonfort, so they met beneath the shade of a tree at noon on March 8, 1856. The president renewed his amnesty offer, and Haro asked for three hours' grace to discuss this matter with his colleagues. He failed to return at the appointed hour, though, and when Comonfort sent a rider to investigate, this scout reported back that the outnumbered and demoralized conservatives were in full retreat back to Puebla.

The liberal army therefore followed and bottled them up inside until the rebels agreed to capitulate two weeks later, on March 23, 1856. Haro was carried off to prison in Mexico City, where he died shortly thereafter, while Osollo and Del Castillo succeeded in escaping, and Miramón remained hidden within Puebla. All the other rebel officers were stripped of their ranks two days afterward and incorporated into the liberal army as privates. Many Church properties in and around Puebla were moreover expropriated to help defray the costs of this campaign, while Bishop Lamadrid was expelled from Mexico, actions that fueled further resentment among the faithful. Comonfort returned to Mexico City on April 3, 1856, parading his army triumphantly through its thronged streets.

Second Conservative Seizure and Defeat (October–December 1856)

Yet another revolt began at 1:00 a.m. on October 20, 1856, when Capt. Leónides Campo arrived unannounced with two captives—the fugitive conservative commanders Miramón and Francisco A. Vélez—awakening the liberal governor of Puebla, Gen. José María García Conde, to request that his prisoners be incarcerated in the same cell as Lt. Col. Luis Reyes. However, when the governor tried to comply, this proved to be a ruse. He was suddenly disarmed by Campo, and the four conservative officers thereupon allowed their fellow conspirator, Col. Joaquín Francisco Orihuela, to enter the palace and assume command over the city garrison.

Learning of this reversal, liberal general Tomás Moreno arrived outside Puebla six days later with 4,000 troops and 30 artillery pieces, laying siege to the city. He was superseded the next month by the 23-year-old brigadier Leandro Valle Martínez before all resistance finally collapsed on December 15, 1856. The conservatives scattered, Orihuela being captured and executed some days later at San Andrés Chalchicomula, while Miramón (an academy classmate of Valle), Vélez, and Manuel Ramírez Arellano were apparently allowed to escape with 100 men toward Toluca.

See also: Ocotlán, Battle of.

Further Reading

"Additional from Mexico: The Puebla Revolution—Conditions of the Surrender." *New York Times*. April 12, 1856.

Álvarez, José J. *Parte general que sobre la campaña de Puebla dirige al ministerio.* Mexico City: Vicente García Torres, 1856.

Bazant, Jan. "La iglesia, el estado y la sublevación conservadora de Puebla en 1856." *Historia mexicana* 35, no. 1 (1987): 93–109.

Bazant, Jan. *México en 1856 y 1857: gobierno del general Comonfort.* Mexico City: INEHRM, 1987.

"Important from Mexico: The Rebels Beaten-Capitulation of Puebla." *New York Times*, April 19, 1856.

Villareal, Florencio. *Parte oficial que dirige al Exmo. Sr. presidente de la República.* Mexico City: J. M. Macías, 1856.

Puebla, Republican Defense of (1862). *See* Cinco de Mayo, Battle of the (1862).

Puebla, French Siege of (1863)

Protracted encirclement and bombardment of this strategically placed city THAT ended with the eventual surrender of its Mexican republican garrison.

Prelude (February–March 1863)

After the repulse of the initial French assault against Puebla on May 5, 1862—the famed Battle of the Cinco de Mayo—Maj. Gen. Charles, Comte de Lorencez, led his bloodied 6,000 troops on a painful retreat back into the city of Orizaba, where his army recuperated and was to be heavily reinforced. An additional 23,000 men arrived from France, the French expeditionary force and their Mexican conservative allies had then resumed their stalled offensive into central Mexico. First, a conservative cavalry brigade under Gen. Antonio Taboada departed Orizaba on February 3, 1863, to begin reconnoitering and securing the road leading inland toward Puebla. Gen. Elie Frédéric Forey's main army—now reorganized into two infantry divisions and a cavalry brigade, totaling 28,800 men—followed on February 22–23, 1863, to be joined en route by other converging French columns under his divisional commanders, Major Generals Charles Abel Douay and François Achille Bazaine.

Progress proved slow but inexorable, as the republicans fell back into the city and prepared to withstand a siege. Forey's 2nd Infantry Division captured Amozoc by March 8, 1863, paving the way for his main body to enter that town two days later.

Siege of Puebla (March–May 1863)

On March 15, 1863, advance French elements occupied Los Álamos Hacienda, then next afternoon their vanguard—comprising the combined 1st and 2nd Infantry Divisions, a Marine battalion, and several squadrons of allied Mexican cavalrymen—began encircling Puebla. Despite the presence of Gen. Ignacio Comonfort's 8,000 troops and 40 artillery pieces among the nearby Uranga Hills, the 25,000-man French Army ascended San Juan Hill unopposed by midday of March 18, 1863, thereby isolating Gen. Jesús González Ortega's 25,000-man, 180-gun garrison within the city below.

Generals Aureliano Carbajal's and Aurelio Rivera Llanos's republican cavalry brigades managed to dash out of the beleaguered city on March 21, 1863, but formal French siege lines and batteries were laid out the next day, and an intense bombardment commenced by March 24th. At dawn four days afterward, three French columns stormed the San Javier Monastery—now strengthened and renamed "Fort Iturbide"—only to be repelled by three battalions of the Zacatecas Regiment. Nonetheless, this strongpoint was carried the next afternoon by a second assault wave that cost 600 French casualties.

After numerous lesser skirmishes, Gen. Tomás O'Horan slipped out of Puebla with 2,500 republican troopers on the night of April 13, 1863, to join Comonfort's army at nearby San Jerónimo. Six days later, the French besiegers once again stormed the southeastern portions of Puebla's defenses, Santa Inés Convent changing hands several times in fierce fighting. On the night of April 20, 1863, Rivera attempted to lead a supply column into Puebla, mistakenly clashing with the 4th Zacatecas Battalion in the darkness. At dawn of April 24th, French sappers detonated mines beneath Santa Inés Convent, and the next morning tried to overrun this stronghold, although they were thrown back by Lt. Col. Jesús Lalanne's Zacatecas Battalion and the 1st Toluca and 2nd Puebla Battalions.

Battle of San Lorenzo (May 8, 1863)

With the republican garrison becoming increasingly hard-pressed, Gen. Ignacio Comonfort marched out of Mexico City with his small *Ejército del Centro* or "Army of the Center," cautiously approaching the French forces out of the east in hopes of diverting the besiegers so Puebla could at least be resupplied. On May 5, 1863, Comonfort's republican army took up position at San Lorenzo, 25 miles southeast of Puebla, hoping to break the siege lines at La Cruz Hill and thus resupply Puebla. After clashing inconclusively against Leonardo Márquez's conservative contingent the next day though, Comonfort's left flank was suddenly driven in at dawn of May 8, 1863, by a surprise French counterattack under Bazaine. This small Mexican army collapsed, suffering 2,000 killed, wounded, or captured, while its demoralized survivors fled in the direction of Tlaxcala. On May 9, 1863, Forey released numerous captives from this battle into Puebla, hoping to thereby spread news of this defeat among its surrounded garrison.

Finally on May 16, 1863, González Ortega requested terms and surrendered at 5:30 next afternoon. Forey proved generous, but in one final act of defiance, the Mexican defenders destroyed their remaining war materiel and attempted to disband their units so as not to be considered prisoners of war. Nevertheless, the French seized 1,000 officers and 16,000 troops upon occupying Puebla—5,000 of whom subsequently joined the victors' ranks.

Aftermath (June 1863)

This protracted siege had cost the French 185 slain officers and soldiers, as well as 1,109 wounded personnel. But with the route inland toward Mexico City now open, Bazaine had departed from Puebla as early as May 26, 1863, with Castagny's brigade, some light infantry, and a body of conservative cavalrymen under Miramón, seizing the vital bridge 20 miles away at Texmelucan by the next day. Bazaine then furthermore detached Márquez on May 28th to occupy the Venta de Córdova and Río Frío, who met with such negligible opposition that his column had even continued as far as Ayutla by June 1st. Bazaine meanwhile contented himself with repairing and holding the bridges at Texmelucan and Río Frío so as to protect these crossings for a resumed advance by Forey's main French Army.

A party of foreign diplomats including the consuls from Spain, Prussia, and the United States entered Puebla on June 2, 1863, bearing a message from the *ayuntamiento* or "municipal government" of Mexico City that informed the French commander-in-chief that President Juárez and his republican government had abandoned the capital for San Luis Potosí at 4:30 p.m. on the afternoon of Sunday, May 31st, leaving

Mexico City defenseless. Forey quickly sent orders to Bazaine to press on toward the national capital while preparing to follow him from Puebla.

A garrison was to be left behind in that battered city under Colonel Brincourt, composed of the 1st Zouave Regiment, a Marine battalion, a squadron of *chasseurs*, and 450 Mexican conservative riders under Chacón and Trujeque. Forey then led his main army out of Puebla on June 5, 1863, leaving behind 1,200 convalescents within various city hospitals, to make its triumphal entry into Mexico City five days afterward.

See also: Bazaine, François Achille; Cinco de Mayo, Battle of the; French Intervention, War of the; González Ortega, José Canuto de Jesús; Márquez Araujo, Leonardo.

Further Reading

González Ortega, Jesús. *Parte general que da al Supremo Gobierno de la Nación respecto de la defensa de la plaza de Puebla, el general Jesús González Ortega*. Mexico City: J. S. Ponce de León, 1871.

"Important from Mexico: Detailed Account of the Surrender of Puebla." *New York Times*, June 13, 1863.

Martin, Charles. *Précis des événements de la campagne du Mexique en 1862*. Paris: Charles Tanera, 1863.

Puebla, Republican Recapture of (1867)

One of the final Mexican triumphs during the War of the French Intervention, occurring shortly before the emperor Maximilian was captured at Querétaro.

Prelude (December 1866– February 1867)

Having recuperated the southern city of Oaxaca from its Franco-imperial occupiers by the end of October 1866, the republican major general Porfirio Díaz then received a shipment of American war surplus armaments in early December 1866, arranged through the offices of Pres. Benito Juárez (whose government was still displaced in northern Mexico). This weaponry allowed Díaz to sortie from Oaxaca toward Tehuacán with his self-proclaimed *Ejército de Oriente* or "Army of the East" on December 19, 1866, so as to begin clearing the Isthmus of Tehuantepec of its last Franco-imperial garrisons.

Maximilian's strength was clearly waning by this point, with French military support being recalled to Europe and outnumbered imperial forces in retreat everywhere. With the fall of San Luis Potosí in early January 1867, only Mexico City, Puebla, Morelia, Querétaro, and Veracruz remained in loyalist hands. The republican generals Mariano Escobedo and Ramón Corona were leading huge armies down out of the north, so the emperor sallied from his capital the next month to mount a defiant last stand at Querétaro. With most imperial forces being concentrated in the Bajío, and the last French troops having departed Puebla on February 16, 1867, Díaz led his small army in an attempt to seize that city.

Siege of Puebla (March 9–April 2, 1867)

On March 9, 1867, Porfirio Díaz arrived at San Juan Hill west of this city with 3,000 republican troops to lay siege to its 3,000-man imperial garrison under Gen. Manuel Noriega. After being reinforced by local contingents and cutting off all communications inland, the republicans began formal siege proceedings.

Within the next couple of weeks, General Carrión seized both San Javier and Penitenciaría redoubts through costly assaults,

as the republicans gradually fought their way into the city limits. However, Díaz was unable to completely subdue the defenders, and on March 31, 1867, received word that Leonardo Márquez had quit Mexico City the preceding day with a relief column of 3,000 imperial troops and 17 fieldpieces.

Reacting swiftly, the republican general gathered three assault columns of 300 men apiece to storm Puebla's main stronghold— El Carmen Convent—plus 13 companies of approximately 100 men each, to stealthily approach other points around the city's defenses. At 2:00 a.m. on April 2, 1867, the three-pronged attack was launched against El Carmen. After an hour and a half of noisy fighting—long enough for Noriega to commit his reserves—Díaz signaled from San Juan Hill, directing his 1,300 hidden soldiers to rise and mount simultaneous attacks. They broke through everywhere, only the Siempreviva trenches and El Carmen Convent offering much resistance before surrendering.

Noriega's remaining defenders sought refuge in the Loreto and Guadalupe Convents, being compelled to capitulate two days later. This assault had cost Díaz 253 dead and 233 wounded, as opposed to much higher casualties among the defenders, plus 2,000 captives. The republican commander quickly detached Colonel Lalane with 900 troopers on April 4, 1867, to monitor the approach of Márquez's imperial relief column.

See also: Díaz Mori, José de la Cruz Porfirio; French Intervention, War of the; Márquez Araujo, Leonardo; Querétaro, Siege of.

Further Reading

"Affairs in Mexico: Reported Capture of Puebla by Gen. Díaz." *New York Times*, March 6, 1867.

Puente de Calderón, Battle of (1811). *See* Calderón Bridge, Battle of (1811).

Puerto de Carretas, Battle of (1858)

Unexpected and unorthodox liberal victory, won during the early stages of the War of the Reform.

Preamble (March 10–April 15, 1858)

This conflict had erupted after a conservative coup removed the moderate president Ignacio Comonfort from office in Mexico City on January 22, 1858, and the succeeding administration thereupon instituted a wholesale revocation of all liberal reforms to Mexico's constitution. Actual fighting began when a large army of regulars advanced north out of the national capital under conservative leadership and scattered the liberal militia contingents that were marshaled near the city of Salamanca in the state of Guanajuato on March 10–11, 1858.

This victorious conservative army then marched on to Guadalajara, from where a division of 2,200 infantrymen, 400 cavalry troopers, and 12 guns was detached under Brig. Gen. Miguel Miramón a few weeks later to continue northeastward and rescue the feeble 1,500-man garrison holding the city of San Luis Potosí, which was being threatened by a descent out of the liberal state of Nuevo León by its *Ejército del Norte* or "Army of the North" under Col. Juan Zuazua.

Miramón and his approaching relief column exited from the town of Salinas on April 15, 1858, and word was carried by 5:00 p.m. next evening into Zuazua's field headquarters at the village of Moctezuma (45 miles north of the city of San Luis

Potosí). Within three hours, the liberal commander instructed his subordinate, Lt. Col. Ignacio Zaragoza, to remain at nearby Venado with the "Army of the North's" infantry and artillery, while Zuazua departed by 8:00 p.m. to lead 1,100 mounted riflemen on a grueling overnight ride to ambush the conservative relief force at a preselected chokepoint: a canyon where the road made a long, exposed ascent in the shadow of two peaks known as *Puerto de Carretas* or "Wagons' Pass."

Battle of Puerto de Carretas (April 17, 1858)

After an 11-hour nocturnal ride, Zuazua and his two brigades totaling 1,100 troopers deployed into hidden positions overlooking this rising roadway at 7:00 a.m. on April 17, 1858. Miramón's 2,600-man column had already resumed its march across the valley below at dawn, and the conservatives' vanguard units began drawing fire around 8:30 a.m., as they began the long climb up into the pass. Consequently, Miramón halted and formed up 1,600 troops to attempt to sweep up the steep incline on the western side of the pass so as to clear its mesa on top of liberal riflemen. Zuazua's self-taught irregulars fought in the guerrilla fashion that they had learned from fighting against native war bands, firing from concealment and giving way as the regulars' firing lines moved closer.

Curiously, both commanders in their after-action reports would overestimate their opponents' strength as well as the outcome of this battle. Zuazua calculated the numbers in the conservative relief column at 4,000 men (almost double their real total) and correctly judged this action to have ended in a liberal victory, given his own scant losses compared to hundreds of conservative casualties—while at the same time acknowledging that Miramón had been able to push past his strongly emplaced force and completed his commission of reinforcing San Luis Potosí.

The conservative brigadier, for his part, overestimated liberal numbers at 3,500 men—almost triple their actual strength—and later falsely claimed that they had "lost half their force, all their ammunition, and an endless number of prisoners" during this confrontation, which because of the unorthodox nature of the liberals' battle tactics he misinterpreted as a victory.

See also: Miramón Tarelo, Miguel Gregorio de la Luz Atenógenes; Reform, War of the; Zaragoza Seguín, Ignacio; Zuazua Esparza, Juan Nepomuceno.

Further Reading
Dávila, Hermenegildo. *Biografía del Sr. General D. Juan Zuazúa*. Monterrey, Nuevo León: Tipografía calle de Dr. Mier, 1892.

García, Luis Alberto. *Guerra y frontera: el Ejército del Norte entre 1855 y 1858*. Monterrey: Fondo Editorial y Archivo General del Estado de Nuevo León, 2006, 83–88,

Puruarán, Battle of (1814). *See* Valladolid, Battle of (1813).

In every town where there were no revolutionists, we were welcomed most
heartily by the people, whom we
found longing for peace and cursing
the French.

> — letter from Maximilian, written
> while riding to his doom at Querétaro,
> February 1867

Querétaro, Siege of (1867)

Ten-week republican encirclement of this
last imperial stronghold, whose fall would
conclude the War of the French Intervention.

Background (February 13–March 5, 1867)

Despite the fact that his French allies had
departed Mexico, Maximilian decided to
remain on its throne, although his regime
was effectively doomed as a groundswell of
support began building toward a restoration
of Benito Juárez's republican government.
The year 1867 had moreover begun with a
string of imperial defeats, as their outnumbered armies and foreign mercenaries were
driven back from the farthest corners of the
country.

Determined to maintain his crown
through battlefield victories, Maximilian
told his personal physician on February 10,
1867, to prepare for a two-week expedition
to Querétaro, having become convinced
that his presence there was required
to counteract the demoralizing effects
from Miramón's defeat at San Jacinto.

The emperor therefore left Mexico City to
ride the 135 miles northwestward three
days later, escorted by 4,000 Mexican
imperial troops and auxiliaries under his
military chief of staff, Maj. Gen. Leonardo
Márquez. Skirmishes against republican
guerrillas under Catarino Fragoso at Lechería and Calpulalpan slowed his progress,
but the emperor nonetheless entered Querétaro six days later with 1,600 troops and a
dozen fieldpieces. The imperial general
José Ramón Méndez furthermore arrived
from Morelia on February 22, 1867, bringing in 3,500 more troops and an artillery
train to augment the city's garrison into a
total of 12,000 men, organized as follows:

- Gen. Severo del Castillo's 1st Division,
  consisting of a 1st Brigade (*Tiradores*
  Battalion, Celaya Light Infantry, and
  the 2nd Line Regiment) and a 2nd
  Brigade (14th Line Regiment, and the
  city's *Guardia municipal* or "Municipal
  Guard")
- Gen. Francisco G. Casanova's 2nd
  Division, subdivided into a 1st Brigade
  (Querétaro Battalion, plus the 7th
  and 12th Line Regiments) and a 2nd
  Brigade (*Cazadores* Battalion, plus the
  15th Line Regiment)
- A cavalry division under Gen. Tomás
  Mejía, again consisting of a 1st Brigade
  (4th and 5th Cavalry Regiments) and
  a 2nd Brigade (2nd and La Frontera
  Cavalry Regiments)
- Gen. Ramón Méndez's reserve, being
  a mixed brigade of the *Emperador*

The ancient, colonial-era Convent of the Capuchinas in the city of Queretaro, where Maximilian was held prisoner prior to being executed in 1867. (Library of Congress)

Battalion, 3rd Line Regiment, and *Emperatriz* Regiment (ex-Belgian Military Legion)
- The 3rd Engineering Company under Col. Mariano Reyes and artillery batteries under Col. Manuel Ramírez de Arellano

Advance republican cavalry units began occupying Estancia de las Vacas and Hacienda de Castillo outside the city on March 6, 1867, being joined two days later by Ramón Corona's column, which seized San Juanico and the Celaya Gate—just as Escobedo's contingent appeared out of the north as well. Together, both generals commanded:

- Gerónimo Treviño's I (Northern) Corps, consisting of two infantry

divisions under Sóstenes Rocha and Francisco Arce plus a cavalry division under Francisco Aguirre
- Corona's II or Western Corps, composed of the Jalisco Infantry Division under Manuel Márquez, the Sinaloa Infantry Division under Félix Vega, the Michoacán Infantry Division under Nicolás Régules, and the Third Division from I Corps under Saturnino Aranda
- An artillery train under Francisco Paz

Eventually, this host would swell to 32,000 troops and 100 guns, requiring the formation of a separate cavalry division under Gen. Amado A. Guadarrama.

Escobedo occupied the hills and roads north of Querétaro, and furthermore detached 5,000 men and 14 guns on March 9, 1867, to strengthen Corona's lines. After several days of positioning his cumbersome and widespread army, the republican commander-in-chief ordered a general probe of the defenses, so a diversionary attack commenced against Las Campanas Hill at 10:00 a.m. of March 14, 1867—quickly followed by a three-pronged drive under Gen. Canuto Antonio Neri against La Cruz Convent, which was serving as Maximilian's headquarters. Its garden and cemetery were overrun, but this assault was eventually driven back when Márquez ordered an imperial infantry battalion and battery to counterattack. Mejía simultaneously sallied from the Pueblito Gate with his imperial cavalry, falling on some republican dragoons opposite and scattering them, in the process capturing 70 and killing 100. Escobedo's lone success after eight hours of heavy fighting was the seizure of San Gregorio Hill to the north of the city, these operations having cost him 1,000 casualties and 4,000 prisoners as opposed to only

250 killed and wounded among the defenders.

Following this bloody setback, the republicans settled down to a protracted siege. On March 17, 1867, Corona launched another assault against La Cruz Convent, yet only to discourage a sortie being contemplated by Miramón. At dawn of March 22, 1867, this general exited with the imperial *Guardia municipal* and *Cazadores* Battalions in his van, supported by a half dozen fieldpieces and a cloud of cavalry. They surprised a republican supply train that had just reached San Juanico Hacienda, capturing and carrying it back into Querétaro with scarcely any losses.

That same night, Márquez and Vidaurri slipped out of the besieged city with two cavalry brigades—1,100 troopers—having been ordered by Maximilian to cut their way through to Mexico City and hasten the dispatch of reinforcements. By sunrise of March 23, 1867, Márquez's contingent was well on its way, but instead of immediately returning with a relief column, he would veer eastward from the capital one week later to rescue the beleaguered imperial garrison at Puebla.

At noon on March 24, 1867, Escobedo—freshly reinforced by 9,000–10,000 men under Generals Vicente Riva Palacio, Vicente Jiménez, and Francisco A. Vélez—attempted a second assault against Querétaro's walls. The main thrust was directed against Casa Blanca and the Alameda by twin columns under Generals Vélez and Joaquín Martínez, supported by numerous diversionary actions. Again, this drive was repelled by timely imperial counterattacks after the republicans had succeeded in penetrating the city. Republican losses totaled 2,000 killed, wounded, and captured, for no gain.

It was the defenders' turn next, as Miramón sortied on April 1, 1867 with eight infantry battalions and 1,000 dragoons to attack the republican siege lines extending from the San Sebastián Convent, northwest of Querétaro. Once more, an initial success was followed by quick containment, the imperial forces eventually retreating back into their defenses. Morale within the city began to sag, especially when two cavalry sallies on April 12th and 16th intended to reestablish contact with Mexico City were both checked.

At 5:00 a.m. of April 27, 1867, Miramón led another sudden exit southward, this time surprising Jiménez's republican troops, who were holding the México Gate and Calleja Hacienda. Brushing them aside, Miramón continued past with 3,000 troops in two columns, defeating Rivera's republican cavalry, who were belatedly hurrying up in Jiménez's support. Then, the imperial forces wrested the Jacal Hacienda from the Sinaloa Regiment, precipitating a wholesale republican flight from their rearmost trenches at Cimatario. In this fashion, Miramón not only seized 21 guns and valuable provisions from supply parks in the republican rear but moreover pierced Querétaro's encirclement. Maximilian personally visited the battlefield to congratulate his general.

However, both the emperor and his military advisers failed to properly exploit this advantage, either by leading their army out of the city or by securing this breach. Instead, it was Escobedo who reacted first, by throwing his Galeana Battalion—armed with repeating rifles—and the San Luis Potosí Chasseurs into this gap, while the Norte Cavalry Regiment recuperated much of the booty being transferred into the city. Naranjo, Guadarrama, and Tolentino thereupon led a massive cavalry movement behind republican lines from the southwest and recovered the Jacal Hacienda with a

3,000-dragoon charge. Maximilian committed the *Emperatriz* Cavalry Regiment in a last-ditch effort to regain his vanishing booty, yet it too was repelled. The disappointed imperial troops streamed back into Querétaro, while Rocha reoccupied the besiegers' original positions at the México Gate and Calleja Hacienda.

At dawn on May 1, 1867, Miramón tried again by unleashing a heavy bombardment of the Calleja Hacienda, followed at 10:00 a.m. by an assault spearheaded by the *Cazadores franco-mexicanos* Battalion, 3rd Line Regiment, and *Guardia municipal* under Colonel Rodríguez. They succeeded in overrunning that hacienda but got no farther before being chased back into the city when Rodríguez was killed. On May 3, 1867, Miramón thrust north toward San Gregorio, breaking through the first two republican siege lines with the 3rd and 13th Line Regiments, plus the *Emperador*, Iturbide, and Celaya Battalions—only to be contained once more and retire. A final imperial breakout was attempted northeast toward San Sebastián on May 5, 1867, yet easily contained.

By this time, the garrison was reduced to only 5,000–6,000 effectives, while civilians were starving. Before sunrise of May 15, 1867, Col. Miguel López, commander of the stronghold of La Cruz, agreed to surrender this crucial imperial redoubt to its republican besiegers in a prearranged piece of treachery. As Vélez's *Supremo Poderes* and the 1st Nuevo León Battalions advanced to seize this building, the emperor was able to escape westward from his sleeping quarters in the darkness and confusion, calling on his supporters to rally atop Las Campanas Hill. But dawn revealed their pathetically small numbers, at which point the last imperial defenders capitulated to Escobedo.

See also: Corona Madrigal, Ramón; Escobedo Peña, Mariano Antonio Guadalupe; French Intervention, War of the; Márquez Araujo, Leonardo; Miramón Tarelo, Miguel Gregorio de la Luz Atenógenes; San Jacinto, Battle of (1867).

Further Reading

de la Peza, Ignacio, and Agustín Pradillo. *Maximiliano y los últimos sucesos del imperio en Querétaro y México.* Mexico City: Imprenta de Ignacio Cumplido, 1870.

Gutiérrez Grageda, Blanca. *Querétaro devastado: fin del segundo imperio.* Querétaro: Universidad Autónoma de Querétaro, 2007.

Moreno, Daniel. *El sitio de Querétaro, según protagonistas y testigos.* Mexico City: Porrúa, 1982.

¿Quién vive?

Generic challenge peremptorily shouted by sentinels at the approach of any unidentified individual that literally means "Who lives?"

This expression had existed for centuries, the usual reply being the name of the ruling monarch or commanding officer. However, Article 186 of the federal army's *Ordenanza General* or "General Ordinances" from January 1912 stated that:

> Any sentinel who is posted in a camp, gate, or place requiring precaution, shall between lights out and the *diana*—unless there are orders to the contrary—give the *¿Quién vive?* to whomever should arrive in its immediate vicinity, either alone or in a group. Having received the reply "*México*," he shall then inquire: *¿Qué gente?* ["What people?"] If no answer is received to this, he shall repeat the question two more times; if they still do not respond or do so incorrectly, he shall command them to halt and summon the Corporal of the Guard so as to arrest and

examine them. Should they flee or continue advancing upon the sentinel, he shall open fire.

In irregular forces such as the revolutionary armies of Pancho Villa or Emiliano Zapata, the correct response to a *¿Quién vive?* challenge was to shout back the name of whatever leader was in command of the encamped soldiers, such as *Viva Villa*, *Viva Zapata*, etc.

Further Reading

González, Manuel. *Ordenanza general para el Ejército de la República Mexicana*. Mexico City: Ignacio Cumplido, 1882.

R

The *rurales* are brave, they are *muy hombres*. *Rurales* are the best fighters Díaz and Huerta ever had. They never desert to the Revolution. They always remain loyal to the established ḡ̣o̱v̱e̱ṟṉm̱e̱ṉṯ,̱ ḇe̱c̱a̱u̱s̱e̱ ṯẖe̱y̱ a̱ṟe̱ p̱o̱ḻi̱c̱e̱.

— Pancho Villa's train master, Col. José "Pepe" Calzado, to John Reed outside of Torreón, March 1914

railroads

A significant factor in the modernization and industrialization of Mexico during the late 19th century, as well as a strategic imperative throughout the military campaigns of the Mexican Revolution.

Evolution (1884–1910)

The country's first functional railway had been completed between the port of Veracruz and Mexico City in 1873, but major construction on a nationwide scale did not really begin until a decade later, once Pres. Porfirio Díaz set about directing government policy to help encourage national modernization by offering incentives and inducements to foreign capitalists to build lines that would radiate into every corner of the country. As a result of his administration's backing, during the quarter century between 1884 and 1910, laid track in Mexico almost quadrupled in extent from some 4,000 miles into a total of more than 15,000.

The spread of these railroads not only invigorated agricultural output, large-scale trade, and manufacturing, it furthermore provided military officers with an effective means for rapidly dispatching federal troops of rurales to any particular trouble spot, after which their operations could be directed or coordinated through another innovation: the telegraph. In this manner, for example, troops were rapidly deployed when a miners' strike erupted at Cananea in 1906, or labor unrest gripped the Río Blanco textile mills the next year, allowing the authorities to quickly suffocate both outbreaks.

Vital Revolutionary Transport (1910–1920)

Confident because of these prewar successes, Porfirian strategists were surprised and overwhelmed by the sheer number of widespread revolts that erupted throughout northern Mexico in late November 1910, too many to send in detachments of troops or *rurales* by rail so as to suppress each individual outburst. Moreover, the mobile revolutionary bands soon learned to gather in concentrations and ambush federal trains, such as occurred in Malpaso Canyon on December 18, 1910, or to unleash runaway locomotives to smash into them headlong as was done at Rellano in March 1912. And when the grassroots revolutionary struggle revived into major battlefield warfare with the aim of removing the usurper Victoriano Huerta from power as of 1913, certain rebel

Carrancista and U.S. troops jointly boarding trains during General Pershing's search for Pancho Villa in 1916. (Library of Congress)

commanders would excel at using railways to their advantage.

Pancho Villa, in particular, quickly mastered their use, using rail transportation to win the Battle of Ojinaga and then departing Chihuahua City to reclaim Torreón in mid-March 1914 with a vanguard division of 8,200 soldiers and 300 gunners for 29 field-pieces aboard a long convoy of 15 trains, which deposited his army on the outskirts of his intended target. These trains then reversed course and returned to various lesser towns and outposts throughout Villista territory, loading and transporting thousands more reinforcements into the 10-day battle for Torreón, providing Villa with a steady stream of fresh troops, which allowed him to overwhelm and defeat its 13,000 federal and *colorado* defenders.

Villa immediately thereafter sent advance elements of his army 32 miles east by rail to engage a second concentration of 6,200 Huertista troops at nearby San Pedro de las Colonias, pulverizing them as well, and would continue to use train convoys to great effect—climaxing with his swift and large-scale assault on the city of Zacatecas in June 1914 by which time the former bandit was routinely traveling on campaigns aboard his own well-outfitted personal train.

Emerging out of northwestern Mexico, the Sonoran general Álvaro Obregón also valued the strategic and logistical advantages of railroads and used them to advance with his compact but potent army down the Pacific coastline. Halted in Tepic by the lack of rail lines through the Sierra Madre range, he took a chance by leading his 14,000 men in a two-week trudge over the mountains and into Jalisco in June 1914, where he secured more trains by smashing Guadalajara's defenders at the Battle of Orendáin. When Huerta subsequently resigned and fled the national capital, Obregón was able to reach Mexico City first because his superior, Venustiano Carranza, was denying coal to the trains of his rival, Villa.

Both commanders transported their armies by rail for an epic showdown the next spring, first clashing at Celaya in April 1915. Villa hurtled from Salamanca with 20,000 men and 22 artillery pieces aboard three huge train columns, only to be defeated by the 11,000 Obregonista defenders. Villa returned almost immediately one week later with 30,000 men and 36 guns aboard an even larger train convoy, to be beaten again. Retreating northward, he fought more circumspectly at the three-week Battle of Trinidad in late May and early June 1915, including a tactic of personally leading 8,000 riders via a circuitous route to surprise Obregón's supply base at Silao and destroy many trains, bridges, and telegraphs in his opponent's rear—a strike that caused Obregón real concern.

Eventually, though, Villa was defeated at Trinidad as well, and Obregón pressed his disintegrating army all the way to the U.S. border where it virtually ceased to exist by year's end. Onlookers and American reporters were impressed by the armored trains that transported Obregón's triumphant constitutionalist troops, which were specially fitted with steel plates, heavy machine guns, and artillery pieces.

See also: Celaya, Battles of; Ejército del Noroeste; Malpaso Canyon, Ambush in; *máquina loca*; Obregón Salido, Álvaro; Orendáin, Battle of; San Pedro de las Colonias, Battle of; Torreón, Villa's Second Capture of (1914); Trinidad, Battle of; Villa, Pancho; Zacatecas, Battle of (1914).

Further Reading

Alessio Robles, Vito. "Reparación de las vías férreas en la última campaña." *Revista del Ejército y de la Marina* 12, no. 9 (September 1911): 161–65.

Jowett, Philip, and Alejandro de Quesada. *The Mexican Revolution, 1910–20*. Oxford: Osprey, 2006, 13, 19–21.

Powell, Fred W. *The Railroads of Mexico*. Boston: Stratford, 1921.

rancho

Historically, a common expression in the Mexican Army for any meal or issue of rations received in the field or in barracks.

Many examples abound of this term's usage in Mexico's military history, such as when Col. Manuel María Giménez reached Santa Anna's defeated army at Agua Nueva with a train of fresh supplies on the morning of February 24, 1847, following its bloody repulse by Gen. Zachary Taylor's army at the Battle of Buenavista only a couple of days earlier. According to Giménez's postwar memoirs, Santa Anna would greet him on that morning before his entire assembled staff with the words: "You have saved these brave men from succumbing to hunger; there have been no *ranchos* for two days, so that no one has eaten anything."

And according to Articles 41 and 42 of the Federal Army's *Ordenanza general* or "General Ordinances" of 1882, *ranchos* were to be issued three times a day to soldiers on active duty, as follows:

- The first in the morning after the *diana* or "reveille" had sounded, consisting of powdered coffee, sugar, spirits, and bread
- The second at noon, composed of fresh meat, *garbanzos* or "chickpeas," vegetables, butter, rice, salt, potatoes, beans, and bread
- The third after *lista* or "roll call" had concluded at six in the evening, being made up of coffee, beans, sugar, and bread

For every day that a serviceman received such rations, 12 *centavos* would be deducted from his pay.

See also: Primary Documents, section titled "Eyewitness Description of Jalisco State Militiamen (March 1854)."

Further Reading

Giménez, Manuel María. *Memorias*. Mexico City: Bouret, 1911, 100.

González, Manuel. *Ordenanza general para el Ejército de la República Mexicana*. Mexico City: Ignacio Cumplido, 1882.

Raousset's Invasion (1852)

Filibustering expedition that attempted to separate the states of Sonora and Baja California from Mexico so as to create an independent republic that could be ruled in favor of private interests.

Having failed to find any riches during California's Gold Rush, the 34-year-old French soldier of fortune Gaston Raoul Raousset, Comte de Boulbon, agreed to recruit and command an armed expedition into Sonora's interior to stake out a huge new claim in this untamed Indian territory for the Franco-Mexican *Restauradora del Mineral de Arizona* Mining Co. Having hired 600 mercenaries at San Francisco (California)—260 of them being French— Raousset arrived at the port of Guaymas on June 1, 1852. After organizing his small army into six infantry companies, plus one each for cavalry and artillerymen, he struck north 12 days later toward Hermosillo.

While encamped at the town of Magdalena, Sonora, Raousset received a message on September 21, 1852, from the new acting governor of that state, Fernando Cubillas, ordering that he and his French followers either adopt Mexican citizenship or leave the country. Knowing this official and Gen. Miguel Blanco, military commander for the state, to be shareholders in a rival mining enterprise, Raousset refused to obey. Instead, he proclaimed Sonora to be an independent country before marching south with his 184 infantrymen, 50 dragoons, and 25 gunners for four small fieldpieces, defeating Blanco on September 30th and occupying the capital of Hermosillo.

Yet after almost four weeks of occupation, Raousset's isolated garrison abandoned Hermosillo on October 26, 1852, retreating south toward the port of Guaymas, hounded by Mexican guerrillas under Blanco. Falling sick with dysentery, Raousset left his army nine miles outside Guaymas on October 29th to sail away for Mazatlán then San Francisco (California). His survivors were allowed to depart undisturbed after surrendering their artillery train to the Mexican authorities in exchange for 11,000 *pesos*.

Having vainly appealed his October 1852 expulsion from Sonora before President Santa Anna in Mexico City, the young adventurer returned to San Francisco by March 1854 and again recruited another 300 volunteers—mostly Frenchmen. Then, after a 35-day voyage, Raousset arrived near Guaymas with this force on June 28, 1854, setting up his temporary headquarters ashore in a cave.

Failing to persuade the local federal commander, Gen. José María Yáñez, to join the ongoing Revolution of Ayutla against Santa Anna, Raousset's contingent was eventually defeated by this Mexican general in a three-hour fight on July 31, 1854, suffering 100 casualties. Captured, Raousset was tried before a military tribunal then executed in Guaymas's La Mole Square at sunrise of August 12, 1854.

Further Reading

La Madeleine, Henri de. *Le compte Gaston de Raousset-Boulbon: Sa vie et ses aventures.* Paris: Poulet-Malassis, 1859.

Lambertie, Charles de. *Le drame de la Sonora: l'état de Sonora, M. Le Comte De Raousset Boulbon et M. Charles De Pindray.* Paris: Chez Ledoyen, 1855.

Wyllys, Rufus Kay. *The French in Sonora, 1850–1854.* Berkeley: University of California Press, 1932.

rayado

Generic word in the Spanish language that, depending on the context in which it is used, can be variously translated as "scored" or "scratched" or "striped"—but that during the latter half of the 19th century was specifically employed by Mexican Army officers to describe the rifling inside of gun barrels.

The technical enhancement of "rifling" had become quite widespread for most armies as of the early 1860s, once it had been proven that helical or spiraling grooves added inside a gun's bore imparted a gyroscopic spin to any projectile fired down its barrel, thus significantly stabilizing the shell's flight and accuracy as well as augmenting its force of impact. As a result, many older-generation smoothbore guns were retooled as of the late 1860s, rifling grooves being scored into their barrels so as to produce this effect.

Mexican Army officers quickly became aware of the advantageous firepower of such weapons and valued them accordingly. For example, in the aftermath of his victory over an imperial army at the Battle of La Carbonera in October 1866, liberal general Porfirio Díaz noted in his official action report to the republican minister of war how his opponents had been equipped with

"six *rayado* cannons of seven centimeter [diameters], of the Austrian system, while my artillery consisted of two smoothbore mountain howitzers."

Reform, War of the (1858–1860)

Climactic showdown between Mexico's liberals and conservatives ending in triumph for the former—although followed almost immediately by the defeated conservatives forging a foreign alliance, thereby continuing their struggle into the War of the French Intervention.

Background (1855–1857)

Ever since Mexico's independence from Spain in 1821, the young nation had become increasingly polarized between

Portrait of the moderate liberal president Ignacio Comonfort, whose attempt to bypass the constitutional reforms of 1857 led to his removal and ignited the War of the Reform. (DeAgostini/Getty Images)

conservative, centrist forces who wished to maintain its old colonial-era institutions largely intact—especially with regard to their own social status, wealth, and privileges, as well as the predominance of the Catholic faith—against liberal, federalist forces who felt that the break with the mother country should have also been accompanied by a loosening of such entrenched restrictions. Both sides remained diametrically opposed, conservatives arguing for retention of a hierarchical social order and the creation of a constitutional monarchy so as to avoid the weakness and anarchy of republican rule, while liberals insisted on true and deeper reforms so more Mexicans might participate and have a vested interest in their country's affairs.

After three decades of conservative intransigence, the liberal cause had finally broken through with the triumph of the Revolution of Ayutla during the summer of 1855, which swept Santa Anna and his aristocratic administration from office for the last time. A new liberal Congress immediately began rewriting and "reforming" Mexico's Constitution, inflaming passions with its very first pronouncement on November 23, 1855, when the 49-year-old justice minister Benito Juárez (a former political prisoner and exile) declared that the exclusive tribunals reserved for members of the military and clergy were to be abolished. Conservative protests quickly erupted under the cry of *¡Religión y fueros!* or "Religion and privileges," although the administration of interim president Ignacio Comonfort was able to crush the major revolts at Puebla in March and December of 1856.

However, the backlash among conservative, Church, and military leaders deepened as yet more constitutional reforms were unveiled in 1857 (some causing dismay among moderate liberals as well), so

still more revolts flared up and had to be stamped out that year. The moderate Comonfort even hesitated to assume office under this "reformed" Constitution as its duly-elected president on December 1, 1857, and consequently staged a "coup" two weeks later—with the connivance of his loyal supporter, Brig. Gen. Félix María Zuloaga—which was intended to leave Comonfort in office, while the more controversial constitutional reforms were to be rescinded and a less radical document could be prepared.

Conservative Seizure of Power (January–February 1858)

Yet Comonfort was overthrown shortly thereafter by a real military coup launched by the Tacubaya garrison on January 11, 1858, departing into exile after freeing the captive Juárez—who promptly fled northwest into Guanajuato and from there claimed the title of president, as he was legally next in line according to the rules of succession. Enjoying the support of most of the liberal state governments in central Mexico, Juárez also began directing preparations for armed resistance, while Zuloaga in the capital was acclaimed as a rival "interim president" by the conservative faction on January 23, 1858, who immediately set about organizing a military force so as to march into the Bajío and disperse any concentrations of liberal militia.

Confident of the loyalty of officers in the regular Mexican Army, conservative brigadier general Miguel Miramón led a vanguard brigade out of the national capital during the second week of February 1858, followed by larger contingent a few days later under the 29-year-old commander-in-chief: one-armed brigadier general Luis G. Osollo. Their combined army passed through undefended Querétaro before detecting more than 7,000 liberal militiamen who were gathering outside the city of Celaya, and subsequently retreated 30 miles farther west into Salamanca.

Conservative Military Victories (March 1858–November 1859)

Osollo's and Miramón's 5,400 regular soldiers and 40 guns easily beat the 7,300 inexperienced liberal militiamen at the Battle of Salamanca on March 10, 1858, marching victoriously on to chase Juárez's government out of Guadalajara as well before that month was out. Yet despite installing army detachments to garrison cities throughout the Bajío, liberal resistance persisted. Guadalajara was almost immediately put under constant pressure by local guerrillas, and although an army of irregulars out of the northern states of Nuevo León and Coahuila was initially defeated at the Battle of Ahualulco de los Pinos in late September 1858, that threat soon rematerialized. The conservative administration struggled to obtain the necessary funds to sustain its disperse armies and realized that it could not rely on its conscript soldiers.

When Miramón took over the title of conservative "substitute president" and led the main army out of Mexico City down to the Gulf coast in February 1859 so as to besiege Juárez's relocated government in the port city of Veracruz, he soon had to hasten back when a 6,000-man liberal force under Gen. Santos Degollado attacked the capital during his absence. Although this particular liberal thrust was repelled at the Battle of Tacubaya, their strength nonetheless continued to grow throughout the Bajío, while Juárez furthermore became recognized by Washington as Mexico's legitimate president and received U.S. assistance as conservative resources dwindled.

Despite being outnumbered by more than two to one, Miramón nevertheless managed to win an unexpected victory at the Battle of Estancia de las Vacas in November 1859, but this battlefield triumph did little more than delay the inevitable end.

Conservative Defeats, Liberal Triumph (1860)

Miramón's second attempt to besiege Veracruz in February 1860 proved equally as fruitless as his first, and although he succeeded in saving Guadalajara's isolated garrison from an assault by 8,000 liberal troops in June 1860, their strength was now so great that he deliberately avoided engaging them afterward. Within a few short weeks, the self-taught liberal general Jesús González Ortega united in Aguascalientes with the talented Ignacio Zaragoza, and their combined 10,000 soldiers chased Miramón out of León, utterly routing his 3,300 demoralized soldiers at the Battle of Silao in August 1860, so the "substitute president" was lucky to ride back into Mexico City with little more than the clothes on his back.

Subsequently, a massive concentration of 20,000 liberals equipped with 125 fieldpieces laid siege to Guadalajara that following month and easily defeated a 3,000-man conservative relief column under Gen. Leonardo Márquez on November 1, 1860, so the isolated garrison surrendered and only the national capital remained in conservative hands. Scraping together every last available man, Miramón marched out of Mexico City with 8,000 troops and 30 guns on the morning of December 19, 1860, taking up position on the high ground overlooking the village of Calpulalpan, 30 miles east of the capital. Three days later, González Ortega beat him there with his 11,000 soldiers and 14 guns, so the "substitute president" fled into European exile and Mexico City was occupied by the triumphant liberals on Christmas Day 1860.

Aftermath (January 1861)

Two days later, González Ortega issued a decree from the National Palace that officially dissolved the Mexican Army, deeming it to have been a "sucker fish [*rémora*] to all social progress in our country, since our political emancipation from the Spanish metropolis." As converging liberal columns continued to arrive in the Valley of Mexico, a grand parade was held on New Year's Day 1861, in which some 30,000 men marched to celebrate the triumph of the liberal cause—Mexico City being firmly in their hands, and no conservative challengers left to contest its ownership. Juárez subsequently departed Veracruz on January 5, 1861, and six days later assumed his duties as president in the capital, officially marking an end to this conflict.

A few conservative diehards such as Márquez, Marcelino Cobos, and Tomás Mejía had withdrawn into the mountains of central Mexico to continue the struggle on behalf of the fugitive conservative "interim president" Zuloaga, eventually coalescing in the vicinity of Izúcar de Matamoros. Still, lacking numbers or resources, these unattached companies could do little more than evade liberal columns and make pinprick raids to secure provisions, so their cause seemed essentially lost. One year later, though, a French military expedition would disembark at Veracruz, and many of these fugitives would help the invaders to install the emperor Maximilian on the throne of Mexico.

See also: Ahualulco de los Pinos, Battle of; Ayutla, Revolution of; Bajío; Calpulalpan, Battle of; Estancia de las Vacas, Battle of; French Intervention, War of the; González Ortega, José Canuto de Jesús; Guadalajara, Sieges of (1858–1860); Márquez Araujo, Leonardo; Miramón Tarelo, Miguel Gregorio de la Luz Atenógenes; Osollo Pancorbo, Luis Gonzaga; Puebla, Conservative Revolt and Liberal Sieges of; Salamanca, Battle of; Silao, Battle of; Tacubaya, Battle of; Veracruz, Conservative Sieges of; Zuazua Esparza, Juan Nepomuceno; Zuloaga Trillo, Félix María.

Further Reading

Cambre, Manuel. *La guerra de Tres Años: apuntes para la historia de la Reforma.* Guadalajara, Jalisco: Biblioteca de Autores Jaliscienses, Gobierno del Estado, 1949.

González Lezama, Raúl. *Reforma liberal: cronología (1854–1876).* Mexico City: INEHRM, 2012.

Haworth, Daniel S. "Civilians and Civil War in Nineteenth-Century Mexico: Mexico City and the War of the Reform, 1858–1861." In *Daily Lives of Civilians in Latin America from the Wars of Independence to the Drug Wars*, edited by Pedro Santoni, 91–122. Westport, CT: Greenwood Press, 2008.

Remington, Frederic Sackrider (1861–1909)

Famed illustrator of the American West, who also visited Mexico and produced accurate, detailed depictions of the soldiers of its Federal Army during the Porfirian era.

He was born in the town of Canton, near the Canadian border in northern New York State on October 4, 1861, the only child of its local newspaper publisher and postmaster, Seth Pierrepont Remington, and his wife, Clara Bascomb Remington (née Sackrider). The entire Remington family was active politically as staunch Republicans, so when Frederic was only four months old, his father left for New York City to recruit for "Scott's 900" of the 11th New

York Volunteer Cavalry Regiment, going on to perform heroically as a colonel during the Civil War before mustering out late in 1864. The small family then moved briefly to Illinois after young Fred's father had been appointed editor of the Bloomington *Republican* but returned to Canton by 1867.

As an only child, Fred was doted on and proved to be an active youngster, large and strong for his age, who loved hunting, swimming, riding, and camping in the countryside of upper New York State. He was a poor student, though, particularly in math, which did not bode well for his father's ambitions for him to attend West Point. When Remington was 11 years old, the family moved to Ogdensburg, New York, where he attended a church-run military school named the Vermont Episcopal Institute before transferring to the Highland Military Academy in Worcester, Massachusetts— where the teenaged Fred proved popular among his classmates, although not deemed to be of soldiery material.

Interested in drawing ever since an early age, Remington instead enrolled in the art school at Yale University, the only male in that faculty during his freshman year. However, he found football and boxing to be more interesting than classroom work, and being big and athletic, soon won a spot as a first-string player on the very competitive Yale varsity football team—but after only three semesters in that university, he dropped out to be at his father's bedside when the elder Remington's tuberculosis reached its final stages and claimed his life by February 1880.

First Western and Artistic Ventures (1882–1888)

Shortly after his father's death, Fred held a series of well-paying clerical jobs in stores in the north country, then as a government clerk in Albany, all arranged through his uncles, although he proved to be unhappy in such work. Upon turning 21 years of age, though, Remington received a $9,000 inheritance from his father's estate in October 1882, which was enough money for him to follow a Yale friend's advice and buy a sheep ranch near Peabody, Kansas. Remington lasted but a year in that lonely occupation, however, before selling his ram, five sheep, and plot of land to pursue other interests that allowed him time to draw.

He therefore became a silent partner in a bar in Kansas City, Missouri, then traveled to Gloversville, New York, to marry his sweetheart, Eva Caten. She returned home to her father after seeing what little Remington was up to in Kansas City, but the couple was reunited and set up a new life in New York City. Legend has it that Remington presented himself to the publisher Henry Harper, decked out in buckskins and professing himself to be an expert on all things western, and thus secured employment as an illustrator—first with *Harper's Weekly*, then with most of the other great New York magazines of that day, who frequently published popular material on western subjects.

Visits to Mexico (1889–1894)

In February 1889, Remington was commissioned by Harper's to travel into Mexico with Thomas A. Janvier so as to prepare illustrations for a forthcoming article that was to be written by Janvier and entitled "The Aztec Treasure-House." During the few weeks that they were in Mexico City though, Remington became fascinated by the Mexican Army and so painted, sketched, and photographed many military figures during his short stay. Almost immediately upon his return home, he wrote enthusiastically on March 14, 1889 to his U.S. Army friend, Lt. Powhatan Clarke:

I am just home from the city of Mexico, where I have been doing the army. They are immensely picturesque and I have some good subjects. In your next letter, write me all the facts you know concerning the operation of the Mex. regular troops in Sonora—their methods—their marching and fighting.

Remington drew on his watercolors and sketches to produce 14 engravings of Mexican Army figures to accompany an article by Janvier in the November 1889 issue of *Harper's New Monthly Magazine* entitled "The Mexican Army" and that featured his finely detailed portraits of:

- A regimental scout
- An artillery sergeant
- An engineer in undress uniform
- A full-dress engineer
- An officer in a French-style uniform
- Drummers and buglers marching up a street
- Soldiers searching a house for deserters
- A lieutenant of the Engineer Battalion
- A bugler of the 2nd Cavalry Regiment
- A mounted gendarme or military policeman
- A soldier of infantry of the line
- A mounted rural policeman
- A mounted trooper of the 5th Cavalry Regiment
- "Stable Call at an Artillery Barrack"

A wood engraving entitled "Mexican Infantry on the March" was also published on page 305 of the April 19, 1890, edition of *Harper's Weekly* with a brief accompanying text by Remington on a separate page. He would always pride himself on the accuracy of his depictions, so his details of Mexican Army uniforms and equipment remain a valuable historical resource.

After making a trip to the Canadian North and to the American West again, Remington returned to Mexico City for a second visit in March 1891, this time accompanied by his wife, Eva, and as guests of U.S. general Nelson A. Miles, to attend a grand review of the Mexican Army. That same September 8, 1891, Remington wrote to his friend Lieutenant Clarke saying that he would be spending the forthcoming winter "devoting myself almost exclusively to American and Mex. military subjects."

After spending their first years of married life in New York City apartments, the Remingtons bought a large home on December 1, 1889, on a three-acre lot in New Rochelle in Westchester County. The home, which they called Endion ("the place where I live" in Ojibwa), was close enough to New York City for Remington to boast that he could get to Times Square with two horses in 30 minutes. It included outbuildings, and Remington built a large studio on the property where most of his artwork was created over the next 18 years.

Remington traveled to Mexico for a third time with his friend John Howard in January 1893, once again on a commission from *Harper's* to write and illustrate articles on the Hacienda de San José Bavicora—a remote 900,000-acre ranch some 225 miles northwest of Chihuahua City, owned by an American named Jack Gilbert. Remington spent four weeks there, sketching and making notes before returning north to Albuquerque in March 1893, where Eva joined him and they continued on together to California. He returned to Texas and Mexico to hunt and sketch in January 1894, returning to New York in February with material for six articles.

Three years later, an author named Maurice Kingsley wrote an article entitled "El Cinco de Mayo" for the May 7, 1892, issue of *Harper's Weekly* for which Remington provided four illustrations. Then early in 1893, Remington visited a huge 900,000 acre American-owned spread named San José de Bavicora for four weeks, 225 miles northwest of Chihuahua City, before traveling to Albuquerque so as to meet his wife Eva. This visit will furnish inspiration for illustrations to accompany three articles in the December 1893 to March 1894 editions of *Harper's Monthly*, as well as other publications, and mark Remington's last visit to Mexico.

See also: Díaz Mori, José de la Cruz Porfirio; Ejército Federal.

Further Reading

Janvier, Thomas A. "The Mexican Army." *Harper's New Monthly Magazine* 79, no. 474 (November 1889): 812–27.

Kingsley, Maurice. "El Cinco de Mayo." *Harper's Weekly* 36, no. 1846 (May 7, 1892): 449.

Remington, Frederic. "Mexican Infantry on the March." *Harper's Weekly* 34, no. 1739 (April 19, 1890): 305.

Revolution, Mexican (1910–1920)

Traumatic upheaval that engulfed Mexico in a decade of bitter warfare so remorselessly that its population contracted by almost 1 million people.

Background (Summer 1910)

Although the country had suffered through previous insurrections and civil wars, this particular conflict—unprecedented in its scope and size, and fought with high-powered weaponry—would be remembered simply as *La Revolución* or "The Revolution." It had originated out of a widespread discontent that accumulated over the 35 years of entrenched rule of Pres. Porfirio Díaz, a prolonged interlude of relative peace during which Mexico had prospered and become more modernized, yet whose greatest benefits were reserved for members of the upper classes and foreign investors. This inflexible Porfirian regime was moreover sustained by federal army garrisons distributed around every region (moving as needed by rail and directed by telegraph), plus mounted police squadrons known as *rurales*, who patrolled the roads and small towns.

During the summer of 1910, Díaz—now approaching 80 years of age—had announced that he would be standing for an eighth term as president, and the wealthy, high-minded northerner Francisco I. Madero declared that he would run against him as head of an "anti-reelectionist" party. Intolerant of even a show of opposition, the president had arranged for Madero to be arrested, and by the time that the primaries were held on June 21, 1910, 5,000 of his challenger's adherents had joined him in prison. When the final elections were held on July 8, 1910, an estimated 60,000 were behind bars, after which the compliant Congress certified the results and duly proclaimed Díaz reelected as president on September 27, 1910—11 days after the celebrations that had marked the centennial of Mexico's uprising against Spanish colonial rule.

Believing the question of the presidential election to be at an end, Madero was allowed to escape from loose confinement at San Luis Potosí on October 4, 1910, riding across the border to gain asylum at San Antonio, Texas. However, incensed at the blatant injustice of Díaz's machinations,

Francisco Madero, third from right, surrounded by supporters in northern Mexico, ca. April 1911. (Library of Congress)

the fugitive issued a call from exile for a nationwide uprising to commence as of November 20, 1910, so as to drive the dictator from power by force of arms.

Overthrow of Porfirio Díaz (November 1910–May 1911)

Numerous outbreaks erupted throughout northern Mexico in late November 1910, almost exclusively confined to remote towns and villages, where rebels overran isolated federal outposts and then defeated the detachments of troops or *rurales* sent in by rail to suppress them. Although larger cities remained firmly under governmental control, there were not enough soldiers available to confront so many widely scattered outbursts, while a coordinated response was further hampered by uncertain telegraphic communications. Popular urban sentiment was already against the regime as well, and would grow even more vocal as weeks went by without the Porfirian authorities being able to contain or curtail the

spread of hit-and-run raids by rebel bands throughout the North.

Then a second popular insurrection exploded in the southern state of Morelos in March 1911, soon spearheaded by the charismatic Emiliano Zapata, fervently demanding *tierra y libertad* or "land and liberty" for his thousands of peasant followers. The following month, Madero managed to marshal some 3,500 of his freelancing northern rebels into a ragtag "army" so as to besiege the 700-man federal garrison holding Ciudad Juárez (opposite El Paso, Texas), whose defenses were finally overwhelmed and carried by storm during the first week of May 1911 by his appointed "general," Pascual Orozco, and "colonel," Pancho Villa.

Having failed to mount any kind of rescue for Ciudad Juarez's doomed federal defenders, the increasingly hard-pressed Díaz proved equally powerless to prevent another 1,700 of his troops from being chased out of the city of Torreón in the state of Coahuila by these same northern rebels on May 15, 1911; or to ensure that the fortified city of Cuautla in the southern state of Morelos did not to fall to Zapata's peasant army six days afterward. Sensing the dictator's weakness, antigovernment riots broke out in the main square of Mexico City outside the Presidential Palace itself on the evening of May 24, 1911, so the octogenarian Díaz finally decided to relinquish the presidency next day and depart for Veracruz, sailing away into European exile aboard the German liner *Ypiranga*.

Troubled Transition under Madero (June 1911–January 1913)

This northern leader—a political figurehead, rather than a field commander—made his triumphal entry into the national capital on June 7, 1911, a few hours after a heavy earthquake had ominously shaken that city and claimed 207 lives. Although major warfare would cease for a brief spell after his arrival, Zapata and his southern peasants nonetheless remained distrustful of this wealthy northern landowner, refusing to disarm until their own recent land reclamations and occupations were recognized as legitimate by the central authorities.

But since Madero had not yet been elected president, the interim administration left temporarily running affairs was under Porfirio Díaz's ex-foreign minister, Francisco León de la Barra, who moved to check any expansion of Zapatista lawlessness beyond the state of Morelos by ordering federal troops under Col. Aureliano Blanquet to attack their unruly occupying force in the city of Puebla in mid-July 1911, killing 80 Zapatistas and wounding 200 in a firefight around its bullring. Then the next month, León de la Barra furthermore dispatched 1,000 more soldiers under hard-bitten general Victoriano Huerta

into Cuernavaca so as to monitor and restrain Zapata's followers through heavy-handed actions.

By the time Madero finally won a special election and assumed the vacant presidency during the first week of November 1911, Zapata was already once again in open rebellion against the central government, and the state of Morelos was being terrorized by brutal federal sweeps. Madero replaced the army commander in that region in early 1912 with the high-minded general Felipe Ángeles, who implemented a much more humane campaign, but the inexperienced president was to be beset by many other difficulties over the ensuing year—beginning with a mutinous challenge to his authority from his disgruntled former subordinate Orozco, who (unhappy at not receiving a plum cabinet appointment) revolted in March 1912 with his large and well-equipped army of *colorados* in Chihuahua, so Madero had to once more rely on Federal Army officers left over from the Porfirian regime to put down this insurrection.

Huerta's Usurpation (February 1913–July 1914)

Given the declining fortunes of Madero's weak and chaotic administration, and its abandonment by many former democratic supporters, a military coup was attempted in Mexico City by Gen. Manuel Mondragón and other conservative officers in February 1913 with the aim of removing his failed reformist movement so as to instead restore the strict law-and-order policies and stability of the Porfirian era. After initially being repulsed, these mutineers engaged in 10 days of heavy gunfire within the crowded confines of the national capital—inflicting so many civilian casualties that this terrible episode would be remembered as the *Decena Trágica* or "Tragic Fortnight"—

before Madero's chosen commander, Huerta, eventually betrayed and murdered the president so as to usurp the office for himself.

Repelled by this crude power grab, the Mexican Revolution was revived with a passion throughout the country, as most factions were united in their hatred of Huerta and his goal of bringing back the old ways. Larger and better-equipped rebel forces began emerging in the north, soon proving to be more than a match for the massive buildup of federal conscripts undertaken by Huerta. A former schoolteacher named Álvaro Obregón developed a small yet potent *Ejército del Noroeste* or "Army of the Northwest" in the state of Sonora by May of 1913, while the former bandit Pancho Villa gathered dozens of bands of riders that same autumn of 1913 into a horde of loosely disciplined irregulars that would become known as the *División del Norte*, eventually traveling in huge train convoys complete with heavy artillery.

Starting in late September 1913, Villa won a string of seven spectacular victories of escalating size at Torreón, Ciudad Juárez, Tierra Blanca, Ojinaga, Torreón again, San Pedro de las Colonias, and Paredón over a span of as many months, pulverizing one Huertista army after another, while Obregón farther west drove inexorably down the Pacific coast into central Mexico. A punitive U.S. expedition furthermore added to Huerta's woes by occupying the main seaport of Veracruz in April 1914, after which his reeling regime was finished off when Villa attacked the main garrison city of Zacatecas with 25,000 rebel troops on June 23, 1914—wiping out almost its entire 12,000-man federal garrison—while Obregón did the same two weeks later, when his 14,000 soldiers crushed the 12,000 *federales* holding Guadalajara at the two-day Battle of Orendáin on July 6–7, 1914. Having lost his two biggest armies in this short span, Huerta resigned the presidency eight days later and fled Mexico City to seek asylum in Spain.

Fratricidal Warfare (1914–1915)

When the victorious Obregón reached the outskirts of Mexico City on August 11, 1914, its surviving federal authorities agreed not only to capitulate but to furthermore dissolve the remnants of the once-proud Federal Army and corps of *rurales*. One week later, these defeated soldiers trudged eastward out of the capital to be disbanded in small groups at rural railway stations, individually wending their way home while behind them, Obregón's 18,000-man Army of the Northwest marched triumphantly into Mexico City to appropriate their vacated bases, armories, ordnance depots, etc.

Obregón's political superior, the revolutionary *primer jefe* or "first chief" Venustiano Carranza also arrived in the capital on August 20, 1914, to assume the office of president the next day. But while everyone was pleased by Huerta's removal, Zapata from his headquarters at Cuernavaca openly defied the haughty Carranza's self-proclaimed accession to the title on September 8, 1914, followed two weeks later by Pancho Villa in the north. A convention held in neutral Aguascalientes to resolve this contentious issue ended in an open break by early November 1914 with Villistas and Zapatistas uniting to drive Carranza from office. Their huge armies quickly began converging on Mexico City from north and south, so the outnumbered Carranza and his loyal general Obregón evacuated it by the last week of that same November 1914, retreating eastward into Veracruz.

Villa and Zapata held an enormous parade of perhaps 50,000 men from their combined armies through the streets of the national capital on December 6, 1914, and posed for photographs sitting in the presidential chair, but neither aspired to the office itself. After a few weeks of token occupation, their forces largely withdrew, so Obregón was able to reclaim Mexico City by January 28, 1915, and prepare his smaller but well-equipped and better-disciplined army to carry the fight northward six weeks later into Villista territory.

Pushing up into Celaya, Obregón's 5,000 infantrymen and 6,000 cavalry troopers, armed with 86 machine guns and 13 cannon, defeated an all-out assault by Villa with 20,000 men and 22 artillery pieces on April 6–7, 1915, driving these more numerous attackers off with heavy losses. After being reinforced by rail and bringing his strength up to 7,000 infantry and 8,000 cavalrymen, Obregón achieved the same decisive result when Villa returned for a second assault against Celaya one week later, this time with 30,000 of his irregulars and 36 guns—leaving behind a further 4,000 dead, 5,000 wounded, 6,000 prisoners, 1,000 fully saddled horses, and all his artillery, in comparison to Obregón's losses of only 138 dead and 276 wounded. Their third confrontation at Trinidad saw an even stronger army of 14,300 infantrymen and 9,400 cavalry troopers under Obregón utterly destroy Villa's last 25,500-man army in May–June 1915, breaking his military power for good.

Obregonista columns were subsequently detached to occupy cities and run down Villista remnants, while Villa himself led a series of diminishing attacks against smaller garrisons before retiring into the mountains in defeat as the winter of 1915–1916 set in. He emerged from hiding to lead 500 riders in a desperate cross-border strike at dawn on March 9, 1916 against Columbus, New Mexico, which galvanized the U.S. government less than a week later into sending 3,000 troops under Brig. Gen. John J. Pershing in pursuit deep into Mexico, yet failed to resurrect Villa's fortunes.

Consolidation (1916–1920)

Following the defeat of Villa's powerful *División del Norte*, no more major setpiece battles had to be fought by the victorious Constitutionalist army, only regional pacification campaigns such as the annihilation of Zapatista resistance in the state of Morelos, which ended with the assassination of its charismatic leader at the Hacienda of San Juan Chinameca on April 10, 1919. Left without any other surviving battlefield opponents, the revolutionary leadership then turned on each other.

When the retired general Álvaro Obregón announced in June 1919 that he intended to run for the presidency, his former chief—the sitting president, Venustiano Carranza—voiced his displeasure and attempted to obstruct Obregón's candidacy. Ordered to appear on a trumped-up charge of treason and conspiracy in mid-April 1920, the one-armed general escaped in disguise and called for a military uprising, which was answered by scores of his former generals. As large Obregonista armies began quickly closing in on Mexico City, Carranza was obliged to abandon his capital at dawn on May 7, 1920, aboard a 15-mile-long train convoy bearing 10,000 adherents and the national treasury. Attacked from every side, the fugitive president was reduced to a few score followers by the time that he rode up into the mountains one week later, to be murdered in a mountain hut on May 21, 1920. Obregón was elected president a few months later, some historians feeling that this event marked an end to the Mexican Revolution, although there is no consensus on this point.

See also: Ángeles Ramírez, Felipe de Jesús; Celaya, Battles of; *Decena Trágica*; Díaz Mori, José de la Cruz Porfirio; División del Norte; Huerta Márquez, José Victoriano; Mondragón Mondragón, Manuel; Obregón Salido, Álvaro; Orendáin, Battle of; *rurales*; Trinidad, Battle of; Villa, Pancho; Zapata Salazar, Emiliano.

Further Reading

Brunk, Samuel. *Emiliano Zapata: Revolution and Betrayal in Mexico*. Albuquerque: University of New Mexico Press, 1995.

Buchenau, Jürgen. *The Last Caudillo: Álvaro Obregón and the Mexican Revolution*. Chichester, England: Wiley-Blackwell, 2011.

Cumberland, Charles C. *Mexican Revolution: The Constitutionalist Years*. Austin: University of Texas Press, 1972.

Johnson, William Weber. *Heroic Mexico: The Violent Emergence of a Modern Nation*. New York: Doubleday, 1968.

Jowett, Philip, and Alejandro de Quesada. *The Mexican Revolution, 1910–20*. Oxford: Osprey, 2006.

McLynn, Frank. *Villa and Zapata: A History of the Mexican Revolution*. New York: Carroll and Graf, 2000.

Scheina, Robert L. *Villa: Soldier of the Mexican Revolution*. Washington, DC: Potomac Books, 2004.

Rexer light machine gun (1905)

British-manufactured copy of the Danish Madsen light machine gun, a less-expensive alternative purchased during the modernization phase of the Porfirian Army.

In 1905, a British firm named the Rexer Arms Company began manufacturing an unlicensed copy of the innovative and highly prized Madsen, and the Porfirian government purchased several dozen of these less-expensive models before Rexer was obliged to halt production because of a lawsuit filed by Madsen. In 1911, the Mexican Army did apparently acquire at least 100 of the M.1911 Madsen light machine guns directly from the Danish manufacturer, although most sources continued to describe all their weapons as "Rexers."

For example, the U.S. military attaché in Mexico City, Capt. Robert M. Campbell, estimated in late April 1918 that the postrevolutionary Mexican Army's machine guns were distributed as follows: one regiment armed with 40 Hotchkiss heavy machine guns; 10 smaller units, each armed with 5 Hotchkiss machine guns apiece; 4 more small units, equipped with 5 Colt machine guns apiece; plus another 10 small units, each armed with 10 Rexer light machine guns—a total of 110 heavy and 100 light machine guns.

See also: *ametralladora*; Colt-Browning heavy machine gun; Hotchkiss heavy machine gun.

Further Reading

Fitzsimmons, Bernard. *Illustrated Encyclopedia of Weapons and Warfare*. London: Phoebus, 1978.

Hughes, James B., Jr. *Mexican Military Arms: The Cartridge Period, 1866–1967*. Houston, TX: Deep River Armory, 1968.

Jowett, Philip, and Alejandro de Quesada. *The Mexican Revolution, 1910–20*. Oxford: Osprey, 2006, 15–16.

"Rexer Automatic Machine Gun." *Scientific American*, August 19, 1905.

Río Blanco Strike (1907)

Major labor stoppage that was broken up by brutal countermeasures taken by the Federal Army on orders from Pres. Porfirio Díaz.

Background (1892–1906)

During the early 1890s, a number of textile factories began to be installed in the Orizaba Valley of the state of Veracruz, the first (and eventually largest) being erected by Franco-Mexican financiers in the municipality of Río Blanco, just west of the city of Orizaba. As output increased over that ensuing decade and a-half, Mexican workers grew resentful over the disparity in wages for their 14-hour workdays: foreign specialists earned 40 *pesos* a week, while Mexican foremen received only 6 and laborers barely made 2. Worse, these meager salaries might further suffer deductions due to tardiness, as well as for purchases made through the company stores, which were known as *tiendas de raya*.

A labor union was therefore secretly organized in the spring of 1906, despite discouragement from the textile companies and a few punitive arrests by the authorities. Eventually, thousands of workers went out on strike on December 4, 1906, and 10 days later sent a public telegram to President Díaz in Mexico City, requesting his mediation. After first attempting to operate their factories with replacement workers, the company management decided to lock out all workers on Christmas Eve of 1906.

Military Suppression (January 7–9, 1907)

When President Díaz issued his verdict (*laudo*) on January 4, 1907, it directed all striking textile workers to return to their labors. On January 7, 1907, a group of hungry strikers stormed the company store in the municipality of Río Blanco (just west of the city of Orizaba in the state of Veracruz), ransacking it and starting a fire, which burned several adjacent buildings. Federal cavalrymen under Gen. Rosalino

Martínez, the undersecretary of war, were consequently rushed in the next day from the nearby city of Orizaba, brutally restoring order by firing point-blank into some mobs, then conducting summary executions of other detainees. Among those shot out of hand was the local garrison commander, Lt. Gabriel Arroyo, as well as his entire company, for having refused to crush the initial outbreak. By the time order was finally restored, some 200 strikers had been killed and the cowed survivors returned to work.

See also: Díaz Mori, José de la Cruz Porfirio; railroads.

Further Reading

Koth, Karl B. " 'Not a Mutiny, but a Revolution': The Río Blanco Labour Dispute, 1906–1907." *Canadian Journal of Latin American and Caribbean Studies* 18, no. 35 (1993): 39–65.

rurales (1879–1914)

Mounted policemen uniformed in traditional *charro*-style dress and commanded by Mexican Army officers, who helped to impose order during the Porfirian era.

Background History (1861–1878)

Given Mexico's perennial problems with banditry, several state governments had begun organizing their own independent *guardia rural* or "rural guard" units during the liberal administrations of the 1850s, led by local militia commanders. The newly installed and hard-pressed president Benito Juárez had furthermore sanctioned the permanent existence of four such *cuerpos* or "corps" with the name of *Policía Rural de la Federación* or "Rural Police of the Federation" in May 1861, their administration being attached as a dependency of the Ministry of War.

Implementation of this measure was soon interrupted by the War of the French Intervention, during which the imperial regime of Maximilian attempted in 1863 to revive the old *Guardia Civil* or "Civil Guard" units, which had been briefly attempted five years previously under Pres. Félix Zuloaga. This imperial effort failed because republican guerrilla bands were by law also regarded as outlaws, clouding the issue and Maximilian's government was left shortly thereafter in control of only a handful of large cities, ending their jurisdiction. Once his French supporters were expelled and peace was restored as of 1867, states were encouraged by the idealistic yet money-strapped liberal administration in Mexico City to resurrect their rural-guard units, some proving more effective than others.

Porfirian Organization (1879–1912)

As early as 1879, the strongman Porfirio Díaz had tried to stamp out Mexico's problem of banditry by upgrading its existing *Guardia Rural* or "Rural Guard," so the federal government assumed its unified direction and organized a new national corps as of June 1880. This was a small force of mounted constabulary who patrolled the countryside. To encourage the nation's peaceful transition into a modern state, he had increased their numbers to more than 2,100 riders. Ten squadrons called *cuerpos* or "corps" comprising three 76-man companies apiece had been created, led by officers seconded from the Mexican Army. Stylish dove-gray uniforms and broad-brimmed hats were issued, modeled on the traditional *charro* dress, complete with silver buckles as well as red and black cravats. Heavier, standardized weaponry had been provided to each trooper: carbines, sabers, and pistols. Telegraph and railway communications had allowed them to concentrate quickly in any troubled area. And the *rurales* were encouraged to apply the notorious *ley fuga*, a ruthless policy whereby any criminal caught in the act could be executed on the spot.

By the first decade of the 19th century, this distinctive body of riders had almost doubled in size and was considered among the most famous police forces in the world, comparable to the Royal Canadian Mounted Police or Texas Rangers. Díaz and his advisers would often parade the glamorous corps on ceremonial occasions and confirm tales about their cruel efficiency so as to reassure foreign investors about the stability of his regime. However, modern research has indicated that the *rurales* were neither as brutal nor omnipresent as once believed but rather were deployed mostly in a few showpiece states, not throughout the country as a whole. Units would moreover be rotated in and out of different theaters so as to give the illusion of greater numbers.

Even such a vehement Porfirian critic as Carlo de Fornaro, after pointing out in 1909 that some lawbreakers were still being tempted from a life of crime by instead "being offered better wages for entering into government service in the corps of *rurales*," would go on to add:

> In this manner, an excellent body of men has been formed, hardened to all fatigues and dangers, so as to maintain order throughout the country.

And perhaps even more tellingly, when the reform-minded Francisco I. Madero would be swept into power by the Mexican Revolution of 1910, the *rurales* were still so highly regarded that he would maintain this force largely intact. It was only after he was betrayed and murdered by his successor, Gen. Victoriano Huerta, that the *rurales* would become transformed into a paramilitary body. As part of his massive military buildup, this new dictotor transferred all 31 regiments of *rurales* from the Secretariat of the Interior to the Ministry of War by a decree dated August 15, 1913, and increased the number of each regiment's riders so as to create an auxiliary *cuerpo de exploradores* or "scout corps" of 12,400 troopers for the Federal Army. In an effort to expand their numbers, standards were lowered and the *rurales'* former pride was lost, their last few units being disbanded by July 1914 as the Huertista regime collapsed.

See also: Huerta Márquez, José Victoriano; Kosterlitzky, Emilio; *ley fuga*; Revolution, Mexican.

Further Reading

Vanderwood, Paul J. "Genesis of the Rurales: Mexico's Early Struggle for Public Security." *Hispanic American Historical Review* 50 (May 1970): 323–44.

Vanderwood, Paul J. "Mexico's Rurales: Reputation versus Reality." *The Americas: Academy of American Franciscan History* 34, no. 1 (July 1977): 102–12.

S

If they're Mexicans, I'll surrender.
If they're gringos, I'll die fighting!
   — Villa's wounded subordinate Pablo
           López as Carrancista troops
           closed in on his hiding place after
           the Columbus raid (1916)

Saint Patrick's Battalion. *See* San Patricio Battalion (1846–1848).

Salamanca, Battle of (1858)

Widely regarded as the opening clash of the War of the Reform or Three Years' War, although hostilities had in fact already commenced by the time that this conservative victory was won.

Background (December 1857–January 1858)

The three months preceding this battle had seen a peacetime backlash among Church and conservative leaders (as well as dismay among certain moderate liberals), against the newly rewritten or "reformed" Constitutional articles that were being unveiled during the autumn of 1857 by Mexico's liberal Congress. The moderate Ignacio Comonfort had even hesitated to assume office as duly elected president under its laws on December 1, 1857, and therefore staged a "coup" two weeks later—with the connivance of his loyal supporter, Brig. Gen. Félix María Zuloaga—which was intended to leave Comonfort in office, while the more controversial articles of the reformed Constitution were to be rescinded and a less radical document prepared.

However, Comonfort had been deposed shortly thereafter by a real military coup sprung by the Mexico City garrison on January 11, 1858, so the legal title of president was consequently claimed by the head of the Supreme Court—the liberal jurist Benito Juárez, author of many of the controversial reforms and next in line to the presidency, according to its chain of succession—who promptly fled to Guanajuato so as to begin raising armed supporters, as he enjoyed the backing of most of the liberal states of central Mexico. Zuloaga meanwhile remained in the national capital and was acclaimed by the conservative mutineers as a rival "interim President," immediately setting about the abolition of the constitutional reforms and preparing the Army for a military offensive.

Preliminary Maneuvers (February 1858)

The conservatives' first overt military act occurred when Brig. Gen. Miguel Miramón led a column due west from the capital toward Toluca, the mere threat of his approach chasing out its liberal garrison by January 26, 1858, so he left behind a detachment and returned to Mexico City. Miramón thereupon marched out of the capital for a second time a fortnight later, departing northwestward with a vanguard brigade of 1,200 regulars on February 5, 1858, so as to spearhead an army that was to coalesce

The youthful, one-armed conservative general Luis G. Osollo. (Library of Congress)

and push up into the Bajío, dispersing any liberal militia forces that might be gathering there in support of Juárez. An even larger conservative contingent followed out of Mexico City a few days later under the usurpers' chosen commander-in-chief— one-armed, 29-year-old brigadier general Luis G. Osollo—whose columns marched in Miramón's wake, and met up along their route with a third brigade under Brig. Gen. Tomás Mejía, who was falling back from San Juan del Río to incorporate his contingent into the main body.

Expecting to be defied by the liberal general José María Arteaga at Querétaro, Osollo and Miramón were surprised to enter that city uncontested on February 12, 1858, Arteaga having withdrawn due westward in the direction of Celaya with his 2,000 troops. Learning that as many as 6,000 liberal militiamen were already marshaling there—only 30 miles from Querétaro— under Gen. Anastasio Parrodi (the governor

of Jalisco), Osollo carefully planned an approach so as to attack this superior force from two directions. It took him until February 24, 1858, to bring his lone division into Apaseo (a town nine miles east of Celaya), while the brigades of his subordinates Francisco García Casanova and Mejía had circled around and were coming down the road from Chamacuero (modern Comonfort), 15 miles to the north of Celaya.

The next day, February 25, 1858, Osollo's scouts exchanged gunfire with the liberal defensive lines some three miles outside Celaya, Parrodi's strength now totaling over 7,000 men, who were dug into strong positions behind the banks of the Laja River. Although the liberal ranks were mostly composed of lightly armed and inexperienced militiamen and volunteers, their sheer numbers and entrenched positioning caused Osollo to wait for his trailing siege train of 40 pieces and supply caravan to close up before attempting to brave their redoubts.

In the prelude to his anticipated assault, a conservative feint on March 7, 1858, tricked some of these liberal brigades into withdrawing from their Laja entrenchments and moving out of their battle line altogether, so Osollo was able to easily push across its vacated stone bridge and drive through this gap directly toward Celaya, while Parrodi's outmaneuvered and split liberal army had to make a hasty retreat by forced marches toward Salamanca, 30 miles farther west, not reaching safety near there until the night of March 8, 1858.

Battle of Salamanca or Arroyo Feo (March 10, 1858)

García Casanova's brigade was the first conservative pursuit column to clash with some liberal cavalrymen resting at the Hacienda de Cerro Gordo on the morning of March 9, 1858, so Parrodi—realizing that Osollo's main body would be coming along close behind—ordered his weary and disorganized army to retrace their steps from their Salamanca encampments to make a stand a half dozen miles away behind a small watercourse known as Arroyo Feo or "Ugly Creek" that traversed the flat landscape. As that afternoon of March 9, 1858, wore on, some 7,300 liberal troops under his subordinates Leandro Valle, Manuel Doblado, and Mariano Moret deployed into a shaky battle line behind its banks, while Osollo's 5,400 regulars arrived on the far side to the west of the Hacienda de Cerro Gordo under Casanova, Miramón, Mejía, and José María Blancarte. As darkness fell, the artillery batteries that were exchanging long-range gunfire fell silent, in anticipation of a major battle next day.

On the morning of March 10, 1858, the gun duel resumed as the conservative infantry closed on the waiting liberal lines with García Casanova's brigade on Osollo's right, Miramón's division in his center, and Antonio Manero's brigade on his left. Parrodi responded by launching a charge around his own left flank with two full cavalry regiments: 1,200 troopers of the Guanajuato, Michoacán, Jalisco 1st Corps, Jalisco Lancers, and Sierra Gorda de Querétaro squadrons under Moret. Watching from his command post, Osollo instructed his artillery commander, Col. Ceferino Rodríguez, to redirect his heavy gunfire so as to break up this mass formation with grapeshot, then a countercharge by Mejía's cavalry chased these broken squadrons back into the liberal left.

Meanwhile, Osollo's regular army infantry continued to steadily close on the liberal militia throng. The Fieles de Guanajuato Battalion was the first liberal unit to give way and run, after which Parrodi's army rapidly disintegrated. Only the liberals' 1st and 5th Line Regiments, 1st Light Infantry Regiment, Tiradores de Guerrero Battalion, Rifleros de Policía Battalion, and parts of their Guanajuato Brigade— 2,800 men in all—managed to trudge off the battlefield in formation, retreating west toward Irapuato with 18 guns and part of their artillery train. Parrodi led these remnants of his army in a further retreat through Silao to Lagos, where they arrived by March 13, 1858, closely shadowed by Mejía's pursuing cavalry.

Aftermath (March–April 1858)

Osollo had been left victorious on the battlefield with another 12 captured liberal guns, and perhaps as many as 4,000 prisoners, plus countless horses and wagons. With no major concentration of militiamen left to oppose him, the conservative general resumed his march and entered the city of León uncontested on March 12, 1858, and the next day received the surrender at Romita of Guanajuato's Manuel Doblado and his 800 survivors from Arroyo Feo.

When news of this crushing defeat at Salamanca reached Guadalajara on the morning of March 13, 1858, Lt. Col. Antonio Landa of the 5th Line Regiment mutinied and seized President Juárez and his liberal cabinet, parading them before a firing squad the next day, only to be spared at the last moment by the eloquence of the minister Guillermo Prieto, who persuaded the soldiers to lower their weapons and spare their lives. Landa's men nonetheless ransacked the palace before decamping on March 15, 1858, the day before the beaten Parrodi brought his surviving troops back home into Guadalajara.

On March 20, 1858, Juárez and his ministers fled toward the Pacific coast with an escort of only 90 liberal troopers, leaving

Parrodi to arrange the surrender of the liberal city next day to Osollo's approaching army. The conservatives occupied it triumphantly on March 23, 1858, and soon after departed to continue campaigning in the state of San Luis Potosí.

See also: Bajío; Miramón Tarelo, Miguel Gregorio de la Luz Atenógenes; Osollo Pancorbo, Luis Gonzaga; Reform, War of the; Zuloaga Trillo, Félix María.

Further Reading
Cambre, Manuel. *La guerra de Tres Años.* Guadalajara, Jalisco: Biblioteca de Autores Jaliscienses, 1949, 45–49.
"Important from Mexico: The Government Gaining Ground-Fall of Salamanca." *New York Times,* April 2, 1858.

San Jacinto, Battle of (1836)

Climactic defeat suffered by Santa Anna's expeditionary force deep inside Texas, resulting in independence for that province as well as the eventual loss of all of Mexico's northern territories.

Preliminary Maneuvers (March 7–April 16, 1836)

Following the defeat and massacre of the defenders of the Alamo on March 6, 1836, the Mexican president and commander-in-chief had resumed his campaign of subduing rebellious Texas by sending out detachments from his encampment at San Antonio to stamp out any remaining pockets of resistance. That very next day his subordinate, Brig. Gen. José de Urrea, had learned at San Patricio that a Texian force under Col. James Fannin was also garrisoning Goliad, so he ventured toward that place with his squadron of 280 Mexican dragoons and Mayo Indian auxiliaries to investigate.

Meanwhile, Brig. Gen. Joaquín Ramírez y Sesma was sent by Santa Anna with another 725 troops to attack the 375 Texians gathering at Gonzales under Gen. Sam Houston, who began a long retreat eastward when this Mexican column approached on March 11, 1836.

Two days later, Urrea clashed against a 120-man Texian detachment under Lt. Col. William Ward at El Refugio Mission, so Santa Anna detached 500 additional troops of the Jiménez and San Luis Potosí Battalions under Col. Juan Morales, plus three fieldpieces, from his main army at San Antonio to reinforce Urrea. These reached him on March 18, 1836, and at 3:30 p.m. the next afternoon, Urrea overtook Fannin's 400 men out on the open plains near Coleto Creek, having torched their fort at Goliad so as to also decamp eastward. After a 24-hour encirclement and gun duel, Fannin surrendered to Urrea next day, the 365 Texian prisoners being marched back to Goliad (where they would be massacred on Santa Anna's express orders on March 27, 1836), while this Mexican brigadier pressed on toward Guadalupe Victoria.

The Texian government of Pres. David G. Burnet had been obliged to abandon its provisional capital at Washington-on-the-Brazos at the approach of a Mexican column on March 17, 1836, while panic-stricken civilians joined in to a wholesale flight that would later be remembered as the "Runaway Scrape." Leaving Maj. Gen. Vicente Filisola in command of his reserves at San Antonio, Santa Anna forged hundreds of miles farther east into Texas and with 900 picked troops attempted to surprise the fugitive government of Burnet at its temporary headquarters in Harrisburg on April 16, 1836, burning this town to the ground after the Texian legislators once again made good their escape.

Battle of San Jacinto (April 21, 1836)

After his long and demoralizing retreat toward the Sabine River, during which he had been openly jeered by Texian settlers and repeatedly ignored commands to stand and fight from the Texian president, Houston was reinforced and at last turned with his 900 troops to seek out Santa Anna's like-sized contingent for battle. After a two-and-a-half-day forced march, the Texian general arrived east of Harrisburg on April 18, 1836, close to where the unsuspecting Mexican commander-in-chief was lying with his detachment. Houston's untested troops were in an ugly mood after their prolonged retreat, and the next day crossed over to the Harrisburg side of Buffalo Bayou to take up a defensive position on the wooded banks of the San Jacinto River by April 20, 1836.

That same morning, Santa Anna countermarched toward Lynch's Ferry, and his scouts discovered Houston's nearby presence. Further probes and skirmishes that same afternoon of April 20, 1836, established that the Texian army had arrived in strength, so Santa Anna encamped his own forces overnight behind an extemporized breastwork of packs and baggage out on the plain, about 1,000 yards opposite Houston's concealed positions. The next morning, the Mexican army was reinforced by the arrival of an additional 500 troops under Col. Martín Perfecto de Cos, bringing their total strength to almost 1,400 men and a single six-pound fieldpiece.

Both contending armies had stood to their arms since that sunrise, but when no action ensued by noon on April 21, 1836, Santa Anna gave the order for his own men to break ranks and rest, intending to fight his battle the next day. Houston, however, conferred with his officers and after sending a stealthy group of riders under the veteran scout Erastus "Deaf" Smith to burn wooden Vince's Bridge, eight miles away—the only available crossing point for any further Mexican reinforcements—the Texian general ordered his small army to silently deploy into four columns at 3:30 p.m. in anticipation of launching a surprise attack.

Smith returned to report that Vince's Bridge had been destroyed, at which point Houston gave the order for his troops to trail arms and silently charge the slumbering Mexican camp at 4:30 p.m. in the following four attack columns:

- The 260-man 2nd Texas Volunteer Regiment of Col. Sidney Sherman and Capt. Juan N. Seguín out on the far left
- The 220 men of the 1st Texas Volunteer Regiment under Col. Edward Burleson in the center
- The 240 troops of the Texas Regular Battalion under Lt. Col. Henry Millard on the right
- Sixty-one cavalrymen under the newly promoted "colonel" Mirabeau Buonaparte Lamar of Georgia, who were to circle far out to the right and take the Mexican heavy cavalry in their flank.

Screened from view by the tall grass, some trees, and a slight ridge that traversed the open ground between both armies, the Texians were within 200 yards of the improvised Mexican breastworks before being detected. Santa Anna's army had maintained a poor watch and so was caught utterly unprepared. Only a few duty companies were armed with muskets and munitions, the remainder having to belatedly retrieve their stacked weapons and try to obtain ammunition in a confused scramble. The cavalrymen did not even have time to saddle their mounts, much less arm themselves, before the Texians were on them.

To the tune of "Will you come to the bower I have shaded for you," the attackers steadied and fired their first volleys, receiving a smattering of shots in return from the few Mexican companies on guard duty. Two six-pounders were wheeled into position by the Texians and unlimbered; donated by citizens of Cincinnati and known as the "Twin Sisters," they were manned by 31 gunners under Maj. George W. Hockley with support from four small infantry companies under Capt. Henry W. Karnes. They opened fire with grapeshot at point-blank range, inflicting fearsome casualties. Within 18 minutes, at a cost of only 9 killed and some 30 wounded (including Houston), Santa Anna's hapless army was decimated, broken, and fleeing in panic. Only Gen. Juan N. Almonte was able to keep about 400 of his troops together in formation so as to formally surrender. To avenge the remorseless Mexican practice of executing their prisoners, the Texians chased down and shot scores of defenseless runaways over the next hour until evening fell, all the while shouting "Remember the Alamo!" and "Remember Goliad!"

Unable to escape because of the destruction of Vince's Bridge, about 730 unarmed Mexican soldiers were rounded up as prisoners of the Texians by next day—including Santa Anna, who had been resting prior to the battle and thus fled without his dress uniform so was not recognized on emerging from the tall grass until he was greeted as *Señor Presidente* by other Mexican captives. An estimated 600–650 of his soldiers had been killed during the battle and the ensuing pursuit of its fugitives, so his army had been completely annihilated.

Aftermath (May 1836)

Santa Anna was compelled to sign an armistice in order to regain his freedom from the vengeful Texians, while his other field commanders retired to Mexico on learning of his capitulation. Eventually, the Mexican government would repudiate this arrangement, insisting it was not valid because its terms had been extorted, yet they are nonetheless powerless to reimpose their will over the Republic of Texas—which was soon recognized by the United States, Britain, France, the Netherlands, and Belgium. Nine years later, in 1845, Texas became part of the United States.

See also: Cos Muñoz, Martín Perfecto; Santa Anna, Antonio López de.

Further Reading

Benson, Nettie Lee. "Texas Viewed from Mexico, 1820–1834." *Southwestern Historical Quarterly* 90, no. 3 (1987): 219–91.

Fluent, Michael. "San Jacinto." *American History Illustrated* 21, no. 3 (1986): 22–31.

Henson, Margaret Swett. "Politics and the Treatment of the Mexican Prisoners after the Battle of San Jacinto," *Southwestern Historical Quarterly* 94, no. 2 (1990):188–230.

Pohl, James W. *The Battle of San Jacinto.* Austin: Texas State Historical Association, 1989.

Pohl, James W. *"The Battle of San Jacinto," April 21, 1836, as Reported by General Santa Anna.* Houston, TX: Union National Bank, 1936.

Tolbert, F. X. *Day of San Jacinto.* Austin: University of Texas Press, 1959.

San Jacinto, Battle of (1867)

One of the final imperial defeats suffered during the War of the French Intervention, shortly before this conflict was concluded by the siege and capture of Querétaro.

Preceding Operations (January 1867)

Having learned of the presence of the republican president Benito Juárez at the city of Zacatecas in early 1867, the Mexican imperial major general Miguel Miramón had sought to reverse his emperor's declining fortunes by leading 2,000 horsemen on a daring 250-mile ride northwestward from Querétaro, bursting into that city five days later—on Sunday, January 27, 1867—only to find that his quarry had been alerted and already decamped from Zacatecas toward Fresnillo.

Miramón had nonetheless remained in possession of Zacatecas with his cavalry, hoping to be joined by the 2,000-man infantry division of Gen. Severo del Castillo, who was marching to his assistance. But a mere four days later, the major general in occupied Zacatecas learned that a republican army of 1,500 troopers, 2,000 infantrymen, and a field battery was drawing near from Mexquitic under Generals Mariano Escobedo and Jerónimo Treviño, so Miramón evacuated that city on the evening of January 31, 1867, retreating toward Aguascalientes in hopes of finding and combining with Del Castillo.

Battle of San Jacinto (February 1, 1867)

Miramón's column had not gotten very far when it was overtaken by Escobedo's pursuing republican cavalry that very next day of February 1, 1867. Knowing his force to be outnumbered and already coming under fire from advancing republican skirmishers, Miramón hurried on past San Francisco de los Adames and Cuisillo Ranch, turning to make a stand and fight on the grounds of the Hacienda de San Jacinto. To anchor his battle line, the imperial commander positioned his best troops at its center, the *Gendarmes de la Emperatriz* or "Mounted Police of the Empress" out of Guadalajara—half of whom were French veterans who had volunteered to remain in Mexico and fight on in the service of Maximilian—and then ordered them to charge the first republican regiment, which they could see was already deploying.

However, these republican troopers turned out to be from the *Cazadores de Galeana*, experienced fighters now armed with 16-shot repeating rifles purchased in the United States, which allowed them to halt this *Gendarme* charge in a hail of bullets. As the imperial troops reeled back into their original starting position, other republican regiments continued to arrive onto the broad plain of the battlefield and opened fire against Miramón's remaining jumble of formations, while still others could be seen maneuvering past to cut off any imperial retreat. The 2nd and 9th Cavalry Regiments, which Miramón had scraped together from diverse *guardia rural* militia contingents, turned and fled in all directions within 10 minutes, leaving him almost alone to fire off a couple of solitary rounds from his unlimbered fieldpieces before mounting up and doing the same.

Accompanied by only 15 loyal officers and cavalrymen, the imperial major general managed to escape from this debacle through the Hacienda de San Marcos by 8:00 p.m. that same evening, riding off into the night to try and find Del Castillo. The next morning, the victorious Escobedo wrote to President Juárez (who was once more reestablished in Zacatecas) and reported how his men had found 96 dead French mercenaries and 46 Mexican conservatives on the battlefield, and more than that wounded—including Miramón's older brother, Joaquín, who was captured while being conveyed toward the rear in a cart, badly wounded in one foot—and the republicans furthermore secured 476 prisoners, of whom 122 were French, plus 21 artillery pieces, 280 draft animals, and the entire supply train. Liberal losses amounted to 18 dead and 16 wounded.

Aftermath (February 2–19, 1867)

Miramón meanwhile located Severo del Castillo's division at Ojuelos but found that it was desperately low on supplies, having been unable to obtain fresh provisions from either Guanajuato or Zacatecas, as well as being closely shadowed by republican cavalry formations. Consequently, Miramón ordered Del Castillo's hungry column to turn back toward Querétaro, while Escobedo encouraged his converging commanders to try to intercept and delay it. As a result, a 600-man republican cavalry brigade under Colonel Herrera y Cairo closed rapidly on Del Castillo's rearguard on February 4, 1867, so this imperial formation wheeled into a battle line on the grounds of the Hacienda de la Quemada. The impetuous republican colonel was killed leading the opening charge, after which a counterattack by the imperial cavalry drove his troopers from the field in some disarray.

When Escobedo heard of this bloody repulse three days later, while resting at the Hacienda de Tepetates, the initial report that he had received suggested that Colonel Herrera and other republican survivors had been summarily executed at Miramón's behest, so Escobedo (who enjoyed a well-deserved reputation for magnanimity toward his captives) angrily ordered a reprisal execution of the imperial general's wounded brother Joaquín and 107 French prisoners. Joaquín Miramón had to be carried to his execution spot at dawn on February 8,

1867, and leaned up against a wall in order to be shot. The Frenchmen were doing their laundry when informed of their own fate and were also killed shortly thereafter in cold blood.

This uncharacteristic cruelty on Escobedo's part was widely deplored, both at home and abroad, and liberal apologists have tried—then and ever since—to explain away this brutal measure. Miramón, for his part, returned to Querétaro to find his prestige greatly diminished by his losses, awaiting the emperor's arrival on February 19, 1867, who appointed his hated rival Márquez over him two days later. Three weeks afterward, Escobedo encircled that city with a huge liberal army, dooming its defenders.

See also: Escobedo Peña, Mariano Antonio Guadalupe; French Intervention, War of the; Miramón Tarelo, Miguel Gregorio de la Luz Atenógenes; Querétaro, Siege of.

Further Reading

Correspondence Relating to Recent Events in Mexico, Executive Documents Number 20. U.S. Congressional Serial Set, Vol. 1308, Washington, D.C: U.S. Government Printing Office, 1868, 176–80.

"The Execution of Prisoners of War by Escobedo." *New York Times*, April 14, 1867.

San Juan de Ulúa

Ancient harbor castle that has guarded the anchorage at Veracruz since colonial times and also served as a customshouse, barracks, depot, prison, etc.

Historical Background (1550s–1820)

Its construction had commenced as long ago as the 1550s, being erected and expanded in stages over the ensuing centuries, atop a

Lithograph depicting the U.S. squadron and garrison in San Juan de Ulúa firing a celebratory salute, as the American flag is hoisted over the capitulated city of Veracruz on March 29, 1847. (Library of Congress)

low-lying islet set amid a group of reefs that act as a collective breakwater to help enclose Veracruz's harbor. The fort rises out of the water about a half mile offshore from the mainland, directly opposite the city. It initially served as the clearing-house for the annual trans-Atlantic plate fleets from Spain, whose galleons would be moored to great iron rings anchored in the fort's walls and unload their cargoes to be inspected and taxed at the royal customs-house inside the compound. These goods would then be ferried ashore to warehouses in the city, to be transported inland by mule trains.

Since Veracruz served as the principal seaport for the viceroyalty of New Spain throughout the entire colonial era, San Juan de Ulúa's original defenses had been slowly built up by numerous construction projects over its 250-year history. A sprawling stone stronghold measuring 725 feet by 450 feet had been gradually erected so as to better

protect the vessels lying beneath the protection of its guns, as well as to shelter them from storms. Officially classified as a *castillo* or "castle" (a fortress that can act as a residence for its commander), San Juan de Ulúa's administration remained completely separate from that of the city of Veracruz opposite—being governed by a military officer appointed from Madrid to serve as its *castellano*, while a civilian governor administered the city on the mainland.

Surrounded by reefs and shallows, bristling with scores of heavy guns, the fortress of San Juan de Ulúa was never threatened, much less attacked, throughout Mexico's 11-year War of Independence. However, monarchist fortunes eventually waned in the interior of the country, especially after the Creole royalist colonel Agustín de Iturbide issued a surprising proclamation from his military base at Iguala in late February 1821, laying out a proposed union between Mexican insurgents and loyalists to jointly achieve independence. A wave of switched allegiances deprived the few Crown officials and regiments of their Mexican militia supporters in the viceroyalty, leaving them outnumbered and isolated.

Royalist Holdout (1821–1825)

During this period of defections, the youthful turncoat lieutenant colonel Antonio López de Santa Anna attempted to surprise the city of Veracruz with a sudden strike during a rainstorm at 4:00 a.m. on July 3, 1821, only to be checked by its still-loyal garrison under Spanish general José María Dávila and ejected at a cost of half of Santa Anna's 500–600 troops. A tight siege of the city was nonetheless imposed, so when Juan O'Donojú arrived from Spain three weeks later as the new viceroy-designate, he realized that New Spain was essentially lost and so procured safe conduct from Santa Anna to proceed inland and conclude a treaty with Iturbide, which recognized Mexican independence by mid-September 1821.

General Dávila, however, refused to comply with O'Donojú's arrangement, instead crippling the heavy artillery in the city of Veracruz before retiring across the bay with 200 loyal Spanish troops, ample ammunition, and the royal treasury on the night of October 25–26, 1821, so as to continue resisting from within the impregnable fortress of San Juan de Ulúa. Mexican troops soon took over the city of Veracruz, but its port traffic naturally remained a standstill with merchantmen being diverted into other Mexican anchorages.

After Iturbide assumed the mantle of Mexico's emperor, he promoted Santa Anna to the brigadier general and placed him in command of the garrison at Veracruz as of September 25, 1822, with orders to secure San Juan de Ulúa from its stubborn

Spanish holdouts. Santa Anna at first attempted to negotiate terms with Dávila during the second week of October 1822, but this Spanish officer was soon relieved in favor of the more intractable brigadier general Francisco Lemaur.

Santa Anna consequently tried to deceive the latter into believing that he was prepared to switch allegiances back to the Crown and allow the Spaniards to reclaim Veracruz, so a flotilla of boats from San Juan de Ulúa approached the city waterfront at dawn on October 27, 1822. Santa Anna's plan was to capture this 400-man Spanish landing force after they entered behind Veracruz's walls to seize the Concepción and Santiago Bastions, then use their uniforms and boats to venture back out to Ulúa and take its defenders by surprise; but the suspicious boatloads of Spanish troops opened fire without disembarking and a two-hour exchange of gunfire ensued before they retired back out to the harbor castle without ever setting foot ashore.

Although Santa Anna ordered public celebrations to honor his "victory" (claiming that he had repulsed a Spanish sneak attack), Iturbide's "imperial captain general" for that district—Mexican general José Antonio de Echávarri—secretly informed Iturbide that the planned deception of the Spaniards had been deliberately sabotaged by Santa Anna. Iturbide therefore attempted to arrest Santa Anna the next month at Jalapa, directing him to accompany the emperor back into Mexico City.

Santa Anna put off this instruction and instead rose in revolt on December 6, 1822, so the hapless city of Veracruz—its harbor still controlled by the Spanish garrison offshore—was now furthermore invested by a 3,000-man imperial army that appeared outside its walls in January 1823. These Mexican commanders quickly agreed to switch over to Santa Anna's republican cause by February 1st, though, being joined by other disgruntled units throughout central Mexico, so Iturbide was compelled to abdicate the next month.

Veracruz nonetheless remained stagnant because of San Juan de Ulúa's occupiers. The insurgent war hero Guadalupe Victoria mounted yet another effort to dislodge its stubborn Spanish holdouts on September 21, 1823, but that unfortunately produced nothing more than a damaging exchange of artillery rounds over the next four days, which inflicted further harm on Veracruz. An English visitor estimated that the battered city's populace had by then dwindled to a mere 7,000 inhabitants, their misery not abating until San Juan de Ulúa's obstinate Spanish holdouts finally capitulated on November 23, 1825.

Subsequent Attacks (1838–1914)

A dozen years later, the elderly fortress was to endure a heavy battering with modern weaponry during the so-called War of the Cakes. After seven months' blockade, a French squadron under rear admiral Charles Baudin delivered an ultimatum in late November 1838 for compensation from the Mexican authorities for economic losses suffered by French citizens in Mexico's civil wars. This was refused, and after two Mexican officers boarded his flagship *Néréide* with an unsuccessful last-minute offer on November 27, 1838, the frigates *Néréide*, *Iphigénie*, and *Gloire*, corvette *Créole*, and bombs *Cyclope* and *Vulcain* opened fire on San Juan de Ulúa's 1,186-man garrison, using newly developed Paixhans explosive shells.

This exchange persisted until 6:00 p.m., when the bombardment slackened and finally ceased two hours later, after garrison commander Antonio Gaona requested a truce to attend to his wounded. During the course of this single afternoon, the French squadron had suffered 4 killed and 39 injured—in contrast to San Juan de Ulúa's 224 casualties and 20 dismounted guns. Overnight, the French informed the Mexican garrison commander that his fortress would be leveled if he did not surrender it, so he agreed to capitulate at 8:00 a.m. on November 28, 1838, as well as surrendering a corvette, two sloops, and three brigs that were moored beneath its walls. The castle would remain in French hands for more than three months, until a peace treaty was finally concluded in March 1839.

A mere eight years afterward, San Juan de Ulúa was battered and captured again by foreign invaders, this time during the Mexican-American War. Having already penetrated the northern portion of Mexico out of Texas, a second U.S. expedition was then dispatched by sea to disembark at Veracruz and press inland, so as to threaten Mexico City. The first vessels began arriving on March 4, 1847, disgorging an 8,600-man American army under Gen. Winfield Scott five days later at Collado Beach, three miles southeast of Veracruz, which encircled and besieged the city. During this operation, its offshore castle of San Juan de Ulúa was bombarded on several occasions by U.S. warships, until its 1,000-man garrison was evacuated when the city was surrendered on March 29, 1847.

The castle was not engaged during the conservative sieges of Veracruz in the War of the Reform from 1858 to 1860, nor was any resistance made to the arrival of more foreign forces in December 1861, whose occupation of San Juan de Ulúa and the city inaugurated the War of the French Intervention. The development of increasingly powerful high-explosive artillery shells during the latter half of the 19th century rendered stone fortresses like Ulúa completely obsolete, so that the castle became used more as a regional headquarters, naval base, prison, and warehouse than a viable military defense. The size of its garrison contracted with the withdrawal of most of its heavy guns, so that when an American battleship squadron arrived to seize the port as a punitive measure on April 21, 1914, rear admiral Frank F. Fletcher forewarned Mexican commodore Alejandro Cerisola of these impending hostilities, so that he could withdraw Ulúa's 160-man garrison without any losses.

See also: Cakes, War of the; Independence, War of; Santa Anna, Antonio López de; Veracruz, American Occupation of; Veracruz, U.S. Bombardment and Occupation of.

Further Reading

Aquino Sánchez, Faustino A. *Intervención francesa, 1838–1839: la diplomacia mexicana y el imperialismo del librecambio.* Mexico City: INAH, 1997.

"France and Mexico." *Niles' National Register*, 5th series, 55, no. 26 (February 23, 1839): 404–5.

Klier, Betje. " 'Peste, Tempestad, & Patisserie': The Pastry War, France's Contribution to the Maintenance of Texas' Independence." *Gulf Coast Historical Review* 12, no. 2 (1997): 58–73.

San Lorenzo, Battle of (1863)

Quick-strike French victory that broke the last Mexican hopes of relieving their besieged republican garrison within Puebla early during the War of the French Intervention.

Prelude (March–May 1863)

On March 16, 1863, advance elements of a 25,000-man French Army that had pressed inland from Orizaba under Maj. Gen. Élie Frédéric Forey began encircling this city. Their formal siege lines and batteries were laid out by March 22, 1863, and a prolonged bombardment commenced two days afterward. Throughout this encirclement and its ensuing siege operation, the French remained aware of Gen. Ignacio Comonfort's 8,000-man *Ejército del Centro* or "Army of the Center," which was based out of the city of Tlaxcala and probing among the nearby Uranga Hills, observing the invaders' efforts and looking for opportunities to assist Gen. Jesús González Ortega's defenders.

After almost two months of isolation, supplies and morale had dwindled within battered Puebla, so a relief was contemplated by the republican forces—and soon detected by the French. On May 5, 1863, General Forey was informed that Comonfort's disperse formations had begun concentrating for some kind of movement. Then, a strong force of republican cavalry ventured out from Tlaxcala into San Pablo del Monte, after which Comonfort deployed 6,000 troops in three division onto its surrounding plains, about 25 miles southeast of Puebla.

The next day, May 6, 1863, the French also noticed that infantry were massing within the trenches of Puebla, opposite La Cruz Hill—evidently with the intent of supporting an imminent thrust by Comonfort to pierce through the siege lines in a combined attack around that point and slip supplies into its exhausted garrison. However, this hill was strongly defended by a Mexican conservative contingent under Gen. Leonardo Márquez, and a daylong bombardment by the French artillery cleared the republican trenches of waiting infantrymen by nightfall.

Austrian cavalryman serving the Emperor Maximilian in Mexico, ca. 1865; an original watercolor-and-ink drawing attributed to J. Höchle. (Anne S. K. Brown Military Collection, Brown University Library)

Battle of San Lorenzo (May 8, 1863)

When nothing further occurred on May 7, 1863, Forey ordered Maj. Gen. François Achille Bazaine that same Thursday evening to take four select battalions of French infantry from the 51st Line Regiment, 3rd Zouaves, and *Tirailleurs algériens*; four cavalry squadrons from the 2nd Regiment de Marche; and eight fieldpieces, on a nocturnal march so as to surprise Comonfort's distant army next dawn. Departing the French encampment via the road leading toward Mexico City at 1:00–2:00 a.m. on May 8, 1863, Bazaine moved swiftly but silently through the night before veering right and coming within sight of the first republican encampment at 5:00 a.m.

Comonfort had installed his 1st Division under Gen. Ignacio Echegaray at the hamlet of San Lorenzo Almecatla; his 2nd Division under Gen. Ángel Trías Álvarez at nearby Panzacola; and his 3rd Division under Gen. Plácido Vega Daza at Santo Toribio. The French were less than a mile away from San Lorenzo when the republican 1st Division finally spotted them in the early morning light, hastily standing to their guns and opening fire. Behind covering fire from their own fieldpieces, Bazaine's infantry double-timed into action, breaking the overmatched 1st Division, which after a brave stand reeled back from San Lorenzo toward Panzacola. There, the 2nd Division was also mauled, after which the 3rd Division was directed to cover the retreat of both shattered formations toward the city of Tlaxcala. Márquez furthermore descended from San Juan Hill with some of his conservative troops to complete Comonfort's rout.

Bazaine reported that there were some 800–900 dead or wounded republicans left on the battlefield before he immediately returned toward Puebla (having ordered his own personal field tent to be set up and left behind at San Lorenzo so as to provide some shelter for the republican wounded until they could be rescued). French losses were 11 eleven dead and 89 injured, thanks largely to the element of surprise and their superior weaponry.

Aftermath (late May 1863)

Returning to base camp, Bazaine presented Forey with more than 1,000 prisoners, along with eight guns, three flags, and the entire supply train that had been intended to relieve Puebla's republican garrison. The next day, May 9, 1863, Forey had many of these prisoners released into the city so as to provide convincing proof of Comonfort's defeat. All hopes of rescue having been dashed, González Ortega requested terms one week later and Puebla's capitulation was consummated by 5:30 p.m. on the afternoon of May 17, 1863. Some 1,000 republican officers and 16,000 troops surrendered, of whom 5,000 subsequently joined the victors' ranks.

After his defeat, Comonfort had ridden back into Mexico City to be relieved of his command in favor of Gen. Juan José de la Garza. Bazaine was rewarded with the title of Knight Grand Cross in the Legion of Honor.

See also: Bazaine, François Achille; French Intervention, War of the; Márquez Arrajo, Leonardo; Puebla, Siege of (1863).

Further Reading

García, Genaro. *El sitio de Puebla en 1863, según los archivos de d. Ignacio Comonfort*. Mexico City: Viuda de C. Bouret, 1909.

González Ortega, Jesús. *Parte general que da al Supremo Gobierno de la Nación respecto de la defensa de la plaza de Puebla*. Mexico City: J. S. Ponce de León, 1871.

"Important from Mexico: Detailed Account of the Surrender of Puebla." *New York Times*, May 23, 1863.

"Important from Mexico: French Oficial News." *New York Times*, June 2, 1863.

San Lorenzo, Battle of (1867)

One of the final defeats suffered by Maximilian's imperial regime, which helped to bring about the end of the War of the French Intervention.

Preamble (March 22–April 7, 1867)

After the imperial general Leonardo Márquez had escaped with more than 1,000 dragoons from the republican siege of Querétaro on March 22, 1867, intending to ride to Mexico City and return with reinforcements so as to relieve the emperor's beleaguered garrison, the republican siege commander Mariano Escobedo detached 8,000 troopers of Maj. Gen. Amado Antonio Guadarrama's three divisions one week later, so as to follow and hinder Márquez's return. However, after learning that this imperial general might actually be contemplating a strike due eastward first from the national capital in an apparent bid to relieve the city of Puebla (whose imperial garrison was also under assault by the *Ejército de Oriente* or "Army of the East" under Porfirio Díaz), these republican riders had pursued so as to overtake Márquez.

Upon reaching Polotitlán on April 1, 1867, they learned that the imperial general had already departed Mexico City with some 4,000 mixed troops—Austro-Hungarians, Poles, and Mexicans, half being infantry and half cavalry—plus 18 guns organized into three field batteries, heading east rather than northwestward. Continuing their search for this small but potent imperial force, Guadarrama's cavalrymen entered Tepejí del Río by April 3, 1867, meeting 600 republican troopers and 600 infantrymen there under Col. Jesús Lalanne, who were marching to Díaz's assistance. The next day, both formations continued into Zumpango.

Márquez had confused republicans and imperialists alike by heading still farther east, circling around Puebla in the direction of Veracruz, rather than making any attempt to fight his way back northwest toward Querétaro, as had been his original commission. Díaz had meanwhile overwhelmed Puebla's imperial garrison by April 4, 1867, and the next day set out with his cavalry in search of Márquez, followed by his infantry and artillery. His republican riders located the imperial column on the morning of April 6, 1867, en route from the Hacienda of San Diego Notario toward Huamantla, their intended destination for that day's march.

Díaz deployed his almost 6,000 cavalrymen for battle, but any charges against the imperial artillery or infantry would have been suicidal, while the well-armed Austrian and Polish troopers inflicted considerable casualties with their disciplined maneuvers. After clashing in mid-morning and again in mid-afternoon on April 6, 1867, Díaz reported that he had suffered "48 men dead and many wounded," along with scores of horses killed or lamed, to little gain. But although the small imperial army remained unbroken, Márquez and his officers were distressed to learn from prisoners that Puebla had already fallen, so before dawn the next morning they reversed their heading and began marching back from whence they had come, toward Mexico City.

Díaz retired through Tlaxcala, while sending messages overnight to all his field commanders instructing them to delay Márquez's escape if possible, so he might overtake the retreating imperialists with his entire Ejército de Oriente. The imperial column consequently camped at the Hacienda of Guadalupe once more on April 7, 1867, before proceeding west the next morning toward the Hacienda de San Lorenzo, near Apizaco in the state of Puebla.

Battle of San Lorenzo (April 8–10, 1867)

With the aim of slowing Márquez's escape, the next day republican Colonel Lalanne decided to engage the larger and better-armed imperial force with only his small brigade as it approached the Hacienda de San Lorenzo on April 8, 1867, the republicans emerging badly mauled yet having checked Márquez's movement. More republican formations continued to appear, allowing Diaz to catch up and deploy his main army into an extended line and commence a long-range bombardment on April 9, 1867, to pin down the imperial troops until Guadarrama could additionally join with his large body of cavalry.

Knowing his forces to be doomed, Márquez ordered a desperate retreat started the next dawn, April 10, 1867, only to then encounter Guadarrama's mass of cavalry barring his path at the Hacienda of San Cristóbal. Losing all hope, the imperial general ordered most of his artillery cast into a ravine and supply carts burned, before leading his small army on a forced march up into the mountains. His Austrian infantry officers sent repeated requests forward to Márquez at the head of this fleeing column, begging for a pause to rest, which he ignored. As his foreign auxiliaries lagged out of weariness that, the imperial general spurred on ahead with his staff, callously abandoning them to their fate. The Austro-Mexican infantry and Hungarian cavalry nonetheless completed a brave fighting retreat from San Lorenzo through San Cristóbal into Texcoco, against overwhelming odds, albeit suffering 300 killed and 1,000 captured during this exhausting ordeal.

See also: Díaz Mori, José de la Porfirio; French Intervention, War of the; Márquez Araujo, Leonardo; Querétaro, Siege of.

Further Reading

Díaz, Porfirio. *Memorias, 1830–1867.* Mexico City: Secretaría de Educación Pública, 1994, vol. 1, chaps. 84–85.

Salm-Salm, Felix. *My Diary in Mexico in 1867.* London: Richard Bentley, 1868, 2: 291–302.

San Patricio Battalion (1846–1848)

Unit of foreign volunteers incorporated into the Mexican Army, formed around a company of mostly Irish soldiers who had originally deserted from the U.S. Army prior to the outbreak of the Mexican-American War. Although commonly referred to today as a "battalion," 19th-century records would suggest that this unit's strength only ever rose to that of a couple of companies, 100 or so men in total.

Desertion into Matamoros (April 1846)

On March 28, 1846—four weeks before a declaration of war from either side—Brig. Gen. Zachary Taylor reached the northern banks of the Río Grande with 2,200 American soldiers, having pushed down from Corpus Christi to erect an advance base that would be dubbed "Fort Texas," directly opposite the Mexican city of Matamoros. Its commander protested against this unilateral relocation of the border, and within a week several thousand Mexican troops were marching to reinforce his city garrison. Brig. Gen. Pedro de Ampudia arrived in Matamoros with the first 2,500 of these troops on April 11, 1846, and soon after demanded that Taylor withdraw back to the Nueces River. The U.S. general refused, and tensions escalated.

It was during this standoff that about 50 soldiers—mostly Irishmen—deserted in a single group from the U.S. forces, crossing over the river into Mexico. *Niles' National Register,* in its edition of May 9, 1846 (vol. 70, pages 132 and 160), republished a story taken from the *New Orleans Bulletin* newspaper that reported "that about thirty of the American troops had deserted, ten or twelve of whom were shot in endeavoring to make their escape," while a second story from the *New Orleans Tropic* stated that:

> About fifty of the American army have deserted, and swam the river for the Mexican camp, but a number of them were shot as deserters while in the water.

In fact, this group—led by Sgt. Jon Riley of the 5th U.S. Infantry Regiment—seemed to have reached Matamoros intact, having been moved to desert because of their shabby treatment and the anti-Catholic prejudices that were rife in the American army.

Its four dozen members were welcomed by General Ampudia and, because of their military training, they were assigned as an artillery company in Matamoros with Riley acting as their lieutenant. When a cross-river bombardment of Fort Texas erupted at dawn on May 3, 1846, the deserters manned some of the 14 Mexican guns and helped maintain this desultory and ineffectual shelling over the next six days until the sight of hundreds of Mexican soldiers fleeing back across the river on the evening of May 9, 1846, after losing the Battle of Resaca de la Palma brought a halt to this bombardment. When Taylor then arrived with his victorious army and pushed across the Río Grande in strength eight days later, the Irish deserters had already marched off deeper into Mexico with Matamoros's retreating garrison.

Defense of Monterrey (September 1846)

After a grueling 45-day trek through the northern wastelands, this Mexican army reached Linares on June 29, 1846, resting there for a couple of weeks. It is possible that the detachment of Irish artillerymen subsequently accompanied Ampudia to San Luis Potosí, where it was to be properly constituted as a unit in the Mexican Army, and even presented with a beautiful green banner on which "glittered a silver cross and a golden harp, embroidered by the fair nuns" of that city.

The *San Patricio* or "Saint Patrick" Company presumably then marched back as part of Ampudia's 3,500 reinforcements for the northern city of Monterrey, arriving there by the end of August 1846. Once again, the Irish artillerymen were assigned to man some of the Mexican guns, working them to great effect throughout the four days of stubborn resistance against General Taylor's assault on September 20–23, 1846. According to the terms of capitulation, the *San Patricios* were among the thousands of Mexican troops allowed to march out of that city with their arms and six guns over a period of several days, retreating beyond Rinconada Pass to observe a two-month cessation of offensive operations. Some American soldiers were offended at the sight of these deserters, now serving in the ranks of their enemies.

Battle of Buena Vista (February 1847)

Once more stationed in San Luis Potosí, the San Patricio Company was bolstered by a trickle of more deserters from the U.S. Army (as well as other foreign volunteers in Mexico's service) after Santa Anna reached that city on October 8, 1846, to begin a major, four-month reconcentration and overhaul that would produce a better-organized 21,500-man *Ejército del Norte* or "Northern Army" by early the next year. Then, learning that regiments were being withdrawn from Taylor's American occupation forces at Monterrey and Saltillo so as to inaugurate a second southern front under Maj. Gen. Winfield Scott by a landing at Veracruz, Santa Anna decided to strike while his northern opponent was debilitated.

Therefore, the vanguard of his improved Northern Army—its artillery train—marched out of San Luis Potosí on January 28, 1847, prominently including the San Patricio artillerymen (now some 80 strong). Of the 20,000 Mexican troops who set out on this grueling three-week trek to Encarnación, only 14,000 arrived with 17 guns by February 17, 1847, the remainder having fallen by the wayside. Three days later, this huge force bore down on Taylor's 4,800 men at Agua Nueva, who hastily retreated to La Angostura—a high, narrow pass on Buena Vista Hacienda, six miles south of Saltillo. The battle began with a clash out on the flanks on February 22, 1847, and became fully joined the next day, when Riley and about 80 San Patricios deployed their three 16-pounder guns onto a piece of high ground—their presence later described by an American historian as "a strong Mexican battery … moved … by dint of extraordinary exertions, … [which] commanded the entire plateau."

Mexican Army records indicated that Riley's company suffered 2 sergeants and 17 men killed at the Battle of Buena Vista, during which they performed heroically. However, their small numbers meant they were powerless to affect the battle's outcome, and so the San Patricios retreated with Santa Anna's other survivors back into Central Mexico. Their commander-in-chief still regarded them so highly that they were amongst the best units ordered to march once again, so as to contest the penetration inland from Veracruz by Gen. Winfield Scott's disembarked army.

On June 7, 1847, Lt. John Riley and Sub-Lt. Raymond Bachelor of the *Compañía de Voluntarios de Tiradores de San Patricio* were awarded commendations by the Mexican Army's high command for their participation in the Battle of La Angostura on February 22–23, 1847. And an order issued on July 9, 1847, by Santa Anna—in his capacity as "interim president" of Mexico—furthermore instructed the general-in-chief of the *Ejército de Oriente* or "Army of the East" to retain the *Compañía de Infantería Activa de San Patricio* or "Active Infantry Company of San Patricio" in that army's 3rd Brigade, to serve under the orders of Brig. Gen. Joaquín Rangel.

Battle of Churubusco (August 1847)

Although present in one of the forward Mexican positions at the Battle of Cerro Gordo on April 17-18, 1847, Santa Anna's 12,000-man army was outflanked when the Americans circled around and struck it in the rear, so that the San Patricios were never closely engaged and thus managed to retire in the chaos following this defeat.

Reassembled around the national capital, Santa Anna's forces had to wait for a few months before the invaders resumed their offensive and closed in on Mexico City, when the Irish company would fight their final battle.

Assigned to defend one of the causeways leading into the capital from inside a fortified convent at Churubusco, the San Patricios fought fiercely against the Americans attack on August 20, 1847, only to be overwhelmed. Official Mexican Army returns for the 5th Infantry Brigade, compiled the next day confirmed that two sublieutenants, four sergeants, six corporals, and 23 soldiers of the "San Patricio Companies" had been slain during the fighting at Churubusco with "the rest prisoners or dispersed."

Executions (September 1847)

Eighty-five of the Irishmen had fallen into the hands of a vengeful U.S. army, whose members regarded them as traitors who had taken up arms against their former comrades on behalf of a foreign enemy, yet could only try 72 of them for desertion. Despite the ongoing drive to penetrate Mexico City, two courts-martial were quickly convened: one at Tacubaya on August 23, 1847, and the other three days later at San Angel. All 72 men were convicted and condemned to death, although several were pardoned by General Scott for a variety of reasons, including one who was only 15 years old, and in the end only 50 were hanged: 16 at San Angel on September 10, 1847, four more next day at Mixcoac, and the final 30 at Mixcoac on September 13th, as Chapultepec Castle fell and the road into Mexico City was opened.

John Riley and a few others had technically deserted before any official declaration of war had benn made between the two nations, and so could not legally be put to death. Instead, they were cruelly lashed and branded with a "D" for deserter on their faces or hips, Riley himself being branded twice on the face after the first brand was "accidentally" applied upside-down. The hatred and scorn which was visited upon all of these unfortunates by their American captors horrified Mexican onlookers, so that the Irish survivors (including Riley) were rewarded after the war with government pensions and lands, and are still remembered today.

See also: Buena Vista, Battle of; Churubusco, Battle of; Mexican-American War; Monterrey, Battle of.

Further Reading

Hogan, Michael. *The Irish Soldiers of Mexico.* Mexico City: Fondo Editorial Universitario, 1998.

Miller, Robert Ryal. *Shamrock and Sword: The Saint Patrick's Battalion in the U.S. Mexican War.* Norman: University Press of Oklahoma, 1989.

Stevens, Peter F. *The Rogue's March: John Riley and the St. Patrick's Battalion, 1846–1848.* London: Brassey's, 2000.

Tucker, Spencer C. *The Encyclopedia of the Mexican-American War.* Santa Barbara, CA: ABC-CLIO, 2013.

San Pedro de las Colonias, Battle of (1914)

Hard-fought victory won by Pancho Villa's División del Norte immediately after having secured Torreón for the second time over a concentration of federal relief columns that had begun arriving nearby by rail in the vain hope of relieving that city's garrison.

Prelude (March 1914)

Having already conquered the state of Chihuahua, Villa departed its capital city with the main 10,000-man corps of his revolutionary army aboard fifteen trains on March 16, 1914, traveling southeastward through the neighboring state of Durango and reaching the rural Bermejillo railway station six days later—20 miles from Torreón, which lay just across the Nazas River in the state of Coahuila. This city and its satellite towns on the Durango side of the river were serving as headquarters for some 7,000 federal soldiers of the so-called *División del Nazas* or *División de la Laguna* under Maj. Gen. J. Refugio Velasco, supported by 6,000 or so *colorado* irregulars and local auxiliaries. Villa had immediately launched a headlong assault against Torreón's sister city of Gómez Palacio that same March 22, 1914, and after four days of bloody fighting—during which his División del Norte had been further reinforced by at least 5,000 more troops—Gómez Palacio's surviving federal defenders had escaped across the river into Torreón proper, whose garrison had then become very hard-pressed as well.

Two flanking Villista brigades had meanwhile seized the rail hub farther to the east of Torreón at Sacramento and left behind an occupying force under Col. Toribio de los Santos, who set about destroying long stretches of track so as to prevent any possible relief for Velasco's beleaguered garrison from two federal divisions that were rumored to be hastening across from Monterrey: the 1,700-man "Federal División del Norte" under Maj. Gen. Carlos García Hidalgo, and 1,300-man *División del Bravo* out of Tamaulipas under the engineer brigadier general Joaquín Maass Águila (a nephew of the dictator Victoriano Huerta).

A third division of 1,700 soldiers under Maj. Gen. Javier de Maure, which was also approaching by rail from Saltillo, was actually the first to reach the rural station at San Pedro de las Colonias (only 32 miles east of Torreón) on March 28, 1914, where it was forced to halt after skirmishing against Colonel de los Santos's Villista detachment farther to its west at Sacramento and discovering that the railway line in between had been destroyed. A force of 1,500 additional troops was furthermore following De Maure from Mexico City under Col. Francisco Cárdenas, including mixed elements of the 6th Infantry Regiment and 4th, 5th, and 6th Cavalry Regiments; 250 *rurales*; a mounted military police squadron; the 43rd Irregular Regiment under its *colorado* commander Marcelo Caraveo; plus a battalion of Juchitecan auxiliaries under militia "general" Rodrigo Paliza with a few 80mm field howitzers.

Immediately upon learning of the appearance of De Maure's vanguard at San Pedro de las Colonias, Villa had detached his subordinates Rosalío Hernández and Toribio Ortega on March 29, 1914, with two brigades totaling 2,000 men from his main assault force outside of Torreón so as to check this new threat. The federal divisions out of Monterrey and Tamaulipas under García Hidalgo and Maass subsequently detrained at San Pedro to join De Maure as well, so a federal concentration of 6,200 troops encamped and began digging in around the rural station and town that normally serviced the sprawling Hacienda San Pedro de las Colonias (former peacetime estate of the murdered president Francisco I. Madero).

Eventually, Velasco managed to escape out of Torreón under cover of a dust storm on the evening of April 2, 1914, yet could reassemble only some 4,000 surviving troops at the municipality of Viesca, who were low on ammunition, supplies, and morale. The victorious Villa, not wishing this defeated force to merge with the *federales* already encamped at San Pedro de las

Colonias so as to present him with a stronger, combined foe, instantly dispatched the brigades of his subordinates José Isabel Robles and Col. Raúl Madero from smoldering Torreón that very next day—April 3, 1914—so as to prepare to engage these reinforcements under the overall direction of his trusted brigadier general Tomás Urbina, while he followed as quickly as possible with the remainder of the División del Norte and its heavy artillery train.

Battle of San Pedro de las Colonias (April 5–13, 1914)

Urbina detrained and assembled his troops, marching eastward along the tracks as early as April 5, 1914, to engage the federal concentration waiting at San Pedro, his army's center comprising his own brigade plus those of Rosalío Hernández, José Rodríguez, and Maclovio Herrera. This initial thrust pushed within a third of a mile of San Pedro de las Colonias's railway station by nightfall, where Urbina's assault force remained held in check by the close-range counterfire from federal soldiers entrenched behind rows of thick cotton bales. These exchanges continued into the next day, when Urbina's right wing—comprising another four brigades under Calixto Contreras, José Isabel Robles, Eugenio Aguirre Benavides, and Raúl Madero—began an enveloping maneuver out of the south, while his left wing—made up of the three brigades of Toribio Ortega, Miguel González, and Toribio de los Santos—did the same around to the north.

However, unnoticed by the attacking Villistas, a column of irregular cavalrymen under the *colorado* commander Benjamín Argumedo rode into San Pedro out of its east that same April 6, 1914, bringing a message from General Velasco to the effect that he had reassembled his surviving 4,000 troops only 10 miles south of San Pedro at Viesca, yet needed to have his ammunition and supplies replenished before attempting to fight his way in to join the federal concentration. A supply convoy was consequently prepared and Argumedo tried to lead it out of San Pedro the next morning, April 7, 1914, along the same route that he had used to enter the previous day—only to discover that the Villista encirclement had since been extended, so he and this train convoy were driven back into San Pedro by heavy gunfire from new Villista positions established at Santa Elena and La Candelaria.

The *federales* strengthened the escort of Argumedo's convoy overnight by adding De Maure's division and Paliza's battalion, more than 2,000 additional men in total, and then made a concerted effort to break it out of San Pedro again on the morning of April 8, 1914. Even so, this second attempt was also beaten back at first by the Villista besiegers until Maass's division intervened and helped the convoy to finally exit on a third try, albeit at a cost of some 500 federal casualties. And when Villa personally reached his división headquarters from Torreón with the remainder of his brigades and heavy artillery on April 9, 1914, and learned that 2,000 defenders had temporarily departed with Argumedo to bring in Velasco, he ordered an all-out assault against San Pedro for the next day, hoping to crush the depleted *federales* before the detached formation and Velasco's survivors could reappear.

A broad attack consequently erupted at dawn on April 10, 1914—Good Friday on the Church calendar—in which some 7,000–8,000 Villista troops stormed defenses being held by about 3,500 Huertistas. However, Maass put up a tenacious resistance along San Pedro's western and northern sectors, while the small cemetery to its southeast was equally well defended by García Hidalgo. Eventually, the Villista artillery fire began to slacken as their ammunition stockpiles ran down after 3:00 p.m., and shortly thereafter it was learned that Velasco's vanguard had arrived from the Hacienda de la Soledad and was entering the Buenavista suburb, fighting its way into San Pedro along with De Maure's, Paliza's, and Argumedo's contingents between 6:00 and 9:00 p.m. on that same evening.

Yet despite being temporarily elated by this relief, San Pedro's outnumbered soldiers had nonetheless endured more than 1,000 casualties during their desperate daylong defense and were now completely surrounded. The 9,000 *federales* and *colorados* furthermore remained low on ammunition and supplies, and realized that no more reinforcements were on their way—unlike Villa, who brought in several thousand more men over the next couple of days so as to bring his total number up to 16,000 troops, and then carefully planned yet another huge assault for 3:30 a.m. on April 13, 1914. His initial predawn attack pressed in from all directions, but a special column thrust straight in to within 60 yards of the combined federal headquarters at San Pedro's main railway station, so alarmingly close that staff officers began using their drawn pistols to beat runaway soldiers back into the firing line.

The defenders nonetheless managed to steady and even mounted a heroic counterattack, which succeeded in recovering much of their lost ground by 10:000 a.m. on that same April 13, 1914, although at a prohibitive cost in lives and expended ammunition. One hour later, Velasco was wounded in his left arm and García Hidalgo took over command, ordering that preparations should begin to be made around 3:00 p.m. for a headlong escape east toward Tizoc after nightfall. The trapped garrison's predicament had grown so acutely dire that numerous suicides were reported among the officers and wholesale desertions by distantly placed companies, while García Hidalgo's order to Argumedo to prepare to lead his riders on a diversionary flanking maneuver found his *colorados* "disorganized and many of them drunk."

Villa himself noted that toward late afternoon on April 13, 1914, smoke columns began to multiply throughout San Pedro as fires were being lit as a smokescreen, while Argumedo's cavalry attempted a feeble flanking maneuver around to the south and Almazán made a much better effort around to the north, "and as all the enemy guns at that same time redoubled their fire, I comprehended that these were preparations for an evacuation." Federal morale collapsed as trains ran the gauntlet after nightfall, leaving many soldiers or *colorados* to flee in any direction or to surrender.

Aftermath

The victorious Villa entered San Pedro by the light of its flames after nightfall on April 13, 1914, to find "heaps of wounded" left behind—at least 600 abandoned in one single warehouse alone, "whose floor was soaked with blood." He estimated Huertista losses to have totaled at least 3,500 dead, wounded, captured, or desertions, compared to 650 casualties among his own men. The shattered federal divisions limped off eastward in the direction of Saltillo, eventually tearing up 12 miles of track between the rural Saucedo and Amargos railway stations so as to shakily reassemble 6 miles beyond this broken segment at the Paredón station.

Given his string of impressive victories, Villa hoped to be rewarded by having his División del Norte belatedly accorded the

status of an army by the constitutionalist political figurehead, *primer jefe* or "first chief" Venustiano Carranza, as well as to be allowed to drive southward through Zacatecas toward the national capital. However, neither wish was granted; for after the more feeble constitutionalist *Ejército del Noreste* or "Army of the Northeast" under Gen. Pablo González had failed to push 60 miles southwest from Monterrey to take Saltillo, Carranza ordered Villa to veer his victorious División del Norte eastward out of Torreón to take care of this matter.

One month after his triumph at San Pedro de las Colonias, Villa would rout the remnants of its defeated Huertista army at the Battle of Paredón with contemptuous ease—the *federales'* resolve so badly shaken that they would break and flee by the thousands within 15 minutes of his opening charge.

See also: Ángeles Ramírez, Felipe de Jesús; División del Norte; Huerta Márquez, José Victoriano; Paredón, Battle of; Revolution, Mexican; *rurales*; Torreón, Federal Abandonment of; Torreón, Villa's First Capture of; Torreón, Villa's Second Capture of; Villa, Pancho.

Further Reading

Aguirre Benavides, Luis and Adrián. *Las grandes batallas de la División del Norte al mando del general Francisco Villa.* Mexico City: Diana, 1967.

Guzmán, Martín Luis. *Memoirs of Pancho Villa.* Austin: University of Texas Press, 1976 translation.

Santa Anna, Antonio López de (1794–1876)

Military officer who emerged from Mexico's early governmental chaos to become its strongman and who would dominate its national politics for a quarter century.

A head-and-shoulders portrait of Gen. Antonio López de Santa Anna, president of Mexico, ca. 1847. (Library of Congress)

Antonio de Padua María Severino López de Santa Anna Pérez de Lebrón was born during the late-colonial era in the city of Jalapa on February 21, 1794, the second child and first son of a royal notary named Antonio López de Santa Anna Pérez de Acal and his wife, Manuela Pérez de Lebrón Cortés. His father saw that his young son became apprenticed to a merchant in Veracruz, but the high-spirited Antonio soon indicated that preferred a military calling, so—against his parents' wishes—he was enrolled on July 6, 1810, as a 16-year-old *subteniente* in the Fixed Infantry Regiment of Veracruz under the command of its newly promoted colonel Joaquín de Arredondo y Muñiz.

Early Military Experiences (1811–1821)

When Mexico's war for independence had exploded that same autumn, Santa Anna had experienced his first taste of combat when Arredondo was sent with 500 troops in mid-March 1811 to put down insurrections in Tamaulipas and Texas. Two-and-a-half years of wide-ranging campaigns had ensued. The young subaltern was wounded in the left forearm by an Indian arrow in San Luis Potosí, then was promoted to second lieutenant as of February 1812. The Texans were finally crushed at Atascoso outside San Antonio on August 12, 1813. It is believed that Arredondo's ruthless execution of beaten foes and torching of towns would help to shape Santa Anna's own harsh attitudes.

Singled out for bravery in battle, he was returned to Veracruz that same autumn as a military instructor. As the viceroy had ordered new companies raised for that port city's regiment, Santa Anna was promoted to first lieutenant of its 2nd Grenadier Battalion. Then the next year, he became an aide to the royalist governor and garrison commander, Gen. José Dávila, and patrolled local highways. In March 1816, Santa Anna was promoted to captain and served in Arredondo's pursuit of Francisco Mina during the summer of 1817.

Santa Anna's next few years were spent quietly, relocating displaced loyalists around Veracruz. had also acquired a few properties as well as considerable debts through gambling. In his provincial backwater, he remained loyal to the Crown until the very closing phases of the War of Independence. Belatedly switching allegiances in the spring of 1821, he became one of many insurgent lieutenant colonels vying for attention. After a few small local victories, he was promoted to command of the 11th Division, yet lost half of his men in a failed assault against Dávila's royal garrison in Veracruz before independence was at last secured on September 27, 1821.

Failed Attempt Against San Juan de Ulúa (September–October 1822)

Santa Anna's first major military assignment came after Iturbide promoted him to brigadier general in May 1822 and placed him in command of the imperial garrison holding the city of Veracruz as of September 25, 1822—with orders to secure its offshore island fortress of San Juan de Ulúa from its stubborn Spanish holdouts. Santa Anna at first attempted to negotiate terms with the castle's commander, General Dávila, during the second week of October 1822, but this Spanish officer was promptly relieved in favor of the more intractable brigadier general Francisco Lemaur.

Santa Anna consequently deceived the latter into believing that he was prepared to switch allegiances and allow the Spaniards to reclaim Veracruz as well, so a flotilla of boats from San Juan de Ulúa approached the city waterfront at dawn on October 27, 1822. Santa Anna's plan was to capture this 400-man Spanish landing force as they entered into the Concepción and Santiago Bastions, then use their uniforms to venture out to Ulúa and take its defenders by surprise; however, the suspicious Spanish troops opened fire without disembarking from their boats and, after a two-hour exchange of gunfire, retired back out to their harbor castle without ever setting foot ashore. Although Santa Anna ordered public celebrations to honor his "victory" (claiming that he had repulsed a Spanish sneak attack), Iturbide's "imperial captain-general" for that district—Mexican general José Antonio de Echávarri—secretly informed Iturbide that the planned deception of the Spaniards had been deliberately sabotaged by Santa Anna.

The emperor therefore proposed to award medals to Santa Anna and his officers, and summoned him to a gala reception next month in Jalapa, when he further intended to offer Santa Anna a new posting in Mexico City—where he might be quietly arrested afterward for harboring republican sentiments. However, upon seeing the public euphoria from the *veracruzanos* as their favorite son Santa Anna entered Jalapa on a white horse, Iturbide promptly informed his suspect general that he was being removed from military command and must accompany the emperor's party back to the capital.

Revolt Against Iturbide (December 1822–March 1823)

Santa Anna insisted on first disposing of his personal affairs, so after Iturbide departed from Jalapa on December 1, 1822, he immediately galloped back to Veracruz and the next day proclaimed himself in revolt against the garish imperial regime. Counting initially on the support of only the 400 soldiers of his 8th Infantry Regiment, Santa Anna then further issued a *pronunciamiento* on December 6, 1822, explaining that he had risen against the absolutism of Iturbide and in favor of more democratic principles for Mexico, in hopes of garnering broader support.

Santa Anna vainly tried to strike a deal with General Lemaur out on San Juan de Ulúa, releasing his Spanish captives and permitting the sale of provisions to that isolated royal outpost in hopes that some sea traffic might be allowed and no attacks made in his rear, while Santa Anna marched with his small rebel force to "liberate" Orizaba from its imperial administration in mid-December 1822. Orizaba's leaders refused to join his movement, although Santa Anna did gather up several hundred more recruits from that city as well as when he routed an imperial force at Plan del Río on December 19, 1822.

Yet upon trying to push into Jalapa two days later with his 800 unruly men, Santa Anna found Gen. José María Calderón opposed to his entry, so his assault became bogged down and trapped within San José Church on the city outskirts. Deserted by many of his recent recruits and low on ammunition after exchanging gunfire with Calderón's defenders from 5:00 until 11:00 a.m. on the morning of December 21, 1822, Santa Anna had no choice but to lead a desperate flight out of Jalapa and march his survivors back into Veracruz to become besieged there. With only 600 men to defend that port, his garrison was soon invested by 3,000 imperial troops who arrived outside under Generals Echávarri and José Gabriel de Armijo.

Nevertheless, resentment against the autocratic misrule of Agustín I broke out elsewhere in the state of Veracruz as well with such famous figures as Nicolás Bravo and Vicente Guerrero also rising against the emperor. Despite their rebel contingents being initially bested at Almolonga during the last week of January 1823 by Armijo's imperial subordinate, Brig. Gen. Epitacio Sánchez, sentiment against Iturbide continued to mount. Santa Anna was relieved when Echávarri and Armijo agreed to lift their siege of Veracruz on February 1, 1823, formalizing their adhesion to the anti-imperial rebellion in support of Bravo by signing the "Plan of Casamata."

Now led by senior commanders, this mutiny quickly spread to most every other Mexican Army unit, including virtually all troops in Mexico City, so Iturbide was obliged to shift his headquarters to Ixtapalucan by February 12, 1823, while the congressmen whom he had imprisoned were released. Five weeks later, with armies closing in on him from several directions, the emperor agreed to abdicate and go into European exile, being temporarily replaced by a triumvirate of Nicolás Bravo, Guadalupe Victoria, and Pedro Celestino Negrete, which would rule the country until a republican constitution could be drafted.

Debate in Congress soon splintered into two contending factions: those favoring a strong central authority (known as *escoceses* or "Scots"), opposed by those wishing for a looser federal system (*yorkinos* or "Yorkists"). When Santa Anna issued a demand from San Luis Potosí on June 5, 1823, for a federal system of government, he was recalled to Mexico City and briefly incarcerated for his temerity.

Uprising Against Gómez Pedraza (September–December 1828)

The national elections held in August 1828 failed to reflect the popular will. The insurgent hero Vicente Guerrero had been the clear choice of a majority of voters, yet because he was a mulatto who had once toiled as a lowly teamster, he was deemed unworthy to occupy the presidency by the Creole elites who dominated all public institutions—and since raw voting results had to be weighed by each state legislature before casting their decisive electoral votes, the final outcome proved unexpected: the former royalist officer and sitting minister of war, Gómez Pedraza, received 11 out of 36 electoral votes; only 8 went to Guerrero; and the remainder were split up amongst Anastasio Bustamante and two other candidates. Gómez Pedraza was proclaimed the winner on September 1, 1828, with Guerrero relegated to serving as his vice president.

A couple of days afterward, Santa Anna (now vice governor of Veracruz) began engineering another revolt, first by persuading the municipal government of its state capital of Jalapa to challenge the electoral vote cast by the Veracruzan legislature in favor of Pedraza, against the popular returns. Suspended from office in retaliation as of September 5, 1828, Santa Anna openly rebelled two days thereafter by assuming command over Lt. Col. Mariano Arista's 80 men of the 2nd Cavalry Regiment and Lt. Col. José Antonio Heredia's 500 soldiers of the 5th Permanent Infantry Regiment (whose commander, Col. Juan M. Azcárate—a brother-in-law of President-elect Gómez Pedraza—was furthermore arrested while attempting to leave the San José barracks).

Santa Anna then sent out calls for support from his regional allies and marched his small force—including two small fieldpieces and 150 militiamen from Jalapa—out of that city on the night of September 11–12, 1828, heading toward the strategic Fort of Perote. Riding on ahead with an advance party of only eight riders, he persuaded its 290-man garrison to arrest their *pedrazista* commander, Lt. Col. José Manuel Arechega and admit his rebel brigade on September 13, 1828, thereby joining Santa Anna's rebellion.

From Perote, he subsequently issued a *pronunciamiento* on September 16, 1828—Mexico's Independence Day—addressed to the "peoples of Anáhuac" in the name of his so-called *Ejército Libertador* or Liberating Army calling for the annulment of Gómez Pedraza's installation as president, the immediate substitution of Guerrero, as well as enactment of effective legislation to remove all Spaniards from Mexican soil. Some small units joined Santa Anna at Perote and supportive uprisings ensued at Acapulco, Chalco, and Apám, but not the broad-based national insurrection that he had been expecting.

Instead, the Gómez Pedraza administration remained firmly in control of most major garrisons and cities, quickly declaring Santa Anna an outlaw and dispatching an army of almost 3,000 men under Brig. Gen. Manuel Rincón from Mexico City to invest the rebels within Perote. This army approached by the afternoon of September 28, 1828, and dug in nearby. Santa Anna sallied from Perote shortly after midnight on October 1–2, 1828, capturing an 800-man *pedrazista* detachment under Col. Pablo Unda that was holding Aguatepec, most of whom thereupon deserted from government service. Santa Anna wrote to fellow conspirators in Mexico City, encouraging them to foment an uprising, while continuing to make feints from Perote in hopes of goading Rincón into mounting a costly assault with his larger army, to no avail. Finally, one rebel sortie on October 13–14, 1828, was bloodied by Rincón's cavalry, so the mutineers persuaded Santa Anna to escape from Perote toward Oaxaca City in a bid to spread their insurrection.

Leaving behind 150 troops, 40 gunners, and 63 convalescents to hold Perote, Santa Anna slipped out with 626 troopers and infantrymen at 7:00 p.m. on October 19, 1828, making for San Andrés Chalchicomula. He arrived there two days later, sending out couriers to Orizaba, Córdoba, and Oaxaca in hopes of raising money and supporters. Allowed passage through the Pass of Cuicatlán into Oaxaca by Col. Pedro Pantoja, Santa Anna was eventually able to enter its state capital uncontested on November 6, 1828, as its *pedrazista* governor fled, bringing his total strength to 1,400 rebel troops and four guns. Rincón had meanwhile accepted the submission of Perote and followed Santa Anna at a slow pace, arriving outside Oaxaca City one week later.

Both generals met at San Juan and seemingly agreed to allow the mutiny to be resolved peaceably before the legislature, but Santa Anna failed to evacuate his defenses as promised, so Rincón assaulted Oaxaca on November 14, 1828, defeating the rebel forces and driving Santa Anna back into its stone Santo Domingo Convent to become besieged once more.

Acordada Mutiny (November 30–December 3, 1828)

Finally, the unpopular administration of President Gómez Pedraza was challenged directly in Mexico City, when the urban militia captain Lucas Balderas declared himself in favor of Guerrero assuming the Presidency from the Inquisition building on the evening of November 30, 1828, and a body of mutineers under Col. Santiago García of the Tres Villas Battalion and militia Col. José María de la Cadena seized the old Acordada tribunals, which housed a large arsenal of weaponry and ammunition. Although well armed because of this coup, the rebels remained very disorganized, falling into disputes among themselves after Brig. Gen. José María Lobato arrived and tried to assume command over their movement, only to be rebuffed—at which point Colonel de la Cadena left to rejoin the government ranks.

However, Gómez Pedraza's supporters were likewise gripped with uncertainty and confusion, so no confrontation immediately ensued. Eventually, after two chaotic days, the fugitive governor of the neighboring state of Mexico—40-year-old Dr. Lorenzo de Zavala—took charge of the mutineers, instructing Lobato to assume command over the *Ciudadela* or "Citadel," while Colonel García led probes through the city streets toward the *pedrazista* loyalists holding the Presidential Palace as well as other adjoining buildings. They opened fire on these rebel patrols at noon on December 2, 1828, some heavy exchanges of gunfire ensuing which killed Colonel García as well as cavalry Col. Gaspar López on the government side.

Vice President Guerrero, who had exited Mexico City and been monitoring the progress of events from its outskirts, thereupon departed toward Tláhuac, while Gómez Pedraza remained ensconced in the Presidential Palace for only one more day before resigning from office and departing toward Guadalajara on the evening of December 3, 1828. With the capital devoid of authorities the next morning, a mob chanting *Mueran los españoles* or "Death to the Spaniards" broke into the padlocked commercial stalls of the Parián in the city center, stripping them bare.

Order was gradually restored, although Guerrero was not officially voted into office as president by the reconvened Congress until January 12, 1829, and the precedent had been set for many future revolts.

In November 1833, Santa Anna requested a leave of absence from his position as president from Mexico's Congress so as to recuperate his "broken health" at his Manga de Clavo estate. This furlough was granted, and a month afterward the liberal administration of his replacement—Vice President Gómez Farías—passed yet another in a series of bills deemed hostile to Church prerogatives, which many bishops threatened to disobey on its becoming law and so appealed to Santa Anna for relief. He consequently reappeared in Mexico City a couple of months early from his leave, on April 24, 1834—the very day on which this controversial new law was scheduled to go into effect. Declaring himself neutral in the mounting confrontation between liberal and conservative factions,

Santa Anna refused to mobilize any military forces in support of Congress and instead called uon its leaders to act with more moderation.

Alarmed, a liberal delegation visited him for clarification on his stand, and when none was forthcoming, Congress suspended its sessions entirely on May 15, 1834. The next day, a conservative-backed uprising erupted in Jalapa and Coatepec acclaiming Santa Anna as the "Protector of the Catholic Religion," soon followed by a *pronunciamiento* at Cuernavaca and a wave of dissension in other towns. When the Congress subsequently tried to reconvene in the capital, deputies found their chamber's doors locked and guarded by soldiers.

Punishment of Zacatecas (May 1835)

On February 14, 1835, the federal Congress in Mexico City passed a law restricting each state's militia forces to just one soldier for every 500 inhabitants, a reduction ordered by Santa Anna so as to curtail the frequent regional uprisings. The state of Zacatecas, with 4,000 men already under arms and another 16,000 in reserve, was one of several states that refused to comply with this decree, instead increasing its armaments production and appointing Gen. Francisco García Salinas as its state militia commander in expectation of a conflict.

Having anticipated just such a reaction, Santa Anna suddenly materialized in the Tolosa Hills less than nine miles east of the city of Zacatecas with 4,000 federal troops on May 10, 1835. The next day, he easily defeated García Salinas near Guadalupe, killing 81 of his state militiamen and making a wholesale capture of some 2,700 others. The president's army thereupon marched into the defenseless city on May 17, 1835, celebrating a *Te Deum* in its cathedral before stripping many of its

buildings of valuables in a calculated act of punishment and then departing 10 days later on a campaign that would eventually take him as far north as Texas.

San Jacinto Defeat and U.S. Imprisonment (March 1836–February 1837)

Following the massacre of the Alamo's defenders, Santa Anna resumed his campaign to subdue the rest of rebellious Texas by sending out detachments to stamp out any remaining pockets of resistance. Apparently seeking to terrorize its thinly spread population into submission, he ruthlessly ordered wholesale massacres of hundreds of prisoners, and left Filisola in command of his main encampment at San Antonio to personally lead a column hundreds of miles farther east into Texas so as to run down the fugitive Texian government of Pres. David G. Burnet. With 900 picked troops, Santa Anna attempted to surprise these Texian legislators at their temporary headquarters in Harrisburg on April 16, 1836, burning this town to the ground after they escaped him once again.

Four days later, the Mexican president countermarched toward Lynch's Ferry, and his scouts discovered the nearby presence of Texian troops. Further probes and skirmishes that same afternoon of April 20, 1836, established that Gen. Sam Houston had arrived with his small army, so Santa Anna encamped his own forces overnight behind an extemporized breastwork of packs and baggage out on the plain, about 1,000 yards opposite the Texians' concealed positions. The next morning, he was reinforced by the arrival of an additional 500 Mexican troops under Cos, bringing Santa Anna's total strength to almost 1,400 men and a single six-pound fieldpiece.

Since both contending armies had stood to their arms since sunrise, Santa Anna gave the order by noon of April 21, 1836, for his men to break ranks and rest, himself retiring for a *siesta*. Houston, however, silently charged in four columns at 4:30 p.m., taking the slumbering Mexican camp completely by surprise. Within the span of 18 minutes, at a cost of only 9 Texians killed and some 30 wounded, Santa Anna's hapless army was destroyed and he fled, being captured the next morning. His army had been annihilated, suffering an estimated 600–650 dead and 730 prisoners—virtually its entire strength.

The captive Santa Anna was compelled to issue orders to his subordinate Filisola to withdraw all remaining Mexican troops from Texas as of May 26, 1836, while he himself returned to Veracruz on February 21, 1837, aboard the brand-new U.S. Navy barque *Pioneer* (described in the September 1837 *Navy List* as an "exploring vessel" built in Boston). Disgraced, he retired out of the limelight to his Manga de Clavo estate.

Honor Restored at Veracruz (November 1838–July 1839)

In April of 1838, a French squadron imposed a naval blockade on the port of Veracruz, to exact compensation for economic losses suffered by French citizens during Mexico's recent turmoil. After seven months of this exercise, the blockaders then increased their pressure by bombarding its harbor castle of San Juan de Ulúa on November 27, 1838, which surrendered next day and a temporary truce was arranged. In this moment of national crisis, the government of Pres. Anastasio Bustamante authorized Santa Anna to rush to the scene from his nearby estate, until reinforcements could arrive from the interior of Mexico under Gen. Mariano Arista.

When the Mexican Congress formally declared war against France shortly thereafter, Santa Anna was informed on the night of December 3, 1838, and given command over the 700–800 soldiers remaining in the city. Informing the French that hostilities would resume on the morning of December 5, 1838, he was almost captured in his quarters in Veracruz by a descent at dawn (in which Arista was taken by the French). Santa Anna subsequently formed about 200 men into a makeshift company and attacked the French landing force as it was retiring, during which he received a blast from a French boat-gun which killed nine of his men and blew off Santa Anna's left leg below the knee, as well as a finger from his right hand.

Because of the severity of his wounds, he was considered a national hero and as a reward for this sacrifice, the convalescent Santa Anna would even be transported from Manga de Clavo to Mexico City by February 21, 1839, to be honored with temporarily occupying the presidency as of mid-March of that year, while Bustamante marched northward with an army to confront the federalist revolt that had been started at Tampico by Gen. José Antonio Mexía. Once the latter was defeated, Santa Anna relinquished the office to Nicolás Bravo by mid-July 1839 and returned home to Manga de Clavo, gradually regaining his strength and plotting to return to power.

Return to Power (1841–1844)

Finally, in a prearranged coup, brigadier general Mariano Paredes—military commander at Guadalajara—rose against President Bustamante on August 8, 1841, being joined shortly thereafter by Santa

Anna at Veracruz. Paredes marched on the city of Guanajuato with 600 men and received the defection of Brig. Gen. Pedro Cortázar, and they then proceeded together toward Querétaro to incorporate Gen. Julián Juvera's garrison into their ranks, swelling rebel numbers to 2,200 men.

Santa Anna meanwhile occupied the Castle of Perote with a few hundred troops, while General Valencia mutinied with another 1,200 inside Mexico City itself, seizing the Ciudadela and Acordada Barracks. The beleaguered president fought back with 2,000 loyal troops and a dozen guns, calling for reinforcements from the countryside, while civilians fled out of the line of fire. Although his following eventually numbered 3,500 men, Bustamante was driven out of the capital by September 20, 1841, resigning nine days later to go into exile in Europe.

A mere three years later, Santa Anna would share this same fate. On October 30, 1844, his ex-collaborator Paredes—while in Guadalajara, en route to taking up a new command in Sonora—agreed to spearhead a revolt against his former co-conspirator. This revolt was joined within one week by the garrison at Aguascalientes, then at Mazatlán on November 7, 1844, plus Zacatecas and Colima the next day, as well as Durango and Querétaro by November 10th.

Santa Anna exited Mexico City on November 22, 1844, marching northwest toward San Juan de los Lagos with a small army to confront Paredes, who had reached Mochiltic in the state of Querétaro with 4,000 troops. During Santa Anna's absence, the capital's *Batallón de Reemplazos* or "Reserves Battalion" also revolted in its Acordada Barracks, sparking a general uprising against his "interim president," Gen. Valentín Canalizo, who was detained and replaced the next day by Gen. José Joaquín de Herrera.

By early January 1845, Santa Anna had given up all hopes of reclaiming power, and so departed from his shrunken army toward Veracruz with a small cavalry escort. He disguised himself as a muleteer but was recognized on reaching Naolinco so was detained in Perote Castle until he could be banished toward Cuba on June 3, 1845, aboard the gunboat *Victoria*.

Role in the Mexican-American War (1846–1847)

July 5, 1846: Cmdr. Alexander Slidell Mackenzie visited Havana, meeting the exiled Santa Anna two days later to enumerate Polk's terms for a peace in case the Mexican strongman should regain power.

August 16, 1846: Santa Anna returned to Veracruz from Cuba aboard the British mail packet *Arab*, which was allowed to enter by its U.S. naval blockaders because Washington believed that he would help conclude a peace.

September 15, 1846: Santa Anna appeared outside Mexico City on the eve of its Independence Day celebrations, entering the next morning to a tumultuous reception escorted by Salas's troops.

September 28, 1846: Santa Anna departed Mexico City northward with a small body of troops, arriving at San Luis Potosí by October 8th to begin amassing an army to confront Taylor.

December 6, 1846: The polarized Senate in Mexico City voted 11–9 to offer the presidency to Santa Anna and vice presidency to the civilian Valentín Gómez Farías; the former remained at San Luis Potosí training his army, leaving the latter to assume office alone on December 23rd.

December 18, 1846: Taylor learned that Santa Anna was moving north from San

Luis Potosí to assail the small American garrison holding Saltillo, so he ordered it reinforced and redeployed his units, causing Santa Anna to cancel his operation

January 13, 1847: An American courier carrying a copy of Scott's campaign plans inland to Taylor was killed between Ciudad Victoria and Monterrey, this intelligence being forwarded to Santa Anna at San Luis Potosí.

January 28, 1847: Realizing that the strength of Taylor's army was being diminished to help Scott, Santa Anna ordered his 20,000 men to begin marching northward from San Luis Potosí to rendezvous south of Saltillo and surprise his American opponent.

March 21, 1847: Having led 10,500 survivors of his shattered army back from Buena Vista into San Luis Potosí, Santa Anna appeared with his two best divisions at the Guadalupe suburb north of Mexico City, then ended the dispute between General Peña and Vice President Gómez Farías by deposing the latter in favor of 51-year-old general and congressman Pedro María Anaya.

April 3, 1847: Santa Anna departed Mexico City, traveling east to assume command over the three infantry divisions, one cavalry brigade, and 2,000 militiamen guarding the Veracruz highway under Canalizo.

Revolution of Ayutla and Final Removal from Office (1854–1855)

Santa Anna was to be reinstalled as president of Mexico one last time in April 1853, following a military coup in the capital engineered by Gen. Manuel María Lombardini. His conservative backers hoped that their strongman's return would restore some semblance of order to a country that remained wracked and angry in the wake of its defeat by the United States. However, its weak and bankrupt central government meant that Santa Anna would initially experience difficulties raising sufficient funds through traditional tax measures, while his authority was furthermore being openly flouted or ignored by some state or regional leaders. Simultaneously, Santa Anna had to negotiate territorial claims being pressed by the U.S. ambassador, James Gadsen, increasing worries among Mexicans about more concessions being demanded of their national sovereignty.

Santa Anna prepared to meet such challenges by recalling and promoting many loyalists into high-ranking military positions and starting to rebuild the army's strength before at last blatantly assuming dictatorial powers as of December 16, 1853—when he proclaimed that he would henceforth dispense with any kind of legislature, abolish all political parties, create an order of nobility, and demand to be addressed as "Most Serene Highness."

Two weeks afterward he signed the Gadsen Treaty, which granted the United States free passage for mail, merchandise, and troops across the Isthmus of Tehuantepec, as well as added a readjustment to the boundaries established earlier by the Treaty of Guadalupe Hidalgo, giving Washington almost 30,000 more square miles of territory in New Mexico and Arizona—in exchange for 10 million desperately needed dollars, which Santa Anna used to help finance his massive military buildup.

The Mexican public was outraged by Santa Anna's actions, for both assuming an imperial crown as well as signing away more Mexican territory, so various mutinies flared up in protest. Among these insurrections, one at Ayutla in March 1854 called not only for Santa Anna's removal but for a complete replacement of the limited democracy that had been imposed on the nation ever since colonial days in favor of a more inclusive form of liberal republican government. Having already anticipated such resistance in Guerrero, Santa Anna had earlier stationed 3,000 troops at Chilpancingo plus directed another couple of brigades to converge on that state. He personally marched out of Mexico City at the head of 5,000 additional troops on March 16, 1854, to wend through the Sierra Madre range down to the Pacific shores and stamp out this uprising. But as he pushed deeper into rebel territory a month later, he found his supply lines being cut off and came within sight of Acapulco on April 20, 1854, with his soldiers suffering from thirst, hunger, disease, and exhaustion in the oppressive heat. Unable to discomfit the mutineers inside Fort San Diego, Santa Anna broke camp six days later to make a painful retreat to Chilpancingo, leaving his broken army there while he returned, humiliated, into Mexico City by May 16, 1854.

Soon other revolts erupted elsewhere because of his failure to crush this initial insurrection, while his overexpanded army proved unmotivated and ill-suited for running down elusive guerrilla bands. A second major sweep led by Santa Anna into Michoacán in the spring of 1855 also failed to bring any enemy formations to battle, despite his proclamations of victory as he returned empty-handed into Mexico City once again on June 9, 1855—to scant enthusiasm.

Santa Anna quietly appointed three men to temporarily assume his presidential duties on August 8, 1855, then at 3:00 a.m. the next morning slipped out of Mexico City with a regiment of lancers as his escort, heading toward Veracruz. He paused at Perote to issue a public proclamation on August 12,

1856, formally resigning from the presidency, and six days later sailed away from Veracruz aboard the ship *Iturbide* toward Cuba, to return into exile at Turbaco in Colombia.

Later Life (1857–1876)

On February 27, 1864, the ex-dictator Santa Anna returned from his Colombian exile, arriving at Veracruz aboard the British vessel *Conway*. Bazaine, commander of the French occupation forces, allowed him ashore after extracting a loyalty oath to the new conservative government, while Santa Anna furthermore promised not to take part in any political activity. However, after almost immediately issuing a call to his adherents through the *Indicador* newspaper, the ex-president was deported once again aboard the 130-man, six-gun, 1,300-ton French corvette *Colbert,* being deposited at Havana by March 12th, from where he continued back toward Colombia.

In 1869, Santa Anna was living in exile in Staten Island, New York, vainly trying to raise money for an army to return to power in Mexico. During his time in New York City, he is credited with bringing in the first shipments of *chicle*, which he planned to try using to replace rubber in carriage tires, without success. He also chewed it sweetened with sugar and mint, so that Thomas Adams—the American assigned to aid Santa Anna while he was in the United States—bought one ton of *chicle* from Santa Anna and eventually used it to found the chewing-gum industry with a product that he called "Chiclets." Santa Anna meanwhile he took advantage of a general amnesty and returned to Mexico in 1874, although crippled and almost blind from cataracts, he was ignored by the liberal republican government. Two years later, Santa Anna died in Mexico City on

June 21, 1876, and was buried in the Panteón del Tepeyac.

See also: Alamo, Siege of the; Buena Vista, Battle of; Mexican-American War; Perote, Fort of; San Jacinto, Battle of (1836).

Further Reading

Fowler, Will. *Santa Anna of Mexico.* Lincoln: University of Nebraska Press, 2009.

"Interesting from Mexico: Santa Anna's Return to the Capital." *New York Times*, June 3, 1854.

Santa Gertrudis, Battle of (1866)

Imperial defeat in northern Mexico during the War of the French Intervention that began to unravel the military fortunes of the emperor Maximilian's regime.

After having originally fought their way up from the Gulf coast, past the city of Puebla to capture the national capital by June 1863, the French invaders and their Mexican conservative allies had then begun fanning out so as to subdue the remainder of the country. Slowly but inexorably, they had penetrated into almost every region and taken city after city, although their military effectiveness diminished as their lines of communication grew stretched, extending farther and thinner into the remotest corners of Mexico.

Consequently, within a month of a Franco-conservative column under Gen. Tomás Mejía having occupied the border town of Matamoros (opposite Brownsville, Texas) in September 1864, its imperial garrison had become subjected to a loose siege by local republican guerrillas, who harassed and raided its overland routes. Provisions could still reach Matamoros's isolated defenders by ship, yet communication inland with the main conservative

stronghold more than 180 miles inland at Monterrey remained sporadic and difficult because of repeated ambushes, especially as travel through this harsh desert landscape required moving from one watering hole to the next.

Preliminary Maneuvers (June 7–14, 1866)

Mejía having failed to stamp out this guerrilla resistance, despite numerous sweeps over almost two years, the imperial authorities decided to make one last attempt at pacifying Mexico's northeastern corner in June 1866 before France's military support would be withdrawn altogether in response to mounting diplomatic pressures out of Washington. Hoping to leave this region more secure for the emperor's adherents upon their departure, French strategists decided to send two heavily escorted wagon trains through this republican-controlled territory from opposite directions: one traveling inland from Matamoros toward Monterrey, the other heading eastward out of Monterrey toward Matamoros so as to meet up at the halfway point of Mier. The objective of this coordinated operation was not merely to deliver supplies at both ends but more importantly for these forces to once again scour the lonely stretches of desert in between of republican contingents while installing imperial garrisons at crucial villages and watering holes so as to prevent any enemy return.

An expedition of 2,000 men therefore began preparing to sally from the imperial base at Monterrey in early June 1866, this force consisting of two battalions of French Foreign Legionnaires under Lt. Col. Louis Adrien de Tuce, numerous Belgian mercenaries, plus Mexican auxiliaries from the Guardia Rural and a cavalry squadron from the Regimiento de la Emperatriz, backed by six fieldpieces. This army intended to strike out across the desert east-northeastward, traveling initially along three separate roads before reuniting at the advance imperial outpost of Cerralvo, then proceeding on to the riverside town of Mier to rendezvous with the other like-sized convoy—which in the meantime would have been approaching out of Matamoros, along the banks of the Río Grande.

Republican general Mariano Escobedo had heard rumors of these planned joint marches at his headquarters in Linares, and although not entirely crediting such reports, nonetheless directed a division of his infantry to begin marshaling at the hamlet of China, while his 2nd Cavalry Brigade was to concentrate at Paso del Zacate, and the 1st Brigade to assemble about 25 miles east of Cerralvo. His men—almost all militia volunteers—were by now quite well armed and disciplined, seasoned after two years of repetitive raids and campaigns, as well as being intimately familiar with the desert terrain.

Shortly thereafter, Escobedo learned from the recently promoted brigadier general Gerónimo Treviño that the first Franco-conservative columns had begun departing Monterrey on the night of June 7–8, 1866, so he joined the 1st Brigade a couple of days later at its advance assembly point to assume command in the field and observe the enemy's arrival at Cerralvo. The three Franco-imperial columns reached that garrisoned town by June 12, 1866, and on that same day saw the dust clouds out in the desert that signaled the movements of large republican formations. This threat caused Tuce's imperial army to dig in at Cerralvo, anticipating an assault, rather than continuing with their trek eastward.

When Escobedo learned from an intercepted message that this French expedition out of Monterrey had no intention of venturing further until Tuce received word that the other wagon train out of Matamoros had reached Mier, the republican general decided to leave these 2,000 men pinned down in Cerralvo—by detaching a screen of 600 republican dragoons under Lt. Col. Ruperto Martínez to maintain the illusion of an impending assault, while sending another 300 cavalrymen under Col. Pedro Martínez to also threaten Saltillo so as to discourage any additional reinforcements out of that imperial base.

Battle of Santa Gertrudis (June 13–15, 1866)

Meanwhile, Escobedo wheeled his remaining 1,500 troops and three mountain howitzers about and hastened almost 30 miles eastward on a forced march, arriving at Derramaderos near Santa Gertrudis two days later, atop the mesa southeast of Camargo. He had chosen this particular spot to observe the other imperial wagon train as it approached from Matamoros, hoping to determine which of two roads it would take up into the Santa Gertrudis Hills, as he knew that its 2,000 Austrian and Mexican auxiliary troops under Gen. Feliciano Olvera—accompanied by 200 wagons with hundreds of mounts and 2,000 mules—would have to travel at a measured pace from one watering hole to the next, so Escobedo hoped to confront and delay them in between.

Having identified his opponents' route, Escobedo furthermore tried to ensure the element of surprise by dividing his brigade up into six smaller contingents, which would be easier to conceal:

- A mixed force of 250 infantrymen under Colonels J. Alonso Flores and Luis G. Cáceres

- A like number from the Zaragoza and Hidalgo Infantry Battalions under Col. Miguel Palacios and Lt. Col. Edelmiro Mayer
- Three hundred men of the "Rifleros de Naranjo" and "Rifleros de China" Battalions under Colonels Francisco Naranjo and Adolfo Garza
- Three hundred Tamaulipas riflemen under Colonels Servando Canales and Julián Cerda
- A hundred or so riders from the Legión del Norte under Col. Joaquin Garza Leal, and Carabineros de Lampazos under Lt. Col. Higinio Villareal, with General Treviño among their midst
- Three hundred men in reserve under Col. Salvador F. de la Cabada and Lt. Col. Vicente Mariscal

These formations hid close to one another in the draws around the hill folds, hoping to draw the imperial troops into close range before engaging them, where their superior European weaponry might not prove so decisive.

However, a small detachment of Escobedo's irregulars revealed themselves prematurely to the approaching imperial vanguard on the afternoon of June 15, 1866, apparently losing the element of surprise. Yet Olvera mistook the sighting of a single republican band as nothing more than a small guerrilla ambush so encamped overnight and resumed his advance along the winding road toward the watering place at 6:00 a.m. on the morning of June 16, 1866—his wagons safely protected in the rear and a line of skirmishers advancing out front, pausing occasionally to fire off artillery volleys from a pair of howitzers so as to scare off any guerrillas.

In the early morning gloom, the imperial commander failed to realize that Escobedo was lying in wait for him with a full brigade, hundreds of republican infantrymen lying prone on the ground and cavalrymen concealed behind thickets of trees as the imperial column drew nearer. Suddenly, these concealed foot soldiers rose and charged in a mass, opening up a withering fire once they came within close range of the main imperial body. Olvera's surprised officers attempted a counterenvelopment around the republican left, but this was hit by a devastating charge in the flank from the hidden republican cavalry.

Within less than an hour, the Battle of the Mesa de Santa Gertrudis was over. By 7:00 a.m. on that June 16, 1866, the victors were counting up 396 imperial dead, 165 wounded, plus 1,001 prisoners (of whom more than 800 Mexican troops would join the republican ranks, leaving only a few dozen conservative officers and 145 Austrian mercenaries as actual captives), along with 1,200 firearms and eight working field-pieces. Republican casualties totaled 155 killed and 78 wounded. Olvera had fled the battlefield with about 100 riders, riding back into Matamoros to report on his utter rout and the complete loss of his valuable expedition.

Aftermath (June 1866)

News of such a wholesale defeat finished off any imperial hopes of retaining a foothold in northeastern Mexico. Four days later, Escobedo's victorious army began marching eastward out of Camargo, pushing slowly through heavy rains toward understrength Matamoros. Its garrison commander Mejía knew that he could mount scant resistance from within the half-starving city, so he handed its administration over to a couple of local Mexican leaders who had been living as exiles in the United States, then decamped with his 600 remaining imperial soldiers through Santa Cruz toward Bagdad on June 22, 1866, making way for Tampico.

The French Foreign Legion commander Tuce also waited with his own halted expedition at Cerralvo for a few more days before ordering a retreat back into Monterrey by June 28, 1866, so as to prepare to evacuate that city as well one month later. The port of Tampico was then furthermore surprised by a republican assault on August 1, 1866, all of its imperial Mexican defenders switching allegiance and joining the attackers' ranks, after which the French Marine detachments left holding out in its harbor forts agreed to withdraw by sea one week afterward. Even Saltillo was abandoned by its Franco-imperial garrison as of August 4, 1866.

Escobedo's victory at Santa Gertrudis had started this wave of retirements, enhancing his military prestige among his commanders and peers, while attracting ever more recruits to serve under his leadership. Within seven months, he would arrive outside the city of Querétaro in central Mexico at the head of an army 10,000 strong to besiege, defeat, and execute Maximilian himself.

See also: Escobedo Peña, Mariano Antonio Guadalupe; French Foreign Legion in Mexico; French Intervention, War of the.

Further Reading
Message of the President of the United States of January 29, 1867, Relating to the Present Condition of Mexico. Washington, DC: U.S. Government Printing Office, 1867, 225–33.

Santa Rosa, Battle of (1913)

First set-piece victory won by the self-taught Sonoran militia colonel Álvaro Obregón over an army of federal regulars in the field.

A youthful militia colonel Álvaro Obregón, seated in full uniform at lower left, with some of his Sonoran officers, ca. May 1913. (Library of Congress)

By mid-April 1913, the acting state governor of Sonora, Ignacio L. Pesqueira, not only had defied the seizure of presidential power in Mexico City by Gen. Victoriano Huerta, but had furthermore authorized the capture or removal of all federal garrisons from Sonora's northern towns of Nogales, Cananea, Agua Prieta, and Naco. Once accomplished, the state militia under Obregón had then begun edging south as well, toward the seaport of Guaymas, which served as the main regional headquarters for Gen. Miguel Gil's 1st Military Zone and was garrisoned by the 1,400 remaining regulars of his "División del Yaqui"—about half their original number of 2,650 men—plus another 150 federal irregulars, and about 400 local recruits.

Huertista Countermoves (April 22– May 7, 1913)

Concerned that this garrison at Guaymas might also fall to the Sonoran militia, the usurper Huerta ordered a brigade of nearly 1,200 reinforcements under newly promoted brigadier general Luis Medina Barrón (a commander of *rurales* with previous experience campaigning against the Yaquis), armed with five artillery pieces, two machine guns, and 1.5 million rounds of ammunition, to depart Mexico City by train on April 22, 1913. They reached Manzanillo three days later and commenced going aboard the transport ship *Pesqueira*, weighing for Guaymas by April 28, 1913, escorted by the gunboats *Morelos* and *Guerrero*, arriving on May 1st and completing their troop disembarkation next day.

Quite a number of these 1,200 new soldiers had deserted during transit, yet Gil nonetheless received telegraphed orders to launch an immediate offensive inland, so the gunboat *Guerrero* shelled the advance Sonoran militia outposts at the nearby Empalme railway junction that same May 2, 1913, causing them to retreat and its civilian population to flee. Col. Manuel F. Santibáñez thereupon exited Guaymas with 300 men of his 14th Infantry Battalion and occupied abandoned Empalme, after which a scouting force probed nine miles farther north up its tracks on May 4, 1913, reaching the rural Maytorena railway station without encountering any signs of the Sonoran militia.

Three days later, General Gil was recalled by telegraph to Mexico City, turning over command of Guaymas's entire federal division to Medina Barrón, while senior general Pedro Ojeda was to arrive so as to act as overall commander and military governor for the 1st Military Zone.

Battle of Santa Rosa (May 8–11, 1913)

Medina Barrón, who had campaigned in Sonora four years previously, quickly implemented a more aggressive strategy than Gil's—starting as of May 8, 1913, when Medina Barrón sent Col. Luis F. Eguiluz with 400 men of his 28th Infantry Battalion to reinforce Santibáñez's federal vanguard at Maytorena station with orders to push on together five miles farther up its tracks and take up defensive positions at the next rural station of Santa Rosa. Medina Barrón would in the meantime bring his main force out of Guaymas so as to follow in their wake.

As Colonels Eguiluz and Santibáñez arrived at the Santa Rosa station, they found a Sonoran rearguard waiting there under Maj. Jesús Trujillo, which promptly withdrew at this first contact with the *federales*. Yet Obregón himself set up an observation post less than a mile away and prepared to attack these two unsuspecting federal battalions with his main army the next dawn. First, however, he stealthily sent a detachment to occupy El Aguajito, a spring located in the Santa Ursula Canyon just to the west of Santa Rosa station, plus another Sonoran detachment to hold the road running three miles eastward from the station to the Hacienda de Santa Maria—the only two viable water sources in the immediate vicinity.

Obregón then unleashed his attack at 5:00 a.m. on the morning of May 9, 1913, sending three columns charging against the *federales* encamped around Santa Rosa station. Their pickets gave them some advance warning of this onslaught, and both sides settled down to heavy exchanges of gunfire. Medina Barrón, having already exited from Guaymas with his main army and followed inland as far as Maytorena station, learned of his vanguard's predicament and hastened his troops forward to assist. The dust columns churned up by his approaching 300 cavalrymen, plus 1,200 infantry and gunners trudging along with 8 fieldpieces and 12 machine guns, were plainly visible and so gave ample warning to Obregón. As Medina Barrón's relief force drew near to Santa Rosa station, ambushes by Sonoran sharpshooters took a considerable toll, especially among the mounted federal troopers, who proved easy targets.

Medina Barrón nonetheless joined Eguiluz's and Santibáñez's vanguard units and deployed their combined forces into a battle line that extended for about a half mile from the cluster of houses around Santa Rosa station, and both armies exchanged gunfire over the next two days. As evening fell on the second night of May 10, 1913, the Sonorans managed to capture a prominence west of the rail line and repulsed three separate counterattacks that the *federales* mounted into the darkness with heavy losses. Fire slackened throughout May 11, 1913, as both sides grew increasingly weary and low on ammunition until the Sonoran right flank under Col. Manuel M. Diéguez managed a daring maneuver at about 4 p.m. that brought them to within 100 yards of the federal batteries, obliging the latter to redeploy into a more crowded and untenable position.

Bloodied, exhausted, thirsty, and almost out of ammunition, Medina Barrón's army retired from Santa Rosa station as darkness fell that same evening of May 11, 1913. Obregón would report that they left behind 422 dead and 180 prisoners, as well as six machine guns, 200 Mauser rifles, 230 saddles, 40 horses, 25 mules, etc. His own forces had suffered nine officers and 33 troops killed, plus 10 officers and 79 men wounded.

Aftermath (May–June, 1913)

Although a shipment of a half million rounds reached the victorious Sonorans at dawn on May 12, 1913, Obregón knew that his men were too spent to pursue the defeated *federales*, who were regrouping at Maytorena station in anticipation of withdrawing still further back into Empalme and Guaymas. Upon reporting on his success to Governor Pesqueira, Obregón was recommended on May 21, 1913, for promotion to brigadier general (which was conferred by the constitutionalist government of Venustiano Carranza on June 29th). By that time, Obregón had lured a second federal army under Ojeda into another disastrous defeat at the Battle of Santa María, leaving the surviving federal garrison helpless and besieged within Guaymas.

See also: Huerta Márquez, José Victoriano; Máuser; Obregón Salido, Álvaro; Revolution, Mexican; *rurales*; Yaqui War.

Further Reading

Barragán Rodríguez, Juan. *Historia del Ejército y de la Revolución Constitucionalista.* Mexico City: Instituto Nacional de Estudios Históricos de la Revolución Mexicana, 1985, 1: 147–48, 659–71.

Obregón, Álvaro. *Ocho mil kilómetros en campaña.* Mexico City: Viuda de Charles Bouret, 1917, 86–93.

Sánchez Lamego, Miguel A. *Historia militar de la Revolución constitucionalista.* Mexico City: Biblioteca del INEHRM, 1956, primera parte, 1: 141–62.

Santos Degollado. Nickname for the liberal general who was born on October 30, 1811, and baptized two days later as José Nemesio Francisco Degollado Sánchez— but because that particular baptismal date of November 1st coincided with the *día de Todos los Santos* or "All Saints Day" on the

Church calendar, the young child would become more commonly known as Santos Degollado throughout his lifetime.

For his full biographical entry, *see* Degollado Sánchez, José Nemesio Francisco (1811–1861).

Schneider-Canet 75mm field gun

French-built artillery piece, several dozen of which were purchased by Mexico's Federal Army in the first decade of the 20th century as part of its modernization efforts under the regime of Pres. Porfirio Díaz.

In particular, the version bought by Mexico was the "Model 1907" or "M.1907," only one in a series of numerous different models and calibers of field-guns that had been designed for manufacture by the armaments firm of Schneider et Compagnie of Le Creusot by its design engineer Gustave Canet, so that they were commonly referred to as "Schneider-Canet" guns. These simple, sturdy weapons proved to be the standard artillery piece for the Porfirian Army, and many were also captured by their revolutionary foes such as Pancho Villa and Álvaro Obregón. Although nowhere near as powerful or accurate as the Mondragón 75mm gun, they were more plentiful and reliable.

In late April 1918, the U.S. military attaché in Mexico City—Capt. Robert M. Campbell—estimated that the Mexican Army had four heavy field artillery regiments in total, each one armed with 16 Schneider-Canet 75mm guns, plus an assortment of other pieces and mountain howitzers operated by six further regiments and 28 detached field batteries.

See also: Díaz Mori, José de la Cruz Porfirio; Mondragón 75mm field gun.

Further Reading

Estudio comparativo de los cañones de 75mm. de tiro rápido, Schneider-Canet, St. Chamond-Mondragón y Krupp. Mexico City: Secretaría de la Defensa Nacional, 1902.

Sedgwick's Intervention (1866)

Unauthorized cross-border venture by the regional U.S. Army commander stationed at Brownsville, Texas, an action that was quickly disavowed by the authorities in Washington.

Following the defeat and withdrawal in June 1866 of the Mexican imperial army, which had been garrisoning the border city of Matamoros in the northeastern state of Tamaulipas during the War of the French Intervention, the republican colonel

Portrait of U.S. major general John Sedgwick, ca. 1864. (Library of Congress)

Servando Canales Molano had subsequently secured the title of its governor through local machinations by mid-August 1866, prompting a sharp objection from the government of Pres. Benito Juárez. Brig. Gen. Santiago Tapia had been sent with 1,500 soldiers to arrest Canales and assume the governorship, although he was denied entry into Matamoros on November 3, 1866, and so set up a siege camp outside—where he died of cholera eight days afterward.

Gen. Mariano Escobedo, commander-in-chief of the republican *Cuerpo del Ejército del Norte* or "Corps of the Army of the North," was thereupon ordered to take another 1,500 troops and join this initial besieging force, so as to remove Canales from office to be tried as a rebel. Escobedo arrived at the existing siege camp outside Matamoros on the evening of November 19, 1866, and was surprised to be greeted with an invitation to visit with the U.S. brevet brigadier general Thomas D. Sedgwick across the river in Brownsville.

In the interim, this U.S. general had occupied Matamoros from Brownsville, citing fears for the safety of American citizens. Fortunately, Escobedo reacted reasonably to this unilateral intervention onto Mexican soil, and senior American officials would soon be recalling Sedgwick. Escobedo nonetheless prepared to storm Matamoros' walls at dawn of November 27, 1866, so as to comply with his original instructions for arresting Canales. After a half-hour bombardment, republican columns fought their way into the city until a ceasefire was requested by both the Americans and mutineers. Escobedo agreed, withdrawing to instead institute a close siege. Canales subsequently surrendered on November 30,

1866, the Americans evacuated, and Escobedo entered Matamoros.

See also: Escobedo Peña, Mariano Antonio Guadalupe; French Intervention, War of the.

Further Reading

Escobedo, Mariano. *Parte general dado al Supremo Gobierno sobre los sucesos de Matamoros, con documentos importantes.* Matamoros, Tamaulipas: Imprenta del Gobierno, 1866.

Message of the President of the United States of January 29, 1867, Relating to the Present Condition of Mexico. Washington, DC: U.S. Government Printing Office, 1867, 543–55.

Silao, Battle of (1860)

Liberal victory during the closing stages of the War of the Reform that helped to hasten the final collapse of conservative resistance and bring about an end to this three-year-old conflict.

Preliminary Maneuvers (August 1–9, 1860)

Faced with a growing number of ever-stronger liberal forces that had begun appearing throughout central Mexico and were closing in on his depleted army from various directions, the conservative "substitute president" and commander-in-chief—28-year-old major general Miguel Miramón—retreated southeastward out of the city of León in early August 1860, withdrawing in the direction of Querétaro in hopes of making a stand there so as to bar their path into the national capital. However, while still only 20 miles along on the first phase of this retreat, Miramón was overtaken while resting his 3,300 demoralized soldiers, 1,300 militia auxiliaries, and

18 guns on the grounds of the Hacienda de la Noria, on the northern outskirts of the small city of Silao in the state of Guanajuato.

The vanguard of Gen. Jesús González Ortega's pursuing liberal army crested the nearby Lomas de las Ánimas high ground at 1:00 p.m. on August 9, 1860, clashing with some conservative patrols, whose main army could be clearly discerned a few miles behind them in the distance. Having thus established contact with his retreating enemy, Ortega directed his able subordinate, Brig. Gen. Ignacio Zaragoza, to begin marshaling the liberal regiments that were continuing to arrive along the highway into a battle-ready formation while Ortega and his cavalry commander, Brig. Gen. Antonio Carbajal, searched for a good spot in which to encamp their army overnight. Selecting a stretch of ground due west of Silao, the 8,000 liberal soldiers and their 38 fieldpieces were ensconced into defensive positions and eating their dinners by 4:30 p.m. without any interference from the watching Miramón, who merely rearranged his own army into an extended line behind the banks of a small stream.

However, a reconnaissance made by Ortega that same evening revealed that the intervening terrain consisted mostly of muddy plains around the city, which were almost impassable due to repeated summer rains. Therefore, he and Zaragoza quietly and skillfully moved 21 liberal artillery pieces through the rain after midnight on August 9–10, 1860, into concealed emplacements only 700 yards from the conservative lines, beside the highway running in from León into Silao, whose packed earth provided the firmest footing around. These batteries were to each be supported by a full infantry division and cavalry brigade on their flanks, a total of 3,000 troops who were to spearhead the assault against the conservative army the next morning—but until then lying prone in the early morning darkness, waiting to be called on to rise and charge behind covering fire from their artillery.

And even before this main thrust went forward, liberal brigadier general Manuel Doblado was supposed to begin making feints at dawn from his headquarters at the Hacienda del Sauz out on the far right, and Brig. Gen. Felipe Berriozábal was to do the same out on the far left so as to divide and dilute conservative resistance.

Battle of Silao (August 10, 1860)

First light on that drizzly Friday morning, August 10, 1860, revealed the newly redeployed liberal positions to the waiting conservatives, whose frantic *toques* or "bugle calls" from their frontline units—signaling "enemy in front, in great numbers"—could be plainly heard by the liberal assault troops lining prone in the grass. Miramón ordered his own artillery to open up a counterfire as early as 5:55 a.m., and an intense gun duel ensued over the next couple of hours, producing such a towering column of smoke that it could be seen as far away as León, 21 miles distant.

Shortly before 8:00 a.m., Zaragoza informed Ortega that his prone assault columns were starting to suffer some casualties from this protracted artillery exchange, so the liberal commander finally gave the order for his guns to redouble their fire and for his infantry to rise and proceed with their attack. Zaragoza personally led the Zacatecas Division on the liberal right with his own Del Centro Division advancing on the left, both columns of soldiers roaring out *Viva la libertad!* or "Long live liberty!" before moving up at double-time behind their screens of cavalrymen.

Having anticipated such a charge into his central battle line, Miramón had massed a body of conservative lancers out on his right flank under his trusty subordinate, Gen. Tomás Mejía, who was to strike the liberals from the side as they rushed past. But Zaragoza's advance proved to be so measured and steady with regular pauses to fire well-aimed volleys into any defensive concentration and then reload before proceeding, that conservative units—beginning with the Carabineros Battalion and 5th Line Regiment—began throwing down their weapons and fleeing toward the rear. This contagion of fear quickly spread, so within 20 minutes the conservative army was broken and dissolving into wholesale panic. Mejía's formation of lancers out on the right was abruptly abandoned by their own support battery, whose gunners simply ran away at the sight of this liberal onslaught, so Mejía's lancers scattered too with the liberal cavalry in hot pursuit.

Many of Miramón's infantrymen rushed back into the streets of Silao, desperately seeking a means of escaping toward Querétaro. Unable to reorganize them into any kind of cohesive military formation, the conservative commander became engulfed himself by 9:00 a.m. in this chaos and gave up all attempts to continue giving unheeded orders. The liberal colonel Jesús Lalanne would later publish a newspaper account in which he described how Miramón was intercepted in this confusion by a body of liberal irregulars known as the *cosacos* or "Cossacks," but who failed to recognize him in their eagerness to secure his magnificent palomino stallion, named the *Dorado* or "Golden One." While trying to corner this beautiful horse among some stone fences at Aguas Buenas Ranch, they did not notice the conservative commander jumping over

a nearby fence, during which action he dropped his plumed general's hat. When the *cosacos* subsequently learned whom they had let escape, they "pulled their hair out by fistfuls, desperate because of the prize which they had let slip away, simply in order to seize his mount."

González Ortega reported that his men found over 70 dead and 207 wounded conservative soldiers on the battlefield in the immediate aftermath of the battle, along with all their artillery and baggage trains (which had been stripped of their draft horses and mules by the deserting troops, stealing them as mounts so as to ride away). The victorious liberal general estimated his own casualties at more than 100 men, while incorporating the captured guns into his own batteries. González Ortega moreover treated his vanquished prisoners magnanimously, releasing most of the rank-and-file conscripts the next day after simply accepting their paroles that they would play no further role in the war.

Aftermath (August 12–September 7, 1860)

Miramón somehow managed to gallop away from Silao with a handful of men, but his whereabouts remained unknown for a couple of days, during which it began to be rumored that he had been killed. The former conservative president Félix M. Zuloaga, who had been traveling as a captive in Miramón's train, managed to regain the national capital and attempted to reclaim the office of president, only to fail because of his utter lack of conservative support. In any event, Miramón reappeared in Mexico City by the night of August 12, 1860, and although temporarily obliged to relinquish office as "substitute president" was restored to power by a vote of confidence two days later and desperately began seizing money and men so as to raise a new army.

But the victorious liberals would not immediately close in on Mexico City. González Ortega gained the city of Querétaro against scant opposition, only to then install a garrison of 4,000 men and 14 artillery pieces under Generals Berriozábal and Benito Quijano before reversing his main army and marching back westward on September 7, 1860—in obedience of Degollado's orders, as "general-in-chief of the Federal [constitutionalist] Army"—to first subdue Guadalajara, the last major conservative-held stronghold before commencing any final push toward the national capital.

See also: Degollado Sánchez, José Nemesio Francisco; González Ortega, José Canuto de Jesús; Miramón Tarelo, Miguel Gregorio de la Luz Atenógenes; Reform, War of the; Zaragoza Seguín, Ignacio; Zuloaga Trillo, Félix María.

Further Reading

Cambre, Manuel. *La guerra de Tres Años*. Guadalajara, Jalisco: Biblioteca de Autores Jaliscienses, Gobierno del Estado, 1949, 468–80.

Doblado, Manuel. *La guerra de Reforma*. San Antonio, TX: Lozano, 1930.

"Important from Mexico: Details of Miramón's Defeat." *New York Times*, September 25, 1860.

soldaderas

Name for the wives or female companions who trailed behind 19th- and early 20th-century Mexican armies, preparing meals whenever their companies encamped, tending to any injuries or wounds, washing laundry, etc.

In his *Reminiscences of the Mexican Revolution*, the transplanted Irishman Patrick A. O'Hea recalled the appearance at his remote hacienda outside of Torreón, in the northern state of Coahuila, by a crack federal cavalry regiment under the aristocratic general Aureliano Blanquet late in 1911:

> Even before their unexpected arrival, there reached us the vanguard of the *soldaderas*, wives or camp-followers, that were indispensable even to Mexican regular troops for lack of commissariat.
>
> These little Indian women, with their wrap-around or bunched skirts in dark figured stuff topped by embroidered blouses or chemises, often with a baby slung in the invariable *rebozo* or shawl, with black hair parted, beribboned and braided, with feet free of footwear, at a short-stepping trot had no fear of failure to keep up with the cavalry on its regular marches. Like locusts they descended upon the outraged villagers, robbing the roosts, capturing squawking fowls and even squealing piglets, gathering the scanty sticks for the fire over which to have a black pot simmering and flat maize tortillas heating on the embers, as soon as the dust-masked troopers might be ready for their fare.

Over the many decades of warfare in Mexico, observers would speak admiringly of the unwavering strength, loyalty, and compassion displayed by such women, on which the young rank-and-file soldiers very much depended.

See also: *adelitas*.

Further Reading

Salas, Elizabeth. *Soldaderas in the Mexican Military: Myth and History*. Austin: University of Texas Press, 1990.

Mexican privates of the 14th Battalion in Torreón, early 1914; within a few weeks, their unit would be pulverized by Pancho Villa's attack. (Library of Congress)

soldado raso

Expression in Mexico for the lowest rank of soldier, equivalent to the American term "buck private."

The adjective *raso* can be generally used in the Spanish language to identify anything flat or smooth or bare, as in *terreno raso* for "flat ground," *cielo raso* for "clear sky," *vuelo raso* for "low-level flight," etc. In the particular case of a *soldado raso*, this term is meant to denote an individual without any military rank or title whatsoever, being simply a "plain soldier." The 19th-century Mexican Army considered the next rank up from *soldado raso* to be *soldado de guardia* or "guard private," in other words a soldier with sufficient basic training and experience to be entrusted with manning a guard post. Next highest was *soldado de primera clase* or "private first-class," followed by *cabo* or "corporal," etc.

Many famous insurgent and liberal commanders began their military careers as *soldados rasos*—men such as Juan N. Álvarez, Mariano Escobedo, Ignacio Zaragoza—in contrast with their royalist or conservative foes, whose aristocratic births meant that they entered military service as junior officers. In one particularly telling example, the mutinous conservative officers who surrendered to the victorious liberal army at Puebla in March of 1856 were punished by being demoted to *soldados rasos* and made to march in the soldiers' ranks back into Mexico City, carrying their own backpacks.

The designation was also quite commonly recognizable and used in everyday speech, such as when the Zacatecan major general Pedro Hinojosa wrote to liberal governor Santiago Vidaurri of Nuevo León in February 1859, following their unexpected defeat at the hands of the conservatives: "I shall do whatever is in my power, be it as even a mere *soldado raso*, to reconquer the glories which through a fatality we lost at Ahualulco."

See also: Ahualulco de los Pinos, Battle of; *escalafón general*; Escobedo Peña, Mariano Antonio Guadalupe; Puebla, Conservative Revolt and Liberal Sieges of; Zaragoza Seguín, Ignacio.

Further Reading

Martínez Cárdenas, Leticia. *Para efectos de la guerra: correspondencia Santiago Vidaurri-Pedro Hinojosa, 1855–1864.* Monterrey, Nuevo León: Archivo General del Estado de Nuevo León, 2000, 25.

The troops, who had been through much fighting, descended into a period of listlessness, during which their officers could scarcely make themselves be obeyed.

— federal major general Eutiquio Munguía, describing the final terrible hour before the fall of Torreón (October 1913)

Tacubaya, Plan de (December 1857)

Conservative proclamation intended to repudiate the reforms made to Mexico's Constitution by its liberal Congress, while leaving the moderate president Ignacio Comonfort in office—although this *pronunciamiento* was backed by a staged coup that would unwittingly pave the way for a real military mutiny, thereby launching the so-called War of the Reform.

Mounting Tensions (February–November 1857)

In the wake of Santa Anna's expulsion from the presidency for the final time in August 1855 and the crushing of armed conservative outbursts throughout Puebla in 1856, liberal politicians set about rewriting and modernizing Mexico's Constitution, an opportunity that they had been seeking for decades. Upon the promulgation of their first few "reformed" articles on February 5, 1857, some of which either curtailed or did away with traditional privileges left over since colonial times, an angry reaction began to develop among certain sectors. Many Church leaders, in particular, expressed resentment against these proposed changes, railing publicly against these and future "radical" measures that might do away with even more traditional values and thus threatening to excommunicate any government official who might be sworn into office under the authority of this "reformed" Constitution.

As public disapproval began to mount, moderates such as Comonfort (who had been serving over the previous two years as Mexico's "provisional president") grew uneasy. He therefore secretly entered into talks in hopes of reaching an accommodation with select statesmen from both liberal and conservative factions, meeting in the archbishopric of Tacubaya on the outskirts of Mexico City as of November 15, 1857, a couple of weeks prior to assuming office as duly elected president. Even after being sworn in on December 1, 1857, Comonfort continued to seek an escape from adhering to this controversial new body of laws until rumors began to circulate six days later that his trusted subordinate, Brig. Gen. Félix María Zuloaga, was sounding out military commanders about a possible coup. A hearing to look into this seditious matter was convened by the newly seated republican Congress on December 14, 1857, but nothing was uncovered before the conspirators struck.

Pronunciamiento (December 17, 1857)

At 6:00 a.m. on December 17, 1857, a 21-gun salute was fired in Tacubaya and Zuloaga—in the presence of Comonfort,

Gov. Juan José Baz of Mexico City's Federal District, and other conservative leaders—announced the "Plan of Tacubaya" from its archbishopric (a document that had been drawn up by Comonfort's own son-in-law, Manuel Siliceo, among others). Its six brief points called for Comonfort to remain in office as interim president for another three months, ruling with a cabinet of appointed ministers, while the liberal Constitution would be suspended immediately until a new Congress could be convened so as to draft a more moderate replacement "in keeping with the national will." Zuloaga marched that same day unopposed from Tacubaya into Mexico City's *Ciudadela* or "Citadel" at the head of his brigade, consisting of 1,200 troops of the 1st Engineer Battalion under Col. Domingo Nava, the Activo "México" Light Infantry Battalion under Col. Marco Esnaurrízar, and two batteries of artillery under Col. Zeferino Rodríguez, to be joined there by other units.

The Plan of Tacubaya was simultaneously telegraphed to every state governor, winning approval over the next few days from Puebla, Tlaxcala, Veracruz, the state of Mexico, Chiapas, Tabasco, and San Luis Potosí. After feigning reluctance for two days, Comonfort himself accepted and publicly swore adhesion to the plan's six terms on December 19, 1857, issuing a lengthy nationwide circular to explain his reasons. On this same date, some conservative ministers furthermore resigned from his cabinet as well so as to trigger the dissolution of the liberal Congress, while prominent opponents such as the president of the Republican Congress, Isidoro Oltivo, and president of the Supreme Court, Benito Juárez, languished in jail.

Second Conservative Coup (January 11, 1858)

However, resistance to the conservatives' forced revocation of the Constitution in the national capital quickly caused numerous liberal states to begin mobilizing for war. Comonfort vainly tried to patch up these differences by steering a course that appeased liberals and conservatives alike, to no avail. After three weeks of confused indecision, conservative general José de la Parra led the Tacubaya garrison in a second coup on January 11, 1858, this time intending to remove the ineffectual Comonfort from office altogether in favor of the figurehead Zuloaga.

These mutineers seized the Ciudadela and San Agustín Church, while Comonfort held out in the Presidential Palace with perhaps 3,000 men, and independent liberal forces occupied the Santísima and San Francisco Churches as their separate strongholds. After 10 days, this tense three-sided standoff was broken when the youthful conservative colonels Luis G. Osollo and Miguel Miramón successfully assaulted Comonfort's positions at dawn on January 21, 1857, defeating his last disheartened followers and driving him completely from office. Before departing Mexico City that same day, the disgraced Comonfort ordered Juárez released from prison, who—being legally next in line to the succession of that office—traveled clandestinely to the city of Guanajuato, proclaimed himself president shortly thereafter, and began organizing liberal resistance against the conservatives.

Meanwhile, an extemporized body of 22 leading conservative figures dubbed the *Junta de Notables* convened in Mexico City and elected Zuloaga as "interim president" on January 22, 1857, with Parra as his minister of war, who in turn promoted both Osollo and Miramón to brigadier generals. Within a few weeks, both young military officers would lead a conservative army northward into the Bajío, and the War of the Reform would erupt in full force.

See also: Bajío; Miramón Tarelo, Miguel Gregorio de la Luz Atenógenes; Osollo Pancorbo, Luis Gonzaga; *pronunciamiento*; Puebla, Conservative Revolt and Liberal Sieges of; Reform, War of the; Zuloaga Trillo, Félix María.

Further Reading

"Additional from Mexico: Formidable Coalition against the Dictator—Bloody Civil War in Prospect—Distracted Condition of the Republic." *New York Times*, January 19, 1858.

Cambre, Manuel. "Civil War in Mexico." *New York Times*, January 19, 1858.

"Later and Important from Mexico: Pronunciamientos against Comonfort—Fighting Taken Place—Confusion Supreme." *New York Times*, January 27, 1858.

Cambre, Manuel. *La guerra de Tres Años: apuntes para la historia de la Reforma.* Guadalajara, Jalisco: Gobierno del Estado, 1949, 1–19, 28–30.

"Resistance in Northern Mexico," *New York Times*, January 27, 1858.

Tacubaya, Battle of (1859)

Major victory for Mexico's conservative centralists, won during the second year of the War of the Reform against a liberal federalist army that had arrived to invest the national capital.

Prelude (March 22–April 2, 1859)

The main conservative army under Maj. Gen. and "substitute president" Miguel Miramón having marched out of Mexico City one month previously, to trudge hundreds of miles down out of the central highlands and besiege the exiled liberal government of Pres. Benito Juárez within the coastal city of Veracruz, a number of liberal forces had combined during this temporary absence under Gen. José Santos Degollado in the Bajío so as to threaten the lightly defended national capital. Pushing through the states of Guanajuato and Querétaro, Degollado's liberal forces materialized outside Mexico City by March 22, 1859, occupying its satellite communities of Tacubaya and Chapultepec with more than 6,000 troops, while 2,400 trailing conservatives of the División del Norte under Brigadier Generals Gregorio del Callejo and Tomás Mejía—who had been harrying this liberal offensive ever since it exited Querétaro—managed to circle around and enter the capital as well two days afterward, augmenting the strength of Maj. Gen. Antonio Corona's garrison to 4,000 defenders.

Degollado soon realized that his liberals were insufficient in numbers to fully encircle the capital, and—lacking any heavy artillery—he was reluctant to storm its defenses directly. Corona's conservative garrison therefore remained safely ensconced behind strongpoints around Mexico City's perimeter, heartened by news that Brig. Gen. Leonardo Márquez was coming from Guadalajara to their relief. In vain did the liberal commander Degollado wait for an insurrection to erupt among the capital's populace so as to facilitate its fall until he finally authorized a military probe in strength.

Shortly before dawn on April 2, 1859, his subordinate, Brig. Gen. Ignacio Zaragoza, stealthily approached with 1,500 men to test the conservative detachments holding the Tlaxpana suburb and San Cosme *garita* or "guard station," failing to surprise these outposts at 4:00 a.m. due to the defenders' high state of watchfulness. Zaragoza was instead compelled to fall back into San Francisco Church under heavy fire, having suffered some 40 dead and 60 wounded during his initial assault, then slipping away southwestward after nightfall so as to return into the main liberal encampment at Tacubaya.

Conservative Relief and Victory (April 7–11, 1859)

Five days later, Márquez entered the beleaguered capital with his conservative relief column from Guadalajara and felt ready to counterattack the besiegers by April 10, 1859. First, he and his second-in-command, Brig. Gen. Tomás Mejía, held a mass review at 6:00 a.m. that Sunday morning in its Zocalo or main square, then led out 10 infantry battalions organized into three brigades under Brigadier Generals Francisco Vélez, José Quintanilla, and Ignacio Orihuela, plus two cavalry brigades for a total of 5,500 soldiers and 22 guns, against the liberal forces. Exiting through San Cosme Gate, Márquez's conservative army passed through Hacienda de los Morales and wound its way around the foothills so as to emerge from the woods beside Chapultepec Hill, cresting the western ridge overlooking Tacubaya by 4:00 p.m. Half an hour later, Márquez opened up a long-range bombardment against the distant liberal entrenchments below with some 20 pieces, who replied—equally ineffectually—with their fewer number of guns. Firing ceased on both sides as evening fell.

The next dawn, Monday, April 11, 1859, Márquez paraded his troops at 6:00 a.m., then one hour later launched a column of some 2,000 soldiers behind heavy covering fire from his batteries toward the Molino de Valdés, a liberal strongpoint "in the highest part of Tacubaya." Degollado's few artillery pieces could make little response to this shelling, the liberals instead waiting until their advancing foes had come within close range before checking this opening charge with their rifle fire. A second conservative infantry assault against this stronghold met the same fate, so Márquez shifted his batteries farther forward to Molino del Rey, into the folds of Chapultepec Hill and into La Condesa.

His resumed bombardments from this closer range, plus the inexorable pressure from his infantry, finally wore down liberal resistance over the next three hours, so their lines began to waver by 10:00 a.m. and gave way entirely an hour later. The liberal militia's retirement from the battlefield quickly turned into a rout, fragmented companies streaming southwestward out of the Valley of Mexico to flee haphazardly back toward Jalisco and Michoacán. Márquez wrote immediately from his field headquarters in Chapultepec Castle to General Corona within Mexico City, reporting on his victory in the following terms:

The arms of the Supreme Government have triumphed completely over the bandits who were threatening the capital of the Republic. The brave troops whom I am proud to command, have obtained this victory, fighting hand-to-hand over the ground and not only defeating the enemy, but also wrenching from them all their artillery, ammunition, wagons, armaments, and other war-implements, including the tunic with a Major-General's insignia worn shamelessly by the infamous Degollado, who has never served the nation, nor even belonged to the noble calling of the arms.

Among the prisoners which were taken, are the ex-[army] General Marcial Lazcano and many other officers, who have already paid at the execution-spot [*patíbulo*] for the crime which they have committed.

Márquez's directive that every high-ranking liberal captive be executed—including medical personnel, plus civilian and foreign detainees, among these at least three American neutrals—would mar his reputation and earn him the sobriquet of the *Tigre de Tacubaya* (an expression roughly equivalent to the "Beast of Tacubaya" in the English language), although years later he would rather unconvincingly insist that this brutal order had been issued without his knowledge or consent by the conservative president Miramón during his inspection tour of the field after fighting ceased.

Miramón had in fact belatedly regained the Valley of Mexico that same Monday afternoon, having traveled on ahead of his main conservative army, which was marching back to help defend the capital after being withdrawn from its siege of Veracruz. Entering Mexico City with a few staff officers aboard the stagecoach from Puebla, Miramón immediately secured a mount and galloped to the scene of the Battle of Tacubaya, just after this engagement had concluded, to find the liberal prisoners already executed and their survivors streaming off into the distance in defeat. His own army being still many miles away, Miramón was annoyed to discover that his old rival Márquez would reap all the accolades for defeating Degollado and rescuing the national capital.

Aftermath (April 12–19, 1859)

Shortly past noon on Tuesday, April 12, 1859, Márquez led a triumphal parade back into the cheering capital by his victorious army and even received the "blue band" signifying promotion to the rank of major

general from the hands of Miramón himself. Meanwhile, the defeated Degollado—escorted by his loyal subordinate, Brig. Gen. Leandro Valle, and the Lanceros de Jalisco cavalry regiment—overtook Zaragoza's retreating División del Norte that same Tuesday, being the only liberal formation that had managed to escape intact from the disaster. Together, both formations continued retiring and reabsorbing scattered liberal fragments as they trudged through Villa del Carbón, Niguini, Teocatitlán, and Jordana until they reached Maravatío, where Degollado ordered Zaragoza to split off for Guanajuato with his northern contingent, while Degollado continued toward Morelia with his western forces.

Márquez did not emerge from Mexico City in pursuit until one week later, on April 17, 1859, pushing uncontested into Morelia with his 3,000 soldiers 12 days afterward, long after Degollado had passed through that city (and whose 2,000-man liberal garrison commander, Brig. Gen. Epitacio Huerta, would simply exit and then reclaim Morelia once the conservative army proceeded on toward Guadalajara). Although eventually driven as far back as Colima following his resounding defeat at Tacubaya, Degollado would nonetheless console his liberal supporters by pointing out that their failed thrust toward the national capital had at least obliged Miramón to lift his siege of Veracruz, while Márquez's departure from Guadalajara with a sizeable rescue force had weakened the conservative grip on Jalisco, leading to a liberal revival.

See also: Degollado Sánchez, José Nemesio Francisco; Márquez Araujo, Leonardo; Miramón Tarelo, Miguel Gregorio de la Luz Atenógenes; Reform, War of the; Veracruz, Conservative Sieges of; Zaragoza Seguín, Ignacio.

Further Reading

Cambre, Manuel. *La guerra de Tres Años: apuntes para la historia de la Reforma.* Guadalajara, Jalisco: Gobierno del Estado, 1949, 237–41.

"The Massacre at Tacubaya." *Harper's Weekly*, 3, no. 127, June 4, 1859, front page.

"The News from Mexico." *New York Times*, 8, no. 2377, May 3, 1859, front page.

Tecoac, Battle of (1876)

Unexpected victory that would sweep Porfirio Díaz into the presidency of Mexico for the first time, a position that he would then dominate over the next 34 years.

Background (January–October 1876)

Dissatisfied after learning that Benito Juárez's liberal successor, Sebastián Lerdo

Porfirio Díaz late in life, photographed some 35 years after the Battle of Tecoac. (Library of Congress)

de Tejada, was intending to run for a second presidential term in 1876, Díaz had issued his "Plan of Tuxtepec" on January 10th of that same year, calling for an anti-reelectionist revolt in southern Mexico—but that failed to shake the Lerdista administration's firm grip on power. Instead, its able minister of war, Gen. Ignacio Mejía, had quickly taken effective countermeasures that smothered Díaz's uprising in the south, and then checked a second attempt made by him to cross back into the country from Brownsville, Texas, so as to personally foment another insurrection in the north. Despite his defeats in both theaters, and his followers' lack of heavy weaponry or materiel, Díaz and his allies had nonetheless maintained a series of guerrilla raids and strikes against isolated army detachments that sustained an undercurrent of unrest throughout the nation.

As a result, the financially pressed Lerdista authorities were constrained to gradually increase local taxation and impose other unpopular measures over the summer months in order to meet their mounting military expenditures, while vainly pursuing their elusive foes. And a few weeks after the disputed election itself, Lerdo de Tejada was unexpectedly declared the winner by Mexico's pliant Congress on September 26, 1876—a controversial decision that prompted José María Iglesias, head of the Supreme Court (and therefore next in line to the presidency), to void this result as having been illegally obtained and instead claim the office of president for himself.

Compelled to flee the national capital because of threats from Lerdista loyalists, Iglesias had taken sanctuary among his supporters in Guanajuato, from where he then trumpeted his legal right to the presidency as of October 31, 1876, calling for the removal of Lerdo de Tejada by force of arms.

Battle of Tecoac (November 16, 1876)

Díaz (who had already revised the terms of his original Plan de Tuxtepec on a couple of occasions so as to accommodate to these changing circumstances) was among the first to heed this call and hastened to rejoin his reassembling forces in the region of Tlaxcala and Puebla. As early as November 2, 1876, rebels under his faithful northern subordinate, one-armed general Manuel González, had seized the railroad station at tiny Apizaco, Puebla, and begun dismantling its rails and trestle bridge so as to cut communications from the national capital. Two days afterward, González's 2,000 men had absorbed 700 troops under Gen. Francisco Tolentino's command, who were defecting from the government cause.

President Lerdo and his ministry of war, now under the direction of Gen. Mariano Escobedo, had responded to these developments by dispatching 600 additional soldiers from Mexico City to Tepeaca, Puebla, so as reinforce the regional commander, Gen. Ignacio R. Alatorre, with orders to confront these upstarts in a battle. Díaz cabled González from Acatlán on November 8, 1876, advising him that he was drawing near, which in turn prompted Alatorre to break camp two days later and march in quest of the rebels, now knowing them to be close. One week later, Díaz's 4,000 lightly armed irregulars—an agglomeration that he had grandly titled the *Ejército Regenerador de la República Mexicana* or "Regenerative Army of the Mexican Republic"—encamped on the evening of November 15, 1876, on the rolling farmland of the Hacienda de Tecoac, a ranch located just north of the small town of San Luis Huamantla in the state of Tlaxcala within sight of the Malinche Volcano.

Alatorre's 3,000 government troops rested that same night near Huamantla and the next morning bore down confidently on the more numerous but less powerful rebel army. Díaz positioned his men atop some nearby hills and sent messengers to urge González to hasten from Tlaxco to his support, allowing Alatorre to occupy the hacienda uncontested to serve as his field headquarters. The better-armed government forces advanced and long-range firing erupted at 10:00 a.m., gradually wearing down the rebels over the next five hours, although neither body of troops fought with any great resolve.

Still, Díaz seemed to be teetering on the brink of defeat by 3:00 p.m. when he suddenly heard two guns being fired in the distance, signaling the timely arrival of his reinforcements. Over that ensuing hour, four rebel columns appeared: one of 1,000 riders under González; another under Brig. Gen. Juan N. Méndez; a third under Quartermaster Gen. Juan Crisóstomo Bonilla; plus a force of rural Tlaxcaltecan militiamen under Gen. Luis León. Their combined strength of 3,800 men so significantly bolstered the crumbling rebel lines that their arrival turned the tide of battle.

Confronted by ever-larger numbers of fresh opponents emerging opposite them, the morale of the federal army broke. With only a half-hearted commitment to the Lerdo administration to begin with, Alatorre's companies and regiments soon began to give up. Casualties had been relatively modest on both sides, yet the wholesale surrender of the federal army presented Díaz with a couple of thousand captives (who would likely switch allegiances), plus all their military-grade weaponry, artillery train, and supplies.

Aftermath (Late November 1876)

Dismayed by the scope of his army's abrupt collapse and defeat, Alatorre rode away from the battlefield toward Santa Anna Chiautempan as night fell with only a small group of staff officers and escorts, returning to Mexico City by November 19, 1876. In the meantime, news of more and more army units beginning to defect to the rebel cause was already being received by President Lerdo de Tejada, so two hours past midnight on that very same night of November 19–20, 1876, he slipped out of the sleeping capital to flee west toward Acapulco with only his cabinet ministers and a few hundred militia troopers, eventually sailing away into exile in the United States—much to everyone's surprise when it was discovered the next morning that he had absconded.

In the resultant vacuum of power, political detainees were freed and Mexico City's garrison commander, Gen. Francisco Loaeza, sent a messenger to personally greet the approaching Díaz at nearby Tepexpan, assuring him that there would be no resistance to his entry into the capital. Indeed, the rebel commander was greeted with ringing church bells when his train pulled into Buena Vista station at 3:15 p.m. on the afternoon of November 23, 1876, although public reaction was muted.

See also: Díaz Mori, José de la Cruz Porfirio; Escobedo Peña, Mariano Antonio Guadalupe.

Further Reading

"Another Mexican Revolution: Porfirio Diaz Defeats the Government Forces, Drives Out Lerdo de Tejada, and Assumes the Office of Provisional President." *New York Times*, December 8, 1876.

Esposito, Matthew D. "The Politics of Death: State Funerals as Rites of Reconciliation in Porfirian Mexico, 1876–1889." *The Americas* 62, no. 1 (July 2005): 65–94.

Telaraña, Operación (1971)

One phase of an increasingly ruthless series of counterinsurgency campaigns conducted by the Mexican Army in the state of Guerrero to run down the elusive leftist guerrilla leader Lucio Cabañas.

Operation *Telaraña* (Summer 1971)

Inspired by Mexico's revolutionary past and other contemporary 20th-century Marxist heroes such as Che Guevara, Cabañas and a few score armed followers from his *Partido de los Pobres* or "Party of the Poor" had begun kidnapping or robbing wealthy victims, then disappearing with their proceeds into the rugged Atoyac range, where they enjoyed a great deal of grassroots support. Determined to crush this small movement before it could spread, the administration of newly inaugurated president Luis Echeverría Álvarez secretly authorized his secretary of defense, Gen. Hermenegildo Cuenca Díaz, to begin implementing a stepped-up military operation code-named *Telaraña* or "Cobweb" as of May 1, 1971. (This name had been deliberately chosen to underscore its intelligence-gathering purpose, representing a spider spinning its web and then waiting for one of its extended tendrils to quiver as a victim passed over it.)

Officers headquartered at Acapulco and responsible for the Mexican Army's *27a. Zona Militar* or "27th Military Zone"—which encompassed the entire state of Guerrero—had already been vainly trying to capture Cabañas for a couple of years. This new operation allowed them to establish a frontline base at El Ticui and deploy at least 3,100 soldiers to hunt for their quarry, assisted by three helicopters operated by the federal police. Extralegal detentions and abuse of scores of family members or associates of Cabañas and his older mentor, Genaro Vázquez, failed to produce any results beyond alienating the civilian populace and generating negative publicity in the press. Within a few months, this particular army operation ended without having located any of the wily guerrilla's hideouts.

Continual Hunts (1972–1973)

The search for Cabañas would continue for another three years, going through at least another dozen operational code names, but *Telaraña* was the one that stuck in the public mind. Cabañas and 20 guerrilla companions ambushed a Mexican Army convoy at Arroyo Las Piñas near San Andrés de la Cruz, Guerrero, killing 10 soldiers and wounding 18 on June 25, 1972. Another attack at nearby Arroyo Oscuro on August 23, 1972, which left 18 more soldiers dead, 9 wounded, and 11 captured, goaded the army into deploying five fresh infantry battalions, as well as thousands of state policemen, who inflicted ever-more brutal reprisals throughout the region in another vain effort to capture his band, which they estimated must number at least 150 guerrillas.

That following year, faced with increased hostility from Cabañas's growing guerrilla movement in the Atoyac range, the Mexican Army launched yet another operation by pushing in columns to relieve its isolated garrisons. On November 11, 1973, one such 300-man convoy was ambushed and suffered 4 soldiers killed between the hamlets of Yerbasantita and Las Compuertas, so the authorities replied by initiating yet another sweep code-named *Operación Luciérnaga* or "Operation Firefly," which involved sending a trio of heavily armed, mobile columns into remote areas. But Cabañas merely shifted from one jungle camp to another

with his 100–150 followers, so after a week of fleeting skirmishes against their elusive quarry, the army also wound down this particular operation.

The next summer, Cabañas seized the senator (and soon to be elected governor of the state of Guerrero) Rubén Figueroa Figueroa on June 2, 1974, holding him for ransom. This act sparked yet one more massive military operation and cruel roundups throughout the region, which again failed to corner Cabañas or his core of 60 faithful fighters, so Gen. Salvador Rangel Medina was relieved of command as of August 5, 1974, and replaced by Gen. Eliseo Jiménez Ruiz. The large-scale operation was terminated and a ransom of 50 million *pesos* was eventually paid for the captive Figueroa, although 60 elite troops under Lt. Col. Juan López Ruiz then intercepted his guerrilla guards as they approached El Huicón to release the senator on September 8, 1974, killing three and scattering the remainder.

Conclusion (Autumn 1974)

With his hostage freed and his personal followers located, the manhunt for Cabañas was renewed by 5,000 Mexican troops in one final operation, surprising the wily guerrilla leader and 14 of his companions shortly after noon on October 11, 1974, near Los Toronjos in the Tecpan range. Making his escape over the Achotla Mountain after nightfall, Cabañas was nonetheless left with only a group of four companions, while his mother, wife, and three-week-old daughter were captured two weeks later at Tixtla by an army detachment.

Eventually, Mexican troops of the 19th Battalion under Capt. Pedro Bravo Torres— guided by a captive—overtook Cabañas's small fugitive band near El Ototal, 12 miles northwest of Tecpan de Galeana, at 9:00 a.m. on December 2, 1974, who killed himself rather than being taken alive. Two soldiers were slain and five wounded during the exchanges of gunfire, which virtually ended all revolutionary activity in the mountains of Guerrero. During the protracted campaign to hunt him down, at least 650 civilian captives had lost their lives at the hands of the authorities, such a toll in human lives that this "dirty war" would long be remembered in the public mind—although curiously as Operation *Telaraña*, the name of only its opening phase.

See also: Cabañas Barrientos, Lucio.

Further Reading

Blacker, O'Neill. "Cold War in the Countryside: Conflict in Guerrero, Mexico." *The Americas* 66, no. 2 (October 2009): 181–210.

Montemayor, Carlos. *Guerra en el paraíso.* Mexico City: Seix Barral, 2008.

Suárez, Luis. *Lucio Cabañas: el guerrillero sin esperanza.* Mexico City: Grijalbo, 1976.

Teoloyucan, Treaties of (1914)

Accord reached during the Mexican Revolution that not only surrendered the national capital to the advancing forces of Gen. Álvaro Obregón but furthermore dissolved Mexico's entire federal army.

Collapse of the Huertista Regime (June–July 1914)

His regime already crumbling and beset by victorious foes on all sides, the usurper president Victoriano Huerta's sevent17een-month-old administration proved too weak to even raise a token resistance against the American occupation of Veracruz in late April 1914. His last major armies were then pulverized at the Battle of Zacatecas by Pancho Villa on June 23, 1914, and outside Guadalajara by Obregón at the Battle of Orendáin on July 7, 1914, so a mere eight days afterward, the failed dictator resigned from office and fled Mexico City toward Veracruz, along with his minister of war, Gen. Aureliano Blanquet, so as to both sail away into exile in Europe.

The reins of the defeated Huertista administration were temporarily assumed by the next in line to the presidential succession—the head of the Supreme Court and minister of foreign relations, the civilian lawyer Francisco S. Carvajal—who sought to simply arrange a peaceful surrender of the government and national capital to the rapidly approaching *Cuerpo del Ejército Constitucionalista del Noroeste* or "Corps of the Constitutionalist Army of the Northwest" under the victorious Obregón.

The latter's revolutionary subordinate Alfredo Robles Domínguez duly met with the interim minister of war, Maj. Gen. José Refugio Velasco, as early as August 9, 1914, persuading him to withdraw the federal garrison from Mexico City without attempting to mount a fight against such overwhelming odds. Two days later, after Carbajal had formally stepped down as acting president, the military governor Eduardo Iturbide of Mexico City, accompanied by diplomats from Brazil, France, Great Britain, Guatemala, and the United States, was driven out toward the revolutionary encampment at Teoloyucan and—halfway between Cuautitlán and that town in the state of Mexico, on the fender of a mud-spattered car—signed a preliminary agreement with Obregón.

The formal "treaties of Teoloyucan" were actually signed in the Ejército del Noroeste camp on August 13, 1914 by Generals Obregón, Lucio Blanco, and Othón P. Blanco on behalf of the *primer jefe* or "first chief" of the constitutionalist movement, Venustiano

Carranza, and by federal generals Velasco, Lauro Villar, and Gustavo A. Salas for the capitulating regime. This agreement was to become known by the pluralized name of "treaties of Teoloyucan," as it encompassed two separate agreements: one detailing the conditions for the peaceful surrender and occupation of Mexico City, another laying out the terms for the remnants of its defending garrison to evacuate the capital and for the entire federal army to be thereupon dissolved.

The next dawn, the remnants of the once proud federal army exited their bases and shuffled disconsolately through the streets to board various trains, then were transported eastward in the direction of Puebla and dropped off by the thousands at different remote stations with vouchers to simply find their best ways home. Meanwhile, Obregón's triumphant Army of the Northwest—now 18,000 strong—paraded into the capital at noon on August 15, 1914, occupying the vacated federal quarters and arsenals by nightfall.

See also: Huerta Márquez, José Victoriano; Obregón Salido, Álvaro; Orendáin, Battle of; Revolution, Mexican; Zacatecas, Battle of.

Further Reading

Ramírez Rancaño, Mario. *El ejército federal, 1914: semblanzas biográficas.* Mexico City: Universidad Nacional Autónoma de México, 2012.

Sáenz, Aarón. *Los históricos tratados de Teoloyucan.* Mexico City: Patronato de la Historia de Sonora, 1964.

Texas, Insurgency in Spanish (1811–1813)

Antimonarchist rebellion that flared up a few times over the span of three years, yet failed to wrest this remote borderland from Crown control.

When Fr. Miguel Hidalgo's initial insurrection against Spanish Peninsular rule erupted in central Mexico on September 16, 1810, Texas was a vast yet sparsely populated province on the distant northeastern fringe of the viceroyalty of New Spain. Word of Hidalgo's inflammatory rhetoric nonetheless spread among its populace, and the royal Spanish governor Manuel María de Salcedo soon began to suspect that the loyalty of his militia officers was becoming subverted.

Short-Lived Casas Revolt (January 1811)

After arresting a couple of junior officers, Salcedo found that when he ordered his militiamen at San Antonio to prepare to march south in mid-January 1811 so as to preemptively check the spreading insurgency at the Rio Grande, his command was met with mutinous grumbling. The garrison was unhappy at the prospect of leaving their families unprotected against Indian hostilities and facing starvation without hunting parties, just to mount border patrols during wintertime, while San Antonio's *alcaldes* did not wish to be pressed into military duties during the militia's absence. A couple of delegates consequently called on Juan Bautista de las Casas, a retired militia captain, asking him to assume command over the garrison.

The next morning, January 22, 1811, Casas led the rebellious militia in arresting the Spanish governor and his military commander, as well as ordering the release of the two detained subalterns. Casas then furthermore began incarcerating *gachupines* or European-born Spaniards in the district and confiscating their properties, while dispatching 80 troops to establish a similar insurgent government at Nacogdoches as well. This contingent reached there on February 1,

1811, succeeding in their commission and returning with more prisoners and booty. Casas, who had grown increasingly autocratic, had some participants from this expedition briefly detained for pocketing confiscated items and neglected to inform the insurgent government in Coahuila of this force's achievement. The slighted revolutionaries subsequently began conspiring with the remaining royalists in San Antonio and found a leader in the licentious subdeacon and militia lieutenant colonel Juan Manuel Zambrano.

Events came to a head when Hidalgo's subordinate, Ignacio Aldama, reached San Antonio with a retinue at the end of February 1811 on a commission to proceed into the United States with a substantial sum of money and silver so as to buy weapons that would better arm insurgent troops. After determining that Aldama would not remove Casas from the governorship, Zambrano and his fellow conspirators spread the rumor that Aldama was actually a Napoleonic agent. Then on the evening of March 1, 1811, 10 men gathered in Zambrano's home some miles outside San Fernando and proceeded into San Antonio, where they persuaded the garrison overnight to support their cause. Early the next morning, the group formed a 12-member junta with Zambrano as their president, swearing an oath "to religion, King Ferdinand VII, and the country." When Casas and Aldama realized that these counterrevolutionaries controlled the 400 troops, they surrendered and were sent to Monclova for trial, conviction, and execution. Less than three weeks later, Hidalgo, Allende, and the other rebel figureheads were treacherously arrested by retired militia captain Francisco Ignacio Elizondo at Acatita de Baján on March 21, 1811, and likewise handed over to Governor de Salcedo at Monclova next day in exchange for a royalist reward.

Gutiérrez-Magee Expedition (Winter of 1812–1813)

Prior to his betrayal and capture, the insurgent leader Hidalgo had dispatched a second emissary to seek help from the American government, colonel José Bernardo Gutiérrez de Lara. His meetings with officials in Washington in December 1811 having received only vague offers of help, this insurgent officer sailed to New Orleans with a letter of introduction to Gov. William C. C. Claiborne, who provided assistance in raising a force of armed adventurers near Natchitoches, Louisiana.

On August 8, 1812, colonel Gutiérrez de Lara recrossed the Sabine River into east Texas with 130 American volunteers, the ex-U.S. Army lieutenant Augustus W. Magee acting as the expedition's lieutenant colonel. This so-called Republican Army of the North seized undefended Nacogdoches four days later, a couple of hundred more recruits being added, while royalist support collapsed throughout the eastern portion of Texas. Trinidad was easily overrun by mid-September 1812, where the invaders remained encamped for more than a month.

On November 2, 1812, royalist governor de Salcedo and Col. Simón de Herrera sallied east from San Antonio with 1,500 troops, deploying them along the Guadalupe River. Learning of this move, Gutiérrez de Lara's and Magee's army (now numbering 800 men) slid south-southwest, overwhelming the tiny Spanish coastal keep at Bahía del Espíritu Santo [modern Goliad] on November 7th. De Salcedo thereupon pursued and trapped the outnumbered insurgents within this place, bombarding its ramparts with 14 fieldpieces; but after three failed assaults, a protracted siege ensued.

Before any decisive action could take place, Magee died of disease on February 6,

1813, being succeeded in command by Samuel Kemper. Four days later, Salcedo attempted to storm the walls, only to be driven back; a second assault on February 13, 1813 fared no better, the Mexican royalists having endured some 300 casualties in total. Salcedo and Herrera therefore decamped for San Antonio on February 19, 1813, followed two days afterward from Espíritu Santo by Gutiérrez de Lara at a safe distance.

Battle of Rosillo (March 28, 1813)

Kemper moved out in a belated pursuit a month later with 800 men, including volunteers from Nacogdoches, deserters from the Spanish army, and Indian warriors. Royalist Col. Simón de Herrera challenged their advance with 1,500 regulars, 1,000 militiamen, and 12 artillery pieces at Rosillo (nine miles southeast of the Texan provincial capital, on a ridge along the banks of Salado Creek). The Americans, cleverly using their Indian allies to charge directly into the Spanish cavalry, quickly outflanked the royalist infantry and defeated them in 15–20 minutes, inflicting 330 deaths and capturing 60 prisoners. Insurgent losses totaled six killed and 26 wounded.

On April 1, 1813, Governor de Salcedo sent out his terms for San Antonio's capitulation to the victorious Gutiérrez de Lara at Concepción Mission, who refused and even detained the emissaries. The next morning, the Texan capital was occupied and the captive De Salcedo and Herrera were murdered at Rosillo along with a dozen other royalists on April 3, 1813, by their insurgent escort under Antonio Delgado. The *República del Norte* or "Republic of the North" was subsequently proclaimed three days later, symbolized by a green flag. The execution of the royalist officers caused many American volunteers to abandon the enterprise at once; a few days later, having lost confidence in Gutiérrez and his provisional government, Kemper led more than 100 Americans back to Louisiana on "furlough."

Battle of Alazán Creek (June 20, 1813)

Organization of the Spanish effort to recover Texas for the Crown fell to Col. Joaquín de Arredondo and his subordinate, Lt.-Col. Francisco Ignacio Elizondo. Acting more or less independently, the latter invaded Texas with a detachment of 3,000 badly trained Mexican conscripts in early June 1813, intent on avenging the insurgent deposal and murder of Governor de Salcedo by Gutiérrez de Lara. Although under orders from his superior Arredondo to advance no farther north than the Frío River, Elizondo progressed to the very outskirts of San Antonio, camping with 900 men on the banks of Alazán Creek by June 16, 1813, and challenging its republican army to battle. Reuben Ross, successor to Kemper in command of the remaining Americans, advised a retreat; but when a council of war refused to support him, he resigned and was followed in office by Henry Perry.

Although outnumbered, the new American leader Perry led the defenders out after nightfall on June 19, 1813, charging across the Alazán next dawn with the sun behind him to crush the royalists in a four-hour fight, and returned into San Antonio with considerable booty. Elizondo sustained 400 casualties and fled to Laredo, trying to rally his scattered forces while Arredondo was marching to supersede him. A month and a half later, the unpopular Gutiérrez de Lara would be overthrown as insurgent leader by his Cuban rival José María Álvarez de Toledo, with support from the American diplomat William Shaler.

Battle of Atascoso (August 18, 1813)

Álvarez de Toledo arrived at Bexar on August 1, 1813, and Gutiérrez left for Natchitoches five days afterward, at which time Shaler's substitution plot was put into effect. Most of the Americans supported the new commander, Álvarez de Toledo; but several Mexicans, led by Col. José Menchaca, attempted to prevent Toledo from moving promptly against Arredondo's advancing royalist forces and avoid his junction with Elizondo.

His small army badly demoralized by these intrigues, Álvarez de Toledo's 850 American troops and 600 Cochate Indian allies marched out of San Antonio on August 15, 1813, taking up a defensive position on the Medina River two days later. They encountered a 180-man cavalry patrol under Lieutenant Colonel Elizondo, who engaged and retreated back across the Medina, drawing the insurgents on toward Colonel Arredondo's main body. About five miles away at Atascoso Creek, the pursuers found 1,200 royalist riders and 700 infantrymen drawn up with their artillery. A four-hour battle ensued, in which Arredondo routed the republicans and their American filibuster allies, brutally executing 112 prisoners, including numerous Americans.

Aftermath

Álvarez de Toledo, Perry, and other republican leaders fled toward Louisiana, effectively ending the insurgent rebellion in Texas. Arredondo entered San Antonio and inaugurated a harsh pacification policy, royalist firing-squads shooting 327 persons dead in that city, while one of his lieutenants carried out a similar bloody purge in Nacogdoches. Yet despite the military triumph of the royalists, complete peace could not be restored in Texas. The province would remain subject to plots or fears of invasion, until Agustín de Iturbide finally brought the War of Independence to an end.

See also: *gachupín*; Hidalgo y Costilla Gallaga, Miguel Gregorio Antonio Ignacio; Independence, War of; Peninsular.

Further Reading

Almaráz, Félix D., Jr. *Tragic Cavalier: Governor Manuel Salcedo of Texas, 1808–1813*. Austin: University of Texas Press, 1971.

Chabot, Frederick Charles, ed. *Texas in 1811: The Las Casas and Sambrano Revolutions*. San Antonio, TX: Yanaguana Society, 1941.

Texas Revolution (1835–1836)

Modern name for the insurrection against centralist Mexican rule that resulted in the creation of the breakaway Republic of Texas.

Background (June 1834–July 1835)

Disapproving of the liberal reforms that had been enacted by his civilian vice president Valentín Gómez Farías and the Mexican Congress during his six-month leave of absence from the presidency, Santa Anna reassumed office and dissolved that legislative body by mid-June 1834. Calling for new elections, he set about rescinding many liberal measures that had been based on the federalist Constitution of 1824 and instead directed his political machinations toward imposing a strong centralist government over the disordered young republic—monopolistic measures that would be resented in many outlying provinces such as Texas.

In February 1835, Santa Anna's new conservative Congress passed a law reducing each state's militia forces to just one soldier for every 500 inhabitants, thus ensuring that his regular army would be the

1835; Mexican Dragoons in Texas War.

An ink-and-watercolor drawing of a Mexican dragoon during the Texas campaign of 1835, by Francisco Ferrer Llull. (Anne S. K. Brown Military Collection, Brown University Library)

preeminent military force in the nation. Zacatecas, the best-armed state with 4,000 militiamen under arms and another 16,000 in reserve, openly defied this decree and began to prepare for a military confrontation. But Santa Anna struck fast, suddenly materializing with 4,000 soldiers less than nine miles from the Zacatecan capital on May 10, 1835, easily defeating its army and sacking the defenseless city as punishment.

Alarmed by reports of this swift strike against Zacatecas, federalist officials of the combined government of Coahuila and Texas fled from their capital of Monclova into Texas on May 21, 1835, leaving Col. Martín Perfecto de Cos (a longtime retainer

of Santa Anna) in command of the centralist garrison at Saltillo. He would soon be reinforced and ordered to Matamoros by the beginning of July 1835, to prepare to lead an expedition into Texas and stamp out its anticentralist dissenters.

Texian Defiance (September–December 1835)

Cos disembarked with 500 soldiers at the tiny port of Copano, about 30 miles north of present-day Corpus Christi, on September 20, 1835, pushing some 50 miles up the San Antonio River to occupy the small presidio town of Goliad by October 2, 1835. Leaving behind a garrison of 30 soldiers, he then pressed on with his main force into San Antonio. The arrival of his expedition brought to a head the long-held grievances from its Texian settlers, whose original expectations upon receiving citizenship in this Mexican province had been eroded over the years and were now about to be submerged altogether by this arbitrary imposition of authoritarian rule from Mexico City.

Therefore, Cos's detachment at Goliad was surprised and overwhelmed one week afterward by 50 Texian volunteers from nearby Victoria under George M. Collinsworth, and by the end of October 1835 a small Texian army under Stephen F. Austin—after a few minor clashes—imposed a loose siege on Cos's unhappy garrison, composed of a battalion of regulars and five companies of conscripts.

On November 3, 1835, a Texian convention at San Felipe resolved to oppose the dictatorship of Santa Anna as loyal Mexican citizens, upholding its federal constitution of 1824, while furthermore calling on other Mexican states to oppose his rule. One month later, militia colonel Benjamin R. Milam led the Texian besiegers in an assault into the very streets of San Antonio,

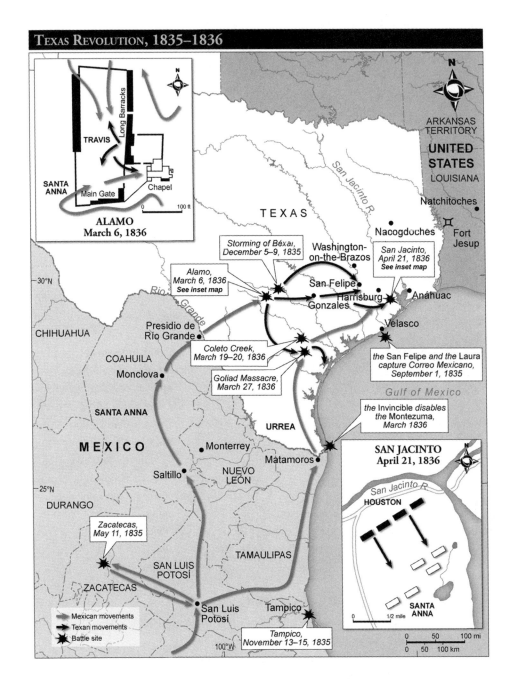

TEXAS REVOLUTION, 1835–1836

ALAMO
March 6, 1836

Storming of Béxar,
December 5–9, 1835

Alamo,
March 6, 1836
See inset map

San Jacinto,
April 21, 1836
See inset map

San Felipe
Harrisburg
Gonzales

Washington-
on-the-Brazos

Nacogdoches

Anáhuac

Velasco

Coleto Creek,
March 19–20, 1836

Goliad Massacre,
March 27, 1836

Presidio de
Río Grande

the San Felipe and the Laura
capture Correo Mexicano,
September 1, 1835

CHIHUAHUA

COAHUILA

Monclova

SANTA ANNA

MEXICO

Monterrey

URREA

Matamoros

the Invincible disables
the Montezuma,
March 1836

SAN JACINTO
April 21, 1836

HOUSTON

SANTA
ANNA

Saltillo

NUEVO
LEÓN

DURANGO

Zacatecas,
May 11, 1835

ZACATECAS

SAN LUIS
POTOSÍ

San Luis
Potosí

TAMAULIPAS

Tampico

Tampico,
November 13–15, 1835

Mexican movements
Texan movements
Battle site

Gulf of Mexico

ARKANSAS
TERRITORY

UNITED
STATES

LOUISIANA

Natchitoches

Fort
Jesup

pressing Cos's men back into the Alamo by December 5, 1835. Four days afterward, Cos sued for terms, and soon more than 1,100 Mexican troops would begin evacuating Texas. Winter now having set in, many of the victorious Texians decamped in the erroneous belief that the campaign was over.

Santa Anna's Descent
(January–March 1836)

However, the Mexican president reached Saltillo on January 7, 1836, and quickly began organizing a large army so as to invade Texas and impose his dictates. Within three weeks, Santa Anna was heading north with one cavalry and two infantry brigades, plus a siege train, to join Brig. Gen. Joaquín Ramírez y Sesma's army, which was already operating near the Río Grande. A total of 6,050 soldiers comprised the invasion force, heavily outnumbering Texas's defenders. News of Santa Anna's swift approach was received at San Antonio by February 11, 1836, but a heavy snowfall two days later was expected to delay him. The Mexican commander-in-chief nevertheless drove his men on hard, and the first 1,500 mounted elements were sighted only a mile and a half outside San Antonio at dawn on February 23, 1836, much sooner than anticipated.

The 150 surprised Texian defenders and 25 noncombatants sent a courier requesting help from James W. Fannin's force at Goliad before gathering inside the fortified Alamo. They were invested that same afternoon by the vanguard of Mexican cavalrymen, and although reinforced by 32 more volunteers from Gonzales after midnight of February 29–March 1, 1836, were wiped out by a four-pronged assault by 1,700 Mexican soldiers on the morning of March 6, 1836.

Following this massacre, Santa Anna began sending out detachments the next day from his San Antonio encampment, resuming his campaign to subdue all of rebellious Texas. Brig. Gen. José de Urrea chased the small Texian garrison out of Goliad, who were later captured and murdered, while Ramírez y Sesma set off in pursuit of the 375 Texians at Gonzales under Gen. Sam Houston, who began a long eastward retreat when this Mexican column appeared on March 11, 1836. The Texian government of Pres. David G. Burnet also fled, along many panic-stricken civilians.

Reversal of Fortunes (April–May 1836)

Leaving Maj. Gen. Vicente Filisola in command of his reserves at San Antonio, Santa Anna personally pressed hundreds of miles farther east into Texas and with 900 picked troops attempted to surprise the fugitive Texian government at its temporary headquarters in Harrisburg on April 16, 1836, burning this town to the ground when it was found empty. Shortly thereafter, Houston turned with 900 troops to seek battle, and in a completely unexpected outcome, routed Santa Anna and his resting army at San Jacinto on the afternoon of April 21, 1836, capturing the dictator along with 730 of his surviving troops.

With the Mexican president and general-in-chief in their power, the Texians were able to demand the withdrawal of the centralist expedition back south of the Río Grande, which Filisola obeyed as of May 26, 1836. However, the government in Mexico City repudiated any arrangements extorted from the captive Santa Anna and refused to acknowledge the demands for autonomy proposed by Texian representatives. Soon, the province would instead break away to become the Republic of Texas and by 1845 a state of the United States.

See also: Alamo, Siege of the; Cos Muñoz, Martín Perfecto; San Jacinto, Battle of (1836); Santa Anna, Antonio López de.

Further Reading
Benson, Nettie Lee. "Texas Viewed from Mexico, 1820–1834." *Southwestern Historical Quarterly* 90, no. 3 (1987): 219–91.

Binkley, William C. *The Texas Revolution.* Baton Rouge: Louisiana State University Press, 1979.

Hardin, Stephen L. *Texian Iliad: A Military History of the Texas Revolution.* Austin: University of Texas Press, 1994.

Lack, Paul D. *The Texas Revolutionary Experience: A Political and Social History.* College Station: Texas A&M University Press, 1992.

Thord-Gray, Ivor (1878–1964)

Swedish-born adventurer who served as a soldier of fortune during the Mexican Revolution, proving a valuable member on the staff of Gen. Álvaro Obregón.

He was born on April 17, 1878, as Thord Ivar Hallström, in the Södermalm district of central Stockholm, the second of three sons of a schoolteacher named August Hallström and his wife, Hilda. Thord's older brother, Gunnar August, would become a well-known artist, while his younger brother, Gustaf, would achieve some fame as an archeologist.

Young Thord had completed only a few years of his own schooling, when he joined the merchant marine at the age of 15 and sailed away aboard a steamer in 1893. After serving on a couple of other vessels, he went ashore in December 1895 at Cape Town, to remain in South Africa for more than a decade.

Early Military Career (1897–1909)

He first served briefly as a prison guard in 1896 on Robben Island and then enlisted the next April as a 19-year-old private in the mixed-race Cape Mounted Riflemen, fighting in both the Bechuanaland and Pondoland campaigns that same year of 1897. Anglicizing his surname into "Gray," Hallström continued to serve in this regiment throughout the Second Boer War of 1899–1902 and afterward became a corporal in the South African Constabulary in July 1902, quickly rising to lieutenant by February 1903. He was promoted to captain of the Lydenburg Militia in the Transvaal during 1904–1905 and after his offer to raise a Schutztruppe to serve in German Southwest Africa (modern Namibia) was rebuffed, became a captain in Royston's Horse by July 1906. This unit of irregular cavalry had participated in the fighting against the Natal Rebellion and been accused of killing five Zulu prisoners in cold blood, so were disbanded shortly thereafter.

Before that year was out, Gray had traveled to Kenya and enlisted with the Nairobi Mounted Police in November 1906, then proceeded to the American-controlled Philippines to become a member of its constabulary by December 1907. A few years later, the adventurous Gray learned of the outbreak of the Mexican Revolution in late 1910, so traveled across the Pacific to the American Southwest in hopes of enlisting with one of its factions.

Service in Mexico (1911–1914)

He introduced himself to Pancho Villa shortly after that revolutionary's seizure of Ciudad Juárez (opposite El Paso, Texas) in mid-November 1913, and upon proving himself capable of replacing the missing firing pins for the rebels' two captured 75mm Mondragón field-guns, was appointed first captain of Villa's artillery. Gray fought them during the subsequent Battle of Tierra Blanca and was rewarded by promotion to major in the revolutionary army as of Christmas Day 1913. It has further been recorded that Villa named a nearby railway junction *El Sueco* or "The Swede" in his honor, which it still bears today.

However, Gray moved into Mexico's northwestern state of Sonora a few months later, taking up service with the more studious general Álvaro Obregón with the rank of lieutenant colonel as of March 10, 1914. He fit in well with Obregón's compact but disciplined *Ejército del Noroeste* or "Army of the Northwest," recruiting fierce Yaqui warriors as his personal troop and rising to colonel as Obregón drove down through Guadalajara toward Mexico City. He even dispatched Gray on a special mission with a message for Emiliano Zapata before the Swede learned of the outbreak of World War I in Europe and departed to participate in that conflict.

Later Years (1914–1964)

Gray served as an officer in the Northumberland Fusiliers for much of World War I, then joined the Canadian Expeditionary Force sent into Russia as a lieutenant colonel in October 1918. Switching into the Russian imperial cavalry as a colonel of the Siberian Storm Division in February 1919, then as a Cossack major general by late November 1919, he was entrusted with a trainload of gold bullion during the dying days of the Romanoff dynasty, which ensured his fortune. Leaving behind his military career, Gray traveled to New York City and established a brokerage and bank, becoming extremely wealthy. Late in life, having retired to Florida, he would write a valuable Tarahumara-English dictionary as well as his memoirs about serving in Mexico.

See also: Ejército del Noroeste; Obregón Salido, Álvaro; Revolution, Mexican; Tierra Blanca, Battle of; Villa, Pancho; Yaqui War; Zapata Salazar, Emiliano.

Further Reading

Bojerud, Stellan. *Soldat Under 13 Fanor.* Stockholm: Sivart Förlag, 2008.

Thord-Gray, Ivor. *Gringo Rebel: Mexico, 1913–1914.* Coral Gables: University of Florida Press, 1960.

Three Guarantees (1821)

Common principles enunciated by the royalist officer Agustín de Iturbide so as to bring insurgents and monarchists together with the purpose of ending Mexico's War of Independence on mutually agreeable terms.

Background (1820)

By 1820, the viceroyalty of New Spain was exhausted by its decade-long struggle to throw off Crown rule from Madrid. Insurgents dominated the countryside and small towns but were too poorly armed and disorganized to defeat the few Spanish regiments and loyalist militiamen who held all of the major cities. However, the support of many Creole royalists was shaken after an army mutiny in Spain had reimposed a liberal constitution on Mexico's viceregal administration as of the spring of 1820, including certain provisions aimed at curtailing aristocratic, clerical, and military prerogatives. This development seemingly undermined loyalist hopes of retaining their traditional values and privileged status intact, so many began to waver and consider some measure of separation from Madrid.

Late that same year, the royalist colonel Agustín de Iturbide—a pitiless commander in the past, who had executed hundreds of insurgent prisoners that fell into his hands—had been recalled from suspension and given the thankless task of campaigning during the winter months of 1820–1821 against Vicente Guerrero's elusive guerrilla bands in the lowlands of southern Mexico. After a few failures, Iturbide unexpectedly contacted that insurgent chieftain on January 10, 1821, to suggest that they suspend hostilities and instead forge a coalition to achieve Mexico's independence on terms that would satisfy rebels and loyalists alike.

Three Guarantees (1821)

Guerrero initially suspected a trap, yet Iturbide issued a public proclamation from his base at Iguala on February 24, 1821, that incorporated broad principles that most of the divided viceroyalty's antagonists could accept. Although a lengthy document, the main tenets of Iturbide's *Plan de Iguala* could be simply summarized as consisting of three focal points or "guarantees":

- Religion—meaning a continued predominance of the Catholic faith
- Independence—calling for a separation from Spain
- Union—signifying the consensus required from all Mexican factions

In practical terms, the ex-royalist colonel believed that conservative values would be maintained by declaring the Catholic Church the paramount religious institution of the newly emergent nation, while furthermore specifying the creation of a constitutional monarchy to govern it, which in turn would recognize and respect already-existing colonial titles regarding land grants, wealth, etc. Insurgent aims would be satisfied by declaring outright independence from Spain and then convening a congress of Mexicans to draft a national constitution, which could address such questions as individual rights and impose limits on the powers of the new constitutional monarchy.

Although bitterly denounced and disavowed by the Spanish viceroy Juan Ruiz de Apodaca in Mexico City, Iturbide's proposal soon turned into an unstoppable movement, in part because of the easily memorable appeal of its core message—the *Tres Garantías* or "Three Guarantees"—which even became incorporated into its new tricolor flag, whose white segment was supposed to represent religion, while green stood for independence, and red for the union of all Mexicans.

See also: Ejército Trigarante; Guerrero Saldaña, Vicente Ramón; Independence, War

of; Iturbide Arambúru, Agustín Cosme Damián de.

Further Reading

Anna, Timothy E. *Forging Mexico: 1821–1835*. Lincoln: University of Nebraska Press, 1998, 85–89.

Di Tella, Torcuato. *National Popular Politics in Early Independent Mexico, 1820–1847*. Albuquerque: University of New Mexico Press, 1996.

Rodriguez O., Jaime E. *"We Are Now the True Spaniards": Sovereignty, Revolution, Independence, and the Emergence of the Federal Republic of Mexico, 1808–1824*. Stanford, CA: Stanford University Press, 2012.

Three Guarantees, Army of the (1821–1822).

See Ejército Trigarante (1821–1822), as well the Appendix in the section titled "Independent Mexico's 'Ejército Trigarante' in September 1821."

Three Years, War of the (1858–1860).

In Spanish, the *Guerra de los Tres Años*, another name for the 19th-century conflict between liberals and conservatives known as the War of the Reform or Reforma. *See* Reform, War of the (1858–1860).

Tierra Blanca, Battle of (1913)

First significant military victory won by Pancho Villa's emergent new army in a pitched battle against a major federal force—rather than in mere hit-and-run strikes against detached units or outposts—thus signaling his rise to real power during the Mexican Revolution.

Prelude (August–November 1913)

An uneducated former bandit who had recently escaped from imprisonment into the United States, Villa had joined the renewed round of antigovernment fighting after Gen. Victoriano Huerta betrayed and murdered Pres. Francisco I. Madero in the national capital in February 1913, seizing the presidency for himself. Six months later, Villa had raised a following of 700 lightly armed riders, whom he led in a successful string of guerrilla raids against isolated Huertista garrisons in the northern state of Chihuahua. Because of these victories, he had attracted even more rebel chieftains to his side, who then agreed to coalesce into a united force under his command on September 26, 1913, merging their diverse regional bands into 19 "brigades," with Villa as their chosen commander-in-chief. This patchwork army was dubbed the *División del Norte Constitucionalista* or "Constitutionalist Division of the North"—a rival to the long-standing federal force that was already operating officially on behalf of Huerta in Chihuahua with the designation of "División del Norte."

Although numerous, Villa's undisciplined horde had proven incapable of dislodging the main Huertista garrison holding the state capital of Chihuahua City under its military governor, Gen. Salvador R. Mercado, despite repeated assaults made over the course of four days in early November 1913. Villa therefore feinted southward before doubling back and leading his army north on November 13, 1913, chancing to intercept a civilian coal train that same afternoon at El Cobre, between the rural Cruz and Terrazas railway stations, as it was cautiously venturing down the tracks toward Chihuahua City from the border town of Ciudad Juárez (opposite El Paso, Texas).

Villa terrified its conductor into telegraphing back to his dispatcher, reporting that the tracks into the state capital had been destroyed, so the train was ordered to return.

Villa thereupon emptied its hoppers of coal and hid with some 2,000 troops aboard its 18 empty cars, ordering another 2,500 riders to trail along behind this train by following its tracks. Securing each successive telegraph station that they reached, Villa compelled their operators to maintain a stream of false messages northward indicating that all was well until his train came gliding into unsuspecting Ciudad Juárez shortly past midnight on November 14–15, 1913. Two columns of *villistas* were immediately sent from the station into the sleeping city under Maclovio Herrera and José Rodríguez to surprise its Huertista garrison under Brig. Gen. Francisco Castro, plus the local *colorado* militia auxiliaries. Ciudad Juárez was secured within less than two hours, Castro escaping across the river into internment in Texas with some 300 regulars from his 23rd Infantry Battalion, while Villa sent Rodolfo Fierro back southward with two trains of flatcars so as to bring in his reinforcements and artillery under Col. Martiniano Servín.

Ciudad Juárez's Villista occupiers meanwhile seized all the heavy weaponry and armaments found in its federal arsenal, relieved its private gambling establishments of millions in currency, and conducted several hundred summary executions (despite Villa's personal leniency in many cases). Only the commander of the local Huertista irregulars, the *colorado* militia general José Inés Salazar—responsible for security along the very railway line that Villa had so cunningly breached—made any attempt to defend Ciudad Juárez before escaping into its neighboring district with some of his men.

Battle of Tierra Blanca
(November 1913)

Upon learning that Ciudad Juárez had been seized by Villa, General Mercado—in his capacity as the state's military governor—issued orders on November 20, 1913, for a large convoy of 11 trains to be prepared and hasten northward up the single track in staggered departures from Chihuahua City, bearing a mixture of regular soldiers under his subordinate federal brigadier generals José Jesús Mancilla and Manuel Landa, plus contingents of mounted *colorado* irregulars under Marcelo Caraveo, Antonio Rojas, Rafael Flores Alatorre, Benjamín Argumedo, and Blas Orpinel—almost 5,500 men in total, backed by 8 artillery pieces and 10 machine guns. Their instructions apparently were to detrain and deploy the federal troops and heavy weaponry into battle formation so as to help Ciudad Juárez's displaced *colorado* commander, Salazar, launch a second attempt at reclaiming the city, while the mounted irregulars were to pursue the Villista occupiers as they tried to flee with their booty.

However, rather than dispersing—as had been the common practice up until then by rebel forces—Villa instead chose to stand and fight a pitched battle when informed that this relief column was on its way. The *El Paso Herald* newspaper reported in its weekend edition of Saturday, November 22, 1913, how Villa had exited Ciudad Juárez at 9:00 a.m. that same morning aboard a locomotive, running about 15 miles south to reconnoiter the terrain and choose a battleground before instructing Rosalío Hernández to hold a position between the rural Bauche railway station and hamlet of Samalayuca with his brigade while Villa returned into Ciudad Juárez by 11:00 a.m. He immediately directed almost 3,500 more troops to board five trains, along with 10 artillery pieces (including 2 captured Mondragón 75mm field guns) and a dozen machine guns, leaving Juan N. Medina in command of the city with a garrison of some 1,500 Revolutionaries, plus another eight guns and a machine gun battery left behind in reserve.

By early afternoon on November 22, 1913, Villa was detraining about 10 miles south of Ciudad Juárez, deploying his 5,000 men and 10 guns into a ragged 7-mile battle line between the Bauche station and hamlet of Tierra Blanca so as to make his stand there. This terrain was well chosen, his army taking up positions atop a ridge of low hills that overlooked an open expanse of sandy dunes below known locally as *Tierra Blanca* or "White Ground," which would hamper any enemy charge, with Villa's command post established atop the Mesa high point at its center.

- On his left, Villa stationed the Brigada "Morelos" under José Rodríguez and Brigada "Leales de Camargo" under Rosalío Hernández.
- Next came the Villista artillery under Servín, the two heavy 75mm's captured at Ciudad Juárez being worked on the day of battle by the Swedish-born soldier-of-fortune Ivor Thord-Gray with the temporary rank of "first captain."
- In the center were the Brigada "Villa" under Toribio Ortega and Brigada "González Ortega" under Porfirio Ornelas.
- On the right were Maclovio Herrera's Brigada "Juárez" and the Brigada "Zaragoza" under Eugenio Aguirre Benavides.

Hernández had already been skirmishing throughout much of that Saturday afternoon against Salazar's displaced *colorados*, and the first federal train appeared from Chihuahua City to begin disgorging its vanguard of troops at dawn on Sunday, November 23, 1913. Their scouts moved toward Villa's lines, probing and gradually discovering from exploratory thrusts that the revolutionaries intended to fight where they stood, so after testing Villa's center and right, these attackers waited until their main body could come up. Villa in turn telegraphed Medina in Ciudad Juárez as evening fell on that November 23, 1913, instructing him to bring his cavalry to the battlefield the next morning, which the garrison's infantry marched west to Flores Ranch.

The Battle of Tierra Blanca became fully joined when two more large train convoys were sighted at 4:00 p.m. the next afternoon, November 24, 1913, the action intensifying and spreading as these *federales* detrained and mounted piecemeal attacks at various different points, only to be thrown back. Both sides were inexperienced in such large set-piece battles and included so many individualistic *colorado* and revolutionary commanders in the field that coordinated strikes proved impossible. Villa himself, lacking any formal military training, had not held back sufficient reserves to take advantage of any openings and instead weakened sections of his own battle line in order to shore up others.

Eventually, though, the battle was decided the next morning, November 25, 1913, as the federal forces at last exhausted themselves. No clear picture was recorded later by commanders on either side, but the artilleryman Thord-Gray would describe events from his own perspective of the battlefield:

> From out of nowhere, appeared a body of mounted men, like a cohort of Roman cavalry, some 300 strong on the Federals' left flank, which was pushing our right to the limit. The commander of this regiment was a remarkably clear-headed and resourceful young man. He saw the extended order of the enemy, and his mounted infantry without the slightest hesitation charged, without saber...This young Lieutenant-Colonel, an uneducated half-breed Apache, was a cavalry leader to be admired.

Some accounts attributed this timely charge to Maclovio Herrera, and it broke the *federales'* resolve, starting a retreat back toward their waiting trains.

Villa's henchman Rodolfo Fierro, an ex-railway brakeman, completed this rout by unleashing a locomotive loaded with dynamite to smash into the federal convoy, sowing panic in their ranks. The attackers broke and fled, leaving behind more than 1,000 dead, plus valuable military booty that included four surviving locomotives, several artillery pieces, high-powered rifles, 400,000 rounds of ammunition, and 350 horses.

Aftermath (December 1913)

Villa's victory completely reversed the strategic balance in Chihuahua. Salazar reeled southeastward, leading his survivors from Tierra Blanca toward the border town of Ojinaga (opposite Presidio, Texas)—where he would surprisingly be joined very shortly thereafter by the 2,900-man Huertista garrison from Chihuahua City as well, which was preemptively evacuated by its rattled governor Mercado, rather than await the inevitable Villista descent. Several thousand civilians furthermore joined Mercado's flight from the state capital, despite the perils of traversing the desert during wintertime (which could be accomplished only by detraining partway, and walking the remaining miles on foot). The victorious Villa consequently made an orderly, uncontested entry into half-empty Chihuahua City by December 8, 1913, to assume office as governor.

All of Mexico had been shocked by the revelation at Tierra Blanca of the northern rebels' newfound military power, Villa's scruffy and despised bandit groups having proven themselves now capable of defeating federal armies on the battlefield and taking over the administration of an entire state. By the end of December 1913, he would detach his subordinates Pánfilo Natera and Toribio Ortega with 3,000 troops to finish off Mercado's and Salazar's frightened remnants altogether, an operation that the government of Pres. Victoriano Huerta would prove powerless to prevent.

See also: Bierce, Ambrose Gwinett; División del Norte; Huerta Márquez, José Victoriano; *maquina loca*; Ojinaga, Battle of; Revolution, Mexican; Thord-Gray, Ivor; Villa, Pancho.

Further Reading

Guzmán, Martín Luis. *Memoirs of Pancho Villa*. Austin: University of Texas Press, 1976 translation.

"Rebels Quit Juárez to Battle Federals Only 15 Miles Away." *El Paso Herald*, November 22, 1913, weekend edition, section A, front page.

Thord-Gray, Ivor. *Gringo Rebel*. Coral Gables, FL: University of Miami Press, 1960, 21–53.

Tlatelolco Massacre (1968)

Repressive action undertaken by Mexican Army units, on government orders, against civilian protestors in the national capital.

Military Deployments (September 18–30, 1968)

The summer months of 1968 had witnessed a rising tide of student protests throughout Mexico, partly in emulation of outbursts by young anarchists in Europe, as well as because it was felt that the Mexican authorities could not resort to harsh countermeasures with the country about to become the focus of global attention as host of the Olympic Games. When student protesters took over the campus of the National Autonomous University, 1,500 troops (including the elite Paratroop Battalion under brigadier general José Hernández Toledo) were sent in on September 18, 1968, and all classes suspended. Further protests five days later at the Instituto Politécnico Nacional degenerated into armed clashes against police that left four people dead, so that several hundred more troops were sent into its widespread campus as well on the morning of September 24, 1968, clearing buildings in the Casco de Santo Tomás and Zacatenco areas. About 300 arrests were made and numerous weapons confiscated, before these troops withdrew that same evening.

Scattered incidents of street violence and vandalism ensued all throughout Mexico City on September 25, 1968, and some 700 soldiers with 25 armored cars were used to break up a crowd of protesters gathering outside the Museum of Anthropology on Paseo de la Reforma. Tensions then eased over the next few days, so that the 1,500 troops and 25 military vehicles were withdrawn from the campus of the National Autonomous University by noon on September 30, 1968. Student leaders soon resumed their protests, calling for a major march into the center of Mexico City for Wednesday,

October 2, 1968, only 10 days' time from the opening ceremonies of the Olympic Games.

Tlatelolco Massacre (October 2, 1968)

Around midday, a coordinated series of protest marches begin converging from various directions on the central core of the capital, the advancing throngs of people being diverted into the Plaza de las Tres Culturas in the nearby Tlatelolco district, where after numerous speeches and harangues by a variety of speakers, the demonstrations finally began to wind down for the day—without any violence, notwithstanding considerable chaos and tension throughout that Wednesday.

By 6:15 p.m. in the evening on that October 2, 1968, only some 5,000 hard-core demonstrators remained in the plaza, who in the fading light unexpectedly found themselves surrounded by hundreds of troops of the Paratroop Battalion and 44th Infantry Battalion emerging from the adjoining streets, backed by armored cars and even a few tanks. A shot rang out and gunfire quickly erupted, the paratroopers' brigadier Hernández Toledo being among the first wounded, while many hapless civilians were mowed down or trampled in the ensuing stampede and confusion. By the time shooting stopped, estimates of the dead ranged between 200 and 300 people with thousands more being wounded, beaten, or arrested. Government sources later cited only 4 dead and 20 wounded, a figure that was widely disbelieved.

Apparently fearful of suffering embarrassment before worldwide television audiences during the forthcoming Olympics, Pres. Gustavo Díaz Ordáz had resorted to the expedient of ordering the army to crush this student movement through an exemplary reprisal, which is still remembered today as the "Tlatelolco Massacre." The

Olympics went off successfully a fortnight later, without incident.

Further Reading

Brewster, Claire. "The Student Movement of 1968 and the Mexican Press: The Cases of *Excélsior* and *¡Siempre!*" *Bulletin of Latin American Research* 21, no. 2 (April 2002): 171–90.

Scherer García, Julio, and Carlos Monsiváis. *Parte de guerra, Tlatelolco 1968: documentos del general Marcelino García Barragán, los hechos y la historia.* Mexico City: Nuevo Siglo/Aguilar, 1999.

Shapira, Yoram. "Mexico: The Impact of the 1968 Student Protest on Echeverria's Reformism." *Journal of Interamerican Studies and World Affairs* 19, no. 4 (November 1977): 557–80.

tocar generala

Ancient Spanish military expression, the phrase "play *generala*" meaning to have drummers and buglers beat for assembly at "general quarters," indicating that all soldiers should immediately arm themselves and stand to their battle stations.

Many examples abound from Mexico's early military history, especially during the first half of the 19th century, although this expression seems to have gradually faded from common usage as the 1800s progressed. For instance, the Spanish general Pascual de Liñán—while his royal regiments were encamped at Xalapa in March 1822, awaiting their evacuation to Spain—experienced an outburst by the Mexican colonel Antonio López de Santa Anna in which, angered because of some minor incident, he ordered the *generala* played so his Mexican troops armed for battle before Liñán was able to smooth this matter over without bloodshed.

A quarter century later, the historian Heriberto Frías described how the renewal of hostilities after a two-week truce with the invading U.S. Army of Gen. Winfield Scott was announced in Mexico City on September 6, 1847:

> The war was renewed! The military bands played *Generala*, and the church bells pealed freely (*a rebato*), while preparations to resist were resumed, the garrisons at the guard stations (*garitas*) were reinforced, as the American army which occupied Tlalpan, Coyoacán, and Tacubaya was mobilizing to advance upon the capital.

Further Reading

Frías, Heriberto. *Episodios militares mexicanos: segunda parte, invasion norteamericana*. Mexico City: Viuda de C. Bouret, 1901, 217.

Torreón, Federal Abandonment of (1911)

Uncontested rebel occupation of this small northern city during the early months of the Mexican Revolution, which was marred by a senseless massacre of Chinese civilians.

By late April 1911, much of the region around this rail hub had been overrun by bands of irregulars, operating in the name of Francisco I. Madero to overthrow the regime of Pres. Porfirio Díaz. The lines to Monterrey and Saltillo had already been severed by these rebels when the 1,700 federal troops holding Torreón under elderly general Emiliano Lojero repulsed an attack on May 9, 1911, by approximately 4,000 revolutionaries who had coalesced out of the followings of such diverse leaders as Sixto Ugalde Guillén and Benjamín Argumedo of Matamoros, as well as Orestes Pereyra, Gregorio García, and Jesús Agustín Castro. However, after various more probes by revolutionary contingents, the defenders' three battalions withdrew through Huarache Canyon at dawn on Sunday, May 15, 1911, leaving the city defenseless so as to be overrun by the unruly *maderistas.*

This easy rebel victory was quickly marred by looting and the massacre of 303 unarmed Chinese civilians, about half the total number living in the city at that time. Emilio Madero, the nominal rebel commander for this district, finally restored order when he entered Torreón with his troops at 10:00 a.m. (The Maderista government would later agree to pay the Chinese government a 3.1 million-*peso* indemnity for this massacre, although the President himself was killed before these funds could actually be disbursed.)

Further Reading

Dambourges Jacques, Leo M. "The Chinese Massacre in Torreón (Coahuila) in 1911." *Arizona and the West* 16, no. 3 (Autumn 1974): 233–46.

Torreón, Villa's First Capture of (1913)

Pair of military assaults launched by Pancho Villa's emergent army, both of which captured this small but strategic city during the Mexican Revolution.

Torreón had not been in existence for very long, having been created only during the late 1880s as a waystation for the central railway line that was to run north toward the American border, as part of a new national network. Its construction crews reached what was then the lonely "ranch of Torreón" in September 1883 before

Maj. Gen. José Refugio Velasco inspecting paraded federal troops at Torreón, early 1914; his army would soon be obliterated by Pancho Villa's second great attack against that northern city. (Library of Congress)

continuing to lay track northward. Even before any rail traffic could commence, a group of German investors had bought up all the farmland around its temporary station three years later, to lay out the trace for a city. And after the first trains actually arrived in March 1888, its population would boom from a scant 200 permanent residents in 1892 to 5,000 only three years later. Driving out spur lines to fertile pockets throughout its surrounding district, provided a hub for an expanding volume of agricultural exports (especially cotton), so the town had become a city with a population of 34,000 residents by 1910, the year in which the Revolution exploded.

First Battle of Torreón (September–October 1913)

Having sallied from the city with 1,000 men, the Huertista Generals Campa and Álvarez probed Villa's huge encampment with a long-range bombardment on September 29, 1913, hoping to scatter his ill-disciplined following—now swollen to 10,000 men, boasting four fieldpieces and a few machine guns, and dubbed the *División del Norte* or "Northern Division." Instead, Villa ordered a general advance eastward against Torreón in three columns: his own "Villa Brigade" under Col. Toribio Ortega driving along the southern bank of the Nazas River toward Áviles; Maclovio Herrera and the "Juárez Brigade" following its northern bank toward the twin towns of Lerdo and Gómez Palacio; while Urbina's "Morelos Brigade" covered Villa's right. The "Zaragoza" and Benjamín Yuriar's brigades were to remain behind as a reserve.

The formidable *colorado* commander Argumedo appeared atop La Cruz Hill with his Huertista cavalry, yet could not stem the Villista onrush despite launching repeated countercharges. Within an hour, the outnumbered Huertistas were falling back. The hamlet of Áviles was carried by Urbina and Pereyra after four hours of heavy fighting, during which the Huertista general Álvarez was slain, while Campa was driven out of Lerdo by Herrera and Contreras. The victors quickly began executing some 500 prisoners gathered at Áviles before being ordered to stop by Villa, who continued on through Huarache Canyon toward Torreón with 6,000–7,000 men of the Villa and Morelos Brigades, while his reserve Zaragoza and Yuriar Brigades were to circle around.

The 63-year-old federal brigadier general Eutiquio Munguía braced to receive this onslaught by detaching Huertista units to entrench themselves atop Polvorera, Calabazas, and Unión Hills outside the city, as well as within its two principal factories—solidly built of brick—while the civilian population fled en masse. The first long-range skirmishes erupted on the evening of September 30, 1913, Calabazas and Polvorera Hills being taken overnight. Amid intense fighting the next day, Villa personally led the final charge that carried the revolutionaries into Torreón on October 1, 1913, despite heavy losses. Some 232 Huertista defenders lay dead—a total of 800 having been killed over the past three days—while another 109 were captured, along with 11 cannon, 5 machine guns, and almost 40 trains. Fires consumed many of the city buildings, while Munguía escaped eastward.

By October 4, 1913, Munguía had managed to reassemble 1,700 survivors from his shattered Nazas Division, whom he led to the rural Tizoc railway station and then handed them over to the command of Gen. Fernando Trucy Aubert, who headed a 7,000-man Huertista concentration around Monterrey. Munguía meanwhile proceeded to Mexico City, arriving to find himself denounced as a coward and being arrested to face a court-martial. Villa extorted a forced loan from Torreón, executed Yuriar for insubordination, and then left his subordinate, Calixto Contreras, in command of a

relatively small garrison to hold the gutted city, while leading a train convoy northwestward in late October 1913, to launch a series of assaults against Chihuahua City that would fail to dislodge its Huertista garrison under Gen. Salvador R. Mercado.

Federal Recuperation (November–December, 1913)

A week after Villa had departed Torreón with his main force, the highly regarded and recently promoted major general José Refugio Velasco—who had been assembling and training a large federal army around Saltillo—began moving his forces in the direction of Torreón by early November 1913, although planning on gradually encircling its garrison by seizing outlying towns and severing its railway communications before launching any direct assault.

Velasco captured his first outpost outside the city on November 9, 1913, then patiently spent the remainder of that month occupying and securing a chain of more outposts, as his army spread its operations out of Coahuila and into Durango as well. Finally, he launched a direct assault against Torreón on December 9, 1913, so its Villista occupiers retired northwestward the next day with most of their equipment and material intact. President Huerta was nonetheless delighted by the news of the recapture of this vital rail hub, so his minister of war—Gen. Aureliano Blanquet—sent a circular around to all federal commanders ordering them to publicize and celebrate this event.

Velasco meanwhile sent detachments to recuperate more towns deeper inside Durango and began erecting defenses and digging trenches around Torreón, as well as its smaller sister cities of Gómez Palacio and Lerdo on the western banks of the Nazas River, to defend against the inevitable revolutionary response. His garrison's strength consisted of some 7,000 federal soldiers organized into two infantry brigades and a cavalry brigade of a reconstituted *División del Nazas* (sometimes called the *División de la Laguna*), supported by a score of artillery pieces, 11 heavy and 24 light machine guns, plus some 6,000 *colorado* irregulars and local auxiliaries who served as scouts and light cavalrymen.

Early the next year, after learning details about Villa's triumphs in Chihuahua and preparations for a renewed offensive southward, Velasco sent a lieutenant colonel from his staff toward Mexico City in late January 1914 to personally appeal for greater reinforcement of Torreón—but this officer, after reaching Saltillo, was obliged to detour through Galveston, New Orleans, and Veracruz merely to reach the national capital because of the frequent disruptions to rail traffic. In the meantime, the U.S. government had raised its arms embargo on Mexico as of February 3, 1914, so Villa was able to purchase ample amounts of ammunition and equipment from across the border and prepared to depart with his rearmed host.

See also: Ángeles Ramírez, Felipe de Jesús; División del Norte; Revolution, Mexican; *rurales*; Villa, Pancho.

Further Reading

Guzmán, Martín Luis. *Memoirs of Pancho Villa*. Austin: University of Texas Press, 1976 translation.

Katz, Friedrich. *The Life and Times of Pancho Villa*. Stanford, CA: Stanford University Press, 1998, 215–18.

Torreón, Villa's Second Capture of (1914)

Major military operation launched by the emergent revolutionary chieftain, climaxing in an epic 12-day battle before overrunning that small northern city.

Approach by Rail (March 16–19, 1914)

His prestige bolstered by his victories at the Battles of Tierra Blanca and Ojinaga, Villa's División del Norte was now swelling into a powerful force of 15,000-plus troops, as more and more volunteers kept joining his ranks. Consequently, he left Chihuahua City with a very large corps on Monday, March 16, 1914, intending to return southeastward so as to reclaim Torreón and its rich Comarca Lagunera region, which had been reoccupied during his absence by a large federal army under Maj. Gen. José Refugio Velasco. [*See* preceding entry "Torreón, Villa's First Capture of (1913)."]

Upon clearing Chihuahua to mount this second assault, the 8,200 soldiers of Villa's main body consisted of nine cavalry and infantry brigades under their chosen revolutionary chieftains, plus two artillery regiments of 300 gunners and 29 pieces under the former federal brigadier general Felipe Ángeles and Col. Martiniano Servín. They left the capital of Chihuahua aboard a long convoy of 15 trains, reaching the town of Santa Rosalía de Camargo before the next sunrise. Villa's trusted subordinate Tomás Urbina would meanwhile lead a couple thousand more riders overland out of Nieves, along a parallel but circuitous route through Pelayo, La Cadena, and Dinamarca, intending to surprise the mining town of Mapimí out of its west, while a half dozen other Villista brigades waited in reserve to be summoned from various different railheads.

By the evening of Wednesday, March 18, 1914, Villa's main body had detrained at the rural station at Yermo, and the next day advanced in full battle array toward the

Gen. Felipe Ángeles (center, facing camera) and Villista troops awaiting the order to attack Gómez Palacio outside of Torreón, possibly on the morning of March 23, 1914. (Library of Congress)

next station down the line at Conejos without encountering any federal detachments.

Warning Clashes (March 20–21, 1914)

It was not until the Villistas overran the tiny outpost at Peronal and chased a few hundred *rurales* and *colorados* of the *3er. Grupo Explorador* or "3rd Scout Group" out of Bermejillo station on Friday, March 20, 1914, that their enemy even realized that the full weight of the constitutionalist División del Norte was now bearing down on Torreón. Ángeles and Villa themselves surprised Velasco, the senior federal commander within the city, when they phoned his headquarters from Bermejillo to propose terms for a capitulation—a suggestion that went nowhere.

The next dawn, March 21, 1914, Villa was informed at Bermejillo that Urbina's detached column of riders had taken Mapimí from its 800 *colorado* defenders under Benjamín Argumedo, so Villa ordered this victorious subordinate to continue riding on toward Santa Clara station with his "Morelos" Brigade so as to rejoin the main body as Villa continued his drive through there toward Torreón.

That same Saturday afternoon, Villa furthermore instructed the 1,500-man "Zaragoza" Brigade of Brig. Gen. Eugenio Aguirre Benavides—which had been detached from the main body earlier to seize the railhead at Tlahualito or Tlahualillo from the 12th and 21st *colorado* Scout Groups—to push southward down its spur line and also take the vital hub at Sacramento, which was being held (along with the station farther east at San Pedro de las Colonias) by the 7th and 26th Scout Groups under the young *colorado* "general" Juan Andrew Almazán.

The latter, although his few hundred men were driven back inside the stout buildings of the Hacienda de Sacramento by Aguirre Benavides's sudden assault at 5:45 p.m. that same Saturday evening of March 21, 1914, nonetheless put up such fierce resistance that Villa had to further detach Rosalío Hernández's brigade at 11:00 p.m. to ride overland in the night and support Aguirre Benavides's ongoing attack. It would take this combined Villista force several hours to overwhelm Almazán's outnumbered defenders, in the process killing some 300 *colorados* and capturing another 40, at a cost of 50 Villistas dead and 95 wounded.

Villa meanwhile shook an additional 1,500 unattached volunteers out of his train convoy the next morning (Sunday, March 22, 1914) and absorbed them as replacements into his ranks, leaving 500 of these men behind to garrison Bermejillo while his main army resumed its movement once again, advancing in a battle formation that stretched out six miles wide, pushing down the rail line toward Gómez Palacio, a satellite city resting on the western banks of the Nazas River opposite Torreón.

Struggle for Gómez Palacio (March 22–26, 1914)

The Villista scouts found the tracks torn up after the station at Noé and began drawing cannon fire from the federal garrison occupying Gómez Palacio itself as evening fell on that Sunday, March 22, 1914. Having been instructed to halt and dismount a mile and a half short of their objective so as to then close in on its defenders afoot in skirmish lines behind covering fire from Ángeles's artillery, 6,000 of Villa's undisciplined troops instead charged impetuously on horseback straight at the federal positions

in response to these first artillery rounds, suffering at least 70 dead and 200 wounded in their initial onrush before becoming pinned down in Gómez Palacio's outskirts overnight, where Ángeles's 25 guns could not assist them for fear of striking their own men in the darkness.

This precipitate attack was revealed as a tactical blunder the next dawn, when Villa and his officers could discern federal emplacements bristling with four field howitzers and eight heavy machine guns atop the half-mile-wide La Pila Hill, as well as other defenders inside stout, stone strongpoints such as *La Jabonera* soap factory and the *Casa Redonda* or railway "Round-House," whose cross-fires had already cost the attackers at least 125 killed and 315 wounded. Ángeles therefore repositioned one of his batteries onto the slopes of San Ignacio Hill, and another beside the rail line so as to counter the federal artillery and allow the pinned-down Villistas to withdraw.

In the meantime, Maclovio Herrera dismounted his riders farther to the west and launched a flanking attack against Gómez Palacio's westernmost suburb (called Lerdo) shortly before 9:00 a.m. on March 23, 1914. This second attack also became temporarily bogged down until Herrera was able to renew his assault after nightfall and carry Lerdo once darkness fell. Desultory exchanges of gunfire continued throughout most of Tuesday, March 24, 1914, as Aguirre Benavides and Hernández rejoined the main Villista body, and Villa summoned his five reserve brigades to begin moving by train toward his stalled División.

At 4:00 p.m. the next afternoon, March 25, 1914, Ángeles's artillery resumed its gun duel against the federal emplacements atop La Pila Hill, preparing for an assault by Herrera's, Urbina's, and

José Rodríguez's three brigades. These 2,400 men charged at 8:45 p.m. that same night and suffered more than 200 killed in overrunning two of La Pila's five strongpoints, but the hill's 500 defenders continued to resist and were reinforced the next dawn, launching a counterattack of their own at 9:00 a.m. on March 26th that recuperated their lost positions. The bloodied Villistas had to retreat with only two heavy machine guns and a light Rexer machine gun as consolation prizes.

Then, a relocated federal battery began threatening Ángeles's guns and also drove back the attackers' pair of flatcar-mounted heavy guns, nicknamed "El Niño" and "Chavalito." Federal artillery salvoes continued raining down on the Villista lines ineffectually for the remainder of that Thursday, March 26, 1914, before falling silent at 4:00 p.m. as a large body of cavalry emerged from Gómez Palacio and inspected the Villista positions from a distance before wheeling about and disappearing back into the battle-damaged city. Villa prepared a massive force for a renewed nocturnal assault against its defenses, but upon advancing to the attack that same Thursday evening, discovered that its federal survivors had evacuated Gómez Palacio unseen and vanished back into Torreón. It was estimated that up until this time, federal casualties totaled a combined 1,500 men lost at Bermejillo, Sacramento, Lerdo, and Gómez Palacio.

Battle for Torreón (March 27–April 2, 1914)

The next morning on Friday, March 27, 1914, Villa began deploying his brigades into new advance positions (in spite of federal artillery fire raining down from Santa Rosa Hill), as well as sending a diplomatic note into Torreón with the British consul Cunard Cummins at mid-afternoon, vainly proposing capitulation terms once again to General Velasco. On Saturday evening, Villa sent in attack columns to seize some of the surrounding hilltops after dark, first light of Sunday, March 29, 1914, revealing that some strongholds had been taken atop Santa Rosa and Calabazas Hills, as well as overlooking Huarache Canyon—although the *federales* promptly counterattacked that same Sunday at dawn out of Torreón and recouped their lost ground.

Very shortly thereafter, a strong column of about 2,000 federal troopers and *colorado* riders tried to clear a passage through Huarache Canyon for two trains to escape out of Torreón at 7:00 a.m. that same Sunday morning, although this attempt was foiled and beaten back into the city. One hour later, Herrera in turn managed to lead his Villista brigade into Torreón out of the east, fighting his way in as far as its Alameda Central before becoming pinned down. Villa was meanwhile distracted by news that three train convoys of *federales* from Monterrey had arrived as close as Benavides station, seeking to relieve their colleagues within Torreón, so Villa detached Brig. Gen. Toribio Ortega with two brigades (2,000 men) from his main army so as to check this new threat at San Pedro de las Colonias.

Exchanges of gunfire continued in and around Torreón on March 30 and March 31, 1914, until further reinforcements began reaching Villa on April 1st and were thrown into another major assault against the *federales* that very same evening. Dawn of Thursday, April 2, 1914, revealed that Calabazas and Polvorera Hills overlooking the city had been taken overnight, along with Torreón's La Fortuna neighborhood, and when the defenders launched their usual early morning counterattacks to recuperate Calabazas Hill and the San Joaquín neighborhood, they failed in these attempts.

Realizing that his exhausted men were now low on ammunition and in danger of being completely overwhelmed, Velasco took advantage when a huge *tolvanera* or "dust storm" began to blow around 4:00 p.m. on that Thursday afternoon to give the order an hour later for his surviving troops to escape eastward aboard trains or on horseback, enveloped in its poor visibility so as to head toward the municipality of Viesca.

Aftermath (April 3–4, 1914)

It was not until 1:00 a.m. on April 3, 1914, that the Villistas noticed there were no longer any replies being made to their artillery salvoes, yet they waited until daylight before pushing into the city ruins, warily probing for mines. The *federales* had indeed evacuated and the ferocious Second Battle for Torreón was ended, Villa having lost approximately 650 dead and 3,200 wounded. Velasco's 7,000-man federal garrison had suffered 1,890 dead, 2,200 wounded, 1,400 desertions, 250 prisoners, plus the loss of seven artillery pieces and 240 horses, while about half of their 6,000 *colorado* auxiliaries had simply vanished. His retreating column consisted of 4,000 disorganized, demoralized soldiers and militiamen with scarcely 20,000 rounds of ammunition and little materiel left between them, limping away in hopes of joining the concentration of federal relief columns at San Pedro de las Colonias.

The presence of these 6,200 federal reinforcements at San Pedro de las Colonias, only 32 miles east of shattered Torreón, meant that Villa did not celebrate his hardfought triumph. Wishing to prevent this disjointed enemy force from uniting with

Velasco's survivors and coalescing into a stronger military threat, Villa instead dispatched the brigades of Brig. Gen. José Isabel Robles and Col. Raúl Madero from Torreón to help contain the enemy formations that very same day of April 3, 1914, then followed the next day with his main *División del Norte* and its heavy artillery train, launching into the Battle of San Pedro de las Colonias by April 5th.

See also Ángeles Ramírez, Felipe de Jesús; División del Norte; Revolution, Mexican; Rexer light machine gun; *rurales*; San Pedro de las Colonias, Battle of; Villa, Pancho.

Further Reading

Guzmán, Martín Luis. *Memoirs of Pancho Villa*. Austin: University of Texas Press, 1976 translation.

O'Hea, Patrick A. *Reminiscences of the Mexican Revolution*. Mexico City: Centro Anglo-Mexicano del Libro, 1966.

Reed, John. *Insurgent Mexico*. New York: Appleton, 1914, 175–259.

treinta-treinta. Nickname in Mexico for the Model 1894 Winchester repeating rifle, a very popular lightweight firearm sold primarily for hunting and sport but that was used by many rebel soldiers during the early phases of the Mexican Revolution.

For a more detailed account, *see* Carabina 30-30.

Tres Años, Guerra de los. Literally translated as "The War of the Three Years," this was another name given during the 19th century to what is more commonly remembered today as the War of the Reform or Reforma. *See* Reform, War of the (1858–1860).

Tres Palos, Battle of (1811)

One of the earliest insurgent victories won during the War of Independence by the rebel priest turned guerrilla chieftain José María Morelos.

Background (November–December 1810)

A former student of Fr. Miguel Hidalgo, who initiated the insurrection against Spanish rule in Guanajuato as of September 16, 1810, the 45-year-old Morelos had joined his mentor's cause five weeks later near Indaparapeo on October 20, 1810, during which he had been commissioned by Hidalgo to "raise troops on the southern coast, acting in accordance with the verbal instructions which I have given him." Intimately familiar with that Pacific coastal region and its people, having spent a decade of his youth traveling its highways as a teamster, Morelos materialized in the vicinity of the port of Acapulco with a couple of hundred lightly armed followers by early November 1810 to raise the banner of revolt.

Joined by local contingents under such leaders as the brothers José and Antonio Galeana, Morelos had threatened the royal force garrisoning lonely Fort San Diego at Acapulco on November 7 and again on December 1, 1810, while attracting thousands of adherents into his ranks, who cut off all communications inland and waylaid royalist patrols. Less than two weeks later, though, Morelos's subordinate Julián de Ávila ambushed a monarchist relief column at Paso Real de la Sabana on December 13, 1810, that had been dispatched into this district by the Crown authorities in Mexico City so as to break the rebel siege of the viceroyalty's main Pacific seaport before the expected annual arrival of the rich "Manila galleon" from the distant Philippines. This relief force consisted of the 5th Oaxaca Militia Division under Capt. Francisco Paris, which was to be reinforced by local levies.

Battle of Tres Palos (January 5, 1811)

Shrewdly judging the low morale and inexperience of Captain Paris's conscript army, Morelos and his lieutenants, José and Antonio Galeana, led slightly more than 1,000 rebels in a bold attack against the 3,000 royalist irregulars on the night of January 4–5, 1811, as they lay encamped at Tres Palos Ranch near Acapulco. Despite outnumbering their attackers by three to one, the monarchist commanders would later complain that the "seduction" of this charismatic guerrilla leader had swayed the loyalty of their native levies.

According to a letter penned eight days after the battle by Capt. Domingo de Larrea, a Spanish officer who survived this encounter, Morelos's predawn attack created considerable confusion in the royalist camps with some of their units mistakenly firing on each other in the darkness. The insurgent chieftain further bewildered the Mexican levies by loudly calling out to them as his forces advanced

> that he was coming in peace, that he did not wish to injure any of them, and so exhorted them not to shoot to kill, because they were Christians, but rather to shoot into the air.

As confusion spread and monarchist resolve weakened, a hoarse bellow of ¡Viva nuestra señora de Guadalupe! or "Long live Our Lady of Guadalupe!" was suddenly heard, at which a royalist artillery piece could be seen slewing around in the gloom and being aimed into their own ranks. The threat of a devastating blast of grapeshot at such close range sparked a panic-stricken stampede with hundreds of pressed local militiamen fleeing to simply return into their homes, while the unwilling Oaxacan militiamen dispersed as well, to reassemble and begin walking back leaderless in the direction of their distant homes.

Aftermath (February 1811)

At a cost of 200 killed and wounded during this nocturnal clash at Tres Palos, the outnumbered Morelos had inflicted 400 casualties among the royalists and taken a further 700 prisoners, including numerous Spanish officers—plus, more importantly, 700 muskets, five artillery pieces, ammunition, and supplies. In the wake of this defeat, the few monarchists throughout the region remained too frightened to even travel its roads (despite the royalist victory that was won only a few days afterward over Miguel Hidalgo's main Army of America at Calderón Bridge, outside Guadalajara).

Morelos's insurgent force was greatly bolstered, so he attempted another surprise attack against Acapulco's Fort San Diego on February 8, 1811, and was not deterred when this assault was repulsed.

See also: Acapulco, Insurgent Siege of; Calderón Bridge, Battle of; Hidalgo y Costilla Gallago, Miguel Gregorio Antonio Ignacio; Independence, War of; Morelos Pavón, José María Teclo.

Further Reading

Ibarra, Ana Carolina. *El cabildo catedral de Antequera, Oaxaca y el movimiento insurgente*. Morelia: El Colegio de Michoacán, 2000, 128–30.

Trigarante, Ejército (1821–1822). *See* Ejército Trigarante (1821–1822) as well the Appendix in the section titled

"Independent Mexico's 'Ejército Trigarante' in September 1821."

Trinidad, Battle of (1915)

One of the biggest encounters in Mexico's military history, being the third and decisive clash between the revolutionary rivals Álvaro Obregón and Pancho Villa, which broke Villa's power forever.

Background (April–May 1915)

Having already mauled Villa's División del Norte at the twin Battles of Celaya in the state of Guanajuato in early and mid-April 1915, Obregón resumed his advance from Irapuato deeper into Villista territory before that same month was out, gaining the small city of Silao by April 28, 1915. The next day, his scouts contacted some Villista patrols farther to its northwest, who—now grown leery because of the heavy toll of casualties that had been inflicted on them earlier by their well-armed, professional foes—only skirmished cautiously against Obregón's advance outposts, buying time for Villa to regroup and resurrect his fighting strength for a third time, now around his new supply depot at León.

Having withdrawn their garrisons from Guadalajara, Monterrey, and Saltillo so as to marshal in full strength, the recuperating Villistas were being continually reinforced at León throughout this interval, so their camps soon sprawled for more than 20 miles—from Rodolfo Fierro's division stationed at San Juan de los Lagos, to Tomás Urbina's and Pánfilo Natera's contingents resting at San Miguel de Allende. Having lost his first two meetings against Obregón so decisively, Villa now hoped to lure his opponent out into the flat Trinidad plains between Silao and León, where the

One-armed General Obregón and his staff at the Ciudad Juárez railway station, May 4, 1916. (Library of Congress)

Villistas' numerical superiority in cavalry might work to his advantage.

Battle of Trinidad or Santa Ana del Conde (May 12–June 5, 1915)

Himself eager to bring matters to a head, Obregón pushed his own vanguard northwestward from Silao on May 7, 1915, reaching the lonely Trinidad railway station out in the plains to begin entrenching his infantry into a defensive line, which initially stretched between the nearby haciendas of Santa Ana del Conde and more distant Otates. Then the next day, Obregón furthermore directed his cavalry to clear Villista picket units from atop Capilla and La Cruz hills so his entire constitutionalist army of 14,300 infantrymen and 9,400 cavalry troopers might deploy fully into a huge square, eventually extending for 10 miles from corner to corner. Obregón's infantry held the northwestern and southeastern lines of this huge square, while his cavalry covered both flanks in between.

Villa, in turn—having amassed 19,500 riders and 6,000 infantrymen of his own at León—left a sizeable garrison behind while launching an initial strike with only 8,000 cavalrymen against Obregón's lines on May 12, 1915. Then after 10 days of probes and long-range exchanges, Villa added a bold new variant by leaving his artillery commander, Gen. Felipe Ángeles, to maintain this pressure on Obregón's main army, while personally leading another 8,000 fresh riders through the hills via a circuitous route to surprise the main Obregonista supply base at Silao, thus destroying numerous trains, bridges, and telegraphs in his opponent's rear.

Obregón found this disruption worrisome, especially after he learned that Villa had returned into Duarte by the morning of June 2, 1915, to prepare for an all-out assault with his entire strength. The Obregonistas braced to receive this onslaught, and when the first Villista wave of three infantry battalions broke cover the next morning and charged directly at Santa Ana del Conde Hacienda, behind an artillery barrage laid down by Ángeles's batteries, Obregón was unexpectedly wounded—his right arm being shredded by a shell. However, his army's discipline nonetheless remained intact, his second-in-command, Gen. Benjamín Hill, immediately taking over and decimating Villa's advancing columns with counterfire from well-placed machine guns and strongly entrenched troops.

After exhausting their strength and ammunition in repeated yet fruitless assaults over the next two days, Villa and Ángeles finally gave the order at dawn of June 5, 1915, for their depleted forces to begin retiring by train from Duarte toward León. Hill launched a massive pursuit by ordering Brigadier Generals Cesáreo Castro and Francisco Murguía to chase the routed Villistas with their 7,000 troopers along both flanks, while Diéguez led the infantry straight up the center into León itself. Having sustained 8,000 casualties—triple

those of the Obregonistas—Villa was powerless to prevent the utter disintegration of his army, abandoning all of his materiel before drawing off northward into Aguascalientes in defeat.

See also: Ángeles Ramírez, Felipe de Jesús; Celaya, Battles of; División del Norte; Obregón Salido, Álvaro; Revolution, Mexican; Villa, Pancho.

Further Reading

Aguirre Benavides, Luis and Adrián. *Las grandes batallas de la División del Norte al mando del general Francisco Villa.* Mexico City: Diana, 1967.

Jowett, Philip, and Alejandro de Quesada. *The Mexican Revolution, 1910–20.* Oxford: Osprey, 2006.

Knight, Alan. *The Mexican Revolution.* New York: Cambridge University Press, 1986.

Obregón, Álvaro. *Ocho mil kilómetros en campaña.* Mexico City: Viuda de Charles Bouret, 1917, chap. 7.

"Villa Repulse in North Is Complete." *El Paso Herald* Extra, June 8, 1915, front page.

V

Our misfortunes are not caused by the enemy, but by the anarchy, falseness, and other defects of liberal leaders.

— Santiago Vidaurri, liberal governor
of Nuevo León and Coahuila, April 1859

Valladolid, Battle of (1813)

Unexpected royalist triumph that inflicted a dramatic military reversal on the fortunes of the insurgent generalissimo José María Morelos.

Preliminary Maneuvers (November–December 1813)

Fresh from presiding over a rebel Congress at Chilpancingo from mid-September through early November 1813—a conference also known as the Congreso de Anáhuac, which would cap three years of struggle by optimistically declaring independence from the Spanish Crown, abolishing slavery, eliminating class privileges, etc.—the insurgent chieftain had begun gathering forces at its conclusion for a renewed military offensive, intending to advance northwest through Mezcala, Cutzamala, Huetamo, and Tzitzio on his native city of Valladolid (modern Morelia, Michoacán) with 5,600–5,700 rebel cavalrymen and infantrymen, plus some 30 guns, so as to conquer that city to serve as the capital for his new government.

The viceroy Félix María Calleja learned of this insurgent design in Mexico City and countered by issuing orders on December 8, 1813, for Lt. Col. Domingo Landázuri to exit with 1,000 troops and coalesce with the so-called *Ejército del Norte* or Army of the North, which comprised another 2,000 troops of the combined Toluca Division under Brig. Gen. Ciriaco de Llano and Guanajuato Division under Col. Agustín de Iturbide so as to race westward together through Ixtlahuaca, Acámbaro, Maravatío, and Indaparapeo to reinforce the outnumbered royalist defenders of the threatened city of Valladolid.

Upon drawing near to this objective, De Llano sent Landázuri on ahead with a vanguard detachment of 800 men so as to immediately bolster the city's small garrison until his remaining 2,200 troops could complete their march. Meanwhile, the regional insurgent commander, Ramón López Rayón, advised Morelos of the approach of this monarchist relief army, so the generalissimo instructed him to fight a delaying action against De Llano's main body, giving him time to carry out his assault on Valladolid; but when López Rayón subsequently clashed with the royalists at Jerécuaro on December 21, 1813, he was badly beaten.

Battle of Valladolid (December 22–25, 1813)

Morelos and his ill-disciplined host began appearing the next day among the hills around the village of Santa María de la Asunción, just south of Valladolid. The next morning, December 23, 1813, while his troops were still moving down onto the plains to assemble into assault columns, the insurgent generalissimo sent a message in to Landázuri, demanding the capitulation of the city's outnumbered garrison within three hours. The royalist commander ignored this demand, bracing for an attack while sending couriers to ask De Llano to hasten his approach with the main body.

Shortly thereafter, Morelos's subordinates Hermenegildo Galeana and Nicolás Bravo attempted to seize Valladolid's outlying Zapote *garita* or "guard station" so as to prevent the entry of any royalist reinforcements, which were known to be approaching. However, this rebel attempt was repelled by a series of flanking counterattacks by the city garrison, which beat off the assault columns and inflicted some 700 casualties (the Spanish defenders later reporting that 230 of the prisoners that they had taken "were all shot on the edges of the ditches where their bodies were to be buried").

Valladolid's royalist garrison was consequently strengthened by the entry of De Llano's and Iturbide's combined divisions on the morning of December 24, 1813. That same afternoon, another of Morelos's subordinates—the ex-priest Mariano Matamoros—paraded and reviewed all the rebel infantry on the plain between the city and the Santa María Hills before attempting another assault, which was driven back out of the city. And while the insurgents were retiring back into their encampments on the heights above as evening fell, Iturbide slipped out of Valladolid with 190 cavalrymen and an infantry company, stealing up on the unwary insurgents as darkness fell. In a brilliant stroke, he launched a nocturnal attack that startled them so badly the rebels began mistakenly firing into each other's ranks in the darkness and eventually dissolved into panic-stricken flight.

Disaster at Puruarán (January 4–5, 1814)

His army having disintegrated, Morelos fled through Chupio with a handful of followers, hoping to regroup his forces around the Hacienda de Santa Lucía at Puruarán, 60 miles southwest of Valladolid. De Llano did not exit in pursuit until dawn on December 30, 1813, and at first marched mistakenly toward Tacámbaro. During this lull, Morelos insisted on making a stand with his reassembled followers at Puruarán, against his subordinates' advice. Matamoros finally convinced the generalissimo to retire toward safety, leaving him to command the shaken, underarmed insurgent force.

Once again, the demoralized and disorganized insurgents were surprised on the night of January 4–5, 1814, by the arrival of De Llano's pursuing cavalry, being utterly routed when the main royalist body arrived the next morning, which took their remaining 25 guns, 1,000 muskets, etc. Among the hundreds of prisoners captured was Matamoros himself, caught while attempting to escape across the Puruarán River, who was held in chains until he could be sent toward Valladolid on January 8, 1814, taking a week to arrive. There, he was stripped of his religious orders by Bishop Manuel Abad y Queipo and humiliated in the public square, while Morelos wrote from Coyuca with an offer to exchange 200 Spanish prisoners for his second-in-command. This proposition was ignored, Matamoros being marched to the Ecce Homo Gate in Valladolid and executed by a firing squad at 11:00 a.m. on February 3, 1813, his corpse being left exposed to public view for the next four hours before at last being taken away for burial.

Aftermath (mid-January–March 1814)

In the wake of these twin defeats, the insurgent Congress sitting at Chilpancingo voted to remove Morelos from his position as chief executive on January 17, 1814, assuming many of his powers and prerogatives for themselves, while furthermore appointing his rival, Ignacio López Rayón, as commander-in-chief of the surviving insurgent garrisons at Tecpan and Oaxaca. Unaware of his demotion, Morelos learned about Matamoros's execution on February 3, 1813, and angrily retaliated by ordering the deaths of his 203 Spanish prisoners. A royalist column under Gabriel Armijo subsequently proceeded toward Chilpancingo and defeated the troops of Victor and Miguel Bravo, thereby crushing all insurgent hopes of resuming any kind of military offensive, instead having to scatter.

See also: Calleja, Félix María, Independence, War of; Iturbide Arambúru, Agustín Cosme Damián de; Morelos Pavón, José María Teclo.

Further Reading

Ibarra, Ana Carolina. *El cabildo catedral de Antequera, Oaxaca y el movimiento insurgente.* Morelia: El Colegio de Michoacán, 2000.

Lemoine, Ernesto. *Morelos: su vida revolucionaria a través de sus escritos y otros testimonios de la época.* Mexico City: Universidad Nacional Autónoma de México, 1991.

Veracruz, Spanish Retention of (1821–1825)

Protracted military occupation of Mexico's main seaport by the defeated royal forces, even after the nation had won its War of Independence.

Background (1810–1821)

Throughout the three centuries of Spanish colonial rule, the offshore island fortress of San Juan de Ulúa had guarded Veracruz's partially sheltered port, the best of the few anchorages available along hundreds of miles of exposed Gulf coastline. A half mile across the water from Ulúa's garrison, on the mainland opposite, a small city had sprung up to receive and dispatch the annual plate fleets from Spain—although because of its torrid climate and pestilential diseases, Veracruz and its infertile district were busy only during these seasonal visits, otherwise having relatively few permanent residents.

When the struggle for independence against Spanish rule had erupted with Fr. Miguel Hidalgo's revolt deep inside the highlands of central Mexico in mid-September 1810, the Crown was able to retain its hold over this isolated coastal city and its harbor castle thanks to its fixed royalist regiments. However, communication inland to the viceregal capital and other centers of commerce was to become seriously impaired as of April 1812 by the depredations of insurgent guerrilla bands who menaced its highways. The reality of this threat was underscored when the young chieftain Nicolás Bravo ambushed a strongly escorted royalist mule train traveling toward Puebla on August 20, 1812, slaughtering most of its 360 guards under Lt. Col. Juan Labaqui.

Merchants consequently took to bribing partisan chieftains so as to ensure safe passage for their goods through rebel territory, but the overall volume of imports naturally dwindled; and as this commercial traffic withered, more and more civilians began to forsake Veracruz, so its population had fallen to roughly 11,000 residents by 1820. With royalist fortunes clearly declining in the interior of Mexico, a youthful ex-monarchist officer named Lt. Col. Antonio López de Santa Anna—who had himself served for years in the Crown regiment of

Aerial view of the Castle of San Juan de Ulúa, ca. May 1914, under American occupation. (Library of Congress)

Veracruz—attempted to surprise the port's garrison under Gen. José María Dávila, his former commander.

Launching a sudden strike during a rainstorm at 4:00 a.m. on July 3, 1821, Santa Anna's assault was checked in the city streets and ejected at a cost of half of his 500–600 Mexican troops. A tight siege was nonetheless imposed by his rebel forces, so when Juan O'Donojú arrived from Spain three weeks later as Mexico's latest viceroy-designate, this official realized that with insurgents in control of the entire viceroyalty except for Veracruz, Mexico City, and Acapulco—and only 4,200 widely scattered Spanish troops remaining available to the Crown—New Spain was essentially lost. O'Donojú therefore procured a safe conduct from Santa Anna to proceed inland

and conclude a treaty with the top insurgent commander, Agustín de Iturbide, that recognized Mexico's de facto independence by mid-September 1821.

Royalist Holdouts (1821–1825)

However, General Dávila refused to comply with O'Donojú's arrangement on September 18, 1821, and entirely disavowed his authority altogether two-and-a-half weeks later. Instead, the Spanish general decided to cripple the city of Veracruz's artillery before retiring across the bay with his 200 royal troops of the Regimiento de Mallorca, ample ammunition, and the royal treasury on the night of October 25–26, 1821, so as to continue resisting from within the impregnable fortress of San Juan de Ulúa until Madrid should signal its acceptance or rejection of these terms. Almost immediately, Mexican *trigarante* troops took over the city of Veracruz, but its port traffic remained at a standstill as the Spanish government flatly refused to accept Mexico's independence and began making plans to attempt a *reconquista* or "reconquest," so Dávila was instructed to hold on to Ulúa and reinforced from Havana with 400 additional soldiers of the Cataluña Regiment and 50 artillerymen on December 30, 1821.

All merchant traffic consequently had to be diverted into other Mexican anchorages, and Veracruz became moribund. After several more months of this stalemate, its municipal authorities attempted to bribe the sergeants of San Juan de Ulúa's royal garrison into switching sides with a secret shipment of gold on August 22, 1822, but this attempt was detected and rebuffed by Dávila. Iturbide having by now crowned himself "emperor" of Mexico placed Santa Anna in command of his imperial garrison in Veracruz as of September 25, 1822, with orders to secure San Juan de Ulúa from its stubborn Spanish holdouts. At first, Santa Anna simply attempted to negotiate terms with Dávila, during the second week of October 1822; but the Spanish general was promptly relieved in favor of the more intractable brigadier general Francisco Lemaur.

Santa Anna consequently deceived the latter into believing that he was prepared to switch allegiances and allow the Spanish Crown to reclaim Veracruz as well, so it was secretly arranged for a flotilla of boats from Ulúa to approach the city waterfront at dawn on October 27, 1822. Santa Anna's plan was to capture this 400-man Spanish landing force as they entered into the Concepción and Santiago Bastions, then use their uniforms and boats to venture out to Ulúa and take its defenders by surprise; but

the suspicious Spaniards instead opened fire from their boats and a two-hour exchange of gunfire ensued before they retired back out toward their harbor castle without ever setting foot ashore.

Iturbide's imperial "captain-general" for the entire coastal district, Gen. José Antonio de Echávarri, informed the emperor that the planned deception had been deliberately sabotaged by Santa Anna, so he was summoned to a gala reception in Jalapa the next month to be awarded a medal and offered a new posting in Mexico City—where he might then be quietly arrested for harboring republican sentiments. But upon being informed that he was being removed from military command to accompany Iturbide's party back to the capital, Santa Anna insisted on first attending to his personal affairs, so after the emperor departed on December 1, 1822, he galloped back to Veracruz and the next day proclaimed a revolt.

The issue of Veracruz's harbor still being controlled by a Spanish garrison in Ulua, was now further complicated by the arrival of an imperial Mexican army outside its walls in January 1823 and instituted a land siege. These Mexican commanders quickly agreed to switch over to Santa Anna's republican cause by February 1st, though, being joined by other disgruntled units throughout central Mexico, so Iturbide was compelled to abdicate the next month.

Veracruz nonetheless remained stagnant because of San Juan de Ulúa's occupiers. The insurgent war hero Guadalupe Victoria mounted yet another effort to dislodge its stubborn Spanish holdouts on September 21, 1823, but that unfortunately produced nothing more than a damaging exchange of artillery rounds over the next four days, which inflicted further harm on Veracruz. An English visitor estimated that the battered city's populace had by then dwindled to a mere 7,000 inhabitants, their misery not abating until San Juan de Ulúa's obstinate Spanish holdouts finally capitulated on November 23, 1825.

Immediate Aftermath (1826–1827)

Despite being free to receive oceangoing ships once again, Veracruz would struggle to revive economically as its colonial-era monopoly was no longer in force, having to instead compete with rival seaports along both coasts. The young republic would also remain handicapped by its uncertain political and financial footing with the city's governor revolting against the state governor Miguel Barragán on July 30, 1827, while Santa Anna arrested Barragán during a similar insurrection that same Christmas.

See also: Independence, War of; Santa Anna, Antonio López de.

Further Reading

Anna, Timothy E. *The Fall of Royal Government in Mexico City.* Lincoln: University of Nebraska Press, 1978.

"Oficios del Consulado de Veracruz: capitulación de la ciudad el 26 de octubre de 1821." *Revista de Historia Militar* [Spain] 34, no. 68 (1990): 225–28.

Ortiz Escamilla, Juan. *Veracruz, la guerra por la Independencia de México, 1821–1825.* Jalapa, Veracruz: Comisión Estatal del Bicentenario de la Independencia, 2008.

Rivera, Manuel. *Historia antigua y moderna de Jalapa y de las revoluciones del estado de Veracruz.* Mexico City: Ignacio Cumplido, 1869.

Veracruz, French Blockade and Assault on (1838–1839)

Year-long closure of this city's seaport by a naval squadron dispatched by Paris to exact compensation for losses sustained in troubled Mexico by its nationals.

In the chaotic decades immediately following Mexico's independence from Spain, foreign traders and investors often suffered economic losses due to the many insurrections, military coups, and lawless unrest that plagued the young republic, in turn complaining about these to their home governments. A French plenipotentiary had consequently traveled through Veracruz in 1837 to demand satisfaction from the government of Pres. Anastasio Bustamante in Mexico City for the sacking of French businesses and the extortion of forced loans during recent disturbances. Obtaining no resolution from his representations, this diplomat took ship again from Veracruz on January 16, 1838—only to return with 10 French warships by March 21, 1838, anchoring off Sacrificios Island to send an ultimatum inland from its flagship, now demanding 600,000 *pesos'* compensation for a long list of grievances.

Blockade (April 15, 1838– November 26, 1838)

When no response to this ultimatum was forthcoming by April 15, 1838, the French squadron imposed a limited naval blockade on Veracruz, restricting entry for many items so as to deprive the Mexican government of the revenues that their traffic generated. After six months of this blockade, the French set another communication ashore on October 21, 1838, leading to a face-to-face meeting at the inland town of Jalapa with the Mexican foreign minister on November 17, 1838—who was willing to concede to most points until the French representative demanded an additional 200,000 *pesos* to compensate his government for its expeditionary costs, so these talks broke off four days later.

Bombardment of San Juan de Ulúa (November 27, 1838)

At 9:00 a.m. on November 27, 1838, two Mexican officers went aboard Baudin's flagship *Néréide* with a last-minute offer from Minister Cuevas to renew negotiations, only to have the French admiral dismiss this proposal five-and-a-half hours later. A mere five minutes later—while these officers were still being rowed ashore—the frigates *Néréide*, *Iphigénie*, and *Gloire*, corvette *Créole*, and bombs *Cyclope* and *Vulcain* opened fire on Veracruz's 153-gun harborcastle of San Juan de Ulúa, using newly developed Paixhans explosive shells. This exchange persisted until 6:00 p.m., when the bombardment slackened and finally ceased two hours later, after its garrison commander, Antonio Gaona, requested a truce to attend to his wounded. During the course of this single afternoon, thanks to their superior ordnance, the French squadron had inflicted 224 casualties and dismounted 20 of San Juan de Ulúa's guns, while suffering 4 four killed and 39 injured aboard their warships.

Overnight, the French informed Gaona that his fortress would be leveled if he did not surrender, so after consulting with Gen. Manuel Rincón in Veracruz at 3:30 a.m. on November 28, 1838, the garrison commander agreed to capitulate at 8:00 a.m. that same morning. By midday, the French were in possession of San Juan de Ulúa, and Rincón—with the intervention of Santa Anna, who had arrived from his nearby Manga de Clavo estate—agreed to a general cessation of hostilities. Baudin's vessels would be allowed to refresh their provisions ashore, while French citizens were promised some measure of compensation and the blockade was to be lifted for eight months while a diplomatic resolution to each nation's grievances was worked out.

Assault on Veracruz (November 30, 1838)

But when news of Rincón's and Gaona's capitulation reached Mexico City on November 30, 1838, an infuriated government ordered both officers arrested and their agreement voided, then took a vote that declared that a state of war existed against France. Santa Anna was informed of this rejection on the night of December 3, 1838, and given command over the 700–800 soldiers remaining in the city (out of a nominal garrison of 1,353 men) with orders to resist the French invaders. The next morning, he informed Baudin of this rejection of the truce, and both leaders agreed to refrain from a resumption of hostilities until 8:00 a.m. on December 5, 1838.

That same night, Gen. Mariano Arista entered Veracruz, having ridden on ahead of an 871-man relief-column that he had left encamped a few miles away at Santa Fe, so as to consult with Santa Anna. The latter ordered Arista's contingent to plan on advancing on Veracruz's outlying town of Los Pocitos by dawn before both commanders went to bed at 2:00 a.m. A few hours later, they were awakened by gunfire, as Baudin swept down on Veracruz's waterfront in a three-pronged assault. Boatloads of French marines and sailors occupied the Santiago and Concepción Bastions at the city's southeastern and northwestern corners, spiking their few guns, while other French forces advanced from the wharf into the city's main square.

Santa Anna narrowly escaped from his headquarters at the corner of Coliseo and Damas Streets, but Arista was taken, surrendering his sword to the prince of Joinville. Baudin then besieged Veracruz's garrison within their fortress-like barracks in La Merced Square, vainly firing on its doors with the small artillery pieces that he had brought along in a bid to gain entry. After an hour of fruitless bombardment though, the French decided to retreat, hoisting a white flag to call for a truce, which the Mexicans refused to honor.

Baudin managed to fight his way back to the wharf with his wounded by 10:00 a.m., beginning his reembarkation. Santa Anna arrived on the scene an hour later with 200 men that he had hastily formed up into a company, only to receive a blast from a French boat gun covering the beach, which killed 9 of his men and blew off Santa Anna's left leg below the knee, as well as a finger from his right hand. Baudin, having suffered 8 men killed and 60 wounded during his foray ashore, retired to his warships and continued bombarding Veracruz for another two hours, while the Mexicans retreated out of the devastated city that afternoon to take up safer positions in the dunes beyond.

Diplomatic Settlement (December 1838–March 1839)

With passions at last beginning to cool on both sides after this bloodletting, Baudin two weeks later dismissed part of his blockading squadron from outside Veracruz on December 16, 1838, and six days afterward the British ambassador Richard Pakenham arrived to help mediate a settlement of the extended Franco-Mexican dispute. Eventually, a meeting was arranged between Baudin and the Mexican delegates Manuel Eduardo de Gorostiza and Guadalupe Victoria on March 7, 1839, a peace treaty being signed two days later whereby Mexico agreed to pay the original 600,000-*peso* compensation, while the French restored San Juan de Ulúa to Mexican control and Veracruz's harbor was once more opened for trade.

See also: Cakes, War of the.

Further Reading

Aquino Sánchez, Faustino A. *Intervención francesa, 1838–1839: la diplomacia mexicana y el imperialismo del librecambio.* Mexico City: INAH, 1997.

"France and Mexico." *Niles' National Register,* 5th series, 55, no. 26 (February 23, 1839): 404—5.

Giménez, Manuel María. *Memorias.* Mexico City: Bouret, 1911, 59–75.

Klier, Betje. "'Peste, Tempestad, & Patisserie': The Pastry War, France's Contribution to the Maintenance of Texas' Independence." *Gulf Coast Historical Review* 12, no. 2 (1997): 58–73.

Veracruz, U.S. Bombardment and Occupation of (1847)

Seizure of Mexico's largest seaport so as to allow Maj. Gen. Winfield Scott to land his invasion force and open up a "second front" during the Mexican-American War.

Having already invaded the northern portion of Mexico successfully out of Texas, with Gen. Zachary Taylor's army seizing the cities of Monterrey, Saltillo, and Tampico, the American government found its efforts stalemated by early 1847, with the administration of President Santa Anna refusing to come to the bargaining table. A separate seaborne expedition was therefore organized under Gen. Winfield Scott, designed to disembark a second U.S. army at Veracruz, so as to press inland and directly threaten Mexico City.

After marshalling his convoy off Lobos Island southeast of Tampico, Scott's steamer *Massachusetts* gave the signal on March 2, 1847, to get under way for Antón Lizardo. His 8,600-man army, traveling aboard 40 transports, was divided into three divisions under Brigadier Generals William J. Worth and David E. Twiggs, and Maj. Gen. Robert Patterson. The first vessels began arriving near Veracruz two days later, anchoring between Antón Lizardo and Salmedina Island, so as to begin preparing for a disembarkation.

Scott himself went aboard *Petrita* along with his senior staff on March 6, 1847 (including Captains Robert E. Lee and Joseph E. Johnston, plus Lieutenants Pierre G. T. Beauregard and George G. Meade) to view the proposed landing site at Collado Beach, three miles southeast of Veracruz. The steamer was unexpectedly shelled by the big guns at San Juan de Ulúa, though, compelling it to withdraw. After a one-day delay, during which the American troops were transshipped from transports aboard navy vessels, commodore David Conner's men-of-war stood toward Sacrificios Island at 11:00 a.m. on March 9, 1847, detaching a line of gunboats closer inshore by 3:30 p.m. to provide covering fire at Collado Beach. The gunboats opened up their bombardment at 5:00, an hour before Worth's 2,600-man 1st Division began disembarking. This landing met no opposition, so was soon followed by Twiggs's 2nd Division, then Patterson's 3rd. By nightfall, all 8,600 American soldiers were ashore, along with a 1,200-man naval contingent, being joined the next morning by Scott and his headquarters staff.

Before sunrise of March 10, 1847, Conner directed Tattnall's *Spitfire* to mount a brief diversionary attack against San Juan de Ulúa, while the American troops fanned out at daylight to begin investing the city proper. Veracruz (population: 15,000) was defended by 3,360 Mexican troops—about two-thirds being regulars—with 86 guns under Maj. Gen. Juan Morales, while their offshore island fortress of San Juan de Ulúa boasted an additional 1,030 men and 135 artillery pieces. However, the ill-prepared defenders offered no resistance to the invaders' progress, preferring to wait behind their ramparts.

Shortly after midday on March 13, 1847, Twiggs's movement reached the sea northwest of Veracruz, thus entirely cutting off the city. Patterson had meanwhile taken up position in the center with Worth farther southeast, after which the Americans began building formal siege works. By noon of March 21, 1847, their first heavy batteries were ready to open fire, Scott calling for Morales's capitulation the next afternoon. Upon being rejected, a concerted bombardment commenced, seconded by Perry's warships offshore.

The besiegers increased their rate of fire until dawn of March 26, 1847, when Gen. José Juan Lander—the new garrison commander inside Veracruz, in place of Morales, who had fallen ill—requested terms. The city officially capitulated three days afterward, along with San Juan de Ulúa, all the defenders being paroled and their officers allowed to retain their sidearms, mounts, and personal effects. At a cost of 14 American dead and 59 wounded, Scott had gained a secure supply base for his advance inland.

Aftermath (March 30–April 11, 1847)

On the afternoon of March 30, 1847, Scott furthermore detached Quitman's brigade to march southeast from Veracruz along the coast and seize the port of Alvarado, supported by a naval squadron offshore. When the three-gun, 60-man, 230-ton, twin-propeller steamer *Scourge* of Lt. Charles G. Hunter bombarded La Vigía Battery that next morning, he discovered Alvarado already abandoned by its Mexican garrison, so immediately occupied the place and pushed upriver as far as Tlacotalpan, capturing three vessels and burning a fourth.

After a brief occupation, Quitman's brigade rejoined Scott at Veracruz, leaving the U.S. Navy to garrison both Alvarado and Tlacotalpan under Capt. Isaac Mayo. One week later, Scott's vanguard departed Veracruz under Twiggs on April 8, 1847, consisting of 2,600 infantrymen, a dragoon squadron, two light field batteries, and a dozen heavier pieces. He was to be followed up the national highway toward Jalapa by Patterson's division before Scott himself emerged from Veracruz on April 11, 1847, with the balance of his forces.

See also: Mexican-American War.

Further Reading

Bauer, Karl Jack. *Surfboats and Horse Marines: U.S. Naval Operations in the Mexican War, 1846–1848.* Annapolis, MD: U.S. Naval Institute Press, 1969.

Johnson, Timothy D. *A Gallant Little Army: The Mexico City Campaign.* Lawrence: University Press of Kansas, 2007.

McCaffrey, James M., and George Sanders. "America's First Day: The Veracruz Landing of 1847." *Military History of the West* 25, no. 1 (1995): 51–68.

Tucker, Spencer C. *The Encyclopedia of the Mexican-American War.* Santa Barbara, CA: ABC-CLIO, 2013.

Veracruz, Conservative Sieges of (1859–1860)

Two failed attempts by General (and "substitute president") Miguel Miramón to capture this port city while it was hosting Benito Juárez's displaced federal government during the War of the Reform.

After escaping from western Mexico through the Pacific port of Manzanillo with his cabinet on April 11, 1858, the liberal president had circled around through Panama and Havana to New Orleans, where he boarded the steamer *Tennessee* on May 1st and appeared off Veracruz three days later. His arrival having been anticipated, the liberal state governor Manuel Gutiérrez Zamora went aboard this vessel and accorded Juárez a warm welcome, escorting him and his exiled ministers ashore amid a 21-gun salute as night fell that same May 4, 1858, through city streets that were thronged with cheering well-wishers. The next day, the liberal government was formally reconstituted in Veracruz and messages duly sent out to their constitutionalist supporters throughout Mexico.

First Stillborn Conservative Siege (1859)

Distracted by already ongoing campaigns to retain Guadalajara and San Luis Potosí in central Mexico, as well as by having to resolve an attempted coup in Mexico City around Christmas 1858, the conservative champion Miramón was prevented from marching down from the national capital to invest the liberal administration in its new transplanted headquarters until nine months after its relocation. Eventually, though, the conservatives' Reserve Division of their *Ejército de Oriente* or "Army of the East" began departing Mexico City with a few mortars on February 14, 1859, followed two days later by Miramón. Passing through Puebla, they reached Orizaba by February 24, 1859, where they rendezvoused with other converging battalions. Miramón combined these forces into two infantry divisions under Generals Carlos Oronoz and Francisco Casanova, plus a cavalry brigade under Gen. José María Cobos.

This conservative force of 5,000 men, accompanied by 46 artillery pieces and 123 wagons, began departing Orizaba in four separate segments as of March 2, 1859, so as to march down out of the central highlands into Veracruz's torrid coastal zone in manageable groups, against liberal opposition. Miramón's vanguard was repulsed when it tried to fight its way across Jamapa Ravine three days later, defended by Generals Pedro Ampudia and Ignacio de la Llave. However, this liberal contingent withdrew at dawn on March 8, 1859, upon learning that another conservative column was maneuvering around it in the distance. Miramón's progression was then slowed for a second time when he discovered that the bridges at Atoyac and Chiquihuite had been destroyed (allegedly by a volunteer American engineer serving in the liberal ranks, who was caught and executed at Soledad a few days later).

After resting for four days at Soledad while these bridges were being repaired, Miramón resumed his advance on March 16, 1859, reaching Tejería—only nine miles short of Veracruz—with a single brigade after nightfall. On the morning of March 18, 1859, the conservative "substitute president" rode toward the city with his staff, drawing fire from a score of its heavy guns when he appeared atop the Encanto Dune to study Veracruz's defenses through his glass from three-quarters of a mile away. All the gates had been sealed up, and its liberal garrison consisted of 539 gunners, 2,000 infantrymen, and a few hundred auxiliaries; Ampudia furthermore commanded a division of another 2,600 troops, who were prowling through the nearby maze of dunes in hopes of threatening the conservatives' lines of communication.

Miramón therefore rested his brigade at Tejería for six days while more and more conservative battalions continued to stagger in from their cross-country treks, many moving at night in order to avoid the scorching heat of day. Soon, disease began thinning their ranks as well. Finally the investment of Veracruz was supposed to start when a conservative column under Casanova made a diversionary strike against Alvarado on the morning of March 24, 1859, while Miramón's vanguard simultaneously advanced to begin establishing siege camps in the dunes right outside the city, moving in so close as to even draw fire from its batteries—only to then do an abrupt about-face and retreat back into Tejería, as information had been received that Miramón's vital powder and supply trains had never departed Mexico City.

Now desperately short of provisions, the conservatives broke camp and began drawing off toward Orizaba the next day, moving out of the region with some difficulty, pursued from a safe distance by the relieved liberals. Veracruz's militiamen were discharged from their duties by March 30, 1859, and the city gates reopened. The U.S. government representative Robert M. McLane had reached the port immediately after Miramón had lifted his siege and officially recognized the legitimacy of Juárez's government on April 1, 1859.

This provoked violent criticism from Mexico's conservatives, knowing that Washington would expect territorial and commercial concessions from Juárez in exchange for their assistance. And McLane indeed signed a treaty with the liberal foreign minister Melchor Ocampo on December 14, 1859, whereby the United States would provide the liberal government with $4 million in exchange for free passage for rail lines across both the Isthmus of Tehuantepec and northwestern Mexico to be guarded by American troops. However, this MacLane-Ocampo Treaty eventually did not win ratification in the U.S. Senate.

Second Failed Conservative Siege (1860)

Miramón marched out of Mexico City again with a large army on February 8, 1860, to proceed down to the Gulf coast and besiege Juárez once more within Veracruz. Despite repeated guerrilla assaults, the conservative general established his headquarters southeast of his objective at Antón Lizardo by March 6, 1860, when secret help appeared: thanks to covert financing from the Spanish government, conservative Rear Adm. Tomás Marín had been allowed to hire the vessels *General Miramón* and *Marqués de la Habana* at Havana so as to blockade Veracruz in support of Miramón's besieging army.

However, when these ships sailed menacingly past the liberals' island fortress of San Juan de Ulúa without displaying any national ensign, representatives of the Juárez government ashore declare them to be piratical craft, thereby subjecting them to capture by any vessel, either domestic or foreign. Availing himself of this excuse, Cmdr. Thomas Turner of the U.S. sloop of war *Saratoga*—stationed at Veracruz as part of Washington's ongoing support for the exiled liberal government against French, Spanish, and British backers of the conservative cause—immediately sortied and captured both hired vessels that same night after a brisk exchange of gunfire. In addition to depriving Miramón of his blockaders, this action cost the conservatives two mortars, 1,000 shells, and 4,000 rifles, which were being brought from Cuba, although the ships themselves were eventually returned to Cuba after adjudication by the U.S. federal court in New Orleans.

On March 15, 1860, Miramón began a desultory bombardment of Veracruz but soon ran out of heavy ammunition and was once more compelled to withdraw toward Mexico City six days later.

See also: Ampudia Grimarest, Pedro; Miramón Tarelo, Miguel Gregorio de la Luz Atenógenes; Reform, War of the.

Further Reading

"Further from Mexico: The Retreat of Miramón." *New York Times*, April 15, 1859.

"Mexico: The March of Miramón upon Vera Cruz." *New York Times*, March 15, 1859.

"Our Mexican Relations." *New York Times*, March 21, 1860.

Ramírez de Arellano, Manuel. *Apuntes de la campaña de Oriente*. Mexico City: Navarro, 1859.

Sitio de Veracruz por Miguel Miramón. Mexico City: Editorial Citlalpétel, 1968.

Veracruz, American Occupation of (1914)

Punitive landing and seizure executed by a U.S. naval expedition with the aim of chastising the regime of Mexico's usurper president, Gen. Victoriano Huerta.

Background (April 9–14, 1914)

After an unarmed boat party from a U.S. Navy vessel had been briefly detained by mistake on April 9, 1914, near Tampico—the city being held by a Huertista garrison under Gen. Ignacio Morelos Zaragoza and besieged by rebels—they were soon released with an apology for any inconvenience. But Rear Adm. Henry Thomas Mayo, in command of the 4th Division of the U.S. Atlantic Fleet, which was stationed off Mexico's Gulf coast to protect American interests, refused to be mollified by this gesture and (without clearance from Washington) insisted that the Mexican general

U.S. Army troops marching through the streets of Veracruz on April 29, 1914, to supplement the landing force of Marines and sailors that had seized the city eight days earlier. (Library of Congress)

punish the offending soldiers, issue a formal apology in writing, and hoist the American flag ashore, saluting it with a 21-gun salvo.

The refusal to comply with this latter demand provoked a diplomatic showdown, so Pres. Woodrow Wilson (who disliked Huerta for his brutal path to power) ordered the U.S. Atlantic Fleet five days later to begin concentrating off of Mexico, so Rear Adm. Charles J. Badger's battleship squadron sailed from Hampton Roads that same evening of April 14, 1914.

Occupation (April 21–November 13, 1914)

April 21, 1914: Wishing to punish Huerta by intercepting a shipment of 200 machine guns and 15 million rounds of ammunition that were scheduled to arrive aboard the Hamburg-America liner *Ypiranga*, Wilson authorized 58-year-old rear admiral Frank Friday Fletcher to disembark his forces and seize Veracruz (population: 40,000).

The American commander first advised his British counterpart, 52-year-old rear admiral Sir Christopher G. F. M. "Kit" Craddock aboard the 680-man, 9,800-ton armored cruiser HMS *Essex*, plus the captain of the antique, 9,200-ton Spanish armored cruiser *Emperador Carlos V*—whose warships lay in the roadstead—of these impending hostilities. Mexican commodore Alejandro Cerisola, commander of the 160-man garrison on the offshore island fortress of San Juan de Ulúa, was also forewarned.

At 11:00 a.m., 800 American seamen and Marines headed inshore under Capt. William R. Rush of the USS *Florida* and Marine Lt. Col. Wendell C. "Buck" Neville, while Gen. Gustavo Maass Flores—the

60-year-old military commander for the city of Veracruz proper and a brother-in-law of Huerta—was advised not to offer any resistance with his 18th and 19th Battalions (600 regulars under Brigadiers Luis B. Becerril and Francisco Figueroa, respectively). The latter withdrew 10 miles inland by train to Tejería, but civilian snipers and 90 cadets from the Mexican Naval Academy opened fire around noon, as the invaders began moving through city streets. Some 100 reinforcements were therefore rushed ashore from USS *Utah* and subdued all resistance by 3:00 p.m., 4 Americans being killed and 20 wounded.

The 8,100-ton *Ypiranga* was detained on its arrival at 2:00 p.m., its armaments proving to have originated not in Germany but rather from the Remington Company in the United States. Admiral Badger's battleships *Arkansas*, *New Hampshire*, *South Carolina*, *Vermont*, and *New Jersey* arrived after midnight of April 21–22, setting an additional 1,500 bluejackets and Marines ashore the next dawn. (Eventually, as more U.S. warships joined, 3,300 sailors and 2,500 Marines entered Veracruz.) Sporadic sniper fire resumed, yet the city was firmly under U.S. control by 11:00 a.m. of April 23rd, when Col. John J. Lejeune disembarked from USS *Hancock* to assume temporary command over its Marine occupiers. Some 126 Mexicans died, and another 195 were injured during this operation, compared to 17 American dead and 63 wounded.

Although directed against Huerta, this invasion was resented by all Mexicans. At Tampico, crews from the neutral HMS *Essex* and German cruiser *Dresden* were to evacuate American civilians under a flag of truce. Meanwhile, San Juan de Ulúa capitulated to the Americans by April 26th and was actually occupied by a Marine company from the battleship *North Dakota* two days

later. Shortly before midnight of April 27th, Brig. Frederick Funston arrived from Texas City with the 5th Reinforced Brigade (4th, 7th, 19th, and 28th Infantry Regiments) aboard the transports *Kilpatrick*, *Meade*, *Sumner*, and *McClellan* to garrison Veracruz.

U.S. forces would remain in possession of the city throughout most of that year, as Washington was bewildered by the rapid-fire changes in Mexican administrations: Huerta being succeeded by Carranza, who in turn was challenged and driven out of the national capital by Villa and Zapata. Eventually, Secretary of State Bryan simply announced on November 13, 1914, that Veracruz would be unilaterally evacuated.

See also: *Decena Trágica*; Huerta Márquez, José Victoriano.

Further Reading

Eisenhower, John S. D. *Intervention!: The United States and the Mexican Revolution, 1913–1917*. New York: W. W. Norton & Company, 1993.

Foreman, Michael A. "A Storm in Veracruz." *American History Illustrated* 29, no. 1 (March 1994): 28–37, 72.

Villa, Pancho (1878–1923)

Lowly bandit who would become a charismatic leader of vast armies during the Mexican Revolution before eventually being defeated on the battlefield and dying by assassination.

He was born on June 5, 1878, and baptized one month later as Doroteo Arango Arámbula, the first of five children of Agustín Arango Vela and his wife, Micaela Arámbula Álvarez (another two sons and two daughters would follow over the next five years). The Arango family was poor,

Pancho Villa posing with a Schneider-Canet 75mm gun, ca. March 1914, resting his hand on the shoulder of his diminutive artillery commander, Col. Martiniano Servín. (Library of Congress)

living on a ranch named Río Grande near the hamlet of San Juan del Río in the arid northern state of Durango. Young Doroteo never received any formal education, and after his father's death—being the eldest— supported his mother and four younger siblings by working as a woodsman and itinerant salesman in the Sierra Madre range. Big, strong, and a natural horseman, he would always possess the common touch among Mexico's poor.

Outlaw (1894–1910)

Legend has it that in 1894, at the age of 16, Doroteo Arango had returned home to find that his younger sister Martina had been seduced and abandoned by Agustín López Negrete, son of the owner of Gogojito Hacienda near Canatlán. In a fit of rage, Arango had wounded him with a gunshot, then in the aftermath to this confrontation, had stolen a horse and fled into the

mountains. After a couple of years, he joined a gang of rustlers and thieves led by Ignacio Parra, choosing to forsake his real name of Doroteo Arango to instead adopt the pseudonym of Francisco "Pancho" Villa—an infamous local bandit who had recently been hanged by the authorities.

When Parra was subsequently slain in a police ambush, Villa had temporarily assumed leadership over the surviving outlaws before the gang disintegrated. Roaming into the adjacent state of Chihuahua, Villa had found occasional work as a manual laborer at El Verde mine and as a bricklayer in Chihuahua City before he once more reverted to a life of crime, taking to the hills with a new gang. More than a decade would elapse in this fugitive existence, Villa living for spells in different towns under assumed names before having to go on the run again. This nomadic life changed when his friend and fellow outlaw, Eleuterio

Soto, introduced Villa during the summer of 1910 to the political agitator Abraham González, who believed that a revolution was needed in order to sweep away Mexico's Porfirian dictatorship and oppressive class system.

Maderista Commander (1910–1912)

Although never having been formally educated, Villa embraced González's doctrine wholeheartedly and agreed as of October 4, 1910, to head up a bodyguard of 15 armed men (including Tomás Urbina) who would protect this wanted agitator from being discovered in Chihuahua City by the *rurales* or police. Six weeks later, González sent Villa as part of a detachment of two dozen riders under the command of Cástulo Herrera, up into the Sierra Azul mountains on the night of November 17, 1910, to join the impending revolt in support of the defrauded presidential challenger, Francisco I. Madero.

Herrera and Villa captured the small town of San Andrés on November 21, 1910, and repulsed the handful of federal soldiers who arrived by train that same afternoon, in a vain attempt to reclaim it. Their group quickly grew in numbers, in no small part thanks to Villa's popularity. Brave, well armed, willing to share any hardship, and used to living rough, the 32-year-old ex-bandit proved a natural leader and was furthermore such a noteworthy rider that he would eventually become nicknamed the *Centauro del Norte* or "Centaur of the North." By the first weeks of December 1910, Herrera and Villa were leading perhaps 500 riders and even probed the defenses at Chihuahua City. However, it was not until more insurrections erupted and the government forces became beset from many directions that the revolutionaries could directly mount a major assault.

With Pascual Orozco serving as a "general" and Villa as a "colonel," Madero personally led some 3,000 ill-disciplined rebels in a drive during the first week of April 1911 to besiege the border town of Ciudad Juárez (opposite El Paso, Texas). Orozco and Villa were disappointed at not being allowed to immediately assault its 700-man federal garrison under Gen. Juan N. Navarro, as Madero instead arranged a 10-day truce on April 23, 1911, and entered into negotiations with plenipotentiaries sent from Mexico City by President Díaz. Tiring of this, Orozco and Villa planned for their besiegers to initiate an exchange of gunfire with the *federales* on May 8, 1911, while they were both visiting El Paso. This fighting soon spiraled out of control, so Madero had no choice but to agree to an all-out assault that pushed the outnumbered defenders back inside their cavalry barracks, where they capitulated two days later.

The dictator Díaz resigned from office and went into exile before that same month was out, allowing Madero to enter Mexico City in triumph by June 7, 1911, and prepare to run again in a new presidential election. Idealistic and inexperienced, this youthful figurehead tried to reward his backers such as Villa with appointments as militia auxiliaries, but few were satisfied with this unfamiliar role. When the disgruntled Pascual Orozco rose in rebellion against Madero's presidency in Chihuahua City on March 3, 1912, and defeated an army sent against him at Rellano Station, Villa formed part of a new Maderista force organized under the command of the hard-bitten ex-Porfirian professional, general Victoriano Huerta.

Near-Execution, Imprisonment, Escape (June–December 1912)

Villa was given the honorary title in this new formation of "brigade general" of his own contingent of 300 riders, but soon angered his commander. After overlooking some minor excesses committed by his ill-disciplined troops, Huerta ordered Villa arrested on the evening of June 3, 1912, for ignoring a direct order to restore some stolen horses. Standing before a firing squad next dawn, Villa begged for his life, and so was sent off in chains aboard a train to Mexico City, to stand trial before a military tribunal.

He arrived at the national capital and was incarcerated in Lecumberri Penitentiary on June 7, 1912, remaining incarcerated there for five months until he was transferred on November 7, 1912, to the military prison at Santiago Tlatelolco. With a court employee as his accomplice, Villa managed to file through the iron mesh on the door leading from that prison into the courtroom during Christmas recess on December 24, 1912, don civilian clothing and a pair of dark glasses, then exit the building into a waiting automobile. Driven to Toluca, he took a train to Guadalajara and then on to Manzanillo; a ship to Mazatlán; and finally another train until he at last crossed the border safely into Nogales, Arizona, on January 2, 1913.

Renewed Campaign (April 1913)

The fugitive Villa traveled to El Paso, Texas, writing secretly from there to Gov. Abraham González of Chihuahua, who sent him some money and advised him to remain in the United States until González could personally intercede on Villa's behalf with Madero. However, the president was betrayed and murdered in Mexico City in February 1913, followed shortly thereafter by González himself, after which the new federal regime under Gen. Victoriano Huerta apparently contacted the U.S. authorities in early March 1913, requesting Villa's extradition. Concerned that he might be arrested and deported, Villa received 1,000 *pesos* from the wealthy supporter José María Maytorena in Tucson, Arizona, which he used to purchase some weapons and slip back across the border with seven men on March 9, 1913.

Within a month, Villa had secured a military commission from Coahuila's anti-Huertista governor Venustiano Carranza and was operating in the mountains of neighboring Chihuahua. His first significant victory occurred when Villa's guerrilla band was overtaken at the rural Hacienda de Bustillos railway station on June 13, 1913, by a pursuing pair of military trains under federal colonel Jesús Mancilla, bearing a combined total of 500 men from the 33rd Battalion and their *colorado* auxiliaries. Villa was able to defeat this force, suffering only 1 dead and 7 wounded, while killing at least 54 attackers and retaining one of their locomotives, then proceeded to batter another federal contingent at Nueva Casas Grandes station five days afterward—for which feats Carranza promoted him to *general de brigada* or "brigade general" (the rank above brigadier; *see escalafón general*).

Two months later, Villa's large following won an even more impressive victory: learning while resting at Namiquipa that 1,000 *colorados* under Gen. Félix Terrazas were detraining at nearby San Andrés to ride in his pursuit, Villa surprised this brigade by attacking them at dawn on August 26, 1913. The Orozquistas were beaten and dispersed, suffering 72 killed and 237 captured (all of whom were executed), while leaving behind two 75mm Mondragón cannons, 412 high-powered rifles, and 20,000 rounds of ammunition. In light of this triumph, Villa was invited to assume command over the numerous rebel bands that were operating in the neighboring state of Coahuila so as to together overrun its strategic railway hub at Torreón.

Leaving a sizeable detachment to maintain watch on Chihuahua City, Villa took his 1,200-man "brigade" aboard three trains, along with his two captured Mondragón artillery pieces and some machine guns, so as to meet up with an additional 400 riders under Maclovio Herrera at Santa Rosalía de Camargo on September 15, 1913. This combined force then proceeded together, being joined en route by another 600 under Tomás Urbina at Ciudad Jiménez, to the Hacienda de la Loma on the banks of the Nazas River (15 miles west of Torreón). There they found more local bands awaiting them, and more continuing to arrive,

Year of Victories (1913–1914)

Starting in late September 1913, Villa began winning a string of victories that escalated in size, mushrooming his reputation and military power. First, he led the 10,000 or so men of his newly created *División del Norte* in a headlong assault against Torreón, carrying that city after a two-day battle that left thousands of casualties. One month later, he departed from there northwestward with the bulk of his forces aboard a large train convoy to conquer the state of Chihuahua—initially failing to drive the main federal concentration out of its capital but slipping shortly thereafter into its northern border city of Ciudad Guzmán (opposite El Paso, Texas) with a couple of his "brigades" concealed aboard a coal train, shortly past midnight on November 14–15, 1913. They completely surprised and overwhelmed its garrison; and upon learning that a mixed force of 5,500 federal regulars and mounted *colorado* auxiliaries were hastening north from Chihuahua City to recuperate Ciudad Guzmán, Villa—rather than dispersing with his booty, as had been the common rebel practice—instead deployed his 6,200 men into a ragged battle line near the hamlet of

Tierra Blanca and routed these *federales* in a pitched battle as they detrained.

Villa followed up this unexpected victory by traveling back southward from Tierra Blanca to occupy half-empty Chihuahua City on December 8, 1913, and assume office as "governor." When the 3,000 troops that he subsequently detached at year's end under his subordinates Pánfilo Natera and Toribio Ortega failed to expel some 3,000 federal soldiers and 2,000 *colorado* irregulars who were cornered in the border town of Ojinaga (opposite Presidio, Texas), Villa himself brought over more reinforcements and drove these terrified defenders across the river into U.S. internment within 30 minutes of launching his opening charge on the afternoon of January 10, 1914.

His prestige now soaring, and his División del Norte swelling into a powerful force of 15,000-plus troops as more and more volunteers kept joining, Villa then quit Chihuahua City with a convoy of 15 trains on March 16, 1914, returning southeast so as to reclaim Torreón from the 7,000 federal soldiers and 6,000 *colorado* irregulars who had reoccupied it during his absence. Six days later, his vanguard charged into the defenses outside its satellite city of Gómez Palacio, pushing that detachment back across the Nazas River into Torreón proper by the night of March 26–27, 1914, with heavy losses inflicted on both sides. More Villista brigades continued joining as at least 5,000 more reinforcements arrived by rail, though, so despite suffering almost 4,000 total casualties, he was able to beat the federal garrison to pieces, only 4,000 demoralized defenders with scarcely any ammunition left managing to flee eastward under cover of a dust storm on the night of April 2–3, 1914.

Villa swiftly followed this retreating force and three days afterward engaged yet another 6,200-man federal concentration only 32 miles east of Torreón, dug in around the rural San Pedro de las Colonias railway station. After a week of heavy fighting during which he inflicted another 3,500 casualties on these *federales*, their shattered divisions limped away eastward in the direction of Saltillo, as he inspected the ruins after nightfall on April 13, 1914.

Given his string of impressive victories, Villa hoped to be rewarded by having his División del Norte accorded the status of an army by the constitutionalist political figurehead, *primer jefe* or "first chief" Venustiano Carranza, as well as to be allowed to drive southward through Zacatecas toward the national capital, but neither wish was granted. Instead, Carranza ordered Villa to press eastward from Torreón to annihilate the last federal remnants around Saltillo, while the constitutionalist general Álvaro Obregón was to be accorded the honor of penetrating into central Mexico with his *Ejército del Noroeste* or "Army of the Northeast" to capture the capital.

One month after his triumph at San Pedro de las Colonias, Villa would rout the remnants of its defeated Huertista army at the Battle of Paredón on May 17, 1914, with contemptuous ease—these 5,000 *federales'* resolve already so badly shaken that they would break and flee by the thousands within 15 minutes of his opening cavalry charge at the head of 6,000 riders. Saltillo was subsequently abandoned without a fight by its 15,000-man federal garrison, leaving Villa in uncontested control of the region.

Carranza thereupon ordered Brig. Gen. Pánfilo Natera to initiate an assault against Zacatecas with his 6,000 troops on June 10, 1914, even though that city was defended by at least 12,000 regulars and auxiliaries, backed by 11 fieldpieces and 90 machine guns. Once repulsed, Carranza telegraphed Villa and instructed him to begin detaching brigades from his own much larger and better-equipped División del Norte at Torreón so as to send these as reinforcements to Natera. Having already expressed an interest in conducting an attack against Zacatecas, Villa instead reiterated his request for permission to lead his own troops personally, which Carranza spitefully refused.

Angry, Villa disobeyed and struck out southward with his main army on June 16, 1914, joining Natera at Fresnillo. Six days later, Villa had 25,000 troops and 50 guns massed all around Zacatecas and launched a massive assault at 10:00 a.m. on June 23, 1914. By evening, its federal garrison had been slaughtered and the shattered city was in his hands. Yet two weeks afterward, Obregón smashed the 12,000-man federal garrison holding Guadalajara at the Battle of Orendáin, so—while Villa's División del Norte was sidelined, denied the necessary coal by Carranza to continue moving— Obregón was able to advance upon Mexico City as the dictator Huerta fled the country, and parade triumphantly into the national capital by August 15, 1914.

Villa and Zapata were deeply dissatisfied when Carranza followed a few days later and proclaimed himself president, so that Villa engineered a political convention at Aguascalientes which refused to recognize this title, and ended in rancorous rupture by mid-November 1914. Obregón loyally declared war against Villa from Mexico City on November 19, 1914, although his army was heavily outnumbered by the combined *villistas* and *zapatistas*. He did not resist as their huge armies quickly began converging upon Mexico City from north and south, instead retreating eastward into Veracruz.

At the peak of his power, Villa and Zapata staged an enormous parade of perhaps 50,000 armed men into the streets of the national capital on December 6, 1914, and posed for photographs sitting in the Presidential Chair, although neither aspired to occupy the office itself. After a few weeks of token occupation, their forces largely withdrew, each retiring into their own territories and allowing Obregón to reclaim Mexico City without a fight by January 28, 1915, and prepare to carry the fight to them.

Year of Defeats (1915)

Obregón spent five weeks assembling a new field force in and around Mexico City that was to be officially designated as the *Ejército de Operaciones* or "Operational Army" of the constitutionalist government, then sent a vanguard unit probing northward on March 7, 1915, which soon clashed with three Villista cavalry brigades near the rural Peón railway station in the state of Querétaro. Obregón followed this pathfinder unit three days later with his main body, heading up into the mountainous central region of Mexico aboard a stream of trains in a direct challenge to Villa for a showdown.

Reaching the small city of Celaya in the state of Guanajuato by April 4, 1915, Obregón learned that Villa had indeed hastened south from Torreón to meet him, eager for battle. Villa quickly closed the distance between both armies, departing Salamanca on the morning of April 6th with 20,000 men and 22 artillery pieces aboard three train columns, hurtling across the final 20 miles against the entrenched constitutionalists. Although Obregón commanded only 6,000 cavalrymen and 5,000 infantrymen, his smaller army was much better disciplined and had greater firepower than Villa's unwieldy mass, especially as Celaya's defensive lines featured 86 heavy machine gun emplacements.

The Villistas began detraining 10 miles west of the city that same afternoon of April 6, 1915, and spent the next 24 hours enduring heavy losses in repeated but fruitless charges against Obregón's infantry, who were well dug in. Finally, he unleashed the unengaged constitutionalist cavalry, sending them on a vast prearranged encircling move, so when their closing pincers began materializing in Villa's rear on the afternoon of April 7th, the attackers broke and fled in panic toward their trains, leaving behind 1,800 dead, 3,000 wounded, 500 prisoners, plus heaps of abandoned materiel. Obregón's losses totaled 558 killed and 365 injured in this, the First Battle of Celaya.

Shrewdly judging his opponent's impulsive character, Obregón remained in Celaya, resting his victorious troops while calling in fresh formations to bolster his army's strength to 7,000 infantrymen and 8,000 cavalry troopers now that he had come to grips with the enemy. Villa spent the next few days feverishly rebuilding his battered army as well by summoning large detachments into his marshaling area at Salamanca. Finally, Villa ordered a mass parade of a new army of 30,000 men on Monday, April 12, 1915, and the next dawn began sending out his infantry and guns aboard trains toward Celaya once again while his masses of cavalry rode along beside the rails. Having been bloodied previously, the Villistas took several hours to unlimber their artillery five miles west of the city and form up into proper attack columns before advancing across the arid landscape toward Celaya.

The result was nonetheless the same: despite their two-to-one superiority in numbers, the attackers spent themselves over the next two days in costly attacks against

Obregón's well-positioned infantry until his cavalry emerged from concealment in a forest to his rear on April 15, 1915, and launched another massive envelopment to the north, which caused Villa's disheartened followers to break and flee westward by that same nightfall, leaving behind a further 4,000 dead, 5,000 wounded, 6,000 prisoners, 1,000 saddled horses, and all their artillery. Obregón, in comparison, had lost only 138 officers and soldiers killed, plus another 276 wounded.

Bested once more in this Second Battle of Celaya, Villa disappeared northward to León, so after resting for a fortnight, Obregón pressed ever deeper into Villista territory in pursuit. Grown more cautious, Villa now hoped to lure his opponent out into the flat Trinidad plains between Silao and León, where the Villistas' numerical advantage in cavalry might work to his advantage. Obregón obliged by pushing northwest from Silao on May 7, 1915, reaching the lonely Trinidad railway station and entrenching his 14,300 infantrymen and 9,400 cavalry troopers into a huge defensive square over the next few days, which extended for 10 miles from corner to corner.

Villa was reduced to commanding only 19,500 riders and 6,000 infantrymen on this occasion, his numerical edge having been eroded. He used 8,000 of his cavalrymen to make an initial strike against Obregón's lines on May 12, 1915, and after 10 days of probes and long-range exchanges left his artillery commander, Gen. Felipe Ángeles, to maintain pressure on Obregón's main army, while personally leading another 8,000 fresh riders through the hills to surprise the main constitutionalist supply base at Silao, destroying numerous trains, bridges, and telegraphs in his opponent's rear. Obregón found this disruption worrisome, especially after he learned that Villa had returned to Duarte by the morning of June 2, 1915, and was preparing to an all-out assault with his entire strength.

And when the first Villista wave of three infantry battalions broke cover the next morning and charged directly at Santa Ana del Conde Hacienda, behind an artillery barrage laid down by Ángeles's batteries, Obregón was unexpectedly wounded—his right arm being shredded by a shell. Yet his second-in-command Hill immediately took over and decimated the advancing Villistas with counterfire from well-placed machine guns and sharp-shooting troops. After two days of exhausting their strength and ammunition in fruitless charges, Villa and Ángeles finally gave the order to retreat at dawn on June 5, 1915, their army disintegrating during the resultant pursuit, suffering 8,000 casualties—triple those of the Obregonistas, whose discipline remained intact despite their leader's grievous wound—and the loss of all their materiel.

Despite having the remnants of his right forearm surgically amputated, Obregón resumed command over his army after only a one-month convalescence, continuing to drive northward in pursuit of Villa. His forces defeated Villa's rearguard at Calvillo Ravine on July 8, 1915, then occupied the city of Aguascalientes two days later. Almost three weeks afterward, a detachment of 4,000 riders under Villa's henchman Rodolfo Fierro—retiring northward after a successful raid into central Mexico—blundered into Obregón's army in the Mariscala Hills near the city of Querétaro and were badly beaten at Jerécuaro.

Obregón seized Saltillo during the first week of September 1920, while Villa desperately tried campaigning in his home state of Sonora, being defeated at every turn.

After his lengthy and demoralizing retreat northward, Villa tried to divert Obregón from his relentless pursuit by leading his remaining 6,000 Villista troops into his opponent's home state of Sonora to make some attacks. However, four nocturnal assaults against 6,500 fresh Carrancista troops under Plutarco Elías Calles at Agua Prieta on November 2, 1915, ended in disaster for Villa. He suffered some 600 casualties among his half-starved following, after which another 400 deserted as he shifted southwest the next day toward the Sonoran capital of Hermosillo.

His 5,000 survivors fared no better there, first fighting an inconclusive yet costly battle at Alamito outside that city against a superior Carrancista force under Manuel M. Diéguez on November 18, 1915. Then four days later, Villa launched an all-out, 30-hour assault against the garrison within Hermosillo proper, during which his last troops were annihilated. He thereupon retired eastward into the mountains with only 1,400 survivors, eventually reaching Chihuahua City and disbanding his bedraggled column. Villa disappeared from there on Christmas Eve 1915, eight days before the Carrancista general Treviño arrived to reoccupy Chihuahua City. Now 37 years of age, Villa had been reduced once more to living like an outlaw in the mountains.

Columbus Raid and Pursuits (1916–1919)

On January 16, 1916, Villa's subordinates Pablo López and Rafael Castro attacked a train at Santa Isabel, bound from Chihuahua City toward the Cusihuiriáchi mining camp, in the process massacring 16 American passengers, provoking outrage in neighboring Texas. Then two months later, Villa emerged and reunited at Las Cruces with his subordinates Candelario Cervantes, Francisco Beltrán, and Pablo and Martín López on March 3, 1916, leading some 300–400 riders through Ojitos Ranch three days afterward and reaching Boca Grande to encamp by

the afternoon of March 8, 1916—with the intent of striking across the U.S. border the next dawn against the small American town of Columbus, New Mexico.

Villa's motivation for this unprovoked attack has never been clearly explained. Contemporary accounts suggested that he wished to precipitate a diplomatic crisis between the governments of Presidents Venustiano Carranza and Woodrow Wilson by giving the lie to the Carrancista claim of having pacified the war-torn neighboring country. During any resultant military pursuit, Villa could once again begin patriotically rallying followers so as to replenish his ranks, while denigrating his opponents as collaborators with the Americans. Modern research has furthermore suggested that his raid may have been encouraged as well by German agents as a means of diverting the American public's interest away from joining the ongoing World War I in Europe, but the real reasoning behind Villa's thinking has never been firmly established.

In May 1916, U.S. troops skirmished against a small Villista force at Ojos Azules Ranch, which quickly disappeared. Early the next month, though, Villa emerged from hiding to overrun the Carrancista garrison of Gen. José Cavazos in the town of Guerrero in the state of Chihuahua, being wounded in his right leg. He consequently ordered his men to disperse once again and reassemble at San Juan Bautista on the Durango border on July 6, 1916, while he himself retired into a cave to convalesce.

On the agreed date, Villa rejoined his followers—now numbering 1,000 strong—at this rendezvous, first leading them northward to forage for supplies.

The previous night, Villa had infiltrated 1,000 riders into Chihuahua City, then at 3:00 a.m. on September 16, 1916—Mexico's Independence Day—he surprised its Carrancista garrison under Treviño. Seizing much booty, he gave a speech from the municipal balcony and recruited an additional 1,500 men before disappearing as suddenly as he had materialized. Two months afterward, he took Chihuahua City again on November 23, 1916, this time occupying it for a week before emerging to confront Gen. Francisco Murguía's approaching Carrancista army on Horcasitas Plain. In a seven-hour engagement on December 1, 1916, Villa was badly beaten and compelled to abandon a trainload of provisions while retreating toward Satevo.

Surprising the Carrancista garrison at Torreón with perhaps as many as 5,000 riders three weeks later, Villa overran its defenses from three different directions and killed two generals on December 22, 1916, while driving a third to suicide. After extorting a 1-million-*peso* loan from the city's inhabitants and destroying all printing presses "so that they won't speak ill of him," he and his raiders abruptly departed five days later. But after a brutal raid on January 7, 1917, against Santa Rosalía, Coahuila, during which he massacred 300 Carrancista prisoners and Chinese civilians, Villa faded from the limelight.

Militarily spent and bereft of financial backing, he was reduced to a negligible role on the national scene, living like a fugitive and conducting operations that were little more than large-scale banditry. In June 1919, Villa and Ángeles captured the border city of Ciudad Juárez, only to be easily driven out by U.S. troops from adjacent El Paso, Texas–an intervention that again provoked a downturn in relations between Mexico City and Washington.

Surrender and Assassination (1920–1923)

Tired of this fruitless campaigning, Villa abruptly reappeared and occupied the town of Sabinas, Coahuila, with 700 riders on July 22, 1920—after first destroying its rail lines so as to prevent any surprise counterattacks by government forces—then telegraphed Pres. Adolfo de la Huerta in Mexco City, requesting amnesty. The latter agreed, deeding Villa the 25,000-acre vacant estate of Canutillo on the Durango-Chihuahua border, and paying off all of his followers so as to allow Villa to retire into private life.

However, the consequences from the many people who had died by his orders eventually caught up with him. At 7:20 a.m. on July 20, 1923, while driving his Dodge touring car back toward his hacienda of Canutillo from Parral, Villa and six companions were ambushed and killed at the corner of Zaragoza and Gabino Barreda Streets by eight assassins led by Melitón Lozoya—allegedly hired by the vengeful local landowner Jesús Salas Barrazas (with the connivance of Obregón's interior minister, Plutarco Elías Calles).

See also: Ángeles Ramírez, Felipe de Jesús; Columbus Raid; División del Norte; Huerta Márquez, José Victoriano; Madero, Obregón Salido,Álvaro; Ojinaga, Battle of; Paredón, Battle of; *rurales*; Revolution, Mexico; San Pedro de las Colonias, Battle of; Tierra Blanca, Battle of; Torreón, Villa's First Capture of; Torreón, Villa's Second Capture of.

Further Reading

Aguirre Benavides, Luis and Adrián. *Las grandes batallas de la División del Norte al mando del general Francisco Villa.* Mexico City: Diana, 1967.

Guzmán, Martín Luis. *Memoirs of Pancho Villa.* Austin: University of Texas Press, 1976 translation.

"Pancho Villa, from Bandit to Military Dictator." *El Paso Herald*, December 6, 1913, weekend edition, comic Section, 3.

Sosa, Francisco. *Biografías de mexicanos distinguidos.* Mexico City: Porrúa, 2006.

It is very sad, the predicament of the defeated; it is very bitter, the dying agony of governments, amid the laments of their supporters, and the laughter of their enemies.

— private observation after the flight of President Sebastián Lerdo de Tejada, November 1876

Walker, William (1824–1860)

American Southern filibuster who attempted to establish a proslavery enclave in Mexico,

He was born on May 8, 1824, in Nashville, Tennessee, the eldest of five children. His Scottish father, James Walker, owned a 752-acre farm next to Indian Creek in Shelby County, while his mother, Mary Norvell, was a member of a well-connected political family. Her brother John was a senator for Michigan and founded the *Philadelphia Inquirer*. Raised amid comfort and privilege, young William had also proven so precocious as to graduate summa cum laude from the University of Nashville by the age of 14. His family was wealthy enough to send him abroad to study medicine at the Universities of Edinburgh and Heidelberg before he returned to obtain his medical degree from the University of Pennsylvania in 1843.

Restless Frontiersman (1845–1852)

After briefly practicing medicine in Philadelphia, the restless young man moved to New Orleans in 1845 to study law. Admitted to the Louisiana bar the next year, Walker worked as a law clerk. He then co-owned and edited *The Crescent* newspaper and strongly upheld the proslavery views of the Deep South. Saddened by the death of his deaf-mute fiancée, Ellen Martin, and attracted by reports of the California Gold Rush, Walker had sold his interest in *The Crescent* and moved on to make a fresh start, arriving in San Francisco by 1850. He initially worked for a brief time as a journalist, been wounded twice in three duels, then relocated to Marysville to dabble in law.

Finally, Walker decided to put his Southern convictions into action. He and many other proponents of slavery not only believed in America's "Manifest Destiny" to expand into Mexican and Caribbean territories, they wished that any gains might be admitted into the Union as proslavery states. The Frenchman Raousset's 1852 foray into Mexico had seemingly threatened to impinge on this design, so Walker visited Mexico himself, hoping to secure governmental permission to create his own colony before any second French attempt might be launched.

Refused, Walker returned to San Francisco to begin selling land grants in his future Mexican colony. He used these funds to raise and arm a force of like-minded Southern volunteers and also chartered the brig *Arrow* as transport before the U.S. Army commander at San Francisco, Gen. Ethan A. Hitchcock, arrested him and impounded the vessel.

Mexican Adventure (October 1853–May 1854)

Walker nonetheless slipped away on October 15, 1853, as the self-proclaimed "colonel" of 45 followers aboard the schooner *Caroline*, disembarking at La Paz, Baja California, by November 3rd. He raised a flag with two stars, ostensibly signifying the union of Baja California and Sonora, and promulgated his newfangled "Republic of Lower California," with himself as president and a constitution modeled on the laws of Louisiana (permitting slavery).

Street fighting erupted 10 days later, though, obliging Walker and his men to retreat north into Ensenada, just south of Tijuana, which he designated as his new capital. Despite receiving reinforcements from nearby California, Walker's hold soon weakened further when he came into conflict with Ensenada's major local landowner, Antonio María Meléndez. Walker nevertheless set out east-northeastward in March 1854 with 100 American filibusters, hoping to push overland into northern Sonora, but after crossing the Colorado River into that state on April 4, 1854, he was obliged to turn back.

Now harassed by Mexican guerrillas, Walker was finally defeated by Lt. Col. Javier Castillo Negrete in a skirmish at La Grulla near Santo Tomás Mission, southeast of Ensenada, compelling him to flee northward across the border into California with his 33 remaining followers on May 8, 1854. Surrendering to U.S. military authorities, he was subsequently tried in San Francisco on a charge of violating the United States' neutrality laws, although he was acquitted that same October 1854 after the jury deliberated for only eight minutes.

Central American Campaigns and Death (1855–1860)

Walker would again escape the U.S. authorities with another small force in May 1855, this time to seize power in war-torn Nicaragua. With support from the tycoon Cornelius Vanderbilt, who wished to build a railway across Central America, Walker's conquest would even be recognized by Washington in May 1856. But he would be driven from that Central American country within a year and fail in two more attempts to reestablish himself. Finally, he would die before a Honduran firing squad, at 36 years of age.

See also: Mexican-American War.

Further Reading

May, Robert E. *Manifest Destiny's Underworld: Filibustering in Antebellum America.* Chapel Hill: University of North Carolina Press, 2002.

Stout, Joseph A., Jr. *Schemers and Dreamers: Filibustering in Mexico, 1848–1921.* Fort Worth: Texas Christian University Press, 2002.

Woll, Adrián (1795–1875)

French-born adventurer who rose to become a high-ranking officer in the Mexican Army, serving over four decades.

Early Career and American Service (1813–1816)

He was born in Saint-Germain-en-Laye, a small town located some six miles west of Paris on December 2, 1795, and was raised by his godfather, a certain "Count Nicolas." Young Adrian had distinguished himself during his early studies at the Lycée of Dijon, and his military career had apparently begun involuntarily, when he (along with many other well-to-do young men who had previously enjoyed deferments) were pressed into service by the Napoleonic authorities in 1813, amid the desperate circumstances following the emperor's disastrous defeat in Russia of that previous winter.

Woll therefore served as an 18-year-old "distinguished private" in the 2nd National Guard Regiment during the defense of Paris against the converging enemies of Napoleon I until the surrender of that city on March 31, 1814. And a mere eight days after the French emperor abdicated on April 6, 1814, Woll was promoted to sub-lieutenant and three days thereafter was transferred to the 4th Battalion of the 10th National Guard Legion (his godfather's unit) and elevated to captain on April 17, 1814, being retained in service with that rank upon the restoration of King Louis XVIII to the throne.

However, when Napoleon escaped the next spring from his exile on the isle of Elba and launched his final "100 Days" campaign, Woll evidently rejoined the emperor's ranks, so when Napoleon was finally defeated at Waterloo and surrendered to the British in early July 1815, Woll was obliged to resign his commission as captain that following month as a Bonapartist sympathizer who had proven disloyal to the king. Armed only with a letter of introduction to Gen. Winfield Scott from his godfather, Woll had sailed for the United States in late 1815.

Scott welcomed the 20-year-old French refugee kindly, attaching Woll to his staff at Baltimore, Maryland, with the rank of sergeant major over the next several months. However, when the young Spanish adventurer Francisco Xavier Mina then reached that port the next summer, seeking to recruit

volunteers to help him revive the faltering antimonarchist rebellion in Mexico, the American general encouraged Woll to enlist in that expedition.

Service with Mina (1816–1817)

Thanks to Scott's endorsement, Woll was welcomed by Mina and appointed as a lieutenant colonel on his staff as of July 3, 1816, sailing with him to Saint Thomas in the Virgin Islands, Port-au-Prince, Galveston, and New Orleans before finally landing at Soto la Marina with 500 hired mercenaries to commence their antimonarchist campaign in the viceroyalty of New Spain on April 15, 1817. Shortly thereafter, Woll was sent back to New Orleans with the vessel *Congress Mexicano* to bring more volunteers and supplies, but by the time that he returned, Mina had already moved into Mexico's interior and the rebel fort at Soto la Marina was in Spanish hands.

Woll therefore converted *Congreso Mexicano* into a raider, making a few privateering cruises before going ashore at New Orleans and working his way into northern Mexico, where he lived as a civilian until independence was won a few years later.

Entry into Mexican Service (1823–1832)

In 1823, Woll applied to the Mexican government to have Mina's commission as a lieutenant colonel of infantry recognized simply so as to be entitled to wear a uniform and be protected by the military exemption laws without receiving any pay. This petition did not prosper until three years afterward, when he was at last acknowledged as a "retired" lieutenant colonel in the Mexican Army and attached as an unpaid aide-de-camp to the staff of Gen. Jose María Lobato. Woll was at this officer's side when Lobato participated in Acordada Mutiny in Mexico

City in late November 1828, being rewarded at its successful conclusion with appointment as lieutenant colonel of an *activo* battalion on July 22, 1829.

Three weeks later, Woll was called up on active duty on August 15, 1829, as part of the general mobilization to repel the disembarkation of a Spanish expeditionary force under Gen. Isidro Barradas in the state of Tamaulipas. During this campaign, Woll managed to get himself attached to the staff of Brig. Gen. Antonio López de Santa Anna and was wounded during the final assaults against the invaders' fortifications on September 11, 1829, for which he was promoted to full colonel.

In 1832, Woll served as second-in-command of the Jalisco Division under Gen. José de la Cuesta, helping to carry the city of Zamora by storm, then hastening immediately thereafter with 200 men to the relief of the Guadalajara garrison where he defeated a superior enemy force on November 13, 1832—for which action he was promoted to the rank of general effective as of that date.

Santa Anna Loyalist (1833–1842)

In October 1833, Woll commanded a brigade in Santa Anna's army, helping besiege the mutinous Generals Mariano Arista and Gabriel Durán in the city of Guanajuato. After capturing Mellando Point, he moved on to Jalisco where he was appointed commandant general of Colima and later military commandant of Tepic and San Blas. In 1835, he was appointed commandant general of Querétaro and marched as part of Santa Anna's army against the militia of Zacatecas, who were defeated in May 1835 at the town of Guadalupe.

Woll continued serving the next year as the quartermaster general of Santa Anna's expedition into Texas, being present at the siege of the Alamo and participating in the subsequent pursuit of Gen. Sam Houston's retreating Texian army. Woll was not present at the defeat at San Jacinto but subsequently rode into the Texian camp under a flag of truce on April 30, 1836, to learn the terms of surrender. Briefly detained, he was released in time to rejoin the remnants of the Mexican army on June 12, 1836, as they departed from Texas.

As an associate of the disgraced Santa Anna, he remained unemployed over the next couple of years and offered to resign his commission in Mexico's army when a French squadron bombarded Veracruz during the "War of the Cakes" in the winter of 1838–1839, although this offer was rejected and he was simply placed on inactive duty. He was restored and sent to purchase military supplies from New Orleans in November 1840 and the next month assigned to frontier duty in northern Mexico. Appointed in June 1842 as second-in-command of Gen. Isidro Reyes's *Ejército del Norte* or "Army of the North," Woll led his 2nd Division across the border into Texas on August 30, 1842, making a rapid strike against San Antonio before being driven back into Coahuila three weeks later. His foray was nonetheless deemed a success, winning him promotion to major general and receipt of the Cross of Honor.

He succeeded to command of the Army of the North in February 1843 and attempted to arrange a truce between Mexico and Texas, but negotiations were broken off on June 19, 1844, after the Mexican government learned of the Texans' contacts with Washington about annexation. When his Army of the North joined the revolt against Santa Anna in December 1844, Woll was deposed from command and arrested, being released from imprisonment under a general amnesty promulgated on May 24, 1845, after Santa Anna had departed into exile. Woll did not actively fight against U.S. forces during the Mexican-American War of 1846–1848, although he did not actually take a leave of absence and sail for Europe until after Santa Anna had been defeated and resigned the presidency.

Woll remained absent for six years before rejoining Santa Anna in Cuba and accompanying him when he reassumed the presidency in the summer of 1853. Santa Anna appointed him as *comandante general* of Tamaulipas, but Woll was swept away with the rest of the *santannista* regime by the Revolution of Ayutla so returned to Europe in 1855.

Last Conservative Commands (1859–1860)

After another four-year absence, Woll landed at Mocambo with several other prominent conservative exiles on March 22, 1859, reporting to Maj. Gen. and "substitute president" Miguel Miramón at Veragua and receiving a military appointment to serve in the ongoing War of the Reform. He managed to defeat the liberal general Santos Degollado near León on August 30, 1859, and helped to recuperate Zacatecas that same November. Woll's last battlefield participation occurred in May 1860 when he successfully directed the 2,700-man garrison of Guadalajara in its resistance against a major liberal assault until relieved by Miramón. Wounded during this action, Woll departed a couple of days afterward to convalesce in California and did not return to Mexico.

Retired from public life, he lived as of 1861 at his estate of Chantilly near Montauban in France but offered his services at the beginning of 1863 to imperialist general Juan N. Almonte with his last rank and commission. He was included in the Committee of Notables that offered the imperial crown of Mexico to Archduke Maximilian of Hapsburg and served him as a senior adviser. Sent to France on a special commission in mid-1865, he never again returned to Mexico. He stayed on in Montauban, dying peacefully in bed early in 1875 at 80 years of age.

See also: Alamo, Siege of the; French Intervention, War of the; Guadalajara, Sieges of; Mina's Expedition; Texas Revolution; Zacatecas, Sack of.

Further Reading

"Militärische Schattenrisse von Mexiko." *Militär-Zeitung* [Vienna] 17, no. 32 (April 20, 1864): 250–51.

Nance, Joseph M. "Brigadier General Adrian Woll's Report of His Expedition into Texas in 1842." *Southwestern Historical Quarterly* 58, no. 4 (April 1955): 523–52.

Sosa, Francisco. *Biografías de mexicanos distinguidos*. Mexico City: Porrúa, 2006.

Fortune does not always accompany Justice.

— republican brigadier general Ignacio Zaragoza, reporting on his setback at the Battle of Barranca Seca, May 20, 1862

Yaqui War (1885–1900)

Orchestrated series of military campaigns during the Porfirian era that opened up this stark northwestern region for settlement, by either slaying or deporting many of its semi-nomadic tribesmen into slavery.

Historical Background (1821–1884)

Since colonial times, the seminomadic tribes of this stark mountainous region and its foothills had resisted assimilation, so only a few Mexican settlements had ever been established along the coasts of the Sea of Cortés or Gulf of California. An uneasy truce prevailed for many decades between the Mexican residents of these coastal pockets and the various inland tribes of the district called *El Yaqui*, occasionally flaring into open warfare as different bands fought against one another or resisted territorial encroachments, during which they often attacked each other's allies as well. Fierce warriors who spoke Tarahumara, they were feared by the Mexicans, just as the natives in turn mistrusted and resented the coastal strangers' incomprehensible demands and designs.

As Mexico began to modernize and prosper during the last quarter of the 19th century under Pres. Porfirio Díaz, unscrupulous local developers tried to expand their claims inland by selling titles to agricultural properties on apparently unused native lands—which the developers had had legally reclassified before compliant Mexican courts as *tierra baldía* or "empty wasteland." The affected Yaqui nomad bands challenged these incursions into their traditional territories, refusing to sign away their rights as various treaties were presented to them by Sonoran officials and thus remaining a threat to the scattered farms and settlements that were being sold and cleared ever farther inland from the coast.

Renewed Hostilities (January 1885–June 1886)

At midnight on January 28, 1885, a raiding party led by Loreto Molina—which had been transported upriver from Guaymas aboard boats secretly provided by elements within the Sonoran state government—attacked the Guamúchil Ranch near Pótam owned by Molina's bitter rival, the "captain-general for the Yaqui and Mayo": 47-year-old José María Leyva or "Cajeme." However, finding this chieftain absent, the attackers instead beat his family, looted and torched his house, and carried away several captives. Furious, Cajeme declared war against these rival tribesmen and furthermore seized the Guayman boats that had brought them on their murderous mission, demanding ransoms from the state authorities for their release.

Many recent settlers throughout this stark, lonely region soon began fleeing into towns,

446

fearful of visitations from the aroused Yaqui war bands that would be moving across its deserts; and as reports of depredations and violence began to multiply, Gen. Col. Bonifacio Topete sallied from Hermosillo on February 23, 1885, with 50 cavalry troopers and 80 infantrymen to protect a group of civilians who had fortified themselves within the Hacienda de la Misa. Five days later, the secretary of war in Mexico City ordered Brig. Gen. José Guillermo Carbó to lead troop reinforcements into that theater, the Porfirian administration having decided to authorize the use of military force to quiet this troubled region and restore public confidence, while state authorities began raising large numbers of local militiamen and hiring mercenaries.

An initial thrust under Topete into the Sierra Madre Range was checked by a fortified Yaqui mountain-fast named El Añil near Vicam, Sonora, obliging this Mexican expedition to retreat by July 1885. A peace conference with Yaqui and Mayo spokesmen at Pótam in early December 1885, also failed to reach an accord with the suspicious Cajeme. Gen. Ángel Martínez then arrived at Álamos next month to assume command over all Mexican forces in Sonora and Sinaloa, which were significantly reinforced and used to pacify the Mayo, before penetrating into the Yaqui heartland.

In late April 1886, some 3,700 troops in four columns pressed up into the mountains, driving Cajeme's Yaqui garrison out of their stronghold of El Añil by May 5th, who escaped northeastward. Six days later, another huge mountain stronghold was encountered at Buatachive, 10 miles north of Tórim in the Bacatete range. Martínez assaulted it with 1,400 troops at dawn on May 6, 1886, supported by artillery. The Yaqui defenders were defeated in a one-sided struggle, suffering 100–200 dead and more than 2,000 noncombatants captured, while Cajeme again escaped deeper into the mountains.

A number of Yaqui and Mayo chieftains consequently submitted to the Mexican authorities at Tórim on May 27, 1886, while Cajeme emerged one month later with 1,500 warriors to be defeated in an attempt to surprise Gen. Juan Hernández's garrison at Médano on June 22, 1886, in the vain hope of securing some desperately needed weapons. This loss effectively ended organized Yaqui resistance under Cajeme, who was betrayed to the Mexican authorities while living under an assumed name in Guaymas in April 1887, and publicly executed. His second-in-command Anastasio Cuca was also extradited from Tucson, Arizona, on May 20, 1887, to share this same fate.

Marginalization (1887–1900)

Believing the Yaquis to be pacified, general Martínez withdrew his federal troops from this theater by June 1887, although some resistance would continue under their new tribal leader Juan Maldonado or "Tetabiate." Next month, the general's subordinate colonel Lorenzo Torres was also appointed as governor of Sonora, although he would delegate most of his duties to the wealthy and corrupt local landowner, Ramón Corral, who would eventually abuse this power for his own ends.

After a year and a half of countering sporadic Yaqui raids, the newly appointed military commander for this district—Gen. Julio M. Cervantes—offered the rebels a general amnesty in February 1889, which was ignored. When Cervantes was replaced by Gen. Marcos Carrillo in March 1890, the latter soon ended the truce by resuming the Mexican Army's patrols against rebel Yaqui bands high up in the mountains of

Sonora and Sinaloa. Under Corral's direction, military efforts were now aimed at driving natives deeper inland so as to commercially develop the pockets of fertile coastal lands, while condemning any captives (and their families) to toil as slaves in the henequen plantations of distant Yucatán. When a federal army wiped out the rebellious town of Tomóchic in Chihuahua on October 29, 1892, killing or enslaving all of its helpless inhabitants, many young officers and soldiers would be haunted for years afterward by the memories of that pitiless massacre.

Finally, Col. Francisco Peinado, commander of the 5th Cavalry Regiment, began a correspondence in December 1896 with the renegade Yaqui chieftain Tetabiate up in the Sierra Madre range, proposing an armistice. Four months later, this chief and 400 of his warriors accepted the colonel's amnesty, meeting at La Cieneguita between Bacatete and Tetacombiate to finalize terms. They were then escorted from La Misa to a special ceremony celebrated at Ortiz station outside of Guaymas on May 15, 1897, where Tetabiate's rebel band formally submitted to Gov. Luis E. Torres.

See also: Buatachive, Campaign of.

Further Reading

"A Butchery: The Mexican Victory Over Chief Cajeme and the Yaquis." *Daily Alta California* 40, no. 13, 424 (May 29, 1886): 5.

Holden, William C., et al. "Studies of the Yaqui Indians of Sonora, Mexico." *Texas Technological College Bulletin* 7, no. 1 (January 1936): 13–133.

Hernández, Fortunato. *Las razas indígenas de Sonora y la guerra del Yaqui*. Mexico City: Elizalde, 1902.

Moisés, Rosalio. *A Yaqui Life: The Personal Chronicle of a Yaqui Indian*. Lincoln,

Nebraska: University of Nebraska Press, 1991 reedition.

Troncoso, Francisco de Paula. *Las guerras con las tribus yaqui y mayo del Estado de Sonora*. Mexico City: Departamento de Estado Mayor, 1905.

Yucatán, Separation of (1841–1848)

Brief secession by this inaccessible eastern state that was resisted by the federal authorities in Mexico City.

Previous Secession (1829–1834)

During colonial times, communication with the Yucatán Peninsula had been possible only via ships sailing between the seaports of Veracruz and Campeche as the intervening terrain was marshy and crisscrossed with numerous rivers and streams, making the construction of roads and bridges very difficult. The remote province was also quite poor, having few wealthy resources and so had been only quite sparsely populated by Spanish settlers, who exported their small amounts of commercial produce through Campeche to both Veracruz and Cuba.

After independence from Spain had been won in central Mexico, the Intendancy of Yucatán agreed to join the newly emergent Mexican Republic in 1823, although seeking to retain a considerable degree of autonomy. A minor rebellion against the government of Pres. Vicente Guerrero occurred on November 6, 1829, and the breakaway state was temporarily brought back under centralist control when the garrison at Campeche under Francisco de Paula Toro (one of Antonio López de Santa Anna's brothers-in-law) mutinied on July 26, 1834, marching inland to bloodily defeat a Yucatecan force at Calkiní then push into the capital of Mérida nine days later to restore federal rule. Toro served as interim governor from August 10, 1834, to January 3, 1835, and again from September 10, 1835, to February 15, 1837, although his militarily backed administration was resisted so he was eventually obliged to step down.

A more vigorous anticentralist movement arose when a leader called Santiago Imán arrived to besiege the town of Tizimín on May 29, 1839, finally carrying that place by November 11, 1839. After a monthlong occupation, though, his followers were dispersed eastward into the jungles. Then the rebel colonel Sebastián López de Llergo arrived outside Yucatán's capital of Mérida on February 17, 1840, and three days later was allowed inside that city by the defection of Col. Anastasio Torrens's garrison in the San Benito Barracks. The resultant combination of López de Llergo's and Torrens's regiments so emboldened the separatist movement that the state legislature severed relations with Mexico City shortly thereafter.

López de Llergo and Imán meanwhile appeared outside the seaport of Campeche with a small military force on April 2, 1840, laying siege to its garrison of centralist troops, who requested terms by June 6, 1840, and capitulated 10 days afterward.

October 1, 1841: Yucatán contemplated declaring independence from Mexico, while furthermore signing peace and commercial treaties with the Republic of Texas—which reciprocated by sending armed gunboats to help protect Yucatán's coastline.

May 7, 1842: Having failed to reach a reconciliation with Yucatán, Mexico's Congress severed relations with this breakaway province.

Mexican Invasion (1842–1843)

Resorting to war, an expedition dispatched from Veracruz by Santa Anna's centralist government arrived off the Gulf port of El Carmen on August 22, 1842, escorted by the British-built steamers *Guadalupe* and *Moctezuma*, as well as the captured *Yucateco*, with orders to begin a military campaign aimed at subduing both the breakaway provinces of Campeche and Yucatán. A 1,300-man vanguard under Gen. Juan D. Morales was disembarked and compelled El Carmen's small garrison under Clemente Trujillo to surrender by August 30, 1842, after which a 3,000-man division under Gen. José Vicente Miñón furthermore landed and began slowly pushing northeastward from Champotón through Seybaplaya and Lerma without encountering any resistance until they were ambushed while coming within sight of this latter town.

However, Miñón was reinforced with a couple thousand more Mexican troops from Veracruz by early November 1842 and so forged on toward Campeche with some 6,000 men to find the Yucatecans awaiting his army's arrival. Gov. Santiago Méndez had left his inland capital of Mérida to personally assume command at this vital seaport and employed his time well in assembling 4,500 defenders (of whom only 650 were regulars, though). His subordinate Pedro Lemus abandoned the fortified heights southwest of Campeche without a fight, so Miñón's artillerists were able to install guns on top that commanded the city center, resulting in Lemus being replaced by the more competent colonel Sebastián López de Llergo. (Banished on suspicion of treason, Lemus would subsequently join the Mexican forces.)

Yet the strength of Campeche's colonial-era walls meant that Miñón settled in with

450 | Yucatán, Separation of

his army for a lengthy siege, eventually being recalled because of this inactivity on January 29, 1843, and replaced by Matías de la Peña Barragán. Four days later, he sent an 800-man detachment under General Andrade five miles east into the town of Chiná, only to be surprised by 500 separatist troops under Lt. Col. Manuel Oliver. In a ferocious exchange, some 400 men were slain on both sides, plus many others wounded before the separatists retreated back into Campeche.

The turncoat Lemus thereupon persuaded the new commander that since Campeche could not be pounded or starved into submission, it would be better to transport a detachment up the coast and march inland so as to threaten its unfortified capital of Mérida from the rear. De la Peña duly withdrew 2,500 troops from his festering siege camp outside Campeche and transferred them aboard ships, disembarking at the tiny northern port of Telchac by March 25, 1843. Probing into the interior, he was able to secure Motul before discovering that Colonel López de Llergo had also withdrawn 1,600 men from the garrison at Campeche, and moved to intercept this new threat.

De la Peña had dug in with his division at Tixcocob on April 10, 1843, and the next day weathered a heavy attack by López de Llergo. Although casualties were considerable on both sides, the Yucatecans fell back, allowing the Mexicans to tentatively resume their drive toward Mérida. However, De la Peña limped to a halt at an hacienda on its outskirts and sent in an offer to discuss terms. Apparently misled as to the defenders' strength, he then tried to retreat back into Tixcocob, only to become trapped two weeks later in the village of Tixpéhual by three converging Yucatecan columns and compelled to capitulate. According the

terms of his surrender, De la Peña departed from Chicxulub with his division by May 26, 1843, sailing away for Veracruz while leaving behind hostages to assure that his force would not rejoin the besiegers at Campeche.

In the wake of this humiliating defeat, Santa Anna replaced De la Peña with the 39-year-old general Pedro Ampudia, who had grown up in Campeche as a boy. Yet despite arriving outside that beleaguered city with 500 fresh troops and better guns, Ampudia could not reduce it either and was soon distressed by the appearance of Texan warships out in the Gulf, which attacked his vessels as allies of the Yucatecans. The Mexican commander consequently entered into discreet talks with Governor Méndez, agreeing to end the siege and withdraw if the separatist Yucatecan government would send a delegation to Mexico City to resume negotiations toward reincorporation into the republic. This deal was struck, so Ampudia retreated back out to sea from Campeche toward El Carmen on June 26, 1843, and hostilities ceased.

December 17, 1846: In order to cut the clandestine trade entering Mexico through the neutral state of Yucatán, Perry set sail from Antón Lizardo with *Mississippi* (flag), *Vixen*, *Bonita*, and *Petrel* to capture the border outpost of El Carmen.

See also: Ampudia Grimarest, Pedro; Mexican-American War; Santa Anna, Antonio López de.

Further Reading

Dumond, Don E. *The Machete and the Cross: Campesino Rebellion in Campeche*. Lincoln: University of Nebraska Press, 1997.

Rugeley, Terry. *Rebellion Now and Forever: Mayas, Hispanics, and Caste War Violence in Yucatan, 1800–1880*. Stanford, CA: Stanford University Press, 2009.

Z

The seven kilometers of road between Zacatecas to Guadalupe and its environs, were strewn with bodies on every side, so thickly that carriages could not get through.

> — from the diary of revolutionary general Felipe Ángeles, June 24, 1914

Zacatecas, Sack of (1835)

Punitive strike by Santa Anna against this small but wealthy mining city whose federalist state leaders were opposed to the centralist policies being implemented by his regime.

Zacatecas was but one of several states that resented his efforts to abrogate the liberal Constitution of 1824 and restore many of the monopolistic restrictions of colonial times onto the semiautonomous, fractious regions. On February 14, 1835, Santa Anna's compliant federal Congress in Mexico City passed a law restricting each state's militia forces to just one soldier for every 500 inhabitants, a reduction intended to ensure the national army's predominance and discourage local uprisings. The state of Zacatecas, with 4,000 men already under arms and another 16,000 in reserve, was one of several states that refused to comply with this decree, instead increasing its armaments production and appointing Gen. Francisco García Salinas as state militia commander.

Having anticipated just such a reaction, Santa Anna suddenly materialized in the Tolosa Hills less than nine miles east of the city of Zacatecas with 4,000 federal troops on May 10, 1835. The next day, he easily defeated García Salinas near Guadalupe, killing 81 of his state militiamen and capturing 2,700. The president's army thereupon marched into the defenseless city on May 17, 1835, celebrating a *Te Deum* in its cathedral before unleashing his troops to strip many buildings of valuables in a calculated act of punishment and then departing 10 days later on a campaign which would eventually take him as far as East Texas.

See also: Alamo, Siege of the; Texas Revolution.

Further Reading

Chartrand, René. *Santa Anna's Mexican Army 1821–48*. Oxford: Osprey, 2004.

Di Tella, Torcuato. *National Popular Politics in Early Independent Mexico, 1820–1847*. Albuquerque: University of New Mexico Press, 1996.

Fowler, Will. *Santa Anna of Mexico*. Lincoln: University of Nebraska Press, 2009.

Memoria del Secretario de Estado y del Despacho de Guerra y Marina, leída a las cámaras del Congreso General Mexicano en marzo de 1835. Mexico City: Ignacio Cumplido, April 1835.

Wasserman, Mark. *Everyday Life and Politics in Nineteenth Century Mexico: Men, Women, and War*. Albuquerque: University of New Mexico Press, 2000.

Zacatecas, Battle of (1914)

Last spectacular victory won by Pancho Villa's División del Norte, helping to bring down the regime of Victoriano Huerta.

Previous Attacks (June and October 1913)

The small but wealthy mining center of Zacatecas was a major waystation along the railway lines running from Mexico City as far north as Texas with a peacetime population recorded in 1907 as slightly less than 35,000 inhabitants. However, as much of the state became overrun by rebel bands on the outbreak of the Revolution, refugees crowded into the city to escape their depredations. Its outskirts were stormed at dawn of June 5, 1913, by 1,500 riders under Pánfilo Natera (a former corporal in the *rurales*), being repelled by Zacatecas's 400-man federal garrison and four fieldpieces under Col. Miguel Rivero. But the next dawn, Natera's second wave succeeded in penetrating into the city, massacring its federal troops while they attempted to escape from their stronghold atop La Bufa Hill toward Aguascalientes.

This rebel success goaded the recently installed government of Huerta into sending Gen. José Refugio Delgado with 1,300 federal soldiers to reclaim Zacatecas, who entered it unopposed two weeks later. Natera, after being promoted to "brigadier" by the revolutionary presidential pretender Venustiano Carranza, threatened the city once more in late October 1913 with his 2,500–3,000 lightly-armed guerrillas, circling it at a distance and firing on its outer ring of defenses for 24 hours before finally being chased away by Delgado's artillery. The military engineer brigadier general Alberto Canseco subsequently arrived to assume office as governor on November 1, 1913, fortifying the city, but fighting between revolutionary and federal forces remained confined farther north over the next seven months.

Carrancista Probe (June 14, 1914)

It was not until Pancho Villa had crushed the major federal concentrations in Chihuahua and Coahuila during the spring of 1914 that both sides began building up their strength for a major showdown over Zacatecas, as the hapless city stood directly in the path of any advance by the northern rebels along the railway line leading toward the national capital. Finally, Carranza ordered Natera on June 10, 1914, to once again push southeast from Fresnillo and assail Zacatecas with the 15,000 poorly equipped troops of his *División del Centro* or "Central Division." His irregular cavalry probed the defenses in its encircling hills for four days until Gen. Luis G. Medina Barrón's garrison was reinforced by yet more *colorado* auxiliaries from San Luis Potosí under Gen. Benjamín Argumedo, who bloodied an ill-coordinated rebel thrust against the city's Guadalupe suburb on June 14, 1914.

Natera gingerly resumed his probing attacks the next day, but with Zacatecas's defenders now totaling more than 12,000 *federales* and *colorados*, backed by 13 artillery pieces and 90 machine guns, greater strength would be required. Carranza therefore telegraphed Villa at Torreón and ordered him to send reinforcements to Natera from his own much larger, better-equipped *División del Norte* or "Northern Division." Villa did not wish to divert any of his men to another general's command so suggested that he personally spearhead the assault against Zacatecas. When Carranza spitefully refused, Villa ignored his nominal "commander-in-chief" and began moving his entire *División del Norte* southward aboard 18 trains on June 16, 1914.

Battle of Zacatecas (June 19–23, 1914)

Three days later, the Villista vanguard under Gen. Felipe Ángeles appeared outside Zacatecas and began bombarding its outer ring of defenses at dawn of June 20, 1914, providing a screen for the main body under Gen. Tomás Urbina to detrain and deploy into battle formation over the next two days. By the time Villa personally arrived on the afternoon of June 22, 1914, his subordinates had already massed 25,000 troops and 50 guns around the city, most of their infantrymen and cavalry riders being concentrated east of Zacatecas at Guadalupe or to its south-southwest, while the main artillery batteries were emplaced at Vetagrande to its northeast. The defenders' guns under Huertista artillery general Guillermo Rubio Navarrete included a mobile 80mm piece nicknamed *El Niño* or "The Boy," mounted on a railway flatcar.

At 10:00 a.m. of June 23, 1914, Villa launched a massive assault by directing an artillery barrage against the federal strongpoints atop La Bufa, Loreto, and La Sierpe heights, while his main force advanced against the fortified El Grillo Hill. This isolated federal outpost west of Zacatecas began to run low on ammunition by 1:00 p.m. and was carried half an hour later. Santa Clara, La Sierpe, Cantarranas, and La Cebada were then rolled up an hour afterward, followed by Bolsas and Clérigos, while the lynchpin redoubt atop La Bufa Hill fell at 4:00 p.m. Such an inexorable series of losses created a panic-stricken stampede of defeated *federales* through the city, which worsened when demolition charges began leveling public buildings at 4:30 p.m. The revolutionaries entered an hour and a half later amid considerable slaughter, total losses being estimated later at 6,000 dead Huertistas, 5,000 captured (2,500 of whom were wounded), plus almost 2,000 civilians slain. Wounded in his left leg, Medina Barrón was lucky to escape southward into Soledad with only 14 men.

Villa's casualties came to 1,500 dead and 2,500 wounded, and he furthermore executed 60 of his own men the next day in an attempt to stem the pillaging of the helpless, smoldering city. Stacks of bodies were burned to prevent outbreaks of disease before Villa boarded his own personal train at Guadalupe station on June 26, 1914, to resume his advance southeastward, delegating Lt. Col. Manuel Carlos de la Vega to be Zacatecas's new revolutionary "governor." The battered city remained under martial law for the next two years, painstakingly repairing its worst damages while handicapped by a typhoid epidemic, drought, and economic paralysis.

See also: Ángeles Ramírez, Felipe de Jesús; División del Norte; Villa, Pancho.

Further Reading

Aguirre Benavides, Luis and Adrián. *Las grandes batallas de la División del Norte al mando del general Francisco Villa*. Mexico City: Diana, 1967.

Ángeles, Felipe. *La batalla de Zacatecas: descripción tomada del diario del general Felipe Ángeles*. Chihuahua City, Chihuahua: Imprenta del Gobierno, 1914.

Brenner, Anita. *The Wind That Swept Mexico: The History of the Mexican Revolution of 1910–1942*. Austin: University of Texas Press, 1996.

Cumberland, Charles C. *Mexican Revolution: The Constitutionalist Years*. Austin: University of Texas Press, 1972.

Guzmán, Martín Luis. *Memoirs of Pancho Villa*. Austin: University of Texas Press, 1976.

Katz, Friedrich. *The Life and Times of Pancho Villa*. Stanford, CA: Stanford University Press, 1998.

Knight, Alan. *The Mexican Revolution*. New York: Cambridge University Press, 1986.

"Reports Rout of Rebels." *New York Times*, June 16, 1914.

Zapata Salazar, Emiliano (1879–1919)

Inspirational southern leader during the Mexican Revolution of 1910 whose legend still lives on today.

Emiliano Zapata at center, with his brother Eufemio seated on his right-hand side, in the Hotel Coliseo in Mexico City on June 24, 1911, about a month after Porfirio Díaz's flight into exile. (Library of Congress)

Early Life and Military Conscription (1879–1910)

He is believed to have been born on August 8, 1879, in San Miguel Anenecuilco, in the lush valleys of the state of Morelos south of Mexico City, the fourth son and ninth of 10 children of Gabriel Zapata and Cleofas Salazar. As a member of an ancient family of small-time ranchers, he had not endured desperate poverty or manual labor as a child. Instead, young Emiliano had grown up to run a small property of his own, on land leased from the wealthy Ignacio de la Torre y Mier, and he furthermore enjoyed a considerable reputation as a talented horse trainer. However, young Emiliano had also developed a genuine sympathy for the poor peasants of Morelos, who were being displaced by ever-larger commercial *haciendas* or "estates." Fluent in the Indian language of Náhuatl, as well as Spanish, he had been elected head of his village's "defense committee," and contested various illegal land expropriations.

After one such action, the 31-year-old Zapata found himself abruptly consigned on February 11, 1910, as a *reemplazo* or "replacement" for the 9th Infantry Regiment stationed at Cuernavaca, his name supposedly having been drawn "by lot" from among the names of eligible military-age villagers—although most likely deliberately submitted to the army bureaucracy, in retaliation for his growing activism. Through the intervention of Ignacio de la Torre, who was Pres. Porfirio Díaz's son-in-law, Zapata managed to get discharged from service in the Mexican Army six weeks later so he might instead work as a groom attending to De la Torre's fine stable of horses.

Revolutionary Firebrand (March–May 1911)

Frustrated by the corruption of local officials and the indifference of federal authorities in the distant capital, Zapata had embraced the Revolution a few months after its eruption in northern Mexico. On March 10, 1911, a local leader named Pablo Torres Burgos led 72 peasants out of Anenecuilco in revolt, striking out southward through the district's sugar plantations to gather greater strength. Two weeks later, they overran Tlaquiltenango and then Jojutla, at which point Torres Burgos—dismayed by the brutalities perpetuated by some of his followers—resigned from the movement. While riding back toward Moyotepec with his two sons, though, they were all killed by a detachment of *federales* from Gen. Javier Rojas's battalion, so command of the 800 revolutionaries that had been raised devolved on Zapata.

Charismatic and of humble origins himself, Zapata quickly harnessed a torrent of ragtag rebels with his simple rallying cry of *Tierra y libertad* or "Land and Liberty." Gathered into a so-called *Ejército Libertador del Sur* or Liberation Army of the South, Zapata's insurrection gained such strength that his peasant army on May 12, 1911, attacked and besieged the federal garrison headquartered in Cuautla, composed of some 300 troopers of the 5th Cavalry Regiment (known as the *Regimiento de Oro* or "Golden Regiment") under Col. Eutiquio Munguía, plus 30 *rurales* under Maj. Gil Villegas. After six days of fierce fighting, the Zapatistas managed to fight their way into this burning city, only to discover that the surviving *federales* had escaped that

same dawn. Numerous excesses were thereupon committed by the victors before Zapata could restore order.

His capture of Cuautla on May 19, 1911, closed the road leading into Mexico City and also prompted the federal garrison at Cuernavaca to evacuate that city as well two days afterward, which was occupied by Zapata without any resistance. Some rioting erupted shortly thereafter in Mexico City's main square on the evening of May 24, 1911, causing Díaz to resign the presidency the next day and sail away from Veracruz toward Europe aboard the German liner *Ypiranga*. Foreign Min. Francisco León de la Barra became interim president until proper elections could be held.

Hostility against Madero and Huerta (1911–1915)

Yet despite the dictator's departure and cessation of warfare for a brief spell, Zapata nonetheless remained distrustful of the new federal administration that was to be created under the northern reformer (and wealthy landowner) Francisco I. Madero. When he proved unable to convince this new president-in-waiting to grant small plots to his thousands of peasant adherents, relations soured and Zapata refused to disarm his army until their recent land reclamations were recognized as legitimate by the central authorities.

But since Madero had not yet been elected president, the interim administration that had been left running affairs was under Porfirio Díaz's ex-foreign minister, Francisco León de la Barra, who moved to check any expansion of Zapatista lawlessness beyond the state of Morelos by ordering federal troops under Col. Aureliano Blanquet to attack their unruly occupying force in the city of Puebla in mid-July 1911, killing 80 Zapatistas and wounding 200 in a firefight around its bullring. Then the next month, León de la Barra furthermore dispatched 1,000 more soldiers under hard-bitten Gen. Victoriano Huerta into Cuernavaca so as to monitor and contain Zapata's followers through heavy-handed actions.

By the time Madero finally won a special election and assumed the vacant presidency during the first week of November 1911, Zapata was already once again in open rebellion against the central government and the state of Morelos was being terrorized by brutal federal sweeps. Madero replaced the army commander in that region early in 1912 with the high-minded general Felipe Ángeles, who implemented a much more humane campaign, but the inexperienced president was to be beset by many other difficulties over the ensuing year until he was finally deposed and murdered by Gen. Victoriano Huerta in February 1913.

Widely hated, Zapata's rebellion grew even stronger during the 15-month unified national struggle against the usurper Huerta. But while pleased by that despot's removal in August 1914, the southern leader rejected the presumption of the northern *primer fefe* or "first chief" Venustiano Carranza, who entered the capital under the protection of Gen. Álvaro Obregón's victorious army to assume the presidency. Although never aspiring to high office himself, Zapata denounced the haughty Carranza's self-proclaimed accession from his headquarters at Cuernavaca on September 8, 1914, followed two weeks later by Pancho Villa in the north. A convention held in neutral Aguascalientes to resolve this contentious issue ended in an open break by early November 1914 with Villistas and Zapatistas uniting to drive Carranza from office.

Their huge armies quickly began converging on Mexico City, so the outnumbered Obregón evacuated it before that same month was out, retreating eastward into Veracruz. Zapata and Villa held an enormous parade of perhaps 50,000 men from their combined armies through the streets of the national capital on December 6, 1914, and posed for photographs with Villa sitting in the presidential chair. But after a few weeks of token occupation, their forces largely withdrew, allowing Obregón to reclaim Mexico City by January 28, 1915, and prepare his smaller but well-equipped and better-disciplined army to drive northward six weeks later and rout Villa's army in three epic battles.

Carrancista Counterinsurgency (1916–1919)

With his northern foe defeated, President Carranza unleashed his general Pablo González to conduct a difficult and pitiless operation to break the Zapatista grip on Morelos. In June 1916, one of its early offensives managed to overrun Tlaltizapán— Zapata's main hideaway, located south of Cuernavaca—in the process slaughtering 286 unarmed men, women, and children. Despite being militarily weakened by this and other sweeps, a Zapatista column nonetheless counterattacked against the Carrancista garrison holding Tlayacapan on July 16, 1916, retiring after six hours of heavy fighting to also vainly attempt to carry Tlaltizapán the next day, failing in both assaults because of their inferior weaponry.

Unable to relieve his despairing followers in Morelos, Zapata consequently pushed over the mountains in late September 1916 to inaugurate a diversionary offensive which threatened Mexico City itself—an act that prompted the Carrancista colonel Jesús María Guajardo to execute 180 captives at Tlaltizapán as punishment and burn much of its surrounding district to the ground. Zapata meanwhile managed to seize the pumping station at Xochimilco on October 4, 1916, thereby cutting off much of the capital's water supply before furthermore destroying the railway lines at Peña Pobre and retiring back into Morelos.

His battered forces were fortuitously able to recuperate Tlaltizapán on December 1, 1916, and launch a major offensive that regained control over much of Morelos but only because González's occupation forces had been temporarily weakened by disease—7,000 Carrancistas reportedly lying sick of malaria. By the next spring though, they had recovered and were once more eroding Zapatista strength, their fortified garrisons controlling all the large towns and roads leading out of the state, stifling commercial activity and preventing any significant guerrilla concentrations. As Zapata's military fortunes faded, support began to melt away, his longtime subordinate Leonardo Vázquez being executed at Buenavista de Cuellar on May 7, 1917, for turning against his former chief, the same fate befalling Zapata's secretary and mentor Otilio Montaño 11 days afterward. Even Zapata's brother Eufemio, his most trusted lieutenant, was murdered by a turncoat at Cuautla on June 18, 1917.

With the return of cooler autumnal weather, González's army resumed its heavy-handed operations, shelling and recapturing Cuautla by November 19, 1917, then shortly thereafter overwhelming the Zapatista strongholds of Jonacatepec and Zacualpan de Amilpas as well. Powerless to defeat his enemy in battle, Zapata could only harass Carrancista outposts or patrols and avoid capture for another year. González advanced out of Cuautla once again with 11,000 Carrancista troops in October 1918, sweeping through Zapatista strongholds laid low by starvation and disease (mostly due to the recent outbreak of Spanish influenza). Yautepec, Jojutla, Cuernavaca, Tetecala, and Tlaltizapán all fell in quick succession, obliging Zapata to flee into the mountains with a few hundred adherents.

Murder and Myth (April 1919)

His military power finally broken by González's pitiless offensive of that previous autumn, Zapata was reduced by the spring of 1919 to living a nomadic existence, moving about ceaselessly throughout the familiar hinterland of Morelos with only an escort of loyal riders. However, he nonetheless maintained a series of guerrilla strikes against Carrancista detachments, while the government steadily lost men, money, and materiel in their unavailing attempts to find him.

Then in early April 1919, Zapata learned that Colonel Guajardo had been found drunk while on garrison duty at Cuautla by Pablo González, so was censured and facing further charges.

In a prearranged plot, Pablo González departed Cuautla for Mexico City, and that same night his supposedly disgruntled subordinate colonel Jesús M. Guajardo mutinied with the 600-man 5th Cavalry Regiment, deserting toward the southeast. Reaching Jonacatepec by the night of April 8–9, 1919, Guajardo seemingly confirmed his switched allegiance by attacking and killing a dozen Carrancista defenders, while losing seven of his own men. He then furthermore executed 59 followers of the ex-Zapatista Victoriano Bárcenas at Mancornadero before being approached—15 miles south of Jonacatepec, at the rural Pastor railway station—by Zapata himself (who had begun corresponding with Guajardo about possibly joining the revolutionary cause).

Both contingents continued to ride on together, Guajardo and his cavalrymen encamping overnight at the Hacienda of San Juan Chinameca while Zapata remained in nearby Tepalcingo with his own troops. The next morning, a false alarm caused the rebel chieftain to send 140 of his mounted men on patrol, so when he was invited to dine with Guajardo at Chinameca at 1:30 p.m. on April 10, 1919, Zapata arrived with only a 10-man cavalry escort. The 5th Regiment's musicians and color guard, drawn up in the hacienda courtyard to receive the guerrilla leader—rather than firing a salute—blasted a volley directly into Zapata, killing him instantly.

Guajardo subsequently had Zapata's body loaded onto a mule, and cleared out of Chinameca with his entire regiment by 4:00 p.m. on that same April 10, 1919, carrying the corpse back into Cuautla to be triumphantly presented to González by 9:00 p.m. and put on public display. For this murderous action, Guajardo was rewarded by González with promotion to brigadier general, plus 50,000 *pesos*—which the colonel shared among his troopers.

Yet Zapata's romantic appeal would not end with his death. Even modern Mexican governments observe his memory by making token land distributions among the poor. And peasants still believe that he rides alone through the forests of Ajusco Mountain on a white horse.

See also: Revolution, Mexican; Villa, Pancho.

Further Reading

Brunk, Samuel. *Emiliano Zapata: Revolution and Betrayal in Mexico*. Albuquerque: University of New Mexico Press, 1995.

Sosa, Francisco. *Biografías de mexicanos distinguidos*. Mexico City: Porrúa, 2006.

Womack, John, Jr. *Zapata and the Mexican Revolution*. New York: Alfred A. Knopf, 1969.

Zaragoza Seguín, Ignacio (1829–1862)

Humbly born, bespectacled young soldier who rose from the ranks to become a talented republican general, only to tragically die of disease at 33 years of age.

Birth and Education (1829–1850)

Born on March 24, 1829, at the Presidio de la Bahía del Espíritu Santo (modern Goliad, Texas), he was the second son of an infantry sublieutenant named Miguel G. Zaragoza Valdés and his wife, María de Jesús Seguín Martínez. Zaragoza's father had arrived in Texas four years previously from Veracruz, as a member of the 12th Line Battalion, and had married María at San Fernando on July 5, 1826, while stationed at San Antonio de Béjar. They would eventually have three more daughters and another son together, for a total number of six children. The family's early years were spent at various military bases as the battalion in which his father served was sent variously to San Luis Potosí, Michoacán, and Guanajuato.

Promoted to lieutenant, Zaragoza's father fought in Santa Anna's campaign into Texas in 1836, and—once the victorious American settlers of that province had won their independence—was assigned to garrison duty in the border town of Matamoros for the next eight years. Young Ignacio attended its San Juan School as of 1837, and upon his father being reassigned to Monterrey as a captain in 1844, his 15-year-old son had been enrolled in its Seminario Conciliar to study for the priesthood.

The bespectacled young liberal general Ignacio Zaragoza, ca. 1860. (Library of Congress)

But when the Mexican-American War had interrupted his studies and Brig. Gen. Zachary Taylor's invading U.S. Army threatened that city two years later, his life would take a different course. After the capitulation and evacuation of Monterrey, Zaragoza petitioned on October 23, 1846, to be enlisted in the Hussar Regiment as a cadet—a request that was apparently ignored as the regional forces were in considerable disarray following that defeat. His father was subsequently reassigned to the city of Zacatecas and then discharged from the Mexican Army altogether once hostilities ceased in 1848, returning to Monterrey the next year with his family and helping his 19-year-old son Ignacio obtain a job in the store of Felipe Sepúlveda.

Early Military Career (1851–1857)

Small, bookish, and wearing glasses, Ignacio Zaragoza was finally able to enlist in a militia fusilier company of the *Guardia Nacional* or "National Guard" at Monterrey, being promoted to first sergeant as of March 12, 1851—three months before his 44-year-old father died on June 11, 1851. Intelligent and disciplined, Zaragoza had risen to the rank of captain by 1853 and was serving as acting major on detached garrison duty with the Batallón Activo de Monterrey at the seaport of Tampico, when the liberal leader Santiago Vidaurri and his military subordinate Juan Zuazua—inspired by the Revolution of Ayutla—toppled the conservative *santannista* administration back home in Nuevo León in May 1855. With considerable skill, Zaragoza managed to extract and bring his own company of 120 men safely home to Monterrey without suffering so much as a single loss during their long and perilous march across the desert.

Almost immediately upon returning home, he was assigned to participate in Colonel Zuazua's offensive against the 2,000-man *santannista* concentration that had gathered at Rancho de las Varas outside Saltillo under Gen. Francisco Güitián. The liberal army came within sight of that city by July 22, 1855, and under cover of darkness, three columns led by Zaragoza, Mariano Escobedo, and Pedro Hinojosa mounted a coordinated assault that same night that captured almost its entire garrison and their armaments. For this success, Zaragoza was promoted to the rank of commander, although he still had scarcely four years of military experience to his credit. Toward the end of 1855, he was furthermore detached to reestablish a Mexican military presence around the border town of Piedras Negras, which had been burned to the ground by the "Callahan Expedition," an independent assignment that the 26-year-old Zaragoza performed so responsibly that he was promoted to lieutenant colonel.

Then, Nuevo León's cantankerous governor Vidaurri annexed Coahuila in February 1856, angrily rebuffing all objections against this unilateral expropriation that were raised by the fledgling national government under interim president Ignacio Comonfort. The latter finally authorized the use of military force to remove Vidaurri from office on August 8, 1856, so two armies began converging on Nuevo León: one out of Tamaulipas to its east, advancing in twin columns through Villagrán and Mier under the overall direction of Gen. Juan José de la Garza; plus a second army out of San Luis Potosí to its south, under Gen. Vicente Rosas Landa.

Zaragoza was sent with a detachment of infantry and artillery in late September 1856 to reinforce the town of Villagrán in support of 100 cavalrymen who had already arrived there under Lieutenant Colonel Escobedo. Subsequently, Zaragoza was ordered to shift his men over into Camargo and ride back into Monterrey with only his staff officers so as to begin organizing the capital's defense against the approach by De la Garza's main army through the town of Mier. This force appeared outside Monterrey on November 1, 1856, calling on Zaragoza to surrender, who refused. Having only a single militia company from Parras and an assortment of volunteers to defend the city, he fortified himself inside its *Ciudadela* or "Citadel," withstanding repeated bombardments and assaults until his outnumbered force was relieved by the timely arrival of Zuazua's army on November 3, 1856.

De la Garza's besiegers retired only briefly toward Saltillo, instead uniting there with Rosas Landa's column before returning to the attack. They were checked short of Monterrey at Cuesta de los Muertos by Zuazua's army, at which time a peace agreement was worked out to bring an end to these hostilities. A couple of months later, Zaragoza would marry Rafaela Padilla in Monterrey on January 21, 1857.

Opening Campaign in the War of the Reform (1858)

Almost one year afterward, Zaragoza happened to be in Mexico City on private business when Brig. Gen. Félix M. Zuloaga suddenly launched a mutiny aimed at keeping moderate president Ignacio Comonfort in office while rejecting the constitutional reforms that had recently been voted into law by Mexico's liberal Congress. When conservative forces then subsequently removed Comonfort from office altogether in a second coup on January 11, 1858, Zaragoza and a half dozen of his northern colleagues volunteered to fight on behalf of the deposed president, helping defend the San Pedro y San Pablo Church during a brief outburst of fighting around Mexico City's *Ciudadela* or "Citadel" before Comonfort finally gave up this struggle and departed 10 days later.

Zaragoza thereupon returned north to Monterrey to find its liberal government already mobilizing for war. He raised a company of *rifleros* or "riflemen" and joined the *Ejército del Norte* or "Army of the North" under Zuazua, whose state-issued "uniforms" consisted simply of red tunics with matching hatbands, plus a general directive for all troopers to keep their trousers thrust into their boot tops. The War of the Reform officially began when a large conservative army advanced out of Mexico City and scattered the liberal forces that were attempting to marshal outside the city of Salamanca in the central state of Guanajuato on March 10–11, 1858. These victorious conservatives then veered westward into Guadalajara, while Zuazua led his "Army of the North" cautiously down from

Monterrey to distantly threaten the city of San Luis Potosí.

Because of this penetration, conservative brigadier general Miguel Miramón was detached from Guadalajara with a division of 2,200 infantrymen, 400 cavalry troopers, and 12 guns to reinforce the beleaguered 1,500-man garrison holding San Luis Potosí. Made aware of this movement, Zuazua ordered Zaragoza to remain in position with the liberal infantry and artillery at Venado (some 50 miles north of the city of San Luis Potosí), while he dashed away with 1,100 mounted riflemen on the evening of April 16, 1858, making an overnight ride to ambush and bloody Miramón's relief column the next day as it came through *Puerto de Carretas* or "Wagons' Pass."

The conservative brigadier nonetheless pushed through and entered San Luis Potosí with his 2,000 surviving troops, bracing for a liberal assault. But Zuazua deceived him by instead disappearing westward with his army and surprising the city of Zacatecas on April 27, 1858, after which Miramón departed the region and San Luis Potosí also fell by the end of June. Zaragoza participated as a subordinate officer in both operations, after which Governor Vidaurri arrived at occupied San Luis Potosí with even more contingents on August 13, 1858, to personally assume overall command.

One month later, the 5,000-man liberal army withdrew out of San Luis Potosí at the approach of 4,000 conservative soldiers under Miramón and took up a strong defensive position at a tiny rural hamlet a few miles beyond Puerto de Carretas named Ahualulco de los Pinos. With Vidaurri in overall command and Zuazua (who had been accidentally wounded in a brawl) temporarily replaced as field commander by the American mercenary Col. Edward H. Jordan, the liberals suffered a humiliating defeat in a three-day battle that climaxed on September 29, 1858. Zaragoza, who had been positioned out on the far right of the liberal battle line throughout that debacle, managed to escape with his two companies and a few fieldpieces intact.

Foray to Mexico City (1859)
Withdrawing toward Zacatecas, Zaragoza was soon given command of a new regiment of *rifleros* raised in Nuevo León and promoted to full colonel. Vidaurri having returned to Monterrey in disgrace, Gen. Santos Degollado emerged as the new liberal field commander for that region, so Zaragoza was attached to his army for a renewed counteroffensive into the Bajío early the next year. Ten days after Degollado had taken the city of León in the state of Guanajuato on February 18, 1859, Zaragoza overtook and bested a retreating conservative column, which won him promotion to brigadier. His men then performed well when two more retiring conservative units were intercepted at the Hacienda de Calamanda on March 11, 1859, seizing the high ground atop Tecolote Hill after a hard-fought action.

But the overconfident Degollado had thereupon marched his army straight on to attempt the national capital, arriving on its western outskirts 10 days later to discover that his 6,000 troops were insufficient to surround it while he lacked the heavy artillery necessary to discomfit its 4,000 conservative defenders. After waiting for a fortnight in hopes that its civilian population might rise against the city garrison, Degollado ordered Zaragoza to attempt a surprise assault. He led 1,500 men through the darkness shortly before dawn on April 2, 1859, to attack the conservative companies holding the Tlaxpana suburb and San Cosme *garita* or "guardhouse," without any success due to the defenders' high state of alertness. Zaragoza was obliged to fall back into San Francisco Church under heavy fire, having suffered some 40 dead and 60 wounded during his initial assault before eventually slipping back southwestward after nightfall to return to the main liberal encampment at Tacubaya.

Five days later, a conservative relief column reached the capital under Gen. Leonardo Márquez, who emerged to give battle with 5,500 soldiers and some 40 guns on April 10, 1859. Degollado's liberal army had dug in around Tacubaya, where it was engaged the next dawn and defeated before noon. Zaragoza had been put in command of the liberal right flank, his battle line extending between the town of Chapultepec and the Casamata, so his brigade was not directly engaged by Márquez's thrust into the liberal center. Instead, Zaragoza's formation was depleted by constant demands for reinforcements until, when finally called on to intervene, he had almost no men left to make a difference.

In the aftermath of this defeat, Zaragoza gathered up what survivors he could and marched away to Morelia, eventually meeting up with Gen. Jesús González Ortega's liberal army at Irapuato before proceeding back into San Luis Potosí. In a subsequent reassessment and restructuring of liberal strength in the Bajío, Zuazua was appointed general-in-chief of their main *ejército de operaciones* or "operational army" on April 25, 1859, with Zaragoza as his second-in-command—although this arrangement was soon voided because of bitter disputes that arose between the two former leaders, Vidaurri and Degollado.

Liberal Infighting (September 1859–April 1860)

After a summer of increasingly shrill complaints from the sidelined Vidaurri, he publicly proclaimed an order on September 5, 1859—in his political capacity as Governor of Nuevo León and Coahuila—which would have recalled both states' troops from serving with the main liberal armies. Degollado deemed this proclamation to be an act of treason because the war was still ongoing against the conservatives (who were backed by regular army units), so Degollado sent Zaragoza on the thankless commission of either soothing or deposing Vidaurri.

Upon reaching the state capital of Monterrey, Zaragoza at first tried reasoning with the irate governor—his longtime commander and superior—before eventually turning to the governor's political opponents in order to bring him down. Escobedo, having also fallen out with Vidaurri previously such that he had retired to his headquarters at Galeana, offered to help Zaragoza by pretending to lead a threatening force out of Villa de los Rayones toward Monterrey. As expected, this movement caused Brigadier Zuazua, Vidaurri's loyal subordinate, to exit the capital with the bulk of its garrison to confront Escobedo's apparent challenge, so—during his absence—Zaragoza was able to penetrate into the governor's sleeping quarters with a few officers on the night of September 24–25, 1859, arresting and deporting him toward exile in the United States.

However, the loyal Zuazua learned of this deposal and rode to Lampazos to rescue the captive governor en route, then furthermore managed to evade Zaragoza's troops and slip into Monterrey on November 29, 1859, to persuade its state Congress to set aside Vidaurri's substitution by Gen. José Silvestre Aramberri so the issue might instead be decided by an election between both men. Vidaurri won and was restored into office by April 11, 1860, but subsequently antagonized the state legislature by refusing to relinquish his two-year-old emergency powers.

The victorious liberal general José López Uraga issued a proclamation from San Luis Potosí, calling on as many regiments as possible to rendezvous at San Juan de los Llanos by May 8, 1860, so as to join him in a major offensive against either Guadalajara or Mexico City. Degollado incorporated his forces under López Uraga's command, along with his subordinate Zaragoza, who became López Uraga's adjutant.

Zaragoza was not given a field command again until González Ortega promoted him to major general of a division. Despite his mild appearance, Zaragoza had proven such an intelligent and determined commander that he had a meteoric rise through liberal ranks. He would always display a rare talent for understanding and inspiring confidence among his soldiers.

A 31-year-old brigadier by May 1860, he had assumed command over the 8,000-man army besieging Guadalajara and led them successfully throughout the remaining months of the War of the Reform.

Secretary of War (April–December 1861)

He was rewarded by being named as Juárez's secretary of war in April 1861, resigning effective December 10th of that same year to depart Mexico City 11 days afterward and assume command over the division that was being assembled at San Luis Potosí in anticipation of hostilities against the French. Tragically, his young wife, Rafaela, died unexpectedly in the capital on January 13, 1862, leaving Zaragoza a widower.

Defense of Puebla (February–May 1862)

With the foreign occupiers who were temporarily holding the port city of Veracruz threatening to push inland in search of healthier cantonments, Zaragoza was officially appointed by Juárez's republican government on February 6, 1862, to begin organizing and to assume command over an *Ejército de Oriente* or "Eastern Army" so as to contest any deeper penetrations into the interior. Thousands more French troops continued to disembark that ensuing month, after which Maj. Gen. Charles, Comte de Lorencez, struck inland from his foothold in the city of Córdoba on April 19, 1862, with an army of 6,800 French soldiers and marines, expecting to be reinforced by conservative contingents as he advanced into Mexico.

Rather than challenge these well-armed invaders in that distant coastal zone, Zaragoza chose a strategy of meeting them after they had ascended into the central highlands, when their supply lines would be extended for a couple hundred miles. So his troops would not be overmatched by superior French firepower, he began digging them into defensive positions around the city of Puebla to make his stand there. In order to buy more time so as to complete these dispositions, he personally led the 2nd Infantry Division of his 29-year-old subordinate, Gen. José María Arteaga, in a foray that ambushed Lorencez's approaching column from atop the heights overlooking the highway winding up out of the town of Acultzingo on April 28, 1862.

Yet the 6,100-man French Army continued its advance, entering the town of Amozoc—only 12 miles short of Puebla—by the afternoon of May 4, 1862. With disease appearing in his ranks, Lorencez decided to drive due west along the highway straight into Puebla's defenses the next dawn, May 5th—in Spanish, the *cinco de mayo*—piercing through in a single stroke thanks to his troops' superior firepower.

Waiting were some 6,000 republican defenders that Zaragoza had ensconced into various strongpoints east of the city, his command post being at the monastery of Los Remedios, a cluster of stone buildings directly beside the highway from Amozoc. Lorencez appeared at 10:45 a.m. on that Monday morning, May 5, 1862, allowing his troops to rest for about three-quarters of an hour before wheeling two Zouave battalions and a Marine Fusilier battalion over onto his right at 11:30 a.m. and deploying 10 fieldpieces around Rementería Ranch.

In the wake of his defeat, Lorencez recuperated for two days atop the nearby Amalucan heights, still hoping to be reinforced from distant Matamoros de Izúcar by his Mexican conservative allies. When none appeared by the third morning, he began leading his 6,000 survivors on the long trudge back east toward the safety of Orizaba, so Zaragoza emerged from behind Puebla's defenses that same afternoon of May 8, 1862, to trail after the invaders—cautiously and with some difficulty—with his own 7,500 ill-supplied soldiers. (Annoyed by the lack of support that he had received from the wealthy inhabitants of that conservative city upon exiting in pursuit of the French, Zaragoza angrily noted the next day: "How good it would be to burn Puebla!")

He slowly followed his retreating opponents for several days over roads waterlogged by heavy rain before Zaragoza paused on May 17, 1862, to rest his weary and hungry troops around San Andrés Chalchicomula in anticipation of being joined by the Zacatecas Division under Brig. Gen. Jesús González Ortega. That same evening, Lorencez was surprised to learn that 2,500 of his allied conservative riders had arrived nearby under Gen. Leonardo Márquez, and Zaragoza's vanguard was unable to prevent their passage the next day at the Battle of Barranca Seca so as to join the French within Orizaba.

Final Operations and Death (June–September 1862)

After being reinforced by González Ortega's 6,000 troops, Zaragoza exited from Acultzingo on June 10, 1862, to attempt to surprise the French in Orizaba. Approaching three days later with his 14,000 men divided up into twin columns, Zaragoza quietly occupied Borrego or Tlalchichilco Hill. However, Lorencez learned of this enemy presence and sent a 150-man company under Capt. Paul Alexandre Détrie of the 99th Line Regiment to reconnoiter, who ascended this height in the predawn darkness of June 14, 1862, and discovered sleeping sentinels from the 4th Zacatecas Battalion.

A skirmish thereupon erupted, after which a second 99th company joined this nocturnal clash. The raw Mexican troops—despite heavily outnumbering their opponents—fired wildly on each other in the darkness, suffering 250 casualties and 200 captured. At dawn, Lorencez furthermore skirmished against Zaragoza's main body outside La Angostura Gate leading into Orizaba, prompting the latter to withdraw his entire army toward El Retiro having lost the element of surprise. French losses totaled only 7 killed and 28 wounded from this failed operation, while Zaragoza suffered a further several hundred desertions during his subsequent retreat toward Puebla.

More French troops began joining Lorencez's idled expeditionary force from across the Atlantic as of late August 1862, so Zaragoza did not mount any further strikes before suddenly sickening and dying of typhoid fever in Puebla on September 8,

1862, being succeeded in command of the Army of the East by González Ortega.

See also: Ahualulco de los Pinos, Battle of; Bajío; Barranca Seca, Battle of; Cinco de Mayo, Battle of the; Cumbres de Acultzingo, Battle of the; Degollado Sánchez, José Nemesio Francisco; Lorencez, Charles Ferdinand Latrille, Comte de; Márquez Araujo, Leonardo; Miramón Tarelo, Miguel Gregorio de la Luz Atenógenes; Reform, War of the; Tacubaya, Battle of; Zuazua Esparza, Juan Nepomuceno; Zuloaga Trillo, Félix María.

Further Reading

Arroyo Llano, Rodolfo. *Ygnacio Zaragoza: defensor de la libertad y la justicia.* Puebla: Colegio de Puebla and Gobierno del Estado de Puebla, 2012 reedition.

Cambre, Manuel. *La guerra de Tres Años: apuntes para la historia de la Reforma.* Guadalajara, Jalisco: Gobierno del Estado, 1949.

Gómez, Manuel Z. *Biografía del Gral. de división C. Ignacio Zaragoza.* Mexico City: Imprenta de Vicente García Torres, 1862.

Sosa, Francisco. *Biografías de mexicanos distinguidos.* Mexico City: Porrúa, 2006.

Zetas (1997–present)

Name of a notorious modern drug gang whose founders were deserters from elite units of the Mexican Army.

Although the precise details are only obscurely known, it is believed that this criminal enterprise had its origins in the power struggle that ensued after the arrest of Juan García Abrego, leader of the Gulf Cartel, in mid-January 1996. With his subordinates left to dispute the leadership of this organization between various different factions, while furthermore fighting off attempted takeovers and territorial encroachments from outside their border state of Tamaulipas by rival gangs, one such claimant to power within the cartel—Osiel Cárdenas Guillén—turned to recruiting disgruntled military commandos to serve him as personal bodyguards and gunmen throughout this struggle. He would soon find a few dozen willing recruits from among the thousands of highly trained, yet modestly paid young daredevils who made up such elite Mexican Army units as the *Grupo Aeromóvil de Fuerzas Especiales* or "Aeromobile Group of Special Forces" (GAFE), or the *Brigada de Fusileros Paracaidistas* or "Brigade of Parachutist Fusiliers"—two units that were often employed in armed interventions during antidrug sweeps or in making difficult arrests.

It is believed that Cárdenas Guillén first came into contact with 20-year-old lieutenant Arturo Guzmán Decena while the latter was in charge of border security at the tiny town of Ciudad Alemán, Tamaulipas (opposite Roma, Texas). Presumably, the young officer had been accepting occasional bribes from the Gulf Cartel to turn a blind eye to cross-border movements, a not uncommon practice among underpaid subalterns, but the beleaguered drug lord must have realized Guzmán Decena's potential value as a fearless and ruthless marksman, trained in both the United States and Israel in the handling of a wide variety of modern weaponry.

Through conversations, Cárdenas Guillén managed to persuade the young lieutenant to join his organization so as to head up his armed guards and hit squads operating out of Matamoros (directly opposite Brownsville, Texas). Guzmán Decena consequently resigned his commission from the Mexican Army effective on September 27, 1997, and furthermore took with him about 13 likeminded members of the 70th Infantry Battalion, 15th Motorized Cavalry Regiment, and paratroopers to compose his new shadowy group of criminal mercenaries.

Militarization of Drug Warfare (1998–2003)

Adapting standard Army security practices, Guzmán assumed the code name of "Z-1" (in Spanish, *zeta-uno*) as his pseudonym, while assigning similarly numbered aliases to his initial band of followers, a practice that was to be continued as other members were recruited into the Zetas. Although few in numbers, this first generation of mercenaries immediately proved their worth, being fit young marksmen who were much more lethal assassins than the typical thug *pistoleros* or "pistol men" employed by other gangs. The Zetas' training allowed them to strike quickly and brazenly, armed with the most sophisticated military-grade machine guns and assault rifles, proving such formidable combatants that they did not fear encountering rival gangs, policemen, or even Mexican Army units.

Delighted, Cárdenas Guillén asked Guzmán as early as 1998 to start recruiting more Zetas, most of this second group of mercenaries being drawn from among GAFE-trained members of the 15th Infantry Battalion stationed at Tampico. Virtually all of this entire first generation of original Zetas would be drawn from the lower ranks of the Mexican armed forces, authorities later identifying 31 of the less than 40 *Zetas Viejos* or "Old Zetas" who had deserted as including five ex-lieutenants, four sublieutenants, three sergeants, three corporals, and the remainder privates. Popular opinion throughout the Mexican Army—even among officers or soldiers with corrupt propensities—held that forsaking one's oath to become a "narco-mercenary" put such turncoats beyond the pale, so they would be hunted down by their fellow soldiers with vindictive zeal. (By 2011, 7 of these 31 identified defectors would be dead and 15 others in prison.)

Nonetheless, the Zetas' skill and ferocity allowed Cárdenas Guillén to secure the leadership of the Gulf Cartel. In July 1999, he invited his equal partner, Ángel Salvador "El Chava" Gómez Herrera, to attend the baptism of Cárdenas's daughter in Matamoros. Upon exiting the church after this ceremony, Cárdenas as host offered "El Chava" a ride in his Dodge Durango. Both men chatted and joked amiably as they drove along until Cárdenas signaled to Guzmán in the backseat, who fired a bullet into Gómez's head. His ex-partner's body was thereupon callously dumped and not found until several days later, decaying on the outskirts of Matamoros, so Cárdenas became widely known as the *Mata Amigos* or "Friend Killer."

The raw fear engendered by the young Zetas' cruelty gave the drug lord a brazen new strength, personally witnessed by two undercover FBI and DEA operatives during a standoff in November 1999 in the streets of Matamoros. Having crossed the bridge from Brownsville in a vehicle with diplomatic plates, the U.S. agents were driving around that Mexican city, discreetly spying on drug sites with the help of a local reporter when they were spotted and chased. Hemmed in by a dozen vehicles within yards of Matamoros's police headquarters, the Americans were menaced in broad daylight by heavily armed gunmen—several wearing police uniforms—while other policemen nearby redirected civilian traffic away from the scene. Cárdenas arrived with his entourage and a gold-plated AK-47 to pound on the hood of the agents' car and demand that the reporter be handed over for execution. After 20 minutes of tense argument, the agents were allowed to escape back over the border with their informant, shaken by this naked display of criminal power.

As Cárdenas's trusted lieutenant, Guzmán would lead the Zetas over the next three years in a wave of assassinations and vicious attacks on behalf of the Gulf Cartel, who remained locked in a bitter fight against the larger Sinaloa Cartel and other organizations for dominance over the lucrative American drug trade. Because of their firepower, the Gulf Cartel's rivals soon began to acquire heavier-grade military ordnance of their own, such as AK-47s, AR-15s, and grenade launchers to match the Zetas, so the violence and casualties being inflicted on both sides (including the civilian population) grew proportionally worse.

And to make up for their lack of numbers, the Zetas were given free rein to visit frightful psy-op terrors on their opponents, resorting to savage beheadings and public executions during their attacks so as to spread fear even more widely among government functionaries, policemen, journalists, and the public at large.

New Depths of Violence (2003–Present)

Conditions became even more appalling after 26-year-old Guzmán Decena (Z-1) was killed on the night of November 21–22, 2002, after leaving a Matamoros restaurant to visit his mistress. Having ordered his henchmen to block off her street and divert traffic, an anonymous tip was phoned in to the police, so a party of Mexican soldiers surprised Guzmán Decena and he died in a hail of bullets. Less than four months later, on March 14, 2003, his cartel boss, Cárdenas Guillén, was also captured, being extradited to the United States four years later and sentenced to 25 years' incarceration in Colorado.

Although most of its original members were by then in prison or dead, the Zetas had nonetheless continued to recruit and grown to number more than 300 vicious young gunmen, expanding their activities to include heartless extortions and kidnappings for ransom. They struck out on their own, dissolving their association with the Gulf Cartel to expand into other states, either through allying themselves or absorbing subsidiary gangs. Despite no longer attracting deserters from elite army units, their level of violence with high-powered weaponry remained appalling, the struggle between the allied Zeta group *La Línea* and the Sinaloa Cartel for control over Ciudad Juárez resulting in at least 5,000 deaths between 2007 and 2010.

The Zetas are currently considered the dominant cartel in eastern Mexico, while the more powerful Sinaloa Cartel controls western Mexico, both groups often clashing either directly or through surrogates. But the once-feared Zetas themselves, no longer more highly trained or better armed than their opponents, have recently been subjected in Veracruz to mass killings and humiliating executions posted on social media by a group that goes by the name of the *Mata Zetas* or "Zeta Killers."

See also: Drug War.

Further Reading

Grayson, George W., and Samuel Logan. *The Executioner's Men: Los Zetas, Rogue Soldiers, Criminal Entrepreneurs, and the Shadow State They Created.* Piscataway, NJ: Transaction, 2012.

The War on Mexican Cartels: Options for U.S. and Mexican Policy-Makers. Cambridge, MA: Harvard University Institute of Politics, September 2012.

Zouaves (1862–1867)

World-famous regiment of elite troops who would see almost five years of service in Mexico during the War of the French Intervention.

Romanticized lithograph by Victor Adam, depicting French Zouaves breaching the Mexican defenses at Puebla in May 1863. (Anne S. K. Brown Military Collection, Brown University Library)

Origins and Early History (1830–1860)

When France had initiated its struggle to subdue Algeria in North Africa in 1830, Berber natives of the Zouaoua mountain tribe in its Jurjura range—who had previously served the country's distant Turkish Ottoman rulers—shifted their allegiance so as to perform similar service for the new French invaders. By that same October 1830, two battalions of "Zouaves" had been formed as French auxiliaries, uniformed in their traditional garb of bright baggy trousers, short jackets, and fezes. The exceptional courage and daring displayed by these colorful Berber warriors had led to the raising of an additional battalion by 1837 so as to constitute a full "1st Zouave Infantry Regiment" five years afterward. When all of the Muslim troops in Algeria had been regrouped shortly thereafter into a separate formation of light infantry designated as the *Tirailleurs Algériens* or "Algerian Sharpshooters," the Zouaves had become transformed into a purely French body.

Troops who volunteered for the lengthy tours in this elite regiment not only retained its distinctive uniform, but also displayed a conspicuous fearlessness and dash in battle. By 1854, there were four Zouave Regiments in the French Army, who served with great gallantry during the Crimean War, as well as the Franco-Austrian War of five years later. Their stylish appearance and bravery attracted much attention from newspaper reporters, making the Zouaves world famous.

Britain, Spain, Portugal, Italy, and even the Papal States had created their own

Zouave units, yet perhaps no country embraced the "Zouave craze" as fully as the United States. Both before and during the Civil War, more than 50 Zouave regiments were formed by American volunteers, mostly in the Union states of the northeast.

French Zouaves in Mexico (1862–1867)

As some of the best-armed and -disciplined formations in France's army, two battalions of the 2nd Zouave Infantry Regiment totaling 1,800 men were included among the units assigned in November 1861 to Brig. Gen. Charles, Comte de Lorencez's initial expedition to Mexico. These battalions sailed from Oran two-and-a-half months apart, aboard the warships *Masséna* and *Fontenoy*, to be reunited under the command of Col. Pierre Guillaume Eugène Gambier outside the port of Veracruz by late March 1862.

They were one of the main components of the 6,100-man army that Lorencez led inland from the occupied city of Córdoba at dawn on April 19, 1862, expecting to be joined by Mexican conservative forces and greeted as liberators as they marched toward Puebla. Instead, they found the countryside deserted and were harried by republican scouts, while no conservative reinforcements appeared. After pushing past a republican division defending the Cumbres de Acultzingo on April 28, 1862, the weary French columns entered the silent town of Amozoc on the afternoon of May 4, 1862, only 12 miles from the city of Puebla.

With disease spreading in his ranks, Lorencez decided to risk an all-out assault against its 6,000 republican defenses the next morning rather than settle down to a protracted siege. The 2nd Zouaves were therefore sent sweeping up Guadalupe Hill twice in extended battle lines on May 5, 1862—the celebrated Battle of the Cinco de Mayo—enduring heavy losses in its

maze of defensive trenches before Lorencez finally called a halt and retreated as evening fell. It would take his army almost two weeks to regain the safety of their base at Orizaba, where the 2nd Zouave Regiment would rest over the next few months.

With this initial penetration into central Mexico having been repelled, thousands of reinforcements were sent out from France, including two more Zouave regiments from North Africa. The 1,850 troops and 200 horses of the 1st Zouave Regiment departed Algiers aboard the warships *Eylau* and *Impérial* in late June 1862, reaching Veracruz by August 23, 1862, to be followed by another 1,800 men of the 3rd Zouave Regiment later that same year and into early 1863, together forming an integral part of a much larger army in Mexico under a new commander, Maj. Gen. Elie Frédéric Forey.

The Zouaves naturally served prominently during the siege of Puebla in the spring of 1863, and after the capitulation of that city on May 17, 1863, the 1st Zouave Regiment remained there for almost another year as the main component of its occupying garrison, occasionally sending out detachments to patrol the region's roads and pursue guerrilla bands. The 2nd Zouave Regiment, meanwhile, participated in Maj. Gen. Charles Douay's epic 300-mile march from the national capital to pacify the mountainous Bajío of central Mexico, entering the city of Querétaro by November 19, 1863; Zamora by December 22nd; Uruapan on New Year's Day, 1864; the capital of Zacatecas by March 12, 1864; Pinos on May 8, 1864; Valparaíso two weeks later; etc.

Having been transferred from Puebla into Guadalajara, the 1st Zouave Regiment took part in Douay's subsequent sweep through Jalisco as far as Colima during the latter half of October and the first two weeks of November 1864. A couple of months afterward, two battalions of the 3rd Zouave Regiment formed the core of Marshal Bazaine's 5,800-man army that besieged the city of Oaxaca and captured its republican garrison under Gen. Porfirio Díaz in January and February 1865.

However, trained and equipped for large-scale field-battles, the dashing Zouaves found the years of garrison-duty as an occupation force in Mexico, unsatisfying and wearing on their morale. Some companies of mounted Zouaves were even extemporized, as a means of coming to grips with the Mexican guerrilla riders who made highways and the countryside dangerous for supporters of the emperor. But the Zouaves saw no major battlefield action during the last two years of the War of the French Intervention and were not displeased to see the last of Mexico when they sailed away in early 1867.

See also: Cinco de Mayo, Battle of the; French Intervention, War of the; Lorencez, Charles Ferdinand Latrille, Comte de.

Further Reading

Charpy, Manuel, and Claire Fredj, eds. *Lettres du Mexique: Itinéraires du zouave Augustin-Louis Frélaut, 1862–1867*. Paris: Éditions Nicolas Philippe, 2003.

Chartrand, René. *The Mexican Adventure, 1861–67*. Oxford: Osprey, 1994.

Descoubès, Ernest. *Historique du 1er Régiment des Zouaves*. Paris: Librairie militaire de Berger-Levrault, 1882, 159–82.

Montbarbut Du Plessis, Jean-Marie. *L'armée de Napoléon III au Mexique, 1862–1867*. Paris: Éditions Nouvelles, 2009.

Zuazua Esparza, Juan Nepomuceno (1820–1860)

Self-taught militia commander who distinguished himself as a liberal general during the War of the Reform.

He was born toward the very end of Mexico's colonial era—on January 6, 1820, in the northern town of Punta de Lampazos, in a province that was then still known as the *Nuevo Reino de León* or "New Kingdom of León" but is today called the state of Nuevo León. He was the sixth and final child of his Spanish father, Juan de Zuazua Mendía, and Mexican mother, María Luisa Esparza Guajardo, having been preceded by two brothers and three sisters. However, he was orphaned in his infancy and so received only a rudimentary education at Lampazos's municipal school before being sent to the Hospicio in Villaldama and then studying briefly at the Seminario Conciliar in the city of Monterrey.

Despite proving a bright student, Zuazua returned to his native town while still a teenager so as to try to earn a living through business and agriculture. He also remained an avid reader, studying military tactics and history in addition to other more practical subjects.

Service against the U.S. Invasion (1846–1848)

When Maj. Gen. Mariano Arista, a former president of Mexico, was ordered to begin organizing an "Army of the North" at Monterrey in April 1846 so as to confront the peacetime push by Brig. Gen. Zachary Taylor's army down to the banks of the Río Bravo, Zuazua went to Monterrey with his older brother Carlos to enlist. Having had some education, plus militia experience against native tribesmen, both brothers were given the rank of *alférez* or "ensign" and became incorporated into a formation of mounted auxiliary irregulars that accompanied Arista's army northeastward to Matamoros.

The next month, Zuazua saw action at both the Battles of Palo Alto and Resaca de la Palma, serving with enough distinction during these two defeats as to receive a field promotion to militia captain. He subsequently accompanied the disgraced Arista all the way back to San Luis Potosí (where the defeated general was to be court-martialed) before being returned northward in August 1846 as part of Gen. Pedro Ampudia's army to reinforce Monterrey and fight in its desperate yet unsuccessful defense against Taylor's assault.

Unattached following the surrender and evacuation of this city, Zuazua led a small group of riders into the state of Tamaulipas, where they joined a guerrilla force under the Alderete brothers. These in turn became incorporated during the winter of 1846–1847 into a larger formation that coalesced around the "Fieles de Guanajuato" and "Libres de Jalisco" militia cavalry regiments under Gen. Juan José Urrea, who had arrived to harass the American supply lines leading into Monterrey. And when Pres. Antonio López de Santa Anna brought a huge army northward in February 1847 to attack Taylor's occupying army, Zuazua's company were among the local contingents who fought as his auxiliaries at the Battle of Buena Vista—which ended in defeat, Santa Anna's retreat into central Mexico, and the local militiamen's dispersal.

Although Zuazua technically remained under arms for the remaining year of the Mexican-American War, he saw no more action and returned into private life embittered at the poor quality and self-interest of national leadership, which had bought peace by surrendering every northern province from Texas to California to the Americans.

Champion of Nuevo León (1855–1857)

When the full weakness of the conservative dictatorship of Santa Anna became revealed seven years later by its failure to crush the liberal Revolution of Ayutla, Zuazua provided the military backing for his own fellow citizen from Lampazos—the well-placed, 45-year-old politician Santiago Vidaurri—to seize power in the state of Nuevo León. On May 12, 1855, they proclaimed Vidaurri's revolt simultaneously, after which Zuazua marched from Lampazos toward the capital city of Monterrey with a small force. Arriving outside it 10 days later, his rebels were joined by many volunteers, and Zuazua carried the city in an almost-bloodless assault on May 23, 1855, so Vidaurri was able to supplant the *santannista* general Gerónimo Cardona as state governor.

Vidaurri furthermore claimed the titles of military commander for Nuevo León (as well as of neighboring Coahuila) and regional commander-in-chief of the so-called *Ejército Restaurador de la Libertad* or Restorer of Liberty Army, the name of southern general Juan N. Álvarez's armed Ayutla movement that was coalescing to drive Santa Anna from power. Vidaurri promoted Zuazua to the top militia rank of colonel and a few weeks later sent him on an offensive against a 2,000-man *santannista* concentration that had gathered under Gen. Francisco Güitián at Rancho de las Varas outside Saltillo. The liberal forces came within sight of that city by July 22, 1855, and under cover of darkness that same night, three columns under Captains Ignacio Zaragoza, Mariano Escobedo, and Pedro Hinojosa mounted a coordinated assault that dispersed these *santannistas* and captured almost the entire city garrison and its armaments.

Less than a month later, after Santa Anna had resigned the presidency and fled from Mexico, the conservative generals Anastasio Parrodi and Güitián tried on August 16, 1855, to acclaim Gen. Antonio Haro y

Tamariz—military governor of San Luis Potosí—as a new challenger for this vacated office, rather than see it go to the lowborn Álvarez. Zuazua marched on San Luis Potosí to contest this *pronunciamiento*, so Parrodi emerged from that city and engaged the liberal army awaiting him atop a hill outside the hamlet of Morterillos on the afternoon of September 12, 1856. Three conservative charges between 1:00 and 6:00 p.m. failed to dislodge Zuazua's force, though, after which he instructed Escobedo to remain with his 5th and 6th Cavalry Squadrons to keep Parrodi busy while Zuazua circled around with the main liberal army to surprise the small garrison left holding San Luis Potosí. Confronted by Zuazua with 800 riders right outside his city gates, Haro agreed to capitulate by September 27, 1855.

After a five months' lull, Zuazua was recalled to active duty when Nuevo León's cantankerous governor, Vidaurri, annexed Coahuila in February 1856 and rebuffed every objection raised against this unilateral expropriation by the fledgling national government under interim president Ignacio Comonfort. The latter finally authorized the use of military force to remove Vidaurri from office on August 8, 1856, so two armies began converging on Nuevo León: one out of Tamaulipas to its east, advancing in twin columns through Villagrán and Mier under the overall direction of Gen. Juan José de la Garza; plus a second one out of San Luis Potosí to its south, under Gen. Vicente Rosas Landa.

Zuazua reached Mier with his main body on September 28, 1856, continuing on into Camargo to repulse the enemy column under Gen. Guadalupe García. But with pressures closing in from several directions, Zuazua could not subsequently prevent García from joining De la Garza at Villagrán and driving on together so as to invest Monterrey itself by November 1, 1856. Through forced marches, Zuazua was able to rescue the capital's beleaguered garrison under Capt. Ignacio Zaragoza two days later and drive this attacking force off toward Saltillo. But having united there with Rosas Landa, this combined government army then returned to threaten Monterrey again, although their approach was checked by Zuazua at Cuesta de los Muertos. Rather than prolong the hostilities, though, Vidaurri agreed to resign as governor and recognize the authority of the national government while leaving the issue of Coahuila's statehood to be decided by a plebiscite among its citizens.

Service in the War of the Reform (Summer 1858)

Naturally, Vidaurri did not resign, and so his northern states were among the first to reject the conservative coup a couple of months later that deposed Comonfort in the national capital on January 22, 1858, and set about rescinding all liberal reforms to Mexico's constitution. Zuazua and his militiamen were recalled to active duty in early February 1858, being organized into a new *Ejército del Norte* or "Army of the North." Their state-issued "uniforms" consisted of simple red tunics with matching hatbands, plus a general directive to all troopers to thrust their trousers into their boot tops (such a casual style of dress that they would be looked down on as amateurs by officers of the regular Mexican Army).

The War of the Reform officially began when a large army of regulars advanced north out of Mexico City under conservative commanders and scattered the liberal militia units that were marshaling outside the city of Salamanca in the state of Guanajuato on March 10–11, 1858. These victors then marched on to Guadalajara while Zuazua led his smaller "Army of the North" a couple of weeks later down into the state of San Luis Potosí, threatening the feeble 1,500-man conservative garrison holding its capital city.

A division of 2,200 infantrymen, 400 cavalry troopers, and 12 guns was consequently detached in early April 1858 from Guadalajara under conservative brigadier general Miguel Miramón to proceed northeastward and rescue the imperiled garrison. This relief column exited from the town of Salinas on the last stage of its march on April 15, 1858, and word was carried by 5:00 p.m. the next evening into Zuazua's field headquarters at the village of Moctezuma (located about 45 miles north of the city of San Luis Potosí). Within three hours, he instructed his subordinate, Lt. Col. Ignacio Zaragoza, to remain at nearby Venado with the liberal army's infantry and artillery, while Zuazua departed by 8:00 p.m. to lead 1,100 mounted riflemen on a grueling overnight ride and ambush the conservative relief force at a preselected chokepoint: a canyon where the road made a long, exposed ascent known as *Puerto de Carretas* or "Wagons' Pass."

Arriving after an 11-hour nocturnal ride, Zuazua deployed his two brigades into hidden positions overlooking this rising roadway at 7:00 a.m. on April 17, 1858, and an hour and a half later opened fire on the conservatives' vanguard. Miramón halted and formed up 1,600 of his 2,600 troops so as to sweep up the steep incline and clear its top of liberal riflemen. Zuazua's irregulars fired from concealed positions and gave way as the regulars' firing lines moved closer to them, so Miramón was able to push through and gain San Luis Potosí with his relief column, despite having suffered several hundred casualties. He then braced his 2,000 surviving men to withstand a liberal assault.

But Zuazua instead materialized unexpectedly outside of the city of Zacatecas on Tuesday, April 27, 1858, his cavalry charging the conservative positions atop La Bufa Hill at 10:00 a.m. The defenders nonetheless managed to fend off these 2,000 mounted liberal riflemen all day until Col. Pedro Hinojosa arrived late in the afternoon with his liberal infantry battalion and their concentrated firepower allowed Zuazua's attackers to carry La Bufa by 8:00 p.m. Fighting then continued on in the city itself, Zacatecas's stone *ciudadela* or "citadel," *parroquia* or "parish church," and San Agustín and Santo Domingo convents all falling in the darkness until shooting finally ceased by midnight. The next morning revealed that the liberals had captured conservative general Antonio Manero, along with 60 of his officers and 420 soldiers. (Manero would complain bitterly to Zuazua about the unorthodox tactics employed by his *blusas*, "crawling on the ground and jumping around" while emitting Comanche war whoops rather than being formed up in erect firing lines.)

The liberal commander felt so confident after this victory that he even detached Col. Miguel Blanco and Lt. Col. Mariano Escobedo to ride farther south into Jalisco with 800 mounted riflemen and seven fieldpieces in early May 1858 so as to reinforce its allied commander in that region, Gen. Santos Degollado. Meanwhile, Vidaurri was raising and equipping more volunteers in Nuevo León in anticipation of a renewed attempt against San Luis Potosí. Its conservative garrison became reduced when Miramón departed with a large force a couple of weeks later so as to rescue Guadalajara; then the 1,500 defenders and 16 guns left behind in San Luis Potosí under youthful major general Luis G. Osollo, were suddenly left leaderless when he died of typhoid fever on June 18, 1858, and Zuazua decided to strike.

He appeared outside San Luis Potosí with 3,400 *blusas* on June 29, 1858, hailing its garrison commander at 10:00 a.m. and giving him two hours to surrender. Rebuffed, Zuazua surrounded the city and attacked simultaneously from several different directions at 9:00 a.m. the next morning so as to dissipate the strength of its 1,500 defenders. Masked by these feints, the liberal commander directed his principal thrust at the stone strongholds represented by the city's *alhóndiga* or "granary," as well as the Refugio and San Juan de Dios convents in Maltas Street, concentrating two-thirds of his men and almost all of his artillery (under the American mercenary, Col. Edward P. Jordan) into penetrating the defenses through that sector.

Zuazua's soldiers fought their way into the city center by 4:00 p.m. on that June 30, 1858, at which time considerable looting and pillaging broke out. Once order was restored, he recorded that the defenders had suffered 103 dead, a like number wounded, along with the capture of their commanding general, 17 officers, and 403 soldiers (the remainder having either deserted or switched allegiances). The liberals, in contrast, had—according to Zuazua—"sustained but a small loss, for which we are very grateful."

In the wake of this capture, the 62-year-old bishop Pedro Barajas was expelled into the United States in July 1858 along with most of San Luis Potosí's clergy, while Aramberri was sent on ahead with a detachment to enter the city of Guanajuato uncontested on July 15, 1858. Two weeks later, Governor Vidaurri departed Monterrey with hundreds more reinforcements and several artillery pieces, arriving in San Luis Potosí by August 13, 1858, to personally assume

command. Over the ensuing month, he also imposed forced loans on that city and expelled all Spanish-born citizens.

When news arrived that a 4,000-man conservative army was approaching under Miramón, the 5,000 liberals evacuated San Luis Potosí on September 10, 1858, to take up a strong defensive position behind the Bocas River near the tiny rural hamlet of Ahualulco de los Pinos. The conservative army arrived opposite 15 days later but could not fight its way across the fast-flowing river, so searched for a way of circling around farther to the east. It was before any final confrontation could occur that Zuazua had an altercation with a scout from Col. Juan Espíndola's contingent, during which the latter commander wounded the liberal general with a sword thrust, so Zuazua was recuperating from this injury and thus unable to command the liberal army at the Battle of Ahualulco. Vidaurri instead entrusted the command to the American Jordan, and the engagement ended in a resounding defeat.

Liberal Infighting and Death (September 1859–July 1860)

Zuazua was one of the few commanders who remained loyal to the discredited Vidaurri in the wake of this disastrous setback. The next year, the governor became bitterly embroiled in a dispute with his rival, Gen. Santos Degollado, to the point of publicly proclaiming an order on September 5, 1859, that would have recalled all troops of Nuevo León and Coahuila serving in the main liberal army. Degollado deemed this to be an act of treason because of that force's ongoing operations against their conservative foes and the regular army so sent Brig. Gen. Ignacio Zaragoza on the thankless commission of deposing Vidaurri.

Reaching the state capital of Monterrey, Zaragoza at first tried reasoning with the irate governor before turning to his political opponents and then acting. Col. Mariano Escobedo, having previously fallen out with Vidaurri and retired to his headquarters at Galeana, helped Zaragoza by pretending to lead a threatening force out of Villa de los Rayones toward Monterrey. Zuazua in turn exited the capital with the bulk of its garrison to confront Escobedo's apparent challenge, so during his absence—Zaragoza was able to penetrate into the governor's sleeping quarters with a few officers on the night of September 24–25, 1859, and deport him toward exile in the United States.

However, when the loyal Zuazua learned of this deposal, he rode to Lampazos and rescued the captive governor. Zuazua then furthermore managed to evade Zaragoza and slip into Monterrey on November 29, 1859, persuading its state Congress to set aside his substitution by Gen. José Silvestre Aramberri so the issue could instead be decided by an election between both men. Vidaurri won and was restored into office by April 11, 1860, but subsequently antagonized the state legislature by refusing to relinquish his two-year-old emergency powers.

After dissolving the state Congress, Vidaurri's rule was challenged once again in June 1860 by Aramberri and Escobedo. The governor and Zuazua marched out of Monterrey with a small army, and Vidaurri and his escort rode on ahead to rest at the Hacienda de San Gregorio for the night of July 30–31, 1860. When his enemies chanced to learn of this, they stealthily sent a small cavalry detachment to make a nocturnal attack without realizing that Zuazua had also arrived with his staff after nightfall. The trusty general emerged from his room into the moonlight upon hearing the first shots and was instantly killed by a round to the head, leaving behind a widow and seven children.

See also: Ampudia Grimarest, Pedro; Ayutla, Revolution of; *blusas*; Degollado Sánchez, José Nemesio Francisco; Escobedo Peña, Mariano Antonio Guadalupe; Márquez Araujo, Leonardo; Mexican-American War; Miramón Tarelo, Miguel Gregorio de la Luz Atenógenes; Monterrey, Battle of; Palo Alto, Battle of; *pronunciamiento*; Puerto de Carretas, Battle of; Reform, War of the; Zaragoza Seguín, Ignacio.

Further Reading

Cambre, Manuel. *La guerra de Tres Años: apuntes para la historia de la Reforma.* Guadalajara, Jalisco: Gobierno del Estado, 1949.

Dávila, Hermenegildo. *Biografía del Sr. General D. Juan Zuazúa.* Monterrey, Nuevo León: Tipografía calle de Dr. Mier, 1892.

García, Luis Alberto. *Guerra y frontera: el Ejército del Norte entre 1855 y 1858.* Monterrey: Fondo Editorial y Archivo General del Estado de Nuevo León, 2006.

"Important from Mexico." *Dallas Herald* 7, no. 6, August 7, 1858, front page.

Sosa, Francisco. *Biografías de mexicanos distinguidos.* Mexico City: Porrúa, 2006.

Zuloaga Trillo, Félix María (1813–1898)

Military officer turned politician who briefly and unsuccessfully occupied the presidency of Mexico.

He was born in colonial times, on March 31, 1813, in a house named Altos de Bojórquez in the northern mining town then known as Real de los Álamos (modern Álamos, Sonora). He was the fourth son and fifth child of Manuel José de Zuloaga Orendáin, a Mexican of Basque descent, and

Mariana Trillo Muñoz de Olvera. His parents would have two more daughters after Félix's birth, for a total of seven children. When this large family moved to Chihuahua City, Félix began his formal education, proving to be such an apt pupil that as a teenager he was enrolled in a seminary in Mexico City, although he soon dropped out so as to return home when his father died in 1832.

Early Military Career (1834–1845)

Two years later, Zuloaga enlisted at the age of 21 in the *Milicia Civica* or "Civic Militia" of Chihuahua, campaigning over the next three years against the Comanches and Apaches (presumably under his older brother José, who was nine years his senior and a captain at the Janos *presidio*). Then in 1838, Félix wrote an exam in Mexico City that won him admittance into the national army as a sublieutenant of engineers. In this rank, he would serve that same year in a minor capacity during the War of the Cakes against the French, and then in July 1840 he fought as a captain in support of the liberal president Anastasio Bustamante against the military coup that was attempted by Gen. Juan José Urrea in Mexico City.

One year later, Zuloaga would switch his allegiances over to Santa Anna, who promoted him and sent the young officer in 1842 to campaign for a year against the separatists in Campeche and Yucatán, a miserable siege operation that ended in fiasco. Before departing Mexico City on that commission, Zuloaga had married María Palafox Garibi—the daughter of a general from Jalisco—with whom he would eventually have two sons and a daughter.

Service during the Mexican-American War (1846–1848)

By the spring of 1846, Zuloaga was a veteran 33-year-old lieutenant colonel of engineers and a member of Maj. Gen. Mariano Arista's army in the northern border town of Matamoros when that force advanced across the Río Bravo, only to be defeated at the Battles of Palo Alto and Resaca de la Palma by the American invaders under Brig. Gen. Zachary Taylor. After retreating back out of Matamoros on a grueling 45-day trek through Mexico's northern wastelands and reaching Linares by June 29, 1846, Arista—in one of his final acts as commander of the *Ejército del Norte* or "Army of the North"—ordered Zuloaga to proceed on into Monterrey with Lt. Col. Mariano Reyes's sappers so as to begin fortifying that city against its inevitable American assault.

Zuloaga's and Reyes's defensive labors were further accelerated after Gen. Pedro de Ampudia reinforced Monterrey with 3,500 fresh soldiers at the end of August 1846, so the city was able to put up a stout resistance when Taylor's army finally arrived on September 19, 1846, and mounted its assault. After three days of heavy fighting, Ampudia requested terms and Taylor agreed to permit the Mexican defenders to march out with their arms and six guns over a number of days, retreating beyond Rinconada Pass, after which both sides would observe a two-month cessation of offensive operations. Zuloaga was subsequently employed in fortification work at Saltillo before being transferred to serve south of Mexico City in 1847, helping to attempt fend off Gen. Winfield Scott's advance on the national capital.

Santa Anna Loyalist (1853–1855)

Following Mexico's defeat and the signing of a peace treaty with the Americans, Zuloaga obtained a three-year furlough from the army as of 1848, during which he served a term as both *regidor* or "alderman" and *alcalde* or "mayor" of Chihuahua City. When the peacetime Mexican Army was resurrected and reconstituted in 1851, he resumed his commission and, like other former Santa Anna loyalists (such as Leonardo Márquez), was promoted and became fully employed after Gen. Manuel María Lombardini engineered a coup in the national capital that temporarily seized the presidency as of February 7, 1853, and held it against Santa Anna's return from exile in Colombia to reassume power.

Promoted to full colonel upon the restoration of this regime, Zuloaga was further appointed in December 1853 as *presidente* or "chief presiding officer" of the *Consejo de Guerra de la Plaza de México*, the court in charge of all military tribunals, and would see active duty in Santa Anna's support when the liberal Revolution of Ayutla erupted in the state of Guerrero the next spring. Having failed to crush this rebellion during its initial stages with his offensive of April–May 1854, Santa Anna subsequently proclaimed that all of that region's inhabitants would be subjected to the full rigors of martial law and instructed Maj. Gen. Ángel Pérez Palacios to unleash detachments from his advance base at Chilpancingo to punish both its rebels and noncombatants alike.

Zuloaga was placed in command of one of the first such punitive expeditions, leading a flying column of 1,500 men and two fieldpieces that arrived below the rebel fortifications atop Limón Hill outside the town of Iguala and carried it by storm on July 12, 1854. Its defeated rebel chieftain Faustino Villalba was thereupon executed and his head left exposed in an iron cage at Mezcala, winning Zuloaga promotion to brigadier from a grateful Santa Anna.

Then Gen. Severo del Castillo was sent with two brigades—one of them being Zuloaga's—to destroy the remote Hacienda de la Providencia, home and headquarters for the rebel leader Álvarez. This expedition forged its way with great difficulty through the hot wilderness terrain and arrived to find that estate empty, leaving these two brigades deep inside enemy territory and faced with the prospect of having to exit while being subjected to thirst, hunger, disease, desertions, and vengeful pursuers.

Zuloaga was consequently ordered by Del Castillo to split off in November 1854 and proceed with his lone brigade toward Coyuca de Benítez—even deeper inside rebel territory, south of the Balsas River—as that town's capture would supposedly cut off the provisions sustaining the insurgent garrison at Acapulco. But after fighting past a rebel force under Brig. Gen. Tomás Moreno that was entrenched at El Calvario near Petatlán on December 9, 1854, Zuloaga turned away from his objective in weary distress, instead making for the relative safety of Tecpan.

But he and his 1,000 surviving men and five fieldpieces became cornered four days later in the Hacienda de Nuxco by a convergence between Álvarez and Moreno that left the *santannistas* surrounded by 4,000 rebels. After holding out for 37 days, well beyond any reasonable hope of rescue, Zuloaga's officers and soldiers surrendered to the besiegers on January 18, 1855, most choosing to join the rebel ranks while Zuloaga himself would remain a prisoner for the next four months.

Comonfort Supporter (1855–1857)

Eventually, the captive Zuloaga was won over by one of the principal leaders of the liberal Revolution of Ayutla, Ignacio Comonfort, and agreed to serve under him as of May 1855. Zuloaga even acted as a representative from Chihuahua at the *Junta de Representantes* or "Congress of Representatives" that met in Cuernavaca that same autumn to decide the issue of liberal succession to the presidency, once Santa Anna had been expelled from Mexico for the final time in August 1855. This office was eventually occupied on an interim basis by Comonfort as of December 12, 1855, while a new Constitution was drafted, and Zuloaga remained faithful to this liberal administration in its two military campaigns to put down conservative mutinies in the state of Puebla in 1856.

However, when the first reforms to Mexico's Constitution began to be announced by the liberal legislature as of early February 1857, some of which curtailed traditional privileges left over since colonial times, moderates such as Comonfort and Zuloaga were shaken by the angry reaction from Church leaders against these supposedly "radical" changes. As public disapproval was fanned by certain factions, Comonfort secretly entered into talks in hopes of reaching an accommodation with select statesmen from the liberal and conservative sides, meeting in the archbishopric of Tacubaya on the outskirts of Mexico City as of November 15, 1857, a couple of weeks prior to assuming office as duly-elected president.

Even after being sworn in on December 1, 1857, Comonfort still continued to seek an escape from adhering to this controversial new body of reformed constitutional laws, so a plot was consequently hatched whereby his trusted subordinate Zuloaga would lead a "mutiny" with his brigade (which was stationed in Tacubaya just outside of Mexico City) aimed at leaving his patron in place as president while rescinding the liberal Constitution and dissolving the "radical" Congress. Within days, rumors began to circulate that Zuloaga was sounding out other military commanders about a possible coup, so a hearing was convened by the newly seated Congress to look into this

seditious matter on Monday, December 14, 1857, although nothing was uncovered before the conspirators struck three days later.

Conservative Coups (December 1857–January 1858)

At 6:00 a.m. on December 17, 1857, a 21-gun salute was fired in Tacubaya and Zuloaga—in the presence of Comonfort, Gov. Juan José Baz of Mexico City's Federal District, and other conservative allies—announced the "Plan of Tacubaya" from that suburb's archbishopric. This document's six brief points called for Comonfort to remain in office as provisional president for another three months, ruling with a cabinet of appointed ministers, while the liberal Constitution was to be suspended forthwith until a new Congress could be elected and draft a replacement that would be more "in keeping with the national will." Zuloaga thereupon marched that same day from Tacubaya into Mexico City's *Ciudadela* or "Citadel" at the head of his brigade, consisting of 1,200 troops of the 1st Engineer Battalion under Col. Domingo Nava, the Activo "México" Light Infantry Battalion under Col. Marco Esnaurrízar, and two batteries of artillery under Col. Zeferino Rodríguez, to be joined there by other units.

The Plan of Tacubaya was simultaneously telegraphed to every state governor, winning approval over the next couple of days from only seven of them, at which point Comonfort publicly swore adhesion to the plan himself on December 19, 1857, and dissolved the liberal Congress, while prominent opponents such as the president of the Supreme Court, Benito Juárez, languished in jail. However, resistance to this forced revocation of the Constitution by reactionaries in the national capital proved to be deep-seated, as numerous liberal states began to mobilize their militias for war. Comonfort vainly tried to patch up the differences by steering a course that appeased liberals and conservatives alike, to no avail.

After three weeks of confused indecision, conservative general José de la Parra led the Tacubaya garrison in another, but this time authentic, mutiny on January 11, 1858, intending to remove the ineffectual Comonfort entirely from office so as to make way for a new administration. These mutineers seized the Ciudadela and San Agustín Church, but Comonfort continued to hold out in the Presidential Palace with perhaps 3,000 men, while independent liberal forces occupied the Santísima and San Francisco Churches as their own separate strongholds. After 10 days, this tense three-sided standoff was broken when the youthful conservative colonel Luis G. Osollo and Lt. Col. Miguel Miramón assaulted Comonfort's positions at dawn on January 21, 1857, defeating his last disheartened followers and driving him out of the country.

Figurehead President (January–December 1858)

That very next day, an extemporized body of 22 leading conservatives dubbed the *Junta de Notables* convened in Mexico City and selected Zuloaga as "interim president" on January 22, 1857, with Parra as his minister of war, who in turn would reward Osollo and Miramón with promotion to brigadier general. Zuloaga, until recently a Comonfort loyalist, was apparently chosen to be president as a more broadly acceptable and mature leader than the two young military officers who would actually be commanding in the field, although his lack of renown in army circles would make it almost impossible for Zuloaga to lead the conservative movement—proving to be little more than

an *hombre de paja* or "strawman" throughout his tenure in office.

Within a few weeks, Osollo and Miramón marched northward into the Bajío at the head of a large army and garnered all the accolades and prestige of initially defeating the liberal forces that had marshaled in support of the fugitive liberal contender for the presidency, Benito Juárez. Yet after Osollo's unexpected death from disease in June 1858, Miramón—despite winning repeated military victories and installing conservative garrisons into major cities—could not stamp out such widespread resistance, so new liberal armies continued to appear.

Zuloaga played no active role in these campaigns, instead being confined to ceremonial duties, so his influence dwindled to almost nothing while military officers sneered about his service being confined to attending Masses.

Humiliation (December 1858–December 1860)

As the War of the Reform was about to enter into its second year without any resolution yet in sight, Gen. Miguel María Echegaray revolted at Ayotla in the state of Mexico on December 20, 1858, seconded three days later by Manuel Robles Pezuela in the national capital, who deposed the powerless Zuloaga. During the brief interlude in which these two mutinous commanders controlled Mexico City, they issued the so-called *Plan de Navidad* or Christmas Plan in hopes of finding an end to the civil war but soon had to submit because of their lack of support.

In the wake of this embarrassing overthrow, the conservative *Junta de Notables* offered the presidency to the victorious Miramón, who had just finished recuperating Guadalajara and driving the liberal forces out of Jalisco again by early

January 1859—but he refused the title. As a result, the now thoroughly discredited Zuloaga was reinstalled as "interim president" on January 24, 1859, but stepped aside a mere five days later so as to name Miramón as his "substitute president," who reached Mexico City to accept the mantle by February 2, 1859 (and departed 12 days afterward at the head of a large army to besiege Juárez's rival government down in Veracruz).

Zuloaga remained sidelined in Mexico City for more than a year, trying to improve his standing in conservative circles, while the military situation deteriorated. In April 1860, amid a renewed round of liberal offensives throughout the entire Bajío, he anonymously financed the publication of a pamphlet that criticized Miramón's conduct of the war and then grew so emboldened as to issue an "official" decree on May 9, 1860—in his long-neglected capacity as "interim president"—in which he revoked his January 29, 1859, appointment of Miramón to serve as his "substitute president."

Miramón, who was closeted that day of May 9, 1860, with his field commanders in preparation for marching at the head of 6,000 troops to relieve Guadalajara, sent an officer to summon Zuloaga from his Mexico City home to a meeting in the Presidential Palace that same evening. After keeping the ex-president waiting for several hours in an anteroom, Miramón emerged from his staff conference after midnight to contemptuously inform Zuloaga that he would be taking him along as a prisoner on this campaign so as to "show him how the presidential chair is won."

Zuloaga had no choice but to endure the humiliation of being led around the country as a captive in Miramón's train over the next three months until he managed to escape on the night of August 2–3, 1860, while the conservative army was resting in León, Guanajuato. Miramón himself was routed one week later at the Battle of Silao, disappearing in the chaos immediately following this defeat, it being rumored that he had been killed. Zuloaga managed to regain the national capital and made a bid to reclaim the office of president, only to fail because of his utter lack of conservative support. Instead, Miramón reappeared in Mexico City on the night of August 12, 1860, and although temporarily obliged to relinquish his title as "substitute president," was restored to power by a vote of confidence two days later before the *Junta de Notables* and desperately began raising a new army.

Following the final conservative defeat at the Battle of Calpulalpan atop the rim overlooking the Valley of Mexico on December 22, 1860, and the triumphal liberal entry into the national capital three days later on Christmas Day, Zuloaga fled to Iguala so as to continue fighting on behalf of his cause. While roaming as a refugee, he managed to get himself recognized as the "legitimate" president of Mexico on May 23, 1861, by such conservative diehards as Marcelino Cobos, Juan Vicario, and even the widely detested Leonardo Márquez, accompanying the latter in surprising Mexico City's liberal garrison by suddenly materializing with 2,600 troops and five small guns along its San Cosme *calzada* or "causeway" on June 24, 1861, only to be driven away by hastily converging liberal forces.

Pursued by González Ortega's 5,000-man liberal division, this small conservative force was overtaken while resting at the town of Jalatlaco on August 13, 1861, Zuloaga and Márquez riding away with a few retainers, abandoning their troops to their fate. The conservative leadership managed to escape up into the mountains of Querétaro, finding shelter with partisans commanded by the skilful general Tomás Mejía.

Exile and Withdrawal from Public Life (1862–1898)

When a French expeditionary force disembarked at Veracruz in February 1862, accompanied by Gen. Juan N. Almonte who claimed to be acting president, many conservative commanders initially refused to take service with the French, claiming Zuloaga as their true figurehead. He nonetheless had no influence over events, so Zuloaga finally went to Orizaba in the summer of 1862 (after the invaders' defeat at the Battle of the Cinco de Mayo outside Puebla) and obtained a passport to depart Mexico altogether for exile in Cuba.

He remained on that Caribbean island until 1873, when—following the death of Benito Juárez—he returned to Mexico and quietly dedicated himself to a modest business of imported tobaccos that he established at the corner of Del Puente and San Francisco Streets in the national capital before dying quietly in the capital on February 11, 1898, a few weeks short of his 85th birthday.

See also: Ampudia Grimarest, Pedro; Ayutla, Revolution of; Cakes, War of the; Márquez Araujo, Leonardo; Monterrey, Battle of; Reform, War of the; Santa Anna, Antonio López de; Tacubaya, Plan of; Yucatán, Separation of.

Further Reading

Bancroft, Hubert H. *History of Mexico*. San Francisco: Bancroft & Company, 1885, 5: 729–34.

"From Mexico: The Attempt of Zuloaga to Seize the Presidency." *New York Times*, June 13, 1860.

"Later from Mexico: Zuloaga Elected President." *Daily Alta California* 10, no. 57, February 27, 1858.

Sosa, Francisco. *Biografías de mexicanos distinguidos*. Mexico City: Porrúa, 2006.

Tucker, Spencer C. *The Encyclopedia of the Mexican-American War*. Santa Barbara, CA: ABC-CLIO, 2013.

Primary Documents

Last Royalist Messages from Guanajuato (11:00 a.m., September 28, 1810)

Miguel Hidalgo's call for a general uprising against Spanish rule from his remote, rural parish on September 16, 1810, unleashed a torrent of hatred against Crown officials and Peninsular Spaniards. Thousands of adherents quickly swelled his popular insurrection, so masses of unruly men were soon preceding his entry into town after town, joining vindictive locals in a purge of any and all Spaniards, often culminating in their deaths. This frightening tide of angry rebels swept through the province unchecked, a torrent headed toward its small capital of Guanajuato.

With only a few hundred poorly armed militiamen of uncertain loyalty available to defend his city, its Spanish intendant Juan Antonio Riaño y Bárcena (a personal acquaintance of Hidalgo, having dined at his table in the past) wrote beseechingly for help from Col. Félix María Calleja at distant San Luis Potosí on September 26, 1810:

Towns have been voluntarily giving themselves up to the insurgents. They have already done so at Dolores, San Miguel, Celaya, Salamanca, Irapuato; Silao is about to do so next. Here, their seductions are everywhere, with a lack of security, a lack of confidence. I have fortified myself in the most ideal place in this city [*Guanajuato's new stone granary, named the*

Alhóndiga de Granaditas], and shall fight to the death, if I am not abandoned by the 500 men who shall be at my side. I have little gunpowder, as absolutely none can be found, and cavalry who are poorly-mounted and with swords that shatter like glass, and infantry with mended weapons; soldiers who it is far from impossible, could easily be seduced. The insurgents beset me: provisions cannot get in, mails are intercepted. Mr. Abarca works most energetically, and if Your Lordship [*Vuestra Señoría; i.e., Calleja*] and he are in agreement, fly to my rescue, because I fear being attacked from one moment to the next. I write no more, because since the 17th I have not rested or undressed, and over these past three days have not slept beyond an hour at a time.

Riaño's worst fears would be realized only two days later, when the dark mass of Hidalgo's 20,000–25,000 rebels began cresting the ridgetop above Guanajuato on the morning of September 28, 1810. As they came pouring around Cuarto and San Miguel Hills in endless numbers so as to descend into the city, the Spanish intendant scrawled one last despairing plea for help and dispatched it to Calleja with a trusted rider at 11:00 a.m. on that fateful day:

I am going to fight, because I shall be attacked at any moment. I shall resist as much as I can, because I am honest. Fly, Your Lordship, to my rescue, to my rescue.

As the tide of insurgents came swarming up Nuestra Señora de Guanajuato Avenue by 1:00 p.m., Riaño locked himself inside the Alhóndiga with a few score of loyal troops plus all of Guanajuato's Peninsula-born Spaniards.

They resisted until nightfall, when the building's wooden doors gave way to a fire and the mobs surged inside to pitilessly slaughter the intendant and virtually everyone else—some 600 monarchist men, women, the elderly, etc.—by dawn of September 29, 1810. Such acts of brutish violence would frighten and alienate many people throughout the viceroyalty who might otherwise have embraced the insurgent cause.

Source: de Bustamante, Carlos María. *Campañas del general D. Félix María Calleja.* El Salvador: Imprenta del Aguila, Dirigida por José Ximenes, 1828, 19–20. English translation by the author. Available online at: https://archive.org/details/campaas delgener00bustgoog.

Iturbide's "Plan of Iguala" (February 24, 1821)

This proclamation managed to resolve a decade of bitter hostilities between royalist garrisons holding Mexico's cities and insurgent bands controlling its countryside and roads after the struggle for independence had bogged down into a stalemate. Col. Agustín de Iturbide—a conservative monarchist from Michoacán who had been disappointed by Spain's reintroduction of its liberal constitution of 1812 and also knew firsthand just how difficult it could prove to stamp out Mexico's guerrilla resistance—combined a number of broadly held aspirations into a single plan so as to bring both sides together for a common purpose: independence from Spain.

According to Iturbide's design, traditional conservative values would be upheld by declaring that the Catholic Church would remain the paramount religious institution of the newly independent nation, while furthermore specifying that a constitutional monarchy was to govern it, which in turn would respect all colonial-era titles regarding land grants, private property, etc. Insurgent demands would in turn be met by declaring outright independence from Spain and immediately convening a cortes *or congress of Mexicans to draft a national constitution, which could address such matters as individual rights and impose limits upon the powers of the new constitutional monarchy.*

This exposition, published by Iturbide at his military base of Iguala on February 24, 1821, was intended to persuade royalist and insurgent commanders alike to cease fighting against one another and instead subscribe to his proposed new army. After a preamble addressed to all "Americans" (which Iturbide clarified as meaning not only persons born in the Americas but also "Europeans, Africans, and Asians who reside here"), he went on to argue that unification between all the contending groups was "the only solid basis upon which our common happiness can rest." Mexicans, he pointed out, shared many links of friendship, common interests, education, and language,

so that our union can be the powerful hand that emancipates America, without the need of foreign help. At the head of a powerful and resolved Army, I have proclaimed the Independence of North America! It is now free, it is now its own master, it no longer recognizes or depends upon Spain, or any other nation.

Although no such army existed yet, Iturbide claimed that he and any soldiers who chose to follow his lead would not be inspired "by any other desire than to keep pure the Holy Religion which we profess, and to preserve the general happiness," going on to enumerate two dozen principles on which his plan was to be founded, namely that:

1. The religion of New Spain is and shall be Catholic, Apostolic, and Roman, without sovereignty of any other.
2. New Spain is independent of the Old [*Spain*] and any other power, even from our own continent.

3. [*Mexico's*] government shall be a limited monarchy, according to a constitution crafted uniquely for this realm.

4. Its Emperor shall be Ferdinand VII, but in case that he should not present himself personally to be sworn in within the time allotted by the [*Mexican*] Cortes, there shall be summoned as his alternates the Most Serene Infante Don Carlos, or Don Francisco de Paula, the Archduke Carlos, or any other member of the ruling-house deemed appropriate by the Cortes.

. . .

7. Until Ferdinand VII should arrive at Mexico City to be sworn in, a Junta shall govern in His Majesty's name, by virtue of a loyalty oath which it will swear to the nation; while any orders that it might emit before giving such an oath, shall be deemed null.

8. If Ferdinand VII should not condescend to come to Mexico City, the [*Mexican*] Junta or Regency shall govern in name of the nation, until it is decided who should be crowned as its Emperor.

9. This [*new imperial Mexican*] government shall be upheld by the Army of the Three Guarantees, of which more shall be said here below.

10. The Cortes shall decide how long the Junta rules, or whether it should be supplanted by a Regency, until the arrival of the person to be crowned.

11. The Cortes shall immediately thereafter establish the constitution of the Mexican empire.

12. All inhabitants of New Spain, without distinction between Europeans, Africans, or Indians, are citizens of this monarchy with right to any position, according to their merits and virtues.

13. The persons of every citizen and their properties, shall be respected and protected by the government.

14. The laic and secular clergy shall retain all their *fuero* privileges and pre-eminences.

15. The Junta shall ensure that all branches of the State [*i.e., the viceroyal Spanish administration*] remain without the slightest alteration, and that all political, ecclesiastical, civilian, and military employments remain the same as today.

16. A protective army will be formed, which shall be called of the Three Guarantees, which will take under its protection:

first, the conservation of the Catholic, Apostolic, Roman religion, co-operating to the full extent of its resources so that no other sect might become intermingled, and any enemies who might seek to harm it shall be opportunely attacked;

and second, [*Mexico's*] independence under the stated [*imperial*] system;

and third, a complete union of Americans and Europeans;

because to guarantee bases which are so fundamental to the happiness of New Spain, rather than consent to any infraction of any of them, the first to the very last member [*of this army*] shall willingly sacrifice their lives.

17. The troops of this Army shall maintain the strictest discipline, exactly according to the ordinances, and their leaders and officers shall retain the same ranks as they have today; . . .

18. The troops of said Army shall be considered as of the line [*i.e., regulars*].

19. The same shall be true of those who adhere forthwith to this Plan. Those who defer; those from the [*viceregal*] system existing prior to independence who immediately thereafter join this Army; and those country irregulars who intend to join, shall be deemed troops of the National Militia, their organization so as to protect the interior and exterior of this country to be decided by the Cortes.

20. Positions shall be given based upon true merit, drawing upon reports from superiors, and being made provisionally in the name of the nation.

21. Until the Cortes can be established, crimes shall be prosecuted in strict accordance with the Spanish Constitution.

The military component of Iturbide's proposal was crucial, for every Mexican royalist commander or battalion that switched allegiance from the Crown to adhere to his plan—even if they did not actively campaign on his behalf— was one less unit to support the dwindling number of Spanish regiments and viceregal authorities seeking to stem the rising tide for independence.

Source: Villa de Iguala (The Plan of Iguala), February 24, 1821. Mexican National Archives. English translation by the author.

Agreement of Velasco and a Supplementary Secret Treaty, Signed by the Captive Santa Anna in Texas (May 14, 1836)

His disastrous rout at the Battle of San Jacinto on April 21, 1836, had left Mexico's president and commander-in-chief in the hands of his Texan opponents, who extracted several promises from him in order to grant his release—specifically, that the large Mexican Army, which still remained intact and unbeaten in Texas, should be withdrawn south of the Rio Grande and not resume any offensive operations, as described in the following "public agreement":

Articles of an agreement entered into between His Excellency David G. Burnet, President of the Republic of Texas of the one part, & His Excellency General Antonio Lopez de Santa Anna, President General in Chief of the other part:

Article 1st.- General Antonio Lopez de Santa Anna agrees that he will not take up arms, nor will he exercise his influence to cause them to be taken up, against the People of Texas during the present War of Independence.

2nd.- All hostilities between the Mexican & Texian troops will cease immediately, both on land & water.

3rd.- The Mexican troops will evacuate the territory of Texas, passing to the other side of the Rio Grande del Norte.

4th.- The Mexican Army in its retreat, shall not take the property of any person without his consent & just indemnification, using only such articles as may be necessary for its subsistence; in cases when the owner may not be present & remitting to the Commander-in-Chief of the Army of Texas or to the Commissioners to be appointed for the adjustment of such matters, an account of the value of the property consumed, the place where taken & the name of the owner, if it can be ascertained.

5th.- That all private property including cattle, horses, negro slaves, or indentured persons of whatever denomination, that may have been captured by any portion of the Mexican Army, or may have taken refuge in the said Army since the commencement of the late invasion, shall be restored to the Commander of the Texian Army or to such other persons as may be appointed by the Government of Texas to receive them.

6th.- The troops of both armies will refrain from coming into contact with each other, & to this end the Commander-in-Chief of the Army of Texas will be careful not to approach within a shorter distance of the Mexican Army than five leagues.

7th.- The Mexican Army shall not make any other delay on its march than that which is necessary to take up their hospitals, baggage, & cross the rivers; any delay not necessary to these purposes, to be considered as an infraction of this agreement.

8th.- By express to be immediately dispatched, this agreement shall be sent to Gen'l Filisola [*at San Antonio*] & to Gen'l T. J. Rusk, Commander of the Texian Army, in order that they may be apprised of its stipulations; & to this, they will exchange engagements to comply with the same.

9th.- That all Texian prisoners now in possession of the Mexican Army, be forthwith released & furnished with free passports to return to their homes, in consideration of which a corresponding number of [*Mexican*] rank-&-file now in possession of the Government of Texas, shall be immediately released; the remainder of the Mexican prisoners that continue in possession of the

Government of Texas, to be treated with due humanity, any extraordinary comforts that may be furnished them to be at the charge of the Government of Mexico.

10th.- Gen'l Antonio Lopez de Santa Anna will be sent to Vera Cruz, as soon as it shall be deemed proper.

The contracting parties sign this instrument for the above-mentioned purposes, by duplicate at the Port of Velasco [*modern Freeport*] this 14th day of May 1836.

[*signed*] David G. Burnet
Antonio Lopez de Santa Anna
James Collinsworth, Sec'y of State
Bailey Hardiman, Sec'y of Treasury
P. H. Grayson, Attorney-Gen'l

A second "secret treaty" was simultaneously signed between both parties in which Santa Anna agreed to "prepare matters" in Mexico City so that a Texan delegation might subsequently negotiate toward independence, as follows:

Antonio Lopez de Santa Anna, General in Chief of the Army of Operations and President of the Republic of Mexico, before the Government established in Texas, solemnly pledges himself to fulfill the stipulations contained in the following Articles, so far as concerns himself.

Art. 1st.- He will not take up arms, nor cause them to be taken up, against the People of Texas during the present War of Independence.

Art. 2nd.- He will give his Orders, that in the shortest time the Mexican Troops may leave the Territory of Texas.

Art. 3rd.- He will so prepare matters in the Cabinet of Mexico, that the Mission that may be sent thither by the Government of Texas may be well received, and that by means of negotiations all differences may be settled, and the Independence that has been declared by the Convention may be acknowledged.

Art. 4th.- A treaty of Commerce, Amity, and Limits will be established between Mexico and Texas, the territory of the latter not to extend beyond the Rio Bravo del Norte.

Art. 5th.- The prompt return of Gen'l. Santa Anna to Vera Cruz being indispensable for the purpose of effecting his solemn engagements, the Government of Texas will provide for his immediate embarkation for said port.

Art. 6th.- This instrument being Obligatory on one part as well as on the other, will be signed by duplicate, remaining folded and sealed until the negotiation shall have been concluded, when it will be restored to His Excellency General Santa Anna; no use of it to be made before that time, unless there should be an infraction by either of the Contracting parties.

Port of Velasco [*modern Freeport*], May 14, 1836.

[*signed*] David G. Burnet
Antonio Lopez de Santa Anna
James Collinsworth, Sec. of State
Baily Hardiman, Sec. of Treasury
P. H. Grayson, Atty. Genl.

Santa Anna duly issued the order to Filisola to withdraw the remaining Mexican forces from Texas, who obeyed as of May 26, 1836 (although later Filisola was brought up on charges by the Mexican government, for having obeyed a command extorted from his captive commander). Yet with little faith that he would honor his other pledges, Santa Anna was not immediately released by the Texans back into Mexico, but rather held prisoner for several months before finally being sent to U.S. Pres. Andrew Jackson in Washington, D.C.

Source: Archivo Historico Militar, Secretaria de Defensa Nacional (Sedena Mexico), Expediente XI/481.3/1146, 852 fojas.

Eyewitness Account of the Spread of the Liberal Plan de Ayutla (March 1854)

Like most other uprisings in 19th-century Mexico, the revolt against Santa Anna's autocratic regime launched by Col. Florencio

Villarreal in the tiny, remote garrison town of Ayutla in the coastal state of Guerrero on March 1, 1854, was accompanied by a **pronunciamiento** *enunciating his "plan"—a public declaration of Villarreal's principles and aims in instigating this rebellion in hopes that others would be drawn to join and uphold his cause. Such plans were commonly circulated throughout the country, despite restrictions imposed by government authorities in a vain attempt to discourage their dissemination, knowing full well that they would be debated (either covertly or openly) as to their merits.*

Villarreal's "Plan of Ayutla," for example, clearly explained in its very preamble how considering:

That the permanence of Don Antonio López de Santa Anna in power constitutes a constant threat to public liberties, given that with the greatest scandal, under his government, individual guarantees which are respected in all the most civilized nations, have been hollowed out;

That having the obligation to preserve the territorial integrity of the Republic, he has sold a considerable part of it [*to the United States*], sacrificing our brothers along the northern border, who heretofore shall be foreigners in their own land, eventually being expelled, as happened to the Californios;

That our Nation cannot continue any longer without constituting itself in a stable and permanent fashion, not depending for its political existence upon the capricious will of a single man.

It had been received and embraced within a fortnight of its promulgation by the 500-man garrison stationed at Acapulco, an early conversion that helped spark what would eventually become known as the Revolution of Ayutla, a national movement that would drive Santa Anna from office for the final time.

An anonymous American visitor who happened to be in that Pacific port when word of this initial insurrection reached there wrote a detailed description of its effects in a letter to a friend in Louisiana, which read as follows:

Acapulco, Wednesday, March 15, 1854.

Dear Pic:

Having stopped here a few days on my way to San Francisco, I have had a good opportunity to see the chiefs and ascertain the designs of the revolutionists, who are headed by Generals [*Juan N.*] Álvarez and Comanfort [*sic: Col. Ignacio Comonfort*], and as you will no doubt receive all kinds of false reports through the Mexican press, which is under influences averse to this movement, I think it worthwhile to send you what I deem a correct view of it.

The *plan politico* of Acapulco was signed on the 11th inst. [*March 1854*], by Gen. Comonfort, and all the officers and noncommissioned officers of the garrison and of the national militia; and Gen. C. was elected Governor of the town and fortress. The *plan* comprises ten articles, which, in substance, are as follows:

1. Gen. Santa Anna, having forfeited the confidence of the nation, is dismissed, with all the employees whom he has placed in power.
2. When the majority of the nation shall have adopted the present *plan*, a President *ad interim* shall be elected by a Congress of one representative for each State and Territory, convoked by the Commander-in-Chief of the revolutionary forces at such place as he shall deem proper; this Congress to serve as a Council of State during the short term of the *ad interim* President.
3. The President-elect shall have power to reform all the branches of public administration; to provide for the security and independence of the nation; and to promote its prosperity, without other restriction than that of an inviolable respect of individual rights.
4. The Departments and Territories adopting this *plan* shall be governed by a provisional code, to be promulgated by the

chief of the forces and a council of five persons of good standing, within one month after their meeting; the basis of which code shall be the integrity, indivisibility, and independence of the nation.

5. The President *ad interim* shall, within fifteen days, convoke Congress on the basis of the law of 10th December, 1841, which shall meet within four months, and shall exclusively attend to the reorganization of the nation under the republican, popular representative form of government, and to the revision of the power conferred upon the President by the second article of this plan.

6. The army, being the defender of independence and the support of public order, the Provisional Government shall preserve and care for it.

7. Commerce demands the immediate care of the Government, and the Provisional Government shall immediately attend to the granting to it of all possible liberty and privileges, forming a new tariff; and in the meantime, the new tariff promulgated by President Cabellos [*sic: Juan Bautista Ceballos, a moderate liberal in office for only a month between January 6 and February 8, 1853, before being deposed to make way for Santa Anna's return from exile*] shall rule; the new tariff to be, under no circumstances, less liberal in its provisions.

8. The existing laws of conscription, passports, capitation tax, excise duties, and all others which are repugnant to a republican system, are abolished.

9. The opposers of the principles of this plan to be held as enemies of the national independence, and Gens. [*Nicolás*] Bravo, Álvarez, and [*Tomás*] Moreno are invited to lead the liberating forces.

10. The majority of the nation to have full authority to alter or modify this plan.

The foregoing plan is, in effect, the same as that promulgated by Col. Villarreal, the *comandante* of Costa Chica, in Ayutla a short time since, with a few modifications which were suggested by Gen. Comonfort, on accepting the command tendered him by the [*Acapulco*] garrison.

On assuming the [*governorship*], Gen. C. immediately issued a proclamation to the citizens and to the troops, in which he declares that in doing so, his only motive is to secure the property and social rights of the citizens from the attacks of a barbarous system of Government, under the will of one man, and to reinstate a free system of Government; and that the three Generals named in the ninth article of the plan, will undoubtedly embrace the command offered them.

The people here are very unanimously in favor of the movement, and the leaders whom I have met seem brave and very intelligent men. I had heard much about Gen. Álvarez being an Indian, (a Pinto), and an ignorant man; but he has displayed great acumen and energy of character here, and his intelligence certainly compares favorably with that of Santa Anna, in the fact that the first measure of the latter was to suppress the press, while that of the former was to establish complete freedom therein.

He [*Álvarez*] has now about 5,000 men fairly equipped, and a portion of them well drilled, and is posted in the mountain passes between here and the city of Mexico, where he awaits Santa Anna.

Among the recent visitors here was Col. [*Chatham R.*] Wheat, of your city [*New Orleans*], so well known on the Texan frontier in connection with Caravajal [*sic: the Mexican secessionist Col. José María Carvajal*]. He had several interviews with Gen. Comonfort, who tendered him a command in the Revolutionary army. What arrangements were made, I know not, but Wheat has gone on to San Francisco in the steamer, and it is openly said here that he will soon return, with some "boys" to back him.

Yours truly,
"MEXICAN"

Source: "Letter from Southern Mexico." Correspondence of the New-Orleans Picayune. *New York Times*, April 14, 1854, page 5. Transcribed and corrected by the author.

Dissolution of the Mexican Army (December 27, 1860)

Five days after winning the final victory of the War of the Reform at the Battle of Calpulalpan outside of Mexico City on December 22, 1860, and subsequently entering the national capital with his triumphant army to claim the vacant Presidential Palace on Christmas Day, the liberal general-in-chief Jesús González Ortega used his temporary powers from Pres. Benito Juárez in Veracruz to issue a decree from that august building on December 27, 1860, dissolving the defeated Mexican Army.

In his terse dictate, the liberal field commander (a former journalist) referred to the regular army as having long been the "remora" of Mexico's social progress—an allusion to the sucker fish that attach themselves unbidden to sharks or other sea creatures so as to cling and feed endlessly. His decree annulling this institution consisted of the following words in its entirety:

Jesús G. Ortega, General-in-Chief of the Federal Army, temporarily in charge of both political and military commands, to the inhabitants of the Republic: know ye that

Considering that the Mexican Army, which has dubbed itself *permanente*, has been the hindrance [*rémora*] to all social progress in our country, since our political emancipation from the Spanish metropolis.

That due to the malicious constitution which [*this permanent army*] has been given, it has served no other purpose over a period of forty long years than to constantly disrupt the public order, guided by purely personal interests, to the detriment of the principles of progress and civilization.

That having opposed the national will and rebelled, in an immoral and scandalous manner, against the fundamental code of the Republic, it

has spread grief and tears over Mexican soil during the struggle which it has sustained against its people over the past three years.

And lastly, that its existence has been a constant threat to public liberties and the rights of the people. [*Therefore*], resorting to the broad powers with which I have been invested, I have been pleased to decree the following:

First Article.- The permanent Army which has taken up arms and rebelled against the political Constitution of the Republic, is hereby discharged from service. It shall be replaced, in order to protect our ports and borders, by permanent bodies from the [*liberal*] Federal Army, or others which shall be accorded veteran status by the Supreme Government [*of President Juárez*].

Second Article.- Those Army individuals who, having served in the reactionaries' ranks, shifted their allegiance over to the defenders of the Constitution and performed valuable services, can obtain employment in the [*new*] Mexican Army once they have become rehabilitated by justifying their services before the Supreme Government or Sovereign Congress, if the latter should be in session.

Third Article.- Those military men who remained neutral during the recent civil war, shall not be allowed any employment in the [*new*] Mexican Army.

Consequently, I order that this decree be printed, published, and circulated among all concerned parties, and be given due implementation.

National Palace of Mexico, December 27, 1860.
— *Jesús G. Ortega*

Source: Archivo Historico Militar, Secretaria de Defensa Nacional (Sedena Mexico), Expediente XI/481.3/4266, 25 fojas.

General Zaragoza's "Cinco de Mayo" Telegrams from Puebla (May 5, 1862)

With the republican administration of Pres. Benito Juárez, and virtually all of Mexico, breathlessly awaiting news of the defense of the city of Puebla by the 6,000-man army of 33-year-old Maj. Gen. Ignacio Zaragoza, that officer managed—during breaks in the action—to dictate a series of telegrams to the minister of war in the capital that succinctly described the evolution of events upon the battlefield. These telegrams appear translated here below, in the same sequence in which they were being received in Mexico City on that fateful day:

(Received Mexico City, 10:45 a.m., May 5, 1862)

Enemy has encamped three-quarters [*of a league*] from this City's *garita*, in its suburbs in the same direction as my camp. The body of [*my*] Army is ready to fight and resist. General O'Horan informs me that he fought yesterday at Atlixco against 1,200 reactionaries, which town they abandoned after some resistance. It seems that the rest of the reactionary gangs are at [*Izúcar de*] Matamoros, preparing to march in this direction. — *I. Zaragoza*

(Received Mexico City, 12:28 past noon, May 5, 1862)

It is high noon and cannon fire has erupted on both sides. — *Zaragoza*

(Received Mexico City, 4:15 p.m., May 5, 1862)

From the battlefield at 2:30: we have fought for two-and-a-half hours. The enemy has fired countless shells. Their [*assault*] columns have been repulsed from Loreto and Guadalupe Hills, having attacked with at least 4,000 men. Their entire thrust was against this hill. At this moment, their columns are retiring, and ours are advancing upon them. A heavy rainfall is commencing. — *I. Zaragoza*

(Received Mexico City, ? p.m., May 5, 1862)

At four in the afternoon: the enemy is commencing to retire, having just started at this moment. Their entire force, as is to be expected, is acting as rearguard for their [*supply*] trains. Fifteen hundred horse which I managed to assemble, I detached yesterday to take them in the rear. At this hour, they are at Amozoc. — *Zaragoza*

(Received Mexico City, 5:49 p.m., May 5, 1862)

The arms of the Supreme Government have covered themselves in glory. The enemy has made a supreme effort to seize Guadalupe Hill, attacking it out of the east from right to left for three hours. He was repulsed three times in complete disarray, and at these moments is formed up in a battle-line 4,000 strong, opposite the hill but out of range. I cannot attack him, as I would wish, because the Government knows that I do not have sufficient strength. I calculate the enemies' losses, who managed to scale as high as the Guadalupe pits during their attack, at 600 or 700 dead and wounded; we have suffered 400 [*casualties*]. Please inform the Citizen President of this report. — *I. Zaragoza*

(Addressed to Juárez from Puebla at 7:03 p.m., May 5, 1862)

Mister President: I am very pleased with the conduct of my generals and soldiers. They all performed well. The French have carried away a severe lesson, but in truth I must say, that they fought very bravely [*como bravos*], a great portion of them dying in the pits among the Guadalupe trenches. May it be for the best, Mister President. I wish that our beloved Fatherland, which today knows such misfortune, should become happy and respected by all nations. — *I. Zaragoza*

Source: Echenique, Rafael. *Batalla del 5 de Mayo de 1862 en Puebla: telegramas oficiales relativos a la mencionada batalla.* Mexico: E. Sanchez, 1894. English translation by the author.

Eyewitness Description of Jalisco State Militiamen, as Recorded by an American Visitor (1869)

The San Francisco newspaper columnist and amateur militiaman "Col." Albert S. Evans— listed in that city's 1869 directory as the pay- master general for California's state militia, a part-time political appointment that required only service on the administrative staff of Gov. Henry H. Haight at Sacramento, rather than being an active-duty soldier—attached himself to the party that was to accompany U.S. Secre- tary of State William H. Seward when that federal official exited California that same autumn to make a diplomatic tour through the neighboring Republic of Mexico on his return voyage toward Washington, D.C.

Departing San Francisco Bay aboard the steamship Golden City *on September 30, 1869, the American visitors disembarked one week later at the Mexican port of Manzanillo and proceeded inland to a warm welcome for this high-ranking U.S. dignitary. Precisely because of Seward's prominent status, an escort of 100 mounted troopers was provided by the state authorities of Jalisco, who met and rode with this diplomatic party from the morning that they left the city of Colima and penetrated into Jalisco on October 13, 1869. Evans, who a couple of years later would pub- lish a travel account of this tour entitled* Our Sister Republic: A Gala Trip through Tropical Mexico, *recorded the following detailed observations about this cavalry squadron on pages 79–81 of his book:*

Our military guard was an object of no little curiosity and admiration. They belong to a force of eight hundred picked men, armed, equipped, and put into the field by the State of Jalisco, to free the roads from robbers and maintain public order. Col. Sabás Lomelí, their commander, is a splendid-looking man, tall, stout built, quite fair-complexioned, with long whiskers and moustaches, *a la Americana*, and is not only remarkably good- looking, but has the air and carriage of a soldier. He is said to be a very brave and

accomplished officer, and the fact that within a few months his command has practically cleared the roads of the great State of Jalisco of robbers, and captured or killed nearly two hundred of the banditti who had made travel- ing very dangerous, speaks well for his energy.

He is accompanied by a major, captain, and the company lieutenants, all of whom are uni- formed with dark-blue jackets, trimmed with broad silver bullion and large silver buttons, bright scarlet pantaloons with silver lace, and top-boots of enamelled leather. Their caps are nearly the same in form as the regular United States fatigue cap, but with green trimmings, and with a white linen cover having a cape, which when let down, protects the shoulders from sun and rain.

The soldiers have caps, blue coats and pan- taloons with green trimmings, and the panta- loons are foxed with dark leather. They carry swords, Colt's revolvers, and Springfield mus- kets, and are mounted on small, but very spir- ited and quick-traveling horses, of which they take excellent care. The officers carry swords and Colt's revolvers, and wear broad, red sashes thrown carelessly over their shoulders. Their uniform is very brilliant and pictu- resque. The force of one hundred men have only three pack-mules to carry all their bag- gage. They take no tents or cooking utensils, and can get over the ground with twice or thrice the speed attained by our troops in the United States. One hundred miles within thirty hours is no great march for them, and the infantry can keep up with them. The common soldiers are all of Indian blood, small in size, but active and admirably fitted for rapid marches, and the guerrilla style of warfare.

I never saw so well-behaved, quiet, and orderly men. They receive thirty-seven and one-half cents per day in coin. Of this, twelve and one-half cents is paid them daily, and the remainder at, or near, the end of the month. They get no rations, but live easily on the twelve and one-half cents. They will gallop up to a road-side shop, and with three cents purchase a dozen tortillas and a piece of the sour-milk cheese of the country, which serves them for lunch. For breakfast, an ear of soft-boiled com will serve them admirably, and for supper a few frijoles and tortillas are sufficient. In camp or at garrison duty, they get rations, and are charged for them. Col. Lomelí wears a magnificent diamond ring and gold watch, and is splendidly mounted, a silver-ornamented saddle setting off to great advantage the fine black horse which he rides.

Source: Evans, Albert S. *Our Sister Republic: A Gala Trip through Tropical Mexico.* Hartford, CT: Columbian Book Company, 1873, 79–81.

Near-Execution of Pancho Villa (June 1912)

On April 12, 1912, the veteran ex-Porfirian general Victoriano Huerta arrived at Torreón, Coahuila, to take over command of a Maderista division that had failed in its recent attempt to put down a rebellion in the neighboring state of Chihuahua led by Pascual Orozco. A stern disciplinarian, Huerta promptly reorganized this defeated force and within a month's time was pushing northward into Orozquista territory with 4,000 men, five batteries of field artillery, and four machine guns.

Among this division was a "brigade" of 300 mounted irregulars to act as scouts under Pancho Villa, who held the honorary rank of "general." Huerta overlooked some minor excesses being committed by these ill-disciplined auxiliaries for a couple of weeks, but when Villa ignored a direct order to restore some stolen horses, the federal general angrily ordered him arrested on the evening of June 3, 1912.

Standing before a firing squad the next dawn, Villa begged for and received a last-minute reprieve, so was taken before Huerta—who decided to send him off to stand trial in Mexico City, accompanied by the following report:

En estos momentos parte el tren llevando, con carácter de procesado, debidamente escoltado, hasta la capital, al general Villa. El motivo que he tenido para mandarlo con el carácter de preso a disposición del Ministerio de la Guerra, es el hecho de haber cometido faltas graves en la división a mi mando, como

son apoderarse sin derecho alguno de bienes ajenos; y además, hay la circunstancia de que el ordenarle yo la devolución a sus dueños de caballos y algunas otras cosas, vino a su cuartel general y armó a toda la fuerza de su mando, advirtiendo a sus soldados que estuvieran preparados para desobedecer las órdenes de marcha hacía Santa Rosalía. La división estaba lista para marchar a las 5 a.m., y por una desobediencia de Villa aún se halla aquí tomando rancho y lista para emprender la marcha dentro de una hora.

Los 300 hombres de Villa los he desarmado y han ido a engrosar las filas de los diversos cuerpos de la división, con la orden de que aquel que manifieste desagrado por la determinación del cuartel general sea pasado por las armas en el acto. A Villa le he perdonado la vida, estando dentro del cuadro que debía ejecutarlo, por razón de haberme suplicado que lo oyera antes de ser pasado por las armas, de cuya entrevista resultó que yo resolviera abrir una averiguación poniéndolo a disposición de la Secretaría de Guerra.

Personalmente estimo a Villa y es un hombre sumamente útil; pero como general en jefe de la división a mi mando, creo que es un hombre peligroso a la división, que a cada paso tiende a relajar la disciplina, cosa que es altamente perjudicial a la división.

General V. Huerta

Source: Diario de los debates de la Camara de Diputados, no. 21 (November 8, 1966), section XI.

Dissolution of Mexico's Federal Army, According to the Terms Laid Out in the Treaties of Teoloyucan (August 1914)

After having mushroomed the federal army's size from 63,500 to perhaps 100,000 men in a six-month span through the forceful recruitment of thousands of raw conscripts in the vain hope of smothering the Revolution through sheer weight of numbers, the overextended and hated regime of Pres. Victoriano Huerta collapsed by the summer of 1914. Pancho Villa destroyed

*one of the last major federal armies at the Battle
of Zacatecas on June 23, 1914, after which
Álvaro Obregón pulverized another at the Battle
of Orendáin outside of Guadalajara on July 7,
1914, before continuing his drive against feeble
opposition directly toward Mexico City.*

*A mere eight days later, the failed dictator
resigned from office and fled along with his
minister of war, Gen. Aureliano Blanquet,
leaving the vestiges of power to the interim
civilian president, Francisco S. Carvajal,
with the defeated Maj. Gen. José Refugio
Velasco as his minister of war. Carvajal used
the few weeks before Obregón's 18,000-man
Ejército del Noroeste or "Northeastern
Army" drew close to the capital to reduce the
overall size of the federal army back down to
a more manageable 38,500 men through dis-
charging thousands of unwilling conscripts
and slashing military expenditures.*

*But when the victorious Obregón halted at
Teoloyucan outside Mexico City and delivered
his terms through intermediaries to the
remaining federal authorities on behalf of his
incumbent president, Venustiano Carranza,
these included a demand for the complete
dissolution of the federal army. With no
other choice than to comply, the defeated
commanders signed the Draconian "treaties
of Teoloyucan" on August 13, 1914, whose
conditions called for:*

I Las tropas dejarán la plaza de
México, distribuyéndose en las poblaciones a lo largo del ferrocarril de
México a Puebla, en grupos no may-
ores de cinco mil hombres. No lle-
varán artillería ni municiones de
reserva. Para el efecto de su desarme,
el nuevo Gobierno mandará representaciones que reciban el armamento.

II Las guarniciones de Manzanillo,
Córdoba, Jalapa y jefatura de
Armas en Chiapas, Tabasco, Campeche y Yucatán, serán disueltas y
desarmadas en esos mismos lugares.

III Conforme vayan retirándose las tropas federales, las constitucionalistas
ocuparán las posiciones desocupadas
por aquéllas.

IV Las tropas federales que guarnecen
las poblaciones de San Ángel, Tlalpan, Xochimilco y demás, frente a
los zapatistas, serán desarmadas en
los lugares que ocupan, tan luego
como las fuerzas constitucionalistas
las releven.

V Durante su marcha, las tropas federales no serán hostilizadas por los
constitucionalistas.

VI El jefe del Gobierno nombrará las
personas que se encarguen de los
gobiernos de los Estados con guarnición federal, para los efectos de la
recepción del armamento.

VII Los establecimientos y oficinas militares continuarán a cargo de emplea-
dos que entregarán, a quien se
nombre, por medio de inventarios.

VIII Los militares que por cualquier
motivo no puedan marchar con la
guarnición, gozarán de toda clase
de garantías, de acuerdo con las
leyes en vigor, y quedarán en las
mismas condiciones que las estipula-
das en la cláusula décima.

IX El general Obregón ofrece, en representación de los jefes constitucionalistas, proporcionar a los soldados
los medios de llegar a sus hogares.

X Los generales, jefes y oficiales del
Ejército y de la Armada, quedarán a
disposición del Primer jefe de las
fuerzas constitucionalistas, quien, a
la entrada a la capital queda investido con el carácter de Presidente
provisional de la República.

XI Los buques de guerra que se encuen-
tran en el Pacífico, se concentrarán
en Manzanillo, y los del Golfo en
Puerto México, donde quedarán a
disposición del Primer jefe del Ejército Constitucionalista, quien, como
se ha dicho, a la entrada a la capital,
queda investido con el carácter de
Presidente provisional de la República.

Por lo que respecta a las demás dependen-
cias de la Armada en ambos litorales, como
en el Territorio de Quintana Roo, quedarán
en sus respectivos lugares, para recibir
iguales instrucciones del mismo Primer
Funcionario.

Source: Aguirre Berlanga, Manuel, compiler and
ed. *Reforma y Revolucion.* Mexico City: Imprenta
Nacional, 1918, Book I, 65–66.

Appendices

Viceroyal Mexico's Spanish and Loyalist Forces, September 1816

Six years after the violent eruption of Miguel Hidalgo's insurgency against Crown rule from Spain, this initial rebellion had been contained, if not yet defeated. Gen. Félix María Calleja had succeeded in stabilizing the monarchists' military situation during his three-and-a-half-year tenure as viceroy; so he relinquished office to his successor Adm. Juan Ruiz de Apodaca on September 19, 1816, claiming that royalist fortunes had been restored throughout Central Mexico with 39,436 Spanish soldiers and Mexican militiamen under arms, ready to defend the viceroyalty in the following deployments (Table 1).

Yet the admiral's own progression inland from the seaport of Veracruz had been a difficult and perilous trek, his convoy—escorted by 1,000 troops—being shadowed and repeatedly harassed by large formations of insurgent guerrillas. Apodaca would soon discover that the paper strength of this army depended upon its minority of Spanish

Table 1. Spanish and Loyalist Units in Mexico, September 1816

Mexico City Division	The viceroy	2,660
Apan Division	Col. Manuel de la Concha	1,310
Huejutla Detachment	Lt. Col. Alejandro Álvarez de Güitián	151
Ejército del Sur ("Army of the South")	Brig. Gen. Ciriaco de Llano	6,699
Veracruz Division	Mariscal José García Dávila	6,482
Detachments for highway escort	Col. Francisco Hevia	968
Isla del Carmen garrison	Col. Cosme de Urquiola	339
Acapulco Division	Col. José Gabriel de Armijo	2,651
Toluca Detachment	Col. Nicolás Gutiérrez	282
Ixtlahuaca Division	Col. Matías Martín y Aguirre	787
Tula Division	Col. Cristóbal Ordóñez	888
Querétaro Division	Brig. Gen. Ignacio García Rebollo	991
Ejército del Norte ("Army of the North")	Col. José Castro	3,803
Ejército de Reserva ("Reserve Army")	Mariscal José de la Cruz	3,363
San Luis Potosí Division	Brig. Gen. Manuel María de Torres	614
Provincias Internas de Oriente Division	Brig. Gen. Joaquín Arredondo	3,987
Provincias Internas de Occidente Division	Mariscal Bernardo Bonavia	279
Antigua (Baja) California	Captain Arguello	109
Nueva (Alta) California	Lt. Col. Pablo Sola	3,665

soldiers, with royalist Mexican militiamen inclined to be more loyal to their native district or territory than to the Crown.

Source: The above list has been published in numerous Spanish-language editions, this particular version being translated, corrected, and augmented by the author from page 311 of Mariano Torrente's *Historia de la independencia de Mexico*, freely available online from the Mexican Senate's website.

Independent Mexico's "Ejército Trigarante" in September 1821

During the four years between 1816 and 1819, the struggle for independence had dwindled into a stalemate between royalist formations who garrisoned most major cities and the more weakly armed and disperse guerrilla bands that outnumbered them, controlled much of the intervening countryside, and threatened any movements along its roadways. However, after an army mutiny in Spain had reimposed a liberal constitution upon the viceroyalty in May 1820 containing certain provisions that were aimed at curtailing or eliminating outdated prerogatives enjoyed by the aristocracy, clergy, and military, many Creole royalist leaders—who up until the spring of 1820 had remained steadfastly committed to the Crown—began to waver in their loyalty and openly consider separation from Madrid as a means of retaining their traditional conservative values and privileged status intact.

Consequently, the royalist Creole officer, Col. Agustín de Iturbide—having failed to subdue Vicente Guerrero's guerrilla bands in southern Mexico during the winter of 1820–1821—instead suddenly proposed an alliance with the insurgents in February 1821 that would bring about Mexico's independence on three broad conditions or "guarantees": continued predominance of the Catholic faith, controlled separation from Spain, and unity among all Mexican factions.

Although disavowed by the Spanish viceroy Apodaca in Mexico City, Iturbide's plan turned into an unstoppable movement over the next several months, as most royalist Creole militia commanders and insurgent guerrilla leaders agreed to join his notional "Army of the Three Guarantees" under its new tricolor flag. And since hardly any troops remained loyal to Spain by the time that the new viceroy-designate, Juan O'Donojú, arrived from across the Atlantic to assume office in late summer of 1821, this lone official felt that he had no choice but to agree to Iturbide's terms and sign a treaty at Córdoba that recognized Mexican independence (albeit still retaining some links to Spain)—an arrangement that was to be rejected out of hand by Madrid.

The coalition of diverse ex-royalist regiments, insurgent battalions, and irregular formations that had subscribed to the Ejército Trigarante converged upon Mexico City to celebrate a grand parade marking their almost-bloodless victory on September 27, 1821, its units being recorded as:

Infantry
(Total: 7,416 foot soldiers)

First Section
Regimiento de la Corona 453
Regimiento de Celaya 490
Granaderos Imperiales 258

Second Section
Regimiento de las Tres Villas 368
Batallón de Guadalajara 134
Batallón de Santo Domingo 162

Third Section
Cazadores de San Luis 47
Regimiento de Fernando VII 382
Batallón Ligero del Imperio 153

Fourth Section
Regimiento Ligero de Querétaro 318
Batallón Segundo de Libertad 195

Fifth Section
Batallón de San Fernando 239
Batallón Ligero de Morelos 129
Batallón Segundo de la Unión 176
Regimiento Primero de la Libertad 485

Sixth Section
Batallón Fijo de Puebla 265
Cazadores de la Patria 62
Batallón de Comercio de Puebla 157
Batallón de Tlaxcala 64

Seventh Section
Batallón de la Lealtad 205
Batallón de Guanajuato 91
Batallón de Zacualtipán 94

Eighth Section
Batallón de Comercio de México 339
Batallón Primero Americano 359

Ninth Section
Regimiento Fijo de México 519

Tenth Section
Batallón Constancia 100
Batallón del Potosí 200

Eleventh Section
Batallón Primero de la Unión 220
Batallón Segundo de México 270

Twelfth Section
Irregular infantry under Father
Izquierdo 500

Artillery
**(Total: 763 gunners for 68 pieces
of various calibers)**

Cavalry
(Total: 7,955 troopers)

First Section
Escolta de Iturbide 300

Second Section
Regimiento de Dragones de México 305
Caballería de Echávarri 186
Dragones de Santander 190

Third Section
Regimiento Fieles de Potosí 300
Regimiento de Dragones del Rey 159
Regimiento de la Sierra Gorda 155

Fourth Section
Regimiento de San Carlos 310
Provinciales de México 80

Fifth Section
Regimiento de Dragones de Valladolid 448
Regimiento Moncada 240

Sixth Section
Regimiento de Toluca 250
Irregular cavalry of Father Izquierdo 300

Seventh Section
Regimiento de Querétaro 283
Regimiento del Príncipe 241

Eighth Section
Regimiento de Dragones de Puebla 119
Regimiento de Dragones de Tulancingo 324
Regimiento de Apán 132

Ninth Section
Regimiento de Dragones de la Libertad 400

Tenth Section
Dragones de Atlixco 83
Regimiento de Dragones de la Unión 389
Regimiento de Voluntarios del Valle 130
Regimiento de Voluntarios Nacionales 247

Eleventh Section
Regimiento de Dragones de América 150
Regimiento de Dragones de Guanajuato 263
Dragones de la Sierra 37

Twelfth Section
Regimiento de Dragones de San Miguel 126
Regimiento de Chilpancingo 124
Regimiento de Dragones del Sur 92

Thirteenth Section
Regimiento de Dragones los
Campeones 166
Regimiento de Santa Rita 130
Compañías del Sur 60
Escolta del general Guerrero 146

Fourteenth Section
Flanqueadores 87
Montealto, Tehuacán y Tehuantepec 189

Fifteenth Section
Regimiento de Dragones de
Azcapotzalco 260
Regimiento de Dragones de Xilotepec 114

Sixteenth Section
Regimiento de Dragones de San Luis 500

And although these 16,134 men had been drawn from every part of Central Mexico, this mass of disparate regional units did not yet constitute a national army for the new country, which at that time had a population of some 5.9 million inhabitants.

Source: The above list has been translated and slightly amended by the author from pages 750–51 of Julio Zárate's 1889 book *Mexico a traves de los siglos.*

Spain's Royal Troops Awaiting Evacuation from Independent Mexico, December 1821

Three months after the cessation of hostilities and triumphal parade into the capital to celebrate national independence, more than 4,200 Spanish officers and soldiers still remained encamped at seven bases throughout central Mexico (at San Miguel el Grande, Toluca, San Joaquín, Tacuba, Cuautitlán, Puebla, and Coatepec), awaiting the arrival of the transport ships that were to repatriate them to Spain. Their commander, Pascual de Liñán, filed a year-end return from Mexico City on December 10, 1821, informing the Ministry of War in Madrid that while his troops were being left undisturbed and were receiving their regular rations, they nonetheless "anxiously awaited the desired moment" when Spanish ships would arrive to carry them home (Table 2).

Mexico's Armed Forces in 1835

In March of 1835, the secretary of war, José María Tornel, informed the national Congress sitting in session in Mexico City

Table 2. Spanish Regiments Awaiting Evacuation from Mexico, December 1821

Officers	NCOs	Men	Total
Regimiento de Fernando VII	26	67	93
Regimiento de la Reina	28	223	251
Regimiento del Infante D. Carlos	44	294	338
Regimiento de Zamora	43	303	346
Regimiento de Murcia	33	277	310
Regimiento de Extremadura	28	374	402
Regimiento de Zaragoza	75	614	689
Regimiento de Órdenes Militares	75	591	666
Regimiento de Castilla	36	337	373
Regimiento de Barcelona	30	306	336
Artillery Corps	37	178	215
Naval Companies	5	77	82
Assorted *piquetes*	63	58	121

how all army, navy, and militia formations were being reconstituted into a more efficient organization, in the process shedding an excess of almost 11,000 men from their combined rosters. As a result of these reforms, the reconstituted army was to henceforth consist of:

10 *permanente* battalions of infantry, totaling 8,620 regulars;

8 *fijo* or "fixed" companies of infantry, totaling another 952 soldiers;

1 battalion of invalids or pensioners, representing 417 retirees

14 *activo* battalions of infantry, totaling 12,066 militiamen;

7 active "coast-guard" battalions, totaling 2,800 militiamen;

3 "fixed companies" at El Carmen and Colima, totaling 276 militiamen

6 permanent cavalry regiments, totaling 3,648 regular troopers

1 squadron each at Durango and Yucatán, 302 more troopers

1 company at Tabasco, another 64 regular troopers

1 active cavalry regiment apiece for the states of Mexico

and San Luis Potosí, totaling 1,216 militia troopers

1 active squadron each for Veracruz, Tlaxcala,

Guanajuato, and Morelia, totaling 1,280 militia troopers

2 active cavalry companies at San Blas, totaling another 158 militia troopers

1 active cavalry company apiece at Tampico

and Acayucan, for another 158 militia troopers

29 *compañías presidiales* to patrol the "interior states" along

the northern borderlands, totaling 2,492 regular soldiers

15 active companies for this same region, totaling 1,500 militiamen

6 more *compañías presidiales* for the Californias, totaling another 422 soldiers

An artillery corps comprising 1,437 regular gunners for two brigades of siege artillery and two companies of field artillery

52 military engineers

455 sappers

400 cadets enrolled in the *Colegio Militar* or "Military College"

In all, a grand total of 38,715 men under arms—10,919 less than in the previous army establishment.

The navy, in comparison, consisted of a mere 80 men employed in a couple of arsenals and shore establishments supporting the patrols of four small vessels:

60 officers and seamen aboard the brig-of-war *Veracruzano*, and another

50 manning the schooner *Moctezuma*, both vessels operating out of the port of Veracruz

24 officers and sailors aboard the corvette *Morelos*, and another 14 on the schooner *Mercado*, sailing out of the Pacific port of San Blas

By this year, Mexico's population had grown to approximately 6.75 million inhabitants.

Source: The above list has been culled, compiled, and translated by the author from Tornel's original *Memoria* presented to the Mexican Congress in March 1835.

Mexico's Reconstituted Army, 1851

After the defeat of Santa Anna by U.S. armies in both North and Central Mexico during the Mexican-American War of 1846–1848, followed by the collapse of his regime and a foreign occupation of the national capital for months on end, the Mexican Army had virtually ceased to exist. Its hierarchical structure had been decimated, its logistical system vanished, and its officers and men left unpaid, unsupplied, dispersed, and abandoned.

Once peace was reestablished and the nation began its slow, painful revival, the administration of Pres. and Maj. Gen. Mariano Arista turned to the task of restoring and reconstituting its armed forces as well, on a properly organized footing. On April 22, 1851, his minister of war—the military engineer Manuel Robles Pezuela—presented the Congress in Mexico City with the Ley de 22 de abril de 1851 sobre arreglo del Ejército, a decree complete with specific details and budgetary allotments so as to begin the process of resurrecting the Mexican Army as a functioning force. All branches of the service were to be included in the president's proposal, which called for an establishment of:

Ten *permanente* infantry battalions, each of these 630-man formations to be composed of:

A lieutenant colonel
An adjutant (*jefe de detalle*)
A second adjutant (lieutenant)
A subadjutant
A chaplain
A quartermaster
A drum major
An armorer
A corporal of trumpeters
A corporal of sappers
6 sappers
8 bandsmen

6 captains (1 for each company)
6 lieutenants
12 sublieutenants
6 first sergeants

24 second sergeants
12 drummers or trumpeters
66 corporals
474 soldiers

16 pack animals

A 1,938-man *permanente* cavalry regiment subdivided into six corps, each 323-man corps consisting of:

A lieutenant colonel
A squadron commander
A subadjutant (*lieutenant*)
2 ensigns (*portas* or "couriers")
A chaplain
A quartermaster
A saddler
An armorer
A bugle major
A marshal (*mariscal*)
A corporal of buglers
2 grooms
5 bandsmen

4 captains (one for each squadron of a corps)
4 lieutenants
8 ensigns
4 first sergeants
16 second sergeants
36 corporals
8 buglers
224 troopers

24 pack animals

An additional 34 militia cavalry squadrons totaling 1,836 troopers of the *Guardia Nacional Móbil* or "Mobile National Guard" were to be sustained nationwide, each squadron having:

A captain
A lieutenant

2 ensigns
A first sergeant
3 second sergeants
A bugler
6 corporals
39 troopers

3 pack mules

A 561-man regular battalion of siege artillery, composed of:

A lieutenant colonel
A division chief (*jefe de división*)
A first adjutant
A second adjutant
A sub adjutant
A chaplain
A quartermaster
A drum major
A corporal of trumpeters
10 musicians
An armorer
A marshal (*mariscal*)

6 captains (1 for each battery)
6 lieutenants
12 sublieutenants
6 first sergeants
36 second sergeants
12 trumpeters
78 corporals
384 artillerymen

12 pack animals

(An artillery train would also have to be hired to move these weapons overland, consisting of 240 teamsters, 6 grooms, and 6 saddlers for 492 mules.)

Six divisions totaling 925 heavy garrison artillerymen, each division's two batteries consisting of:

A division chief (*jefe de división*)
A first adjutant
A subadjutant
A quartermaster

2 captains (1 for each battery)
2 lieutenants
4 sublieutenants
2 first sergeants
12 second sergeants
4 trumpeters
26 corporals
128 artillerymen
An armorer

Two batteries of light field artillery, operated by 188 men organized as:

A division chief (*jefe de división*)
A first adjutant
A subadjutant
A quartermaster
An armorer
A marshal (*mariscal*)

2 captains (one for each battery)
2 lieutenants
4 ensigns
2 first sergeants
12 second sergeants
26 corporals
6 buglers
128 artillerymen

180 mounts
8 pack animals

(An artillery train would also have to be hired to move these weapons overland, consisting of 76 teamsters, 2 grooms, 2 saddlers, and 4 laborers for 164 draft horses.)

Four 100-man companies of sappers, each composed of:

A captain

A lieutenant

2 sublieutenants

A first sergeant

4 second sergeants

13 corporals

78 sappers

2 pack animals

Including the 75 or so high-ranking officers and subordinates who comprised its *estado mayor* or "general staff," as well as 4 major generals and 12 brigadier generals with active field commands; plus 8 infantry colonels, 3 cavalry colonels, 4 artillery colonels, and another 50 assorted staff officers on active service; the complement of the Mexican Army that was to be revived as of 1851 would total 687 officers and 11,455 soldiers, slightly more than 12,100 men in all. The population of the country had by then reached roughly 7.6 million inhabitants.

Upon Santa Anna's return from exile a couple of years later, he would find that only about half of this number of men had actually been put into service by Arista's hard-pressed, bankrupt administration. Santa Anna would therefore squander much of the 10 million American dollars that he received from the U.S. government for signing the Gadsen Treaty in late December 1853 to almost quadruple the size of the 12,000-man army envisioned by Arista—a massive buildup that would turn out to be both costly and ineffective, as Santa Anna's grand force failed to perform during the Revolution of Ayutla.

Source: The above list has been culled, compiled, and translated by the author from Pezuela's original *Ley* presented to the Mexican Congress in April 1851.

The Imperial (Combined Franco-Mexican) Army under Maximilian, June 1864

When the Austrian archduke Maximilian disembarked at the port of Veracruz in late May 1864 to begin his ceremonial two-week progression inland to be crowned as emperor in Mexico City, all major cities throughout the central portions of the country had already been secured by detachments from the French expeditionary force under Maj. Gen. Achille Bazaine. The number and distribution of units from this 35,500-man French army were recorded as follows upon Maximilian's arrival:

1st Infantry Division under Brig. Gen. Armand Alexandre de Castagny, headquartered in the city of Querétaro and composed of a total of 10,439 men (9,290 actually under arms), divided between two brigades:

1st Brigade under Gen. Alexis de Bertier, 5,250 men (4,755 under arms) headquartered in the city of San Luis Potosí, consisting of the following units:

  7th Chasseur Battalion—at San Luis Potosí

  51st Line Regiment—with companies dispersed around Guanajuato, Silao, León, Irapuato, and Salamanca

  62nd Line Regiment—at San Luis Potosí

2nd Brigade under Col. Léon Mangin, 5,189 men (4,535 under arms) headquartered at Querétaro, comprising the following:

  20th Chasseur Battalion—with companies in Querétaro and San Luis de la Paz

95th Line Regiment—at Querétaro, San Juan del Río, Arroyo Zarco, Tepejí, Pachuca, and San Luis de la Paz

3rd Zouave Regiment—at Mexico City

2nd Infantry Division under Maj. Gen. Charles Abel Douay, headquartered at Guadalajara and comprising a total of 10,176 men (9,272 under arms), divided between two brigades:

1st Brigade under Brig. Gen. Edmond l'Heriller, 5,096 men (4,583 under arms) headquartered in the city of Zacatecas, consisting of the following units:

1st Chasseur Battalion—at Zacatecas and Jeréz

2nd Zouave Regiment—at Zacatecas, Malpaso, Salinas, and Fresnillo

99th Line Regiment—at Aguascalientes, Lagos, and Encarnación

2nd Brigade under Brig. Gen. Charles-Louis Camille, Baron Neigre, 5,080 men (4,689 under arms) headquartered in Guadalajara, consisting of the following units:

18th Chasseur Battalion—at Guadalajara

1st Zouave Regiment—at Guadalajara and its environs

81st Line Regiment—distributed between Guadalajara, Tepatitlán, San Juan de los Lagos, and Tololotlán

Algerian Tirailleurs Battalion—patrolling the road to Acapulco

Reserve Brigade under General de Maussion, headquartered in the city of Orizaba, comprising a total of 2,919 men (2,783 under arms), and consisting of the following units:

7th Line Regiment—distributed from Orizaba to Córdoba, La Cañada, Tehuacán, Río Frío, Chapultepec, and Mexico City

2nd African Light Infantry Battalion —with companies at Paso del Macho, Palo Verde, Camarón, Cotaxtla, and Córdoba

Foreign Legion Regiment under Col. Pierre Joseph Jeanningros, a total of 2,682 men (2,263 under arms) who were stationed in the city of Puebla, with detachments at San Juan de los Llanos, Zacatlán, Tlaxcala, Tepejí de la Seda, and Acatlán

Cavalry Brigade under Col. Hippolyte Reynaud Boulogne de Lascours, a total of 2,449 troopers (2,206 under arms), whose three regiments were scattered throughout the country as follows:

1st Régiment de marche (constituted by the 1st and 3rd chasseurs d'Afrique), with two squadrons stationed at San Luis Potosí, one squadron at Puebla, and two squadrons at Querétaro

2nd Régiment de marche (comprising the 2nd chasseur d'Afriques and 5th Hussars), whose four squadrons operated out of Mexico City into its surrounding territory

12th Chasseur Regiment, with three squadrons patrolling out of Guadalajara into its district and one squadron stationed in the city of Zacatecas

In addition to these infantrymen and cavalrymen, there were another 2,709 artillerymen; 684 engineers; 609 medical personnel; two companies (159 men) of naval "colonial engineers" at the cities of Veracruz and La Soledad; 1,981 teamsters; plus some 575 administrative personnel, for a grand total of 35,500 members of the French expeditionary force in Mexico— 32,000 actively under arms.

This force was furthermore backed by an estimated 20,000 Mexican imperial troops, as well as 8,500 *guardias rurales* or "rural guards" who policed their local districts and roads. In addition, the young emperor would attract some 6,000 Austrian and 1,300 Belgian auxiliaries into his service, who proved to be well armed and loyal to his cause.

Source: The above lists have been culled and translated by the author from Noix's 1874 book *Expedition du Mexique.*

The Mexican Army under a Liberal Administration, 1873

Following the death of Pres. Benito Juárez in July 1872, his successor, Sebastián Lerdo de Tejada, continued the liberal administration's policies, supported throughout this turbulent transition by the able major general Ignacio Mejía, who had been retained in his capacity as minister of war. One year later, Mejía would report upon the state of the Mexican Army in June 1873—which although boasting a nominal complement of almost 34,000 officers and soldiers, had been allowed to fall almost 10,000 men below strength.

Mejía pointed out that during the budgetary period running from July 1, 1870, to June 30, 1871, the assigned complements of regular infantry battalions had been reduced from 800 to 600 men apiece, and cavalry corps likewise down from 400 to 320 troopers each, so when revolts subsequently erupted in San Luis Potosí and Zacatecas, the understrength field units

had struggled to contain these insurrections. To compensate for such deficiencies, an executive order had been issued on December 1, 1871, that increased the size of regular infantry battalions back up to 820 men and cavalry corps up to 430 troopers.

And because of the revolts, 13 auxiliary infantry battalions and 4 cavalry corps had also been authorized to operate on a temporary basis in the states of Jalisco, Guerrero, Puebla, San Luis Potosí, Chihuahua, Baja California, and the Federal District, plus 7 smaller infantry companies and a dozen auxiliary cavalry squadrons in Tabasco, Teotitlán, Tepejí, Acatlán, Jalisco, Veracruz, Zacatecas, Durango, etc. Three *batallones de reemplazos* or "replacement battalions" had furthermore been temporarily created in Querétaro, Guanajuato, and San Luis Potosí so as to funnel fresh recruits into any units deployed in the field.

By June of 1873, Mejía could report that only two auxiliary infantry battalions (the 1st Battalions of Guanajuato and Celaya), plus a pair of auxiliary cavalry squadrons under Lieutenant Colonels Práxedis Núñez and Andrés Rosales, remained temporarily in service in the mountain ranges of Querétaro. Otherwise, the Mexican Army had resumed its nominal peacetime complement of:

26 infantry battalions with 820 rank-and-file regulars each

15 cavalry corps with 430 regular troopers apiece

Table 3. Nominal and Actual Table of Strength of the Mexican Army, 1873

	Allotted	Actual	Understrength
Jefes or high command	297	310	—
Field officers	1,674	1,359	315
Troops	31,952	22,311	9,641
Mounts	6,719	4,794	1,925
Pack animals	3,833	2,235	1,598

A single engineering battalion with 880 sappers
3 artillery branches composed of roughly 3,300 gunners in total

However, the problem of chronically understrength units still remained an issue, so rather than its allotted number of 31,952 soldiers, the Mexican Army in reality had only 22,311 troops on active duty by the summer of 1873 (Table 3).

At this time, Mexico had a total population of some 8.8 million inhabitants.

Source: The above list has been compiled and translated by the author from Mejia's original *Memoria* presented to the Mexican Congress in 1873.

The Federal Army of Porfirio Díaz, 1900

The prolonged rule of Díaz, who had assumed power after a successful revolt as long ago as the autumn of 1876, stabilized Mexico's military establishment and even allowed for its overall numbers to contract so as to better conduct operations with only a core of properly trained, armed, and organized regulars deployed on active duty. According to the official *Memoria* presented by Gen. Felipe O. Berriozábal for the year 1900, the peacetime army's strength at the dawn of the 20th century consisted of:

- 28 infantry battalions, each composed of roughly 30 officers and 575 soldiers
- 4 detached infantry companies or *cuadros* of another 10 officers and 140 men apiece
- 14 cavalry regiments, each made up of approximately 30 officers and 425 troopers

- 4 detached cavalry squadrons or *cuadros* of some 12 officers and 150 troopers apiece
- 5 artillery battalions, each consisting of 30 officers and roughly 350 gunners apiece

Budgetary figures indicated that the Porfirian Army's actual numbers for 1900 stood at 989 staff officers, 2,430 field officers, and 27,401 soldiers in total, distributed among the following branches:

High command: 1,320 senior officers, administrators, etc.

Military justice: 134 officers serving as judges, prosecutors, *defensores*, jailers, etc.

Infantry: 85 staff officers, 813 field officers, and 17,526 foot soldiers

Cavalry: 50 staff officers, 433 field officers, and 6,669 troopers

Artillery: 14 staff officers, 133 field officers, and 1,602 gunners

Sappers: 3 staff officers, 27 field officers, and 642 sappers

Medical corps: 79 staff officers, 58 field officers, 235 medics

Military college: 14 officer instructors for 267 student cadets

Engineer park: 2 staff officers, 11 field officers, and 45 mechanics

Construction battalion: 11 staff officers, 56 field officers, and 287 laborers

Veterinary service: 4 staff officers and 10 field officers.

Administratively, the country was divided into 11 existing *zonas militares* or "military zones" (the eighth having been suppressed), each listed here below with the respective state in which their regional army detachment was to be headquartered:

1a. *Zona militar*: Sonora
2a. *Zona militar*: Chihuahua
3a. *Zona militar*: Nuevo León
4a. *Zona militar*: Tamaulipas
5a. *Zona militar*: Jalisco
6a. *Zona militar*: San Luis Potosí
7a. *Zona militar*: Guanajuato
9a. *Zona militar*: Puebla
10a. *Zona militar*: Oaxaca
11a. *Zona militar*: Oaxaca
12a. *Zona militar*: Yucatán

During the forthcoming decade from 1900 to 1910, these forces would be further improved by purchases of advanced weaponry abroad, such as thousands of high-powered Mauser rifles and dozens of Hotchkiss or Colt heavy machine guns, while their scattered garrisons could respond ever more swiftly to local outbreaks of violence by the dispatch of mounted contingents by rail, whose subsequent movements could be coordinated and directed in the field by telegraph.

Yet despite all of these advantages, the Porfirian Army would be overwhelmed by the sheer number of minor rebellions that exploded on all sides against the government in November 1910, so the regime fell within six months' time. And despite the massive military escalation that was then attempted by Gen. Victoriano Huerta three years later, this Federal Army would be pulverized by more powerful revolutionary battlefield forces under Pancho Villa and Álvaro Obregón and pass out of existence by August 1914.

Chronology

Interrupted Royal Rule (1808–1810)

Early March 1808 — Weary of his ineffectual Spanish allies, Napoleon sends a French army into northern Spain to occupy its major cities and seize its royal family.

March 19, 1808 — Charles IV of Spain abdicates in favor of his son, Ferdinand VII, but both Bourbon monarchs are soon imprisoned in France.

June 7, 1808 — Joseph Bonaparte is installed upon the throne in Madrid, a dynastic change that is dismissed by most Spanish-American subjects.

September 16, 1808 — A coup by Peninsular Spaniards in Mexico City deposes the viceroy José de Iturrigaray in favor of the elderly field marshal Pedro de Garibay, believed to be more firmly loyal to the Bourbon cause.

September 25, 1808 — A liberal *junta* or "council" is formed at Aranjuez in Spain to spearhead resistance against the French occupation and uphold its incarcerated monarchs.

War of Independence (1810–1821)

September 16, 1810 — Miguel Hidalgo calls for an insurrection at his rural church of Dolores, leading several hundred adherents on a march toward Guanajuato, whose ranks soon swell into the thousands.

September 28, 1810 — Twenty to twenty-five thousand of Hidalgo's rebels storm into Guanajuato, massacring its few hundred Peninsular Spaniards in the Alhóndiga de Granaditas.

October 17, 1810 — Hidalgo enters Michoacán's capital of Valladolid unopposed with tens of thousands of followers.

October 30, 1810 — In a mountain pass leading from Toluca toward Mexico City, Hidalgo's 80,000 insurgents defeat a much smaller royalist force at Monte de las Cruces but are so mauled that they turn away northwest rather than assault the defenseless viceregal capital.

November 7, 1810 — Hidalgo's unwieldy throng is surprised at Aculco by a royalist army under Gen.

Félix María Calleja and scattered in confusion.

November 25, 1810 Calleja recuperates Guanajuato from its insurgent occupiers.

January 17, 1811 Calleja defeats Hidalgo's army at Calderón Bridge, dispersing his followers and reclaiming Guadalajara four days later.

Early February 1811 Hidalgo and Allende retreat north from Zacatecas with the remnants of their army, pursued by Calleja's monarchist army.

March 16, 1811 Hidalgo and Allende continue north from Saltillo with 1,300 insurgents, hoping to reach the United States. They are treacherously arrested five days afterward at Acatita de Baján and presented to the Crown authorities in Monclova on March 22nd for a reward.

May 10–19, 1811 A royalist expedition out of Veracruz under Col. Joaquín de Arredondo recuperates Tamaulipas for the Crown.

May 26, 1811 Hidalgo's former pupil, José María Morelos, defeats 1,500 royalists at Tixtla.

July 30, 1811 Hidalgo is executed in Chihuahua City, his head being pickled and sent to Guanajuato to be displayed on the Alhóndiga de Granaditas.

August 18, 1811 Morelos drives the last demoralized royalist troops out of the southwestern theater.

Early November, 1811 Morelos launches a three-pronged insurgent offensive inland, sending one column toward Oaxaca and another toward Taxco, with himself occupying Izúcar.

Christmas Day, 1811 Morelos occupies Cuautla de Amilpas.

January 2, 1812 Calleja's 5,000-strong royalist army fights its way into the insurgent "capital" of Zitácuaro, inflicting thousands of casualties before burning it to the ground.

February 17, 1812 Calleja's army lays siege to Morelos within Cuautla, who eventually fights his way clear with a few starved survivors on May 2nd; the insurgent cause nonetheless remains alive.

March 1812 The *Cortes* or legislative assembly in Cadiz promulgates Spain's first ever constitution, a liberal document that generates much enthusiasm throughout large segments of the empire because of its promises of limited self-rule and other reforms.

April 5, 1812 Royalist lieutenant colonel Francisco Caldelas lays siege to the insurgent garrison holding Huajuapan with more than 2,000 men and 14 guns. After three-and-a-half months, Morelos arrives with a reconstituted insurgent army to relieve its defenders.

November 25, 1812 Morelos surprises and takes Oaxaca City.

February 7, 1813 Morelos leads a division out of Oaxaca to invest the unessential royal garrison at Acapulco, rather than challenge the weakened viceregal administration in central Mexico.

March 4, 1813 Because of his military successes, General Calleja is appointed viceroy of New Spain and sets about reconcentrating and improving its weakened royal armies.

August 20, 1813 After a four-and-a-half month siege, Acapulco surrenders to Morelos.

September 13, 1813 Morelos opens a "constitutional congress" at Chilpancingo, which formally declares independence from Spain (while retaining the Catholic faith) and begins laying out the structure for a Mexican government.

November 6, 1813 The congressional deputies conclude their creation of an independent government, and their commander-in-chief, Morelos, begins gathering forces to capture the city of Valladolid (modern Morelia) to serve as its new capital.

December 8, 1813 Viceroy Calleja in Mexico City learns of Morelos's plan so orders Gen. Ciriaco de Llano and Col. Agustín de Iturbide to rush with 3,000 royalist troops and reinforce Valladolid's garrison.

December 22, 1813 Morelos arrives outside Valladolid, whose royalist garrison is reinforced by De Llano and Iturbide at the last minute, defeating and scattering the undisciplined insurgent throng two days later.

January 4–5, 1814 Having regrouped his fleeing insurgent army at Puruarán, Morelos is persuaded to leave them under his second-in-command, Mariano Matamoros, who is defeated and captured.

January 17, 1814 Morelos is stripped of his command by the insurgent Congress, returning to Acapulco with only 100 demoralized survivors by early March 1814, only to disappear into the mountains shortly thereafter and resume his guerrilla strikes.

September 25, 1815 Zacatlán falls to the royalists, prompting the insurgent Congress to flee Uruapan four days later, escorted by Morelos.

November 3, 1815 The fugitive congressional caravan is detected crossing the Mezcala River at Tenango, being overtaking two days later by royalist cavalry at Tezmalaca. Among the 29 prisoners taken is Morelos, who is sent to Mexico City.

December 15, 1815 Guerrero forces the surrender of the royalist garrison

	holding Acatlán under Antonio Flon, conde de la Cadena, but monarchist reinforcements arrive shortly thereafter under Lamadrid and put Guerrero's band to flight.
December 22, 1815	Stripped of his religious orders, Morelos is shot by a firing squad at San Cristóbal Ecatepec; the demoralized Congress will disband before this year is out.
April 21, 1816	The insurgent commander Osorio is beaten at Venta de Cruz by Manuel de la Concha and again two days later at San Felipe.
September 13, 1816	Royalist forces recuperate Janitzio Island in Michoacán's Lake Pátzcuaro.
November 25, 1816	The royalists recover Mezcala Island in Lake Chapala.
December 10, 1816	Royalists reoccupy Fort Cuiristarán.
January 7, 1817	The insurgents holding out in Fort San Pedro Cóporo, outside Jungapeo in Michoacán, surrender to the royalists.
January 20, 1817	The insurgent Mier y Terán surrenders to royalist forces at Cerro Colorado, near Tehuacán.
February 9, 1817	Royalist forces wrest San Juan Coscomatepec from the insurgents in Veracruz.
February 17, 1817	Huatusco is reconquered by the royalists.
March 10, 1817	The fortified pass of Mesa de los Caballos, near San Felipe

	in Guanajuato, is recuperated from the insurgents.
April 15, 1817	The young Spanish antimonarchist Francisco Javier Mina disembarks at Soto la Marina in Veracruz with 500 foreign mercenaries to bolster the Mexican insurgency's flagging fortunes. He erects a fort on the eastern side of Soto la Marina's plaza, armed with artillery from his ships, then strikes inland with 300 men on May 24, 1817, to join forces with other insurgents.
June 8, 1817	Having seized 700 horses, Mina emerges into the Valle del Maíz in Central Mexico and defeats a force of 152 royalists.
June 11, 1817	A 1,500-man royalist expedition from Veracruz besieges Mina's fort at Soto la Marina, compelling its 93 defenders to surrender.
June 15, 1817	Continuing his march toward San Luis Potosí, Mina defeats 2,000 royalists under Col. Benito Armiñán at Peotillos Hacienda.
June 19, 1817	Mina's small army occupies Real de Pinos in Zacatecas after a surprise night attack, then three days later links up with some Mexican insurgents, reaching Fort Sombrero in the Comanja Range by June 24th to unite with the guerrilla chieftains Pedro Moreno and Encarnación "El Pachón" Ortiz.

June 29, 1817 Mina and Moreno sortie from Fort Sombrero with 330 followers, mauling a royalist force at Ferrero Ranch.

August 1, 1817 After unsuccessfully attacking the city of León, Mina and Moreno are besieged within Fort Sombrero by 3,500 royalists under Pascual Liñán. Mina and Moreno slip out with part of their small army on August 8th but cannot rescue their colleagues, so reinstall themselves at Fort Remedios near Pénjamo.

October 10, 1817 While returning from a raid against San Luis de la Paz, Mina and Moreno are bested in a clash at the Caja Hacienda by royalists under Col. Francisco Orrantia.

October 25, 1817 Mina, Moreno, and other leaders attempt to attack the royalist garrison in the city of Guanajuato with their combined 1,400 men, only to be repulsed. Two days later, while asleep at Venadito Ranch, both leaders are surprised by a monarchist column under Orrantia, Mina being carried into Liñán's encampment near Fort Remedios to be shot on November 11th.

December 21, 1817 The insurgent chieftain Nicolás Bravo is captured and his Fort Cóporo occupied by royalist forces; transferred into Mexico City on October 9, 1818, he will be pardoned two years later.

March 6, 1818 The insurgent stronghold of Fort Jaujilla, located on an island in Zacapu Lake, surrenders to the royalists.

September 15, 1818 Guerrero defeats his royalist pursuer Armijo at Tamo, wresting away sufficient arms and ammunition to equip 1,800 guerrillas.

January 1, 1820 Near the port of Seville in Spain, Col. Rafael del Riego mutinies against Ferdinand VII rather than take ship with his Asturias Regiment for the Americas, calling instead for the restoration of the liberal constitution of March 1812. Other contingents of the 14,000-man expeditionary force preparing to reconquer the River Plate emulate this example, until popular support compels the king to accept this resolution by March 9th.

May 24, 1820 Veracruz's merchants organize a battalion called the "Fernando VII Volunteers" and compel its garrison commander, José Dávila, to proclaim the liberal constitution of 1812; similar demonstrations occur at Jalapa and other Mexican towns.

August 22, 1820 In Mexico City, a general pardon is offered to all insurgents.

November 16, 1820 The royalist Iturbide departs Mexico City for Teloloapan, having been restored to field command in New Spain's difficult southern district with orders to subdue the guerrilla activities of Guerrero and Pedro Ascencio Alquisiras.

January 2, 1821
Guerrero defeats a small loyalist detachment at Zapotepec, and Ascencio does the same three days later at Tlatlaya.

January 10, 1821
Iturbide contacts Guerrero, proposing that they forge a new alliance to achieve Mexico's independence.

February 24, 1821
Iturbide proclaims his Plan of Iguala whereby the nation can gain its independence from Spain, subject to three conditions or "guarantees."

March 10, 1821
Guerrero and Iturbide meet at Acatempan, agreeing to merge forces into a new *Ejército Trigarante* or "Army of the Three Guarantees" representing Catholicism, independence, and union.

March 24, 1821
Insurrectionist generals Luis de Cortazar and Anastasio Bustamante capture the city of Guanajuato.

April 25, 1821
Insurrectionist general José Joaquín de Herrera is defeated at Tepeaca by loyalist colonel Francisco Hevia, but after being reinforced by Santa Anna, they succeed in taking Jalapa.

May 1, 1821
Iturbide's *Ejército Trigarante* enters the city of León, having marched uncontested from Teloloapan to Acámbaro, as

Field Marshal Liñán refuses to stir from his Cuernavaca headquarters with the loyalist southern army.

May 20, 1821
Valladolid (modern Morelia) surrenders to Iturbide.

July 1, 1821
Bravo besieges the city of Puebla.

July 5, 1821
Most of New Spain having adhered to Iturbide's Plan of Iguala, Spanish general Francisco Novella mutinies in the isolated viceregal capital, deposing the seemingly ineffectual viceroy Ruiz de Apodaca and deporting him toward Spain, while preparing to defend the city with some 5,000 remaining soldiers.

July 7, 1821
Santa Anna fails to carry loyalist Veracruz in a surprise assault, then imposes a tight siege.

July 30, 1821
Lt. Gen. Juan O'Donojú reaches Veracruz as New Spain's viceroy-designate to find that only this port and two other cities—Mexico City and Acapulco—remain loyal to Madrid. He therefore obtains a safe conduct from Santa Anna to travel inland and three weeks later signs the Treaty of Córdoba recognizing Mexico's independence (which agreement the Spanish government will later refuse to ratify).

Early September 1821: Mexican forces under Isidro Montes de Oca and Juan N. Alvarez besiege the royalist garrison within Fort San Diego at Acapulco, while Santa Anna occupies the fortress of Perote near Jalapa.

September 13, 1821 Meeting with Iturbide and O'Donojú at the Pateza Hacienda near Mexico City, the Spanish general Novella agrees to surrender the capital without a fight.

September 27, 1821 The 9,000 infantry and 7,000 cavalry of Iturbide's *Ejército Trigarante* parade triumphantly into Mexico City, effectively ending Spanish rule. Nicaragua declares its independence next day, followed by El Salvador on September 29th.

October 15, 1821 Juan N. Alvarez accepts the surrender of Fort San Diego at Acapulco.

October 25, 1821 General Dávila, still loyal to Spain, retires from the city of Veracruz into its offshore island fortress of San Juan de Ulúa to hold it for the Crown.

November 12, 1821 Learning that Chiapas wishes to become incorporated into Mexico, Iturbide dispatches 5,000 soldiers to ensure the peaceful fulfillment of this goal.

November 22, 1821 Juan Lindo, the Honduran leader, announces his country's incorporation into Mexico.

December 29, 1821 Factions in Guatemala City and Quezaltenango request to become incorporated into Mexico.

Turbulent Early Years (1822–1835)

January 9, 1822 The former Spanish captain general of Guatemala, Gabino Gaínza, announces the union of all of Central America.

May 8, 1822 The United States recognizes the independence of Argentina, Chile, Colombia, Mexico, and Peru.

May 18, 1822 In a staged act, troopers from the 1st Cavalry Regiment parade before Iturbide's residence in Mexico City and urge him to assume the mantle of emperor. After a show of reluctance, he consents and Congress is bullied into ratifying this arrangement next morning.

June 1822 A small Mexican army under the Italian-born brigadier general Vicente Filisola arrives in Guatemala with orders from Iturbide to secure Central America.

July 21, 1822 Iturbide (like Napoleon) crowns himself emperor in Mexico City's cathedral and proposes to create an order of Mexican nobility to be known as the "Order of Guadalupe."

August 26, 1822 Numerous military officers are arrested throughout Mexico on suspicion of plotting to overthrow Agustín I.

September 1822 Iturbide dispatches Brig. Gen. Juan José Zenón Fernández from San Luis Potosí to put down a republican mutiny in Tamaulipas led by Brig. Gen. Felipe de la Garza.

October 27, 1822 Santa Anna, now in command at Veracruz, attempts to lure a Spanish force from occupied San Juan de Ulúa to land at the city waterfront, but his ambush fails when the suspicious Spaniards turn back.

October 31, 1822 Iturbide dissolves Congress with the help of Gen. Luis de Cortazar's troops, replacing the legislators with a *junta* appointed by himself.

December 2, 1822 Threatened with demotion and arrest for his failed ambush of October 27th, Santa Anna mutinies with Veracruz's garrison against the imperial regime, issuing a call four days later for a republican form of government.

Late December 1822 Santa Anna's 600 defenders are besieged within Veracruz by 3,000 imperial troops under Generals Echávarri and José Gabriel de Armijo.

January 23, 1823 More anti-imperial rebels under Bravo and Guerrero are defeated in a two-day fight at Almolonga, Veracruz, by Armijo's subordinate, Brig. Gen. Epitacio Sánchez, yet anti-Iturbide sentiment continues to mount.

February 1, 1823 Echávarri and Armijo lift their siege of Veracruz, instead switching allegiances over to Bravo.

February 12, 1823 With mutinies erupting on every side, Iturbide shifts his headquarters out of the capital to Ixtapalucan.

March 19, 1823 Iturbide abdicates, being escorted to Antigua in the state of Veracruz under Bravo's protection, then deported two months later.

March 29, 1823 Learning of Iturbide's removal, Filisola convenes a constitutional congress in Guatemala City to decide Central America's fate before departing with his Mexican army. This body will opt for full independence by July 1st, only Chiapas choosing to remain as part of Mexico.

March 31, 1823 Mexico's Congress decides that a triumvirate composed of Bravo, Guadalupe Victoria, and Pedro Celestino Negrete will temporarily rule the country until a republican constitution can be drafted.

June 1823 Bravo marches into Jalisco with 2,000 men to calm disturbances in that state.

January 31, 1824 Mexico's new constitution is promulgated, establishing a republican form of government.

June 1824 Bravo marches into Jalisco with 4,000 men because of its continued political unrest.

July 1824 After a year in Italy and England, Iturbide returns to Mexico, only to be taken prisoner and executed in Tamaulipas.

October 10, 1824 The insurgent hero Guadalupe Victoria is sworn into office as Mexico's first elected president.

December 23, 1827 Col. Manuel Montaño leads an uprising at Otumba, soon joined by Vice President Bravo at Tulancingo, who assumes command over the rebel forces.

January 7, 1828 Guerrero defeats Bravo, who is exiled to Ecuador, although pardoned the next year.

September 1, 1828 Popular voting returns are ignored in the presidential election, when the highborn general Gómez Pedraza is proclaimed as winner, with the lowborn Guerrero relegated to vice president. Eleven days later, Santa Anna revolts and seizes the fortress of Perote in the state of Veracruz, calling for the annulment of these results. Within a few weeks, he will be obliged to retreat into Oaxaca.

November 30, 1828 A mutiny in favor of Guerrero seizes the Acordada garrison in Mexico City, and street fighting erupts two days later, driving Gómez Pedraza from the presidency by December 3rd.

March 20, 1829 Guerrero orders all Spaniards expelled from Mexico.

April 1, 1829 Guerrero is officially inaugurated as president, with Anastasio Bustamante as vice president and Santa Anna as governor of Veracruz.

July 26, 1829 A transport fleet appears off Cape Rojo, the next day disembarking 3,500 Spanish troops under Brig. Gen. Isidro Barradas to attempt the reconquest of Mexico by fomenting an insurrection against republican rule. No uprising occurs, though, so the invaders are contained around Tampico by thousands of Mexican troops, and compelled to reembark by late September.

November 6, 1829 Yucatán rebels against Guerrero's administration.

December 4, 1829 Vice President Bustamante mutinies against President Guerrero at Jalapa with the large army that has been raised to repel the Spanish invasion. Within two weeks, Guerrero flees the national capital to mount a guerrilla resistance in southern Mexico, allowing Bustamante to assume the presidency as of January 1, 1830.

January 15, 1831 After a year of successful guerrilla attacks, Guerrero is lured aboard the Genoese brigantine *Colombo* at Acapulco, then sailed to Huatulco in the state of Oaxaca and handed over to be executed on February 14th.

January 2, 1832 Santa Anna rises in revolt with the Veracruz garrison

	against Bustamante, calling for a restoration of the exiled president Gómez Pedraza. Despite a halting start, this rebellion will gradually spread throughout central Mexico.
March 19, 1832	Gov. Francisco Vital Fernández of Tamaulipas also revolts against the government in Mexico City but flees upon the approach of Mier y Terán's loyal troops.
July 8, 1832	Mier y Terán, humiliated by his inability to put down another revolt at Tampico, commits suicide by falling upon his sword at Padilla.
August 14, 1832	Bustamante is obliged to march out of Mexico City at the head of his army to battle the spreading antigovernment revolts throughout Central Mexico.
August 1832	In the state of Guerrero, Gen. Juan Nepomuceno Álvarez rises against Bustamante.
September 17, 1832	Bustamante defeats a rebel concentration at Gallinero Pass near Dolores Hidalgo in the state of Guanajuato but must then retrace his steps toward Puebla to intercept Santa Anna's army, which is advancing inland from Veracruz.
October 5, 1832	Gómez Pedraza reaches Veracruz from his exile in France, becoming the figurehead for Santa Anna's movement.
December 21, 1832	Santa Anna's army clashes with Bustamante's near Puebla, then two days later an armistice is signed at Zavaleta Hacienda whereby the latter resigns as president in favor of Gómez Pedraza.
January 3, 1833	Gómez Pedraza and Santa Anna enter Mexico City triumphantly, the former temporarily reoccupying the presidency, although as little more than a puppet. When elections are held a couple of months later, Santa Anna becomes president, officially taking office as of April 1st.
June 2, 1833	Santa Anna marches out of Mexico City at the head of his army to put down a minor insurrection at Cuautla Amilpas.
March 5, 1834	General Álvarez defeats Bravo's conservative followers at Chilapa.
November 9, 1834	Álvarez rises in revolt against Santa Anna at Tecpan, eventually besieging Acapulco and clashing with Bravo.
February 14, 1835	Determined to curtail the frequent regional uprisings against his centralist aims, Santa Anna's Congress in Mexico City passes a law restricting each state's militia forces to just one soldier for every 500 inhabitants, a reduction that will be contested by the state of Zacatecas.

May 10, 1835 Santa Anna suddenly materializes with 4,000 troops in the Tolosa Hills, less than nine miles east of the city of Zacatecas, easily defeating its state militia next day and sacking the city.

Loss of Texas (1835–1836)

May 21, 1835 Alarmed by the news of Santa Anna's swift strike against Zacatecas, federalist officials of the combined states of Coahuila and Texas flee north from their capital of Monclova into Texas.

Early July 1835 Santa Anna's trusted subordinate, Brig. Gen. Martín Perfecto de Cos, arrives at Matamoros with instructions to lead an expedition into restive Texas and stamp out its anticentralist dissent.

September 20, 1835 Cos disembarks with 500 soldiers north of Corpus Christi, pushing upriver to occupy the small presidio of Goliad by October 2nd and continuing toward San Antonio.

October 9, 1835 Cos's 40-man detachment at Goliad is surprised by 50 Texian volunteers under George Collingsworth, and a small Texian army under Stephen F. Austin (only recently released from a long imprisonment in Mexico City) imposes a loose siege on Cos's unhappy Mexican garrison at San Antonio, comprising the Morelos Battalion and five companies of conscripts.

November 3, 1835 A Texian convention at San Felipe resolves to oppose Santa Anna as loyal Mexican citizens, upholding its federal constitution of 1824 while calling upon other states to oppose his dictatorship.

December 5, 1835 An assault on San Antonio by Texian forces under Col. Benjamin R. Milam presses Cos's men back into the Alamo, so he sues for terms four days later. More than 1,100 Mexican troops will soon begin marching south out of Texas as winter sets in.

January 7, 1836 Santa Anna reaches Saltillo and quickly begins organizing a large army so as to invade Texas and reimpose his rule.

Late January 1836 Santa Anna moves north from Saltillo with one cavalry and two infantry brigades, plus a siege train, to join two other divisions already operating near the Río Grande under Brigadier Generals Joaquín Ramírez y Sesma and Juan José Urrea, for a combined total of 6,050 soldiers.

February 11, 1836 News is received at San Antonio of Santa Anna's unexpected approach, although a heavy snowfall two days later gives its 150 defenders hope that his march will be delayed.

February 23, 1836 Sooner than anticipated, Santa Anna's vanguard of 1,500 troopers is sighted a mile and a half outside San Antonio, so

150 Texian defenders and 25 noncombatants gather inside its fortified Alamo. After a 13-day siege, they are wiped out by a three-pronged assault.

March 7, 1836

The victorious Santa Anna immediately sends columns from his San Antonio encampment to attack the Texian garrisons at Goliad and Gonzales.

March 11, 1836

Houston abandons Gonzales with his 375 followers and a large number of refugees, retreating eastward.

March 17, 1836

The Texian government of Pres. David G. Burnet, which has declared independence from Mexico, is obliged to abandon its provisional capital at Washington-on-the-Brazos because of the approach of a Mexican column, while thousands of American settlers flee east toward Louisiana.

March 27, 1836

On Santa Anna's express orders, 365 Texian prisoners are marched a short distance out of Goliad and shot by Urrea's troops, only 30 surviving this massacre.

April 16, 1836

Having pursued for hundreds of miles into East Texas, Santa Anna with 900 picked troops attempts to surprise the fugitive Texian government at its temporary headquarters in Harrisburg, only to find them gone.

April 18, 1836

Having been reinforced and countermarched with 900 troops to seek out Santa Anna for battle, Houston arrives east of Harrisburg and the next day crosses over Buffalo Bayou to take up a defensive position on the wooded banks of the San Jacinto River.

April 21, 1836

Encamped opposite and joined by Cos with additional troops, Santa Anna waits until noon for action to commence, then orders his 1,400 men to stand down in anticipation of fighting next day. Instead, Houston's small army silently charges the slumbering Mexican camp at 4:30 p.m., killing some 650 and capturing 730 prisoners, including Santa Anna.

May 14, 1836

The captive Mexican president is compelled to agree to an armistice and order all his troops back south of the Río Grande within 12 days' time.

February 21, 1837

After being held for months in Texas and Washington, Santa Anna is returned to Veracruz aboard a U.S. Navy barque, retiring in disgrace to his estate of Manga de Clavo.

War of the Cakes (1838–1839)

September 1837

A French plenipotentiary arrives in Mexico to demand compensation from the government of Pres. Anastasio Bustamante for economic losses suffered by French businesses during recent disturbances. After more than three months of fruitless talks, the plenipotentiary departs in January 1838.

March 21, 1838 The French plenipotentiary returns with 10 French warships, which anchor off Veracruz and send a renewed ultimatum ashore.

April 16, 1838 No satisfaction having been received, the French squadron imposes a limited naval blockade on Veracruz, restricting entry for certain items so as to deprive the Mexican government of revenues.

November 17, 1838 After six months' blockade, the French admiral has a face-to-face meeting with the Mexican foreign minister at Jalapa without reaching any resolution.

November 27, 1838 The French warships open fire on Veracruz's harbor castle of San Juan de Ulúa, using newly developed Paixhans explosive shells that inflict 224 casualties and dismount 20 of its guns by nightfall. Its garrison capitulates the next morning and a local cessation of hostilities is reached, seemingly promising a resolution for each nation's grievances.

November 30, 1838 Angered by this bombardment, the government in Mexico City rejects the temporary truce and instead declares that a state of war exists against France.

December 3, 1838 The disgraced ex-president Santa Anna is given command of Veracruz's garrison and the next day informs the French admiral of the rejection of the truce by Mexico's government.

December 5, 1838 The French launch a surprise attack on Veracruz's waterfront at dawn, occupying its bastions and spiking a few guns. Santa Anna narrowly escapes from his headquarters, but Gen. Mariano Arista is captured. Santa Anna returns to attack the French reembarkation, losing a leg to a gun blast.

December 16, 1838 As passions cool, the French admiral dismisses part of his blockading squadron, and a British ambassador arrives six days afterward to mediate a truce.

March 9, 1839 Mexican and French representatives sign a peace accord, bringing an end to the dispute.

Turmoil (1839–1845)

May 3, 1839: The rebel northeastern general José Antonio Mexía is defeated by President Bustamante at San Miguel de la Blanca and executed that same evening at Acajete.

May 18, 1839 Angered by centralist tendencies and increased taxation imposed by the government in Mexico City, a brief revolt occurs in the state of Jalisco, being quickly suppressed.

May 29, 1839
Another anticentralist uprising also erupts in Yucatán, its leader Santiago Imán besieging and finally carrying the town of Tizimín by November 11th before his followers are dispersed a month later into the jungles.

February 17, 1840
The rebel colonel Sebastián López de Llergo arrives outside Yucatán's capital of Mérida, being allowed inside three days later by the defection of Col. Anastasio Torrens's garrison, so emboldening the separatist cause that the state legislature severs relations with Mexico City shortly thereafter.

April 2, 1840
A small Yucatecan separatist expedition besieges Campeche's centralist garrison, who request terms by June 6th and capitulate 10 days later.

July 15, 1840
The imprisoned general Juan José Urrea is broken out of confinement at dawn, then leads mutinous troops in an assault against Bustamante's palace, capturing that president in bed. However, a loyalist counterattack from the Ciudadela results in gunfire, during which Bustamante cuts his way free, so after a fortnight of street fighting that inflicts many civilian casualties, Urrea is compelled to surrender and retire to Durango.

August 8, 1841
Gen. Mariano Paredes, military commander at Guadalajara, rises against President Bustamante, joined by Santa Anna out of Veracruz plus Generals Pedro Cortázar and Julián Juvera. Their 2,200 combined men reinforce another 1,200 mutineers at Mexico City, seizing the Ciudadela and Acordada Barracks. Bustamante fights back with 2,000 loyal troops, receiving 1,500 reinforcements from the countryside, but is driven out of the capital by September 20th and resigns nine days later.

March 5, 1842
Refusing to acknowledge Texas's separation from Mexico, Brig. Gen. Rafael Vásquez appears outside San Antonio with 700 troops, which is evacuated by its outnumbered defenders. Vásquez remains two days then withdraws.

May 7, 1842
Having failed to reach an accommodation with the separatist forces in Yucatán, Santa Anna's Congress will sever relations with this breakaway state and send an expeditionary force that same August 1842 to assail its principal seaport of Campeche, besieging it for many months without success.

September 11, 1842
Gen. Adrián Woll occupies San Antonio, Texas, with 1,200 troops, fighting off a couple of Texian relief

columns before retiring back toward Mexico on September 20th.

October 19, 1842 Under a mistaken belief that hostilities have erupted, the U.S. naval commodore Thomas ap Catesby "Tac" Jones drops anchor off Monterey, California, and demands the surrender of its Mexican garrison, landing 150 men before discovering his error.

February 4, 1843 In a bid to reinvigorate the stalled siege of Campeche, newly appointed centralist general Matías de la Peña Barragán sends an 800-man detachment five miles east into the town of Chiná, where it is surprised by 500 separatist troops and a ferocious exchange ensues, some 400 men being slain on both sides and many others wounded, until the separatists retreat back into Campeche.

March 25, 1843 De la Peña disembarks 2,500 centralist troops at the port of Telchac, hoping to surprise Yucatán's capital of Mérida from the rear. He is checked at Tixcocob by López de Llergo on April 10th, then requests terms two weeks later, sailing away in defeat with his army from Chicxulub by May 26th.

June 26, 1843 Centralist general Pedro de Ampudia lifts the siege of the separatist garrison within Campeche, retreating by sea to El Carmen.

October 30, 1844 In Guadalajara, Paredes agrees to spearhead a revolt against Santa Anna's regime, being joined one week later by the Aguascalientes garrison and several others.

November 22, 1844 Santa Anna marches northwest out of Mexico City with a small army to confront Paredes and his 4,000 rebel troops in the state of Querétaro.

December 6, 1844 The Reserve Battalion also revolts in its Acordada Barracks in the capital against Santa Anna, sparking a general uprising against his handpicked "interim president," Gen. Valentín Canalizo, who is arrested and replaced the next day byGen. José Joaquín de Herrera.

Early January 1845 Santa Anna gives up all hope of reclaiming power so departs with his shrunken army to ride toward Veracruz with a small escort. Detained upon reaching Naolinco, he is held in the Fortress of Perote Castle until banished toward Cuba on June 3, 1845.

Mexican-American War (1846–1848)

March 1, 1845 The U.S. Congress in Washington votes to accede to American settlers' wishes and annex the Republic of Texas. The ambassador, Gen. Juan N. Almonte, departs in protest five days later, as Mexico still regards Texas as a breakaway province, and severs diplomatic relations by the end of this same month.

June 3, 1845 The incarcerated Santa Anna is banished toward Cuba aboard the gunboat *Victoria*.

July 4, 1845 Anglo-Texans accept the American government's terms for annexation.

July 23, 1845 To match Mexico's military buildup near the mouth of the Río Grande, brevet brigadier general Zachary Taylor departs Fort Jesup in Louisiana with 1,500 troops, disembarking two days later at Aransas inlet. His force will be encamped by July 31st at Corpus Christi, near the Nueces River mouth— traditionally regarded by Mexicans as marking the Texan border.

August 24, 1845 Three hundred troopers join Taylor at Corpus Christi, having traveled overland from Louisiana via San Antonio. By late October, Taylor's contingent will consist of 3,500 regulars: four infantry regiments, one of dragoons, and four artillery regiments, half the peacetime U.S. Army.

October 31, 1845 In order to help reconcile with Mexico, a U.S. naval squadron is withdrawn from near Veracruz.

November 29, 1845 The ex-Louisiana congressman John C. Slidell arrives at Veracruz to reopen a diplomatic dialogue with the Mexican government.

December 14, 1845 Frustrated in his attempts to mobilize an effective fighting force at San Luis Potosí, Gen. Mariano Paredes revolts against Pres. José Joaquín de Herrera and marches upon Mexico City with his small army. Herrera is abandoned by his troops, so Paredes enters the capital uncontested on January 2, 1846, to be acclaimed as the new president.

March 8, 1846 Having been authorized to move his 3,500 troops south from Corpus Christi, deeper into disputed territory, Taylor orders his first brigade to depart, following with his main body in segments over the next few days. His vanguard sights Point Santa Isabel by March 24th, finding supply ships awaiting them in the Gulf of Mexico plus the town of El Frontón torched and abandoned by its 280-man Mexican garrison.

March 28, 1846 Taylor's army reaches the northern banks of the Río Grande to a frosty reception from Col. Francisco Mejía, commander in Matamoros opposite, who considers this American advance to be an invasion of Mexican territory. Yet despite commanding 3,000 troops, Mejía is not empowered to do anything more than observe as Taylor erects a 2,200-man, star-shaped camp named Fort Texas.

March 30, 1846 Having failed to reach any agreement with the Mexican government, Slidell departs Veracruz.

April 4, 1846 Mexico's war minister, José María Tornel, appoints Maj. Gen. and former president Mariano Arista to organize an "Army of the North" and confront Taylor, who sets out from Monterrey with various bodies of troops for Matamoros.

April 11, 1846 Arista's vanguard, 1,000 cavalry troopers and 1,500 infantrymen under Gen. Pedro de Ampudia, reaches Matamoros and two days later Ampudia orders Taylor to begin retiring north toward Corpus Christi within 24 hours. The American general refuses and in turn directs his warships out in the Gulf to blockade the Río Grande, cutting off seaborne supplies for the Mexican army.

April 17, 1846 Two schooners approaching Matamoros with provisions from New Orleans for the Mexican forces but are turned back by U.S. blockaders, so Ampudia lodges a protest five days later.

April 23, 1846 Paredes declares a "defensive war" against the American penetration, and Arista orders Gen. Anastasio Torrejón to cross the Río Grande a few miles upstream of Taylor's encampment with 1,600 cavalrymen. The American general responds by dispatching a patrol of 63 dragoons, which is ambushed at Carricitos the next day by 200 Mexican troopers, suffering 16 killed and the remainder captured.

April 29, 1846 Capt. Samuel Walker's 77 volunteer "Texas Rangers" clash with Mexican irregulars, suffering 10 killed.

May 1, 1846 Fearful that he is about to be encircled by a flanking maneuver, Taylor leaves an infantry regiment and two batteries to hold Fort Texas while commencing a 30-mile forced march northeast with his remaining 2,300 men to bolster his contingent at Point Santa Isabel.

This same day, Arista's army slips east-southeast out of Matamoros to cross the Río Grande and unite with Torrejón's cavalry behind American lines.

May 3, 1846 The Mexican artillery in Matamoros opens fire against Fort Texas, exchanging salvoes across the Río Grande for the next several days.

May 8, 1846 Returning to relieve Fort Texas, Taylor defeats Arista's and Torrejón's 3,200 combined troops at the Battle of Palo Alto, then beats them again next day at a new defensive position at Resaca de la Palma.

May 11, 1846 President Polk requests an official declaration of war

	from the U.S. Congress, which is passed the next day.
May 17, 1846	Taylor pushes across the Río Grande and occupies Matamoros without resistance the next day.
May 20, 1846	Amid growing dissatisfaction with Paredes's handling of affairs, a revolt erupts in Guadalajara, its governor and garrison commander being arrested.
June 12, 1846	The first half of a 6,000-man army arrives to besiege the liberal rebels within Guadalajara, and a protracted encirclement ensues.
August 5, 1846	As President Paredes is preparing to depart Mexico City to invigorate his besiegers outside the rebel city of Guadalajara, Gen. José Mariano Salas mutinies at the capital's *Ciudadela* or "Citadel," arresting and deposing him.
August 14, 1846	In California, organized Mexican resistance ends with the surrender of Gen. José María Castro's army and capture of most prominent officials at San Luis Obispo, although guerrilla strikes will continue.
August 16, 1846	Santa Anna returns to Veracruz from Cuba aboard a British mail packet, which is allowed to enter by its U.S. naval blockaders because Washington believes that he will help conclude a peace.
August 18, 1846	Santa Fe, New Mexico, is occupied without a fight by a 1,400-man U.S. expedition under brevet brigadier general Stephen W. Kearny, while Gov. Manuel Armijo retires toward Albuquerque with his Mexican troops.
August 19, 1846	Taylor advances west out of Camargo toward Mier and Cerralvo with his 3,200 U.S. Army regulars and 3,000 best volunteers, leaving behind 4,700 of the latter as a garrison.
September 15, 1846	Santa Anna arrives outside Mexico City on the eve of Independence Day, entering the next morning to a tumultuous reception escorted by Salas's troops.
September 19, 1846	Taylor's 6,600-man army comes within sight of the northern city of Monterrey, subduing it after four days of heavy fighting, after which Ampudia's defenders are allowed to exit and both sides observe a two-month cessation of offensive operations.
September 28, 1846	Santa Anna departs Mexico City northward with a small body of troops, arriving at San Luis Potosí by October 8th to begin amassing an army to confront Taylor.
October 21, 1846	Tampico is evacuated by its Mexican garrison as part of Santa Anna's concentration of forces at San Luis Potosí.

November 13, 1846	Taylor pushes southwest out of Monterrey with a portion of his army, occupying the undefended town of Saltillo three days later without resistance.
November 23, 1846	Vacated Tampico is garrisoned by U.S. forces.
November 30, 1846	U.S. major general Winfield Scott set sails from New York for Brazos de Santiago to begin organizing a second expeditionary force, Washington having decided to bring the Mexican government to the bargaining table by invading nearer to their capital.
December 6, 1846	The polarized Senate in Mexico City votes 11–9 to offer the presidency to Santa Anna and vice presidency to the civilian Valentín Gómez Farías; the former remains at San Luis Potosí training his army, leaving the latter to assume office alone on December 23rd.
December 18, 1846	Taylor learns that Santa Anna is moving north from San Luis Potosí to assail the small American garrison holding Saltillo so orders it reinforced and redeploys his units, causing Santa Anna to cancel his operation.
December 25, 1846	Having pushed south from Valverde, New Mexico, Col. Alexander W. Doniphan's 850 mounted infantrymen easily best 1,200 poorly armed Mexican irregulars

	north of El Paso, Texas, and occupy that city.
December 27, 1846	Scott arrives at Brazos de Santiago to begin assembling his expeditionary force to open a second front through Veracruz, which will entail stripping 8,000 infantrymen, 1,000 cavalry troopers, and two field batteries from Taylor's army.
January 4, 1847	Taylor enters abandoned Ciudad Victoria, detaching a division east to link up with the American garrison already holding the Gulf port of Tampico.
January 10, 1847	U.S. forces make a triumphal entry into Los Angeles, securing the last Mexican stronghold in California.
January 13, 1847	An American courier carrying a copy of Scott's campaign plans inland to Taylor is killed between Ciudad Victoria and Monterrey, this intelligence being forwarded to Santa Anna at San Luis Potosí.
January 28, 1847	Realizing that the strength of Taylor's army is being diminished to help Scott, Santa Anna orders his 20,000 men to begin marching northward from San Luis Potosí to rendezvous south of Saltillo and surprise his American opponent.
February 15, 1847	Scott departs Brazos de Santiago for Tampico to then proceed farther southeast to

his expedition's rendezvous off Lobos Island.

February 17, 1847 Santa Anna's first division reaches Encarnación, only 14,000 of his troops and 17 guns completing the grueling trek from San Luis Potosí to surprise the unwary Taylor at nearby Agua Nueva, Coahuila.

February 20, 1847 On this evening, an American patrol sights the vanguard of Santa Anna's huge approaching army and warns Taylor the next morning. With only 4,800 troops under his command, the U.S. general hastily falls back into a narrow pass known as La Angostura, six miles south of Saltillo, and succeeds in exhausting Santa Anna's efforts over the two-day Battle of Buena Vista.

February 27, 1847 Mexico City's garrison revolts against the liberal vice president Gómez Farías, who has introduced some new taxes on Church properties, both factions appealing to the absent Santa Anna for resolution.

February 28, 1847 Doniphan smashes an ill-armed throng of 4,100 Mexican volunteers north of Chihuahua, and the next day occupies that city.

March 9, 1847 Scott disembarks his 8,600 troops and a 1,200-man naval contingent southeast of Veracruz, besieging the city's 4,400 defenders, who capitulate 20 days later.

March 21, 1847 Santa Anna appears with his two best divisions at Guadalupe, just north of Mexico City, ending the political dispute by replacing Vice President Gómez Farías with the general and congressman Pedro María Anaya.

April 3, 1847 Santa Anna exits Mexico City eastward to assume command over the three infantry divisions, one cavalry brigade, and 2,000 militiamen guarding the highway from Veracruz.

April 8, 1847 Scott's vanguard marches inland from Veracruz toward Jalapa, defeating Santa Anna's waiting army 10 days later at the Battle of Cerro Gordo.

May 6, 1847 From Jalapa, Scott sends a division on ahead to seize Puebla, while at the same time losing seven of his volunteer regiments, totaling 3,000 men, whose terms of enlistment have expired and so return toward the coast.

May 15, 1847 Scott's vanguard under Brig. Gen. William J. Worth occupies Puebla without opposition, being joined 13 days later by Scott's main body, although their combined strength totals only 5,820 effectives—too few to push on toward Mexico City so they will have to await reinforcements for three months before resuming their offensive into central Mexico.

July 8, 1847 Scott is reinforced at Puebla by 4,500 American troops.

July 27, 1847 Gen. Gabriel Valencia arrives outside Mexico City from San Luis Potosí with 4,000 veteran troops of Santa Anna's northern army.

August 6, 1847 Another 2,400 reinforcements reach Scott's army at Puebla, with 1,000 more following along behind, bringing his total numbers to 14,000 troops (of whom 3,000 are temporarily sick or convalescent). He therefore launches his long-anticipated offensive against Mexico City by dispatching his vanguard division the next day.

August 10, 1847 Learning that the Americans are at last moving out of Puebla, Anaya's brigade marches 10 miles east of Mexico City to begin fortifying El Peñón de los Baños with 7,000 troops and 30 cannon, in accordance with Santa Anna's strategy for defending the capital.

August 16, 1847 Rather than approach the Mexican defenses at El Peñón head-on, the American divisions double back and slip southwestward around various strongpoints, while Santa Anna redeploys his divisions to confront them.

August 19–20, 1847 The advancing Americans maul Valencia's division at the Padierna crossroads near Contreras, then rout Santa

Anna's main army at Churubusco, inflicting 4,000 casualties and capturing 3,000 prisoners. The next day, the Mexican president proposes a truce for a discussion of terms, to which Scott agrees, hoping that it might lead to an armistice.

September 6, 1847 After two weeks of fruitless talks, Scott informs Santa Anna that hostilities will resume the next day, and a concentration of Mexican troops is defeated at the Battle of Molino del Rey, with heavy losses on both sides.

September 13, 1847 Scott's army assaults and overruns Chapultepec Castle, sweeping past toward the capital's western gates, which Santa Anna abandons overnight.

September 14, 1847 Penetrating into Mexico City's main square by noon, the U.S. occupiers restore some semblance of order after a couple of days of riotous looting.

September 15, 1847 At the suburb of Guadalupe, Santa Anna resigns the presidency in favor of Mexico's chief justice, Manuel de la Peña y Peña.

September 21, 1847 Santa Anna appears outside of American-occupied Puebla, his arrival raising the strength of its Mexican besiegers to 3,200 irregular cavalrymen and 2,500 militiamen, so he storms its defenses the next day without success.

October 8, 1847	Santa Anna's pickets are chased back into his camp at Huamantla by a party of "Texas Rangers," and his army is defeated and dispersed next day by a 3,000-man brigade under Maj. Gen. Joseph P. Lane.
October 12, 1847	Lane's army lifts the siege of Puebla, proving to be the last major action of the war. Shortly thereafter, Santa Anna is informed by President Peña that he is to turn over military command to Gen. Manuel Rincón so as to stand trial for his conduct of Mexico's defense.
November 18, 1847	Delegates from eight Mexican states agree to seek a peace agreement with the Americans.
February 2, 1848	Following fitful negotiations between U.S. representatives and the faction-plagued rump of Mexico's government, the Treaty of Guadalupe Hidalgo is signed. By its terms, the provinces of California, Nevada, Utah, Colorado, Arizona, and New Mexico are ceded to the Americans, while all claims to Texas are abandoned. The American government will pay $15 million in compensation for these lands while assuming responsibility for an additional $3.5 million in legal claims.
March 10, 1848	The Treaty of Guadalupe Hidalgo is ratified by the U.S.

Congress, and by Mexico's on May 19th.

June 11, 1848	The port of Veracruz is restored to Mexican control, the last of 18,300 American occupation troops departing through there by July 31st.

War of the Reform (1858–1861)

January 11, 1858	Gen. José de la Parra leads the Tacubaya garrison in a mutiny aimed at removing the collapsed administration of Comonfort. After a 10-day standoff, the young conservative colonels Luis G. Osollo and Miguel Miramón scatter Comonfort's disheartened followers and he flees into exile.
January 22, 1858	A body of 22 leading conservatives dubbed the *Junta de Notables* appoint Zuloaga as "interim president," with Parra as minister of war, who in turn promotes Osollo and Miramón to brigadier generals.
January 26, 1858	Miramón leads a column to secure the nearby city of Toluca, then returns to Mexico City.
February 5, 1858	Miramón departs the capital with a vanguard brigade of 1,200 regulars to spearhead an army that is to push up into the Bajío and disperse liberal militia forces gathering in support of the liberal presidential contender Benito Juárez.

March 10, 1858	The main 5,400-man conservative army, united under Osollo's command, defeats 7,300 green liberal militiamen under Gen. Anastasio Parrodi at the Battle of Salamanca.
March 20, 1858	Juárez quits Guadalajara with his fugitive liberal government, and Osollo enters triumphantly three days later, departing shortly thereafter to continue campaigning in the state of San Luis Potosí.
April 11, 1858	Juárez clears from Manzanillo, Colima, aboard the American steamer *John L. Stephens*, accompanied by four cabinet ministers.
April 17, 1858	While hastening from Guadalajara to relieve San Luis Potosí, threatened by a northern liberal army under Col. Juan Zuazua, Miramón's 2,600 troops endure hundreds of casualties while fighting past an ambush in *Puerto de Carretas* or "Wagons' Pass."
April 27, 1858	Rather than launching the anticipated assault against San Luis Potosí, Zuazua instead surprises and captures the city of Zacatecas.
May 4, 1858	After passing through Panama, Havana, and New Orleans, Juárez and his fugitive liberal cabinet reach Veracruz aboard an American steamer, installing their government.
May 21, 1858	A liberal division under Generals Santos Degollado and Pedro Ogazón arrived to lay siege to Guadalajara.
June 13, 1858	The poorly armed liberals raised their siege of Guadalajara at the approach of Miramón's returning column.
June 18, 1858	Having reinforced San Luis Potosí and detached Miramón to relieve Guadalajara, the youthful conservative commander-in-chief Osollo dies unexpectedly of typhoid fever.
June 30, 1858	Zuazua and 3,400 *blusas* overwhelm the 1,500 conservative troops garrisoning San Luis Potosí.
July 2, 1858	Miramón fights a heavy but indecisive action against various liberal commanders at the bottom of Atenquique Ravine (near modern Ciudad Guzmán, Jalisco).
July 21, 1858	Liberal forces once again raise their siege of Guadalajara, as Miramón returns from his southern foray.
July 28, 1858	The conservative brigadier general Leonardo Márquez sets out from Querétaro with three brigades totaling 4,000 men to reclaim San Luis Potosí. As his initial progress is slow, Miramón convinces the conservative leadership in Mexico City to put him in command of this campaign.

September 18, 1858 With Miramón once again absent from Guadalajara, its conservative garrison commander exits with 1,500 troops and seven guns, only to be routed three days later so the triumphant liberals reimpose a siege.

September 29, 1858 Miramón defeats a large liberal army outside San Luis Potosí, at the Battle of Ahualulco de los Pinos.

October 15, 1858 A small liberal army from Morelia, having advanced through the Valley of Toluca, assaults the outskirts of Mexico City, only to be beaten off.

October 26, 1858 The conservative garrison holding Villahermosa de Tabasco is besieged by liberal forces out of Tabasco and Chiapas, surrendering 12 days later.

December 14, 1858 After defeating Guadalajara's liberals in a series of clashes along the banks of the Santiago River, Miramón reclaims the city and drives the liberal army completely out of Jalisco by Christmas.

December 23, 1858 The conservative "interim president" Zuloaga is deposed in Mexico City by Generals Miguel María Echegaray and Manuel Robles Pezuela, who must soon submit for lack of support.

Early January 1859 By a narrow vote, the conservative leadership in Mexico City offers the vacant presidency to 27-year-old Miramón in Jalisco, who refuses. The now thoroughly discredited Zuloaga is reinstalled on January 24th, who appoints Miramón as his "substitute president" one week later. Miramón reaches Mexico City by February 2nd to be sworn in.

February 16, 1859 Miramón leaves the capital to personally march 5,000 soldiers and 46 artillery pieces down to the coast to attack the liberal administration of President Juárez in Veracruz. It will take this army five weeks to reach its destination.

February 18, 1859 With Miramón's main army departing from the Valley of Mexico, the liberal general Santos Degollado overruns León, and the city of Guanajuato 11 days later, driving on through Querétaro to draw Miramón away from his venture against Veracruz by threatening the capital.

March 22, 1859 Degollado appears outside Mexico City with more than 6,000 liberal troops but is unable to carry its defenses. Márquez arrives from Guadalajara with a relief column by April 7th and four days later defeats the liberals at the Battle of Tacubaya.

April 1, 1859 The American representative Robert H. MacLane reaches Veracruz and five days later recognizes the legitimacy of Juárez's government.

November 12, 1859	With a growing number of liberal forces materializing in the Bajío, General Degollado approaches the city of Querétaro with 6,000 troops and 29 fieldpieces, obliging Miramón to emerge next morning with 2,600 soldiers and 19 guns for a battle at nearby Estancia de las Vacas—which against all odds the conservative commander-in-chief wins.
November 19, 1859	Miramón reaches Guadalajara and shortly thereafter has Márquez arrested on a vindictive charge of misappropriation of funds.
December 14, 1859	MacLane signs a treaty with the liberal foreign finister Melchor Ocampo at Veracruz, promising $4 million in exchange for building rail lines across the Isthmus of Tehuantepec and northwestern Mexico to be guarded by American troops. This MacLane-Ocampo Treaty eventually fails to win ratification in the U.S. Senate.
December 24, 1859	Miramón successfully concludes a long pursuit of liberal forces in Jalisco.
February 8, 1860	Miramón marches out of Mexico City at the head of a large army to attempt a second siege of Juárez's government in Veracruz. Despite having secretly hired two blockaders at Havana, these vessels are promptly captured by the U.S. warship *Saratoga* as suspected

"pirates," so the conservative president is compelled to withdraw by March 21st.

May 11, 1860	The liberal general Ogazón threatens Guadalajara once more with 3,000 men and 15 fieldpieces, while a division of 5,000 additional men under Gen. José López Uraga marches from Lagos de Moreno to assist. Miramón races from Mexico City with 6,000 troops, arriving just in time to interrupt the liberal assault upon that city on May 24th.
June 8, 1860	After sortieing from Guadalajara with his 6,000 troops in pursuit of the liberal army, Miramón finds it dug in along Zapotlán Crest between Ciudad Guzmán and Sayula but still so strong (7,500 men and 40 guns) that he hesitates to attack.
June 15, 1860	The liberal general Jesús González Ortega leads 10,000 men to victory over Gen. Silverio Ramírez's 3,000-man conservative army at the Hacienda of Peñuelas in the state of Aguascalientes, who have been moving southwest to reinforce Miramón at Guadalajara.
June 27, 1860	Miramón installs a 5,000-man garrison under conservative general Severo del Castillo to hold Guadalajara, then hastens into Lagos de Moreno three days later to concentrate his dwindling strength for a showdown in Central Mexico.

Early July 1860 — Miramón shifts his small army from Lagos de Moreno into León, prompted by news of a liberal division under Zaragoza approaching from his southwestern flank to reinforce González Ortega. The two liberal contingents meet at vacated Lagos and continue to press back Miramón.

August 10, 1860 — In full-blown retreat from León toward Querétaro, Miramón's 4,600 men are overtaken by 8,000 liberals under González Ortega and Zaragoza and pulverized in the Battle of Silao.

August 12, 1860 — On this night, Miramón returns to Mexico City with only a handful of retainers, being temporarily obliged to relinquish the presidency by the conservative leadership, although restored to power by a vote of confidence two days afterward.

September 7, 1860 — Having occupied the city of Querétaro, González Ortega leaves behind a garrison and reverses his main army back westward on Degollado's orders to first subdue Guadalajara before commencing any final drive upon the national capital.

September 22, 1860 — González Ortega's liberal army arrives near Guadalajara, being joined four days later by Ogazón's corps, bringing their combined strength to 20,000 men and 125 fieldpieces, their siege commencing by September 27th.

November 1, 1860 — A relief column of 3,000 conservative soldiers under Márquez surrenders at Tepetates Ranch near Zapotlanejo, so Guadalajara's garrison also capitulates two days later.

December 8, 1860 — With liberal armies closing in upon Mexico City from every direction, Miramón surprises the forward-most liberal division of Generals Degollado and Felipe Berriozábal at Toluca, capturing both officers along with 1,400 of their men.

December 22, 1860 — González Ortega's 11,000-man liberal army defeats Miramón's 8,000 troops at the Battle of Calpulalpan, closing in upon the national capital as the conservatives flee.

December 25, 1860 — González Ortega's victorious army enters Mexico City.

May 23, 1861 — Various fugitive conservative leaders such as Márquez, Marcelino Cobos, Juan Vicario, and others reunite and recognize Zuloaga as the "legitimate" president of Mexico, vowing to continue their resistance.

June 1, 1861 — A band of conservative guerrillas capture the retired liberal foreign minister Melchor Ocampo at his rural home and carry him before Márquez and Zuloaga for execution.

June 24, 1861 Márquez surprises Mexico City's liberal garrison by an undetected approach with 2,600 troops and five small guns, only to be driven away by hastily converging liberal forces.

War of the French Intervention (1862–1867)

July 17, 1861 the bankrupt administration of President Juarez suspends all payments on Mexico's 82.2-million-*peso* foreign debt for two years, 70 million of which is owed to British, 9.4 million to Spanish, and 2.8 million to French interests.

August 13, 1861 Márquez's small conservative force is overtaken while resting at the town of Jalatlaco and decimated by González Ortega's 5,000-man liberal division.

October 20, 1861 Another small force under the conservative diehards Márquez, Mejía, and Zuloaga is defeated at Mineral del Chico, just beyond Pachuca in the state of Hidalgo.

October 31, 1861 Leaders in London, Paris, and Madrid sign a pact to send a joint expedition to occupy Veracruz and garnishee customs dues until Mexico's obligations are met.

December 14, 1861 A Spanish-led expedition calls for the surrender of Veracruz, and 5,800 soldiers under Gen. Manuel Gasset occupy the city three days later without resistance.

January 7, 1862 British and French contingents join the Spaniards at Veracruz, and a joint offer is sent inland to Mexico City one week later hinting at a resolution. However, excessive demands by the French delegation hamper any diplomatic progress, while they secretly help Mexican conservative exiles to contact sympathizers in the interior calling for revolts against Juárez.

February 2, 1862 With disease thinning the foreign occupiers' ranks, Mexico's republican authorities are informed that the joint expedition will have to advance inland to healthier cantonments; this threat leads to a renewal of negotiations.

February 19, 1862 A preliminary accord is signed at Orizaba and sent to Europe for ratification.

February 25, 1862 Without waiting for the Orizaba accord to be approved, the 1,800-man French contingent moves inland from Veracruz.

March 6, 1862 Forty-five hundred more French troops land under Gen. Charles Ferdinand Latrille, Comte de Lorencez, and push inland to Córdoba.

April 9, 1862 After lengthy consultations, the British and Spaniards dissolve their association with the French, who are now openly pursuing their own separate agenda for the installation of a puppet regime in Mexico.

April 19, 1862

Lorencez strikes inland from Córdoba with 6,800 troops, occupying Orizaba without resistance the next day. Continuing their march inland one week later, the French are ambushed by a Mexican republican division just past Acultzingo as they push up its steeply winding highway on April 28th.

May 5, 1862

Hoping to fight his way into the city of Puebla, Lorencez charges into the heart of its republican trenches, being repulsed by 6,000 defenders under Gen. Ignacio Zaragoza in the Battle of the Cinco de Mayo.

May 18, 1862

While retreating back toward Orizaba, Lorencez's army is joined by 2,500 conservative Mexican cavalrymen under Gen. Leonardo Márquez, who fight their way past a republican formation at Barranca Seca.

June 10, 1862

Reinforced by republican general Jesús González Ortega, Zaragoza marches out of Acultzingo with 14,000 men to attack Lorencez's army ensconced in Orizaba. The republicans' approach three nights later ends in confusion and retreat after their defeat at Borrego Hill, leaving the invaders waiting in Orizaba to be reinforced from France.

August 28, 1862

Two thousand more French troops arrive at Veracruz to be followed by thousands more over the next several months.

September 8, 1862

Zaragoza dies of typhoid fever in Puebla, being succeeded in command of the republicans' Eastern Army by González Ortega.

September 22, 1862

Gen. Elie Frédéric Forey arrives at Orizaba, having been appointed to succeed Lorencez as commander-in-chief of the French expeditionary force.

Late September 1862

A detachment of 5,400 French troops occupy Jalapa, brushing aside 2,000 mounted Mexican irregulars called *chinacos* under Salvador Díaz Mirón.

November 23, 1862

A French naval squadron raids Tampico, searching for mules and cattle to supply their army farther south.

February 3, 1863

Conservative general Antonio Taboada departs Orizaba with his cavalry brigade to reconnoiter the road leading inland toward Puebla in advance of Forey's main army.

February 22–23, 1863

Forey quits Orizaba with 28,800 men, striking inland behind two advance French columns under his divisional commanders Charles Abel Douay and François Achille Bazaine.

March 16, 1863

Forey's army begins encircling Puebla, isolating

González Ortega's 25,000-man garrison two days later. French siege lines and batteries are laid out, and seven weeks of bombardments and assaults ensue.

April 30, 1863 A company from the newly landed French Foreign Legion fights to the last man against overwhelming odds at the Battle of Camerone.

May 8, 1863 A republican relief force attempting to resupply Puebla is defeated at the Battle of San Lorenzo, and Forey releases numerous prisoners into the starving city to spread this demoralizing news.

May 16, 1863 González Ortega requests terms and surrenders Puebla's garrison the next day; 1,000 republican officers and 16,000 troops are captured (of whom 5,000 will join the victors' ranks).

May 31, 1863 President Juárez and his republican administration abandon Mexico City for San Luis Potosí.

June 4, 1863 Forey's vanguard reaches San Lázaro, just outside of Mexico City, and Márquez's conservative contingent is allowed to lead its triumphal occupation six days later.

June 15, 1863 A new administrative body known as the "Superior Junta" is created and instructed by Forey the next day to appoint Gen. Juan N. Almonte as "provisional president" of Mexico.

July 5, 1863 A French detachment occupies Toluca.

July 10, 1863 Under Forey's guidance, the Superior Junta elevates the country's status into a "Catholic empire" and votes to offer its crown as emperor to the Austrian archduke Maximilian.

July 29, 1863 A Franco-conservative column occupies Cuernavaca.

August 6, 1863 A French landing force takes the port of Tampico.

October 1, 1863 As a reward for his services, Forey is promoted to field marshal and succeeded as commander-in-chief of the French expeditionary forces by Bazaine.

October 3, 1863 In Europe, a Mexican delegation officially offers the throne to Maximilian, who requests that a plebiscite be held to ensure that it truly reflects the Mexican people's will.

October 10, 1863 The conservative Mexican general Tomás Mejía defeats a republican force at Actopan, Hidalgo.

October 23, 1863 Franco-conservative forces occupy Jalapa.

October 27, 1863 A 7,000-man republican army under Gen. Porfirio Díaz overruns the rich mining town of Taxco.

Late October 1863 Douay marches north with a French division from Mexico City toward Querétaro to take control of the Bajío.

November 12, 1863	A French squadron seizes the Pacific port of Mazatlán without opposition. However, a probe inland is repelled 11 days later at Higueras.
November 24, 1863	After clashing with some republican guerrillas near Maravatío, Gen. Armand Alexandre de Castagny's 1st Infantry Division occupies Acámbaro, then Morelia six days later.
December 1, 1863	Culminating a long march, Díaz's footsore republican army establishes itself in his native city of Oaxaca.
December 9, 1863	The cities of Guanajuato, Celaya, and San Miguel Allende are occupied by the French.
December 18, 1863	Republican general José López Uraga's forces attack the conservative garrison under Márquez at Morelia, being repelled and driven south into Jalisco with heavy losses.
December 20, 1863	Threatened by Castagny's and Mejía's parallel drives northward, Juárez abandons his provisional capital of San Luis Potosí in favor of Saltillo. Five days later, San Luis Potosí is occupied by the invaders.
December 27, 1863	Mejía repels an attempt by republican general Miguel Negrete against San Luis Potosí.
January 6, 1864	Guadalajara falls to Franco-conservative forces under Bazaine.
January 15, 1864	The port of Campeche is jointly invested by a French naval squadron and a small Yucatecan army under conservative general Felipe Navarrete, capitulating 11 days later to become incorporated into Yucatán as part of Mexico's new conservative administration.
February 2, 1864	The city of Aguascalientes is occupied by Franco-conservative forces, followed by Zacatecas five days later.
February 27, 1864	Santa Anna returns to Veracruz from his lengthy exile in Colombia, being allowed ashore by Bazaine after promising not to take part in any political activity. However, after almost immediately publishing an appeal to his adherents, the former dictator is deported to Havana aboard the French corvette *Colbert*.
March 29, 1864	Juárez deposes Gov. Santiago Vidaurri of Coahuila and Nuevo León for having hinted at switching to the conservative cause.
April 3, 1864	Juárez temporarily reestablishes his government in the northern city of Monterrey.
April 9, 1864	Maximilian renounces all claims to the Austrian throne and the next day formally accepts the offer of Mexico's crown. Napoleon promises to support him for three years, gradually reducing the size of

the French expeditionary force from 38,000 down to 20,000 men.

May 17, 1864 Mejía and the French colonel Edouard Alphonse Antoine, Baron de Aymard, destroy a republican force under Gen. Manuel Doblado at Matehuala.

May 28, 1864 Maximilian and his Belgian-born consort, Charlotte, reach Veracruz, aboard the Austro-Hungarian frigate *Novara*.

June 3, 1864 The port of Acapulco is captured by five French warships.

June 12, 1864 Maximilian enters Mexico City to a generally warm reception, although many conservatives will soon be offended by some of their idealistic young monarch's liberal notions, while republicans reject him as a foreign puppet.

August 1, 1864 Franco-imperial forces inaugurate a four-pronged offensive against Oaxaca, but its republican defender, Gen. Porfirio Díaz, slips between two French columns and attacks San Antonio Teotitlán in their rear, obliging them to turn back to relieve this town by August 17th. Upon resuming their penetration, the French furthermore learn that Nochixtlán has been heavily fortified, so Bazaine in Mexico City orders the attack columns to retire to their original bases.

December 12, 1864 With the advent of cooler winter weather,

Franco-imperial forces mount a new three-pronged offensive against Oaxaca. Etla is occupied with little difficulty by December 18th.

January 6, 1865 Conservative general Taboada is arrested in Mexico City, suspected of plotting against the emperor.

January 17, 1865 Bazaine reaches Etla to personally assume command over the Franco-imperial army closing in on the city of Oaxaca. A siege is imposed and Díaz surrenders by February 8th, being carried off into captivity.

April 9, 1865 Saltillo is retaken by 3,000 republican troops under Negrete, followed by Monterrey three days later, which has been abandoned by its imperial garrison.

April 23, 1865 Republican colonel Pedro Méndez occupies the border town of Ciudad Victoria, Tamaulipas, while Col. Francisco Naranjo seizes Piedras Negras (opposite Eagle Pass, Texas).

April 30, 1865 Negrete's 4,000 republican troops threaten Mejía's 2,000-man imperial garrison in Matamoros (opposite Brownsville), only to retire the next day because of the disembarkation of French reinforcements at nearby Bagdad plus the possible intervention of defeated Confederate forces out of Texas.

Spring 1865 Notwithstanding the assassination of Pres. Abraham Lincoln, the end of the American Civil War will free Washington to begin increasing diplomatic pressure against the presence of French armed forces in neighboring Mexico as well as supplying weapons to their republican opponents.

May 25, 1865 Fifteen hundred Franco-imperial troops under Foreign Legion general Pierre-Jean Joseph Jeanningros reach San Buenaventura, Coahuila, part of a pincer operation to break up republican concentrations around Saltillo under Negrete and Escobedo. One week later, the Legionnaires encounter the republicans at La Angostura, who repulse Jeanningros's initial assaults and slip away on the night of June 6–7, before Brincourt's pincer can close from Parras.

June 18, 1865 Republican general Arteaga overruns Uruapan, Michoacán, executing its imperial garrison commander and other officials as traitors to Mexico.

September 21, 1865 Republican general Porfirio Díaz escapes from confinement at Puebla, a 1,000-*peso* reward being offered for his recapture.

October 3, 1865 The imperial government decrees that all republican soldiers or guerrillas should be considered as bandits and summarily executed if found under arms. Eighteen days later, General Arteaga and four of his republican officers are executed in reclaimed Uruapan in compliance with this new policy.

October 23, 1865 Escobedo with several thousand men assaults Mejía's imperial garrison in Matamoros, being checked and so settling down to a formal siege until November 14th when the republicans withdraw.

November 23, 1865 Escobedo appears outside Monterrey with his small army, almost overwhelming its Mexican imperial garrison two days later, only to be interrupted by the unexpected arrival of a relief column of French Foreign Legionnaires from Saltillo.

Early January 1866 One thousand French and 1,200 imperial troops sortie from the port of Mazatlán in another vain attempt to chase away the republican guerrillas under Corona who have been hampering their communications inland.

January 4, 1866 Escobedo's republican troops overrun the Gulf port of Bagdad below Matamoros, and because looting threatens American goods, 150 black U.S. Army regulars are dispatched across the border to restore order. They withdraw three weeks later after protests from the Mexican imperial and French authorities.

January 22, 1866	In Paris, Napoleon—under increasing domestic and international pressure to withdraw from Mexico—declares the intervention a success then dispatches a delegation to Maximilian to discuss accelerating French troop withdrawals. In order to make up for their loss, Austrian and Belgian mercenaries are encouraged to volunteer for the imperial cause.
February 12, 1866	Republican forces seize the town of Parras, only to be chased out eight days later by four companies of French Foreign Legionnaires; but when two of these companies subsequently try to surprise the republican camp on February 28th, only a single Legionnaire out of 182 returns alive.
March 4, 1866	At Río Frío, a Belgian delegation is attacked by republican guerrillas—who kill General Forey, who is accompanying these visitors.
April 1, 1866	Escobedo attacks Matehuala and then sends a detachment to loot the rich mining camp of Real de Catorce.
April 11, 1866	Republican general Nicolás Régules surprises and overwhelms the Belgian garrison holding Tacámbaro, Michoacán.
June 1, 1866	In anticipation of making an orderly withdrawal from Mexico, French units begin to be recalled from outposts throughout the interior to reassemble around the capital.
June 16, 1866	Having already checked one Franco-imperial column of 2,000 troops from Monterrey, Escobedo annihilates a second like-size force from Matamoros at the Battle of Santa Gertrudis.
June 22, 1866	Mejía abandons Matamoros with 600 remaining imperial troops.
July 8, 1866	The empress Carlota departs Mexico City for Paris to beseech Napoleon to maintain his French army in Mexico.
July 26, 1866	The French Foreign Legion commander Jeanningros abandons Monterrey.
August 1, 1866	Tampico is taken by a surprise republican assault.
September 14, 1866	The French evacuate the port of Guaymas, Sonora.
October 3, 1866	Republican general Porfirio Díaz defeats a pursuing Franco-imperial force at the Battle of Miahuatlán, allowing him to lay siege to the few remaining defenders of Oaxaca City. He then defeats a second Franco-imperial relief column at the Battle of La Carbonera on October 18th, leading to the capitulation of the city by month's end.
October 21, 1866	Washington recognizes Juárez's republican government as the sole

legitimate representative of the Mexican people. This same day, Maximilian reaches Orizaba to meet an aide-de-camp from Napoleon sent to persuade him to abdicate the Mexican throne and return to Europe.

November 12, 1866 Corona's republican forces occupy the evacuated port of Mazatlán.

December 1, 1866 Swayed by such conservative leaders as Márquez and Miramón, Maximilian decides to remain on as emperor, even though the French military will soon withdraw completely. Five days later, he offers any Austro-Belgian volunteers the option of joining his imperial Mexican army with higher ranks rather than departing.

December 19, 1866 Porfirio Díaz sorties from Oaxaca City to clear the Isthmus of Tehuantepec of its Franco-imperial garrisons.

Early January 1867 San Luis Potosí is reoccupied without opposition by an advancing republican army under Gen. Jerónimo Treviño.

January 10, 1867 The French general Castelnau receives orders from Paris to begin reembarking the final units (Foreign Legion, Austrian and Belgian contingents, etc.) for their return toward Europe; within a month, most will be going aboard ship at Veracruz.

Mexican Revolution (1910–1924)

September 27, 1910 Eighty-year-old president Porfirio Díaz's latest reelection is certified by his compliant Congress, despite having been won through orchestrating the detention of his high-minded northern challenger, Francisco I. Madero, and 60,000 of his adherents.

October 4, 1910 With the issue of the presidential election apparently decided, Madero is allowed to escape from loose confinement at San Luis Potosí and ride across the border into asylum at San Antonio, Texas, from where he issues a call for a nationwide uprising to commence on November 20th.

November 20, 1910 Numerous outbreaks erupt throughout northern Mexico with rebels overrunning isolated federal outposts in remote towns and villages and then defeating the small detachments of troops or *rurales* sent in by rail to suppress them.

November 27, 1910 A rebel force under ex-teamster Pascual Orozco ambushes a federal column under Gen. Juan N. Navarro at Pedernales then descends upon Ciudad Guerrero, capturing it after a brief siege.

December 18, 1910 Orozco's rebels ambush two trains bearing almost 600 *federales* in Malpaso Canyon, Chihuahua, driving them back with heavy losses and creating

February 2, 1911
Orozco threatens Ciudad Juárez (opposite El Paso, Texas) with three trainloads of rebels, withdrawing when federal reinforcements arrive three days later.

February 4, 1911
A small revolutionary band takes the Zacatecan town of Nieves, and more attacks ensue in this state and neighboring Durango as the Revolution spreads.

March 6, 1911
Madero personally leads 800 men in an attack against the depleted federal garrison at Casas Grandes, Chihuahua, only to be wounded and repulsed; other rebel leaders will nonetheless rally to his side.

Late March 1911
A second major insurrection breaks out in the southern state of Morelos, soon to be led by the charismatic Emiliano Zapata.

April 19, 1911
Madero arrives to besiege the 700-man federal garrison holding the border town of Ciudad Juárez under Gen. Juan N. Navarro, with 3,500 ill-disciplined revolutionaries (Orozco serving as a "general" and the former bandit Pancho Villa as a "colonel" among this throng). After two weeks of talks, the impatient Orozco and Villa precipitate a firefight that allows them to

a sensation throughout Mexico by diminishing the regime's aura of invincibility.

overwhelm its defenses surrender by May 10th. Three days later, they fall out with Madero for not permitting the execution of Navarro.

May 12, 1911
Zapata's peasant army besieges the federal garrison at Cuautla, Morelos, fighting their way inside after six days of fierce fighting.

May 15, 1911
Maderista forces chase the 1,700-man federal garrison out of Torreón, Coahuila, more than 300 Chinese civilians being massacred during the ensuing rebel entry.

May 21, 1911
Cuernavaca, Morelos, is evacuated by its federal garrison.

May 24, 1911
Anti-Díaz riots break out in the main square of Mexico City, so the octogenarian dictator finally decides to relinquish office the next day and depart for Veracruz, sailing away into European exile.

May 26, 1911
A 500-man revolutionary force enters the city of San Luis Potosí, deposing its governor the next day.

May 31, 1911
The revolutionary "colonel" Benigno N. Zenteno occupies the state capital of Tlaxcala at the head of 3,000 men.

June 7, 1911
A few hours after a heavy earthquake has killed 207 people in Mexico City, Madero makes a triumphal entry into the shaken capital.

June 12, 1911 Madero visits the state of Morelos, where Zapata has refused to disarm his revolutionary followers or restore any captured lands.

June 22, 1911 Orozco's army triumphantly enters Chihuahua City, transforming it into his headquarters.

July 13, 1911 After Zapatista troops stationed in Puebla begin arresting civilians, federal troops under Col. Aureliano Blanquet attack the Zapatista encampment, killing 80 and wounding 200 of these unruly occupiers.

August 8, 1911 The former Porfirian general Victoriano Huerta is dispatched into Cuernavaca with 1,000 federal troops to keep an eye on Zapata, who grudgingly demobilizes part of his peasant army.

August 22, 1911 The new governor of Morelos, appointed by interim federal authorities, executes 70 Zapatistas in Jojutla.

August 31, 1911 Ignoring Madero's calls for restraint, Huerta occupies Cuautla and orders Zapata's arrest, who flees into the hills.

October 10, 1911 Zapata reoccupies Cuautla with 1,500 followers.

November 6, 1911 Having won a special presidential election, Madero officially assumes office in Mexico City.

November 11, 1911 Zapata narrowly escapes capture by federal troops and once again flees from Cuautla.

November 27, 1911 Zapata publicly disavows Madero's presidency because of his apparent unwillingness to cede land to the peasants.

December 13, 1911 The former Porfirian general Bernardo Reyes crosses the border from Texas, calling for a conservative uprising against Madero although surrendering to the authorities at Linares, Nuevo León, by Christmas Day.

February 6, 1912 Zapata's subordinate, Genovevo de la O, launches a series of attacks against Cuernavaca to which its federal garrison retaliates by razing the town of Santa María Ahuacatitlán.

February 10, 1912 Federal troops seize Zapata's mother-in-law, one of his sisters, and several brothers-in-law to serve as hostages.

February 15, 1912 Gen. Juvencio Robles, newly appointed federal commander for the state of Morelos, launches a terror campaign against Zapatista resistance by ordering the town of Nexpa to be burned followed by a half dozen others over the next few days.

March 3, 1912 The disaffected Orozco rises in Chihuahua City against Madero, accusing him of failing to carry out the Revolution's promise although actually resentful at being passed over for preferment. A few days later, he will begin moving southward with 7,000 well-equipped irregulars aboard several trains to confront Gen. José González Salas—a relative of Madero by marriage, who has resigned his position as war minister to put down this revolt.

March 25, 1912
Near Rellano station in southern Chihuahua, González's vanguard is devastated by a runaway Orozquista locomotive sent flying down the track filled with dynamite by Emilio P. Campa, then the trapped Maderistas are decimated as they detrain. Wounded and despondent, González orders a retreat into Torreón and commits suicide at Bermejillo.

April 1, 1912
Zapatista forces occupy Tepoztlán, and Jonacatepec five days later.

April 12, 1912
Huerta reaches Torreón to assume command over González Salas's defeated army. Tightening its organization, he advances northward into Chihuahua to inflict a series of defeats on Orozco in a summerlong campaign, which culminates with this rebel leader being wounded during an assault against the garrison holding the border town of Ojinaga on September 11th and seeking refuge in the United States.

April 26, 1912
Col. Pedro León's "Sierra Juárez" Battalion mutinies against Madero in Oaxaca City, attempting to take over this capital a few days later,

only to be driven out into the countryside and its commander executed by June.

October 16, 1912
Brig. Gen. Félix Díaz, nephew of the departed dictator Porfirio Díaz, leads the Veracruz garrison in a conservative rebellion against Madero, only to be checked by loyal forces within a week and arrested on October 23rd.

February 9, 1913
Generals Manuel Mondragón and Gregorio Ruiz mutiny against Madero in Mexico City, setting off 10 days of fighting that will claim 5,000 civilian lives and be remembered as the *Decena Trágica* or "Tragic Fortnight." Eventually, Madero is betrayed and murdered by Huerta on February 22nd, who usurps the office of president.

February 24, 1913
Many officials and noteworthy guerrilla chieftains in northern Mexico rise in revolt against the usurper Huerta, including Venustiano Carranza, the 53-year-old governor of Coahuila.

March 13, 1913
The Sonoran militia colonel Álvaro Obregón carries the border town of Nogales by assault, driving its 100-man Huertista garrison and 300 *rurales* under Col. Emilio Kosterlitzky into internment in Arizona.

March 17, 1913
In Chihuahua, the renegade Orozco accepts the rank of brigadier general in command

of *colorado* auxiliaries assisting Huerta's federal army.

April 15, 1913
After heavy fighting at Naco and Agua Prieta, Sonora, Obregón and Manuel M. Diéguez defeat all remaining Huertista forces along the U.S. border, thereby facilitating the purchase of more arms and ammunition.

April 17, 1913
Several months of peace are shattered in Morelos when General Robles deposes its state government and assumes office as Huerta's military governor. Zapata furthermore surprises the Huertistas garrisoning Jonacatepec, whose commander defects to the rebel cause after a day and a half of desperate fighting.

April 18, 1913
Pánfilo Natera, an ex-corporal in the *rurales*, surprises Jerez in the state of Zacatecas with 400 riders, absorbing its 100-man federal garrison into his ranks.

April 23, 1913
Zapata besieges the Huertista garrison in Cuautla yet is unable to subdue its defenders because of a lack of artillery. A fortnight later, some of his revolutionaries will blow up a military train and kill 100 federal troops, provoking brutal reprisals against civilians.

May 8, 1913
Natera circles Fresnillo, Zacatecas, and is joined by almost all of its federal garrison.

May 9, 1913
After witnessing the arrival of 3,000 Huertista reinforcements at the Pacific port of Guaymas, Obregón's small revolutionary army retreats north and makes a stand at Santa Rosa on May 12th, defeating the pursuing *federales* next day.

June 1, 1913
Natera takes the city of Zacatecas, although it will be recaptured two weeks later by Huertista general José Delgado.

June 4, 1913
Pablo González's small revolutionary army seizes the border town of Matamoros (opposite Brownsville, Texas).

June 18, 1913
The revolutionary "colonel" Tomás Urbina seizes the city of Durango.

June 20, 1913
Obregón defeats a Huertista force at Santa María, Sonora, then does the same one week later at San Alejandro, driving his beaten foes back inside Guaymas and besieging them.

August 19, 1913
Huertista troops overrun Zapata's base at Huautla, Morelos, but the rebel chieftain escapes into the hills.

August 26, 1913
With 700 riders, Villa wins his first independent victory by defeating Gen. Félix Terrazas's 1,300-man Huertista force at San Andrés, near Riva Palacio, southwest of the state capital of Chihuahua.

September 15, 1913
Villa's 700 riders incorporate Maclovio Herrera's 400 at Santa Rosalía de Camargo,

then Urbina's 600 at Jiménez, being further reinforced by contingents under Orestes Pereyra and Calixto Contreras as they press on for a joint attempt against the beleaguered 3,500 Huertistas and *colorados* holding Torreón.

September 29, 1913

Villa's following, now swollen to 10,000 men and dubbed the *División del Norte* or "Northern Division," advance upon Torreón in an unstoppable wave and overrun that city by October 1st, heavy losses being suffered on both sides.

Late October 1913

Leaving Contreras to garrison Torreón, Villa leads a train convoy north to launch repeated assaults against Chihuahua City without being able to subdue its Huertista defenders under Gen. Salvador R. Mercado.

November 14, 1913

Obregón's newly created *Ejército del Noroeste* or "Army of the Northwest" captures Culiacán and cuts off the Huertista-held port of Mazatlán, gathering further strength for a major spring offensive into central Mexico.

November 15, 1913

Villa glides undetected into Ciudad Juárez with 2,000 men hidden aboard a captured train, capturing the city with ease.

November 18, 1913

Pablo González's small *Ejército del Noreste* or "Army of the Northeast" captures Ciudad Victoria, Tamaulipas,

followed by Nuevo Laredo and Guerrero.

November 23, 1913

Villa's 6,200-man *División del Norte* fights a set-piece battle at the Tierra Blanca railway station south of Ciudad Juárez, defeating the 5,500 *federales* and *colorados* sent as a relief force from Chihuahua City.

December 8, 1913

Villa occupies Chihuahua City unopposed.

December 10, 1913

A Huertista army under Maj. Gen. José Refugio Velasco reclaims Torreón.

January 10, 1914

Villa pulverizes the defeated *federales* and *colorados* reconcentrated in the border town of Ojinaga, ending all Huertista resistance in the state of Chihuahua.

March 12, 1914

Zapata arrives to besiege Cuautla with 5,000 revolutionaries, overwhelming its Huertista garrison 11 days later.

March 16, 1914

Villa departs Chihuahua City with a vanguard contingent of 8,200 men aboard 15 trains to reconquer Torreón. He surprises its 7,000 federal defenders and 6,000 *colorado* irregulars 4 days later, overwhelming its suburb of Gómez Palacio and the city itself after 11 days of bloody combat.

March 23, 1914

Zapata captures Chilpancingo, Guerrero.

April 5, 1914

Villa proceeds 32 miles east of shattered Torreón and in

another week of heavy fighting defeats 6,200 federal reinforcements who have been joined by the survivors from his triumph at Torreón.

April 8, 1914   Zapata captures Iguala, followed shortly thereafter by Taxco, bringing all of Morelos under his control.

April 21, 1914   Wishing to punish Huerta by intercepting an arms shipment scheduled to arrive from Europe, U.S. president Woodrow Wilson authorizes the disembarkation of a naval landing force to seize Veracruz.

May 16, 1914   Villa routs the remnants of Velasco's defeated Huertista army at Paredón, Coahuila.

June 22, 1914   Villa arrives with 25,000 troops and 50 guns to assault Zacatecas, annihilating its 12,000 Huertista defenders in a ferocious battle the next day.

July 6, 1914   Obregón engages a portion of Guadalajara's 12,000 Huertista defenders at Orendáin, utterly routing them over two days of wide-ranging fighting.

July 14, 1914   Following the twin disasters at Zacatecas and Orendáin, Huerta resigns the presidency and flees, appointing Francisco S. Carvajal as his interim successor.

July 20, 1914   Pablo González's Army of the Northeast takes the city of San Luis Potosí without opposition.

August 1, 1914   Obregón's Army of the Northwest unites at Querétaro with Pablo González's Army of the Northeast, together driving toward Mexico City.

August 13, 1914   At Teoloyucan outside of Mexico City, Obregón signs a treaty with representatives from the federal government that officially dissolves the Huertista administration as well as much of the regular 30,000-man Mexican Army and 10,000 *rurales*. Only those troops deployed south of the capital to contain Zapata's peasant revolutionaries are to temporarily remain in position.

August 18, 1914   Obregón's 18,000-man Army of the Northwest enters Mexico City in triumph, followed two days later by the "first chief" Carranza, who unilaterally assumes office as president.

August 22, 1914   The disgruntled governor of Sonora, José María Maytorena, approaches the border town of Nogales with 2,000 men, obliging its Carrancista garrison under Gen. Benjamín Hill and Col. Plutarco Elías Calles to evacuate. Maytorena enters Nogales triumphantly the next day, so Villa and Obregón subsequently travel by train through El Paso, Texas, to meet with Maytorena on August 28th in an unsuccessful bid to mediate this dispute.

September 5, 1914 Carranza, who has refused Zapata access to Mexico City, furthermore rejects the revolutionary leader's land claims on behalf of his peasant followers, so Zapata openly defies Carranza's self-proclaimed rule from Cuernavaca three days later.

September 22, 1914 Villa refuses to acknowledge Carranza as president, so neither Villistas nor Zapatistas will attend the constitutional convention held in Mexico City on October 1st.

November 6, 1914 The constitutional convention, transferred out of Mexico City into neutral Aguascalientes, recognizes "general" and former mine foreman Eulalio Gutiérrez as interim president of Mexico. Carranza refuses to accept this nomination, so he is labeled a rebel four days later, and Gutiérrez appoints Villa as "head of military operations" to drive Carranza out of Mexico.

November 12, 1914 Zapata also declares war against Carranza.

November 13, 1914 American secretary of state Bryan announces that Veracruz will be evacuated by its U.S. occupiers within 10 days.

November 18, 1914 Threatened by the simultaneous advance of Villa's División del Norte plus Zapata's guerrillas out of the southwest, Carranza quits his temporary Orizaba encampment for Veracruz, establishing his provisional government there eight days later.

November 23, 1914 The last American troops depart Veracruz, Gen. Cándido Aguilar's division arriving to reestablish Mexican control.

November 24, 1914 After Obregón's depleted 4,000-man garrison abandons Mexico City for Veracruz, Zapata occupies its southern suburbs without opposition two days later.

December 1, 1914 Villa appears at Mexico City's northern suburb of Tacuba and three days later meets Zapata at Xochimilco. On December 6th, their combined armies—numbering perhaps as many as 50,000 men—parade through the capital.

December 12, 1914 Carrancista general Diéguez evacuates Guadalajara for Ciudad Guzmán, allowing a Villista contingent to occupy the city uncontested five days later.

December 17, 1914 The conventionalist general Ángeles departs Mexico City at the head of 5,500 troops to reclaim the northern city of Monterrey. He will be joined en route by an additional 4,500 men at Torreón, eventually commanding 11,000 troops that brush aside a Carrancista formation under Gen. Antonio I. Villarreal at Ramos Arizpe and gain Monterrey by January 5, 1915.

January 5, 1915 After defeating a depleted Zapatista garrison at

Tecamachalco, Obregón (now "general-in-chief" of Carranza's armies) takes the city of Puebla with his 12,000 troops.

January 17, 1915 Having united with Murguía, Diéguez leads 9,000 Carrancistas north to assault Guadalajara, defeating its 10,000 Villista defenders in a two-day battle.

January 28, 1915 Obregón reenters Mexico City—which has been abandoned earlier by both its Villista and Zapatista occupiers—with 9,000 troops.

January 30, 1915 Guadalajara is struck by 3,500 Villista raiders, who are ejected by its Carrancista garrison, leaving behind 400 dead.

February 11, 1915 Because of mounting pressure from Villa, Diéguez evacuates Guadalajara for Ciudad Guzmán.

March 5, 1915 A Villista column under General Chao attacks Pablo González's Carrancista garrison, which is holding the seaport of Tampico, only to be repelled.

March 10, 1915 Obregón abandons starving Mexico City and the next day reaches Tula, Hidalgo, massing his forces to press deeper into central Mexico and challenge Villa to a pitched battle.

April 1, 1915 Obregón occupies the city of Querétaro, then Celaya three days later, learning that Villa's army has just entered Irapuato, 30 miles to the west.

April 6, 1915 Villa departs Salamanca with 20,000 men and 22 artillery pieces, smashing into Obregón's 5,000 infantrymen and 6,000 cavalry troopers who arc dug in at Celaya with 86 machine guns and 13 cannon. After an epic two-day battle, Villa reels back in defeat.

April 13, 1915 Villa makes a second huge attack with 30,000 men against Obregón in Celaya, whose own strength has been increased to 15,000 men, and once again inflicts a stinging defeat on the Villistas.

April 19, 1915 Obregón occupies Salamanca, then Irapuato two days later, while Villa's shattered *División del Norte* retreats northwestward.

April 25, 1915 An Obregonista column occupies Guanajuato City.

April 28, 1915 Obregón enters Silao with his main army and the next day contacts Villista forces again, farther to its northwest.

May 7, 1915 Obregón reaches the rural Trinidad railway station and entrenches his 14,300 infantry and 9,400 cavalry on the open plains, receiving Villa's opening attacks five days later. Wary because of his recent defeats and with only 19,500 riders and 6,000 foot soldiers under his command, Villa proceeds cautiously, yet (despite Obregón losing an arm to an artillery round) the

Villistas are nonetheless routed and in full retreat by June 5th.

June 3, 1915
Oaxaca declares itself to be a sovereign state, refusing to acknowledge the authority of Carranza or any other federal leader.

June 8, 1915
Villista general Máximo García evacuates Ciudad Victoria, Tamaulipas.

June 24, 1915
Huerta and Orozco are arrested by U.S. authorities in El Paso, Texas, for violating American neutrality laws by plotting to rejoin the fighting in Mexico.

July 2, 1915
As Villa's defeated División del Norte limps northward, his henchman Rodolfo Fierro begins a series of raids in the Obregonista rear, slowing their pursuit of the retreating Villistas.

July 6, 1915
After a brief convalescence, Obregón resumes command over his army, driving northward in pursuit of Villa.

July 8, 1915
Obregón defeats Villa's rearguard at Calvillo Ravine, then occupies the city of Aguascalientes two days later.

July 28, 1915
Fierro's 4,000 riders blunder into Obregón's army in the Mariscala Hills near the city of Querétaro, being badly beaten two days later at Jerécuaro.

July 30, 1915
A Zapatista contingent under Gen. Amador Salazar is defeated near Mexico City.

August 10, 1915
Obregón's subordinate, Pablo González, reoccupies Mexico City.

August 30, 1915
Outside El Paso (Texas), the exiled Orozco is murdered along with four companions.

September 4, 1915
Obregón wins a clash at La Angostura and shortly thereafter reoccupies Saltillo.

October 19, 1915
The United States, Argentina, Bolivia, Brazil, Chile, Guatemala, and Uruguay recognize Carranza as de facto president of Mexico.

November 2, 1915
Villa's 6,000 remaining troops are easily beaten in four failed nocturnal assaults against Calles's 6,500 fresh Carrancista defenders at Agua Prieta, Sonora.

November 8, 1915
Seeking to reassert federal rule over the breakaway state of Oaxaca, Carrancista general Jesús Agustín Castro departs Chiapas with the 21st Division and seizes Salina Cruz, soon followed by other contingents.

November 18, 1915
Villa's 5,000 survivors fight a costly battle against a superior Carrancista force outside Sonora's capital of Hermosillo and are almost annihilated four days later in another all-out assault, so Villa retires eastward with only 1,400 followers, eventually reaching Chihuahua City to disband his división.

December 24, 1915
Villa disappears from Chihuahua City, eight days before

Carrancista general Treviño arrives to reoccupy this state capital.

March 2, 1916 After pushing inland from Puerto Ángel, a small Carrancista army under Generals Macario M. Hernández and Juan José Baños defeats a separatist force at Ocotlán then three days later occupies deserted Oaxaca City.

March 9, 1916 Villa emerges from hiding to make a lightning raid against Columbus, New Mexico, then immediately flees back across the border.

March 15, 1916 Two columns of 3,000 U.S. troops cross the border at Palomas, Chihuahua, to pursue Villa, inaugurating a protracted yet fruitless penetration that will become known as the Pershing Expedition.

May 2, 1916 The Carrancista general Pablo González launches an offensive—complete with air support—against the Zapatistas in Morelos by bringing in 30,000 troops occupy almost all major towns over the next four days then further establishing concentration camps to stifle guerrilla resistance.

May 8, 1916 González's subordinate, Rafael Cepeda, executes 225 Zapatista prisoners in Jiutepec.

May 15, 1916 Félix Díaz—nephew of Oaxaca's native son, former president Porfirio Díaz—returns from exile and joins this state's separatist movement. His grandly named *Ejército Reorganizador Nacional* or "National Reorganizer Army" is promptly defeated by Carrancista forces at Yucucundo in June, then Tlalcolula in July, obliging Díaz to retreat northeast toward the Chiapas-Veracruz border.

June 1916 González's forces overrun Tlaltizapán—Zapata's main hideaway, south of Cuernavaca (Morelos)—slaughtering 286 unarmed men, women, and children.

July 6, 1916 Villa rejoins his followers—now 1,000 strong—at San Juan Bautista on the Chihuahua-Durango border then leads them northward to forage for supplies.

July 16, 1916 Despite being seriously weakened by González's offensive, a Zapatista column attacks the Carrancista garrison at Tlayacapan (Morelos), retiring after six hours' heavy fighting to assault Tlaltizapán the next day.

August 1, 1916 Carranza calls out troops to put down a general strike in Mexico City.

September 16, 1916 The previous night, Villa infiltrated 1,000 riders into Chihuahua City then at 3:00 a.m. on September 16th—Mexico's Independence Day—surprised its Carrancista garrison under Treviño. After seizing much booty, giving a speech from the municipal balcony, and recruiting an additional 1,500 men, Villa disappears as suddenly as he has materialized.

Late September 1916   In order to relieve his despairing followers in Morelos, Zapata advances across the mountains to threaten Mexico City, in turn prompting Carrancista colonel Jesús María Guajardo to execute 180 captives in Tlaltizapán and raze much of its surrounding district.

October 4, 1916   Zapata seizes the Xochimilco pumping station, cutting off much of Mexico City's water supply, then retires after destroying the railway lines at Peña Pobre.

November 7, 1916   Zapatista guerrillas blow up a train, killing more than 400 passengers.

November 23, 1916   Villa again captures Chihuahua City, occupying it for a week before emerging to confront Murguía's approaching Carrancista army on Horcasitas Plain. In a seven-hour engagement on December 1st, Villa is badly beaten and compelled to abandon a trainload of provisions while retreating toward Satevo.

December 1, 1916   With González's occupation forces now grown weak due to neglect, desertion, and disease—7,000 Carrancistas reportedly lying sick of malaria—Zapata's battered forces are able to recuperate Tlaltizapán then launch a major offensive to regain control over the state of Morelos.

December 22, 1916   Villa with perhaps as many as 5,000 riders surprises the Carrancista garrison at Torreón, overrunning its defenses and looting the city before departing five days later.

January 7, 1917   Zapata reoccupies Jonacatepec, followed by Yautepec, Cuautla, and numerous other towns, including Cuernavaca.

January 28, 1917   The U.S. government announces its withdrawal of the Pershing Expedition, and eight days later the last American troops depart Chihuahua.

May 1, 1917   After holding an election in which he received 198,000 of 250,000 votes cast (out of 3 million potential voters throughout Mexico) Carranza assumes the presidency, while his top general, Obregón, retires modestly into private life at his birthplace of Navojoa, Sonora.

May 7, 1917   Zapata's longtime subordinate, Leonardo Vázquez, is executed at Buenavista de Cuellar for turning against his former chief, the same fate befalling Zapata's secretary and mentor, Otilio Montaño, 11 days later.

June 18, 1917   With Zapatista support melting away, Zapata's brother,

Eufemio, is murdered by a turncoat at Cuautla.

November 19, 1917 Pablo González shells and recaptures Cuautla then shortly thereafter overwhelms the Zapatista garrisons at Jonacatepec and Zacualpan de Amilpas.

February 8, 1918 After being captured at San Bernardino, Oaxaca, separatist general Alberto Córdova is executed in the state capital by a Carrancista firing squad.

October 1918 González advances out of Cuautla with 11,000 Carrancista troops, sweeping through Zapatista strongholds now laid low by starvation and disease—mostly due to the outbreak of Spanish influenza—so Zapata is obliged to flee into the mountains with a handful of adherents.

December 11, 1918 Ex-Porfirian general Felipe Ángeles returns from exile in the United States, attempting to organize yet another revolutionary uprising with Villa.

April 10, 1919 In a prearranged plot, Zapata is lured into a meeting at the Hacienda of Chinameca and murdered by a sudden volley.

May 31, 1919 Separatist governor José Inés Dávila is defeated and killed at Ixtayutla (Oaxaca), his head being displayed in the state capital.

June 1, 1919 In Nogales (Sonora), Obregón announces he will contest the presidency in Mexico's forthcoming elections, running against Carranza's handpicked successor, Ignacio Bonillas. The president—already jealous of Obregón's popularity—actively obstructs his campaign.

June 17, 1919 Zapatista resistance having ceased with the death of their chieftain, Pablo González departs Morelos for Puebla, leaving occupation duties to his subordinates.

June 1919 Villa and Ángeles capture the border city of Juárez, only to be driven out by U.S. troops from adjacent El Paso (Texas)—an intervention that again provokes a downturn in relations between Mexico City and Washington.

November 15, 1919 Ángeles is captured in hiding near Balleza (Chihuahua) and executed 11 days later in its state capital on Carranza's orders, despite widespread pleas for clemency.

December 27, 1919 Meixueiro, one of the last remaining separatist leaders in Oaxaca, surrenders to Pablo González.

January 1920 Pablo González announces that he too will run for president, on the *Liga Democrática* or "Democratic League" ticket.

Early April 1920 Obregón is made to appear before a military tribunal in Mexico City, falsely accused of conspiring to overthrow Carranza's government.

World War II (1941–1945)

April 19, 1941
Rear Adm. Luis Hurtado de Mendoza, on orders from Pres. Manuel Ávila Camacho, sends Marines from the 31st Battalion to impound nine Italian vessels idled at Tampico plus another three German merchantmen lying at Veracruz.

September 4, 1941
Washington orders implementation of "Western Hemisphere Defense Plan Number 4," which among other dictates authorizes U.S. Navy escorts to include non-American vessels in their convoys.

December 9, 1941
Germany and Italy, Japan's Axis partners in Europe, declare war against the United States.

December 11, 1941
Cuba joins the United States and declares war against the Axis powers.

January 12, 1942
German U-boats begin sinking Allied vessels off of North America and in the next month expand their offensive in Caribbean waters as well.

May 13, 1942
While sailing past Miami, the neutral Mexican oil tanker *Potrero del Llano* is sunk by a German submarine, with the loss of 15 of its 35-man crew. The Mexican government lodges a protest with Berlin, which is ignored.

May 20, 1942
The 6,000-ton Mexican tanker *Faja de Oro*, returning in ballast toward its home port of Tampico, Tamaulipas, after making a delivery at Marcus Hook, Pennsylvania, is torpedoed near Key West at 4:21 a.m. by the German submarine *U-106* of Capt. Lt. Hermann Rasch, resulting in the death of 8 of the tanker's 36-man crew.

May 22, 1942
Mexico declares a "state of war" with the Axis powers.

Modern Era (1950–Present)

June 24, 1953
Having failed to capture the Moncada Barracks in Santiago de Cuba with a rebel assault, the young political agitator Fidel Castro Ruz is exiled to Mexico by the regime of Gen. Fulgencio Batista.

December 1, 1956
Castro sails from the small port of Tuxpan, Veracruz, with 82 adherents aboard the yacht *Granma*, including the young Argentine medical student Ernesto "Che" Guevara, to mount a second successful guerrilla campaign against Cuba's Batista regime.

September 15, 1961
On this evening in San Luis Potosí's main square, several followers of the upstart gubernatorial candidate Dr. Salvador Nava Martínez are shot dead, after which soldiers detain him and destroy the *Tribuna* newspaper office so as to maintain the PRI Party's stranglehold on power.

May 18, 1967

In the impoverished town of Atoyac de Álvarez, Guerrero, a teachers' protest led by the 30-year-old union organizer Lucio Cabañas is dispersed with gunfire, five protesters being slain. Cabañas flees into the mountains to begin creating a grassroots rebel movement called the *Partido de los Pobres* or "Party of the Poor."

October 2, 1968

Amid mounting political turmoil in Mexico City, which is about to host the Summer Olympic Games, a protest march by university students ends at the Plaza de las Tres Culturas, where over 200 are killed and thousands injured by gunfire from army troops, being remembered as the "Tlatelolco Massacre."

November 14, 1968

Mexican troops begin counterguerrilla sweeps through the rugged Atoyac Range of Guerrero, vainly searching for the tiny bands led by Lucio Cabañas and Genaro Vázquez. Army morale is low on account of poor pay, rusting equipment, and public disapproval.

Mid-December 1969

While attending horse races in Mexico City, Panamanian strongman Omar Torrijos is deposed by a military coup back home, returning on December 16th aboard a private plane lent to him by Nicaraguan dictator Anastasio Somoza to reclaim his office.

July 25, 1970

Having failed to locate Cabañas's and Vázquez's guerrilla bands, the Mexican Army launches a new "hearts and minds" campaign dubbed *Operación Amistad* or "Operation Friendship" in the Atoyac range in hopes of gaining local collaborators. Within weeks, it is abandoned as an abject failure.

May 1, 1971

The government of newly inaugurated president Luis Echeverría authorizes his defense secretary, Gen. Hermenegildo Cuenca Díaz, to implement *Operación Telaraña* or "Operation Cobweb": the extralegal detention of scores of family members or associates of the guerrilla leaders Cabañas and Vázquez so as to help find and kill them. Some 24,000 troops—a third of the active-duty Mexican Army—will be committed to Guerrero in support of these sweeps, failing to produce any results beyond alienating the civilian populace.

June 10, 1971

To quell a wave of violent leftist street protests gripping Mexico City, Echeverría also unleashes a shadowy paramilitary group nicknamed the *Halcones* or "Hawks," secretly raised and trained by Col. Manuel Díaz Escobar. They kill 23 and injure some 200–300 protesters in a clash photographed by newsmen, so Colonel Díaz's group is quickly disavowed and dissolved.

June 25, 1972
Cabañas and 20 companions ambush a Mexican Army convoy at Arroyo Las Piñas near San Andrés de la Cruz, Guerrero, killing 10 soldiers and wounding 18.

August 23, 1972
A second ambush by Cabañas at nearby Arroyo Oscuro results in 18 more soldiers dead, 9 wounded, and 11 captured, goading the army into a series of brutal reprisals throughout the region with five fresh infantry battalions and thousands of state policemen.

November 11, 1973
Another ambush by Cabañas on a 300-man army convoy between Yerbasantita and Las Compuertas leaves four soldiers dead. The authorities launch *Operación Luciérnaga* or "Operation Firefly," sending a trio of heavily armed, mobile columns in pursuit of the guerrilla, who avoids this chase, which is soon wound down.

June 2, 1974
After three days of secret negotiations between Cabañas and Sen. Rubén Figueroa Figueroa of Guerrero, the guerrilla chieftain seizes his guest and holds him for ransom. This sparks massive military roundups and sweeps throughout the region, which fail to corner Cabañas.

August 5, 1974
Gen. Salvador Rangel Medina is relieved of command in

Guerrero and replaced by Gen. Eliseo Jiménez Ruiz.

September 8, 1974
Having received a ransom of 50 million *pesos* for the captive Figueroa, 60 elite troops under Lt. Col. Juan López Ruiz intercept his guerrilla guards as they approach El Huicón to release him, killing 3 and scattering the rest.

October 11, 1974
Chased by 5,000 Mexican troops since the freeing of Senator Figueroa, Cabañas and 14 companions are surprised near Los Toronjos in the Tecpan Range, Guerrero. Escaping over Achotla Mountain after nightfall, he is left with only four followers, while his mother, wife, and three-week-old daughter will also be captured two weeks later at Tixtla.

December 2, 1974
Guided by a captive, soldiers of the 19th Battalion under Capt. Pedro Bravo Torres overtake Cabañas's fugitive band at 9:00 a.m. near El Ototal, 12 miles northwest of Tecpan de Galeana, killing him along with his three remaining followers. Two soldiers are slain and five wounded during the exchange of gunfire, which virtually ends all revolutionary movement in the mountains of Guerrero.

January 1, 1994
Timed to embarrass Mexico's government by coinciding with that nation's entry into the North American Free

Trade Agreement, guerrilla bands of the heretofore-unknown *Ejército Zapatista de Liberación Nacional* or "Zapatista Army for National Liberation" (EZLN) seize government offices in the impoverished southern border state of Chiapas. Thousands of troops are rushed into the region but cannot find the elusive 2,000 guerrillas, who have disappeared into jungle hideaways.

January 12, 1994 Pres. Carlos Salinas de Gortari calls a halt to military operations in Chiapas and instead sends his foreign minister, Manuel Camacho Solís, to enter into talks with the mysterious rebel leader, Subcomandante Marcos.

February 9, 1995 The newly installed president, Ernesto Zedillo, orders the army to resume its offensive against the rebel stronghold of Guadalupe Tepeyac, deep within the Lacandona jungles, and moreover identifies the rebel leader as a university graduate named Rafael Sebastián Guillén. Five days later, military operations are halted once again, and negotiations produce an accord by February 16, 1996.

February 18, 1997 Maj. Gen. Jesús Gutiérrez Rebollo, head of Mexico's federal drug agency, is arrested and it is revealed that he has actually been directing his antidrug efforts so as to benefit his covert cartel backer, Amado Carrillo Fuentes.

September 1997 Osiel Cárdenas Guillén, locked in a power struggle for leadership of the Gulf Cartel, begins hiring a group of highly trained deserters from Mexico's Special Forces to become his personal bodyguards and hit men. Their skill with sophisticated modern weaponry, and cruel ferocity under their code name of *Los Zetas*, will terrify and defeat larger gangs.

December 1, 2000 The new president, Vicente Fox, orders the army withdrawn from Chiapas altogether, even allowing Subcomandante Marcos to tour the country giving leftist speeches.

October 29, 2006 After five months' occupation of the city of Oaxaca by thousands of supporters of the state's 70,000 striking teachers, their barricades are breached by armored cars and an estimated 4,000 federal policemen under the command of an army general, although with only 1 protester killed and 50 others arrested.

December 1, 2006 Felipe Calderón, elected president by the narrowest of margins, inaugurates his administration by authorizing a pay raise for the Mexican Army and federal police, and 10 days later begins the deployment of what will eventually total almost 50,000 soldiers (fully one-quarter of the army's fighting strength) and 10,000 federal police officers in a bid to rein in cartel violence.

December 16, 2009

Five days after narrowly escaping capture, about 200 Mexican Marines backed by a pair of Mi-17 helicopters kill the alleged drug cartel leader Arturo Beltrán Leyva and four body-guards during a shootout at a luxurious apartment complex in Cuernavaca, Morelos.

August 2010

Mexican forces discover the bodies of 72 migrants murdered by members of the Zeta drug cartel in northern Mexico.

Mid-May 2012

Three high-ranking military officers—Major Generals Tomás Ángeles Dauahare and Ricardo Escorcia Vargas, and Brig. Gen. Roberto Dawe González—are arrested on charges of colluding with the Beltrán Leyva Cartel.

October 7, 2012

One of the founders of the Zeta drug cartel, Heriberto "El Lazca" Lazcano Lazcano (Z-3), is killed during a fire-fight in Progreso, Coahuila, with Mexican Marines. Initially unaware of his true identity, his body was delivered to a funeral home in Sabinas from where it was subsequently stolen by masked gunmen.

November 2012

After six years of ill-defined patrols against the drug gangs, it is estimated that 43,800 soldiers have deserted from the army during this interlude.

January 10, 2013

The Mexican Army announces that during the previous two months, nine soldiers have died in operations against criminal elements, in which they in turn killed 161 suspects and helped arrest another 1,356, in 13 different states (the most violent being Tamaulipas).

December 12, 2013

The Mexican Navy orders construction at Tampico of its fifth 140-foot patrol boat, contracted from the Dutch maritime firm Damen.

December 19, 2013

After two-and-a-half years of treatment for prostate cancer, the incarcerated general Gutiérrez Rebollo dies in the Hospital Central Militar in Mexico City.

July 15, 2013

The Zeta leader Miguel Ángel Treviño Morales (Z-40) is captured in Nuevo Laredo, Tamaulipas, by special forces of the Mexican Navy.

January 14, 2014

In a half dozen separate shootouts between army troops and cartel gunmen in the northern states of Nuevo León and Tamaulipas, 18 criminals are killed and 7 captured, along with armored vehicles, explosives, and a considerable arsenal of weaponry.

Glossary

Academia de Cadetes: Name given in 1822 to the first temporary school established for instructing Mexico's cadets, which would eventually evolve into the modern *Colegio Militar* or "Military College"; for a more comprehensive description, see full entry under "Academia de Cadetes (1822–1823)" in the main text.

acémila: Generic Spanish term for a "pack animal" or "beast of burden" and that, for purposes of transportation in the 19th- and early-20th-century Mexican Army, almost invariably referred to *burros* or "donkeys."

activo: Nineteenth-century designation for Mexican militia battalions that were raised and maintained for defense by various different states, regions, or cities, as opposed to *permanente* regiments, which comprised Mexico's standing national army and were sustained by its federal government; for a more comprehensive description, see full entry under "*activo*" in the main text.

adelita: Nickname derived from a song that became popular early during the Mexican Revolution and came to be applied to all women who accompanied soldiers on their campaigns, especially those serving with rebel forces out of the north; for a more comprehensive description, see full entry under "*adelita*" in the main text.

Alhóndiga de Granaditas: Name meaning the "Granary of Granaditas" that was given to the huge new royal warehouse completed in the city of Guanajuato just a few months before the eruption of Miguel Hidalgo's insurrection against Spanish colonial rule in mid-September 1810; for a more comprehensive account of its sorry place in history, see full entry under "Alhóndiga de Granaditas, Assault on the (1810)" in the main text.

ametralladora: Generic designation for a "machine gun" in the Spanish language, derived from the same Latin root origin as the French term*mitrailleuse*; for a more comprehensive explanation, see full entry under "*ametralladora*" in the main text.

Angostura, Battle of La: Name in Mexico for the encounter known to American military history as the "Battle of Buena Vista."

Arango Arámbula, Doroteo: Real name of Pancho Villa, who adopted the latter pseudonym when he became an outlaw; for a more comprehensive explanation, see entry under "Villa, Pancho (1878–1923)" in the main text.

aspillera: Generic word in the Spanish language for a gun slit, a loophole, or an embrasure in a fort or defensive emplacement; for an example of this term's usage, see full entry under "*aspillera*" in the main text.

baboso: Mild pejorative term in the Spanish language meaning "fool" or "idiot," derived from the noun *baba*, which signifies "drool," so a *baboso* would imply a person behaving like a "drooling idiot."

Bajío: Historic name for the vast expanse of fertile, flat farmland enclosed by the mountain ranges of central Mexico, which encompasses parts of the modern states of Aguascalientes, Guanajuato, Querétaro, Jalisco, and northern Michoacán; for a more comprehensive description, see full entry under "Bajío" in the main text.

blusas: Nickname that translated literally means "blouses" or "tunics" and during the 19th century was applied to irregular militiamen fighting on behalf of the northern states of Nuevo León and Coahuila; for a much more comprehensive description, see full entry under *blusas* in the main text.

boina: Generic Spanish word for "beret," a type of headgear widely adopted by the Mexican Army during the last few decades of the 20th century.

caja: Generic word in the Spanish language for any kind of "box" but that in military parlance is used as the nickname for a drum; for an example of its usage, see full entry under "caja" in the main text.

Camisas Doradas: "Gold Shirts," a fascist paramilitary group that emerged during Mexico's troubled 1930s, similar to the "Black Shirts" of Mussolini's Italy or "Brown Shirts" of Hitler's Germany, although the Camisas Doradas never attained any significant numbers or political power.

campechana: Nineteenth-century Mexican artillerymen's slang expression for a special combination of a canister shell double-loaded atop a round prior to being fired; for a more comprehensive description, see full entry under "*campechana*" in the main text.

cangrejos: Derisive nickname meaning "crabs" that was applied to conservatives during Mexico's War of the Reform by the liberal satirist Guillermo Prieto; for a more fulsome explanation as to the origin of this expression, see full entry under "Cangrejos, Marcha de los (1854–1867)" in the main text.

cantimplora: Generic term in the Spanish language for a soldier's "canteen" or drinking flask.

carabina 30-30: Mexican nickname for a Winchester .30-30 rifle, a lightweight weapon designed for hunting small game but that was carried into battle by many rebel soldiers during the early stages of the Mexican Revolution in 1910; for a more comprehensive description, see full entry under "carabina 30-30" in the main text.

cartilla: Generic name for Mexico's modern national identity card certifying that one has completed the requisite year of part-time military training.

Centauro del Norte: Nickname that literally means the "Centaur of the North" and was popularly applied during the Mexican Revolution to Pancho Villa, renowned for his skillful horsemanship.

Cerro de las Campanas: Geographic name meaning "Hill of the Bells," famous throughout Mexico as the spot on the outskirts of the city of Querétaro where the foreign-born emperor Maximilian and his Mexican imperial generals Miguel Miramón and Tomás Mejía were executed by a republican firing squad in 1867; for a more fulsome explanation, see entries under "Maximilian" or "Querétaro, Siege of" in the main text.

chaco: Phonetic spelling in the Spanish language for the term "shako," the designation for the military headgear typically worn during the 19th century, which in later decades would be superseded by the smaller kepi; for an example of its usage, see full entry under "chaco" in the main text.

chapín: Common Mexican nickname for any person or object originating from Guatemala.

charretera: Generic term in the Spanish language for a military "epaulet," the gilt or brass adornment worn atop the shoulder of an officer's dress uniform on parade or other ceremonial occasions.

chinacos: Lower-caste Mexican horsemen who provided excellent irregular cavalry for both liberal and conservative commanders alike throughout the mid-19th century.

chivo: Among many other meanings, a slang expression among Mexican soldiers for their salary or wages.

Chucho or Chuy: Common Mexican nickname for anyone whose first name is "Jesús."

ciudadano: Word that simply denotes a "citizen" but has become an honorific embellishment used by military officers to underscore their egalitarianism and acceptance of civilian rule, by inserting the initial "C." before their rank in all official documents; for a more comprehensive explanation, see the full entry under "ciudadano" in the main text.

ciudadela: Generic term in Spanish for a "citadel," typically defined in military architecture as a small stronghold in or near a city intended to prolong resistance against an attacking enemy.

clarín de órdenes: Literally the "clarion of orders," a military designation for a staff trumpeter who served as "command bugler" in 19th-century Mexican armies, relaying signals to units in the field or deployed upon a battlefield by playing certain prearranged *toques* or "calls"; for a more expansive description, see entry under "clarín de órdenes" in the main text.

cocona: Slang expression that appeared during the early 20th century for a heavy machine gun and was to be used by federal soldiers and rebel irregulars alike throughout the Mexican Revolution, being derived from the mythical childhood ogre known as *El Coco* or "The Boogeyman" who would carry the dying off into the night, never to return (the male and female versions of this figure being called *el coco y la cocona*).

colorados: Literally the "Reds" or "Red Ones," a nickname during the Mexican Revolution for followers of Pascual Orozco in northern Mexico who often flew a red flag or sported red bandanas as identification.

combates de Celaya: Popular name in Mexico for the two major battles fought outside this small city in the state of Guanajuato during the Mexican Revolution between the powerful armies of Pancho Villa and Álvaro Obregón in April 1915.

consejo de guerra: Generic expression in the Spanish language for a military tribunal charged with conducting courts-martial and resolving other army-related legal matters. The modern Mexican Army maintains *consejos de guerra ordinarios* or "ordinary" tribunals comprising five officers who sit permanently to hear and review cases regarding military discipline as well as occasionally convening *consejos de guerra extraordinarios* or "extraordinary" tribunals on an emergency basis.

constitucionalistas: Name that translates simply as "constitutionalists" and has been used more than once in Mexican history:

for example, to describe the followers of Pres. Benito Juárez's liberal government during the War of the Reform or the followers of Venustiano Carranza's self-proclaimed government during the Mexican Revolution of 1910.

convencionalistas: After celebrating an anti-Carrancista convention in the city of Aguascalientes during the autumn of 1914, which designated someone other than Venustiano Carranza as president of Mexico, the armies of Pancho Villa and Emiliano Zapata fought as "conventionalists" against the "constitutionalist" forces of general Álvaro Obregón who supported Carranza's claim.

corneta de órdenes: Literally the "cornet of orders," the military designation for a staff trumpeter who served as "command bugler" in 19th-century Mexican armies, relaying signals to units in the field or deployed upon a battlefield by playing certain prearranged *toques* or "calls"; for an example of its usage, see full entry under "*corneta de órdenes*" in the main text.

corridos: Popular songs played by Mexican street performers during the 19th and early 20th centuries near such public gathering spots as taverns, restaurants, or markets that often narrated stories about noteworthy events or figures of the day; for a more comprehensive description, see full entry under "*corridos*" in the main text.

criollo: Designation in colonial times for a person of Spanish ancestry born in Mexico as opposed to *peninsulares* or *gachupines* who were Spaniards born in Spain; resentment against the special status and privileges enjoyed in the Mexican viceroyalty by this minority of Peninsula-born Spaniards, who help fuel the War of Independence.

cristeros: Nickname for the rebels who rose (mostly in rural areas) against the anticlerical legislation introduced by Pres. Plutarco Elías Calles in June 1926. As these campaigners often shouted the words *Viva Cristo rey!* or "Long live Christ the King!" as their rallying cry, they soon became more popularly known as *cristeros*; for a more comprehensive description, see full entry under "Cristero Rebellion" in the main text.

cuartelazo: Expression used in modern Mexico and throughout Latin America to denote a military mutiny or coup, being derived from the noun *cuartel*, which signifies "barracks" or "quarters"; for a more comprehensive description, see full entry under "*cuartelazo*" in the main text.

cuerno: Literally the "horn" of any animal but that in contemporary Mexican slang is the nickname for an AK-47 assault rifle, which features a distinctively curved magazine shaped like a horn on its underside.

diana: Centuries-old Spanish name for a trumpet flourish, usually referring to the tune played at dawn to announce reveille, although also used by 19th- and early 20th-century Mexican armies to highlight special moments or events throughout the day.

dirty war: In Spanish, *guerra sucia*, the nickname given by Mexican journalists to the covert operations carried out by Mexican Army units on government orders starting in the 1960s, to combat subversive elements through the illegal detention, torture, and oftentimes execution of suspects, as well their family members, friends, and associates.

Dorados: Nickname that literally means the "Golden Ones" or "Golden Men" but during the Mexican Revolution came to be applied to a select troop of cavalrymen who served as a personal escort for Pancho Villa; for a more comprehensive description, see full entry under "Dorados" in the main text.

Ejército invicto: Nickname meaning the "Undefeated Army," sometimes applied to the revolutionary *Ejército del Noroeste* or "Army of the Northwest" of Gen. Álvaro Obregón that helped to eradicate the Federal Army created under Porfirio Díaz and then evolved into the main constitutionalist field force that defeated Pancho Villa's huge División del Norte in 1915, eventually emerging as the foundation for the modern Mexican Army.

escoceses: Literally, "Scots," the nickname in the immediate postindependence era of followers of the Masonic "Scottish rite," a political faction opposed during the 1820s by observers of the "York rite" or *yorquinos.*

fuero militar: In medieval times, a *fuero* was the name for any body of Spanish laws that applied exclusively to one particular territory, municipality, or social group, so the *fuero militar* referred to laws that could be applied only by military tribunals against serving officers or soldiers, effectively placing their offenses beyond the jurisdiction of civilian courts.

gabacho: Modern Mexican nickname for any person or object originating from the United States, having largely supplanted the older expression of *gringo.*

gachupín: Pejorative Mexican slang expression for any Peninsular Spaniard; for a more comprehensive description, see full entry under "*gachupín*" in the main text.

gavilla: Generic noun denoting a "group" or "bunch" in the Spanish language, although often used by Mexican authorities or army officers to describe a lawless "gang"; for a more comprehensive description, see full entry under "*gavilla*" in the main text.

guerra sucia: Expression that translates literally as "dirty war" used to describe the antiguerrilla campaigns conducted by the Mexican Army during the 1960s and 1970s, which included many unmilitary tactics such as extralegal arrests, brutal tortures, rapes, and murders to break suspected subversive elements and their sympathizers.

Halcones: Code name meaning "Hawks" given to a strong-arm squad covertly raised in the early 1970s by the administration of Pres. Luis Echeverría to break up antigovernment protests; for a more comprehensive description, see full entry under "*Halcones*" in the main text.

héroe de las derrotas: Derisive nickname that can be translated literally as "hero of the defeats" given during the War of the Reform to the liberal general Santos Degollado, who persistently raised new armies and returned to the battlefield despite his frequent military setbacks.

jarocho: Mexican nickname for any person or object originating from the state of Veracruz.

joven Macabeo: Nickname given to the youthful general Miguel Miramón by his ardent conservative backers meaning the "young Maccabee"; for a more complete description, see full entry under "joven Macabeo" in the main text.

leva: Ancient term meaning "conscription" or the forceful recruitment of men for a military unit, long practiced in Mexico's many wars.

levita: Name for a 19th-century "frock coat" often associated with the simple tunics worn by soldiers, as in the mournful *corrido* from the Mexican Revolutionary era entitled *Soldado de levita;* see full entry under "*corridos*" in the main text.

ley fuga: Mexican euphemism for the ruthless police practice of summarily executing a criminal suspect or detainee, its very name (which translates literally as "law of flight") implicitly justifying such an extra-legal death as a case of a prisoner being "killed while attempting to escape"; for a more comprehensive description, see full entry under "*ley fuga*" in the main text.

***loco loca*:** Rhyming-slang expression for *locomotora loca*—literally meaning a "crazy locomotive"—that in military terms referred to the tactic employed during the Mexican Revolution of unleashing a runaway locomotive filled with explosives against an enemy train or rail yard; for a more comprehensive description, see full entry under "*máquina loca*" in the main text.

Macabeo: Nickname given to the youthful general Miguel Miramón by his ardent conservative backers referring to the biblical warrior Judah Maccabee; for a more complete description, see full entry under "joven Macabeo" in the main text.

***macana*:** Uniquely Mexican nickname for a policeman's riot stick, billy club, truncheon, nightstick, cudgel, etc.

***manco de Celaya*:** Literally the "one-armed man of Celaya," a popular nickname for the revolutionary general Álvaro Obregón, who had had the lower portion of his right arm blown off during an epic battle against Pancho Villa—although curiously enough, it was well known throughout Mexico that Obregón had lost his arm during the Battle of Trinidad, not during either of his two previous victories over Villa at Celaya. For a more comprehensive description, see full entry under "*manco de Celaya*" in the main text.

***máquina loca*:** Colloquialism that translated literally means a "crazy machine" but was specifically used during the Mexican Revolution of 1910 to describe the tactic of deliberately unleashing a runaway locomotive so as to smash into an enemy target; for a more comprehensive description, see full entry under "*máquina loca*" in the main text.

***mochila*:** Generic term in the Spanish language for a leather "bag" often used to describe an infantryman's "knapsack" or pluralized into *mochilas* for a cavalry trooper's "saddlebags."

Nacho: Common nickname in Mexico for anyone whose first name is "Ignacio."

Niños Héroes: Literally the "Boy Heroes," six young cadets who died helping to defend their Military College in Chapultepec Castle against the American invasion in 1847; for a more comprehensive description, see full entry under Niños Héroes in the main text.

***nombre de pila*:** Mexican term for a person's first name (or names) given upon being baptized at the *pila* or "baptismal font," not including the paternal surnames. For example, the one-armed Mexican conservative general Luis G. Osollo had originally been baptized as José Luis Silverio Pascual (his *nombre de pila*), but he was to be commonly called Luis or Luis Gonzaga during his youth to the point of always signing his name as Luis G. Osollo throughout the remainder of his short life.

***obregonista*:** Name given to the followers of the revolutionary general Álvaro Obregón.

***orejón*:** A nickname roughly equivalent to "jug ears," sometimes applied during the Mexican Revolution to the *colorado* leader Benjamín Argumedo—although presumably with a certain measure of caution, given his fearsome reputation.

***orozquista*:** Name given to the followers of the northern *colorado* leader Pascual Orozco during the Mexican Revolution.

Padierna, Battle of: Mexican name for the encounter during the Mexican-American War that was called the "Battle of Contreras" by the U.S. invaders; see a full description of this action in the main text under "Contreras, Battle of (1847)."

Pancho: Common nickname in Mexico for anyone whose first name is "Francisco"; in Spain, the contraction "Paco" is more usually applied.

paredón: Euphemism that translates literally as the "big wall" but in fact refers to an execution wall before which prisoners would be made to stand so as to be shot down by firing squads.

parte oficial: Designation long employed in the Mexican bureaucracy to refer to any "official report." In the army, every commander in the field was expected to submit a *parte oficial* at the conclusion of a major action or campaign, whether successful or not, which reports were then often published for widespread circulation; for a more comprehensive description, see full entry under "*parte oficial*" in the main text.

Pasteles, Guerra de los: Term that translates literally as the "War of the Cakes," the derisory name given by Mexicans to the French blockade and bombardment of Veracruz during the winter of 1838–1839; for a much more comprehensive description, see full entry under "Cakes, War of the (1838–1839)" in the main text.

patente: Generic term for an officially issued certificate, in the Mexican Army applied to the "commission" given to officers upon being promoted to a new rank; for a more comprehensive description, see full entry under "*patente*" in the main text.

pecho a tierra: Expression that translates literally as "chest to ground" used by soldiers to indicate a prone position; for an example of its usage, see full entry under "*pecho a tierra*" in the main text.

pedrazistas: Nickname for supporters of the ex-minister of war, Gen. Manuel Gómez Pedraza, who was controversially elected president of Mexico and deposed by the Acordada Mutiny.

pelón: Generic expression for anyone having been "shorn" or sporting a very short haircut, often applied derisively to rank-and-file soldiers of the Mexican Army who routinely received buzz cuts for health and discipline reasons; for examples of its usage, see full entry under "*pelón*" in the main text,

Peninsular: Expression during the late colonial and early independence eras used to describe Spanish-born subjects who were from the Iberian Peninsula, as opposed to native-born Mexican *criollos* or "Creoles"; for a more ample description, see full entry under "Peninsular" in the main text.

Pepe: Common nickname in the Spanish language for anyone whose first name is José or "Joseph."

perfumao: Contraction of the adjective *perfumado* or "perfumed one," a derisive nickname used by soldiers or country folk to describe fashionable city dwellers; for a more expansive description, see entry under "*perfumao*" in the main text.

pienso y agua: Common horseman's or cavalryman's expression simply meaning the "feed and water" provided for their mounts; for an example of its usage, see full entry under "*pienso y agua*" in the main text.

pintos: Originally a derisive nickname used by Santa Anna to dismiss the coastal natives in Guerrero who had risen in revolt against his regime in 1854 and whose faces were often dappled or "painted" with colored splotches left over from tropical diseases; for a much more expansive description, see entry under "*pintos*" in the main text.

"Pípila," El: Personal nickname of a young miner named Juan José María Martínez in the city of Guanajuato who crawled through a hail of gunfire with a stone slab tied protectively to his back in September 1810 so as to set alight the wooden doors of the stone granary called the Alhóndiga de Granaditas and admit a storming party of Miguel Hidalgo's insurgents. For a more expansive description, see full entry under " 'Pípila,' " "El (1810)" in the main text.

polainas: Generic Spanish word for gaiters or puttees, referring to the leggings usually made out of heavy canvas or leather that are worn like protective spats around their ankles by soldiers or hikers in the field.

pronunciamiento: A word that simply means "pronouncement," yet in 19th- and early 20th-century Mexican military history referred to a public "declaration of principles" issued by any insurrectionist group intended to attract adherents to their cause; for a more expansive description, see entry under "*pronunciamiento*" in the main text.

quema ropa: An expression that can be translated literally as "clothes burning," a euphemism signifying "point-blank range"—it being understood that the discharge from any shot fired so close to a victim often ignited a small blaze in their clothing.

¿Quién vive?: Generic challenge peremptorily shouted by sentinels at the approach of any unidentified individuals that literally means "Who lives?" The correct response is to shout back the name of whatever leader is upheld by the encamped soldiers, such as *Viva Villa*, *Viva Zapata*, etc.

quinceuñas: Mocking nickname used by political opponents of Santa Anna that translates literally as "Fifteen Nails" and alluded to his missing foot—which "His Most Serene Highness" had had exhumed and reburied in a grand religious ceremony attended by hundreds of his courtiers.

quintar: In military parlance, a synonym for "decimating," referring to the brutal Roman practice of executing every tenth man as punishment for the misdeeds of a regiment or unit, although *quintar* actually means to extract the fifth part of the value of anything.

rancho: A common expression in the Mexican Army for any meal or issue of rations received either in the field or in barracks; for some examples of its usage, see the entry under "*rancho*" in the main text.

rayado: Generic word that (depending upon its context) can be variously translated as "scored" or "scratched" or "striped" but during the second half of the 19th century was used by Mexican Army officers to denote the rifling inside of gun barrels; for a more expansive description, see entry under "*rayado*" in the main text.

reconquista: Literally, the "reconquest," an avowed policy of the Spanish Crown in the immediate aftermath of Mexico having attained its independence in 1821, whereby Madrid hoped to land an expeditionary force and reclaim its former colony with the help of royalists and sympathizers who remained loyal.

reemplazos: Term that translates literally as "replacements" but has long been part of the Mexican Army's lexicon used to describe its military "reserves."

regiomontano: Common Mexican nickname for any person or object originating from the city of Monterrey, Nuevo León.

revista de comisario: Military expression which can be translated literally as a "marshal's review," signifying a full and formal inspection of a unit, usually conducted once a week or so.

Sedena: Modern acronym that stands for *Secretaría de Defensa Nacional* or "Secretariat of National Defense," the equivalent of the American DoD or Department of Defense.

sicario: Nickname in modern Mexico for a drug cartel hit man or assassin, taken directly from the ancient Latin word *sicarius*, which in biblical times literally meant a "dagger man."

siesta de San Jacinto: Derisive Mexican nickname for the *batalla de San Jacinto* or "Battle of San Jacinto" of 1836, infamous because Gen. Antonio López de Santa Anna and his army were taken by surprise while having their afternoon *siesta* or "nap" and thus were easily defeated by their Texian opponents.

soldaderas: Generic name for the wives or female companions who trailed behind Mexican armies, preparing meals whenever the troops encamped, tending to their injuries or wounds, washing their laundry, etc.; for a more expansive description, see entry under "*soldaderas*" in the main text.

soldado raso: Expression for the lowest rank of soldier, equivalent to the American term "buck private"; for a more complete explanation, see entry under "*soldado raso*" in the main text.

tapatío: Common Mexican nickname for any person or object originating from the state of Jalisco.

tierra y libertad: "Land and liberty," the rallying cry of Emiliano Zapata's insurrection in the downtrodden state of Morelos in March 1911 that encapsulated the desires and grievances held by his peasant followers against decades of government callousness.

Tigre de Tacubaya: Pejorative term, roughly equivalent to the "Beast of Tacubaya" in the English language, that was applied to the conservative general Leonardo Márquez for having ordered the wholesale execution of all liberal captives—including medical personnel, unarmed civilians,

foreign neutrals, etc.—in the wake of his victory over a besieging army just outside of Mexico City in April 1859; for a more comprehensive description, see the full entry under "Tacubaya, Battle of (1859)" in the main text.

toque de silencio: Military expression that can be loosely translated as "call for silence" and is equivalent to the "last post" in English, being the final notes played to mark the conclusion of retreat in an army base or camp, signaling "lights out" for the remainder of the night.

traqueteo: Onomatopoeic word used since the early 20th century by revolutionary and federal soldiers alike to describe the chattering roar of machine guns or automatic weapons being fired.

treinta-treinta: Words literally meaning "thirty-thirty," the most common nickname in Mexico for the Model 1894 Winchester repeating rifle, a very popular lightweight firearm sold primarily for hunting and sport but that would be carried on campaigns by many peasant soldiers during the Mexican Revolution.

zapatista: Originally the name given to any follower of Emiliano Zapata during the Mexican Revolution of 1910 but that in modern times has been co-opted by many government opponents to indicate a militant believer in Zapata's ideals: i.e., an activist interested in securing social justice for the poorest classes.

Zetas: Name of a vicious modern drug gang whose founders were deserters from elite Special Forces units of the Mexican Army and who for reasons of anonymity chose to identify themselves with the letter "Z"—in Spanish, *zeta*—coupled with a numeral (as in Z-1, Z-2, etc.) during their criminal careers; for a more comprehensive description, see the full entry under "Zetas" in the main text.

Bibliography

General Histories

Calderón Quijano, José Ignacio. *Historia de las fortificaciones en Nueva España*. Seville: Escuela de Estudios Hispano-Americanos, 1953.

Casasola, Gustavo. *Anales gráficos de la historia militar de México: 1810–1991*. Mexico City: Secretaría de Educación Pública, 1991.

Chávez Marín, Clever Alfonso. *Memoria del Primer Simposio Internacional de Historia Militar de México*. Mexico City: Asociación Internacional de Historia Militar, 2001.

Fallaw, Ben, and Terry Rugeley, eds. *Forced Marches: Soldiers and Military Caciques in Modern Mexico*. Tucson: University of Arizona Press, 2012.

Hefter, Joseph. *Crónica del traje militar en México, del siglo XVI al XX*. Mexico City: Artes de México (issue no. 102), 1968.

Iglesias González, Román, compiler. *Planes políticos, proclamas, manifiestos y otros documentos de la Independencia al México moderno, 1812–1940*. Mexico City: Instituto de Investigaciones Jurídicas de la Universidad Nacional Autónoma de México, 1998.

Salmón, Roberto Mario. "A Thankless Job: Mexican Soldiers in the Spanish Borderlands." *Military History of the Southwest* 21, no. 1 (1991): 1–19.

Sánchez Lamego, Miguel A. *Generales de ingenieros del Ejército Mexicano, 1821–1914*. Mexico City: n.p., 1952.

War of Independence (1810–1821)

Archer, Christon I., ed. *The Wars of Independence in Spanish America*. Wilmington, DE: Scholarly Resources, 2000.

Archer, Christon I. "The Royalist Army of New Spain, 1810–1821: Militarism, Praetorianism, or Protection of Interests?" *Armed Forces and Society* 17, no. 1 (Fall 1990): 99–116.

Archer, Christon I. "Las tropas expedicionarias españolas en la guerra de independencia de México, 1810–1822." In *Revisión histórica de la guerra de Independencia en Veracruz, 1810–1822*, 197–228. Veracruz: Universidad Veracruzana, 2008.

Archer, Christon I. "La revolución militar de México: estrategia, tácticas y logística durante la guerra de independencia, 1810–1821." In *Interpretaciones de la independencia de México*, 156–76. Mexico City: Nueva Imagen, 1997.

Frías, Heriberto. *Episodios militares mexicanos: primera parte, guerra de Independencia*. Mexico City: Viuda de C. Bouret, 1901.

González, Luis. *Once ensayos de tema insurgente*. Zamora, Mexico: El Colegio de Michoacán, 1985.

Guzmán, Moisés. "Fabricar y luchar . . . para emancipar: la tecnología militar insurgente en la independencia de México." *Fronteras de la Historia [Instituto Colombiano de Antropología e Historia]* 15, no. 2 (July–December 2012): 245–81.

Hamnett, Brian R. *Roots of Insurgency: Mexican Regions, 1750–1824.* Cambridge, MA: Cambridge University Press, 1986.

Hamnett, Brian R. "Mexico's Royalist Coalition: The Response to Revolution, 1808–1821." *Journal of Latin American Studies* 12, no. 1 (1980): 55–86.

Henderson, Timothy J. *The Mexican Wars for Independence.* New York: Hill and Wang, 2009.

Hernández y Dávalos, Juan Evaristo, compiler and ed. *Colección de documentos para la historia de la guerra de independencia de México de 1808 a 1821.* 6 vols. Mexico City: imprenta de José Maria Sandoval, 1877–1882.

Landavazo, Marco Antonio. "El asesinato de gachupines en la guerra de independencia mexicana." *Estudios mexicanos* 23, no. 2 (Summer 2007): 253–82.

Marchena Fernández, Juan. *Oficiales y soldados en el ejército de América.* Seville: Escuela de Estudios Hispano-americanos, 1983.

McFarlane, Anthony. *War and Independence in Spanish America.* New York: Routledge, 2014.

Montiel, Rosalba, ed. *Documentos de la guerra de independencia en Oaxaca.* Oaxaca City: Archivo General del Estado de Oaxaca, 1986.

Munguía Cárdenas, Federico. *La Guerra de Independencia en Jalisco.* Guadalajara: Unidad Editorial, Secretaría General del Gobierno de Jalisco, 1986.

Navarro y Rodrigo, Carlos. *Vida de Agustín de Iturbide y memorias de Agustín de Iturbide.* Madrid: Editorial América, 1919.

Pérez Verdía, Luis. *Apuntes históricos sobre la guerra de Independencia en Jalisco.* Guadalajara: BiblioBazaar, 2010 reedition of privately printed original from 1886.

Real ordenanza para el establecimiento e instrucción de intendentes de ejército y provincia en el reino de la Nueva España. Mexico City: Instituto de Investigaciones Históricas de la Universidad Nacional Autónoma de México, 1984 reedition.

Rodriguez O., Jaime E. *"We Are Now the True Spaniards": Sovereignty, Revolution, Independence, and the Emergence of the Federal Republic of Mexico, 1808–1824.* Stanford, CA: Stanford University Press, 2012.

Van Young, Eric, compiler. *Colección documental sobre la independencia mexicana.* Mexico City: Universidad Iberoamericana, 1998.

Van Young, Eric. "Islands in the Storm: Quiet Cities and Violent Countrysides in the Mexican Independence Era." *Past and Present* 118 (February 1988: 120–56.

Van Young, Eric. *The Other Rebellion: Popular Violence, Ideology, and the Mexican Struggle for Independence, 1810–1821.* Stanford, CA: Stanford University Press, 2001.

Vázquez, Josefina Zoraida, ed. *Interpretaciones de la independencia de México.* Mexico City: Nueva Imagen, 1997.

Initial Insurrection by Hidalgo and Morelos (1810–1815)

Almaráz, Félix D., Jr. *Tragic Cavalier: Governor Manuel Salcedo of Texas, 1808–1813.* Austin: University of Texas Press, 1971.

Archer, Christon I. "Bite of the Hydra: The Rebellion of Cura Miguel Hidalgo, 1810–1811." In *Patterns of Contention in Mexican History*, edited by Jaime E. Rodriguez O., 69–93. Wilmington, DE: Scholarly Resources, 1992.

Archer, Christon I. "Royalist Scourge or Liberator of the Patria? Agustín de Iturbide and Mexico's War of Independence, 1810–1814." *Estudios Mexicanos* 24, no. 2 (Summer 2008): 325–61.

Archer, Christon I. "Years of Decision: Félix Calleja and the Strategy to End the Revolution of New Spain." In *The Birth of Modern Mexico*, edited by Christon I. Archer, 125–49. Wilmington, DE: Scholarly Resources, 2003.

Bustamante, Carlos María de. *Campañas del general D. Félix María Calleja, comandante en jefe del ejército real de operaciones, llamado del Centro*. Mexico City: Imprenta del Águila, 1828.

Chabot, Frederick Charles, ed. *Texas in 1811: The Las Casas and Sambrano Revolutions*. San Antonio, TX: Yanaguana Society, 1941.

Correspondencia y diario militar de don Agustín de Iturbide, 1810–1813. Mexico City: Imprenta de Manuel León Sánchez, 1923, for the Archivo General de la Nación, Serie "Documentos para la Historia de la Independencia de México," Vol. IX, Tomo 1.

Gonzalez Betancourt, Jorge, ed. *Batalla del Monte de las Cruces: relación histórica de la ocupación del Valle de Toluca por el ejército del cura Hidalgo, batalla de las Cruces y acontecimientos militares ocurridos en la ciudad de Lerma desde aquella época hasta el 27 de septiembre del año de 1821, escrita por un lermeno imparcial, por noticias fidedignas y como testigo ocular en su mayor parte y la que tuvo en uno que otro de los acontecimientos en el tiempo a que se refiere, y otros documentos publicados*. Mexico City: Comisión Nacional para las Celebraciones del 175º. Aniversario de la Independencia Nacional, 1985 reedition.

Guedea, Virginia. "Las primeras elecciones populares en la ciudad de México, 1812–1813." *Estudios Mexicanos* 7, no. 1 (1991): 128.

Guzmán, Moisés. "Miguel Hidalgo y la artillería insurgente." *Revista Ciencia [Academia Mexicana de Ciencias]* 61, no. 3 (July–September 2010): 30–39.

Hamill, Hugh M., Jr. *The Hidalgo Revolt: Prelude to Mexican Independence*. Gainesville: University of Florida Press, 1966.

Hamill, Hugh M., Jr. "Royalist Counterinsurgency in the Mexican War for Independence: The Lessons of 1811." *Hispanic American Historical Review* 53, no. 3 (August 1973): 470–89.

Herrejón Peredo, Carlos. *Morelos: vida preinsurgente y lecturas*. Zamora, Michoacán: Colegio de Michoacán, 1984.

Herrejón Peredo, Carlos, ed. *Hidalgo: razones de la insurgencia y biografía documental*. Mexico City: Secretaria de Educación Pública, 1987.

Ibarra, Ana Carolina. *El cabildo catedral de Antequera, Oaxaca y el movimiento insurgente*. Morelia: El Colegio de Michoacán, 2000.

Lemoine, Ernesto. *Morelos: su vida revolucionaria a través de sus escritos y otros testimonios de la época*. Mexico City: Universidad Nacional Autónoma de México, 1991.

Lemoine, Ernesto. *Morelos y la revolución de 1810*. Mexico City: Universidad Nacional Autónoma de México, 1990 reedition.

Meyer, Jean A. *Los tambores de Calderón*. Mexico City: Editorial Diana, 1993.

Ortiz Escamilla, Juan. "Las elites de las capitales novohispanas ante la guerra civil de 1810." *Historia Mexicana* 46, no. 2 (1996): 32–57.

Pompa y Pompa, Antonio. *Proceso inquisitorial y militar seguidos a D. Miguel Hidalgo y Costilla*. Morelia: Colegio de Michoacán, 1984.

Ramírez Flores, José. *El gobierno insurgente en Guadalajara, 1810–1811*. Guadalajara: Publicaciones del Ayuntamiento, 1969; republished by the Unidad Editorial of the Gobierno de Jalisco in 1980.

Soriano, Cristina. "La huerta del colegio de San Gregorio, asiento del taller de Manuel Tolsá y su transformación en fundición de cañones, 1796–1815." *Historia Mexicana* 59, no. 4 (2010): 1401–31.

Terán Fuentes, Mariana. "Por lealtad al rey, a la patria y a la religión: los años de transición en la provincia de Zacatecas, 1808–1814." *Mexican Studies/Estudios Mexicanos* 24, no. 2 (Summer 2008): 289–323.

Van Young, Eric. "Millennium on the Northern Marches: The Mad Messiah of Durango and Popular Rebellion in Mexico,

1800–1815."*Comparative Studies in History and Society* 28, no. 3 (July 1986): 385–413.

Vizcaya Canales, Isidro. *En los albores de la independencia: las provincias internas de oriente durante la insurrección de don Miguel Hidalgo y Costilla, 1810–1811*. Monterrey, 1976.

Mina's Expedition (1817)

Díaz Thomé, Hugo. "La Guerra de Independencia: expedición de Mina." *Boletín del Archivo General de la Nación* [Mexico], 1st series, 20, no. 3 (July–September 1949): 365–77.

Guzmán R., José R. "Francisco Javier Mina en la isla de Gálveston y Soto la Marina." *Boletín del Archivo General de la Nación* [Mexico], 2nd series, 7, no. 4 (October–December 1966): 898–1081.

Guzmán R., José R. "La correspondencia de don Luis de Onís sobre la expedición de Javier Mina." *Boletín del Archivo General de la Nación* [Mexico], 2nd series, 9, nos. 3–4 (July–December 1968): 509–44.

Ortuño Martínez, Manuel, ed. *Brush, Webb, Bradburn y Terrés. Diarios: Expedición de Mina, México (1817)*. Mexico City: Trama Editorial, 2011.

Ortuño Martínez, Manuel. *Expedición a Nueva España de Xavier Mina*. Pamplona: Universidad Pública de Navarra, 2006.

Royalist Counterinsurgency and Rebel Triumph (1816–1821)

Anna, Timothy E. *The Fall of Royal Government in Mexico City*. Lincoln: University of Nebraska Press, 1978.

Anna, Timothy E. "Francisco Novella and the Last Stand of the Royal Army in New Spain." *Hispanic American Historical Review* 51, no. 1 (1971): 92–111.

Archer, Christon I. " 'La Causa Buena': The Counterinsurgency Army of New Spain and the Ten Years' War." In *The Independence of Mexico and Creation of the New Nation*, edited by Jaime E. Rodriguez O.,

85–108. Los Angeles: UCLA Latin American Center, 1989.

Archer, Christon I. "Years of Decision: Félix Calleja and the Strategy to End the Revolution of New Spain." In *The Birth of Modern Mexico*, edited by Christon I. Archer, 125–49. Wilmington, DE: Scholarly Resources, 2003.

Hamnett, Brian R. "Royalist Counterinsurgency and the Continuity of Rebellion: Guanajuato and Michoacán, 1813–1820." *Hispanic American Historical Review* 62, no. 1 (1982): 19–48.

"Oficios del Consulado de Veracruz: capitulación de la ciudad el 26 de octubre de 1821." *Revista de Historia Militar* [Spain] 34, no. 68 (1990): 225–28.

Turbulence (1822–1834)

Anna, Timothy E. *Forging Mexico: 1821–1835*. Lincoln: University of Nebraska Press, 1998.

Anna, Timothy E. "Inventing Mexico: Provincehood and Nationhood After Independence." *Bulletin of Latin American Research* [UK] 15, no. 1 (January 1996): 7–17.

Anna, Timothy E. *The Mexican Empire of Iturbide*. Lincoln: University of Nebraska Press, 1990.

Anna, Timothy E. "The Rule of Agustin de Iturbide: A Reappraisal." *Journal of Latin American Studies* 17, no. 1 (May 1985): 79–110.

Arrom, Sylvia M. "Popular Politics in Mexico City: The Parián Riot, 1828." *Hispanic American Historical Review* 68, no. 2 (May 1988): 245–68.

Benson, Nettie Lee. "Texas Viewed from Mexico, 1820–1834." *Southwestern Historical Quarterly* 90, no. 3 (1987): 219–91.

Brister, Louis E., and Robert C. Perry. "La derrota de Santa Anna en Tolomé, una relación crítica y personal." *Historia mexicana* 34, no. 4 (1985): 715–16.

Chartrand, René. *Santa Anna's Mexican Army 1821–48*. Oxford: Osprey, 2004.

DePalo, William A., Jr. *The Mexican National Army, 1822–1852.* College Station: Texas A&M University Press, 1997.

Di Tella, Torcuato. *National Popular Politics in Early Independent Mexico, 1820–1847.* Albuquerque: University of New Mexico Press, 1996.

Ducey, Michael Thomas. *Nation of Villages: Riot and Rebellion in the Mexican Huasteca, 1750–1850.* Tucson: University of Arizona Press, 2004

Fowler, Will. *Celebrating Insurrection: The Commemoration and Representation of Nineteenth-Century Mexican Pronunciamiento.* Lincoln: University of Nebraska Press, 2012.

Fowler, Will. "El pronunciamiento mexicano del siglo XIX: hacia una nueva tipología." *Estudios de historia moderna y contemporánea de México* 38 (2009): 5–34.

Fowler, Will. *Forceful Negotiations: The Origins of the* Pronunciamiento *in Nineteenth-Century Mexico.* Lincoln: University of Nebraska Press, 2010.

Fowler, Will. "Joseph Welsh: A British *Santanista* (Mexico, 1832)." *Journal of Latin American Studies* 36, no. 1 (February 2004): 29–56.

Fowler, Will, ed. *Malcontents, Rebels, and* Pronunciados: *The Politics of Insurrection in Nineteenth-Century Mexico.* Lincoln: University of Nebraska Press, 2012.

Fowler, Will. *Military Political Identity and Reformism in Independent Mexico: An Analysis of the Memorias de Guerra (1821–1855).* London: Institute for Latin American Studies, 1996.

Fowler, Will. *Santa Anna of Mexico.* Lincoln: University of Nebraska Press, 2009.

Fowler, Will. "Valentín Gómez Farías: Perceptions of Radicalism in Independent Mexico, 1821–1847." *Bulletin of Latin American Research [UK]* 15, no. 1 (1996): 39–62.

Giménez, Manuel María. *Memorias del coronel Manuel María Giménez, ayudante de campo del general Santa Anna.* Mexico City: Viuda de Ch. Bouret, 1911.

Griffen, William B. *Utmost Good Faith: Patterns of Apache-Mexican Hostilities in Northern Chihuahua Border Warfare, 1821–1848.* Albuquerque: University of New Mexico Press, 1988.

Guerra, François-Xavier. "El pronunciamiento en México: prácticas e imaginarios." *Travaux et recherches dans les Amérique du Centre* 37 (June 2000): 15–26.

Hamnett, Brian R. "Partidos políticos mexicanos e intervención militar, 1823–1855." In *America Latina dallo stato coloniale allo stato nazione*, 1: 573–91. Milan: Franco Angeli, 1987.

Hernández López, Conrado. " 'Espíritu de cuerpo' y el papel del ejército permanente en el surgimiento del estado-nación, 1821–1860." *Ulúa* 8 (July–December 2006): 129–54.

Kahle, Günter. *El ejército y la formación del Estado en los comienzos de la independencia de México.* Mexico City: Fondo de Cultura Económica, 1997 translated reedition by María Martínez Peñaloza of 1969 German original *Militär und Staatsbildung in den Anfängen der Unabhängigkeit Mexikos.*

Lozoya, Jorge Alberto. "Un guión para el estudio de los ejércitos mexicanos del siglo diecinueve." *Historia Mexicana* 17, no. 1 (April–June 1968): 553–68.

Memoria del Secretario de Estado y del Despacho de Guerra y Marina, leída a las cámaras del Congreso General Mexicano en marzo de 1835. Mexico City: Ignacio Cumplido, abril de 1835.

Moctezuma, Esteban. *Detall que el señor general D. Estévan Moctezuma dirije al Exmo. Señor D. Antonio López de Santa Anna, general de división y en gefe del ejército libertador: relativo a la acción que el 3 de agosto de 1832 se dió en el Pozo de los Carmeles.* Mexico City: Imprenta Liberal, a cargo del ciudadano José Guadalupe Amacosta, 1832.

Ortiz Escamilla, Juan, compiler. *Veracruz, la guerra por la Independencia de México, 1821–1825: antología de documentos.* Jalapa, Veracruz: Comisión Estatal del Bicentenario de la Independencia, 2008.

Reglamento para el ejercicio y maniobras de la caballería. Mexico City: Reimpreso en la oficina a cargo de Martín Rivera para el Ministerio de Guerra y Marina, 1824.

Reglamento para el ejercicio y maniobras de la infantería, mandado a observar en la República Mexicana. Mexico City: Imprenta de Galván a cargo de Mariano Arévalo para el Ejército de Tierra, 1829.

Rivera, Manuel. *Historia antigua y moderna de Jalapa y de las revoluciones del estado de Veracruz.* Mexico City: Imprenta de Ignacio Cumplido, 1869.

Robertson, William Spence. *Iturbide of Mexico.* Durham, NC: Duke University Press, 1952.

Rodriguez O., Jaime E, ed. *The Independence of Mexico and Creation of the New Nation.* Los Angeles: UCLA Latin American Center, 1989.

Rodriguez O., Jaime E. "The Origins of the 1832 Rebellion." In *Patterns of Contention in Mexican History*, 145–62. Wilmington, DE: Scholarly Resource Books, 1992.

Rodriguez O., Jaime E. "The Struggle for the Nation: The First Centralist-Federalist Conflict in Mexico." *The Americas* [Academy of American Franciscan History] 49, no. 1 (1992): 1–22.

Rodriguez O., Jaime E. *"We Are Now the True Spaniards": Sovereignty, Revolution, Independence, and the Emergence of the Federal Republic of Mexico, 1808–1824.* Stanford, CA: Stanford University Press, 2012.

Samponaro, Frank N. "Santa Anna and the Abortive Anti-federalist Revolt of 1833 in Mexico." *Americas* [Academy of American Franciscan History] 40, no. 1 (1983): 95–107.

Serrano Ortega, José Antonio. "El ascenso de un caudillo en Guanajuato: Luis de Cortázar, 1827–1832." *Historia Mexicana* 43, no. 1 (July–September 1993): 49–80.

Serrano Ortega, José Antonio. *El contingente de sangre: los gobiernos estatales y departamentales y los métodos de reclutamiento del ejército permanente mexicano, 1824–1844.* Mexico City: Instituto Nacional de Antropología e Historia, 1993.

Solares Robles, Laura. *Bandidos somos y en el camino andamos: bandidos, caminos y administración de justicia en el siglo XIX, 1821–1855, el caso de Michoacán.* Morelia: Instituto Michoacano de Cultura, Instituto de Investigaciones Dr. José Maria Luis Mora, 1999.

Stevens, Donald F. *Origins of Instability in Early Republican Mexico.* Durham, NC: Duke University Press, 1991.

Stevens, Donald F. *Instability in Mexico from Independence to the War of the Reform.* Chicago: University of Chicago Press, 1984.

Vázquez, Josefina Zoraida. *Dos décadas de desilusiones: en busca de una fórmula adecuada de gobierno (1832–1854).* Mexico City: El Colegio de México, Instituto de Investigaciones Dr. José María Luis Mora, 2009.

Vázquez, Josefina Zoraida. "El modelo de pronunciamiento mexicano, 1820–1823." *Ulúa* 7 (January–June 2006): 31–52.

Vázquez, Josefina Zoraida. "Los pronunciamientos de 1832: aspirantismo político e ideología." In *Patterns of Contention in Mexican History*, edited by Jaime E. Rodríguez O., 163–86. Wilmington, DE: Scholarly Resource, 1992.

Vázquez, Josefina Zoraida. "Political Plans and Collaboration between Civilians and the Military, 1821–1846." *Bulletin of Latin American Research* [UK] 15, no. 1 (January 1996): 19–38.

Victoria Ojeda, Jorge. "Planes de reconquista del Yucatán independiente: el proyecto de Manuel de Mediavilla." *Revista Complutense de Historia de América* [Spain] 22 (1996): 275–85.

Wasserman, Mark. *Everyday Life and Politics in Nineteenth Century Mexico: Men, Women, and War.* Albuquerque: University of New Mexico Press, 2000.

Barradas's Invasion (1829)

Culebrina bien cargada para la cachupinada. Puebla: Oficina Nacional, 1832.

Frasquet, Ivana. "Milicianos y soldados: la problemática social mexicana en la invasión de 1829." In *Las ciudades y la guerra, 1750–1898*, edited by Salvador Broseta Perales, 115–32. Castelló de la Plana: Universitat Jaume, 2002.

Langrod, Witold. "The Ups and Downs of Charles Beneski: An Attempt to Reconstruct a Distant Life History." *Polish Review* 26, no. 2 (1981): 64–75.

Los pueblos toman armas; la ley de expulsión esperan. Puebla: Imprenta del Patriota, 1827.

Sánchez Lamego, Miguel A. *La invasión española de 1829.* Mexico City: Editorial Jus, 1971.

Sims, Harold D. *The Expulsion of Mexico's Spaniards, 1821–1836.* Pittsburgh, PA: University of Pittsburgh Press, 1990.

Sims, Harold D. *La reconquista de México: la historia de los atentados españoles, 1821–1830.* Mexico City: Fondo de Cultura Económica, 1984.

Loss of Texas (1835–1836)

Chartrand, René. *Santa Anna's Mexican Army 1821–48.* Oxford: Osprey, 2004.

Davis, William C. *Three Roads to the Alamo: The Saga of Davey Crockett, Jim Bowie, and William Travis.* New York: Harper Collins, 1998.

de la Peña, José Enrique. "¡Recuerda el Álamo!" *American Heritage* 26, no. 6 (October 1975): 57–61, 92–93.

de la Peña, José Enrique. *With Santa Anna in Texas: A Personal Narrative of the Revolution.* College Station: Texas A & M University Press, 1975 translation by Carmen Perry.

de Palo, William A., Jr. *The Mexican National Army, 1822–1852.* College Station: Texas A & M University Press, 1997.

Dimmick, Gregg J. "A Newly Uncovered Alamo Account: By Pedro Ampudia, Commanding General of the Mexican Army over Texas Artillery." *Southwestern Historical Quarterly* 114, no. 4 (April 2011): 379–86.

Filisola, Vicente. *Representación dirigida al supremo gobierno por el general Vicente Filisola, en defensa de su honor y aclaración de sus operaciones como general en jefe del ejército sobre Tejas.* Mexico City: Ignacio Cumplido, 1836.

Fluent, Michael. "San Jacinto." *American History Illustrated* 21, no. 3 (1986): 22–31.

Fowler, Will. *Santa Anna of Mexico.* Lincoln: University of Nebraska Press, 2009.

Gaddy, J. J. *Texas in Revolt.* Fort Collins: Colorado State University Press, 1973.

Hardin, Stephen L. *Texian Iliad: A Military History of the Texas Revolution.* Austin: University of Texas Press, 1997.

Haythornthwaite, Philip. *The Alamo and the War of Texan Independence, 1835–1836.* London: Osprey, 1986.

Henson, Margaret Swett. "Politics and the Treatment of the Mexican Prisoners after the Battle of San Jacinto." *Southwestern Historical Quarterly* 94, no. 2 (1990): 188–230.

Marshall, Bruce. *Uniforms of the Republic of Texas and the Men That Wore Them, 1836–1846.* Atglen, PA: Schiffer, 1999.

Nofi, Albert A. *The Alamo and the Texas War of Independence, September 30, 1835 to April 21, 1836: Heroes, Myths, and History.* Conshohocken, PA: Combined Books, 1992.

Ramsdell, Charles. "The Storming of the Alamo." *American Heritage* 12, no. 2 (February 1961): 30–33, 90–92.

Santos, Richard G. *Santa Anna's Campaign Against Texas, 1835–1836: Featuring the Field Commands Issued to Major General*

Vicente Filisola. Salisbury, NC: Documentary Publications, 1982.

"The Battle of San Jacinto" April 21, 1836, as Reported by General Santa Anna, etc. Houston, TX: Compliments of the Union National Bank, 1936.

Todish, Tim and Terry S. *The Alamo Sourcebook, 1836: A Comprehensive Guide to the Alamo and the Texas Revolution*. Austin, TX: Eakin Press, 1997.

Tolbert, F. X. *Day of San Jacinto*. Austin: University of Texas Press, 1959.

Tornel y Mendivil, José Maria. "Relations between Texas, the United States of America, and the Mexican Republic." In *The Mexican Side of the Texas Revolution*, edited by Carlos E. Castañeda, 358–61, 370–71. Dallas, TX: 1928 translation.

Urrea, José. *Diario de las operaciones militares de la división que al mando del general José Urrea hizo la campaña de Tejas; publícalo su autor con algunas observaciones para vindicarse ante sus conciudadanos*. Victoria de Durango: Imprenta del gobierno a cargo de Manuel González, 1838.

Vázquez, Josefina Z. "Santa Anna y el reconocimiento de Texas." *Historia Mexicana* 36, no. 3 (1987): 553–62.

War of the Cakes (1838–1839)

Aquino Sánchez, Faustino A. *Intervención francesa, 1838–1839: la diplomacia mexicana y el imperialismo del librecambio*. Mexico City: Instituto Nacional de Antropología e Historia, 1997.

Blanchard, P., and A. Dauzatz. *San Juan de Ulúa ou Relation de l'Expédition française au Mexique sous ordres de M. le Contre-amiral Baudin*. Paris, 1839.

De la Peña y Reyes, Antonio. *La primera guerra entre México y Francia*. Vol. 23. Mexico City: "Archivo Histórico Diplomático Mexicano," Secretaría de Relaciones Exteriores, 1927.

"France and Mexico." *Niles' National Register*, 5th series, 55, no. 26 (February 23, 1839): 404–5.

Hello, J. M. *Relation de l'Expédition de la Corvette " La Créole " au Mexique en 1838 et 1839*. Paris, 1839.

Klier, Betje. " 'Peste, Tempestad, & Patisserie': The Pastry War, France's Contribution to the Maintenance of Texas' Independence." *Gulf Coast Historical Review* 12, no. 2 (1997): 58–73.

Maissin, Eugène. *The French in Mexico and Texas, 1838–1839*. Salado, TX, 1961 edition and translation by James L. Shepherd III.

Muñoz, Rafael Felipe. *La guerra de los pasteles*. Mexico City: Secretaría de Educación Pública, 1981.

Internal Turmoil (1840–1845)

Arista, Mariano. *Teoría para el manejo del sable a caballo por el general de brigada del Ejército mexicano C. Mariano Arista, con ocho láminas litográficas*. Mexico City: Impreso por Juan Ojeda, 1840.

Costeloe, Michael P. *The Central Republic in Mexico, 1835–1846: Hombres de Bien in the Age of Santa Anna*. Cambridge: University of Cambridge Press, 1993.

Costeloe, Michael P. "Los generales Santa Anna y Paredes y Arrillaga en México, 1841-1843: rivales por el poder, o una copa más." *Historia Mexicana* 39, no. 2 (October–December 1989): 417–40.

Costeloe, Michael P. "Generals versus Politicians: Santa Anna and the 1842 Congressional Elections in Mexico." *Bulletin of Latin American Research* 8, no. 2 (1989): 257–274.

Costeloe, Michael P. "The Triangular Revolt in Mexico and the Fall of Anastasio Bustamante, August–October 1841." *Journal of Latin American Studies* 20, no. 2 (November 1988): 337–60.

Costeloe, Michael P. "A *Pronunciamiento* in Nineteenth Century Mexico: '15 de julio de 1840.' " *Mexican Studies/Estudios Mexicanos* 4, no. 2 (Summer 1988): 245–64.

Dumond, Don E. *The Machete and the Cross: Campesino Rebellion in Campeche*. Lincoln: University of Nebraska Press, 1997.

Fowler, Will. *Santa Anna of Mexico*. Lincoln: University of Nebraska Press, 2009.

Hefter, Joseph. *El soldado mexicano. Organización. Vestuario. Equipo/The Mexican Soldier. Organization. Dress. Equipment. 1837–1847*. Mexico City: Ediciones Nieto, Brown, Hefter, 1958.

Ordenanza militar para el régimen, disciplina, subordinación y servicio del Ejercito, aumentada con las disposiciones relativas, anteriores y posteriores a la Independencia, con las tarifas de haberes, formularios de la plana mayor, &c., &c. 2 vols. Mexico City: Imprenta de José M. Lara, 1842.

Ortíz Escamilla, Juan. "El pronunciamiento federalista de Gordiano Guzmán, 1837–1842." *Historia Mexicana* 38, no. 2 (October–December 1988): 241–82.

Rodríguez García, Martha. *La guerra entre bárbaros y civilizados: el exterminio del nómada en Coahuila, 1840–1880*. Saltillo: CESHAC, 1998.

Santoni, Pedro. *Mexicans at War: Puro Federalists and the Politics of War, 1845–1848*. Fort Worth: Texas Christian University Press, 1996.

Santoni, Pedro. "A Fear of the People: The Civic Militia in Mexico, 1845." *The Hispanic American Historical Review* 68, no. 2 (1988): 269–88.

Vázquez, Josefina Z. *Dos décadas de desilusiones: en busca de una fórmula adecuada de gobierno (1832–1854)*. Mexico City: El Colegio de México, Instituto de Investigaciones Dr. José María Luis Mora, 2009.

Wasserman, Mark. *Everyday Life and Politics in Nineteenth Century Mexico: Men, Women, and War*. Albuquerque: University of New Mexico Press, 2000.

Cross-Border Frictions with Texas (1842–1844)

Friend, Llerena B. "Sidelights and Supplements on the Perote Prisoners." *Southwestern Historical Quarterly* 68 (January–April 1965): 366–74, 489–96; 69 (July–October 1965): 88–95, 224–30; and 69 (January–April 1966): 377–85, 516–24.

Friend, Llerena B. "Thomas W. Bell Letters." *Southwestern Historical Quarterly* 63 (April 1960): 589–99.

Green, Thomas J. *Journal of the Texian Expedition against Mier*. Austin: Steck, 1935 reedition of 1845 original published by Harper in New York.

Haynes, Sam W. *Soldiers of Misfortune: The Somervell and Mier Expeditions*. Austin: University of Texas Press, 1997.

Nance, Joseph M., trans. and ed. "Brigadier General Adrian Woll's Report of His Expedition into Texas in 1842." *Southwestern Historical Quarterly* 58, no. 4 (April 1955): 523–52.

Sánchez Lamego, Miguel A. *The Second Mexican-Texas War, 1841–1843*. Waco, Texas: Texian Press, 1972.

Stapp, William P. *The Prisoners of Perote: A First-Hand Account of the Mier Expedition*. Austin: "Barker Texas History Center Series," University of Texas Press, 1977 reedition of the journal published in 1845 by Zieber of Philadelphia.

Mexican-American War (1846–1848)
General Histories (1846–1848)

Bauer, Karl Jack. *The Mexican War, 1846–1848*. New York: Macmillan, 1974 [also reprinted by the University of Nebraska Press, 1992].

Butler, Stephen R., ed. *A Documentary History of the Mexican War*. Richardson, TX: Descendants of Mexican War Veterans, 1995.

Eisenhower, John S. D. *So Far from God: The U.S. War with Mexico, 1846–1848*. New York: Random House, 1989.

Field, Ron. *Mexican-American War, 1846–1848*. London: Brassey's, 1997.

Fowler, Will. *Santa Anna of Mexico*. Lincoln: University of Nebraska Press, 2009.

Fredriksen, John C. "Colonel Childs and His Quadrant: Reflections on the Career of a Distinguished American Soldier." *Military Collector and Historian* 39, no. 3 (1987): 122–25.

Frías, Heriberto. *Episodios militares mexicanos: segunda parte, invasión norteamericana*. Mexico City: Viuda de C. Bouret, 1901.

Goetzmann, William F. "Our First Foreign War." *American Heritage* 17, no. 4 (June 1966): 18–27, 85.

Levinson, Irving. *Wars within Wars: Mexican Guerrillas, Domestic Elites, and the United States of America, 1846–1848*. Fort Worth: Texas Christian University Press, 2005.

Miller, Robert Ryal. *Shamrock and Sword: The Saint Patrick's Battalion in the U.S. Mexican War*. Norman: University of Oklahoma Press, 1989 and 1997 reedition.

Roa Bárcena, José María. *Recuerdos de la invasión norteamericana, 1846–1848, por un joven de entonces*. 3 vols. Mexico City: Porrúa, 1993 reedition of 1883 original published by the Librería Madrileña de Juan Buxó.

Santoni, Pedro. *Mexicans at Arms: Puro Federalists and the Politics of War, 1845–1848*. Fort Worth: Texas Christian University Press, 1996.

Stevens, Peter F. *The Rogue's March: John Riley and the St. Patrick's Battalion, 1846–1848*. London: Brassey's, 2000.

Tucker, Spencer C., ed. *The Encyclopedia of the Mexican-American War: A Political, Social, and Military History*. 3 vols. Santa Barbara, CA: ABC-CLIO, 2013.

Wasserman, Mark. *Everyday Life and Politics in Nineteenth Century Mexico: Men, Women, and War*. Albuquerque: University of New Mexico Press, 2000.

Northern Theater of Operations (1846–1847)

Dana, Napoleon Jackson Tecumseh. *Monterrey Is Ours! The Mexican War Letters of Lieutenant Dana, 1845–1847*. Lexington: University Presses of Kentucky, 1990 edition by Robert H. Ferrell.

Dilworth, Rankin. *The March to Monterrey: The Diary of Lt. Rankin Dilworth*, eds. Lawrence R. Clayton and Joseph F. Chance. El Paso: Texas Western University Press, 1996.

Dishman, Christopher D. *A Perfect Gibraltar: The Battle for Monterrey, Mexico, 1846*. Norman: University of Oklahoma Press, 2010.

Katcher, Philip R. N. *The Mexican-American War, 1846–1848*. London: Osprey, 1976.

McCaffrey, James M. *Army of Manifest Destiny: The American Soldier in the Mexican War, 1846–1848*. New York: New York University Press, 1992.

Rocha, Sóstenes. *Enquiridión para los sargentos y cabos del ejército mexicano*. Vol. 7. Mexico City: Imprenta de "El Combate," 1892.

Salisbury, Richard V. "Kentuckians at the Battle of Buena Vista." *Filson Club History Quarterly* 61, no. 1 (1987): 34–53.

Spurlin, Charles. "Texas Volunteers in the Monterrey Campaign." *Military History of Texas and the Southwest* 16, no. 1 (1980): 5–22 and no. 2, 137–42.

Southern Theater of Operations (1847–1848)

Bauer, Karl Jack. *Surfboats and Horse Marines: U.S. Naval Operations in the Mexican War, 1846–1848*. Annapolis: U.S. Naval Institute Press, 1969.

Denham, James M. and Keith L. Huneycutt. "With Scott in Mexico: Letters of Captain James W. Anderson in the Mexican War, 1846–1847." *Military History of the West* 28, no. 1 (1998): 19–48.

Frías, Heriberto. *La batalla de Padierna*. Mexico City: Fondo de Cultura Económica, 2000 reedition.

Harlow, Neal. *California Conquered: War and Peace on the Pacific, 1846–1850*. Berkeley: University of California Press, 1982.

Holt, Thaddeus. "Checkmate at Mexico City." *MHQ: The Quarterly Journal of Military History* 2, no. 3 (Spring 1990): 82–93.

Johnson, Timothy D. *A Gallant Little Army: The Mexico City Campaign*. Lawrence: University Press of Kansas, 2007.

McCaffrey, James M., and George Sanders, eds. "America's First Day: The Veracruz Landing of 1847." *Military History of the West* 25, no. 1 (1995): 51–68.

Michael, Steven. "A Year's Campaign: Dewitt C. Loudon's Mexican War." *Timeline* 9, no. 2 (April–May 1992): 18–33.

Smith, Robert P., Jr. "Impossible Campaign Attempted." *Military History* 10, no. 1 (April 1993): 92–96.

Solares Robles, Laura. "Gómez Farías y Santa Anna: correspondencia en tiempos de crisis, 1847." *Secuencia* [Mexico] 19 (1991): 109–22.

Stokes, G. P. "Naked Sword in Hand." *Military History* 8, no. 2 (August 1991): 44–49.

Watkins, T. H. "The Taking of California." *American Heritage* 24, no. 2 (February 1973): 4–7, 81.

Winders, Richard B. "Puebla's Forgotten Heroes." *Military History of the West* 24, Number 1 (Spring 1994): 1–23.

Caste War (1847–1855)

Alexander, Rani T. *Yaxcabá and the Caste War of the Yucatán: An Archaeological Perspective*. Albuquerque: University of New Mexico Press, 2004.

Lapointe, Marie. *Los mayas rebeldes de Yucatán*. Zamora: Colegio de Michoacán, 1983.

Reed, Nelson. *The Caste War of Yucatán*. Stanford, CA: Stanford University Press, 1964.

Rugeley, Terry. *Rebellion Now and Forever: Mayas, Hispanics, and Caste War Violence in Yucatan, 1800–1880*. Stanford, CA: Stanford University Press, 2009.

Rugeley, Terry. "Rural Political Violence and the Origins of the Caste War." *The Americas: Academy of American Franciscan History* 53, no. 4 (April 1997): 469–96.

Rugeley, Terry. *Yucatán's Maya Peasantry and the Origins of the Caste War*. Austin: University of Texas Press, 1996.

Filibusterism (1852–1854)

La Madeleine, Henri de. *Le compte Gaston de Raousset-Boulbon: Sa vie et ses aventures (d'après ses papiers, et sa correspondance)*. Paris: Poulet-Malassis, 1859.

Lambertie, Charles de. *Le drame de la Sonora: l'etat de Sonora, M. Le Comte De Raousset Boulbon et M. Charles De Pindray*. Paris: Chez Ledoyen, 1855.

May, Robert E. *Manifest Destiny's Underworld: Filibustering in Antebellum America*. Chapel Hill: University of North Carolina Press, 2002.

Stout, Joseph A., Jr. *Schemers and Dreamers: Filibustering in Mexico, 1848–1921*. Fort Worth: Texas Christian University Press, 2002.

Wyllys, Rufus Kay. *The French in Sonora, 1850–1854*. Berkeley: University of California Press, 1932.

Wyllys, Rufus Kay. "The Republic of Lower California, 1853–1854." *Pacific Historical Review* 2 (1933): 194–213.

Revolution of Ayutla (1854–1855)

Cuentas de la comisaría y sub-comisaría del Ejército Restaurador de la Libertad, que manifiestan los ingresos y egresos que han tenido, en las fechas que mencionan. Mexico City: Imprenta de Vicente García Torres, 1856.

De la Cueva, Mario, compiler and ed. *Plan de Ayutla: conmemoración de su primer centenario*. Mexico City: Ediciones de la Facultad de Derecho, Universidad Nacional Autónoma de México, 1954.

Escalafón general que comprende a los Exmos. Sres. capitán general, generales de división, a los de brigada efectivos y graduados, a los Sres. coroneles de todas armas: tenientes coroneles de infantería y caballería, comandantes de batallón y escuadrón, primeros ayudantes de infantería y caballería, capitanes y subalternos de una y otra arma, en servicio e ilimitados, gefes y oficiales del cuerpo especial de Estado Mayor, detalles de plaza, cuerpo médico, cuerpos nacionales de ingenieros y artillería. Mexico City: Imprenta de Ignacio Cumplido, 1854.

González Lezama, Raúl. *Reforma liberal: cronología (1854–1876).* Mexico City: Instituto Nacional de Estudios Históricos de las Revoluciones de México, 2012.

Haworth, Daniel S. "Insurgencia y contrainsurgencia en la Revolución de Ayutla, 1854–1855." In *Fuerzas Militares en Iberoamérica, Siglos XVIII y XIX*, coordinated by Juan Ortiz Escamilla, 293–300. Mexico City: Colegio de México-Centro de Estudios Históricos, Colegio de Michoacán, Universidad Veracruzana, 2005.

Historia de la revolución de México contra la dictadura del general Santa-Anna, 1853–1855. Durango, Durango: Imprenta del Gobierno a cargo de Manuel González, 1859.

Johnson, Richard A. *The Mexican Revolution of Ayutla, 1854–1855: An Analysis of the Evolution and Destruction of Santa Anna's Last Dictatorship.* Westport, CT: Greenwood Press, 1974 reedition of original Augustana College Library Publication no. 17, from 1939.

Lambert, Dean P. "Regional Core-Periphery Imbalance: The Case of Guerrero, Mexico, since 1821." *Yearbook of the Conference of Latin Americanist Geographers* 20 (1994): 59–71.

La Revolución de Ayutla: los caudillos y la frontera: cartas Santiago Vidaurri, Juan Álvarez, 1855. Monterrey: Universidad Autónoma de Nuevo León, Dirección General de Investigaciones Humanísticas, 1978.

Muñoz y Pérez, Daniel. *El general don Juan Álvarez: ensayo biográfico seguido de una selección de documentos.* Mexico City: Academia Literaria, 1959.

Portilla, Anselmo de la. *Historia de la revolución de México contra la dictadura del general Santa Anna, 1853–1855.* Mexico City: Vicente García Torres, 1856.

Prieto, Guillermo. *Viajes de orden suprema: años de 1853, 1854 y 1855.* Mexico City: Bibliófilos Mexicanos, 1968.

Robles Pezuela, Manuel. *Ley de 22 de abril de 1851 sobre arreglo del Ejército: disposiciones reglamentarias del Gobierno para su cumplimiento.* Mexico City: Vicente García Torres, 1851.

Suárez y Navarro, Juan. *Historia de México y del general Antonio López de Santa Anna.* Mexico City: Ignacio Cumplido, 1859.

Trueba Urbina, Alberto. *Centenario del Plan de Ayutla.* Mexico City: Manuel Porrúa, 1957.

Vázquez Mantecón, Carmen. *Santa Anna y la encrucijada del Estado: la dictadura, 1853–1855.* Mexico City: Fondo de Cultura Económica, 1986.

Imposing Liberal Reforms (1856–1857)

Álvarez, José J. *Parte general que sobre la campaña de Puebla dirige al ministerio de la Guerra el Sr. general ayudante general D. José J.Álvarez, segundo jefe de estado mayor, cuartel maestre general del ejército de operaciones, por orden del Exmo. Sr. D. Ignacio Comonfort, presidente sustituto de la República y general en jefe de dicho ejército.* Mexico City: Imprenta de Vicente García Torres, 1856.

Bazant, Jan. *México en 1856 y 1857: gobierno del general Comonfort.* Mexico City: Instituto Nacional de Estudios Históricos de la Revolución Mexicana, 1987.

Bazant, Jan. *Antonio Haro y Tamariz y sus aventuras políticas, 1811–1869.* Mexico City: El Colegio de México, 1985.

Bazant, Jan. "La iglesia, el estado y la sublevación conservadora de Puebla en 1856." *Historia mexicana* 35, no. 1 (1987): 93–109.

Berry, Charles R. *The Reform in Oaxaca, 1856–57: A Microhistory of the Liberal Revolution.* Lincoln: University of Nebraska Press, 1981.

De la Portilla, Anselmo. *Méjico en 1856 y 1857: gobierno del general Comonfort.* New York City: S. Hallet, 1858.

García, Genaro, ed. *Documentos inéditos o muy raros para la historia de México: los gobiernos de Álvarez y Comonfort según el archivo del general Doblado.* Mexico City: Porrúa, 1974.

Guevara Ramírez, Héctor. *El Estado de México: desarrollo y repercusiones políticas y sociales de la Constitución Federal de 1857.* Coacoalco: Gobierno del Estado de México, 2010.

Hamnett, Brian. "The Comonfort Presidency, 1855–1857." *Bulletin of Latin American Research [UK]* 15, no. 1 (January 1996): 81–100.

Haworth, Daniel S. "The Mobile National Guard of Guanajuato, 1855–1858: Military Hybridization and Statecraft in Reforma Mexico." In *Forced Marches: Soldiers and Military Caciques in Modern Mexico*, edited by Ben Fallaw and Terry Rugeley, 49–80. Tucson: University of Arizona Press, 2012.

Martínez Cárdenas, Leticia, compiler and editor. *Para efectos de la guerra: correspondencia Santiago Vidaurri-Pedro Hinojosa, 1855–1864.* Monterrey, Nuevo León: Archivo General del Estado de Nuevo León, 2000.

McGowan, Gerald L. *Prensa y poder, 1854–1857: la revolución de Ayutla, el congreso constituyente.* Mexico City: El Colegio de México, 1978.

Ribes Iborra, Vicente. "El bandolerismo en el centro de México durante la Reforma." *Quinto centenario* 7 (1985): 121–60.

Tena Ramírez, Felipe. *Comonfort, los moderados y la Revolución de Ayutla.* Mexico City, 1954.

Thomson, Guy P. C., with David G. LaFrance. *Patriotism, Politics, and Popular Liberalism in Nineteenth-Century Mexico: Juan Francisco Lucas and the Puebla Sierra.* Wilmington, DE: Scholarly Resources, 1999.

Villareal, Florencio. *Parte oficial que dirige al Exmo. Sr. presidente de la República y general en jefe del ejército de operaciones, como su segundo el de división D. Florencio Villareal, de la batalla del día ocho del presente en el puerto de Montero y San Francisco Ocotlán (San Javier en Puebla, marzo 19 de 1856).* Mexico City: Imprenta de J. M. Macías, 1856.

Villegas Revueltas, Silvestre. "Santannismo, reforma liberal y las campañas de Puebla en 1856." *Estudios de Historia Moderna y Contemporánea de México* 40 (July–December 2010): 13–52.

War of the Reform or Three Years' War (1858–1860)

Apuntes biográficos del ciudadano Jesús González Ortega. Mexico City: Imprenta de Manuel Castro, 1861.

Blázquez, Carmen. *Veracruz liberal, 1858–1860.* Mexico City: El Colegio de México, 1985.

Cambre, Manuel. *La guerra de Tres Años: apuntes para la historia de la Reforma.* Guadalajara, Jalisco: Biblioteca de Autores Jaliscienses, Gobierno del Estado, 1949 reedition of 1904 original published by J. Cabrera; also reissued in 1986 by the Universidad de Guadalajara.

Cerutti, Mario. *Economía de guerra y poder regional en el siglo XIX: gastos militares, aduanas y comerciantes en años de Vidaurri.* Monterrey: Archivo General del Estado de Nuevo León, 1983.

Daran, Victor. *Le général Miguel Miramon: notes sur l'histoire du Mexique.* Rome: Edoardo Pereno, 1886.

Dávila, Hermenegildo. *Biografía del Sr. General D. Juan Zuazúa.* Monterrey, Nuevo León: Tipografía calle de Dr. Mier, 1892.

Detall^e de la acción que el día 20 de octubre de 1861 la Brigada mixta del mando del ciudadano general Santiago Tapia libró en la sierra intermedia de Pachuca al Mineral del Monte: derrotando al ejército reaccionario al mando de sus principales caudillos Márquez, Mejía,

Zuloaga, Zires, Herrera y Lozada, &c. Mexico City: Vicente García Torres for the Secretaría de Guerra y Marina, 1861.

Doblado, Manuel. *La guerra de Reforma: según el archivo del General D. Manuel Doblado, 1857–1860.* Vol. 3 of the series *Nuevos documentos inéditos o muy raros para la historia de México.* San Antonio, TX: Volume 3 of the Series "Nuevos documentos inéditos o muy raros para la historia de México," Casa editorial Lozano, 1930.

Galeana, Patricia. "Los conservadores en el poder: Miramón." *Estudios de Historia Moderna y Contemporánea de México* 14 (1991): 67–87.

Gálvez Medrano, Arturo. *Regionalismo y gobierno general: el caso de Nuevo León y Coahuila, 1855–1864.* Monterrey: Archivo General del Estado de Nuevo León, 1993.

García, Genaro, ed. *Causa mandada formar a D. Leonardo Márquez por desobediencia e insubordinación como general en jefe del primer cuerpo del Ejército de Operaciones, diciembre de 1859.* Vol. 8. Mexico City: Librería de la Vda. de Ch. Bouret, Serie "Documentos inéditos o muy raros para la historia de México," 1906.

García, Luis Alberto. *Guerra y frontera: el Ejército del Norte entre 1855 y 1858.* Monterrey, Nuevo León: Fondo Editorial y Archivo General del Estado de Nuevo León, 2006.

Haworth, Daniel S. "Civilians and Civil War in Nineteenth-Century Mexico: Mexico City and the War of the Reform, 1858–1861." In *Daily Lives of Civilians in Latin America from the Wars of Independence to the Drug Wars,* edited by Pedro Santoni, 91–122. Westport, CT: Greenwood Press, 2008.

Haworth, Daniel. "Desde los baluartes conservadores: la Ciudad de México y la Guerra de Reforma, 1857–1860." *Relaciones* 84, no. 21 (Fall 2000): 95–131.

Hernández Rodríguez, Rosaura. *El general conservador Luis G. Osollo.* Mexico City: Editorial Jus, 1959.

Hernández Rodríguez, Rosaura. "Leonardo Márquez: de cadete a capitán," *Estudios de historia moderna y contemporánea de México* 5 (1976): 53–62.

"Important from Mexico: Particulars of the Engagement between Vidaurri and Miramón." *New York Times,* October 25, 1858.

Morado Macías, César, compiler and ed. *Monterrey en guerra: hombres de armas tomar, Santiago Vidaurri–Julián Quiroga, 1858–1865.* Monterrey: Archivo General del Estado de Nuevo León, 2000.

Ramírez de Arellano, Manuel. *Apuntes de la campaña de Oriente: 1859, febrero, marzo y abril.* Mexico City: Navarro, 1859.

Pérez Gallardo, Basilio. *Breve reseña de los sucesos de Guadalajara y de las Lomas de Calderón; diario de las operaciones y movimiento del ejército federal, después de la batalla de Silao … con un apéndice en que se refieren los sucesos de las lomas de San Miguelito y ocupación de la capital de la República.* Mexico City: Imprenta de Ignacio Cumplido, 1861.

Sitio de Veracruz por Miguel Miramón. Mexico City: Editorial Citlalpétel, 1968 edition of the original *Diario de los sucesos de Veracruz durante los días en que está amagada la plaza por los facciosos acaudillados por D. Miguel Miramón.*

Stevens, Donald F. *Instability in Mexico from Independence to the War of the Reform.* Chicago: University of Chicago Press, 1984.

Taylor Hanson, Lawrence D. "Voluntarios extranjeros en los ejércitos liberales mexicanos, 1854–1867." *Historia Mexicana* 37, no. 2 (1987): 205–37.

Teixidor, Felipe, ed. *Memorias de Concepción Lombardo de Miramón.* Mexico City: Editorial Porrúa, 1980.

Torre Villar, Ernesto de la. *El triunfo de la república liberal, 1857–1860.* Mexico City: Fondo de Cultura Económica, 1960.

Valdés, Manuel. *Memorias de la guerra de Reforma: diario del coronel Manuel Valdés.* Mexico City: Sociedad Mexicana de Geografía y Estadística de la Secretaría de Fomento, 1913.

Wasserman, Mark. *Everyday Life and Politics in Nineteenth Century Mexico: Men, Women, and War.* Albuquerque: University of New Mexico Press, 2000.

War of the French Intervention (1862–1867)

General Histories

Bassols Batalla, Ángel. *Temas y figuras de la intervención.* Mexico City: Sociedad Mexicana de Geografía y Estadística, Sección de Historia, 1963.

Charpy, Manuel, and Claire Fredj, eds. *Lettres du Mexique: Itinéraires du zouave Augustin-Louis Frélaut, 1862–1867.* Paris: Éditions Nicolas Philippe, 2003.

Chartrand, René. *The Mexican Adventure, 1861–67.* Men at Arms series. Oxford: Osprey, 1994.

Dabbs, Jack Autrey. *The French Army in Mexico, 1861–1867: A Study in Military Government.* The Hague: Mouton & Co., 1963.

Escalante, Constantino, and Hesiquio Iriarte. *Las glorias nacionales: el álbum de la guerra.* Puebla: Gobierno del Estado de Puebla y Secretaría de Educación Pública, 2012 reedition by Arturo Aguilar Ochoa [also issued in a separate publication this same year in Mexico City by the Instituto Nacional de Antropología e Historia, in a reedition by María de Lourdes González Cabrera and Juan Carlos Franco Montes de Oca].

French, John D. "Commercial Foot Soldiers of the Empire: Foreign Merchant Politics in Tampico, Mexico, 1861–1866." *The Americas [Academy of American Franciscan History]* 46, no. 3 (January 1990): 291–314.

Hanna, Alfred J. and Kathryn A. *Napoleon III and Mexico: American Triumph over Monarchy.* Chapel Hill: University of North Carolina Press, 1971.

Lecaillon, Jean-François. *Napoléon III et le Mexique: Les illusions d'un grand dessein.* Paris: L'Harmattan, 1994.

León Toral, Gen. Jesús de. *Historia militar: la intervención francesa en México.* Mexico City: Sociedad Mexicana de Geografía y Estadística, 1962.

Meyer, Jean. *Yo, el francés.* Puebla: El Colegio de Puebla, Gobierno del Estado de Puebla, and SEP Puebla, 2012.

Montbarbut Du Plessis, Jean-Marie. *L'armée de Napoléon III au Mexique, 1862–1867.* Paris: Éditions Nouvelles, 2009.

Papers Relative to Mexican Affairs, Communicated to the Senate, June 16, 1864. Washington, DC: U.S. Government Printing Office, 1864.

Pola, Ángel. *Manifiestos (el imperio y los imperiales) por Leonardo Márquez, lugarteniente del imperio.* Mexico City: F. Vázquez, 1904.

Rivera Cambas, Manuel. *Historia de la intervención europea y norteamericana en México y del imperio de Maximiliano de Hapsburgo.* Mexico City: Instituto Nacional de Estudios Históricos de la Revolución Mexicana, 1987.

Santibáñez, Manuel. *Reseña histórica del Cuerpo del Ejército de Oriente.* Vol. 1. Mexico City: Tipografía de la Oficina Impresora del Timbre, 1892.

Tarragó M., Ernesto. *La intervención francesa.* Mexico City: Sociedad Mexicana de Geografía y Estadística, Sección de Historia, 1963.

Thomas, Lately. "The Operator and the Emperors." *American Heritage* 15, no. 3 (April 1964): 4–23, 83–88.

Opening French Campaign (1862)

A cien años del 5 de mayo de 1862. Mexico City: Secretaría de Hacienda y Crédito Público, 1962.

Arroyo Llano, Rodolfo. *Ygnacio Zaragoza: defensor de la libertad y la justicia.* Puebla:

"Biblioteca 5 de Mayo," El Colegio de Puebla and Gobierno del Estado de Puebla, 2012 reedition.

Barker, Nancy N. *The French Experience in Mexico, 1821–1861: A History of Constant Misunderstanding*. Chapel Hill: University of North Carolina Press, 1979.

Bibesco [or Bibescu], prince Georges. *Au Mexique 1862: combats et retraite des six mille*. Paris: E. Plon, Nourrit, et Cie., 1887.

Bibesco [or Bibescu], prince Georges. *Le corps Lorencez devant Puebla 5 mai 1862: retraite des cinq mille*. London: British Library, Historical Print Editions, 2011 reedition of an abbreviated extract originally published in 1868 and then again in 1876.

Castañeda Batres, Óscar. *La convención de Londres (31 de octubre de 1861)*. Mexico City: Sociedad Mexicana de Geografía y Estadística, Sección de Historia, 1962.

Cunningham, Michele. *Mexico and the Foreign Policy of Napoleon III*. New York: Palgrave, 2001.

Detall de la acción que el día 20 de octubre de 1861 la Brigada mixta del mando del ciudadano general Santiago Tapia libró en la sierra intermedia de Pachuca al Mineral del Monte: derrotando al ejército reaccionario al mando de sus principales caudillos Márquez, Mejía, Zuloaga, Zires, Herrera y Lozada, &c. Mexico City: Vicente García Torres for the Secretaría de Guerra y Marina, 1861.

Echenique, Rafael. *Batalla del 5 de Mayo de 1862 en Puebla: telegramas oficiales relativos a la mencionada batalla*. Mexico City: Eusebio Sánchez, 1894.

Gómez, Manuel Z. *Biografía del Gral. de división C. Ignacio Zaragoza*. Mexico City: Imprenta de Vicente García Torres, 1862.

González Lezama, Raúl. *Cinco de mayo: las razones de la victoria*. Mexico City: Instituto Nacional de Estudios Históricos de las Revoluciones de México, 2012.

Hayes-Bautista, David. *El Cinco de Mayo: An American Tradition*. Berkeley and Los Angeles: University of California Press, 2012.

List Arzubide, Germán. *Guía conmemorativa del centenario de la batalla del cinco de mayo de 1862*. Mexico City: Secretaría de Educación Pública, 1962.

Norris, David A. "The Origin of Cinco de Mayo." *History Magazine* 14, no. 4 (April–May 2013): 40–43.

Palou, Pedro Ángel. *5 de mayo, 1862*. Puebla: Benemérita Universidad Autónoma de Puebla, 2007 bilingual reedition of 1994 original published by the H. Ayuntamiento de Puebla.

Pérez de Acevedo, Javier. *Europa y México, 1861–1862: ambiciones y codicias, liberalismo y teocracia, la expedición europea, retirada de Prim; monografía histórica, diplomática*. Mexico City: Imprenta Rambla, Bouza y cía., 1935.

Ramos, Patricio. *Descripción de la batalla del 5 de mayo de 1862*. Puebla: "Biblioteca 5 de Mayo," El Colegio de Puebla, Gobierno del Estado de Puebla, and INAH Puebla, 2012 reedition.

Salazar Exaire, Celia. *Los fuertes de Loreto y Guadalupe*. Puebla: "Biblioteca 5 de Mayo," El Colegio de Puebla, Gobierno del Estado de Puebla, and INAH Puebla, 2012.

Sánchez Lamego, Miguel A. "El combate de Barranca Seca." *Historia Mexicana* 14, no. 3 (January–March 1965): 469–87.

French Conquest and Imperial Installation (1863–1865)

Anderson, William M. *An American in Maximilian's Mexico, 1865–1866: The Diaries of William Marshall Anderson*. San Marino, CA: Huntington Library, 1959 reedition by Ramón Eduardo Ruiz.

Blasio, José Luis. *Maximiliano íntimo*. Mexico City: Editora Nacional, 1973.

Descoubès, Ernest. *Historique du 1er Régiment des Zouaves*. Paris: Librairie militaire de Berger-Levrault, 1882, 159–82.

Dunn, John. "Africa Invades the New World: Egypt's Mexican Adventure, 1863–1867." *War in History* [UK] 4, no. 1 (January 1997): 27–34.

García, Genaro, compiler and editor. *El sitio de Puebla en 1863, según los archivos de d. Ignacio Comonfort . . . y de d. Juan Antonio de la Fuente.* Mexico City: Viuda de C. Bouret, 1909.

González Ortega, Jesús. *Parte general que da al Supremo Gobierno de la Nación respecto de la defensa de la plaza de Puebla, el general Jesús González Ortega.* Mexico City: J. S. Ponce de León, 1871.

Hernández, Juan A. *Memorias del Gral. de División Juan A. Hernández sobre la Guerra de Intervención en el occidente y el centro de la República.* Mexico City: Sociedad Mexicana de Geografía y Estadística, Sección de Historia, 1962.

Hill, Richard L. *A Black Corps d'Elite: An Egyptian Sudanese Conscript Battalion with the French Army in Mexico, 1863–1867, and Its Survivors in Subsequent African History.* East Lansing: Michigan State University Press, 1995.

La Bédollière, Émile de. *Histoire de la guerre du Mexique 1861 à 1866.* Paris: Georges Barba, 1866.

Martin, Charles L. A. *Précis des événements de la campagne du Mexique en 1862.* Paris: Charles Tanera, Librairie pour l'art militaire, 1863.

Mayer, Edelmiro. *Campaña y guarnición: memorias de un militar argentino en el ejército de Benito Juárez.* Mexico City: Secretaría de Hacienda y Crédito Público, Dirección General de Prensa, Memoria, Bibliotecas y Publicaciones, 1972.

Ollivier, Émile. *Expedición de México.* Mexico City: Cámara de Diputados, 1972 translation by Manuel Puega y Acal of the 1922 French original.

Páez Brotchie, Luis. *Valiosos documentos tapatíos sobre la intervención francesa.* Mexico City: Sociedad Mexicana de Geografía y Estadística, Sección de Historia, 1963.

Pitner, Ernst. *Maximilian's Lieutenant: A Personal History of the Mexican Campaign, 1864–7.* Trans. and ed. Gordon Etherington-Smith. Albuquerque: University of New Mexico Press, 1993.

Rickards, Colin. *Hand of Captain Danjou: Camerone and the French Foreign Legion in Mexico, 30 April 1863.* Marlborough, Wilshire, England: Crowood Press, 2008.

Ryan, James W. *Camerone: The French Foreign Legion's Greatest Battle.* New York: Praeger, 1996.

Tapia, Santiago. *Diario de prisionero (1864–1865).* Puebla: Instituto Poblano de Antropología e Historia, 1970.

Imperial Defeats and Republican Triumph (1866–1867)

Arias, Juan de Dios. *Reseña histórica de la formación y operaciones del cuerpo de Ejército de Norte durante la intervención francesa, sitio de Querétaro y noticias oficiales sobre la captura de Maximiliano, su proceso íntegro y su muerte.* Mexico City: Imprenta de Nabor Chávez, 1867.

Báez Macías, Eduardo. "Pintura militar: entre lo episódico y la acción de masas." *Anales del Instituto de Investigaciones Estéticas de la Universidad Nacional Autónoma de México* 78 (2001): 129–47.

Beltrán y Puga, Emilia. *Apuntes biográficos del general de división Ramón Corona.* Mexico City: Tipografía "Diario del Hogar," 1885.

Causa de Fernando Maximiliano de Hapsburgo y sus generales Miguel Miramón y Tomás Mejía. Guadalajara: Instituto Jalisciense de Historia y Antropología, 1967.

Correspondence Relating to Recent Events in Mexico, Executive Documents Number 20, U.S. Congressional Serial Set, Vol. 1308. Washington, DC: U.S. Government Printing Office, 1868.

De la Peza, Ignacio, and Agustín Pradillo. *Maximiliano y los últimos sucesos del imperio en Querétaro y México: opúsculo en que se refutan las memorias redactadas por Félix de Salm Salm.* Mexico City: Imprenta de Ignacio Cumplido, 1870.

Escobedo, Mariano. *Parte general dado al Supremo Gobierno sobre los sucesos de Matamoros, con documentos importantes.* Matamoros, Tamaulipas: Imprenta del Gobierno a cargo de Segura y Ambros, 17 de diciembre de 1866.

Gutiérrez Grageda, Blanca. *Querétaro devastado: fin del segundo imperio.* Querétaro: Universidad Autónoma de Querétaro, 2007.

Hernández López, Conrado. "Querétaro en 1867 y la división en la historia (sobre una carta enviada por Silverio Ramírez a Tomás Mejía el 10 de abril de 1867)." *Historia Mexicana* 57, no. 4 (April–June 2008): 1201–14.

Márquez, Leonardo. *Refutación hecha por el general de división Leonardo Márquez al libelo del general de brigada don Manuel Ramírez de Arellano: publicado en Paris el 30 de diciembre de 1868 bajo el epígrafe de "Ultimas horas del imperio."* New York: privately printed, 1869.

Message of the President of the United States of March 20, 1866, Relating to the Condition of Affairs in Mexico, in Answer to a Resolution of the House of December 11, 1865; Executive Document No. 73, Parts I and II. Washington, D.C.: Government Printing Office, 1866.

Message of the President of the United States of January 29, 1867, Relating to the Present Condition of Mexico, in Answer to a Resolution of the House of December 4, 1866; Executive Document No. 76. Washington, DC: U.S. Government Printing Office, 1867.

Miller, Robert R. "Arms Across the Border: United States Aid to Juarez During the French Intervention in Mexico." *Transactions of the American Philosophical Society,* New Series, 63, no. 6 (December 1973): 1–68.

Moreno, Daniel, ed. *El sitio de Querétaro, según protagonistas y testigos.* Mexico City: Editorial Porrúa, 1982.

Paz, Ireneo, ed. *Datos biográficos del general de división C. Porfirio Díaz, con acopio de documentos históricos.* Mexico City: Imprenta de Ireneo Paz, 1884.

Ramírez de Arellano, Manuel. *Últimas horas del imperio.* Mexico City: Tipografía Mexicana, 1869.

Salm-Salm, Felix. *My Diary in Mexico in 1867, Including the Last Days of the Emperor Maximilian.* 2 vols. London: Richard Bentley, 1868.

Liberal Republic Restored (1867–1875)

Aguilar Rivera, José Antonio. "Oposición y separación de poderes: la estructura nacional institucional del conflicto, 1867–1872."*Metapolítica* 2, no. 5 (January–March 1998): 69–92.

Balbontín, Manuel. *Apuntes sobre un sistema militar para la República: obra dedicada al supremo gobierno nacional.* Mexico City: Ignacio Cumplido, 1867.

Díaz Zermeño, Héctor, and Javier Torres Medina, compilers and eds. *México del triunfo de la República al Porfiriato: antología, textos de la historia.* Mexico City: Universidad Nacional Autónoma de México, 2005.

Evans, Col. Albert S. "Our Military Escort." In *The Age of Porfirio Díaz: Selected Readings*, edited by Carlos B. Gil, 15–17. Albuquerque: University of New Mexico Press, 1977.

Mejía, Ignacio. *Memoria que el C. General de División Ignacio Mejía, Ministro de Guerra y Marina, presenta al 7°. Congreso Constitucional.* Mexico City: Imprenta del Gobierno, en Palacio, 1873.

Parte oficial de la toma de Tampico por las fuerzas del supremo gobierno al mando del C. general S[óstenes] Rocha. Mexico City: Imprenta del Gobierno, en Palacio, 1871.

Reglamento para el establecimiento de las colonias militares en la frontera del norte ... diciembre de 1868. Mexico City: Imprenta del Gobierno, 1869.

Trujillo Bretón, Jorge Alberto. "En el Camino Real: representaciones, prácticas y biografías de bandidos en Jalisco, México, 1867–1911." *Letras Históricas* 2 (Spring–Summer 2010): 105–32.

Vanderwood, Paul J. "Genesis of the Rurales: Mexico's Early Struggle for Public Security." *Hispanic American Historical Review* 50 (May 1970): 323–44.

Wasserman, Mark. *Everyday Life and Politics in Nineteenth Century Mexico: Men, Women, and War.* Albuquerque: University of New Mexico Press, 2000.

Porfirian Army (1876–1910)

Carreño, Alberto María. *Archivo del general Porfirio Díaz: memorias y documentos.* Mexico City: Serie "Colección de obras históricas mexicanas." Editorial Elede, 1955.

Didapp, Juan Pedro. *Gobiernos militares de México: los ataques al ejército y las maquinaciones políticas del partido científico para regir los destinos nacionales.* Mexico City: Tipografía de J. I. Guerrero y Comp., 1904.

Domingo y Barrera, Francisco. *Ligero estudio sobre higiene de cuarteles e indicaciones de las condiciones que guardan los de la Capital.* México City: Tipografía Literaria de Filomeno Mata, 1880.

Escalafón general del Ejército: cerrado hasta 30 de junio de 1910. Mexico City: Secretaría de Estado y del Despacho de Guerra y Marina, 1910.

Escalafón general del Ejército y Armada nacionales; Departamento de Estado Mayor, Secretaría de Guerra y Marina. Mexico City: Tipografía de la Oficina Impresora del Timbre, 1897.

Escobar, Alberto. *Manual de higiene militar.* Mexico City: Imprenta de Ignacio Escalante, 1887.

Esposito, Matthew D. "The Politics of Death: State Funerals as Rites of Reconciliation in Porfirian Mexico, 1876–1889." *The Americas* 62, no. 1 (July 2005): 65–94.

Estudio comparativo de los cañones de 75mm. de tiro rápido, Schneider-Canet, St. Chamond-Mondragón y Krupp. Mexico City: Secretaría de la Defensa Nacional, 1902.

Figueroa, Agustín García. *Higiene militar: causas de la frecuencia de la sífilis en el ejército y medios de disminuirla.* Mexico City: Imprenta de Ignacio Escalante, 1874.

Fornaro, Carlo de. *México tal cual es.* New York: International Publishing Company, 1909.

Fuentes, Ernesto. *Historia patria, obra adoptada por la Secretaría de Guerra y Marina para servir de todo en las escuelas de tropa del Ejército Nacional.* Mexico City: Secretaría de Fomento, 1909.

Gantús, Fausta. "La inconformidad subversiva, entre el pronunciamiento y el bandidaje: un acercamiento a los movimientos rebeldes durante el tuxtepecanismo, 1876–1888." *Estudios de Historia Moderna y Contemporánea de México* 35 (January–June 2008): 49–74.

González, Manuel. *Ordenanza general para el Ejército de la República Mexicana.* 4 vols. Mexico City: Imprenta de Ignacio Cumplido, 1882.

Gutiérrez Santos, Daniel. *Historia militar de México, 1876–1914.* Mexico City: Ateneo Press, 1955.

Hernández Chávez, Alicia. "Origen y ocaso del Ejército Porfiriano." *Historia Mexicana* 39, no. 1 (1989): 257–96.

Hughes, James B., Jr. *Mexican Military Arms: The Cartridge Period, 1866–1967.* Houston, TX: Deep River Armory, Inc., 1968.

Janvier, Thomas A. "The Mexican Army." *Harper's New Monthly Magazine* 79, no. 474 (November 1889): 812–27.

Kingsley, Maurice. "El Cinco de Mayo." *Harper's Weekly* 36, no. 1846 (May 7, 1892): 449.

Koth, Karl B. " 'Not a Mutiny, But a Revolution': The Rio Blanco Labour Dispute, 1906–1907." *Canadian Journal of Latin*

American and Caribbean Studies 18, no. 35 (1993): 39–65.

Mellichamp, Robert A. *A Gun for All Nations: The 37mm Gun and Ammunition.* Houston, TX: Privately published, 2010.

Memoria de la Secretaría de Estado y del Despacho de Guerra y Marina. Mexico City: Secretaría de Guerra y Marina, 1878.

Memoria de la Secretaría de Estado y del Despacho de Guerra y Marina, presentada al Congreso de la Unión por el secretario del ramo, General de División Bernardo Reyes; comprende del 1º de julio de 1901 al 31 de diciembre de 1902, (Anexos). Mexico City: Oficina Impresora de Estampillas, Palacio Nacional, 1903.

Memoria de la Secretaría de Estado y del Despacho de Guerra y Marina, presentada al Congreso de la Unión por el secretario del ramo, General de División Manuel González Cosío; comprende del 1º de julio de 1906 al 15 de julio de 1908, (Anexos). Mexico City: Talleres del Departamento de Estado Mayor, Palacio Nacional, 1909.

Neufeld, Stephen. "Behaving Badly in Mexico City: Discipline and Identity in the Presidential Guards, 1900–1911." In *Forced Marches: Soldiers and Military Caciques in Modern Mexico*, edited by Ben Fallaw and Terry Rugeley, 81–108. Tucson: University of Arizona Press, 2012.

Ortega, Leopoldo. *Breves consideraciones sobre algunos puntos de higiene militar.* Mexico City: Imprenta de Ignacio Cumplido, 1882.

Powell, Fred W. *The Railroads of Mexico.* Boston: Stratford Company, 1921.

Ramírez Rancaño, Mario. "La logística del ejército federal: 1881–1914." *Estudios de Historia Moderna y Contemporánea de México* 36 (July–December 2008): 183–219.

Reglamento provisional para el servicio de los cañones de 75mm S. Schneider-Canet tipo ligero. Mexico City: Tipografía del Departamento de Estado Mayor, Secretaría de Guerra y Marina, 1904; republished by Nabu Press in 2012.

Remington, Frederic. "Mexican Infantry on the March." *Harper's Weekly* 34, no. 1739 (April 19, 1890): 305.

Reyes, Bernardo. *Conversaciones militares escritas para las academias del 6º regimiento de caballería permanente, por el jefe del mismo, coronel C. Bernardo Reyes, San Luis Potosí, 1879; 3rd ed., corregida por el autor.* Monterrey: Imprenta del Gobierno en Palacio, a cargo de Viviano Flores, 1886.

Reyes, Bernardo. *Ensayo sobre un nuevo sistema de reclutamiento para el ejército y organización de la Guardia Nacional.* San Luis Potosí, S.L.P.: Imprenta de Dávalos, 1885.

Rocha, Sóstenes. *Estudios sobre la ciencia de la guerra.* Mexico City: Imprenta y librería Pablo Dupont, 1878.

Sánchez Rojas, Luis Ignacio. "La educación en el ejército porfiriano, 1900–1910." *Tzintzun: Revista de Estudios Históricos* 54 (July–December 2011): 93–127.

Sánchez Rojas, Luis Ignacio. "La prensa y las armas nacionales: la visión del ejército mexicano en la opinión pública en 1900." *Letras Históricas* 3 (Autumn–Winter 2010): 163–90.

Schiff, Warren. "German Military Penetration into Mexico during the Late Díaz Period." *Hispanic American Historical Review* 39, no. 4 (1959): 568–79.

Súarez Pichardo, Jorge. *Hechos ilustres de la clase de tropa del Ejército mexicano.* Mexico City: D. Hernández Mejía, 1909.

Troncoso, Francisco P. *Proyecto de decreto de organización general del ejército.* Mexico City: Imprenta del timbre, Palacio Nacional, 1896.

Truett, Samuel. "Transnational Warrior: Emilio Kosterlitzky and the Transformation of the U.S. Mexico Borderlands." In *Continental Crossroads: Remapping U.S. Mexico Borderlands History*, edited by

Samuel Truett and Elliott Young, 241–70. Durham, NC: Duke University Press, 2004.

Wells, Allen, and G. M. Joseph. *Summer of Discontent, Seasons of Upheaval: Elite Politics and Rural Insurgency in Yucatan, 1876–1915.* Stanford, CA: Stanford University Press, 1996.

Rurales (1879–1914)

Kitchens, John W. "Some Considerations on the *Rurales* of Porfirian Mexico." *Journal of Inter-American Studies* 9, no. 3 (July 1967): 441–55.

Ramírez, Francisco M., compiler and ed. *Colección de decretos, reglamentos y circulares referentes a los cuerpos rurales de la Federación: desde su fundación hasta la fecha.* Mexico City: Tipografía "El Lápiz de Águila," 1900.

Smith, Cornelius Cole, Jr. *Emilio Kosterlitzky: Eagle of Sonora and the Southwest Border.* Glendale, CA: A. H. Clark Company, 1970.

Vanderwood, Paul J. *Los rurales mexicanos.* Mexico City: Fondo de Cultura Económica, 1981.

Vanderwood, Paul J. "Mexico's Rurales: Reputation versus Reality." *The Americas: Academy of American Franciscan History* 34, no. 1 (July 1977): 102–12.

Yaqui War (1885–1900)

Balbás, Manuel. *Recuerdos del Yaqui: principales episodios durante la campaña de 1899 a 1901.* Mexico City: Sociedad de Edición y Librería Franco Americano, 1927.

Frías, Heriberto. *The Battle of Tomochic: Memoirs of a Second Lieutenant.* New York: Oxford University Press, 2006 translated edition by Barbara Jamison of 1893 original.

Hernández, Fortunato. *Las razas indígenas de Sonora y la guerra del Yaqui.* Mexico City: Elizalde, 1902.

Holden, William C., et al. "Studies of the Yaqui Indians of Sonora, Mexico." *Texas Technological College Bulletin* 7, no. 1 (January 1936): 13–133.

Hu-deHart, Evelyn. "Development and Rural Rebellion: Pacification of the Yaquis in the Late Porfiriato." *The Hispanic-American Historical Review* 54, no. 1 (February 1974): 72–93.

Hu-deHart, Evelyn. *Yaqui Resistance and Survival: The Struggle for Land and Autonomy, 1821–1910.* Madison: University of Wisconsin Press, 1984.

Troncoso, Brig. Gen. Francisco de Paula. *Las guerras con los pueblos yaqui y mayo del Estado de Sonora.* 2 vols. Mexico City: Secretaría de Estado y Despacho de Guerra y Marina, 1903–1905.

Vanderwood, Paul J. *The Power of God Against the Guns of Government: Religious Upheaval in Mexico at the Turn of the Nineteenth Century.* Stanford, CA: Stanford University Press, 1998.

Mexican Revolution (1910–1924)
General Histories (1910–1920)

Almada, Francisco R. *Diccionario de historia, geografía y biografía sonorenses.* Hermosillo: Gobierno de Sonora, 1983 reedition.

Blasco Ibáñez, Vicente. *Mexico in Revolution.* New York: E. P. Dutton & Company, 1920.

Brading, D. A., ed. *Caudillo and Peasant in the Mexican Revolution.* Cambridge: Cambridge University Press, 1980.

Brenner, Anita. *The Wind That Swept Mexico: The History of the Mexican Revolution of 1910–1942.* Austin: University of Texas Press, 1996, 1984, and 1971 reeditions of 1943 original.

Britton, John A. *Revolution and Ideology: Images of the Mexican Revolution in the United States.* Louisville: University Press of Kentucky, 1995.

Chávez M., Armando B., and Francisco R. Almada. *Visión histórica de la frontera norte de México, tomo V: de la Revolución a la Segunda Guerra Mundial.* Mexicali:

Universidad Autónoma de Baja California y Editorial Kino, 1994.

Chilcote, Ronald, ed. *Mexico at the Hour of Combat: Sabino Osuna's Photographs of the Mexican Revolution*. Laguna Beach, CA: Laguna Wilderness Press, 2012.

Cosío Villegas, Daniel. *Historia de la Revolución Mexicana*. 8 vols. Mexico City: El Colegio de Mexico, 1977–1995.

Cumberland, Charles C. *Mexican Revolution: The Constitutionalist Years*. Austin: University of Texas Press, 1972.

Dorado Romo, David. *Ringside Seat to a Revolution: An Underground Cultural History of El Paso and Juárez, 1893–1923*. El Paso, TX: Cinco Puntos Press, 2005.

Fabela, Isidro and Josefina E. de, eds. and compilers. *Documentos históricos de la revolución mexicana*. 27 vols. Mexico City: Editorial Jus and Fondo de Cultura Económica, 1960–1976.

Garciadiego Dantan, Javier, compiler and ed. *La Revolución Mexicana: crónicas, documentos, planes y testimonios*. Mexico City: Universidad Nacional Autónoma de México, 2005.

Hall, Linda B., and Don M. Coerver. *Revolution on the Border: The United States and Mexico, 1910–1920*. Albuquerque: University of New Mexico Press, 1988.

Hanrahan, Gene Z., ed. 9 vols. in 13 tomes. *Documents on the Mexican Revolution*. Salisbury, NC: Documentary Publications, 1976–1985.

Jacobs, Ian. *Ranchero Revolt: The Mexican Revolution in Guerrero*. Austin: University of Texas Press, 1982.

Johnson, William Weber. *Heroic Mexico: The Violent Emergence of a Modern Nation*. New York: Doubleday, 1968.

Jowett, Philip, and Alejandro de Quesada. *The Mexican Revolution, 1910–20*. Elite series, no. 137. Oxford: Osprey, 2006.

Knight, Alan. *The Mexican Revolution*. Cambridge Latin American Studies series. Vols. 54–55. New York: Cambridge University Press, 1986.

LaFrance, David G. *Revolution in Mexico's Heartland: Politics, War, and State Building in Puebla, 1913–1920*. Wilmington, DE: Scholarly Resources, 2003.

Langle Ramírez, Arturo. *Vocabulario, apodos, seudónimos, sobrenombres y hemerografía de la Revolución*. Mexico City: Instituto de Investigaciones Históricas de la Universidad Nacional Autónoma de México, 1966.

Lieuwen, Edwin. *Mexican Militarism: The Political Rise and Fall of the Revolutionary Army, 1910–1940*. Albuquerque: University of New Mexico Press, 1968.

Lozoya, Jorge Alberto. *El ejército mexicano, 1911–1965*. Mexico City: El Colegio de México, 1970.

Quirk, Robert E. *The Mexican Revolution and the Catholic Church, 1910–1919*. Bloomington: Indiana University Press, 1973.

Raat, W. Dirk. *The Mexican Revolution: An Annotated Guide to Recent Scholarship*. Boston: G. K. Hall, 1982.

Records of the Department of State Relating to the Internal Affairs of Mexico, 1910–1920. Washington, DC: U.S. National Archives, 1961.

Ruíz, Ramón Eduardo. *The Great Rebellion: Mexico, 1905–1924*. New York: W. W. Norton & Company, 1980.

Sarber, Mary A. *Photographs from the Border: The Otis A. Aultman Collection*. El Paso, TX: El Paso Public Library Association, 1977.

Vanderwood, Paul J., and Frank N. Samponaro. *Border Fury: A Picture Postcard Record of Mexico's Revolution and U.S. War Preparedness, 1910–1917*. Albuquerque: University of New Mexico Press, 1988.

Wasserman, Mark. *Persistent Oligarchs: Elites and Politics in Chihuahua, Mexico, 1910–1940*. Durham, NC: Duke University Press, 1993.

Toppling the Porfirian Regime (1910–1911)

Alessio Robles, Vito. "Reparación de las vías férreas en la última campaña." *Revista del Ejército y de la Marina* 12, no. 9 (September 1911): 161–65.

Blanco, Mónica. *Revolución y contienda política en Guanajuato, 1908–1913.* Mexico City: El Colegio de México, 1995.

Dambourges Jacques, Leo M. "The Chinese Massacre in Torreón (Coahuila) in 1911." *Arizona and the West* 16, no. 3 (Autumn 1974): 233–46.

Hanrahan, Gene Z., editor. *Documents on the Mexican Revolution.* Vols. 1–3. Salisbury, NC: Documentary Publications, 1976–1979.

McNeely, John H. "Origins of the Zapata Revolt in Morelos." *Hispanic American Historical Review* 46, no. 2 (May 1966): 153–69.

Pineda Gómez, Francisco. *La irrupción zapatista, 1911.* Mexico City: Ediciones Era, 1997.

Portilla, Santiago. *Una sociedad en armas: insurrección antireelecionista en México, 1910–1911.* Mexico City: Centro de Estudios Históricos del Colegio de México, 1995.

Ramírez Flores, José. *La revolución maderista en Jalisco.* Mexico City: Universidad de Guadalajara and the Centre d'études mexicaines et centroaméricaines, 1992.

Sánchez Lamego, Miguel A. *Historia militar de la revolución mexicana en la época maderista.* 3 vols. Mexico City: Instituto Nacional de Estudios Históricos de la Revolución Mexicana, 1976–1977.

Vanderwood, Paul J. "Response to Revolt: The Counter-Guerrilla Strategy of Porfirio Díaz." *Hispanic American Historical Review* 56, no. 4 (November 1976): 551–79.

Major Personages (1910–1920)

Ángeles Contreras, Jesús. *Felipe Ángeles: su vida y su obra.* Pachuca, Hidalgo: Universidad Autónoma del Estado de Hidalgo, 1996.

Benavides Hinojosa, Artemio. *Bernardo Reyes, vida de un liberal porfirista.* Mexico City: Tusquets, 2009 reedition of 1998 original published in Monterrey, Nuevo León, by Ediciones Castillo.

Brunk, Samuel. *Emiliano Zapata: Revolution and Betrayal in Mexico.* Albuquerque: University of New Mexico Press, 1995.

Buchenau, Jürgen. *The Last Caudillo: Álvaro Obregón and the Mexican Revolution.* Chichester, England: Wiley-Blackwell, 2011.

Gil, Feliciano. *Biografía y vida militar del general Álvaro Obregón.* Hermosillo, Sonora: Editorial M. F. Remo, 1914.

Gilly, Adolfo, compiler. *Felipe Ángeles en la Revolución.* Mexico City: Ediciones Era, 2005.

Guzmán, Martín Luis. *Memoirs of Pancho Villa.* Austin: University of Texas Press, 1976 translation by Virginia H. Taylor of 1936 original.

Hall, Linda B. *Álvaro Obregón: Power and Revolution in Mexico, 1911–1920.* College Station: Texas A&M University Press, 1981.

Katz, Friedrich. *The Life and Times of Pancho Villa.* Stanford, CA: Stanford University Press, 1998.

McLynn, Frank. *Villa and Zapata: A History of the Mexican Revolution.* New York: Carroll and Graf Publishing, 2000.

Mena Brito, Bernardino. *El lugarteniente gris de Pancho Villa (Felipe Ángeles).* Mexico City: Casa M. Coli, 1938.

Meyer, Michael C. *Huerta: A Political Portrait.* Lincoln: University of Nebraska Press, 1972.

Naranjo, Francisco. *Diccionario biográfico Revolucionario.* Mexico City: Imprenta Editorial "Cosmos," 1935.

Niemeyer, Eberhardt V., Jr. *El general Bernardo Reyes.* Monterrey: Gobierno del estado de Nuevo León, Centro de Estudios

Humanísticos de la Universidad de Nuevo León, 1966.

Obregón, Álvaro. *Ocho mil kilómetros en campaña*. Paris and Mexico City: Librería de la Viuda de Charles Bouret, 1917 [republished by the Fondo de Cultura Económica in 1970, plus numerous other times].

O'Hea, Patrick A. *Reminiscences of the Mexican Revolution*. Mexico City: Centro Anglo-Mexicano del Libro, 1966; republished in 1981 by Sphere.

Osorio, Rubén, editor. *La correspondencia de Francisco Villa: cartas y telegramas de 1911 a 1923*. Chihuahua City: Talleres Gráficos del Gobierno del Estado de Chihuahua, 2004 reedition.

Palou, Pedro Ángel. *Zapata*. Mexico City: Editorial Planeta Mexicana, 2006.

Ramírez Rancaño, Mario. "La renuncia y huida de Victoriano Huerta." *Escenarios XXI* 1, nos. 5–6 (November–December 2010): 23 pp.

Ramos, Miguel S. *Un soldado: Gral. José Refugio Velasco*. Mexico City: Ediciones Oasis, 1960.

Rausch, George J., Jr. "The Early Career of Victoriano Huerta." *Americas: Academy of American Franciscan History* 21, no. 2 (October 1964): 136–45.

Reed, John. *Insurgent Mexico*. New York: Simon and Schuster, 1969, reedition of 1914 original published by D. Appleton and Company.

Rosovsky, Mirta, Guadalupe Tolosa, and Laura Espejel, compilers and eds. *Documentos inéditos sobre Emiliano Zapata y el Cuartel General, seleccionados del archivo de Genovevo de la O, que conserva el Archivo General de la Nación*. Mexico City: Archivo General de la Nación, 1979.

Sánchez Lamego, Miguel A. *Generales de la Revolución*. 2 vols. Mexico City: Biblioteca del Instituto Nacional de Estudios Históricos de la Revolución Mexicana, 1979–1981.

Scheina, Robert L. *Villa: Soldier of the Mexican Revolution*. Washington, DC: Potomac Books, 2004.

Womack, John, Jr. *Zapata and the Mexican Revolution*. New York: Alfred A. Knopf, 1969.

Orozquista Rebellion (1912)

Meyer, Michael C. *Mexican Rebel: Pascual Orozco and the Mexican Revolution, 1910–1915*. Lincoln: University of Nebraska Press, 1967.

Tablada, Juan José. *La defensa social: historia de la campaña de la División del Norte*. Mexico City, Universidad Iberoamericana, 2010 reedition by Rubén Lozano Herrera of 1913 original.

Decena Trágica (1913)

Aguilar, Jose Ángel. *La decena tragica*. 2 vols. Mexico City: Biblioteca del Instituto Nacional de Estudios Historicos de la Revolucion Mexicana, no. 89, 1981–1982.

Haley, P. Edward. *Revolution and Intervention: The Diplomacy of Taft and Wilson with Mexico, 1910–1917*. Cambridge, MA: MIT Press, 1970.

Hanrahan, Gene Z., ed. *Documents on the Mexican Revolution, Volume 4: The Murder of Madero and Role Played by U.S. Ambassador Henry Lane Wilson*. Salisbury, NC: Documentary Publications, 1981.

Hidalgo, Dennis R. "The Evolution of History and the Informal Empire: La Decena Trágica in the British Press." *Mexican Studies/Estudios Mexicanos* 23, no. 2 (Summer 2007): 317–54.

LaFrance, David G. "Germany, Revolutionary Nationalism, and the Downfall of President Francisco I. Madero: The Covadonga Killings."*Mexican Studies/Estudios Mexicanos* 2, no. 1 (1986): 53–82.

Olguín Mosqueda, Socorro. *La decena trágica vista por dos embajadores*. Mexico City: Universidad Nacional Autónoma de México, 1965.

Torrea, Juan Manuel. *La decena trágica.* Mexico City: "*Serie de divulgación cultural,*" Volume 2, Academia Nacional de Historia y Geografía, 1963.

Urquizo, Francisco Luis. *La decena trágica.* Mexico City: Serie "Cuadernos mexicanos," Number 23, Secretaría de Educación Pública, 1980s reedition of the *Asonada militar de 1913* originally published by Ediciones Joloco in 1939.

Urquizo, Francisco Luis. *La ciudadela quedo atras; escenas vividas de la decena trágica.* Mexico City: B. Costa-Amic, 1965.

Villalpando César, José Manuel. *La decena trágica.* Mexico City: Editorial Diana, 2009.

Great Battles (1913–1915)

Aguirre Benavides, Luis and Adrián. *Las grandes batallas de la División del Norte al mando del general Francisco Villa.* Mexico City: Editorial Diana, 1967 reedition.

Ángeles, Felipe. *La batalla de Zacatecas: descripción tomada del diario del general Felipe Ángeles.* Chihuahua City, Chihuahua: Imprenta del Gobierno, 1914.

Arredondo Torres, Agur. *Los valientes de Zapata: guerrilleros de la zona sur del estado de Morelos y del norte de Guerrero.* Cuernavaca, Morelos: Unidad de Culturas Populares e Indígenas del Instituto de Cultura de Morelos, 2002.

Barragán Rodríguez, Juan. *Historia del ejército y de la revolución constitucionalista.* 2 vols. Mexico City: Stylo, 1946; republished in 1985 by the Instituto Nacional de Estudios Históricos de la Revolución Mexicana.

Bojerud, Stellan. *Soldat Under 13 Fanor.* Stockholm, Sweden: Sivart Förlag, 2008.

Elam, Earl. "Revolution on the Border: The U.S. Army in the Big Bend and the Battle of Ojinaga, 1913–1914." *West Texas Historical Association Yearbook* (1990): 5–25.

Espejel López, Laura. *El cuartel general zapatista, 1914–1915: documentos del Fondo Emiliano Zapata del Archivo General de la Nación.* 2 vols. Mexico City: Instituto Nacional de Antropología e Historia, 1995.

Espejel López, Laura. Francisco Pineda, and Fernando Robles. *Emiliano Zapata, como lo vieron los zapatistas.* Mexico City: Ediciones Tecolote, 2006.

Gilliam, Ronald R. "Turning Point of the Mexican Revolution." *MHQ: The Quarterly Journal of Military History* 15, no. 3 (Spring 2003): 40–51.

González, Manuel W. *Contra Villa: relatos de la campaña 1914–1915.* Mexico City: Ediciones Botas, 1935.

González, Manuel W. *Con Carranza: episodios de la Revolución Constitucionalista, 1913–1914.* Monterrey, Nuevo León: Talleres J. Cantú Leal, 1933.

Jaurrieta, José María. *Con Villa (1916–1920), memorias de campaña.* Mexico City: Consejo Nacional para la Cultura y las Artes, 1997.

López González, Valentín. *La muerte del general Emiliano Zapata.* Mexico City: Cuadernos Zapatistas, Ediciones del Gobierno del Estado Libre y Soberano de Morelos, 1979.

MacGregor, Josefina, and Guillermina Palacios Suárez. *Ejército Libertador del Sur (1911–1923).* Mexico City: Cuadernos del Archivo Histórico de la UNAM, no. 9, 1988.

Magaña, Gildardo. *La toma de Cuernavaca.* Mexico City: Cuadernos Zapatistas, Ediciones del Gobierno del Estado Libre y Soberano de Morelos, 1979.

Manifesto Addressed by General Francisco Villa to the Nation, and Documents Justifying the Disavowal of Venustiano Carranza as First Chief of the Revolution. Chihuahua City[?]: Headquarters, Division of the North, Constitutionalist Army, 1914.

Meyer, Michael C. "The Militarization of Mexico, 1913–1914." *Americas: Academy of American Franciscan History* 27, no. 3 (January 1971): 283–306.

Muro, Luis, and Ulloa, Berta. *Guía del Ramo Revolución Mexicana, 1910–1920, del Archivo Histórico de la Defensa Nacional y de otros repositorios del Gabinete de Manuscritos de la Biblioteca Nacional de México.* Mexico City: Centro de Estudios Históricos del Colegio de México, 1997.

Obregón, Álvaro. *Partes oficiales de las batallas de Celaya: 6, 7, 13, 14 y 15 de abril de 1915.* Celaya, Guanajuato: Confederación Revolucionaria, 1915.

Ortiz, Orlando. *Los dorados: Pancho Villa y la División del Norte.* Mexico City: Editorial Nueva Imagen, 1982.

Páez López, Joaquín. *Cuatro meses de vacaciones con Zapata.* Cuernavaca, Morelos: Cuadernos Históricos Morelenses, 1999.

Pineda Gómez, Francisco. *La Revolución del Sur, 1912–1914.* Mexico City: Ediciones ERA, 2005.

Ramírez Rancaño, Mario. *El ejército federal, 1914: semblanzas biográficas.* Mexico City: Universidad Nacional Autónoma de México, 2012.

Raun, Gerald G. "Refugees or Prisoners of War: The Internment of a Mexican Federal Army after the Battle of Ojinaga, December 1913–January 1914." *Journal of Big Bend Studies* 12 (2000): 133–65.

Sáenz, Aarón. *Los históricos tratados de Teoloyucan.* Mexico City: Patronato de la Historia de Sonora, 1964.

Salmerón, Pedro. *Los carrancistas: la historia nunca contada del victorioso Ejército del Noroeste.* Mexico City: Planeta, 2010.

Salmerón, Pedro. *La División del Norte: la tierra, los hombres y la historia de un ejército del pueblo.* Mexico City: Editorial Planeta Mexicana, 2006.

Sánchez Lamego, Miguel A. *Historia militar de la revolución constitucionalista.* 5 vols. Mexico City: Talleres Gráficos de la Nación for the Biblioteca del Instituto Nacional de Estudios Históricos de la Revolución Mexicana, 1956–1960.

Sánchez Lamego, Miguel A. *Historia militar de la revolución mexicana en la época de la convención.* Mexico City: Instituto Nacional de Estudios Históricos de la Revolución Mexicana, 1983.

Sánchez Lamego, Miguel A. *Historia militar de la Revolución zapatista bajo el régimen huertista.* Mexico City: Instituto Nacional de Estudios Históricos de la Revolución Mexicana, 1979.

Swanson, Julia. "Murder in Mexico." *History Today* 54, no. 6 (June 2004): 38–45.

Thord-Gray, Ivor. *Gringo Rebel.* Coral Gables, FL: University of Miami Press, 1960.

Vargas Arreola, Juan Bautista. *A sangre y fuego con Pancho Villa.* Mexico City: Fondo de Cultura Económica, 1988.

Whitt, E. Brondo. *La División del Norte 1914: por un testigo presencial.* Chihuahua, Chihuahua: Centro Librero La Prensa, 1996 reedition of 1940 original published by Editorial Lumen in Mexico City.

U.S. Occupation of Veracruz (1914)

Alexander, J. H. "Roots of Deployment: Vera Cruz, 1914." *Marine Corps Gazette* 66, no. 11 (1982): 71–79.

Eisenhower, John S. D. *Intervention!: The United States and the Mexican Revolution, 1913–1917.* New York: W. W. Norton & Company, 1993.

Foreman, Michael A. "A Storm in Veracruz." *American History Illustrated* 29, no. 1 (March 1994): 28–37 and 72.

Haverstock, Mike. "Waiting in Veracruz, 1914." *Américas* [Organization of American States] 35, no. 6 (1983): 34–39.

Owsley, Frank L., Jr., and Wesley Phillip Newton. "Eyes in the Skies." *U.S. Naval Institute Proceedings* (1986 Supplement): 17–25.

Quirk, Robert E. *An Affair of Honour: Woodrow Wilson and the Occupation of Veracruz.* Knoxville: Published for the Mississippi Valley Historical Association by the University of Kentucky Press, 1962.

Sweetman, Jack. *Landing at Veracruz, 1914: The First Complete Chronicle of a Strange Encounter in April 1914, When the United States Navy Captured and Occupied the City of Veracruz, Mexico.* Annapolis: U.S. Naval Institute Press, 1968.

Vanderwood, Paul J. "The Picture Postcard as Historical Evidence: Veracruz, 1914." *Americas* (Academy of American Franciscan History) 45, no. 2 (1988): 201–25.

Columbus Raid and the Pursuit of Pancho Villa (1917)

Anderson, Mark Cronlund. *Pancho Villa's Revolution by Headlines.* Norman: University of Oklahoma Press, 2000.

Braddy, Haldeen. *Pancho Villa at Columbus: The Raid of 1916.* El Paso: Texas Western College Press, 1965.

Calzadías Barrera, Alberto. *Villa contra todo y contra todos.* Mexico City: Editores Mexicanos Unidos, 1963.

Clendenen, Clarence C. *Blood on the Border: The United States Army and the Mexican Irregulars.* New York: Macmillan, 1969.

Clendenen, Clarence C. *The United States and Pancho Villa: A Study in Unconventional Diplomacy.* Ithaca, NY: Cornell University Press, 1961.

de Quesada, Alejandro. *The Hunt for Pancho Villa: The Columbus Raid and Pershing's Punitive Expedition, 1916–17.* London: "Raid" Series, no. 29, Osprey, 2012.

Eisenhower, John S. D. *Intervention!: The United States and the Mexican Revolution, 1913–1917.* New York: W. W. Norton & Company, 1993.

Harris, Larry A. *Pancho Villa and the Columbus Raid.* El Paso, TX: McMath, 1949.

Hurst, James W. *Pancho Villa and Black Jack Pershing: The Punitive Expedition in Mexico.* Westport, CT: Greenwood, 2008.

Katz, Friedrich. "Pancho Villa and the Attack on Columbus, New Mexico." *American Historical Review* 58, no. 1 (February 1978): 101–30.

Mason, Herbert M. *The Great Pursuit.* New York: Random House, 1970.

Salinas Carranza, Alberto. *La expedición punitiva.* Mexico City: Ediciones Botas, 1936.

Sandos, James A. "German Involvement in Northern Mexico, 1915–1916: A New Look at the Columbus Raid." *Hispanic American Historical Review* 50, no. 1 (February 1970): 70–89.

Smythe, Donald. *Guerrilla Warrior: The Early Life of John J. Pershing.* New York: Charles Scribner's Sons, 1973.

Stout, Joseph A., Jr. *Border Conflict: Villistas, Carrancistas, and the Punitive Expedition, 1915–1920.* Fort Worth: Texas Christian University Press, 1999.

Thomas, Robert S., and Invez V. Allen. *The Mexican Punitive Expedition under Brigadier General John J. Pershing, United States Army, 1916–1917.* Washington, DC: Office of the Chief of Military History, Department of the Army, 1954.

Tompkins, Frank. *Chasing Villa: The Story Behind the Story of Pershing's Expedition into Mexico.* Harrisburg, PA: Military Service Publishing, 1934.

Vanderwood, Paul J., and Frank N. Samponaro. *Border Fury: A Picture Postcard Record of Mexico's Revolution and U.S. War Preparedness, 1910–1917.* Albuquerque: University of New Mexico Press, 1988.

Welsome, Eileen. *The General and the Jaguar: Pershing's Hunt for Pancho Villa, a True Story of Revolution and Revenge.* New York: Little, Brown, and Co., 2006.

Wolff, Leon. "Black Jack's Mexican Goose Chase." *American Heritage* 13, no. 4 (June 1962): 22–27, 100–106.

Soldaderas or Women Soldiers (1910–1920)

Arrizon, Alicia. "Soldaderas and the Staging of the Mexican Revolution." *The Drama Review* 42, no. 1 (1998): 90–112.

Cuesy, Silvia L., ed. *Diario de Elodia: la revolución zapatista contada por una adolescente de la época (1914–1916).* Mexico City: Colección "Diarios Mexicanos," Editorial Planeta, 2003.

Fuentes, Andrés R. "Battleground Women: Soldaderas and Female Soldiers in the Mexican Revolution." *The Americas: Academy of American Franciscan History* 51, no. 4 (April 1995): 525–53.

Macias, Anna. "Women and the Mexican Revolution, 1910–1920." *The Americas: Academy of American Franciscan History* 37, no. 1 (July 1980): 53–82.

Salas, Elizabeth. *Soldaderas in the Mexican Military: Myth and History.* Austin: University of Texas Press, 1990.

Music (1910–1920)

De María y Campos, Armando. *La Revolución mexicana a través de los corridos populares.* 2 vols. Mexico City: Instituto Nacional de Estudios Históricos de la Revolución Mexicana, 1962.

Mendoza, Vicente T. *El corrido mexicano.* Mexico City: Fondo de Cultura Económica, 1954.

Sánchez, Enrique. *Corridos de Pancho Villa.* Mexico City: Editorial de Magisterio, 1952.

De la Huerta Revolt (1923–1924)

Castro, Pedro. "La intervención olvidada: Washington en la rebelión delahuertista." *Secuencia* 34 (January–April 1996): 63–91.

Llerenas, Fidelina G., and Tamayo, Jaime. *El levantamiento delahuertista: cuatro rebeliones y cuatro jefes militares.* Guadalajara, Jalisco: Universidad de Guadalajara, 1995.

Machado, Manuel A., Jr. "The United States and the De la Huerta Rebellion." *Southwestern Historical Quarterly* 75, no. 3 (January 1972): 303–24.

Peterson, Edward J. *The Role of the United Status in the De la Huerta Rebellion in Mexico, 1923–1924.* Austin: University of Texas Press, 1965.

Cristero Rebellion (1926–1929)

Bailey, David C. *Viva Cristo Rey! The Cristero Rebellion and the Church-State Conflict in Mexico.* Austin: University of Texas Press, 1974.

Butler, Matthew. *Popular Piety and Political Identity in Mexico's Cristero Rebellion: Michoacán, 1927–29.* New York: Oxford University Press, 2004.

Castillo Girón, Víctor Manuel. "La cristiada: desarrollo y efectos en el suroeste de Jalisco." *Estudios jaliscienses* 18 (November 1994): 47–62.

Jrade, Ramón. "Inquiries into the Cristero Insurrection against the Mexican Revolution." *Latin American Research Review* 20, no. 2 (1985): 53–69.

Meyer, Jean A. *The Cristero Rebellion: The Mexican People between Church and State, 1926–1929.* New York: Cambridge University Press, 1976.

Purnell, Jennie. *Popular Movements and State Formation in Revolutionary Mexico: The Agraristas and Cristeros of Michoacán.* Durham, NC: Duke University Press, 1999.

Quirk, Robert E. *The Mexican Revolution and the Catholic Church, 1910–1929.* Bloomington: Indiana University Press, 1973.

Tuck, Jim. *The Holy War in Los Altos: A Regional Analysis of Mexico's Cristero Rebellion.* Tucson: University of Arizona Press, 1982.

Postrevolutionary Entrenchment (1930–1941)

Bazant de Saldaña, Mílada, et al. *La evolución de la educación militar de México.* Mexico City: Secretaría de la Defensa Nacional, 1997.

Camp, Roderic Ai. *Generals in the Palacio: The Military in Modern Mexico.* New York: Oxford University Press, 1992.

Hall, Linda B. *Oil, Banks, and Politics: The United States and Postrevolutionary Mexico, 1917–1924.* Austin: University of Texas Press, 1995.

Informe del Secretario de la Defensa Nacional. Mexico City: Secretaría de la Defensa Nacional, 1938.

Loyo Camacho, Martha Beatriz. *Joaquín Amaro y el proceso de institucionalización del Ejército Mexicano, 1917–1931*. Mexico City: Universidad Nacional Autónoma de México, 2003.

Lozoya, Jorge Alberto. *El ejército mexicano (1911–1965)*. Mexico City: El Colegio de México, 1984 reedition of 1970 original published by the Centro de Estudios Internacionales.

Ortiz Rubio, Pascal. *Los alojamientos militares en la República Mexicana*. México: Dirección de Talleres Gráficos, 1921.

Ramírez Rancaño, Mario. "Una discusión sobre el tamaño del ejército mexicano, 1876–1930." *Estudios de historia moderna y contemporánea de México* 32, no. 32 (2009): 35–71.

Rath, Thomas G. *Myths of Demilitarization in Postrevolutionary Mexico, 1920–1960*. Chapel Hill: University of North Carolina Press, 2013.

Urquizo, Francisco Luis. *De la vida militar mexicana*. Mexico City: Herrero Hermanos Sucesores, 1920.

Urquizo, Francisco Luis. *Tropa vieja*. Mexico City: SEDENA, 1984 reedition of 1921 original.

World War II (1942–1945)

Cárdenas de la Peña, Enrique. *Gesta en el golfo: la Segunda Guerra Mundial y México*. Mexico City: Primicias, 1966.

González Luna, Efraín. *Servicio militar: derechos del soldado*. Mexico City: Acción Nacional, 1943.

Knight, Alan. "México y Estados Unidos, 1938–1940: rumor y realidad." *Secuencia* 34 (January–April 1996): 129–53.

Niblo, Stephen R. *War, Diplomacy, and Development: The United Status and Mexico, 1938–1954*. Wilmington, DE: Scholarly Resources, 1995.

Paz Salinas, María Emilia. *Strategy, Security, and Spies: Mexico and the U.S. as Allies in World War II*. University Park: Pennsylvania State University Press, 1997.

Prewitt, Virginia. "The Mexican Army." *Foreign Affairs* 19, no. 3 (April 1941): 609–20.

Rodríguez Aviñoá, Pastora. "La prensa nacional frente a la intervención de México en la Segunda Guerra Mundial." *Historia Mexicana* 29, no. 2 (1979): 252–300.

Torres, Blanca. *Historia de la Revolución Mexicana, período 1940–1952: México en la segunda guerra mundial*. Mexico City: El Colegio de México, 1979.

Dirty War (1968–1980)

Adler Hellman, Judith. *Mexico in Crisis*. New York: Holmes & Meier, 1978.

Aguayo Quezada, Sergio. *Los archivos de la violencia*. Mexico City: Grijalbo, 1998.

Aguayo Quezada, Sergio. *La charola: una historia de los servicios de inteligencia en México*. Mexico City: Grijalbo, 1978.

Álvarez Garín, Raúl. *La estela de Tlatelolco*. Mexico City: Itaca, 1998.

Bartra, Armando. *Guerrero bronco: campesinos, ciudadanos y guerrilleros en la Costa Grande*. Mexico City: Era, 2000.

Blacker, O'Neill. "Cold War in the Countryside: Conflict in Guerrero, Mexico." *The Americas* 66, no. 2 (October 2009): 181–210.

Brewster, Claire. "The Student Movement of 1968 and the Mexican Press: The Cases of *Excélsior* and *¡Siempre!*" *Bulletin of Latin American Research* 21, no. 2 (April 2002): 171–90.

Carpenter, Victoria. "The Echo of Tlatelolco in Mexican Protest Poetry." *Bulletin of Latin American Research* 24 (2005): 496–512.

Castellanos, Laura. *México armado, 1943–1981*. Mexico City: Era, 2007.

Estrada Correa, Francisco. *La "guerra sucia" contra la democracia: apuntes para la otra historia de México*. Mexico City, 2006.

Hodges, Donald, and Ross Gandy. *Mexico Under Siege: Popular Resistance to Presidential Despotism.* New York: Zed, 2002.

Moksnes, Heidi. "Factionalism and Counterinsurgency in Chiapas: Contextualizing the Acteal Massacre." *Revista Europea de Estudios Latinoamericanos y del Caribe* 76 (April 2004): 109–17.

Montemayor, Carlos. *Guerra en el paraíso.* Mexico City: Seix Barral, 2008.

Morales Hernández, José de Jesús. *Memorias de un guerrillero: la guerra sucia del México de los 70's.* Zapopan: Jalisco, 2006.

Moreno Barrera, Jorge. *La guerra sucia en México: el toro y el lagarto, 1968–1980.* Mexico City: Libros para Todos, 2002.

Poniatowska, Elena. *La noche de Tlatelolco.* Mexico City: Ediciones Era, 1999 reedition.

Scherer García, Julio, and Monsiváis, Carlos. *Los patriotas: de Tlatelolco a la guerra sucia.* Mexico City: Aguilar, 2004.

Scherer García, Julio, and Carlos Monsiváis. *Parte de guerra, Tlatelolco 1968: documentos del general Marcelino García Barragán, los hechos y la historia.* Mexico City: Nuevo Siglo/Aguilar, 1999.

Schmidt, Samuel. *The Deterioration of the Mexican Presidency: The Years of Luis Echeverria.* Tucson: University of Arizona Press, 1991.

Shapira, Yoram. "Mexico: The Impact of the 1968 Student Protest on Echeverria's Reformism." *Journal of Interamerican Studies and World Affairs* 19, no. 4 (November 1977): 557–80.

Solomon, Joel. *Systemic Injustice: Torture, "Disappearance," and Extrajudicial Execution in Mexico.* New York: Human Rights Watch, 1999.

Suárez, Luis. *Lucio Cabañas: el guerrillero sin esperanza.* Mexico City: Grijalbo, 1976.

Ulloa Bornemann, Alberto. *Surviving Mexico's Dirty War: A Political Prisoner's Memoir.* Trans. Arthur Schmidt and Aurora Camacho de Schmidt. Philadelphia: Temple University Press, 2007.

Velediaz, Juan. *El general sin memoria: una crónica de los silencios del ejército mexicano.* Mexico City: Debate, 2010.

Young, Dolly J. "Mexican Literary Reactions to Tlatelolco 1968." *Latin American Research Review* 20, no. 2 (1985): 71–85.

Drug War (1980s–Present)

Andreas, Peter. *Border Games: Policing the U.S. Mexico Divide.* Ithaca, NY: Cornell University Press, 2009 reedition of original from 2000.

Campbell, Howard. *Drug War Zone: Frontline Despatches from the Streets of El Paso and Juárez.* Austin: University of Texas Press, 2009.

Díez, Jordi, and Ian Nicholls. *The Mexican Armed Forces in Transition.* Carlisle, PA: Strategic Studies Institute, January 2006.

Garduño Valero, Guillermo J. R. *El ejército mexicano, entre la guerra y la política.* Mexico City: Universidad Autónoma Metropolitana, Unidad Iztapalapa, División de Ciencias Sociales y Humanas, 2008.

Grayson, George W., and Samuel Logan. *The Executioner's Men: Los Zetas, Rogue Soldiers, Criminal Entrepreneurs, and the Shadow State They Created.* Piscataway, NJ: Transaction, 2012.

Payan, Tony. *The Three U.S. Mexico Border Wars: Drugs, Immigration, and Homeland Security.* Westport, CT: Praeger, 2006.

The War on Mexican Cartels: Options for U.S. and Mexican Policy-Makers. Cambridge, MA: Harvard University Institute of Politics, September 2012.

Index

Note: Page numbers in **bold** font indicate main entries.

About the Author

David F. Marley is a historian who lived in Mexico City for more than three decades, researching and teaching at such institutions as the Colegio de Mexico and Instituto Nacional de Antropologia e Historia. His published works include ABC-CLIO's *Wars of the Americas* and *Historic Cities of the Americas*.

DATE DUE